THE GOOD
BIRD
GUIDE

A species-by-species guide to finding Europe's best birds

Keith Marsh

CHRISTOPHER HELM
LONDON

Published 2005 by Christopher Helm,
an imprint of A&C Black Publishers Ltd,
37 Soho Square, London W1D 3QZ

ISBN 0-7136-6848-2

A CIP catalogue record for this book is available from
the British Library

A&C Black uses paper produced with elemental
chlorine-free pulp, harvested from managed
sustainable forests.

www.acblack.com

Typeset and designed by Tina Tong

Printed and bound in Wales by Creative Print and Design,
Ebbw Vale

10 9 8 7 6 5 4 3 2 1

Contents

List of species covered

Acknowledgements

A book of this kind is inevitably heavily dependent on a huge number of information sources. While many personal observations are included, these are in the minority. The bulk of the information has been gleaned from the numerous detailed site guides now available (many of which are listed in the bibliography), as well as articles in the various birding magazines and correspondence with fellow travelling birders. I also owe a debt of gratitude to the scores of authors of trip reports posted on the internet. This is an invaluable source of up-to-the-minute information on where to see birds and how to get there – essential preparation for any birding trip.

From Christopher Helm Publishers, I would like to thank Nigel Redman for the original idea and title for the book, and Julie Bailey for her valuable assistance in the latter stages of the book's production. However, special thanks must go to Marianne Taylor, without whose encouragement and help this project would never have got off the ground. In addition to her ideas on the content and format of the book, Marianne also contributed the many illustrations, for which I am exceedingly grateful.

Special mention must also go to Guy Kirwan who provided much-needed corrections and guidance, especially relating to birds in Turkey, to Vasil Ananian for help with Armenia, and to Ewan Urquhart for his numerous suggestions, and assistance with Biscay and many other areas.

Last, but certainly not least, this book is dedicated to my partner Jane, without whose support this book would never have reached completion.

Introduction

In the last 30 years the popularity of birding has grown enormously and interest in travelling to see birds has increased to such an extent that it is possible to travel the globe on guided birding holidays. At one time the majority of British birders, or birdwatchers as they were then known, seldom moved far from their 'local patches' except for the occasional day-trip to some reserve or migration hotspot. However, the introduction of guides covering European as well as British birds whetted many appetites, and the publication of *Where to Watch Birds in Britain and Europe* by John Gooders in 1970 undoubtedly encouraged many birders to pack their binoculars and head abroad.

Today birders can join organised tours to the Arctic or Antarctic, the Australian outback or the Amazon, but the Western Palearctic region still holds a special importance for many. Covering the area from Iceland and the Azores east to the Urals and Caspian Sea, this region includes such diverse habitats as the Russian taiga and Sahara desert, the mountains of the Pyrenees, Alps and Caucasus, and the bird-rich deltas of the Coto Doñana, Camargue, Danube and Volga. The birds of the Western Palearctic are probably the best studied of any region in the world, and travel and birding in most of the countries is easy and safe. There are, of course, exceptions and Foreign Office advice should be sought before visiting countries where the political situation is unstable or which have sensitive border areas. However, every year sees the bird tour companies travelling to new areas, and pioneering work is undertaken by a few intrepid independent birders. Once a foundation has been laid and a few key sites are established for the more exciting species, new areas quickly join the birding circuit and attract interest from local ornithologists, which may, in turn, lead to important sites gaining protection. There is still a great deal to be discovered about the birds of the Western Palearctic, both in more remote countries and in regularly visited areas. Many birders now contribute to the store of knowledge by placing trip reports on the Internet, and this is an ideal way to research and plan a trip.

This book is aimed at all birders, but especially those who wish to see the more sought-after birds of the region. Many do not have the resources or time to join organised tours or to go on a purely birding holiday. Fortunately, some superb birding sites are close to popular holiday areas, particularly around the Mediterranean, enabling the birder on a family holiday to take a day or two away from the pool or beach and venture into nearby hills or to a local wetland in search of birds not found at home. There are birding site guides to many parts of Europe, North Africa and the Middle East, but this book takes the opposite approach, taking the bird as the starting point. The aim is to direct the reader to the most likely sites within the Western Palearctic for the region's most sought-after birds.

This book covers 435 special birds: endemics, species of restricted range or small population within the region, and those that, for whatever reason, are difficult to find. Compared with other regions, the Western Palearctic has few endemics, i.e. species that occur nowhere else, although recent taxonomic changes have increased this number slightly. Among the endemics are three nuthatches: one on Corsica, another in Algeria and a third almost confined to Turkey. There are also endemic finches, with the Citril Finch of Iberia and the Alps, the recently split Corsican Finch on Corsica and Sardinia, the Syrian Serin confined to parts of the Middle East and the Canary on the north-east Atlantic Islands. The Scottish Crossbill, currently Britain's only endemic bird, may be about to lose its specific status, but the Red Grouse of Britain and Ireland may once again be considered a full species. Recent splits have resulted in species status being afforded to Iberian and Canary Islands Chiffchaffs, Canary Island Kinglet and African Blue Tit, which is found in North Africa and the Canaries. These islands, as well as Madeira and the Azores, are home to races of more widespread species of landbird that are potential future splits, and host important populations of rare seabirds very difficult to see elsewhere including Zino's, Fea's and Bulwer's Petrels, shearwaters and storm-petrels. Further south, at the far south-western limit of the Western Palearctic, the Cape Verde Islands also host endemic species and rare seabirds such as Brown Booby, Red-billed Tropicbird and Magnificent Frigatebird. The Mediterranean has two highly sought-after near-endemics, Eleonora's Falcon and Audouin's Gull, both of which, although scarce, are fairly easily found. North Africa has several endemics as well as some species with very limited Western Palearctic ranges but which are widespread south of the Sahara, e.g. Dark Chanting-goshawk, Double-spurred Francolin and Black-crowned Tchagra. Egypt is now very popular amongst travelling birders with various Afrotropical species in the far south around Lake Nasser and seabird specialities of the Red Sea such as Sooty and White-eyed Gulls. Some of these can also be observed off Eilat, in Israel, one of the best migration watchpoints in the entire region. Turkey is one of the best countries in the region for birds, with a diverse

species list and montane specialities such as Caucasian Black Grouse and Caspian Snowcock. These and other Caucasian birds can also be seen in Armenia, and trips elsewhere in the Caucasus may become possible in the near future. Most East European countries possess excellent forest birding and there are fishpond complexes in many areas that are regularly visited by birders for their fine selection of wetland birds. European Russia is virtually unexplored ornithologically but holds enormous promise. Scandinavia, although expensive, has become popular with birders for its owls and woodpeckers, which are now usually located with the help of local ornithologists, and for the Arctic species to be seen at Varanger Fjord. Iceland hosts two ducks which occur elsewhere in the region only as rare vagrants, and holds some of the most impressive seabird colonies in the Atlantic. The British Isles are also famous for their seabird colonies and for rarity hotspots, where virtually any migrant bird, including North American and Siberian vagrants, can occur. It is assumed that most of the readers of this book will be British-based and some widespread species covered here occur only as rare migrants in Britain, including such birds as Red-breasted Flycatcher, Woodchat Shrike and Ortolan Bunting, which are fairly easy to find on the Continent but hold a special interest for British birders.

It is hoped that this book will provide much enjoyment to birders of all levels, as well as helping to plug a few gaps in their lists. The selection of sites included in the book is inevitably constrained by space limitations but readers are invited to submit corrections or omissions so that future editions can be improved. Please send your comments to the author, c/o Christopher Helm Publishers, 37 Soho Square, London, W1D 3QZ.

How to use this book

This book is divided into two main sections: Species accounts and Site accounts. Readers can look up a species they would like to see in the first section, and find information about its range, geographical variation (if any) and tips on how to look for it. This is followed by a listing of a selection of sites arranged by country or region.

Full details of the sites themselves are given in the second section, the Site accounts, which are arranged alphabetically by country/region. This section can also be used on its own as a simple site guide.

Species Accounts

Taxonomy broadly follows *The Birds of the Western Palearctic: Concise Edition* (1998), but with the addition of some recent splits. These include forms such as Canary Islands Chiffchaff, Atlas Flycatcher and African Blue Tit.

The sequence of species does not adopt the latest official recommendations, thus keeping it more in line with current field guides. English names of birds largely follow the *'British Birds' List of Birds of the Western Palearctic* (2004). In keeping with standard field guides, such as the *Collins Bird Guide* (1999), English names are kept as simple as possible, with prefixes omitted if there are no confusable species in the region (e.g. Capercaillie). However, alternative English names, and 'international' names with prefixes, are given in brackets in the main species accounts, e.g. Capercaillie (Western Capercaillie).

Symbols in the top line of each account cover the preferred habitats for each species and its status (resident, migrant etc). Habitat symbols in brackets indicate a habitat of secondary importance or irregular use. Status symbols in brackets indicate the status for part of

the population, or seasonal changes (e.g. altitudinal migrants).

The **Range** section provides distribution information, including when a species is present in the breeding range and the peak passage months for migrants. **Subspecies** details some of the races found in the Western Palearctic, but mainly those that are potential future splits. The **Tips** section gives fuller details of preferred habitats and how, where and when to search for each species. This is followed by the **Sites** section, which lists the best sites in each country or region. The star ratings offer a rough guide to the likelihood of seeing the species at each site and guide the reader to the better sites within each country. Of course few species can be 100% guaranteed at any site due to vagaries of timing, weather and viewing conditions, observer competence, etc. However, at a site marked with three stars there is roughly a 75% chance or more of seeing the species if visited at the appropriate season, two stars represent a 50-75% chance and one star a 25-50% chance. No star means a less than 25% chance, i.e. the species is far from guaranteed but is a distinct possibility, at least more so than at other sites. However, any species could conceivably turn up at any site, which is the very nature of birding and provides much of its appeal.

Site Accounts

Almost 550 sites are covered in the site section, which covers 64 countries and regions within the Western Palearctic.

Each country has a brief introduction, followed by an entry for each of the best sites. The number of sites per country varies widely as some, such as Spain and Turkey, hold many more of the selected species. Some areas, mainly islands and island groups, are dealt with separately from their mother countries, and most are small enough to be covered from a single base and so are not split into individual sites.

Brief details of habitats and some of the special birds to be seen at each site are provided, along with information as to when to visit and, where available, access details. The accounts are necessarily brief but many are covered in detail elsewhere in regional site guides, while for others information is currently rather limited. The sites have been chosen for the special birds they hold and, to a lesser extent, ease of access, although most can be visited either as part of an organised tour or independently.

Most countries in Europe, North Africa and the Middle East are covered but there are exceptions. The current conflict in Iraq will prevent birding there for some time to come, but when visits are possible it will be of immense interest to see which species, if any, survive in the formerly extensive marshes of the south. Libya is rarely visited and virtually no birding information is available. However, the recent improvement in the political situation between Libya and the rest of the world may lead to increased travel to this potentially interesting country. Mauritania, in the far south-west of the region, is currently rarely visited despite having one of the most important shorebird areas in the world, the Banc d'Arguin. Birding tours to this area are just starting to become available and it looks set to become one of the great destinations of the future, but independent travel is still difficult. In addition to shorebirds, Mauritania also hosts some sub-Saharan birds at the northern limits of their ranges that cannot be observed elsewhere in the Western Palearctic. The countries comprising the former Yugoslavia are included, albeit using possibly rather outdated information, as the current state of some sites is unknown.

As stated above, information on some sites and some countries, particularly in the east of the region, is currently very limited. It is hoped that this book will encourage visits to some of the more remote sites and thus improve our knowledge of their birds and how to see them.

Abbreviations

Habitats:

CF	Coniferous forest/woodland
MF	Mixed forest/woodland
DF	Deciduous forest/woodland
SH	Scrub, moorland and heathland
T	Tundra
D	Desert
SD	Semi-desert
M	Mountains and inland cliffs
FG	Farmland and grassland
FW	Freshwater wetlands, marshes, reedbeds, rivers, lakes, reservoirs, etc.
BW	Brackish water, lagoons, saltpans
Sea	Offshore/pelagic
C	Cliffs and rocky coasts
ES	Estuaries and shorelines
I	Small islands and islets
U	Urban areas

Status :

Res	Resident
Mig	Migrant
AMig	Altitudinal migrant
PMig	Partial migrant
Nom	Nomadic
Dis	Dispersive
Irr	Irruptive

Other abbreviations:

N	North
S	South
E	East
W	West
C	Central
NP	National Park
NR	Nature Reserve
Mt/Mts	Mount/Mountains
I/Is	Island/Islands
ad/ads	adult/adults
imm/imms	immature/immatures
juv/juvs	juvenile/juveniles

Star ratings for sites in the species accounts:

***	75% chance or more of seeing the species at the appropriate season
**	50-75% chance of seeing the species at the appropriate season
*	25-50% chance of seeing the species at the appropriate season
no star	less than 25% chance of seeing the species at the appropriate season

Black-throated Diver
Gavia arctica

Range: Breeds in NW Scotland and the Hebrides, over much of Scandinavia except extreme S Sweden, across Russia S to about 55°N, and patchily in the Baltic states and N Belarus. Winters from N Scandinavia to Biscay, and on inland lakes of C and E Europe, the N Mediterranean, Black and Caspian Seas. Departs breeding range in Sep–Oct, returning Apr–mid May.

Tips: Breeds on medium–large lakes with islands, larger than those used by Red-throated Diver. Listen for the wailing call at likely waters in summer, and often calls at night. Passage and winter birds occur on inshore seas and bays, and on large inland fresh waters.

Sites:

BELARUS Belovezhskaya Pushcha NP* (summer).

BULGARIA Albena-Golden Sands*** (passage, winter), Burgas area*** (passage, winter), Cape Emine*** (passage, winter), Cape Kaliakra*** (passage, winter), Lake Durankulak*** (passage, winter), Lake Shabla*** (passage, winter), Lake Srebarna*** (passage, winter), Ropotamo NP*** (passage, winter).

CORSICA Biguglia Lake* (winter).

CROATIA Cres*** (winter), Mljet*** (winter).

CZECH REPUBLIC Nové Mlýny** (passage, winter).

DENMARK Amager* (winter), Bornholm-Christiansø*** (passage, winter), Hanstholm** (passage, winter), Møn-Falster*** (passage, winter), Ringkøbing Fjord* (passage, winter), Rømø* (passage, winter), Skagen*** (passage, winter), Skallingen-Blåvandshuk*** (passage, winter), Stignæs** (passage, winter).

ESTONIA Matsalu Bay*** (passage), Nigula NR*** (summer).

FINLAND Åland Is*** (summer), Kolvanan Uuro*** (summer), Kuusamo*** (summer), Liminganlahti*** (summer), Linnansaari NP*** (summer), Maltio NR*** (summer), Oulanka NP*** (summer), Parikkala*** (summer), Patvinsuo NP*** (summer), Vesijako NP*** (summer), Viikki*** (passage).

FRANCE Baie de Vilaine* (passage, winter), Baie du Mont-St-Michel* (passage, winter), Cap Gris Nez*** (passage), Golfe du Morbihan** (winter), Lac du Der-Chantecoq* (winter), Leucate** (winter), Ouessant* (passage, winter), Somme Estuary* (passage, winter).

GREECE Axios-Aliakmonas Deltas* (winter), Evros Delta* (winter).

GREAT BRITAIN Anglesey** (passage, winter), Dungeness* (passage, winter), Flamborough Head*** (passage, winter), Islay*** (passage), Minsmere* (passage, winter), N Norfolk coast** (passage, winter), Orkney Is* (passage), Outer Hebrides*** (summer, passage), Portland*** (winter), Rhum** (passage), St Ives Bay*** (passage, winter), Spurn Peninsula* (passage, winter).

GREEK IS Lesvos* (winter).

HUNGARY Danube Bend** (passage, winter), Kis-balaton* (passage, winter), Lake Fertö* (passage, winter), Lake Velence* (passage, winter).

IRELAND Belfast Lough* (passage, winter), Strangford Lough* (winter), Tacumshin Lake* (spring).

ISRAEL Eilat (winter).

ITALY Circeo NP** (winter), Gargano Peninsula*** (winter), Maremma Regional

Park*** (winter), Monte Conero*** (passage, winter), Orbetello Reserve*** (winter).
LATVIA Cape Kolka*** (passage, winter), Lake Pape*** (passage, winter).
LITHUANIA Kirsiu Peninsula*** (passage, winter).
NORWAY Hardangervidda NP*** (summer), Lista*** (passage), Lofoten Is*** (passage), Øvre Pasvik NP*** (summer), Slettnes*** (summer, passage), Stabbursdalen NP*** (summer), Utsira*** (passage), Varanger** (summer).
POLAND Gdańsk Bay*** (passage, winter), Siemianówka Reservoir** (passage), Szczecin Bay area** (passage).
ROMANIA Bicaz* (passage), Danube Delta** (winter), Dobrudja** (passage, winter).
RUSSIA Kola Peninsula*** (summer).
SLOVAKIA Orava Reservoir*** (passage), Senné Fishponds*** (passage), Zemplínská Reservoir** (passage, winter).

SPAIN Aiguamolls de l'Empordá* (winter), Ebro Delta* (winter), Llobregat Delta* (winter).
SWEDEN Abisko NP*** (summer), Falsterbo*** (passage), Färnebofjärden*** (summer), Getterön*** (passage, winter), Gotland*** (passage, winter), Holmöarna*** (summer, passage), Kristianstad*** (passage, winter), Lake Ånnsjön*** (summer), Muddus NP*** (summer), Öland*** (passage, winter), Padjelanta NP*** (summer), Ripakaisenvuoma*** (summer), Sarek NP*** (summer), Stockholm archipelago*** (summer), Store Mosse NP*** (summer), Tarnasjön*** (summer), Tyresta NP*** (summer).
SWITZERLAND Fanel NR* (passage), Grangettes** (passage, winter).
TURKEY İstanbul*** (winter), Kızılırmak Delta*** (winter).
UKRAINE Dunay Delta* (winter), Syvash Bay*** (winter).

Great Northern Diver
Gavia immer

FW ES Sea Mig

Range: Breeds regularly only in Iceland, and occurs rarely in summer on Bear I, Jan Mayen and the Faroes. Regular in small numbers off Shetland and elsewhere in N Scotland but breeding is rare. Departs breeding grounds in Sep–Oct to winter around Iceland, in the North Sea from N Norway to the Channel, and in small numbers in the Bay of Biscay. Leaves wintering areas from Apr and returns to breeding lakes in May–Jun.

Tips: Breeds on medium–large lakes in tundra, often with islands, listen for the characteristic call at likely waters, and calls day and night. Winters on sheltered seas but often some distance offshore. Sometimes seen on large fresh waters on passage or after severe weather.

Sites:
DENMARK Hanstholm* (passage), Rømø* (passage, winter), Skagen** (passage, winter), Skallingen-Blåvandshuk*** (passage, winter).
FAROE IS* (passage, winter).
FRANCE Cap Gris Nez*** (passage), Golfe du Morbihan* (winter), Lac du Der-Chantecoq* (winter), Ouessant* (passage, winter), Somme Estuary* (passage, winter).
GREAT BRITAIN Anglesey*** (passage, winter), Dungeness* (winter), Flamborough Head*** (passage, winter), Islay*** (passage), Minsmere* (passage, winter), N Norfolk coast**

(passage, winter), Orkney Is*** (passage, winter), Outer Hebrides*** (passage, winter, sometimes summer), Pembrokeshire Is*** (passage), Portland*** (passage, winter), Rhum** (passage, winter), St Ives Bay*** (passage, winter), Scilly*** (winter), Shetland Is*** (passage, winter), Spurn Peninsula*** (passage, winter).
ICELAND Lake Mývatn*** (summer), Breiðafjörður***, Northwest Peninsula***, Olfusar Delta*** (passage, winter), Skagafjörður*** (summer), Thingvellir NP***, Westmann Is*** (winter).

IRELAND Belfast Lough*** (passage, winter), Cape Clear Is*** (passage, winter), Galley Head*** (passage, winter), Kinsale*** (passage, winter), Mullet Peninsula*** (passage, winter), North Bull*** (winter), North Slob*** (passage, winter), Strangford Lough*** (passage, winter), Tacumshin Lake** (passage, winter).
NORWAY Lista*** (passage), Lofoten Is* (winter), Slettnes** (passage), Utsira** (winter).
SPAIN Ebro Delta (winter).
SWEDEN Getterön* (winter), Holmöarna (passage), Öland* (passage).

Yellow-billed Diver (White-billed Diver)
Gavia adamsii   FW ES Sea Mig

Range: In our region breeding recorded only on Novaya Zemlya, and possibly on the Kola Peninsula, Ostrov Kolguyev and Ostrov Vaygach. Often present in summer in the Varanger area of Norway and may have bred. North Sea wintering population probably numbers *c.*200 birds and winters from the Kola Peninsula to S Norway (Oct–May). Very small numbers are regular in N Scotland (Apr–May), particularly off Shetland, rarely off the E coast of England (Jan–Mar). May also winter in the Bay of Biscay as passage birds have occasionally been recorded off seawatching points in the English Channel. Present in wintering areas Oct–May, bulk passage at Scandinavian migration watchpoints late Apr–early Jun (particularly May) and Sep–Dec.
Tips: Breeds on tundra lakes (avoiding forest areas) and feeds at sea. Coastal on passage and in winter, found on inshore seas, bays and estuaries.

Sites:
DENMARK Skagen* (passage), Skallingen-Blåvandshuk* (passage, winter).
FINLAND Viikki* (passage)
GREAT BRITAIN Flamborough Head (passage, winter), Orkney Is (passage), Shetland Is* (passage, winter).
NORWAY Lista (passage), Lofoten Is*** (passage, winter), Slettnes*** (passage),

Varanger*** (mainly winter but also in summer).
RUSSIA Kola Peninsula*** (mainly winter).
SWEDEN Getterön** (passage, winter), Gotland* (passage, winter), Holmöarna** (passage), Öland** (passage, winter).

Red-necked Grebe
Podiceps grisegena FW Sea ES Mig

Range: Main range is from Denmark and S Sweden E to Russia and the Caspian and S to the Black Sea. Also breeds throughout much of S Finland and at scattered sites in SE Europe and Turkey. Has bred or attempted to breed in Britain, France and the Netherlands. Winters from the British Isles and S Scandinavia to Biscay, also on some C European lakes and in the N Adriatic. Present on wintering grounds Oct–Mar.

Tips: Breeds on small–medium, well-vegetated fresh waters, shy and often difficult to see well but can be very vocal in spring. On passage and in winter mainly on estuaries and sheltered seas but regular in small numbers on large inland waters, and reservoirs and gravel pits are worth checking.

Sites:

ARMENIA Armash Fishponds*** (winter).
BELARUS Belovezhskaya Pushcha NP*** (summer), Berezinsky Reserve*** (summer), Pripyatsky NP*** (summer).
BULGARIA Albena-Golden Sands*** (passage), Burgas area** (passage), Cape Emine*** (passage), Cape Kaliakra** (passage), Lake Durankulak*** (summer, passage), Lake Shabla*** (summer, passage), Lake Srebarna*** (summer, passage).
CZECH REPUBLIC Nové Mlýny** (passage), Poodří*** (summer).
DENMARK Amager** (summer, passage), Hanstholm** (passage), Møn-Falster*** (passage), Ringkøbing Fjord*** (summer), Rømø*** (summer, passage), Skagen***, Skallingen-Blåvandshuk*** (passage), Stignæs** (summer, passage).
FINLAND Åland Is*** (passage), Kuusamo*** (summer), Liminganlahti*** (summer), Parikkala*** (summer), Viikki*** (passage).
FRANCE Baie de Vilaine** (winter), Baie du Mont-St-Michel* (passage, winter), Cap Gris Nez** (passage), Fôret d'Orient*** (passage), Lac du Der-Chantecoq** (passage, winter), Ouessant* (passage), Somme Estuary** (passage, winter), Teich Reservoir** (winter).

GERMANY Berchtesgaden NP* (winter), Kuhkopf*** (summer), Mecklenburg Lakes*** (summer), Rügen*** (summer).
GREAT BRITAIN Anglesey** (passage, winter), Dungeness** (winter), Flamborough Head** (passage, winter), Minsmere** (passage, winter), N Norfolk coast** (passage, winter), Portland*** (passage, winter), St Ives Bay* (winter), Shetland Is* (passage, winter), Spurn Peninsula** (passage, winter).
GREECE Amvrakiko's Gulf*** (passage), Lake Kerkini* (passage), Mikrí Prespa NP*, Porto Lagos area** (summer, passage).
GREEK IS Lesvos* (winter).
HUNGARY Biharugra* (summer), Hortobágy NP*** (summer), Kis-balaton* (summer), Lake Fertö*** (summer), Lake Velence** (summer).
IRELAND Strangford Lough* (winter).
ITALY Circeo NP* (passage), Gargano Peninsula*** (passage, winter), Orbetello Reserve** (winter), Po Delta** (passage, winter).
LATVIA Cape Kolka*** (passage, winter), Lake Engure*** (summer), Lake Lubana*** (summer), Lake Pape*** (passage).
LITHUANIA Kirsiu Peninsula*** (passage, winter).
MACEDONIA Lakes Ohrid and Prespa** (passage).

NETHERLANDS Lauwersmeer*** (winter), Oostvaadersplassen*** (winter), Terschelling*** (winter), Texel*** (winter).
NORWAY Lista*** (passage), Slettnes** (passage), Varanger* (passage).
POLAND Białystok Fishponds*** (summer), Biebrza Marshes*** (summer), Gdańsk Bay*** (summer, passage), Milicz Fishponds*** (summer), Siemianówka Reservoir*** (summer), Słońsk*** (summer), Szczecin Bay area** (passage).
ROMANIA Danube Delta*** (summer), Dobrudja*** (summer, passage).
RUSSIA Kalmykia** (summer), Kola Peninsula*** (summer), Volga Delta*** (summer).

SLOVAKIA Orava Reservoir**, Senné Fishponds*** (summer, passage), Zemplínská Reservoir** (passage).
SWEDEN Falsterbo*** (passage, winter), Gammelstadsviken*** (summer), Gotland*** (passage), Hornborgasjön*** (summer), Kristianstad** (summer, passage), Kvismaren*** (summer), Lake Krankesjön*** (summer), Öland*** (passage), Store Mosse NP*** (summer), Tåkern*** (summer).
SWITZERLAND Grangettes** (passage, winter).
TURKEY Dalyan* (summer, passage), Sultan Marshes*** (summer, passage), Van Gölü** (summer, passage).
UKRAINE Dunay Delta** (summer).
YUGOSLAVIA Obedska bara (summer).

Slavonian Grebe (Horned Grebe)
Podiceps auritus   FW Sea ES Mig

Range: Very patchily distributed, with main breeding range from C and S Sweden, S Finland and the Baltic states E across Russia. Also breeds in Iceland (rarely the Faroes), C and NW Scotland (mainly at Loch Ruthven Royal Society for the Protection of Birds Reserve), and coastal Norway, with sporadic nesting in Germany, Poland, Belarus, Ukraine and Moldova. Winters off SW Iceland, the British Isles and from Norway to Brittany, also in the N Adriatic and Black Seas. Generally present in breeding areas May–Oct.
Tips: In summer occurs on well-vegetated freshwaters, is colonial and often breeds in association with Black-headed Gulls. Also breeds on more open waters, e.g. in Iceland, and on brackish waters in the Baltic. In winter on reservoirs, estuaries and sheltered seas.

Sites:
BELARUS Belovezhskaya Pushcha NP** (passage), Pripyatsky NP*** (summer).
BULGARIA Burgas area** (passage, winter), Cape Emine* (passage), Cape Kaliakra* (passage), Lake Durankulak* (passage).
DENMARK Bornholm-Christiansø*** (passage, winter), Hanstholm** (passage), Møn-Falster*** (passage), Ringkøbing Fjord** (passage), Rømø*** (passage), Skagen*** (passage), Skallingen-Blåvandshuk*** (passage).

FINLAND Åland Is*** (summer), Liminganlahti*** (summer), Parikkala*** (summer), Viikki*** (passage).
FRANCE Camargue** (winter), Cap Gris Nez*** (passage), Fôret d'Orient** (passage), Golfe du Morbihan** (passage, winter), Lac du Der-Chantecoq*** (passage, winter), Leucate*** (winter), Ouessant* (passage), Somme Estuary* (passage).

GREAT BRITAIN Anglesey*** (passage, winter), Dungeness** (winter), Flamborough Head*** (passage, winter), Islay* (winter), Minsmere** (passage, winter), N Norfolk coast*** (passage, winter), Orkney Is* (winter), Portland*** (passage, winter), St Ives Bay* (passage, winter), Shetland Is* (passage, winter).

HUNGARY Danube Bend** (passage, winter), Hortobágy NP** (passage, winter).

ICELAND Breiðafjörður*** (summer), Lake Mývatn*** (summer), Northwest Peninsula*** (summer), Olfusar Delta*** (passage), Skagafjörður*** (summer).

IRELAND Belfast Lough* (winter), North Bull* (passage, winter), North Slob** (passage, winter), Strangford Lough** (winter).

ITALY Circeo NP** (winter), Gargano Peninsula* (passage, winter), Monte Conero*** (passage, winter), Orbetello Reserve** (winter), Po Delta** (passage, winter).

LATVIA Lake Engure*** (summer), Lake Lubana*** (summer), Lake Pape*** (passage),

LITHUANIA Kirsiu Peninsula*** (passage).

NETHERLANDS Lauwersmeer*** (winter), Oostvaadersplassen*** (winter), Terschelling*** (winter), Texel*** (winter).

NORWAY Lista** (passage), Lofoten Is* (summer), Slettnes* (passage).

POLAND Białystok Fishponds*** (summer).

ROMANIA Bicaz** (winter).

SLOVAKIA Zemplínská Reservoir* (passage, winter).

SWEDEN Abisko NP*** (summer), Falsterbo*** (summer, passage), Gammelstadsviken*** (summer), Getterön*** (passage), Gotland*** (summer, passage), Hjälstaviken*** (summer), Hornborgasjön*** (summer), Kristianstad** (passage), Kvismaren*** (summer), Muddus NP*** (summer), Öland*** (summer, passage), Store Mosse NP*** (summer), Tåkern*** (summer).

SWITZERLAND Grangettes** (passage, winter).

UKRAINE Syvash Bay*** (passage, winter).

Black-necked Grebe
Podiceps nigricollis

FW Sea ES Mig

Range: Main breeding range is from Denmark and Germany E to C and S Russia and S to the Black Sea. Also breeds at widely scattered localities in many European countries including Spain, France, Great Britain and the Netherlands, also Turkey and has bred on Cyprus. Formerly bred in N Africa but probably now only a winter visitor. Present on breeding lakes Apr–Oct but in southern parts of range may remain all year. Winters from the southern North Sea to NW Africa, in the Mediterranean, Black and Caspian Seas, and on many C European lakes.

Tips: Breeds on densely vegetated fresh waters, often in association with gulls or terns, but colonies often abandon established sites for no apparent reason. Winters on reservoirs, estuaries and sheltered seas. More often seen on fresh waters than Slavonian Grebe, which generally prefers saltwater.

Sites:
ALBANIA Lake Shkodra*** (winter).   **ALGERIA** El Kala NP* (winter).

ARMENIA Armash Fishponds***.

AUSTRIA Lake Neusiedl*** (summer).

AZERBAIJAN Kyzylagach Bay*** (winter).

BALEARIC IS Formentera*** (mainly winter), Mallorca** (passage, winter), Menorca** (passage, winter).

BELARUS Belovezhskaya Pushcha NP** (passage), Pripyatsky NP*** (summer).

BELGIUM Kalmthoutse Heide* (summer).

BULGARIA Albena-Golden Sands*** (passage), Burgas area*** (winter), Cape Emine*** (passage), Cape Kaliakra*** (passage), Lake Durankulak*** (summer, passage), Lake Shabla*** (summer, passage), Lake Srebarna*** (summer, passage), Strandja Mts*** (passage).

CANARY IS ** (winter).

CORSICA Biguglia Lake*** (winter).

CYPRUS * (winter).

CZECH REPUBLIC Nové Mlýny*** (passage), Poodří*** (summer), Třeboňsko*** (summer).

DENMARK Amager*** (summer, passage), Møn-Falster*** (passage), Ringkøbing Fjord** (passage), Rømø** (passage), Skagen***, Skallingen-Blåvandshuk*** (passage).

EGYPT Abu Simbel*** (passage, winter), Aswan*** (passage, winter), Faiyum* (winter), Luxor*** (passage, winter), Nile Delta*** (winter), Sharm el Sheikh*** (winter), Zaranik*** (winter).

FRANCE Camargue*** (winter), Cap Gris Nez*** (passage), Dombes*** (summer), Fôret d'Orient** (passage), Golfe du Morbihan*** (passage, winter), La Brenne***, Lac du Der-Chantecoq*** (passage, winter), Leucate*** (winter), Lorraine NP***, Sologne***, Somme Estuary* (passage), Teich Reservoir*** (winter).

GEORGIA Kolkheti*** (passage, winter).

GERMANY Federsee*** (summer), Oder Valley*** (summer), Tiroler Achen*** (summer).

GREAT BRITAIN Anglesey*** (passage, winter), Dungeness** (passage, winter), Minsmere* (passage, winter), N Norfolk coast** (passage, winter), Portland*** (passage, winter), St Ives Bay* (passage, winter).

GREECE Amvrakiko's Gulf*** (passage, winter), Axios-Aliakmonas Deltas** (winter), Lake Kerkini**, Mikrí Prespa NP***, Porto Lagos area***.

GREEK IS Corfu*** (passage, winter), Crete*** (passage, winter), Kos*** (winter), Lesvos*** (winter).

HUNGARY Biharugra*** (summer), Hortobágy NP*** (summer), Kis-balaton*** (summer), Lake Fertö*** (summer), Lake Velence** (summer), Tihany** (winter).

IRELAND North Bull* (passage).

ISRAEL Arava Valley* (winter), Bet Shean Valley*** (winter), Eilat*** (winter), Hula Reserve*** (passage, winter), Jezreel Valley*** (winter), Ma'agan Mikhael*** (passage, winter).

ITALY Circeo NP** (winter), Gargano Peninsula*** (passage, winter), Monte Conero*** (passage, winter), Orbetello Reserve*** (winter), Po Delta***.

JORDAN Aqaba* (winter), Azraq** (passage, winter), Ghadir Burqu' (passage).

LATVIA Lake Engure*** (summer), Lake Lubana*** (summer).

LEBANON Aamiq Marshes*** (passage, winter), Qaraoun Lake*** (winter).

LITHUANIA Kirsiu Peninsula*** (passage).

MACEDONIA Lakes Ohrid and Prespa*** (winter).

MALTA * (passage).

NETHERLANDS Lauwersmeer*** (winter), Oostvaadersplassen*** (winter), Terschelling*** (winter), Texel*** (winter), Zwanenwater** (passage).

POLAND Białystok Fishponds*** (summer), Gdańsk Bay*** (summer, passage), Milicz Fishponds*** (summer), Siemianówka Reservoir*** (summer), Słońsk*** (summer), Szczecin Bay area*** (summer, passage).

PORTUGAL Castro Marim*** (passage, winter), Ria Formosa*** (passage, winter), Sado Estuary*** (winter), Santo Andre Lagoon*** (winter), Tagus Estuary*** (winter).

ROMANIA Danube Delta*** (summer), Dobrudja*** (summer, passage), Lake Călăraşi*** (summer), Satchinez*** (summer).

RUSSIA Kalmykia*** (summer), Volga Delta*** (summer).

SARDINIA Cagliari wetlands*** (winter), Oristano wetlands*** (passage, winter).
SICILY Vendicari*** (passage, winter).
SLOVAKIA Senné Fishponds*** (summer, passage), Záhorie*** (summer), Zemplínská Reservoir* (summer, passage).
SPAIN Cabo de Gata*** (winter), Cádiz Lagoons***, Coto Doñana***, Ebro Delta***, Guadalhorce Estuary***, La Serena*** (winter), Santa Pola*** (passage, winter), Tablas de Daimiel***.
SWEDEN Hornborgasjön** (summer), Kristianstad* (summer), Kvismaren* (summer), Lake Krankesjön*** (summer), Tåkern** (summer).

SWITZERLAND Fanel NR***, Grangettes*** (passage, winter), Klingnau Reservoir*** (winter).
SYRIA Baath Lakes** (passage, winter), Bahrat Homs*** (passage, winter), Dayr al-Zawr*** (passage), Lake Assad*** (passage, winter), Sabkhat al-Jubbal*** (passage, winter).
TUNISIA Cap Bon Peninsula*** (passage, winter), Lake Ichkeul*** (winter), Tunis*** (passage, winter).
TURKEY Bafa Gölü***, Göksu Delta***, Kulu Gölü***, Sultan Marshes***, Uluabat Gölü***, Van Gölü*** (passage).
UKRAINE Dunay Delta** (summer), Syvash Bay*** (passage).
YUGOSLAVIA Lake Skadar*** (winter), Obedska bara (summer).

Zino's Petrel (Madeiran Petrel or Freira)
Pterodroma madeira   I M Sea Mig

Range: Breeds only in the mountains of Madeira, in the Curral das Freiras. Population is probably fewer than 45 pairs.
Tips: Nests in small colonies in burrows on inland cliffs, to 1,600m in C Madeiran mountains and present mid Mar–early Apr until Sep–early Oct; easiest to locate in May–Jun, otherwise at sea. Comes to land under cover of darkness and by day usually more than 3km from land. Sometimes seen between Madeira and Porto Santo in Apr–Oct, especially Oct, but not recorded outside Madeiran waters. The breeding grounds can only be visited with an official guide when can be heard and brief moonlight flight views are possible.

Site:
MADEIRA**.

Fea's Petrel (Cape Verde Petrel or Gon-gon)
Pterodroma feae   I Sea Mig

Range: Breeds on Bugio, the most southerly of the Desertas, with larger numbers on São Tiago, Fogo, Santo Antão and São Nicolau in the Cape Verde Is. Has been trapped in the Azores and may breed but status there unclear.

Subspecies: Nominate race is found in the Cape Verde Is and *deserta* in the Desertas.

Tips: Present on Bugio late May–Feb and nests in burrows, mainly at the S end of this arid windswept island. A winter breeder on Cape Verde Is, *c.*1,000 pairs are present Sep–May, nesting on high cliffs. Outside the breeding season found at sea around nesting islands, and often seen during inter-island boat-trips, associates with Cape Verde Shearwater and sometimes follows ships. Recorded between Madeira and Porto Santo and Madeira and the Desertas and from Ponta das Gaviotas, the E tip of Madeira. Annually recorded in small numbers off the SW British Isles, often with Cory's Shearwaters, and probably regular in the Azores and Canaries.

Sites:
AZORES*.
CANARY IS Gomera* (summer, autumn),
Tenerife*.
CAPE VERDE IS**.

GREAT BRITAIN Scilly (autumn).
IRELAND Cape Clear Is (autumn), Galley Head (autumn), Kinsale (autumn).
MADEIRA*.

Bulwer's Petrel
Bulweria bulwerii   I Sea Mig

Range: Breeds on Porto Santo, the Desertas and Selvagems, and the Canaries off Lanzarote, in the Azores on Santa Maria, Graciosa and perhaps São Jorge, and in the Cape Verde Is on Cima and Raso. Migrants have been recorded in the Atlantic off NW Africa and it winters in the tropical Atlantic.

Tips: Nests in rocky crevices on islands and is nocturnal at colonies. Most are present in breeding range Apr–Sep but has been recorded in the Cape Verde Is in Jan. Most easily seen from the Tenerife–Gomera ferry, in the Canaries, in May–Sep, and regular between Madeira and Porto Santo (common in summer from Jun onwards), and Madeira and the Azores. Usually seen singly, flying low over the sea in fast, circling flight with short glides interspersed with a few quick wingbeats. Does not normally follow ships.

Sites:

AZORES*** (summer, autumn).
CANARY IS El Hierro*** (summer), Fuerteventura*** (summer), Gomera*** (summer), La Palma** (summer), Lanzarote*** (summer), Tenerife*** (summer).

CAPE VERDE IS**.
MADEIRA*** (summer).
MOROCCO Agadir and the Sous Plain (passage), Oued Massa (passage).

Cory's Shearwater
Calonectris diomedea   I Sea Mig

Range: Breeds on the Azores, Madeira and Porto Santo, the Selvagems, Desertas and Canaries, and on many islands in the Mediterranean from the Balearics to the Aegean. Winters in the Atlantic from the SW British Isles southwards and throughout the Mediterranean, regular in the North Sea and N Red Sea. Sometimes enters the Black Sea in small numbers in autumn.

Subspecies: Nominate race, Scopoli's Shearwater, breeds in the Mediterranean, *borealis* in the Atlantic (although it has been recorded at Scopoli's colonies in the Mediterranean). These races may be treated as full species in the future.

Tips: Breeds mainly on islands, in burrows and rock crevices, generally nocturnal at colonies where present Feb–Oct. Common in most of range, often seen from inter-island ferries; although it gathers around fishing boats, it rarely follows ships. In good years hundreds can be seen from an autumn Biscay ferry trip.

Sites:

AZORES***.
BALEARIC IS Formentera***, Ibiza***, Mallorca***, Menorca***.
BAY OF BISCAY*** (autumn).
BULGARIA Cape Emine* (autumn).
CANARY IS El Hierro*** (summer), Fuerteventura*** (summer), Gomera*** (summer), Gran Canaria*** (summer), La Palma*** (summer), Lanzarote*** (summer), Tenerife*** (summer).
CORSICA Bonifacio***, Cap Corse***, Scandola***.
CROATIA Cres*** (summer), Mljet*** (summer).
EGYPT Zaranik* (passage).
FRANCE Camargue***, Ouessant** (autumn).
GIBRALTAR*** (passage).

GREAT BRITAIN Flamborough Head* (autumn), N Norfolk coast (autumn), St Ives Bay*** (autumn), Scilly** (autumn).
GREECE Porto Lagos area*** (summer, passage).
GREEK IS Corfu***, Crete***, Kos*** (summer, passage), Lesvos** (summer, passage), Náxos*** (summer, passage), Rhodes*** (summer, passage).
IRELAND Cape Clear Is*** (autumn), Galley Head***, (autumn), Kinsale** (autumn).
ISRAEL Eilat** (summer, passage), Tel Shiqmona*** (autumn).
ITALY Circeo NP*** (summer), Gargano Peninsula*** (summer), Tuscan archipelago*** (summer, passage).
JORDAN Aqaba** (summer, passage).

LEBANON Palm Is*** (passage, winter).
MADEIRA*.
MALTA* (summer, passage).
MOROCCO Agadir and the Sous Plain** (passage), Oualidia** (passage), Oued Massa* (passage).
PORTUGAL Berlenga Is*** (summer, passage), Cape St Vincent*** (autumn), Castro Marim*** (passage).
SARDINIA San Pietro I*** (summer, passage).

SICILY Pelagie Is*** (summer, passage), Strait of Messina*** (spring).
SPAIN Aiguamolls de l'Empordá*** (passage), Cabo de Gata*** (summer, passage), Coto Doñana*** (summer, passage), Ebro Delta***, Guadalhorce Estuary*** (passage), Llobregat Delta** (passage), Santa Pola*** (passage).
TUNISIA Cap Bon Peninsula*** (passage).
TURKEY Göksu Delta** (summer, passage), İstanbul* (passage).

Cape Verde Shearwater
Calonectris edwardsii   I Sea Mig

Range: Formerly considered a race of Cory's Shearwater. Endemic to the Cape Verde Is, breeding on São Tiago, Brava, Santo Antão, Branco, Raso and São Nicolau, and possibly on Sal and Boa Vista. Winters further S in the Atlantic and is principally present in Cape Verdean waters late Feb–Nov. Recently reported off eastern North America so vagrancy is clearly a possibility.
Tips: Breeds in rock crevices on sea- and inland cliffs, on offshore stacks and islets. Nocturnal at colonies where present early Mar–early Nov. At sea sometimes follows ships.

Sites:
CAPE VERDE IS*.   **MOROCCO** Oued Massa* (passage).

Great Shearwater
Puffinus gravis   Sea Mig

Range: Breeds in the S Atlantic then moves N, some as far as Iceland, before moving E then S through W European seas.
Tips: Peak numbers reach European waters in late Jul–Oct and most occur off the W British Isles in early Aug–late Sep (the Cork–Swansea ferry can be partic-ularly good), also in Biscay and off the Atlantic coast of Iberia. Small numbers regularly reach the North Sea. Often seen far from shore and much scarcer than Sooty Shearwater at coastal watch-points. Sometimes follows ships and hundreds can be seen from the Biscay ferries in late Aug–early Sep.

Sites:

AZORES* (autumn).
BAY OF BISCAY* (autumn).
CANARY IS Gomera* (autumn), Tenerife* (autumn).
CAPE VERDE IS* (autumn).
FRANCE Ouessant* (autumn).
GREAT BRITAIN Flamborough Head* (autumn), St Ives Bay* (autumn), Scilly*** (autumn).

IRELAND Cape Clear Is*** (autumn), Galley Head*** (autumn), Kinsale* (autumn), Mullet Peninsula** (autumn).
MADEIRA* (passage).
MOROCCO Agadir and the Sous Plain* (autumn).
PORTUGAL Cape St Vincent* (autumn).

Sooty Shearwater
Puffinus griseus   Sea Mig

Range: Migrates to Western Palearctic waters from breeding islands in the southern hemisphere, and occurs off W European coasts with small numbers regular in the North Sea and English Channel, and even off the Mediterranean coast of Israel.

Tips: Departs breeding range in Mar–May and undertakes a huge loop migration reaching as far as Iceland. On return passes W Europe in Aug–Sep, often close inshore and follows fishing vessels. The Biscay ferries can be guaranteed to produce this species, although it is regularly seen by seawatchers from many headlands in the W of the region.

Sites:

AZORES (autumn).
BAY OF BISCAY* (autumn).
CANARY IS Gomera* (autumn), Tenerife* (autumn).
CAPE VERDE IS* (autumn).
FRANCE Cap Gris Nez* (passage), Ouessant* (autumn).
GREAT BRITAIN Anglesey* (autumn), Dungeness* (autumn), Flamborough Head** (autumn), Islay** (autumn), N Norfolk coast* (autumn), Orkney Is* (autumn), Outer Hebrides** (autumn), Pembrokeshire Is* (autumn), Portland* (autumn), Rhum*

(autumn), St Ives Bay*** (autumn), Scilly** (autumn), Shetland Is* (autumn), Spurn Peninsula* (autumn).
ICELAND Reykjanes Peninsula* (autumn).
IRELAND Cape Clear Is*** (autumn), Galley Head*** (autumn), Kinsale** (autumn), Mullet Peninsula*** (autumn), Rathlin Is* (autumn).
ISRAEL Eilat** (summer).
JORDAN Aqaba (summer).
MOROCCO Agadir and the Sous Plain* (autumn), Oualidia* (autumn).
NORWAY Utsira (passage). Getterön* (passage).

Manx Shearwater
Puffinus puffinus   I Sea Mig

Range: Breeds on the Westmann Is off Iceland, the Faroes and the N and W British Isles, on the Channel Is and off Brittany, the Azores and Madeira and in the Canaries. Winters at sea off S America.

Tips: Nests colonially, in burrows on grassy slopes of islands and visits burrows after dark. Adults present at colonies Feb–Aug, young until Sep. Passage birds are seen off many western headlands but also in the North Sea and English Channel. Sightings are usually recorded from the Biscay ferries in autumn. Does not normally follow ships but is sometimes attracted to trawlers.

Sites:

AZORES** (summer, autumn).
BAY OF BISCAY*** (autumn).
CANARY IS La Palma* (summer, passage), Tenerife* (summer, passage).
CAPE VERDE IS* (passage).
DENMARK Hanstholm** (passage), Skallingen-Blåvandshuk** (autumn).
FAROE IS*** (summer).
FRANCE Cap Gris Nez*** (passage), Ouessant*** (summer, passage), Sept Îles*** (summer).
GREAT BRITAIN Anglesey*** (summer, passage), Dungeness** (passage), Flamborough Head*** (passage), Islay*** (passage), N Norfolk coast** (passage), Orkney Is*** (summer, passage), Outer Hebrides*** (autumn), Pembrokeshire Is*** (summer), Portland** (summer, passage), Rhum*** (summer), St Ives Bay*** (passage), Scilly*** (summer, autumn), Shetland Is*** (summer, autumn), Spurn Peninsula** (passage).
ICELAND Reykjanes Peninsula*** (summer), Westmann Is*** (summer).
IRELAND Cape Clear Is*** (passage), Galley Head*** (passage), Ireland's Eye*** (summer, passage), Kinsale*** (summer, passage), Mullet Peninsula*** (passage), Rathlin Is*** (summer, passage), Saltee Is*** (summer, passage), Strangford Lough** (passage).
MADEIRA* (summer).
MOROCCO Agadir and the Sous Plain*** (passage).
NORWAY Mølen** (passage), Utsira*** (passage).
SWEDEN Getterön** (passage).

Yelkouan Shearwater (Levantine Shearwater)
Puffinus yelkouan   I Sea Dis

Range: Breeds widely in the Mediterranean, on islets from S France and Sardinia E to the Aegean, and probably in the Bosphorus–Dardanelles area. Recently discovered to breed alongside Balearic Shearwater on Menorca. Post-breeding occurs throughout the Mediterranean and Black Seas. Occurs off NE Spain in some numbers and regularly reaches Gibraltar, but only recently recorded in the Atlantic off Spain, and may occasionally wander N to Britain. Formerly considered to be race of Manx Shearwater.

Tips: Colonial breeder in burrows on steep hillsides, otherwise at sea. Occurs in mixed flocks with Balearic Shearwater off NE Spain.

Sites:

BALEARIC IS Mallorca* (winter), Menorca* (summer, winter).
BULGARIA Albena-Golden Sands*** (passage), Cape Emine*** (passage), Cape Kaliakra*** (passage), Lake Durankulak*** (passage), Lake Shabla*** (passage), Ropotamo NP*** (passage).
CORSICA Bonifacio***, Cap Corse***, Scandola***.
CROATIA Cres*** (summer, passage), Mljet*** (summer, passage).
CYPRUS** (passage, winter).
EGYPT Zaranik** (passage).
FRANCE Camargue* (winter).
GREECE Nestos Delta*** (autumn, winter), Porto Lagos area*** (summer, passage).
GREEK IS Corfu***, Crete*** (summer, passage), Kos*** (summer, passage),

Lesvos*** (summer, passage), Náxos*** (summer, passage), Rhodes*** (summer, passage).
ISRAEL Ma'agan Mikhael***, Tel Shiqmona*** (summer, passage).
ITALY Gargano Peninsula*** (summer), Tuscan archipelago*** (summer, passage).
LEBANON Palm Is*** (passage).
MALTA** (summer, passage).
ROMANIA Dobrudja** (passage, winter).
SARDINIA San Pietro I*** (summer, passage).
SICILY Strait of Messina*** (spring).
SPAIN Aiguamolls de l'Empordá* (passage, winter), Llobregat Delta* (passage, winter).
TUNISIA Cap Bon Peninsula***.
TURKEY Göksu Delta** (summer, passage), İstanbul*** (passage), Kızılırmak Delta*** (passage, winter).

Balearic Shearwater
Puffinus mauretanicus   I Sea Mig

Range: Breeds in the Balearics and disperses into the W Mediterranean, particularly off Catalonia and Valencia, and into the adjacent Atlantic, mainly from Biscay to Morocco, with smaller numbers reaching Ireland and the English Channel. Stragglers regularly reach the North Sea. Peak passage at Gibraltar occurs in mid Jun. Treated as a race of Yelkouan Shearwater by some authorities and formerly included in Manx Shearwater.

Tips: Breeds colonially in burrows on steep hillsides, otherwise at sea. Possible from the Biscay ferries in late Aug–early Sep.

Sites:

BALEARIC IS Formentera***, Ibiza***, Mallorca***, Menorca***.
BAY OF BISCAY** (autumn).

CANARY IS Gomera* (autumn), Tenerife* (autumn).
FRANCE Baie de Vilaine** (autumn), Baie du

Mont-St-Michel* (summer, autumn), Camargue**, Cap Gris Nez** (passage), Île d'Oléron*** (autumn), Leucate**, Ouessant*** (summer, autumn).
GREAT BRITAIN Anglesey* (autumn), Dungeness* (autumn), Flamborough Head* (autumn), Pembrokeshire Is* (autumn), Portland* (summer, passage), St Ives Bay*** (passage), Scilly** (autumn).
GIBRALTAR** (passage).
IRELAND Cape Clear Is*** (autumn), Galley Head** (autumn), Kinsale* (autumn).

MOROCCO Agadir and the Sous Plain** (passage), Oualidia** (passage), Oued Massa* (passage).
PORTUGAL Berlenga Is*** (passage), Cape St Vincent*** (autumn), Castro Marim*** (passage).
SPAIN Aiguamolls de l'Empordá*** (passage, winter), Cabo de Gata*** (passage, winter), Coto Doñana*** (passage, winter), Ebro Delta*** (passage, winter), Guadalhorce Estuary*** (passage, winter), Llobregat Delta** (passage, winter), Santa Pola*** (passage, winter).
TUNISIA Cap Bon Peninsula* (passage).

Little Shearwater
Puffinus assimilis   I Sea Dis (Mig)

Range: Colonies throughout the Cape Verde Is and on the Azores (mainly on islets off Graciosa and Santa Maria), the Desertas and Selvagems, and in the Canaries on Alegranza, Montana Clara and Graciosa. Most move into adjacent seas after breeding, although the species is probably regular in small numbers as far N as SW Ireland.
Subspecies: The race *baroli* breeds on the Azores, Desertas, Selvagems and Canaries and *boydi* on the Cape Verde Islands but both forms have been treated as full species at times. However, *boydi* is considered a race of Audubon's Shearwater *P. lherminieri* by some authorities and recent DNA analysis suggests *baroli* is also better placed within this species, with the true *assimilis* confined to Australasia and the Southern Ocean.
Tips: Breeds on undisturbed islands, often at some distance inland and post-breeding stays at sea close to colony, sometimes visiting nest site during non-breeding period. Often seen from the Tenerife–Gomera ferry and off seawatching points in the W Canaries. Ferries across Biscay sometimes produce this species and careful searching of passage flocks of Manx Shearwater can result in the occasional Little Shearwater; look for the smaller size and more fluttering flight with quicker wingbeats and shorter glides.

Sites:
AZORES** (summer, autumn).
BAY OF BISCAY** (autumn).
CANARY IS El Hierro***, Fuerteventura***, Gomera***, Lanzarote***, Tenerife***.
CAPE VERDE IS**.

FRANCE Ouessant* (autumn).
IRELAND Cape Clear Is* (autumn).
MADEIRA** (present all year).
MOROCCO Oualidia (passage).

Wilson's Storm-petrel
Oceanites oceanicus **Sea Mig**

Range: An Antarctic breeder which migrates N and was formerly considered a rare vagrant to our region. Now known to be regular in some numbers far offshore in late summer in the Western Approaches off southern Ireland and SW England, and off Iberia. Also recorded off the Canaries, Madeira and the Cape Verde Is, and off NW Africa in May–Nov, rarely also in the western Mediterranean.

Subspecies: Nominate breeds in the subantarctic and *exasperatus* in the Antarctic, and both migrate into the N Atlantic.

Tips: At sea usually far from land but often follows ships in small flocks. Pelagics or shark-fishing trips from Scilly offer the best chance to see this species although it can be seen from the Biscay ferries but good views are rare. Look for swallow-like flight and habit of pattering feet on sea surface.

Sites:
BAY OF BISCAY** (autumn).
CAPE VERDE IS** (autumn).
FRANCE Ouessant (autumn).
GREAT BRITAIN Scilly* (autumn).
MOROCCO Agadir and the Sous Plain (passage), Oualidia (passage).
PORTUGAL Berlenga Is** (autumn), Cape St Vincent** (autumn).

White-faced Storm-petrel (Frigate Petrel)
Pelagodroma marina **I Sea Mig Dis**

Range: Breeds on Selvagem Grande and Selvagem Pequena, in the Selvagems, and in the Cape Verde Is, on Cima, Branco, Laje Branca and Pássaros. Also breeds in small numbers in the Canaries, on Montana Clara off Lanzarote and possibly elsewhere.

Subspecies: Race *hypoleuca* breeds on the Selvagems and *eadesi* on the Cape Verde Is.

Tips: Breeds in burrows on arid islands, otherwise at sea. Rarely follows ships and only occasionally seen at sea, usually singly and flying low in erratic, weaving flight. A winter breeder, present on the Selvagems Feb–Sep, and on the Cape Verde Is in Nov–Jun. Dispersing birds recorded off the Canaries, Madeira (rarely seen with early spring the most likely time), Portugal and NW Africa. Nocturnal at breeding sites, although one can sometimes be found at the entrance to its burrow in daylight. Perhaps most easily seen well on land on the tiny islet of Ilhéu dos Pássaros off the E coast of Boa Vista in the Cape Verdes.

European Storm-petrel
Hydrobates pelagicus   I Sea   Mig Dis

Range: Breeds on islands from S Iceland and the Lofotens to the N and W British Isles, NW France and Spain, the Canaries and in the Mediterranean E to Malta and probably also in the Adriatic and Aegean. Winters in the Mediterranean and off W and S Africa, occasional in the Black Sea.

Tips: Nocturnal when visiting burrow, present at colonies Apr–Sep, rarely Oct. Otherwise difficult to see from shore except from some western headlands. Often follows ships in swallow-like flight. Pelagic trips off SW England and the Biscay ferries in autumn guarantee this species, otherwise visit known colonies and listen for the purring call from burrows.

Sites:

BALEARIC IS Formentera*** (summer), Ibiza*** (summer), Mallorca** (summer).
BAY OF BISCAY* (autumn).
DENMARK Skallingen-Blåvandshuk** (passage).
CANARY IS El Hierro*** (summer, passage), Fuerteventura*** (summer, passage), Gomera*** (summer, passage), Lanzarote*** (summer, passage), Tenerife*** (summer, passage).
CAPE VERDE IS (passage).
CROATIA Cres (passage).
FAROE IS* (summer).
FRANCE Cap Gris Nez* (passage), Île d'Oléron* (autumn), Ouessant*** (summer, passage), Sept Îles*** (summer).
GREAT BRITAIN Anglesey* (autumn), Flamborough Head* (autumn), Islay** (passage), N Norfolk coast* (autumn), Orkney Is*** (summer, passage), Outer Hebrides** (passage), Pembrokeshire Is*** (summer), Portland* (passage), Rhum* (summer), St Ives Bay** (passage), Scilly*** (summer, autumn), Shetland Is*** (summer, passage), Spurn Peninsula* (passage).
GIBRALTAR* (passage).
ICELAND Reykjanes Peninsula*** (summer), Westmann Is*** (summer).
IRELAND Cape Clear Is*** (passage), Galley Head*** (passage), Ireland's Eye* (passage), Kinsale*** (passage), Mullet Peninsula*** (summer, passage), Strangford Lough* (passage).
MADEIRA* (passage).
MALTA* (summer).
MOROCCO Agadir and the Sous Plain* (passage), Oualidia (passage).
NORWAY Lofoten Is*** (summer), Runde*** (summer), Utsira* (summer, passage), Varanger* (passage).
PORTUGAL Berlenga Is (autumn), Cape St Vincent** (autumn).
SARDINIA Pelagie Is*** (summer), San Pietro I** (summer).
SPAIN Cabo de Gata* (summer, passage), Coto Doñana* (passage), Santa Pola** (summer).
SWEDEN Getterön** (passage).

Leach's Storm-petrel
Oceanodroma leucorhoa   I Sea Mig

Range: Breeds on the Westmann Is off Iceland, on Mykines in the Faroes, the Lofotens off Norway, islands off N and W Scotland and at one site in Ireland (Stags of Broadhaven off Co. Mayo). Present at breeding colonies late Apr–Nov and winters in the tropical Atlantic.

Tips: Breeds on remote islands, in rocky crevices, visiting colonies only at night. Pelagic when not breeding, rarely follows ships but can be attracted to 'chum'. Passage recorded from many western headlands in late autumn and this is by far the most likely storm-petrel to be driven inland by severe weather.

Sites:

BAY OF BISCAY*** (autumn).
CAPE VERDE IS* (passage).
DENMARK Skallingen-Blåvandshuk* (passage).
FAROE IS*** (summer).
FRANCE Cap Gris Nez* (passage), Île d'Oléron* (autumn), Ouessant** (autumn).
GREAT BRITAIN Anglesey* (autumn), Flamborough Head* (autumn), N Norfolk coast* (autumn), Orkney Is* (autumn), Outer Hebrides*** (autumn), Portland* (autumn), St Ives Bay** (passage), Shetland Is** (summer, autumn), Spurn Peninsula* (passage).

GIBRALTAR* (passage, winter).
ICELAND Reykjanes Peninsula*** (summer), Westmann Is*** (summer).
IRELAND Cape Clear Is*** (passage), Galley Head** (passage), Mullet Peninsula** (passage).
MADEIRA (passage).
NORWAY Lofoten Is*** (summer).
PORTUGAL Berlenga Is (passage), Cape St Vincent* (autumn).
SPAIN Coto Doñana (passage).
SWEDEN Getterön* (passage).

Swinhoe's Storm-petrel
Oceanodroma monorhis   I Sea Mig

Range: Widespread in the N Pacific and in our region breeds on the Cape Verde Is, probably on Selvagem Grande in the Selvagems (recorded several times in burrows of Madeiran Storm-petrels), and possibly the Azores. Otherwise a rare but increasing vagrant, to Norway, NW France, the Balearics and the Gulf of Aqaba. In addition, there have been several Jul records from the NE coast of England.

Tips: Pelagic in warm oceanic waters when not breeding.

Sites:

CAPE VERDE IS*.   **MADEIRA.**

Madeiran Storm-petrel
Oceanodroma castro I Sea Dis

Range: Breeds on islets off Graciosa and Santa Maria in the Azores, on islets off E Madeira, Porto Santo, the Desertas and Selvagems, the Canaries, the Farilhões and Berlengas off Portugal, and on Rombo, Branco, Raso and Boa Vista in the Cape Verde Is. Winters in local seas but some may disperse across the Atlantic. On Graciosa, in the Azores, there are two genetically distinct populations with different nesting periods, suggesting that they are perhaps separate species.

Tips: A winter breeder that spends most of the year at sea but may visit land outside the breeding season. Breeds in rock crevices on remote islands. Possible from the Biscay ferries in late Aug–early Sep but not normally attracted to ships. Most easily seen from the Madeira–Porto Santo ferry. May occur more frequently in European seas but identification can be very difficult.

Sites:
AZORES**.
BAY OF BISCAY (autumn).
CANARY IS El Hierro**, Fuerteventura**, Gomera**, Lanzarote**, Tenerife**.
CAPE VERDE IS**.

MADEIRA**.
MOROCCO Oualidia (passage).
PORTUGAL Berlenga Is** (summer, passage), Cape St Vincent* (autumn).

Magnificent Frigatebird
Fregata magnificens I Sea Res Dis

Range: Breeds widely in tropical oceans but now very rare in our region, breeding only in the Cape Verde Is on the Ilhéu de Curral Velho off the S coast of Boa Vista. Larger numbers breed in the Caribbean and off S America, and these areas are likely to be the origin of vagrants to Europe. Adults are largely sedentary but immatures may disperse some distance.

Tips: Found in tropical and subtropical oceans, breeding on trees on islands, occurs far from land and close inshore, and often attracted to ships. Any vagrant frigatebird should be identified with great care as several other species could possibly occur.

Site:
CAPE VERDE IS*.

Red-billed Tropicbird
Phaethon aethereus   I Sea Dis

Range: Breeds in the Cape Verde Is, on São Tiago and Raso, possibly on other islands, and on islands in the N Red Sea off Egypt. Has bred in the Azores and probably the Canaries in recent years. Disperses to local seas post-breeding. Rare and declining in both known breeding areas, and the Cape Verde Is population numbers fewer than 100 pairs. Recently recorded off Cornwall and Scilly and the increase in pelagic trips, from Great Britain and elsewhere, is likely to produce more sightings.

Tips: Breeds on islands, otherwise at sea, sometimes far from land.

Sites:

AZORES.

CAPE VERDE IS**.

EGYPT Hurghada*, Sharm el Sheikh*.

ISRAEL Eilat (passage).

MADEIRA.

Brown Booby
Sula leucogaster   I Sea Dis

Range: Breeds in the Cape Verde Is, on São Tiago, Brava, Rombo, Raso and islets off Boa Vista, and in the Red Sea on islets in the mouth of the Gulf of Suez; Gezira Ashrafi, Gezira Qeisum, Gezira Umm el Heimat and Gezira Umm Qamar. May occur regularly on the Banc D'Arguin, of Mauritania, and is an occasional visitor to Eilat.

Subspecies: Nominate race occurs on the Cape Verde Is and *plotus* in the Red Sea.

Tips: Present close to breeding islands all year but immatures may disperse more widely. Breeds colonially on the ground on undisturbed islands.

Sites:

CAPE VERDE IS***.

EGYPT Hurghada***, Sharm el Sheikh***.

ISRAEL Eilat**.

JORDAN Aqaba*.

Pygmy Cormorant
Phalacrocorax pygmaeus   FW (BW) (ES) Dis Mig

Range: After a long period of decline, this species was confined to the SE of the region with breeding mainly limited to the Danube and Dnestr Deltas, a few large lakes in the S Balkans and N Greece, and at a few colonies in Turkey. However, a recent range expansion N and W has led to breeding in Hungary, N Italy and Slovakia. Small numbers also breed in Israel and vagrancy throughout the region is increasing. Present at colonies Mar–Sep.

Tips: Search heronries for this species, as it often breeds in association with herons, egrets and Glossy Ibis, beside fresh waters, but is also seen on brackish lagoons in winter.

Sites:
ALBANIA Drini Delta*** (summer, passage), Karavasta Lagoon*** (passage), Lake Shkodra***.
ARMENIA Armash Fishponds*** (summer).
AZERBAIJAN Kura Valley Salt-lakes***, Kyzylagach Bay***.
BOSNIA-HERZEGOVINA Hutovo blato (summer).
BULGARIA Belene** (summer), Burgas area*** (passage), Cape Kaliakra* (passage), Lake Durankulak***, Lake Shabla*** (passage, winter), Lake Srebarna***, Ropotamo NP**, Strandja Mts*** (passage).
CROATIA Kopački Rit** (summer).
CYPRUS* (winter).
GEORGIA Javakheti Plateau*** (passage, winter).
GREECE Amvrakikós Gulf*** (passage, winter), Axios-Aliakmonas Deltas*** (passage, winter), Evros Delta** (passage, winter), Lake Kerkini***, Mikrí Prespa NP***, Nestos Delta**, Porto Lagos area***.
GREEK IS Corfu* (passage), Lesvos* (winter).
HUNGARY Hortobágy NP*** (summer), Kis-balaton*** (summer, passage), Kiskunság NP*** (summer), Lake Fertö*** (summer).

ISRAEL Bet Shean Valley***, Hula Reserve*** (passage, winter), Ma'agan Mikhael* (winter).
ITALY Isonzo Regional Park* (winter), Po Delta**.
LEBANON Aamiq Marshes* (passage, winter), Qaraoun Lake* (passage, winter).
MACEDONIA Lakes Ohrid and Prespa***.
MOLDOVA Balatina**, Manta Floodplain***.
ROMANIA Danube Delta*** (summer), Dobrudja*** (summer, passage), Lake Călăraşi** (summer).
RUSSIA Volga Delta*** (summer).
SLOVAKIA Senné Fishponds* (summer).
SYRIA Baath Lake**, Lake Assad* (passage), Dayr al-Zawr* (passage).
TURKEY Bafa Gölü***, Birecik-Halfeti***, Bulanik**, Dalyan*** (summer, passage), Göksu Delta**, Kızılırmak Delta** (passage, winter), Kocaçay Delta* (passage), Manyas Gölü**, Sultan Marshes***, Uluabat Gölü***, Van Gölü (summer, passage).
UKRAINE Dunay Delta***.
YUGOSLAVIA Carska bara**, Đerdap NP**, Lake Skadar***.

Long-tailed Cormorant
Phalacrocorax africanus

FW BW ES   Dis

Range: Widespread and common in sub-Saharan Africa but in our region confined to the extreme southern limits, where breeds only in the Banc d'Arguin of Mauritania, although vagrants have reached Morocco. Formerly bred in the Nile Delta and Valley of Egypt but nowadays an uncommon, but apparently increasing, visitor to Lake Nasser.

Tips: Declining in Mauritania but increasingly recorded at Abu Simbel. Found on fresh and saltwater, along rivers and lakes, in mangroves, estuaries and on rocky coasts. Like Pygmy Cormorant, often associates with herons, egrets and storks. Swims very low in the water, often with only the head and neck above the surface and perches in waterside trees.

Site:
EGYPT Abu Simbel* (summer).

White Pelican
Pelecanus onocrotalus

FW BW ES   Mig

Range: Breeding now confined to a few sites in the SE, with scattered colonies in the Volga Delta and on the N shores of the Black Sea, the Danube Delta, Bulgaria, Greece and Turkey. Also breeds in the far SW of the Western Palearctic, in the Banc d'Arguin of Mauritania. Most migrate to Israel or sub-Saharan Africa, formerly Egypt where now scarce. Occurs on passage over Greece, Turkey, Cyprus, the Middle East and Egypt.

Tips: Breeds on large, shallow fresh waters with dense vegetation, at other times may use brackish or saline waters in estuaries and lagoons.

Sites:
ALBANIA Karavasta Lagoon** (passage).
ARMENIA Armash Fishponds** (passage, passage).
AZERBAIJAN Kyzylagach Bay* (winter).
BULGARIA Albena-Golden Sands*** (passage), Burgas area*** (passage), Cape Emine*** (passage), Cape Kaliakra*** (passage), Lake Durankulak*** (passage), Lake Shabla*** (passage), Lake Srebarna*** (summer, passage), Ropotamo NP*** (passage).

CYPRUS ** (passage).
EGYPT Abu Simbel*** (passage, winter), Aswan*** (passage), Hurghada*** (passage), Luxor*** (passage), Sharm el Sheikh*** (passage), Suez area*** (passage), Zaranik*** (passage).
GEORGIA Javakheti Plateau*** (summer, passage).
GREECE Amvrakikós Gulf*** (passage, winter), Evros Delta*** (passage), Lake Kerkini***

(passage), Mikrí Prespa NP***, Porto Lagos area** (passage).
GREEK IS Lesvos* (passage).
ISRAEL Eilat*** (passage), Bet Shean Valley*** (passage, winter), Hula Reserve*** (passage), Jezreel Valley*** (passage, winter), Ma'agan Mikhael*** (passage, winter). **LEBANON** Aamiq Marshes*** (passage), Palm Is* (passage), Qaraoun Lake** (passage). **MACEDONIA** Lakes Ohrid and Prespa** (passage).
ROMANIA Danube Delta*** (summer), Dobrudja*** (summer, passage), Lake Călăraşi** (summer, passage).

RUSSIA Volga Delta*** (summer).
SYRIA Bahrat Homs*** (passage, winter), Lake Assad*** (passage).
TURKEY Bafa Gölü** (passage), Bulanik* (passage), Göksu Delta*** (summer, passage), Kocaçay Delta*** (passage), Kulu Gölü*** (summer, passage), Manyas Gölü*** (passage), Sultan Marshes*** (summer, passage), Uluabat Gölü*** (mainly passage), Van Gölü** (passage).
UKRAINE Dunay Delta*** (summer), Tiligul Liman*** (passage).

Dalmatian Pelican
Pelecanus crispus

FW BW ES   Mig Res

Range: A declining and globally threatened species with breeding in our region now confined to the SE. Breeds in the Danube Delta and at a few sites in the S Balkans, Greece and Turkey, with scattered colonies along the N shores of the Black Sea. Some are resident, others disperse and winter in E Greece and S Turkey, but now rare in Egypt, more easterly populations winter in Iraq. Passage occurs across SE Europe, the Middle East and Egypt. Present in the Danube Delta Mar–Aug.

Tips: Found on large shallow lakes and deltas, also along coastlines and in lagoons and estuaries on passage and in winter. Passage is generally earlier than White Pelican.

Sites:
ALBANIA Karavasta Lagoon*** (summer, passage), Lake Shkodra***(summer, passage).
ARMENIA Armash Fishponds** (passage), Lake Sevan* (passage).
AZERBAIJAN Kura Valley Salt-lakes*** (passage, winter), Kyzylagach Bay*** (winter).
BULGARIA Albena-Golden Sands** (passage), Burgas area*** (passage, winter), Cape Emine* (passage), Cape Kaliakra* (passage), Lake Durankulak*** (passage), Lake Shabla*** (passage), Lake Srebarna*** (summer, passage), Strandja Mts** (passage).
EGYPT Zaranik* (passage).

GEORGIA Javakheti Plateau*** (summer, passage).
GREECE Amvrakikós Gulf***, Axios-Aliakmonas Deltas** (passage), Evros Delta* (passage), Lake Kerkini***, Mikrí Prespa NP***, Nestos Delta*** (passage, winter), Porto Lagos area*** (passage, winter).
GREEK IS Corfu* (passage).
LEBANON Aamiq Marshes* (passage), Palm Is (passage), Qaraoun Lake* (passage).
MACEDONIA Lakes Ohrid and Prespa** (passage).
MOLDOVA Manta Floodplain** (passage).

ROMANIA Danube Delta*** (summer), Dobrudja*** (summer, passage), Lake Călăraşi* (summer, passage).
RUSSIA Volga Delta*** (summer).
SYRIA Lake Assad** (passage).
TURKEY Bafa Gölü***, Dalyan (passage), Göksu Delta** (passage, winter), Kızılırmak Delta***, Manyas Gölü*** (summer, passage), Sultan Marshes* (passage), Uluabat Gölü** (mainly passage).
UKRAINE Dunay Delta** (summer, passage).
YUGOSLAVIA Lake Skadar**.

Pink-backed Pelican
Pelecanus rufescens FW (ES) Mig (Dis)

Range: Widespread in sub-Saharan Africa but in our region a rare but regular visitor to S Egypt where most frequent at Abu Simbel. There is a small population of free-flying birds on the Mediterranean coast of France, now numbering more than 20 birds and escapes occur widely across Europe.

Tips: Abu Simbel is *the* place for this species, although care must be taken, as White Pelican may also be present. Found on lakes, rivers and floodplains in much of Africa, coastal in some areas being seen in bays and harbours, on islands and in mangroves.

Site:
EGYPT Abu Simbel** (summer).

Great Bittern
Botaurus stellaris FW Res Mig

Range: Breeds widely but at very scattered localities in W and E Europe, in E and NW England, parts of France, Iberia and N Italy. Main range extends from S Sweden and Finland, Denmark, N Germany and the Low Countries E to the Baltic states and Russia. Patchily distributed in the SE, with scattered populations in the Balkans and Turkey. Very small numbers breed around the Mediterranean, in the Balearics and Sardinia and perhaps in NW Africa. A summer visitor to E of range, but resident elsewhere, although dispersive in severe weather, and is more widespread around the Mediterranean in winter.

Tips: Occurs mainly in extensive reedbeds, also densely vegetated swamps with open water. Best located by 'booming' of male in late winter and spring. Rarely seen in the open but more visible in winter when frequents disused gravel pits and reservoirs. Most often seen in early morning or late evening in flight over reedbeds.

Sites:

ALBANIA Lake Shkodra*.

AUSTRIA Lake Neusiedl***.

AZERBAIJAN Kura Valley Salt-lakes***, Kyzylagach Bay***.

BALEARIC IS Mallorca**.

BELARUS Belovezhskaya Pushcha NP** (summer), Berezinsky Reserve*** (summer), Pripyatsky NP*** (summer).

BELGIUM Blankaart Reserve*.

BOSNIA-HERZEGOVINA Hutovo blato. **CROATIA** Kopački Rit**.

CZECH REPUBLIC Lednice**, Pohořelice Fishponds*, Poodři*, Třeboňsko***.

DENMARK Amager* (winter), Møn-Falster* (summer), Ringkøbing Fjord***, Rømø***.

EGYPT Nile Delta* (winter).

ESTONIA Emajõgi Floodplain*** (summer), Lake Endla** (summer), Matsalu Bay*** (summer), Vilsandi NP** (summer).

FINLAND Åland Is** (summer), Liminganlahti*** (summer), Parikkala*** (summer), Viikki** (passage).

FRANCE Camargue*** (winter), Cap Gris Nez** (winter), Dombes**, La Brenne***, Lac du Der-Chantecoq***, Lorraine NP***, Romelaere NR* (winter), Sologne***, Somme Estuary**, Trunvel Reserve***.

GERMANY Dummer*, Federsee**, Kuhkopf*, Mecklenburg Lakes***, Oder Valley***, Schweinfurt***, Tiroler Achen***.

GREAT BRITAIN Anglesey** (winter), Dungeness (winter), Minsmere***, N Norfolk coast**, Portland* (winter).

BULGARIA Burgas area***, Lake Durankulak***, Lake Shabla***, Lake Srebarna***, Ropotamo NP**.

GREECE Amvrakikós Gulf** (winter), Axios-Aliakmonas Deltas* (winter), Evros Delta* (winter), Lake Kerkini* (winter), Mikrí Prespa NP** (winter), Nestos Delta* (winter), Porto Lagos area* (winter).

GREEK IS Crete* (passage, winter), Lesvos* (passage, winter).

HUNGARY Biharugra***, Hanság**, Hortobágy NP***, Kis-balaton***, Kiskunság

NP***, Lake Fertö***, Lake Velence***, Ócsa**, Szeged Fishponds***.

ISRAEL Ma'agan Mikhael* (winter).

ITALY Isonzo Regional Park* (winter), Lake Massaciuccoli***, Maremma Regional Park**, Orbetello Reserve** (autumn, winter), Po Delta***.

LATVIA Lake Engure*** (summer), Lake Lubana*** (summer), Lake Pape*** (summer).

LEBANON Aamiq Marshes* (winter).

LITHUANIA Kirsiu Peninsula*** (summer), Lake Kretuonas* (summer), Zuvintas NR*** (summer).

MACEDONIA Lakes Ohrid and Prespa***.

MALTA* (passage).

NETHERLANDS Lauwersmeer**, Naardermeer**, Oostvaadersplassen***, Zwanenwater**.

POLAND Białystok Fishponds*** (summer), Biebrza Marshes*** (summer), Chełm Marshes*** (summer), Gdańsk Bay*** (summer), Milicz Fishponds*** (summer), Słońsk*** (summer), Szczecin Bay area** (summer).

PORTUGAL Ria Formosa* (winter), Sado Estuary*.

ROMANIA Danube Delta***, Dobrudja***, Lake Călăraşi***, Satchinez**.

RUSSIA Volga Delta***.

SARDINIA Oristano wetlands** (passage, winter).

SICILY Lago di Lentini** (winter).

SLOVAKIA Senné Fishponds***, Záhorie*, Zemplínská Reservoir*.

SPAIN Aiguamolls de l'Empordá*, Coto Doñana*, Ebro Delta*, Llobregat Delta*.

SWEDEN Falsterbo* (autumn), Gammelstadsviken*** (summer), Getterön*** (passage), Hjälstaviken*** (summer), Hornborgasjön*** (summer), Kristianstad*** (summer), Kvismaren*** (summer), Lake Krankesjön*** (summer), Tåkern*** (summer).

SWITZERLAND Fanel NR** (passage, winter), Grangettes* (winter).

SYRIA Bahrat Homs* (passage).

TURKEY Dalyan* (winter), Göksu Delta** (principally winter), Kızılırmak Delta***, Uluabat Gölü**, Van Gölü*.

UKRAINE Dunay Delta**, Shatsk NP***, Syvash Bay***.
YUGOSLAVIA Lake Skadar*, Carska bara.

Little Bittern
Ixobrychus minutus

FW Mig

Range: Very patchy range across S Europe from Iberia to the S Urals and Caspian, ranging N to the Baltic coast. In the Mediterranean breeds on Mallorca, Sardinia and Sicily and in N Africa breeds in Morocco, N Algeria and N Tunisia, also in the Nile Delta and Valley. Some winter in the Nile Delta but most migrate to sub-Saharan Africa, vacating breeding range in Aug–Sep and returning mid Mar–Apr. Passage occurs throughout the Mediterranean, the Middle East and N Africa.

Tips: Usually seen in flight over reedbeds, most often in late afternoon or evening. Less shy than Great Bittern but can be very difficult to see well in dense vegetation. Occurs in swamps and reedbeds with scattered willows and other scrub.

Sites:
ALBANIA Lake Shkodra** (summer).
ALGERIA El Kala NP*** (summer).
ARMENIA Armash Fishponds*** (summer).
AUSTRIA Lake Neusiedl*** (summer), Marchauen-Marchegg Reserve*** (summer).
AZERBAIJAN Kura Valley Salt-lakes*** (summer), Kyzylagach Bay*** (summer).
BALEARIC IS Formentera* (passage), Mallorca*** (summer, rare in winter), Menorca* (passage).
BELARUS Belovezhskaya Pushcha NP** (summer), Berezinsky Reserve*** (summer), Pripyatsky NP*** (summer).
BELGIUM Blankaart Reserve** (summer).
BOSNIA-HERZEGOVINA Hutovo blato (summer).
BULGARIA Albena-Golden Sands*** (summer, passage), Burgas area*** (summer), Lake Durankulak*** (summer, passage), Lake Shabla*** (summer, passage), Lake Srebarna*** (summer, passage), Ropotamo NP*** (summer), Strandja Mts*** (summer, passage), Tissata NR* (passage).

CANARY IS Fuerteventura* (passage).
CORSICA Biguglia Lake** (summer), Cap Corse** (passage).
CROATIA Kopački Rit** (summer), Neretva Delta*** (summer), Pokupsko Depression*** (summer).
CYPRUS* (passage).
CZECH REPUBLIC Lednice*** (summer, passage), Pohořelice Fishponds*** (summer), Poodří*** (summer), Soutok*** (summer).
EGYPT Abu Simbel***, Aswan***, Faiyum* (summer), Luxor***, Nile Delta***, Sharm el Sheikh*** (passage), Zaranik*** (passage).
FRANCE Baie de Bourgneuf* (summer), Camargue***, Dombes*** (summer), Fôret d'Orient*** (summer), Gruissan*** (summer), La Brenne*** (summer), Lac du Der-Chantecoq** (summer), Leucate*** (summer), Lorraine NP** (summer), Marais Poitevin*** (summer), Romelaere NR* (summer), Sologne*** (summer), Trunvel Reserve*** (summer).
GEORGIA Javakheti Plateau*** (summer), Kolkheti*** (summer).

GERMANY Dummer* (summer), Federsee*** (summer), Kuhkopf*** (summer), Mecklenburg Lakes*** (summer), Oder Valley** (summer), Schweinfurt** (summer).

GREECE Amvrakikós Gulf*** (summer), Axios-Aliakmonas Deltas*** (summer), Evros Delta** (summer, passage), Lake Kerkini*** (summer), Mikrí Prespa NP*** (summer), Nestos Delta*** (summer), Porto Lagos area*** (summer).

GREEK IS Corfu*** (summer, passage), Crete*** (passage), Kos*** (passage), Lesvos*** (summer, passage), Rhodes** (passage).

HUNGARY Aggtelek NP*** (summer), Biharugra*** (summer), Hanság*** (summer), Hortobágy NP*** (summer), Kis-balaton*** (summer), Kiskunság NP*** (summer), Lake Fertö*** (summer), Lake Velence*** (summer), Ócsa*** (summer), Szeged Fishponds*** (summer), Tihany*** (summer), Zemplén Hills*** (summer).

ISRAEL Arava Valley*** (passage), Bet Shean Valley*** (passage), Eilat*** (passage), Hula Reserve*** (passage).

ITALY Circeo NP*** (summer), Gargano Peninsula*** (summer, passage), Isonzo Regional Park*** (summer, passage), Lake Massaciuccoli*** (summer), Monte Conero*** (summer, passage), Orbetello Reserve*** (summer), Po Delta*** (summer), Tuscan archipelago** (passage).

JORDAN Azraq** (passage).

LATVIA Lake Engure*** (summer), Lake Lubana*** (summer).

LEBANON Aamiq Marshes*** (passage), Palm Is* (passage), Qaraoun Lake* (passage).

LITHUANIA Kirsiu Peninsula*** (summer).

MACEDONIA Lakes Ohrid and Prespa*** (summer).

MALTA** (passage, rare breeder).

MOROCCO Dayet Aaoua*** (summer, passage), Oualidia*** (passage), Oued Massa*** (summer, passage).

NETHERLANDS Naardermeer* (summer), Oostvaadersplassen (summer).

POLAND Białystok Fishponds*** (summer), Biebrza Marshes*** (summer), Chełm Marshes*** (summer), Gdańsk Bay*** (summer), Milicz Fishponds*** (summer), Słońsk*** (summer), Szczecin Bay area** (summer).

PORTUGAL Baixo Alentejo** (summer), Boquilobo*** (summer), Castro Marim*** (passage), Ria Formosa*** (summer), Sado Estuary*** (summer), Santo André Lagoon*** (summer), Tagus Estuary*** (summer).

ROMANIA Danube Delta*** (summer), Dobrudja*** (summer, passage), Lake Călăraşi*** (summer), Satchinez*** (summer).

RUSSIA Volga Delta*** (summer).

SARDINIA Cagliari wetlands*** (summer), Giara di Gesturi* (passage), Oristano wetlands*** (summer, passage), San Pietro I** (passage).

SICILY Lago di Lentini*** (summer, passage).

SLOVAKIA Senné Fishponds*** (summer), Slovenský Kras* (summer), Záhorie*** (summer), Zemplínská Reservoir** (summer).

SLOVENIA Lake Cerknica* (summer), Ljubljansko Moor** (summer).

SPAIN Aiguamolls de l'Empordá*** (summer), Cabo de Gata** (passage), Cáceres-Trujillo Steppes** (summer), Cádiz Lagoons*** (summer), Coto Doñana*** (summer), Ebro Delta*** (summer), Guadalhorce Estuary*** (summer, passage), La Serena** (summer), Llobregat Delta*** (summer), Santa Pola*** (summer), Serrania de Ronda* (summer), Tablas de Daimiel*** (summer).

SWITZERLAND Fanel NR*** (summer), Grangettes* (passage), Leuk** (summer).

SYRIA Baath Lake*** (summer), Bahrat Homs*** (summer), Dayr al-Zawr*** (summer).

TUNISIA Cap Bon Peninsula*** (passage), Kelbia Lake** (summer), Lake Ichkeul*** (summer, passage).

TURKEY Bafa Gölü*** (summer, passage), Birecik-Halfeti* (summer, passage), Bulanik* (summer, passage), Dalyan*** (summer, passage), Göksu Delta*** (summer), Kulu Gölü*** (summer), Manyas Gölü*** (summer), Sultan Marshes*** (summer, passage), Uluabat Gölü*** (summer), Van Gölü*** (summer, passage).

UKRAINE Dunay Delta*** (summer), Syvash Bay*** (summer).

YUGOSLAVIA Carska bara* (summer), Lake Skadar*** (summer), Obedska bara* (summer).

Black-crowned Night Heron
Nycticorax nycticorax   FW (BW ES) Mig

Range: Breeds at scattered localities from Iberia E to Turkey and the Middle East, and N to southern Russia, with an isolated breeding population in the Netherlands. In the Mediterranean breeds on Mallorca, Sardinian and Sicily. Also breeds in N Africa, in N Morocco, Algeria and Tunisia, and the Nile Delta. Passage birds occur throughout S Europe, N Africa and the Middle East. Departs breeding range late Jul–Oct and returns mid Mar–mid Apr.

Tips: Usually crepuscular, but can be seen by day. Breeds colonially, often in mixed heronries, and roosts in trees in wooded swamps and well-vegetated margins of lakes and rivers. Passage and winter birds often seen in more open habitats, including brackish lagoons and estuaries.

Sites:
ALBANIA Lake Shkodra*** (summer).
ALGERIA El Kala NP*** (summer).
ARMENIA Armash Fishponds*** (summer).
AUSTRIA Lake Neusiedl*** (summer), Marchauen-Marchegg Reserve*** (summer).
AZERBAIJAN Kura Valley Salt-lakes*** (summer), Kyzylagach Bay*** (summer).
BALEARIC IS Formentera** (passage), Mallorca***, Menorca*** (summer, passage).
BOSNIA-HERZEGOVINA Hutovo blato (summer).
BULGARIA Albena-Golden Sands*** (summer, passage), Belene*** (summer), Burgas area*** (summer, passage), Lake Durankulak*** (passage), Lake Shabla*** (passage), Lake Srebarna*** (summer, passage), Strandja Mts** (summer, passage), Tissata NR* (passage).
CANARY IS Fuerteventura*** (passage).
CORSICA Biguglia Lake*** (passage), Cap Corse** (passage).
CROATIA Kopački Rit** (summer), Pokupsko Depression*** (summer).

CYPRUS* (passage).
CZECH REPUBLIC Lednice*** (summer, passage), Pohořelice Fishponds** (passage), Třeboňsko*** (summer, passage).
EGYPT Abu Simbel*** (passage, winter), Faiyum* (winter), Aswan*** (passage, winter), Luxor*** (passage), Nile Delta** (passage, winter), Sharm el Sheikh*** (passage), Zaranik*** (passage).
FRANCE Camargue*** (summer), Dombes** (summer), Gruissan*** (passage), La Brenne*** (summer), Leucate*** (passage), Marais Poitevin*** (summer), Sologne*** (summer), Teich Reserve*** (summer).
GREECE Amvrakikós Gulf*** (summer, passage), Axios-Aliakmonas Deltas*** (summer), Dadiá-Soufli Forest*** (summer), Evros Delta** (passage), Lake Kerkini*** (summer), Mikrí Prespa NP*** (summer), Nestos Delta*** (summer), Porto Lagos area*** (summer).
GREEK IS Corfu*** (passage), Crete*** (passage), Kos*** (passage), Lesvos*** (passage), Rhodes** (passage).

HUNGARY Biharugra*** (summer), Hanság*** (summer), Hortobágy NP*** (summer), Kis-bal-aton*** (summer), Kiskunság NP*** (summer), Lake Fertö*** (summer), Lake Velence*** (summer), Ócsa* (summer), Szeged Fishponds*** (summer), Tihany*** (summer), Zemplén Hills*** (summer).

ISRAEL Arava Valley*** (passage), Bet Shean Valley*** (passage), Eilat*** (passage), Hula Reserve*** (passage, winter), Ma'agan Mikhael*** (summer, passage).

ITALY Circeo NP*** (passage), Gargano Peninsula*** (summer, passage), Isonzo Regional Park*** (summer, passage), Orbetello Reserve*** (summer), Po Delta*** (summer), San Giuliano Reserve*** (summer, passage), Tuscan archipelago** (passage).

JORDAN Aqaba*** (passage), Azraq** (passage), Ghadir Burqu'* (passage).

LEBANON Aamiq Marshes*** (summer, passage), Palm Is.** (passage), Qaraoun Lake*** (passage).

MACEDONIA Lakes Ohrid and Prespa*** (summer).

MALTA* (passage).

MOLDOVA Balatina** (summer).

MOROCCO Agadir and the Sous Plain** (passage), Dayet Aaoua* (summer), Oualidia*** (passage), Oued Massa*** (passage).

NETHERLANDS Oostvaadersplassen (passage).

PORTUGAL Baixo Alentejo*** (summer), Boquilobo*** (summer), Castro Marim*** (passage), Ria Formosa** (passage), Santo André Lagoon*** (passage).

ROMANIA Danube Delta*** (summer), Dobrudja*** (passage), Lake Călăraşi* (summer), Satchinez*** (summer).

RUSSIA Volga Delta*** (summer).

SLOVAKIA Senné Fishponds*** (summer), Záhorie*** (passage), Zemplínská Reservoir** (passage).

SLOVENIA Ljubljansko Moor** (summer).

SPAIN Aiguamolls de l'Empordá*** (summer), Cabo de Gata*** (passage), Cádiz Lagoons** (passage), Coto Doñana*** (summer), Ebro Delta*** (summer), Guadalhorce Estuary*** (summer, passage), La Serena* (summer), Llobregat Delta** (summer), Monfragüe NP*** (summer), Santa Pola*** (summer, passage), Tablas de Daimiel*** (summer).

SWITZERLAND Fanel NR** (passage), Grangettes* (passage), Klingnau Reservoir** (passage), Leuk** (passage).

SYRIA Baath Lake* (passage), Bahrat Homs*** (summer), Dayr al-Zawr*** (passage, winter). **TUNISIA** Cap Bon Peninsula*** (passage), Kelbia Lake** (passage), Lake Ichkeul*** (summer, passage).

TURKEY Bafa Gölü*** (passage), Birecik-Halfeti*** (summer), Bulanik* (passage), Dalyan** (passage), Göksu Delta*** (summer), Kulu Gölü* (passage), Manyas Gölü*** (summer), Sultan Marshes*** (summer), Uluabat Gölü*** (summer), Van Gölü*** (summer, passage).

UKRAINE Dunay Delta*** (summer), Syvash Bay*** (summer).

YUGOSLAVIA Carska bara* (summer), Lake Skadar*** (summer), Obedska bara* (summer).

Striated Heron (Green-backed Heron)
Butorides striatus

FW BW ES Res (Dis)

Range: Coasts of the N Red Sea in Egypt, Sinai and N Saudi Arabia, and increasingly recorded in the Nile Valley. Rarely wanders outside breeding range but does occur at Eilat and Aqaba, where recently also found breeding.
Tips: Red Sea birds are entirely marine, being found on reefs, lagoons, mudflats and mangroves, and in the Nile Valley occurs in densely vegetated swamps and river-banks where often shy and difficult to see.

Sites:
EGYPT Aswan***, Hurghada***, Luxor***, Sharm el Sheikh***.

ISRAEL Eilat***.
JORDAN Aqaba*.

Squacco Heron
Ardeola ralloides

FW Mig

Range: Patchy breeding range, in NW Africa and across S Europe from Iberia to the Balkans and N Greece, Ukraine and S Russia. Also breeds at very scattered localities in Turkey, the Middle East and in the Nile Delta and Valley of Egypt. Recently bred in the Balearics. Present in breeding range Apr–Sep and most winter in sub-Saharan Africa with small numbers in N Africa. Passage noted throughout the Mediterranean in Jul–Oct and Apr–May.
Tips: Freshwater swamps and ponds, reedbeds with scattered willows. Shy and often difficult to see until white wings are revealed on taking flight.

Sites:
ALBANIA Lake Shkodra** (summer).
ALGERIA El Kala NP*** (summer).
ARMENIA Armash Fishponds** (summer).
AUSTRIA Lake Neusiedl*** (summer).
AZERBAIJAN Kura Valley Salt-lakes*** (summer), Kyzylagach Bay*** (summer).
BALEARIC IS Formentera* (passage), Mallorca** (summer, passage), Menorca* (passage).
BOSNIA-HERZEGOVINA Hutovo blato (summer).

BULGARIA Albena-Golden Sands* (passage), Belene*** (summer), Burgas area*** (summer, passage), Lake Durankulak*** (passage), Lake Shabla*** (passage), Lake Srebarna*** (summer), Ropotamo NP*** (summer), Strandja Mts*** (passage), Tissata NR* (passage).
CORSICA Biguglia Lake* (passage), Cap Corse* (passage).
CROATIA Kopački Rit** (summer).
CYPRUS* (passage).

EGYPT Abu Simbel***, Aswan***, Faiyum* (passage, winter), Luxor***, Nile Delta***, Sharm el Sheikh*** (passage), Suez area* (passage), Wadi el Natrun*** (passage), Zaranik*** (passage).

FRANCE Camargue*** (summer), Dombes** (summer), Gruissan*** (passage), Leucate** (passage).

GEORGIA Javakheti Plateau** (summer).

GREECE Amvrakikós Gulf*** (summer, passage), Axios-Aliakmonas Deltas*** (summer), Evros Delta* (summer, passage), Lake Kerkini*** (summer), Mikrí Prespa NP*** (summer), Nestos Delta*** (summer), Porto Lagos area*** (summer).

GREEK IS Corfu*** (summer, passage), Crete*** (summer, passage), Kos*** (passage), Lesvos*** (passage), Rhodes** (passage).

HUNGARY Hortobágy NP*** (summer), Kisbalaton*** (summer), Kiskunság NP*** (summer), Lake Fertö*** (summer), Lake Velence*** (summer), Szeged Fishponds*** (summer), Tihany*** (summer).

ISRAEL Arava Valley*** (passage), Bet Shean Valley*** (passage), Eilat*** (passage), Hula Reserve*** (summer, passage), Ma'agan Mikhael*** (summer, passage).

ITALY Circeo NP*** (passage), Gargano Peninsula** (summer, passage), Isonzo Regional Park** (passage), Orbetello Reserve*** (summer), Po Delta*** (summer), San Giuliano Reserve*** (summer, passage), Tuscan archipelago** (passage).

JORDAN Aqaba*** (passage), Azraq*** (passage).

LEBANON Aamiq Marshes*** (passage), Palm Is** (passage), Qaraoun Lake** (passage).

MACEDONIA Lakes Ohrid and Prespa*** (summer).

MALTA*** (passage).

MOROCCO Asilah and Oued Loukkos*** (summer), Lac de Sidi Bourhaba*** (passage), Merja Zerga** (passage), Oualidia*** (passage, Oued Massa*** (passage).

PORTUGAL Baixo Alentejo* (summer), Boquilobo** (summer), Castro Marim*** (passage), Ria Formosa*** (passage), Santo André Lagoon* (passage).

ROMANIA Danube Delta*** (summer), Dobrudja*** (summer, passage), Lake Călăraşi*** (summer), Satchinez*** (summer).

RUSSIA Volga Delta*** (summer).

SARDINIA Giara di Gesturi* (passage), San Pietro I* (passage).

SICILY Lago di Lentini*** (summer, passage).

SLOVAKIA Senné Fishponds* (passage), Zemplínská Reservoir** (passage).

SPAIN Aiguamolls de l'Empordá*** (summer), Cádiz Lagoons* (passage), Coto Doñana*** (summer), Ebro Delta*** (summer), Guadalhorce Estuary*** (summer, passage), Llobregat Delta*** (summer), Santa Pola** (summer), Tablas de Daimiel*** (summer).

SWITZERLAND Fanel NR* (passage), Leuk* (passage).

SYRIA Baath Lake*** (summer), Bahrat Homs*** (summer), Dayr al-Zawr*** (summer).

TUNISIA Cap Bon Peninsula*** (passage), Kelbia Lake** (summer, passage), Lake Ichkeul** (passage).

TURKEY Bafa Gölü*** (summer, passage), Bulanik* (passage), Dalyan** (passage), Göksu Delta*** (summer), Kulu Gölü*** (summer), Manyas Gölü*** (summer), Sultan Marshes*** (summer), Uluabat Gölü*** (summer), Van Gölü** (summer, passage).

UKRAINE Dunay Delta*** (summer).

YUGOSLAVIA Carska bara* (summer), Lake Skadar** (summer), Obedska bara (summer).

Cattle Egret
Bubulcus ibis

Range: Discontinuous but expanding range in the Western Palearctic. Main range is in S Iberia and NW Africa but also breeds in the Canaries and in S and W France (as far N as Lac de Grand Lieu, Brittany), N Italy and Sardinia, the N and W shores of the Caspian and in Egypt. Sporadic breeding or summering occurs in the Cape Verde Is, the Balearics, Turkey and in various Middle Eastern countries. Large numbers winter in S Iberia and NW Africa.

Tips: Freshwater margins and open grasslands. Often associates with livestock and will follow tractors. Frequently seen close to habitation. Breeds colonially in trees and reedbeds, and in Iberia often breeds on cliffs and sea stacks.

Sites:

ALGERIA El Kala NP***.

ARMENIA Armash Fishponds*** (summer), Lake Sevan*** (summer).

AZERBAIJAN Kyzylagach Bay*** (summer).

BALEARIC IS Mallorca***, Menorca*** (winter).

BELGIUM Het Zwin* (summer).

BULGARIA Burgas area** (summer).

CANARY IS Lanzarote***, Tenerife***.

CAPE VERDE IS.

CORSICA Biguglia Lake* (passage).

CYPRUS** (passage).

EGYPT Abu Simbel***, Aswan***, Luxor***, Nile Delta* (passage, winter), Sharm el Sheikh***, Suez area***.

FRANCE Camargue*** (summer), Dombes*** (summer), Golfe du Morbihan** (passage, winter), Gruissan***, La Brenne*** (summer), Leucate*** (passage), Marais Poitevin* (summer), Somme Estuary* (summer).

GREECE Axios-Aliakmonas Deltas**.

GREEK IS Crete* (passage, winter).

ISRAEL Arava Valley*** (passage), Bet Shean Valley*** (passage), Eilat*** (passage), Hula Reserve***, Jezreel Valley***, Ma'agan Mikhael***, Mt Hermon* (winter), Urim** (winter).

ITALY Maremma Regional Park*** (summer), Orbetello Reserve*** (summer), Po Delta*** (summer).

JORDAN Aqaba* (passage), Azraq* (passage).

MOROCCO Agadir and the Sous Plain***, Asilah and Oued Loukkos***, Dayet Aaoua***, Lac de Sidi Bourhaba***, Merja Zerga***, Oualidia***, Oued Massa***, Zaër***.

PORTUGAL Baixo Alentejo***, Boquilobo***, Cape St Vincent***, Castro Marim***, Ria Formosa***, Sado Estuary***, Santo André Lagoon***, Tagus Estuary***.

RUSSIA Volga Delta** (summer).

SARDINIA Cagliari wetlands***.

SPAIN Aiguamolls de l'Empordá***, Cabo de Gata*** (winter), Cáceres-Trujillo Steppes***, Cádiz Lagoons***, Coto Doñana***, Ebro Delta***, Guadalhorce Estuary*** (winter), La Serena***, Llobregat Delta*** (winter), Monfragüe*** (summer), Santa Pola***, Serrania de Ronda***, Tablas de Daimiel***.

SYRIA Baath Lake*, Bahrat Homs**, Dayr al-Zawr*.

TUNISIA Cap Bon Peninsula*** (passage), Kelbia Lake**, Lake Ichkeul***.

TURKEY Bulanik* (passage), Göksu Delta*** (passage), Van Gölü* (passage).

Western Reef Egret (Western Reef Heron)
Egretta gularis

ES   Res (Dis)

Range: In our region confined as a breeder to coasts of the N Red Sea and the Banc d'Arguin of Mauritania. Possibly a regular non-breeding visitor to the Cape Verde Is and a fairly frequent vagrant to Europe, particularly to Spain, France and Italy, including long-staying, practically resident individuals, and there have been occasional breeding attempts by mixed pairs of Western Reef Egret and Little Egret. Some European records probably refer to escaped birds.

Subspecies: West African birds belong to nominate *gularis* and those from the Red Sea to *schistacea*, sometimes given specific status as Arabian Reef Egret.

Tips: Strictly coastal, often on offshore islands. Look for this species on sandy and rocky shores, mudflats and lagoons; breeds colonially, often in mangroves.

Sites:
EGYPT Hurghada***, Sharm el Sheikh***, Suez area***.
FRANCE Camargue.

ISRAEL Eilat***.
JORDAN Aqaba***.
SPAIN Coto Doñana, Ebro Delta.

Great Egret (Great White Egret)
Ardea alba

FW (BW) (ES)   Res PMig

Range: Breeds in E and SE Europe, in Austria, Hungary, Romania, Ukraine and E across S Russia to the Caspian, also in the S Balkans, Turkey and Transcaucasia. Has expanded range in recent decades and now breeds sporadically W to N Italy, France and Spain, and regularly in small numbers in Netherlands. More widespread in winter in SE Europe, Turkey, the Middle East and N Africa and now regular W to Italy and W and S France, with more than 100 recorded wintering in the Camargue.

Tips: Lakes, marshes and wet grasslands, breeding in dense vegetation, especially reedbeds. On passage and in winter also on estuaries and brackish lagoons.

Sites:
ALBANIA Karavasta Lagoon** (passage), Lake Shkodra*** (winter).
ARMENIA Armash Fishponds*** (summer, passage).
AUSTRIA Lake Neusiedl*** (summer, passage).

AZERBAIJAN Kura Valley Salt-lakes***, Kyzylagach Bay*** (winter).
BALEARIC IS Mallorca** (passage, winter), Menorca* (passage).
BELARUS Belovezhskaya Pushcha NP* (summer), Berezinsky Reserve*** (passage).

BULGARIA Burgas area***, Lake Durankulak*** (passage, winter), Lake Shabla*** (passage, winter), Lake Srebarna***, Ropotamo NP**, Strandja Mts* (passage), Studen Kladenetz* (passage, winter), Tissata NR* (passage).

CORSICA Biguglia Lake (passage, winter).

CROATIA Kopački Rit** (summer), Pokupsko Depression** (summer, passage).

CYPRUS* (passage).

CZECH REPUBLIC Lednice**, Nové Mlýny*** (passage, winter), Třeboňsko*** (passage).

EGYPT Aswan** (passage, winter), Faiyum* (winter), Luxor*** (passage), Hurghada* (passage), Nile Delta*** (passage, winter), Sharm el Sheikh*** (passage, winter), Zaranik** (passage).

FRANCE Camargue*** (winter), Dombes* (passage), Fôret d'Orient* (winter), Golfe du Morbihan* (winter), La Brenne*** (summer), Lac du Der-Chantecoq* (winter), Somme Estuary* (passage, winter).

GEORGIA Kolkheti*** (passage).

GREECE Amvrakikós Gulf*** (passage, summer), Axios-Aliakmonas Deltas** (passage, winter), Evros Delta* (winter), Lake Kerkini** (winter), Mikrí Prespa NP**, Nestos Delta** (winter), Porto Lagos area**.

GREEK IS Crete* (passage, winter), Kos* (passage), Lesvos*** (winter), Rhodes* (passage).

HUNGARY Biharugra*** (summer), Csákvár*** (summer), Hanság***, Hortobágy NP*** (summer), Kis-balaton***, Kiskunság NP*** (summer), Lake Fertö*** (summer, passage), Lake Velence*** (summer, passage), Szeged Fishponds*** (summer), Zemplén Hills** (summer).

ISRAEL Arava Valley*** (passage), Bet Shean Valley*** (winter), Eilat*** (passage, winter), Hula Reserve*** (passage, winter), Jezreel Valley*** (winter), Ma'agan Mikhael*** (passage, winter).

ITALY Circeo NP*** (passage, winter), Gargano Peninsula*** (passage, winter), Isonzo Regional Park*** (winter), Lake Massaciuccoli*** (passage), Maremma Regional Park*** (winter), Orbetello Reserve*** (passage, winter), Po Delta***, San Giuliano Reserve*** (passage).

JORDAN Aqaba* (passage), Azraq* (passage).

LATVIA Lake Engure* (summer).

LEBANON Aamiq Marshes** (passage, winter).

MACEDONIA Lakes Ohrid and Prespa**.

MOLDOVA Balatina**.

NETHERLANDS Lauwersmeer* (summer), Naardermeer* (summer), Oostvaadersplassen*** (summer).

POLAND Biebrza Marshes* (summer), Milicz Fishponds*** (autumn), Siemianówka Reservoir** (summer, passage), Słońsk** (passage).

ROMANIA Danube Delta***, Dobrudja*** (passage), Lake Călăraşi*** (passage).

RUSSIA Kalmykia*** (passage), Volga Delta*** (summer).

SARDINIA Cagliari wetlands*** (passage, winter).

SICILY Lago di Lentini*** (passage, winter).

SLOVAKIA Orava Reservoir*** (passage), Senné Fishponds*** (summer), Záhorie*** (passage, winter), Zemplínská Reservoir** (passage).

SPAIN Aiguamolls de l'Empordá*** (passage), Coto Doñana**, Ebro Delta*** (passage and winter, rare in summer).

SWITZERLAND Fanel NR* (passage, winter), Grangettes* (passage, winter), Klingnau Reservoir* (autumn).

SYRIA Baath Lake* (passage), Bahrat Homs** (passage, winter), Lake Assad** (passage, winter), Dayr al-Zawr** (summer, passage).

TUNISIA Cap Bon Peninsula** (passage, winter), Kelbia Lake* (passage).

TURKEY Bulanik* (summer, passage), Dalyan* (passage, winter), Göksu Delta*** (summer), İstanbul*** (passage), Kızılırmak Delta*** (winter), Kulu Gölü** (passage), Soğuksu NP* (passage, winter), Sultan Marshes*** (summer, passage), Uluabat Gölü*** (winter), Van Gölü* (passage).

UKRAINE Dunay Delta*** (summer, passage), Tiligul Liman*** (passage), Syvash Bay*** (summer).

YUGOSLAVIA Carska bara*, Lake Skadar*** (winter).

Purple Heron
Ardea purpurea   FW   Mig

Range: Breeds widely but discontinuously across S Europe, in Iberia, C and S France, parts of Italy and much of SE Europe and S Russia. Also at a few scattered sites in NW Africa, Turkey, the Middle East and Transcaucasia. An isolated population breeds in the Netherlands and there are very small numbers in the Cape Verde Is. Departs breeding range in Aug–Oct to winter in sub-Saharan Africa, returning in Apr–May. Small numbers winter in the S of the region, particularly in the Nile Valley. A frequent vagrant outside range and recorded annually in Britain.

Subspecies: Nominate over most of range, with the very rare *bournei* in the Cape Verde Is, where it occurs on São Tiago (but only nine nests were found in 2002). This race is considered a full species, **Cape Verde Heron**, by some authorities.

Tips: Shallow fresh waters with reedbeds, where usually breeds. More skulking than Grey Heron and far more difficult to see: search likely reedbeds in early morning and evening, but most often seen in flight.

Sites:

ALBANIA Lake Shkodra** (summer).
ALGERIA El Kala NP*** (summer).
ARMENIA Armash Fishponds*** (summer).
AUSTRIA Lake Neusiedl*** (summer), Marchauen-Marchegg Reserve*** (summer).
AZERBAIJAN Kura Valley Salt-lakes*** (summer), Kyzylagach Bay***(summer).
BALEARIC IS Mallorca*** (summer, passage), Menorca** (passage).
BELGIUM Het Zwin* (passage).
BOSNIA-HERZEGOVINA Hutovo blato (summer).
BULGARIA Albena-Golden Sands*** (summer, passage), Belene*** (summer), Burgas area*** (summer, passage), Lake Durankulak*** (summer, passage), Lake Shabla*** (summer, passage), Lake Srebarna*** (summer), Ropotamo NP*** (summer), Strandja Mts*** (passage), Tissata NR* (passage).
CANARY IS * (passage).
CAPE VERDE IS *.
CORSICA Biguglia Lake*** (summer, passage), Cap Corse* (passage).
CROATIA Kopački Rit** (summer).

CYPRUS *** (passage).
CZECH REPUBLIC Lednice*** (summer, passage), Nové Mlýny*** (summer), Pohořelice Fishponds*** (summer), Soutok*** (summer), Třeboňsko*** (summer).
EGYPT Abu Simbel** (passage, winter), Aswan*** (passage, winter), Faiyum* (passage), Luxor*** (passage), Nile Delta** (passage), Sharm el Sheikh*** (passage), Suez area* (passage), Wadi el Natrun*** (passage), Zaranik*** (passage).
FRANCE Camargue*** (summer), Cap Gris Nez* (passage), Dombes*** (summer), Gruissan*** (summer), Île d'Oléron* (summer), La Brenne*** (summer), Lac du Der-Chantecoq*** (summer), Leucate*** (passage), Lorraine NP*** (summer), Marais Poitevin*** (summer), Sologne*** (summer), Somme Estuary* (passage), Trunvel Reserve*** (summer).
GERMANY Federsee*** (summer).
GREAT BRITAIN Minsmere (passage).
GREECE Amvrakikós Gulf*** (summer, passage), Axios-Aliakmonas Deltas*** (summer,

passage), Evros Delta* (summer, passage), Lake Kerkini*** (summer), Mikrí Prespa NP*** (summer), Nestos Delta*** (summer), Porto Lagos area*** (summer).

GREEK IS Corfu*** (passage), Crete*** (summer, passage), Kos*** (passage), Lesvos*** (passage), Rhodes** (passage).

HUNGARY Biharugra*** (summer), Hanság*** (summer), Hortobágy NP*** (summer), Kisbalaton*** (summer), Kiskunság NP*** (summer), Lake Fertö*** (summer), Lake Velence*** (summer), Szeged Fishponds*** (summer), Tihany*** (summer), Zemplén Hills*** (summer).

ISRAEL Arava Valley*** (passage), Bet Shean Valley*** (passage), Eilat** (passage), Hula Reserve*** (passage), Ma'agan Mikhael*** (summer, passage).

ITALY Circeo NP*** (summer), Gargano Peninsula*** (summer, passage), Isonzo Regional Park*** (summer), Lake Massaciuccoli*** (summer), Maremma Regional Park*** (summer), Orbetello Reserve*** (summer, passage), Po Delta*** (summer), San Giuliano Reserve*** (summer, passage), Tuscan archipelago** (passage).

JORDAN Aqaba (passage), Azraq* (passage).

LEBANON Aamiq Marshes*** (passage), Palm Is** (passage), Qaraoun Lake** (passage).

MADEIRA (passage).

MALTA ** (passage).

MOROCCO Agadir and the Sous Plain*** (passage), Dayet Aaoua* (summer), Lac de Sidi Bourhaba*** (passage), Merja Zerga** (passage), Oualidia*** (passage), Ouarzazate** (passage), Oued Massa*** (passage).

NETHERLANDS Naardermeer** (summer), Oostvaadersplassen*** (summer).

POLAND Milicz Fishponds*** (summer).

PORTUGAL Baixo Alentejo*** (summer), Boquilobo*** (summer), Cape St Vincent*

(passage), Castro Marim*** (passage), Ria Formosa*** (summer), Sado Estuary*** (summer), Santo André Lagoon*** (summer), Tagus Estuary*** (summer).

ROMANIA Danube Delta*** (summer), Dobrudja*** (summer, passage), Lake Călăraşi*** (summer), Satchinez*** (summer).

RUSSIA Kalmykia*** (passage), Volga Delta*** (summer).

SARDINIA Cagliari wetlands*** (summer), Oristano wetlands*** (summer, passage).

SICILY Vendicari** (passage).

SLOVAKIA Senné Fishponds*** (summer), Zemplínská Reservoir* (passage).

SPAIN Aiguamolls de l'Empordá*** (summer), Cabo de Gata*** (passage), Cádiz Lagoons*** (summer), Coto Doñana*** (summer), Ebro Delta*** (summer), Guadalhorce Estuary*** (passage), Llobregat Delta** (summer), Monfragüe*** (summer), Santa Pola*** (summer), Serrania de Ronda* (summer), Tablas de Daimiel*** (summer).

SWITZERLAND Fanel NR** (summer), Grangettes* (passage), Leuk** (passage).

SYRIA Baath Lake*** (summer), Bahrat Homs*** (summer), Dayr al-Zawr*** (summer).

TUNISIA Cap Bon Peninsula*** (passage), Kelbia Lake** (passage), Lake Ichkeul*** (summer, passage).

TURKEY Bafa Gölü** (passage), Birecik-Halfeti** (summer), Bulanik* (passage), Dalyan*** (summer, passage), Göksu Delta*** (summer), İstanbul*** (summer, passage), Kızılırmak Delta*** (summer), Kulu Gölü*** (summer), Manyas Gölü*** (summer), Uluabat Gölü*** (summer), Van Gölü** (summer).

UKRAINE Dunay Delta*** (summer), Syvash Bay*** (summer).

YUGOSLAVIA Carska bara* (summer), Lake Skadar** (summer), Obedska bara* (summer).

Yellow-billed Stork
Mycteria ibis

FW (BW) (ES) Dis

Range: Found throughout sub-Saharan Africa and a rare but regular non-breeding visitor to the Banc d'Arguin, in Mauritania. Once again regularly recorded in S Egypt, mainly on Lake Nasser. Vagrants or escapes occasionally occur elsewhere in the region and there have now been *c.*20 records for Israel.

Tips: Occurs in swamps and at the margins of lakes and large rivers, sometimes on coastal mudflats and alkaline lakes. Increasingly seen at Abu Simbel, where formerly a regular visitor.

Site:
EGYPT Abu Simbel** (summer).

Black Stork
Ciconia nigra

DF FW FG Mig (Dis)

Range: Main breeding range is in C and E Europe to Russia, from Germany E across Russia reaching the Baltic states in the N and extending S to the S Balkans and N Greece. Also breeds in parts of Turkey and over much of the Caucasus. Isolated populations breed further W in C and E France and C Iberia. Present all year in Iberia and perhaps parts of SE Europe, but most migrate across the E Mediterranean although wintering in Israel has increased in recent years. Small numbers are seen at Gibraltar and a few in spring in Tunisia. Most leave Europe early Aug–Sep, peak period at the Bosphorus is late Sep–early Oct. Returning birds arrive in Europe in late Mar–May, mainly in Apr.

Tips: Shy and retiring when breeding, which occurs mainly in mature undisturbed forest, but in Spain, the Carpathians and the Caucasus also on rocky crags. Passage birds form small flocks and stop to feed on open wetlands. On both migrations peak passage is 2–4 weeks later than that of White Stork and often associates with passage raptors.

Sites:
ARMENIA Armash Fishponds** (passage).
AUSTRIA Lake Neusiedl** (summer), Marchauen-Marchegg Reserve*** (summer), Wienerwald* (summer).
BALEARIC IS Mallorca* (passage).
BELARUS Belovezhskaya Pushcha NP*** (summer), Berezinsky Reserve*** (summer), Pripyatsky NP*** (summer).

BELGIUM Croix-Scaille NR* (summer).
BULGARIA Albena-Golden Sands** (passage), Burgas area*** (passage), Cape Emine* (passage), Cape Kaliakra*** (passage), Lake Durankulak*** (passage), Lake Shabla*** (passage), Lake Srebarna** (passage), Ropotamo NP** (summer, passage), Rusenski Lom NP*** (summer), Strandja Mts*** (sum-

mer, passage), Studen Kladenetz*** (summer), Trigradski Gorge** (summer, passage), Tissata NR* (passage).

CORSICA Biguglia Lake (passage), Cap Corse* (passage).

CROATIA Kopački Rit* (summer), Plitvice* (summer), Pokupsko Depression*** (summer).

CZECH REPUBLIC Beskydy Mts*** (summer), Jeseníky Mts** (summer), Krkonoše NP*** (summer), Lednice* (summer), Poodří** (summer), Soutok*** (summer), Šumava NP*** (summer), Třeboňsko*** (summer).

DENMARK Møn-Falster* (passage).

EGYPT Hurghada*** (passage), Sharm el Sheikh* (passage), Suez area** (passage), Zaranik*** (passage).

ESTONIA Lake Endla*** (summer), Matsalu Bay** (passage), Nigula NR*** (summer).

FRANCE Fôret d'Orient* (summer, passage), Gruissan* (passage), Leucate* (passage), Lorraine NP* (summer, passage), Marais Poitevin* (passage), Organbidexka*** (passage).

GEORGIA Iori Steppes** (summer), Javakheti Plateau** (passage), Kolkheti*** (passage, rare in summer).

GERMANY Oder Valley*** (summer), Mecklenburg Lakes*** (summer), Vessertal* (summer).

GIBRALTAR** (passage).

GREECE Avas Gorge** (summer), Dadiá-Soufli Forest*** (summer), Evros Delta** (summer, passage), Lake Kerkini*** (summer, passage), Mikrí Prespa NP*** (summer), Mt Olympus NP** (summer).

GREEK IS Crete* (passage), Lesvos*** (summer, passage), Rhodes* (passage).

HUNGARY Aggtelek NP*** (summer), Biharugra** (passage), Hanság* (summer), Hortobágy NP* (summer), Kiskunság NP*** (summer), Lake Fertö* (summer), Ócsa* (summer), Zemplén Hills* (summer).

ISRAEL Arava Valley*** (passage), Bet Shean Valley*** (passage), Eilat*** (passage), Ein Gedi*** (passage), Hula Reserve*** (passage, winter), Jezreel Valley*** (passage), Ma'agan Mikhael*** (passage, winter), Nizzana*** (passage).

ITALY Circeo NP*** (passage), Gargano Peninsula*** (passage), Monte Conero*** (passage), San Giuliano Reserve*** (passage), Tuscan archipelago* (passage).

JORDAN Aqaba* (passage), Azraq** (passage).

LATVIA Cape Kolka** (summer), Lake Engure*** (summer), Lake Lubana*** (summer), Lake Pape** (passage).

LEBANON Aamiq Marshes*** (passage), Qaraoun Lake** (passage).

LITHUANIA Cepkeliai NR* (summer), Kirsiu Peninsula*** (passage), Zuvintas NR*** (summer).

MACEDONIA Babuna Gorge* (summer), Crna Gorge** (summer), Demir Kapija Gorge** (summer).

MALTA* (passage).

MOLDOVA Balatina** (passage).

POLAND Białowieża Forest*** (summer), Białystok Fishponds* (summer), Biebrza Marshes*** (summer), Bieszczady NP*** (summer), Chełm Marshes** (summer), Gdańsk Bay** (summer), Kampinos NP* (summer), Milicz Fishponds*** (summer), Siemianówka Reservoir*** (summer), Słońsk** (summer), Szczecin Bay area** (summer).

PORTUGAL Baixo Alentejo***, Cape St Vincent*** (autumn), Castro Marim** (passage), International Douro*** (summer), International Tagus*** (summer), Montesinho* (summer).

ROMANIA Danube Delta*** (passage), Dobrudja*** (passage).

RUSSIA Teberdinskiy Reserve*** (summer, passage), Volga Delta*** (passage).

SICILY Strait of Messina*** (spring), Vendicari** (passage).

SLOVAKIA High Tatras NP* (summer), Malá Fatra*** (summer), Malé Karpaty*** (summer), Nízke Tatry NP*** (summer), Orava Reservoir*** (summer, passage), Senné Fishponds** (passage), Slanské Hills*** (summer). Slovenský Kras** (summer), Vihorlatske

Hills*** (summer), Záhorie (summer),
Zemplínská Reservoir** (passage).
SLOVENIA Krakovski Forest* (summer),
Ljubljansko Moor (summer).
SPAIN Aiguamolls de l'Empordá* (passage),
Cabo de Gata* (passage), Cáceres-Trujillo
Steppes* (summer, passage), Coto Doñana*
(passage), Guadalhorce Estuary* (passage),
La Serena** (summer, passage), Monfragüe***
(summer), Picos de Europa*** (summer),
Sierra de Gredos*** (summer), Sierra de
Guadarrama* (summer), Tablas de Daimiel**
(passage).
SWEDEN Falsterbo* (autumn).
SWITZERLAND Col de Bretolet* (passage),
Klingnau Reservoir* (passage).

SYRIA Bahrat Homs** (passage, winter), Dayr
al-Zawr*** (passage, winter).
TUNISIA Cap Bon Peninsula* (passage).
TURKEY Göksu Delta** (passage), İstanbul***
(passage), Kızılırmak Delta*** (summer),
Kocaçay Delta*** (summer), Soğuksu NP***
(summer), Sultan Marshes** (summer),
Uluabat Gölü*** (passage).
UKRAINE Carpathians*** (summer) Dunay
Delta** (passage).
YUGOSLAVIA Carska bara (summer), Đerdap
NP** (summer, passage), Fruška Gora NP
(summer), Obedska bara* (summer, passage).

White Stork
Ciconia ciconia   FW FG U   Mig (Dis)

Range: Widespread breeder in Iberia, except much of
the Mediterranean coast, and NW Africa from S Morocco
to N Tunisia. Main range is from Denmark and
Germany E across Russia and S to Greece, Turkey and
Transcaucasia. Small numbers occur in W and C France,
the Netherlands, N Italy and Sardinia. The majority of
Western Palearctic breeders migrate to sub-Saharan
Africa or India, but small numbers remain in S Iberia all
year. Most migrate via Gibraltar or the Bosphorus in Aug–Sep and return in Mar–Apr.
Tips: Breeds in tall trees and, often, on buildings or large pylons close to wet meadows and
marshes. Urban nesters are rigorously protected and various reintroduction programmes
are underway but the species is still in decline.

Sites:
ALGERIA Djebel Babor***, El Kala NP***.
ANDORRA** (passage).
ARMENIA Armash Fishponds*** (summer,
passage).
AUSTRIA Lake Neusiedl*** (summer),
Marchauen-Marchegg Reserve*** (summer),
Wienerwald*** (summer).
BALEARIC IS Mallorca* (passage).
BELARUS Belovezhskaya Pushcha NP***
(summer), Berezinsky Reserve*** (summer),
Pripyatsky NP*** (summer).

BULGARIA Albena-Golden Sands*** (pas-
sage), Burgas area*** (passage), Cape
Emine*** (passage), Cape Kaliakra*** (pas-
sage), Lake Durankulak*** (summer), Lake
Shabla*** (passage), Lake Srebarna*** (sum-
mer, passage), Rila Mts*** (summer),
Ropotamo NP*** (passage), Rusenski Lom
NP*** (summer), Strandja Mts*** (summer,
passage), Studen Kladenetz*** (summer),
Tissata NR*** (summer).
CANARY IS* (passage).

CORSICA Biguglia Lake* (passage), Cap Corse** (passage).

CROATIA Kopački Rit*** (summer), Pokupsko Depression*** (summer).

CZECH REPUBLIC Beskydy Mts** (summer), Lednice*** (summer), Nové Mlýny*** (summer), Pálava Hills*** (summer), Pohořelice Fishponds*** (summer), Soutok*** (summer), Šumava NP*** (summer), Třeboňsko*** (summer).

DENMARK Møn-Falster*** (passage), Ringkøbing Fjord*** (passage), Skagen*** (summer, passage).

EGYPT Abu Simbel*** (passage), Aswan*** (passage), Hurghada*** (passage), Luxor*** (passage), Sharm el Sheikh*** (passage), Suez area*** (passage), Zaranik*** (passage).

ESTONIA Lake Endla*** (summer), Matsalu Bay*** (summer).

FRANCE Camargue*** (summer, passage), Dombes*** (summer), Gruissan*** (passage), Leucate*** (passage), Marais Poitevin*** (summer, passage), Organbidexka*** (passage), Somme Estuary*** (passage), Teich Reserve*** (summer).

GEORGIA Javakheti Plateau*** (summer), Kolkheti*** (passage).

GERMANY Berchtesgaden NP*** (passage), Dummer*** (summer), Federsee*** (summer), Mecklenburg Lakes*** (summer), Oder Valley*** (summer, passage), Rügen*** (summer), Vessertal*** (summer).

GIBRALTAR** (passage).

GREECE Amvrakikós Gulf*** (summer, passage), Axios-Aliakmonas Deltas*** (summer, passage), Dadiá-Soufli Forest*** (summer), Evros Delta*** (summer, passage), Lake Kerkini*** (summer, passage), Mikrí Prespa NP*** (summer), Nestos Delta*** (summer), Porto Lagos area*** (summer), Vikos-Aoos NP*** (summer).

GREEK IS Corfu*** (passage), Crete* (passage), Kos*** (passage), Lesvos*** (summer, passage), Rhodes** (passage).

HUNGARY Aggtelek NP*** (summer), Biharugra*** (summer, passage), Danube Bend*** (summer), Hanság*** (summer), Hortobágy NP*** (summer), Kis-balaton*** (summer), Kiskunság NP*** (summer), Lake Fertö*** (summer), Lake Velence*** (summer), Ócsa*** (summer), Zemplén Hills*** (summer).

ISRAEL Arava Valley*** (passage), Bet Shean Valley*** (passage), Eilat*** (passage), Ein Gedi*** (passage), Golan Heights*** (summer, passage), Hula Reserve*** (passage), Jezreel Valley*** (passage), Ma'agan Mikhael*** (passage, winter), Mt Hermon*** (passage), Nizzana*** (passage), Urim*** (passage, winter).

ITALY Circeo NP*** (summer, passage), Gargano Peninsula*** (passage), Monte Conero*** (passage), Orbetello Reserve*** (summer), Po Delta*** (summer), San Giuliano Reserve*** (passage), Tuscan archipelago*** (passage).

JORDAN Aqaba* (passage), Azraq** (passage), Wadi Dana-Fidan* (passage).

LATVIA Cape Kolka*** (summer), Lake Engure*** (summer), Lake Lubana*** (summer), Lake Pape*** (summer, passage).

LEBANON Aamiq Marshes*** (passage), Barouk Cedars*** (passage), Qaraoun Lake** (passage).

LITHUANIA Kirsiu Peninsula*** (summer, passage), Zuvintas NR*** (summer).

MACEDONIA Babuna Gorge** (summer), Lakes Ohrid and Prespa*** (summer).

MALTA* (passage).

MOLDOVA Balatina*** (passage).

MOROCCO Agadir and the Sous Plain***, Asilah and Oued Loukkos***, Boumalne***, Lac de Sidi Bourhaba*** (passage), Merja Zerga***, Oualidia***, Ouarzazate***, Oued Massa***, Tafilalt* (passage), Zaër*** (summer).

NETHERLANDS Veluwe** (summer).

POLAND Białowieża Forest*** (summer), Białystok Fishponds*** (summer), Biebrza Marshes*** (summer), Bieszczady NP*** (summer), Chełm Marshes*** (summer), Gdańsk Bay*** (summer), Kampinos NP*** (summer), Milicz Fishponds*** (summer), Siemianówka Reservoir*** (summer), Słońsk*** (summer), Szczecin Bay area*** (summer).

PORTUGAL Baixo Alentejo***, Boquilobo***, Cape St Vincent*** (autumn), Castro Marim***, International Douro*** (summer), International Tagus*** (summer), Montesinho*** (summer), Ria Formosa***, Sado Estuary***, Santo André Lagoon*** (mainly summer), Tagus Estuary*** (summer).

ROMANIA Danube Delta*** (summer), Dobrudja*** (summer, passage), Lake Călăraşi*** (summer), Satchinez*** (summer).

RUSSIA Teberdinskiy Reserve*** (summer, passage).

SICILY Lago di Lentini***, Strait of Messina*** (spring), Vendicari*** (passage).

SLOVAKIA High Tatras NP*** (summer), Malé Karpaty*** (summer), Nízke Tatry NP*** (summer), Orava Reservoir*** (summer, passage), Senné Fishponds*** (summer, passage), Slanské Hills*** (summer), Slovenský Kras*** (summer), Vihorlatske Hills*** (summer), Záhorie*** (summer), Zemplínská Reservoir*** (passage), Zlatná na Ostrove*** (summer).

SLOVENIA Krakovski Forest** (summer).

SPAIN Aiguamolls de l'Empordá*** (reintroduced), Cabo de Gata*** (passage), Cáceres-Trujillo Steppes*** (summer), Cádiz Lagoons*** (passage), Coto Doñana***, Guadalhorce Estuary*** (summer, passage), La Serena*** (summer), Llobregat Delta***, Monfragüe*** (summer), Picos de Europa*** (summer), Santa Pola*** (passage), Sierra de Gredos*** (summer), Sierra de Guadarrama*** (summer), Serrania de Ronda***, Tablas de Daimiel*** (summer), Zaragoza Steppes*** (summer).

SWEDEN Falsterbo* (passage), Kristianstad*** (summer, reintroduced), Öland* (passage).

SWITZERLAND Fanel NR*** (passage), Klingnau Reservoir* (passage).

SYRIA Aqra Mts*** (passage), Jabal Slenfeh*** (passage), Dayr al-Zawr*** (passage).

TUNISIA Cap Bon Peninsula*** (passage), Chott el Djerid* (passage), Kelbia Lake** (summer, passage), Lake Ichkeul*** (summer, passage).

TURKEY Birecik-Halfeti*** (summer), Dalyan*** (summer, passage), Demirkazik*** (summer), Göksu Delta*** (summer, passage), İstanbul*** (passage), Kızılırmak Delta*** (summer), Kocaçay Delta*** (summer), Kulu Gölü*** (summer), Manyas Gölü*** (summer, passage), Uluabat Gölü*** (summer, passage), Van Gölü* (summer, passage).

UKRAINE Crimean Mts*** (summer), Dunay Delta*** (summer), Syvash Bay*** (summer).

YUGOSLAVIA Carska bara* (summer), Đerdap NP** (passage), Fruška Gora NP* (summer), Obedska bara* (summer).

Glossy Ibis
Plegadis falcinellus   FW (BW) (ES)   Mig (Dis)

Range: Breeds mainly in SE Europe, particularly the Volga and Danube deltas, and in Ukraine. Smaller numbers breed at scattered sites in the Balkans, N Greece, Turkey and Morocco. Has recently bred in France, in the Camargue, in the Ebro Delta of Spain, Sardinia and in mainland Italy. May also breed sporadically in the Middle East and N Africa but nesting sites change frequently throughout range. Most winter in tropical Africa with smaller numbers around the Mediterranean, mainly in Morocco and Tunisia. Departs breeding areas in Sep and returns late Mar–Apr.

Tips: Breeds colonially in trees, in swamps and around lakes, often roosting and nesting alongside herons, egrets and Pygmy Cormorants. In winter on shallow lagoons, estuaries and shorelines.

Sites:

ALBANIA Lake Shkodra** (summer, passage).
ARMENIA Armash Fishponds*** (summer), Lake Sevan** (passage).
AZERBAIJAN Kura Valley Salt-lakes*** (summer), Kyzylagach Bay*** (summer).
BALEARIC IS Mallorca* (passage).
BULGARIA Albena-Golden Sands** (passage), Belene* (summer, passage), Burgas area*** (summer, passage), Lake Durankulak** (passage), Lake Shabla*** (passage), Lake Srebarna*** (summer, passage).
CORSICA Biguglia Lake (passage). **CYPRUS*** (passage).
EGYPT Aswan** (passage, winter), Luxor*** (passage, winter), Hurghada* (passage), Nile Delta* (passage), Sharm el Sheikh* (passage), Suez area** (passage), Wadi el Natrun*** (passage), Zaranik** (passage).
FRANCE Camargue**.
GEORGIA Javakheti Plateau** (passage), Kolkheti** (passage).
GREECE Amvrakikós Gulf*** (summer, passage), Axios-Aliakmonas Deltas*** (summer, passage), Evros Delta** (passage), Lake Kerkini*** (passage), Mikrí Prespa NP*** (summer, passage), Nestos Delta* (passage), Porto Lagos area*** (passage).
GREEK IS Corfu* (passage), Crete*** (passage), Kos*** (passage), Lesvos*** (passage), Rhodes* (passage).
HUNGARY Hortobágy NP*** (summer), Kisbalaton** (summer, passage), Szeged Fishponds* (summer, passage).
ISRAEL Arava Valley*** (passage), Bet Shean Valley*** (passage), Eilat*** (passage), Hula Reserve***, Jezreel Valley*** (passage, winter), Ma'agan Mikhael***.
ITALY Circeo NP** (passage), Gargano Peninsula*** (summer, passage), Isonzo Regional Park** (passage), Lake Massaciuccoli*** (passage), Maremma Regional Park* (passage), Po Delta*** (summer, passage), San Giuliano Reserve** (passage).
JORDAN Azraq* (passage).
LEBANON Aamiq Marshes (passage), Qaraoun Lake* (passage).
MACEDONIA Lakes Ohrid and Prespa*** (passage).
MOLDOVA Balatina** (passage).
MOROCCO Agadir and the Sous Plain*** (passage), Asilah and Oued Loukkos*** (passage), Lac de Sidi Bourhaba*** (passage), Merja Zerga*** (passage), Oued Massa*** (passage).
PORTUGAL Castro Marim* (winter), Ria Formosa** (passage, winter), Santo André Lagoon*** (passage).
ROMANIA Danube Delta*** (summer), Dobrudja*** (summer, passage), Lake Călăraşi** (summer, passage).
RUSSIA Volga Delta*** (summer).
SARDINIA Cagliari wetlands*** (summer, passage), Oristano wetlands*** (passage).
SICILY Lago di Lentini*** (passage, winter), Vendicari*** (passage, winter).
SPAIN Aiguamolls de L'Empordá** (passage, winter), Coto Doñana*** (passage), Ebro Delta** (summer, passage), Santa Pola* (passage).
SYRIA Bahrat Homs*** (summer).
TUNISIA Cap Bon Peninsula** (passage), Chott el Djerid** (winter), Kelbia Lake** (passage).
TURKEY Bafa Gölü** (passage), Bulanik*** (summer, passage), Dalyan** (passage), Göksu Delta*** (summer, passage), Kızılırmak Delta*** (passage), Kocaćay Delta*** (passage) Kulu Gölü*** (summer, passage), Manyas Gölü*** (passage), Sultan Marshes*** (summer, passage), Uluabat Gölü*** (summer).
UKRAINE Dunay Delta*** (summer), Syvash Bay*** (summer, passage).
YUGOSLAVIA Lake Skadar* (summer), Obedska bara (summer).

Bald Ibis (Waldrapp)
Geronticus eremita   M C Mig Dis

Range: Survives in Morocco (*c.*300 birds) and there is a population of *c.*75 free-flying birds in SE Turkey, part of a captive-breeding programme. Passage birds are still occasionally seen in Saudi Arabia, Yemen and Israel, which led to suggestions that there may be another breeding site somewhere in the Middle East, and this was confirmed in spring 2002 when three pairs were rediscovered in the mountains of C Syria. There is a reintroduction scheme underway in N Italy. Turkish birds were migratory and wintered in Ethiopia but Moroccan birds are merely dispersive.

Tips: Breeds on rock ledges on cliffs in arid country or on coasts. Feeds in dry wadis and semi-desert, meadows and sometimes along shores. The famous Turkish colony at Birecik became extinct (as a wild population) in 1989, although there have been recent suggestions that some genuine wild birds may still be present. The small Syrian population should not be searched for without assistance and permission from the relevant conservation authorities.

Sites:
MOROCCO Agadir and the Sous Plain* (winter), Oued Massa***.

SYRIA Tadmur and Sabkhat Muh (summer).
TURKEY Birecik-Halfeti*** (semi-captive).

Eurasian Spoonbill
Platalea leucorodia   FW BW ES Mig Dis

Range: Very scattered range, with breeding populations in S Iberia, W France, the Netherlands, Austria, Hungary, parts of the Balkans and Turkey. Some expansion of range has taken place in the W and the species has recently bred in Morocco, Italy, Germany, Denmark and Britain. Most Spoonbills in the region are summer visitors, departing in Aug–Sep and returning in Mar–Apr, but Spanish birds are more or less resident. Immatures often undertake dispersive movements and some adults remain N in winter, many winter around the Mediterranean and on the Atlantic coast of NW Africa.

Tips: Search shallow fresh, brackish or saltwater for a large creamy white bird, rather than the pure white of egrets. Occurs more often on brackish and estuarine waters on passage and in winter.

Sites:
ARMENIA Armash Fishponds*** (summer, passage), Lake Sevan** (summer, passage).

AUSTRIA Lake Neusiedl*** (summer), Marchauen-Marchegg Reserve*** (summer).

AZERBAIJAN Kura Valley Salt-lakes*** (summer).
BALEARIC IS Mallorca** (passage).
BELGIUM Het Zwin** (passage).
BULGARIA Albena-Golden Sands* (passage), Belene*** (summer, passage), Burgas area*** (summer, passage), Lake Durankulak*** (passage), Lake Shabla*** (passage), Lake Srebarna*** (summer, passage), Ropotamo NP** (passage), Strandja Mts*** (passage).
CANARY IS Tenerife* (passage, winter). **CROATIA** Kopački Rit** (passage), Neretva Delta** (passage).
CYPRUS* (passage).
CZECH REPUBLIC Nové Mlýny** (passage), Soutok*** (summer, passage), Třeboňsko*** (passage).
EGYPT Abu Simbel*** (passage), Aswan*** (passage, winter), Faiyum* (passage, winter), Hurghada***, Luxor*** (passage, winter), Nile Delta* (passage, winter), Sharm el Sheikh*** (passage, winter), Suez area*** (passage), Zaranik*** (passage).
FRANCE Baie du Mont-St-Michel** (passage), Cap Gris Nez** (passage), Golfe du Morbihan*** (passage), Marais Poitevin* (passage), Somme Estuary* (passage), Teich Reserve*** (passage, winter).
GREAT BRITAIN Dungeness* (passage), Minsmere** (summer, passage), N Norfolk coast** (summer, passage), Portland** (passage).
GREECE Amvrakikós Gulf*** (summer, passage), Axios-Aliakmonas Deltas*** (summer, passage), Evros Delta** (passage), Lake Kerkini*** (summer, passage), Mikrí Prespa NP*** (summer, passage), Porto Lagos area*** (summer, passage).
GREEK IS Crete* (passage), Lesvos** (passage).
HUNGARY Biharugra*** (summer), Hortobágy NP*** (summer), Kis-balaton*** (summer), Kiskunság NP*** (summer), Lake Fertö*** (summer), Lake Velence*** (summer), Szeged Fishponds*** (summer, passage).
ISRAEL Bet Shean Valley*** (passage), Hula Reserve*** (passage, winter), Ma'agan

Mikhael*** (passage, winter).
ITALY Circeo NP*** (passage), Gargano Peninsula*** (summer, passage), Isonzo Regional Park*** (passage), Orbetello Reserve*** (passage, winter), Po Delta***, San Giuliano Reserve** (passage).
LEBANON Aammiq Marshes (passage), Palm Is* (passage).
MACEDONIA Lakes Ohrid and Prespa*** (passage).
MOROCCO Agadir and the Sous Plain*** (passage, winter), Asilah and Oued Loukkos*** (passage, winter), Essaouira* (passage, winter), Lac de Sidi Bourhaba*** (passage, winter), Merja Zerga*** (passage, winter), Oualidia*** (passage, winter), Ouarzazate*** (passage, winter), Oued Massa*** (passage, winter).
NETHERLANDS Lauwersmeer*** (summer, passage), Oostvaardersplassen*** (summer), Terschelling*** (summer), Texel*** (summer), Zwanenwater*** (summer).
PORTUGAL Boquilobo*** (summer), Castro Marim*** (passage, winter), Ria Formosa*** (passage, winter), Sado Estuary*** (passage, winter), Santo André Lagoon*** (passage, winter), Tagus Estuary*** (passage, winter).
ROMANIA Danube Delta*** (summer), Dobrudja*** (summer, passage), Lake Călăraşi (summer, passage).
RUSSIA Volga Delta*** (summer).
SARDINIA Cagliari wetlands*** (passage, winter), Oristano wetlands*** (passage, winter).
SICILY Lago di Lentini*** (passage, winter), Vendicari*** (passage, winter).
SLOVAKIA Orava Reservoir** (passage), Senné Fishponds*** (summer), Záhorie*** (passage).
SPAIN Aiguamolls de l'Empordá*** (passage), Cabo de Gata** (passage), Cádiz Lagoons***, Coto Doñana***, Ebro Delta*** (passage, winter), Monfragüe*** (passage, winter), Santa Pola** (passage, winter).
SYRIA Sabkhat al-Jubbal*** (passage).
TUNISIA Cap Bon Peninsula** (passage), Kelbia Lake** (passage, winter), Lake Ichkeul*** (passage, winter).

TURKEY Bafa Gölü** (passage), Bulanik*** (summer, passage), Dalyan** (passage), Göksu Delta*** (summer), Kızılırmak Delta*** (summer), Kulu Gölü*** (passage), Manyas Gölü*** (summer, passage), Sultan Marshes*** (summer, passage), Uluabat Gölü*** (summer).

UKRAINE Dunay Delta*** (summer), Syvash Bay*** (summer).
YUGOSLAVIA Carska bara (passage), Obedska bara (summer).

Greater Flamingo
Phoenicopterus roseus   BW (ES)   Mig Dis

Range: Breeding is often irregular at the few known sites in S Spain and the Camargue in France, C Turkey and at scattered localities in N Africa. Has bred in Portugal and C Spain, Sardinia, Italy and Sinai. More widespread in winter in Iberia and N Africa, Mallorca, Sardinia, Sicily and Cyprus. Non-breeders are often present on wintering grounds all year.

Tips: Requires large open, shallow waters, usually saline lakes and coastal lagoons, sometimes on tidal mudflats. Exceptionally, prone to abandon breeding and wintering sites.

Sites:
ARMENIA Armash Fishponds* (passage).
AZERBAIJAN Kura Valley Salt-lakes*, Kyzylagach Bay** (winter).
BALEARIC IS Formentera** (passage, winter), Ibiza* (passage), Mallorca*** (passage, winter).
CORSICA Biguglia Lake (passage). **CYPRUS*** (passage, winter).
EGYPT Abu Simbel** (passage, winter), Aswan*** (passage, winter), Faiyum* (passage), Hurghada*** (passage, winter), Luxor*** (passage), Nile Delta*** (passage, winter), Sharm el Sheikh*** (passage, winter), Suez area* (passage), Zaranik**.
FRANCE Camargue***, Gruissan**, Leucate***.
GIBRALTAR* (passage).
GREECE Axios-Aliakmonas Deltas** (passage, winter), Evros Delta**, Nestos Delta***, Porto Lagos area***.
GREEK IS Crete* (passage, winter), Kos*** (passage), Lesvos*** (winter).
ISRAEL Bet Shean Valley** (passage, winter), Eilat*** (passage, winter), Hula Reserve** (passage, winter), Ma'agan Mikhael*** (winter).

ITALY Circeo NP** (passage), Gargano Peninsula* (passage), Maremma Regional Park* (passage, winter), Orbetello Reserve** (mainly passage), Po Delta* (passage).
MOROCCO Agadir and the Sous Plain*** (passage, winter), Lac de Sidi Bourhaba*** (passage), Merja Zerga*** (passage, winter), Oualidia*** (passage, winter), Ouarzazate*** (passage, winter), Oued Massa***, Tafilalt** (winter).
NETHERLANDS Lauwersmeer* (feral), Oostvaardersplassen** (feral).
PORTUGAL Castro Marim*** (passage, winter), Ria Formosa*** (passage, winter), Sado Estuary*** (passage, winter), Santo André Lagoon*** (passage, winter), Tagus Estuary*** (passage, winter).
SARDINIA Cagliari wetlands*** (mainly passage, winter), Oristano wetlands*** (passage, winter), San Pietro I** (passage, winter).
SICILY Vendicari*** (passage, winter).
SPAIN Aiguamolls de l'Empordá*** (passage, winter), Cabo de Gata***, Cádiz Lagoons***,

Coto Doñana*** Ebro Delta***, Guadalhorce Estuary***, Llobregat Delta*** (passage), Santa Pola**.

SYRIA Bahrat Homs*** (passage, winter, may also occur in summer), Sabkhat al-Jabbul*** (passage, winter, possible in summer), Tadmur and Sabkhat Muh* (winter).

TUNISIA Cap Bon Peninsula*** (passage, winter), Chott el Djerid (irregular), Kelbia Lake** (passage, winter), Lake Ichkeul*** (passage, winter), Tunis*** (passage, winter).

TURKEY Göksu Delta*** (winter), Kulu Gölü*** (summer, passage), Manyas Gölü*** (passage, winter), Sultan Marshes*** (passage, winter), Van Gölü*** (autumn).

Bewick's Swan (Tundra Swan)
Cygnus (columbianus) bewickii

Summer **FW** winter **FG (ES)** **Mig**

Range: Breeds in coastal Arctic Russia and on Ostrov Kolguyev and Novaya Zemlya, with small numbers summering in the Baltic. Migrates through the White Sea and Baltic to winter in NW Europe. Wintering range mainly the southern British Isles, the Netherlands and Denmark, with smaller numbers in N France, Belgium and Germany, and regular in Bulgaria and Romania. Main passage periods Mar–Apr and Oct–Nov. Usually considered a race of Tundra Swan *C. columbianus*.

Tips: Breeds beside tundra lakes or the coast, on passage occurs on lakes, rivers and coasts, and in winter at wetlands with open water and flooded fields. Wintering and passage sites are traditional, but may wander widely in severe weather. Small numbers often associate with large flocks of Whooper Swan in winter.

Sites:
BELGIUM Blankaart Reserve*** (winter). **BULGARIA** Burgas area* (winter).
DENMARK Bornholm-Christiansø*** (passage), Møn-Falster** (passage, winter).
ESTONIA Emajõgi Floodplain*** (passage), Matsalu Bay*** (passage), Vilsandi NP*** (passage).
FRANCE Camargue** (winter), Forêt d'Orient** (winter), Lac du Der-Chantecoq*** (winter), Somme Estuary* (winter).
GERMANY Oder Valley*** (passage, winter).
GREAT BRITAIN Anglesey*** (winter), Dungeness*** (winter), Minsmere*** (winter), N Norfolk coast** (winter), Portland* (winter), Tregaron Bog* (winter).
GREECE Evros Delta* (winter).
IRELAND Akeragh Lough*** (winter), North

Slob*** (passage, winter), Tacumshin Lake*** (winter).
LATVIA Lake Engure*** (passage), Lake Lubana*** (passage), Lake Pape*** (passage).
LITHUANIA Kirsiu Peninsula*** (passage, winter).
NETHERLANDS Lauwersmeer*** (winter), Oostvaardersplassen*** (winter), Texel*** (winter).
NORWAY Varanger* (passage).
POLAND Gdańsk Bay** (passage, winter), Milicz Fishponds* (passage, winter), Słońsk** (winter), Szczecin Bay area** (passage).
ROMANIA Danube Delta (winter), Dobrudja* (winter).
SWEDEN Falsterbo** (passage, winter), Gotland*** (passage), Getterön*** (passage,

winter), Hornborgasjön** (passage), Kristianstad*** (passage), Öland*** (passage, winter), Store Mosse NP* (passage).

SWITZERLAND Klingnau Reservoir*** (winter).

Whooper Swan
Cygnus cygnus

Summer **FW** winter **FG (ES)**   **Mig**

Range: Breeds in Iceland, coastal N Norway, in much of Sweden and Finland, and across Arctic Russia, with smaller numbers breeding in Scotland, Poland, the Baltic States and Belarus. Icelandic birds winter mainly in Scotland and Ireland. Continental birds winter in eastern England and from Norway to the Baltic and E to NE France, C Europe, around the E Mediterranean, and the Black and Caspian Seas. Departs breeding grounds mid Sep–Oct and return movement commences Mar–Apr, arriving on the breeding grounds in May.

Tips: Breeds on forest or tundra lakes, in winter occur in coastal areas or on lakes and large rivers, often grazing in winter cereal fields. Usually winters in traditional areas but wanders widely in severe weather. Check large flocks of Mute Swans as the two species often associate in winter.

Sites:
ARMENIA Armash Fishponds*** (winter), Lake Sevan** (winter).
AZERBAIJAN Kura Valley Salt-lakes*** (winter), Kyzylagach Bay*** (winter).
BELARUS Belovezhskaya Pushcha NP* (summer, passage), Berezinsky Reserve*** (winter).
BULGARIA Burgas area*** (winter), Lake Durankulak*** (winter), Lake Shabla*** (winter).
DENMARK Amager** (winter), Hanstholm** (winter), Møn-Falster** (passage), Ringkøbing Fjord*** (passage, winter), Skagen*** (passage), Stignæs*** (winter).
ESTONIA Matsalu Bay*** (passage), Vilsandi NP*** (passage).
FINLAND Åland Is*** (summer), Kuusamo*** (summer), Lake Inari*** (summer), Lemmenjoki NP*** (summer), Liminganlahti*** (summer, passage), Oulanka NP*** (summer), Pallas-Ounastunturi NP*** (summer), Parikkala*** (summer, passage), Patvinsuo NP*** (summer), Ruissalo*** (passage), Urho Kekkonen NP*** (summer), Viikki*** (passage).

FRANCE Forêt d'Orient** (winter), Lac du Der-Chantecoq*** (winter), Somme Estuary* (winter).
GERMANY Oder Valley*** (passage, winter).
GREAT BRITAIN Islay*** (winter), Anglesey*** (winter), Dungeness* (winter), Islay*** (winter), Minsmere* (winter), N Norfolk coast** (winter), Orkney Is*** (passage, winter), Outer Hebrides*** (passage, winter, often also in summer), Portland* (winter), Rhum** (passage), Shetland Is*** (passage, winter), Spurn Peninsula* (passage), Tregaron Bog*** (winter).
GREECE Evros Delta* (winter).
HUNGARY Hortobágy NP* (winter), Kis-balaton* (winter).
ICELAND Breiðafjörður***, Lake Mývatn***, Northwest Peninsula***, Olfusar Delta***, Reykjanes Peninsula***, Skagafjörður*** (summer, passage), Thingvellir NP*** (passage).
IRELAND Akeragh Lough*** (winter), Mullet Peninsula*** (winter), North Slob** (winter), Strangford Lough*** (winter), Tacumshin Lake*** (winter).

LATVIA Cape Kolka*** (summer, passage), Lake Engure*** (passage), Lake Lubana*** (passage), Lake Pape*** (passage).
LITHUANIA Kirsiu Peninsula*** (passage), Zuvintas NR*** (passage).
MOLDOVA Balatina** (passage), Manta Floodplain** (passage).
NETHERLANDS Lauwersmeer*** (winter), Oostvaardersplassen*** (winter), Texel*** (winter).
NORWAY Lofoten Is*** (passage), Øvre Pasvik NP*** (summer), Slettnes* (passage).
POLAND Białystok Fishponds* (summer), Biebrza Marshes*** (passage), Gdańsk Bay*** (passage, winter), Milicz Fishponds*** (mainly passage, winter but also summer), Słońsk*** (passage, winter), Szczecin Bay area*** (summer).

ROMANIA Danube Delta*** (winter), Dobrudja*** (winter).
RUSSIA Kola Peninsula*** (summer), Volga Delta*** (winter).
SWEDEN Falsterbo* (passage, winter), Färnebofjärden*** (passage), Getterön** (passage, winter), Gotland*** (passage, winter), Hornborgasjön*** (summer, passage), Kristianstad*** (passage, winter), Lake Krankesjön*** (passage), Muddus NP*** (summer), Öland*** (passage), Ripakaisenvuoma*** (summer), Sarek NP*** (summer), Store Mosse NP*** (summer, passage), Tåkern*** (passage), Tärnasjön*** (summer).
SWITZERLAND Fanel NR** (winter), Klingnau Reservoir*** (winter).
TURKEY Kızılırmak Delta (winter).
UKRAINE Dunay Delta* (winter).

Taiga Bean Goose
Anser (fabalis) fabalis Summer **CF (DF)** winter **FW FG   Mig**

Range: Scattered small numbers breed in N and C Norway, Sweden and N Finland, and across Arctic Russia. Winters from the Netherlands to Germany and in scattered areas across C Europe, with the majority in Austria and Hungary. Small numbers winter in Iberia and France, but now very scarce in Great Britain with just one regular site in England and one in Scotland. Departs breeding areas in Sep–Nov, returning in Mar–May.

Tips: Breeds in coniferous forest and birch woodland, but winters on pastures and stubble fields with nearby lakes or estuaries. Mixes freely with Tundra Bean Goose on passage and in winter, and larger flocks often contain both forms.

Sites:
AUSTRIA Lake Neusiedl*** (passage, winter).
BELARUS Belovezhskaya Pushcha NP* (passage), Berezinsky Reserve* (passage), Prypyatsky NP** (passage).
BELGIUM Blankaart Reserve*** (winter), Het Zwin*** (winter).
CROATIA Kopački Rit** (passage).

CZECH REPUBLIC Lednice*** (passage, winter), Nové Mlýny*** (passage, winter), Pohořelice Fishponds*** (passage, winter), Třeboňsko*** (passage, winter).
DENMARK Bornholm-Christiansø*** (passage), Hanstholm** (passage), Møn-Falster*** (passage), Ringkøbing Fjord*** (passage, winter), Skagen*** (passage), Skallingen-

Blavandshuk*** (passage), Stignæs*** (winter), Vadehavet*** (passage, winter).

ESTONIA Emajõgi Floodplain*** (passage), Matsalu Bay*** (passage), Nigula NR*** (passage), Vilsandi NP*** (passage).

FINLAND Kuusamo*** (summer), Liminganlahti*** (passage), Oulanka NP*** (summer), Patvinsuo NP*** (summer, passage), Ruissalo*** (passage), Viikki*** (passage).

FRANCE Forêt d'Orient*** (passage, winter), La Brenne* (winter), Lac du Der-Chantecoq*** (passage, winter), Somme Estuary* (passage, winter).

GERMANY Dummer*** (winter), Mecklenburg Lakes*** (passage, winter), Oder Valley*** (passage, winter), Rügen*** (passage, winter).

GREAT BRITAIN Minsmere* (winter), N Norfolk coast* (winter).

HUNGARY Biharugra*** (passage), Csákvár*** (passage, winter), Danube Bend*** (passage, winter), Hortobágy NP*** (passage), Kardoskút*** (passage), Kis-balaton*** (passage, winter), Kiskunság NP*** (passage, winter), Lake Fertö*** (passage, winter), Lake Velence*** (passage, winter), Szeged Fishponds*** (passage, winter).

LATVIA Cape Kolka*** (passage), Lake Engure*** (passage), Lake Lubana*** (passage), Lake Pape*** (passage).

LITHUANIA Kirsiu Peninsula*** (passage), Zuvintas NR*** (passage).

NETHERLANDS Lauwersmeer*** (passage, winter), Oostvaardersplassen*** (passage, winter), Terschelling*** (passage), Texel*** (winter),

NORWAY Lofoten Is*** (passage), Øvre Pasvik NP*** (summer), Stabbursdalen NP** (passage), Varanger*** (passage).

POLAND Gdańsk Bay*** (passage), Milicz Fishponds*** (passage), Słońsk*** (passage, winter), Szczecin Bay area*** (passage).

RUSSIA Kola Peninsula*** (summer).

SLOVAKIA Senné Fishponds** (passage), Záhorie** (passage), Zemplínská Reservoir** (passage).

SWEDEN Falsterbo** (passage), Getterön*** (passage), Gotland*** (passage), Hjälstaviken*** (passage) Hornborgasjön*** (passage), Kristianstad*** (passage, winter), Kvismaren*** (passage), Lake Ånnsjön*** (summer, passage), Lake Krankesjön*** (passage, winter), Öland*** (passage), Padjelanta NP*** (summer), Ripakaisenvuoma*** (summer), Sarek NP*** (summer), Store Mosse NP*** (passage), Tåkern*** (passage).

UKRAINE Dunay Delta** (passage), Shatsk NP*** (passage).

Tundra Bean Goose
Anser (fabalis) rossicus Summer **T** winter **FW FG** **Mig**

Range: Breeds across Arctic Russia from the Kanin Peninsula to Taimyr. Main wintering range is in Iberia and France, Italy and the Balkans, but often occurs in C Europe. Rare and irregular winter visitor to Britain. Considered a race of *A. fabalis* by many authorities.

Tips: Breeds on tundra but winters on pastures and stubble fields with nearby lakes or estuaries. Mixes freely with Taiga Bean Goose on passage and in winter, and flocks are worth checking for both forms.

Sites:
AUSTRIA Lake Neusiedl** (passage, winter).
BELARUS Belovezhskaya Pushcha NP* (passage), Berezinsky Reserve* (passage), Prypyatsky NP** (passage, winter).
BELGIUM Het Zwin* (winter).
CROATIA Kopački Rit** (passage).
ESTONIA Emajõgi Floodplain*** (summer), Matsalu Bay*** (passage), Nigula NR*** (summer), Vilsandi NP*** (passage).
FINLAND Viikki*** (passage).
FRANCE Forêt d'Orient*** (passage, winter), La Brenne* (winter), Lac du Der-Chantecoq*** (passage, winter), Somme Estuary* (passage, winter).
GERMANY Dummer* (winter), Mecklenburg Lakes* (passage, winter), Oder Valley*** (summer), Rügen*** (passage).
HUNGARY Biharugra*** (passage), Csákvár* (passage), Danube Bend* (passage), Hortobágy NP** (passage), Kardoskút* (passage), Kis-balaton** (passage, winter), Kiskunság NP*** (passage, winter), Lake Fertő*** (passage, winter), Lake Velence*** (passage, winter), Szeged Fishponds** (passage, winter).

LATVIA Cape Kolka*** (passage), Lake Engure*** (passage), Lake Lubana*** (passage), Lake Pape*** (passage).
LITHUANIA Kirsiu Peninsula*** (passage), Zuvintas NR*** (passage).
NETHERLANDS Lauwersmeer** (passage, winter), Oostvaardersplassen*** (passage, winter), Terschelling*** (passage), Texel*** (winter).
NORWAY Lofoten Is*** (passage), Stabbursdalen NP** (passage), Varanger*** (passage).
POLAND Gdańsk Bay*** (passage), Milicz Fishponds*** (passage), Słońsk*** (passage), Szczecin Bay area*** (passage).
RUSSIA Volga Delta* (passage).
SLOVAKIA Senné Fishponds** (passage), Záhorie** (passage), Zemplínská Reservoir** (passage).
SWEDEN Falsterbo* (passage), Getterön* (passage), Gotland* (passage), Hjälstaviken* (passage), Kristianstad* (passage), Kvismaren* (passage), Lake Krankesjön* (passage), Öland* (passage), Tåkern* (summer).
SWITZERLAND Fanel NR** (passage, winter).

Pink-footed Goose
Anser brachyrhynchus   Summer **T** winter **FG FW ES   Mig**

Range: Breeds in C Iceland and Svalbard, and outside the region in Greenland. Winters in Britain (mainly Scotland and N and E England), Belgium, the Netherlands, Denmark and Germany. Departs breeding grounds in late Sep–late Oct and returns from mid Apr to mid May. Formerly considered a race of *A. fabalis*.

Tips: Breeds on tundra and in winter feeds on grassland, stubble and crop fields close to estuaries, lakes and reservoirs, which are used for roosting and swims well. More strictly coastal than other grey geese and winters at traditional sites although seldom forms mixed flocks with other species.

Sites:
BELGIUM Blankaart Reserve*** (winter), Het Zwin*** (winter).

DENMARK Bornholm-Christiansø*** (passage), Møn-Falster* (passage), Ringkøbing Fjord***

(passage, winter), Rømø*** (passage, winter), Skallingen-Blåvandshuk*** (passage), Stignæs** (passage, winter), Vadehavet*** (passage, winter).
FRANCE Golfe du Morbihan** (winter), Ouessant** (autumn).
GREAT BRITAIN Anglesey* (winter), Islay* (passage), N Norfolk coast*** (winter), Orkney Is* (passage), Outer Hebrides** (passage), Rhum** (passage), Shetland Is*** (autumn), Spurn Peninsula* (passage).
ICELAND Lake Mývatn*** (summer), Olfusar Delta*** (passage), Skagafjörður*** (summer, passage).

IRELAND North Slob** (passage, winter).
NETHERLANDS Lauwersmeer*** (winter), Oostvaardersplassen*** (winter), Terschelling*** (passage), Texel*** (passage).
NORWAY Lofoten Is*** (passage), Utsira* (passage), Varanger* (passage).
SVALBARD* (summer).
SWEDEN Getterön* (passage), Gotland* (passage), Hjälstaviken* (passage), Hornborgasjön** (passage), Kristianstad* (passage, winter), Kvismaren* (passage), Öland* (passage), Tåkern* (passage).

White-fronted Goose (Greater White-fronted Goose)
Anser albifrons   Summer **T** winter **FW FG   Mig**

Range: Breeds in Arctic Russia from the Kanin Peninsula and S Novaya Zemlya eastwards. In winter, Russian breeders occur mainly from S Great Britain and W and N France to Denmark and Germany, as well as in C and SE Europe, in Austria and Hungary, along the Danube and the W shores of the Black Sea, in parts of Turkey and on the W shore of the Caspian. Smaller numbers are regular in NW Africa. Greenland breeders occur on passage in Iceland and winter (Oct–Apr) in Ireland and W Scotland, sometimes also in Wales.
Subspecies: Nominate race breeds in Siberia; *flavirostris*, which is sometimes considered a full species, breeds in western Greenland and is known as **Greenland White-fronted Goose**.
Tips: Breeds on lowland tundra often close to the nest of a raptor. On passage and in winter on steppe, pastures, cultivated areas and bogs. Check flocks of this species for individuals of scarcer grey geese.

Sites:
AUSTRIA Lake Neusiedl*** (passage, winter).
AZERBAIJAN Kyzylagach Bay*** (winter).
BELARUS Belovezhskaya Pushcha NP* (passage), Berezinsky Reserve* (passage), Prypyatsky NP*** (passage, winter).
BELGIUM Blankaart Reserve*** (winter), Het Zwin*** (winter).
BULGARIA Burgas area*** (winter), Lake Durankulak*** (winter), Lake Shabla*** (winter), Lake Srebarna*** (winter).

CZECH REPUBLIC Lednice*** (passage, winter), Nové Mlýny*** (passage, winter).
DENMARK Bornholm-Christiansø*** (passage), Møn-Falster*** (passage), Ringkøbing Fjord*** (passage, winter), Skagen*** (passage), Skallingen-Blåvandshuk*** (passage), Stignæs** (passage), Vadehavet*** (passage).
ESTONIA Emajõgi Floodplain*** (passage), Matsalu Bay*** (passage), Nigula NR*** (passage), Vilsandi NP*** (passage).

FINLAND Liminganlahti*** (passage), Ruissalo*** (passage), Viikki*** (passage).

FRANCE Baie du Mont-St-Michel** (passage, winter), Camargue* (winter), Forêt d'Orient** (passage, winter), Lac du Der-Chantecoq*** (passage, winter), Marais Poitevin* (winter), Somme Estuary* (passage, winter).

GERMANY Dummer* (winter), Mecklenburg Lakes*** (passage, winter), Oder Valley*** (passage, winter).

GREAT BRITAIN Anglesey* (winter), Dungeness** (winter), Islay*** (winter), Minsmere* (autumn, winter), N Norfolk coast** (winter), Orkney Is*** (winter), Outer Hebrides** (passage), Rhum* (passage), Pembrokeshire Is* (autumn), Portland* (winter), Shetland Is* (autumn).

GREECE Evros Delta** (passage, winter), Lake Kerkini* (passage), Mikrí Prespa NP* (passage), Nestos Delta** (passage, winter), Lesvos* (winter).

HUNGARY Biharugra* (passage), Danube Bend* (passage, winter), Hortobágy NP*** (passage), Kardoskút*** (passage), Kis-balaton*** (passage, winter), Kiskunság NP*** (passage, winter), Lake Fertö*** (passage, winter), Lake Velence*** (passage, winter), Szeged Fishponds* (passage).

ICELAND Olfusar Delta*** (passage).

IRELAND Mullet Peninsula*** (passage, winter), North Slob*** (passage, winter).

ISRAEL Hula Reserve* (winter).

ITALY Gargano Peninsula** (passage, winter), Maremma Regional Park** (winter).

LATVIA Cape Kolka*** (passage), Lake Engure*** (passage), Lake Lubana*** (passage), Lake Pape*** (passage).

LITHUANIA Kirsiu Peninsula*** (passage), Zuvintas NR*** (passage).

MACEDONIA Lakes Ohrid and Prespa** (passage).

MOLDOVA Manta Floodplain** (passage).

NETHERLANDS Lauwersmeer*** (passage, winter), Oostvaardersplassen*** (passage, winter), Terschelling*** (passage), Texel*** (passage, winter).

NORWAY Varanger*** (passage).

POLAND Gdańsk Bay*** (passage), Milicz Fishponds*** (passage), Słońsk*** (passage, winter), Szczecin Bay area** (passage).

ROMANIA Bicaz*** (autumn), Danube Delta*** (winter), Dobrudja*** (winter), Satchinez*** (winter).

RUSSIA Oka Valley*** (passage), Volga Delta*** (passage).

SLOVAKIA Senné Fishponds*** (passage), Zemplínská Reservoir*** (passage).

SWEDEN Falsterbo** (passage), Getterön*** (passage, winter), Gotland*** (passage), Hjälstaviken*** (passage), Hornborgasjön*** (passage), Kristianstad*** (passage, winter), Kvismaren*** (passage), Lake Krankesjön*** (passage, winter), Öland*** (passage), Tåkern*** (passage).

SWITZERLAND Fanel NR*** (passage, winter).

SYRIA Baath Lakes*** (winter), Bahrat Homs** (winter), Dayr al-Zawr*** (winter), Lake Assad*** (winter), Sabkhat al-Jubbal*** (winter).

TURKEY Göksu Delta*** (winter), İstanbul*** (winter), Kulu Gölü*** (passage, winter), Sultan Marshes*** (passage, winter).

UKRAINE Askania-Nova*** (passage, winter), Dunay Delta*** (winter), Tiligul Liman*** (passage, winter), Syvash Bay*** (passage).

Lesser White-fronted Goose
Anser erythropus   Summer **T** winter **FG   Mig**

Range: breeds in the mountains of N Norway E to the Kola Peninsula and across Arctic Russia. Very rare in Scandinavia with very few remaining wild birds, and reintroductions are underway in Norway, Sweden and Finland. Western birds migrate through Scandinavia and E Europe to winter very locally in the Balkans and Greece, with the Evros Delta one of the best sites. Eastern birds winter around the Caspian Sea, in Iran and on the Euphrates in Iraq. Attempts are being made to encourage reintroduced birds (fostered by semi-wild Barnacle Geese) to winter in the safer Netherlands rather than further E in Europe, and this now appears to be succeeding with 78 birds wintering in 2003. These arrive in Nov and remain until spring.

Tips: Present in breeding range May to late Aug or early Sep but shy and difficult to see. Breeds on tundra and in birch and willow scrub in montane areas, but on passage and in winter occurs on meadows, pasture and vegetable fields, often in more arid areas than other geese. Away from main wintering areas, search flocks of Bean Geese or Greater White-fronts (particularly at Slimbridge WWT) to locate vagrants of this species, which can often be picked out by their more rapid rate of feeding.

Sites:

ARMENIA Armash Fishponds* (passage), Lake Sevan** (winter).
AUSTRIA Lake Neusiedl* (passage).
AZERBAIJAN Kyzylagach Bay* (winter).
BELARUS Belovezhskaya Pushcha NP* (passage), Prypyatsky NP* (passage).
BULGARIA Lake Durankulak*** (winter), Lake Shabla*** (winter), Lake Srebarna** (winter).
DENMARK Møn-Falster* (passage), Skallingen-Blåvandshuk*** (passage).
ESTONIA Matsalu Bay** (passage).
FINLAND Liminganlahti*** (passage), Kilpisjärvi Saana* (summer).
GEORGIA Javakheti Plateau** (passage), Kolkheti* (winter).
GERMANY Wattenmeer** (passage).
GREECE Evros Delta** (passage, winter), Lake Kerkini* (passage), Nestos Delta* (passage, winter), Porto Lagos Area** (passage, winter).
HUNGARY Hortobágy NP** (passage), Kardoskút* (passage), Kiskunság NP* (passage), Lake Fertö* (passage).

LATVIA Lake Engure (passage), Lake Lubana* (passage), Lake Pape* (passage).
MOLDOVA Balatina* (passage), Manta Floodplain (passage).
NETHERLANDS Lauwersmeer** (winter), Oostvaardersplassen** (winter).
NORWAY Slettnes** (passage), Stabbursdalen NP* (passage), Varanger* (passage).
POLAND Milicz Fishponds (passage).
ROMANIA Danube Delta (autumn, winter), Dobrudja** (winter).
RUSSIA Kola Peninsula* (summer), Volga Delta* (passage).
SLOVAKIA Senné Fishponds* (passage), Zemplínská Reservoir* (passage).
SWEDEN Hjälstaviken* (passage), Hornborgasjön (passage), Kristianstad* (passage), Kvismaren* (passage), Öland* (passage), Padjelanta NP* (summer), Sarek NP* (summer), Tåkern* (passage).
UKRAINE Syvash Bay*** (passage).
YUGOSLAVIA Carska bara (winter).

Barnacle Goose
Branta leucopsis　　　　　　　　　Summer **M I ES** winter **FG FW ES　Mig**

Range: In the Western Palearctic, breeds on Svalbard and Novaya Zemlya, with more recently established populations in Iceland, Franz Josef Land, Norway, around the Baltic, in Denmark and Germany. Some of these populations may originate from escapees, and the species now breeds ferally in Great Britain and elsewhere. Present on breeding grounds mid May to mid Sep. Greenland breeders winter in Ireland and W Scotland, birds from Svalbard winter on the Solway Firth of Scotland, and those from Novaya Zemlya winter in the Netherlands, northern Germany and southern Denmark.

Tips: A colonial breeder on cliffs and crags, sometimes on islands, often near gull colonies or the nest of a raptor. In winter grazes on coastal pastures, roosting on lakes and rivers.

Sites:

DENMARK Bornholm-Christiansø*** (passage), Møn-Falster*** (passage, winter), Ringkøbing Fjord*** (passage, winter), Rømø*** (passage, winter), Skagen*** (passage), Skallingen-Blåvandshuk*** (passage), Stignæs** (passage), Vadehavet*** (passage, winter).

ESTONIA Matsalu Bay*** (summer, passage), Vilsandi NP*** (summer, passage).

FINLAND Ruissalo*** (summer, passage), Viikki*** (passage).

FRANCE Baie du Mont-St-Michel* (passage, winter), Lac du Der-Chantecoq (winter).

GERMANY Rügen*** (passage, winter), Wattenmeer*** (passage, winter).

GREAT BRITAIN Islay*** (winter), N Norfolk coast* (passage, winter), Orkney Is*** (winter), Outer Hebrides*** (passage, winter), Rhum** (passage), Shetland Is** (autumn).

HUNGARY Lake Fertö* (passage, winter).

ICELAND Lake Mývatn* (passage), Skagafjördur*** (passage).

IRELAND Mullet Peninsula*** (passage, winter), North Bull* (passage), North Slob* (passage, winter).

LATVIA Cape Kolka*** (passage), Lake Pape*** (passage).

LITHUANIA Kirsiu Peninsula*** (passage).

NETHERLANDS Lauwersmeer*** (winter), Oostvaardersplassen*** (passage, winter), Terschelling*** (passage), Texel** (passage, winter).

NORWAY Lofoten Is** (passage), Slettnes* (passage), Utsira** (passage), Varanger* (passage).

POLAND Gdańsk Bay* (passage), Milicz Fishponds* (passage).

SVALBARD* (summer).

SWEDEN Falsterbo*** (passage), Gotland*** (summer, passage), Holmöarna*** (passage), Hornborgasjön** (passage), Kristianstad** (passage), Öland*** (summer, passage), Tåkern* (passage).

Dark-bellied Brent Goose
Branta (bernicla) bernicla　　　　　Summer **T ES** winter **ES**　**Mig**

Range: Breeds in Arctic Russia, mainly outside Western Palearctic. Departs breeding grounds late Aug–early Sep, moving W to the White Sea, then overland to the Baltic. Winters on coasts, from Denmark and N Germany to W France, and on S and E coasts of England.

Tips: Breeds on tundra and on rivers and coasts. Winters on coastal mudflats, feeding on eel-grass and grazing on adjacent grasslands. Often occurs in association with Eurasian Wigeon *Anas penelope* but rarely mixes with larger geese. Check flocks of Dark-bellied Brents for small numbers of Pale-bellied Brent and the occasional, but increasingly recorded, Black Brant *B. (b). nigricans.*

Sites:

DENMARK Bornholm-Christiansø*** (passage), Møn-Falster*** (passage, winter), Ringkøbing Fjord*** (passage, winter), Rømø*** (passage, winter), Skagen*** (passage), Skallingen-Blåvandshuk*** (passage), Stignæs** (passage), Vadehavet*** (passage, winter), Viikki*** (passage).

FRANCE Baie de Bourgneuf*** (passage, winter), Baie de Vilaine*** (passage, winter), Baie du Mont-St-Michel*** (passage, winter), Cap Gris Nez*** (passage, winter), Golfe du Morbihan*** (passage, winter), Île d'Oléron* (passage, winter), Marais Poitevin*** (passage, winter), Somme Estuary*** (passage, winter), Teich Reserve*** (winter).

GERMANY Wattenmeer*** (passage, winter).

GREAT BRITAIN Dungeness*** (passage), Flamborough Head*** (passage), Minsmere*** (passage, winter), N Norfolk coast*** (passage, winter), Portland*** (passage, winter), St Ives Bay* (winter), Spurn Peninsula*** (passage, winter).

LATVIA Cape Kolka*** (passage), Lake Pape*** (passage).

LITHUANIA Kirsiu Peninsula*** (passage).

NETHERLANDS Lauwersmeer** (passage), Oostvaardersplassen** (passage), Terschelling*** (passage), Texel*** (passage, winter).

NORWAY Lista*** (passage), Lofoten Is** (passage), Utsira* (passage), Varanger* (passage).

POLAND Gdańsk Bay** (passage).

SWEDEN Falsterbo*** (passage), Getterön*** (passage), Gotland*** (passage), Holmöarna*** (passage), Kristianstad*** (passage), Öland*** (passage), Stockholm archipelago*** (passage).

Pale-bellied Brent Goose
Branta (bernicla) hrota Summer **M I ES** winter **FG FW ES Mig**

Range: Two populations, which breed and winter in separate areas. One breeds in the Canadian Arctic and Greenland and migrates through Iceland to winter in Ireland, where present from mid Oct to mid Apr. The other population breeds on Svalbard and Franz Josef Land and winters in Denmark, with smaller numbers in NE England, present late Sep to mid May. Usually considered a race of Dark-bellied Brent but may be afforded full species status in the future.

Tips: Breeds on tundra with pools, along rivers and on Arctic coasts. Winters on coastal mudflats feeding on eel-grass, and grazes on adjacent grasslands. Most sites with large numbers of Dark-bellied Brent Geese attract a few of this form.

Sites:

DENMARK Ringkøbing Fjord*** (passage, winter), Rømø*** (passage, winter), Skagen*** (passage), Skallingen-Blåvandshuk*** (passage), Stignæs** (passage), Vadehavet*** (passage, winter).
FRANCE Baie du Mont-St-Michel** (passage, winter), Cap Gris Nez* (passage), Somme Estuary* (passage).
GERMANY Wattenmeer** (passage).
GREAT BRITAIN Islay*** (passage, winter), N Norfolk coast* (passage, winter), Spurn Peninsula* (passage, winter).
ICELAND Breiðafjörður*** (passage), Northwest Peninsula*** (passage), Olfusar

Delta*** (passage), Reykjanes Peninsula*** (passage).
IRELAND Belfast Lough*** (passage, winter), Ireland's Eye*** (winter), Mullet Peninsula*** (passage), North Bull*** (passage, winter), North Slob*** (passage, winter), Strangford Lough*** (passage, winter), Tacumshin Lake*** (passage, winter).
NETHERLANDS Oostvaardersplassen** (passage), Terschelling* (passage), Texel* (passage, winter).
SVALBARD* (summer).

Red-breasted Goose
Branta ruficollis Summer **M T FW** winter **FG FW Mig**

Range: Breeds on the Taimyr Peninsula and winters in lowland areas on the N and W shores of the Black Sea. Leaves breeding range in Sep and most now winter from Nov onwards in the Dobrudja region of Romania, with smaller numbers in N Bulgaria and Hungary, sometimes in NE Greece and Turkey. Returns to breeding grounds in early Jun.

Tips: Breeds in small, loose colonies on cliffs or rocky outcrops in tundra, usually near water and close to nest of a raptor or large gull. On passage and in winter occurs on open steppe, pastures and crop fields, usually near large shallow waters. Away from regular wintering areas search flocks of other geese for this species and vagrants annually recorded in western Europe.

Sites:

AZERBAIJAN Kyzylagach Bay* (winter).
BULGARIA Burgas area** (winter), Cape Kaliakra* (winter), Lake Durankulak*** (winter), Lake Shabla*** (winter), Lake Srebarna** (winter).
GEORGIA Kolkheti* (winter).
GREECE Evros Delta* (winter), Nestos Delta* (winter), Porto Lagos Area** (winter).
HUNGARY Hortobágy NP* (passage, winter), Kardoskút* (passage), Kiskunság NP*** (passage, winter).
ISRAEL Hula Reserve (winter).

MOLDOVA Manta Floodplain** (passage).
NETHERLANDS Lauwersmeer* (winter), Oostvaardersplassen* (winter), Terschelling (winter).
POLAND Milicz Fishponds (passage).
ROMANIA Danube Delta** (winter), Dobrudja*** (winter).
RUSSIA Volga Delta* (passage).
SWEDEN Öland* (passage).
UKRAINE Askania-Nova** (passage), Dunay Delta*** (winter), Syvash Bay* (passage, winter), Tiligul Liman* (passage, winter).

Egyptian Goose
Alopochen aegyptiaca   FW (FG)   Res (Dis)

Range: A widespread and common African goose that breeds in the Western Palearctic only in the Nile Valley of Egypt and as an introduced species in Great Britain and Belgium, the Netherlands and Germany, and more recently in S France. In S Egypt, where still fairly common, it is a resident or dispersive species that is recorded further N in winter. The British population is centred on Norfolk, with occasional birds breeding elsewhere. The Belgian population of over 250 pairs is mainly found around Brussels and in Flanders. More than 1,300 pairs now breed in the Netherlands and from here the species has spread to Nordhein-Westfalen in Germany, where several hundred pairs are now established.
Tips: In Africa found on rivers, lakes and pools in a range of habitats, in Great Britain mainly on lowland farmland, open woodland and parkland.

Sites:
EGYPT Abu Simbel***, Aswan***, Luxor***.
GREAT BRITAIN Breckland***, N Norfolk coast***.

Ruddy Shelduck
Tadorna ferruginea   FW BW   Res (Mig) (Dis)

Range: Breeds in the Middle Atlas of NW Africa and in larger numbers on the Black Sea coasts of Romania and Bulgaria, in N Greece and Turkey, and E to the Caspian. Reintroduction programmes are underway in Bulgaria and Ukraine, and it now breeds ferally in the Netherlands and Germany. More widespread in Turkey in winter, and also reaches the Middle East and Egypt at this season. Moroccan breeders formerly wintered in southern Spain but numbers are now very low and little movement seems to occur.

Tips: Search for this species beside rivers and saline lakes in open country, although spends much time on land in pairs or small parties. Most records in N and W Europe probably refer to feral birds, rather than genuine vagrants, although this species can be prone to irruptions.

Sites:

ARMENIA Armash Fishponds*** (summer, passage), Lake Sevan*** (summer, passage).
AZERBAIJAN Kura Valley Salt-lakes*** (winter), Kyzylagach Bay*** (summer).
BULGARIA Burgas area*** (summer, passage), Cape Kaliakra* (summer, passage), Lake Durankulak** (summer, passage), Lake Shabla*** (summer, passage), Lake Srebarna*** (summer), Rusenski Lom NP* (summer), Strandja Mts* (summer, passage).
CANARY IS Fuerteventura**(probably introduced).
CYPRUS ** (passage, winter).
GREECE Evros Delta**, Nestos Delta*** (summer), Porto Lagos Area*** (passage).
GREEK IS Kos***, Lesvos***.
ISRAEL Arava Valley* (passage), Bet Shean Valley** (passage), Hula Reserve*** (passage), Jezreel Valley** (passage, winter), Ma'agan Mikhael* (winter).

MOROCCO Agadir and the Sous Plain* (passage, winter), Merja Zerga*** (winter), Oued Massa***, Tafilalt** (passage, winter).
NETHERLANDS Oostvaardersplassen*** (feral, passage).
ROMANIA Danube Delta*** (summer), Dobrudja*** (summer).
RUSSIA Kalmykia*** (summer), Volga Delta*** (summer).
SYRIA Bahrat Homs**, Dayr al-Zawr***, Sabkhat al-Jubbal***.
TUNISIA Chott el Djerid** (irregular), Lake Ichkeul* (winter).
TURKEY Bulanik***, Göksu Delta***, Kocaćay Delta*** (summer), Kulu Gölü***, Soğuksu NP* (summer), Sultan Marshes*** (summer), Van Gölü*** (summer, passage).
UKRAINE Askania-Nova*** (winter), Dunay Delta* (passage), Syvash Bay** (summer), Tiligul Liman*** (passage).

Marbled Duck
Marmaronetta angustirostris   **FW (BW)   Res Mig Dis**

Range: Rare and local with widely separated breeding areas in the south-west and south-east of the region. A declining breeder in S Spain, mainly in Andalucia and Valencia, and probably still in NW Africa in Morocco and Tunisia, possibly also in Algeria. In the E breeds in S and E Turkey, and Transcaucasia. Probably breeds regularly in Syria and Jordan, perhaps elsewhere in the Middle East, and has recently bred in Mallorca and Sicily. Virtually resident in parts of range, migratory and dispersive in others, but with little discernable pattern. Occurs in Israel and Egypt in winter and then more widespread and numerous in Morocco. Increasingly recorded further N in Europe but most are generally regarded as escapes.

Tips: Usually seen on small densely vegetated fresh waters, sometimes reservoirs and brackish lagoons and usually sociable, breeding in loose colonies. Generally shy and difficult to see, particularly when breeding as it often remains hidden in vegetation and most active during early morning and evening.

Sites:
ALGERIA El Kala NP***.
ARMENIA Armash Fishponds*** (summer).
AZERBAIJAN Kura Valley Salt-lakes***, Kyzylagach Bay*** (winter).
BALEARIC IS Mallorca*.
CANARY IS Fuerteventura*.
EGYPT Luxor** (winter).
GEORGIA Javakheti Plateau** (passage).
ISRAEL Golan Heights* (winter), Hula Reserve** (mainly winter), Jezreel Valley*** (passage, winter), Ma'agan Mikhael** (winter).
JORDAN Azraq (passage).
MOROCCO Agadir and the Sous Plain* (summer, passage), Asilah and Oued Loukkos***, Lac de Sidi Bourhaba***, Merja Zerga***

(passage, winter), Oualidia*** (passage, winter), Oued Massa*** (passage, winter), Tafilalt* (winter).
SPAIN Cádiz Lagoons*** (passage, winter), Coto Doñana***, Guadalhorce Estuary** (passage, winter), Santa Pola***.
SYRIA Bahrat Homs** (passage), Dayr al-Zawr*** (summer, passage), Sabkhat al-Jubbal* (summer, passage).
TUNISIA Cap Bon Peninsula**, Chott el Djerid***, Kelbia Lake**, Lake Ichkeul***.
TURKEY Göksu Delta***, Kulu Gölü*** (summer, passage), Sultan Marshes** (summer), Van Gölü*** (summer, passage).

Red-crested Pochard
Netta rufina Summer **FW** winter **FW (BW) (ES) Mig Dis**

Range: Very patchily distributed across S Europe, breeding at scattered localities in Iberia and S France, N to the Netherlands and Germany and E to the N Black Sea and the Caspian. Also breeds sporadically in Morocco, in the Mediterranean on Mallorca (reintroduced), Corsica and Sardinia, and more widely in Turkey and Transcaucasia. Breeds ferally in Great Britain and can be virtually guaranteed at Cotswold Water Park in autumn and winter. More widespread in winter around the Mediterranean and Black Seas, with concentrations in the Ebro, Camargue and Danube deltas, Turkey and Egypt.

Tips: Breeds on fairly deep fresh waters with dense marginal vegetation, on passage and in winter on reservoirs, brackish lagoons and estuaries. Forms large flocks on favoured wintering waters.

Sites:

ARMENIA Armash Fishponds*** (summer), Lake Sevan*** (passage, winter).

AUSTRIA Lake Neusiedl***.

AZERBAIJAN Kura Valley Salt-lakes***, Kyzylagach Bay*** (winter).

BALEARIC IS Mallorca***.

BULGARIA Lake Durankulak**, Lake Srebarna*** (summer).

CORSICA Biguglia Lake (winter).

CYPRUS* (passage, winter).

CZECH REPUBLIC Lednice*** (summer, passage), Nové Mlýny*** (summer, passage), Pohořelice Fishponds*** (summer, passage), Soutok*** (summer), Třeboňsko** (summer, passage).

EGYPT Luxor*** (winter), Nile Delta*** (passage, winter).

FRANCE Camargue***, Dombes***, Gruissan*** (passage), Lac du Der-Chantecoq** (winter).

GERMANY Mecklenburg Lakes*** (summer), Tiroler Achen***.

GREAT BRITAIN Dungeness* (passage, winter), N Norfolk coast* (passage, winter).

GREECE Mikrí Prespa NP*** (passage).

HUNGARY Kis-balaton** (summer), Lake Fertö*** (summer, passage), Lake Velence*** (summer, passage).

ISRAEL Hula Reserve** (passage, winter), Jezreel Valley** (passage, winter).

ITALY Po Delta**.

MACEDONIA Lakes Ohrid and Prespa*** (winter).

MOROCCO Asilah and Oued Loukkos* (winter), Lac de Sidi Bourhaba*** (passage), Merja Zerga*** (passage, winter), Oued Massa*** (passage, winter).

NETHERLANDS Oostvaardersplassen* (passage).

PORTUGAL Baixo Alentejo*** (passage, winter), Boquilobo**, Castro Marim***, Ria Formosa***, Santo André Lagoon*** (mainly winter), Tagus Estuary***.

ROMANIA Danube Delta***, Dobrudja*** (passage, winter).

RUSSIA Kalmykia*** (summer), Volga Delta*** (summer, passage).

SARDINIA Cagliari wetlands***, Oristano wetlands***.

SICILY Vendicari**.

SLOVAKIA Záhorie* (summer), Zemplínská Reservoir* (passage).

SPAIN Cádiz Lagoons***, Coto Doñana***, Ebro Delta***, Guadalhorce Estuary*** (passage, winter), La Serena**, Llobregat Delta**, Santa Pola***, Tablas de Daimiel***.

SWITZERLAND Fanel NR*** (passage, winter, rare in summer), Grangettes** (passage, winter), Klingnau Reservoir*** (winter). **SYRIA** Bahrat Homs*** (passage, winter).

TURKEY Göksu Delta***, Kızılırmak Delta***, Kulu Gölü***, Sultan Marshes***. **UKRAINE** Dunay Delta***, Syvash Bay***.

Ferruginous Duck
Aythya nyroca   FW (BW) Mig

Range: Main breeding range is from Germany, Poland and SE Europe E to the Caspian, with isolated populations in S Spain and Morocco, Italy and Turkey. More widespread around the Mediterranean and Black Seas in winter, particularly in Egypt. In decline over much of the region, particularly in the W.

Tips: Freshwater lakes and marshes with abundant vegetation, in winter on larger, more open waters, sometimes brackish lakes. Often keeps to marginal vegetation, particularly during the breeding season and most active during early morning and evening.

Sites:
ALBANIA Lake Shkodra*** (summer, passage). **ARMENIA** Armash Fishponds***, Lake Sevan*** (passage, winter). **AUSTRIA** Lake Neusiedl*** (summer). **AZERBAIJAN** Kura Valley Salt-lakes*** (summer). **BALEARIC IS** Mallorca*. **BELARUS** Belovezhskaya Pushcha NP* (summer, passage), Prypyatsky NP*** (summer). **BOSNIA-HERZEGOVINA** Hutovo blato (summer). **BULGARIA** Burgas area*** (summer), Lake Durankulak*** (summer, passage), Lake Shabla***, Lake Srebarna*** (summer, passage), Ropotamo NP*** (summer, passage). **CORSICA** Biguglia Lake* (winter). **CROATIA** Kopački Rit** (summer), Pokupsko Depression*** (summer). **CYPRUS** (passage, winter). **CZECH REPUBLIC** Nové Mlýny* (summer), Pohořelice Fishponds* (summer, passage). **EGYPT** Aswan** (winter), Luxor*** (winter), Nile Delta*** (passage, winter), Suez area* (passage).

FRANCE Camargue* (winter), Dombes** (passage), La Brenne* (winter), Lac du Der-Chantecoq* (passage, winter), Sologne* (autumn). **GEORGIA** Javakheti Plateau** (summer, passage), Kolkheti*** (passage). **GREECE** Amvrakikós Gulf*** (summer, passage), Axios-Aliakmonas Deltas*** (passage), Evros Delta* (summer, passage), Lake Kerkini*** (summer, passage), Mikrí Prespa NP*** (summer), Nestos Delta*** (summer), Porto Lagos Area**. **GREEK IS** Corfu* (passage), Crete* (winter, spring), Lesvos* (passage). **HUNGARY** Biharugra** (summer), Hanság* (summer), Hortobágy NP*** (summer), Kis-balaton*** (summer), Kiskunság NP*** (summer, passage), Lake Fertö*** (summer, passage), Lake Velence** (summer, passage), Ócsa*** (summer), Tihany*** (summer). **ISRAEL** Bet Shean Valley*** (passage, winter), Hula Reserve*** (passage, winter), Jezreel Valley*** (passage, winter). **ITALY** Circeo NP*** (winter), Gargano Peninsula*** (winter), Isonzo Regional Park*

(winter), Lake Massaciuccoli*** (summer, passage), Maremma Regional Park* (winter), Orbetello Reserve** (passage), Po Delta***, San Giuliano Reserve** (passage).
LATVIA Lake Engure* (summer).
LEBANON Aammiq Marshes*** (winter), Qaraoun Lake**.
LITHUANIA Lake Kretuonas (summer).
MACEDONIA Lakes Ohrid and Prespa***.
MOLDOVA Balatina** (summer), Manta Floodplain**.
MOROCCO Asilah and Oued Loukkos*** (winter), Lac de Sidi Bourhaba*** (passage, winter), Merja Zerga** (winter), Oued Massa*** (winter).
POLAND Biebrza Marshes*** (summer), Chełm Marshes** (summer), Gdańsk Bay** (summer), Milicz Fishponds*** (summer).
ROMANIA Danube Delta*** (summer), Dobrudja*** (summer, passage), Lake Călăraşi** (summer), Satchinez*** (summer).
RUSSIA Kalmykia** (summer), Volga Delta*** (summer).
SARDINIA Cagliari wetlands** (winter), Oristano wetlands***.
SICILY Lago di Lentini***, Vendicari***.

SLOVAKIA Senné Fishponds*** (summer), Slovenský Kras* (summer), Záhorie** (summer, passage), Zemplínská Reservoir** (summer, passage).
SLOVENIA Lake Cerknica* (summer).
SPAIN Cádiz Lagoons** (passage, winter), Coto Doñana**, Guadalhorce Estuary** (passage, winter), Llobregat Delta** (passage, winter), Tablas de Daimiel***.
SWITZERLAND Fanel NR** (passage, winter), Grangettes* (passage, winter).
SYRIA Bahrat Homs** (passage, winter), Dayr al-Zawr** (passage, winter, rare in summer).
TUNISIA Cap Bon Peninsula*** (passage, winter), Chott el Djerid* (winter), Kelbia Lake* (winter), Lake Ichkeul** (winter).
TURKEY Göksu Delta***, Kızılırmak Delta*** (summer), Kocaçay Delta*** (summer), Kulu Gölü***, Manyas Gölü*** (passage), Sultan Marshes*** (summer, passage), Uluabat Gölü*** (summer), Van Gölü*** (summer, passage).
UKRAINE Dunay Delta** (summer), Shatsk NP*** (summer), Syvash Bay**.
YUGOSLAVIA Carska bara (summer), Lake Skadar*** (summer), Obedska bara* (summer).

King Eider
Somateria spectabilis

Summer **T Sea** winter **Sea   Mig**

Range: In summer found on Svalbard, Novaya Zemlya, Ostrov Kolguev and Ostrov Vaygach, and on coasts and inland areas of Arctic Russia. Winters from the White Sea to N Scandinavian coasts and around Iceland. Rare but regular in N Scotland and the S Baltic.
Tips: Breeds on tundra, winters at sea, normally in Arctic regions, and not confined to inshore waters. Search flocks of Common Eider carefully, vagrant King Eiders usually associate with this species and can be easily overlooked, particularly females.

Sites:
DENMARK Bornholm-Christiansø* (winter).
GREAT BRITAIN Shetland Is* (winter).

ICELAND Northwest Peninsula** (summer), Reykjanes Peninsula** (winter).

NORWAY Lofoten Is*** (passage, winter), Slettnes*** (passage), Stabbursdalen NP** (passage), Varanger***.
POLAND Gdańsk Bay* (passage, winter).
RUSSIA Kola Peninsula*** (mainly winter).

SVALBARD* (summer).
SWEDEN Getterön** (passage), Gotland** (passage), Holmöarna*** (passage), Öland*** (passage, winter).

Steller's Eider
Polysticta stelleri

Summer **T Sea** winter **Sea** **Mig**

Range: Rarely breeds in the Western Palearctic, but small numbers regular in summer in N Norway and Estonia, around the Kola Peninsula and S Novaya Zemlya. Winters off N Norway and in small numbers in the Baltic, particularly around the Åland Is, rarely off Poland and Germany. Non-breeders sometimes summer in wintering areas.

Tips: Breeds beside tundra pools and rivers, on passage and in winter found in coastal waters, present all year off N Norway.

Sites:

DENMARK Bornholm-Christiansø* (winter).
ESTONIA Nigula NR* (passage), Vilsandi NP*** (passage).
FINLAND Åland Is*** (passage, winter), Ruissalo* (passage), Viikki* (passage).
LITHUANIA Kirsiu Peninsula* (passage).

NORWAY Lofoten Is* (winter), Slettnes** (passage), Varanger*** (mainly winter but also summer).
POLAND Gdańsk Bay (passage, winter).
RUSSIA Kola Peninsula*** (mainly winter).
SWEDEN Gotland*** (winter), Holmöarna*** (passage), Öland** (passage, winter).

Harlequin Duck
Histrionicus histrionicus

Summer **FW (Sea)** winter **Sea** **Dis**

Range: In the Western Palearctic range restricted to Iceland, where widespread, moving to coastal areas in winter but rarely further.

Tips: Breeds beside montane rivers and streams, in winter off exposed rocky coasts. Gathers in bays and river mouths in spring and in late Apr–May moves upriver to breeding areas. Immatures and non-breeders remain on coasts all year.

Long-tailed Duck
Clangula hyemalis

Summer **T FW** winter **Sea (FW)** **Mig**

Range: Breeds in Iceland, Svalbard and Novaya Zemlya, in N and montane Scandinavia, and across Arctic Russia, with small isolated populations in S Finland. In winter occurs from Iceland and N Scandinavia to the N and E British Isles, the southern North Sea and S Baltic. Regular in small numbers inland on C European lakes and in the N Adriatic.

Tips: Breeds beside pools on tundra, otherwise usually found at sea, mainly offshore but in small numbers close to shore, rarely seen inland but sometimes occurs on reservoirs after severe weather. Sociable outside breeding season and flocks often sexually segregated.

Sites:

BELGIUM Het Zwin* (winter).
DENMARK Amager** (winter), Bornholm-Christiansø*** (winter), Hanstholm*** (passage), Møn-Falster*** (passage, winter), Ringkøbing Fjord*** (passage, winter), Rømø*** (passage, winter), Skagen*** (passage, winter), Skallingen-Blåvandshuk*** (passage, winter), Stignæs*** (winter), Vadehavet*** (winter).
ESTONIA Matsalu Bay*** (passage), Vilsandi NP*** (passage).
FINLAND Åland Is*** (passage, winter), Kilpisjärvi Saana*** (summer), Oulanka*** (summer), Pallas-Ounastunturi NP*** (summer), Ruissalo*** (passage, winter), Viikki*** (passage).
FRANCE Baie de Bourgneuf* (winter). Baie de Vilaine** (winter), Baie du Mont-St-Michel* (winter), Cap Gris Nez** (passage), Golfe du Morbihan*** (winter), Île d'Oléron* (winter), Somme Estuary* (winter).
GEORGIA Kolkheti** (winter).

GREAT BRITAIN Anglesey* (winter), Dungeness* (winter), Flamborough Head*** (passage, winter), Islay* (winter), Minsmere* (autumn, winter), N Norfolk coast*** (winter), Orkney Is*** (passage, winter), Outer Hebrides** (winter), Portland** (passage, winter), Scilly*** (winter), Shetland Is*** (passage, winter), Spurn Peninsula*** (passage, winter).
HUNGARY Danube Bend** (passage, winter), Tihany* (winter).
ICELAND Breiðafjörður***, Lake Mývatn*** (summer), Northwest Peninsula***, Olfusar Delta***, Reykjanes Peninsula*** (winter), Thingvellir NP*** (passage), Westmann Is*** (winter).
IRELAND Belfast Lough*** (winter), Galley Head* (passage, winter), Mullet Peninsula*** (winter), North Bull** (winter), North Slob** (winter), Strangford Lough* (winter).
ITALY Gargano Peninsula*** (winter), Isonzo Regional Park*** (winter), Orbetello Reserve** (winter).

LATVIA Cape Kolka*** (passage, winter), Lake Engure*** (winter), Lake Pape*** (passage, winter).

LITHUANIA Kirsiu Peninsula*** (passage, winter).

NETHERLANDS Lauwersmeer*** (winter), Oostvaardersplassen* (winter), Terschelling*** (winter), Texel*** (winter).

NORWAY Dovrefjell NP*** (summer), Hardangervidda NP*** (summer), Lista*** (passage), Lofoten Is***, Slettnes*** (summer, passage), Stabbursdalen NP*** (summer), Utsira*** (passage, winter), Varanger***.

POLAND Gdańsk Bay*** (passage, winter), Szczecin Bay area*** (passage, winter).

RUSSIA Kola Peninsula***.

SPAIN Llobregat Delta* (winter).

SVALBARD* (summer).

SWEDEN Abisko NP*** (summer), Ammarnäs*** (summer), Falsterbo*** (passage, winter), Gotland*** (passage, winter), Lake Ånnsjön*** (summer), Öland*** (passage, winter), Padjelanta NP*** (summer), Sarek NP*** (summer), Stockholm archipelago*** (winter).

SWITZERLAND Fanel NR* (winter), Grangettes* (passage, winter), Klingnau Reservoir* (winter).

Velvet Scoter
Melanitta fusca   Summer **FW** winter **Sea   Mig**

Range: Breeds in montane and N Scandinavia, around the Baltic and across N Russia. In winter occurs from Norway S to Biscay, regular in small numbers on lakes in C Europe and the N Mediterranean. A small, isolated population of the nominate race persists in E Turkey and Transcaucasia, which winters on the E and S coasts of the Black Sea.

Subspecies: Nominate race breeds in the Western Palearctic and both the Asian *stejnegeri* and N American *deglandi* have occurred as vagrants. These forms are variously treated as races of *M. fusca*, combined under *M. deglandi* as a full species, or considered two further individual species.

Tips: Breeds beside freshwater lakes, often in forests, on passage on large fresh waters and estuaries, and in winter offshore. Check flocks of Common Scoter or eiders for this species. Occurs in smaller flocks than Common Scoter, often off rockier coasts. Birds from the isolated population in the S are best seen at Nemrut Daği near Van Gölü in Turkey and on the Javakheti Plateau in Georgia.

Sites:
DENMARK Amager** (winter), Bornholm-Christiansø*** (passage), Hanstholm** (passage), Møn-Falster** (passage, winter), Ringkøbing Fjord*** (passage, winter), Rømø** (passage, winter), Skagen*** (passage, winter), Skallingen-Blåvandshuk*** (passage, winter), Stignæs** (passage), Vadehavet*** (winter).

ESTONIA Matsalu Bay*** (passage), Vilsandi NP*** (passage).

FINLAND Åland Is*** (summer), Kuusamo*** (summer), Lake Inari*** (summer), Liminganlahti*** (summer), Pallas-Ounastunturi NP*** (summer), Ruissalo*** (passage), Viikki*** (passage).

FRANCE Baie de Vilaine** (passage, winter), Baie du Mont-St-Michel* (passage, winter),

Cap Gris Nez* (passage), Forêt d'Orient* (winter), Île d'Oléron** (passage, winter), Lac du Der-Chantecoq* (winter), Somme Estuary** (passage, winter).
GEORGIA Javakheti Plateau*** (summer), Kolkheti** (passage).
GREAT BRITAIN Dungeness** (passage, winter), Flamborough Head** (passage, winter), Minsmere** (passage, winter), N Norfolk coast*** (passage, winter), Orkney Is** (autumn, winter), Portland** (passage), Shetland Is** (autumn, winter), Spurn Peninsula* (passage, winter).
HUNGARY Danube Bend** (passage, winter).
IRELAND Belfast Lough* (passage, winter), Galley Head* (passage), North Slob** (passage, winter), Rathlin Is** (passage).
ITALY Gargano Peninsula** (passage), Isonzo Regional Park*** (winter), Maremma Regional Park** (passage, winter), Monte Conero** (passage, winter), Orbetello Reserve*** (passage, winter).
LATVIA Cape Kolka*** (passage, winter), Lake Pape*** (passage, winter).
LITHUANIA Kirsiu Peninsula*** (passage, winter).
NETHERLANDS Terschelling*** (passage, winter), Texel*** (passage, winter).

NORWAY Dovrefjell NP*** (summer), Hardangervidda NP*** (summer), Lista*** (passage), Lofoten Is* (passage), Slettnes*** (passage), Stabbursdalen NP*** (summer, passage), Utsira* (passage), Varanger*** (summer).
POLAND Gdańsk Bay*** (passage, winter), Szczecin Bay area*** (passage, winter).
ROMANIA Danube Delta* (winter), Dobrudja* (winter).
RUSSIA Kola Peninsula*** (summer).
SPAIN Aiguamolls de L'Empordá* (winter), Coto Doñana (winter), Ebro Delta* (winter), Guadalhorce Estuary (winter), Llobregat Delta* (winter).
SWEDEN Abisko NP*** (summer), Ammarnäs*** (summer), Falsterbo** (passage, winter), Gotland*** (passage), Getterön* (passage), Holmöarna*** (passage), Lake Ānnsjön*** (summer), Öland*** (summer, passage), Padjelanta NP*** (summer), Sarek NP*** (summer), Stockholm archipelago***, Tärnasjön*** (summer).
SWITZERLAND Fanel NR* (winter), Grangettes* (passage, winter), Klingnau Reservoir* (winter).
TURKEY Kızılırmak Delta*** (winter), Van Gölü*** (summer).

Barrow's Goldeneye
Bucephala islandica Summer **FW** winter **(Sea)** **Res (Dis)**

Range: Western Palearctic range restricted to Iceland, main range is in North America. Locally cómmon in Iceland, particularly in the River Laxa/Lake Myvatn area. Some reach coastal areas in winter.
Tips: Search small lakes and rivers inland, nests in rocky crevices, dense scrub or nestboxes. Some move to larger lakes and sheltered coasts in winter.

Sites:
ICELAND Lake Mývatn***, Olfusar Delta*** (winter), Reykjanes Peninsula** (winter), Thingvellir NP***.

Smew
Mergellus albellus

Summer **FW** winter **FW (ES)** **Mig**

Range: Main range lies in N Scandinavia and across N Russia, with isolated outposts in S Finland and Belarus. Very patchy winter range from S England and N France to the Baltic and S to the Mediterranean, Black and Caspian Seas.

Tips: Breeds in tree holes beside lakes, pools and rivers in forested areas. In winter, look on larger fresh waters, including reservoirs and gravel pits, estuaries and sometimes sheltered seas. Gathers into small flocks in winter, rarely reaching 100 birds, and often associates with Common Goldeneye. Severe winters bring the highest numbers to Great Britain and western Europe.

Sites:

ALBANIA Lake Shkodra** (winter).
ARMENIA Armash Fishponds** (winter).
BELGIUM Het Zwin** (winter).
CZECH REPUBLIC Nové Mlýny*** (winter).
DENMARK Amager*** (winter), Møn-Falster*** (winter), Ringkøbing Fjord*** (passage, winter), Skagen*** (passage), Skallingen-Blåvandshuk*** (passage), Stignæs** (passage).
ESTONIA Emajõgi Floodplain*** (passage), Matsalu Bay*** (passage), Vilsandi NP*** (passage).
FINLAND Kilpisjärvi Saana*** (summer), Kuusamo*** (summer), Lake Inari*** (summer), Lemmenjoki NP*** (summer), Liminganlahti*** (summer, passage), Oulanka NP*** (summer), Pallas-Ounastunturi NP*** (summer), Parikkala*** (summer), Ruissalo*** (passage), Urho Kekkonen NP*** (summer), Viikki*** (passage).
FRANCE La Brenne** (winter), Cap Gris Nez** (passage), Forêt d'Orient*** (winter), Lac du Der-Chantecoq*** (winter), Sologne** (winter), Somme Estuary** (winter).
GEORGIA Kolkheti*** (winter).
GERMANY Mecklenburg Lakes*** (winter), Oder Valley*** (winter).
GREAT BRITAIN Dungeness** (winter), Minsmere* (winter), N Norfolk coast* (winter), Portland* (winter), Spurn Peninsula* (winter).

BULGARIA Burgas area** (winter), Lake Durankulak** (winter), Lake Srebarna*** (winter).
HUNGARY Danube Bend*** (winter), Hortobágy NP*** (winter), Lake Fertö** (winter), Lake Velence** (winter), Tihany* (winter).
ITALY Orbetello Reserve** (winter).
LATVIA Cape Kolka*** (passage, winter), Lake Lubana*** (passage), Lake Pape*** (passage, winter).
LITHUANIA Kirsiu Peninsula*** (passage, winter).
NETHERLANDS Lauwersmeer*** (winter), Oostvaardersplassen*** (winter), Terschelling*** (winter), Texel*** (passage, winter).
NORWAY Øvre Pasvik NP*** (summer), Varanger* (summer).
POLAND Gdańsk Bay*** (winter), Milicz Fishponds*** (winter), Siemianówka Reservoir* (winter), Szczecin Bay area** (winter).
ROMANIA Danube Delta*** (winter), Dobrudja*** (winter).
RUSSIA Kola Peninsula* (summer), Volga Delta*** (winter).
SLOVAKIA Zemplínská Reservoir** (passage, winter).
SWEDEN Falsterbo*** (winter), Getterön*** (winter), Gotland*** (passage, winter),

Holmöarna*** (passage), Hornborgasjön*** (passage, winter), Kristianstad*** (passage, winter), Lake Krankesjön*** (winter), Öland*** (passage, winter), Ripakaisenvuoma*** (summer), Store Mosse NP*** (passage, winter).
SWITZERLAND Fanel NR*** (winter), Grangettes*** (winter).

TURKEY İstanbul*** (winter), Kızılırmak Delta*** (winter), Manyas Gölü*** (winter), Uluabat Gölü*** (winter).
UKRAINE Dunay Delta** (winter), Syvash Bay** (winter).
YUGOSLAVIA Đerdap NP*** (winter), Lake Skadar* (winter).

White-headed Duck
Oxyura leucocephala   FW (BW)   Res PMig

Range: Very patchy range, breeding in S Spain and in NW Africa in N parts of Morocco, Algeria and Tunisia, in C and E Turkey, and in parts of S Russia possibly including the Volga Delta. Recently reintroduced to Lake Biguglia in Corsica and Albufera in Mallorca. More widespread in winter, particularly in NW Africa, Turkey and the Middle East. Spanish population is threatened by hybridisation with closely related Ruddy Duck *O. jamaicensis*, a North American species introduced to Great Britain which has now begun to reach Spain.
Tips: Search well-vegetated freshwater pools and brackish lagoons in known areas of occurrence. Where migratory it is present on breeding lakes late Apr–early Oct.

Sites:
ALBANIA Karavasta Lagoon** (passage, winter).
ALGERIA El Kala NP***.
ARMENIA Armash Fishponds*** (summer), Lake Sevan (summer).
AZERBAIJAN Kura Valley Salt-lakes*** (winter).
BALEARIC IS Mallorca* (reintroduced).
BULGARIA Burgas area*** (winter), Lake Durankulak** (winter).
CORSICA Biguglia Lake*** (reintroduced).
CYPRUS* (winter).
GEORGIA Javakheti Plateau* (passage), Kolkheti* (winter).
GREECE Evros Delta* (winter), Lake Kerkini** (winter), Nestos Delta** (winter), Porto Lagos Area*** (winter).

ISRAEL Hula Reserve*** (winter), Jezreel Valley*** (winter).
ROMANIA Danube Delta (winter), Dobrudja* (winter).
RUSSIA Volga Delta (summer).
SPAIN Cabo de Gata* (winter), Cádiz Lagoons*** (winter), Coto Doñana*, Tablas de Daimiel*.
SYRIA Bahrat Homs*** (passage, winter), Dayr al-Zawr* (summer), Sabkhat al-Jubbal** (passage).
TUNISIA Cap Bon Peninsula*, Kelbia Lake**, Lake Ichkeul***.
TURKEY Kızılırmak Delta*** (mainly winter), Kulu Gölü*** (summer, passage), Sultan Marshes*** (summer), Van Gölü*** (summer).

Black-shouldered Kite
Elanus caeruleus DF FG Res (Dis)

Range: Breeds in S Portugal and C Spain, in NW Africa (mainly W and N Morocco, in coastal Algeria and a small area of N Tunisia), and in the Nile Valley of Egypt. In decline in North Africa but increasing in Iberia and has recently begun to breed in SW France.

Tips: Search open areas with scattered trees and woodland edges in cultivated areas, commonly seen in olive and palm groves and evergreen oak woodland. Sometimes hovers like a kestrel or quarters like a harrier, but spends much time perched on a tree or telephone pole, often cocking tail.

Sites:
EGYPT Aswan***, Faiyum**, Luxor***, Nile Delta***, Suez area, Wadi el Natrun.
MOROCCO Agadir and the Sous Plain***, Lac de Sidi Bourhaba***, Merja Zerga***, Zaër***.
PORTUGAL Baixo Alentejo***, Boquilobo*, Cape St Vincent* (autumn), International Tagus***, Ria Formosa* (autumn, winter), Sado Estuary***, Santo André Lagoon***, Tagus Estuary***.
SPAIN Cáceres-Trujillo Steppes***, Coto Doñana** (winter), La Serena***, Monfragüe***.
TUNISIA Cap Bon Peninsula***.

Black Kite
Milvus migrans DF FW FG (U) Mig (Res)

Range: Widespread and common breeder from Iberia to the Urals, also on the Cape Verde Is, in NW Africa, Egypt, Sinai and Turkey. Absent from the British Isles and most of Scandinavia, but breeds N to the S shores of the Baltic and SE Finland. Small numbers winter in S Europe but most are migratory and in Aug–Oct concentrate at the Gibraltar and Bosphorus. Also seen in significant numbers at Borçka in NE Turkey and on passage through Italy. The same routes are used in spring, with peak movements in Mar–Apr.

Subspecies: Nominate race occurs over most of Western Palearctic including the now very rare Cape Verde Is population which was formerly separated as *tenebrosus*. Resident birds from Egypt and Sinai belong to *aegyptius* which is sometimes lumped with sub-Saharan *parasitus* and given specific status under the name Yellow-billed Kite

Tips: Usually seen close to water, and in parts of range, especially the S, closely associated with man. Breeds in tall trees in open or sparsely wooded country. Usually gregarious, particularly on migration.

Sites:

ALGERIA El Kala NP*** (summer).

ANDORRA*** (passage).

ARMENIA Arapan Area* (passage).

AUSTRIA Lake Neusiedl*** (summer), Marchauen-Marchegg Reserve*** (summer).

BALEARIC IS Formentera*** (passage), Ibiza** (passage), Mallorca*** (passage), Menorca*** (passage).

BELARUS Belovezhskaya Pushcha NP*** (summer), Berezinsky Reserve*** (summer), Prypyatsky NP*** (summer).

BELGIUM Croix-Scaille NR* (passage), Lesse et Lomme NR* (passage).

BULGARIA Albena-Golden Sands*** (passage), Burgas area*** (passage), Cape Emine*** (passage), Cape Kaliakra*** (passage), Lake Durankulak*** (summer, passage), Lake Shabla*** (summer, passage), Lake Srebarna*** (summer), Rusenski Lom NP*** (passage), Strandja Mts*** (summer, passage), Studen Kladenetz*** (summer, passage), Tissata NR*** (passage).

CANARY IS* (passage).

CAPE VERDE IS**.

CORSICA Bonifacio** (autumn), Cap Corse** (passage).

CROATIA Kopački Rit** (summer).

CYPRUS** (passage).

CZECH REPUBLIC Lednice* (summer), Soutok** (summer), Třeboňsko*** (summer).

DENMARK Skagen* (passage).

EGYPT Abu Simbel***, Aswan***, Hurghada***, Luxor***, Sharm el Sheikh***, Suez area***, Wadi el Natrun***, Zaranik**.

FRANCE Baie de Bourgneuf*** (summer), Camargue*** (summer), Cévennes NP*** (summer), Dombes*** (summer), La Brenne*** (summer, passage), Écrins NP*** (summer), Forêt d'Orient*** (summer), Golfe du Morbihan* (summer), Gruissan*** (summer, passage), Île d'Oléron*** (summer), Lac du Der-Chantecoq*** (summer), Leucate*** (summer, passage), Lorraine NP*** (summer), Marais Poitevin** (summer, passage), Organbidexka*** (passage), Pyrenees NP***

(summer), Sologne*** (summer), Teich Reserve*** (summer).

GEORGIA Iori Steppes*** (passage), Kolkheti*** (passage), Mt Kazbek** (summer).

GERMANY Federsee*** (summer), Kuhkopf*** (summer), Mecklenburg Lakes*** (summer), Oder Valley*** (summer), Schweinfurt** (summer), Vessertal*** (summer).

GIBRALTAR*** (passage).

GREECE Amvrakikós Gulf*** (summer, passage), Avas Gorge*** (summer), Dadiá-Soufli Forest*** (summer), Evros Delta*** (summer), Lake Kerkini*** (summer), Mikrí Prespa NP** (summer), Mt Olympus NP*** (summer), Nestos Delta*** (summer).

GREEK IS Crete** (passage, mainly spring), Kos* (passage), Lesvos* (passage).

HUNGARY Börzsöny NP** (summer), Danube Bend** (summer, passage), Hanság** (summer), Hortobágy NP* (passage), Lake Fertö*** (summer), Pilis Hills** (summer), Zemplén Hills*** (summer).

ISRAEL Arava Valley*** (passage), Bet Shean Valley*** (passage, winter), Eilat*** (passage), Ein Gedi*** (passage), Hula Reserve*** (passage, winter), Jezreel Valley*** (passage, winter), Ma'agan Mikhael*** (passage), Mt Hermon*** (passage), Urim*** (passage, winter).

ITALY Abruzzo NP*** (summer), Circeo NP*** (summer), Gargano Peninsula*** (summer), Lake Massaciuccoli*** (summer, passage), Maremma Regional Park*** (summer), Monte Conero*** (passage), Orbetello Reserve*** (summer), San Giuliano Reserve*** (summer), Tuscan archipelago*** (passage).

JORDAN Aqaba*** (passage), Azraq*** (passage), Ghadir Burqu'** (passage), Petra*** (passage), Wadi Dana-Fidan*** (passage), Wadi Rum*** (passage).

LATVIA Cape Kolka*** (summer, passage), Lake Lubana*** (summer), Lake Pape** (passage).

LEBANON Aammiq Marshes*** (passage), Barouk Cedars*** (passage), Qaraoun Lake** (passage).

LITHUANIA Kirsiu Peninsula*** (passage), Lake Kretuonas (summer).

MACEDONIA Bregalnica Valley** (summer), Crna Gorge** (passage), Demir Kapija Gorge** (summer), Galicica NP** (spring), Lakes Ohrid and Prespa** (spring), Mavrovo NP** (summer).

MADEIRA (passage).

MALTA (passage).

MOROCCO Agadir and the Sous Plain*** (summer), Asilah and Oued Loukkos*** (passage), Boumalne*** (passage), Dayet Aaoua*** (summer), Goulimine to Tan-Tan*** (summer), Lac de Sidi Bourhaba*** (summer,), Merja Zerga*** (summer), Ouarzazate*** (passage), Tafilalt*** (passage), Zaër*** (summer).

POLAND Białowieża Forest*** (summer), Biebrza Marshes*** (summer), Chełm Marshes*** (summer), Milicz Fishponds*** (summer), Słońsk*** (summer), Szczecin Bay area**.

PORTUGAL Baixo Alentejo*** (summer), Boquilobo*** (summer), Cape St Vincent*** (autumn), Castro Marim*** (summer), International Douro*** (summer), International Tagus*** (summer), Montesinho*** (summer), Peneda Gêres NP*** (summer), Ria Formosa*** (summer), Sado Estuary*** (summer), Santo André Lagoon*** (summer, passage), Tagus Estuary*** (summer).

ROMANIA Danube Delta*** (summer), Dobrudja*** (summer), Lake Călăraşi*** (summer).

RUSSIA Kalmykia*** (summer), Teberdinskiy Reserve*** (summer, passage), Volga Delta*** (summer).

SARDINIA Giara di Gesturi** (passage), San Pietro I*** (passage).

SICILY San Vito Peninsula*** (passage), Strait of Messina*** (spring).

SLOVAKIA Malé Karpaty*** (passage), Senné Fishponds*** (passage), Záhorie*** (summer).

SPAIN Aiguamolls de L'Empordá*** (summer), Aigües Tortes NP*** (summer), Cabo de Gata*** (summer), Cáceres-Trujillo Steppes*** (summer), Cádiz Lagoons*** (summer), Coto Doñana*** (summer), Ebro Delta*** (summer), Guadalhorce Estuary*** (passage), Jaca*** (summer), La Serena*** (summer), Monfragüe*** (summer), Ordesa NP*** (summer), Picos de Europa*** (summer), Serrania de Ronda*** (summer), Sierra de Gredos*** (summer), Sierra de Guadarrama*** (summer), Tablas de Daimiel*** (summer), Zaragoza Steppes*** (summer).

SWEDEN Falsterbo* (passage), Öland* (passage).

SWITZERLAND Clos-du-Doubs*** (summer), Col de Bretolet*** (passage), Fanel NR*** (summer), Grangettes*** (summer, passage), Klingnau Reservoir*** (passage), Monte Generoso*** (summer), Niderholz*** (summer).

SYRIA Bahrat Homs*** (passage), Dayr al-Zawr** (passage), Jabal Slenfeh*** (passage), Tadmur and Sabkhat Muh*** (passage).

TUNISIA Ain Draham*** (summer), Cap Bon Peninsula*** (passage), Kelbia Lake** (summer, passage), Lake Ichkeul*** (summer, passage), Zaghouan** (summer).

TURKEY Bafa Gölü* (summer, passage), Birecik-Halfeti* (passage), Borçka*** (passage), Dalyan* (summer, passage), Demirkazik* (summer), Göksu Delta* (passage), İstanbul*** (summer, passage), Soğuksu NP** (summer, passage).

UKRAINE Askania-Nova*** (summer), Carpathians*** (summer), Dunay Delta** (summer), Shatsk NP** (passage).

YUGOSLAVIA Carska bara* (summer), Fruška Gora NP** (summer), Obedska bara* (summer).

Red Kite
Milvus milvus

Range: Breeds in Iberia and from France E to Belarus and Ukraine, and around the W Mediterranean. Reaches Denmark and S Sweden in N of range. In Great Britain long confined to C Wales but recent reintroductions have led to breeding in Scotland, particularly the Black Isle, and in the Chiltern Hills in England. In the Mediterranean, breeds on Mallorca, Corsica, Sardinia and Sicily, but now very rare in NW Africa, breeding only in N Morocco, recently extinct in the Canaries and close to extinction in the Cape Verde Is. Birds from N and E of range are migratory and small numbers are regular at the major migration watchpoints.

Subspecies: Nominate race occurs over most of range, those on the Cape Verde Is have been regarded as a race of Red Kite, *fasciicauda*, as hybrids between Red and Black Kites, or as a separate species. However they are classified, this form is now extremely rare and only four were found on Boa Vista during a search in 2001 (although two were reported from São Vicente in 2000).

Tips: Favours hill country with mature deciduous woodland and open fields. Much less common than Black Kite throughout range.

Sites:

AUSTRIA Lake Neusiedl*** (summer), Marchauen-Marchegg Reserve*** (summer).
BALEARIC IS Formentera* (passage), Mallorca**, Menorca***.
BELARUS Belovezhskaya Pushcha NP*** (summer).
BELGIUM Croix-Scaille NR*, Hautes Fagnes Natural Park***.
BULGARIA Albena-Golden Sands* (passage), Burgas area* (passage), Lake Durankulak* (passage), Lake Shabla* (passage, winter), Lake Srebarna* (passage, winter), Studen Kladenetz* (passage).
CAPE VERDE IS*.
CORSICA Asco Valley***, Bonifacio**, Cap Corse***, Restonica Valley***.
CROATIA Cres* (passage), Plitvice**.
CZECH REPUBLIC Lednice***, Soutok**, Třeboňsko***, Znojmo*.
DENMARK Bornholm-Christiansø*** (passage), Hellebæk*** (passage), Møn-Falster*** (passage), Skagen** (passage), Skallingen-Blåvandshuk* (passage), Stevns Klint*** (passage), Stignæs*** (passage).

EGYPT Suez area* (passage).
FRANCE Camargue*** (winter), Cévennes NP***, Dombes***, Forêt d'Orient***, Gruissan** (passage, winter), La Brenne***, Lac du Der-Chantecoq***, Leucate*** (passage), Lorraine NP***, Organbidexka***, Pyrenees NP***.
GEORGIA Kolkheti (passage).
GERMANY Federsee***, Kuhkopf***, Mecklenburg Lakes***, Oder Valley***, Rügen*** (summer), Schweinfurt***, Vessertal***.
GIBRALTAR*** (passage).
GREAT BRITAIN Tregaron Bog***.
GREECE Dadiá-Soufli Forest* (passage).
ISRAEL Bet Shean Valley* (passage), Hula Reserve* (passage).
ITALY Gargano Peninsula**, San Giuliano Reserve**.
LEBANON Barouk Cedars (passage), Qaraoun Lake (passage).
MOROCCO Dayet Aaoua*.

POLAND Biebrza Marshes*** (summer), Milicz Fishponds** (summer), Słońsk** (summer), Szczecin Bay area**.
PORTUGAL Baixo Alentejo***, Cape St Vincent** (autumn), International Douro***, International Tagus***, Montesinho***, Ria Formosa** (passage, winter), Tagus Estuary** (passage).
ROMANIA Dobrudja* (passage).
SARDINIA Capo Marargiu***, Giara di Gesturi** (passage, winter).
SICILY Strait of Messina** (spring).
SLOVAKIA Malé Karpaty*, Záhorie***.
SPAIN Aigües Tortes NP***, Cáceres-Trujillo Steppes***, Cádiz Lagoons** (winter), Coto

Doñana***, Jaca***, La Serena**, Monfragüe***, Ordesa NP***, Serrania de Ronda** (winter), Sierra de Gredos***, Sierra de Guadarrama***, Zaragoza Steppes***.
SWEDEN Falsterbo*** (passage), Kristianstad*** (summer), Lake Krankesjön***, Store Mosse NP* (summer).
SWITZERLAND Clos-du-Doubs***, Col de Bretolet*** (passage), Klingnau Reservoir***, Niderholz***.
TUNISIA Cap Bon Peninsula** (passage), Zaghouan**.
TURKEY Borçka* (passage), İstanbul* (passage), Kızılırmak Delta* (passage).

White-tailed Eagle
Haliaeetus albicilla   C FW   Res (Mig)

Range: Breeds in W Iceland, coastal Scandinavia and around parts of the Baltic, and across E Europe from Germany to the Urals and Caspian. Isolated pockets persist in the Balkans, Greece and Caucasus, possibly Turkey, and successfully reintroduced to Scotland where 25 pairs are now established and can be seen most easily on Rhum and Mull. Also reintroduced in Bohemia. More widespread in winter, particularly around the Baltic, also at lakes in C Europe and around the Black Sea, and now regularly winters in NE France.
Tips: Nests on sea-cliffs in N of range but uses trees elsewhere. Spends much time perched motionless on a crag or in a large tree. Away from sea-cliffs occurs along large rivers, around lakes and in extensive marshes.

Sites:
ALBANIA Karavasta Lagoon (winter).
AUSTRIA Marchauen-Marchegg Reserve* (winter).
AZERBAIJAN Kura Valley Salt-lakes** (winter), Kyzylagach Bay*** (winter).
BELARUS Belovezhskaya Pushcha NP**, Berezinsky Reserve***, Prypyatsky NP***.
BULGARIA Albena-Golden Sands* (passage), Burgas area*** (passage, winter), Lake Durankulak* (winter), Lake Shabla** (winter), Lake Srebarna* (winter), Ropotamo NP* (winter), Studen Kladenetz* (passage).

CROATIA Kopački Rit**, Pokupsko Depression***.
CZECH REPUBLIC Lednice*** (winter), Nové Mlýny***, Pohořelice Fishponds** (passage, winter), Soutok* (passage), Třeboňsko***.
DENMARK Amager* (winter), Bornholm-Christiansø*** (winter), Hellebæk** (passage), Møn-Falster*** (passage, winter), Ringkøbing Fjord* (winter), Skagen** (passage), Skallingen-Blåvandshuk** (passage, winter), Stevns Klint*** (passage), Stignæs*** (winter).

ESTONIA Emajõgi Floodplain*** (summer), Lake Endla*** (summer), Matsalu Bay*** (summer, passage).

FINLAND Åland Is***, Liminganlahti** (passage), Linnansaari NP*** (passage), Oulanka**, Ruissalo*** (passage), Viikki** (passage).

FRANCE Dombes* (passage), Forêt d'Orient*** (passage, winter), La Brenne* (winter), Lac du Der-Chantecoq*** (passage, winter), Lorraine NP* (winter).

GEORGIA Iori Steppes*, Kolkheti**.

GERMANY Mecklenburg Lakes**, Oder Valley*** (winter), Rügen***.

GREAT BRITAIN Outer Hebrides*, Rhum***.

GREECE Amvrakiko's Gulf* (passage), Axios-Aliakmonas Deltas** (winter), Dadiá-Soufli Forest** (mainly winter), Evros Delta* (winter), Lake Kerkini** (passage, winter), Mikrí Prespa NP**, Nestos Delta** (passage, winter), Porto Lagos Area** (passage, winter).

GREEK IS Corfu* (passage).

HUNGARY Biharugra** (winter), Hanság*** (winter), Hortobágy NP***, Kardoskút* (winter), Kis-balaton***, Kiskunság NP*, Szeged Fishponds*.

ICELAND Breiðafjörður***, Northwest Peninsula***.

ISRAEL Hula Reserve** (passage, winter).

ITALY Orbetello Reserve (winter).

LATVIA Cape Kolka** (passage), Lake Engure***, Lake Lubana***, Lake Pape*** (passage, winter).

LITHUANIA Cepkeliai NR***, Kirsiu Peninsula***.

MACEDONIA Galicica NP*, Lakes Ohrid and Prespa*.

MOLDOVA Balatina* (passage), Manta Floodplain** (passage).

NETHERLANDS Lauwersmeer* (winter), Oostvaardersplassen* (winter).

NORWAY Lofoten Is***, Mølen* (passage), Øvre Pasvik NP***, Runde***, Slettnes* (passage), Stabbursdalen NP*, Varanger**.

POLAND Białowieża Forest (passage), Biebrza Marshes**, Chełm Marshes*, Gdańsk Bay**, Milicz Fishponds***, Siemianówka Reservoir***, Słońsk*** (winter), Szczecin Bay area***.

ROMANIA Danube Delta***, Dobrudja*** (passage).

RUSSIA Kalmykia*** (winter), Kola Peninsula*** (summer), Oka Valley***, Volga Delta***.

SLOVAKIA Orava Reservoir** (passage), Senné Fishponds** (passage), Záhorie** (passage, winter), Zemplínská Reservoir** (passage, winter).

SLOVENIA Kocevje*, Lake Cerknica* (passage).

SWEDEN Abisko NP*, Ammarnäs*, Falsterbo* (passage), Färnebofjärden*, Getterön** (passage, winter), Gotland*** (passage, winter), Hjälstaviken*** (passage), Holmöarna** (passage), Hornborgasjön* (passage), Kristianstad*** (passage, winter), Kvismaren*** (winter), Lake Krankesjön*** (winter), Öland*** (passage, winter), Padjelanta NP*** (summer), Ripakaisenvuoma*** (summer), Sarek NP*** (summer), Stockholm archipelago***, Store Mosse NP*** (passage, winter), Tåkern*** (passage, winter), Tarnasjön***.

TURKEY Bafa Gölü**, Borçka* (passage), Dalyan* (passage), Göksu Delta** (passage, winter), İstanbul* (passage), Kızılırmak Delta* (winter).

UKRAINE Dunay Delta**, Shatsk NP* (passage).

YUGOSLAVIA Carska bara, Đerdap NP**, Obedska bara.

Lammergeier
Gypaetus barbatus　　　　　　　　　　　　　　　　　　　　M　Res (Dis)

Range: Breeds in the Pyrenees, in Greece and the N Caucasus, and in very small numbers in the Balkans, Corsica and Crete. More widespread but local in Turkey and the Caucasus, with relict populations in Sinai and on the Red Sea coast of Egypt, NW Africa (High Atlas of N Morocco), and possibly still Israel and Jordan. Successfully reintroduced to the Alps, with birds released in Austria, Switzerland, France and Italy. Regular in all these countries and wanderers have been recorded as far as the Atlantic coast of France, the Netherlands and the German coast.

Subspecies: Nominate race is found in Morocco and *aureus* in remainder of Western Palearctic range.

Tips: Search areas with deep valleys and high ridges, usually seen at 1,000–2,000m. Ads are resident but imms may wander and are occasionally seen at migration watchpoints such as Gibraltar.

Sites:

ANDORRA*.

ARMENIA Khosrov Preserve**, Pambak Mts***, Vedi Hills*.

AUSTRIA Hohe Tauern NP*.

AZERBAIJAN Turianchai Reserve***, Zakataly**.

CORSICA Asco Valley***, Cap Corse*, Restonica Valley***.

EGYPT Suez area* (passage).

FRANCE Mercantour NP*, Organbidexka***, Prats-de-Mollo*, Pyrenees NP***, Vanoise NP**.

GEORGIA Iori Steppes*, Mt Kazbek***.

GREECE Dadiá-Soufli Forest**, Mt Olympus NP*, Mt Parnassós NP*, Vikos-Aoos NP***.

GREEK IS Crete***.

ITALY Gran Paradiso NP, Stelvio NP.

JORDAN Aqaba, Wadi Rum.

MACEDONIA Babuna Gorge, Crna Gorge, Demir Kapija Gorge, Mavrovo NP, Sara Mts.

MOROCCO Agadir and the Sous Plain, Boumalne*, Oukaimeden*.

RUSSIA Teberdinskiy Reserve***.

SPAIN Aigües Tortes NP**, Jaca***, Ordesa NP***.

SWITZERLAND Col de Bretolet*, Swiss NP*** (reintroduced).

TURKEY Borçka***, Demirkazik***, Sivrikaya***, Soğuksu NP***, Uludağ NP***.

Egyptian Vulture
Neophron percnopterus   M Mig

Range: Rare and local around the Mediterranean, breeding in Iberia and Menorca (small numbers also on Mallorca), S France and S Italy, Sicily, the Balkans, Greece and Turkey. To the E, breeds in Moldova, Crimea, the Caucasus and the Middle East. Widespread in N Africa, from S Morocco to N Libya and in E Egypt and Sinai, also breeds on the Canaries and Cape Verde Is. Most European birds pass through Gibraltar on migration, with smaller numbers at Cap Bon and the Bosphorus, although wintering in southern Europe is increasing. Numbers at Gibraltar peak in Sep and return movement occurs from Feb to mid Apr.

Tips: Found mainly in mountains in the Western Palearctic, nesting on cliffs, often seen beside rivers and at refuse tips in some areas, particularly in N Africa.

Sites:

ANDORRA** (summer).

ARMENIA Khosrov Preserve** (summer), Vedi Hills* (summer).

AZERBAIJAN Turianchai Reserve*** (summer).

BALEARIC IS Mallorca**, Menorca***.

BULGARIA Albena-Golden Sands* (passage), Burgas area* (passage), Rusenski Lom NP** (summer), Strandja Mts*** (summer, passage), Studen Kladenetz*** (summer), Tissata NR*** (summer, passage).

CANARY IS Fuerteventura***, Lanzarote**.

CAPE VERDE IS***.

EGYPT Abu Simbel***, Aswan***, Hurghada** (passage), Suez area*** (passage), Zaranik** (passage).

FRANCE Camargue** (summer), Cévennes NP** (summer), Les Alpilles*** (summer), Organbidexka** (summer, passage), Pyrenees NP** (summer).

GEORGIA Iori Steppes** (summer), Kolkheti** (passage).

GIBRALTAR*** (passage).

GREECE Avas Gorge*** (summer), Dadiá-Soufli Forest*** (summer), Mikrí Prespa NP*** (summer), Mt Olympus NP*** (summer), Mt Parnassós NP*** (summer), Valia Kalda NP*** (summer), Vikos-Aoos NP*** (summer).

GREEK IS Crete* (passage), Lesvos* (passage).

ISRAEL Arava Valley*** (summer, passage), Bet Shean Valley*** (passage), Eilat*** (summer, passage), Ein Gedi*** (summer, passage), Golan Heights*** (summer), Mt Hermon*** (summer), Jezreel Valley*** (passage), Wadi Ammud-Mt Arbel*** (summer).

ITALY Gargano Peninsula* (summer, passage), San Giuliano Reserve* (passage).

JORDAN Azraq* (passage), Petra** (passage), Wadi Dana-Fidan* (passage), Wadi Rum**.

LEBANON Aammiq Marshes** (passage), Barouk Cedars* (passage), Qaraoun Lake** (passage).

MACEDONIA Babuna Gorge** (summer), Bregalnica Valley** (summer), Crna Gorge** (summer), Demir Kapija Gorge** (summer), Mavrovo NP** (summer).

MALTA (passage).

MOROCCO Agadir and the Sous Plain** (summer), Dayet Aaoua* (summer), Tafilalt* (summer).

PORTUGAL Baixo Alentejo*** (summer), Cape St Vincent** (autumn), International Douro*** (summer), International Tagus*** (summer), Montesinho** (summer).

ROMANIA Dobrudja** (summer).

RUSSIA Teberdinskiy Reserve* (passage).
SICILY Strait of Messina* (spring).
SPAIN Cáceres-Trujillo Steppes* (summer), Cádiz Lagoons** (summer), Coto Doñana**, Jaca*** (summer), La Serena* (summer), Monfragüe*** (summer), Ordesa NP*** (summer), Picos de Europa*** (summer), Serrania de Ronda*** (summer), Sierra de Gredos*** (summer), Zaragoza Steppes*** (summer).
SYRIA Jabal al-Bishri*** (summer), Jabal Slenfeh** (passage), Tadmur and Sabkhat

Muh* (summer), Wadi al-Qarn-Burqush** (summer).
TUNISIA Cap Bon Peninsula** (passage), Zaghouan*.
TURKEY Birecik-Halfeti*** (summer), Borçka** (passage), Demirkazik*** (summer), Göksu Delta** (summer),İstanbul*** (passage), Soğuksu NP*** (summer), Sultan Marshes** (summer), Uludağ NP*** (summer), Van Gölü** (summer).
UKRAINE Crimean Mts (summer).

Griffon Vulture
Gyps fulvus   M (FG)   Res (Dis)

Range: Breeds over much of Spain but rare in Portugal, in Sardinia, the Balkans, Greece (including Crete) and Turkey. Reintroduced to the the Massif Central of France and the Italian Alps. More widespread in the Caucasus, and also breeds in Cyprus and parts of the Middle East. Now very rare in NW Africa with breeding perhaps limited to Algeria with very small numbers possibly surviving in Morocco. Basically sedentary in Spain but imms may wander widely or move S to N Africa in autumn, and small numbers are regular at Gibraltar in Jul–Nov with a return movement in Apr–May. More migratory in Turkey and occurs at the Bosphorus Sep–Oct and Apr–May. Increasing in Spain but in decline elsewhere in the Western Palearctic, .

Tips: Nests colonially on cliff ledges in mountainous country and requires carrion of livestock or wild ungulates. Usually seen soaring in thermals. **Rüppell's Vulture** *Gyps rueppellii* increasingly recorded in S Spain in recent years, presumably birds that have joined migrant Griffons in Africa and returned N with them. Records include three birds in Aug–Dec 1987, and several reports of small groups in the 1990s and 2000–01. In 1998, one was seen, apparently nesting, within a Spanish Griffon colony, and in Oct 2001, one was recorded at Cape St Vincent in Portugal. Check passage vultures carefully in S Spain and search Griffon colonies for this species.

Sites:
ANDORRA**.
ARMENIA Khosrov Preserve***, Pambak Mts***, Vedi Hills**.
AUSTRIA Hohe Tauern NP*** (summer).
AZERBAIJAN Turianchai Reserve***, Zakataly**.

BALEARIC IS Mallorca (one bird present since the early 1980s).
BOSNIA-HERZEGOVINA Sujetska NP.
BULGARIA Burgas area* (passage), Studen Kladenetz***, Tzarichina NR*.
CROATIA Cres***, Paklenica NP**.
CYPRUS***.

EGYPT Hurghada** (passage), Sharm el Sheikh** (passage), Suez area*** (passage), Zaranik** (passage).
FRANCE Cévennes NP***, Pyrenees NP***.
GEORGIA Iori Steppes***, Kolkheti* (passage), Mt Kazbek***.
GIBRALTAR** (passage).
GREECE Akarnanika Mts***, Avas Gorge***, Dadiá-Soufli Forest***, Delphi*, Mt Olympus NP***, Mt Parnassós NP***, Valia Kalda NP***, Vikos-Aoos NP***.
GREEK IS Crete***, Náxos***.
ISRAEL Bet Shean Valley** (passage), Eilat*** (passage), Ein Gedi***, Golan Heights***, Hula Reserve* (winter), Jezreel Valley** (passage), Mt Hermon***, Wadi Ammud-Mt Arbel***.
JORDAN Azraq* (passage), Petra** (passage), Wadi Dana-Fidan***, Wadi Rum**.
LEBANON Aammiq Marshes** (passage), Barouk Cedars*** (passage), Qaraoun Lake* (passage).
MACEDONIA Babuna Gorge*, Bregalnica Valley**, Crna Gorge**, Demir Kapija Gorge**, Mavrovo NP**, Sara Mts**.

MOROCCO Agadir and the Sous Plain**.
PORTUGAL Baixo Alentejo*, Cape St Vincent* (autumn), Castro Marim* (passage), International Douro***, International Tagus***, Ria Formosa* (passage).
RUSSIA Teberdinskiy Reserve***.
SARDINIA Capo Marargiu***.
SPAIN Aigües Tortes NP***, Cáceres-Trujillo Steppes***, Cádiz Lagoons* (passage), Coto Doñana** (passage), Jaca***, La Serena***, Monfragüe***, Ordesa NP***, Picos de Europa***, Serrania de Ronda***, Sierra de Gredos***, Sierra de Guadarrama***, Zaragoza Steppes*.
SYRIA Aqra Mts*, Bahrat Homs*, Dayr al-Zaer*, Jabal al-Bishri***, Jabal Slenfeh*, Lake Assad***, Sabkhat al-Jubbal*, Tadmur and Sabkhat Muh*, Wadi al-Qarn-Burqush**, Yarmuk Valley***.
TURKEY Borçka, Demirkazik, Sivrikaya, Soğuksu NP.
UKRAINE Crimean Mts**.

Lappet-faced Vulture
Torgos tracheliotus   D SD M   Res (Dis)

Range: Widespread and common in sub-Saharan Africa, but very rare in the Western Palearctic. Has bred, and may still do so irregularly, in Western Sahara, possibly also in Mauritania, Chad and extreme SE Egypt. Formerly bred in the Negev desert of Israel (and probably adjacent Jordan), but this population is now extinct in the wild. Small numbers are regularly seen in S Egypt, especially between Aswan and Abu Simbel.

Subspecies: This species is often regarded as monotypic but birds from Israel are sometimes separated as *negevensis*. The latter race still occurs in Arabia.

Tips: Inhabits arid steppes, deserts and mountain areas. Loosely colonial in some areas, but a solitary breeder in others. Nest is constructed atop an acacia or on a cliff ledge.

Sites:
EGYPT Abu Simbel** (summer), Aswan** (summer).

Black Vulture (Monk or Cinereous Vulture)
Aegypius monachus   M FG   Res (Dis)

Range: Rare in our region, breeding in C and S Spain and Mallorca, N Greece and perhaps Macedonia, Turkey, Crimea and the Caucasus (mainly Azerbaijan with smaller numbers in Armenia and Georgia). Recently began breeding again in E Portugal and a reintroduction programme that commenced in 1993 has re-established the species in France, where *c.*50 birds can be seen in the Grands Causses, S of the Massif Central. Rare but regular in the Rodopi Mts of S Bulgaria.

Tips: Hills and mountains, sometimes lowlands, with wooded and open areas. Searches for carrion over open areas with livestock or wild ungulates. Young birds disperse and the Guadalquivir marismas are a regular winter haunt. Formerly regular in very small numbers at the Bosphorus in autumn. Often seen soaring in thermals with Griffon Vultures. The reintroduced French birds are regularly seen at the Gorge du Tarn and Gorge de la Jonte, and have wandered to Spain, Switzerland and Germany.

Sites:

ARMENIA Khosrov Preserve***, Vedi Hills*.
AZERBAIJAN Turianchai Reserve***, Zakataly**.
BALEARIC IS Mallorca***.
BULGARIA Studen Kladenetz*.
EGYPT Suez area* (passage).
FRANCE Cévennes NP**.
GEORGIA Iori Steppes***, Mt Kazbek*.
GREECE Avas Gorge***, Dadiá-Soufli Forest***, Mt Olympus NP***.
ISRAEL Golan Heights**, Hula Reserve* (passage, winter).
JORDAN Ghadir Burqu'.

MACEDONIA Babuna Gorge, Crna Gorge, Demir Kapija Gorge.
PORTUGAL Baixo Alentejo*, International Tagus***.
RUSSIA Kalmykia, Teberdinskiy Reserve*.
SPAIN Cáceres-Trujillo Steppes***, Coto Doñana* (winter), La Serena** (winter), Monfragüe***, Serrania de Ronda**, Sierra de Gredos***, Sierra de Guadarrama**.
SYRIA Tadmur and Sabkhat Muh (winter).
TURKEY Soğuksu NP***.
UKRAINE Crimean Mts***.

Short-toed Eagle
Circaetus gallicus   DF SH M   Mig

Range: A summer visitor to Iberia, C and S France, Italy and SE Europe. Range extends E across Russia to the S Urals and Caspian, and N to the Baltic states and Belarus. Widespread in Greece and Turkey, with small numbers in the Middle East and breeds in NW Africa from S Morocco to N Tunisia. Follows major migration routes, appearing in some numbers at Gibraltar, the Bosphorus and Borçka. In autumn this movement peaks in late Sep–early Oct, with the return in late Mar. Smaller numbers also use the Sicily–Cap Bon route.

Tips: Look for this species on dry and warm hillsides with abundant reptile prey. Often hovers over hilly country with woodland or scattered trees, heathlands and maquis, and rocky terrain.

Sites:

ALGERIA El Kala NP*** (summer).

ANDORRA** (summer, passage).

ARMENIA Arapan Area*** (passage), Armash Fishponds** (summer, passage), Khosrov Preserve* (summer), Lake Sevan*** (passage).

AUSTRIA Lake Neusiedl** (summer).

AZERBAIJAN Turianchai Reserve** (summer).

BELARUS Albena-Golden Sands** (passage), Belovezhskaya Pushcha NP* (summer), Berezinsky Reserve* (summer).

BULGARIA Albena-Golden Sands** (passage), Burgas area** (passage), Cape Emine*** (passage), Cape Kaliakra*** (passage), Lake Durankulak*** (passage), Lake Shabla** (passage), Lake Srebarna* (passage), Rila Mts*** (summer), Rusenski Lom NP*** (summer), Strandja Mts*** (summer, passage), Studen Kladenetz** (summer), Trigradski Gorge*** (summer), Tissata NR*** (summer).

CROATIA Cres*** (summer), Mljet* (passage), Neretva Delta*** (summer), Paklenica NP** (summer).

EGYPT Abu Simbel* (passage), Aswan* (passage), Hurghada* (passage), Luxor** (passage), Sharm el Sheikh** (passage), Suez area*** (passage), Zaranik** (passage).

FRANCE Camargue*** (summer), Cévennes NP*** (summer), Écrins NP*** (summer), La Brenne** (summer), Gruissan*** (summer, passage), Île d'Oléron* (summer), Les Alpilles*** (summer), Leucate*** (passage), Marais Poitevin* (summer), Mercantour NP* (summer), Organbidexka*** (passage), Prats-de-Mollo*** (summer), Pyrenees NP*** (summer), Sologne*** (summer), Teich Reserve** (summer), Vanoise NP* (summer).

GEORGIA Iori Steppes*** (summer, passage), Kolkheti*** (passage).

GIBRALTAR** (passage).

GREECE Akarnanika Mts*** (summer), Amvrakiko's Gulf*** (passage), Avas Gorge*** (summer), Axios-Aliakmonas Deltas* (passage), Dadiá-Soufli Forest*** (summer), Delphi*** (summer), Evros Delta* (summer), Lake Kerkini*** (summer), Mikrí Prespa NP*** (summer), Mt Olympus NP*** (summer), Mt Parnassós NP*** (summer), Porto Lagos Area** (passage), Vikos-Aoos NP*** (summer).

GREEK IS Crete* (passage), Kos* (passage), Lesvos*** (summer).

HUNGARY Aggtelek NP*** (summer), Börzsöny NP*** (summer), Csákvár*** (summer), Hortobágy NP** (passage), Pilis Hills** (summer), Zemplén Hills*** (summer).

ISRAEL Bet Shean Valley*** (passage), Eilat*** (passage), Ein Gedi** (passage), Golan Heights*** (summer), Hula Reserve*** (passage), Jezreel Valley*** (passage), Ma'agan Mikhael** (passage), Mt Hermon*** (summer), Nizzana** (passage), Wadi Ammud-Mt Arbel*** (summer).

ITALY Gargano Peninsula*** (summer), Maremma Regional Park** (summer), Monte Conero*** (passage), Orbetello Reserve*** (summer), Tuscan archipelago** (passage).

JORDAN Aqaba** (passage), Azraq* (passage), Petra** (summer, passage), Wadi Dana-Fidan** (summer, passage), Wadi Rum** (passage).

LATVIA Cape Kolka** (summer), Lake Pape* (passage).

LEBANON Aammiq Marshes*** (passage), Barouk Cedars** (passage).

MACEDONIA Babuna Gorge* (summer), Bregalnica Valley** (summer), Crna Gorge** (summer), Demir Kapija Gorge** (summer), Galicica NP*** (summer), Lakes Ohrid and Prespa** (summer), Mavrovo NP* (summer).

MALTA (passage).

MOROCCO Agadir and the Sous Plain** (summer), Dayet Aaoua* (summer), Ouarzazate*** (passage), Oukaimeden** (summer, passage), Tafilalt** (summer, passage), Zaër** (summer).

POLAND Białowieża Forest* (summer), Biebrza Marshes* (summer), Bieszczady NP** (summer), Szczecin Bay area** (summer).

PORTUGAL Baixo Alentejo*** (summer), Boquilobo** (summer), Cape St Vincent*** (autumn), Castro Marim*** (passage), International Douro*** (summer), International Tagus*** (summer), Montesinho** (summer), Peneda Gêres NP*** (summer), Ria Formosa*** (summer), Sado Estuary*** (summer), Santo André Lagoon* (passage), Tagus Estuary*** (summer).

ROMANIA Danube Delta*** (summer), Dobrudja*** (summer, passage), Lake Călăraşi** (summer).

SICILY Strait of Messina* (passage).

SLOVAKIA Malé Karpaty** (summer), Slanské Hills** (summer), Slovenský Kras** (summer), Vihorlatske Hills* (summer), Záhorie* (summer).

SPAIN Aiguamolls de L'Empordá*** (summer), Aigües Tortes NP*** (summer), Cáceres-Trujillo Steppes*** (summer), Cádiz Lagoons*** (summer), Coto Doñana*** (summer), Ebro Delta*** (summer), Jaca*** (summer), La Serena*** (summer), Monfragüe***, Ordesa NP*** (summer), Picos de Europa*** (summer), Serrania de Ronda*** (summer), Sierra de Gredos*** (summer), Sierra de Guadarrama*** (summer), Tablas de Daimiel*** (summer), Zaragoza Steppes*** (summer).

SWITZERLAND Leuk (passage).

SYRIA Aqra Mts*** (summer), Jabal Slenfeh*** (passage), Wadi al-Qarn-Burqush** (summer).

TUNISIA Ain Draham*** (summer), Cap Bon Peninsula*** (passage), Lake Ichkeul** (summer, passage), Zaghouan* (summer).

TURKEY Bafa Gölü** (summer, passage), Birecik-Halfeti*** (summer), Borçka*** (passage), Dalyan*** (summer), Demirkazik*** (summer), Göksu Delta** (summer), İstanbul*** (passage), Soğuksu NP*** (summer), Uluabat Gölü** (summer), Uludağ NP*** (summer), Van Gölü*** (summer, passage).

UKRAINE Carpathians** (summer), Crimean Mts*** (summer), Dunay Delta* (summer, passage), Shatsk NP (passage).

YUGOSLAVIA Durmitor NP* (summer).

Pallid Harrier
Circus macrourus

FG Mig (Irr)

Range: Breeds in S Belarus, Ukraine and across S Russia, sometimes in Moldova and NE Romania. Irruptive, frequently appearing and even nesting far outside normal range in Scandinavia and C Europe. Small numbers winter in Tunisia, Egypt and Greece, and elsewhere in the Middle East, sometimes the southern Balkans. Present in our region late Apr–Sep, and occurs on passage throughout SE Europe, the Middle East and N Africa. Seen on passage at Borçka in Turkey in Sep–Oct, but return movement westerly, with small numbers taking the Cap Bon–Sicily route.

Tips: Breeds on dry steppes, on passage and winter also found in grasslands and cornfields, usually in drier habitats than Montagu's Harrier.

Sites:

ALBANIA Karavasta Lagoon** (passage).
ARMENIA Arapan Area*** (passage), Armash Fishponds** (passage), Lake Sevan*** (passage), Mt Aragats** (passage).
BELARUS Prypyatsky NP*** (summer).
BULGARIA Albena-Golden Sands* (passage), Burgas area** (passage), Cape Emine* (passage), Cape Kaliakra*** (passage), Lake Srebarna*** (summer), Rusenski Lom NP* (passage), Studen Kladenetz* (passage), Tissata NR* (passage).
CYPRUS* (passage).
DENMARK Hellebæk* (passage), Skagen* (passage).
EGYPT Abu Simbel* (passage), Aswan* (passage), Hurghada** (passage), Luxor* (passage), Sharm el Sheikh** (passage), Suez area*** (passage), Zaranik*** (passage).
GEORGIA Iori Steppes*** (passage, winter), Javakheti Plateau** (passage), Kolkheti* (passage).
GREECE Amvrakiko's Gulf* (passage, mainly spring), Evros Delta** (passage, mainly spring).
GREEK IS Corfu** (spring), Crete* (spring), Lesvos** (spring).
HUNGARY Hortobágy NP* (passage), Kiskunság NP* (autumn).
ISRAEL Arava Valley (passage), Bet Shean Valley*** (passage, winter), Eilat*** (passage), Ein Gedi** (passage), Hula Reserve*** (passage, winter), Jezreel Valley*** (passage), Nizzana*** (passage, winter), Urim*** (passage, winter).
ITALY Gargano Peninsula* (passage), Monte Conero** (passage).
JORDAN Azraq* (passage, winter), Ghadir Burqu'* (passage), Wadi Dana-Fidan* (passage).
LEBANON Aammiq Marshes* (passage), Qaraoun Lake* (passage).
MALTA (passage).
ROMANIA Danube Delta* (passage), Dobrudja* (summer, passage).
RUSSIA Kalmykia*** (summer), Teberdinskiy Reserve*** (passage), Volga Delta*** (summer, passage).
SARDINIA San Pietro I.* (passage).
SICILY Strait of Messina** (spring).
SYRIA Dayr al-Zawr*** (passage, winter), Tadmur and Sabkhat Muh** (passage).
TUNISIA Cap Bon Peninsula* (passage), Chott el Djerid* (winter).
TURKEY Borçka* (passage), Bulanik (passage), Dalyan (passage), İstanbul* (passage), Kulu Gölü** (passage), Van Gölü (passage).
UKRAINE Askania-Nova*** (summer), Dunay Delta** (passage).

Montagu's Harrier
Circus pygargus   FW FG (SH) Mig

Range: Widespread but very patchily distributed across Europe, from Spain and France E to the Urals and Caspian. Small numbers breed in Great Britain, S Scandinavia, Turkey and in coastal areas of NW Africa. Generally rare in western Europe with highest numbers in Spain and France, much more numerous in the E of the region. Occurs on passage across the southern half of the region, with birds concentrated at the usual watchpoints and particularly Gibraltar. Present in breeding range from Apr until mid Oct.
Tips: Found in marshes, reedbeds and cornfields, also heathland and rough grassland. Sometimes breeds in young conifer plantations and other areas of low scrub.

Sites:

ARMENIA Arapan Area*** (passage), Armash Fishponds*** (summer, passage), Lake Sevan*** (passage), Mt Aragats** (passage).
AUSTRIA Lake Neusiedl*** (summer), Marchauen-Marchegg Reserve*** (summer).
AZERBAIJAN Kura Valley Salt-lakes*** (summer).
BALEARIC IS Mallorca*** (passage). **BELARUS** Belovezhskaya Pushcha NP*** (summer), Berezinsky Reserve*** (summer), Prypyatsky NP*** (summer).
BULGARIA Albena-Golden Sands** (passage), Burgas area*** (passage), Cape Emine*** (passage), Cape Kaliakra*** (passage), Lake Durankulak*** (summer, passage), Lake Shabla*** (summer, passage), Lake Srebarna*** (summer, passage), Rusenski Lom NP** (passage), Strandja Mts*** (summer, passage), Studen Kladenetz* (passage), Tissata NR* (passage).
CANARY IS* (passage).
CORSICA Bonifacio* (autumn), Cap Corse** (passage).
CROATIA Cres** (passage), Mljet* (passage).
CYPRUS* (passage).
CZECH REPUBLIC Třeboňsko* (summer).
DENMARK Hellebæk* (passage), Rømø** (summer), Skagen*** (summer, passage), Vadehavet* (summer).

EGYPT Abu Simbel** (passage), Aswan* (passage), Faiyum* (passage), Hurghada** (passage), Luxor* (passage), Sharm el Sheikh** (passage), Suez area*** (passage), Zaranik** (passage).
ESTONIA Emajõgi Floodplain*** (summer), Lake Endla*** (summer), Matsalu Bay*** (summer).
FINLAND Liminganlahti*** (summer).
FRANCE Baie de Bourgneuf*** (summer), Baie du Mont-St-Michel* (passage), Camargue*** (summer), Cévennes NP*** (summer), Dombes*** (summer), La Brenne*** (summer), Golfe du Morbihan** (summer), Gruissan*** (passage), Île d'Oléron*** (summer), Leucate*** (passage), Marais Poitevin*** (summer), Organbidexka*** (passage), Ouessant** (summer), Sologne*** (summer).
GEORGIA Iori Steppes*** (passage), Javakheti Plateau*** (summer), Kolkheti*** (passage).
GERMANY Dummer* (summer), Federsee* (summer), Mecklenburg Lakes*** (summer).
GIBRALTAR* (passage).
GREAT BRITAIN N Norfolk coast** (passage), Portland* (passage), Spurn Peninsula* (passage).
GREECE Amvrakikós Gulf* (passage), Mikrí Prespa NP* (passage), Nestos Delta** (passage), Porto Lagos Area** (summer).

GREEK IS Corfu*** (passage), Crete** (spring), Kos*** (passage), Lesvos*** (passage), Rhodes** (passage).

HUNGARY Biharugra*** (summer), Csákvár*** (summer), Hanság*** (summer), Hortobágy NP*** (summer), Kis-balaton*** (summer), Kiskunság NP*** (summer), Lake Velence*** (summer), Ócsa*** (summer).

ISRAEL Bet Shean Valley*** (passage), Eilat*** (passage), Ein Gedi*** (passage), Hula Reserve*** (passage), Jezreel Valley*** (passage), Nizzana* (passage), Urim*** (passage).

ITALY Circeo NP*** (passage), Gargano Peninsula** (passage), Lake Massaciuccoli** (passage), Maremma Regional Park** (summer), Monte Conero** (passage), Orbetello Reserve*** (summer, passage), Po Delta* (summer), Tuscan archipelago** (passage).

JORDAN Aqaba*** (passage), Azraq*** (passage, mainly autumn), Ghadir Burqu'*** (passage), Wadi Dana-Fidan* (passage), Wadi Rum*** (passage).

LATVIA Cape Kolka*** (spring), Lake Lubana*** (summer), Lake Pape*** (summer, passage).

LEBANON Aammiq Marshes** (passage), Barouk Cedars** (passage), Qaraoun Lake* (passage).

LITHUANIA Kirsiu Peninsula*** (passage).

MACEDONIA Bregalnica Valley*** (summer), Galicica NP*** (passage), Lakes Ohrid and Prespa*** (passage).

MALTA * (passage).

MOROCCO Lac de Sidi Bourhaba*** (passage), Merja Zerga*** (summer), Oualidia*** (passage), Ouarzazate*** (passage), Tafilalt*** (passage), Zaër*** (summer).

NETHERLANDS Lauwersmeer** (summer), Oostvaardersplassen*** (summer, passage), Terschelling** (summer), Texel* (summer), Veluwe** (summer).

POLAND Białowieża Forest*** (summer), Biebrza Marshes*** (summer), Chełm Marshes*** (summer), Gdańsk Bay*** (summer), Milicz Fishponds** (summer), Siemianówka Reservoir*** (summer), Słońsk*** (summer), Szczecin Bay area*** (summer).

PORTUGAL Baixo Alentejo*** (summer), Cape St Vincent*** (autumn), Castro Marim*** (summer, passage), International Douro*** (summer), International Tagus*** (summer), Montesinho*** (summer), Peneda Gêres NP*** (summer), Ria Formosa*** (summer, passage), Sado Estuary*** (summer), Santo André Lagoon** (passage), Tagus Estuary*** (summer).

ROMANIA Danube Delta*** (summer), Dobrudja*** (summer, passage), Lake Călăraşi*** (summer).

RUSSIA Kalmykia*** (summer), Teberdinskiy Reserve*** (summer), Volga Delta*** (summer).

SARDINIA Giara di Gesturi* (passage), Oristano wetlands*** (summer), San Pietro I** (passage).

SICILY Strait of Messina*** (spring), Vendicari*** (passage).

SLOVAKIA Malé Karpaty** (passage), Senné Fishponds** (summer), Vihorlatske Hills*** (summer), Záhorie** (summer), Zlatná na Ostrove* (summer).

SPAIN Aiguamolls de L'Empordá*** (summer), Cabo de Gata*** (summer), Cáceres-Trujillo Steppes*** (summer), Cádiz Lagoons*** (summer), Coto Doñana*** (summer, passage), Ebro Delta*** (summer, passage), Guadalhorce Estuary*** (passage), Jaca* (summer), La Serena*** (summer), Monfragüe*** (summer), Ordesa NP*** (summer), Picos de Europa*** (summer), Santa Pola*** (passage), Tablas de Daimiel*** (summer), Zaragoza Steppes*** (summer).

SWEDEN Falsterbo* (passage), Gotland* (summer, passage), Hjälstaviken** (summer), Hornborgasjön** (summer), Kristianstad** (summer), Öland** (summer, passage).

SWITZERLAND Col de Bretolet** (passage), Klingnau Reservoir* (passage), Leuk* (passage).

SYRIA Tadmur and Sabkhat Muh** (passage).

TUNISIA Cap Bon Peninsula** (passage).

TURKEY Borçka** (passage), Bulanik*** (summer, passage), Dalyan (passage), Göksu Delta* (passage), İstanbul* (passage), Kulu Gölü** (summer, passage), Uluabat Gölü* (summer, passage).

UKRAINE Askania-Nova*** (summer), Dunay Delta*** (summer), Shatsk NP*** (summer, passage).
YUGOSLAVIA Obedska bara (summer).

Dark Chanting-goshawk
Melierax metabates   SD   Res (Dis)

Range: Very rare in the Western Palearctic, where it is one of the most sought after raptors of the region. Found only in a tiny area of Morocco, this very isolated and small population (endemic race *theresae*) is confined to the Sous Plain. Even here, the species can be very difficult to locate, with most recent sightings coming from the area between Taroudannt and Aoulouz. The area around Igoudar was a regular site in early spring in the early 1990s, but there have been few sightings from anywhere on the plain in recent years.

Tips: Look for this species in dry savanna and semi-desert, cultivated areas and plantations in known areas, although sightings are far from guaranteed. Requires trees for nesting and uses termite-hills, fenceposts and treetops as lookout posts from which makes short stoops at prey.

Sites:
MOROCCO Agadir and the Sous Plain, Ouarzazate, Oued Massa.

Northern Goshawk
Accipiter gentilis   CF MF DF winter (FG)   Res (Mig) (Dis)

Range: Widespread breeder, from Iberia E to the Black Sea and Caucasus, and N to Scandinavia and Arctic Russia. In the Mediterranean, breeds on Corsica and Sardinia, possibly also Cyprus. Rare and local in Turkey and the N Middle East, and there is a small and rarely seen population in Morocco. Rare but increasing in Great Britain with the breeding population thought to originate, in part, from escaped falconers' birds and most easily seen in Breckland and the Forest of Dean. Northernmost birds move southwards in autumn, elsewhere merely dispersive but small numbers are regular at the major migration watchpoints.

Subspecies: Nominate race is found over most of Europe with *arrigonii* on Corsica and Sardinia and *buteoides* in northern Scandinavia. Iberian and Moroccan birds are sometimes separated as race *kleinschmidti* and the North American race *atricapillus* has been recorded as a vagrant in Great Britain.

Tips: Forest interspersed with open areas, often hunting over more open country in winter. In Morocco found in cork oak woodlands and cedar forests. A difficult bird to find, as it occurs at low density and is generally rather secretive, best seen when indulging in its spectacular display flights in Feb–Mar.

Sites:

ANDORRA**.

ARMENIA Pambak Mts***.

AUSTRIA Hohe Tauern NP*** Hohe Wand*, Karwendel Reserve***, Lake Neusiedl**, Schneeburg Mts***.

BELARUS Belovezhskaya Pushcha NP***, Berezinsky Reserve***, Prypyatsky NP***.

BELGIUM Croix-Scaille NR**, Hautes Fagnes***, Het Zwin** (winter), Kalmthoutse Heide*, Lesse et Lomme NR**.

BOSNIA-HERZEGOVINA Sujetska NP***.

BULGARIA Albena-Golden Sands* (passage), Burgas area** (passage), Cape Emine** (passage), Cape Kaliakra** (passage), Rila Mts***, Ropotamo NP***, Rusenski Lom NP***, Strandja Mts***, Studen Kladenetz***, Trigradski Gorge***, Tissata NR* (passage), Tzarichina NR***.

CORSICA Asco Valley***, Restonica Valley***.

CROATIA Cres**, Paklenica NP***, Plitvice***.

CYPRUS**.

CZECH REPUBLIC Beskydy Mts***, Lednice***, Pálava Hills***, Šumava NP***.

DENMARK Amager** (passage, winter), Bornholm-Christiansø*** (passage), Hellebæk***, Møn-Falster** (passage), Skagen*** (passage), Skallingen-Blåvandshuk* (passage), Stevns Klint*** (passage), Stignæs*** (passage, winter).

ESTONIA Emajõgi Floodplain***, Lake Endla***, Nigula NR***.

FINLAND Åland Is***, Kevo NR***, Kolvanan Uuro***, Kuusamo***, Lake Inari***, Oulanka NP***, Parikkala***, Patvinsuo NP***, Pyhä-Häkki NP***, Urho Kekkonen NP***, Vesijako NP***, Viikki***.

FRANCE Cévennes NP***, Dombes***, Fontainebleau***, Forêt d'Orient***, La Brenne***, Lac du Der-Chantecoq***, Lorraine NP***, Mercantour NP***, Organbidexka** (passage), Prats-de-Mollo***, Pyrenees NP***, Queyras NP***, Sologne***, Vanoise NP***.

GEORGIA Iori Steppes***, Kolkheti* (passage), Mt Kazbek***.

GERMANY Ammer Valley***, Bayerischer Wald NP***, Berchtesgaden NP***, Federsee***, Kuhkopf***, Mecklenburg Lakes***, Vessertal***.

GIBRALTAR*** (passage).

GREAT BRITAIN Breckland**.

GREECE Dadiá-Soufli Forest***, Evros Delta*, Lake Kerkini**, Mikrí Prespa NP***, Mt Olympus NP***, Mt Parnassós NP***, Nestos Delta**, Valia Kalda NP***, Vikos-Aoos NP***.

GREEK IS Crete* (passage, winter), Lesvos*.

HUNGARY Aggtelek NP***, Börzsöny NP***, Buda Hills*, Bükk Hills***, Csákvár***, Danube Bend**, Hanság**, Hortobágy NP* (passage), Lake Fertő***, Lake Velence**, Pilis Hills***, Zemplén Hills***.

ISRAEL Eilat* (passage), Mt Hermon* (winter).

ITALY Abruzzo NP***, Gargano Peninsula**, Gran Paradiso NP***, Maremma Regional Park**, Sibillini NP***, Stelvio NP***.

LATVIA Cape Kolka***, Lake Engure***, Lake Lubana***, Lake Pape***.

LITHUANIA Kirsiu Peninsula*** (passage).

MACEDONIA Bregalnica Valley**, Demir Kapija Gorge**, Galicica NP***, Lakes Ohrid and Prespa**, Mavrovo NP***, Sara Mts***.

MOROCCO Agadir and the Sous Plain

NETHERLANDS Lauwersmeer**, Naardermeer**, Oostvaardersplassen***, Veluwe***.

NORWAY Hardangervidda NP***, Mølen** (passage), Slettnes* (passage), Stabbursdalen NP***, Utsira* (passage, winter).

POLAND Białowieża Forest***, Biebrza Marshes***, Bieszczady NP***, Chełm Marshes***, Gda_sk Bay***, Milicz Fishponds***, Siemianówka Reservoir***, Szczecin Bay area***.

PORTUGAL Baixo Alentejo***, Cape St Vincent* (autumn), International Douro***, International Tagus***, Montesinho***, Peneda Gêres NP***, Tagus Estuary** (winter).

ROMANIA Bicaz***, Dobrudja**, Gurghiu Mts***, Poiana Braşov***, Retezat NP***, Turda Gorge***.

RUSSIA Kola Peninsula***, Teberdinskiy Reserve***.

SARDINIA Giara di Gesturi*, Monte Arcuso***.

SLOVAKIA High Tatras NP***, Malá Fatra***, Malé Karpaty***, Nízke Tatry NP***, Orava Reservoir***, Senné Fishponds***, Slanské Hills***, Slovenský Kras***, Vihorlatske Hills***.

SLOVENIA Kocevje***, Triglav NP***.

SPAIN Aigües Tortes NP***, Garraf Massif**, Jaca***, Monfragüe***, Ordesa NP***, Picos de Europa***, Serrania de Ronda***, Sierra de Gredos***, Sierra de Guadarrama***.

SWEDEN Ammarnäs***, Falsterbo*** (passage, winter), Färnebofjärden***, Gammelstadsviken***, Getterön***, Gotland***, Hjälstaviken***, Hornborgasjön***, Kristianstad***, Kvismaren***, Lake Ånnsjön***, Lake Krankesjön***, Muddus NP***, Öland***, Padjelanta NP***, Ripakaisenvuoma***, Store Mosse NP***, Tåkern***, Tyresta NP***.

SWITZERLAND Aletschwald***, Clos-du-Doubs***, Col de Bretolet***, Fanel NR***, Flims***, Klingnau Reservoir** (passage), Monte Generoso***, Niderholz***, Swiss NP***.

SYRIA Aqra Mts*.

TURKEY Borçka* (passage), İstanbul* (passage), Soğuksu NP*, Uludağ NP.

UKRAINE Carpathians***, Crimean Mts**, Shatsk NP***.

YUGOSLAVIA Ðerdap NP**, Fruška Gora NP*.

Levant Sparrowhawk
Accipiter brevipes   DF (FG)   Mig

Range: Breeds in the SE of our region, in Moldova and S Ukraine, across Russia to Kazakstan, and in scattered areas of SE Europe, through most of the Balkan countries and Greece, as well as in Turkey and the Caucasus. Has bred in southern Hungary. Passage occurs across Turkey, the Middle East and Egypt, and the species is numerous on migration at the Bosphorus and, particularly, Eilat. Main passage period mid Aug–early Oct, peaking in mid–late Sep, with the return in mid–late Apr. Passage is concentrated and most of the population moves through the Bosphorus in a few days in dense flocks with much smaller numbers in NE Turkey.

Tips: Search dry hilly or lowland areas with open and scattered woodlands, sometimes nests in trees in open cultivated land.

Sites:

ARMENIA Arapan Area*** (passage), Khosrov Preserve*** (summer), Lake Sevan*** (passage), Meghri Area*** (summer), Pambak Mts*** (summer), Vedi Hills*** (summer).
AZERBAIJAN Zakataly*** (summer).
BULGARIA Albena-Golden Sands*** (passage), Burgas area*** (summer, passage), Cape Emine*** (summer, passage), Cape Kaliakra*** (summer, passage), Lake Durankulak*** (passage), Lake Shabla* (passage), Lake Srebarna** (summer), Ropotamo NP*** (summer, passage), Rusenski Lom NP*** (summer), Strandja Mts*** (summer, passage), Studen Kladenetz*** (summer), Tissata NR*** (passage).
CYPRUS* (passage).
EGYPT Hurghada*** (passage), Sharm el Sheikh** (passage), Suez area*** (passage), Zaranik*** (passage).
GEORGIA Iori Steppes*** (passage), Kolkheti*** (passage).
GREECE Amvrakiko's Gulf* (passage), Avas Gorge*** (passage), Axios-Aliakmonas Deltas* (summer, passage), Dadiá-Soufli Forest***

(summer), Delphi** (passage), Evros Delta** (passage), Lake Kerkini* (summer), Mt Olympus NP*** (summer), Nestos Delta*** (summer, passage), Valia Kalda NP*** (summer).
GREEK IS Lesvos* (summer, passage).
ISRAEL Arava Valley*** (passage), Eilat*** (passage), Ein Gedi*** (passage), Hula Reserve*** (passage), Jezreel Valley*** (passage), Mt Hermon*** (passage).
JORDAN Aqaba*** (passage), Azraq** (passage), Petra*** (passage), Wadi Dana-Fidan** (passage), Wadi Rum*** (passage).
LEBANON Aammiq Marshes*** (passage), Barouk Cedars*** (passage), Qaraoun Lake** (passage).
MACEDONIA Babuna Gorge* (summer), Demir Kapija Gorge** (summer).
ROMANIA Danube Delta* (passage), Dobrudja*** (summer, passage).
RUSSIA Volga Delta* (passage).
SYRIA Jabal Slenfeh*** (passage), Tadmur and Sabkhat Muh* (passage).
TURKEY Borçka*** (passage), İstanbul*** (passage).

Long-legged Buzzard
Buteo rufinus D SD FG Mig Res

Range: Rare in the Balkans, N Greece and Cyprus, but breeds more commonly across interior Turkey, the Caucasus and S Russia bordering the Caspian. Also breeds over much of the Middle East and in NW Africa from S Morocco to N Libya. Has recently begun to breed regularly in Hungary. More widespread in Turkey, the Middle East and Egypt in winter, and increasingly recorded in S France at this season. Small numbers occur on passage at the Bosphorus and Borçka, with rather more at Suez. Autumn movements are in late Aug–Oct and the return in Feb–Apr.

Subspecies: North African birds belong to race *cirtensis* with remainder of range occupied by the nominate race and it has been suggested that the two should be regarded as separate species. Interestingly, it has also been recently proposed that the Common Buzzard population of the Cape Verde Is (formerly race *bannermani* but now usually lumped with nominate *buteo*) may be better placed with Long-legged Buzzard and that Long-legged Buzzards from C Turkey are in fact *menetriesi* race Common Buzzards.

Tips: A bird of desert and steppe, wooded hillsides and cliffs near open country. Spends more time perched than Common Buzzard, but is the ecological replacement of that species in N Africa.

Sites:

ALGERIA Djebel Babor***, El Kala NP***.

ARMENIA Arapan Area*** (passage), Khosrov Preserve*** (summer), Lake Sevan*** (passage), Mt Aragats*** (summer), Pambak Mts*** (summer), Vedi Hills*** (summer).

AZERBAIJAN Turianchai Reserve*** (summer).

BULGARIA Albena-Golden Sands*** (summer, passage), Burgas area*** (summer, passage), Cape Emine*** (passage), Cape Kaliakra*** (summer, passage), Rusenski Lom NP*** (summer), Strandja Mts* (summer, passage), Studen Kladenetz*** (summer), Tissata NR*** (summer), Tzarichina NR*** (summer).

CYPRUS (passage).

EGYPT Aswan*** (passage, winter), Faiyum** (winter), Hurghada** (passage), Luxor** (passage, winter), Nile Delta* (winter), Sharm el Sheikh*** (passage), Suez area*** (passage), Zaranik** (passage).

FRANCE Camargue* (winter).

GEORGIA Iori Steppes***, Kolkheti* (passage).

GREECE Amvrakiko's Gulf** (passage), Avas Gorge*** (summer), Dadiá-Soufli Forest*** (summer), Evros Delta** (summer, passage), Lake Kerkini*** (summer), Mikrí Prespa NP*** (summer).

GREEK IS Crete* (passage, mainly spring), Kos***, Lesvos***, Náxos***, Rhodes***.

HUNGARY Hortobágy NP** (summer, passage), Kiskunság NP* (autumn).

ISRAEL Bet Shean Valley*** (passage, winter), Eilat*** (passage), Ein Gedi***, Golan Heights***, Hula Reserve*** (passage), Jezreel Valley*** (passage), Mt Hermon*** (passage), Nizzana***, Wadi Ammud-Mt Arbel***, Urim***.

ITALY Gargano Peninsula (passage).

JORDAN Azraq***, Ghadir Burqu'***, Petra***, Wadi Dana-Fidan***, Wadi Rum***.

LEBANON Aammiq Marshes*** (passage), Barouk Cedars* (summer), Qaraoun Lake**.

MACEDONIA Babuna Gorge* (summer), Bregalnica Valley** (summer), Crna Gorge* (summer), Demir Kapija Gorge** (summer), Galicica NP* (summer).

MOROCCO Agadir and the Sous Plain***, Boumalne***, Dayet Aaoua***, Goulimine to Tan-Tan***, Merja Zerga*** (passage), Ouarzazate***, Oukaimeden*, Tafilalt***, Zaër***.

PORTUGAL Cape St Vincent (autumn).

ROMANIA Dobrudja*** (summer, passage), Lake Călăraşi* (passage).

RUSSIA Kalmykia*** (summer), Teberdinskiy Reserve*** (passage), Volga Delta*** (summer).

SICILY Strait of Messina* (spring).

SYRIA Dayr al-Zawr** (passage), Jabal al-Bishri***, Jabal Slenfeh** (passage), Tadmur and Sabkhat Muh***, Wadi al-Qarn-Burqush***, Yarmuk Valley***.

TUNISIA Ain Draham***, Cap Bon Peninsula***, Chott el Djerid***, Kelbia Lake**, Lake Ichkeul** (mainly winter), Tataouine***, Zaghouan***.

TURKEY Akseki*, Bafa Gölü*, Birecik-Halfeti**, Borçka** (passage), Bulanik** (passage), Dalyan*, Demirkazik** (summer), Göksu Delta*, İstanbul* (passage), Kulu Gölü*** (summer), Van Gölü*** (summer).

UKRAINE Askania-Nova*** (summer).

Rough-legged Buzzard
Buteo lagopus   Summer **T CF** winter **FG   Mig**

Range: Breeds in Scandinavia (except S Sweden and Finland) and across N Russia, and in years of rodent abundance may nest further S than usual. Winters on the E coast of Great Britain (scarce but fairly regular in East Anglia and N Kent) and from Belgium E to the Caspian, ranging S to the Adriatic and Black Seas. Variable numbers pass through Falsterbo in Aug–Oct and Feb–Apr.
Tips: Breeds on cliffs in tundra or in trees at taiga edge, on passage and in winter hunts over open farmland, moors and marshes.

Sites:

AUSTRIA Lake Neusiedl*** (winter).
BELARUS Belovezhskaya Pushcha NP*** (winter), Berezinsky Reserve*** (winter). **BULGARIA** Cape Kaliakra* (passage), Lake Shabla* (passage, winter), Lake Durankulak** (passage, winter), Lake Srebarna** (winter). **CZECH REPUBLIC** Znojmo** (winter).
DENMARK Amager*** (passage, winter), Bornholm-Christiansø*** (passage), Hellebæk*** (passage), Møn-Falster*** (passage), Ringkøbing Fjord*** (winter), Rømø*** (winter), Skagen*** (passage, winter), Skallingen-Blåvandshuk*** (passage, winter), Stevns Klint*** (passage), Stignæs*** (passage, winter), Vadehavet*** (winter).
ESTONIA Matsalu Bay*** (passage).
FINLAND Åland Is*** (passage), Kevo NR*** (summer), Kilpisjärvi Saana*** (summer), Kuusamo*** (summer), Lake Inari*** (summer), Lemmenjoki NP*** (summer), Oulanka NP*** (summer), Pallas-Ounastunturi NP*** (summer), Pyhätunturi NP*** (summer), Ruissalo*** (passage), Urho Kekkonen NP*** (summer), Viikki*** (passage), Somme Estuary* (winter).
GEORGIA Iori Steppes* (passage), Kolkheti (passage).
GERMANY Mecklenburg Lakes** (winter), Oder Valley** (winter).
GREAT BRITAIN Fair Isle* (autumn), Minsmere* (passage, winter), N Norfolk coast** (autumn, winter), Orkney Is* (passage, winter).

HUNGARY Biharugra*** (winter), Csákvár*** (winter), Danube Bend** (passage, winter), Hanság*** (winter), Hortobágy NP*** (passage, winter), Kardoskút*** (winter), Kis-balaton*** (winter), Kiskunság NP*** (winter), Lake Fertö*** (winter), Lake Velence*** (winter), Ócsa*** (summer), Zemplén Hills*** (winter).
LATVIA Cape Kolka*** (passage), Lake Lubana** (passage), Lake Pape*** (passage).
LITHUANIA Kirsiu Peninsula*** (passage).
NETHERLANDS Lauwersmeer*** (winter), Oostvaardersplassen*** (winter), Terschelling*** (winter), Texel*** (winter).
NORWAY Dovrefjell NP*** (summer), Fokstumyra*** (summer), Hardangervidda NP*** (summer), Lista*** (passage), Lofoten Is*** (summer), Mølen*** (passage), Øvre Pasvik NP*** (summer), Rondane NP*** (summer), Slettnes*** (summer), Stabbursdalen NP*** (summer), Utsira** (passage), Varanger*** (summer).
POLAND Gdańsk Bay*** (passage, winter), Szczecin Bay area** (passage, winter).
ROMANIA Danube Delta*** (winter), Dobrudja*** (passage, winter), Satchinez*** (winter).
RUSSIA Kalmykia*** (winter), Kola Peninsula*** (summer), Volga Delta*** (winter).
SLOVAKIA Zlatná na Ostrove*** (winter).
SWEDEN Abisko NP*** (summer), Ammarnäs*** (summer), Falsterbo*** (pas-

sage, winter), Gotland*** (passage), Hjälstaviken*** (passage, winter), Hornborgasjön*** (winter), Kristianstad*** (passage, winter), Kvismaren*** (winter), Lake Ånnsjön*** (summer), Lake Krankesjön*** (winter), Padjelanta NP*** (summer), Öland*** (passage, winter), Ripakaisenvuoma*** (summer), Sarek NP*** (summer), Tåkern*** (winter), Tarnasjön*** (summer).
TURKEY Kızılırmak Delta (winter).
UKRAINE Askania-Nova*** (winter), Crimean Mts** (winter), Dunay Delta*** (winter), Shatsk NP*** (passage, winter).

Lesser Spotted Eagle
Aquila pomarina   CF MF DF (FG) (FW) Mig

Range: Breeds from NE Germany and Poland to the Baltic states and S to Ukraine, with isolated pockets in E and SE Europe including Romania and Bulgaria, Turkey and the Caucasus. Occurs on passage across SE Europe, Turkey and the Middle East. Many thousands pass through the Bosphorus during mid Aug to mid Oct and return in late Mar to late Apr. Smaller numbers regular at Borçka and Sicily–Cap Bon.

Tips: Breeds in forests and woodlands with clearings and lakes, often hunting over grassland outside breeding season. Less tied to water than Greater Spotted Eagle and often seen at higher altitudes.

Sites:
ARMENIA Arapan Area*** (passage), Khosrov Preserve*** (summer, passage), Lake Sevan*** (passage), Mt Aragats** (summer), Pambak Mts*** (summer), Vedi Hills* (summer).
AUSTRIA Lake Neusiedl** (summer), Marchauen-Marchegg Reserve*** (summer).
AZERBAIJAN Turianchai Reserve*** (summer).
BELARUS Belovezhskaya Pushcha NP*** (summer), Berezinsky Reserve*** (summer), Prypyatsky NP*** (summer).
BULGARIA Albena-Golden Sands*** (passage), Burgas area*** (passage), Cape Emine*** (summer, passage), Cape Kaliakra*** (summer, passage), Lake Srebarna*** (passage), Rila Mts*** (summer), Ropotamo NP*** (summer, passage), Rusenski Lom NP*** (summer), Strandja Mts*** (summer, passage), Studen Kladenetz*** (summer, passage),

Tissata NR** (passage), Tzarichina NR*** (summer).
CROATIA Pokupsko Depression*.
CZECH REPUBLIC Beskydy Mts* (summer), Krkonoše NP* (summer), Šumava NP** (summer).
DENMARK Stevns Klint* (passage).
EGYPT Abu Simbel** (passage), Aswan** (passage), Hurghada** (passage), Luxor** (passage), Sharm el Sheikh** (passage), Suez area*** (passage), Zaranik** (passage).
ESTONIA Lake Endla*** (summer), Matsalu Bay*** (passage), Nigula NR*** (summer).
FRANCE Camargue* (passage, winter).
GEORGIA Iori Steppes*** (summer, passage), Kolkheti*** (passage).
GERMANY Mecklenburg Lakes*** (summer), Oder Valley*** (summer).
GREECE Amvrakiko's Gulf** (passage), Dadiá-Soufli Forest*** (summer), Evros Delta**

(passage), Lake Kerkini*** (summer), Mikrí Prespa NP*** (summer), Mt Olympus NP*** (summer, passage).
GREEK IS Lesvos* (passage).
HUNGARY Aggtelek NP*** (summer), Börzsöny NP*** (summer), Bükk Hills NP*** (summer), Danube Bend* (summer), Hortobágy NP*** (passage), Kiskunság NP* (passage), Lake Fertö* (summer), Pilis Hills** (summer), Zemplén Hills*** (summer).
ISRAEL Arava Valley*** (passage), Bet Shean Valley*** (passage, winter), Eilat*** (passage), Ein Gedi*** (passage), Hula Reserve*** (passage), Jezreel Valley*** (passage), Nizzana*** (passage), Urim*** (passage).
ITALY Monte Conero* (passage).
JORDAN Aqaba*** (passage), Azraq*** (passage), Ghadir Burqu'* (passage), Petra** (passage), Wadi Dana-Fidan* (passage), Wadi Rum* (passage).
LATVIA Lake Engure*** (summer), Lake Lubana*** (summer, passage), Lake Pape*** (passage).
LEBANON Aammiq Marshes*** (passage), Barouk Cedars*** (passage), Qaraoun Lake** (passage).
LITHUANIA Kirsiu Peninsula*** (passage), Lake Kretuonas** (summer).
MACEDONIA Mavrovo NP* (summer).
MOLDOVA Balatina** (summer).
POLAND Białowieża Forest*** (summer), Biebrza Marshes*** (summer), Bieszczady NP*** (summer), Gdańsk Bay*** (summer), Kampinos NP** (summer), Siemianówka Reservoir*** (summer), Słońsk*** (summer), Szczecin Bay area** (summer).
ROMANIA Danube Delta*** (summer), Dobrudja*** (summer, passage), Gurghiu Mts*** (summer), Lake Călăraşi** (summer), Retezat NP*** (summer).
RUSSIA Teberdinskiy Reserve*** (passage).
SICILY Strait of Messina* (spring).
SLOVAKIA High Tatras NP** (summer), Malá Fatra*** (summer), Malé Karpaty** (summer), Nízke Tatry NP*** (summer), Orava Reservoir*** (summer), Slanské Hills*** (summer), Slovensk_ Kras*** (summer), Vihorlatske Hills*** (summer).
SLOVENIA Krakovski Forest** (summer). Falsterbo* (passage).
SYRIA Dayr al-Zawr* (passage), Jabal Slenfeh*** (passage).
TUNISIA Cap Bon Peninsula* (passage).
TURKEY Borçka*** (passage), Dalyan (passage), İstanbul*** (passage), Kızılırmak Delta** (summer), Kocaçay Delta** (summer), Soğuksu NP (passage), Uluabat Gölü** (summer), Uludağ NP* (summer).
UKRAINE Carpathians*** (summer), Dunay Delta* (passage), Shatsk NP*** (summer, passage).
YUGOSLAVIA Đerdap NP* (summer), Fruška Gora NP (summer), Obedska bara (summer).

Greater Spotted Eagle (Spotted Eagle)
Aquila clanga   CF MF DF (FW)   Mig (PMig)

Range: A rare breeder in N Russia and Ukraine E to the Urals, with few pairs in Latvia and Lithuania, NE Poland, Moldova and Belarus. Small numbers winter in N Greece and Turkey, the Middle East and Egypt. Also occurs in winter in the Po Valley of Italy and the Camargue of S France, rarely further W to Spain and Morocco. A broad-front migrant in Sep–Oct and does not concentrate at the major migration watchpoints. Although very small numbers occur at the Bosphorus, most migrate along the E coast of the Black Sea. Return movement occurs in Mar–Apr.

Tips: Look for this species in forested areas with marshes, lakes and clearings, and in more open areas on passage. In severe decline and now extinct in many parts of former range, occurs at low density over much of remainder.

Sites:

ALBANIA Karavasta Lagoon* (winter).
ARMENIA Pambak Mts* (passage).
AUSTRIA Lake Neusiedl* (passage).
AZERBAIJAN Turianchai Reserve* (passage), Kyzylagach Bay** (winter).
BELARUS Belovezhskaya Pushcha NP* (summer), Berezinsky Reserve* (passage).
BULGARIA Albena-Golden Sands* (passage), Burgas area* (passage), Ropotamo NP* (winter), Tissata NR* (passage).
CROATIA Kopački Rit* (winter).
EGYPT Aswan* (passage), Hurghada* (passage), Luxor* (passage), Sharm el Sheikh* (passage), Suez area*** (passage), Zaranik* (passage).
ESTONIA Emajõgi Floodplain*** (summer), Nigula NR* (summer).
FINLAND Parikkala* (summer).
FRANCE Camargue* (passage, winter), Dombes* (winter).
GEORGIA Iori Steppes** (passage), Kolkheti*** (passage).
GREECE Amvrakiko's Gulf** (passage, winter) Axios-Aliakmonas Deltas* (winter), Dadiá-Soufli Forest** (passage, winter), Evros Delta* (passage, winter), Lake Kerkini** (passage, winter), Nestos Delta** (passage, winter), Porto Lagos Area** (passage, winter).
GREEK IS Lesvos** (winter).
HUNGARY Hortobágy NP* (passage), Kis-balaton* (passage), Kiskunság NP* (passage).

ISRAEL Bet Shean Valley*** (passage, winter), Eilat (passage), Ein Gedi** (passage), Hula Reserve*** (passage, winter), Jezreel Valley** (passage), Ma'agan Mikhael* (passage), Urim** (winter).
ITALY Circeo NP* (passage), Gargano Peninsula* (passage).
JORDAN Aqaba (passage), Azraq (passage), Petra (passage).
LATVIA Cape Kolka (summer, passage), Lake Lubana** (summer, passage).
LEBANON Aammiq Marshes* (passage), Barouk Cedars (passage), Qaraoun Lake* (passage).
MOLDOVA Balatina* (summer), Manta Floodplain** (passage).
POLAND Białowieża Forest* (summer), Biebrza Marshes*** (summer), Bieszczady NP* (summer).
ROMANIA Danube Delta** (passage).
RUSSIA Oka Valley*** (summer), Volga Delta* (summer).
SARDINIA Cagliari wetlands (winter).
SPAIN Coto Doñana (winter).
SWEDEN Falsterbo* (passage).
TURKEY Borçka* (passage), Dalyan* (winter), Göksu Delta** (winter), İstanbul* (passage), Kızılırmak Delta** (winter).
YUGOSLAVIA Carska bara (winter), Fruška Gora NP (passage).

Tawny Eagle
Aquila rapax

M CF DF SD   Res

Range: Very rare in our region, breeding in SC Morocco and perhaps still in a small area of N Algeria, but common and widespread S of the Sahara. Probably sedentary in N Africa but vagrants have been recorded in Tunisia, Egypt and Israel.

Tips: Nests in small trees, in rocks and ruins, and occurs in a wide range of habitats from montane forests to semi-desert.

Sites:
MOROCCO Agadir and the Sous Plain*, Goulimine to Tan-Tan***, Oued Massa*, Tafilalt**.

Steppe Eagle
Aquila nipalensis

FG SD   Mig

Range: Breeds in the extreme E of the region, from the N Caucasus to N of the Caspian. Formerly bred in Romania and Moldova and probably now extinct as a breeding species in Ukraine. Small numbers winter in Israel, occasionally in Greece and Turkey but most migrate to sub-Saharan Africa. Rather scarce on passage through Turkey and the northern Middle East but regular in some numbers in Israel, Sinai and Egypt.

Tips: Lowland steppe, semi-desert and arid foothills.

Sites:
ARMENIA Arapan Area*** (passage), Armash Fishponds** (passage), Khosrov Preserve*** (passage), Lake Sevan*** (passage), Mt Aragats** (passage), Vedi Hills* (passage).
BULGARIA Albena-Golden Sands* (passage), Burgas area* (passage).
EGYPT Aswan** (passage), Hurghada** (passage), Luxor** (passage), Sharm el Sheikh** (passage), Suez area*** (passage), Zaranik** (passage).
GEORGIA Iori Steppes** (passage), Kolkheti** (passage).

GREECE Dadiá-Soufli Forest*** (passage).
ISRAEL Arava Valley*** (passage), Bet Shean Valley** (passage, winter), Eilat*** (passage), Ein Gedi* (passage), Hula Reserve* (passage), Jezreel Valley** (passage), Nizzana** (passage, winter), Urim*** (winter).
JORDAN Aqaba** (passage), Azraq* (passage), Ghadir Burqu'** (passage), Petra** (passage), Wadi Dana-Fidan*** (passage), Wadi Rum** (passage), Wadi as Sir** (passage).

LEBANON Aammiq Marshes*** (passage), Barouk Cedars** (passage), Qaraoun Lake** (passage).
RUSSIA Kalmykia*** (summer), Teberdinskiy Reserve*** (passage), Volga Delta*** (summer).

SYRIA Dayr al-Zawr* (passage), Tadmur and Sabkhat Muh** (passage).
TURKEY Borçka*** (passage), İstanbul (passage).
UKRAINE Askania-Nova* (summer).

Eastern Imperial Eagle
Aquila heliaca CF MF DF FG Res Mig

Range: Breeds in scattered pockets across E Europe, from Slovakia and Hungary E to Ukraine and S Russia, and S to N Greece and Turkey. Recently bred in the Czech Republic and Austria for the first time. Formerly bred in Cyprus but no recent reports. Hungarian birds are mainly resident but others move S, and the species is more widespread in winter in the Balkans, Greece, parts of Turkey, the Middle East and Egypt. Tiny numbers are annual on passage at the Bosphorus and Borçka, Eilat and Suez. Autumn passage is in Aug–Oct and the return in late Feb–Apr.

Tips: Occurs in open lowland areas with scattered trees or wooded patches, often close to water.

Sites:

ARMENIA Mt Aragats* (summer).
AZERBAIJAN Turianchai Reserve*** (summer).
BULGARIA Albena-Golden Sands* (passage), Burgas area* (passage), Lake Srebarna* (passage), Rila Mts* (summer, passage), Strandja Mts* (summer), Studen Kladenetz** (summer, passage), Tissata NR* (passage).
CYPRUS (passage).
CZECH REPUBLIC Pálava Hills* (summer).
EGYPT Aswan** (passage, winter), Hurghada** (passage), Luxor* (passage), Sharm el Sheikh** (passage, winter), Suez area*** (passage), Zaranik*** (passage).
GEORGIA Iori Steppes** (passage), Kolkheti* (passage).
GREECE Amvrakiko's Gulf* (passage), Avas Gorge*, Dadiá-Soufli Forest** (passage), Evros Delta* (passage), Lake Kerkini* (passage, winter), Mikrí Prespa NP*, Nestos Delta*

(winter), Porto Lagos Area* (passage), Valia Kalda NP**.
HUNGARY Aggtelek NP* (summer), Börzsöny NP* (summer), Bükk Hills NP** (summer), Csákvár** (summer), Hortobágy NP** (passage), Pilis Hills* (passage), Zemplén Hills** (summer).
ISRAEL Arava Valley*** (passage, winter), Eilat*** (passage), Bet Shean Valley** (passage, winter), Ein Gedi* (passage), Hula Reserve** (passage, winter), Jezreel Valley* (passage), Urim** (winter).
JORDAN Aqaba* (passage), Azraq* (passage, winter), Ghadir Burqu'* (passage, winter), Petra* (passage), Wadi Dana-Fidan* (passage), Wadi Rum (passage).
LEBANON Aammiq Marshes* (passage), Barouk Cedars** (passage).
MACEDONIA Babuna Gorge (summer, passage), Bregalnica Valley* (summer), Crna

Gorge (passage), Demir Kapija Gorge* (summer), Mavrovo NP* (summer).
ROMANIA Danube Delta** (passage), Dobrudja** (summer, passage).
RUSSIA Teberdinskiy Reserve*** (passage), Volga Delta** (passage).
SLOVAKIA Malé Karpaty** (summer), Slanské Hills** (summer), Slovenský Kras** (summer),

Vihorlatske Hills*** (summer).
TURKEY Borçka* (passage), Göksu Delta* (winter), İstanbul* (passage), Soğuksu NP (rare in summer).
UKRAINE Crimean Mts***, Dunay Delta (passage).
YUGOSLAVIA Đerdap NP* (passage), Fruška Gora NP (summer).

Spanish Imperial Eagle
Aquila adalberti   FG DF   Res (Dis)

Range: A Western Palearctic endemic (recently separated from the Eastern Imperial Eagle). Breeds in C and SW Spain, with strongholds in the Extremadura region Coto Doñana. Bred in Portugal in 2004 after an absence of 25 years and nesting recently confirmed in Morocco, where formerly regular. Occasionally observed at Gibraltar and wanders to the Pyrenees, with vagrants recorded in the Balearics.

Tips: Mainly lowland open country and foothills with scattered trees and wooded patches, particularly pine and oak.

Sites:
PORTUGAL Baixo Alentejo*.
SPAIN Cáceres-Trujillo Steppes***, Cádiz Lagoons** (passage, winter), Coto Doñana***,

Monfragüe***, Serranía de Ronda*, Sierra de Gredos***, Sierra de Guadarrama***.

Golden Eagle
Aquila chrysaetos   M (CF) (MF) (DF)   Res (Dis)

Range: Breeds in N Great Britain and Scandinavia and from N Poland and Estonia across Russia. Further S breeds in Spain, montane parts of S Europe, Corsica, Sardinia, Sicily and Crete, much of Turkey and scattered parts of the Middle East S to Sinai. In NW Africa breeds in mountains from S Morocco to N Tunisia and also NW and NE Libya. Recently bred for the first time in Jordan and Denmark. Northernmost populations are migratory and winter in SE and E Europe and across southern Russia. Throughout range imms wander to some extent and the species is regular at the major raptor migration watchpoints.

Subspecies: Nominate race occurs over most of our region with *homeyeri* in Iberia, N Africa and the Middle East.

Tips: Mountainous country but also in lowlands where not persecuted; watch forest edges, open grassland or heather moors in the mountains for this species. The long-established breeding birds at Haweswater, in the English Lake District, could be viewed without disturbance from a Royal Society for the Protection of Birds observation point equipped with telescopes but unfortunately one of the pair has recently died.

Range: Current status in our region difficult to determine, but probably breeds regularly in very small numbers in SW Jordan, S Sinai and extreme SE Egypt. Irregularly wanders to Eilat and elsewhere in S Israel.

Sites:

ANDORRA*.

ARMENIA Arapan Area*, Khosrov Preserve**, Pambak Mts***, Vedi Hills*.

AUSTRIA Hohe Tauern NP***, Hohe Wand*, Karwendel Reserve***, Schneeberg Mts***.

AZERBAIJAN Turianchai Reserve***, Zakataly**.

BELARUS Belovezhskaya Pushcha NP**, Berezinsky Reserve*.

BOSNIA-HERZEGOVINA Sujetska NP***. **BULGARIA** Rila Mts***, Rusenski Lom NP***, Strandja Mts***, Studen Kladenetz***, Trigradski Gorge***, Tissata NR**, Tzarichina NR*.

CORSICA Asco Valley**, Cap Corse**, Restonica Valley***.

CROATIA Cres**, Neretva Delta**, Paklenica NP**, Plitvice**.

DENMARK Hellebæk* (passage), Stevns Klint* (passage).

EGYPT Suez area* (passage).

ESTONIA Lake Endla***, Matsalu Bay***, Nigula NR***.

FINLAND Kilpisjärvi Saana***, Kuusamo***, Lemmenjoki NP***, Oulanka NP***, Pallas-Ounastunturi NP***, Patvinsuo NP***, Urho Kekkonen NP***.

FRANCE Cévennes NP***. Écrins NP***, Forêt d'Issaux**, Mercantour NP***, Organbidexka***, Prats-de-Mollo***, Pyrenees NP***, Queyras NP***, Vanoise NP***.

GEORGIA Iori Steppes* (passage), Javakheti Plateau*, Mt Kazbek***.

GERMANY Ammer Valley***, Berchtesgaden NP***.

GREECE Akarnanika Mts***, Avas Gorge**, Dadiá-Soufli Forest***, Delphi***, Lake

Kerkini**, Mikrí Prespa NP***, Mt Olympus NP***, Mt Parnassós NP***, Valia Kalda NP***, Vikos-Aoos NP***.

GREAT BRITAIN Cairngorms and Speyside***, Islay***, Outer Hebrides***, Rhum***.

GREEK IS Corfu*, Crete***.

HUNGARY Aggtelek NP*, Börzsöny NP** (winter), Hortobágy NP*** (passage), Zemplén Hills***.

ISRAEL Arava Valley***, Eilat***, Ein Gedi***, Hula Reserve* (winter), Mt Hermon***, Urim** (winter).

ITALY Abruzzo NP***, Gran Paradiso NP***, Sibillini NP***, Stelvio NP***.

JORDAN Azraq* (passage), Ghadir Burqu'**, Petra**, Wadi Rum*.

LATVIA Cape Kolka***, Lake Pape** (passage).

LEBANON Aammiq Marshes* (passage), Barouk Cedars (passage).

LITHUANIA Kirsiu Peninsula*** (passage).

MACEDONIA Babuna Gorge, Bregalnica Valley**, Crna Gorge**, Demir Kapija Gorge**, Galicica NP**, Lakes Ohrid and Prespa*, Mavrovo NP**, Sara Mts**.

MOLDOVA Balatina*.

MOROCCO Agadir and the Sous Plain*, Boumalne**, Goulimine to Tan-Tan*, Oukaimeden**, Zaër**.

NORWAY Dovrefjell NP***, Hardangervidda NP***, Mølen* (passage), Rondane NP**, Slettnes* (passage), Stabbursdalen NP***.

POLAND Biebrza Marshes***, Bieszczady NP***, Tatra NP**.

PORTUGAL Baixo Alentejo*, International Douro***, International Tagus***, Montesinho**, Peneda Gêres NP**.

ROMANIA Bicaz***, Gurghiu Mts***, Poiana Braşov***, Retezat NP***, Turda Gorge***.
RUSSIA Kola Peninsula*** (summer), Teberdinskiy Reserve***.
SARDINIA Monte Arcuso***.
SICILY Strait of Messina* (spring).
SLOVAKIA High Tatras NP**, Malá Fatra***, Malé Karpaty* (passage), Nízke Tatry NP***, Slanské Hills***, Vihorlatske Hills*.
SLOVENIA Triglav NP***.
SPAIN Aiguamolls de L'Empordá (winter), Aigües Tortes NP***, Cáceres-Trujillo Steppes**, Jaca***, La Serena**, Monfragüe***, Ordesa NP***, Picos de Europa***, Serrania de Ronda**, Sierra de Gredos***, Sierra de Guadarrama***, Zaragoza Steppes*.
SWEDEN Abisko NP***, Ammarnäs***, Falsterbo* (passage), Färnebofjärden** (winter), Gotland***, Hjälstaviken*** (winter), Hornborgasjön* (passage), Kristianstad* (passage, winter), Kvismaren*** (winter), Lake Krankesjön** (winter), Muddus NP***, Öland*** (passage, winter), Padjelanta NP***, Ripakaisenvuoma*** (summer), Sarek NP*** (summer), Store Mosse NP** (winter), Tärnasjön***.
SWITZERLAND Aletschwald***, Col de Bretolet***, Flims***, Monte Generoso***, Swiss NP***.
SYRIA Aqra Mts***, Tadmur and Sabkhat Muh**.
TUNISIA Zaghouan**.
TURKEY Borçka***, Dalyan, Demirkazik***, İstanbul (passage), Sivrikaya***, Soğuksu NP***, Uludağ NP**, Van Gölü**.
UKRAINE Carpathians** (summer).
YUGOSLAVIA Durmitor NP*, Fruška Gora NP, Obedska bara.

Verreaux's Eagle
Aquila verreauxi   M Res

Tips: Search gorges in mountains and rocky areas in deserts for this very localised species. Preys predominantly on hyrax and rarely occurs where these mammals are absent.

Sites:
ISRAEL Eilat.
JORDAN Wadi Rum.

Booted Eagle
Hieraaetus pennatus   M CF MF DF (FG) Mig

Range: Breeds in Iberia (including the Balearics), NW Africa from northern Morocco to NW Tunisia, and parts of C and S France, E Europe, Belarus and Russia, Turkey and the Caucasus. Small numbers winter in S France, E Spain and the Balearics, S Greece and Cyprus but most migrate S to sub-Saharan Africa via Gibraltar, the Bosphorus and through the Caucasus. Occurs at Gibraltar late Aug–early Oct, peaking in mid Sep, with the return in early Mar–May, peaking early Apr. Generally uncommon over most of range and probably most numerous in Spain.

Tips: Search hilly country or mountains where open areas alternate with mature woodland, the species is often seen over warm sunny slopes. Hunts in soaring flight or in short stoops to the ground from trees.

Sites:

ALGERIA El Kala NP** (summer).
BALEARIC IS Mallorca***, Menorca***.
BELARUS Belovezhskaya Pushcha NP** (summer).
BULGARIA Albena-Golden Sands* (passage), Burgas area** (passage), Cape Emine** (passage), Cape Kaliakra** (passage), Lake Durankulak** (passage), Lake Srebarna* (passage), Rila Mts*** (summer), Ropotamo NP** (summer, passage), Rusenski Lom NP** (summer), Strandja Mts*** (summer, passage), Studen Kladenetz** (summer, passage), Tissata NR* (passage), Tzarichina NR** (summer).
CROATIA Cres* (passage).
EGYPT Hurghada** (passage), Sharm el Sheikh** (passage), Suez area*** (passage), Zaranik** (passage).
FRANCE Camargue* (passage, winter), Gruissan** (passage), Lac du Der-Chantecoq* (summer), Leucate** (passage), Lorraine NP* (summer), Organbidexka*** (passage), Prats-de-Mollo* (summer), Pyrenees NP* (summer), Sologne** (summer).
GEORGIA Iori Steppes*** (passage), Kolkheti*** (passage).
GIBRALTAR* (passage).

GREECE Amvrakiko's Gulf* (passage), Avas Gorge** (summer), Dadiá-Soufli Forest*** (summer), Lake Kerkini** (summer), Mikrí Prespa NP*** (summer), Mt Olympus NP*** (summer), Nestos Delta** (summer, passage), Vikos-Aoos NP*** (summer).
GREEK IS Crete** Lesvos* (passage).
HUNGARY Hortobágy NP* (passage), Pilis Hills* (passage), Zemplén Hills** (summer).
ISRAEL Bet Shean Valley*** (passage), Eilat*** (passage), Ein Gedi* (passage), Hula Reserve*** (passage), Jezreel Valley** (passage).
ITALY Monte Conero* (passage).
JORDAN Aqaba* (passage), Azraq* (passage), Wadi Dana-Fidan* (passage), Wadi Rum** (passage).
LEBANON Aammiq Marshes** (passage), Barouk Cedars (summer).
MACEDONIA Babuna Gorge* (summer), Crna Gorge* (summer), Demir Kapija Gorge (summer), Mavrovo NP* (summer).
MOLDOVA Balatina* (summer).
MOROCCO Agadir and the Sous Plain** (summer), Dayet Aaoua* (summer), Ouarzazate** (passage), Oued Massa** (summer, passage), Tafilalt** (passage), Zaër** (summer).

POLAND Białowieża Forest* (summer), Biebrza Marshes* (summer), Bieszczady NP* (summer).

PORTUGAL Baixo Alentejo*** (summer), Boquilobo** (summer), Cape St Vincent*** (autumn), Castro Marim*** (passage), International Douro*** (summer), International Tagus*** (summer), Peneda Gêres NP* (summer), Ria Formosa***, Sado Estuary*** (summer), Santo André Lagoon** (summer).

ROMANIA Danube Delta*** (summer), Dobrudja*** (summer, passage), Lake Călăraşi* (summer, passage).

RUSSIA Teberdinskiy Reserve*** (passage).

SICILY Strait of Messina** (spring).

SLOVAKIA Slanské Hills** (summer), Vihorlatske Hills* (summer).

SPAIN Cabo de Gata** (summer), Cáceres-Trujillo Steppes*** (summer), Cádiz Lagoons*** (summer), Coto Doñana*** (summer), Ebro Delta** (summer), Guadalhorce Estuary** (passage, rare in winter), Jaca*** (summer), La Serena** (summer), Llobregat Delta* (passage, winter), Monfragüe*** (summer), Ordesa NP*** (summer), Picos de Europa** (summer, passage), Santa Pola** (passage), Serrania de Ronda*** (summer), Sierra de Gredos*** (summer), Sierra de Guadarrama*** (summer), Tablas de Daimiel*** (summer).

SYRIA Yarmuk Valley* (passage).

TUNISIA Ain Draham***, Cap Bon Peninsula* (passage), Lake Ichkeul** (summer, passage), Zaghouan**.

TURKEY Borçka** (passage), Dalyan** (summer), Demirkazik*** (summer), İstanbul** (passage).

UKRAINE Carpathians* (summer), Dunay Delta* (passage), Shatsk NP (passage).

YUGOSLAVIA Đerdap NP* (summer), Fruška Gora NP (summer).

Bonelli's Eagle
Hieraaetus fasciatus   M CF MF DF SH Res (Dis)

Range: Mainly resident around the Mediterranean, breeding in Morocco, N Algeria and Tunisia, Iberia and SW France, Italy, Greece, parts of Turkey, very locally in the Middle East (mainly Israel), and on Sardinia, Sicily, Crete and Cyprus. Most frequent in Spain and NW Africa but decreasing throughout range. Imms wander to some extent and occur outside breeding range but highly territorial ads usually remain in breeding areas.

Tips: Search montane and hilly areas with open woodland, forest edge and maquis, and outside breeding season often hunts over wetlands. Often noted around desert cliffs in N Africa. Usually seen in flight, soaring over hillsides, rarely observed at rest and often perches in shade.

Sites:

ALGERIA Djebel Babor**.

AZERBAIJAN Turianchai Reserve*.

CROATIA Cres*.

CYPRUS.

EGYPT Hurghada* (passage), Sharm el Sheikh* (passage), Suez area* (passage), Zaranik* (passage).

FRANCE Gruissan* (passage), Prats-de-Mollo***, Pyrenees NP**, Les Alpilles***.

GREECE Akarnanika Mts***, Dadiá-Soufli Forest**, Porto Lagos Area* (passage).

GREEK IS Corfu**, Crete***, Kos**, Lesvos**, Náxos**.

ISRAEL Bet Shean Valley* (passage), Ein Gedi*, Golan Heights***, Mt Hermon**.
JORDAN Amman NP (passage), Petra**, Wadi Dana-Fidan***, Wadi Rum.
LEBANON Barouk Cedars (passage).
MACEDONIA Crna Gorge* (summer).
MOROCCO Agadir and the Sous Plain**, Boumalne**, Ouarzazate, Oued Massa*, Oukaimeden**, Tafilalt*, Zaër**.
PORTUGAL Baixo Alentejo*** , Cape St Vincent** (autumn), Castro Marim* (winter), International Douro***, International Tagus***, Montesinho**, Tagus Estuary* (passage).

SARDINIA Capo Marargiu***, Monte Arcuso***.
SICILY San Vito Peninsula***, Strait of Messina (passage).
SPAIN Aiguamolls de L'Empordá*, Cabo de Gata**, Cáceres-Trujillo Steppes*, Coto Doñana* (winter), Garraf Massif***, Jaca***, La Serena***, Monfragüe***, Ordesa NP***, Picos de Europa***, Serrania de Ronda**, Sierra de Gredos***, Sierra de Guadarrama***.
TUNISIA Ain Draham*, Cap Bon Peninsula***, Kelbia Lake* (passage), Zaghouan***. **TURKEY** Birecik-Halfeti**, Borçka* (passage), Dalyan, Soğuksu NP.

Lesser Kestrel
Falco naumanni   FG SD U Mig

Range: Patchily distributed around the Mediterranean, breeding in NW Africa, from Morocco to NW Libya, in C and S Iberia, S France, Sardinia, Sicily and S Italy, the southern Balkans, Greece, Turkey and scattered parts of the Middle East. More widespread in Ukraine and across S Russia. A broad-front migrant but regularly seen at Gibraltar and small numbers winter in S Spain, N Africa and S Turkey. Most leave Europe in Aug–Sep and return late Feb–Apr, with largest numbers seen in spring travelling in loose flocks sometimes mixed with other small falcons. Small numbers may remain in southernmost breeding range in winter.

Tips: Usually seen in dry open country, semi-desert, grassland and farmland, and nests in rocky gorges and on ruined buildings. A colonial breeder, often nesting in towns, and provision of nest boxes has increased populations in Spain and France. Over 1,000 pairs nest in a colony in the S Italian town of Matera.

Sites:
ARMENIA Arapan Area*** (passage), Armash Fishponds*** (passage), Lake Sevan*** (passage).
AZERBAIJAN Turianchai Reserve*** (summer).
BULGARIA Albena-Golden Sands* (summer, passage), Burgas area* (summer), Cape Emine* (passage), Cape Kaliakra** (passage), Rila Mts* (passage), Rusenski Lom NP*** (summer), Studen Kladenetz** (summer,

passage), Trigradski Gorge*** (summer), Tissata NR*** (summer, passage).
CORSICA Bonifacio* (passage), Cap Corse** (passage).
CROATIA Cres** (passage), Mljet* (passage).
EGYPT Abu Simbel*** (passage), Aswan*** (passage), Hurghada* (passage), Luxor** (passage), Sharm el Sheikh** (passage), Suez area*** (passage), Zaranik** (passage).
FRANCE Camargue*** (summer, passage).

GEORGIA Iori Steppes** (passage), Kolkheti* (passage).

GIBRALTAR* (passage).

GREECE Akarnanika Mts* (summer), Amvrakiko's Gulf* (passage), Avas Gorge*** (summer), Dadiá-Soufli Forest*** (summer), Evros Delta**(passage), Lake Kerkini** (passage), Mikrí Prespa NP*** (summer), Nestos Delta** (passage), Porto Lagos Area* (passage).

GREEK IS Corfu** (passage), Crete** (summer, passage), Kos** (summer, passage), Lesvos*** (summer, passage), Rhodes** (summer, passage).

ISRAEL Arava Valley*** (passage), Eilat*** (passage), Ein Gedi** (passage), Hula Reserve*** (summer), Jezreel Valley*** (passage), Ma'agan Mikhael** (passage), Mt Hermon*** (passage), Nizzana*** (passage), Wadi Ammud-Mt Arbel*** (summer).

ITALY Gargano Peninsula** (summer, passage), Monte Conero** (passage), Orbetello Reserve** (summer), San Giuliano Reserve*** (summer).

JORDAN Aqaba* (passage), Azraq** (passage, mainly spring), Petra*** (summer, passage), Wadi Dana-Fidan** (summer, passage), Wadi Rum** (passage).

LEBANON Aammiq Marshes** (passage), Barouk Cedars** (passage), Qaraoun Lake* (passage).

MACEDONIA Babuna Gorge** (summer), Crna Gorge** (summer), Demir Kapija Gorge** (summer), Galicica NP** (summer), Lakes Ohrid and Prespa*** (summer).

MALTA* (passage).

MOROCCO Agadir and the Sous Plain** (summer), Asilah and Oued Loukkos** (passage), Dayet Aaoua** (summer), Oualidia* (passage), Zaër** (summer).

PORTUGAL Baixo Alentejo*** (summer), Cape St Vincent** (summer, autumn), International Douro* (summer), International Tagus*** (summer), Tagus Estuary* (passage).

ROMANIA Danube Delta** (passage), Dobrudja*** (passage).

RUSSIA Teberdinskiy Reserve*** (passage), Volga Delta* (summer, passage).

SARDINIA Capo Marargiu*** (summer), Oristano wetlands** (summer).

SICILY Strait of Messina*** (spring), Vendicari** (passage).

SLOVENIA Ljubljansko Moor** (summer).

SPAIN Aiguamolls de L'Empordá** (reintroduced, summer), Cabo de Gata** (summer), Cáceres-Trujillo Steppes*** (summer), Cádiz Lagoons** (summer), Coto Doñana*** (summer), La Serena*** (summer), Monfragüe*** (summer), Serrania de Ronda*** (summer), Sierra de Guadarrama*** (summer), Tablas de Daimiel** (summer), Zaragoza Steppes*** (summer).

SYRIA Tadmur and Sabkhat Muh*** (summer).

TUNISIA Cap Bon Peninsula*** (passage), Zaghouan** (summer).

TURKEY Bafa Gölü*** (summer, passage), Birecik-Halfeti* (summer), Borçka** (passage), Dalyan*** (summer), Göksu Delta** (passage), İstanbul*** (passage), Kulu Gölü*** (summer, passage), Manyas Gölü* (summer), Soğuksu NP* (summer, passage), Uluabat Gölü** (summer), Van Gölü*** (summer).

UKRAINE Dunay Delta* (passage), Tiligul Liman*** (summer).

Red-footed Falcon
Falco vespertinus   FG (DF) (FW)   Mig (Irr)

Range: Breeds from Belarus and Ukraine E across Russia with small numbers in the Czech Republic, Slovakia and Hungary, Moldova and the northern Balkans. Sometimes breeds outside main range in Sweden, Poland and elsewhere. Winters almost entirely in southern Africa and passage birds occur throughout Europe (mainly in the E but sometimes W to Spain), Turkey, the Middle East and Egypt. A broad-front migrant, departs breeding areas mid Sep to early Oct, and return begins in Mar, with larger numbers then seen further W and regular in NW Africa. Irruptive, often occurring outside main breeding and passage areas, and frequently wanders W to Great Britain in spring.

Tips: Look for this species in steppe country with woodlands, on farmland, along forest edges and clearings; breeds colonially, often in rookeries. May hunt over wetlands on passage, sometimes hovers or perches on roadside wires like a shrike.

Sites:
ARMENIA Arapan Area*** (passage), Armash Fishponds*** (passage), Lake Sevan*** (passage).
AUSTRIA Lake Neusiedl*** (passage).
BALEARIC IS Mallorca* (passage), Menorca* (passage).
BELARUS Belovezhskaya Pushcha NP*** (summer).
BELGIUM Kalmthoutse Heide* (passage).
BULGARIA Albena-Golden Sands*** (passage), Burgas area*** (passage), Cape Emine*** (passage), Cape Kaliakra*** (summer, passage), Lake Durankulak*** (summer, passage), Lake Shabla*** (summer, passage), Lake Srebarna*** (passage), Rila Mts** (passage), Ropotamo NP*** (passage), Strandja Mts*** (passage), Studen Kladenetz*** (passage).
CORSICA Biguglia Lake*** (spring).
CYPRUS** (passage).
DENMARK Hellebæk* (passage), Møn-Falster** (passage), Skagen* (passage), Stevns Klint* (passage).
EGYPT Hurghada** (passage), Sharm el Sheikh** (passage), Suez area*** (passage), Zaranik** (passage).

FRANCE Camargue** (passage), Leucate** (passage).
GEORGIA Iori Steppes** (summer, passage), Kolkheti* (passage).
GREECE Amvrakiko's Gulf*** (passage, mainly spring), Axios-Aliakmonas Deltas*** (passage, mainly spring), Dadiá-Soufli Forest*** (passage, mainly spring), Evros Delta*** (passage, mainly spring), Lake Kerkini*** (passage, mainly spring), Mikrí Prespa NP*** (passage, mainly spring), Nestos Delta*** (passage, mainly spring), Porto Lagos Area*** (passage, mainly spring).
GREEK IS Corfu*** (passage, mainly spring), Crete*** (passage, mainly spring), Kos*** (passage, mainly spring), Lesvos*** (passage), Náxos*** (passage, mainly spring), Rhodes***.
HUNGARY Biharugra*** (summer), Hortobágy NP*** (summer, passage), Kiskunság NP*** (summer, passage), Szeged Fishponds*** (summer), Tihany* (summer).
ISRAEL Bet Shean Valley*** (passage), Jezreel Valley*** (passage), Nizzana*** (passage), Urim*** (passage).
ITALY Circeo NP*** (passage), Gargano Peninsula*** (passage), Monte Conero***

(passage), Tuscan archipelago*** (passage, mainly spring).
JORDAN Aqaba* (passage), Azraq** (passage), Petra* (passage), Wadi Rum** (passage).
LATVIA Lake Pape*** (passage).
LEBANON Aammiq Marshes** (passage), Barouk Cedars* (passage), Palm Is** (passage), Qaraoun Lake* (passage).
MACEDONIA Babuna Gorge** (passage), Crna Gorge** (passage), Galicica NP*** (passage), Lakes Ohrid and Prespa*** (passage).
MALTA* (passage).
POLAND Gdańsk Bay*** (passage), Siemianówka Reservoir*** (passage).
ROMANIA Danube Delta*** (summer), Dobrudja*** (summer, passage), Lake Călăraşi*** (summer).
RUSSIA Kalmykia*** (summer), Teberdinskiy Reserve*** (passage), Volga Delta*** (summer).
SICILY Lago di Lentini** (passage), San Vito Peninsula*** (spring), Strait of Messina*** (spring).

SLOVAKIA Malé Karpaty*** (passage), Senné Fishponds*** (summer), Záhorie*** (summer, passage), Zlatná na Ostrove** (summer).
SPAIN Aiguamolls de L'Empordá (spring).
SWEDEN Falsterbo* (spring), Holmöarna (spring), Kristianstad* (spring), Öland* (spring), Store Mosse NP* (spring).
SWITZERLAND Leuk (passage).
SYRIA Aqra Mts** (passage), Dayr al-Zawr** (passage).
TUNISIA Cap Bon Peninsula*** (spring), Kelbia Lake* (spring).
TURKEY Bafa Gölü** (passage), Birecik-Halfeti (passage), Borćka* (passage), Dalyan** (passage), İstanbul*** (passage), Kızılırmak Delta*** (passage), Kocaćay Delta** (passage), Kulu Gölü*** (passage), Manyas Gölü*** (passage), Soğuksu NP (passage), Uluabat Gölü*** (passage).
UKRAINE Askania-Nova*** (summer), Carpathians* (summer).
YUGOSLAVIA Dunay Delta*** (passage), Shatsk NP (passage), Tiligul Liman*** (passage).

Eleonora's Falcon
Falco eleonorae   I C (FW) (Sea)   Mig

Range: Confined to the Western Palearctic as a breeder, with the bulk of the world population (fewer than 5,000 pairs) found in the Mediterranean. Small numbers breed in the Atlantic, on islets off Lanzarote in the Canaries, and off NW Morocco. In the W Mediterranean, breeds on the Balearics, Sardinia and Sicily, Algeria and Tunisia. Rare in the Adriatic but more than half of the world population breeds on the Greek islands, with most on the Cyclades and around Crete. Small numbers breed on Cyprus, and probably on islands off Turkey. Present mid Apr-Oct, with unconfirmed reports of wintering in the Aegean which may involve late migrants. Passage birds are regularly seen on the coasts of many Mediterranean countries, and sometimes reach well inland, even to the Black Sea coast.
Tips: A late-summer breeder that feeds its young on migrant passerines and nests colonially on rocky cliffs of undisturbed islands and islets. Usually seen hunting over the sea but also over fresh waters and usually gregarious.

Sites:

BALEARIC IS Formentera*** (summer, autumn), Ibiza*** (summer, autumn), Mallorca*** (summer, autumn), Menorca*** (summer, autumn).
BULGARIA Cape Kaliakra* (summer). **CANARY IS** Lanzarote*** (summer, autumn). **CORSICA** Bonifacio** (passage).
CROATIA Mljet*** (summer).
CYPRUS* (summer, autumn).
EGYPT Hurghada* (passage), Suez area** (passage), Zaranik* (passage).
FRANCE Gruissan* (passage).
GIBRALTAR* (passage).
GREECE Dadiá-Soufli Forest*** (passage), Lake Kerkini*** (passage), Mt Olympus NP** (summer, autumn), Nestos Delta*** (summer, autumn).
GREEK IS Corfu*** (summer, autumn), Crete*** (summer, autumn), Kos*** (summer, autumn), Lesvos*** (summer, autumn), Náxos*** (summer, autumn), Rhodes*** (summer, autumn).
ISRAEL Jezreel Valley** (passage).

ITALY Gargano Peninsula*** (passage), Monte Conero** (passage), Tuscan archipelago*** (passage).
JORDAN Aqaba (passage).
MALTA* (passage).
MOROCCO Essaouira*** (summer).
PORTUGAL Berlenga Is (autumn), Cape St Vincent* (autumn).
SARDINIA San Pietro I*** (summer, passage).
SICILY Pelagie Is*** (summer, autumn), San Vito Peninsula*** (passage), Strait of Messina** (spring, summer).
SPAIN Aiguamolls de l'Empordá* (summer, passage), Cabo de Gata* (passage), Ebro Delta* (passage).
SYRIA Aqra Mts* (summer).
TUNISIA Cap Bon Peninsula*** (passage), Lake Ichkeul** (autumn).
TURKEY Bafa Gölü* (spring), Birecik-Halfeti (passage), Dalyan*** (summer, passage), Göksu Delta*** (summer, autumn), Kocaćay Delta** (passage).

Sooty Falcon
Falco concolor   D I C Mig

Range: Western Palearctic breeding range little known, but currently thought to breed at scattered oases in Libya and W Egypt, on the Red Sea coast of Egypt, S Sinai, S Jordan and S Israel. A late-summer breeder, feeding its young on migrating passerines, before departing S in Oct–Nov, and returning in Apr. Winters in E Africa and Madagascar.
Tips: Breeds in stony deserts with rocky outcrops and on arid rocky islands. Most active at dawn and dusk in hottest parts of range.

Sites:

EGYPT Abu Simbel*** (summer), Aswan** (summer), Hurghada*** (summer, autumn), Luxor** (summer), Suez area*** (summer, passage), Sharm el Sheikh*** (summer, autumn).
ISRAEL Arava Valley*** (summer), Eilat*** (summer, passage), Ein Gedi*** (summer).

JORDAN Aqaba* (summer, passage), Petra** (summer), Wadi Dana-Fidan** (summer), Wadi Rum*** (summer, autumn).

Lanner Falcon
Falco biarmicus   FG D SD C M   Res (Dis)

Range: In Europe, breeds in S Italy and Sicily, the southern Balkans, N Greece, Crete, Lesvos and possibly Rhodes, and further E at a few scattered Turkish localities mainly in the NE, in the Caucasus. In the Middle East probably breeds in C and S Syria, S Israel and S Jordan, perhaps also Sinai. More numerous and widespread in N Africa, breeding in Morocco, N and C Algeria, Tunisia, N and C Libya and in Egypt mainly in the Nile Valley and on the Red Sea coast. Ads are largely sedentary but imms may wander widely, particularly those from N of range.

Subspecies: Race *feldeggii* occurs from Italy to Turkey, *erlangeri* in NW Africa and *tanypterus* in NE Africa and the Middle East.

Tips: A bird of dry steppe and savanna, rocky desert and semi-desert, also cliffs, rocky sea coasts, ruins and rugged mountains. Now very rare in Europe with the bulk of the population in Italy, particularly on Sicily.

Sites:

EGYPT Abu Simbel**, Aswan**, Hurghada***, Luxor**, Suez area* (passage), Zaranik* (passage).

FRANCE Camargue* (winter).

GEORGIA Iori Steppes*.

GREECE Avas Gorge** (passage), Axios-Aliakmonas Deltas* (passage), Dadiá-Soufli Forest***, Mt Olympus NP**, Mt Parnassós NP***, Valia Kalda NP***, Vikos-Aoos NP***.

GREEK IS Corfu** (passage), Crete*, Kos*, Lesvos*, Rhodes*.

ISRAEL Arava Valley** (passage), Bet Shean Valley* (winter), Eilat***, Ein Gedi***, Nizzana***, Urim***.

ITALY Circeo NP* (passage), Gargano Peninsula**, Maremma Regional Park* (passage), Sibillini NP**.

JORDAN Aqaba*, Azraq** (passage), Ghadir Burqu'** (passage, winter), Petra*, Wadi Dana-Fidan* (passage).

LEBANON Qaraoun Lake* (passage).

MACEDONIA Babuna Gorge*, Crna Gorge*, Demir Kapija Gorge*, Mavrovo NP*.

MOROCCO Agadir and the Sous Plain***, Boumalne***, Goulimine to Tan-Tan***, Oualidia* (passage), Ouarzazate* (passage), Tafilalt***, Zaër**.

SARDINIA San Vito Peninsula*.

SICILY Lago di Lentini* (passage, winter), Strait of Messina* (passage).

SYRIA Bahrat Homs* (passage), Sabkhat al-Jubbal* (passage), Tadmur and Sabkhat Muh**, Wadi al-Qarn-Burqush** (passage).

TUNISIA Cap Bon Peninsula**, Chott el Djerid***, Kelbia Lake** (passage) Lake Ichkeul**, Tataouine***, Zaghouan***.

TURKEY Birecik-Halfeti, Göksu Delta, İstanbul (passage), Soğuksu NP.

Saker Falcon
Falco cherrug   CF MF DF FG (C)   Res Mig

Range: A rare breeder in E Europe from the Czech Republic and Slovakia across S Russia. Also breeds in Moldova, Romania and Bulgaria and in scattered parts of C and E Turkey. Generally in decline but breeding or recolonisation has recently occurred in Poland, Germany and Austria. Northern birds are migratory, departing the breeding areas in late Sep–early Oct and returning in Mar–early Apr. More widespread in winter when young birds in particular, occur more widely around the Mediterranean, Turkey, the Caucasus and the Middle East. In spring and autumn small numbers formerly occurred at the Bosphorus and it remains regular at Cap Bon in spring.

Subspecies: Breeding birds belong to the nominate race but the C Asian *milvipes* has wandered to the east of the region .

Tips: Often seen hunting over farmland close to forested areas, also over marshes and coasts in winter and frequently perches on pylons. Hortobágy, in Hungary, is the most reliable site in Europe for this species.

Sites:

ARMENIA Arapan Area* (passage).
AUSTRIA Lake Neusiedl*, Marchauen-Marchegg Reserve*.
BULGARIA Albena-Golden Sands* (passage), Burgas area* (passage), Cape Kaliakra* (summer, passage), Lake Srebarna* (passage), Rusenski Lom NP*** (summer), Strandja Mts*.
CROATIA Kopački Rit*.
CZECH REPUBLIC Lednice*, Soutok**, Znojmo* (winter).
GEORGIA Iori Steppes*.
GREECE Axios-Aliakmonas Deltas* (passage), Dadiá-Soufli Forest** (passage, winter), Evros Delta* (winter).
HUNGARY Börzsöny NP*, Bükk Hills NP**, Csákvár**, Hortobágy NP**, Kiskunság NP**, Ócsa*, Pilis Hills*, Zemplén Hills**.
ISRAEL Ein Gedi* (passage), Hula Reserve* (passage), Nizzana** (winter), Urim** (winter).
JORDAN Azraq* (passage), Ghadir Burqu'** (passage, winter), Wadi Rum (passage, winter).

LEBANON Barouk Cedars (passage), Qaraoun Lake (passage).
MACEDONIA Bregalnica Valley, Demir Kapija Gorge
POLAND Bieszczady NP.
ROMANIA Danube Delta, Dobrudja*.
RUSSIA Kalmykia***, Teberdinskiy Reserve* (passage), Volga Delta**.
SICILY Strait of Messina (passage).
SLOVAKIA Malé Karpaty**, Senné Fishponds** (reintroduced), Slanské Hills***, Slovenský Kras**, Záhorie*.
SYRIA Tadmur and Sabkhat Muh** (passage).
TUNISIA Cap Bon Peninsula (passage).
TURKEY Akseki, Borćka* (passage), Bulanik, Demirkazik*, Göksu Delta, İstanbul (passage), Van Gölü*.
UKRAINE Crimean Mts**, Shatsk NP (passage).
YUGOSLAVIA Fruška Gora NP, Obedska bara.

Gyr Falcon
Falco rusticolus

T C (FW) (FG) Mig Res Dis

Range: Breeds in Iceland, N Scandinavia and Arctic Russia, albeit scarce throughout range. Some, particularly juvs, disperse and in winter the species ranges S to S Norway, C Finland and Russia, mainly in late Oct–Mar. Annually recorded in Great Britain in very small numbers, usually involving white-morph birds from Greenland, which are extremely rare elsewhere in Europe.

Tips: Breeds on cliffs in mountains or tundra river valleys, also on coasts. Migrants and vagrants may hunt over open steppes, coasts, marshes or cultivated land. Spends much time perched on a prominent rock.

Sites:
FINLAND Kevo NR*, Kilpisjärvi Saana***, Lemmenjoki NP**, Pallas-Ounastunturi NP**.
ICELAND Breiðafjörður*** (summer), Jökulsárgljúfur NP*** (summer), Lake Mývatn*** (summer), Northwest Peninsula*** (summer), Thingvellir NP*** (summer), Westmann Is** (winter).
NORWAY Dovrefjell NP*, Hardangervidda NP**, Lista (passage), Lofoten Is** (winter),
Mølen (passage), Øvre Pasvik NP*** (summer), Rondane NP*, Slettnes* (passage), Stabbursdalen NP** (summer), Utsira* (passage), Varanger** (summer).
RUSSIA Kola Peninsula***.
SWEDEN Abisko NP***, Ammarnäs*, Holmöarna* (passage), Öland* (winter), Padjelanta NP***, Sarek NP***, Tarnasjön***.

Barbary Falcon
Falco pelegrinoides

C D SD Res Dis

Range: Patchy and little–known range in the Western Palearctic, breeding in scattered pockets in N Africa in Morocco, N Algeria, Tunisia, and in the Nile Valley and Red Sea coast of Egypt, probably also in Libya. Also breeds in Sinai, Jordan and Israel. Occurs on Tenerife and Lanzarote in the Canaries, but now rare and current status on other islands is unclear.

Tips: Nests on cliffs or ruined buildings in desert and semi-desert, often in mountains. Sometimes occurs on coasts inviting confusion with Peregrine which tends to be more strictly coastal in N Africa.

Sites:
CANARY IS Fuerteventura***, Gomera, Gran Canaria, Lanzarote**, Tenerife**.
EGYPT Abu Simbel***, Aswan**, Hurghada***,
Luxor**, Suez area* (passage), Sharm el Sheikh***.
ISRAEL Arava Valley***, Eilat***, Ein Gedi***.

JORDAN Aqaba**, Azraq*, Petra***, Wadi Dana-Fidan***, Wadi Rum**.
MOROCCO Agadir and the Sous Plain***, Boumalne**, Goulimine to Tan-Tan***, Oued Massa***, Ouarzazate*, Oukaimeden***.

TUNISIA Chott el Djerid*, Lake Ichkeul** (passage, winter).

Hazel Grouse (Hazelhen)
Bonasa bonasia   CF MF DF (M) Res

Range: Scandinavia and from the Baltic states and E Poland across much of Russia to the Urals. Scattered populations in persist in E France, S Belgium and W Germany, also in the Alps and mountains of SE Europe S to N Greece. Long considered extinct in the French Pyrenees but breeding confirmed in the 1990s and recently rediscovered in the Massif Central.

Subspecies: Several races have been described from the Western Palearctic, the nominate *bonasia* being the most widespread, from Norway to the Urals where it meets *sibirica*. The race *rupestris* occurs from eastern France to Poland and south to Bulgaria and birds from northern Sweden are sometimes separated as *griseonota*.

Tips: Look for this bird in mature undisturbed forest, often conifers with a dense birch and alder understorey, and frequently near streams. A notoriously difficult bird to see well, usually staying in dark, dense undergrowth and seen only briefly when flushed. Best located by whistling call and wing-beating display in Mar–Apr and Sep. Early spring mornings are often best.

Sites:
AUSTRIA Hohe Wand*, Karwendel Reserve**.
BELARUS Belovezhskaya Pushcha NP***, Berezinsky Reserve***, Prypyatsky NP***.
BELGIUM Croix-Scaille NR*, Lesse et Lomme NR*.
BOSNIA-HERZEGOVINA Sujetska NP***.
BULGARIA Rila Mts***, Tzarichina NR***.
CROATIA Plitvice**.
CZECH REPUBLIC Beskydy Mts***, Jeseníky Mts***, Šumava NP***, Třeboňsko*.
ESTONIA Lake Endla***, Nigula NR***, Taevaskoja***.
FINLAND Åland Is***, Kolvanan Uuro***, Kuusamo***, Oulanka NP***, Pallas-Ounastunturi NP***, Patvinsuo NP***, Pyhähäkki NP***, Urho Kekkonen NP***, Vesijako NP***.

FRANCE Cévennes NP*, Écrins NP***, Vanoise NP***.
GERMANY Ammer Valley***, Bayerischer Wald NP**, Berchtesgaden NP**.
GREECE Mikrí Prespa NP**.
HUNGARY Aggtelek NP**, Börzsöny NP*, Bükk Hills NP*, Zemplén Hills*.
ITALY Gran Paradiso NP**, Stelvio NP***.
LATVIA Cape Kolka***, Lake Engure***.
MACEDONIA Crna Gorge, Galicica NP, Mavrovo NP*, Sara Mts**.
NORWAY Stabbursdalen NP***.
POLAND Białowieża Forest***, Bieszczady NP***, Tatra NP**.
ROMANIA Bicaz***, Gurghiu Mts***, Retezat NP***.
RUSSIA Kola Peninsula***, Oka Valley***.

SLOVAKIA High Tatras NP**, Malá Fatra***, Nízke Tatry NP***, Orava Reservoir***, Slanské Hills**, Slovenský Kras***, Vihorlatske Hills**. **SLOVENIA** Triglav NP**.

SWEDEN Ammarnäs***, Färnebofjärden***, Lake Ånnsjön***, Ripakaisenvuoma***, Store Mosse NP***, Tyresta NP***. **SWITZERLAND** Flims***, Swiss NP***. **UKRAINE** Carpathians***.

Willow Grouse (Willow Ptarmigan)
Lagopus lagopus   T M CF Res (Irr)

Range: Resident in Scandinavia, Estonia and N Belarus and across N Russia including Ostrov Kolguev. Rare in Latvia and may still breed in N Lithuania.

Subspecies: Several races occur in the region with the nominate *lagopus* in Fenno-Scandia and Russia north of 60° and *rossicus* further south in Russia. **Red Grouse** *scoticus*, usually considered a race of Willow Grouse, is treated separately. Birds from islands in the Trondheim area of Norway, race *variegatus*, are intermediate between *scoticus* and *lagopus*.

Tips: Tundra and moorland where heather is abundant. Also bogs in boreal forest, birch woodland and willow scrub, particularly in winter.

Sites:
BELARUS Berezinsky Reserve***.
FINLAND Kilpisjärvi Saana***, Kuusamo***. Lake Inari***, Lemmenjoki NP***, Oulanka NP***, Pallas-Ounastunturi NP***, Patvinsuo NP***, Pyhätunturi NP***, Urho Kekkonen NP***.

NORWAY Dovrefjell NP***, Fokstumyra***, Hardangervidda NP***, Lofoten Is***, Rondane NP***, Slettnes*, Stabbursdalen NP***, Varanger***.
RUSSIA Kola Peninsula***.
SWEDEN Abisko NP***, Ammarnäs***, Lake Ånnsjön***, Ripakaisenvuoma***.

Red Grouse
Lagopus (lagopus) scoticus   SH M Res

Range: Usually considered a race of the Willow Grouse, but may be treated as a full species again in the future. Found over much of mainland Scotland and many of the islands. In the Outer Hebrides occurs on Lewis, Harris and North Uist, but scarce or absent from Benbecula southwards, and in the Inner Hebrides breeds on all of the main islands except Coll and Tiree. In Shetland small numbers occur on Mainland (introduced), and in the Orkneys it is found on all but the northernmost islands. Also occurs on moors of N England

and N and C Wales, and there are very small and declining (introduced) populations on Dartmoor and Exmoor in SW England. Widespread in Ireland, occurring over much of the country except the E.

Subspecies: *L.l.scoticus*, is found in Scotland, most of the Scottish islands, England and Wales, with birds in the Outer Hebrides and Ireland sometimes separated as race *hibernicus*.

Tip:s Characteristic bird of moorland with heather up to about 900m, most numerous on drier moors of E Scotland and NE England. Usually only seen when flushed when explodes from the heather on whirring wings.

Sites:
GREAT BRITAIN Cairngorms and Speyside***, Islay***, Orkney Is**, Outer Hebrides***, Rhum***, Shetland Is**, Tregaron Bog***.

Ptarmigan (Rock Ptarmigan)
Lagopus mutus   M T Res (Irr)

Range: Resident in Iceland and N and W Scotland, in the mountains and far N of Scandinavia, the Kola Peninsula, Svalbard and Franz Josef Land, and the N Urals. Isolated populations in the French and Spanish Pyrenees and throughout most of the Alps. Introduced population in the Faroe Is is now considered extinct.

Subspecies: Various races occur in the region but differences between them are slight; *hyperboreus* is found on the Arctic islands, nominate *mutus* breeds from Norway to the Kola Peninsula, *nelsoni* in the northern Urals, *islandorum* in Iceland and *millaisi* in Scotland. Isolated in the south are *pyrenaicus* in the Pyrenees and *helveticus* in the Alps. The introduced birds on the Faroes belonged to the race *saturatus*.

Tips: Rocky, often rather barren slopes in mountains in S of range, found at 200–1,200m in Scotland and 2,000–2,500m or more in the Alps. In far N of range occurs at much lower levels on rocky moss and lichen tundra, often near pools.

Sites:
ANDORRA.

AUSTRIA Hohe Tauern NP**, Hohe Wand*, Karwendel Reserve***, Schneeberg Mts***.

FINLAND Kevo NR***, Kilpisjärvi Saana***, Lemmenjoki NP***, Pallas-Ounastunturi NP***, Urho Kekkonen NP***.

FRANCE Écrins NP***, Mercantour NP***, Prats-de-Mollo***, Pyrenees NP***, Queyras NP***, Vanoise NP***.

GERMANY Ammer Valley**, Berchtesgaden NP**.

GREAT BRITAIN Cairngorms and Speyside***.

ICELAND Breiðafjörður***, Jökulsárgljúfur NP*** (summer), Lake Mývatn***, Northwest Peninsula***, Skaftafell NP***, Thingvellir NP***.

ITALY Gran Paradiso NP***, Stelvio NP***.

NORWAY Dovrefjell NP***, Fokstumyra***, Hardangervidda NP***, Rondane NP***, Slettnes***, Varanger***.

RUSSIA Kola Peninsula***.

SLOVENIA Triglav NP***.

SPAIN Aigües Tortes NP***, Jaca**, Ordesa NP***.
SVALBARD*.

SWEDEN Abisko NP***, Ammarnäs***, Lake Ånnsjön***, Sarek NP***.
SWITZERLAND Aletschwald***, Flims***, Swiss NP***.

Black Grouse
Tetrao tetrix

CF SH M   Res

Range: Main range lies from Scandinavia and E and S Poland to the Urals, and in the Alps. Small and scattered populations persist, some verging on extinction, in N and W Great Britain (mainly Scotland, now rare in N England and Wales), E France, Belgium, and the Netherlands, Germany, the Czech Republic, Slovakia and N Romania. Resident over most of range but local movements may occur.

Subspecies: Nominate race *tetrix* is found over most of Europe with *britannicus* in Great Britain, and *viridanus* in SE Russia.

Tips: Occurs at forest edges and in clearings, usually conifer or birch, swampy heathland, and moorland with scattered trees. Gathers at traditional communal lekking sites, and best seen early morning or evening. However, now rare in much of range and great care should be taken to avoid undue disturbance at leks; best searched for in autumn and winter when often in single sex flocks.

Sites:

AUSTRIA Hohe Tauern NP**, Hohe Wand*, Karwendel Reserve**, Schneeberg Mts**.
BELARUS Belovezhskaya Pushcha NP***, Berezinsky Reserve***,Prypyatsky NP***.
BELGIUM Hautes Fagnes Natural Park***.
CZECH REPUBLIC Jeseníky Mts***, Krkonoše NP***, Poodří**, Šumava NP***, Třeboňsko*.
ESTONIA Emajõgi Floodplain***, Lake Endla***, Nigula NR***, Taevaskoja***.
FINLAND Åland Is***, Kuusamo***, Lemmenjoki NP***, Oulanka NP***, Patvinsuo NP***, Pyhä-Häkki NP***, Urho Kekkonen NP***, Vesijako NP***.
FRANCE Cévennes NP*, Écrins NP***, Mercantour NP***, Queyras NP***, Vanoise NP**.
GERMANY Ammer Valley***, Bayerischer Wald NP*, Berchtesgaden NP**, Federsee*, Tiroler Achen**, Vessertal**.

GREAT BRITAIN Cairngorms and Speyside**, Islay**.
ITALY Gran Paradiso NP***, Stelvio NP***.
LATVIA Cape Kolka***, Lake Engure***, Lake Pape***.
LITHUANIA Cepkeliai NR***, Lake Kretuonas*.
NETHERLANDS Veluwe**.
NORWAY Rondane NP***.
POLAND Białowieża Forest*, Biebrza Marshes***.
ROMANIA Retezat NP**.
RUSSIA Kola Peninsula***, Oka Valley***.
SLOVAKIA High Tatras NP**, Malá Fatra***, Nízke Tatry NP***, Orava Reservoir**.
SLOVENIA Triglav NP***.
SWEDEN Ammarnäs***, Färnebofjärden***, Gotland***, Holmöarna***, Hornborgasjön***, Lake Ånnsjön***, Stockholm archipelago***, Store Mosse NP***, Tyresta NP***.

SWITZERLAND Aletschwald***, Col de Bretolet***, Flims***, Swiss NP***.

UKRAINE Carpathians**.

Caucasian Black Grouse
Tetrao mlokosiewiczi   M CF   Res (AMig)

Range: Confined to the Greater and Lesser Caucasus Mts and the Pontics of NE Turkey. In the Caucasus, breeds in S Russia, Georgia, Armenia and Azerbaijan, and range also extends into N Iran.

Tips: A highly sought after species with a very restricted Western Palearctic range. Found in high meadows, rhododendron thickets and willow and birch scrub, usually at 2,000–3,000m, sometimes as low as 1,500m, and in severe winters below 1,000m. Often seen at forest edge and displays on south-facing grassy slopes with azalea scrub in late Apr to mid May, sometimes until Jun. The most accessible area for this species is Sivrikaya in Turkey.

Sites:

ARMENIA Pambak Mts**.
AZERBAIJAN Zakataly**.
GEORGIA Mt Kazbek***.

RUSSIA Teberdinskiy Reserve***.
TURKEY Sivrikaya***.

Capercaillie (Western Capercaillie)
Tetrao urogallus   CF MF M   Res

Range: Resident from Scandinavia, the Baltic states and Belarus across Russia to the Urals, with scattered populations elsewhere in Europe, mainly in montane areas. Breeds in Scotland (reintroduced), in the Cantabrian Mts, Pyrenees and Alps, the Dinaric Alps and Carpathians, with smaller pockets in various other upland areas.

Subspecies: Nominate race is present over much of range, including reintroduced Scottish population, *aquitanicus*, in the Pyrenees and Cantabrians, *rudolfi* in the Carpathians and *taczanowskii* in S of the Russian range.

Tips: Found in forests with clearings, at 1,000–1,500m in the Alps, up to 2,000m in the Pyrenees and to 450m in Scotland. Cantabrian birds are found mainly in holly woodlands. Now rare or locally extinct in many areas, particularly in S of range, and care should be taken to avoid excessive disturbance early in the breeding season. Most easily found in early spring but best looked for in Aug–Sep.

Sites:
ANDORRA**.

AUSTRIA Hohe Wand*, Karwendel Reserve**, Schneeberg Mts**.

BELARUS Belovezhskaya Pushcha NP***, Berezinsky Reserve***, Prypyatsky NP***.

BOSNIA-HERZEGOVINA Sujetska NP*. **BULGARIA** Rila Mts***, Tzarichina NR*. **CROATIA** Plitvice*.

CZECH REPUBLIC Beskydy Mts**, Jeseníky Mts**, Krkonoše NP**, Šumava NP***, Třeboňsko*.

ESTONIA Lake Endla***, Nigula NR***, Taevaskoja***.

FINLAND Åland Is*, Kolvanan Uuro**, Kuusamo***, Lake Inari**, Lemmenjoki NP***, Oulanka NP***, Pallas-Ounastunturi NP***, Patvinsuo NP***, Pyhähäkki NP***, Urho Kekkonen NP***, Vesijako NP***.

FRANCE Cévennes NP*, Écrins NP**, Mercantour NP**, Prats-de-Mollo**, Pyrenees NP**, Vanoise NP**.

GERMANY Ammer Valley**, Bayerischer Wald NP*, Berchtesgaden NP**, Vessertal*.

GREAT BRITAIN Cairngorms and Speyside**.

ITALY Gran Paradiso NP*, Stelvio NP**.

LATVIA Cape Kolka***.

MACEDONIA Sara Mts.

NORWAY Øvre Pasvik NP***, Rondane NP***, Stabbursdalen NP***.

POLAND Białowieża Forest, Tatra NP**.

ROMANIA Bicaz***, Gurghiu Mts***, Retezat NP***.

RUSSIA Kola Peninsula***, Oka Valley***.

SLOVAKIA High Tatras NP***, Malá Fatra***, Nízke Tatry NP***.

SLOVENIA Triglav NP***.

SPAIN Aigües Tortes NP**, Jaca*, Ordesa NP***, Picos de Europa**.

SWEDEN Ammarnäs***, Färnebofjärden***, Hornborgasjön***, Lake Ånnsjön***, Muddus NP***, Store Mosse NP***, Tyresta NP***.

SWITZERLAND Swiss NP***.

UKRAINE Carpathians**.

Caucasian Snowcock
Tetraogallus caucasicus   M   Res (AMig)

Range: Confined to the Caucasus Mts, from Mt Oshten to Mt Babadag, and occurs in Russia, Georgia and Azerbaijan. An altitudinal migrant that sometimes reaches the Dagestan steppes in winter.

Tips: A Western Palearctic endemic and one of the region's most sought after birds, best located by listening for its curlew-like whistle. Very difficult to approach closely as found on rocky slopes and screes, cliffs and grassy slopes with rocky outcrops, at 1,700–4,300 m, usually above 2,500 m, but lower in winter. Often attracted to melting snow patches. When disturbed tends to fly downhill then returns upslope.

Sites:
AZERBAIJAN Zakataly**.

GEORGIA Mt Kazbek***.

RUSSIA Teberdinskiy Reserve***.

Caspian Snowcock
Tetraogallus caspius M Res (AMig)

Range: An uncommon to rare species, with isolated populations in S and E Turkey, in the Armenia/Azerbaijan border area, and in extreme N Iraq on the border with Iran. Most numerous in Turkey where it occurs in the Taurus Mts in the S, the Pontics in the N, and various montane areas further E.

Subspecies: Race *tauricus* is found in Turkey and intergrades with nominate *caspius* in Armenia and Azerbaijan.

Tips: Shy and difficult to approach, but, given its range, far easier to see than the Caucasian Snowcock. Found on steep rocky slopes and in ravines at 1,800–3,000m, sometimes up to 4,000m, with limited altitudinal movements. Often occurs in more vegetated areas than Caucasian Snowcock, including rhododendron scrub and open grassy areas, and often attracted to patches of late-lying snow. Like Caucasian species has a habit of flying on stiff wings downhill and then running back upslope.

Sites:
ARMENIA Khosrov Preserve*, Mt Aragats**, Pambak Mts**.
GEORGIA Javakheti Plateau***.
TURKEY Demirkazik***, Sivrikaya***.

Chukar Partridge
Alectoris chukar FG D M Res (AMig)

Range: Breeds in S Bulgaria and N Greece, on Crete and many Aegean islands including Crete and Rhodes, in Turkey, the Caucasus and introduced into the Crimea. Also occurs on Cyprus and in the Middle East in Syria, Lebanon, Israel, Jordan and Sinai. Widely introduced in Europe and hybrids with Red-legged Partridge *A. rufa* may persist in some areas.

Subspecies: Five races occur in the Western Palearctic; *kleini* in Bulgaria, N Greece and the N Aegean islands across N Turkey to the Caucasus, *cypriotes* in the S Aegean islands, S Turkey and Cyprus, *kurdestanica* in SE Turkey, Transcaucasia and N Iraq; *werae* in E Iraq and *sinaica* from Syria to Sinai.

Tips: A bird of dry grassland, desert and sparsely vegetated rocky slopes from sea level to 4,500 m.

Sites:

ARMENIA Khosrov Preserve***.
AZERBAIJAN Turianchai Reserve***, Zakataly***.
BULGARIA Strandja Mts***, Studen Kladenetz***.
CYPRUS***.
EGYPT Santa Katharina Monastery***.
GEORGIA Iori Steppes***, Javakheti Plateau**, Mt Kazbek**.
GREECE Dadiá-Soufli Forest***, Evros Delta*.
GREEK IS Crete***, Kos***, Lesvos***, Náxos***, Rhodes***.
ISRAEL Arava Valley***, Bet Shean Valley***, Ein Gedi***, Ma'agan Mikhael***, Mt

Hermon***, Nizzana***, Urim***, Wadi Ammud-Mt Arbel***.
JORDAN Amman NP***, Azraq*, Ghadir Burqu'***, Petra***, Wadi Dana-Fidan***, Wadi Rum**, Wadi as Sir***.
LEBANON Aammiq Marshes**, Barouk Cedars***.
RUSSIA Teberdinskiy Reserve***.
SYRIA Bahrat Homs***, Jabal Slenfeh***, Sabkhat al-Jubbal***.
TURKEY Birecik-Halfeti**, Dalyan**, Demirkazik***, Göksu Delta**, Sivrikaya**, Van Gölü**, Yeşilce***.
UKRAINE Crimean Mts***.

Rock Partridge
Alectoris graeca   M FG   Res (AMig)

Range: Endemic to the Western Palearctic and found in the Alps, Apennines, C Sicily and throughout most upland areas of the Balkans S to S Greece including the Ionian Is. Introduced to Lebanon and may have become established there.

Subspecies: Nominate race occurs in Albania, S Bulgaria and Greece, *whitakeri* on Sicily, and the remainder of the range is covered by *saxatilis*, although Apennine birds are sometimes separated as *orlandoi*.

Tips: Look for this species on dry, south-facing, rock-strewn slopes with scattered bushes and grassy areas, sometimes with open woodland and cultivated land. Found at 500–2,500 m in the Alps and 1,000–2,300 m in Greece, sometimes at lower levels in winter. In areas of overlap generally occurs at higher elevations than Chukar Partridge.

Sites:

ALBANIA Drini Delta**, Lake Shkodra***.
AUSTRIA Hohe Tauern NP***, Karwendel Reserve***.
BOSNIA-HERZEGOVINA Sujetska NP***.
BULGARIA Rila Mts***, Trigradski Gorge***, Tissata NR***, Tzarichina NR***.
CROATIA Cres***, Neretva Delta***, Paklenica NP***.
FRANCE Écrins NP**, Mercantour NP***, Queyras NP**, Vanoise NP***.

GREECE Akarnanika Mts***, Mikrí Prespa NP***, Mt Olympus NP***, Mt Parnassós NP***, Valia Kalda NP***, Vikos-Aoos NP***.
GREEK IS Corfu***.
ITALY Abruzzo NP***, Gran Paradiso NP***, Sibillini NP***, Stelvio NP***, Tuscan archipelago***.
LEBANON Barouk Cedars*.
MACEDONIA Babuna Gorge***, Crna Gorge***, Demir Kapija Gorge***, Galicica

NP***, Lakes Ohrid and Prespa**, Mavrovo NP**, Sara Mts***.
SICILY San Vito Peninsula***, Strait of Messina***.

SLOVENIA Karst RP*, Triglav NP***.
SWITZERLAND Aletschwald***, Leuk* (winter), Monte Generoso***, Swiss NP***.
YUGOSLAVIA Durmitor NP**, Lake Skadar***.

Barbary Partridge
Alectoris barbara   D SD FG Res

Range: Widespread in NW Africa, from Morocco to NE Libya, possibly still in NW Egypt, and also on Gibraltar and adjacent S Spain, Sardinia, and several of the Canaries, probably as a result of introductions.
Subspecies: Nominate *barbara* is found in Sardinia and Gibraltar, Morocco, Algeria and Tunisia, *spatzi* in the W Sahara, Canarian birds resemble those from north-west Morocco and are usually grouped together as *koenigi*.
Most distinct race is geographically isolated *barbata* from NE Libya and NW Egypt.
Tips: Occurs in desert, semi-desert, dry grassland and rocky slopes up to 3,500m, in some areas in woodland clearings. Shy and often keeps in cover, running when threatened but rarely taking flight. On Gibraltar best seen at dawn and dusk, and usually located by call.

Sites:
ALGERIA Djebel Babor***.
CANARY IS Fuerteventura***, Gomera**, La Palma**, Lanzarote***, Tenerife***.
GIBRALTAR*.
SARDINIA Cagliari wetlands**, Giara di Gesturi**, Oristano wetlands**, San Pietro I***.

MOROCCO Agadir and the Sous Plain***, Asilah and Oued Loukkos***, Boumalne***, Essaouira***, Merja Zerga***, Oued Massa***, Oukaimeden***, Tafilalt***, Zaers***, Zeida**.
TUNISIA Cap Bon Peninsula***, Lake Ichkeul***, Zaghouan***.

See-see Partridge
Ammoperdix griseogularis   D SD M FG Res

Range: A local breeder in SE Turkey between Gaziantep and the Tigris, and N to Diyarbakir, as well as in adjacent Syria, and recently discovered at one site in Armenia. Range does not overlap that of Sand Partridge.
Tips: Arid open areas with rocks in foothills and mountains, semi-desert and bare plateaux up to 2,000 m, and usually found close to a water source. Very reluctant to fly and usually escapes by running. Best located by its characteristic call uttered from a prominent rock during early morning.

Sites:
ARMENIA Meghri Area*.
SYRIA Lake Assad***.
TURKEY Birecik-Halfeti***, Cizre**, Yeşilce*.

Sand Partridge
Ammoperdix heyi   D SD   Res

Range: Found in E Egypt, between the Nile and the Red Sea, in Sinai and in the Middle East in N Saudi Arabia, S Israel, W Jordan and S Syria. Rare in far N of range.

Subspecies: Three races occur in our region; nominate *heyi* from Israel, Jordan, Sinai and N Saudi Arabia, *nicolli* in NE Egypt and *cholmleyi* in SE Egypt.

Tips: Desert and semi-desert, on sparsely vegetated, steep, rocky slopes and wadis up to 2,000m. Runs when disturbed and difficult to see amongst rocks.

Sites:
EGYPT Hurghada***, Santa Katharina Monastery***, Sharm el Sheikh***.
ISRAEL Arava Valley***, Eilat***, Ein Gedi***, Nizzana***.

JORDAN Azraq**, Ghadir Burqu'***, Petra***, Wadi Dana-Fidan***, Wadi Rum***.
SYRIA Jabal al-Bishri***.

Black Francolin
Francolinus francolinus   D SD   Res

Range: Occurs in Cyprus and scattered areas of S Turkey, in Azerbaijan, Georgia and a small area of Armenia, and in the Middle East in Syria, Israel, W Jordan and Iraq. Introduced widely around the Mediterranean, but today probably established only in Tuscany although recently reported in the N Algarve in Portugal where may be established.

Tips: Found in dense vegetation, in wadis, grassland, crops and reedbeds, often near water, in Cyprus often in dense juniper scrub. Best located by strident call of male, uttered mainly in early morning and evening, but the species can be very difficult to see well.

Sites:
ARMENIA Meghri Area*.
AZERBAIJAN Kura Valley Salt-lakes***.

CYPRUS*.
GEORGIA Iori Steppes*.

ISRAEL Bet Shean Valley***, Hula Reserve***.   **TURKEY** Birecik-Halfeti***, Cizre***, Göksu
SYRIA Dayr al-Zawr***.   Delta***.

Double-spurred Francolin
Francolinus bicalcaratus   FG S Res

Range In the Western Palearctic confined to tiny areas of Morocco (endemic race *ayesha*) where now extremely rare and current range little known. In recent decades reported from Sous and Essaouira but now thought to be extinct in the Forest of Mamora.

Tips: Found at woodland edges in coastal lowlands, in vegetated wadis, cultivated land and palm groves. Usually observed in small parties, sometimes perches in trees and calls from a mound or post at dawn or dusk, but usually very shy and difficult to see. The Sidi Bettache and Sidi Yahya area of the Zaër is the best and now perhaps the only locality in the Western Palearctic guaranteed to produce this species, although it was recorded at Oued Sous in Feb 2004.

Sites:
MOROCCO Agadir and the Sous Plain*, Zaër***.

Helmeted Guineafowl
Numida meleagris   FG SH Res

Range: Extremely rare, if not already extinct, as a wild bird in the Western Palearctic. An introduced population on the Cape Verde Is is declining and now found only on Fogo, Maio, São Nicolau and São Tiago. Also introduced to Tenerife in the Canaries and on Madeira, and the species may now be established in S France and in SW Bulgaria around Rupite as a result of escapes.

Subspecies: Recently extinct Moroccan birds belonged to endemic race *sabyi* and those in the Cape Verde Is to W African race *galeata*.

Tips: Formerly found in grassland and forest edge, wadis and hillsides, roosting in trees, and usually close to a water source. May occur ferally in Morocco but there have been very no reliable records of wild birds since the 1970s.

Sites:
CANARY IS***.
CAPE VERDE IS**.
MADEIRA*.

Small Button-quail (Andalusian Hemipode)
Turnix sylvatica

FG SH   Res

Range: Very rare and localised and one of the region's most sought after birds. Endemic race *sylvatica* may still occur in S Portugal, though there are no recent records, and very small numbers probably still present in S Spain, in the Guadalquivir marismas, but rarely seen and precise range unknown. Formerly more widespread in N Africa, from about Essaouira in Morocco to NW Libya, but there have been very few recent records. In Morocco, formerly known from the Atlantic coast with records from Oualidia and Casablanca, and on the Mediterranean coast near the mouth of Wadi Moulouya. There are also 1970s records from Algeria, at the mouth of Oued Zour, and N of Sousse in Tunisia.

Tips Found on sandy plains with palmetto scrub and asphodel, in stubble fields and abandoned farmland. Extremely rare and little known in our region, and probably crepuscular, making it one of the most difficult birds in the Western Palearctic to find. It may be worth watching field edges and tracks in suitable habitat, and listening for the distinctive and oft-repeated low crooning call of the female at dawn.

Site:
SPAIN Coto Doñana.

Spotted Crake
Porzana porzana

FW   Mig (PMig)

Range: Widespread but patchily distributed from Spain to Scandinavia and E to the Urals. Breeds sporadically over much of its range, including Britain, where otherwise a rare passage migrant. Much more numerous in E of range particularly Russia, Belarus, Ukraine and Romania. Small numbers winter in the region, mainly in Iberia, N Africa and the Middle East, with a few individuals further N. However, the majority are summer visitors, present Apr–Sep and passage birds occur throughout the S of the region.

Tips: A highly secretive bird of marshes and swamps, usually those with sedges rather than purely reeds, flooded fields and densely vegetated margins of lakes and rivers. Not easily observed and best located by its characteristic call heard on warm summer evenings. A dusk visit to a known site provides the best chance of seeing the species.

Sites:
ARMENIA Armash Fishponds** (passage),
Lake Sevan*** (summer, passage).

AUSTRIA Lake Neusiedl*** (summer).
BALEARIC IS Mallorca*** (summer).

BELARUS Belovezhskaya Pushcha NP*** (summer), Berezinsky Reserve*** (summer), Pripyatsky NP*** (summer).

BELGIUM Kalmthoutse Heide* (summer, passage).

BULGARIA Burgas area*** (summer, passage), Lake Durankulak*** (summer), Lake Shabla*** (summer, passage), Lake Srebarna*** (summer, passage), Ropotamo NP*** (summer), Strandja Mts* (summer, passage).

CANARY IS Fuerteventura* (passage).

CORSICA Biguglia Lake* (summer), Cap Corse** (passage).

CROATIA Kopački Rit** (summer).

CYPRUS* (passage).

CZECH REPUBLIC Pohořelice Fishponds*** (summer), Poodří*** (summer), Soutok*** (summer), Třeboňsko*** (summer).

DENMARK Bornholm-Christiansø*** (passage), Møn-Falster*** (summer, passage), Ringkøbing Fjord*** (summer), Rømø** (summer), Skagen*** (summer, passage).

EGYPT Abu Simbel* (passage), Aswan* (passage), Faiyum* (passage), Luxor* (passage), Nile Delta** (passage, winter), Sharm el Sheikh** (passage), Wadi el Natrun** (passage), Zaranik* (passage).

ESTONIA Emajõgi Floodplain*** (summer), Lake Endla*** (summer), Matsalu Bay*** (summer).

FINLAND Åland Is*** (summer), Liminganlahti*** (summer), Parikkala*** (summer), Viikki*** (passage).

FRANCE Camargue*** (summer), Dombes*** (summer), Golfe du Morbihan* (summer), La Brenne*** (summer), Lorraine NP* (summer), Sologne*** (summer), Somme Estuary** (summer), Teich Reserve*** (summer).

GERMANY Dummer** (summer), Federsee*** (summer), Kuhkopf*** (summer), Mecklenburg Lakes*** (summer), Oder Valley*** (summer), Schweinfurt*** (summer).

GREAT BRITAIN Minsmere* (summer, autumn), N Norfolk coast* (autumn), Scilly*** (autumn).

GREECE Amvrakiko's Gulf*** (summer, passage), Axios-Aliakmonas Deltas** (summer), Evros Delta* (summer), Lake Kerkini*** (summer), Mikrí Prespa NP** (summer), Nestos Delta** (summer), Porto Lagos area*** (summer).

GREEK IS Corfu*** (passage), Crete** (passage), Kos* (passage), Lesvos*** (passage).

HUNGARY Biharugra* (summer), Csákvár*** (summer), Hortobágy NP*** (summer), Kis-balaton*** (summer), Kiskunság NP*** (summer), Lake Fertö*** (summer), Lake Velence*** (summer), Ócsa** (summer).

ISRAEL Arava Valley*** (passage), Bet Shean Valley*** (passage, winter), Eilat*** (passage), Hula Reserve*** (passage, winter), Jezreel Valley*** (passage, winter).

ITALY Lake Massaciuccoli*** (summer, passage), Gargano Peninsula* (summer, passage), Po Delta*** (summer, passage).

JORDAN Azraq (passage).

LATVIA Lake Engure*** (summer), Lake Lubana*** (summer), Lake Pape*** (summer).

LEBANON Aamiq Marshes** (passage), Palm Is* (passage), Qaraoun Lake* (passage).

LITHUANIA Kirsiu Peninsula*** (summer), Zuvintas NR*** (summer).

MOROCCO Oued Massa** (passage).

NETHERLANDS Lauwersmeer* (summer), Oostvaadersplassen** (summer), Terschelling** (summer), Zwanenwater** (summer).

POLAND Białowieża Forest*** (summer), Biebrza Marshes*** (summer), Chełm Marshes*** (summer), Gdańsk Bay*** (summer), Milicz Fishponds*** (summer), Siemianówka Reservoir*** (summer), Słoňsk*** (summer), Szczecin Bay area** (summer).

ROMANIA Danube Delta*** (summer), Dobrudja*** (summer, passage), Satchinez*** (summer).

RUSSIA Volga Delta*** (summer).

SLOVAKIA Orava Reservoir** (summer), Senné Fishponds*** (summer), Slovenský Kras** (summer), Záhorie*** (summer), Zemplínská Reservoir* (summer).

SLOVENIA Lake Cerknica* (summer).

SPAIN Aiguamolls de l'Empordá** (passage), Cabo de Gata* (passage), Coto Doñana***, Ebro Delta*** (summer), Guadalhorce

Estuary** (passage), Llobregat Delta** (summer).

SWEDEN Falsterbo** (summer), Getterön* (passage), Gotland*** (summer), Hornborgasjön*** (summer), Kristianstad*** (summer), Kvismaren*** (summer), Öland*** (summer, passage), Store Mosse NP*** (summer), Tåkern*** (summer).

SWITZERLAND Fanel NR*** (passage), Klingnau Reservoir*** (passage).

TUNISIA Cap Bon Peninsula* (passage), Kelbia Lake (passage), Lake Ichkeul* (passage).

TURKEY Bulanik (summer, passage), Dalyan* (passage), Göksu Delta*** (summer, passage), Kızılırmak Delta*** (passage), Kocaćay Delta* (passage), Kulu Gölü* (summer, passage), Van Gölü*** (passage).

UKRAINE Dunay Delta* (summer), Shatsk NP*** (summer).

YUGOSLAVIA Carska bara (summer), Obedska bara* (summer).

Little Crake
Porzana parva   FW Mig (PMig)

Range: Main breeding range is in E Europe, from E Germany and Poland to Ukraine and S Russia. Very fragmented distribution elsewhere in Europe, breeding at scattered sites in Iberia and from France and the Netherlands to Greece. Also breeds in S Finland. Occurs on passage in Sep–Oct and Mar–May throughout the S of the region, and small numbers probably winter around the Mediterranean.

Tips: A very secretive and probably often overlooked bird of freshwater wetlands with dense vegetation. Watch suitable areas at dusk from a concealed vantage point and crakes may wander out to feed on open mud or swim across short stretches of water.

Sites:
ARMENIA Lake Sevan** (summer).
AUSTRIA Lake Neusiedl*** (summer).
BALEARIC IS Mallorca* (summer, passage).
BELARUS Belovezhskaya Pushcha NP** (summer), Berezinsky Reserve* (summer), Pripyatsky NP*** (summer).
BULGARIA Burgas area** (summer), Lake Durankulak*** (summer), Lake Shabla*** (summer), Lake Srebarna*** (summer), Ropotamo NP*** (summer).
CANARY IS Fuerteventura* (passage).
CORSICA Biguglia Lake* (summer), Cap Corse* (passage).
CYPRUS* (passage).
CZECH REPUBLIC Poodří** (summer), Soutok*** (summer), Třeboňsko** (summer).

EGYPT Abu Simbel** (passage), Aswan** (passage), Faiyum** (passage), Luxor** (passage), Nile Delta**, Wadi el Natrun** (passage, winter), Zaranik* (passage).
ESTONIA Lake Endla** (summer), Matsalu Bay*** (summer).
FINLAND Parikkala* (summer).
FRANCE Camargue* (summer), La Brenne* (summer), Lorraine NP* (summer), Sologne* (summer), Somme Estuary* (summer).
GERMANY Federsee* (summer), Kuhkopf** (summer), Oder Valley** (summer), Schweinfurt* (summer).
GREECE Amvrakiko's Gulf*** (summer, passage), Axios-Aliakmonas Deltas** (summer), Evros Delta* (summer), Lake Kerkini***

(summer), Mikrí Prespa NP** (summer), Nestos Delta*** (summer, passage), Porto Lagos area*** (summer).

GREEK IS Corfu* (passage), Crete*** (passage, winter), Kos** (passage), Lesvos*** (passage).

HUNGARY Biharugra** (summer), Csákvár** (summer), Hortobágy NP*** (summer), Kis-balaton*** (summer), Kiskunság NP*** (summer), Lake Fertö*** (summer), Lake Velence*** (summer), Ócsa** (summer).

ISRAEL Arava Valley*** (passage), Bet Shean Valley*** (passage, winter), Eilat*** (passage), Hula Reserve*** (passage, winter), Jezreel Valley** (passage), Ma'agan Mikhael*** (passage, winter).

ITALY Gargano Peninsula* (passage), Po Delta** (summer, passage).

JORDAN Azraq** (passage).

LATVIA Lake Engure*** (summer), Lake Lubana*** (summer), Lake Pape*** (summer).

LEBANON Aamiq Marshes* (passage), Palm Is (passage).

LITHUANIA Kirsiu Peninsula*** (summer), Zuvintas NR*** (summer).

MACEDONIA Lakes Ohrid and Prespa** (summer).

MALTA (passage).

MOROCCO Oued Massa** (passage), Tafilalt* (passage).

POLAND Białowieża Forest** (summer), Białystok Fishponds** (summer), Biebrza Marshes*** (summer), Chełm Marshes*** (summer), Gdańsk Bay*** (summer), Milicz Fishponds*** (summer), Siemianówka Reservoir*** (summer), Słońsk* (summer), Szczecin Bay area* (summer).

PORTUGAL Ria Formosa* (summer).

ROMANIA Danube Delta*** (summer), Dobrudja*** (summer, passage), Satchinez** (summer).

RUSSIA Volga Delta*** (summer).

SLOVAKIA Senné Fishponds*** (summer), Záhorie** (summer).

SLOVENIA Lake Cerknica* (summer).

SPAIN Aiguamolls de l'Empordá*** (summer), Coto Doñana***, Ebro Delta*** (summer, passage), Llobregat Delta* (summer, passage).

SWEDEN Kvismaren* (summer), Öland (passage).

SWITZERLAND Fanel NR* (passage), Klingnau Reservoir** (passage).

SYRIA Dayr al-Zawr* (passage).

TUNISIA Cap Bon Peninsula (passage), Kelbia Lake (passage), Lake Ichkeul (passage).

TURKEY Göksu Delta** (summer, passage), Kızılırmak Delta* (passage), Kocaćay Delta* (passage), Kulu Gölü** (summer, passage), Van Gölü* (passage).

UKRAINE Dunay Delta* (summer), Shatsk NP*** (summer).

YUGOSLAVIA Carska bara (summer), Obedska bara* (summer).

Baillon's Crake
Porzana pusilla   FW   Mig (PMig)

Range: Main range is from Belarus and Ukraine to the Urals and Caspian, but breeds at scattered localities in W and C Europe including Spain and Portugal, France, the Netherlands and Sardinia. Probably also breeds in Turkey, parts of the Middle East and in N Africa in Morocco and the Nile Valley of Egypt. Some may winter around the Mediterranean but status at this season poorly known, migration periods are late Aug–Nov and Mar–May.

Subspecies: Race *intermedia* occurs over most of Western Palearctic range with *pusilla* in S Russia.

Tips: Like all crakes, this is a little-known, very secretive and rarely observed bird of marshes and swamps. Prefers sedges and rushes rather than reeds, and is sometimes found in tall vegetation in drier situations. Watch suitable areas at dawn and dusk from a concealed vantage point and seeing a crake in the open may be possible.

Sites:

ARMENIA Armash Fishponds** (passage), Lake Sevan* (passage).

AUSTRIA Lake Neusiedl** (summer).

BALEARIC IS Mallorca (passage).

CYPRUS (passage).

EGYPT Abu Simbel* (passage), Aswan* (passage), Faiyum* (passage), Luxor* (passage), Nile Delta*, Zaranik* (passage).

FRANCE La Brenne* (summer), Sologne** (summer).

GREECE Amvrakiko's Gulf* (summer, passage), Axios-Aliakmonas Deltas* (summer), Evros Delta* (summer), Lake Kerkini* (summer), Mikrí Prespa NP* (summer), Porto Lagos area** (summer, passage).

GREEK IS Crete* (passage), Kos* (passage), Lesvos** (passage).

HUNGARY Biharugra* (summer), Csákvár*** (summer), Hortobágy NP*** (summer), Kis-balaton* (summer), Kiskunság NP** (summer), Lake Fertö* (summer), Lake Velence* (summer), Ócsa* (summer).

ISRAEL Arava Valley** (passage), Bet Shean Valley*** (passage, winter), Eilat** (passage), Jezreel Valley** (passage, winter), Ma'agan Mikhael*** (passage).

ITALY Po Delta (passage).

JORDAN Azraq** (passage, may also breed).

LEBANON Aamiq Marshes** (passage), Qaraoun Lake* (passage).

MACEDONIA Lakes Ohrid and Prespa* (summer).

MALTA (passage).

MOROCCO Oued Massa* (passage), Tafilalt* (passage).

PORTUGAL Boquilobo** (summer), Santo André Lagoon* (summer), Tagus Estuary* (summer).

ROMANIA Danube Delta** (summer), Dobrudja* (passage).

RUSSIA Volga Delta*** (summer).

SPAIN Aiguamolls de l'Empordá* (summer), Cabo de Gata* (passage), Cádiz Lagoons** (summer), Coto Doñana** (summer), Ebro Delta**, Llobregat Delta* (summer).

SWEDEN Kvismaren* (summer), Öland (passage).

SYRIA Dayr al-Zawr* (passage).

TUNISIA Cap Bon Peninsula (passage), Kelbia Lake (passage), Lake Ichkeul (passage).

TURKEY Göksu Delta** (summer, passage), Kızılırmak Delta* (passage), Kulu Gölü* (passage), Van Gölü (passage).

UKRAINE Dunay Delta* (summer).

YUGOSLAVIA Carska bara (summer).

Corn Crake
Crex crex

FG (FW)   Mig

Range: Declining in much of the Western Palearctic due to development of modern farming methods. Breeds in Ireland, N and W Scotland, Orkney and the Hebrides, and across Europe from N Spain and France, N to C Scandinavia and E to the Urals. Also breeds in Turkey and in the Caucasus. Numbers are highest in the E of the region where traditional farming methods are still practised. Attempts are underway to reintroduce the species to E England and breeding first occurred in 2004. Autumn passage occurs late Aug–early Nov, peaking in Sep, and the return in late Mar to mid–May. Very small numbers may winter in N Africa but most cross the Sahara.

Tips: Often secretive and difficult to flush, but easily located by its unique call, given most frequently early in the breeding season, and patient watching may result in a sighting. Calls mainly at night and early morning, with 03.00 often the peak time. In some areas less secretive and may call from a perch and appear in the open. Inhabits grasslands, both natural and man-made, as well as drier marshes with reeds or other dense vegetation.

Sites:
AUSTRIA Lake Neusiedl** (summer), Marchauen-Marchegg Reserve*** (summer), Wienerwald* (summer).

BELARUS Belovezhskaya Pushcha NP*** (summer), Berezinsky Reserve*** (summer), Prypyatsky NP*** (summer).

BELGIUM Hautes Fagnes Natural Park* (summer), Lesse et Lomme NR* (summer).

BOSNIA-HERZEGOVINA Sujetska NP*** (summer).

BULGARIA Burgas area** (summer), Lake Shabla*** (summer), Strandja Mts** (passage).

CROATIA Kopački Rit** (summer), Pokupsko Depression** (summer).

CYPRUS* (passage).

CZECH REPUBLIC Beskydy Mts** (summer), Jeseníky Mts* (summer), Krkonoše NP** (summer), Poodří** (summer), Soutok*** (summer), Šumava NP** (summer), Třeboňsko*** (summer).

DENMARK Bornholm-Christiansø*** (summer), Ringkøbing Fjord* (summer), Skagen** (passage).

EGYPT Zaranik*** (passage).

ESTONIA Emajõgi Floodplain*** (summer), Lake Endla*** (summer), Matsalu Bay*** (summer), Nigula NR*** (summer), Vilsandi NP*** (summer).

FINLAND Åland Is*** (summer), Parikkala* (summer), Patvinsuo NP** (summer), Viikki** (passage).

FRANCE Écrins NP* (summer), Marais Poitevin* (summer), Vanoise NP* (summer).

GEORGIA Iori Steppes*** (summer), Javakheti Plateau*** (summer).

GERMANY Dummer* (summer), Federsee** (summer), Kuhkopf*** (summer), Mecklenburg Lakes** (summer), Oder Valley*** (summer), Schweinfurt** (summer), Tiroler Achen* (summer).

GREAT BRITAIN Islay*** (summer), Orkney Is* (summer, passage), Outer Hebrides*** (summer), Shetland Is* (passage).

GREEK IS Lesvos* (passage).

HUNGARY Aggtelek NP** (summer), Hanság* (summer), Hortobágy NP*** (summer), Kis-balaton*** (summer), Kiskunság NP*** (summer), Lake Fertö*** (summer), Lake Velence* (summer), Ócsa** (summer), Zemplén Hills* (summer).

IRELAND Mullet Peninsula** (summer).

ISRAEL Eilat*** (passage), Ein Gedi** (passage), Hula Reserve*** (passage), Jezreel Valley*** (passage), Ma'agan Mikhael** (passage).

JORDAN Aqaba* (passage), Azraq** (passage).

LATVIA Cape Kolka*** (summer), Lake Engure*** (summer), Lake Lubana*** (summer), Lake Pape*** (summer).

LEBANON Palm Is* (passage).

LITHUANIA Cepkeliai NR** (summer), Kirsiu Peninsula** (summer), Lake Kretuonas* (summer), Zuvintas NR** (summer).

MALTA (passage).

MOLDOVA Balatina** (summer), Manta Floodplain** (passage).

POLAND Białowieża Forest*** (summer), Biebrza Marshes*** (summer), Bieszczady NP*** (summer), Chełm Marshes*** (summer), Gdańsk Bay*** (summer), Kampinos NP*** (summer), Milicz Fishponds*** (summer), Siemianówka Reservoir*** (summer), Słoňsk** (summer), Szczecin Bay area** (summer).

ROMANIA Danube Delta*** (summer), Satchinez*** (summer).

RUSSIA Oka Valley*** (summer), Volga Delta*** (summer).

SLOVAKIA High Tatras NP** (summer), Malá Fatra** (summer), Malé Karpaty*** (summer), Nízke Tatry NP*** (summer), Orava Reservoir*** (summer), Senné Fishponds*** (summer), Slanské Hills* (summer), Slovenský Kras*** (summer), Vihorlatske Hills** (summer), Záhorie** (summer), Zlatná na Ostrove** (summer).

SLOVENIA Lake Cerknica*** (summer), Ljubljansko Moor*** (summer), Triglav NP* (summer).

SWEDEN Getterön* (passage), Gotland* (summer, passage), Hornborgasjön** (summer), Kristianstad* (summer), Kvismaren** (summer), Öland** (summer, passage), Tåkern* (summer).

SWITZERLAND Swiss NP* (summer).

TURKEY Göksu Delta (passage).

UKRAINE Dunay Delta* (summer), Shatsk NP** (summer).

YUGOSLAVIA Carska bara* (summer), Đerdap NP* (summer), Durmitor NP* (summer).

Purple Swamphen (Purple Gallinule)
Porphyrio porphyrio   FW BW   Res (Dis)

Range: Rare and very local in the Western Palearctic, breeding in S Iberia, NW Africa and Sardinia, the Volga Delta, Azerbaijan, S Turkey and the Nile Valley. Reintroduced to Albufera, on Mallorca, and the Aiguamolls de L'Empordá, in Spain. Increasing under protection and recent range expansion has led to breeding in S France, the Extremadura region of Spain, and Israel.

Subspecies: Nominate race breeds in the W Mediterranean, *madagascariensis* in Egypt and *caspius* from Turkey to the Caspian; these are considered full species by some authorities.

Tips: Secretive and rarely seen in the open, as found in marshes and swamps, often in reeds and reedmace and frequently in brackish areas. Spends much time in dense vegetation but occasionally swims across open water or clambers up reeds. Best seen early morning and evening.

Sites:

ALGERIA El Kala NP***.
ARMENIA Armash Fishponds* (passage).
AZERBAIJAN Kura Valley Salt-lakes***,
Kyzylagach Bay*.
BALEARIC IS Mallorca*** (reintroduced).
EGYPT Aswan***, Faiyum**, Luxor***, Nile
Delta***, Suez area**.
ISRAEL Bet Shean Valley*.
MOROCCO Asilah and Oued Loukkos***.
PORTUGAL Boquilobo*, Ria Formosa***.

RUSSIA Volga Delta*** (summer).
SARDINIA Cagliari wetlands***, Oristano
wetlands***.
SPAIN Aiguamolls de l'Empordá*** (reintro-
duced), Cádiz Lagoons***, Coto Doñana***,
Ebro Delta***, Tablas de Daimiel***.
SYRIA Bahrat Homs*, Dayr al-Zawr***.
TUNISIA Kelbia Lake**, Lake Ichkeul***.
TURKEY Göksu Delta***.

Crested Coot (Red-knobbed Coot)
Fulica cristata   FW (BW)   Res (Dis)

Range: Rare at a few sites in S Spain, more numerous and locally common in N Morocco. Rarely seen outside restricted range, but there are occasional records from Portugal. Reintroduction programmes are extending range in S Spain.

Tips: Shyer than Common Coot, keeps more to cover and less often seen on land. Easily observed at known sites, although this may still involve searching large flocks of Common Coot. Found on fresh waters, rarely on small ponds but often on reed-fringed lagoons, even with brackish water.

Sites:

MOROCCO Asilah and Oued Loukkos***, Dayet
Aaoua, Lac de Sidi Bourhaba***, Merja Zerga**
(winter).

PORTUGAL Santo André Lagoon (winter).
SPAIN Cádiz Lagoons***, Coto Doñana**,
Llobregat Delta*** (reintroduced).

Common Crane
Grus grus   FG FW   Mig

Range: Breeds widely across NE Europe, from Scandinavia and E Germany to the Urals, and in small numbers in C and E Turkey, Georgia and Armenia. In recent years has become re-established in Britain and the first breeding in France and the Netherlands has occurred. Most are migratory and winter in S Iberia, N Africa, Turkey and the Middle East, with a regular winter-ing site in NE France. Occurs on passage over most of

Europe, N Africa and the Middle East, with regularly used staging areas including Öland in Sweden, Matsalu Bay in Estonia and Hortobágy in Hungary.

Subspecies: Nominate form occurs over most of our region with very similar *lilfordi* breeding in the extreme E in the Urals and perhaps also Turkey.

Tips: Breeds in wet meadows and marshes, usually close to forest or on drier steppes in S of range. Often found on cultivated land in winter. Prefers traditional sites on passage and in winter, where sightings are virtually guaranteed. The very small British population in Norfolk can be seen in the Waxham area and near Horsey Mere but should not be disturbed during the breeding season.

Sites:

BALEARIC IS Mallorca* (passage).

BELARUS Belovezhskaya Pushcha NP*** (passage), Berezinsky Reserve*** (summer), Pripyatsky NP*** (summer).

BELGIUM Hautes Fagnes Natural Park** (passage).

BULGARIA Albena-Golden Sands** (passage), Burgas area*** (passage), Cape Kaliakra*** (passage), Lake Durankulak*** (passage), Lake Shabla*** (passage), Lake Srebarna*** (passage).

CROATIA Kopački Rit** (passage).

CYPRUS* (passage).

DENMARK Amager*** (passage), Bornholm-Christiansø*** (summer, passage), Hanstholm* (summer), Hellebæk***(passage), Skagen*** (passage), Skallingen-Blåvandshuk** (passage).

EGYPT Abu Simbel*** (passage), Aswan*** (passage), Hurghada*** (passage), Luxor*** (passage), Sharm el Sheikh*** (passage, winter), Zaranik*** (passage).

ESTONIA Emajõgi Floodplain*** (summer, passage), Lake Endla*** (summer), Matsalu Bay*** (passage), Nigula NR*** (summer), Vilsandi NP*** (summer, passage).

FINLAND Åland Is* (summer), Kuusamo*** (summer), Lake Inari*** (summer), Lemmenjoki NP*** (summer), Liminganlahti*** (summer, passage), Oulanka NP*** (summer), Pallas-Ounastunturi NP*** (summer), Parikkala*** (summer, passage), Patvinsuo NP*** (summer), Pyhä-Häkki NP*** (summer), Urho Kekkonen NP*** (summer), Viikki** (passage).

FRANCE Fôret d'Orient*** (passage, winter), La Brenne** (passage), Lac du Der-Chantecoq*** (passage, winter), Marais Poitevin* (passage), Organbidexka*** (passage), Sologne*** (autumn).

GEORGIA Iori Steppes*** (passage), Javakheti Plateau*** (summer, passage).

GERMANY Dummer** (passage), Kuhkopf** (passage), Mecklenburg Lakes*** (summer, autumn), Oder Valley*** (summer, autumn), Rügen*** (passage).

HUNGARY Biharugra* (passage), Hortobágy NP*** (passage), Kardoskút*** (passage), Kiskunság NP*** (passage), Lake Fertö*** (passage), Szeged Fishponds*** (passage).

ISRAEL Arava Valley*** (passage, winter), Eilat*** (passage), Ein Gedi*** (passage), Golan Heights*** (winter), Hula Reserve*** (passage, winter), Jezreel Valley*** (passage, winter), Nizzana*** (passage), Urim*** (passage, winter).

ITALY Circeo NP*** (passage), Gargano Peninsula*** (passage), Orbetello Reserve** (passage).

JORDAN Azraq*** (winter), Ghadir Burqu'*** (winter).

LATVIA Cape Kolka*** (summer, passage), Lake Engure*** (summer), Lake Pape*** (summer, passage).

LEBANON Aamiq Marshes* (passage), Qaraoun Lake* (passage).

LITHUANIA Cepkeliai NR*** (summer), Kirsiu Peninsula*** (passage), Zuvintas NR*** (summer).

MALTA* (passage).

MOROCCO Asilah and Oued Loukkos*** (winter), Merja Zerga*** (winter), Oued Massa*** (winter).

NORWAY Dovrefjell NP*** (summer), Fokstumyra** (summer), Hardangervidda NP*** (summer), Øvre Pasvik NP*** (summer), Rondane NP*** (summer).

POLAND Białowieża Forest*** (summer), Biebrza Marshes*** (summer), Kampinos NP*** (summer), Milicz Fishponds*** (summer, passage), Siemianówka Reservoir*** (summer), Słońsk*** (summer, passage), Szczecin Bay area** (summer, passage).

PORTUGAL Baixo Alentejo*** (winter).

ROMANIA Danube Delta*** (summer, passage), Dobrudja** (passage).

RUSSIA Kalmykia*** (passage), Kola Peninsula*** (summer), Volga Delta** (passage).

SARDINIA Cagliari wetlands*** (passage), Oristano wetlands*** (passage).

SICILY Vendicari* (passage).

SLOVAKIA Malé Karpaty** (passage), Senné Fishponds*** (passage), Záhorie* (passage), Zemplínská Reservoir*** (passage).

SPAIN Aiguamolls de l'Empordá* (passage), Cáceres-Trujillo Steppes*** (winter), Coto Doñana*** (winter), La Serena*** (winter), Monfragüe*** (winter), Tablas de Daimiel*** (passage, winter), Zaragoza Steppes** (winter).

SWEDEN Falsterbo*** (passage), Färnebofjärden*** (summer, passage), Gammelstadsviken*** (passage), Getterön*** (passage), Gotland*** (summer, passage), Holmöarna*** (summer, passage), Hornborgasjön*** (summer, passage), Kristianstad*** (summer, passage), Kvismaren*** (passage), Öland*** (summer, passage), Store Mosse NP*** (summer), Tåkern*** (summer).

SYRIA Bahrat Homs*** (winter), Sabkhat al-Jubbal*** (winter), Tadmur and Sabkhat Muh** (winter).

TUNISIA Cap Bon Peninsula*** (passage), Kelbia Lake** (passage, winter), Lake Ichkeul*** (passage, winter).

TURKEY Bulanik*** (summer), Göksu Delta*** (passage, winter), Kızılırmak Delta*** (summer, passage), Van Golu* (passage).

UKRAINE Askania-Nova*** (passage), Dunay Delta*** (passage), Shatsk NP*** (summer), Syvash Bay*** (passage).

Siberian Crane
Grus leucogeranus   FW Mig

Range: Breeds E of the Urals in Siberia and winters in SE China with very small numbers in N India and N Iran. However, none has appeared at the Indian site, Bharatpur, in recent winters, and the tiny western population is now confined to Iran in winter, where six birds were present in 2004. In the Western Palearctic, occurs on passage in the Astrakhan Reserve, in the Volga Delta, but numbers are very low with c.10 birds usually recorded, although in some years none are seen. Another possible site is Lenkoran in Azerbaijan. Most records are in late Mar to mid April or Aug–Sep, sometimes later. In Oct 2001 only three were reported in the Volga Delta and another three, or possibly the same, were seen in Jordan.

Tips: On passage occurs at river mouths and lakes, always near water rather than on cultivated land, as in other cranes. The world population numbers fewer than 3,000 birds and this is one of the region's most difficult birds to see.

Site:
RUSSIA Volga Delta* (passage).

Demoiselle Crane
Anthropoides virgo

FW FG Mig

Range: Breeds in S Ukraine and Crimea and across S Russia to the Caspian, with tiny numbers in E Turkey, and perhaps also still in Morocco, where very small numbers were present in the Middle Atlas in the mid 1980s. On migration passes through the Middle East and NE Africa, but few are actually seen except in Cyprus. Some hundreds pass over the island in mid Aug to early Sep with much smaller numbers in late Mar to mid Apr. Rare on passage through Turkey, but several thousands are sometimes observed at Lake Sevan in Armenia. Occasionally reported elsewhere in the region, with most birds considered escapes, although a record of one in Spain with Russian-ringed Common Cranes in winter 2003/2004 probably involved a wild bird.

Tips: Breeds in flooded grassland, beside lakes and rivers in steppe, and in winter also occurs on cultivated land. Moroccan birds breed on montane plateaux.

Sites:

ARMENIA Lake Sevan** (passage).
CYPRUS ** (passage).
EGYPT Suez area* (passage).
GEORGIA Iori Steppes** (passage).
MOROCCO Dayet Aaoua.
ROMANIA Dobrudja (passage).

RUSSIA Kalmykia*** (summer), Volga Delta* (summer).
TURKEY Bulanik** (summer).
UKRAINE Askania-Nova*** (summer), Syvash Bay*** (summer).

Little Bustard
Tetrax tetrax

FG Mig Res

Range: Fragmented range in the W with breeding populations in Iberia and Morocco, W, C and S France, Sardinia and SW Italy. More widespread in the E from S Ukraine and Turkey (where very rare as a breeder) across S Russia to the Caspian. Northern breeders are migratory wintering in Iberia and S France in the W and Transcaucasia in the E.

Tips: A very shy bird of open habitats, mainly grasslands, but also cereal and clover fields, and in winter on airfields. Crouches or runs when disturbed and only flies very reluctantly. Most easily seen in jumping display with clicking calls in late Apr–early May. Migrants gather in flocks from Aug and depart breeding areas in Sep–Oct, returning Mar–Apr.

Sites:

AZERBAIJAN Kyzylagach Bay*** (winter).
BULGARIA Lake Durankulak* (winter).
FRANCE Camargue***, Cévennes NP** (summer), La Brenne** (summer), Les Alpilles*, Marais Poitevin* (winter).
GEORGIA Iori Steppes** (passage), Javakheti Plateau** (passage).
ISRAEL Bet Shean Valley*** (autumn, winter), Golan Heights*** (winter), Hula Reserve** (passage, winter).
ITALY Gargano Peninsula.
MACEDONIA Bregalnica Valley.
MOROCCO Asilah and Oued Loukkos*** (winter), Merja Zerga (winter).
PORTUGAL Baixo Alentejo***, Cape St Vincent**, Castro Marim**, International

Tagus**, Ria Formosa* (winter), Santo André Lagoon* (passage), Tagus Estuary***.
ROMANIA Satchinez**.
RUSSIA Kalmykia***, Volga Delta* (passage).
SARDINIA Giara di Gesturi*.
SPAIN Cabo de Gata**, Cáceres-Trujillo Steppes***, Coto Doñana*, La Serena***, Monfragüe***, Sierra de Guadarrama* (autumn), Tablas de Daimiel**, Zaragoza Steppes***.
SYRIA Jabal al-Bishri* (winter), Tadmur and Sabkhat Muh** (winter).
TURKEY Bulanik (autumn).
UKRAINE Askania-Nova*** (summer).

Houbara Bustard
Chlamydotis undulata   SD FG Dis

Range: Declining through persecution, this species is now absent or scarce over much of its range. Widespread but rare in N Africa and also breeds in the Canaries, on Fuerteventura and in smaller numbers on Lanzarote (and also recorded on Graciosa).
Subspecies: Nominate race breeds in N Africa, *fuertaventurae* in the Canaries (which may be given full species status in the future).
Tips: Search arid sandy and stony semi-deserts and cultivated land. The easiest place to find Houbara is probably now the Canaries.

Sites:
CANARY IS Fuerteventura***, Lanzarote**.
MOROCCO Boumalne*, Tafilalt*.
TUNISIA Chott el Djerid.

Macqueen's Bustard
Chlamydotis macqueenii

SD FG   Res (Dis)

Range: Like the closely related Houbara, of which this is considered a race by some authorities, this species is declining due to hunting and is now rare in many parts of its range. Breeds in NE Sinai and N Saudi Arabia, the Negev of Israel, parts of Jordan, and perhaps also in Syria. **Tips:** Search arid steppe and semi-desert with sparse vegetation, especially Artemisia; in winter also cultivated land.

Sites:
ISRAEL Arava Valley* (winter), Nizzana***, Urim***.
JORDAN Azraq, Ghadir Burqu'.

SYRIA Bahrat Homs*, Dayr al-Zawr**, Jabal al-Bishri***, Sabkhat al-Jubbal***, Tadmur and Sabkhat Muh**.

Great Bustard
Otis tarda

FG   Mig Res

Range: Rare with fragmented range, breeding in Iberia and N Morocco, in parts of C Europe and C and E Turkey (where recently discovered to be much rarer than previously thought), and more extensively in Ukraine across S Russia and Kazakhstan. In winter more widespread in Ukraine, Turkey and Transcaucasia, with small numbers probably wintering regularly in the Middle East. Plans are once again underway to reintroduce this species to Salisbury Plain in England.
Tips: Shy and wary, but when displaying can be quite obvious from some distance. Found in open grassland, steppes and areas of extensive, low-intensity cultivation.

Sites:
AUSTRIA Lake Neusiedl** (summer).
BULGARIA Cape Kaliakra* (winter), Lake Durankulak* (winter).
CZECH REPUBLIC Znojmo**.
GEORGIA Iori Steppes* (passage, winter), Javakheti Plateau** (passage).
HUNGARY Biharugra**, Hanság*, Hortobágy NP***, Kardoskút**, Kiskunság NP***, Lake Fertö**.
ISRAEL Golan Heights (winter).

MOROCCO Asilah and Oued Loukkos*** (winter).
PORTUGAL Baixo Alentejo***, International Tagus*, Tagus Estuary* (passage).
RUSSIA Kalmykia*** (winter), Volga Delta* (winter).
SLOVAKIA Zlatná na Ostrove***.
SPAIN Cáceres-Trujillo Steppes***, La Serena***, Tablas de Daimiel**, Zaragoza Steppes*.

SYRIA Tadmur and Sabkhat Muh* (winter).
TURKEY Bulanik**, Kulu Gölü.

UKRAINE Askania-Nova***, Syvash Bay***
(mainly passage).

Painted Snipe (Greater Painted-snipe)
Rostratula benghalensis   FW   Res (Dis)

Range: In our region found only in the Nile Delta and lower Nile Valley, Wadi el Natrun and Faiyum. Bred at Hadera in Israel in 1995 and found breeding on Lake Nasser in Egypt in 2000. Vagrants have been recorded in Sinai, Jordan, and particularly Israel.

Tips: Crepuscular, occurs in swamps with dense vegetation and open muddy areas, reedbeds and paddyfields. Freezes if disturbed and flies only on close approach. Often feeds in open grassland and ploughed areas at dawn and dusk, and this probably offers the best chance of seeing the species.

Sites:
EGYPT Luxor**, Faiyum*, Nile Delta***, Sharm el Sheikh*, Wadi el Natrun**.

Black-winged Stilt
Himantopus himantopus   FW BW ES   Mig Dis Res

Range: Breeds at scattered localities around much of the Mediterranean, in W France, Ukraine and S Russia, and much of Turkey. An opportunistic species that frequently breeds outside main range, and particularly in the Netherlands in recent years. Many are migratory but present year-round in parts of the Mediterranean.

Tips: Occurs on fresh or brackish shallow water with mud or sand margins, often in estuarine and delta areas. Loosely colonial when breeding. On approach makes its presence obvious by loud calls.

Sites:
ARMENIA Armash Fishponds*** (summer).
AUSTRIA Lake Neusiedl*** (summer).
AZERBAIJAN Kura Valley Salt-lakes***
(summer), Kyzylagach Bay*** (summer).
BALEARIC IS Formentera***, Ibiza***,
Mallorca***.

BULGARIA Burgas area*** (summer), Lake Durankulak** (passage), Lake Shabla*** (summer, passage), Ropotamo NP*** (passage).
CANARY IS Fuerteventura**, Lanzarote***.
CORSICA Biguglia Lake* (summer, passage).
CYPRUS* (summer, passage).

EGYPT Abu Simbel*** (passage), Aswan*** (passage, winter), Hurghada*** (passage), Luxor*** (passage), Nile Delta* (passage), Sharm el Sheikh*** (passage), Zaranik** (passage).

FRANCE Baie de Bourgneuf*** (summer), Camargue***, Dombes*** (summer), La Brenne** (summer), Golfe du Morbihan*** (summer), Gruissan** (passage), Žle d'Oléron*** (summer), Marais Poitevin*** (summer), Sologne* (summer), Somme Estuary* (summer).

GREECE Amvrakiko's Gulf*** (summer), Axios-Aliakmonas Deltas*** (summer), Evros Delta*** (summer), Lake Kerkini*** (summer), Nestos Delta*** (summer), Porto Lagos area*** (summer).

GREEK IS Crete*** (passage), Kos*** (summer, passage), Lesvos*** (summer, passage), Náxos*** (summer).

HUNGARY Hortobágy NP*** (summer), Kiskunság NP*** (summer), Szeged Fishponds** (summer).

ISRAEL Bet Shean Valley*** (passage), Eilat*** (passage), Hula Reserve***, Ma'agan Mikhael***, Nizzana** (passage).

ITALY Circeo NP*** (summer, passage), Gargano Peninsula*** (summer), Isonzo Regional Park*** (summer), Lake Massaciuccoli*** (summer), Maremma Regional Park*** (summer), Orbetello Reserve*** (summer), Po Delta*** (summer), San Giuliano Reserve*** (summer).

JORDAN Aqaba* (passage), Azraq*** (summer, passage), Ghadir Burqu'** (passage).

LEBANON Aamiq Marshes** (passage), Palm Is** (passage), Qaraoun Lake* (passage).

MALTA ** (passage).

MOROCCO Agadir and the Sous Plain*** (summer, passage), Asilah and Oued Loukkos***, Dayet Aaoua***, Essaouira** (passage), Lac de Sidi Bourhaba*** (summer, passage), Merja Zerga*** (passage), Oualidia*** (summer, passage), Ouarzazate*** (passage), Oued Massa***, Tafilalt* (passage, winter).

PORTUGAL Boquilobo*** (summer), Cape St Vincent* (passage), Castro Marim*** (summer), Ria Formosa*** (mainly summer), Sado Estuary*** (summer), Santo André Lagoon*** (summer), Tagus Estuary*** (summer).

ROMANIA Danube Delta*** (summer), Dobrudja*** (summer, passage), Lake Călăraşi** (summer).

RUSSIA Kalmykia*** (summer), Volga Delta*** (summer).

SARDINIA Cagliari wetlands***, Oristano wetlands*** (summer, passage).

SICILY Lago di Lentini***, Vendicari***.

SLOVAKIA Senné Fishponds*** (summer).

SPAIN Aiguamolls de l'Empordá*** (summer), Cabo de Gata***, Cáceres-Trujillo Steppes*** (summer), Cádiz Lagoons*** (summer), Coto Doñana***, Ebro Delta*** (summer), Guadalhorce Estuary*** (summer), La Serena*** (summer), Llobregat Delta*** (summer), Santa Pola***, Tablas de Daimiel*** (summer).

SWITZERLAND Fanel NR* (passage).

SYRIA Bahrat Homs*** (summer, passage), Dayr al-Zawr*** (passage), Sabkhat al-Jubbal*** (summer, passage).

TUNISIA Cap Bon Peninsula***, Chott el Djerid*, Kelbia Lake**, Lake Ichkeul***.

TURKEY Bafa Gölü*** (summer), Bulanik*** (summer), Göksu Delta*** (summer), Kızılırmak Delta*** (summer), Kulu Gölü*** (summer), Manyas Gölü*** (passage), Sultan Marshes*** (summer), Uluabat Gölü*** (summer), Van Gölü*** (summer).

UKRAINE Dunay Delta*** (summer), Syvash Bay*** (summer).

Pied Avocet
Recurvirostra avosetta

FW BW ES Mig Dis Res

Range: Highly discontinuous range, breeding in E and SE England, southern coasts of the North Sea and parts of the Baltic, the Biscay coast of France and around parts of the Mediterranean, Black and Caspian Seas. In Turkey breeds mainly in Anatolia, also occurs in Transcaucasia, but N African range confined to Tunisia. Departs breeding areas in N in late Jul–Sep, wintering mainly in Iberia and N Africa, returning Mar–Apr.

Tips: Distinctive, usually gregarious and noisy, and easy to locate at known sites, often lagoons; outside the breeding season also on muddy and sandy shores, and estuaries.

Sites:

ALBANIA Karavasta Lagoon*** (winter).
ARMENIA Armash Fishponds*** (summer).
AUSTRIA Lake Neusiedl*** (summer).
AZERBAIJAN Kura Valley Salt-lakes***, Kyzylagach Bay*** (winter).
BALEARIC IS Mallorca*** (passage).
BELGIUM Blankaart Reserve*** (summer), Het Zwin***.
BULGARIA Albena-Golden Sands*** (passage), Burgas area*** (summer, passage), Lake Durankulak*** (passage), Lake Shabla*** (summer, passage), Ropotamo NP*** (passage).
CANARY IS* (passage, winter).
CORSICA Biguglia Lake** (passage).
CYPRUS* (passage, winter).
DENMARK Amager*** (summer, passage), Bornholm-Christiansø*** (passage), Møn-Falster*** (summer, passage), Ringkøbing Fjord*** (summer, passage), Rømø*** (summer, passage), Skagen*** (summer, passage), Skallingen-Blåvandshuk*** (summer, passage), Vadehavet*** (summer, passage).
EGYPT Aswan*** (passage), Faiyum* (winter), Hurghada*** (passage), Luxor*** (passage), Nile Delta** (passage, winter), (Sharm el Sheikh*** (passage), Zaranik***.
ESTONIA Matsalu Bay*** (summer).
FRANCE Baie de Bourgneuf***, Baie de Vilaine*** (winter), Baie du Mont-St-Michel***

(passage), Camargue***, Cap Gris Nez*** (passage), Golfe du Morbihan***, Gruissan*** (summer), Île d'Oléron***, La Brenne*** (summer), Leucate***, Marais Poitevin***, Somme Estuary*** (summer, passage), Trunvel Reserve** (passage, winter).
GERMANY Rügen*** (summer), Wattenmeer*** (summer).
GREAT BRITAIN Dungeness** (passage), Minsmere***, N Norfolk coast*** (summer, passage), Portland** (passage).
GREECE Amvrakikós Gulf***, Axios-Aliakmonas Deltas***, Evros Delta***, Lake Kerkini***, Nestos Delta***, Porto Lagos area***.
GREEK IS Corfu* (passage), Lesvos***.
HUNGARY Hortobágy NP*** (summer), Kisbalaton*** (summer), Kiskunság NP*** (summer), Lake Fertö*** (summer), Szeged Fishponds*** (summer).
ISRAEL Bet Shean Valley*** (passage), Eilat*** (passage, winter), Hula Reserve*** (winter), Jezreel Valley*** (passage, winter), Ma'agan Mikhael***.
ITALY Circeo NP*** (passage), Gargano Peninsula***, Maremma Regional Park***, Orbetello Reserve***, Po Delta***, San Giuliano Reserve*** (summer).
JORDAN Azraq** (summer, passage).
LEBANON Palm Is* (passage).
MALTA* (passage).

MOROCCO Agadir and the Sous Plain*** (summer, passage), Asilah and Oued Loukkos***, Essaouira*** (passage), Lac de Sidi Bourhaba*** (summer, passage), Merja Zerga*** (passage), Oualidia*** (passage, winter), Ouarzazate*** (passage), Oued Massa***, Tafilalt* (passage).

NETHERLANDS Lauwersmeer*** (summer, passage), Oostvaadersplassen*** (summer, passage), Terschelling*** (summer), Texel*** (summer), Zwanenwater*** (summer).

POLAND Gdaňsk Bay* (passage).

PORTUGAL Castro Marim***, Ria Formosa***, Sado Estuary***, Santo André Lagoon*** (passage, winter), Tagus Estuary*** (passage, winter).

ROMANIA Danube Delta*** (summer), Dobrudja*** (passage).

RUSSIA Kalmykia*** (summer), Volga Delta*** (summer).

SARDINIA Cagliari wetlands***, Oristano wetlands***.

SICILY Lago di Lentini***, Vendicari***.

SLOVAKIA Senné Fishponds*** (summer).

SPAIN Aiguamolls de l'Empordá***, Cabo de Gata***, Cádiz Lagoons***, winter), Coto Doñana***, Ebro Delta***, Guadalhorce Estuary***, Llobregat Delta**, Santa Pola***, Tablas de Daimiel***.

SWEDEN Falsterbo*** (summer, passage), Getterön*** (summer, passage), Gotland*** (summer, passage), Kristianstad*** (summer), Öland*** (summer, passage).

SWITZERLAND Fanel NR* (passage).

SYRIA Bahrat Homs*** (summer), Dayr al-Zawr*** (passage), Sabkhat al-Jubbal*** (summer, passage).

TUNISIA Cap Bon Peninsula***, Kelbia Lake** (passage), Lake Ichkeul***, Tunis***.

TURKEY Bafa Gölü* (summer), Göksu Delta***, Kocaćay Delta*** (passage), Kulu Gölü*** (summer), Sultan Marshes*** (passage), Uluabat Gölü*** (passage), Van Gölü*** (passage).

UKRAINE Dunay Delta*** (summer), Syvash Bay*** (summer, passage).

Stone-curlew
Burhinus oedicnemus   FG SH   Mig

Range: Widespread but scarce, with a very patchy distribution across S Europe from Iberia E to the Urals, and reaching N to S England. Also breeds across much of Turkey and parts of the Middle East, on the Canaries, and in N Africa widespread in the NW, in coastal Libya and Egypt and in the Nile Valley. Present late Mar–Sep in N of range.

Subspecies: Nominate *oedicnemus* is found over most of range, replaced on the smaller Mediterranean islands, Greece, Turkey and N Africa E to Iraq by *saharae* and in S Russia by *harterti*. Race *distinctus* is found in the W Canaries and *insularum* in the E Canaries.

Tips: Found in dry, open country, including stony grassland, sand dunes, heaths and farmland. Chiefly crepuscular or nocturnal, more active during day when feeding young but well camouflaged and difficult to see. Crouches motionless or runs when disturbed, rarely flying.

Sites:

ARMENIA Armash Fishponds*** (summer).
BALEARIC IS Ibiza***, Mallorca***, Menorca***.
BULGARIA Burgas area** (summer), Cape Kaliakra*** (summer), Lake Durankulak*** (summer), Lake Shabla*** (summer), Strandja Mts* (summer).
CANARY IS El Hierro***, Fuerteventura***, Gran Canaria***, La Palma**, Lanzarote***, Tenerife***.
CYPRUS***.
CZECH REPUBLIC Znojmo* (summer).
EGYPT Abu Simbel*, Aswan**, Hurghada*, Luxor***.
FRANCE Camargue*** (summer), Cévennes NP*** (summer), La Brenne*** (summer), Marais Poitevin*** (summer).
GREAT BRITAIN Breckland*** (summer).
GREECE Amvrakikós Gulf*** (summer), Axios-Aliakmonas Deltas*** (summer), Evros Delta** (summer), Lake Kerkini*** (summer), Nestos Delta*** (summer), Porto Lagos area*** (summer).
GREEK IS Crete***, Lesvos*** (summer), Rhodes** (summer).
HUNGARY Hortobágy NP*** (summer), Kiskunság NP*** (summer).
ISRAEL Arava Valley***, Bet Shean Valley***, Ein Gedi***, Jezreel Valley***, Nizzana***, Urim***.
ITALY Gargano Peninsula** (summer), Maremma Regional Park*** (summer), Orbetello Reserve*** (summer), Po Delta*** (summer).
JORDAN Azraq***, Wadi Rum***.

MALTA* (passage).
MOROCCO Agadir and the Sous Plain***, Boumalne***, Essaouira***, Lac de Sidi Bourhaba***, Merja Zerga***, Ouarzazate***, Oued Massa***, Tafilalt***, Zeida**.
PORTUGAL Baixo Alentejo***, Cape St Vincent***, Castro Marim***, International Tagus**, Ria Formosa***, Sado Estuary***, Santo André Lagoon***, Tagus Estuary***.
ROMANIA Danube Delta*** (summer), Dobrudja*** (summer).
RUSSIA Kalmykia*** (summer), Volga Delta*** (summer).
SARDINIA Oristano wetlands*** (summer).
SICILY Lago di Lentini***, Vendicari***.
SPAIN Aiguamolls de l'Empordá***, Cabo de Gata***, Cáceres-Trujillo Steppes***, Cádiz Lagoons***, Coto Doñana***, La Serena***, Monfragüe***, Serrania de Ronda**, Sierra de Guadarrama**, Tablas de Daimiel***, Zaragoza Steppes***.
SYRIA Sabkhat al-Jabbul**, Tadmur and Sabkhat Muh***.
TUNISIA Cap Bon Peninsula***, Chott el Djerid***, Kelbia Lake***, Lake Ichkeul***, Tataouine***.
TURKEY Birecik-Halfeti* (summer), Bulanik*** (summer), Göksu Delta*** (summer), Kızılırmak Delta*** (summer), Kocaćay Delta*** (summer), Kulu Gölü*** (summer), Sultan Marshes*** (summer), Uluabat Gölü*** (summer), Van Gölü* (summer).
UKRAINE Askania-Nova*** (summer), Dunay Delta*** (summer), Syvash Bay*** (summer).

Senegal Thick-knee
Burhinus senegalensis

FG SH FW U   Res

Range: Western Palearctic range confined to the Nile Delta and Valley, possibly elsewhere in Egypt including Wadi el Natrun.

Tips: Less wary and more approachable than Stone-curlew, found in savanna, farmland and wooded clearings, usually near water. Nests on sandbanks and islets in rivers, and even nests colonially on flat rooftops in Cairo.

Sites:
EGYPT Abu Simbel***, Aswan***, Faiyum***, Luxor***, Nile Delta**, Wadi el Natrun**.

Cream-coloured Courser
Cursorius cursor

D SD (FG)   Res PMig (Dis)

Range: Widespread across N Africa and the Middle East, on Lanzarote and Fuerteventura in the Canaries, and on São Tiago, Boa Vista, São Vicente, Sal and Maio in the Cape Verde Is, where now declining. Bred in Spain in 2001.

Subspecies: Nominate race occurs over most of range with *exsul* in the Cape Verde Is.

Tips: A well-camouflaged bird that is difficult to see in its desert and semi-desert habitat. Passage birds and vagrants often occur on cultivated land or at sandy estuaries. Runs rather than flies when disturbed.

Sites:
CANARY IS Fuerteventura***, Lanzarote**.
CAPE VERDE IS*.
CYPRUS (passage).
EGYPT Abu Simbel*, Aswan**, Hurghada***, Luxor**, Suez area***, Wadi el Natrun*, Zaranik** (passage).
ISRAEL Arava Valley***, Eilat***, Nizzana***, Urim***.
JORDAN Azraq*** (summer, passage), Ghadir Burqu'*** (summer), Wadi Rum*** (summer, passage).

MALTA (passage).
MOROCCO Boumalne***, Goulimime to Tan-Tan***, Oued Massa***, Tafilalt***.
SYRIA Bahrat Homs*** (summer), Sabkhat al-Jubbal*** (summer, passage), Tadmur and Sabkhat Muh** (summer).
TUNISIA Chott el Djerid***, Kelbia Lake*.
TURKEY Birecik-Halfeti (summer, passage).

Collared Pratincole
Glareola pratincola　　　　　　　　　　FW BW SD (FG)　Mig

Range: Discontinuous range across the S of the region; breeds in S Iberia and NW Africa, S France, Italy and Sardinia, and more widely in the SE in Greece and Albania, Turkey and on the W and N shores of the Black Sea E to the Caspian. Also breeds in Hungary. Small numbers may winter on Mediterranean coasts but most depart the region in late Aug–Oct and return late Mar–Apr.

Tips: Found on marshes and deltas, arid farmland and semi-deserts. Breeds in noisy colonies, often near water and in E of range may nest alongside Black-winged Pratincole.

Sites:

ALBANIA Karavasta Lagoon*** (summer).
ARMENIA Armash Fishponds*** (summer, passage).
BALEARICS IS Mallorca** (passage).
BULGARIA Burgas area*** (summer), Lake Durankulak** (summer, passage), Lake Shabla* (summer, passage).
CANARY IS* (passage).
CYPRUS* (passage).
EGYPT Hurghada*** (passage), Nile Delta*** (summer), Sharm el Sheikh** (passage), Wadi el Natrun** (passage), Zaranik** (passage).
FRANCE Camargue** (summer).
GREECE Amvrakikós Gulf*** (summer, passage), Axios-Aliakmonas Deltas*** (summer), Evros Delta* (summer), Lake Kerkini** (summer), Mikrí Prespa NP* (passage), Nestos Delta** (summer), Porto Lagos area*** (summer).
GREEK IS Corfu*** (summer, passage), Crete*** (spring), Lesvos*** (passage).
HUNGARY Hortobágy NP*** (summer), Kiskunság NP*** (summer).
ISRAEL Arava Valley*** (passage), Bet Shean Valley*** (passage), Eilat*** (passage), Jezreel Valley** (passage), Nizzana** (passage).
ITALY Circeo NP** (passage), Gargano Peninsula** (summer, passage), Lake Massaciuccoli* (spring), Maremma Regional Park* (passage), Orbetello Reserve** (passage), Po Delta*** (summer).
JORDAN Azraq* (summer, passage), Ghadir Burqu'* (passage).
LEBANON Aamiq Marshes** (passage), Palm Is* (passage), Qaraoun Lake** (passage).
MACEDONIA Lakes Ohrid and Prespa** (passage).
MALTA (passage).
MOROCCO Lac de Sidi Bourhaba*** (passage), Merja Zerga*** (summer, passage), Oualidia*** (summer).
PORTUGAL Baixo Alentejo*** (summer), Castro Marim*** (summer), Ria Formosa* (summer), Sado Estuary*** (summer), Santo André Lagoon* (passage), Tagus Estuary*** (summer).
ROMANIA Danube Delta*** (summer), Dobrudja*** (summer, passage), Lake Călăraşi*** (summer).
RUSSIA Kalmykia* (summer), Volga Delta* (summer).
SARDINIA Cagliari wetlands*** (summer), Oristano wetlands*** (summer).
SICILY Lago di Lentini*** (summer), Vendicari* (passage).
SPAIN Aiguamolls de l'Empordá*** (summer), Cabo de Gata** (passage), Cáceres-Trujillo Steppes** (summer), Cádiz Lagoons*** (sum-

mer), Coto Doñana*** (summer), Ebro Delta*** (summer), Guadalhorce Estuary** (passage), La Serena** (summer), Llobregat Delta** (passage), Tablas de Daimiel*** (summer, passage).
SYRIA Dayr al-Zawr*** (passage), Sabkhat al-Jubbal*** (summer, passage).
TUNISIA Cap Bon Peninsula*** (passage), Kelbia Lake** (summer, passage), Lake Ichkeul*** (summer).

TURKEY Bafa Gölü*** (summer), Bulanik*** (summer), Göksu Delta*** (summer), Kızılırmak Delta*** (summer), Kocaćay Delta*** (summer), Kulu Gölü*** (summer), Sultan Marshes*** (summer), Uluabat Gölü*** (summer).
UKRAINE Dunay Delta*** (summer, passage), Tiligul Liman*** (summer), Syvash Bay*** (summer, passage).
YUGOSLAVIA Lake Skadar** (summer).

Black-winged Pratincole
Glareola nordmanni   FG FW BW   Mig

Range: Breeds in S Ukraine and across S Russia to the Urals and Caspian, occasionally in Hungary, Belarus and Turkey. Departs breeding grounds in Aug–Oct and crosses Middle East and Egypt, but rarely seen on passage except in small numbers in Cyprus, Israel and Egypt. Most arrive in breeding areas in May.

Tips: Breeds on steppes, often in meadows, cultivated fields, Artemisia scrub and at edges of saline lakes. Feeds mostly in morning and evening, both in flight and on ground.

Sites:
ARMENIA Armash Fishponds** (summer, passage).
AZERBAIJAN Kura Valley Salt-lakes*** (summer).
BULGARIA Lake Durankulak* (passage).
CYPRUS** (passage).
EGYPT Sharm el Sheikh* (passage), Zaranik* (passage).
GEORGIA Javakheti Plateau** (passage).
GREEK IS Lesvos* (passage).
HUNGARY Hortobágy NP* (summer, passage), Kiskunság NP* (summer, passage).
ISRAEL Arava Valley* (passage), Bet Shean Valley* (passage), Jezreel Valley* (passage), Ma'agan Mikhael** (passage).

JORDAN Azraq (passage).
LEBANON Aamiq Marshes* (passage), Palm Is (passage), Qaraoun Lake* (passage).
ROMANIA Dobrudja* (summer, passage).
RUSSIA Kalmykia*** (summer), Volga Delta*** (summer).
SYRIA Sabkhat al-Jubbal (passage).
TURKEY Bulanik*** (autumn), Göksu Delta (passage), Kızılırmak Delta (passage), Van Gölü* (passage).
UKRAINE Askania-Nova*** (summer), Dunay Delta (passage), Syvash Bay*** (summer).

Kittlitz's Plover
Charadrius pecuarius

FW BW (FG)   Res

Range: Found in the Nile Delta and in S Egypt in the Nile Valley, breeding on Lake Nasser. Recorded annually in Israel, usually in winter, and twice in Cyprus.

Tip:s Occurs on margins and sandbanks of lakes and rivers, but rarely coastal in Egypt, sometimes on cultivated ground.

Sites:
EGYPT Abu Simbel***, Aswan***, Nile Delta**, Wadi el Natrun***.
ISRAEL Ma'agan Mikhael (winter).

Kentish Plover
Charadrius alexandrinus

ES BW FW   Res Dis

Range: Widespread but scarce and decreasing in the N of the region. Breeds on coasts from Denmark to NW Africa and in the Atlantic on the Azores, Madeira, the Canaries and Cape Verde Is. Breeds throughout the Mediterranean, in the N Red Sea, and around much of the Black Sea. Also occurs inland in some areas, particularly in Iberia. A former breeder in Britain but now a rare migrant with a few S coast records each spring.

Tips: Search sand or shingle beaches, mudflats and estuaries, mainly in coastal areas, but also found at salt lakes and along rivers inland.

Sites:
ARMENIA Armash Fishponds*** (summer).
AUSTRIA Lake Neusiedl*** (summer).
AZORES*.
BALEARIC IS Formentera***, Ibiza***, Mallorca***, Menorca***.
BELGIUM Blankaart Reserve** (summer), Het Zwin** (summer).
BULGARIA Burgas area*** (summer, passage), Lake Durankulak*** (passage, winter), Lake Shabla*** (summer, passage), Ropotamo NP*** (summer, passage).

CANARY IS El Hierro**, Fuerteventura***, Gomera*, Gran Canaria***, Lanzarote***, Tenerife***.
CAPE VERDE IS*.
CORSICA Biguglia Lake***.
CYPRUS*.
DENMARK Rømø* (summer, passage), Skagen** (summer, passage), Skallingen-Blåvandshuk*** (summer, passage).
EGYPT Luxor** (passage, winter), Faiyum***, Hurghada***, Nile Delta***, Sharm el

Sheikh***, Suez area***, Wadi el Natrun***, Zaranik***.

FRANCE Baie de Bourgneuf*** (summer), Baie de Vilaine** (summer), Baie du Mont-St-Michel*** (summer, passage), Camargue***, Golfe du Morbihan*** (summer), Gruissan***, Île d'Oléron*** (summer), Leucate***, Marais Poitevin*** (summer), Somme Estuary*** (summer), Teich Reserve*** (summer), Trunvel Reserve*** (summer).

GEORGIA Javakheti Plateau*** (summer).

GERMANY Wattenmeer*** (summer, passage).

GREAT BRITAIN Dungeness* (passage), Minsmere* (passage), N Norfolk coast* (passage), Portland* (spring).

GREECE Amvrakikós Gulf***, Axios-Aliakmonasas Deltas***, Evros Delta***, Lake Kerkini***, Nestos Delta***, Porto Lagos area***.

GREEK IS Corfu***, Crete** (winter), Kos*** (passage), Lesvos***, Rhodes***.

HUNGARY Hortobágy NP*** (summer), Kiskunság NP*** (summer), Szeged Fishponds*** (summer).

ISRAEL Bet Shean Valley***, Eilat***, Hula Reserve***, Ma'agan Mikhael***.

ITALY Circeo NP***, Gargano Peninsula***, Isonzo Regional Park***, Maremma Regional Park***, Orbetello Reserve***, Po Delta***, San Giuliano Reserve*** (passage).

JORDAN Azraq***, Ghadir Burqu'*.

LEBANON Aamiq Marshes** (passage), Palm Is** (passage), Qaraoun Lake** (passage).

MADEIRA*.

MALTA* (passage).

MOROCCO Agadir and the Sous Plain***, Asilah and Oued Loukkos***, Merja Zerga***, Oualidia*** (passage, winter), Oued Massa*** (passage, winter), Tafilalt* (passage).

NETHERLANDS Lauwersmeer*** (passage), Oostvaadersplassen*** (passage), Terschelling*** (summer), Texel*** (summer), Zwanenwater*** (summer).

POLAND Szczecin Bay area* (passage).

PORTUGAL Cape St Vincent* (autumn), Castro Marim***, Ria Formosa***, Sado Estuary***, Santo André Lagoon***, Tagus Estuary***.

ROMANIA Danube Delta*** (summer), Dobrudja*** (summer, passage).

RUSSIA Kalmykia*** (summer), Volga Delta*** (summer).

SARDINIA Cagliari wetlands***, Oristano wetlands***, San Pietro I***.

SICILY Lago di Lentini***, Vendicari***.

SPAIN Aiguamolls de l'Empordá***, Cabo de Gata***, Cádiz Lagoons***, Coto Doñana***, Ebro Delta***, Guadalhorce Estuary***, Llobregat Delta***, Santa Pola***, Tablas de Daimiel***.

SWEDEN Falsterbo* (summer, passage).

SWITZERLAND Fanel NR* (passage).

SYRIA Dayr al-Zawr***, Sabkhat al-Jabbul***.

TUNISIA Cap Bon Peninsula***, Chott el Djerid***, Kelbia Lake***, Lake Ichkeul***, Tunis***.

TURKEY Göksu Delta***, Kızılırmak Delta*, Kocaçay Delta*, Kulu Gölü*, Manyas Gölü*, Sultan Marshes*, Ulubat Gölü*.

UKRAINE Dunay Delta*** (summer), Syvash Bay*** (summer,

Lesser Sand Plover (Mongolian Plover)
Charadrius mongolus

ES Mig

Range: A rare but regular passage and winter visitor to the Red Sea coast of Egypt from its C Asian breeding grounds.

Subspecies: Birds occurring in the Western Palearctic probably belong to race *pamirensis*, breeding in Tajikistan and Kyrgyzstan and wintering from E Africa to W India.

Tips: Very difficult to see in the Western Palearctic; try sandy shores and mudflats on the Red Sea coast of Egypt, where it may associate with Greater Sand Plover.

Site:
EGYPT Hurghada** (passage, winter).

Greater Sand Plover
Charadrius leschenaultii

Summer **SD FG** passage and winter **ES   Mig**

Range: Main breeding range is in C Asia but isolated populations occur in Turkey, principally in C Anatolia and in the S and E of the country. Has also bred in Armenia, the Middle East and Egypt. Passage and winter birds occur in Egypt and Sinai, the Middle East and Cyprus.

Subspecies: Race breeding in most of Western Palearctic is *columbinus*, replaced by the *crassirostris* around parts of the Caspian coast.

Tips: Small numbers make this a rather difficult species to see in the Western Palearctic. Breeds on salt steppe, semi-desert and dry plateaux; also occurs on sandy shores and estuaries on passage and in winter.

Sites:

ARMENIA Armash Fishponds** (passage).
CYPRUS (passage, winter).
EGYPT Hurghada*** (passage, winter), Nile Delta** (winter), Sharm el Sheikh*** (passage), Suez area*** (passage), Wadi el Natrun*** (passage), Zaranik*** (passage).
GREECE Evros Delta* (passage).
ISRAEL Eilat*** (passage), Ma'agan Mikhael*** (summer, passage), Tel Shiqmona* (winter).

JORDAN Aqaba* (passage), Azraq*** (summer, passage), Ghadir Burqu'* (summer).
LEBANON Palm Is* (passage).
SYRIA Bahrat Homs*** (summer), Sabkhat al-Jubbal*** (summer), Tadmur and Sabkhat Muh** (summer).
TURKEY Göksu Delta*** (summer, passage), Kulu Gölü*** (summer), Sultan Marshes*** (summer).

Caspian Plover
Charadrius asiaticus

SD FG FW   Mig

Range: A rare and sporadic breeder in S Russia, between the Sea of Azov and the Caspian, and in W Kazakhstan but precise range little known. Departs breeding range in late Jul–Aug and returns Feb–Apr. Rarely observed on passage, especially in autumn, which is presumed to be rapid and accomplished with few stopovers. Passage birds recorded in Cyprus, Turkey, Israel, Jordan and Egypt.
Tips: Breeds on salt and Artemisia steppes, often near water, also on riverbanks, lake margins and farmland.

Sites:

CYPRUS (passage).
EGYPT Hurghada* (passage).
ISRAEL Arava Valley* (passage), Eilat* (passage).

JORDAN Aqaba* (passage), Azraq (spring), Ghadir Burqu' (passage).
RUSSIA Kalmykia** (passage), Volga Delta* (passage).
TURKEY Van Gölü (passage).

Dotterel (Eurasian Dotterel)
Charadrius morinellus

Summer **M T** passage **FG**   Mig

Range: Main breeding range is N Scandinavia, the Kola and Kanin peninsulas, in S Novaya Zemlya and the Urals. Isolated populations breed in Scotland, the Netherlands, the C Apennines and C Finland, and breeding occurs irregularly at sites usually used as migration stopovers such as in the Pyrenees and Alps. Present in breeding range mainly May–Sep and migrates in groups known as 'trips', which often pause at traditional sites. Winters in Spain (rare) and from Morocco to the Middle East.
Tips: Breeds on tundra and in mountains, but more easily seen on passage, when regularly stops on farmland, (particularly pea fields), airfields or heaths.

Sites:

ANDORRA** (passage, rare in summer).
CANARY IS* (passage, winter).
CORSICA Asco Valley* (passage).
CZECH REPUBLIC Jeseníky Mts* (summer, passage), Krkonoše NP* (passage).
DENMARK Skagen*** (passage), Skallingen-Blåvandshuk** (passage).

FINLAND Kilpisjärvi Saana*** (summer), Lake Inari*** (summer), Lemmenjoki NP*** (summer), Oulanka*** (summer), Pallas-Ounastunturi NP*** (summer), Urho Kekkonen NP*** (summer).
FRANCE Camargue** (passage), Cap Gris Nez* (passage), Ouessant** (passage), Golfe

du Morbihan* (passage), Marais Poitevin* (passage).

GREAT BRITAIN Cairngorms and Speyside** (summer), N Norfolk coast* (passage), Pembrokeshire Is* (autumn), Portland* (passage), Scilly** (passage), Shetland Is* (passage).

HUNGARY Hortobágy NP** (autumn).

ISRAEL Arava Valley* (passage, winter) Nizzana* (winter), Urim*** (winter).

ITALY Abruzzo NP* (summer), Sibillini NP (summer), Stelvio NP* (passage).

JORDAN Azraq* (winter), Ghadir Burqu' (winter).

LEBANON Aammiq Marshes* (passage), Qaraoun Lake** (passage, winter).

MALTA* (passage).

MOROCCO Oued Massa* (winter).

NETHERLANDS Lauwersmeer* (passage), Oostvaardersplassen** (spring).

NORWAY Dovrefjell NP*** (summer), Fokstumyra*** (summer), Hardangervidda NP*** (summer), Rondane NP*** (summer), Slettnes* (summer), Varanger*** (summer).

POLAND Bieszczady NP* (autumn).

PORTUGAL Cape St Vincent** (autumn).

RUSSIA Kola Peninsula*** (summer).

SPAIN Aiguamolls de L'Empordá* (passage), Coto Doñana* (passage), Zaragoza Steppes** (passage).

SWEDEN Abisko NP*** (summer), Ammarnäs*** (summer), Falsterbo* (autumn), Getterön* (passage).

SWITZERLAND Flims** (autumn), Swiss NP* (passage).

SYRIA Tadmur and Sabkhat Muh*** (winter).

TUNISIA Kelbia Lake** (passage, winter), Lake Ichkeul* (passage).

TURKEY Kızılırmak Delta (passage), Sultan Marshes* (passage), Van Gölü (passage).

UKRAINE Syvash Bay*** (passage).

Spur-winged Lapwing (Spur-winged Plover)
Vanellus spinosus   FW BW (FG) (ES)   Mig Res

Range: Breeds in NE Greece and in scattered pockets in C, S and E Turkey, and N Syria, Israel, W Jordan and the Nile Valley of Egypt. Decreasing in Greece but has recently bred again in Cyprus. Northernmost breeders are migrants, departing in Aug–early Oct to winter in range of southern breeders and returning mid Mar to mid Apr. Small numbers regularly pass through Cyprus and Crete.

Tips: Found at margins of fresh, brackish and saltwater, farmland and, sometimes on islands in estuaries.

Sites:
CYPRUS (summer, passage).

EGYPT Abu Simbel***, Aswan***, Luxor***, Faiyum***, Nile Delta***, Sharm el Sheikh***, Suez area***, Wadi el Natrun***, Zaranik***.

GREECE Evros Delta*** (summer), Nestos Delta*** (summer), Porto Lagos area* (summer).

GREEK IS Lesvos* (passage).

ISRAEL Arava Valley***, Bet Shean Valley***, Eilat**, Hula Reserve***, Jezreel Valley***, Ma'agan Mikhael***, Nizzana***, Urim***.

JORDAN Aqaba**, Azraq*.

LEBANON Palm Is (passage).

SYRIA Bahrat Homs***, Dayr al-Zawr***.

TURKEY Bafa Gölü*** (summer), Birecik-Halfeti* (summer), Bulanik* (summer), Dalyan*** (summer), Göksu Delta*** (summer), Kulu Gölü*** (passage), Manyas Gölü*** (summer), Sultan Marshes*** (summer), Uluabat Gölü*** (summer).

Red-wattled Lapwing
Vanellus indicus   FG FW   Res (Dis)

Range: In the Western Palearctic breeds only along the Tigris and Euphrates rivers in Iraq, and in extreme SE Turkey, in the Cizre area, where discovered in 1983.
Tips: Occurs in open farmland, often near water, and frequently on islands in rivers and in flooded meadows.

Site:
TURKEY Cizre***.

Sociable Lapwing (Sociable Plover)
Vanellus gregarius   FG (FW)   Mig

Range: Breeds in S Russia and Kazakhstan, departing breeding areas in Aug–Nov and crosses Turkey, the Middle East and Egypt, returning late Mar–early May.
Tips: Has declined strongly in recent years. Search dry grassy steppes, cultivated land and Artemisia scrub, often found near water but rarely in coastal areas. Breeds in loose colonies and always gregarious.

Sites:
EGYPT Abu Simbel* (passage).
GREECE Evros Delta* (passage).
ISRAEL Arava Valley* (passage), Bet Shean Valley* (passage, winter), Hula Reserve** (passage, winter), Jezreel Valley* (passage), Urim** (winter).

JORDAN Azraq* (winter).
RUSSIA Kalmykia** (passage), Volga Delta** (passage).
SYRIA Lake Assad** (passage).
TURKEY Kızılırmak Delta (passage), Van Gölü (passage).

White-tailed Lapwing (White-tailed Plover)
Vanellus leucurus   FW BW (FG) Mig

Range: In our region breeds N of the Caspian in Kazakhstan and has recently expanded range westwards with breeding reported in S and C Turkey, C Syria, Armenia and Azerbaijan, occasionally in Jordan, and bred in Romania in 2000–2002. Departs breeding grounds in Sep and is a rare passage migrant through the Middle East. Small numbers winter in the Nile Valley and returns N in Mar–Apr.

Tips: Occurs in areas of sparse vegetation and short grass near fresh, brackish or saltwater and sometimes breeds coloni–ally. Migrates in small flocks of usually fewer than five birds.

Sites:
ARMENIA Armash Fishponds** (summer).
AZERBAIJAN Kura Valley Salt-lakes*** (summer).
EGYPT Abu Simbel** (passage, winter), Aswan**(passage, winter), Faiyum** (passage), Luxor** (passage), Zaranik* (passage).
GREECE Evros Delta* (passage).
ISRAEL Arava Valley* (passage), Bet Shean Valley* (passage), Eilat* (passage).

JORDAN Aqaba (passage), Azraq* (summer, passage).
RUSSIA Kalmykia** (passage), Volga Delta* (passage).
SYRIA Dayr al-Zawr*** (summer).
TURKEY Birecik-Halfeti (passage), Göksu Delta* (summer, passage), Sultan Marshes (passage).

Temminck's Stint
Calidris temminckii   FW (ES) Mig

Range: Breeds widely in N Scandinavia and from the Kola Peninsula eastwards on the Arctic coast of Russia. Very small numbers summer in Scotland but confirmed breeding is rare, and has recently bred in Estonia. Within our region winters around the Mediterranean and in the Nile Valley. Occurs on passage over most of the region but scarce in Britain with c.100 records per annum Adults depart breeding grounds in Jul, juveniles in Aug and most pass through Europe late Jul–late Sep. Return is mainly mid Apr to mid May.

Tips: Breeds on sheltered coasts or by tundra pools, often in willow scrub. On passage and in winter search freshwater margins with open mud and nearby vegetation, in winter also on sheltered estuaries and saltmarshes. Look for characteristic 'towering' flight when flushed, accompanied by distinctive call.

Sites:

ARMENIA Armash Fishponds* (passage), Lake Sevan* (passage).

AUSTRIA Lake Neusiedl*** (passage).

AZERBAIJAN Kura Valley Salt-lakes*** (passage).

BALEARIC IS Mallorca** (passage).

BULGARIA Burgas area*** (passage), Lake Durankulak*** (passage), Lake Shabla*** (passage), Lake Srebarna*** (passage), Ropotamo NP*** (passage).

CANARY IS* (passage).

CORSICA Biguglia Lake* (passage), Cap Corse* (passage).

CZECH REPUBLIC Lednice*** (passage), Nové Mlýny*** (passage), Soutok** (passage), Třeboňsko*** (passage).

DENMARK Amager*** (passage), Bornholm-Christiansø*** (passage), Rømø** (passage), Skagen*** (passage), Skallingen-Blåvandshuk*** (passage), Vadehavet* (passage).

EGYPT Abu Simbel*** (passage), Aswan*** (passage), Faiyum*** (passage), Luxor*** (passage), Nile Delta*** (passage), Suez area*** (passage), Wadi el Natrun*** (passage), Zaranik** (passage).

ESTONIA Matsalu Bay*** (summer, passage).

FINLAND Kevo NR*** (summer), Kilpisjärvi Saana*** (summer), Kuusamo*** (summer), Lake Inari*** (summer), Lemmenjoki NP*** (summer), Liminganlahti*** (summer), Pallas-Ounastunturi NP*** (summer), Patvinsuo NP*** (passage), Urho Kekkonen NP*** (summer), Viikki*** (passage).

FRANCE Camargue** (passage), Dombes** (passage), Fôret d'Orient* (passage), Gruissan** (passage), Île d'Oléron* (passage), La Brenne* (passage), Lac du Der-Chantecoq** (passage), Sologne* (autumn), Somme Estuary** (passage).

GERMANY Kuhkopf** (passage).

GREAT BRITAIN Dungeness* (autumn), Minsmere* (autumn), N Norfolk coast** (autumn), Portland* (autumn).

GREECE Amvrakikós Gulf*** (passage), Axios-Aliakmonas Deltas*** (passage), Evros Delta*** (passage), Lake Kerkini*** (passage), Mikrí Prespa NP*** (passage), Nestos Delta*** (passage), Porto Lagos area*** (summer).

GREEK IS Corfu*** (passage), Crete** (passage), Kos* (passage), Lesvos*** (passage), Rhodes* (passage).

HUNGARY Biharugra*** (passage), Hortobágy NP*** (passage), Kardoskút*** (passage), Kisbalaton*** (passage), Kiskunság NP*** (passage), Lake Fertö*** (passage), Lake Velence*** (passage), Szeged Fishponds*** (passage).

IRELAND Akeragh Lough* (autumn), Tacumshin Lake* (autumn).

ISRAEL Arava Valley*** (passage), Bet Shean Valley*** (passage), Hula Reserve*** (passage), Jezreel Valley*** (passage), Ma'agan Mikhael*** (passage, winter).

ITALY Gargano Peninsula* (passage), Lake Massaciuccoli* (passage), Maremma Regional Park** (passage), Orbetello Reserve** (passage), Po Delta*** (passage).

JORDAN Azraq** (passage).

LATVIA Cape Kolka*** (passage), Lake Engure** (passage), Lake Lubana*** (passage), Lake Pape*** (passage).

LEBANON Aamiq Marshes*** (passage), Palm Is** (passage), Qaraoun Lake** (passage).

LITHUANIA Cepkeliai NR*** (passage), Kirsiu Peninsula*** (passage), Zuvintas NR*** (passage).

MACEDONIA Lakes Ohrid and Prespa*** (passage).

MALTA ** (passage).

MOLDOVA Manta Flooplain** (passage).

MOROCCO Essaouira* (passage), Merja Zerga*** (passage).

NETHERLANDS Lauwersmeer* (passage), Oostvaadersplassen* (passage), Texel* (passage), Zwanenwater (passage).

NORWAY Dovrefjell NP*** (summer), Fokstumyra*** (summer), Hardangervidda NP*** (summer), Rondane NP*** (summer), Slettnes* (summer), Stabbursdalen NP*** (summer), Varanger*** (summer, passage).

POLAND Gdańsk Bay* (passage), Milicz Fishponds* (passage), Szczecin Bay area** (passage).

PORTUGAL Castro Marim* (passage), Ria Formosa* (passage), Sado Estuary** (passage) Santo André Lagoon* (passage), Tagus Estuary** (summer).

ROMANIA Danube Delta*** (passage), Dobrudja*** (passage), Lake Călăraşi*** (passage), Satchinez*** (passage).

RUSSIA Kalmykia*** (passage), Kola Peninsula*** (summer), Volga Delta*** (passage).

SARDINIA Cagliari wetlands* (passage), Oristano wetlands** (passage).

SICILY Lago di Lentini* (passage), Vendicari* (passage).

SLOVAKIA Senné Fishponds** (passage), Zemplínská Reservoir* (passage).

SPAIN Aiguamolls de l'Empordá*** (passage), Cabo de Gata* (passage), Cádiz Lagoons** (passage), Coto Doñana*** (passage), Ebro Delta*** (passage), Guadalhorce Estuary* (passage), Llobregat Delta** (passage), Tablas de Daimiel** (passage).

SWEDEN Abisko NP*** (summer), Ammarnäs*** (summer), Falsterbo** (passage), Getterön*** (passage), Hornborgasjön*** (passage), Kristianstad*** (passage), Kvismaren** (passage), Öland*** (passage), Store Mosse NP** (passage).

SWITZERLAND Fanel NR** (passage), Klingnau Reservoir* (passage).

SYRIA Bahrat Homs* (passage), Dayr al-Zawr** (passage), Sabkhat al-Jubbal** (passage).

TUNISIA Kelbia Lake** (passage), Lake Ichkeul** (passage).

TURKEY Bafa Gölü** (passage), Bulanik (passage), Dalyan** (passage), Göksu Delta*** (passage), Kızılırmak Delta*** (passage), Kulu Gölü*** (passage), Sultan Marshes*** (passage), Uluabat Gölü*** (passage), Van Gölü** (passage).

UKRAINE Dunay Delta*** (passage), Tiligul Liman*** (passage), Syvash Bay*** (passage).

Pectoral Sandpiper
Calidris melanotos   FW (ES) Mig

Range: A N American and Siberian breeder, which occurs in the Western Palearctic as a rare but regular migrant, and has been recorded throughout the region. Most occur in the British Isles, with over 100 noted in some years, mostly in the SW but with significant numbers in the E, suggesting a Siberian origin. Recorded throughout the year but very rare in midwinter and records clearly peak in Sep–Oct. Displaying males have been recorded in the far NE of the Western Palearctic.

Tips: Prefers freshwater habitats, often in coastal areas with damp grassland, marshes and the margins of ponds and lakes with emergent vegetation.

Sites:

AZORES*** (autumn).
CANARY IS (autumn).
GREAT BRITAIN St Ives Bay** (autumn), Scilly*** (autumn).

IRELAND Akeragh Lough*** (autumn), Belfast Lough*(autumn), North Bull* (autumn), Tacumshin Lake** (autumn).
MADEIRA* (passage).
SPAIN Ebro Delta (autumn).

Purple Sandpiper
Calidris maritima   C (ES) Mig (PMig)

Range: Breeds in Iceland, the Faroes and N Scandinavia, the Kola Peninsula, Svalbard, Franz Josef Land and Novaya Zemlya, and has recently bred in Scotland. Winters around the British Isles and from Norway to Biscay.

Tips: In the N breeds in swampy tundra or on rocky islands and in montane regions, often in scrubby habitats. Most easily found outside the breeding season when strictly coastal, found mainly on rocky coasts, as well as on harbours and piers, and often associates with Ruddy Turnstone.

Sites:

DENMARK Bornholm-Christiansø*** (winter), Hanstholm*** (winter), Skagen*** (passage).
FAROE IS* (summer).
FINLAND Kilpisjärvi Saana*** (summer).
FRANCE Baie de Vilaine** (winter), Île d'Oléron*** (passage, winter), Ouessant*** (passage, winter), Sept Îles*** (winter).
GERMANY Heligoland*** (passage).
GREAT BRITAIN Anglesey*** (winter), Flamborough Head*** (winter), N Norfolk coast* (winter), Scilly*** (winter), Orkney Is*** (passage, winter), Outer Hebrides*** (passage, winter), Portland*** (winter), St Ives Bay*** (winter), Shetland Is*** (passage, winter), Spurn Peninsula* (passage, winter).
ICELAND Breiðafjörður*** (summer), Lake Mývatn*** (summer), Northwest Peninsula*** (summer), Olfusar Delta*** (passage, winter), Reykjanes Peninsula***, Westmann Is*** (winter).

IRELAND Belfast Lough*** (passage, winter), Mullet Peninsula*** (passage, winter), North Bull*** (winter), Strangford Lough*** (passage, winter).
NETHERLANDS Lauwersmeer*** (winter).
NORWAY Dovrefjell NP*** (summer), Fokstumyra*** (summer), Hardangervidda NP*** (summer), Lofoten Is*** (winter), Rondane NP*** (summer), Slettnes*** (summer), Utsira*** (passage, winter), Varanger***.
POLAND Gdańsk Bay*** (passage, winter), Szczecin Bay area** (passage, winter).
RUSSIA Kola Peninsula*** (summer).
SPAIN Coto Doñana (passage).
SVALBARD* (summer).
SWEDEN Abisko NP*** (summer), Ammarnäs*** (summer), Falsterbo* (winter), Getterön*** (passage, winter), Gotland*** (passage, winter), Öland*** (passage, winter), Padjelanta NP*** (summer), Tärnasjön*** (summer).

Broad-billed Sandpiper
Limicola falcinellus   FW (ES)   Mig

Range: Breeds in N Scandinavia and adjacent N Russia, and on the Kola and Kanin peninsulas. Migrates through E Europe, especially via the E Mediterranean, the Black and Caspian Seas, in late Jul–Sep. Small numbers are regular in W Europe, mainly in S France, in May and Aug.
Tips: Breeds in extensive bog lands with sedges and cotton-grass and best looked for on breeding grounds in early spring when displaying, otherwise rather a secretive bird. On passage search marshes and muddy pools and lakes, and further south may occur on muddy estuaries.

Sites:

ARMENIA Armash Fishponds** (passage), Lake Sevan** (passage).

BULGARIA Burgas area*** (passage), Lake Durankulak*** (passage), Lake Shabla*** (passage), Ropotamo NP*** (passage).

CYPRUS* (passage).

DENMARK Amager* (passage).

EGYPT Zaranik** (passage, winter).

FINLAND Kevo NR*** (summer), Kilpisjärvi Saana*** (summer), Kuusamo*** (summer), Lake Inari*** (summer), Lemmenjoki NP*** (summer), Liminganlahti*** (passage), Oulanka NP* (summer), Pallas-Ounastunturi NP*** (summer), Patvinsuo NP*** (summer), Urho Kekkonen NP*** (summer), Viikki*** (passage).

FRANCE Camargue* (winter).

GERMANY Rügen** (passage), Wattenmeer* (passage).

GREECE Amvrakikós Gulf* (passage), Axios-Aliakmonas Deltas** (passage), Evros Delta** (passage), Lake Kerkini** (passage), Mikrí Prespa NP* (passage), Nestos Delta*** (passage), Porto Lagos area* (passage).

GREEK IS Kos** (passage), Lesvos** (passage).

HUNGARY Hortobágy NP** (passage), Kiskunság NP* (passage).

ISRAEL Arava Valley* (passage), Bet Shean Valley** (passage), Eilat*** (passage), Ma'agan Mikhael*** (passage).

JORDAN Azraq** (passage).

LITHUANIA Kirsiu Peninsula*** (passage). Manta Floodplain (passage).

NORWAY Øvre Pasvik NP*** (summer), Varanger (passage).

POLAND Gdańsk Bay** (passage), Milicz Fishponds (passage), Szczecin Bay area* (passage).

ROMANIA Danube Delta*** (passage), Dobrudja*** (passage), Lake Călăraşi* (passage), Satchinez* (passage).

RUSSIA Kalmykia*** (passage), Kola Peninsula*** (summer), Volga Delta*** (passage).

SICILY Vendicari* (passage).

SLOVAKIA Senné Fishponds* (passage), Zemplínská Reservoir* (passage).

SPAIN Ebro Delta (passage).

SWEDEN Abisko NP*** (summer), Ammarnäs*** (summer), Falsterbo** (passage), Gammelstadsviken** (passage), Getterön** (passage), Gotland*** (passage), Hornborgasjön* (passage), Kristianstad* (passage), Öland*** (passage), Store Mosse NP* (passage), Tåkern** (passage).

TURKEY Bafa Gölü (passage), Bulanik (passage), Dalyan (passage), Göksu Delta** (passage), Kızılırmak Delta** (passage), Kulu Gölü** (passage), Van Gölü*** (passage).

UKRAINE Dunay Delta*** (passage), Tiligul Liman*** (passage), Syvash Bay*** (passage).

Jack Snipe
Lymnocryptes minimus

CF FW Mig

Range: Breeds in N Scandinavia, possibly the Baltic states, and across N Russia to the Urals, with a small, isolated population in C Sweden. Autumn movements are mainly SW, from mid Sep to mid Nov. In winter found in the British Isles and from S Scandinavia to NW Africa, SE Europe and Turkey. Return movements commence as early as Feb, but generally occur in Apr–May. Scarce on passage throughout most of Europe.

Tips: Breeds in forest bogs and marshy woodland. In winter search wet farmland, muddy margins of lakes and rivers, and the upper reaches of estuaries but the species does not occur in brackish or saltwater. Shy and often crepuscular, usually seen only when flushed, but frequently runs rather than flies. Sometimes flies only when almost trodden on and has short, straight and low flight, unlike zigzagging or towering of Common Snipe.

Sites:

BALEARIC IS Mallorca** (winter).
BELGIUM Het Zwin** (winter).
BULGARIA Burgas area*** (passage, winter), Lake Durankulak*** (passage, winter), Lake Shabla*** (passage, winter), Lake Srebarna*** (passage).
CANARY IS* (passage, winter).
CORSICA Biguglia Lake* (passage).
CYPRUS* (passage).
DENMARK Amager*** (passage, winter), Bornholm-Christiansø*** (passage), Møn-Falster*** (passage, winter), Ringkøbing Fjord*** (passage, winter), Rømø** (passage, winter), Skagen*** (passage), Skallingen-Blåvandshuk*** (passage, winter), Vadehavet* (passage, winter).
EGYPT Aswan** (passage, winter), Faiyum* (passage), Luxor** (passage, winter), Nile Delta* (winter), Sharm el Sheikh* (passage), Wadi el Natrun**(passage, winter), Zaranik** (passage).
ESTONIA Matsalu Bay*** (passage).
FINLAND Kevo NR*** (summer), Kuusamo*** (summer), Lake Inari*** (summer), Lemmenjoki NP*** (summer), Liminganlahti*** (summer), Oulanka NP*** (summer), Pallas-Ounastunturi NP*** (summer), Patvinsuo NP*** (summer),

Urho Kekkonen NP*** (summer), Viikki*** (passage).
FRANCE Baie de Bourgneuf* (winter), Baie du Mont-St-Michel* (winter), Camargue** (passage), Dombes** (passage), Forêt d'Orient*** (passage, winter), Golfe du Morbihan*** (passage, winter), Île d'Oléron* (winter), La Brenne** (passage, winter), Marais Poitevin* (winter), Romelaere NR* (winter), Sologne*** (autumn, winter), Somme Estuary*** (winter), Teich Reserve*** (passage, winter).
GERMANY Kuhkopf* (passage), Rügen*** (passage).
GREAT BRITAIN Dungeness* (autumn, winter), Islay* (winter), Minsmere** (autumn, winter), N Norfolk coast*** (autumn, winter), Outer Hebrides* (winter), Portland* (autumn, winter), Scilly*** (autumn, winter), Shetland Is** (autumn), Spurn Peninsula* (passage, winter).
GREECE Amvrakikós Gulf** (passage), Axios-Aliakmonas Deltas* (passage), Evros Delta* (passage), Lake Kerkini** (passage), Mikrí Prespa NP*** (passage), Nestos Delta*** (passage), Porto Lagos area** (passage).
GREEK IS Kos** (passage), Lesvos** (passage, winter).

HUNGARY Biharugra*** (passage), Hortobágy NP*** (passage), Kardoskút*** (passage), Kisbalaton*** (passage), Kiskunság NP*** (passage), Lake Fertö*** (passage), Lake Velence*** (passage), Szeged Fishponds** (passage).

IRELAND Akeragh Lough* (passage, winter), Belfast Lough** (winter), North Bull** (winter), Strangford Lough* (passage, winter), Tacumshin Lake** (passage, winter).

ISRAEL Arava Valley*** (passage), Bet Shean Valley*** (passage, winter), Jezreel Valley*** (passage, winter), Ma'agan Mikhael*** (passage, winter).

ITALY Circeo NP*** (winter), Gargano Peninsula*** (passage, winter), Maremma Regional Park** (passage), Monte Conero* (passage, winter), Orbetello Reserve** (passage, winter), Po Delta*** (passage, winter).

JORDAN Azraq* (winter).

LATVIA Cape Kolka*** (passage), Lake Lubana*** (passage), Lake Pape*** (passage).

LEBANON Aammiq Marshes*** (passage), Qaraoun Lake** (passage).

LITHUANIA Cepkeliai NR*** (passage), Kirsiu Peninsula*** (passage), Zuvintas NR*** (passage).

MACEDONIA Lakes Ohrid and Prespa* (passage, winter).

MADEIRA (passage).

MALTA* (passage, winter).

MOLDOVA Manta Floodplain** (passage).

MOROCCO Merja Zerga*** (passage, winter), Oualidia** (passage, winter).

NETHERLANDS Lauwersmeer** (passage, winter), Oostvaardersplassen** (passage, winter), Texel* (passage, winter), Zwanenwater* (passage, winter).

NORWAY Lista*** (passage), Øvre Pasvik NP*** (summer), Utsira* (passage), Varanger (summer).

POLAND Biebrza Marshes*** (summer), Gdańsk Bay*** (passage). Milicz Fishponds*** (passage), Słońsk** (passage, winter), Szczecin Bay area** (passage).

ROMANIA Danube Delta*** (passage), Dobrudja*** (passage), Lake Călăraşi*** (passage), Satchinez*** (passage).

RUSSIA Kalmykia* (passage), Kola Peninsula*** (summer), Volga Delta*** (passage).

SARDINIA Cagliari wetlands* (passage, winter), Oristano wetlands* (passage, winter).

SICILY Lago di Lentini* (passage, winter), Vendicari* (passage, winter).

SLOVAKIA Senné Fishponds*** (passage), Zemplínská Reservoir* (passage).

SPAIN Aiguamolls de L'Empordá* (passage), Cádiz Lagoons*** (passage, winter), Coto Doñana*** (passage, winter), Ebro Delta* (passage), Guadalhorce Estuary** (winter), Llobregat Delta* (passage).

SWEDEN Abisko NP*** (summer), Falsterbo* (passage), Gammelstadsviken*** (summer), Getterön*** (passage, winter), Gotland*** (passage), Hornborgasjön*** (passage), Kristianstad*** (passage), Store Mosse NP*** (summer), Tåkern*** (passage).

SWITZERLAND Fanel NR* (passage), Klingnau Reservoir** (passage, winter).

TURKEY Dalyan (passage), Göksu Delta (passage), Kızılırmak Delta* (passage), Kulu Gölü (passage), Van Gölü (passage).

UKRAINE Dunay Delta*** (passage), Tiligul Liman* (passage), Syvash Bay*** (passage).

Great Snipe
Gallinago media   CF FW   Mig

Range: Breeds in montane Scandinavia, and from Belarus and N Ukraine across Russia to the Urals. Also breeds in small numbers in E Poland and the Baltic states. Occurs on passage over much of C and E Europe, but scarce in SW Asia and NE Africa but is generally rarely seen on migration. Departs breeding areas early Aug–Nov and returns in Mar–May.

Tips: Breeds in marshes and grassy areas in wooded tundra and areas of birch and conifer scrub. Visit a traditional lek site, some of which have excellent viewing facilities. Probably the best site for this declining species is the Biebrza Marshes of Poland, where the facilities permit the snipe to be observed without disturbance. Outside the breeding season occurs in wet grassland and marshes, but often on drier ground than Common Snipe. Has brief, low and straight flight when flushed, unlike towering or zigzagging of Common Snipe.

Sites:

BELARUS Belovezhskaya Pushcha NP*** (summer), Berezinsky Reserve*** (summer), Prypyatsky NP*** (summer).
BULGARIA Burgas area*** (passage), Lake Srebarna*** (passage).
CYPRUS** (passage).
EGYPT Wadi el Natrun* (passage).
ESTONIA Emajõgi Floodplain*** (summer), Matsalu Bay** (summer).
GEORGIA Javakheti Plateau* (passage).
GREECE Amvrakikós Gulf* (passage), Axios-Aliakmonas Deltas** (passage), Evros Delta* (passage), Lake Kerkini** (passage, winter), Nestos Delta* (passage, winter), Porto Lagos area* (passage, winter).
GREEK IS Corfu* (passage, winter), Crete*** (winter), Kos* (passage), Lesvos* (passage).
JORDAN Azraq (spring).
LATVIA Cape Kolka** (passage), Lake Pape** (passage), Lake Lubana*** (summer, passage).
LEBANON Aammiq Marshes* (spring), Palm Is* (spring), Qaraoun Lake* (spring).
LITHUANIA Cepkeliai NR*** (summer), Kirsiu Peninsula*** (summer, passage), Lake Kretuonas (summer), Zuvintas NR*** (summer).

MALTA (passage).
MOLDOVA Balatina** (passage), Manta Flooplain** (passage).
NORWAY Dovrefjell NP*** (summer), Fokstumyra*** (summer), Hardangervidda NP** (summer).
POLAND Biebrza Marshes*** (summer), Chełm Marshes*** (summer).
ROMANIA Danube Delta** (passage), Dobrudja** (passage).
RUSSIA Oka Valley*** (summer), Volga Delta** (passage).
SLOVAKIA Zemplínská Reservoir* (passage).
SWEDEN Ammarnäs*** (summer), Falsterbo (passage), Getterön*** (summer), Hornborgasjön** (passage), Kristianstad* (summer, passage), Kvismaren* (passage), Tåkern** (summer, passage), Tarnasjön*** (summer).
TURKEY Bulanik** (passage), Göksu Delta* (passage), Kızılırmak Delta* (passage), Kulu Gölü* (passage), Sultan Marshes* (passage), Ulubat Gölü* (autumn), Van Gölü* (passage).
UKRAINE Dunay Delta* (passage), Syvash Bay*** (passage).

Slender-billed Curlew
Numenius tenuirostris   FW BW ES (FG) Mig

Range: One of the most endangered birds in the world. Breeds in Siberia but precise range unknown, and there have been no recent nesting records. Formerly wintered in Morocco, particularly at Merja Zerga, but few confirmed sightings there since the mid 1990s. A flock of 19 wintered in the Gulf of Manfredonia, in Apulia, Italy, in 1995. Formerly also recorded in winter in Tunisia and was regularly seen on passage throughout SE Europe, Italy and Turkey, most regularly at the Evros Delta in Greece. Recent records in Crete and Hungary, but none anywhere in 2000, although reported from Hungary, in Kiskunság NP, in Apr 2001, and the Hortobágy, in Sep 2002. Very few confirmed records in recent years and the species may be on the very brink of extinction, although one was reported in the Evros Delta in Feb 2004 and another in Mar in Egypt. However, the closely related Eskimo Curlew *N. borealis* continued to be reported long after its supposed extinction, so there may yet be hope.

Tips: Merja Zerga is perhaps still worth checking in winter but it could conceivably turn up at any wetland in SE Europe on passage. Outside the breeding season occurs on fresh, brackish or saline waters, sometimes on drier farmland or estuaries. Vagrants often seen in the company of Eurasian Curlews.

Sites: There are no longer any regular passage or wintering sites but the species has occurred at all of the following sites and it could appear again.

ALBANIA Karavasta Lagoon.
BALEARIC IS Mallorca.
BULGARIA Burgas area.
GREECE Amvrakikós Gulf, Axios-Aliakmonas Deltas, Evros Delta, Nestos Delta, Porto Lagos area.
GREEK IS Kos, Lesvos.
HUNGARY Biharugra Fishponds, Hortobágy NP, Kardoskút, Kiskunság NP.
ITALY Circeo NP, Gargano Peninsula, Lake Massaciuccoli, Maremma Regional Park, Orbetello Reserve.
JORDAN Azraq.

MALTA.
MOROCCO Lac de Sidi Bourhaba (winter), Merja Zerga (winter, mainly Nov to mid Feb), Oualidia (winter), Oued Massa (winter).
ROMANIA Danube Delta, Dobrudja.
RUSSIA Volga Delta.
SICILY Lago di Lentini, Vendicari.
SPAIN Coto Doñana.
TUNISIA Lake Ichkeul.
TURKEY Göksü Delta, Kulu Gölü.
UKRAINE Dunay Delta.
YUGOSLAVIA Carska bara.

TUNISIA   SFAX

Marsh Sandpiper
Tringa stagnatilis   Summer **FW** passage/winter **BW (ES)   Mig**

Range: Main breeding range lies from Belarus and N Ukraine across C Russia to the Urals, but in recent decades has expanded westwards with breeding confirmed in Finland, Latvia and Poland, and Sweden in 2000. A scarce to rare passage migrant across SE Europe, Turkey, the Middle East and NE Africa. Autumn passage occurs Jul–Sep and return movement is in Mar–May. Small numbers winter in Egypt and regularly seen in SW Spain, occasionally in Tunisia.

Tips: Breeds beside freshwater lakes, in marshes and flooded meadows with plentiful grass. Search similar habitats for vagrants, with passage and winter birds also found at brackish sites, but rarely on coasts.

Sites:
AUSTRIA Lake Neusiedl* (passage).
BALEARIC IS Mallorca* (passage).
BULGARIA Burgas area*** (passage), Lake Durankulak*** (passage), Lake Shabla*** (passage), Lake Srebarna*** (passage), Ropotamo NP*** (passage).
CORSICA Biguglia Lake* (passage).
CYPRUS*** (passage).
EGYPT Abu Simbel*** (passage), Aswan*** (passage), Faiyum* (passage), Luxor*** (passage), Nile Delta* (winter), Sharm el Sheikh** (passage), Suez area* (passage), Zaranik* (passage).
FRANCE Camargue* (passage).
GEORGIA Javakheti Plateau** (passage).
GREECE Amvrakikós Gulf* (passage), Axios-Aliakmonas Deltas*** (passage), Evros Delta** (passage), Lake Kerkini** (passage), Nestos Delta** (passage), Porto Lagos area** (passage).
GREEK IS Corfu* (passage), Crete** (passage, mainly spring), Kos* (passage), Lesvos** (passage).
HUNGARY Hortobágy NP** (passage), Kiskunság NP* (passage).
ISRAEL Arava Valley* (passage), Bet Shean Valley** (passage), Eilat*** (passage), Hula Reserve*** (passage), Ma'agan Mikhael*** (passage), Nizzana* (passage).

ITALY Circeo NP** (passage), Massaciuccoli** (passage), Maremma Regional Park** (passage), Orbetello Reserve** (passage), Po Delta** (passage).
JORDAN Aqaba** (passage), Azraq** (passage), Ghadir Burqu' (passage).
LATVIA Lake Lubana* (summer).
LEBANON Aammiq Marshes** (passage), Palm Is* (passage), Qaraoun Lake* (passage).
MALTA* (passage).
NETHERLANDS Oostvaardersplassen (passage).
POLAND Biebrza Marshes* (summer), Gdańsk Bay* (passage), Siemianówka Reservoir* (summer, passage).
PORTUGAL Castro Marim (passage).
ROMANIA Danube Delta*** (passage), Dobrudja*** (summer, passage), Lake Călăraşi** (passage).
RUSSIA Kalmykia** (passage), Oka Valley*** (summer), Volga Delta*** (passage).
SARDINIA Oristano wetlands* (passage).
SICILY Vendicari (passage).
SLOVAKIA Senné Fishponds*** (summer, passage).
SPAIN Aiguamolls de l'Empordá (passage), Cádiz Lagoons* (passage), Coto Doñana* (passage, winter), Ebro Delta (passage), Santa Pola (passage).

SWEDEN Falsterbo (passage).
SYRIA Dayr al-Zawr** (passage).
TUNISIA Cap Bon Peninsula*** (passage), Kelbia Lake** (passage), Lake Ichkeul*** (passage).

TURKEY Göksu Delta*** (passage), Kızılırmak Delta** (passage), Kulu Gölü*** (passage), Van Gölü*** (passage).
UKRAINE Dunay Delta*** (passage), Tiligul Liman*** (passage), Syvash Bay*** (passage).

Terek Sandpiper
Xenus cinereus   Summer **FW** passage/winter **BW ES** **Mig**

Range: Main breeding range is from the Baltic states E across N Russia, with small numbers at the head of Gulf of Bothnia in Finland, and S Belarus and N Ukraine. Occasionally breeds elsewhere in Russia outside main range and has bred in N Norway. There has been a gradual westward expansion since the mid 20th century. A regular migrant through S Russia and Ukraine, rare in the Balkans and a vagrant further W.

Tips: Breeds in marshes and along wooded rivers and lakeshores, post-breeding mainly coastal, usually on estuaries, mudflats and tidal creeks.

Sites:
ARMENIA Armash Fishponds** (passage).
BELARUS Prypyatsky NP** (summer).
EGYPT Hurghada* (passage), Sharm el Sheikh* (passage), Zaranik* (passage).
FINLAND Liminganlahti** (summer).
FRANCE Camargue* (passage).
GEORGIA Javakheti Plateau** (passage).
GREECE Amvrakikós Gulf* (passage), Axios-Aliakmonas Deltas* (passage), Evros Delta* (passage), Nestos Delta** (passage), Porto Lagos area* (passage).
HUNGARY Hortobágy NP* (passage).
ISRAEL Eilat* (passage), Ma'agan Mikhael* (passage).

ITALY Orbetello Reserve* (passage), Po Delta (passage).
LATVIA Lake Lubana (summer).
POLAND Gdańsk Bay* (passage).
ROMANIA Dobrudja* (passage).
RUSSIA Kalmykia* (passage), Oka Valley*** (summer), Volga Delta** (passage).
SICILY Vendicari* (passage).
TURKEY Göksu Delta* (passage), Kulu Gölü** (passage), Van Gölü** (passage).
UKRAINE Tiligul Liman*** (passage), Syvash Bay*** (passage).

Red-necked Phalarope
Phalaropus lobatus

Range: Breeds in Iceland and the Faroes, Shetland and the Outer Hebrides, N Scandinavia and the Arctic coast of Russia. Greenland and Iceland breeders migrate southwards to the W of the British Isles, but wintering grounds unclear, probably off W Africa. Scandinavian birds cross the Gulfs of Finland and Bothnia, then E Europe to the Black and Caspian Seas, wintering in the Indian Ocean. Autumn passage commences late Jun, with juveniles departing Aug–early Sep and often occurs at inland sites.

Tips: Breeds by pools in tundra and montane moors, wintering at sea, often far from land. Away from breeding sites, the best chance of observing the species is to check coastal marshes in autumn or, to a lesser extent, by seawatching from western headlands in the appropriate weather conditions.

Sites:

ARMENIA Armash Fishponds* (passage).
BULGARIA Burgas area** (passage), Lake Durankulak** (passage), Lake Shabla* (passage).
DENMARK Amager* (winter), Hanstholm** (passage), Skallingen-Blåvandshuk* (passage).
EGYPT Hurghada* (passage), Zaranik* (passage).
FAROE IS*** (summer).
FINLAND Kevo NR*** (summer), Kilpisjärvi Saana*** (summer), Kuusamo*** (summer), Lemmenjoki NP*** (summer), Limanganlahti*** (summer), Oulanka NP*** (summer), Pallas-Ounastunturi NP*** (summer), Patvinsuo NP*** (passage), Urho Kekkonen NP*** (summer).
GEORGIA Javakheti Plateau*** (passage).
GREAT BRITAIN Minsmere* (autumn), N Norfolk coast* (autumn), Outer Hebrides* (summer, passage), Shetland Is*** (summer).
GREECE Porto Lagos area* (passage).
HUNGARY Hortobágy NP* (passage), Kiskunság NP* (passage).
ICELAND Breiðafjörður*** (summer), Grímsey** (summer), Jökulsárgljúfur NP*** (summer), Lake Mývatn*** (summer), Northwest Peninsula*** (summer), Olfusar

Delta*** (summer), Reykjanes Peninsula** (summer), Skaftafell NP*** (summer).
IRELAND Mullet Peninsula** (summer, passage).
ISRAEL Bet Shean Valley** (passage).
ITALY Orbetello Reserve* (passage).
JORDAN Azraq* (passage).
LATVIA Cape Kolka*** (passage), Lake Pape*** (passage).
LITHUANIA Kirsiu Peninsula*** (passage).
NETHERLANDS Lauwersmeer* (passage), Oostvaardersplassen* (passage).
NORWAY Dovrefjell NP*** (summer), Fokstumyra*** (summer), Hardangervidda NP*** (summer), Lofoten Is*** (summer, passage), Øvre Pasvik NP*** (summer), Rondane NP*** (summer), Slettnes*** (summer), Varanger*** (summer, passage).
POLAND Biebrza Marshes (passage), Gdańsk Bay** (passage), Szczecin Bay area* (passage).
PORTUGAL Ria Formosa* (passage).
ROMANIA Danube Delta*** (passage), Dobrudja*** (passage).
RUSSIA Kalmykia* (passage), Kola Peninsula*** (summer), Volga Delta*** (passage).

SLOVAKIA Senné Fishponds* (passage).
SPAIN Ebro Delta* (passage).
SVALBARD* (summer).
SWEDEN Abisko NP*** (summer), Ammarnäs*** (summer), Falsterbo** (passage), Gammelstadsviken*** (summer), Getterön*** (passage), Gotland*** (passage), Hornborgasjön** (passage), Öland*** (passage), Padjelanta NP*** (summer), Tärnasjön*** (summer).
TURKEY Kızılırmak Delta** (passage), Kulu Gölü** (passage), Van Gölü*** (passage).
UKRAINE Dunay Delta*** (passage), Syvash Bay*** (passage).

Grey Phalarope (Red Phalarope)
Phalaropus fulicarius

Summer **FW** passage/winter **Sea Mig**

Range: Breeds in Iceland, Svalbard and Novaya Zemlya, but rare and difficult to observe on breeding grounds. Passage entirely maritime and is rarely seen from shore unless storm-driven, usually in Sep–Oct, occasionally Nov. Regular in autumn in Biscay, but a scarce migrant in Britain with fewer than 200 per annum Rarely winters in European waters, being mainly found off W Africa at this season.

Tips: Breeds on tundra, in Iceland on dry, sparsely vegetated ground near pools. Departs breeding areas in Jul–Aug and returns May–Jun. Seawatching from western headlands may produce the species, but pelagic trips from SW England or the Biscay ferries offer the best chance. The Icelandic island of Flatey is the most accessible breeding site but even here a sighting is not guaranteed, and the breeding area is closed to visitors.

Sites:
BAY OF BISCAY* (autumn).
DENMARK Hanstholm* (autumn), Skallingen-Blåvandshuk* (autumn).
FRANCE Ouessant** (autumn).
GREAT BRITAIN Flamborough Head* (autumn), N Norfolk coast* (autumn), Outer Hebrides** (autumn), Portland* (autumn), St Ives Bay*** (autumn), Scilly*** (autumn), Spurn Peninsula* (autumn).
ICELAND Breiðafjörður**(summer), Olfusar Delta* (summer), Reykjanes Peninsula* (summer).
IRELAND Mullet Peninsula** (autumn).
MOROCCO Oualidia* (passage).
PORTUGAL Berlenga Is (autumn), Cape St Vincent* (autumn).
SVALBARD* (summer).

Pomarine Skua
Stercorarius pomarinus

Summer **T Sea** passage/winter **Sea   Mig**

Range: Breeds on coasts of N Russia from the Kanin Peninsula E and on N Novaya Zemlya, and summers on Svalbard and at Varanger in Norway. Small numbers remain in the N Atlantic in winter but most move to seas around the Canaries and Morocco southwards. Passage is mainly through the Atlantic but small numbers are regular in the North and Baltic Seas and in spring in small numbers in the English Channel. Rare in the Mediterranean, the N Red Sea and the Black Sea.

Tips: Breeds on coastal or inland moss tundra but location dependent on fluctuations in lemming population. At sea, outside breeding season, often far from land but seen from many western headlands on passage. Adults depart breeding grounds late Jul–Aug, juveniles in Sep–Oct, passing Britain and W Europe in Aug–Nov, and returning late Apr–May.

Sites:

AZORES** (passage).
BAY OF BISCAY*** (passage).
BULGARIA Burgas area* (passage).
CANARY IS* (passage).
DENMARK Bornholm-Christiansø*** (passage), Hanstholm*** (passage), Møn-Falster*** (passage), Skagen*** (passage), Skallingen-Blåvandshuk*** (passage).
EGYPT Hurghada* (passage), Suez area* (passage), Zaranik** (passage).
FAROE IS*** (passage).
FRANCE Baie de Vilaine* (autumn), Cap Gris Nez** (passage), Île d'Oléron*** (autumn), Ouessant*** (autumn).
GIBRALTAR* (passage).
GREAT BRITAIN Anglesey* (autumn), Dungeness** (spring), Flamborough Head*** (passage), N Norfolk coast*** (passage), Orkney Is** (passage), Outer Hebrides*** (passage), Pembrokeshire Is* (autumn), Portland** (passage), St Ives Bay*** (passage), Scilly*** (passage), Shetland Is** (passage), Spurn Peninsula** (passage).

ICELAND Reykjanes Peninsula*** (autumn).
IRELAND Cape Clear Is*** (passage), Galley Head*** (passage), Kinsale*** (passage), Mullet Peninsula*** (passage).
ISRAEL Eilat** (passage).
ITALY Maremma Regional Park* (passage).
JORDAN Aqaba* (passage).
MADEIRA* (passage).
MALTA (passage).
MOROCCO Oualidia* (passage).
NORWAY Slettnes*** (passage), Varanger*** (passage).
POLAND Gdańsk Bay* (passage).
PORTUGAL Berlenga Is** (autumn), Cape St Vincent** (autumn), Santo André Lagoon* (passage).
RUSSIA Kola Peninsula** (passage).
SICILY Vendicari* (passage).
SPAIN Guadalhorce Estuary (passage).
SVALBARD** (summer).
SWEDEN Falsterbo* (passage), Getterön** (passage), Gotland** (passage), Öland*** (passage), Holmöarna*** (passage).

Arctic Skua
Stercorarius parasiticus

Summer **T C I Sea** passage/winter **Sea   Mig**

Range: Breeds in Iceland and the Faroes, N Scotland, coastal Scandinavia, the Arctic coast of Russia and on Svalbard, Jan Mayen and Novaya Zemlya. Some winter off NW Africa and Iberia but most move further S. Occurs on passage throughout the NW Atlantic, North and Baltic Seas and W Mediterranean, with small numbers in the Black Sea.

Tips: A colonial breeder on lowland wet tundra and rocky islands in N of range and on moors and cliff-tops in the S. At sea, outside breeding season, often far from shore but frequently seen from headlands on passage, mainly in Aug–Sep, occasionally in Oct, and returning Apr–May. Migration is often linked with that of passage Common Terns.

Sites:
AZORES*** (passage).
BAY OF BISCAY*** (passage).
BULGARIA Burgas area*** (passage).
CANARY IS** (passage).
CYPRUS* (passage).
DENMARK Bornholm-Christiansø*** (passage), Hanstholm*** (passage), Møn-Falster*** (passage), Skagen*** (passage), Skallingen-Blåvandshuk*** (passage).
EGYPT Hurghada* (passage), Suez area* (passage), Zaranik** (passage).
FAROE IS*** (summer).
FINLAND Åland Is*** (summer).
FRANCE Baie de Vilaine** (autumn), Cap Gris Nez*** (passage), Île d'Oléron*** (autumn), Ouessant*** (passage), Somme Estuary*** (passage).
GERMANY Heligoland*** (passage).
GIBRALTAR*** (passage).
GREAT BRITAIN Anglesey*** (autumn), Dungeness*** (passage), Flamborough Head*** (passage), Islay*** (passage), Minsmere*** (autumn), N Norfolk coast*** (passage), Orkney Is*** (summer, passage), Outer Hebrides*** (summer, passage), Pembrokeshire Is*** (autumn), Portland*** (passage), Rhum** (passage), St Ives Bay*** (passage), Scilly*** (passage), Shetland Is*** (summer, passage), Spurn Peninsula*** (passage).

ICELAND Breiðafjörður*** (summer), Jökulsárgljúfur NP*** (summer), Lake Mývatn*** (summer), Northwest Peninsula*** (summer), Reykjanes Peninsula*** (summer), Skaftafell NP*** (summer), Westmann Is*** (summer).
IRELAND Cape Clear Is*** (passage), Galley Head*** (passage), Ireland's Eye*** (autumn), Kinsale*** (passage), Mullet Peninsula*** (passage), Saltee Is** (passage).
ISRAEL Eilat** (passage), Ma'agan Mikhael*** (passage), Tel Shiqmona** (autumn).
ITALY Isonzo Regional Park* (passage).
JORDAN Aqaba** (passage).
LATVIA Cape Kolka*** (passage), Lake Pape*** (passage).
LITHUANIA Kirsiu Peninsula*** (passage).
MADEIRA* passage).
MOROCCO Agadir and the Sous Plain** (passage), Oualidia* (passage), Oued Massa* (passage).
NETHERLANDS Terschelling* (passage), Texel* (passage).
NORWAY Lofoten Is*** (summer, passage), Runde*** (summer, passage), Slettnes*** (summer, passage), Utsira*** (summer, passage), Varanger*** (summer).
POLAND Gdańsk Bay** (passage).
PORTUGAL Berlenga Is** (autumn), Cape St

Vincent** (autumn), Castro Marim** (autumn), Santo André Lagoon* (passage).
RUSSIA Kola Peninsula*** (summer, passage), Volga Delta* (passage).
SICILY Vendicari** (passage).
SPAIN Aiguamolls de l'Empordá* (passage), Cabo de Gata* (passage, winter), Coto Doñana* (passage), Ebro Delta* (passage), Guadalhorce Estuary** (passage), Llobregat Delta* (passage), Santa Pola* (passage, winter).
SVALBARD*** (summer).
SWEDEN Falsterbo** (passage), Getterön*** (passage), Gotland** (passage), Holmöarna*** (summer, passage), Öland*** (passage).
SWITZERLAND Grangettes* (passage).
TUNISIA Cap Bon Peninsula*** (passage).
TURKEY Kızılırmak Delta* (passage).

Long-tailed Skua
Stercorarius longicaudus   Summer **T M Sea** passage/winter **Sea   Mig**

Range: Breeds in varying numbers in montane and N Scandinavia and on the Arctic coast of Russia from the Kola Peninsula E, also on Novaya Zemlya and Svalbard. Small numbers sometimes present and may have attempted breeding in N Scotland. Passage occurs throughout NW Atlantic but generally scarce and numbers fluctuate. Uncommon in the Baltic and North Seas with small numbers now regularly recorded moving east in the English Channel in spring. In Britain most occur off the NW in spring and North Sea coast in autumn.

Subspecies Nominate race breeds in Western Palearctic and race *pallescens* from Greenland occurs on passage.

Tips: Nests on tundra above treeline in mountains. Pelagic outside breeding season but many seen from w headlands on passage. Main passage periods are Aug–Sep, fewer in Nov, and again in May. Ferry trips across Biscay in autumn can produce a sighting of this species.

Sites:
BAY OF BISCAY*** (passage).
DENMARK Skagen*** (passage), Skallingen-Blåvandshuk*** (passage).
EGYPT Suez area (passage), Zaranik* (passage).
FAROE IS** (passage).
FINLAND Kevo NR*** (summer), Kilpisjärvi Saana*** (summer), Lake Inari*** (summer), Oulanka NP** (summer), Pallas-Ounastunturi NP*** (summer).
FRANCE Cap Gris Nez* (passage), Ouessant*** (autumn).
GIBRALTAR (passage).
GREAT BRITAIN Anglesey* (autumn), Flamborough Head** (passage), N Norfolk coast* (passage), Orkney Is* (passage), Outer Hebrides** (passage), St Ives Bay* (passage), Scilly** (passage), Shetland Is* (passage), Spurn Peninsula* (passage).
IRELAND Cape Clear Is** (passage), Galley Head* (passage), Mullet Peninsula*** (passage).
ISRAEL Eilat (passage).
JORDAN Aqaba (passage).

MADEIRA* (passage).
NORWAY Hardangervidda NP*** (summer), Lofoten Is*** (summer, passage), Slettnes*** (passage), Stabbursdalen NP* (summer), Varanger*** (summer).
POLAND Gdańsk Bay* (passage).
PORTUGAL Berlenga Is (autumn), Cape St Vincent (autumn).

RUSSIA Kola Peninsula*** (summer, passage).
SPAIN Ebro Delta (autumn).
SVALBARD** (summer).
SWEDEN Abisko NP*** (summer), Ammarnäs*** (summer), Falsterbo* (passage), Getterön* (passage), Padjelanta NP*** (summer), Tärnasjön*** (summer).

Great Skua
Stercorarius skua

Summer **I C Sea** passage/winter **Sea Mig**

Range: Breeding confined to Iceland, the Faroes and in Scotland on many islands and at a few mainland sites. Has bred on Svalbard, in Norway and Russia. Present at colonies late Mar–Sep, wintering in the Atlantic from Biscay to W Africa, with small numbers entering the W Mediterranean and occasional winter records from Europe.

Tips: Breeds on upland moors and grassland, often above high sea-cliffs and near colonies of other seabirds. At sea, outside the breeding season, sometimes far from land but on passage often seen from headlands. Passage occurs off N and W Europe and NW Africa in Aug–Oct and, to a lesser extent, in Mar–Apr. Guaranteed from the Biscay ferries in autumn.

Sites:
BALEARIC IS Mallorca (winter).
BAY OF BISCAY* (passage, winter).
CANARY IS* (winter).
DENMARK Hanstholm*** (passage), Skagen*** (passage), Skallingen-Blåvandshuk*** (passage).
FAROE IS* (summer).
FRANCE Baie de Vilaine** (autumn), Cap Gris Nez*** (passage), Île d'Oléron*** (autumn), Ouessant*** (autumn).
GIBRALTAR**.
GREAT BRITAIN Anglesey*** (autumn), Dungeness*** (passage), Flamborough Head*** (passage), Islay*** (passage), N Norfolk coast*** (passage), Orkney Is*** (summer, passage), Outer Hebrides*** (passage), Pembrokeshire Is*** (autumn), Portland***

(passage), Rhum** (passage), Scilly*** (passage), St Ives Bay*** (passage), Shetland Is*** (summer, passage), Spurn Peninsula*** (passage).
ICELAND Breðafjörður*** (summer), Lake Mývatn* (summer), Northwest Peninsula** (passage), Olfusar Delta*** (summer), Reykjanes Peninsula*** (summer, passage), Skaftafell NP*** (summer), Westmann Is*** (summer).
IRELAND Cape Clear Is*** (passage), Galley Head*** (passage), Ireland's Eye** (autumn), Kinsale*** (passage), Mullet Peninsula*** (passage), Saltee Is** (passage).
MADEIRA* (passage).
MOROCCO Oualidia* (passage), Oued Massa* (passage).

NORWAY Lofoten Is* (passage), Runde*** (summer, passage), Slettnes** (passage), Utsira* (passage), Varanger* (summer). **PORTUGAL** Berlenga Is* (autumn), Cape St Vincent** (autumn), Santo André Lagoon* (passage).

RUSSIA Kola Peninsula* (summer, passage). **SPAIN** Aiguamolls de l'Empordá* (passage, winter), Cabo de Gata* (passage), Coto Doñana*, Ebro Delta* (passage), Guadalhorce Estuary (passage). **SVALBARD**** (summer).

Sooty Gull
Larus hemprichii

I ES U Sea Dis

Range: In our region breeds only on islands in the N Red Sea. A regular non-breeding visitor to the Gulfs of Suez and Aqaba, chiefly in winter but at Eilat has been recorded in May–Jun.

Tips: More coastal than White-eyed Gull, breeding on bare sandy or rocky islands. Often seen around harbours, perching on posts or buoys, and closely associated with man in many areas.

Sites:
EGYPT Hurghada***, Sharm el Sheikh***.
ISRAEL Eilat (passage, winter).
JORDAN Aqaba (passage).

White-eyed Gull
Larus leucophthalmus

I ES Sea (U) Dis

Range: Breeds on islands near Hurghada in the mouth of the Gulf of Suez, Tiran in the Gulf of Aqaba and at 1–2 sites further S but status there unclear. In summer occurs N to the Bitter Lakes and, rarely, the Suez Canal. Most probably disperse S in winter to the Gulf of Aden.

Tips: Strictly marine, found mainly on bare rocky or sandy coasts and islets, breeding colonially on low-lying islands. More maritime than Sooty Gull and spends much time at sea, although it is also seen at harbours and docks.

Sites:
EGYPT Hurghada*** (summer), Suez area*** (summer).

ISRAEL Eilat***.
JORDAN Aqaba***.

Pallas's Gull (Great Black-headed Gull)
Larus ichthyaetus

FW BW Sea Mig

Range: Breeds at scattered sites around the Sea of Azov and in the Volga Delta, and perhaps at lakes midway between the two. Recently discovered breeding further W in Ukraine. In winter occurs in the E Black Sea, Sea of Azov, Caspian Sea and Turkey. Rare in the E Mediterranean and the N Red Sea, but regular in increasing numbers at fish-ponds in Israel and in small numbers in Cyprus.

Tips: Breeds beside lakes and rivers and in deltas, often on islands or in reedbeds. Post-breeding moves to coastal areas, often harbours, following ships into port, sometimes also found on large inland waters, such as reservoirs, at this season. Vagrancy to Europe is increasing and often involves returning and long-staying individuals.

Sites:

ARMENIA Armash Fishponds*** (winter), Lake Sevan*** (winter).
BULGARIA Lake Durankulak* (winter), Lake Shabla* (winter).
CYPRUS** (winter).
EGYPT Faiyum* (passage), Hurghada* (passage), Nile Delta* (winter), Suez area* (passage, winter), Zaranik** (passage, winter).
GEORGIA Javakheti Plateau* (passage).
GREECE Evros Delta* (passage, winter).
GREEK IS Crete* (winter).
HUNGARY Hortobágy NP (passage).

ISRAEL Bet Shean Valley*** (winter), Eilat*** (passage, winter), Hula Reserve*** (passage, winter), Ma'agan Mikhael*** (passage, winter), Tel Shiqmona** (winter).
JORDAN Aqaba** (passage, winter).
LEBANON Palm Is (passage).
ROMANIA Dobrudja (passage, winter).
RUSSIA Volga Delta***.
SYRIA Sabkhat al-Jabbul* (passage).
TURKEY Kızılırmak Delta** (winter).
UKRAINE Syvash Bay*** (summer).

Mediterranean Gull
Larus melanocephalus

FW BW ES Sea Mig Dis

Range: Breeds at very scattered localities in E and SE Europe, the Black Sea and Turkey, but has undergone a recent range expansion and now breeds much more widely around the Mediterranean, Biscay and North Sea. In winter widespread in the Mediterranean and Black Seas, and in smaller numbers N to Denmark and Britain.

Tips: Breeds on estuarine saltmarshes, flooded fields and sparsely vegetated islands. Out of main range search Black-headed Gull or tern colonies for 1–2 pairs of this species. Post-breeding mostly coastal, although some feed on inland grasslands and join mixed gull roosts on inland reservoirs. The most reliable British site is Copt Point, Folkestone, where more than 100 can occur in winter.

Sites:

AUSTRIA Lake Neusiedl* (passage).
BALEARIC IS Mallorca** (passage).
BAY OF BISCAY.
BELGIUM Het Zwin*** (summer).
BULGARIA Albena-Golden Sands*** (passage), Burgas area***, Cape Emine*** (passage), Cape Kaliakra** (passage), Lake Durankulak***, Lake Shabla***, Ropotamo NP***, Strandja Mts*** (passage).
CANARY IS Lanzarote* (passage).
CORSICA Biguglia Lake*** (passage, winter), Cap Corse** (passage).
CROATIA Mljet* (passage).
CYPRUS** (passage, winter).
CZECH REPUBLIC Nové Mlýny*** (summer).
EGYPT Nile Delta* (winter), Zaranik** (passage, winter).
FRANCE Camargue***, Cap Gris Nez* (passage), Gruissan***, Île d'Oléron***, Leucate**, Somme Estuary**.
GEORGIA Kolkheti*** (passage, winter).
GIBRALTAR** (passage, winter).
GREAT BRITAIN Dungeness**, Minsmere**, N Norfolk coast***, Portland**, St Ives Bay**, Spurn Peninsula** (passage).
GREECE Amvrakikós Gulf*** (summer, passage), Axios-Aliakmonas Deltas*** (summer, passage), Evros Delta*** (summer, passage), Lake Kerkini*** (summer, passage), Nestos Delta*** (summer, passage), Porto Lagos area*** (summer, passage).
GREEK IS Corfu***, Crete***, Kos*** (passage, winter), Lesvos*** (passage, winter), Náxos*** (passage), Rhodes*** (passage).
HUNGARY Hortobágy NP*** (summer), Kiskunság NP*** (summer), Szeged Fishponds*** (summer).
IRELAND Belfast Lough* (passage, winter), North Bull* (winter).
ITALY Circeo NP*** (passage, winter), Gargano Peninsula***, Maremma Regional Park*** (passage, winter), Monte Conero*** (passage, winter), Orbetello Reserve*** (passage, winter), Po Delta***.
LEBANON Palm Is** (passage, winter).
MADEIRA (passage).
MALTA** (passage, winter).
MOROCCO Agadir and the Sous Plain** (passage, winter), Essaouira** (passage), Merja Zerga** (passage, winter), Oualidia* (passage, winter), Oued Massa** (passage).
NETHERLANDS Oostvaardersplassen* (passage).
POLAND Gdańsk Bay** (summer, passage), Szczecin Bay area* (summer).
PORTUGAL Cape St Vincent*** (autumn), Castro Marim* (passage), Ria Formosa** (passage, winter), Sado Estuary** (passage, winter), Santo André Lagoon*** (passage), Tagus Estuary*** (passage).
ROMANIA Danube Delta*** (summer, passage), Dobrudja*** (summer, passage).
SICILY Lago di Lentini*** (passage, winter), Vendicari*** (passage, winter).
SLOVAKIA Senné Fishponds** (passage).
SPAIN Cabo de Gata*** (passage, winter), Cádiz Lagoons*** (passage, winter), Coto Doñana*** (passage, winter), Ebro Delta*** (passage, winter), Guadalhorce Estuary***, Llobregat Delta*** (passage, winter), Santa Pola** (passage), Tablas de Daimiel*** (passage).
SWEDEN Falsterbo* (passage).
SWITZERLAND Fanel NR** (passage), Grangettes*** (passage, winter), Klingnau Reservoir** (passage).
SYRIA Lake Assad**.
TUNISIA Cap Bon Peninsula*** (passage), Lake Ichkeul* (winter).
TURKEY Bafa Gölü*** (passage), İstanbul*** (passage), Kulu Gölü*** (summer, passage), Van Gölü (passage).
UKRAINE Dunay Delta*** (passage), Tiligul Liman*** (passage), Syvash Bay*** (summer).

Sabine's Gull
Larus sabini

Range: Breeds in Arctic Siberia, N America and Greenland, and in the Western Palearctic in very small numbers in Svalbard, mainly on Moffen I, and in Franz Josef Land. A scarce passage migrant off Atlantic coasts of NW Europe, with the largest numbers occurring following periods of stormy weather.

Tips: Away from the almost inaccessible tundra breeding areas, this species is pelagic, departing its colonies in late Jul–Aug. It is seen regularly off Ireland and SW England, in smaller numbers in the North Sea, and in Biscay, particularly off Belle Isle. Most are seen in autumn, usually late Aug–early Nov, peaking late Sep–Oct. Some western headlands regularly produce sightings and the species is virtually guaranteed from the Biscay ferries.

Sites:
AZORES* (autumn).
BAY OF BISCAY*** (autumn).
DENMARK Skallingen-Blåvandshuk* (autumn).
FRANCE Baie de Vilaine* (autumn), Cap Gris Nez* (passage), Île d'Oléron* (autumn), Ouessant** (autumn).
GREAT BRITAIN Anglesey* (autumn), Flamborough Head* (autumn), Orkney Is*

(autumn), Portland* (autumn), St Ives Bay*** (autumn), Scilly** (autumn).
IRELAND Cape Clear Is** (autumn), Mullet Peninsula* (autumn).
PORTUGAL Cape St Vincent (autumn).
SVALBARD** (summer).

Slender-billed Gull
Larus genei

Range: Breeds at widely scattered sites around the Mediterranean, Black and Caspian Seas, irregularly in some areas, particularly N Africa, but increasing dramatically in others. Has bred in the Canaries and the Middle East, and recently discovered breeding in Egypt. Present at colonies late Mar–Sep, and post-breeding widespread in the Mediterranean, Black and Red Seas.

Tips: Breeds colonially in river deltas, freshwater lakes and brackish lagoons, also inland salt lakes. Often breeds in association with Gull-billed and Caspian Terns. Mainly coastal outside breeding season.

Sites:

ARMENIA Armash Fishponds*** (summer, passage), Lake Sevan*** (passage).
BALEARIC IS Mallorca* (passage).
BULGARIA Albena-Golden Sands*** (passage), Burgas area***, Cape Emine*** (passage), Cape Kaliakra** (passage), Lake Durankulak** (passage), Lake Shabla*** (passage), Ropotamo NP*** (passage), Strandja Mts*** (passage).
CORSICA Biguglia Lake** (passage, winter).
CYPRUS*** (passage, winter).
EGYPT Aswan** (passage), Faiyum***, Hurghada*** (passage, winter), Luxor** (passage), Nile Delta*** (passage, winter), Sharm el Sheikh*** (passage, winter), Suez area*** (passage, winter), Zaranik***.
FRANCE Camargue*** (summer), Leucate*** (summer).
GREECE Amvrakikós Gulf** (summer, passage), Axios-Aliakmonas Deltas*** (summer, passage), Evros Delta** (passage), Porto Lagos area** (passage).
GREEK IS Corfu* (passage), Lesvos* (passage, winter).
ISRAEL Eilat*** (passage), Ma'agan Mikhael*** (passage, winter), Tel Shiqmona*** (passage).
ITALY Gargano Peninsula***, Po Delta**.

JORDAN Aqaba** (passage), Azraq* (passage, winter).
LEBANON Palm Is* (passage, winter).
MALTA (passage, winter).
MOROCCO Agadir and the Sous Plain*** (passage, winter), Merja Zerga*** (passage, winter), Oued Massa*** (passage, winter).
PORTUGAL Castro Marim* (passage).
ROMANIA Dobrudja** (passage).
RUSSIA Volga Delta*** (summer).
SARDINIA Cagliari wetlands***, Oristano wetlands***, San Pietro I*** (passage, winter).
SICILY Vendicari*** (passage, winter).
SPAIN Cabo de Gata** (passage), Cádiz Lagoons*** (summer), Coto Doñana*** (summer), Ebro Delta***, Santa Pola**.
SYRIA Baath Lake***, Bahrat Homs*** (passage), Dayr al-Zawr** (passage), Lake Assad***, Sabkhat al-Jubbal***.
TUNISIA Cap Bon Peninsula*** (passage, winter), Kelbia Lake** (passage, winter), Lake Ichkeul* (passage), Tunis*** (passage, winter).
TURKEY Dalyan*** (passage), Göksu Delta*** (passage), Kulu Gölü*** (summer, passage), Van Gölü*** (passage).
UKRAINE Dunay Delta*** (summer, passage), Tiligul Liman*** (passage), Syvash Bay*** (summer).

Audouin's Gull
Larus audouinii   I C ES Sea Res Dis (Mig)

Range: Almost endemic to the Mediterranean and, despite a recent population increase and range expansion, one of the world's rarest gulls. Breeds in NW Africa, Spain and the Balearics, off Corsica, the Tuscan archipelago and Sardinia, in the Aegean and Cyprus. Has bred in the Algarve of Portugal since 2001. Winters near breeding colonies, but some disperse to the Atlantic coast of NW Africa. In 2003 recorded for the first time in Britain at Dungeness.

Tips: Look on small islands and, to a lesser extent, mainland cliffs. Coastal outside breeding season, on sandy or rocky shores, sometimes visiting harbours. Migrants pass Gibraltar in Jun-Sep, returning Mar–Apr, but some are usually present all year.

Sites:

BALEARIC IS Formentera***, Ibiza***, Mallorca***, Menorca**.

CANARY IS* (passage, winter).

CORSICA Biguglia Lake* (passage), Cap Corse** (passage), Scandola** (passage).

CYPRUS*.

EGYPT Zaranik* (autumn).

FRANCE Gruissan* (passage), Leucate* (passage).

GIBRALTAR*.

GREECE Evros Delta* (passage), Nestos Delta** (passage), Porto Lagos area* (passage).

GREEK IS Crete***, Kos*** (passage), Lesvos***, Náxos* (passage), Rhodes***.

ITALY Circeo NP** (passage), Monte Conero** (passage), Orbetello Reserve*** (summer, passage), Po Delta* (passage), Tuscan archipelago***.

LEBANON Palm Is (passage).

MOROCCO Agadir and the Sous Plain*** (passage, winter), Essaouira* (passage), Merja Zerga*** (passage, winter), Oualidia* (passage, winter), Oued Massa***.

PORTUGAL Cape St Vincent** (autumn), Castro Marim** (summer, passage).

SARDINIA Cagliari wetlands** (passage, winter), Oristano wetlands*** (passage, winter), San Pietro I***.

SICILY Vendicari*** (passage, winter).

SPAIN Aiguamolls de L'Empordá* (passage), Cabo de Gata*** (passage, winter), Coto Doñana*** (summer, passage), Ebro Delta*** (summer), Guadalhorce Estuary*** (summer, passage), Llobregat Delta*** (summer), Santa Pola***.

TUNISIA Cap Bon Peninsula*** (passage), Lake Ichkeul* (passage).

TURKEY Göksu Delta*** (summer, passage).

Ring-billed Gull
Larus delawarensis   ES Sea Res Dis

Range: A widespread N American species, breeding in C Canada and the NW USA, and on the E coast from Newfoundland to New England, and wintering from Maine to Florida. First recorded in the Western Palearctic in the 1970s and now one of the most frequently seen Nearctic vagrants, especially in the British Isles, NW France and the Azores, but also recorded N to Svalbard, S to Morocco and the Canaries, and E to Bulgaria. Recorded in Britain in all months involving many long-staying, returning individuals but numbers usually peak in winter/early spring. There is now a significant population in the NE Atlantic and breeding is likely to occur in the near future. Hybridisation with Common Gull has been reported.

Tips: The dramatic increase in records is due in part to increased observer awareness but has been assisted by an expanding population in N America. Post-breeding found on lakeshores, riverbanks and coasts. Vagrants often seen at major gull roosts, frequently at harbours, refuse tips and playing fields. Check local birdlines to locate the species.

Sites:

Armenian Gull
Larus armenicus   FW BW ES (Sea)   Dis (Mig)

Range: Formerly considered a race of Herring or Yellow-legged Gull, this form breeds on lakes in C and E Turkey, Georgia and Armenia, particularly on islands in Lake Sevan and at Lake Arpilich. Disperses post-breeding to Middle Eastern coasts, mainly in the E Mediterranean, especially Israel and Egypt. May be regular in Cyprus in winter.

Tips: Breeds on highland lakes but more easily found in winter when occurs on coasts.

Sites:

Iceland Gull
Larus glaucoides   C ES Sea   Mig

Range: Breeds in Greenland and in our region only the W coast of southern Novaya Zemlya, where status little known. A common winter visitor and passage migrant to Iceland and the Faroes, scarce in the British Isles, where mainly found in Scotland but also Ireland and E England, rare in Norway and S to N France.

Subspecies: Nominate race occurs in Europe, *kumlieni*, which breeds on Baffin I and is considered a full species by some, has been recorded as a vagrant.

Tips: A coastal gull that frequently winters at regular haunts, often around fishing harbours and refuse tips. Check local birdlines to locate this species, but much scarcer in Britain than Glaucous Gull.

Sites:

DENMARK Hanstholm** (winter), Ringkøbing Fjord* (winter), Skagen*** (passage, winter), Skallingen-Blåvandshuk* (passage).
FAROE IS* (passage, winter).
GREAT BRITAIN Flamborough Head* (winter), Islay** (winter), Minsmere* (winter), N Norfolk coast** (winter), Orkney Is*** (winter), Outer Hebrides*** (winter), St Ives Bay* (passage, winter), Shetland Is*** (passage, winter), Spurn Peninsula* (winter).

ICELAND Breiðafjörður*** (winter), Reykjanes Peninsula*** (winter), Northwest Peninsula*** (winter), Olfusar Delta*** (winter), Skagafjörður*** (winter).
IRELAND Belfast Lough* (winter), Mullet Peninsula*** (winter).
NORWAY Lofoten Is* (winter), Slettnes* (spring), Varanger* (winter, spring).
POLAND Gdańsk Bay* (winter).
SWEDEN Getterön** (winter).

Glaucous Gull
Larus hyperboreus

I C ES Sea Mig

Range: Breeds in Iceland, Jan Mayen, Bear I and Svalbard, on the N Russian coast and on Novaya Zemlya and Franz Josef Land. In winter occurs around Iceland and from N Norway to the Netherlands, N Scotland and in smaller numbers on the E coast of Britain. Total British wintering population is usually 200–600 birds.
Tips: Breeds in small colonies close to other breeding seabirds. Away from breeding areas, most easily seen at traditional sites, where regular individuals return annually. Mainly coastal but occasionally seen at large inland gull roosts. Check local birdlines to locate this species.

Sites:

DENMARK Hanstholm*** (winter), Ringkøbing Fjord** (winter), Skagen*** (passage, winter), Skallingen-Blåvandshuk** (passage).
FAROE IS* (passage, winter).
FRANCE Île d'Oléron* (winter), Somme Estuary* (winter).
GREAT BRITAIN Dungeness* (winter), Flamborough Head* (winter), Islay** (winter), Minsmere* (winter), N Norfolk coast** (winter), Orkney Is*** (winter), Outer Hebrides*** (winter), St Ives Bay** (passage, winter), Shetland Is*** (passage, winter), Spurn Peninsula* (winter).

ICELAND Breiðafjörður***, Lake Mývatn** (summer), Northwest Peninsula***, Olfusar Delta***, Reykjanes Peninsula***, Skagafjörður***, Westmann Is***.
IRELAND Belfast Lough** (winter), Mullet Peninsula*** (winter).
NORWAY Lofoten Is*** (winter), Slettnes*** (passage), Varanger*** (mainly winter, spring but also in summer).
POLAND Gdańsk Bay* (winter).
RUSSIA Kola Peninsula* (summer, passage).
SWEDEN Getterön** (winter).

Ivory Gull
Pagophila eburnea

I C ES Sea   Mig

Range: Breeds on Svalbard and Franz Josef Land and in small numbers in W and N Novaya Zemlya. Present at breeding colonies late May–Sep, wintering at edge of pack-ice and the southern limits of drift ice in the N Atlantic. Some move south-west in autumn through Norwegian Sea, and possibly rare but regular in Iceland and Faroes. May wander further S than usual by following trawlers.

Tips: The best chance of seeing this Arctic species lies in cruises around Svalbard, otherwise check local birdlines for vagrants, which are usually seen at fishing ports or scavenging along coastlines.

Sites:
FAROE IS* (passage, winter).
ICELAND Grímsey* (winter).
SVALBARD*** (summer).

Gull-billed Tern
Sterna nilotica

FW BW ES (FG)   Mig

Range: Widely scattered breeding sites in Denmark and Germany, Iberia, NW Africa and Italy, more numerous in Greece, Turkey and around the Black Sea. Colonies often changed and sporadic breeding occurs outside main range. Departs breeding areas from late Jun, passage continuing into Sep, rarely early Oct and returns in Apr–May. Passage occurs on North Sea and Atlantic coasts, from Scandinavia to Spain, and in SE Europe, Turkey and the Middle East.

Tips: Breeds on saline steppe lakes, salt or freshwater lagoons, deltas, islands and banks of large rivers or on saltmarshes. Coastal or found at large inland freshwaters on passage, and often feeds over farmland.

Sites:
ARMENIA Armash Fishponds*** (summer).
BALEARIC IS Mallorca** (passage).
BULGARIA Albena-Golden Sands* (passage), Burgas area*** (summer, passage), Lake Durankulak** (passage), Lake Shabla** (passage).

CORSICA Biguglia Lake* (passage).
CYPRUS*** (passage).
DENMARK Rømø* (summer, passage).
EGYPT Abu Simbel*** (passage), Aswan*** (passage), Luxor*** (passage), Nile Delta* (passage), Suez area** (passage).

FRANCE Camargue*** (summer).
GERMANY Wattenmeer* (summer).
GIBRALTAR** (passage).
GREECE Amvrakikós Gulf*** (summer, passage), Axios-Aliakmonas Deltas*** (summer, passage), Evros Delta** (summer, passage), Lake Kerkini** (passage), Nestos Delta* (passage), Porto Lagos area*** (summer, passage).
GREEK IS Corfu*** (passage), Crete** (passage), Kos*** (passage), Lesvos*** (passage).
ISRAEL Bet Shean Valley*** (passage), Eilat*** (passage), Jezreel Valley** (passage).
ITALY Circeo NP** (passage), Gargano Peninsula*** (summer, passage), Po Delta*** (summer, passage).
JORDAN Aqaba** (passage), Azraq** (summer, passage), Ghadir Burqu'* (passage).
MALTA* (passage).
MOROCCO Agadir and the Sous Plain*** (passage), Merja Zerga*** (passage), Oued Massa*** (passage), Tafilalt* (passage).
PORTUGAL Castro Marim*** (passage), Ria Formosa*** (passage), Santo André Lagoon*** (passage), Tagus Estuary*** (passage).
ROMANIA Danube Delta*** (summer), Dobrudja*** (summer, passage).

RUSSIA Kalmykia*** (summer), Volga Delta*** (summer, passage).
SARDINIA Cagliari wetlands*** (summer), Oristano wetlands*** (summer).
SICILY Vendicari*** (passage).
SPAIN Aiguamolls de l'Empordá** (passage), Cabo de Gata* (passage), Cádiz Lagoons*** (summer, passage), Coto Doñana*** (summer), Ebro Delta*** (summer, passage), Guadalhorce Estuary** (passage), La Serena*** (summer), Llobregat Delta*** (summer), Santa Pola** (summer, passage), Tablas de Daimiel*** (summer).
SWEDEN Kristianstad* (passage).
SYRIA Bahrat Homs*** (summer), Sabkhat al-Jubbal*** (summer).
TUNISIA Cap Bon Peninsula*** (passage), Kelbia Lake* (summer, passage), Lake Ichkeul** (passage), Tunis* (passage).
TURKEY Birecik-Halfeti (summer), Bulanik*** (summer), Göksu Delta*** (summer, passage), Kızılırmak Delta* (summer, passage), Kulu Gölü*** (summer), Van Gölü* (summer, passage).
UKRAINE Dunay Delta*** (summer, passage), Tiligul Liman*** (summer), Syvash Bay*** (summer).

Caspian Tern
Sterna caspia

I ES Sea (FW) Mig

Range: Fragmented range in our region, with colonies in the northern Baltic and the SE, around the Black Sea, in C Turkey and the N Red Sea. Occasionally breeds outside main areas, e.g. Ebro Delta, Spain. Departs Baltic colonies in late Jul–Oct, small numbers moving through the North Sea to the Atlantic, but most cross C and E Europe and return in Mar–early May. Small numbers remain around Mediterranean in winter.

Tips: Breeds on coasts and islets in sheltered seas, sometimes on estuaries or coastal lagoons. On passage either coastal or at large inland freshwaters, in winter mainly coastal.

Sites:

AUSTRIA Lake Neusiedl* (passage).
BALEARIC IS Mallorca* (passage).
BULGARIA Albena-Golden Sands** (passage), Burgas area*** (passage, summer), Cape Emine** (passage), Lake Durankulak** (passage), Lake Shabla** (passage), Lake Srebarna* (passage).
CAPE VERDE IS (passage).
CORSICA Biguglia Lake (passage).
CYPRUS* (passage).
DENMARK Amager* (passage), Bornholm-Christiansø** (passage).
EGYPT Hurghada*** , Suez area*** (passage, winter), Sharm el Sheikh*** (passage, winter).
ESTONIA Matsalu Bay*** (summer), Vilsandi NP*** (summer).
FINLAND Åland Is*** (summer), Liminganlahti*** (summer).
FRANCE Camargue** (passage), Marais Poitevin* (passage).
GERMANY Mecklenburg Lakes* (passage), Rügen*** (summer, passage).
GIBRALTAR* (passage).
GREECE Amvrakikós Gulf* (passage), Axios-Aliakmonas Deltas** (passage), Evros Delta* (summer, passage), Lake Kerkini** (passage), Porto Lagos area** (summer, passage).
GREEK IS Corfu* (passage), Crete* (passage, winter), Kos* (passage), Lesvos** (passage).
HUNGARY Kiskunság NP* (passage).
ISRAEL Eilat** (passage).
ITALY Circeo NP** (passage), Isonzo Regional Park** (passage), Orbetello Reserve** (passage), Po Delta* (passage).
JORDAN Aqaba**.
LATVIA Cape Kolka** (passage), Lake Lubana* (passage), Lake Pape* (passage).
MALTA (passage).

MOROCCO Agadir and the Sous Plain*** (passage), Merja Zerga*** (passage, winter), Oualidia*** (passage), Oued Massa*** (passage).
NETHERLANDS Lauwersmeer* (passage), Oostvaardersplassen* (passage).
POLAND Gdańsk Bay** (passage), Szczecin Bay area* (passage).
PORTUGAL Castro Marim** (passage, winter), Ria Formosa** (passage, winter), Tagus Estuary*** (passage).
ROMANIA Danube Delta* (summer), Dobrudja* (passage), Lake Călăraşi** (passage).
RUSSIA Volga Delta*** (passage).
SARDINIA Cagliari wetlands (passage).
SICILY Vendicari*** (passage).
SLOVAKIA Senné Fishponds* (passage), Zemplínská Reservoir (passage).
SPAIN Cabo de Gata* (passage), Cádiz Lagoons*** (winter), Coto Doñana** (passage, winter), Ebro Delta**, Guadalhorce Estuary* (passage), Llobregat Delta* (passage, winter), Santa Pola* (passage).
SWEDEN Falsterbo* (passage), Getterön*** (summer, passage), Gotland*** (summer, passage), Holmöarna*** (summer), Kristianstad** (summer, passage), Öland*** (summer, passage), Tåkern* (passage).
SYRIA Bahrat Homs** (summer, passage), Sabkhat al-Jubbal*** (summer, passage).
TUNISIA Cap Bon Peninsula*** (passage), Kelbia Lake* (passage), Tunis* (passage).
TURKEY Göksu Delta** (summer, passage), Kocaćay Delta** (passage), Manyas Gölü** (passage), Van Gölü** (summer, passage).
UKRAINE Dunay Delta** (summer, passage), Syvash Bay*** (summer).

Greater Crested Tern (Swift Tern)
Sterna bergii   I ES (Sea) Dis

Range: Regular only in the N Red Sea, particularly on islands off Hurghada in Egypt and disperses N to the Gulf of Suez from breeding sites further S.

Tips: Breeds colonially on sandy and rocky islands and mainland coasts, winters at sea sometimes far from land.

Sites:
EGYPT Hurghada***, Suez area***.
ISRAEL Eilat** (passage).
JORDAN Aqaba (passage).

Lesser Crested Tern
Sterna bengalensis   I ES Sea Mig (PMig)

Range: Breeds in the N Red Sea, on islands off Hurghada in Egypt and off S Sinai including Tiran in some years. An isolated population breeds on the islets of Geziret al Elba and Geziret Garah off Libya. Red Sea birds are partial migrants, with most wintering off E Africa, Mediterranean breeders are summer visitors, wintering off W Africa. Passage occurs on the S Mediterranean coast, at Gibraltar and in NW Africa. Rare on the N Mediterranean coast but vagrancy is increasing and breeding occurs sporadically or has been attempted in Greece, Italy, France and Spain, often in mixed pairs with Sandwich Terns.

Subspecies: Mediterranean and Persian Gulf birds belong to race *torresii*, nominate race occurs in the Red Sea.

Tips: Breeds on sparsely vegetated sandy beaches and islands, often with other terns. Coastal on passage, May–Jun and Sep–Nov, and in winter.

Sites:
EGYPT Hurghada***, Suez area***.
GIBRALTAR (passage).
ISRAEL Eilat* (passage).
JORDAN Aqaba (passage).
ITALY Po Delta* (summer).
MOROCCO Agadir and the Sous Plain*** (passage), Merja Zerga*** (passage), Oualidia* (passage), Oued Massa** (passage).
SPAIN Cabo de Gata (spring, summer), Coto Doñana (summer), Ebro Delta* (summer), Guadalhorce Estuary (summer).
TUNISIA Cap Bon Peninsula* (passage).

Roseate Tern
Sterna dougallii

I ES Sea Mig

Range: Breeding is confined to the Atlantic Is, Britain, Ireland and Brittany. More than 50% of the breeding population in our region is in the Azores and Selvagems, and perhaps the Canaries and Madeira. In NW Europe colonies persist around the Irish Sea, most notably on Anglesey in Wales and Rockabill off Ireland. There are further colonies on the E coast of Britain at Inchmickery in the Firth of Forth, and the Farnes and Coquet Island off NE England with small numbers elsewhere at very scattered localities in Ireland, Scotland and on Scilly.

Tips: Breeds mainly on small rocky or sandy islands with some vegetation. More coastal than Common Tern and very rare inland. Occasionally pairs will breed or summer at tern colonies outside main breeding areas. Departs breeding grounds in Aug–Sep but rarely seen on passage, winters off NW and W Africa, returning in Apr–May. Fishing birds can often be picked out by higher flight and faster plunge-dives.

Sites:
AZORES*** (summer).
BELGIUM Het Zwin* (summer).
CANARY IS El Hierro** (summer, passage).
FRANCE Golfe du Morbihan* (passage), Somme Estuary* (passage).
GREAT BRITAIN Anglesey** (summer, passage), Dungeness* (summer, passage), N Norfolk coast* (passage), Portland* (passage), St Ives Bay** (passage), Scilly* (summer), Spurn Peninsula* (passage).
IRELAND Strangford Lough* (summer, passage), Tacumshin Lake** (summer).
MADEIRA** (summer, passage).

White-cheeked Tern
Sterna repressa

I ES Sea Mig

Range: Breeds only in the N Red Sea, in Egypt on islands off Hurghada, off E Sinai including Tiran, and possibly elsewhere. Rarely recorded in the Gulf of Aqaba at Eilat and Aqaba.

Tips: Summer visitor to breeding areas, present Apr–Sep on sandy and rocky islands.

Sites:
EGYPT Hurghada*** (summer).
ISRAEL Eilat* (passage).

JORDAN Aqaba* (passage).

Bridled Tern
Sterna anaethetus

Summer **I Sea** winter **Sea   Dis (Mig)**

Range: Breeds on the Brothers Is and Gumrah in the Red Sea off Egypt. May also occur off NW Africa, as it breeds in Mauritania.

Subspecies: Two races occur in our region; *melanoptera* off NW Africa and very similar *antarctica* in the Red Sea.

Tips: Present at colonies Apr–Sep on rocky islands or sandy and coral islets, sometimes on mainland coasts. Post-breeding moves offshore, often far from land.

Sites:
EGYPT Hurghada***, Sharm el Sheikh**.
ISRAEL Eilat* (passage).
JORDAN Aqaba* (passage).

Whiskered Tern
Chlidonias hybrida

Summer **FW** passage **FW ES   Mig**

Range: Breeds at scattered sites across S Europe, with colonies in C and S Iberia, W, C and S France and NE Italy. More widespread in E Europe, breeding in Hungary, Slovenia, Romania and N Greece, across S Russia to the Volga and in C Turkey. May still breed in NW Africa. Sporadic breeding often occurs outside main range. Passage occurs over much of S Europe, Turkey, the Middle East and N Africa in Jul–Sep and Apr–May.

Tips: Breeds on marshy fresh waters and densely vegetated lakesides, and is also found on estuaries and mudflats on passage.

Sites:
ALBANIA Lake Shkodra*** (summer, passage).
ARMENIA Armash Fishponds*** (summer, passage), Lake Sevan** (passage).
AUSTRIA Lake Neusiedl*** (passage).
BALEARIC IS Formentera** (passage), Mallorca*** (passage), Menorca*** (passage).
BULGARIA Belene*** (summer, passage), Burgas area*** (passage), Lake Durankulak*** (summer, passage), Lake Shabla*** (summer, passage), Lake Srebarna*** (summer, passage).
CANARY IS* (passage).
CORSICA Biguglia Lake (passage).
CROATIA Kopački Rit** (summer), Pokupsko Depression*** (summer).
CYPRUS* (passage).
EGYPT Abu Simbel*** (passage, winter), Aswan*** (passage, winter), Luxor*** (passage, winter), Nile Delta*** (passage, winter), Suez area* (passage), Zaranik*** (passage).

FRANCE Baie de Bourgneuf* (summer, passage), Camargue*** (summer, passage), Dombes*** (summer), La Brenne*** (summer, passage), Gruissan* (passage), Sologne*** (summer, passage).

GREECE Amvrakikós Gulf*** (summer, passage), Axios-Aliakmonas Deltas** (passage), Evros Delta** (passage), Lake Kerkini*** (summer, passage), Mikrí Prespa NP*** (passage), Porto Lagos area*** (summer, passage).

GREEK IS Corfu*** (passage), Crete*** (passage, mainly spring), Kos*** (passage), Lesvos*** (passage).

HUNGARY Biharugra*** (summer), Hortobágy NP*** (summer, passage), Kis-balaton*** (summer, passage), Kiskunság NP*** (summer, passage).

ISRAEL Arava Valley* (passage), Bet Shean Valley*** (passage), Eilat*** (passage), Hula Reserve*** (passage), Jezreel Valley** (passage), Ma'agan Mikhael*** (passage).

ITALY Circeo NP** (passage), Gargano Peninsula** (passage), Lake Massaciuccoli** (passage), Monte Conero** (passage), Orbetello Reserve*** (passage), Po Delta*** (summer, passage), San Giuliano Reserve*** (passage).

JORDAN Azraq** (passage).

LEBANON Aamiq Marshes* (passage), Qaraoun Lake** (passage).

MACEDONIA Lakes Ohrid and Prespa*** (passage).

MOROCCO Agadir and the Sous Plain*** (passage), Essaouira*** (passage), Merja Zerga*** (passage, winter), Oualidia* (passage), Oued Massa*** (passage).

POLAND Białystok Fishponds*** (summer), Biebrza Marshes*** (summer), Chełm Marshes*** (summer), Siemianówka Reservoir*** (summer, passage), Słońsk*** (summer).

PORTUGAL Boquilobo*** (summer), Castro Marim** (passage), Ria Formosa* (passage), Santo André Lagoon*** (summer, passage), Tagus Estuary*** (summer, passage).

ROMANIA Danube Delta*** (summer), Dobrudja*** (summer, passage), Lake Călăraşi*** (summer), Satchinez*** (passage).

RUSSIA Volga Delta*** (summer).

SICILY Vendicari** (passage).

SLOVAKIA Orava Reservoir* (passage), Senné Fishponds*** (summer, passage), Záhorie*** (passage), Zemplínská Reservoir** (passage).

SLOVENIA Lake Cerknica** (passage).

SPAIN Aiguamolls de l'Empordá*** (summer, passage), Cabo de Gata** (passage, Cáceres-Trujillo Steppes** (summer), Cádiz Lagoons***, Coto Doñana***, Ebro Delta***, Guadalhorce Estuary** (passage), Llobregat Delta***, Santa Pola*** (summer, passage), Tablas de Daimiel***.

SWITZERLAND Fanel NR* (passage).

SYRIA Bahrat Homs*** (passage), Dayr al-Zawr*** (summer, passage).

TUNISIA Cap Bon Peninsula*** (passage), Kelbia Lake* (passage), Lake Ichkeul** (passage), Tunis* (passage).

TURKEY Bafa Gölü*** (passage), Dalyan*** (passage), Göksu Delta*** (passage), İstanbul*** (passage), Kızılırmak Delta*** (passage), Kulu Gölü*** (passage), Manyas Gölü*** (passage), Sultan Marshes*** (summer), Uluabat Gölü*** (summer), Van Gölü*** (passage).

UKRAINE Dunay Delta*** (passage), Tiligul Liman*** (passage), Syvash Bay*** (passage).

YUGOSLAVIA Lake Skadar*** (summer, passage).

White-winged Tern (White-winged Black Tern)
Chlidonias leucopterus
Summer **FW** passage **FW ES (FG)** **Mig**

Range: Main breeding range lies from Belarus, Ukraine and the Danube Delta E to the Urals and Caspian. Small numbers breed in C and E Poland, Latvia and Hungary, and breeding has occurred or been attempted in various other European countries. Passage occurs throughout SE Europe, Turkey, the Middle East and N Africa. Scarce in NW Europe but annual in Britain, mainly in E and SE England in Aug–Sep. Autumn passage occurs in late Jul–Oct and the return in Mar–Jun.

Tips: Breeds on densely vegetated lakes, swamps and flooded grasslands. On passage, search rivers and lakes, coastal lagoons and estuaries, and often feeds over farmland.

Sites:

ARMENIA Armash Fishponds*** (summer, passage).

AUSTRIA Lake Neusiedl*** (passage).

AZERBAIJAN Kyzylagach Bay*** (summer).

BALEARIC IS Mallorca** (passage).

BELARUS Belovezhskaya Pushcha NP*** (summer), Berezinsky Reserve*** (summer), Prypyatsky NP*** (summer).

BULGARIA Burgas area*** (passage), Lake Durankulak*** (passage), Lake Shabla*** (passage), Lake Srebarna*** (passage).

CORSICA Biguglia Lake** (passage).

CYPRUS* (passage).

CZECH REPUBLIC Poodří* (autumn).

EGYPT Abu Simbel*** (passage), Aswan*** (passage), Luxor*** (passage), Nile Delta** (passage), Suez area** (passage), Zaranik*** (passage).

FRANCE Camargue*** (passage).

GERMANY Rügen*** (passage).

GREAT BRITAIN Dungeness* (passage).

GREECE Amvrakikós Gulf* (passage), Axios-Aliakmonas Deltas*** (passage), Evros Delta** (passage), Lake Kerkini** (passage), Mikrí Prespa NP*** (passage), Nestos Delta*** (passage), Porto Lagos area*** (passage).

GREEK IS Corfu*** (passage), Crete*** (passage, mainly spring), Kos*** (passage), Lesvos*** (passage).

HUNGARY Hortobágy NP*** (summer, passage), Kis-balaton*** (summer, passage), Kiskunság NP*** (passage).

ISRAEL Bet Shean Valley*** (passage), Eilat*** (passage), Jezreel Valley** (passage), Ma'agan Mikhael* (passage).

ITALY Circeo NP** (passage), Gargano Peninsula** (passage), Lake Massaciuccoli** (passage), Monte Conero** (passage), Orbetello Reserve*** (passage), Po Delta** (passage), San Giuliano Reserve*** (passage).

JORDAN Aqaba** (passage), Azraq** (passage), Ghadir Burqu'** (passage).

LATVIA Lake Lubana*** (summer, passage), Lake Pape*** (passage).

LEBANON Qaraoun Lake** (passage).

MACEDONIA Lakes Ohrid and Prespa*** (passage).

MALTA* (passage).

MOROCCO Agadir and the Sous Plain** (passage), Essaouira** (passage), Merja Zerga** (passage), Oualidia* (passage), Oued Massa** (passage).

NETHERLANDS Oostvaardersplassen* (autumn).

POLAND Biebrza Marshes*** (summer), Chełm Marshes*** (summer), Gdańsk Bay** (passage), Siemianówka Reservoir*** (summer, passage), Słońsk** (summer).

PORTUGAL Ria Formosa* (passage).
ROMANIA Danube Delta*** (summer),
Dobrudja*** (summer, passage), Lake
Călăraşi*** (passage), Satchinez*** (passage).
RUSSIA Oka Valley*** (summer), Volga
Delta*** (summer).
SICILY Vendicari** (passage).
SLOVAKIA Orava Reservoir* (summer), Senné
Fishponds** (summer), Záhorie*** (passage),
Zemplínská Reservoir** (passage).
SLOVENIA Lake Cerknica*** (passage).
SPAIN Aiguamolls de l'Empordá* (passage),
Cabo de Gata* (passage), Cádiz Lagoons*
(passage), Coto Doñana** (passage), Ebro
Delta* (passage), Guadalhorce Estuary*
(passage).

SWEDEN Falsterbo* (passage), Öland
(passage).
SWITZERLAND Fanel NR* (passage).
SYRIA Bahrat Homs*** (passage), Dayr al-
Zawr** (passage).
TURKEY Bafa Gölü*** (passage), Birecik-
Halfeti* (passage), Dalyan*** (passage), Göksu
Delta*** (passage),İstanbul* (passage),
Kızılırmak Delta*** (passage), Kulu Gölü***
(summer, passage), Manyas Gölü*** (pas-
sage), Sultan Marshes*** (passage), Uluabat
Gölü* (passage), Van Gölü*** (summer,
passage).
UKRAINE Dunay Delta*** (passage), Tiligul
Liman*** (passage), Syvash Bay*** (passage).

African Skimmer
Rynchops flavirostris   FW BW ES PMig

Range: Widespread in sub-Saharan Africa, where it is a
partial migrant in response to local rains. Occurs in our
region regularly only in S Egypt in summer and autumn,
mainly on Lake Nasser at Abu Simbel, where breeding
was first confirmed in the late 1980s. Also recorded in the
southern Nile Valley at Kom Ombo and Aswan, and on
the coast at Hurghada in May.

Tips Abu Simbel is the only regular site for this species,
which is not usually coastal, being mainly found along
rivers and lakeshores with sandy banks and islands.

Sites:
EGYPT Abu Simbel*** (summer, autumn),
Aswan* (summer), Hurghada (summer), Luxor*
(summer).

Common Guillemot
Uria aalge   Summer **C I Sea** passage/winter **Sea (ES)   Dis**

Range: Colonies in Iceland and the Faroes, Jan Mayen, Bear I and Svalbard, the N and W British Isles, the Channel Is and Brittany. Also breeds on Heligoland and at a few sites in the Baltic, along the Norwegian and Murmansk coasts, and on Novaya Zemlya. A rare and declining breeder further S, with small numbers in NW Spain and on the Berlenga Is off Portugal. Many remain near breeding areas, but others disperse.

Subspecies: Three races occur in the region; *albionis* breeds from S Britain to Portugal and on Heligoland, nominate race from Iceland, the Faroes and N Britain to the Baltic and *hyperborea* on the Arctic coasts of Europe and the Arctic islands. The bridled form, not a race but a genetic morph, is found in half the population in the N and decreasing in frequency southwards.

Tips: Colonial breeder on sea-cliffs and stacks, wintering at sea, mainly offshore but regularly seen from headlands. Oiled birds occur on beaches and storm-driven birds occasionally appear on inland waters.

Sites:
DENMARK Bornholm-Christiansø***, Hanstholm*** (passage, winter), Skagen*** (passage, winter), Skallingen-Blåvandshuk*** (passage, winter).
FAROE IS* (summer).
FINLAND Åland Is*** (summer).
FRANCE Baie de Vilaine** (passage, winter), Baie du Mont-St-Michel** (passage, winter), Cap Gris Nez*** (passage, winter), Île d'Oléron*** (passage, winter), Ouessant*** (passage, winter), Sept Îles*** (summer).
GERMANY Heligoland***.
GREAT BRITAIN Anglesey***, Dungeness*** (passage, winter), Flamborough Head***, Islay*** (summer, passage), Minsmere* (passage, winter), N Norfolk coast*** (passage, winter), Orkney Is***, Outer Hebrides***, Pembrokeshire Is*** (summer, passage), Portland*** (summer, passage), Rhum***, St Ives Bay*** (passage, winter), Scilly***, Shetland Is***, Spurn Peninsula*** (passage, winter).

ICELAND Breiðafjörður***, Grímsey*** (summer), Northwest Peninsula***, Reykjanes Peninsula***, Skagafjörður*** (summer), Westmann Is***.
IRELAND Cape Clear Is***, Cliffs of Moher***, Galley Head*** (passage, winter), Ireland's Eye***, Kinsale*** (summer, passage), Rathlin I*** (summer, passage), Saltee Is***, Strangford Lough** (passage, winter).
LATVIA Lake Pape*** (passage, winter).
NORWAY Lista*** (passage), Lofoten Is*** (summer, passage), Runde*** (summer), Slettnes*** (passage), Utsira*** (summer, passage), Varanger*** (summer).
PORTUGAL Berlenga Is*** (summer, passage), Cape St Vincent*** (passage).
RUSSIA Kola Peninsula*** (summer).
SVALBARD (summer).
SWEDEN Falsterbo*** (passage), Getterön*** (passage), Gotland*** (summer, passage).

Brünnich's Guillemot
Uria lomvia   Summer **C I Sea** passage/winter **Sea   Mig Dis**

Range: More northerly than Common Guillemot, but overlaps in some areas. Breeds in Iceland, Jan Mayen, Bear I, Svalbard, Franz Josef Land and Novaya Zemlya, the Lofotens and coastal Finnmark, and on the Kola Peninsula. Many remain close to breeding areas, others move S from mid Aug. A rare winter visitor to the Faroes.
Tips: Colonial breeder on sea-cliffs, often with Common Guillemot. Present at breeding cliffs Apr–Sep. Winters at sea, and more oceanic than the previous species. Most of those recorded outside of regular range are found dead or dying.

Sites:
ICELAND Breiðafjörður***, Grímsey*** (summer), Northwest Peninsula***, Reykjanes Peninsula***, Skagafjörður*** (summer), Westmann Is***.
NORWAY Lofoten Is*** (summer), Runde*** (summer), Slettnes*** (passage), Varanger*** (summer).

RUSSIA Kola Peninsula*** (summer).
SVALBARD*** (summer).

Razorbill
Alca torda   Summer **C I Sea** passage/winter **Sea (ES)   Mig Dis**

Range: Colonies in Iceland, the Faroes and the N and W British Isles, Bear I, Jan Mayen, coastal Norway, the Kola Peninsula and the White Sea. Also found in parts of the northern Baltic, the Channel Is and Brittany, and on Heligoland. In winter occurs in the Baltic, North Sea and English Channel S to Morocco and the W Mediterranean.
Subspecies: Race *islandica* breeds from Iceland to the British Isles, Brittany and Heligoland, nominate race elsewhere.
Tips: Breeds colonially on rocky cliffs and islands, present Feb–Aug. At sea post-breeding is usually coastal and seen from many headlands. Storm-driven and oiled birds frequently seen on beaches.

Sites:
BALEARIC IS Mallorca* (winter).
DENMARK Bornholm-Christiansø***, Hanstholm*** (passage, winter), Skagen***

(passage, winter), Skallingen-Blåvandshuk*** (passage, winter).
FAROE IS*** (summer).

FINLAND Åland Is*** (summer).

FRANCE Baie de Vilaine** (passage, winter), Baie du Mont-St-Michel** (passage, winter), Camargue** (winter), Cap Gris Nez*** (passage, winter), Golfe du Morbihan* (winter), Île d'Oléron*** (passage, winter), Ouessant*** (passage, winter), Sept Îles*** (summer).

GERMANY Heligoland***.

GIBRALTAR* (passage, winter).

GREAT BRITAIN Anglesey*** (summer, passage), Dungeness*** (passage, winter), Flamborough Head***, Islay*** (summer, passage), Minsmere* (passage, winter), N Norfolk coast*** (passage, winter), Orkney Is***, Outer Hebrides***, Pembrokeshire Is*** (summer, passage), Portland** (summer, passage), Rhum***, St Ives Bay*** (passage, winter), Scilly***, Shetland Is***, Spurn Peninsula*** (passage, winter).

ICELAND Breiðafjörður***, Grímsey*** (summer), Northwest Peninsula***, Reykjanes Peninsula***, Skaftafell NP*** (summer), Skagafjörður*** (summer), Westmann Is***.

IRELAND Cape Clear Is***, Cliffs of Moher***, Galley Head*** (passage, winter), Ireland's Eye***, Kinsale*** (summer, passage), Rathlin I*** (summer, passage), Saltee Is***, Strangford Lough** (passage, winter).

LATVIA Cape Kolka*** (passage, winter), Lake Pape*** (passage, winter).

LITHUANIA Kirsiu Peninsula*** (passage, winter).

NORWAY Lista*** (passage), Lofoten Is*** (summer, passage), Runde*** (summer), Slettnes*** (passage), Utsira*** (summer, passage), Varanger*** (summer).

PORTUGAL Berlenga Is*** (passage), Cape St Vincent*** (passage), Sado Estuary*** (winter).

RUSSIA Kola Peninsula*** (summer).

SPAIN Aiguamolls de L'Empordá* (winter), Cabo de Gata** (winter), Coto Doñana* (passage, winter), Ebro Delta* (winter), Guadalhorce Estuary* (winter), Llobregat Delta* (winter), Santa Pola* (winter).

SWEDEN Falsterbo*** (passage), Getterön*** (passage, winter), Gotland*** (summer, passage).

Black Guillemot
Cepphus grylle

Summer **C I Sea** winter **Sea   Dis**

Range: Breeds in Iceland and the Faroes, Jan Mayen, Bear I, Svalbard and Franz Josef Land. Also in the N and W British Isles, the N Baltic and islands in the Kattegat, and from S Norway to the coast and islands of Arctic Russia. Most remain close to breeding areas in winter.

Subspecies: Five similar races occur in the region with most distinctive *mandtii* from Jan Mayen, Bear I and Svalbard. Remaining races, nominate *grylle* from the Baltic, *arcticus* from the British Is to Arctic Russia, *faroeensis* from Faroes and *islandicus* from Iceland differ only in minor measurements.

Tips: Breeds colonially in boulders at the base of cliffs and on islands, and post-breeding disperses to sheltered nearby seas.

Sites:
DENMARK Bornholm-Christiansø*** (passage).
FAROE IS*.
FINLAND Åland Is***.

GREAT BRITAIN Anglesey**, Flamborough Head* (passage), Islay***, Orkney Is***, Outer Hebrides***, Rhum***, Shetland Is***.

ICELAND Breiðafjörður***, Northwest Peninsula***, Reykjanes Peninsula***, Skagafjörður*** , Westmann Is***.
IRELAND Belfast Lough***, Cape Clear Is***, Ireland's Eye***, Kinsale***, Mullet Peninsula***, Rathlin I***, Strangford Lough***.
LATVIA Cape Kolka** (winter), Lake Pape** (winter).

NORWAY Lofoten Is***, Utsira***, Runde***, Slettnes*** (summer), Varanger*** (summer).
RUSSIA Kola Peninsula*** (summer).
SVALBARD*** (summer).
SWEDEN Falsterbo (passage, winter), Gotland***, Holmöarna*** (summer).

Little Auk (Dovekie)
Alle alle

Summer **C I Sea** passage/winter **Sea Mig**

Range: Breeds on Svalbard, Franz Josef Land and Novaya Zemlya, with smaller numbers on Grímsey, off Iceland, Bear I and Jan Mayen. Most winter in the Barents and Norwegian Seas, but small numbers are regular off N Scotland and a few reach Ireland and SW England.

Subspecies: Nominate *alle* breeds over much of Western Palearctic range with slightly larger *polaris* on Franz Josef Land.

Tips: Breeds colonially on rocky cliffs and slopes, often some distance from the sea. Leaves colonies from Aug and returns in Apr–May. At sea post-breeding, usually far from land, except when driven inshore or even inland by bad weather. Indeed, it is the most likely of the auks to appear inshore and 'wrecks' involving hundreds of birds frequently occur.

Sites:

DENMARK Hanstholm** (autumn, winter).
FAROE IS** (passage, winter).
FRANCE Cap Gris Nez* (passage, winter).
GREAT BRITAIN Flamborough Head*** (autumn, winter), N Norfolk coast** (passage, winter), Orkney Is** (passage, winter), Portland* (passage, winter), St Ives Bay** (autumn, winter), Shetland Is** (passage, winter), Spurn Peninsula* (passage, winter).

ICELAND Breiðafjörður*** (winter), Grímsey*** (winter, very rare in summer), Northwest Peninsula***, Westmann Is*** (winter).
IRELAND Cape Clear Is* (passage, winter).
NORWAY Lofoten Is* (passage), Slettnes* (passage), Utsira* (passage), Varanger*** (passage, winter).
RUSSIA Kola Peninsula*** (passage, winter).
SVALBARD*** (summer).
SWEDEN Getterön** (autumn).

Puffin (Atlantic Puffin)
Fratercula arctica

Summer **C I Sea** passage/winter **Sea   Mig Dis**

Range: Breeds in Iceland and the Faroes, Jan Mayen, Bear I and Svalbard, the N and W British Isles, Channel Is and NW France. Also from coastal Norway to the Murmansk coast and at a few scattered sites on Novaya Zemlya. Winters from Iceland and the northern North Sea to the Azores and Canaries, NW Africa and the W Mediterranean. Migratory and dispersive, departs colonies in late Jul–Aug and returns from mid Mar, later in the N.

Subspecies: Three very similar races occur in the region, nominate *arctica* from Iceland, northern Norway, Bear Island and S Novaya Zemlya, *grabae* from the Faroes, British Is, France and S Norway and *naumanni* from Svalbard and N Novaya Zemlya.

Tips: Breeds colonially in burrows in sloping, turf-covered cliff-tops, present mid Mar until Aug. Winters at sea, usually further from land than other auks and less commonly seen during seawatches.

Sites:

AZORES* (winter).
BALEARIC IS Mallorca* (winter).
FAROE IS*** (summer).
FRANCE Cap Gris Nez* (passage), Ouessant*** (summer, passage), Sept Îles*** (summer).
GIBRALTAR** (passage, winter).
GREAT BRITAIN Anglesey*** (summer, passage), Dungeness* (passage), Flamborough Head*** (summer, passage), Islay* (passage), Orkney Is*** (summer), Pembrokeshire Is*** (summer), Portland** (summer, passage), Rhum*** (summer), St Ives Bay** (passage), Scilly*** (summer), Shetland Is*** (summer), Spurn Peninsula* (passage).
ICELAND Breiðafjörður*** (summer), Grímsey*** (summer), Northwest Peninsula*** (summer), Reykjanes Peninsula*** (summer), Skagafjörður*** (summer), Westmann Is*** (summer).
IRELAND Cape Clear Is*** (summer, passage), Cliffs of Moher*** (summer), Ireland's Eye*** (summer), Rathlin Is*** (summer), Saltee Is*** (summer).
NORWAY Lofoten Is*** (summer, passage), Slettnes*** (passage), Utsira*** (summer, passage), Runde*** (summer, passage), Varanger*** (summer).
PORTUGAL Cape St Vincent** (passage).
RUSSIA Kola Peninsula*** (summer).
SPAIN Cabo de Gata (winter).
SVALBARD*** (summer).

Lichtenstein's Sandgrouse
Pterocles lichtensteinii　　　　　　　　　　　　　D SD　Res (Nom)

Range: In our region breeds in N Africa in Western Sahara, S Morocco and adjacent W Algeria, also in SE Algeria and extreme SE Egypt. In the Middle East breeds in S Israel and E and S Sinai; probably also occurs in Jordan.

Subspecies: Nominate race occurs in the Middle East with *targius* in the Sahara.

Tips: A nocturnal or crepuscular bird of stony desert and semi-desert, dry acacia scrub, wadis and sparsely wooded rocky hillsides. Difficult to see well and usually flies to waterholes before dawn or after dark, but the site near Eilat can usually be relied upon to provide excellent views of up to 50 birds, and that at Sharm el Sheikh attracts more than 100. Rare in Morocco and regular only in the far S, in stone desert with acacias.

Sites:
EGYPT Sharm el Sheikh***.
ISRAEL Arava Valley***, Eilat***.

Crowned Sandgrouse
Pterocles coronatus　　　　　　　　　　　　　D SD FG　Res (Dis)

Range: Found across large areas of N Africa, in S and E Morocco, C and S Algeria, S Tunisia and N and E Libya. Very patchy range in Egypt, mainly in the E on the Red Sea coast but also recorded near Abu Simbel. Also occurs in Sinai and S Israel, and recently reported from Jordan and N Saudi Arabia. More widespread in Morocco in winter.

Subspecies: Two rather similar races occur in our region, nominate over much of N Africa and *vastitus* in the Middle East.

Tips: Search stony desert and semi-desert, hillsides and sparsely vegetated areas, principally in uplands. Arrive at a known waterhole before dawn and wait, as the birds are usually present during the first hour after dawn.

Sites:
EGYPT Abu Simbel***, Hurghada***, Sharm el Sheikh***.
ISRAEL Arava Valley***, Eilat***, Nizzana*.

JORDAN Wadi Dana-Fidan.
MOROCCO Boumalne**, Goulimime to Tan-Tan***, Oued Massa*, Tafilalt***.

Spotted Sandgrouse
Pterocles senegallus

S SD Res (Nom)

Range: Widespread in N Africa, being found in S and E Morocco, through most of Algeria and S Tunisia to N and C Libya and much of C and E Egypt. Also Sinai and Israel, NE Jordan, N Saudi Arabia and probably Syria. Variable numbers breed in Israel but apparently decreasing in the S.

Tips: Search sandy and rocky deserts, semi-deserts and salt flats, sometimes with fairly dense scrub and often in dry cultivated areas. Usually seen in small flocks flying to or from waterholes, particularly in the morning.

Sites:
EGYPT Abu Simbel***, Luxor***, Hurghada***, Sharm el Sheikh***, Suez area***.
ISRAEL Arava Valley***, Nizzana***, Urim***.
JORDAN Azraq** (mainly autumn), Ghadir Burqu'*, Wadi Dana-Fidan*.

MOROCCO Boumalne, Goulimime to Tan-Tan*, Ouarzazate*, Oued Massa*, Tafilalt**.
TUNISIA Chott el Djerid***.

Black-bellied Sandgrouse
Pterocles orientalis

SD FG Res (PMig) (Nom)

Range: Breeds discontinuously in E and S Portugal and C and S Spain, in the E Canaries, across NW Africa from C Morocco to Tunisia and in NW Libya. In the SE of the region breeds across much of C and E Turkey to Armenia and S Azerbaijan. Small populations persist on Cyprus (at Athlassa Dam) and in C Israel. A partial migrant in E of range and small numbers pass through S Turkey and Cyprus in Apr and Sep–Nov. Wintering birds mainly occur in Syria, Iraq and C Jordan, rarely NE Egypt.

Subspecies: Nominate occurs over much of Western Palearctic range with scarcely distinguishable *arenarius* breeding in the extreme E.

Tips: Search arid, open country with sparse vegetation, particularly saline plains, stony semi-desert and the edges of cultivation, sometimes in uplands. Most often seen in morning and evening, flying to and from waterholes and usually heard before being seen.

Sites:
CANARY IS Fuerteventura***, Lanzarote*.
CYPRUS.
ISRAEL Golan Heights* (winter), Nizzana***.

JORDAN Azraq*, Ghadir Burqu'.
MOROCCO Boumalne***, Goulimime to Tan-Tan***, Ouarzazate*, Oued Massa***, Tafilalt***, Zeida***.

PORTUGAL Baixo Alentejo***, International Tagus**.
RUSSIA Kalmykia**.
SPAIN Cabo de Gata***, Cáceres-Trujillo Steppes***, La Serena***, Zaragoza Steppes***.

TUNISIA Kelbia Lake***.
TURKEY Birecik-Halfeti**, Bulanik**, Kulu Gölü***, Van Gölü*.

Pin-tailed Sandgrouse
Pterocles alchata   SD FG   Res (Nom)

Range: In Europe breeds in scattered parts of C and S Spain, probably still in extreme E Portugal, and a tiny area of S France in the Camargue. In N Africa occurs through-out the Atlas of Morocco and Algeria and in C Tunisia and NW Libya. In the SE breeds in a small area of SE Turkey and in N and E Syria. Isolated populations persist in N Jordan and C Israel and may also breed in N Saudi Arabia.

Subspecies: Nominate breeds in SW Europe with *caudacutus* in N Africa and SW Asia.
Tips: Arid country, but not true desert, often in open sandy and stony areas with sparse vegetation, on sandy riverbanks, sometimes in dry cultivation. Gregarious and arrives in flocks at drinking sites soon after dawn, less commonly near dusk.

Sites:
FRANCE Camargue***.
ISRAEL Nizzana**, Urim***.
JORDAN Azraq* (irregular), Ghadir Burqu', Wadi Dana-Fidan.
MOROCCO Boumalne***, Tafilalt**.
PORTUGAL International Tagus*.

SPAIN Cáceres-Trujillo Steppes***, Coto Doñana**, La Serena***, Tablas de Daimiel**, Zaragoza Steppes***.
SYRIA Baath Lake***, Bahrat Homs***, Jabal al-Bishri***, Dayr al-Zawr***, Sabkhat al-Jubbal***, Tadmur and Sabkhat Muh**.
TURKEY Birecik-Halfeti*.

Trocaz Pigeon (Long-toed Pigeon)
Columba trocaz   M DF MF (FG)   Res

Range: Confined to cloud-covered mountains on Madeira, mainly in the N but with smaller numbers in surviving forest in the S. In decline through loss of habitat and hunting and now numbers fewer than 5,000 birds.
Tips: Occurs in laurel forest or in dense stands of tree heath, often in ravines and along watercourses. Usually nests on rock-faces and cliffs, occasionally in trees and

bushes. Sometimes descends to feed on lower farmland, especially in winter, but generally shy. The most reliable site is Balcoes, Ribeiro Frio.

Site:
MADEIRA***.

Bolle's Pigeon (Dark-tailed Laurel Pigeon)
Columba bollii   M DF MF (FG)   Res

Range: Sometimes treated as a subspecies of Trocaz Pigeon. Confined to the Canaries, breeding on Tenerife, La Gomera; La Palma and El Hierro. Locally common on Gomera; only recently proved to breed on El Hierro, where numbers are very low, and formerly also found on Gran Canaria.

Tips: Found mainly in laurel forest or tree heath, moving to lower farmland in autumn. Spends the hottest part of the day deep in shade, and nests in trees. Usually occurs at higher altitudes than Laurel Pigeon, generally between 1,300 and 1,500m. One of the most reliable sites is the Garajonay National Park on Gomera.

Sites:
CANARY IS El Hierro***, Gomera***, La Palma***, Tenerife***.

Laurel Pigeon
Columba junoniae   M DF MF (FG)   Res

Range: Found only on La Palma, Gomera and Tenerife in the Canaries, perhaps also El Hierro. Locally fairly common on La Palma and Gomera but very rare on Tenerife and breeding only confirmed in the 1990s. In decline through loss of habitat and hunting.

Tips: Search steep mountain slopes covered with mixed forest, laurel and tree heath stands, and scrub-covered crags. Visits lower altitude farmland in autumn when more easily seen but generally a shy forest bird. Nests on cliff-faces. Usually found in lower areas than Bolle's Pigeon.

Sites:
CANARY IS Gomera***, La Palma***, Tenerife***.

African Collared Dove (Pink-headed Turtle Dove)
Streptopelia roseogrisea

SD FG   Res

Range: An African species widespread S of the Sahara in the dry subtropical zone but penetrates our region only in the extreme S, from Mauritania to SE Egypt. Wanders N to the Arava Valley of Israel. Perhaps also regular in extreme S Morocco. The so-called **Barbary Dove** is a domesticated form of this species and a frequent escape, and is now established in the Balearics and Canaries.

Tips: Semi-desert and savanna, particularly fond of tamarisk and acacia scrub. Frequently associated with man, often breeding in towns.

Site:
EGYPT Abu Simbel***.

Laughing Dove (Palm Dove)
Streptopelia senegalensis

U FG SH SD D   Res (Dis)

Range: Breeds at scattered sites in N Africa, the Middle East and Turkey. In N Africa breeds at many Saharan oases and is common in Tunisia, the Nile Delta and Valley, and as a recent colonist in southern Morocco. Also breeds in Sinai, Israel, Jordan and parts of Lebanon and Syria, perhaps also Malta. Occurs throughout urban areas of Turkey as well as in Transcaucasia.

Subspecies: Three races occur in the region; nominate on the southern edge of the Western Palearctic in Africa and in the Middle East, *phoenicophila* from N Algeria to N Libya and, perhaps as a result of introduction, in Turkey and N Syria and *aegyptiaca* from Egypt.

Tips Closely associated with man in many areas and often found in cities such as İstanbul, Beirut and Jerusalem. Also occurs in cultivated areas, orchards and palm groves, in dry scrub and at oases in deserts.

Sites:
EGYPT Abu Simbel***, Aswan***, Faiyum***, Hurghada***, Luxor***, Nile Delta***, Santa Katharina Monastery***, Sharm el Sheikh***, Suez area***, Wadi el Natrun***, Zaranik***.
ISRAEL Arava Valley***, Eilat***, Ein Gedi***, Hula Reserve***, Jezreel Valley***, Ma'agan Mikhael***.

JORDAN Amman NP***, Aqaba***, Azraq***, Petra***, Wadi Dana-Fidan***, Wadi Rum***, Wadi as Sir***.
MOROCCO Agadir and the Sous Plain***, Oued Massa***.
SYRIA Baath Lake***, Bahrat Homs***, Dayr al-Zawr***.

TUNISIA Ain Draham***, Cap Bon Peninsula***, Chott el Djerid***, Kelbia Lake***, Lake Ichkeul***, Zaghouan***.

TURKEY Birecik-Halfeti***, Cizre**, İstanbul***, Van Gölü***.

Namaqua Dove
Oena capensis　　　　　　　　　　　　FG SH SD　Res (Mig)

Range: Rare and local in the region, breeding in the far S of Algeria and Egypt, in N Saudi Arabia and the Arava Valley of Israel. Breeding in Israel first confirmed in 1980. This population is migratory, arriving in Mar–Apr and departing in Sep–Oct. Uncommon but increasing and spreading in Israel and in Egypt now firmly established in the Nile Valley. Recently reported from C Syria and recorded as a vagrant on Cyprus and the Canaries.

Tips: Found in semi-desert and thornbush country, scrub and gardens in some areas.

Sites:
EGYPT Abu Simbel***, Aswan***, Luxor**.
ISRAEL Arava Valley***, Eilat***.

JORDAN Aqaba* (summer).
SYRIA Tadmur and Sabkhat Muh.

Great Spotted Cuckoo
Clamator glandarius　　　　　　　　　DF MF FG SH　Mig (Res)

Range: Breeds in Iberia, S France and W Italy, in Croatia, N Greece and much of W and C Turkey, Cyprus, parts of the Middle East and in the Nile Valley. Has bred in NW Africa, Sardinia and Lebanon. A summer visitor: most adults depart in Jul–Aug, juveniles slightly later, and the main return movement is in mid Apr. Small numbers winter in NW Morocco, and occasionally in S Iberia, although migrants return as early as Jan.

Tips: A noisy and obvious bird of dry savanna, parkland with scrub and scattered trees, open woodland and cork oak groves. Parasitises corvids, mainly Common Magpie.

Sites:
BULGARIA Strandja Mts* (summer).
CYPRUS*** (summer, passage).
EGYPT Aswan* (summer), Luxor** (summer).
FRANCE Camargue* (summer), Gruissan*** (summer), Leucate*** (summer).
GIBRALTAR*** (passage).

GREEK IS Kos* (passage), Lesvos* (passage).
ISRAEL Bet Shean Valley*** (spring), Hula Reserve* (passage), Nizzana*** (summer), Urim*** (summer).
ITALY Circeo NP*** (summer), Maremma Regional Park* (spring), Orbetello Reserve*** (summer).

JORDAN Azraq* (spring).
LEBANON Aamiq Marshes** (summer), Qaraoun Lake* (passage).
MALTA* (passage).
MOROCCO Lac de Sidi Bourhaba**(passage, winter), Oued Massa** (passage), Zaër** (passage).
PORTUGAL Baixo Alentejo*** (summer), Boquilobo** (summer), Cape St Vincent* (autumn), Castro Marim*** (summer), International Douro* (summer), International Tagus*** (summer), Montesinho*** (summer), Peneda Gêres NP** (summer), Ria Formosa*** (summer), Sado Estuary*** (summer), Santo

André Lagoon*** (summer), Tagus Estuary* (passage).
SPAIN Aiguamolls de l'Empordá*** (summer), Cabo de Gata*** (summer), Cáceres-Trujillo Steppes*** (summer), Coto Doñana*** (summer, rare in winter), Garraf Massif*** (summer), La Serena** (summer), Llobregat Delta*** (summer), Monfragüe*** (summer), Sierra de Gredos*** (summer), Tablas de Daimiel*** (summer), Zaragoza Steppes** (summer).
SYRIA Dayr al-Zawr* (passage).
TURKEY Akseki* (passage), Göksu Delta** (summer), Manyas Gölü*** (summer), Van Gölü (passage).

Senegal Coucal
Centropus senegalensis

FG SH FW   Res

Range: In our region confined to the Nile Delta and Valley, where fairly common and probably increasing.
Tips: Inhabits savanna and woodland, reedbeds and dense vegetation beside streams and rivers, grasslands, gardens and cultivated areas. Shy and often difficult to observe, but occasionally seen in clumsy flight over reeds or feeding in the open on the ground.

Sites:
EGYPT Faiyum***, Luxor*, Nile Delta***.

Striated Scops Owl (Bruce's or Pallid Scops Owl)
Otus brucei

FG SD U M   Res (PMig)

Range: Breeds in SE Turkey, Iraq and N Syria, has bred in Israel and may do so regularly but more numerous as a winter visitor. May be a rare resident in Jordan but there are few records and old reports of breeding may refer to Eurasian Scops Owl.
Subspecies: Two similar races occur in our region; *obsoletus* in Turkey, Syria and N Iraq and *exiguus* in Sinai, Israel and S Iraq.

Tips: Search arid, rocky hillsides, cliffs and gorges with scattered trees, cultivated areas and semi-desert, riverine woodland, palm groves and town gardens. Nests in hollow trees. Less strictly nocturnal than Eurasian Scops Owl. The most famous and long-standing site is the tea gardens at Birecik, in Turkey, and the species was still present in 2004, but beware, Eurasian Scops Owl also occurs here.

Sites:
ISRAEL Arava Valley** (winter), Eilat** (winter). **JORDAN** Azraq (spring), Wadi Rum (spring).

SYRIA Dayr al-Zawr**, Sabkhat al-Jubbal** (summer).
TURKEY Birecik-Halfeti***.

Eurasian Scops Owl (Scops Owl)
Otus scops   DF MF FG SH (U) Mig (PMig)

Range: Widespread over much of Iberia and C and S France, throughout Italy, the Balkans, Greece and much of Turkey. Also breeds in parts of Austria, Slovakia and Hungary, Ukraine and across S Russia to the Urals and Caspian but generally much scarcer in N of range. Found on all larger Mediterranean islands, in scattered parts of the Middle East and, in NW Africa, in Morocco, coastal Algeria and Tunisia. A summer visitor over most of range, but some resident in Iberia, the Balearics, Sardinia, Sicily and S Italy, S Greece and Crete, and entirely so on Cyprus. Migrants depart in Sep–Oct and return in Feb–Apr.

Subspecies: Four–six races are recognised within the Western Palearctic; nominate *scops* across most of S Europe and NW Africa, *mallorcae* from the Balearics, *cyprius* from Cyprus and Turkey, *pulchellus* from the Volga eastwards and in the Caucasus and *turanicus* from Iraq. Race *cycladum* from Greece, the Greek islands and S Turkey is now sometimes included in the nominate.

Tips: Strictly nocturnal and superbly camouflaged, this owl is best located by its monotonous and repetitive call, often uttered in duet, although note that Midwife Toad can sound very similar. Listen in dry open woodland, olive groves, almond plantations, vineyards, parks and gardens or the species can be located by tracking mobbing passerines. Usually avoids conifers, except in parts of Russia. Nests in tree holes and in cavities in rocks and walls.

Sites:
ALBANIA Lake Shkodra*** (summer).
ANDORRA ** (summer).
ARMENIA Khosrov Preserve*** (summer).
AZERBAIJAN Zakataly*** (summer).
BALEARIC IS Ibiza***, Mallorca***, Menorca***.
BULGARIA Albena-Golden Sands*** (summer), Cape Emine*** (summer), Lake Durankulak** (summer), Lake Shabla*** (summer), Rila Mts*** (summer), Ropotamo NP*** (summer),

Rusenski Lom NP*** (summer), Strandja Mts*** (summer), Studen Kladenetz*** (summer), Trigradski Gorge*** (summer), Tissata NR*** (summer).
CANARY IS* (passage).
CORSICA Cap Corse*** (summer).
CROATIA Cres*** (summer), Mljet*** (summer), Paklenica NP***.
CYPRUS*.

FRANCE Camargue***, Cévennes NP*** (summer), Gruissan* (summer), Île d'Oléron* (summer), Les Alpilles*** (summer), Leucate** (summer).

GIBRALTAR* (summer, passage).

GREECE Dadiá-Soufli Forest*** (summer), Mikrí Prespa NP*** (summer), Nestos Delta*** (summer), Vikos-Aoos NP*** (summer).

GREEK IS Corfu*** (summer), Crete***, Kos***, Lesvos***, Náxos***, Rhodes***.

HUNGARY Tihany** (summer).

ISRAEL Arava Valley*** (summer, passage), Bet Shean Valley*** (summer), Eilat*** (passage), Urim***.

ITALY Gargano Peninsula*** (summer), Po Delta** (summer).

JORDAN Azraq* (passage), Petra*** (summer), Wadi Dana-Fidan** (summer), Wadi Rum* (passage), Wadi as Sir* (summer).

LEBANON Aamiq Marshes*** (summer), Qaraoun Lake*** (summer).

MACEDONIA Galicica NP*** (summer), Lakes Ohrid and Prespa*** (summer).

MALTA* (passage).

MOROCCO Tafilalt***, Zeida** (summer).

PORTUGAL Baixo Alentejo*** (summer), Castro Marim*** (summer), International Douro*** (summer), International Tagus*** (summer), Montesinho*** (summer), Peneda Gêres NP*** (summer), Ria Formosa*** (summer).

ROMANIA Dobrudja*** (summer).

RUSSIA Volga Delta*** (summer).

SARDINIA San Pietro I*** (summer).

SLOVAKIA Senné Fishponds** (summer).

SLOVENIA Karst RP*** (summer), Kocevje** (summer).

SPAIN Aiguamolls de L'Empordá*** (summer), Cabo de Gata*** (summer), Cáceres-Trujillo Steppes*** (summer), Coto Doñana*** (summer, passage), Ebro Delta*** (summer), Garraf Massif*** (summer), La Serena*** (summer), Jaca*** (summer), Llobregat Delta*** (summer), Monfragüe*** (summer), Serrania de Ronda*** (summer), Sierra de Gredos*** (summer), Sierra de Guadarrama*** (summer), Tablas de Daimiel*** (summer).

TURKEY Akseki*** (summer), Birecik-Halfeti*** (summer), Dalyan*** (summer), Demirkazik*** (summer), İstanbul*** (summer), Manyas Gölü*** (summer), Soğuksu NP*** (summer).

YUGOSLAVIA Durmitor NP** (summer), Fruška Gora NP** (summer), Lake Skadar*** (summer).

Eurasian Eagle Owl (Eagle Owl)
Bubo bubo　　　　　　　　　　　DF MF CF M SD D　Res

Range: Declining and now rare in most of our region due to persecution but breeds over much of Iberia and in isolated pockets in S France and Italy, E to C Europe, the Balkans and Turkey. In the N breeds in Norway and parts of Sweden, much of Finland and from the Baltic states and E Poland across Russia to the Urals and Caspian. To the S breeds over much of N Africa from Mauritania to Libya, in the Nile Valley and elsewhere in Egypt, in Sinai, Israel and Jordan, and perhaps still in Syria. Generally rare but some increase in numbers and range expansion recently, aided by protection and reintroduction schemes. Birds from German reintroductions have bred in Belgium, the Netherlands and Denmark. A pair at Maastricht, in the Netherlands, still present in 2004, have been the most accessible Eagle Owls for British birders for several years.

Subspecies: Races within our region include the nominate *bubo* over much of Europe, *hispanus* from Iberia, *ruthenus* from central European Russia, *sibirica* from the W Urals and *turcomanus* from the Volga steppes. **Desert** or **Pharoah Eagle Owl** *B. ascalaphus* of N Africa and the Middle East is considerably smaller than other races and is sometimes afforded species status. There is DNA evidence suggesting the race *interpositus* from the Crimea, Caucasus and Turkey might also be specifically distinct.

Tips: Generally only occurs where undisturbed by man, in rocky areas with cliffs and gorges, and trees or bushes. Also in forested mountains and in wadis in semi-desert. Most easily located by call and most vocal in very early spring. The best way to see this species is to visit known areas or seek local assistance, but can be found by listening at likely gorges or cliffs at dusk then scanning the same area in daylight.

Sites:

ALBANIA Lake Shkodra*.

ANDORRA.

ARMENIA Khosrov Preserve***.

AUSTRIA Wienerwald*.

AZERBAIJAN Turianchai Reserve*, Zakataly**.

BELARUS Belovezhskaya Pushcha NP**, Berezinsky Reserve**, Pripyatsky NP***.

BOSNIA-HERZEGOVINA Sujetska NP*.

BULGARIA Albena-Golden Sands***, Cape Kaliakra**, Ropotamo NP***, Rusenski Lom NP***, Strandja Mts***, Studen Kladenetz***, Trigradski Gorge**, Tissata NR***, Tzarichina NR***.

CROATIA Cres*, Paklenica NP**, Plitvice*.

CZECH REPUBLIC Beskydy Mts**, Jeseníky Mts*, Krkonoše NP***, Lednice*, Pálava Hills**, Šumava NP***, Třeboňsko***.

EGYPT Abu Simbel***, Aswan***, Sharm el Sheikh***.

ESTONIA Matsalu Bay***, Nigula NR***.

FINLAND Åland Is***, Kuusamo**, Liminganlahti***, Oulanka NP***.

FRANCE Cévennes NP**, Les Alpilles***, Mercantour NP**, Prats-de-Mollo**, Pyrenees NP**, Queyras NP**, Vanoise NP**.

GEORGIA Iori Steppes**, Javakheti Plateau***.

GERMANY Ammer Valley*, Bayerischer Wald NP**, Berchtesgaden NP*.

GREECE Akarnanika Mts**, Avas Gorge*, Dadiá-Soufli Forest**, Lake Kerkini*, Mikrí Prespa NP**, Mt Olympus NP**, Valia Kalda NP*, Vikos-Aoos NP**.

GREEK IS Lesvos*.

HUNGARY Aggtelek NP*, Bükk Hills NP**, Zemplén Hills**.

ISRAEL Arava Valley**, Eilat*, Golan Heights**, Urim***, Wadi Ammud-Mt Arbel**.

ITALY Abruzzo NP**, Gargano Peninsula**, Gran Paradiso NP***, Sibillini NP*, Stelvio NP**.

JORDAN Ghadir Burqu', Wadi Dana-Fidan**, Wadi Rum***.

LATVIA Cape Kolka**, Lake Engure***, Lake Pape**.

LEBANON Aamiq Marshes*.

MACEDONIA Babuna Gorge*, Bregalnica Valley**, Crna Gorge*, Demir Kapija Gorge**, Galicica NP**, Mavrovo NP**, Sara Mts**.

MOROCCO Boumalne**, Tafilalt**.

NORWAY Dovrefjell NP*, Rondane NP**.

POLAND Białowieża Forest***, Biebrza Marshes**, Bieszczady NP**, Chełm Marshes*, Szczecin Bay area*, Tatra NP***.

PORTUGAL Baixo Alentejo*, Cape St Vincent, International Douro***, International Tagus***, Montesinho*, Peneda Gêres NP**.

ROMANIA Bicaz***, Dobrudja*, Gurghiu Mts**, Poiana Brașov*, Retezat NP**, Turda Gorge***.

RUSSIA Kola Peninsula***, Oka Valley**, Teberdinskiy Reserve***, Volga Delta**.

SLOVAKIA High Tatras NP**, Malá Fatra***, Malé Karpaty***, Nízke Tatry NP***, Slanské Hills***, Slovenský Kras***, Vihorlatske Hills***, Zemplínská Reservoir***.

SLOVENIA Triglav NP*.

SPAIN Aigües Tortes NP**, Cabo de Gata*, Cáceres-Trujillo Steppes, Garraf Massif**, Jaca*, La Serena*, Monfragüe NP***, Ordesa NP***, Picos de Europa***, Serrania de Ronda*, Sierra de Gredos***, Sierra de Guadarrama**, Zaragoza Steppes*.
SWEDEN Getterön***, Tärnasjön***.
SWITZERLAND Monte Generoso*, Swiss NP**.

SYRIA Tadmur and Sabkhat Muh**, Wadi al-Qarn-Burqush*.
TURKEY Birecik-Halfeti**, Dalyan*, Demirkazik*, Göksu Delta**, Soğuksu NP**, Van Gölü*.
UKRAINE Carpathians**, Crimean Mts*, Shatsk NP**.
YUGOSLAVIA Đerdap National Park**, Durmitor NP*, Fruška Gora NP, Lake Skadar*.

Brown Fish Owl
Bubo zeylonensis

FW Res

Range: Very rare and quite possibly extinct in the Western Palearctic, making it one of the region's most sought after birds. Perhaps still present in the Taurus Mts of S Turkey, where one was captured in the Adana area in 1990, and plausibly persists in Jordan, in the Yarmuk and Jordan Valleys, but almost certainly extinct in the Golan Heights, where unrecorded since 1975. Formerly bred in N Israel and may yet be discovered elsewhere, as recently reported at several sites in Iran for the first time in several years.

Tips: Search beside lakes, rivers and streams with tree-lined margins in likely areas; the species formerly occurred in shrub-filled wadis in the Golan Heights. Nocturnal and spends much time perched on an overhanging branch or on the ground beside water.

Site:
SYRIA Yarmuk Valley.

Snowy Owl
Nyctea scandiaca

T (FG) Nom (PMig)

Range: Small numbers breed in the uplands of N Scandinavia, and sporadically in the N Kola Peninsula, along the Arctic coast of Russia and on Novaya Zemlya. Regular in summer in Iceland but breeding in 1998 was the first recorded for 25 years. Has bred in Shetland and 1–2 birds sometimes summer there or in the Scottish Highlands. A partial migrant in Russia but more or less nomadic elsewhere, occurring irregularly in winter S to N Scotland, Denmark and Germany, Poland and C Russia. Numbers and range vary and are heavily dependent on fluctuations in lemming populations.

Tips: Breeds on Arctic tundra from sea level to uplands, in winter in open habitats on coasts and islands, and further S on moorland and marshes, over farmland and grassland. Diurnal but with peaks of activity around dawn and dusk and perches prominently on rocks or slight elevations.

Sites:

FINLAND Kilpisjärvi Saana* (irregular), Pallas-Ounastunturi NP** (irregular).
GREAT BRITAIN Cairngorms and Speyside (summer), Shetland Is.
ICELAND Lake Mývatn (irregular).

NORWAY Hardangervidda NP* (summer), Slettnes* (summer, passage), Varanger* (summer).
RUSSIA Kola Peninsula** (summer).
SWEDEN Abisko NP* (irregular), Holmöarna (irregular).

Hawk Owl (Northern Hawk Owl)
Surnia ulula

CF   Dis Nom

Range: In our region breeds in varying numbers in upland and N areas of Norway and Sweden, throughout much of Finland, except the extreme S, and across N Russia. Sometimes breeds far S of usual range, e.g. in S Sweden, S Finland and the Baltic states. Performs irregular southward movements when rodent prey is in short supply.

Tips: Search edges and clearings of coniferous forest and birch woodland in mountains. Mainly diurnal, fearless of man and often perches prominently on treetops. Abisko NP, in Sweden, is one of the most reliable sites, particularly in Jun when the young can be very conspicuous.

Sites:

FINLAND Kuusamo***, Lake Inari***, Lemmenjoki NP***, Liminganlahti* (irregular), Oulanka NP*, Pallas-Ounastunturi NP***, Urho Kekkonen NP***, Vesijako NP*.
NORWAY Øvre Pasvik NP***.

RUSSIA Kola Peninsula***.
SWEDEN Abisko NP***, Getterön* (irregular autumn, winter), Holmöarna** (passage), Tarnasjön***.

Pygmy Owl (Eurasian Pygmy Owl)
Glaucidium passerinum CF Res (Dis) (Irr)

Range: Breeds over much of Scandinavia, although scarce in the far S and absent from the mountains and far N, and from the Baltic states and Belarus across Russia to the Urals. Isolated populations further S in upland areas of C Europe breeding in the Alps and Jura, Erzgebirge and Moravian Heights, Carpathians and Transylvanian Alps. Precise range little known in many areas, particularly in the S, and may breed in Rhodope Mts of Greece and Bulgarisa, and perhaps in the Pyrenees. Heard in the springs of 2001–2003 in Aggtelek NP, in Hungary, but breeding unconfirmed. Mainly resident but with some southward movements in winter and occasionally irruptive. Small numbers are present most winters in Denmark.

Tips: Search forest edges or clearings at dawn and dusk, although often active by day and in Mar–Apr calls from treetops. May also call late Oct–Dec. Main habitat is taiga in the N and coniferous and mixed montane woodland further S and nests in woodpecker holes. In winter also occurs in more open habitats including farmland and has been recorded taking small birds from garden feeding stations.

Sites:

AUSTRIA Hohe Tauern NP**, Karwendel Reserve**.
BELARUS Belovezhskaya Pushcha NP**, Berezinsky Reserve***, Pripyatsky NP***.
BULGARIA Tzarichina NR**.
CZECH REPUBLIC Beskydy Mts**, Krkonoše NP**, Šumava NP***, Třeboňsko***.
ESTONIA Nigula NR***.
FINLAND Liminganlahti***, Pyhähäkki NP***, Vesijako NP***, Viikki** (winter).
FRANCE Écrins NP**, Mercantour NP***, Vanoise NP***.
GERMANY Ammer Valley***, Bayerischer Wald NP***, Berchtesgaden NP***, Vessertal**.
HUNGARY Aggtelek NP.
ITALY Gran Paradiso NP**, Stelvio NP***.

LATVIA Lake Pape***.
NORWAY Hardangervidda NP***, Lista (passage), Mølen* (passage).
POLAND Białowieża Forest***, Bieszczady NP***, Tatra NP***.
ROMANIA Gurghiu Mts***, Retezat NP***.
RUSSIA Kola Peninsula***, Oka Valley***.
SLOVAKIA High Tatras NP**, Malá Fatra***, Nízke Tatry NP***, Slovenský Kras*, Vihorlatske Hills**.
SWEDEN Getterön***, Holmöarna* (passage), Tyresta NP***.
SWITZERLAND Aletschwald**, Flims***, Swiss NP**.
UKRAINE Carpathians**.

Hume's Owl (Hume's Tawny Owl)
Strix butleri

D SD Res

Range: Very local and known from E Egypt, in mountains between the Nile and the Red Sea, S Sinai, Israel and adjacent Jordan. Probably also occurs in parts of Syria and perhaps elsewhere including Lebanon, but range poorly known.

Tips: Inhabits gorges, cliffs and wadis in rocky desert, often near oases and palm groves, sometimes close to human habitation and often hunts along roads. Undoubtedly, most easily found by using local guides, but care should be taken to keep disturbance to a minimum. Strictly nocturnal and best located by listening for calling birds which are most vocal in Feb–Mar.

Sites:
EGYPT Santa Katharina Monastery*.
ISRAEL Eilat*, Ein Gedi.

JORDAN Aqaba, Ghadir Burqu', Petra*, Wadi Dana-Fidan**, Wadi Rum*.

Ural Owl
Strix uralensis

CF MF DF M Res (Dis)

Range: Breeds in SE Norway, N Sweden through C and S Finland and the Kola Peninsula and from Estonia and Belarus across N Russia to the Urals. Small populations persist in forested areas of Poland, the Czech Republic and Slovakia, and further S in upland regions of the Balkans. The species has been reintroduced to Germany. Resident with some local wandering in winter.

Subspecies: In the N of range there are two races, *uralensis* in the E and *liturata* in the W, the southern populations belong to *macroura*.

Tips: Mainly nocturnal but may hunt by day in far N of range, often over open areas close to pine, fir and spruce forest and found in montane beech woodland in S of range. Listen for calling males in Mar–Apr, but the best way to locate the species is to contact local birders. Most visible in Jun, when accompanied by newly fledged young but very aggressive close to the nest.

Sites:
AUSTRIA Marchauen-Marchegg Reserve*.
BELARUS Belovezhskaya Pushcha NP**, Berezinsky Reserve***.
BOSNIA-HERZEGOVINA Sujetska NP**.
BULGARIA Tzarichina NR.

CROATIA Plitvice.
CZECH REPUBLIC Beskydy Mts*, Šumava NP*.
ESTONIA Nigula NR***.
FINLAND Liminganlahti***, Patvinsuo NP***, Pyhä-Häkki NP***, Vesijako NP***.

GERMANY Bayerischer Wald NP*.
HUNGARY Aggtelek NP* (irregular), Zemplén Hills** (irregular).
MACEDONIA Sara Mts.
POLAND Bieszczady NP**.
ROMANIA Bicaz**, Gurghiu Mts*, Poiana Braşov**, Retezat NP**.

RUSSIA Kola Peninsula***.
SLOVAKIA High Tatras NP, Slanské Hills**, Slovenský Kras**, Vihorlatske Hills**, Zemplínská Reservoir**.
SLOVENIA Kocevje**.
UKRAINE Carpathians*.

Great Grey Owl
Strix nebulosa   CF MF (DF)   Res (Nom)

Range: Breeds from NE Sweden, Finland and the S Kola Peninsula across N Russia to the Urals. Recent records, including breeding, from further S including Belarus, Ukraine and the Białowieża Forest, Poland, may involve vagrants but current status of this species outside the main range is little known.

Tips: Search lichen-covered spruce, pine and fir forest edges adjacent to swamps, fields, clearings and other open areas. Often seen by day in summer. Local assistance is often necessary to locate this bird and, like Ural Owl, this species is aggressive towards intruders at the nest which is usually a disused raptor or corvid nest.

Sites:
BELARUS Belovezhskaya Pushcha NP*.
FINLAND Kuusamo*, Lemmenjoki NP**, Liminganlahti**, Oulanka NP***, Pallas-Ounastunturi NP***, Urho Kekkonen NP***.

NORWAY Øvre Pasvik NP**.
POLAND Białowieża Forest.
RUSSIA Kola Peninsula***.
SWEDEN Tärnasjön**, Holmöarna** (passage).

African Marsh Owl
Asio capensis   FG FW   PMig (Dis)

Range: In our region confined as a breeder to a small area of NW Morocco (endemic race *tingitanus*) where decreasing. Formerly occurred in Algeria and vagrants have been recorded in Portugal, Spain and the Canaries.

Tips: Spends much time on the ground in marshes and grassland but also roosts in trees. Prefers wetter habitats than Short-eared Owl and is more nocturnal, although it hunts by day with harrier-like flight, sometimes in small parties. One of the main target species for birders visiting Morocco and can be guaranteed at Merja Zerga, despite current decline. Care should be taken to avoid undue disturbance to this species.

Sites:
MOROCCO Lac de Sidi Bourhaba***, Merja Zerga***.

Tengmalm's Owl (Boreal Owl)
Aegolius funereus

CF MF DF M   Res (Dis) (Irr)

Range: Main breeding range is from Scandinavia and E Poland, the Baltic states and Belarus E to the Urals. Also breeds very patchily in the Pyrenees and Alps, E France, Belgium and the Netherlands, many upland areas of C and SE Europe S to Greece, and the Caucasus. Has bred in the Bükk Hills of Hungary, and is probably more widespread than currently known. Resident in S of range but more nomadic in the N.

Tips: Strictly nocturnal and found mainly in coniferous forest, often Norway Spruce, sometimes mixed forest or birch woodland. Nests in old Black Woodpecker holes or nest boxes, and roosts in dense foliage. Often difficult to see and best located by call at night or by searching for young outside nest by day. Most vocal late Jan–late Apr and rarely located outside this period. Local assistance may be necessary to track down this elusive species, despite being fairly common in parts of range.

Sites:
ANDORRA*.
ARMENIA Khosrov Preserve*.
AUSTRIA Karwendel Reserve**, Marchauen-Marchegg Reserve**.
BELARUS Belovezhskaya Pushcha NP***, Berezinsky Reserve***, Pripyatsky NP***.
BELGIUM Hautes Fagnes Natural Park**.
BOSNIA-HERZEGOVINA Sutjeska NP**.
BULGARIA Tzarichina NR**.
CZECH REPUBLIC Beskydy Mts***, Jeseníky Mts**, Krkonoše NP***, Šumava NP**, Třeboňsko***.
DENMARK Amager* (winter), Bornholm-Christiansø**.
ESTONIA Lake Endla***, Nigula NR***, Taevaskoja***.
FINLAND Åland Is***, Kuusamo***, Liminganlahti***, Oulanka NP***, Patvinsuo NP***, Pyhähäkki NP***, Vesijako NP***.
FRANCE Écrins NP**, Mercantour NP***, Prats-de-Mollo*, Queyras NP**, Vanoise NP**.

GEORGIA Mt Kazbek***.
GERMANY Ammer Valley*, Bayerischer Wald NP**, Berchtesgaden NP**, Vessertal**.
GREECE Mt Olympus NP**.
HUNGARY Zemplén Hills* (irregular).
ITALY Gran Paradiso NP***, Stelvio NP***.
LATVIA Cape Kolka***, Lake Engure***, Lake Pape***.
LITHUANIA Kirsiu Peninsula** (passage).
MACEDONIA Sara Mts.
NORWAY Hardangervidda NP***, Lista (passage), Mølen* (passage).
POLAND Białowieża Forest***, Biebrza Marshes**, Bieszczady NP***, Tatra NP***.
ROMANIA Bicaz**, Gurghiu Mts**, Retezat NP*.
RUSSIA Kola Peninsula***, Teberdinskiy Reserve**.
SLOVAKIA High Tatras NP**, Malá Fatra***, Nízke Tatry NP**, Slovenský Kras*.
SPAIN Aigües Tortes NP**, Ordesa NP***.

SWEDEN Falsterbo* (autumn), Getterön***, Gotland*, Holmöarna***, Tyresta NP***.
SWITZERLAND Aletschwald***, Col de Bretolet**, Flims*, Swiss NP**.

TURKEY Soğuksu NP, Sumela, Uludağ NP.
UKRAINE Carpathians*.

Nubian Nightjar
Caprimulgus nubicus   D SD PMig

Range: In the Western Palearctic breeds only in the Rift Valley of S Israel and probably in adjacent W Jordan N to the Dead Sea. A partial migrant with some birds wintering in Israel but migrants have been recorded on Red Sea coasts. There have been unconfirmed reports of this species in southern Morocco.

Tips: Search rocky desert and semi-desert areas with tamarisk and acacia scrub, and passage birds may be seen in coastal dunes. Nocturnal and crepuscular, flies only a short distance when flushed, compared to Egyptian Nightjar, and often sits on desert roads and tracks at night.

Sites:
ISRAEL Arava Valley*.
JORDAN Azraq (spring).

Red-necked Nightjar
Caprimulgus ruficollis   SH SD Mig

Range: Confined as a breeder to the Western Palearctic, in Spain (except the N), S Portugal and in NW Africa, from C Morocco to N Tunisia. Has bred in S France where normally a vagrant. Fairly common in Iberia but uncommon over much of N African range. Present late Apr–late Oct, sometimes Nov. Passage noted at Gibraltar and in Morocco where some winter, but remainder of W African wintering range is poorly known.

Tips: Search dry open country with bare sandy patches and sparse cover, such as olive groves, arid hillsides and open pinewoods, sometimes semi-desert. Nocturnal and usually solitary when not breeding, and may rest on roads at night and feed on moths attracted to streetlights.

Sites:
ALGERIA Djebel Babor*** (summer).
GIBRALTAR*** (passage).

MOROCCO Agadir and the Sous Plain*** (summer), Merja Zerga*** (summer), Zeida** (summer).

PORTUGAL Baixo Alentejo*** (summer), Boquilobo** (summer), Cape St Vincent** (autumn), Castro Marim*** (summer), International Douro*** (summer), International Tagus*** (summer), Montesinho*** (summer), Ria Formosa*** (summer), Sado Estuary*** (summer), Santo André Lagoon*** (summer), Tagus Estuary*** (summer).

SPAIN Cabo de Gata*** (summer), Cáceres-Trujillo Steppes*** (summer), Cádiz Lagoons*** (summer), Coto Doñana*** (summer), Ebro Delta*** (summer), Monfragüe*** (summer), Serrania de Ronda*** (summer), Sierra de Gredos*** (summer), Zaragoza Steppes** (summer).

Egyptian Nightjar
Caprimulgus aegyptius

D SD   Mig (PMig)

Range: Breeds in S and E Morocco and across N Algeria to C Tunisia, in N Egypt and the Nile Valley. Has bred in Israel and at Azraq in Jordan. Also breeds in Kazakhstan and may occur in extreme SE Russia. Rare over most of our region. Present in breeding range Mar–Oct and mostly migratory, although some remain in the Nile Delta and SE Egypt in winter.

Subspecies: There are two races which are usually separable in the field; nominate race is from N Egypt to Iraq and *saharae* from NW Africa.

Tips: Occurs in desert and semi-desert, often near rivers and in Artemisia scrub, sometimes near palm groves and often sits on roads at night. Nocturnal and crepuscular, resting by day beneath bushes or rocks, and flies a considerable distance when flushed.

Sites:
EGYPT Abu Simbel**, Aswan*, Nile Delta*.
ISRAEL Eilat* (summer).
JORDAN Azraq* (spring, summer), Wadi Rum (spring, summer).

MOROCCO Tafilalt** (summer).
RUSSIA Kalmykia (summer).
TUNISIA Chott el Djerid**.

Cape Verde Swift (Alexander's Swift)
Apus alexandri

M FG C U   Res

Range: Endemic to the Cape Verde Is, where common on most islands, particularly Fogo and Brava, but thought not to breed on São Vicente.

Tips: Common in restricted range, feeding over towns, trees and open country, cliffs and shores, from sea level to 1,600 m in mountains. Nests in crevices in rocks and buildings.

Site:
CAPE VERDE IS***.

Plain Swift
Apus unicolor   M C U PMig

Range: Breeds on Madeira and the Canaries. Common on Madeira and Porto Santo, but status unclear on the Desertas and Selvagems, and may not breed on either. In the Canaries common on Tenerife, Gran Canaria and La Palma, less so on El Hierro, Gomera, Lanzarote and Fuerteventura. Present all year on both archipelagos with smaller numbers remaining to winter. Most migrate in Sep–Oct, to adjacent Africa, particularly in the Agadir–Oued Massa area, but extent of winter range little known, returning Feb–Mar. Has been recorded N to Merja Zerga. Discovered breeding on coastal cliffs in S Morocco in the 1980s, where formerly thought to be merely a vagrant or winter visitor.

Tips: Usually at higher altitudes but also found at sea level, feeding over trees, scrub and open areas. Breeds in rock crevices and caves. One of the best sites is the Garajau Cliffs of

Sites:
CANARY IS El Hierro**, Fuerteventura**, Gomera**, Gran Canaria***, La Palma***, Lanzarote**, Tenerife***.

MADEIRA*.
MOROCCO Agadir and the Sous Plain*, Essaouira, Merja Zerga, Oued Massa* (winter).

Pallid Swift
Apus pallidus   M C U Mig

Madeira. Often associates with Common and Pallid Swifts.

Range: Widespread around the Mediterranean, breeding in Spain, parts of S France and Italy. Rare on Adriatic coasts but breeds commonly in Greece and many Greek islands. Also breeds on the Balearics, Corsica, Sardinia, N Sicily and Cyprus. Rare and local in Turkey and the Rift Valley of Israel and W Jordan, and has bred in Lebanon. Common in NW Africa from Morocco to Tunisia, breeds discontinuously on the Libyan coast and in Egypt mainly in the Nile Delta and Valley. Also breeds on Madeira and the Canaries. Most winter in sub-Saharan Africa, leaving Sep–early Nov and returning in Jan (Canaries) to early Apr (France), although present all year in parts of N Africa.

Subspecies: There are three races present in our region but they are not safely separable in the field. Nominate *pallidus* is found from inland N Africa to the Middle East, *brehmorum* from the Canary Is, coastal N Africa and Iberia to Cyprus and Turkey and *illyricus* from around the eastern Adriatic, although some authorities include birds from Cyprus and NE Africa in this race.

Tips: Often more coastal than Common Swift, but also seen over river valleys. Feeds over open country and towns, and breeds in crevices in buildings or cliffs. The most numerous swift in some Mediterranean towns.

Sites:

ANDORRA*** (summer).

BALEARIC IS Ibiza*** (summer), Mallorca*** (summer, passage), Menorca*** (summer).

BULGARIA Cape Kaliakra* (summer), Rila Mts** (summer), Studen Kladenetz*** (summer), Tissata NR** (summer).

CANARY IS El Hierro** (summer), Fuerteventura** (summer), Gran Canaria** (summer), Lanzarote*** (summer), Tenerife** (summer).

CORSICA Bonifacio*** (summer, passage), Cap Corse** (summer, passage), Scandola*** (summer).

CROATIA Cres*** (summer), Mljet*** (summer).

EGYPT Aswan***, Faiyum* (summer), Luxor***.

FRANCE Camargue*** (summer).

GIBRALTAR*** (summer, passage).

GREECE Delphi*** (summer), Mt Olympus NP*** (summer), Mt Parnassós NP*** (summer).

GREEK IS Corfu*** (summer), Crete** (summer, passage), Kos*** (summer, passage), Lesvos** (summer, passage), Náxos*** (summer).

ISRAEL Arava Valley*** (summer, passage), Eilat*** (passage), Ein Gedi*** (summer, passage), Nizzana*** (summer, passage).

ITALY Circeo NP*** (summer), Gargano Peninsula*** (summer), Monte Conero*** (passage).

JORDAN Aqaba* (passage), Azraq** (passage), Petra*** (summer), Wadi Rum*** (summer).

LEBANON Palm Is** (summer).

MADEIRA** (summer).

MALTA* (passage, summer).

MOROCCO Agadir and the Sous Plain*** (summer), Essaouira*** (summer), Goulimime to Tan-Tan*** (summer), Oualidia*** (passage), Zaër*** (summer).

PORTUGAL Cape St Vincent*** (summer), Castro Marim*** (summer), Ria Formosa*** (summer), Sado Estuary*** (summer), Santo André Lagoon*** (summer), Tagus Estuary*** (summer).

SARDINIA San Pietro I*** (summer).

SICILY San Vito Peninsula*** (summer), Strait of Messina*** (summer).

SLOVENIA Karst RP** (summer), Kocevje* (summer).

SPAIN Aiguamolls de L'Empordá*** (summer, passage), Cabo de Gata*** (summer), Cáceres-Trujillo Steppes*** (summer), Cádiz Lagoons*** (summer), Coto Doñana*** (passage), Ebro Delta*** (summer, passage), Garraf Massif*** (summer), Guadalhorce Estuary*** (summer, passage), Jaca** (summer), Llobregat Delta*** (summer, passage), Santa Pola*** (summer), Serrania de Ronda*** (summer).

SYRIA Aqra Mts*** (summer), Dayr al-Zawr*** (summer).

TUNISIA Tunis*** (summer), Zaghouan*** (summer).

TURKEY İstanbul*** (summer, passage), Uludağ NP*** (summer).

White-rumped Swift
Apus caffer M FG PMig

Range: Widespread in sub-Saharan Africa but also breeds in the Atlas Mts of C Morocco and S Iberia, where first noted in the 1960s. In Spain, occurs in Cádiz, Cordoba and Almería, and recently discovered in Extremadura, and breeding in S Portugal was confirmed in 1995. Numbers breeding in Iberia are still low but increasing and a new breeding site near Seville was discovered in 2002. Mainly a summer visitor to Spain, present May–Oct, although has been recorded in winter, whilst movements of Moroccan population are unknown.

Tips: Feeds over open country, in particular farmland. Breeds in Spain only in old nests of Red-rumped Swallow.

Sites:
MOROCCO Agadir and the Sous Plain** (summer), Ouarzazate* (summer), Oukaimeden** (summer).
PORTUGAL Baixo Alentejo* (summer).

SPAIN Guadalhorce Estuary* (passage), Monfragüe*** (summer), Serrania de Ronda** (summer).

Alpine Swift
Apus melba M U Mig

Range: Widespread and fairly common around the Mediterranean, breeding in Iberia, S France and the Alps, much of Italy, the Balkans and Greece. Also breeds on Mallorca, Corsica, Sardinia, Sicily, many Greek islands and Cyprus. Widespread in Turkey, the Caucasus and Crimea, and local in the Middle East and at scattered sites in in the Atlas Mts of NW Africa. Small numbers have been recorded in winter in N Africa and the Middle east but most migrate to sub-Saharan Africa.

Subspecies: Nominate *melba* occurs over European range and in N Morocco, replaced by *tuneti* in the S Morocco and throughout remainder of N Africa to SW Asia but intermediates occur over large areas.

Tips: Easy to see in most of range, breeding on tall buildings and crevices in cliffs and feeding over towns and open country. Departs breeding areas Sep–early Nov to winter in sub-Saharan Africa, returning in Apr.

Sites:
ANDORRA* (summer).

ARMENIA Khosrov Preserve*** (summer).

AUSTRIA Hohe Tauern NP*** (summer), Hohe Wand*** (summer), Karwendel Reserve*** (summer).
BALEARIC IS Mallorca*** (summer, passage), Menorca*** (summer, passage).
BOSNIA-HERZEGOVINA Sujetska NP*** (summer, passage).
BULGARIA Albena-Golden Sands** (summer), Cape Kaliakra*** (summer), Rila Mts*** (summer), Rusenski Lom NP*** (summer), Studen Kladenetz*** (summer), Trigradski Gorge*** (summer), Tissata NR*** (summer).
CANARY IS Fuerteventura* (passage).
CORSICA Asco Valley*** (summer), Bonifacio*** (summer), Cap Corse*** (summer, passage), Restonica Valley*** (summer) Scandola*** (summer).
CROATIA Cres*** (summer), Mljet*** (summer), Paklenica NP*** (summer).
CYPRUS** (summer, passage).
FRANCE Camargue*** (summer), Cévennes NP*** (summer), Les Alpilles*** (summer), Prats-de-Mollo*** (summer), Pyrenees NP*** (summer), Queyras NP*** (summer).
GEORGIA Mt Kazbek*** (summer).
GIBRALTAR** (summer, passage).
GREECE Delphi*** (summer), Mikrí Prespa NP*** (summer), Mt Olympus NP*** (summer), Mt Parnassós NP*** (summer).
GREEK IS Corfu*** (summer), Crete*** (summer, passage), Kos*** (summer, passage), Lesvos*** (summer, passage), Náxos*** (summer), Rhodes*** (summer).
ISRAEL Arava Valley*** (passage), Eilat*** (passage), Golan Heights*** (summer), Hula Reserve** (passage), Ma'agan Mikhael*** (passage), Wadi Ammud-Mt Arbel*** (summer, small numbers winter).
ITALY Circeo NP*** (summer), Gargano Peninsula*** (summer), Gran Paradiso NP*** (summer), Monte Conero*** (summer), Stelvio NP*** (summer), Tuscan archipelago*** (summer).

JORDAN Azraq* (passage), Petra*** (summer), Wadi Dana-Fidan** (summer, passage).
MACEDONIA Babuna Gorge*** (summer), Galicica NP*** (summer), Lakes Ohrid and Prespa** (summer), Mavrovo NP** (summer).
MALTA* (passage).
MOROCCO Oukaimeden*** (summer).
PORTUGAL Baixo Alentejo*** (summer), Boquilobo* (passage), Cape St Vincent*** (summer), International Douro*** (summer), International Tagus*** (summer), Sado Estuary* (passage), Tagus Estuary* (passage).
ROMANIA Bicaz*** (summer), Dobrudja** (summer), Poiana Braşov*** (summer), Retezat NP*** (summer), Turda Gorge*** (summer).
SARDINIA San Pietro I*** (summer).
SICILY San Vito Peninsula*** (summer), Strait of Messina*** (passage).
SLOVENIA Triglav NP*** (summer).
SPAIN Aiguamolls de L'Empordá*** (summer, passage), Aigües Tortes NP*** (summer), Cabo de Gata*** (summer), Cáceres-Trujillo Steppes*** (summer), Coto Doñana*** (passage), Ebro Delta* (passage), Garraf Massif*** (summer), Jaca*** (summer), La Serena* (summer), Llobregat Delta*** (summer), Monfragüe*** (summer), Ordesa NP*** (summer), Serrania de Ronda*** (summer).
SWITZERLAND Flims*** (summer), Klingnau Reservoir** (passage), Monte Generoso*** (summer), Niderholz*** (summer), Swiss NP*** (summer).
SYRIA Jabal Slenfeh*** (summer), Tadmur and Sabkhat Muh** (summer), Yarmuk Valley*** (summer).
TUNISIA Zaghouan*** (summer).
TURKEY Demirkazik*** (summer), Göksu Delta* (summer),İstanbul*** (summer, passage), Sultan Marshes* (summer, passage), Uludağ NP*** (summer), Van Gölü*** (summer, passage).
UKRAINE Crimean Mts*** (summer).

Little Swift
Apus affinis   M U Res Mig

Range: Breeds in NW Africa, in coastal Morocco from Oued Massa northwards, in the Moroccan Atlas, and in very scattered localities in N Algeria and Tunisia. Also breeds in extreme SE Turkey, possibly in Syria, in N and SC Israel and W Jordan. Suspected of breeding in S Spain in the 1990s and this was confirmed near Cádiz in 2000. N African populations probably resident but Asian birds are summer visitors, especially in Turkey, returning in Feb–Apr.

Tips: Found in towns and around cliffs, often near water, feeding over nearby farmland. Breeds on cliffs or buildings.

Sites:
ISRAEL Ein Gedi*** (summer, passage), Golan Heights*** (summer), Hula Reserve** (passage), Ma'agan Mikhael*** (passage), Mt Hermon*** (summer), Wadi Ammud-Mt Arbel*** (summer).
JORDAN Azraq* (passage).
MOROCCO Agadir and the Sous Plain***, Asilah and Oued Loukkos***, Essaouira***, Oukaimeden***.

SYRIA Tadmur and Sabkhat Muh** (summer), Wadi al-Qarn-Burqush** (summer), Yarmuk Valley*** (summer).
TUNISIA Chott el Djerid***, Tunis***.
TURKEY Birecik-Halfeti*** (summer).

White-breasted Kingfisher (Smyrna Kingfisher)
Halcyon smyrnensis   FW FG (BW) (ES) Res (Dis)

Range: A local breeder in our region, in coastal areas of S Turkey and perhaps N Syria, in Israel and Jordan. Also small numbers in Sinai and the Nile Delta of Egypt.
Tips: Search margins of lakes and rivers with trees and bushes, also wooded areas not necessarily close to water. Sometimes in gardens and plantations and also seashores.

Sites:
EGYPT Nile Delta**, Sharm el Sheik, Zaranik***.
ISRAEL Bet Shean Valley***, Eilat***, Ein Gedi***, Hula Reserve***, Jezreel Valley***, Ma'agan Mikhael***, Urim**.

JORDAN Aqaba*, Wadi as Sir***.
SYRIA Yarmuk Valley***.
TURKEY Dalyan***, Göksu Delta***.

Grey-headed Kingfisher
Halcyon leucocephala   DF FG C   Res

Range: Widespread in sub-Saharan Africa and also found in SW Arabia, but the only Western Palearctic locality is the Cape Verde Is, where the endemic subspecies *acteon* occurs on São Tiago, Brava and Fogo.

Tips: Inhabits dry woodland and open country, rocky ravines, vineyards and often found near human habitation. Common on the Cape Verdes, where it can even be seen in the main square in Praia, on São Tiago.

Site:
CAPE VERDE IS***.

Pied Kingfisher
Ceryle rudis   FW (BW) (ES)   Res (Dis)

Range: Local in S Turkey, N Syria, Israel, Jordan, Sinai and more common in Egypt, in the Nile Delta and Valley. Common in Iraq and extends N along the Tigris and Euphrates Rivers into E Turkey. More widespread in the Middle East during post-breeding dispersal. Irregularly recorded in Cyprus, usually Oct–Apr.

Tips: Conspicuous around lakes, ponds and rivers, and also fishes in estuaries and on sheltered seas.

Sites:
CYPRUS (passage, winter).
EGYPT Aswan***, Faiyum*, Luxor***, Nile Delta***, Sharm el Sheikh***, Suez area***, Zaranik***.
ISRAEL Bet Shean Valley***, Eilat***, Hula Reserve***, Jezreel Valley***, Ma'agan Mikhael***, Urim**.

JORDAN Azraq* (autumn, winter).
SYRIA Baath Lakes***, Bahrat Homs*** (autumn, winter), Dayr al-Zawr***, Sabkhat al-Jubbal** (winter), Yarmuk Valley** (passage, winter).
TURKEY Birecik-Halfeti***, Cizre***.

Little Green Bee-eater
Merops orientalis

FG (DF)   Res (PMig) (Dis)

Range: Breeds in Egypt, mainly in the Nile Delta and Valley, and in the Rift Valley of Israel and adjacent Jordan. A partial migrant in Egypt, with some present all year, and resident or locally dispersive in Israel.

Subspecies: Two distinct races occur in our region; *cleopatra* in Egypt and *cyanophrys* in the Middle East.

Tips: Search cultivated land and open woodland, and it is often seen along tree-lined riverbanks and roadsides.

Sites:

EGYPT Aswan***, Faiyum***, Luxor***, Nile Delta**.

ISRAEL Arava Valley***, Eilat***, Ein Gedi***, Mt Hermon***.

JORDAN Aqaba***, Wadi Dana-Fidan***.

Blue-cheeked Bee-eater
Merops persicus

FG SD (FW)   Mig

Range: In N Africa breeds in Mauritania and locally in SE Morocco, possibly also in W Algeria, and in the Nile Delta. In SW Asia breeds around the Caspian from the Volga Delta southwards, in Armenia, extreme S and E Turkey, adjacent Syria and in Israel. Has bred in Jordan and Lebanon. Most populations are migratory and small numbers move into NW Africa from further S in late summer before departing in Oct. SW Asian birds move through the Middle East and Egypt, mainly in Sep–Oct, returning Mar–May. Rare but regular passage visitor through Cyprus, mainly late Mar–May and Sep.

Subspecies: Two similar races are found in our region; *chrysocercus* is found in NW Africa and *persicus* in SW Asia and Egypt.

Tips: Search dry sandy areas, wadis and gorges with scattered trees, semi-desert and dry steppe with bushes and other vegetation. Often near water and regularly breeds in deltas and along sandy riverbanks.

Sites:

ARMENIA Armash Fishponds*** (summer).
AZERBAIJAN Turianchai Reserve***, Kyzylagach Bay*** (summer).
CYPRUS* (passage).
EGYPT Abu Simbel*** (summer, passage), Aswan*** (summer, passage), Faiyum** (summer), Luxor** (summer, passage), Nile Delta*** (summer), Wadi el Natrun*** (summer).
ISRAEL Arava Valley* (passage), Bet Shean Valley*** (passage), Eilat** (summer, passage).
JORDAN Aqaba** (passage), Azraq** (passage).

MOROCCO Tafilalt** (summer).
RUSSIA Kalmykia*** (summer), Volga Delta*** (summer).

SYRIA Baath Lakes*** (summer), Dayr al-Zawr*** (summer, passage).
TURKEY Birecik-Halfeti* (summer).

European Bee-eater
Merops apiaster   FG DF (FW)   Mig

Range: Fairly common in Iberia (except on the N coast), in S France and parts of Italy, and from the E Adriatic to the Black and Caspian Seas. Found throughout Turkey and the Caucasus, and in parts of the Middle East. In the Mediterranean breeds on the Balearics, Corsica and Sardinia, Crete and Cyprus and is widespread in NW Africa. Departs breeding grounds in Aug–Sep, occurring on passage throughout S Europe and the Middle East, returning Apr–May. Frequently overshoots in spring and is an annual visitor, with occasional breeding, N to Great Britain and Scandinavia.

Tips: Usually seen in flocks, over open country with scattered trees and woodland edges, commonly along rivers and in cultivated areas. Presence often first revealed by call, which can be heard even from high-flying migrants.

Sites:

ALBANIA Drini Delta** (summer), Karavasta Lagoon** (summer), Lake Shkodra*** (summer).

ARMENIA Armash Fishponds*** (summer), Khosrov Preserve*** (summer).

AUSTRIA Lake Neusiedl*** (summer, passage).

BALEARIC IS Ibiza*** (summer, passage), Mallorca*** (summer, passage), Menorca*** (summer, passage).

BULGARIA Albena-Golden Sands*** (summer, passage), Burgas area*** (passage), Cape Emine*** (passage), Cape Kaliakra*** (passage), Lake Durankulak*** (summer, passage), Lake Shabla*** (summer, passage), Lake Srebarna*** (summer), Rusenski Lom NP*** (summer), Strandja Mts*** (summer, passage), Studen Kladenetz*** (summer), Trigradski Gorge** (passage), Tissata NR*** (summer, passage).

CANARY IS Fuerteventura* (passage).

CORSICA Biguglia Lake*** (summer), Cap Corse*** (passage).

CROATIA Cres** (passage), Neretva Delta*** (summer), Paklenica NP*** (summer).

CYPRUS* (summer, passage).

EGYPT Abu Simbel** (passage), Aswan** (passage), Faiyum** (passage), Hurghada*** (passage), Luxor** (passage), Suez area*** (passage), Wadi el Natrun*** (passage), Zaranik** (passage).

FRANCE Camargue*** (summer), Dombes*** (summer), Gruissan*** (summer), La Brenne*** (summer), Leucate*** (passage), Organbidexka*** (passage).

GEORGIA Iori Steppes*** (summer), Mt Kazbek*** (summer).

GIBRALTAR* (passage).

GREECE Avas Gorge*** (summer), Axios-Aliakmonas Deltas*** (summer), Dadiá-Soufli Forest*** (summer), Evros Delta*** (summer), Lake Kerkini*** (summer), Mikrí Prespa NP*** (summer), Mt Olympus NP*** (summer), Nestos Delta*** (summer), Porto Lagos area*** (summer, passage).

GREEK IS Corfu*** (summer, passage), Crete*** (summer, passage), Kos*** (passage), Lesvos*** (summer, passage), Rhodes*** (summer, passage).

HUNGARY Csákvár*** (summer), Hortobágy NP* (summer), Kis-balaton** (summer), Kiskunság NP* (summer), Lake Fertö** (summer), Lake Velence* (summer), Ócsa*** (summer), Pilis Hills** (summer), Zemplén Hills* (summer).

ISRAEL Arava Valley*** (passage), Bet Shean Valley*** (passage), Eilat*** (passage), Ein Gedi*** (passage), Urim*** (passage).

ITALY Circeo NP*** (summer), Gargano Peninsula*** (summer, passage), Lake Massaciuccoli*** (passage), Maremma Regional Park*** (summer, passage), Monte Conero*** (passage), Orbetello Reserve*** (summer), Po Delta*** (summer), San Giuliano Reserve*** (passage), Tuscan archipelago*** (passage).

JORDAN Amman NP*** (summer), Aqaba*** (passage), Azraq*** (passage), Petra*** (passage), Wadi Dana-Fidan*** (passage), Wadi Rum*** (passage), Wadi as Sir** (summer).

LEBANON Aamiq Marshes*** (passage), Palm Is** (passage).

MACEDONIA Galicica NP*** (summer), Lakes Ohrid and Prespa*** (summer).

MADEIRA* (passage).

MALTA* (passage).

MOROCCO Agadir and the Sous Plain*** (summer, passage), Ouarzazate*** (passage), Oued Massa*** (passage), Oukaimeden*** (passage), Tafilalt** (passage), Zaër*** (passage), Zeida** (summer).

PORTUGAL Baixo Alentejo*** (summer), Boquilobo*** (summer), Cape St Vincent*** (summer, passage), Castro Marim*** (summer), International Douro*** (summer), International Tagus*** (summer), Montesinho*** (summer), Peneda Gêres NP* (summer), Ria Formosa*** (summer), Sado Estuary*** (summer), Santo André Lagoon*** (summer), Tagus Estuary*** (summer).

ROMANIA Danube Delta*** (summer), Dobrudja*** (summer, passage).

RUSSIA Kalmykia*** (summer), Volga Delta*** (summer).

SARDINIA Oristano wetlands*** (summer).

SICILY San Vito Peninsula*** (summer, passage), Strait of Messina*** (passage).

SLOVAKIA Malé Karpaty*** (summer).

SPAIN Aiguamolls de L'Empordá*** (summer), Cabo de Gata*** (summer), Cáceres-Trujillo Steppes*** (summer), Cádiz Lagoons*** (summer), Coto Doñana*** (summer), Ebro Delta*** (summer), Garraf Massif*** (summer), Guadalhorce Estuary*** (summer, passage), Jaca*** (summer), La Serena*** (summer), Llobregat Delta*** (summer), Monfragüe*** (summer), Picos de Europa*** (summer), Santa Pola*** (summer), Serrania de Ronda*** (summer), Sierra de Gredos*** (summer), Sierra de Guadarrama*** (summer), Tablas de Daimiel*** (summer), Zaragoza Steppes*** (summer).

SWEDEN Öland (spring).

SYRIA Dayr al-Zawr*** (summer), Tadmur and Sabkhat Muh* (passage).

TUNISIA Cap Bon Peninsula*** (passage), Lake Ichkeul*** (summer, passage), Zaghouan*** (summer).

TURKEY Bafa Gölü** (passage), Birecik-Halfeti*** (summer), Borćka*** (passage), Dalyan** (summer, passage), Demirkazik*** (summer), Göksu Delta*** (summer), _stanbul*** (passage), Kocaćay Delta*** (summer), Kulu Gölü*** (passage), Manyas Gölü*** (summer), Uluabat Gölü*** (summer), Van Gölü*** (summer).

UKRAINE Askania-Nova*** (summer), Crimean Mts** (summer), Dunay Delta*** (summer), Tiligul Liman*** (summer).

YUGOSLAVIA Carska bara* (summer), Fruška Gora NP* (summer).

European Roller
Coracias garrulus   FG DF SD (FW)   Mig

Range: Declining in Europe but still breeds in much of Iberia and S France, Sardinia, Sicily and parts of Italy, and from Slovenia N to Poland and the Baltic states and E to the Urals and Caspian. Occurs throughout Turkey and Cyprus, in N Syria, Israel and Jordan and across much of NW Africa. Departs breeding range in Aug–Oct to winter in E Africa and returns in Apr–May.

Subspecies: Nominate race occurs over most of range with very similar *semenowi* in the far E of the Western Palearctic in Iraq.

Tips: Search open pinewoods and edges and clearings in oak woodland, also trees along canals, rivers and roadsides, in cultivated areas with scattered trees, often in steppe and semi-desert in E of range. Often seen perched on roadside wires or in tumbling display flight.

Sites:

ARMENIA Armash Fishponds*** (summer).

AUSTRIA Lake Neusiedl* (summer).

AZERBAIJAN Turianchai Reserve** (summer).

BALEARIC IS Ibiza* (passage), Mallorca* (passage), Menorca* (passage).

BELARUS Belovezhskaya Pushcha NP* (summer), Berezinsky Reserve* (summer), Pripyatsky NP** (summer).

BULGARIA Albena-Golden Sands* (summer, passage), Burgas area*** (summer), Cape Emine* (passage), Cape Kaliakra*** (passage, summer), Lake Durankulak** (summer, passage), Lake Shabla* (summer, passage), Lake Srebarna*** (summer), Rila Mts** (summer), Rusenski Lom NP*** (summer), Strandja Mts*** (summer, passage), Studen Kladenetz*** (summer), Tissata NR*** (summer, passage).

CORSICA Cap Corse** (passage).

CYPRUS* (summer, passage).

EGYPT Abu Simbel* (passage), Aswan* (passage), Hurghada** (passage), Luxor* (passage), Zaranik* (passage).

FRANCE Camargue*** (summer), Leucate** (passage).

GEORGIA Iori Steppes** (summer).

GIBRALTAR* (passage).

GREECE Avas Gorge*** (summer), Axios-Aliakmonas Deltas*** (summer), Dadiá-Soufli Forest*** (summer), Evros Delta* (summer), Lake Kerkini*** (summer), Mikrí Prespa NP*** (summer), Nestos Delta** (summer), Porto Lagos area** (summer, passage).

GREEK IS Corfu*** (summer, passage), Crete* (passage), Kos* (passage), Lesvos** (passage), Rhodes* (passage).

HUNGARY Hortobágy NP** (summér), Kiskunság NP*** (summer), Ócsa* (summer), Szeged Fishponds* (summer).

ISRAEL Arava Valley** (passage), Bet Shean Valley*** (passage), Eilat** (passage), Nizzana** (passage), Urim** (passage).

ITALY Circeo NP** (summer), Gargano Peninsula*** (summer), Maremma Regional Park*** (summer, passage), Orbetello Reserve*** (summer), Po Delta*** (summer), San Giuliano Reserve*** (passage), Tuscan archipelago*** (passage).

JORDAN Amman NP*** (passage), Aqaba** (passage), Azraq* (passage), Petra* (passage), Wadi Rum** (passage) Wadi as Sir* (passage).

LEBANON Aamiq Marshes** (passage).

LITHUANIA Lake Kretuonas (summer).

MACEDONIA Babuna Gorge*** (summer),

Bregalnica Valley** (summer), Crna Gorge** (summer), Demir Kapija Gorge** (summer), Galicica NP*** (summer), Lakes Ohrid and Prespa*** (summer), Mavrovo NP** (summer).
MADEIRA (passage).
MALTA** (passage).
MOROCCO Agadir and the Sous Plain*** (summer, passage), Dayet Aaoua** (summer), Oued Massa* (passage).
POLAND Białowieża Forest* (summer), Biebrza Marshes* (summer), Milicz Fishponds** (summer), Siemianówka Reservoir* (summer).
PORTUGAL Baixo Alentejo*** (summer), Cape St Vincent** (autumn), Castro Marim** (passage), International Douro*** (summer), International Tagus*** (summer), Peneda Gêres NP* (passage), Sado Estuary* (passage), Santo André Lagoon (passage), Tagus Estuary* (passage).
ROMANIA Danube Delta*** (summer), Dobrudja*** (passage).
RUSSIA Kalmykia*** (summer), Volga Delta*** (summer).

SARDINIA Capo Marargiu*** (passage).
SICILY Strait of Messina** (passage).
SLOVAKIA Senné Fishponds* (summer), Slovenský Kras* (summer), Záhorie* (summer).
SPAIN Aiguamolls de L'Empordá*** (summer), Cabo de Gata*** (summer), Cáceres-Trujillo Steppes*** (summer), Coto Doñana*** (summer), Guadalhorce Estuary* (passage), La Serena*** (summer), Monfragüe*** (summer), Tablas de Daimiel** (summer).
SYRIA Dayr al-Zawr* (summer).
TUNISIA Cap Bon Peninsula* (passage), Zaghouan** (summer).
TURKEY Akseki** (summer), Bafa Gölü** (summer, passage), Birecik-Halfeti*** (summer), Borćka* (passage), Dalyan** (summer, passage), Göksu Delta*** (summer), İstanbul** (passage), Kızılırmak Delta** (summer), Kocaćay Delta*** (summer), Kulu Gölü*** (summer), Manyas Gölü*** (summer), Sultan Marshes*** (summer), Van Gölü*** (summer).
UKRAINE Askania-Nova*** (summer), Dunay Delta*** (summer), Tiligul Liman*** (summer).

Wryneck
Jynx torquilla

CF MF DF SH   Mig (PMig)

Range: Widespread across Europe, from N and E Iberia to the Urals, Caspian and the N Caucasus. Absent from the British Isles but breeds over most of Scandinavia and, in the S, on all of the larger Mediterranean islands and in parts of N Africa. Mainly a summer visitor but a partial migrant in far S of range. Main passage periods are Aug–Oct and Apr–May, and passage birds occur over much of the region.

Subspecies: Nominate race is found over most of Europe replaced by *tschusii* in Corsica, Sardinia, Italy and the Adriatic coast of the Balkans and *mauretanica* in NW Africa.

Tips: An elusive bird of all kinds of open woodland and spends much time on the ground. Search clearings and woodland edges, in orchards, parks and large gardens, and more open habitats on passage.

Sites:

ALBANIA Drini Delta** (summer), Karavasta Lagoon*** (summer), Lake Shkodra*** (summer).

ALGERIA Djebel Babor*** (summer), El Kala NP*** (summer).

ANDORRA** (summer).

ARMENIA Khosrov Preserve*** (summer).

AUSTRIA Lake Neusiedl*** (summer), Marchauen-Marchegg Reserve*** (summer), Wienerwald*** (summer).

BALEARIC IS Ibiza**, Mallorca***, Menorca***.

BELARUS Belovezhskaya Pushcha NP*** (summer), Berezinsky Reserve*** (summer), Pripyatsky NP*** (summer).

BOSNIA-HERZEGOVINA Sujetska NP*** (summer).

BULGARIA Albena-Golden Sands*** (passage), Burgas area*** (summer), Cape Emine*** (summer, passage), Cape Kaliakra*** (passage), Lake Shabla** (summer), Lake Srebarna*** (summer), Rila Mts*** (summer), Ropotamo NP*** (summer), Rusenski Lom NP*** (summer), Strandja Mts*** (summer, passage), Trigradski Gorge*** (summer).

CANARY IS Fuerteventura* (passage).

CORSICA Cap Corse** (passage).

CROATIA Cres*** (summer), Paklenica NP*** (summer).

CZECH REPUBLIC Beskydy Mts*** (summer), Jeseníky Mts*** (summer), Krkonoše NP*** (summer), Lednice*** (summer), Nové Mlýny*** (summer), Pálava Hills*** (summer), Poodří*** (summer), Soutok*** (summer), Třeboňsko*** (summer).

DENMARK Amager* (passage), Bornholm-Christiansø*** (summer, passage), Møn-Falster*** (summer, passage), Skagen*** (passage), Skallingen-Blåvandshuk*** (passage).

EGYPT Abu Simbel** (passage), Aswan** (passage), Hurghada*** (passage), Luxor** (passage), Suez area*** (passage), Zaranik** (passage).

ESTONIA Lake Endla*** (summer), Matsalu Bay*** (summer), Nigula NR*** (summer), Taevaskoja*** (summer).

FINLAND Åland Is*** (summer), Liminganlahti*** (summer), Vesijako NP*** (summer).

FRANCE Baie du Mont-St-Michel* (passage), Camargue*** (summer), Cap Gris Nez* (passage), Cévennes NP*** (summer), Dombes*** (summer), Fontainebleau*** (summer), Golfe du Morbihan*** (summer), Île d'Oléron** (summer), Lac du Der-Chantecoq*** (summer), Lorraine NP*** (summer), Ouessant*** (passage), Pyrenees NP*** (summer), Sologne*** (summer).

GERMANY Ammer Valley*** (summer), Bayerischer Wald NP*** (summer), Berchtesgaden NP*** (summer), Federsee*** (summer), Heligoland*** (passage), Kuhkopf*** (summer), Mecklenburg Lakes*** (summer), Schweinfurt*** (summer), Tiroler Achen*** (summer), Vessertal*** (summer).

GIBRALTAR** (passage).

GREAT BRITAIN Dungeness* (passage), Flamborough Head** (passage), Minsmere** (passage), N Norfolk coast*** (passage), Orkney Is** (passage), Pembrokeshire Is* (autumn), Portland* (passage), Scilly*** (passage), Shetland Is*** (passage), Spurn Peninsula** (passage).

GREECE Dadiá-Soufli Forest*** (summer), Lake Kerkini*** (summer), Mikrí Prespa NP*** (summer), Mt Olympus NP*** (summer), Nestos Delta*** (summer).

GREEK IS Crete*** (summer, passage), Lesvos*** (passage), Rhodes*** (passage).

HUNGARY Aggtelek NP*** (summer), Börzsöny NP*** (summer), Bükk Hills NP** (summer), Buda Hills*** (summer), Csákvár*** (summer), Danube Bend*** (summer), Hortobágy NP*** (summer), Kis-balaton*** (summer), Kiskunság NP*** (summer), Lake Fertö*** (summer), Ócsa*** (summer), Pilis Hills*** (summer), Tihany*** (summer), Zemplén Hills*** (summer).

ISRAEL Arava Valley*** (passage), Eilat*** (passage), Ein Gedi*** (passage), Nizzana** (passage), Urim*** (passage).

ITALY Abruzzo NP*** (summer), Circeo NP*** (summer), Gargano Peninsula*** (summer), Lake Massaciuccoli*** (passage), Maremma Regional Park*** (summer, passage), Orbetello Reserve*** (summer), Po Delta*** (summer), San Giuliano Reserve*** (passage), Sibillini NP*** (summer), Tuscan archipelago*** (passage).

JORDAN Amman NP* (passage), Aqaba*** (passage), Azraq* (passage), Wadi Rum*** (passage).

LATVIA Cape Kolka*** (summer), Lake Lubana*** (summer), Lake Pape*** (summer, passage).

LEBANON Aamiq Marshes*** (passage), Qaraoun Lake** (passage).

MACEDONIA Babuna Gorge** (summer), Galicica NP*** (summer), Lakes Ohrid and Prespa*** (summer), Mavrovo NP** (summer), Sara Mts** (summer).

MALTA** (passage).

MOROCCO Boumalne** (passage), Ouarzazate*** (passage), Oued Massa*** (passage), Tafilalt** (passage).

NETHERLANDS Veluwe*** (summer).

NORWAY Hardangervidda NP** (summer), Utsira* (passage).

POLAND Białowieża Forest*** (summer), Biebrza Marshes*** (summer), Bieszczady NP*** (summer), Chełm Marshes*** (summer), Kampinos NP*** (summer), Milicz Fishponds*** (summer), Siemianówka Reservoir*** (summer), Słońsk*** (summer).

PORTUGAL Baixo Alentejo*** (summer), Cape St Vincent*** (autumn), Castro Marim*** (passage), Montesinho*** (summer), Peneda Gêres NP*** (summer), Ria Formosa*** (passage), Sado Estuary*** (summer), Santo André Lagoon*** (summer), Tagus Estuary*** (summer).

ROMANIA Danube Delta*** (summer), Dobrudja*** (summer, passage), Turda Gorge*** (summer).

RUSSIA Teberdinskiy Reserve*** (summer).

SLOVAKIA High Tatras NP*** (summer), Malá Fatra*** (summer), Malé Karpaty*** (summer), Nízke Tatry NP*** (summer), Senné Fishponds*** (summer), Slanské Hills*** (summer), Slovenský Kras*** (summer), Vihorlatske Hills*** (summer), Záhorie*** (summer).

SLOVENIA Karst RP*** (summer), Kocevje** (summer), Krakovski Forest** (summer), Ljubljansko Moor*** (summer), Triglav NP*** (summer).

SPAIN Aiguamolls de L'Empordá*** (passage), Cabo de Gata** (passage), Cáceres-Trujillo Steppes*** (summer), Cádiz Lagoons*** (passage, rare in winter), Coto Doñana*** (summer, passage), Ebro Delta** (passage), Garraf Massif*** (summer), Jaca*** (summer), La Serena*** (summer), Llobregat Delta*** (summer, passage), Monfragüe*** (summer), Ordesa NP** (summer), Picos de Europa*** (summer), Santa Pola** (passage), Sierra de Gredos*** (summer), Sierra de Guadarrama*** (summer), Tablas de Daimiel*** (summer, passage).

SWEDEN Falsterbo** (summer, passage), Getterön*** (summer), Gotland*** (summer, passage), Kristianstad*** (passage), Kvismaren*** (summer), Tyresta NP*** (summer).

SWITZERLAND Clos-du-Doubs*** (summer), Fanel NR** (passage), Flims* (passage), Leuk*** (summer), Monte Generoso*** (summer), Niderholz*** (summer), Swiss NP*** (summer).

SYRIA Dayr al-Zawr** (passage), Yarmuk Valley* (passage).

TUNISIA Ain Draham** (summer), Cap Bon Peninsula*** (passage), Zaghouan*** (summer).

TURKEY Akseki** (summer), Borćka** (passage), Dalyan** (passage), Demirkazik (passage), İstanbul** (passage), Kızılırmak Delta*** (summer), Soğuksu NP** (summer), Uludağ NP** (summer), Van Gölü* (passage).

UKRAINE Carpathians*** (summer), Crimean Mts*** (summer).

YUGOSLAVIA Durmitor NP** (summer), Fruška Gora NP** (summer), Obedska bara** (summer).

Grey-headed Woodpecker (Grey-faced Woodpecker)
Picus canus   CF MF DF   Res (Dis)

Range: Breeds in S Scandinavia and C and E Europe southwards to N Greece and the Black Sea coast of the Balkans, E to the Urals. Scarce further W, where found in parts of W and C France, S Germany, Switzerland, N Italy and, more widely, in Austria. Recently proven to breed in NE, W and S Turkey and, in Mar 1992, reported in Circeo NP, far S of the previously known Italian range.

Tips: Where both species occur, usually found in smaller woods and higher areas than Green Woodpecker, and drums more frequently than the latter. Often seen in larches, and in Scandinavia occurs in coniferous forest mixed with aspen but in C Europe often found in deciduous and riparian forest, even parks and large gardens. Spends much time feeding on ground but unobtrusive, particularly in spring and best located by call.

Sites:

AUSTRIA Karwendel Reserve**, Lake Neusiedl***, Marchauen-Marchegg Reserve***, Wienerwald***.

BELARUS Belovezhskaya Pushcha NP***, Berezinsky Reserve***.

BELGIUM Croix-Scaille NR*, Hautes Fagnes Natural Park**.

BOSNIA-HERZEGOVINA Sutjeska NP***.

BULGARIA Albena-Golden Sands***, Lake Srebarna***, Rila Mts***, Ropotamo NP***, Strandja Mts***, Trigradski Gorge***, Tzarichina NR***.

CROATIA Paklenica NP**, Plitvice**.

CZECH REPUBLIC Beskydy Mts*, Jeseníky Mts***, Krkonoše NP**, Lednice***, Nové Mlýny***, Pálava Hills***, Pohořelice Fishponds*, Poodří***, Soutok*, Šumava NP***, Třeboňsko***.

ESTONIA Lake Endla***, Matsalu Bay***, Nigula NR***, Vilsandi NP**.

FINLAND Åland Is***, Ruissalo***.

FRANCE Fontainebleau***, Forêt d'Orient***, Lac du Der-Chantecoq***, Lorraine NP***, Sologne***.

GERMANY Ammer Valley***, Bayerischer Wald NP***, Berchtesgaden NP***, Kuhkopf***, Schweinfurt***, Tiroler Achen***, Vessertal***.

GREECE Mt Olympus NP**.

HUNGARY Aggtelek NP***, Börzsöny NP***, Buda Hills**, Bükk Hills NP***, Csákvár***, Danube Bend***, Kis-balaton***, Pilis Hills***, Zemplén Hills**.

ITALY Circeo NP, Stelvio NP***.

LATVIA Cape Kolka***, Lake Pape***.

LITHUANIA Cepkeliai NR***.

NORWAY Hardangervidda NP***.

POLAND Białowieża Forest***, Biebrza Marshes***, Bieszczady NP***, Milicz Fishponds***, Tatra NP***.

ROMANIA Bicaz***, Danube Delta**, Gurghiu Mts***, Retezat NP***, Turda Gorge***.

SLOVAKIA High Tatras NP**, Malá Fatra***, Malé Karpaty***, Nízke Tatry NP***, Orava Reservoir***, Slanské Hills***, Slovenský Kras***, Vihorlatske Hills***, Záhorie***.

SLOVENIA Kocevje**, Krakovski Forest***, Triglav NP***.

SWITZERLAND Clos-du-Doubs**, Fanel NR*, Klingnau Reservoir***, Niderholz**.

TURKEY Akseki**, Borçka***, Soğuksu NP.

UKRAINE Carpathians***.

YUGOSLAVIA Durmitor NP**.

Levaillant's Green Woodpecker
Picus vaillantii CF MF DF Res

Range: Only recently split from Green Woodpecker and still considered a race of it by some authorities. Breeds in C and N Morocco, and across N Algeria to NW Tunisia.

Tips: Search wooded hillsides and warm dry slopes with scattered trees, and often found in cork oak, pines or cedars, from lowlands up to the treeline and sometimes above it. Has been recorded breeding in palm groves. Drums more frequently than Green Woodpecker.

Sites:
ALGERIA Djebel Babor***, El Kala NP***.
MOROCCO Dayet Aaoua***, Oukaimeden***, Zaër***.

TUNISIA Ain Draham***.

Black Woodpecker
Dryocopus martius CF MF DF Res (Dis)

Range: Main range is Scandinavia and from C France and the Alps across Europe to the Urals and Caspian, with small populations in the Pyrenees and Cantabrians, Apennines, the Balkans, Greece, Turkey and the Caucasus. Expanding range in NW Europe, particularly in France and now found as far W as Brittany. Northern birds are partial migrants, otherwise this is a resident species with some dispersal of juvs.

Tips: Search mature forest, preferably mixed; the species nests in large trees, favouring beech, pine or aspen, and often drums from the tallest tree in the area. Frequently feeds on the ground but can be difficult to see, despite large size, and loud call and frequent loud drumming are the best initial indicators of presence.

Sites:
ANDORRA*.
AUSTRIA Hohe Tauern NP***, Hohe Wand**, Karwendel Reserve***, Lake Neusiedl**, Marchauen-Marchegg Reserve***, Wienerwald***.
BELARUS Belovezhskaya Pushcha NP***, Berezinsky Reserve***.

BELGIUM Croix-Scaille NR**, Hautes Fagnes Natural Park**, Kalmthoutse Heide***, Lesse et Lomme NR***.
BOSNIA-HERZEGOVINA Sujetska NP***.
BULGARIA Albena-Golden Sands***, Lake Srebarna***, Rila Mts***, Rusenski Lom NP***, Strandja Mts***, Trigradski Gorge***, Tzarichina NR***.

CROATIA Plitvice***.

CZECH REPUBLIC Beskydy Mts***, Jeseníky Mts***, Krkonoše NP***, Lednice***, Pálava Hills***, Soutok***, Šumava NP***, Třeboňsko***.

DENMARK Bornholm-Christiansø***, Hellebæk***, Møn-Falster***.

ESTONIA Lake Endla***, Matsalu Bay***, Nigula NR***, Taevaskoja***, Vilsandi NP***.

FINLAND Åland Is***, Kuusamo***, Liminganlahti***, Oulanka NP***, Pyhä-Häkki NP***, Ruissalo***, Vesijako NP***.

FRANCE Cévennes NP***, Écrins NP***, Fontainebleau***, Forêt d'Issaux***, Forêt d'Orient***, Golfe du Morbihan***, Lac du Der-Chantecoq***, Lorraine NP***, Mercantour NP***, Prats-de-Mollo***, Pyrenees NP***, Queyras NP***, Sologne***, Vanoise NP***.

GERMANY Ammer Valley***, Bayerischer Wald NP***, Berchtesgaden NP***, Federsee***, Kuhkopf***, Mecklenburg Lakes***, Oder Valley**, Schweinfurt***, Tiroler Achen***, Vessertal***.

GREECE Mikrí Prespa NP***, Mt Olympus NP**, Mt Parnassós NP***, Valia Kalda NP***, Vikos-Aoos NP***.

GREEK IS Kos*.

HUNGARY Aggtelek NP***, Börzsöny NP***, Buda Hills***, Bükk Hills NP***, Csákvár***, Danube Bend***, Hanság*, Kis-balaton***, Kiskunság NP**, Ócsa**, Pilis Hills***, Zemplén Hills***.

ITALY Gargano Peninsula***, Gran Paradiso NP***, Stelvio NP***.

LATVIA Cape Kolka***, Lake Lubana***, Lake Pape***.

LITHUANIA Cepkeliai NR***, Kirsiu Peninsula***, Lake Kretuonas***.

MACEDONIA Galicica NP***, Lakes Ohrid and Prespa***, Mavrovo NP***, Sara Mts***.

NETHERLANDS Oostvaardersplassen***, Veluwe***.

NORWAY Hardangervidda NP***, Øvre Pasvik NP***.

POLAND Białowieża Forest***, Biebrza Marshes***, Bieszczady NP***, Kampinos NP***, Milicz Fishponds***, Szczecin Bay area***, Tatra NP***.

ROMANIA Bicaz***, Dobrudja***, Gurghiu Mts***, Lake Călăraşi**, Retezat NP***, Turda Gorge***.

RUSSIA Kola Peninsula***, Oka Valley***, Teberdinskiy Reserve***.

SLOVAKIA High Tatras NP***, Malá Fatra***, Malé Karpaty***, Nízke Tatry NP***, Orava Reservoir***, Slanské Hills***, Slovenský Kras***, Vihorlatske Hills***, Záhorie***.

SLOVENIA Kocevje***, Krakovski Forest**, Triglav NP***.

SPAIN Aigües Tortes NP***, Jaca***, Ordesa NP***, Picos de Europa***.

SWEDEN Falsterbo**, Getterön***, Gotland***, Holmöarna***, Kristianstad***, Öland***, Tåkern***, Tyresta NP***.

SWITZERLAND Aletschwald***, Clos-du-Doubs***, Flims***, Niderholz***, Swiss NP***.

TURKEY Borćka***, Soğuksu NP***, Sumela**, Uludağ NP***.

UKRAINE Carpathians*, Dunay Delta**.

YUGOSLAVIA Durmitor NP**.

Syrian Woodpecker
Dendrocopos syriacus   DF MF SH (CF) (U) Res (Dis)

Range: Breeds in C and SE Europe from Austria, the Czech Republic and Slovakia to S Russia and S to Greece, Turkey and Transcaucasia, with scattered populations in the Middle East. Formerly confined to Asia but spread into Europe during 20th century and although scarce in many areas it is still expanding range.

Tips: Found mainly in areas with broadleaf trees, particularly oak, and where range overlaps with Great Spotted Woodpecker usually found in more lowland areas. Look in open woodlands, parkland, orchards and farmland with scattered woods. A familiar village bird in SE Europe and often the most easily seen of the woodpeckers.

Sites:

ARMENIA Mt Aragats***.

AUSTRIA Lake Neusiedl***, Marchauen-Marchegg Reserve***.

BELARUS Belovezhskaya Pushcha NP*.

BULGARIA Albena-Golden Sands***, Burgas area***, Cape Emine***, Cape Kaliakra***, Lake Durankulak***, Lake Shabla***, Lake Srebarna***, Rila Mts***, Ropotamo NP***, Rusenski Lom NP***, Strandja Mts***, Studen Kladenetz***, Tissata NR***.

CROATIA Plitvice***.

CZECH REPUBLIC Lednice***, Pálava Hills***, Pohořelice Fishponds***, Znojmo.

GREECE Axios-Aliakmonas Deltas***, Dadiá-Soufli Forest***, Lake Kerkini***, Mikrí Prespa NP***, Nestos Delta***, Porto Lagos area***, Valia Kalda NP***.

HUNGARY Börzsöny NP***, Buda Hills***, Bükk Hills NP***, Csákvár***, Danube Bend***, Hortobágy NP***, Kis-balaton***, Lake Fertö***, Ócsa***, Pilis Hills***, Tihany***, Zemplén Hills***.

ISRAEL Ma'agan Mikhael***, Mt Hermon***, Urim***.

JORDAN Wadi as Sir***.

LEBANON Aamiq Marshes***, Qaraoun Lake**.

MACEDONIA Babuna Gorge***, Galicica NP***, Lakes Ohrid and Prespa***, Mavrovo NP**, Sara Mts**.

POLAND Bieszczady NP***.

ROMANIA Danube Delta***, Dobrudja***, Lake Călăraşi***, Turda Gorge***.

SLOVAKIA Malé Karpaty***, Senné Fishponds***, Slanské Hill***, Slovenský Kras***, Vihorlatske Hills***, Záhorie***, Zemplínská Reservoir***.

TURKEY Akseki***, Birecik-Halfeti***, Dalyan***, Demirkazik***, Göksu Delta***, İstanbul***, Kocaçay Delta***, Manyas Gölü***, Sultan Marshes***, Uludağ NP***, Yeşilce***.

UKRAINE Carpathians**, Dunay Delta***.

YUGOSLAVIA Durmitor NP**, Fruška Gora NP***, Obedska bara**.

Middle Spotted Woodpecker
Dendrocopos medius   DF (MF) Mig (Dis)

Range: Almost confined to the Western Palearctic, breeding from Brittany and C France across Europe to Ukraine and S Russia. In the N reaches the Baltic states and in the S found in the Balkans, Greece, Turkey and the Caucasus. Isolated populations persist in the Pyrenees and Cantabrians and Apennines. Has recently begun to breed in the Netherlands, Latvia and Lithuania, although recently became extinct in S Sweden.

Subspecies: Nominate race is found over most of Europe, replaced by *caucasicus* in N Turkey and the Caucasus and *anatoliae* in W and S Turkey.

Tips: To locate this species, search mature oak and hornbeam woods, also alder, ash and beech, sometimes orchards and olive groves in S of range. Feeds in higher branches and is more restless than Great Spotted Woodpecker, drumming less frequently, which can make the species more difficult to locate. Listen for characteristic nasal call in likely areas in early spring before trees are fully in leaf.

Sites:

ARMENIA Khosrov Preserve***.

AUSTRIA Lake Neusiedl**, Marchauen-Marchegg Reserve***, Wienerwald**.

BELARUS Belovezhskaya Pushcha NP***, Berezinsky Reserve***, Pripyatsky NP***.

BELGIUM Hautes Fagnes Natural Park*, Lesse et Lomme NR**.

BOSNIA-HERZEGOVINA Sujetska NP***.

BULGARIA Albena-Golden Sands*, Rila Mts***, Ropotamo NP***, Rusenski Lom NP***, Strandja Mts***, Tzarichina NR**.

CROATIA Plitvice**.

CZECH REPUBLIC Jeseníky Mts**, Krkonoše NP**, Lednice***, Nové Mlýny***, Pálava Hills**, Poodří**, Pohořelice Fishponds***, Soutok***, Třeboňsko***.

FRANCE Fontainebleau**, Forêt d'Orient**, Lac du Der-Chantecoq***, Lorraine NP***.

GEORGIA Iori Steppes**, Mt Kazbek***.

GERMANY Ammer Valley**, Kuhkopf**, Mecklenburg Lakes**, Schweinfurt***, Vessertal***.

GREECE Akarnanika Mts***, Dadiá-Soufli Forest***, Mikrí Prespa NP**, Mt Olympus NP**, Mt Parnassós NP***, Valia Kalda NP***, Vikos-Aoos NP***.

GREEK IS Lesvos***.

HUNGARY Aggtelek NP***, Börzsöny NP***, Bükk Hills NP***, Buda Hills***, Csákvár***, Danube Bend***, Pilis Hills***, Zemplén Hills***.

ITALY Abruzzo NP***, Gargano Peninsula***, Sibillini NP***.

MACEDONIA Mavrovo NP*.

POLAND Białowieża Forest***, Bieszczady NP***, Milicz Fishponds***.

ROMANIA Dobrudja***, Retezat NP***.

RUSSIA Teberdinskiy Reserve***.

SLOVAKIA High Tatras NP***, Malá Fatra***, Malé Karpaty***, Nízke Tatry NP***, Slanské Hills***, Slovenský Kras***, Vihorlatske Hills***, Záhorie***.

SLOVENIA Krakovski Forest***.

SPAIN Jaca**, Picos de Europa***.

SWITZERLAND Klingnau Reservoir***, Niderholz***.

TURKEY Akseki***, Dalyan***, İstanbul***.

UKRAINE Carpathians**.

YUGOSLAVIA Carska bara***, Fruška Gora NP**, Obedska bara**.

White-backed Woodpecker
Dendrocopos leucotos

DF MF (CF)   Res (Dis)

Range: Very patchy range, breeding in the Pyrenees, S Apennines and parts of the eastern Alps, upland areas of the Balkans, the Carpathians and from Ukraine, E Poland and Belarus E to the Urals. In the N breeds in S Scandinavia and the Baltic states, and also breeds in the Caucasus and at scattered localities in Turkey. Recorded on Corsica but status there uncertain. Decreasing in parts of range but recently bred for the first time in Switzerland.

Subspecies: Nominate race is found over most of range, with *uralensis* in the Urals and the distinctive race *lilfordi* in SE Europe, Turkey and the Caucasus which is sometimes afforded species status.

Tips: This species requires dead and dying trees in open, mainly broadleaf woodland and is absent from heavily managed forests. Most easily found in early morning and before trees are in full leaf in early spring. Search fairly open forest, concentrating on areas with rotten wood, and sometimes found on hillsides with scattered trees. One of the more difficult woodpeckers to locate due to its soft call and relatively weak drumming. Occurs in large areas of woodland at low density.

Sites:

AUSTRIA Karwendel Reserve**, Wienerwald***.

BELARUS Belovezhskaya Pushcha NP***, Berezinsky Reserve***, Prypyatsky NP***.

BOSNIA-HERZEGOVINA Sujetska NP**.

BULGARIA Rila Mts**, Strandja Mts***, Tzarichina NR*.

CROATIA Plitvice*.

CZECH REPUBLIC Beskydy Mts***, Krkonoše NP*, Šumava NP**.

ESTONIA Matsalu Bay***, Nigula NR***, Taevaskoja**.

FINLAND Linnansaari NP***, Parikkala*.

FRANCE Forêt d'Issaux**, Organbidexka*.

GERMANY Ammer Valley**, Bayerischer Wald NP*, Berchtesgaden NP**.

GREECE Mikrí Prespa NP*, Mt Olympus NP**, Mt Parnassós NP***, Valia Kalda NP**, Vikos-Aoos NP***.

HUNGARY Aggtelek NP**, Börzsöny NP***, Bükk Hills NP***, Zemplén Hills***.

ITALY Abruzzo NP***, Gargano Peninsula**, Sibillini NP*.

LATVIA Lake Lubana***.

LITHUANIA Cepkeliai NR***.

MACEDONIA Babuna Gorge, Mavrovo NP*, Sara Mts.

NORWAY Hardangervidda NP***.

POLAND Białowieża Forest***, Biebrza Marshes***, Bieszczady NP***, Kampinos NP*, Milicz Fishponds*, Tatra NP***.

ROMANIA Bicaz***, Dobrudja*, Gurghiu Mts***, Retezat NP***.

SLOVAKIA High Tatras NP**, Malá Fatra***, Malé Karpaty***, Nízke Tatry NP***, Slanské Hills*, Slovenský Kras***, Vihorlatske Hills***.

SPAIN Ordesa NP*.

TURKEY Akseki**, Borçka***, Kocaćay Delta*.

UKRAINE Carpathians***.

Three-toed Woodpecker
Picoides tridactylus

CF (MF) Res (Dis) (Irr)

Range: Main range is from Scandinavia and E Poland, Belarus and the Baltic states across Russia to the Urals. Isolated populations persist in the Alps, Carpathians and the mountains in the Balkans.

Subspecies: Nominate race is found across N Europe, replaced in the Urals by the *crissoleucus* and the distinctive *alpinus* in C Europe and the Balkans.

Tips: In N of range preferred habitat is coniferous forest with abundant dead wood, often around swampy areas, sometimes in birch and willow. In S mainly found in conifers on hillsides. Often unobtrusive and difficult to locate, but drums loudly and often feeds low on tree trunks.

Sites:

AUSTRIA Hohe Tauern NP***, Karwendel Reserve***.

BELARUS Belovezhskaya Pushcha NP***, Berezinsky Reserve***.

BOSNIA-HERZEGOVINA Sujetska NP***.

BULGARIA Rila Mts**.

CROATIA Plitvice**.

CZECH REPUBLIC Beskydy Mts***, Krkonoše NP***, Šumava NP***.

ESTONIA Nigula NR***, Taevaskoja***.

FINLAND Åland Is*, Kuusamo***, Lemmenjoki NP***, Liminganlahti***, Maltio NR***, Oulanka NP***, Patvinsuo NP***, Urho Kekkonen NP***, Vesijako NP***.

FRANCE Vanoise NP***.

GERMANY Ammer Valley**, Bayerischer Wald NP**, Berchtesgaden NP***.

GREECE Mt Olympus NP**, Valia Kalda NP*.

ITALY Gran Paradiso NP**, Stelvio NP***.

LATVIA Cape Kolka***.

LITHUANIA Cepkeliai NR***.

MACEDONIA Mavrovo NP, Sara Mts.

NORWAY Hardangervidda NP***, Øvre Pasvik NP***, Stabbursdalen NP***.

POLAND Białowieża Forest***, Bieszczady NP***, Tatra NP***.

ROMANIA Bicaz***, Gurghiu Mts***, Poiana Braşov***, Retezat NP***.

RUSSIA Kola Peninsula***.

SLOVAKIA High Tatras**, Malá Fatra***, Nízke Tatry NP***, Slovenský Kras*.

SLOVENIA Triglav NP***.

SWEDEN Abisko NP***, Holmöarna***.

SWITZERLAND Aletschwald***, Flims***, Swiss NP***.

UKRAINE Carpathians***.

Black-crowned Finch-lark
Eremopterix nigriceps

SD FG   Res (Dis) (Nom)

Range: In N Africa occurs in our region only in extreme SE Egypt, in Mauritania and recently found breeding in S Morocco, where previously considered to be a vagrant. Also breeds in the Cape Verde Is, where common on São Tiago, Fogo, Boa Vista and Maio, less so on Brava and São Nicolau. Has probably bred in Israel and may do so regularly in the Middle East.

Subspecies: Nominate race occurs in the Cape Verde Islands where fairly common, *albifrons* in the Sahara and *melanauchen* from the Red Sea coast of Egypt to Iraq.

Tips: Difficult to see in the Western Palearctic outside the Cape Verde Is. Try semi-desert and sandy savanna with acacia scrub, or sandy wadis and the edges of cultivated land, where often found in small flocks.

Sites:
CAPE VERDE IS***.

Dunn's Lark
Eremalauda dunni

D SD   Res (Nom)

Range: In the Western Palearctic only breeds regularly in N Saudi Arabia, but has bred in the Arava Valley of Israel, where probably regular, and may also breed in Egypt, Sinai, and Jordan.

Subspecies: African birds belong to nominate *dunni* and Middle Eastern birds to *eremodites*.

Tips: Inhabits stony and sandy deserts and flat semi-desert with sparse vegetation. An active ground-feeder, but less restless than Desert Lark. Unpredictable in its appearances, the Arava Valley is the most likely area for this species.

Sites:
ISRAEL Arava Valley**.
JORDAN Azraq* (irregular), Ghadir Burqu', Wadi Dana-Fidan, Wadi Rum.

SYRIA Tadmur and Sabkhat Muh*.

Bar-tailed Desert Lark
Ammomanes cincturus

D SD Res (Dis) (Nom)

Range: Breeds across inland N Africa from S Morocco to Egypt and in the Middle East in Sinai and Israel, Jordan and N Saudi Arabia. In the Cape Verde Is, breeds on Sal, Boa Vista, Maio, São Tiago and São Nicolau but is rare on Fogo.

Subspecies: The race *arenicolor* is found over most of Western Palearctic range replaced by nominate *cincturus* in the Cape Verde Is.

Tips: Search stony or sandy deserts and semi-desert, usually in flat areas or rolling hills, sometimes with sparse vegetation, but not in rocky uplands. Very active and feeds restlessly, rarely remaining still for long.

Sites:

CAPE VERDE IS***.
EGYPT Hurghada***, Santa Katharina Monastery***, Sharm el Sheikh***, Suez area***.
ISRAEL Arava Valley***, Eilat***, Nizzana**.

JORDAN Azraq**, Ghadir Burqu'***, Wadi Dana-Fidan***, Wadi Rum***.
MOROCCO Boumalne**, Goulimine to Tan-Tan***, Ouarzazate*, Tafilalt***.
SYRIA Tadmur and Sabkhat Muh***.
TUNISIA Chott el Djerid***.

Desert Lark
Ammomanes deserti

D SD Res (Dis)

Range: Widespread across N Africa from Morocco to C Libya, also breeds widely in E Egypt, and in the Middle East breeds in Sinai and from N Saudi Arabia N to Syria. Very small numbers were discovered breeding in SE Turkey in the 1980s.

Subspecies: A number of races have been described from the Western Palearctic differing mainly in colour, but this often varies with the colour of the local soil. They range between the pale and sandy *algeriensis* from Algeria and Tunisia, and the darkest, the sooty-grey, *annae* from the black lava desert of north Jordan. The nominate *deserti* from Egypt, Sinai and Jordan is about midway between the two extremes. However, there is much intergradation and pale birds can be seen together with much darker birds in some areas and many birds cannot be safely assigned to race on plumage alone.

Tips: Look in broken, hilly country with stone-covered slopes, wadis and sparsely vegetated semi-deserts. Perches prominently for long periods and feeds on the ground less restlessly than Bar-tailed Desert Lark.

Sites:

EGYPT Abu Simbel**, Aswan**, Hurghada***, Luxor***, Santa Katharina Monastery***, Sharm el Sheikh***, Suez area***, Wadi el Natrun***.
ISRAEL Arava Valley***, Eilat***, Ein Gedi***, Mt Hermon***, Nizzana***.
JORDAN Aqaba***, Azraq***, Ghadir Burqu'***, Petra***, Wadi Dana-Fidan***, Wadi Rum***, Wadi as Sir***.

MOROCCO Boumalne**, Goulimime to Tan-Tan***, Ouarzazate***, Tafilalt***.
SYRIA Tadmur and Sabkhat Muh***.
TUNISIA Chott el Djerid***, Tatahouine***.
TURKEY Birecik-Halfeti***.

Hoopoe Lark (Bifasciated Lark)
Alaemon alaudipes   D SD Res

Range: Breeds across N Africa (except the NW coastal strip) from S and E Morocco, to N Egypt and the Nile Valley. In the Middle East breeds in Sinai, Israel and W Jordan and S Syria, and also breeds in the Cape Verde Is, on Boa Vista and Maio.

Subspecies: Nominate race is found in N Africa with *doriae* in the Middle East and *boavistae* from the Cape Verde Is.

Tips: Search flat desert and semi-desert, in sparsely vegetated wadis or on sandy shores. Best located by distinctive song, which is most often heard Jan–Jun, and perches prominently on a bush after song-flight. Runs rather than flies when disturbed.

Sites:
CAPE VERDE IS**.
EGYPT Abu Simbel*, Aswan*, Hurghada*, Santa Katharina Monastery**, Sharm el Sheikh***, Suez area***, Wadi el Natrun***, Zaranik***.
ISRAEL Arava Valley***, Eilat***, Nizzana**.

JORDAN Aqaba***, Azraq***, Ghadir Burqu'***, Wadi Dana-Fidan***, Wadi Rum***.
MOROCCO Boumalne***, Goulimine to Tan-Tan***, Ouarzazate**, Tafilalt***.
SYRIA Tadmur and Sabkhat Muh***.
TUNISIA Chott el Djerid***, Tatahouine***.

Dupont's Lark
Chersophilus duponti   FG SD Res (Dis)

Range: Breeds in C and S Spain, in the C Atlas Mts of E Morocco and W Algeria, and in scattered pockets elsewhere in Algeria, C and S Tunisia, N Libya and N Egypt. Commonest in Morocco but even there can be difficult to find.

Subspecies: Two races occur in our region, the nominate in Spain and northern parts of NW Africa, but has occurred as a vagrant in Egypt and *margaritae* in the southern Atlas Mts, S Tunisia and in Libya and Egypt.

Tips: Inhabits flat and dry scrubby areas, usually above 1,000 m and is particularly associated with *Artemisia* scrub. Outside the breeding season often seen in cereal fields. Notoriously difficult to locate, preferring to run rather than fly when disturbed. The best time is late Mar–early Apr when performs high song-flights and is most vocal two hours before dawn until two hours after.

Sites:

MOROCCO Agadir and the Sous Plain, Boumalne*, Zeida**.

SPAIN Cabo de Gata***, Zaragoza Steppes***.
TUNISIA Tataouine*.

Thick-billed Lark
Ramphocoris clotbey

D SD FG Res (Dis)

Range: Breeds in NW Africa from SW Morocco to N Algeria, C Tunisia and NW Libya. In the Middle East occurs in Jordan and has bred in Syria, the Negev Desert of Israel, where possibly regular, and in Egypt in 1996.

Tips: Difficult to find in our region, but try searching stony deserts, grassy wadis, arid cultivated land and rocky hillsides, and look for a fast-running bird with a characteristic upright stance. Gregarious and somewhat nomadic in winter.

Sites:

ISRAEL Arava Valley*, Eilat*, Nizzana.
JORDAN Azraq*, Ghadir Burqu'***.

MOROCCO Boumalne**, Goulimime to Tan-Tan**, Ouarzazate**, Tafilalt***, Zeida**.
TUNISIA Chott el Djerid**.

Calandra Lark
Melanocorypha calandra

FG SH Mig Res (PMig)

Range: Breeds over much of Iberia and in scattered pockets in S France, S Italy, Sardinia and Sicily, discontinuously through the Balkans, and on Crete and Cyprus. Also breeds in much of Ukraine and Russia E to the Caspian, parts of the Caucasus and widely in Turkey. In the Middle East occurs in Syria, Israel and NW Jordan, and in NW Africa from Morocco to Tunisia and NE Libya. Irregular passage migrant on Malta.

Subspecies: Three races occur in the Western Palearctic but there is a great deal of variation within populations and races are rarely separable in the field. Nominate is found over most of range replaced by *hebraica* in Turkey and the Near East and *psam-mochroa* in Iraq.

Tips: Usually found on dry plains and steppe, in cultivation and open, flat areas of scrub. Cereal fields are favoured in winter, often associating with Corn Buntings, and located by the loud jingling call.

Sites:

BULGARIA Albena-Golden Sands***, Burgas area**, Cape Kaliakra***, Lake Durankulak***, Lake Shabla***, Lake Srebarna***, Rila Mts***, Strandja Mts*, Tissata NR***.
CYPRUS*.
EGYPT Nile Delta* (winter).
FRANCE Camargue**.
GREECE Amvrakikós Gulf***, Axios-Aliakmonas Deltas**, Evros Delta**, Lake Kerkini***, Mikrí Prespa NP***, Nestos Delta***, Porto Lagos area***.
GREEK IS Crete* (passage), Lesvos* (passage).
ISRAEL Golan Heights***, Hula Reserve***, Mt Hermon**, Urim***.
ITALY Gargano Peninsula***.
JORDAN Amman NP***, Wadi Rum***.
LEBANON Aammiq Marshes***, Qaraoun Lake***.
MALTA* (passage).
MOROCCO Asilah and Oued Loukkos***, Merja Zerga***, Oualidia***, Zaër***.

PORTUGAL Baixo Alentejo***, Castro Marim***, International Tagus***, Tagus Estuary***.
ROMANIA Danube Delta***, Dobrudja***.
RUSSIA Kalmykia*** (summer), Volga Delta*** (summer).
SARDINIA Giara di Gesturi***, Oristano Wetlands***.
SICILY Lago di Lentini***.
SPAIN Cabo de Gata**, Cáceres-Trujillo Steppes***, Cádiz Lagoons***, Coto Doñana***, La Serena***, Sierra de Gredos***, Sierra de Guadarrama***, Tablas de Daimiel***, Zaragoza Steppes***.
SYRIA Bahrat Homs**, Sabkhat al-Jabbul***.
TUNISIA Cap Bon Peninsula***, Kelbia Lake***, Lake Ichkeul***.
TURKEY Bafa Gölü***, Bulanik***, Kulu Gölü***, Van Gölü***.
UKRAINE Askania-Nova*** (summer), Dunay Delta**, Tiligul Liman*** (passage).

Bimaculated Lark
Melanocorypha bimaculata

M FG Mig

Range: Breeds in C and E Turkey and Transcaucasia, and in Lebanon, S Syria and N Jordan and Israel. Departs breeding grounds in Oct and returns in Mar–Apr. Passage noted in Cyprus, the Middle East and NE Africa.
Subspecies: Nominate race is found in N Turkey and Transcaucasia and *rufescens* further S.
Tips: Often found at higher altitudes and on stonier ground than Calandra Lark, on rocky, scrub-covered mountainsides and in cultivated areas with rocks at 1,200–2,000m.

CYPRUS* (passage).
ISRAEL Arava Valley*** (passage), Eilat*** (passage), Golan Heights*** (summer), Mt Hermon** (summer), Nizzana** (passage), Urim*** (summer).
JORDAN Azraq* (passage).

LEBANON Barouk Cedars** (summer), Qaraoun Lake** (passage, winter).
TURKEY Birecik-Halfeti** (summer), Demirkazik*** (summer), Kulu Gölü** (summer).

White-winged Lark
Melanocorypha leucoptera   FG SD Mig

Range: Breeds in the extreme E of the Western Palearctic, mainly in the Caspian Depression, in Kazakhstan and S Russia to the Urals. Vacates breeding areas in Aug–Oct, sometimes later, returning late Mar to mid Apr. Winters SW of breeding range in Ukraine and Crimea, and in the Caucasus. In severe winters may reach Romania.

Tips: Breeds in arid short-grass steppes, arable areas and semi-desert. Forms large flocks in winter.

Sites:

AZERBAIJAN Kyzylagach Bay*** (winter).
ROMANIA Danube Delta (winter), Dobrudja (winter).

RUSSIA Kalmykia*** (summer), Volga Delta*** (summer).
UKRAINE Dunay Delta (winter).

Black Lark
Melanocorypha yeltoniensis   FG Dis

Range: Breeds in the northern Caspian Depression, Kazakhstan and the S Urals, and winters SW to the N shores of the Black Sea and the N Caucasus. Present all year in southern parts of breeding range.

Tips: Breeds in dry grassland and artemisia steppe, often close to water and usually in wetter areas than White-winged Lark.

Sites:

RUSSIA Kalmykia*** (winter), Volga Delta*** (winter).

Short-toed Lark (Greater Short-toed Lark)
Calandrella brachydactyla

FG SD (ES)   Mig (PMig) (Dis)

Range: Common and widespread in S Europe, breeding in Iberia, at a few scattered localities in W and S France and in much of Italy. Also patchily in the Balkans and Greece, Ukraine and across Russia to the Caspian. In the Mediterranean breeds on the Balearics, Corsica and Sardinia, Sicily, Malta, Crete and many other Greek islands, and Cyprus. Breeds widely in Turkey and the Caucasus, and in the Middle East in Syria, Jordan, Israel and N Sinai. In N Africa breeds from S Morocco to Tunisia. Bred in Finland in 2002. Autumn passage occurs Aug–Oct and the return in Mar–Apr, although some remain in breeding range all year.

Subspecies: A number of races have been recorded in our region but the slight differences in ground colour and markings are mainly clinal and great variation occurs seasonally and within populations.

Tips: Inhabits open steppe, semi-desert and cultivated plains, in winter also on dried salt-marshes and sand dunes. Gregarious and in winter and on passage frequently associates with flocks of other larks and Corn Buntings.

Sites:

ALBANIA Drini Delta** (summer), Karavasta Lagoon** (summer), Lake Shkodra** (summer).
ARMENIA Armash Fishponds*** (summer).
BALEARIC IS Formentera***, Ibiza***, Mallorca***, Menorca***.
BULGARIA Albena-Golden Sands*** (summer), Burgas area*** (summer), Cape Kaliakra*** (summer), Lake Durankulak*** (summer), Lake Shabla*** (summer), Ropotamo NP*** (summer), Tissata NR*** (summer).
CANARY IS** (passage).
CORSICA Biguglia Lake*** (summer).
CROATIA Cres*** (summer).
CYPRUS*** (summer, passage).
EGYPT Abu Simbel** (passage), Aswan*** (passage), Hurghada*** (passage), Luxor** (passage), Wadi el Natrun***, Zaranik***.
FRANCE Baie de Bourgneuf** (summer), Camargue*** (summer), Cévennes NP*** (summer), Gruissan*** (summer), Ouessant* (passage).
GERMANY Leucate*** (summer).
GEORGIA Iori Steppes*** (summer).
GIBRALTAR*** (passage).

GREAT BRITAIN Scilly (spring), Shetland Is (passage).
GREECE Amvrakikós Gulf*** (summer), Axios-Aliakmonas Deltas*** (summer), Evros Delta*** (summer), Lake Kerkini*** (summer), Mikrí Prespa NP*** (summer), Nestos Delta*** (summer), Porto Lagos area*** (summer).
GREEK IS Corfu*** (summer), Crete** (summer), Kos*** (summer, passage), Lesvos*** (summer, passage), Rhodes*** (passage).
HUNGARY Hortobágy NP*** (summer), Kardoskút*** (summer).
ISRAEL Arava Valley*** (passage), Eilat*** (passage), Mt Hermon*** (summer), Nizzana*** (summer), Urim*** (summer).
ITALY Gargano Peninsula*** (summer), Orbetello Reserve*** (summer), Po Delta*** (summer), San Giuliano Reserve*** (summer), Tuscan archipelago*** (passage).
JORDAN Amman NP*** (summer), Azraq** (passage, mainly autumn), Wadi Rum*** (summer).
LEBANON Aammiq Marshes** (summer, passage), Qaraoun Lake**.

MACEDONIA Babuna Gorge** (summer), Galicica NP*** (summer), Lakes Ohrid and Prespa*** (summer).
MALTA* (summer, passage).
MOROCCO Agadir and the Sous Plain*** (summer), Boumalne*** (summer), Goulimine to Tan-Tan*** (summer), Merja Zerga*** (summer), Oualidia*** (summer), Ouarzazate*** (passage), Oued Massa*** (summer), Tafilalt***, Zeida*** (summer).
PORTUGAL Baixo Alentejo*** (summer), Cape St Vincent*** (summer, passage), Castro Marim*** (summer), International Douro*** (summer), International Tagus*** (summer), Montesinho*** (summer), Ria Formosa*** (summer), Santo André Lagoon*** (summer), Tagus Estuary*** (summer).
ROMANIA Dobrudja***.
RUSSIA Kalmykia*** (summer), Volga Delta* (summer).
SARDINIA Oristano Wetlands*** (summer).
SICILY Vendicari*** (summer).

SPAIN Aiguamolls de L'Empordá*** (summer), Cabo de Gata* (summer), Cáceres-Trujillo Steppes*** (summer), Cádiz Lagoons*** (summer), Coto Doñana*** (summer), Ebro Delta*** (summer), Guadalhorce Estuary*** (summer), La Serena*** (summer), Llobregat Delta*** (summer), Santa Pola*** (summer), Sierra de Guadarrama*** (summer), Tablas de Daimiel*** (summer), Zaragoza Steppes** (summer).
SWITZERLAND Leuk* (passage).
SYRIA Dayr al-Zawr** (summer), Sabkhat al-Jabbul*** (summer), Yarmuk Valley** (passage).
TUNISIA Chott el Djerid*** (summer, passage), Kelbia Lake*** (summer), Lake Ichkeul** (summer).
TURKEY Birecik-Halfeti*** (summer), Dalyan*** (summer), Demirkazik*** (summer), Göksu Delta*** (summer), Kulu Gölü*** (summer), Van Gölü*** (summer).
UKRAINE Askania-Nova*** (summer), Tiligul Liman*** (summer, passage).

Asian Short-toed Lark
Calandrella cheleensis   SD   Mig (PMig)

Range: Until recently, this form was usually considered a subspecies of Lesser Short-toed Lark and the taxonomy of this complex remains confused, much debated and seemingly problematic. Breeds in C Turkey and perhaps elsewhere in the Middle East, also in S Kazakhstan and further E. Recorded in Syria, where it may breed. Winters to the SE, mainly in Iraq but also in SE Turkey and W Jordan.

Tips: A bird of salt deserts, often found by saline and soda lakes, in winter on cultivated land and around lakes.

Sites:
TURKEY Kulu Gölü*** (summer), Sultan Marshes (summer).

Lesser Short-toed Lark
Calandrella rufescens   FG SD   Res (Mig) (Dis)

Range: Breeds on the Canaries and in S and E Spain, across NW Africa, in coastal Libya and the Nile Delta. Further E breeds from Ukraine to the Caspian, in E Turkey and the Caucasus, and in the Middle East mainly in Syria, but also in Israel, Jordan and Sinai. Passage noted in Turkey and the Middle East, less commonly in Cyprus and Gibraltar.

Subspecies: About 10 races occur in our region differing in ground colour, strength of markings and bill size.

Tips: Search stony or rocky areas in steppe, semi-desert and open cultivated land with short vegetation. Migratory populations are present in breeding areas Mar–Sep, and on passage is often gregarious, sometimes associating with Short–toed Lark.

Sites:
ARMENIA Armash Fishponds***.

CANARY IS Fuerteventura***, Gran Canaria***, Lanzarote***, Tenerife***.

CYPRUS (passage).

EGYPT Nile Delta***.

ISRAEL Arava Valley***, Eilat*** (passage), Nizzana***.

JORDAN Azraq***, Ghadir Burqu'*, Wadi Rum*.

LEBANON Aammiq Marshes***, Qaraoun Lake** (winter).

MOROCCO Boumalne***, Goulimine to Tan-Tan***, Ouarzazate***, Oued Massa***, Zeida***.

PORTUGAL Baixo Alentejo***, Cape St Vincent*, Castro Marim***.

SPAIN Cabo de Gata***, Cádiz Lagoons***, Coto Doñana***, Ebro Delta***, Santa Pola***, Zaragoza Steppes***.

SYRIA Sabkhat al Jabbul**, Tadmur and Sabkhat Muh***.

TUNISIA Chott el Djerid***, Kelbia Lake***, Lake Ichkeul***.

TURKEY Birecik-Halfeti*, Bulanik***, Kulu Gölü***, Van Gölü***.

Crested Lark
Galerida cristata   FG SD (U)   Res (Mig)

Range: Widespread but decreasing in N of range. Breeds from Iberia to Denmark and E to the Baltic states and Russia. Very patchy in Portugal, France and the Alps, but found along the entire N Mediterranean coast and on Sicily, Crete and other Greek islands, and Cyprus. Also breeds around the Black Sea, throughout Turkey and the Caucasus, and in much of the Middle East. In N Africa found throughout the NW and on coasts from Tunisia to Sinai and in the Nile Valley.

Subspecies: More than 20 races of this highly variable species have been described from the Western Palearctic. They mainly differ in ground colour and strength of markings but there is much variation within races due to amount of light, humidity and soil colour. Generally, N European birds *cristata* are darker and browner, NW African birds paler, plainer and more sandy-coloured, e.g. Tunisian *arenicola*, but birds from Iberia and Morocco may be heavily tinged reddish and *cinnamomina* from Lebanon is rich cinnamon. Towards the E and S birds are usually paler and greyer, e.g. *subtaurica* from Turkey, with especially grey forms in the Caucasus and pale brownish-grey birds on the Greek islands. However, the darkest birds, *nigricans*, occur in the Nile Delta.

Tips: Occurs on waste ground, cultivated land, scrub, roadsides and railway sidings, often near habitation. Also on arid grassy plains and in semi-desert.

Sites:

ALBANIA Drini Delta***, Karavasta Lagoon***, Lake Shkodra***.

ARMENIA Armash Fishponds***.

AUSTRIA Lake Neusiedl***.

BELARUS Belovezhskaya Pushcha NP**.

BELGIUM Blankaart Reserve**.

BULGARIA Albena-Golden Sands***, Lake Shabla***. Lake Srebarna***, Strandja Mts***, Studen Kladenetz***, Trigradski Gorge***.

CROATIA Cres***.

CYPRUS*.

CZECH REPUBLIC Lednice*.

DENMARK Ringkøbing Fjord**, Rømø**, Skagen* (passage).

EGYPT Abu Simbel***, Aswan***, Faiyum***, Hurghada***, Luxor***, Nile Delta***, Santa Katharina Monastery***, Sharm el Sheikh***, Suez area***, Wadi el Natrun***, Zaranik***.

FRANCE Baie de Bourgneuf***, Baie de Vilaine**, Camargue***, Golfe du Morbihan*, Gruissan***, Île d'Oléron***, Leucate***, Marais Poitevin***, Somme Estuary**, Teich Reserve***.

GEORGIA Iori Steppes***.

GIBRALTAR ** (winter).

GREECE Amvrakikós Gulf***, Axios-Aliakmonas Deltas***, Evros Delta***, Lake Kerkini***, Mikrí Prespa NP***, Porto Lagos area***.

GREEK IS Corfu***, Crete***, Kos*** (passage), Lesvos***, Náxos***, Rhodes***.

HUNGARY Buda Hills***, Csákvár***, Hortobágy NP***, Kis-balaton***, Kiskunság NP***, Lake Fertö***, Lake Velence***, Pilis Hills***, Tihany***.

ISRAEL Arava Valley***, Eilat***, Ein Gedi***, Golan Heights***, Hula Reserve***, Jezreel Valley***, Ma'agan Mikhael***, Mt Hermon***, Nizzana***, Urim***.

ITALY Gargano Peninsula***, Orbetello Reserve***, Po Delta***.

JORDAN Amman NP***, Azraq***, Ghadir Burqu'***, Petra***, Wadi Rum***, Wadi as Sir***.

LEBANON Aammiq Marshes***, Barouk Cedars***, Qaraoun Lake***.

MACEDONIA Galicica NP***, Lakes Ohrid and Prespa***.

MOROCCO Agadir and the Sous Plain***, Asilah and Oued Loukkos***, Boumalne***, Dayet Aaoua***, Essaouira***, Goulimine to Tan-Tan***, Merja Zerga***, Oualidia***, Ouarzazate***, Oued Massa***, Tafilalt***, Zeida***.

NETHERLANDS Oostvaardersplassen*, Zwanenwater**.

POLAND Białystok Fishponds***, Siemianówka Reservoir**.

PORTUGAL Baixo Alentejo***, Boquilobo***, Cape St Vincent***, Castro Marim***, International Tagus***, Montesinho***, Peneda Gêres NP***, Ria Formosa***, Sado Estuary***, Santo André Lagoon***, Tagus Estuary***.

ROMANIA Danube Delta***, Dobrudja***.

RUSSIA Kalmykia***, Volga Delta*.

SICILY Lago di Lentini***, Strait of Messina***, San Vito Peninsula***, Vendicari***.

SLOVAKIA High Tatras NP**.

SPAIN Aiguamolls de L'Empordá***, Cabo de Gata***, Cáceres-Trujillo Steppes***, Cádiz Lagoons***, Coto Doñana***, Ebro Delta***, Garraf Massif***, Guadalhorce Estuary***, La Serena***, Llobregat Delta***, Monfragüe***, Santa Pola***, Tablas de Daimiel***, Zaragoza Steppes***.

SYRIA Aqra Mts***, Baath Lake***, Bahrat Homs***, Dayr al-Zawr***, Jabal Slenfeh***,

Lake Assad***, Sabkhat al-Jabbul***, Tadmur and Sabkhat Muh***, Yarmuk Valley.

TUNISIA Cap Bon Peninsula***, Chott el Djerid***, Kelbia Lake***, Lake Ichkeul***, Tataouine***.

TURKEY Birecik-Halfeti***, Bulanik***, Dalyan***, Göksu Delta***, İstanbul***, Kocaçay Delta***, Kulu Gölü***, Soğuksu NP***, Van Gölü***.

UKRAINE Askania-Nova***, Dunay Delta***, Tiligul Liman***.

YUGOSLAVIA Lake Skadar***.

Thekla Lark
Galerida theklae FG SH Res (Dis)

Range: Patchily distributed in Iberia, breeding in S and E Portugal and much of Spain except the N, also on the Balearics and in a tiny area of SW France. In NW Africa occurs throughout Morocco and across N Algeria to Tunisia and N Libya, and also in NW Egypt.

Subspecies: Nominate race *theklae* is found in France and Iberia and 4–5 further races occur in N Africa.

Tips: Found in similar habitats to Crested Lark, but more frequent away from habitation and less common along roadsides and in cultivation. Often at higher altitudes than Crested Lark, on rocky and bush-covered hillsides, and often perches on bushes, which Crested rarely does.

Sites:

BALEARIC IS Formentera***, Ibiza***, Mallorca***, Menorca***.

MOROCCO Agadir and the Sous Plain***, Boumalne***, Dayet Aaoua***, Essaouira***, Goulimine to Tan-Tan***, Ouarzazate***, Oued Massa***, Oukaimeden***, Tafilalt***, Zaër***, Zeida***.

PORTUGAL Baixo Alentejo***, Cape St Vincent***, Castro Marim***, International Douro***, International Tagus***,

Montesinho***, Ria Formosa***, Santo André Lagoon**.

SPAIN Aiguamolls de l'Empordá***, Cabo de Gata***, Cáceres-Trujillo Steppes***, Coto Doñana***, Garraf Massif***, Jaca***, La Serena**, Monfragüe***, Santa Pola***, Serrania de Ronda***, Sierra de Guadarrama***, Tablas de Daimiel***, Zaragoza Steppes***.

TUNISIA Cap Bon Peninsula***, Chott el Djerid***, Kelbia Lake***, Lake Ichkeul***, Zaghouan***.

Wood Lark
Lullula arborea　　　　　　　　　　　　CF MF DF SH FG　Res Mig

Range: Almost confined to our region as a breeder, being found in Iberia and France to European Russia. In the N reaches S England and S Scandinavia. Occurs along the N coast of the Mediterranean and on most islands, except the Balearics, and found throughout Turkey and the Caucasus. Very patchy in Lebanon and Israel and in NW Africa. Northern birds are migratory and winter mainly within range of southern breeders.

Subspecies: Nominate occurs over most of Europe replaced in the S by *pallida*, which is sometimes separable in the field on paler plumage.

Tips: Search woodland edges and clearings, heaths and recently felled woodland, open plains with scattered trees, dunes and scrub. Feeds on short grass and requires trees and bushes for song-posts.

Sites:

ANDORRA**.

AUSTRIA Wienerwald*** (summer), Schneeberg Mts** (summer).

BELARUS Belovezhskaya Pushcha NP*** (summer), Berezinsky Reserve*** (summer), Prypyatsky NP*** (summer).

BELGIUM Croix-Scaille NR*** (summer), Hautes Fagnes Natural Park** (summer), Kalmthoutse Heide*** (summer), Lesse et Lomme NR** (summer).

BULGARIA Albena-Golden Sands***, Burgas area***, Cape Kaliakra***, Rila Mts*** (summer), Rusenski Lom NP*** (summer), Strandja Mts***, Studen Kladenetz***, Trigradski Gorge***, Tissata NR***, Tzarichina NR***.

CORSICA Bonifacio** (passage), Cap Corse** (passage), Restonica Valley***.

CROATIA Cres***.

CYPRUS**.

CZECH REPUBLIC Beskydy Mts*** (summer), Krkonoše NP* (summer), Lednice** (summer), Šumava NP*** (summer), Třeboňsko*** (summer).

DENMARK Møn-Falster*** (summer), Skagen*** (summer), Skallingen-Blåvandshuk** (passage).

EGYPT Nile Delta* (winter).

ESTONIA Matsalu Bay*** (summer).

FRANCE Baie de Bourgneuf***, Baie du Mont-St-Michel**, Camargue***, Écrins NP*** (summer), Fontainebleau***, Golfe du Morbihan***, Île d'Oléron***, La Brenne***, Les Alpilles***, Leucate*** (passage), Sologne*** (summer), Somme Estuary* (passage).

GERMANY Ammer Valley*** (summer), Bayerischer Wald NP*** (summer), Berchtesgaden NP*** (summer), Kuhkopf*** (summer), Mecklenburg Lakes*** (summer), Vessertal*** (summer).

GREAT BRITAIN Breckland***, Dungeness* (passage), Minsmere*** (summer), N Norfolk coast* (passage).

GREECE Dadiá-Soufli Forest***, Mikrí Prespa NP***, Mt Olympus NP***, Mt Parnassós NP**, Vikos-Aoos NP***.

GREEK IS Crete***, Lesvos***, Náxos***, Rhodes***.

HUNGARY Aggtelek NP*** (summer), Buda Hills*** (summer), Bükk Hills NP*** (summer), Csákvár*** (summer), Danube Bend** (summer), Pilis Hills*** (summer), Zemplén Hills*** (summer).

ISRAEL Golan Heights*** (winter), Mt Hermon***.

ITALY Abruzzo NP***, Gran Paradiso NP***, Po Delta* (passage), Stelvio NP***, Sibillini NP***, Tuscan archipelago*** (passage).
JORDAN Amman NP** (winter), Wadi Dana-Fidan* (passage, winter).
LATVIA Cape Kolka*** (summer).
LEBANON Barouk Cedars***, Qaraoun Lake** (passage, winter).
LITHUANIA Kirsiu Peninsula*** (summer, passage).
MALTA (autumn).
MOROCCO Dayet Aaoua***, Oukaimeden*** (summer), Zaër***, Zeida**.
NETHERLANDS Veluwe*** (summer).
POLAND Białowieża Forest*** (summer), Biebrza Marshes*** (summer), Bieszczady NP*** (summer), Gdańsk Bay*** (summer), Kampinos NP*** (summer).
PORTUGAL Baixo Alentejo***, Boquilobo***, Cape St Vincent***, Castro Marim***, International Douro***, International Tagus***, Montesinho***, Peneda Gêres NP***, Ria Formosa***, Sado Estuary***, Santo André Lagoon***, Tagus Estuary***.
ROMANIA Turda Gorge*** (summer).
RUSSIA Teberdinskiy Reserve*** (summer).
SARDINIA Giara di Gesturi***, San Pietro I***.
SLOVAKIA High Tatras NP*** (summer), Malá

Fatra*** (summer), Malé Karpaty*** (summer), Nízke Tatry NP*** (summer), Slanské Hills*** (summer), Slovenský Kras*** (summer), Vihorlatske Hills*** (summer), Záhorie*** (summer).
SPAIN Cabo de Gata**, Cáceres-Trujillo Steppes**, Coto Doñana***, Garraf Massif***, Jaca*** (summer), La Serena***, Monfragüe***, Ordesa NP*** (summer), Picos de Europa***, Serrania de Ronda**, Sierra de Gredos***, Sierra de Guadarrama***, Tablas de Daimiel***.
SWEDEN Falsterbo** (passage), Getterön*** (summer), Gotland*** (summer), Hornborgasjön** (passage), Kristianstad*** (summer), Öland*** (summer), Tyresta NP*** (summer).
SWITZERLAND Col de Bretolet*** (passage), Leuk*** (summer).
SYRIA Jabal Slenfeh***, Wadi al-Qarn-Burqush**.
TURKEY Borçka*** (summer), Dalyan*** (summer), Demirkazik*** (summer), İstanbul*** (passage).
UKRAINE Carpathians*** (summer), Crimean Mts**.
YUGOSLAVIA Durmitor NP**, Fruška Gora NP**.

Oriental Skylark (Small Skylark)
Alauda gulgula   FG SH   Res (Dis)

Range: Breeds in C and E Asia and northern populations are migratory, wintering in Pakistan and NW India. In the Western Palearctic this is a rare but regular winter visitor to the Middle East. There are several recent records from S Sinai and it occasionally occurs in the Caucasus.
Tips: Eilat and the Arava Valley are *the* sites to find this species but it undoubtedly occurs elsewhere. Uses natural and artificial grasslands, mainly steppe and agricultural areas, also wet areas such as flooded fields and in winter on tidal saltmarshes and mudflats. Often occurs within flocks of Skylark, where it can be picked out by the soft buzzing call and shape reminiscent of Wood Lark.

Sites:
EGYPT Sharm el Sheik (passage).
ISRAEL Arava Valley** (passage, winter), Bet
Shean Valley** (autumn, winter), Eilat**

(passage, winter), Nizzana (passage), Urim
(passage).

Raso Lark
Alauda razae   I Res

Range: One of the world's most range-restricted birds,
being found only on part of the 7km² island of Raso, in
the Cape Verde Is, where the population probably numbers fewer than 200 birds.

Tips: Restricted to an arid, windswept plateau with
sparse vegetation in the centre of the island. Sometimes
found in sandy ravines or feeding on rocks close to
the sea.

Site:
CAPE VERDE IS*.

Shore Lark (Horned Lark)
Eremophila alpestris   Breeding **T M** winter **ES FG   Mig Res**

Range: Main breeding range is in montane and extreme
N Scandinavia and on the Arctic coast and islands of
Russia. Isolated populations exist at scattered sites
throughout the Balkans and Greece, upland areas of
Turkey, the Caucasus and on the Volga steppes. More isolated still are populations in the Atlas of C Morocco and
in the mountains of N Israel and Lebanon, and has also
bred in Scotland. Migratory in the N, wintering on the
North Sea coasts of Great Britain and from Denmark to N France, on the German Baltic
coast and inland from Germany and Poland across Europe to the Black Sea. In Great Britain
a scarce and decreasing winter visitor and passage migrant, most numerous on the
English E coast. Southerly populations are resident.

Subspecies: At least seven races have occurred in our region differing in colour of face
and extent of black head and breast markings, ground colour and streaking of upperparts.
Typical examples may be separable in the field. There are two groups of races; 1) *alpestris*
(vagrant from North America), *flava* from Fenno–Scandia and N Russia, *brandti* from the
Volga steppes and *atlas* from Morocco, and; 2) *penicillata* From Turkey and the Caucasus,
balcanicus from Greece and the Balkans, and *bicornis* isolated in the Middle East. In the

latter group the black chest bar is joined to the black of the cheeks, in the former these are separated.

Tips: In the N breeds on tundra and moorland with bare areas, rocks and stony patches, and elsewhere on high barren plateaux and mountain ridges. In winter often found along sandy shores, on saltmarshes and coastal farmland. Unobtrusive and generally seen only when flock takes flight. Often occurs with Snow Buntings in winter.

Sites:

ARMENIA Arapan Area***, Mt Aragats***.
BELGIUM Het Zwin** (winter).
BULGARIA Rila Mts**, Tzarichina NR**.
DENMARK Bornholm-Christiansø*** (passage), Ringkøbing Fjord*** (passage, winter), Rømø*** (passage, winter), Skagen*** (passage), Skallingen-Blåvandshuk*** (passage).
FINLAND Lake Inari*** (summer), Lemmenjoki NP*** (summer), Kilpisjärvi Saana*** (summer), Pallas-Ounastunturi NP*** (summer), Urho Kekkonen NP*** (summer).
FRANCE Baie du Mont-St-Michel* (passage, winter), Somme Estuary** (passage, winter).
GEORGIA Mt Kazbek***.
GREAT BRITAIN Minsmere* (autumn, winter), N Norfolk coast** (passage, winter), Shetland Is* (passage), Spurn Peninsula* (winter).
GREECE Mt Olympus NP**, Mt Parnassós NP**, Valia Kalda NP***.
HUNGARY Hortobágy NP** (winter), Kardoskút*** (winter), Kiskunság NP*** (winter), Lake Fertö* (winter).
ISRAEL Mt Hermon***.
LATVIA Lake Pape** (passage).

LEBANON Barouk Cedars***.
MOROCCO Boumalne***, Dayet Aaoua**, Oukaimeden***, Zeida***.
NETHERLANDS Lauwersmeer** (passage, winter), Oostvaardersplassen* (winter), Terschelling** (passage, winter), Texel** (passage, winter).
NORWAY Dovrefjell NP*** (summer), Fokstumyra*** (summer), Hardangervidda NP*** (summer), Rondane NP*** (summer), Utsira* (passage), Varanger*** (summer).
POLAND Gdańsk Bay* (passage, winter).
ROMANIA Retezat NP*.
RUSSIA Kola Peninsula*** (summer), Teberdinskiy Reserve***.
SWEDEN Abisko NP*** (summer), Ammarnäs* (summer), Falsterbo* (passage, winter), Getterön** (passage, winter), Gotland** (passage), Öland** (passage, winter).
SYRIA Wadi al-Qarn-Burqush**.
TURKEY Demirkazik***, Sivrikaya***, Uludağ NP**, Van Gölü***.
UKRAINE Askania-Nova*** (winter).

Temminck's Horned Lark (Temminck's Lark)
Eremophila bilopha   D SD Res (Dis)

Range: Breeds in N Africa in E Morocco, N Algeria, S Tunisia and N Libya and, probably, Egypt. Also in Sinai and S Israel, W and N Jordan and C and S Syria.
Tips: Generally local and uncommon in lowland desert and semi-desert, dry plains and artemisia steppe, avoids areas of pure sand. In NW Africa altitudinally separated from Horned Lark.

Sites:
ISRAEL Arava Valley***, Nizzana***.
JORDAN Azraq***, Ghadir Burqu'***, Petra***,
Wadi Rum*.

MOROCCO Boumalne***, Goulimine to Tan-
Tan***, Tafilalt***.
SYRIA Tadmur and Sabkhat Muh***.
TUNISIA Tataouine***.

Brown-throated Sand Martin (Plain Martin)
Riparia paludicola   FW Res

Range: In our region found only in a small area of NW Morocco (endemic race *mauritanica*), where resident, perhaps with local dispersive movements. Vagrants have been recorded in Egypt and Israel.

Tips: Breeds colonially in winter (Nov–Feb) in burrows in sandy riverbanks, lakesides and along roadsides, but colonies frequently changed. Gregarious and feeds mainly over water.

Sites:
MOROCCO Agadir and the Sous Plain***,
Essaouira***, Oualidia*, Oued Massa***,
Oukaimeden***.

Rock Martin
Ptyonoprogne fuligula   M D (U) Res (Dis)

Range: Breeds in N Africa and parts of the Middle East, in S and E Morocco and over much of Algeria, Egypt in the Nile Valley and on the Red Sea coast. In the Middle East breeds in S Sinai, Israel and Jordan.

Subspecies: Four similar races have been recorded in the Western Palearctic region; *presaharica* in NW Africa, *spatzi* in S Algeria, *perpallida* from S Iraq and the more distinct *obsoleta* from Israel to Sinai and Egypt which is considered a full species, **Pale Crag Martin**, by some authorities.

Tips: Originally occurred solely in montane and rocky areas, on cliffs and gorges in deserts, but now most easily found near habitation, e.g. around ancient monuments in Jordan and Egypt, and buildings in S Israel. Rare in Morocco and some past claims may have involved Eurasian Crag Martin.

Sites:

EGYPT Abu Simbel***, Aswan***, Luxor***, Santa Katharina Monastery***, Sharm el Sheikh***, Suez area**.
ISRAEL Arava Valley***, Eilat***, Ein Gedi***, Hula Reserve***.

JORDAN Aqaba***, Petra***, Wadi Dana-Fidan***, Wadi Rum***.
MOROCCO Ouarzazate.

Eurasian Crag Martin (Crag Martin)
Ptyonoprogne rupestris   M C (FW)   Res AMig PMig

Range: Widespread in Iberia, C and S France, the Alps, Italy, the Balkans and Greece, and in the Mediterranean breeds on the Balearics, Corsica and Sardinia, Sicily, Crete, some Aegean islands and Cyprus. Also breeds over much of Turkey and the Caucasus, with isolated populations in SW Syria, Lebanon and N Israel. In N Africa breeds in Morocco, N Algeria and Tunisia, and coastal Libya. Northernmost populations are partial migrants, some remaining N of the Mediterranean all year whilst others gather at Gibraltar to winter there or cross into NW Africa.

Tips: Search gorges and cliffs in montane areas up to 2,500m, and sometimes occurs on coastal cliffs. Often feeds over grasslands in summer and fresh water in winter. Mud nests constructed in ravines and on cliff-faces, sometimes on buildings or bridges.

Sites:

ANDORRA* (summer).
AUSTRIA Hohe Tauern NP***, Hohe Wand**, Karwendel Reserve***, Schneeberg Mts***.
BALEARIC IS Ibiza***, Mallorca***, Menorca***.
BULGARIA Rila Mts***, Rusenski Lom NP***, Studen Kladenetz***, Trigradski Gorge***, Tissata NR***.
CORSICA Asco Valley*** (summer), Restonica Valley***, Scandola***.
CROATIA Paklenica NP***.
CYPRUS*.
FRANCE Camargue***, Cévennes NP***, Les Alpilles***, Prats-de-Mollo***, Pyrenees NP***, Queyras NP*** (summer).
GEORGIA Mt Kazbek*** (summer).
GERMANY Ammer Valley*** (summer), Berchtesgaden NP*** (summer).
GIBRALTAR* (passage, winter).

GREECE Avas Gorge***, Dadiá-Soufli Forest***, Delphi***, Lake Kerkini*, Mikrí Prespa NP***, Mt Olympus NP***, Mt Parnassós NP***, Valia Kalda NP***, Vikos-Aoos NP***.
GREEK IS Crete***, Lesvos*, Rhodes*.
ISRAEL Arava Valley*** (passage), Eilat*** (passage), Golan Heights*** (winter), Mt Hermon***, Wadi Ammud-Mt Arbel***.
ITALY Abruzzo NP***, Gran Paradiso NP***, Sibillini NP***, Stelvio NP***.
JORDAN Wadi Rum* (passage).
LEBANON Barouk Cedars** (summer), Palm Is** (summer), Qaraoun Lake** (passage, winter).
MACEDONIA Babuna Gorge*** (summer), Galicica NP***, Lakes Ohrid and Prespa***.
MALTA* (passage, winter).
MOROCCO Boumalne***, Tafilalt**, Oukaimeden***.

PORTUGAL Baixo Alentejo***, Boquilobo* (winter), Cape St Vincent** (winter), International Douro***, International Tagus***, Montesinho***, Peneda Gêres NP***.
ROMANIA Poiana Braşov***.
RUSSIA Teberdinskiy Reserve*** (summer).
SPAIN Aiguamolls de L'Empordá***, Aigües Tortes NP***, Cabo de Gata***, Cáceres-Trujillo Steppes**, Coto Doñana** (passage, winter), Ebro Delta** (winter), Garraf Massif***, Guadalhorce Estuary** (passage, winter), Jaca*** (summer), La Serena**, Llobregat Delta** (winter), Monfragüe***, Ordesa NP*** (summer), Picos de Europa***, Santa Pola*** (winter), Serrania de Ronda***, Sierra de Gredos***, Sierra de Guadarrama***.
SWITZERLAND Aletschwald***, Clos-du-Doubs***, Col de Bretolet***, Flims***, Leuk***, Monte Generoso***, Swiss NP***.
TUNISIA Lake Ichkeul***, Zaghouan***.
TURKEY Borçka*** (summer), Dalyan*** (passage), Demirkazik*** (summer), Doğubeyazit*** (summer), Göksu Delta***, Sumela***, Uludağ NP***, Van Gölü***.

Red-rumped Swallow
Hirundo daurica   M C U   Mig

Range: Summer visitor to Iberia (except N) and SW France, a few scattered sites in N and W Italy, the S Balkans, Greece and W and S Turkey. In the Mediterranean breeds on Crete and many other Greek islands and Cyprus. In the Middle East breeds in Lebanon, W Syria, N Israel and NW Jordan, and in N Africa in Morocco and at a few sites in N Algeria. Has recently expanded northwards, nesting in Hungary in 2002.

Arrives in our region sometimes as early as Feb, usually Mar–Apr and departs in Aug–Oct, occurring throughout the Mediterranean on passage.

Tips: Found around cliffs and rock-faces from sea level to mountains, nesting on cliffs and ravines. Uses coastal cliffs in some areas and urban habitats in others, nesting on buildings and bridges.

Sites:
ALBANIA Drini Delta** (summer), Karavasta Lagoon*** (summer).
BALEARIC IS Mallorca*** (summer, passage).
BULGARIA Albena-Golden Sands*** (summer), Rila Mts*** (summer), Rusenski Lom NP*** (summer), Strandja Mts*** (summer), Studen Kladenetz*** (summer), Trigradski Gorge*** (summer), Tissata NR*** (summer).
CANARY IS* (passage).
CORSICA Cap Corse* (passage).
CYPRUS* (summer, passage).
EGYPT Hurghada* (passage), Suez area** (passage).
FRANCE Camargue* (summer).
GIBRALTAR* (passage).
GREECE Amvrakikós Gulf** (passage), Avas Gorge*** (summer), Axios-Aliakmonas Deltas** (passage), Dadiá-Soufli Forest*** (summer), Delphi*** (summer), Lake Kerkini*** (summer), Mikrí Prespa NP*** (summer), Mt Parnassós NP*** (summer), Nestos Delta** (passage), Porto Lagos area* (passage).
GREEK IS Corfu*** (summer, passage), Crete*** (summer, passage), Kos*** (summer, passage), Lesvos*** (summer, passage), Náxos* (summer), Rhodes*** (summer, passage).

ISRAEL Arava Valley*** (passage), Eilat*** (passage), Golan Heights*** (summer).
ITALY Gargano Peninsula*** (passage), Monte Conero* (passage), Orbetello Reserve*** (summer, passage), Po Delta* (passage), Tuscan archipelago* (passage).
JORDAN Aqaba** (passage), Wadi Rum** (passage), Wadi as Sir** (summer).
LEBANON Qaraoun Lake** (passage).
MACEDONIA Babuna Gorge*** (summer), Demir Kapija Gorge** (summer), Galicica NP*** (summer), Lakes Ohrid and Prespa*** (summer).
MALTA** (passage).
MOROCCO Essaouira*** (summer, passage), Oualidia* (passage), Oued Massa*** (passage), Oukaimeden*** (summer), Zaër*** (summer).
PORTUGAL Baixo Alentejo*** (summer), Boquilobo** (summer), Cape St Vincent*** (passage), Castro Marim*** (summer), International Douro*** (summer), International Tagus*** (summer), Montesinho*** (summer),

Peneda Gêres NP*** (summer), Ria Formosa*** (summer), Sado Estuary*** (summer), Santo André Lagoon*** (passage), Tagus Estuary*** (summer).
SPAIN Aiguamolls de L'Empordá*** (summer, passage), Cabo de Gata*** (summer), Cáceres-Trujillo Steppes*** (summer), Cádiz Lagoons*** (passage), Coto Doñana*** (summer), Ebro Delta*** (summer), Garraf Massif*** (summer), La Serena*** (summer), Monfragüe NP*** (summer), Santa Pola*** (passage), Serrania de Ronda*** (summer), Sierra de Gredos*** (summer), Sierra de Guadarrama*** (summer), Tablas de Daimiel*** (summer).
SYRIA Aqra Mts*** (summer), Yarmuk Valley** (summer, passage).
TUNISIA Cap Bon Peninsula*** (passage), Lake Ichkeul** (passage).
TURKEY Birecik-Halfeti*** (summer), Dalyan*** (summer, passage), Demirkazik*** (summer), Göksu Delta*** (summer), Uludağ NP*** (summer), Yeşilce*** (summer).

Richard's Pipit
Anthus richardi

FG FW   Mig

Range: A scarce but regular passage migrant to many European countries, from Scandinavia to the Mediterranean, the Middle East and N Africa. Main period is late Sep–early Nov, but now overwinters regularly in S France, S Iberia, Italy, the Balearics and perhaps elsewhere. Spring records much rarer than autumn but peak in Apr. More than 100 per annum are recorded in Great Britain, mainly on E and S coasts, most occur in autumn with a few spring records and the occasional wintering bird.

Tips: Migrants are usually seen in open grassland and marshes, often coastal, or on cultivated land. Well-watched coastal migration hotspots provide the best chance of locating this species.

Sites:
BALEARIC IS Mallorca* (winter).
DENMARK Bornholm-Christiansø*** (autumn), Skagen*** (autumn), Skallingen-Blåvandshuk*** (autumn).

EGYPT Sharm el Sheikh* (passage, winter).
FINLAND Åland Is** (autumn).
FRANCE Camargue* (passage, winter), Cap Gris Nez* (autumn), Ouessant*** (autumn).

GERMANY Heligoland*** (passage).
GREAT BRITAIN Flamborough Head*
(autumn), N Norfolk coast** (autumn),
Portland* (passage), Scilly*** (autumn),
Shetland Is** (autumn), Spurn Peninsula*
(autumn).
GREEK IS Crete* (passage).
ISRAEL Arava Valley*** (passage), Bet Shean
Valley** (passage), Eilat*** (passage).
JORDAN Azraq* (passage).
MALTA (autumn, winter).
MOROCCO Oued Massa (winter).

NETHERLANDS Terschelling* (autumn), Texel*
(autumn).
NORWAY Utsira* (autumn).
POLAND Gdańsk Bay* (autumn).
SARDINIA Cagliari* (winter).
SICILY Lago di Lentini (passage).
SPAIN Coto Doñana* (winter).
SWEDEN Falsterbo* (autumn), Gotland**
(autumn), Holmöarna** (autumn), Öland**
(autumn).
TURKEY Kızılırmak Delta* (passage).

Tawny Pipit
Anthus campestris

SH FG   Mig (Res)

Range: Breeds in Iberia, S France and Italy, the Balkans,
Greece and most of Turkey. Also very patchily further N
in Europe, in C and N France, the Netherlands, Germany
and S Sweden E to the Urals, Caspian and Caucasus.
Isolated populations persist in NW Africa and the Middle
East, and has recently bred in Malta. Possibly resident in
Greece and Crete.

Tips: A characteristic bird of dry heaths, roadsides and
cultivated land. Also found in newly cut woodlands, dunes and vineyards. In NW Africa
occurs above the treeline in the Atlas Mts. Outside main range most regular at well-
watched coastal migration sites.

Sites:
ARMENIA Armash Fishponds*** (summer).
AUSTRIA Lake Neusiedl*** (summer).
BALEARIC IS Formentera*** (summer), Ibiza***
(summer), Mallorca*** (summer), Menorca***
(summer).
BELARUS Belovezhskaya Pushcha NP** (sum-
mer), Berezinsky Reserve** (summer),
Prypyatsky NP*** (summer).
BOSNIA-HERZEGOVINA Hutovo blato** (sum-
mer). Sujetska NP** (summer).
BULGARIA Albena-Golden Sands*** (summer),
Burgas area*** (summer), Cape Emine***
(summer, passage), Cape Kaliakra*** (summer,
passage), Lake Durankulak*** (summer), Lake
Shabla*** (summer), Ropotamo NP***

(summer), Rusenski Lom NP*** (summer),
Strandja Mts*** (summer), Studen Kladenetz***
(summer), Trigradski Gorge*** (summer),
Tissata NR*** (summer).
CANARY IS Fuerteventura**(passage).
CORSICA Asco Valley*** (summer),
Bonifacio*** (summer), Cap Corse** (passage).
CROATIA Cres*** (summer), Neretva Delta***
(summer), Mljet*** (summer).
CYPRUS*** (passage).
CZECH REPUBLIC Znojmo** (summer).
DENMARK Skagen** (summer, passage),
Skallingen-Blåvandshuk** (autumn).
EGYPT Abu Simbel** (passage), Aswan**
(passage), Hurghada** (passage), Luxor*

(passage), Sharm el Sheikh*** (passage, winter), Suez area*** (passage), Zaranik** (passage). **FRANCE** Baie de Bourgneuf*** (summer), Baie du Mont-St-Michel* (passage), Camargue*** (summer), Cap Gris Nez* (autumn), Cévennes NP*** (summer), Golfe du Morbihan* (passage), Gruissan*** (summer), Île d'Oléron*** (summer), Les Alpilles*** (summer), Leucate*** (summer), Marais Poitevin** (passage), Ouessant** (passage). **GEORGIA** Iori Steppes*** (summer). **GERMANY** Ammer Valley** (summer). **GIBRALTAR***** (passage). **GREAT BRITAIN** Flamborough Head (autumn), Portland* (autumn), Scilly** (autumn), Spurn Peninsula (autumn). **GREECE** Amvrakikós Gulf*** (summer), Avas Gorge*** (summer), Axios-Aliakmonas Deltas*** (summer), Dadiá-Soufli Forest*** (summer), Delphi*** (summer), Evros Delta*** (summer), Lake Kerkini*** (summer), Mikrí Prespa NP*** (summer), Mt Olympus NP*** (summer), Mt Parnassós NP*** (summer), Nestos Delta*** (summer), Porto Lagos area*** (summer). **GREEK IS** Corfu*** (summer), Crete*** (summer, passage), Kos*** (summer), Lesvos*** (summer, passage), Rhodes*** (summer). **HUNGARY** Hortobágy NP*** (summer), Kis-balaton*** (summer), Kiskunság NP*** (summer), Lake Fertö*** (summer), Lake Velence*** (summer), Tihany*** (summer). **IRELAND** Saltee Is (passage). **ISRAEL** Arava Valley*** (passage), Bet Shean Valley*** (passage), Eilat*** (passage), Jezreel Valley*** (passage), Mt Hermon*** (summer, passage), Nizzana*** (summer, passage), Urim*** (passage). **ITALY** Abruzzo NP*** (summer), Circeo NP*** (summer), Orbetello Reserve*** (summer), Po Delta*** (summer), Tuscan archipelago*** (passage). **JORDAN** Aqaba** (passage), Azraq* (passage), Wadi Rum** (passage). **LATVIA** Cape Kolka*** (summer), Lake Pape** (summer).

LEBANON Palm Is** (passage), Qaraoun Lake** (passage). **LITHUANIA** Kirsiu Peninsula*** (summer). **MACEDONIA** Babuna Gorge*** (summer), Demir Kapija Gorge** (summer), Galicica NP*** (summer), Lakes Ohrid and Prespa*** (summer). **MALTA***** (passage). **MOROCCO** Boumalne*** (passage), Dayet Aaoua*** (summer), Goulimine to Tan-Tan*** (passage), Zeida** (summer). **NETHERLANDS** Veluwe*** (summer). **POLAND** Białowieża Forest** (summer), Biebrza Marshes** (summer), Gdańsk Bay** (summer), Kampinos NP*** (summer), Milicz Fishponds*** (summer), Siemianówka Reservoir*** (summer), Szczecin Bay area** (summer). **PORTUGAL** Baixo Alentejo*** (summer), Cape St Vincent*** (passage), Castro Marim*** (summer), International Tagus*** (summer), Montesinho*** (summer), Peneda Gêres NP*** (summer), Ria Formosa*** (summer), Sado Estuary*** (summer), Santo André Lagoon*** (summer), Tagus Estuary*** (summer). **ROMANIA** Danube Delta*** (summer), Dobrudja*** (summer). **RUSSIA** Kalmykia*** (summer), Volga Delta*** (summer). **SLOVAKIA** Senné Fishponds** (summer), Slovenský Kras** (summer), Záhorie** (summer), Zlatná na Ostrove*** (summer). **SPAIN** Aiguamolls de L'Empordá*** (summer), Cáceres-Trujillo Steppes*** (summer), Coto Doñana*** (summer), Ebro Delta*** (summer), Garraf Massif*** (summer), Jaca*** (summer), La Serena*** (summer), Llobregat Delta*** (summer), Monfragüe*** (summer), Serrania de Ronda*** (summer), Sierra de Guadarrama*** (summer), Tablas de Daimiel*** (summer), Zaragoza Steppes*** (summer). **SWEDEN** Falsterbo* (passage), Getterön* (passage), Kristianstad*** (summer). **SWITZERLAND** Klingnau Reservoir** (passage), Leuk* (summer, passage).

TUNISIA Kelbia Lake** (summer, passage), Lake Ichkeul*** (summer, passage).
TURKEY Demirkazik*** (summer), Göksu Delta*** (summer), İstanbul*** (passage), Kocaçay Delta*** (summer), Kulu Gölü*** (summer), Van Gölü*** (summer).
UKRAINE Askania-Nova*** (summer), Dunay Delta*** (summer), Tiligul Liman*** (summer).

Berthelot's Pipit (Canarian Pipit)
Anthus berthelotii

FG SH   Res

Range: Endemic to the Atlantic islands of Madeira, the Desertas, Selvagems and Canaries. Common on the eastern Canaries, particularly Fuerteventura.

Subspecies: Nominate race is found on the Canaries and *madeirensis* in Madeira.

Tips: Usually easy to locate on rocky, sparsely vegetated plains, hillsides and plateaux from sea level to over 2,000m. Also found in cultivated areas such as vineyards, and in open woodland. Occurs in a range of habitats in the Canaries but found mainly in upland areas of Madeira.

Sites:
CANARY IS El Hierro***, Fuerteventura***, Gomera***, Gran Canaria***, La Palma***, Lanzarote***, Tenerife***.
MADEIRA*.

Long-billed Pipit
Anthus similis

SH FG   Res

Range: In our region restricted to the Middle East, where breeds in parts of Lebanon, S and W Syria, N Israel and W Jordan. May also breed in Egypt.

Tips: Search rocky mountain slopes with sparse vegetation, up to 2,000 m in summer and lower hillsides and plains in winter.

Sites:
ISRAEL Arava Valley, Golan Heights***, Wadi Ammud-Mt Arbel***.
JORDAN Petra, Wadi as Sir**.
LEBANON Barouk Cedars**, Palm Is* (winter).
SYRIA Yarmuk Valley**.

Red-throated Pipit
Anthus cervinus

Summer **T SH** winter **FW FG** **Mig**

Range: Breeds in extreme N Scandinavia, the N Kola Peninsula and the Arctic coast of Russia from the Kanin Peninsula E. Has bred further S in Norway. Departs breeding areas in late Aug–early Oct and returns from Feb, but most reach N of range in late May. Migrates across Europe and passage birds common in the C and E Mediterranean and the Middle East. Small numbers winter in S Turkey and the Middle East, N Africa, especially the Nile Delta, with a few in coastal Morocco and the Canaries. Also regular in very small numbers in SE Italy and Greece.

Tips: Breeds on tundra and in willow and birch scrub, usually near water. On passage and in winter occupies open areas, including marshes and meadows, often with grazing livestock.

Sites:

BALEARIC IS Mallorca** (passage).
CANARY IS Tenerife** (winter).
CYPRUS*** (passage).
DENMARK Amager** (passage), Bornholm-Christiansø*** (passage), Møn-Falster** (passage), Skagen*** (passage), Skallingen-Blåvandshuk*** (passage), Stignæs** (passage).
EGYPT Abu Simbel*** (winter), Aswan*** (winter), Faiyum*** (winter), Hurghada*** (passage), Luxor*** (passage, winter), Nile Delta*** (passage, winter), Sharm el Sheikh*** (passage), Suez area*** (passage), Zaranik*** (passage).
FINLAND Åland Is*** (passage), Kevo NR*** (summer), Kilpisjärvi Saana*** (summer), Pallas-Ounastunturi NP*** (summer), Ruissalo*** (passage), Urho Kekkonen NP*** (summer), Viikki*** (passage).
FRANCE Cap Gris Nez* (passage).
GREAT BRITAIN Flamborough Head* (autumn).
GREECE Axios-Aliakmonas Deltas** (passage), Evros Delta** (passage), Lake Kerkini** (passage), Porto Lagos area*** (passage). **GREEK IS** Corfu*** (passage), Crete*** (passage), Kos*** (passage), Lesvos*** (passage), Náxos*** (passage), Rhodes*** (passage).

HUNGARY Hortobágy NP* (passage), Kis-balaton*** (passage), Kiskunság NP*** (passage).
ISRAEL Arava Valley*** (passage, winter), Bet Shean Valley*** (passage, winter), Eilat*** (passage, winter), Ma'agan Mikhael*** (passage, winter), Nizzana*** (passage, winter), Urim*** (passage, winter).
ITALY Gargano Peninsula* (passage), Maremma Regional Park* (passage), Monte Conero** (passage), Orbetello Reserve* (passage), Po Delta* (passage), Tuscan archipelago* (passage).
JORDAN Aqaba*** (passage, winter), Azraq*** (passage, winter), Petra** (passage), Wadi Rum** (passage).
LEBANON Aammiq Marshes*** (passage, winter), Qaraoun Lake** (passage).
MALTA*** (passage).
MOROCCO Oualidia (passage).
NETHERLANDS Lauwersmeer (passage), Oostvaardersplassen (passage), Terschelling* (passage), Texel* (passage).
NORWAY Lista*** (passage), Mølen** (passage), Slettnes*** (summer), Utsira** (passage), Varanger*** (summer).
POLAND Gdańsk Bay** (passage), Siemianówka Reservoir** (passage), Szczecin Bay area** (passage).

PORTUGAL Castro Marim** (passage).
RUSSIA Kola Peninsula*** (summer).
SICILY Lago di Lentini* (passage), Vendicari* (passage).
SPAIN Aiguamolls de l'Empordá* (spring), Coto Doñana* (passage), Ebro Delta* (spring).
SWEDEN Abisko NP*** (summer), Falsterbo* (autumn), Gotland*** (passage), Hjälstaviken*** (passage), Hornborgasjön** (passage), Kristianstad** (passage), Muddus NP*** (summer), Öland*** (passage).

SWITZERLAND Leuk* (passage).
SYRIA Sabkhat al-Jabbul** (passage), Yarmuk Valley* (passage).
TUNISIA Cap Bon Peninsula** (passage), Lake Ichkeul** (winter).
TURKEY Dalyan** (passage), Göksu Delta*** (passage), İstanbul*** (passage), Kızılırmak Delta** (passage), Kulu Gölü*** (passage), Van Gölü** (passage).
UKRAINE Dunay Delta* (passage), Tiligul Liman** (passage).

Rock Pipit
Anthus petrosus   ES   Res Mig

Range: Confined to the Western Palearctic, breeding in coastal areas of the Faroes, British Isles, Channel Is and W and N France. Also in Denmark, around Scandinavia to the Kola Peninsula. Has bred in Iceland and Estonia. Scandinavian birds are migratory, wintering on coasts of Denmark and Great Britain to Iberia and NW Africa. Occasionally recorded on passage in C Europe and in the Mediterranean E to Sicily and Malta.

Subspecies: Race *kleinschmidti* is found in the Faroes and Shetland Is, *meinertzhageni* in the Outer Hebrides, nominate race in remainder of Great Britain, Ireland and France, and *littoralis* in Scandinavia.

Tips: Search rocky shores and sea-cliffs, in winter harbours, piers and jetties. Rare at inland waters.

Sites:
DENMARK Bornholm-Christiansø*** (passage), Hanstholm*** (winter), Skagen*** (passage, winter), Skallingen-Blåvandshuk*** (passage, winter).
FAROE IS***.
FINLAND Åland Is*** (summer), Ruissalo*** (summer).
FRANCE Golfe du Morbihan***, Île d'Oléron***, Ouessant***, Sept Îles***, Somme Estuary*** (winter).
GREAT BRITAIN Anglesey***, Dungeness** (passage), Flamborough Head** (winter), Islay***, Minsmere* (winter), N Norfolk coast* (passage), Orkney Is***, Outer Hebrides***,

Pembrokeshire Is***, Portland***, Rhum***, St Ives Bay*** (winter), Scilly***, Shetland Is***, Spurn Peninsula* (passage).
IRELAND Rathlin I***, Saltee Is***.
NETHERLANDS Lauwersmeer*** (winter), Oostvaardersplassen*** (winter), Terschelling*** (winter), Texel*** (winter).
NORWAY Lofoten Is*** (summer), Slettnes*** (summer), Utsira*** (summer, passage), Varanger*** (summer).
RUSSIA Kola Peninsula*** (summer).
SWEDEN Falsterbo** (autumn, winter), Gotland*** (passage), Holmöarna*** (summer), Öland*** (summer), Stockholm archipelago*** (summer).

Water Pipit
Anthus spinoletta
Summer **M** winter **FG ES**   **Mig (PMig) (AMig)**

Range: Confined to montane areas of S Europe and SW Asia. Breeds in the Cantabrians and other upland areas of Spain, the Pyrenees and Alps, the Apennines and on Corsica and Sardinia. Further E found in the Carpathians, Dinaric Alps and the Balkan and Rhodope ranges. Also breeds over much of upland Turkey and the Caucasus. In winter occurs from the Netherlands to Spain, Italy and Greece, on many Mediterranean islands and in N Africa. Scarce winter visitor and passage migrant to Great Britain.

Subspecies: Nominate occurs over most of range with *coutelli* in E Turkey and the Caucasus.

Tips: Generally easily seen in mountain meadows with grass or other low vegetation, usually at 1,500–2,500m or above. Sometimes found near glaciers or even above the snowline. Descends in winter, occurring around lakes and in marshy areas, often on coastal farmland and estuaries.

Sites:

ANDORRA*** (summer).

AUSTRIA Hohe Tauern NP*** (summer), Hohe Wand*** (summer), Karwendel Reserve*** (summer), Schneeberg Mts*** (summer).

BALEARIC IS Mallorca** (winter).

BOSNIA-HERZEGOVINA Sujetska NP*** (summer).

CORSICA Asco Valley*** (summer), Restonica Valley*** (summer).

CYPRUS* (winter).

CZECH REPUBLIC Jeseníky Mts*** (summer), Krkonoše NP*** (summer).

DENMARK Skagen*** (passage, winter), Skallingen-Blåvandshuk*** (passage).

EGYPT Faiyum* (winter), Nile Delta** (winter), Sharm el Sheikh*** (winter), Zaranik** (passage, winter).

FRANCE Baie de Vilaine** (winter), Baie du Mont-St-Michel* (winter), Camargue*** (winter), Cévennes NP*** (summer), Écrins NP*** (summer), Forêt d'Issaux*** (summer), Forêt d'Orient** (passage), Lac du Der-Chantecoq*** (winter), Marais Poitevin** (winter), Mercantour NP*** (summer), Ouessant*** (passage), Prats-de-Mollo*** (summer), Pyrenees NP*** (summer), Queyras NP*** (summer), Somme Estuary** (winter), Vanoise NP*** (summer).

GEORGIA Javakheti Plateau*** (summer), Mt Kazbek*** (summer).

GERMANY Ammer Valley*** (summer), Berchtesgaden NP*** (summer).

GREAT BRITAIN Dungeness* (passage), Minsmere* (winter), N Norfolk coast** (passage, winter).

BULGARIA Rila Mts*** (summer), Tzarichina NR*** (summer).

GREECE Mikrí Prespa NP*** (winter).

GREEK IS Lesvos*** (winter).

HUNGARY Hortobágy NP** (passage), Kiskunság NP* (passage).

ISRAEL Arava Valley*** (passage, winter), Bet Shean Valley*** (passage, winter), Eilat*** (passage, winter), Ein Gedi*** (passage), Hula Reserve*** (passage, winter), Ma'agan Mikhael*** (passage, winter), Urim** (passage, winter).

ITALY Abruzzo NP*** (summer), Gran Paradiso NP*** (summer), Po Delta*** (winter), Sibillini NP*** (summer), Stelvio NP*** (summer), Tuscan archipelago* (passage).

JORDAN Aqaba*** (passage, winter), Azraq*** (winter).

LEBANON Aammiq Marshes** (passage), Qaraoun Lake** (passage).

MACEDONIA Galicica NP*** (summer), Lakes Ohrid and Prespa*** (winter).

MALTA* (autumn, winter).

MOROCCO Oukaimeden*** (winter).

NETHERLANDS Lauwersmeer*** (winter), Oostvaardersplassen*** (winter), Texel*** (winter).

POLAND Bieszczady NP*** (summer), Tatra NP*** (summer).

PORTUGAL Baixo Alentejo*** (winter), Boquilobo** (winter), Castro Marim*** (passage, winter), Montesinho***, Peneda Gêres NP*** (winter), Ria Formosa*** (winter), Sado Estuary*** (winter), Santo André Lagoon*** (winter), Tagus Estuary*** (winter).

ROMANIA Bicaz*** (summer), Poiana Braşov*** (summer), Retezat NP*** (summer).

RUSSIA Teberdinskiy Reserve*** (summer).

SLOVAKIA High Tatras NP*** (summer), Malá Fatra*** (summer), Nízke Tatry NP*** (summer).

SLOVENIA Triglav NP*** (summer).

SPAIN Aiguamolls de L'Empordá*** (passage, winter), Aigües Tortes NP*** (summer), Cádiz Lagoons*** (winter), Coto Doñana*** (passage, winter), Ebro Delta*** (winter), Jaca*** (summer), Llobregat Delta*** (passage, winter), Ordesa NP*** (summer), Picos de Europa*** (summer), Santa Pola*** (passage, winter), Sierra de Gredos*** (summer), Sierra de Guadarrama*** (summer), Tablas de Daimiel*** (winter).

SWITZERLAND Aletschwald*** (summer), Col de Bretolet*** (summer), Fanel NR*** (winter), Flims*** (summer), Klingnau Reservoir*** (winter), Monte Generoso*** (summer), Swiss NP*** (summer).

TUNISIA Cap Bon Peninsula*** (passage), Chott el Djerid** (winter), Kelbia Lake** (winter), Lake Ichkeul*** (winter).

TURKEY Borçka*** (summer), Demirkazik*** (summer), Sivrikaya*** (summer), Uludağ NP*** (summer).

UKRAINE Carpathians*** (summer).

Buff-bellied Pipit
Anthus rubescens

FG ES Mig

Range: Breeds in N America and in NC and NE Asia, with Asian birds wintering from Pakistan to Japan and S to SE Asia. Regular on passage and in winter in small but increasing numbers in S Israel, and has been recorded in Lebanon and Syria.

Subspecies: Nominate race breeds in North America (has occurred in Europe as a vagrant) and *japonicus* in N Asia.

Tips: Outside the breeding season found in a range of wet and dry habitats including sparsely vegetated fields and open beaches. Eilat is the place to look for this species, but it undoubtedly occurs elsewhere in the Near East.

Sites:
ISRAEL Arava Valley** (passage, winter), Bet Shean Valley** (passage, winter), Eilat** (passage, winter).

Citrine Wagtail
Motacilla citreola

FW T   Mig

Range: Breeds across N Russia from the Kola Peninsula E and, further S, from C Belarus and Ukraine to the Urals. Small numbers regular in Latvia and range is expanding westwards with first breeding records for Finland, Lithuania, Estonia, Poland, the Czech Republic, Slovakia and Switzerland in recent years. Also now a rather common breeder in C and E Turkey, and has bred in Armenia and attempted to do so in Israel. Small numbers regular on passage through the Middle East. Summer visitor to our region, arriving mid Mar–mid May and mainly departing in Sep. A few winter in Saudi Arabia but the majority move to India and SE Asia at this season.

Subspecies: Nominate occurs across N of range replaced by *werae* further S.

Tips: Breeds in river deltas, in osiers and other waterside vegetation, and on wet tundra, further S in bogs, wet meadows and marshy vegetation. Passage birds occur in similar wetland habitats.

Sites:

CYPRUS** (passage).
EGYPT Sharm el Sheikh* (passage).
GEORGIA Javakheti Plateau** (summer).
GREEK IS Kos* (passage), Lesvos** (passage).
ISRAEL Arava Valley*** (passage, winter), Bet Shean Valley*** (passage, winter), Eilat** (passage, winter), Hula Reserve** (passage, winter), Ma'agan Mikhael** (passage).
JORDAN Azraq* (passage).
LATVIA Cape Kolka* (passage).

LEBANON Aammiq Marshes* (passage).
LITHUANIA Cepkeliai NR* (summer).
POLAND Gdańsk Bay** (summer, passage), Siemianówka Reservoir** (summer, passage).
RUSSIA Kola Peninsula* (summer).
SWEDEN Falsterbo* (autumn).
SYRIA Dayr al-Zawr** (passage).
TURKEY Kızılırmak Delta** (summer, passage), Kulu Gölü*** (summer, passage), Van Gölü** (summer).
UKRAINE Tiligul Liman*** (summer).

African Pied Wagtail
Motacilla aguimp

FW FG   Res

Range: Widespread in tropical Africa but in our region a rare breeder confined to extreme S Egypt on Lake Nasser. Wanders locally in response to changing water levels basically resident.

Tips: Found along riverbanks and lake margins, in some areas common around habitation. Abu Simbel is the only reasonably reliable site for this species.

Site:
EGYPT Abu Simbel**.

White-cheeked Bulbul
Pycnonotus leucogenys

FG U Res

Range: Occurs from Kuwait and Iraq E to Assam, and in the Western Palearctic common and widespread in Iraq from the Gulf to near the Syrian border. Recently recorded spreading NW along the Euphrates into Syria.

Tips: Inhabits open country with bushes and scattered trees, palm groves, orchards and cultivated areas, often near habitation. Only likely to be seen in the Euphrates Valley of Syria, at Dayr al-Zawr, but may occur elsewhere in the valley, and recently reported from Fuerteventura, in the Canaries, where it may be in the process of becoming established.

Sites:
SYRIA Dayr al-Zawr***.

Spectacled Bulbul (Yellow-vented Bulbul)
Pycnonotus xanthopygos

SH D SD U Res

Range: Occurs in S Turkey from about Antalya E, in coastal Syria and Lebanon, Israel and adjacent W Jordan, and parts of N and extreme S Sinai.

Tips: Common near habitation, in palm groves, orchards and gardens, also in wadis and oases and most habitats with trees and bushes.

Sites:
ISRAEL Arava Valley***, Eilat***, Ein Gedi***, Hula Reserve***, Jezreel Valley***, Ma'agan Mikhael***, Mt Hermon***.
JORDAN Amman NP***, Aqaba***, Petra***, Wadi Dana-Fidan***, Wadi Rum***, Wadi as Sir***.

LEBANON Barouk Cedars**, Qaraoun Lake**.
SYRIA Aqra Mts**, Yarmuk Valley***.
TURKEY Birecik-Halfeti**, Göksu Delta***, Yeşilce***.

Common Bulbul
Pycnonotus barbatus

SH D SD U Res

Range: Common in Morocco, coastal Algeria and extreme N Tunisia, and in the Nile Delta and Valley of Egypt. Has also colonised part of the Suez Canal area in recent decades.

Subspecies: Nominate *barbatus* is found in NW Africa and *arsinoe* in Egypt.

Tips: A characteristic bird of urban gardens over most of range, often attracted to berry-bearing bushes and trees, and usually seen near habitation. Also palm groves, orchards and cultivated areas, and remote wadis and oases. The only bulbul in N Africa.

Sites:
ALGERIA El Kala NP***.
EGYPT Abu Simbel***, Aswan***, Luxor***, Nile Delta**.
MOROCCO Agadir and the Sous Plain***, Boumalne***, Essaouira***, Goulimime to Tan-

Tan***, Ouarzazate***, Oued Massa***, Tafilalt***, Zaers***, Zeida***.
TUNISIA Ain Draham***, Cap Bon Peninsula***, Lake Ichkeul***, Tunis***.

Radde's Accentor
Prunella ocularis

M SH AMig

Range: Breeds in the Aladağ region of the Taurus Mts of C Turkey and more widely in E Turkey and the Caucasus. However, precise limits of range unclear and may be more widespread than thought. An altitudinal migrant, moving lower in winter and also further afield, as small numbers are regular in Syria and N Israel, especially in the Mt Hermon area.

Tip: Breeds at 2,000–3,500m in rocky and scrubby areas, especially those with junipers or cedars. In winter descends to 1,000m and often feeds along streams. Shy and secretive, most easily located by voice.

Sites:
ARMENIA Arapan Area***, Mt Aragats***, Pambak Mts***.
GEORGIA Javakheti Plateau** (summer).

ISRAEL Golan Heights* (winter), Mt Hermon* (winter), Wadi Ammud-Mt Arbel (winter).
TURKEY Birecik-Halfeti* (winter), Demirkazik***, Yeşilce* (winter), Van Gölü***.

Alpine Accentor
Prunella collaris

M Res (AMig)

Range: In Iberia breeds in the Cantabrians, Sierra de Gredos, Sierra Nevada and Pyrenees, also throughout the Alps and Apennines and further E in the Carpathians and in scattered localities in the Balkans and N Greece. Occurs over much of S and E Turkey and the Caucasus, in the Mediterranean breeds on Corsica and Crete, and in N Africa in the Moroccan Atlas. More widespread in Iberia and N Africa in winter, when descends lower.

Subspecies: Three races occur in our region but differences are very slight; nominate is found from Iberia and NW Africa E to the Carpathians, *subalpina* in the Balkans, Greece and S Turkey and *montana* in N and E Turkey and the Caucasus.

Tips: Found at 1,800–3,000m in mountains and high plateaux, in open grassy areas and on boulder-strewn slopes. Often feeds around buildings at ski stations but easily overlooked.

Sites:

ANDORRA*.

ARMENIA Mt Aragats***, Pambak Mts***.

AUSTRIA Hohe Tauern NP***, Hohe Wand*, Karwendel Reserve***, Schneeberg Mts***.

BALEARIC IS Mallorca** (winter).

BOSNIA-HERZEGOVINA Sutjeska NP***.

BULGARIA Rila Mts***, Tzarichina NR***.

CORSICA Asco Valley***, Bonifacio* (winter), Restonica Valley***.

CZECH REPUBLIC Jeseníky Mts**, Krkonoše NP***.

FRANCE Cévennes NP* (winter), Écrins NP***, Les Alpilles* (winter), Mercantour NP***, Prats-de-Mollo***, Pyrenees NP***, Queyras NP***, Vanoise NP***.

GEORGIA Javakheti Plateau***, Mt Kazbek***.

GERMANY Ammer Valley***, Berchtesgaden NP***.

GIBRALTAR* (winter).

GREECE Mikrí Prespa NP* (winter), Mt Olympus NP***, Mt Parnassós NP***, Valia Kalda***, Vikos-Aoos NP***.

GREEK IS Crete**.

HUNGARY Buda Hills* (winter), Pilis Hills* (winter).

ISRAEL Wadi Ammud-Mt Arbel* (winter).

ITALY Abruzzo NP***, Gran Paradiso NP***, Sibillini NP***, Stelvio NP***, Tuscan archipelago** (winter).

MACEDONIA Galicica NP* (winter).

MALTA* (winter).

MOROCCO Oukaimeden***.

POLAND Bieszczady NP***, Tatra NP***.

PORTUGAL Baixo Alentejo* (winter), Cape St Vincent** (winter), International Tagus* (winter), Peneda Gêres NP** (winter).

ROMANIA Bicaz***, Poiana Braşov***, Retezat NP***.

RUSSIA Teberdinskiy Reserve***.

SARDINIA San Pietro I.* (winter).

SLOVAKIA High Tatras NP*** (summer), Malá Fatra*** (summer), Nízke Tatry NP*** (summer).

SLOVENIA Triglav NP***.

SPAIN Aiguamolls de L'Empordá* (winter), Aigües Tortes NP*** (summer), Garraf Massif* (winter), Jaca***, La Serena* (winter), Monfragüe* (winter), Ordesa NP***, Picos de Europa***, Serrania de Ronda** (winter), Sierra de Gredos***, Sierra de Guadarrama*** (summer).

SWITZERLAND Aletschwald***, Flims***, Monte Generoso***, Swiss NP***.

TURKEY Borçka***, Demirkazik***, Sivrikaya***, Uludağ NP***.
UKRAINE Carpathians***.

Rufous Bush Robin (Rufous-tailed Scrub Robin)
Cercotrichas galactotes

SD SH   Mig

Range: Breeds in SE Portugal and C and S Spain, the SW Balkans and Greece, W and S Turkey and Transcaucasia. In the Middle East breeds in N and W Syria, Israel and Jordan and is widespread across NW Africa. In Egypt breeds along the Mediterranean coast and the Nile Valley, at a few scattered oases in the interior and in parts of Sinai. Present in N of range Apr–Aug.

Subspecies: Four races occur in our region which may be better treated as two full species. Nominate race from Iberia, N Africa and Israel and *minor* from the Sahara may form a separate species from *syriacus* (Greece and Turkey to Lebanon) and *familiaris* from Transcaucasia.

Tips: Inhabits semi-deserts and wadis, particularly tamarisk scrub, also oases, gardens, orchards, vineyards and palm groves. Often found close to human habitation in N Africa.

Sites:

ARMENIA Armash Fishponds*** (summer).
BALEARIC IS Mallorca* (spring).
BULGARIA Ropotamo NP* (summer).
CYPRUS** (passage).
EGYPT Abu Simbel** (summer), Aswan*** (summer), Hurghada* (summer), Nile Delta** (summer).
GEORGIA Iori Steppes*** (summer), Mt Kazbek*** (summer).
GIBRALTAR*** (passage).
GREECE Avas Gorge*** (summer), Axios-Aliakmonas Deltas*** (summer), Evros Delta** (summer), Nestos Delta*** (summer), Porto Lagos area*** (summer).
GREEK IS Corfu*** (summer), Lesvos*** (summer).
ISRAEL Arava Valley*** (summer, passage), Bet Shean Valley*** (summer), Eilat** (summer), Ein Gedi*** (summer), Urim*** (summer).
JORDAN Amman NP*** (summer), Aqaba** (passage), Azraq*** (summer), Petra** (summer), Wadi Rum** (passage), Wadi as Sir*** (summer).

LEBANON Aammiq Marshes*** (summer), Qaraoun Lake** (summer).
MACEDONIA Demir Kapija Gorge** (summer).
MALTA* (spring).
MOROCCO Agadir and the Sous Plain*** (summer), Boumalne*** (summer), Essaouira*** (summer), Oued Massa*** (summer), Oukaimeden*** (summer), Tafilalt*** (summer), Zaër*** (summer), Zeida*** (summer).
PORTUGAL Baixo Alentejo*** (summer), Cape St Vincent*** (passage), Castro Marim*** (summer), International Tagus*** (summer), Ria Formosa*** (summer).
SPAIN Aiguamolls de L'Empordá* (passage), Cabo de Gata** (summer, passage), Cádiz Lagoons*** (summer), Coto Doñana*** (summer), La Serena*** (summer), Monfragüe*** (summer), Santa Pola*** (summer).
SYRIA Baath Lake** (summer), Dayr al-Zawr*** (summer), Tadmur and Sabkhat Muh** (summer).
TUNISIA Cap Bon Peninsula*** (summer).

TURKEY Bafa Gölü*** (summer), Birecik-Halfeti*** (summer), Dalyan*** (summer), Göksu Delta*** (summer), Kocaçay Delta*** (summer), Manyas Gölü*** (summer), Van Gölü*** (summer), Yeşilce*** (summer).

Black Bush Robin (Black Scrub Robin)
Cercotrichas podobe D SD Res

Range: In the Western Palearctic breeds in Mauritania, and elsewhere occurs regularly only in the Arava Valley of Israel, between mid Mar and mid Jul, mainly in Apr–May. Pairs have been recorded and breeding may occur in the near future.

Tips: Inhabits open, sandy plains with acacia and other dry scrub, wadis and oases, also gardens and cultivation. Generally shy and skulking, often keeping to bushes but also seen running on the ground.

Sites:
ISRAEL Arava Valley* (spring), Eilat* (spring).

Thrush Nightingale
Luscinia luscinia DF Mig

Range: The eastern counterpart of Common Nightingale *L. megarhynchos*, breeding in coastal S Norway, S and E Sweden and S Finland, and from Denmark and N Germany SE to the Danube and E to the Urals. Perhaps also breeds in the Caucasus. Expanding range northwards in Europe, with the first Dutch breeding record in 1995. A summer visitor to our region, present May–Sep, and occurs on passage through SE Europe, Turkey, the Middle East and NE Africa. Winters in E Africa.

Tips: Mainly deciduous woodland, often in riverine and marshy woods, also dense shrubs in cultivated areas, around reedbeds and sometimes orchards. Usually in wetter areas than Common Nightingale.

Sites:
AUSTRIA Marchauen-Marchegg Reserve*** (summer).

BELARUS Belovezhskaya Pushcha NP*** (summer), Berezinsky Reserve*** (summer), Prypyatsky NP*** (summer).

BULGARIA Albena-Golden Sands*** (summer, passage), Burgas area*** (passage), Cape Kaliakra*** (passage).
CYPRUS* (passage).
DENMARK Amager*** (summer), Bornholm-Christiansø*** (summer, passage), Møn-Falster*** (summer, passage), Skagen*** (summer, passage), Skallingen-Blåvandshuk*** (passage).
EGYPT Abu Simbel*** (passage), Aswan*** (passage), Hurghada*** (passage), Luxor*** (passage), Nile Delta* (passage), Sharm el Sheikh*** (passage), Suez area*** (passage), Zaranik*** (passage).
ESTONIA Lake Endla*** (summer), Matsalu Bay*** (summer), Nigula NR*** (summer), Taevaskoja*** (summer), Vilsandi NP*** (summer).
FINLAND Åland Is*** (summer), Kolvanan Uuro*** (summer), Parikkala*** (summer), Ruissalo*** (summer), Viikki*** (summer).
GERMANY Heligoland*** (passage), Mecklenburg Lakes*** (summer), Oder Valley*** (summer), Rügen*** (summer).
GREAT BRITAIN Shetland Is* (passage).
GREECE Amvrakikós Gulf*** (passage), Lake Kerkini** (passage), Porto Lagos area*** (passage).
GREEK IS Corfu*** (passage), Lesvos* (passage).

ISRAEL Arava Valley** (passage), Bet Shean Valley*** (passage), Eilat*** (passage), Ein Gedi*** (passage).
JORDAN Aqaba** (passage), Azraq** (passage), Wadi Rum* (passage).
LATVIA Lake Lubana*** (summer), Lake Pape*** (summer, passage).
LEBANON Aammiq Marshes*** (passage), Qaraoun Lake** (passage).
POLAND Białowieża Forest*** (summer), Biebrza Marshes*** (summer), Chełm Marshes*** (summer), Gdańsk Bay*** (summer), Milicz Fishponds*** (summer), Siemianówka Reservoir*** (summer), Słońsk*** (summer), Tatra NP*** (summer).
ROMANIA Danube Delta*** (summer).
RUSSIA Teberdinskiy Reserve* (passage), Volga Delta** (summer, passage).
SLOVAKIA Senné Fishponds*** (summer), Zemplínská Reservoir*** (summer).
SWEDEN Falsterbo*** (summer, passage), Getterön*** (summer), Gotland*** (summer, passage), Hornborgasjön*** (summer), Kristianstad*** (summer), Kvismaren*** (summer), Lake Krankesjön*** (summer), Öland*** (summer, passage), Tåkern*** (summer).
TURKEY İstanbul** (passage), Van Gölü (passage).
UKRAINE Dunay Delta*** (summer).

Bluethroat
Luscinia svecica

Summer **T CF MF** winter **SH FG FW** **Mig**

Range: Main breeding range is in N and E of our region. Breeds through most of Norway, upland Sweden and N Finland, and from Poland and the Baltic states to the Urals, S to Ukraine. Also in very scattered localities across Europe, from Spain and W France to Hungary, with an isolated population in the Caucasus and NE Turkey. Has bred in Great Britain, Switzerland, Italy and Romania. Migratory over most of range, departing in Aug–Sep to winter around the Mediterranean in small numbers, more commonly in sub-Saharan Africa and the Middle East, and returning in Mar–May. Passage birds occur throughout Europe but it is a scarce but regular migrant in Great Britain.

Subspecies: A number of races occur in our region, some of which are separable in the field, differing in throat colour of breeding male. Red-spotted races include nominate *svecica* over N of the range and *pallidigularis* in S Russia. In the Caucasus, race *magna* has all-blue throat lacking any spot. White-spotted *cyanecula* occurs in C Europe and *namnetum* in W France. However, there is much individual variation and intergradation between races and isolated pockets of red-spotted birds occur within range of *cyanecula*.

Tips: Breeds in wooded tundra, in birch forest and willow scrub, often near water. In the non-breeding season occurs in reedbeds, open grassland and cultivated land, but shy and rarely ventures far from cover.

Sites:

ARMENIA Arapan Area*** (summer), Mt Aragats*** (summer), Pambak Mts*** (summer).

AUSTRIA Lake Neusiedl*** (summer).

BALEARIC IS Mallorca*** (winter).

BELARUS Belovezhskaya Pushcha NP*** (summer), Berezinsky Reserve*** (summer), Prypyatsky NP*** (summer).

BELGIUM Kalmthoutse Heide** (summer).

BULGARIA Albena-Golden Sands** (passage), Burgas area*** (passage), Lake Durankulak*** (passage).

CANARY IS Fuerteventura* (passage).

CORSICA Biguglia Lake*** (passage), Cap Corse** (passage).

CYPRUS* (passage, winter).

CZECH REPUBLIC Krkonoše NP*** (summer), Lednice*** (summer), Nové Mlýny** (summer), Poodří** (passage), Šumava NP*** (summer), Třeboňsko*** (summer).

DENMARK Amager* (passage), Bornholm-Christiansø*** (passage), Møn-Falster*** (passage), Skagen*** (passage), Skallingen-Blåvandshuk*** (passage).

EGYPT Abu Simbel** (passage, winter), Aswan*** (passage, winter), Faiyum** (winter), Hurghada*** (passage, winter), Luxor*** (passage, winter), Nile Delta*** (passage, winter), Sharm el Sheikh*** (passage, winter), Suez area*** (passage), Zaranik*** (passage, winter).

FINLAND Kevo NR*** (summer), Kilpisjärvi Saana*** (summer), Kolvanan Uuro*** (summer), Kuusamo*** (summer), Lemmenjoki NP*** (summer), Liminganlahti*** (summer),

Maltio NR*** (summer), Oulanka NP*** (summer), Pallas-Ounastunturi NP*** (summer), Parikkala*** (summer), Urho Kekkonen NP*** (summer), Viikki*** (passage).

FRANCE Baie de Bourgneuf*** (summer), Cap Gris Nez** (summer, passage), Golfe du Morbihan*** (summer), Île d'Oléron*** (summer), Marais Poitevin** (summer), Ouessant*** (passage), Romelaere NR*** (summer), Somme Estuary** (summer), Teich Reserve*** (summer).

GERMANY Federsee*** (summer), Heligoland*** (passage), Kuhkopf*** (summer), Mecklenburg Lakes*** (summer), Oder Valley*** (summer), Schweinfurt*** (summer), Tiroler Achen*** (summer).

GIBRALTAR* (passage).

GREAT BRITAIN Flamborough Head** (autumn), Minsmere* (passage), N Norfolk coast** (passage), Orkney Is** (passage), Pembrokeshire Is* (autumn), Portland* (passage), Scilly*** (autumn), Shetland Is*** (passage), Spurn Peninsula** (passage).

GREEK IS Corfu* (passage).

HUNGARY Biharugra*** (summer), Hanság*** (summer), Hortobágy NP*** (summer), Kiskunság NP*** (summer), Lake Fertö*** (summer), Lake Velence*** (summer).

ISRAEL Arava Valley*** (passage, winter), Bet Shean Valley*** (passage, winter), Eilat*** (passage, winter), Ein Gedi*** (passage), Hula Reserve*** (passage, winter), Ma'agan Mikhael*** (passage, winter), Mt Hermon** (passage, winter).

ITALY Gargano Peninsula*** (passage), Orbetello Reserve*** (passage), Po Delta*** (passage).

JORDAN Azraq*** (passage).

LATVIA Cape Kolka*** (autumn), Lake Lubana*** (summer), Lake Pape*** (passage).

LEBANON Aammiq Marshes*** (passage, winter), Qaraoun Lake** (passage).

LITHUANIA Kirsiu Peninsula*** (passage).

MALTA* (passage).

MOROCCO Agadir and the Sous Plain*** (passage, winter), Asilah and Oued Loukkos*** (winter), Boumalne* (passage), Oualidia*** (passage, winter), Oued Massa*** (passage, winter), Tafilalt*** (passage).

NETHERLANDS Lauwersmeer** (summer), Naardermeer** (summer), Oostvaardersplassen*** (summer), Terschelling*** (summer, passage), Texel*** (summer, passage), Zwanenwater*** (summer).

NORWAY Dovrefjell NP*** (summer), Fokstumyra*** (summer), Hardangervidda NP*** (summer), Mølen** (passage), Rondane NP*** (summer), Slettnes*** (summer), Utsira*** (passage), Varanger*** (summer).

POLAND Białowieża Forest*** (summer), Biebrza Marshes*** (summer), Chełm Marshes*** (summer), Gdańsk Bay*** (summer), Milicz Fishponds*** (summer), Siemianówka Reservoir*** (summer), Słońsk*** (summer).

PORTUGAL Boquilobo** (passage, winter), Cape St Vincent* (passage), Castro Marim*** (winter), Ria Formosa*** (passage, winter), Sado Estuary*** (passage, winter), Santo André Lagoon*** (passage, winter), Tagus Estuary*** (passage, winter).

ROMANIA Danube Delta*** (summer).

RUSSIA Kola Peninsula*** (summer), Volga Delta*** (passage).

SARDINIA Cagliari Wetlands*** (passage, winter).

SICILY Lago di Lentini** (passage, winter), Vendicari*** (passage, winter).

SLOVAKIA Malé Karpaty* (passage), Senné Fishponds*** (summer, passage), Záhorie*** (summer), Zemplínská Reservoir* (passage).

SPAIN Aiguamolls de L'Empordá* (winter), Cádiz Lagoons*** (winter), Coto Doñana** (passage, winter), Ebro Delta** (winter), Guadalhorce Estuary** (winter), Llobregat Delta** (winter), Picos de Europa* (summer), Santa Pola** (winter), Sierra de Gredos*** (summer), Sierra de Guadarrama** (summer), Tablas de Daimiel** (passage).

SWEDEN Abisko NP*** (summer), Ammarnäs*** (summer), Falsterbo** (passage), Getterön*** (passage), Gotland*** (passage), Hjälstaviken*** (passage), Holmöarna*** (passage), Hornborgasjön*** (passage), Kristianstad***, (passage), Lake Ånnsjön*** (summer), Öland*** (passage), Padjelanta NP*** (summer), Sarek NP*** (summer).

SWITZERLAND Fanel NR*** (passage), Klingnau Reservoir*** (passage).

SYRIA Dayr al-Zawr*** (passage, winter), Tadmur and Sabkhat Muh** (passage), Yarmuk Valley*** (passage).

TUNISIA Cap Bon Peninsula*** (passage), Kelbia Lake** (passage), Lake Ichkeul** (passage).

TURKEY Göksu Delta** (passage), Van Gölü*** (passage).

UKRAINE Dunay Delta*** (summer).

Red-flanked Bluetail
Tarsiger cyanurus   CF (MF) Mig

Range: Breeds widely across N and C Asia but in our region mainly limited to the C Urals and adjacent European Russia. A westward expansion has led to regular breeding in Finland in recent decades, and has bred in Sweden and Estonia, but this now seems to have halted. Migrates, in Sep, to winter in the Himalayas and S China and returns in May–Jun.

Tips: Found mainly in coniferous forest, sometimes mixed, with dense undergrowth. Feeds on the ground less than relatives but shy and skulking, particularly when breeding.

Sites:
FINLAND Kuusamo*** (summer), Oulanka NP*** (summer).

White-throated Robin
Irania gutturalis   M SH SD Mig

Range: In the Western Palearctic breeds in C and S Turkey E to Armenia and in isolated pockets in SW Syria and N Israel, and has bred in Lebanon. Recently recorded breeding on Lesvos. A summer visitor, arriving in mid Apr–early May from wintering grounds in E Africa and departing in Aug–Sep. Passage birds could occur over much of the Middle East.

Tips: Search dry, rocky and stony slopes and gorges with Kermes Oak and juniper scrub, sometimes found in taller trees. Usually at 1,000–2,200m but also occurs lower on passage.

Sites:
ARMENIA Khosrov Preserve*** (summer), Mt Aragats*** (summer).
GEORGIA Iori Steppes*** (summer).
GREEK IS Lesvos* (summer, passage).
ISRAEL Arava Valley* (spring), Mt Hermon** (summer).

JORDAN Azraq* (passage), Wadi Rum (passage).
SYRIA Tadmur and Sabkhat Muh* (passage), Wadi al-Qarn-Burqush*** (summer).
TURKEY Birecik-Halfeti*** (summer), Demirkazik** (summer), Yeşlce*** (summer), Van Gölü*** (summer).

Moussier's Redstart
Phoenicurus moussieri

M SH FG SD Res (AMig)

Range: Endemic to NW Africa: breeds in the Atlas Mts of Morocco and in parts of Algeria and Tunisia, perhaps also in NW Libya. Resident or partial migrant with some short-distance dispersal in winter, chiefly to lower altitudes, when becomes more widespread in Morocco.

Tips: Search scrub-covered hillsides, rocky slopes and upland grasslands. In winter occurs at lower altitudes in plains and semi-desert.

Sites:

ALGERIA Djebel Babor***, El Kala NP***.
MOROCCO Agadir and the Sous Plain***, Boumalne***, Dayet Aaoua***, Essaouira***, Ouarzazate***, Oued Massa***, Oukaimeden***, Tafilalt***, Zeida***.

TUNISIA Ain Draham***, Cap Bon Peninsula***, Chott el Djerid*** (winter), Lake Ichkeul***, Zaghouan***.

Güldenstädt's Redstart
Phoenicurus erythrogaster

M (FG) AMig

Range: Main range lies in C Asia but breeds in the Western Palearctic in a small isolated outpost in the Caucasus, between Mt Elbrus and Mt Kazbek in the Russia–Georgia border area; has been erroneously reported from Armenia and Turkey. Performs altitudinal movements in winter. Although some may remain at high altitudes, most descend to the foothills and others disperse further.

Tips: To find this scarce bird search rocky slopes and screes, ravines and gorges; it usually occurs near flowing water, but is also found in upland cultivated areas and in winter in foothills and plains. Breeds at 2,000-3,000m and descends to c.1,000m in winter. Also descends temporarily to lower altitudes during snowfalls.

Sites:

AZERBAIJAN Zakataly**.
GEORGIA Mt Kazbek**.

RUSSIA Teberdinskiy Reserve*.

Blackstart
Cercomela melanura

M D SD SH   Res (Dis)

Range: Breeds at the southern edge of the Sahara and in Arabia. Local in the Western Palearctic, breeding in Sinai, commonly in Israel and adjacent W Jordan, and in N Saudi Arabia. Probably also breeds in S Syria. Short-distance dispersal in winter extends range to include SW Syria and NE Israel. Also breeds in the extreme S of our region in N Niger and Chad.

Subspecies: Nominate race occurs in Sinai, Israel and adjacent areas with browner *lypura* and *airensis* in the far S of the Western Palearctic in the Sahara.

Tips: Search rocky slopes, ravines and cliff-faces in desert and semi-desert areas. Often found in wadis with scrub and bushes, sometimes in cultivated areas.

Sites:
EGYPT Santa Katharina Monastery***, Sharm el Sheikh***.
ISRAEL Arava Valley***, Eilat***, Ein Gedi***, Mt Hermon***, Nizzana***.

JORDAN Aqaba***, Petra***, Wadi Dana-Fidan***, Wadi Rum*, Wadi as Sir***.
SYRIA Yarmuk Valley**.

Canary Islands Stonechat (Fuerteventura Chat)
Saxicola dacotiae

SH SD (FG)   Res

Range: Endemic to the Canaries and has one of the most restricted ranges of any Western Palearctic bird. Found only on Fuerteventura where fairly common, particularly in the central uplands and the Jandia Peninsula in the S. Has been reported from Lanzarote in recent years, and there are old records from Alegranza and Montaña Clara.

Tips: Occurs from sea level to mountains on sparsely vegetated rocky slopes, hillsides and ravines. Also found on barren volcanic areas and in semi-desert scrub, sometimes on cultivated land.

Sites:
CANARY IS Fuerteventura***.

Isabelline Wheatear
Oenanthe isabellina   FG SD (M) Mig

Range: In our region breeds in Bulgaria and N Greece, interior Turkey and the Caucasus, and in the Middle East in N and SW Syria, Lebanon, parts of Israel and W Jordan. Very small numbers breed in E Romania and range extends from SE Ukraine across S Russia to the Caspian. A summer visitor, present Mar to mid May until Aug–Sep, and winters along the southern edge of the Sahara and from Arabia to NW India. In the Western Palearctic, winters in Egypt, particularly the Nile Valley and on the Red Sea coast, in S Jordan, N Saudi Arabia and Iraq. Regular on passage through Cyprus and Libya, rarer in Tunisia and Algeria, and in recent years regular in small numbers on Sicily in spring.

Tips: Found on barren plateaux and steppes, rocky hillsides, arid stony plains and deserts, as well as grassy slopes up to 3,500m. Also on cultivated land outside breeding season.

Sites:

BULGARIA Burgas area** (passage), Cape Emine** (summer), Cape Kaliakra** (summer, passage), Lake Shabla*** (summer), Strandja Mts*** (summer), Studen Kladenetz*** (summer).

CYPRUS* (passage).

EGYPT Abu Simbel*** (passage, winter), Aswan*** (passage, winter), Faiyum* (winter), Hurghada** (passage, winter), Luxor** (passage, winter), Nile Delta* (winter), Sharm el Sheikh*** (passage, winter), Suez area*** (passage), Zaranik** (passage, winter).

GEORGIA Iori Steppes*** (summer), Mt Kazbek*** (summer).

GREECE Avas Gorge*** (summer), Evros Delta** (summer), Porto Lagos area* (passage).

GREEK IS Crete** (passage, mainly spring), Lesvos** (summer), Náxos* (passage).

ISRAEL Arava Valley*** (summer, passage), Bet Shean Valley*** (passage, winter), Eilat*** (passage), Ma'agan Mikhael*** (passage), Mt Hermon*** (summer), Nizzana*** (summer), Urim*** (winter).

JORDAN Azraq*** (passage), Wadi Rum*** (passage).

LEBANON Aammiq Marshes*** (passage), Qaraoun Lake*** (passage).

MACEDONIA Babuna Gorge* (summer).

MALTA (passage).

RUSSIA Kalmykia*** (summer), Teberdinskiy Reserve* (summer), Volga Delta*** (summer).

SYRIA Sabkhat al-Jabbul** (summer), Tadmur and Sabkhat Muh** (summer, passage).

TURKEY Birecik-Halfeti** (summer), Dalyan* (summer), Demirkazik** (summer), Kulu Gölü*** (summer), Uludağ NP* (summer), Sultan Marshes*** (summer), Van Gölü*** (summer).

UKRAINE Askania-Nova*** (summer).

Pied Wheatear
Oenanthe pleschanka

M SH FG   Mig

Range: Main Western Palearctic range is from the Ukraine to the Urals and Caspian, with isolated populations in E Bulgaria, E Romania, Moldova and Crimea. Has bred in Armenia, Yugoslavia, Greece, Turkey and possibly Syria and Lebanon. Departs breeding areas in Sep–Oct to winter in SW Arabia and E Africa, returning Mar–Apr. Occurs on passage in C and E Turkey, the Middle East and Egypt.

Tips: Search dry, rocky hillsides with scattered bushes, cliff-faces and ravines. Outside breeding season also in cultivated areas, villages and wadis.

Sites:

BULGARIA Albena-Golden Sands*** (summer), Cape Kaliakra*** (summer).
EGYPT Abu Simbel*** (passage, winter), Aswan*** (passage), Hurghada*** (passage), Luxor*** (passage), Sharm el Sheikh*** (passage), Zaranik*** (passage).
GREEK IS Lesvos* (summer, passage).
ISRAEL Eilat* (passage).

JORDAN Wadi Rum*** (passage).
ROMANIA Dobrudja*** (summer).
RUSSIA Kalmykia*** (summer).
TURKEY Kızılırmak Delta* (passage), Van Gölü (summer, passage).
UKRAINE Askania-Nova*** (summer), Crimean Mts*** (summer), Tiligul Liman*** (summer).

Cyprus Pied Wheatear
Oenanthe cypriaca

M SH FG   Mig

Range: Endemic breeder to Cyprus, where very common and widespread; possibly seen at a nest on Rhodes in Jun 2000. Present on Cyprus early Mar–late Sep, rarely into Oct, even Nov. Passage recorded in Syria, Lebanon, Jordan, Israel and Egypt and regularly overshoots in spring to coastal deltas of S Turkey. Winters in Ethiopia and Sudan, with small numbers in Egypt. Formerly considered a race of Pied Wheatear *O. pleschanka*.

Tip: Easily seen in breeding range, on rocky slopes, cliffs and ravines with scattered bushes and trees, from sea level to 3,000m. Often perches prominently on high rocks, posts, pylons and buildings. On passage occurs in more open country, including farmland.

Sites:

CYPRUS* (summer).
EGYPT Abu Simbel** (passage), Aswan** (passage), Luxor* (passage), Sharm el

Sheikh*** (passage), Zaranik** (passage).
ISRAEL Arava Valley** (passage), Eilat* (passage, winter).

JORDAN Azraq* (passage), Wadi Dana-Fidan (passage), Wadi Rum* (passage).

SYRIA Tadmur and Sabkhat Muh* (passage).
TURKEY Göksu Delta** (spring).

Black-eared Wheatear
Oenanthe hispanica   M SH (FG) Mig

Range: Widespread around the Mediterranean, breeding over most of Iberia, in southern France and parts of Italy, throughout the S Balkans and Greece, and most of Turkey. Also breeds in the Caucasus and from coastal Syria to N Israel and NW Jordan. In the Mediterranean breeds on Sicily, Corfu, Crete and other Greek islands, and in N Africa from the Sous in Morocco to Tunisia and NE Libya. Arrives in Mar–Apr from wintering grounds in sub-Saharan Africa and departs in Aug–Sep, rarely remaining until Oct. Occurs on passage on most larger Mediterranean islands.

Subspecies: Two races occur in our region, considered by some to be separate species, both of which have black-throated and pale-throated forms, but pale-throated birds increasingly frequent towards the E. Nominate race breeds from Iberia and N Africa to N Italy, and race *melanoleuca* from S Italy eastwards.

Tips: Generally common on rocky and maquis-covered slopes, in dry, open woodland with rocky outcrops, and often found in areas of oak and juniper. Sometimes noted at the margins of cultivated land, near ruins, roadsides and large gardens, and often perches high on wires or bushes.

Sites:

ALBANIA Lake Shkodra*** (summer).
ARMENIA Khosrov Preserve*** (summer), Lake Sevan*** (summer), Mt Aragats*** (summer), Pambak Mts*** (summer).
BALEARIC IS Formentera*** (passage), Mallorca*** (passage).
BOSNIA-HERZEGOVINA Hutovo blato** (summer). Sujetska NP*** (summer).
BULGARIA Cape Emine*** (summer), Cape Kaliakra*** (summer), Rusenski Lom NP*** (summer), Studen Kladenetz*** (summer), Tissata NR*** (summer).
CORSICA Cap Corse** (passage).
CROATIA Cres*** (summer), Mljet*** (summer), Neretva Delta*** (summer), Paklenica NP*** (summer).
CYPRUS* (passage).

EGYPT Abu Simbel*** (passage), Aswan*** (passage), Luxor*** (passage), Sharm el Sheikh*** (passage), Zaranik** (passage).
FRANCE Camargue*** (summer), Cévennes NP*** (summer), Gruissan*** (summer).
GIBRALTAR* (passage).
GREECE Akarnanika Mts*** (summer), Avas Gorge*** (summer), Axios-Aliakmonas Deltas*** (summer), Dadiá-Soufli Forest*** (summer), Delphi*** (summer), Evros Delta*** (summer), Mikrí Prespa NP*** (summer), Mt Olympus NP*** (summer), Mt Parnassós NP*** (summer), Nestos Delta*** (summer).
GREEK IS Corfu*** (summer), Crete*** (summer, passage), Kos*** (summer, passage), Lesvos*** (summer, passage), Náxos*** (summer, passage), Rhodes*** (summer).

ISRAEL Arava Valley*** (summer, passage), Eilat*** (passage), Ein Gedi*** (summer), Golan Heights*** (summer), Mt Hermon*** (summer), Nizzana*** (summer).
ITALY Gargano Peninsula*** (summer, passage), Maremma Regional Park** (passage), Monte Conero*** (passage), Orbetello Reserve*** (summer), San Giuliano Reserve*** (summer), Tuscan archipelago*** (summer).
JORDAN Amman NP*** (summer), Aqaba*** (passage), Azraq** (passage), Wadi Dana-Fidan*** (passage), Wadi Rum** (passage), Wadi as Sir*** (summer).
LEBANON Aammiq Marshes*** (summer), Barouk Cedars*** (summer), Qaraoun Lake** (passage).
MACEDONIA Babuna Gorge*** (summer), Crna Gorge*** (summer), Galicica NP*** (summer), Lakes Ohrid and Prespa*** (summer).
MALTA* (passage).
MOROCCO Agadir and the Sous Plain*** (summer), Boumalne*** (summer), Dayet Aaoua*** (summer), Essaouira*** (summer), Ouarzazate*** (passage), Oued Massa*** (summer, passage), Tafilalt** (summer), Zeida*** (summer).
PORTUGAL Baixo Alentejo*** (summer), Boquilobo** (passage), Cape St Vincent*** (passage), Castro Marim*** (summer), International Douro*** (summer), International

Tagus*** (summer), Montesinho*** (summer), Peneda Gêres NP*** (summer), Ria Formosa*** (summer), Tagus Estuary*** (summer).
ROMANIA Dobrudja*** (summer).
SARDINIA San Pietro I** (passage).
SICILY Strait of Messina*** (summer, passage), Vendicari** (passage).
SPAIN Aiguamolls de L'Empordá*** (summer), Cabo de Gata*** (summer), Cáceres-Trujillo Steppes*** (summer), Cádiz Lagoons*** (summer), Coto Doñana*** (passage), Garraf Massif*** (summer), Guadalhorce Estuary** (passage), Jaca*** (summer), La Serena*** (summer), Monfragüe*** (summer), Picos de Europa*** (summer), Santa Pola*** (summer), Serrania de Ronda*** (summer), Sierra de Gredos*** (summer), Sierra de Guadarrama*** (summer), Tablas de Daimiel*** (summer, passage), Zaragoza Steppes*** (summer).
SYRIA Yarmuk Valley*** (summer).
TUNISIA Cap Bon Peninsula*** (summer, passage), Kelbia Lake** (summer), Lake Ichkeul*** (summer), Zaghouan*** (summer).
TURKEY Akseki*** (summer), Birecik-Halfeti*** (summer), Dalyan*** (summer), Demirkazik*** (summer), Yeşilce*** (summer), Van Gölü*** (summer).
YUGOSLAVIA Lake Skadar*** (summer).

Desert Wheatear
Oenanthe deserti   SD FG SH   Mig (PMig)

Range: Breeds across NW Africa, from Mauritania to C Tunisia, N Libya, N Egypt and Sinai. In the Middle East breeds in S Syria and in Israel and adjacent Jordan, as well as in N Saudi Arabia. Recently discovered breeding in S Turkey. Northernmost birds tend to be most migratory, and winter range extends from the Sahara to the Horn of Africa, and from Arabia to NW India.

Subspecies: Three races occur but field separation is difficult. N African birds belong to *homochroa*, Middle Eastern birds to *deserti* and those from Transcaucasia to *atrogularis*.

Tips: Search sandy or stony plains and steppes and semi-desert with scrub, often found in areas of abandoned cultivation. In winter also in coastal areas.

Sites:

EGYPT Abu Simbel*** (passage, winter), Aswan*** (passage), Luxor*** (passage), Sharm el Sheikh***, Wadi el Natrun***, Zaranik***.
ISRAEL Arava Valley***, Nizzana*** (autumn, winter), Urim*** (autumn, winter).
JORDAN Aqaba* (passage), Azraq***, Ghadir Burqu'***, Wadi Dana-Fidan***, Wadi Rum***.

LEBANON Qaraoun Lake** (passage).
MOROCCO Boumalne*** (summer), Goulimime to Tan-Tan*** (summer), Tafilalt***, Zeida** (summer).
SYRIA Tadmur and Sabkhat Muh***.
TUNISIA Chott el Djerid***.
TURKEY Birecik-Halfeti (summer).

Finsch's Wheatear
Oenanthe finschii   M SD (FG)   Res (PMig) (AMig)

Range: Breeds in S and E Turkey, Transcaucasia and the E Caucasus, also W Syria, probably in Lebanon and has bred in N Israel. Was thought to have bred on the Black Sea coast of Bulgaria, in 1993, but these birds are now thought to be hybrids between Pied and Black-eared Wheatears. Summer visitor to upland areas, descending in winter. Winter range more extensive in S Turkey, and in many areas of the Middle East, and small numbers regularly winter in Cyprus.

Subspecies: Two similar races occur, nominate *finschii* from S Turkey to Lebanon and *barnesi* in E Turkey and the Caucasus.

Tips: Generally uncommon, best looked for on arid, rocky and stony slopes and hillsides, ravines and valleys in semi-desert areas. Uses low perches on rocks or low walls but mainly terrestrial.

Sites:

ARMENIA Lake Sevan* (summer), Vedi Hills** (summer).
CYPRUS* (winter).
EGYPT Sharm el Sheikh*** (winter), Zaranik** (winter).
GEORGIA Iori Steppes*** (summer).
ISRAEL Arava Valley*** (passage, winter), Golan Heights*** (winter), Mt Hermon** (passage, winter), Nizzana*** (winter), Urim*** (winter), Wadi Ammud-Mt Arbel* (winter).

JORDAN Azraq (passage, winter), Ghadir Burqu'*** (winter), Wadi Rum (winter).
LEBANON Barouk Cedars*** (summer), Qaraoun Lake* (passage).
SYRIA Tadmur and Sabkhat Muh** (winter), Wadi al-Qarn-Burqush** (summer), Yarmuk Valley*** (winter).
TURKEY Birecik-Halfeti***, Demirkazik*** (summer), Van Gölü*** (summer).

Red-rumped Wheatear
Oenanthe moesta D SD SH Res (PMig)

Range: Occurs widely but discontinuously across N Africa, breeding in N Mauritania, S and E Morocco, N Algeria, C Tunisia, parts of Libya and between the Nile and the Red Sea in Egypt. In the Middle East breeds patchily in W Jordan, N Saudi Arabia, and in tiny numbers in Israel. Has bred in Syria and Sinai.

Subspecies: Two similar races occur; nominate in N Africa and *brooksbanki* in the Middle East but differences are very slight.

Tips: Found in flat, often saline plains, edges of desert with tamarisk and other shrubs.

Sites:
JORDAN Azraq**.
MOROCCO Boumalne***, Goulimime to Tan-Tan***, Zeida**.

TUNISIA Chott el Djerid***.

Red-tailed Wheatear (Persian Wheatear)
Oenanthe xanthoprymna M SH (SD) (FG) PMig

Range: Main breeding range is from Iran to Pakistan, but also breeds in E and SE Turkey and the Caucasus. Mainly a summer visitor, wintering in Arabia and Sudan, with small numbers also in Sinai and E Egypt. Observed in small numbers on passage in Israel, Jordan and Syria in Sep–Oct.

Subspecies: Nominate race (also known as Kurdish Wheatear) occurs in SE Turkey and extreme W Iran, with the eastern *chrysopygia* in Transcaucasia. The latter has occurred as a vagrant in Israel and recently also in Turkey and Egypt. Eastern birds are sometimes considered a full species under the name **Rufous-tailed Wheatear**.

Tips: Search rocky and bare hillsides, boulder-strewn areas with scrub; in winter also found on cultivated land and semi-desert areas.

Sites:
ARMENIA Meghri Area*** (summer).
EGYPT Sharm el Sheikh*** (passage, winter).
ISRAEL Arava Valley* (passage).

JORDAN Wadi Rum (passage).
TURKEY Birecik-Halfeti* (summer), Van Gölü (summer), Yeşilce*** (summer).

Mourning Wheatear
Oenanthe lugens

D SD SH   PMig

Range: Discontinuous range in N Africa and the Middle East. Breeds in E Morocco, N Algeria and C Tunisia, N Libya and in Egypt from the Nile Valley to the Red Sea, in Sinai and N Saudi Arabia, Israel, W Jordan and Syria. Most populations are partially migratory but extent of movements little known, although thought to be mainly short distances to the S or SW.

Subspecies: Three races occur in the region; nominate *lugens* is found in the Near East and Egypt, *persica*, breeding in Iran and a rare passage migrant and winter visitor to the Middle East, and *halophila* in N Africa. An all-dark population from the basaltic desert of S Syria and N Jordan was once thought to be a form of Eastern Pied or Variable Wheatear *O. picata* but is now considered to be a morph of nominate *lugens* and referred to as the Basalt Wheatear. This form has been recorded as a vagrant in Israel.

Tips: Inhabits wadis, stony hillsides and boulder-strewn plateaux in desert and semi-deserts with scattered bushes and trees.

Sites:
EGYPT Luxor***, Sharm el Sheikh***, Suez area***.
ISRAEL Arava Valley***, Eilat***, Nizzana***.
JORDAN Azraq***, Ghadir Burqu', Petra***, Wadi Rum***.

MOROCCO Boumalne*, Ouarzazate**, Tafilalt**.
SYRIA Tadmur and Sabkhat Muh***.
TUNISIA Chott el Djerid***.

Hooded Wheatear
Oenanthe monacha

M D SD   Res

Range: Breeds in Israel and adjacent W Jordan, Sinai and N Saudi Arabia, and in Egypt between the Nile and Red Sea. Mainly resident but some may perform short-distance movements.

Tips: Search rocky hillsides, wadis and ravines in desert areas, often without vegetation, in some areas near habitation.

Sites:
EGYPT Hurghada***, Luxor**, Santa Katharina Monastery***, Sharm el Sheikh***.
ISRAEL Arava Valley***, Eilat***, Ein Gedi***.

JORDAN Aqaba**, Wadi Dana-Fidan***, Wadi Rum***.

White-tailed Wheatear (White-crowned Black Wheatear)
Oenanthe leucopyga   D SD (M) Res

Range: Widespread across inland areas of N Africa and the Middle East, breeding in Mauritania, throughout the Atlas of Morocco, over much of Algeria and S Tunisia, discontinuously in Libya and in Egypt breeds at scattered western oases, in the Nile Valley and on the Red Sea coast. Also in Sinai, Israel and adjacent W Jordan and parts of N Saudi Arabia. Mainly resident but some short-distance dispersal in winter.

Subspecies: Nominate race occurs in N Africa W of the Nile Valley, replaced by similar *ernesti* E of the Nile, in Sinai and the Middle East.

Tips: Found in rocky desert and semi-deserts, oases and wadis, sometimes around ruins and settlements. In places up to 3,000m.

Sites:
EGYPT Abu Simbel***, Aswan***, Luxor***, Santa Katharina Monastery***, Sharm el Sheikh***.
ISRAEL Arava Valley***, Eilat***, Ein Gedi***.

JORDAN Aqaba***, Petra***, Wadi Rum***.
MOROCCO Boumalne***, Goulimine to Tan-Tan***, Ouarzazate***, Tafilalt***.
TUNISIA Chott el Djerid***.

Black Wheatear
Oenanthe leucura   M C SH SD Res (AMig)

Range: Breeds in C Portugal and over much of Spain, and perhaps still in very small numbers in extreme SW France, but close to extinction there. In N Africa occurs from N Mauritania across the Atlas Mts to Tunisia and NE Libya. Mainly resident but some altitudinal movements and juveniles are possibly dispersive.

Subspecies: Two similar races occur; nominate *leucura* in France and Iberia and *syenitica* in N Africa.

Tips: Can be difficult to see until it flies, but search cliffs, rocky slopes and hillsides, rocky seacoasts, and around ruined buildings and quarries, usually in very arid habitats with scattered trees.

Sites:
MOROCCO Boumalne***, Dayet Aaoua**, Goulimine to Tan-Tan***, Ouarzazate***, Oukaimeden***, Zeida***.
PORTUGAL Baixo Alentejo*, International Douro***, International Tagus***.

SPAIN Aiguamolls de l'Empordá***, Cabo de Gata***, Garraf Massif***, La Serena***, Monfragüe***, Santa Pola***, Serrania de Ronda***, Sierra de Gredos***, Zaragoza Steppes***.
TUNISIA Chott el Djerid***.

Rock Thrush (Rufous-tailed Rock Thrush)
Monticola saxatilis   M Mig

Range: Patchily distributed in montane and upland areas of Iberia and S France, the Alps and Italy. In the E breeds from S Poland to the Balkans and Greece, Crimea, the Caucasus and Turkey. In the Mediterranean occurs on Mallorca, Corsica, Sardinia and Sicily. Isolated populations in the Atlas Mts of Morocco and Algeria, and very small numbers in N Israel. In decline in many parts of range, especially in the N. Most winter in sub-Saharan Africa but some may remain in N Africa all year. Main passage periods are late Aug–Sep and late Mar–early May.

Subspecies: Usually considered monotypic but birds from E Turkey have been separated as *coloratus*.

Tips: Shy and often difficult to see, best located by call. Found on dry open hillsides with scree and boulder patches, scattered bushes and trees, mainly at 1,500–3,000m, occasionally lower.

Sites:

ANDORRA** (summer).

ARMENIA Khosrov Preserve*** (summer), Mt Aragats***, Pambak Mts*** (summer).

AUSTRIA Hohe Wand* (summer), Schneeberg Mts** (summer).

BALEARIC IS Formentera* (passage), Mallorca*** (summer, passage).

BOSNIA-HERZEGOVINA Sujetska NP*** (summer).

BULGARIA Cape Emine** (summer, passage), Cape Kaliakra* (passage), Rila Mts*** (summer), Rusenski Lom NP*** (summer), Strandja Mts* (summer), Studen Kladenetz*** (summer), Tissata NR*** (summer), Tzarichina NR*** (summer).

CORSICA Asco Valley*** (summer), Restonica Valley*** (summer).

CYPRUS*** (passage).

EGYPT Abu Simbel** (passage), Aswan* (passage), Luxor* (passage), Suez area* (passage).

FRANCE Cévennes NP*** (summer), Écrins NP*** (summer), Leucate* (summer), Prats-de-Mollo*** (summer), Pyrenees NP*** (summer), Queyras NP*** (summer), Vanoise NP*** (summer).

GEORGIA Mt Kazbek*** (summer).

GIBRALTAR*** (passage).

GREECE Mikrí Prespa NP*** (summer), Mt Olympus NP** (summer), Vikos-Aoos NP*** (summer).

GREEK IS Corfu*** (summer), Lesvos** (summer, passage).

HUNGARY Aggtelek NP* (summer), Börzsöny NP* (summer), Bükk Hills NP* (summer), Csákvár* (summer), Pilis Hills* (summer), Zemplén Hills* (summer).

ISRAEL Arava Valley** (passage), Mt Hermon** (summer).

ITALY Abruzzo NP*** (summer), Circeo NP*** (summer), Gargano Peninsula** (summer), Gran Paradiso NP*** (summer), Sibillini NP*** (summer), Stelvio NP*** (summer), Tuscan archipelago*** (summer).

JORDAN Aqaba* (passage), Azraq (passage), Petra* (summer), Wadi Rum* (passage).

MACEDONIA Babuna Gorge** (summer), Crna Gorge** (summer), Galicica NP*** (summer), Lakes Ohrid and Prespa*** (summer).

MALTA* (passage).

MOROCCO Oukaimeden*** (summer).

POLAND Bieszczady NP (summer).

PORTUGAL Cape St Vincent (autumn), Montesinho** (summer), Peneda Gêres NP** (summer).
ROMANIA Dobrudja** (summer, passage), Turda Gorge*** (summer).
RUSSIA Teberdinskiy Reserve*** (summer).
SICILY San Vito Peninsula*** (summer).
SLOVAKIA High Tatras NP** (summer), Malá Fatra*** (summer), Malé Karpaty** (summer), Nízke Tatry NP*** (summer), Slovenský Kras*** (summer), Zemplínská Reservoir** (summer).
SLOVENIA Karst RP*** (summer), Triglav NP*** (summer).
SPAIN Aiguamolls de L'Empordá*** (summer), Aigües Tortes NP*** (summer), Garraf Massif*** (summer), Jaca*** (summer), Ordesa NP*** (summer), Picos de Europa*** (summer), Serrania de Ronda*** (summer), Sierra de Gredos*** (summer), Sierra de Guadarrama*** (summer).
SWITZERLAND Aletschwald*** (summer), Col de Bretolet* (summer), Leuk*** (summer), Monte Generoso*** (summer), Swiss NP*** (summer).
SYRIA Tadmur and Sabkhat Muh* (passage).
TUNISIA Cap Bon Peninsula* (passage).
TURKEY Borçka*** (summer), Demirkazik*** (summer), Uludağ NP*** (summer), Yeşilce*** (summer), Van Gölü*** (summer).
UKRAINE Crimean Mts** (summer).
YUGOSLAVIA Durmitor NP** (summer).

Blue Rock Thrush
Monticola solitarius   M C (U)   Res (AMig)

Range: Breeds in Iberia and the Balearics, S France and patchily in the Alps, much of Italy and from Slovenia to Greece. In the Mediterranean breeds on Corsica, Sardinia, Sicily and Malta, and many Greek islands. Also breeds in Turkey (except C and N areas) to the Caucasus, and in the Middle East in parts of Syria, Israel and W Jordan. In N Africa found in Morocco and N Algeria and Tunisia. Most populations are altitudinal migrants to some extent but others move longer distances and is more widespread in winter in N Africa. Females tend to move further than males in autumn.

Subspecies: Nominate over most of Western Palearctic with *longirostris* in C and S Turkey and Iraq.

Tips: Often easy to locate due to habit of perching conspicuously on exposed rocks, occurs in mountains, on cliff-faces and in ravines, also on ruined buildings, in quarries and, in some areas, on sea-cliffs and in towns. Generally commoner and found at lower levels than Rock Thrush.

Sites:
ANDORRA*.
ARMENIA Khosrov Preserve***, Lake Sevan***, Mt Aragats***, Pambak Mts***.
BALEARIC IS Formentera***, Ibiza***, Mallorca***, Menorca***.

BULGARIA Cape Emine***, Studen Kladenetz***, Tissata NR***.
CORSICA Asco Valley***, Bonifacio***, Cap Corse***, Restonica Valley***, Scandola***.
CROATIA Cres***, Mljet***, Paklenica NP***, Plitvice***.

CYPRUS***.
EGYPT Aswan** (winter), Luxor***.
FRANCE Camargue***, Cévennes NP***, Les Alpilles***, Leucate***, Prats-de-Mollo***.
GIBRALTAR***.
GREECE Akarnanika Mts***, Avas Gorge***, Dadiá-Soufli Forest***, Delphi***, Lake Kerkini***, Mt Olympus NP***, Mt Parnassós NP***.
GREEK IS Corfu***, Crete***, Kos***, Lesvos***, Náxos***, Rhodes***.
ISRAEL Arava Valley***, Eilat*** Golan Heights***, Mt Hermon***, Urim***, Wadi Ammud-Mt Arbel***.
ITALY Abruzzo NP***, Circeo NP***, Gargano Peninsula***, Monte Conero***, Orbetello Reserve**, Sibillini NP***, Tuscan archipelago***.
JORDAN Azraq* (passage, mainly spring), Ghadir Burqu' (passage), Petra***, Wadi Dana-Fidan***, Wadi Rum***, Wadi as Sir***.
LEBANON Aamiq Marshes***, Barouk Cedars***, Qaraoun Lake***.
MACEDONIA Babuna Gorge***, Crna Gorge***.
MALTA***.

MOROCCO Agadir and the Sous Plain***, Boumalne***, Oualidia***, Oued Massa***, Oukaimeden***.
PORTUGAL Baixo Alentejo***, Cape St Vincent***, International Douro***, International Tagus***, Montesinho***, Peneda Gêres NP***.
SARDINIA Capo Marargiu***, San Pietro I***.
SICILY San Vito Peninsula***, Strait of Messina***.
SPAIN Aiguamolls de L'Empordá***, Aigües Tortes NP***, Cabo de Gata***, Cáceres-Trujillo Steppes***, Garraf Massif***, Jaca***, La Serena***, Monfragüe***, Ordesa NP***, Picos de Europa***, Santa Pola***, Serrania de Ronda***, Sierra de Gredos***, Sierra de Guadarrama***, Zaragoza Steppes***.
SWITZERLAND Monte Generoso*.
SYRIA Tadmur and Sabkhat Muh***, Wadi al-Qarn-Burqush***.
TUNISIA Ain Draham***, Cap Bon Peninsula***, Chott el Djerid***, Lake Ichkeul***, Zaghouan***.
TURKEY Birecik-Halfeti***, Borçka***, Dalyan***, Demirkazik***, Doğubeyazit***, Göksu Delta***, Uludağ NP***, Yeşilce***.

Ring Ouzel
Turdus torquatus   M SH MF   Mig (PMig)

Range: Breeds in the N and W British Isles and Brittany, in Scandinavia almost throughout Norway and montane Sweden and N and E Finland and also breeds in N Lativa, SW Estonia and the Kola Peninsula. Further S, breeds in the Cantabrians and Pyrenees, in the uplands of S France, the Alps and Carpathians, Dinaric Alps, the Balkan and Rhodope Mts, and the Pindos of N Greece. Also breeds in the Caucasus, NE Turkey and at scattered upland sites elsewhere in Turkey, and in the Djurdjura area of N Algeria. Most populations are migratory, although some occasionally winter close to breeding areas, but everywhere at lower altitudes. Breeders in the N depart Sep–Oct and move to SW Europe and NW Africa, and return Apr–May.

Subspecies: Three races occur, usually separable in the field. Nominate race is found in Scandinavia, the British Isles and Brittany, replaced by *alpestris* in the mountains of C and

S Europe and *amicorum* in E Turkey and the Caucasus. Alpine race has occurred as a vagrant north to the British Isles and Sweden.

Tips: Found in moorland areas of NW Europe with a few scattered bushes and stunted trees and occasional boulders and rocky crags. In Scandinavia also in open birch woodland and in the Alps in open pine forest. In the Caucasus breeds in juniper and rhododendron scrub. On passage often found in lowlands, on open grassland with hedges, but can be skulking. In winter chiefly found on sparsely vegetated hillsides and mountains.

Sites:

ANDORRA*** (summer).

ARMENIA Mt Aragats** (summer), Pambak Mts*** (summer).

AUSTRIA Hohe Wand** (summer), Karwendel Reserve*** (summer), Schneeberg Mts*** (summer).

AZERBAIJAN Zakataly*** (summer).

BALEARIC IS Mallorca** (passage).

BELGIUM Hautes Fagnes Natural Park* (summer).

BOSNIA-HERZEGOVINA Sujetska NP*** (summer).

BULGARIA Rila Mts*** (summer), Tzarichina NR*** (summer).

CORSICA Cap Corse** (passage).

CYPRUS* (winter).

CZECH REPUBLIC Beskydy Mts*** (summer), Jeseníky Mts** (summer), Krkonoše NP*** (summer), Šumava NP*** (summer).

DENMARK Bornholm-Christiansø*** (passage), Møn-Falster* (passage), Skagen*** (passage), Skallingen-Blåvandshuk*** (passage).

FINLAND Kilpisjärvi Saana*** (summer), Pallas-Ounastunturi NP*** (summer).

FRANCE Cap Gris Nez** (passage), Cévennes NP*** (summer), Écrins NP*** (summer), Forêt d'Issaux*** (summer), Ouessant*** (passage), Prats-de-Mollo*** (summer), Pyrenees NP*** (summer), Queyras NP*** (summer), Vanoise NP*** (summer).

GEORGIA Mt Kazbek*** (summer).

GERMANY Ammer Valley*** (summer), Bayerischer Wald NP*** (summer), Berchtesgaden NP*** (summer).

GIBRALTAR*** (passage).

GREAT BRITAIN Anglesey** (passage), Cairngorms*** (summer), Dungeness* (passage), Flamborough Head** (passage), Minsmere** (passage), N Norfolk coast** (passage), Orkney Is** (summer), Pembrokeshire Is** (spring), Portland** (passage), Rhum*** (summer), Scilly** (passage), Shetland Is** (passage), Spurn Peninsula*** (passage).

GREECE Mikrí Prespa NP*** (summer), Vikos-Aoos NP*** (summer).

HUNGARY Hortobágy NP* (spring), Kiskunság NP** (spring).

ITALY Gran Paradiso NP*** (summer), Monte Conero** (passage), Stelvio NP*** (summer), Tuscan archipelago*** (passage).

MALTA* (passage).

MOROCCO Agadir and the Sous Plain*** (winter), Boumalne*** (winter).

NETHERLANDS Oostvaardersplassen** (passage), Terschelling*** (passage), Texel*** (passage).

NORWAY Fokstumyra** (summer), Utsira*** (passage), Varanger* (summer).

POLAND Bieszczady NP*** (summer), Tatra NP*** (summer).

PORTUGAL Baixo Alentejo*** (winter), Cape St Vincent*** (passage).

ROMANIA Bicaz*** (summer), Gurghiu Mts*** (summer), Poiana Braşov*** (summer), Retezat NP*** (summer).

RUSSIA Kola Peninsula*** (summer), Teberdinskiy Reserve*** (summer).

SARDINIA Capo Marargiu*** (passage), Monte Arcuso** (passage, winter), San Pietro I** (passage).

SLOVAKIA High Tatras NP*** (summer), Malá Fatra*** (summer), Nízke Tatry NP*** (summer).

SLOVENIA Kocevje** (summer), Triglav NP*** (summer).

SPAIN Aigües Tortes NP*** (summer), Cabo de Gata** (winter), Coto Doñana** (passage, winter), Jaca*** (summer), Ordesa NP*** (summer), Picos de Europa*** (passage), Serrania de Ronda** (winter).
SWEDEN Abisko NP*** (summer), Ammarnäs*** (summer), Falsterbo* (passage), Hornborgasjön* (passage), Padjelanta NP*** (summer), Sarek NP*** (summer).
SWITZERLAND Aletschwald*** (summer), Col de Bretolet*** (passage), Flims*** (summer), Monte Generoso*** (passage), Swiss NP*** (summer).
TUNISIA Ain Draham** (winter).
TUNISIA Cap Bon Peninsula** (passage), Lake Ichkeul** (passage, winter).
TURKEY Borçka** (summer), Demirkazik** (summer), İstanbul* (passage), Sivrikaya** (summer).
UKRAINE Carpathians*** (summer).
YUGOSLAVIA Durmitor NP** (summer).

Cetti's Warbler
Cettia cetti   FW SH Res (Mig)

Range: Breeds throughout Iberia and the Balearics, over much of France and patchily in Italy, the Balkans and Greece. Also throughout Turkey, the Caucasus and around the Caspian. In the Mediterranean on Corsica, Sardinia and Sicily, Malta, Cyprus, Crete and many other Greek islands. In NW Africa from the Sous Valley of Morocco to N Tunisia. Isolated populations in S England, Belgium and the Netherlands. Most are resident with some winter movements, especially in Turkey and the Caucasus.
Subspecies: Three similar races occur in our region; nominate in most of range with *orientalis* in the C and E Turkey, the Caucasus and parts of the Middle East, and *albiventris* in the Caspian region
Tips: Easily located by its explosive voice but generally keeps to dense cover and can be very difficult to see. Generally makes brief flights between bushes but also feeds on ground. Better views possible in early morning or when feeding young. Inhabits dense vegetation in swampy areas, ditches and reedbeds, sometimes in drier situations, particularly in E of range. Usually in lowlands but also found in montane valleys above 2,000m.

Sites:
ALGERIA El Kala NP***.
ANDORRA**.
ARMENIA Armash Fishponds***, Lake Sevan***.
BALEARIC IS Ibiza***, Mallorca***, Menorca***.
BELGIUM Blankaart Reserve*.
BOSNIA-HERZEGOVINA Hutovo blato***. **BULGARIA** Albena-Golden Sands***, Burgas Area***, Lake Durankulak***, Lake Shabla***, Ropotamo NP***, Strandja Mts**, Studen Kladenetz***, Tissata NR***.
CORSICA Biguglia Lake***, Bonifacio***, Cap Corse***.
CROATIA Neretva Delta***.
CYPRUS***.
FRANCE Baie de Bourgneuf***, Baie du Mont-St-Michel***, Camargue***, Cap Gris Nez***, Golfe du Morbihan***, Île d'Oleron***, La Brenne***, Marais Poitevin***, Romelaere NR***, Sologne***, Teich Reserve***.
GREAT BRITAIN Dungeness (autumn, winter), Minsmere*, N Norfolk coast*, Portland*.

GREECE Axios-Aliakmonas Deltas***, Dadiá-Soufli Forest***, Evros Delta***, Lake Kerkini***, Mikrí Prespa NP***, Nestos Delta***, Porto Lagos Area***.
GREEK IS Corfu***, Crete***, Kos***, Lesvos***, Naxos***.
ISRAEL Arava Valley***, Bet Shean Valley***, Ein Gedi***, Hula Reserve***, Jezreel Valley***, Ma'agan Mikhael***, Urim***.
ITALY Circeo NP***, Gargano Peninsula***, Isonzo Regional Park***, Lake Massaciuccoli***, Maremma Regional Park***, Monte Conero***, Orbetello Reserve***, Po Delta***, San Giuliano Reserve***.
JORDAN Azraq* (autumn, winter), Petra***, Wadi Dana-Fidan***, Wadi as Sir***.
LEBANON Aamiq Marshes***, Qaraoun Lake***.
MACEDONIA Galicica NP***, Lakes Ohrid and Prespa***.
MALTA***.
MOROCCO Agadir and the Sous Plain***, Asilah and Oued Loukkos***, Boumalne***, Dayet Aaoua***, Essaouira***, Lac de Sidi Bourhaba***, Merja Zerga***, Oualidia***, Ouarzazate***, Oued Massa***, Oukaimeden***, Tafilalt***, Zaers***.
NETHERLANDS Oostvaadersplassen***.

PORTUGAL Baixo Alentejo***, Boquilobo***, Castro Marim***, Montesinho***, Peneda Gêres NP***, Ria Formosa***, Sado Estuary***, Santo André Lagoon***, Tagus Estuary***.
ROMANIA Danube Delta** (summer), Dobrudja** (summer).
RUSSIA Kalmykia*** (summer), Volga Delta*** (summer).
SARDINIA Cagliari wetlands***, Oristano wetlands***, San Pietro I***.
SPAIN Aiguamolls de L'Empordá***, Cabo de Gata***, Cáceres-Trujillo Steppes***, Cádiz Lagoons***, Coto Doñana***, Ebro Delta***, Garraf Massif***, Guadalhorce Estuary***, Jaca***, La Serena***, Llobregat Delta***, Monfragüe***, Picos de Europa***, Santa Pola***, Serrania de Ronda***, Sierra de Gredos***, Sierra de Guadarrama***, Tablas de Daimiel***.
SYRIA Aqra Mts***, Baath Lake***, Dayr al-Zawr***, Lake Assad***, Yarmuk Valley***.
TUNISIA Ain Draham***, Cap Bon Peninsula***, Kelbia Lake***, Lake Ichkeul***.
TURKEY Bafa Gölü***, Birecik-Halfeti***, Dalyan***, Demirkazik***, Göksu Delta***, Kocaçay Delta***, Manyas Gölü***, Sultan Marshes***, Van Gölü***.
UKRAINE Dunay Delta** (summer).

Zitting Cisticola (Fan-tailed Warbler)
Cisticola juncidis FG FW Res (Dis)

Range: Found around much of the Mediterranean, breeding widely in Iberia and the Balearics, in W and S France, on Corsica, Sardinia and Sicily, through much of Italy, Malta, Greece and Crete. Has expanded N in recent decades, with breeding records in N France, Belgium, the Netherlands, Germany, Switzerland and Austria. Also breeds locally in W and S Turkey, Cyprus and the Middle East, in the Nile Delta and Valley, and in NW Africa.
Subspecies: Nominate *juncidis* breeds from S France and Corsica to W Turkey and in Egypt, *cisticola* in western France, Iberia and NW Africa and *neurotica* in Cyprus and the Middle East.

Tips: Found in open habitats with long grasses, often in cereal fields, edges of marshes and rice fields, often near water but rarely in reedbeds. Most easily seen during characteristic song-flights, often from overhead wires and frequently during the hottest part of the day.

Sites:

BALEARIC IS Ibiza***, Mallorca***, Menorca***.
BOSNIA-HERZEGOVINA Hutovo blato***.
CORSICA Biguglia Lake***, Cap Corse***.
CROATIA Neretva Delta***.
CYPRUS*.
EGYPT Aswan***, Faiyum***, Luxor***, Nile Delta***, Suez area***, Wadi el Natrun***.
FRANCE Camargue***, Dombes***, Golfe du Morbihan***, Île d'Oléron***, Marais Poitevin***, Somme Estuary**, Trunvel Reserve***.
GIBRALTAR** (winter).
GREECE Axios-Aliakmonas Deltas***, Evros Delta***, Lake Kerkini***, Nestos Delta***, Porto Lagos area***.
GREEK IS Corfu*, Crete***, Kos***, Lesvos**.
ISRAEL Bet Shean Valley***, Hula Reserve***, Urim***.
ITALY Circeo NP***, Isonzo Regional Park***, Lake Massaciuccoli***, Maremma Regional Park***, Monte Conero***, Orbetello Reserve***, Po Delta***, San Giuliano Reserve***.
LEBANON Aamiq Marshes***, Qaraoun Lake*.

MALTA*.
MOROCCO Agadir and the Sous Plain***, Asilah and Oued Loukkos***, Lac de Sidi Bourhaba***, Merja Zerga***, Oualidia***, Oued Massa***, Zaers***.
PORTUGAL Baixo Alentejo***, Boquilobo***, Cape St Vincent***, Montesinho***, Peneda Gêres NP***, Ria Formosa***, Sado Estuary***, Santo André Lagoon***, Tagus Estuary***.
SARDINIA Cagliari wetlands***, Oristano wetlands***, San Pietro I***.
SPAIN Aiguamolls de L'Empordá***, Cabo de Gata***, Cádiz Lagoons***, Coto Doñana***, Ebro Delta***, Guadalhorce Estuary***, La Serena***, Llobregat Delta***, Santa Pola***, Tablas de Daimiel***.
SYRIA Bahrat Homs***, Lake Assad***, Yarmuk Valley***.
TUNISIA Ain Draham***, Cap Bon Peninsula***, Chott el Djerid***, Kelbia Lake***, Lake Ichkeul***.
TURKEY Bafa Gölü*, Dalyan***, Göksu Delta***, Manyas Gölü***.

Graceful Prinia (Graceful Warbler)
Prinia gracilis   FG SH SD   Res (Dis)

Range: Locally common in the Western Palearctic, breeding in S Turkey, on the Syrian coast and along the Euphrates, in Lebanon, Israel and adjacent W Jordan, in N Sinai and in the Nile Valley in Egypt.

Subspecies: Various races occur in our region with the most widespread being *palestinae* from Syria to E Sinai. Race *deltae* occurs from the Nile Delta to Israel with nominate *gracilis* in the Nile Valley, and *natronensis* from Wadi El Natrun in N Egypt. Race *akyildizi* is found in Turkey and *irakensis* in NE Syria and Iraq.

Tips: Inhabits semi-desert, scrub and cultivation, grasslands, gardens and plantations, in some areas frequent near habitation. Usually found in dense low scrub and rarely feeds on the ground, although small parties may hunt insects at ground level.

Sites:

EGYPT Abu Simbel***, Aswan***, Faiyum***, Luxor***, Nile Delta***, Suez area***, Wadi el Natrun***.

ISRAEL Arava Valley***, Eilat***, Hula Reserve***, Jezreel Valley***, Ma'agan Mikhael*** Mt Hermon***, Wadi Ammud-Mt Arbel***.

JORDAN Aqaba***, Azraq***, Wadi as Sir***.

LEBANON Aammiq Marshes***, Palm Is**, Qaraoun Lake***.

SYRIA Aqra Mts***, Baath Lake***, Bahrat Homs***, Dayr al-Zawr***, Lake Assad***, Sabkha al-Jabbul***, Yarmuk Valley***.

TURKEY Birecik-Halfeti***, Göksu Delta***.

Scrub Warbler (Streaked Scrub-warbler)
Scotocerca inquieta

D SD SH Res

Range: Widespread in N Africa, in Mauritania and S and E Morocco, across the Atlas of Algeria to C and S Tunisia, at scattered localities in N Libya and in E Egypt between the Nile and the Red Sea. Also in C and E Sinai, Israel and W Jordan, N Saudi Arabia and perhaps also in Syria. An altitudinal migrant in parts of range.

Subspecies: Three races occur in our region with the nominate the most widespread and found in the Near East, Sinai and Egypt, *saharae* in the Sahara and *theresae* in Morocco.

Tips: Search rocky and stony deserts, semi-desert, barren hillsides, sandy plains and wadis with scrub and sparse vegetation, especially *Artemisia*. Generally keeps to dense cover but often seen on the ground, unlike Graceful Prinia, and prefers to run than fly when disturbed. Best located by song.

Sites:

EGYPT Santa Katharina Monastery***, Sharm el Sheikh***, Suez area***.

ISRAEL Arava Valley***, Eilat***, Ein Gedi***, Nizzana***.

JORDAN Azraq***, Petra***, Wadi Dana-Fidan***, Wadi Rum***, Wadi as Sir***.

MOROCCO Goulimime to Tan-Tan***, Tafilalt***.

TUNISIA Chott el Djerid***, Tatahouine***.

River Warbler
Locustella fluviatilis

FW Mig

Range: Breeds from C Germany to the Urals, N to S Finland and S to the Black Sea. Range has expanded W during second half of 20th century, and has bred in Denmark and Sweden, and perhaps in Belgium. Departs breeding range in late Jul–Aug with most passing through SE Europe in late Aug to mid Sep. Returns in May. Passage occurs throughout SE Europe, the Middle East and NE Africa.

Tips: Inhabits densely wooded swamps and scrub along rivers, streams and canals. Often sings from an exposed perch such as a bush under the shade of a tree and is then easily seen. Sings mostly at dusk, also nocturnally and at dawn, but is skulking, very difficult to see and keeps to dense cover.

Sites:

ARMENIA Lake Sevan* (summer).

AUSTRIA Lake Neusiedl*** (summer), Marchauen-Marchegg Reserve*** (summer).

BELARUS Belovezhskaya Pushcha NP*** (summer), Berezinsky Reserve*** (summer), Prypyatsky NP*** (summer).

BULGARIA Belene*** (summer), Burgas area** (summer, passage), Cape Kaliakra* (passage), Lake Shabla* (summer), Lake Srebarna** (summer), Rusenski Lom NP** (summer).

CYPRUS (passage).

CZECH REPUBLIC Lednice*** (summer), Poodří*** (summer), Soutok*** (summer), Třeboňsko*** (summer).

ESTONIA Matsalu Bay*** (passage).

FINLAND Åland Is* (summer), Parikkala*** (summer).

GERMANY Mecklenburg Lakes*** (summer), Oder Valley*** (summer), Tiroler Achen*** (summer).

GREECE Porto Lagos Area* (passage). **GREEK IS** Lesvos** (passage).

HUNGARY Aggtelek NP*** (summer), Csákvár*** (summer), Danube Bend** (summer), Hortobágy NP*** (summer), Kis-balaton*** (summer), Kiskunság NP*** (summer), Lake Fertö*** (summer), Lake Velence*** (summer), Ócsa*** (summer), Zemplén Hills*** (summer).

ISRAEL Eilat* (passage).

JORDAN Aqaba (passage), Azraq (passage), Wadi Rum (passage).

LATVIA Lake Lubana*** (summer), Lake Pape*** (summer).

LITHUANIA Kirsiu Peninsula*** (summer).

POLAND Białowieża Forest*** (summer), Białystok Fishponds*** (summer), Biebrza Marshes*** (summer), Bieszczady NP*** (summer), Chełm Marshes*** (summer), Gdańsk Bay*** (summer), Milicz Fishponds*** (summer), Słońsk*** (summer), Szczecin Bay Area** (summer), Tatra NP** (summer).

ROMANIA Danube Delta*** (summer), Dobrudja*** (summer), Satchinez*** (summer).

RUSSIA Volga Delta* (passage).

SLOVAKIA Slovenský Kras*** (summer), Záhorie*** (summer), Zlatná na Ostrove*** (summer).

SWEDEN Getterön* (summer), Gotland* (summer, passage), Holmöarna** (passage), Hornborgasjön** (summer, passage), Kristianstad* (summer, passage), Kvismaren* (summer, passage), Öland* (spring).

TURKEY Dalyan (passage), Kocaçay Delta (passage).

UKRAINE Dunay Delta*** (summer), Shatsk NP*** (summer).

Savi's Warbler
Locustella luscinioides   FW SH Mig

Range: Main breeding range is from E Germany and Poland to the N Caspian region. Also occurs in scattered pockets W to Iberia and W France and S to N Italy and Greece. Beyond Europe occurs in parts of NW Africa, in N Morocco, Algeria and Tunisia, in Turkey, and sporadically in the Middle East, in Syria, Lebanon, Jordan and N Israel, and probably also breeds in Armenia. Formerly a rare breeder in S Great Britain but now a rare migrant with only occasional breeding records. Departs breeding areas in Aug–Sep, returning mid Apr–early Jun.

Subspecies: Nominate occurs over most of Western Palearctic range, *sarmatica* in the European Russia and *fusca* in Turkey.

Tips: Occurs in reeds and other tall dense waterside vegetation including rushes and sedges with scattered bushes and trees. Found beside brackish as well as fresh water. Reeling song is given from an exposed perch, often high on a reed and then easily seen but otherwise keeps to dense cover.

Sites:

ALBANIA Lake Shkodra*** (summer).

ARMENIA Armash Fishponds*** (summer).

AUSTRIA Lake Neusiedl*** (summer), Marchauen-Marchegg Reserve*** (summer).

BELARUS Prypyatsky NP*** (summer).

BELGIUM Blankaart Reserve*** (summer), Lesse et Lomme NR* (summer).

BULGARIA Albena-Golden Sands*** (summer), Burgas area*** (summer), Lake Durankulak*** (summer), Lake Shabla*** (summer), Lake Srebarna*** (summer), Strandja Mts* (summer).

CROATIA Kopački Rit** (summer).

CZECH REPUBLIC Lednice*** (summer), Nové Mlýny*** (summer), Třebońsko*** (summer).

DENMARK Møn-Falster*** (summer).

ESTONIA Matsalu Bay*** (summer).

FRANCE Camargue*** (summer), Cap Gris Nez** (summer), Dombes*** (summer), Golfe du Morbihan** (summer), Île d'Oléron** (summer), La Brenne*** (summer), Romelaere NR*** (summer), Sologne*** (summer), Somme Estuary* (summer).

GERMANY Federsee*** (summer), Mecklenburg Lakes*** (summer), Oder Valley*** (summer).

GREAT BRITAIN Minsmere* (summer, passage), N Norfolk coast* (summer, passage).

GREECE Mikrí Prespa NP*** (summer), Porto Lagos area*** (summer).

GREEK IS Lesvos*** (passage).

HUNGARY Biharugra*** (summer), Csákvár*** (summer), Hanság*** (summer), Hortobágy NP*** (summer), Kis-balaton*** (summer), Kiskunság NP*** (summer), Lake Fertö*** (summer), Lake Velence*** (summer), Ócsa*** (summer), Tihany*** (summer), Szeged Fishponds*** (summer).

ISRAEL Arava Valley*** (passage), Eilat*** (passage), Jezreel Valley*** (passage).

ITALY Isonzo Regional Park* (summer), Lake Massaciuccoli*** (summer), Po Delta*** (summer).

JORDAN Azraq (passage), Ghadir Burqu' (passage), Wadi Rum (passage).

LATVIA Lake Engure*** (summer), Lake Lubana*** (summer), Lake Pape*** (summer).

LEBANON Aammiq Marshes*** (summer), Qaraoun Lake** (summer).

LITHUANIA Kirsiu Peninsula*** (summer).

MACEDONIA Lakes Ohrid and Prespa*** (summer).

MALTA (passage).
MOROCCO Asilah and Oued Loukkos*** (summer), Dayet Aaoua*** (summer), Oued Massa** (summer, passage).
NETHERLANDS Lauwersmeer*** (summer), Naardermeer** (summer), Oostvaardersplassen*** (summer), Zwanenwater*** (summer).
POLAND Białowieża Forest*** (summer), Chełm Marshes*** (summer), Gdańsk Bay*** (summer), Milicz Fishponds*** (summer), Słońsk*** (summer), Szczecin Bay area*** (summer).
PORTUGAL Boquilobo*** (summer), Santo André Lagoon*** (summer), Tagus Estuary*** (summer).
ROMANIA Danube Delta*** (summer), Dobrudja*** (summer), Lake Călăraşi*** (summer), Satchinez*** (summer).
RUSSIA Volga Delta*** (summer).

SLOVAKIA Senné Fishponds*** (summer), Záhorie*** (summer).
SPAIN Aiguamolls de L'Empordá*** (summer), Cádiz Lagoons*** (summer), Coto Doñana*** (summer), Ebro Delta*** (summer), Guadalhorce Estuary*** (summer), Llobregat Delta*** (summer), Santa Pola*** (summer), Tablas de Daimiel*** (summer).
SWEDEN Kristianstad* (summer, passage), Kvismaren* (summer).
SWITZERLAND Fanel NR*** (summer), Grangettes* (summer).
SYRIA Baath Lake*** (summer).
TURKEY Manyas Gölü*** (summer), Sultan Marshes*** (summer), Uluabat Gölü*** (summer), Van Gölü* (passage).
UKRAINE Dunay Delta*** (summer), Shatsk NP*** (summer).
YUGOSLAVIA Carska bara*** (summer), Obedska bara** (summer).

Moustached Warbler
Acrocephalus melanopogon   **FW   Res Mig**

Range: Very local in Europe, breeding on the Mediterranean coasts of Spain and France, and in parts of Italy, in Hungary and along the Danube, and patchily in the Balkans, Greece and Turkey. In the Mediterranean found on Mallorca and Crete, in N Africa in Tunisia and in Israel. More widespread in the E of the region, in the E Ukraine and around the W shores of the Caspian. Has bred in Britain (although disputed), Germany, Slovakia, Switzerland and probably also in Corsica and Morocco. Birds from E of range are migratory; those around the Mediterranean are resident or partial migrants. Passage birds occur widely around the Mediterranean and winter range is more extensive, especially in Greece, the Middle East and NW Africa.

Subspecies: Nominate race is found in S and E Europe, *mimica* from the Caspian region to Turkey and Israel and *albiventris* in the Ukraine.

Tips: Search reedbeds, rushes and sedges around shallow fresh waters, sometimes also found in tamarisk and, in parts of range, along upland streams. Although sometimes sings from exposed reeds, generally shy and remains out of sight for long periods, feeding very low in vegetation close to the water. One of the world's most accessible sites for this species is Albufera, in Mallorca, where large numbers are present all year.

Sites:

ALBANIA Lake Shkodra* (summer).
ARMENIA Armash Fishponds*** (summer).
AUSTRIA Lake Neusiedl***.
BALEARIC IS Mallorca***, Menorca***.
BULGARIA Lake Srebarna** (summer).
CORSICA Biguglia Lake** (mainly winter).
CYPRUS* (passage, winter).
EGYPT Luxor** (winter), Sharm el Sheikh* (winter).
FRANCE Camargue***, Gruissan** (winter), Leucate**.
GREECE Mikrí Prespa NP**.
GREEK IS Corfu*, Crete** (passage), Lesvos** (passage, winter).
HUNGARY Biharugra*** (summer), Hanság*** (summer), Hortobágy NP*** (summer), Kis-balaton** (summer), Kiskunság NP*** (summer), Lake Fertö*** (summer), Lake Velence*** (summer), Ócsa*** (summer), Szeged Fishponds*** (summer).
ISRAEL Bet Shean Valley*** (passage, winter), Eilat** (passage), Hula Reserve*** (winter), Jezreel Valley***, Ma'agan Mikhael*** (winter).
ITALY Circeo NP* (passage), Gargano Peninsula* (passage), Lake Massaciuccoli**, Maremma Regional Park** (passage), Monte Conero* (passage), Orbetello Reserve* (passage, winter), Po Delta***.
JORDAN Wadi Rum (passage).
LEBANON Aammiq Marshes**, Qaraoun Lake**.
MACEDONIA Lakes Ohrid and Prespa**.
MALTA* (passage, winter).
MOROCCO Asilah and Oued Loukkos***, Merja Zerga** (passage, winter), Oued Massa*** (passage, winter).
ROMANIA Danube Delta*** (summer), Dobrudja** (passage), Lake Călăraşi***.
RUSSIA Kalmykia*** (summer), Volga Delta*** (summer).
SPAIN Aiguamolls de L'Empordá**, Cádiz Lagoons*, Coto Doñana*** (passage, winter), Ebro Delta***, Llobregat Delta** (mainly winter), Santa Pola**, Tablas de Daimiel*.
SYRIA Yarmuk Valley*.
TUNISIA Kelbia Lake*, Lake Ichkeul***.
TURKEY Göksu Delta***, Kızılırmak Delta*** (summer), Kulu Gölü*** (summer), Sultan Marshes*** (summer), Van Gölü*** (summer).
UKRAINE Dunay Delta*** (summer).
YUGOSLAVIA Lake Skadar*.

Aquatic Warbler
Acrocephalus paludicola   FW Mig

Range: Breeds locally from Lithuania, E Poland, Belarus and Ukraine to the Urals and also at very scattered localities in W Poland, E Germany and Hungary. Has bred in France, Belgium, the Netherlands, Slovakia, Austria and Italy. Uncommon to rare over most of range. A summer visitor, moving W or SW in Aug–Sep, when occurs in the Netherlands, Belgium, S England and W France, before heading S to winter in W Africa. Most NW Europe records (in autumn) are juveniles. Some 20–40 birds occur annually in Britain, with most on the S coast, particularly in the SW. Spring passage, in late Apr to mid May, is more easterly and the species is then rarely recorded in NW Europe.

Tips: Breeds in marshes and swamps with tussock sedge, yellow iris and reedmace, but less frequently in pure reedbeds. On passage uses reedbeds more frequently, as well as waterside scrub, and sometimes occurs in drier habitats including crops. Spends much time deep in cover and feeds very low in vegetation, sometimes on the ground. Often difficult to see well but males sing from exposed perches or in flight, and often most easily seen at dawn. The Biebrza and Chełm Marshes of Poland and the Pripyatsky Marshes of Belarus are the best sites during the breeding season, whilst most passage records are from trapping sites.

Sites:

BELARUS Belovezhskaya Pushcha NP*** (summer), Pripyatsky NP*** (summer).
BULGARIA Burgas area* (passage).
CZECH REPUBLIC Poodří* (autumn).
FRANCE Marais Poitevin* (autumn), Trunvel Reserve* (autumn).
GERMANY Oder Valley*** (summer), Rügen** (autumn).
GREAT BRITAIN Portland* (autumn).
HUNGARY Hortobágy NP*** (summer).
ITALY Po Delta* (passage).

LATVIA Lake Pape (passage).
LITHUANIA Zuvintas NR** (summer), Kirsiu Peninsula*** (summer).
POLAND Biebrza Marshes*** (summer), Chełm Marshes*** (summer), Słońsk** (summer), Szczecin Bay area*** (summer).
ROMANIA Danube Delta*** (passage), Dobrudja*** (passage).
SLOVAKIA Senné Fishponds* (summer).
UKRAINE Dunay Delta* (passage), Shatsk NP*** (summer).

Paddyfield Warbler
Acrocephalus agricola   FW (SH) Mig

Range: In our region breeds in NE Bulgaria and coastal Romania, S Ukraine and Crimea and across S Russia to the Caspian. Also in Armenia and around Van in E Turkey. Departs breeding areas in Aug–Sep to winter in the Indian subcontinent, returning late Apr–early May. Common in much of range.

Subspecies: Usually considered monotypic but sometimes separated into *septima* over most of range and *capistrata* in the E.

Tips: Found in dense vegetation, often in reeds and reedmace mixed with willows, in or beside fresh or brackish water, but rarely in extensive beds of pure reeds. May occur far from water on passage, in cultivated areas and woodlands, even in steppe and semi-desert areas. Often feeds low in vegetation but not particularly shy, sometimes feeding in the open, and males sing from exposed reeds from early May until late Jul.

Sites:

ARMENIA Armash Fishponds*** (summer).
BULGARIA Lake Durankulak*** (summer), Lake Shabla*** (summer).
LATVIA Lake Pape (summer).
ROMANIA Danube Delta*** (summer), Dobrudja*** (summer, passage).

RUSSIA Kalmykia*** (summer), Volga Delta*** (summer).
TURKEY Van Gölü*** (summer).
UKRAINE Dunay Delta*** (summer), Syvash Bay*** (summer).

Blyth's Reed Warbler

Acrocephalus dumetorum   FW DF SH   Mig

Range: Breeds from S Finland and the Baltic states to E Belarus and across Russia to the Urals. A rare breeder in S Sweden, has attempted to breed in Norway and hybridisation with Marsh Warbler has occurred in the Netherlands. Departs breeding areas in late Jul–Aug and returns early May to mid Jun.

Tips: Found in dense tall vegetation at the edge of marshes and in deciduous riverine woodland. Sometimes occurs in parks, gardens, orchards and hedgerows, and uses trees more than other *Acrocephalus*. Males sing from exposed perches and can then be seen fairly easily.

Sites:

DENMARK Bornholm-Christiansø* (passage).
ESTONIA Matsalu Bay* (summer).
FINLAND Åland Is* (summer), Liminganlahti* (summer), Parikkala*** (summer).

LATVIA Lake Lubana* (summer).
RUSSIA Volga Delta* (passage).
SWEDEN Getterön* (summer), Holmöarna** (summer, passage), Kvismaren* (summer), Öland* (spring).

Clamorous Reed Warbler

Acrocephalus stentoreus   FW   Res (PMig)

Range: A very widespread species, breeding discontinuously from the E Mediterranean to New Guinea and Australia. In our region breeds in Egypt, in the Nile Delta and Valley, and in S Israel and the Yarmuk Valley on the Syria/Jordan border. Largely resident with some local wandering in winter.

Subspecies: Nominate race is found in Egypt, *levantina* in the Middle East and *brunnescens* in S Iraq.

Tips: Found in reedbeds but prefers papyrus swamps, also in mangroves and, sometimes, drier scrub and crops. Spends much time in dense vegetation but occasionally sings from exposed perches in the breeding season.

Sites:

EGYPT Abu Simbel***, Aswan***, Faiyum***, Luxor***, Nile Delta***, Suez area***, Wadi el Natrun***.

ISRAEL Bet Shean Valley***, Eilat***, Hula Reserve***, Ma'agan Mikhael***.
JORDAN Azraq.
SYRIA Yarmuk Valley***.

Cape Verde Warbler (Cape Verde Cane Warbler)
Acrocephalus brevipennis　　　　　　　　　　　　　　　SH FG U　Res

Range: Endemic to the Cape Verde Is: on São Tiago, where generally scarce, the local population probably numbering fewer than 500 pairs, and São Nicolau, where long considered extinct but small numbers were discovered in the NW in 1998. Formerly also on Brava but not recorded since 1969.

Tips: Search reeds and field edges, sugarcane and other crops including banana plantations; the species often occurs close to water, sometimes in gardens. Locally fairly common and widespread, occurring to 1,400 m, but can be difficult to see as it keeps to dense cover for long periods.

Site:
CAPE VERDE IS***.

Western Olivaceous Warbler
Hippolais opaca　　　　　　　　　　　　　　　　SH SD (FG)　Mig

Range: This species, which was until recently considered conspecific with Eastern Olivaceous Warbler, breeds in S Portugal and S Spain and in parts of N and E Spain. Also breeds across NW Africa, from S Morocco to N Tunisia and NW Libya. Generally scarce over much of range. Departs breeding areas in mid July to late Sep to winter in sub-Saharan Africa, and returns in late April–May.

Tips: Search shrubs in dunes, semi-desert and other arid areas and maquis; often seen in tamarisk scrub. Also found in cultivated areas, olive groves and gardens. Less shy and skulking than Eastern Olivaceous Warbler.

Sites:
ALGERIA El Kala NP*** (summer).
BALEARIC IS Mallorca* (passage).
GIBRALTAR*** (passage).
MOROCCO Agadir and the Sous Plain*** (summer), Dayet Aaoua*** (summer), Essaouira*** (summer), Goulimime to Tan-Tan*** (summer), Oued Massa*** (summer, passage), Zaër*** (summer), Zeida** (summer).

SPAIN Aiguamolls de l'Empordá** (passage), Cabo de Gata*** (summer, passage), Coto Doñana*** (passage), Serrania de Ronda*** (summer), Tablas de Daimiel*** (summer).
TUNISIA Ain Draham*** (summer), Kelbia Lake** (summer), Lake Ichkeul*** (summer).

Eastern Olivaceous Warbler
Hippolais pallida   SH SD (FG)   Mig (Res)

Range: Breeds in S Hungary and throughout much of the Balkans, in Greece, Turkey and the Caucasus. Also Crete and other Greek islands, Cyprus, parts of the Middle East and in N Africa in C and S Tunisia, the Sahara and at scattered oases in W Egypt, the Nile Delta and Valley. Departs breeding areas in mid Jul to late Sep to winter in sub-Saharan Africa, returning late April–May. Southernmost populations are resident.

Subspecies: The four races fall into two groups, which may be treated as full species in the future. Race *elaeica* occurs in SE Europe and the Middle East, and the three remaining races in N Africa: *reiseri* in the Moroccan, Algerian and Tunisian Sahara, where it may overlap with Western Olivaceous Warbler; *laeneni* in the far S of our region in N Niger and N Chad; and *pallida* in Egypt.

Tips: Often occurs in drier habitats than other Hippolais warblers, found in semi-desert and other arid scrubby areas, also on cultivated land, in woodlands and sometimes mangroves, gardens and riverside vegetation.

Sites:

ALBANIA Drini Delta*** (summer), Karavasta Lagoon*** (summer), Lake Shkodra*** (summer).

ARMENIA Mt Aragats*** (summer).

BULGARIA Albena-Golden Sands*** (summer), Belene*** (summer), Burgas area*** (summer), Cape Emine*** (summer), Cape Kaliakra*** (summer), Lake Durankulak*** (summer), Lake Shabla*** (summer), Ropotamo NP*** (summer), Strandja Mts*** (summer), Studen Kladenetz*** (summer), Tissata NR** (summer).

CROATIA Cres*** (summer), Mljet*** (summer), Paklenica NP*** (summer).

CYPRUS*** (summer).

EGYPT Abu Simbel*** (summer), Aswan*** (summer), Faiyum*** (summer), Hurghada*** (summer), Luxor** (summer), Nile Delta*** (summer), Suez area*** (passage).

GREECE Akarnanika Mts*** (summer), Amvrakikós Gulf*** (summer, Avas Gorge*** (summer), Axios-Aliakmonas Deltas*** (summer), Dadiá-Soufli Forest*** (summer), Delphi*** (summer), Evros Delta*** (summer), Lake Kerkini*** (summer), Mikrí Prespa NP*** (summer), Mt Olympus NP*** (summer), Mt Parnassós NP*** (summer), Nestos Delta*** (summer), Porto Lagos area*** (summer).

GREEK IS Corfu*** (summer), Crete*** (summer, passage), Kos*** (summer), Lesvos*** (summer), Náxos*** (summer), Rhodes*** (summer).

HUNGARY Szeged Fishponds* (summer).

ISRAEL Arava Valley*** (passage), Eilat*** (passage), Urim*** (summer), Wadi Ammud-Mt Arbel*** (summer).

JORDAN Amman NP*** (summer), Aqaba*** (passage), Azraq** (passage), Petra*** (summer), Wadi Dana-Fidan** (passage), Wadi Rum*** (passage), Wadi as Sir*** (summer).

LEBANON Aammiq Marshes*** (summer), Palm Is** (passage), Qaraoun Lake** (summer).

MACEDONIA Babuna Gorge*** (summer), Galicica NP*** (summer), Lakes Ohrid and Prespa*** (summer).

ROMANIA Danube Delta*** (summer), Dobrudja** (summer, passage).

SYRIA Aqra Mts*** (summer), Baath Lake*** (summer), Dayr al-Zawr*** (summer).
TURKEY Bafa Gölü*** (summer), Birecik-Halfeti*** (summer), Dalyan*** (summer), Demirkazik*** (summer), Göksu Delta*** (summer), İstanbul*** (summer, passage), Kocaćay Delta*** (summer), Manyas Gölü*** (summer), Soğuksu NP*** (summer), Uluabat Gölü*** (summer), Van Gölü* (summer), Yeşilce*** (summer).
UKRAINE Dunay Delta*** (summer).
YUGOSLAVIA Carska bara** (summer), Lake Skadar*** (summer), Obedska bara** (summer).

Booted Warbler
Hippolais caligata   DF SH FG (FW)   Mig

Range: In our region breeds from W Russia to the Urals and S to the Caspian. Expanding W, with first breeding for Estonia in 1998, Finland in 2000 and Estonia in 2002. A summer visitor arriving in late Apr–May and departing in Aug–Sep. Reports of passage birds at Azraq in Jordan are now considered doubtful.
Subspecies: Sykes's Warbler *H. rama*, a vagrant to the Western Palearctic, was formerly considered a race of Booted Warbler but is now usually regarded as a full species.
Tips: Search cultivated land, open woodland, orchards and gardens, and passage birds are usually found in wooded or scrub habitats, often near water and sometimes in reeds. Generally very skulking and most easily located during the breeding season when male sings from a high (although rarely exposed) perch in a bush or tree. Sometimes sings at night.

Sites:
FINLAND Parikkala* (summer).   **RUSSIA** Volga Delta*** (passage).

Upcher's Warbler
Hippolais languida   SH SD FG   Mig

Range: Breeds in C, S and SE Turkey, Armenia and SW Azerbaijan, and further S breeds in Lebanon, Syria, N Israel and W Jordan. Generally scarce over restricted Western Palearctic range. Winters in E Africa, departing breeding areas in late Jul–Sep and returning in late Apr–early May. Probably regular on passage in Sinai.
Tips: Occurs in dry scrub and semi-desert with tamarisks, sand dunes and hillsides with rocks and scrub, orchards, vineyards and cultivated areas, occasionally gardens. Fairly easily observed and often perches prominently on trees or rocks.

Sites:

ARMENIA Armash Fishponds*** (summer), Meghri Area*** (summer), Vedi Hills*** (summer).
GREEK IS Lesvos (passage).
ISRAEL Eilat* (passage), Mt Hermon** (summer).
JORDAN Amman NP*** (summer), Azraq (spring), Wadi Dana-Fidan (summer, passage), Wadi Rum* (passage).

LEBANON Aamiq Marshes** (summer), Qaraoun Lake* (passage).
SYRIA Dayr al-Zawr*** (summer), Tadmur and Sabkhat Muh** (passage), Wadi al-Qarn-Burqush* (summer).
TURKEY Birecik-Halfeti*** (summer), Demirkazik*** (summer), Göksu Delta*** (summer), Yeşilce*** (summer).

Olive-tree Warbler
Hippolais olivetorum   SH DF FG   Mig

Range: Breeds on the W Adriatic coast from Croatia to Albania and Corfu, widely in Greece, on Crete and many other Greek islands, in Macedonia, Bulgaria and S Romania, W and S Turkey and N Syria. Possibly also breeds in Lebanon and very locally in N Israel. Departs breeding areas in late Jul–early Sep and returns late Apr–early May. Passage records are scarce, but seen sometimes in Israel and Egypt, and even more rarely from Cyprus.

Tips: Search hillsides with olive groves, vineyards, open oak woodland and scrub, and is often found in coastal areas and on islands. A local and generally scarce bird that can be difficult to locate due to its rather skulking nature.

Sites:

ALBANIA Drini Delta** (summer), Karavasta Lagoon*** (summer), Lake Shkodra*** (summer).
BOSNIA-HERZEGOVINA Hutovo blato** (summer).
BULGARIA Albena-Golden Sands*** (summer), Burgas area*** (summer), Cape Emine*** (summer), Cape Kaliakra*** (summer), Strandja Mts*** (summer), Studen Kladenetz*** (summer), Ropotamo NP*** (summer), Tissata NR*** (summer).
CROATIA Mljet*** (summer), Neretva Delta*** (summer), Paklenica NP* (summer).
CYPRUS** (passage).
EGYPT Hurghada* (passage), Suez area* (passage), Zaranik* (passage).

GREECE Akarnanika Mts*** (summer), Amvrakikós Gulf*** (summer), Avas Gorge*** (summer), Dadiá-Soufli Forest*** (summer), Delphi*** (summer), Evros Delta*** (summer), Mikrí Prespa NP* (summer), Mt Parnassós NP** (summer). Nestos Delta*** (summer).
GREEK IS Corfu*** (summer), Crete* (passage), Kos*** (summer, passage), Lesvos** (summer, passage), Rhodes* (passage).
ISRAEL Arava Valley* (passage), Eilat* (passage), Mt Hermon* (summer).
JORDAN Aqaba* (passage), Wadi Rum* (passage).
LEBANON Qaraoun Lake** (passage).
MACEDONIA Babuna Gorge** (summer), Galicica NP*** (summer), Lakes Ohrid and Prespa*** (summer).

ROMANIA Dobrudja (summer).
SYRIA Aqra Mts*** (summer).
TURKEY Akseki** (summer), Dalyan*** (summer), İstanbul*** (summer), Kocaćay Delta

(summer), Soğuksu NP* (passage), Yeşilce** (summer).
YUGOSLAVIA Lake Skadar*** (summer).

Marmora's Warbler
Sylvia sarda   SH   Res (PMig)

Range: Locally common on Mallorca, Formentera, Ibiza and many nearby islets (apparently formerly also on Menorca, but now replaced there by Dartford Warbler), Corsica and Sardinia, the Italian islands of Capraia, Elba and Pianosa, and possibly also Montecristo, Giglio, Ponza, Ischia, Capri and, further S, on Pantellaria. Recently found breeding in mainland Italy, at Monte Argentario. Also recorded breeding on Zembra, off Tunisia, but status unclear, and there are unsubstantiated reports of breeding on Náxos and Crete. Mainly resident but regular in winter in NE Algeria, Tunisia and NW Libya. Formerly regular in Sicily at this season but now scarce, and passage and wintering birds have been recorded in S Spain, Morocco, S France and mainland Italy.

Subspecies: The race *balearica* occurs on the Balearics, and nominate *sarda* in rest of range; they have been treated as species by some authorities. The nominate is a rare migrant in the Balearics.

Tips: Search rocky and garrigue-covered cliff-tops and hillsides with low cover such as heather and palmetto, and scattered pines. Less shy and easier to see than Dartford Warbler, and generally occurs at higher levels than Dartford where the two overlap.

Sites:
ALGERIA El Kala NP*** (winter).
BALEARIC IS Formentera***, Ibiza***, Mallorca***.
CORSICA Asco Valley***, Bonifacio***, Cap Corse***, Scandola***.
ITALY Orbetello Reserve* (summer), Tuscan archipelago***.

SARDINIA Capo Marargiu***, Giara di Gesturi***, Monte Arcuso***, San Pietro I***.
SICILY Pelagie Is***.
TUNISIA Ain Draham** (winter), Cap Bon Peninsula* (winter), Chott el Djerid*** (winter), Kelbia Lake* (winter), Lake Ichkeul* (winter).

Dartford Warbler
Sylvia undata   SH (CF)   Res (Dis)

Range: Breeds in S England and the Channel Is, in France, in Brittany and on the W and S coasts, throughout Iberia and, since the mid 1970s, on Menorca. Also breeds on Corsica and Sardinia, in S Italy and NE Sicily, and in coastal N Africa in Morocco, Algeria, and possibly Tunisia. Mainly resident but juveniles wander in winter and then occur on Mallorca and more widely in N Africa.

Subspecies: Nominate race *undata* is found in NE Spain, S France, Italy and the Mediterranean islands, *dartfordiensis* in S England, W France and N Iberia and *toni* from S Iberia and N Africa.

Tips: In N of range found on open heaths with gorse, further S in dense thorn scrub and maquis, sometimes open pinewoods. Most easily seen when singing in early spring or when feeding young but otherwise an elusive bird of dense cover. In Great Britain most easily found in the New Forest or at Arne RSPB reserve in Dorset.

Sites:

ANDORRA**.

BALEARIC IS Mallorca* (mainly winter but breeding recently confirmed), Menorca***.

CORSICA Bonifacio**, Cap Corse***, Scandola***.

FRANCE Baie de Vilaine***, Baie du Mont-St-Michel**, Camargue*** La Brenne***, Fontainebleau**, Gruissan***, Île d'Oléron***, Ouessant***, Teich Reserve***, Trunvel Reserve***, Les Alpilles***, Leucate***.

GIBRALTAR**.

ITALY Gargano Peninsula***, Orbetello Reserve***, Tuscan archipelago***.

MALTA* (winter).

MOROCCO Boumalne***, Tafilalt** (winter).

PORTUGAL Baixo Alentejo***, Cape St Vincent***, Castro Marim***, International Douro***, International Tagus***, Montesinho***, Peneda Gêres NP***, Ria Formosa***, Sado Estuary***, Santo André Lagoon***, Tagus Estuary**.

SARDINIA Capo Marargiu***, Giara di Gesturi***, Monte Arcuso***, San Pietro I***.

SICILY Strait of Messina***.

SPAIN Aiguamolls de l'Empordá***, Cabo de Gata***, Cádiz Lagoons***, Coto Doñana***, Ebro Delta***, Garraf Massif***, Guadalhorce Estuary***, Jaca***, La Serena***, Llobregat Delta***, Monfragüe***, Ordesa NP***, Serrania de Ronda***, Sierra de Gredos***, Sierra de Guadarrama***, Tablas de Daimiel***, Zaragoza Steppes**.

TUNISIA Ain Draham***.

Tristram's Warbler
Sylvia deserticola   SH (MF) (SD)   Res (AMig)

Range: Breeds only in NW Africa, in montane Morocco, N Algeria and NW Tunisia. Mainly resident but also an altitudinal and short-distance migrant, with some moving towards the coast in autumn. Some make longer movements and winter range extends over much of Morocco and Algeria.

Subspecies: Nominate race occurs in Atlas Saharien and Aures in Algeria and in adjacent Tunisia, *maroccana* from the Atlas of W Morocco to NW Algeria. **Meinertzhagen's Warbler** *S. ticehursti*, a very pale form described from a single specimen from the Ouarzazate area of central Morocco, is probably an aberrant individual of Tristram's Warbler; others have considered it a full species.

Tips: Mountain and hill scrub, often juniper, usually at 1,200–2,400 m, sometimes in open oak woodland and cedar forest. In winter in lower, bushy habitats including wadis, oases and desert edges, often in tamarisk scrub. Keeps low in dense cover but males sing from atop bushes during breeding season.

Sites:
MOROCCO Agadir and the Sous Plain**, Boumalne**, Goulimime to Tan-Tan*** (winter), Oukaimeden***, Tafilalt*** (winter), Zeida**.

TUNISIA Ain Draham***, Chott el Djerid** (winter), Tataouine** (winter).

Spectacled Warbler
Sylvia conspicillata   SH (FG)   PMig

Range: Breeds in S, C and E Spain, S France, on the Balearics, Corsica (rare) and Sardinia, in S Italy, Sicily and Malta, and has bred in Switzerland. Further E breeds on Cyprus, in Syria, Lebanon, Israel and Jordan, at one site in SE Turkey, and possibly N Sinai. In the Atlantic occurs on Madeira, the Canaries and Cape Verde Is, and in N Africa in Morocco, N Algeria, C Tunisia, NW Libya and NE Egypt. A partial migrant from Iberia to Italy, with some present all year, resident elsewhere or makes short-distance movements S. More widespread in winter in NW Africa, Egypt, Sinai and Israel.

Subspecies: Birds from the Atlantic islands belong to race *orbitalis*, those on Madeira are sometimes separated as *bella*. The nominate race is found in remainder of range.

Tips: Search open dry and scrubby areas without tall vegetation, arid hillsides and lowland plains, cultivated areas and salt flats with *Salicornia*. Often feeds along low walls, in low bushes and on the ground. Fairly skulking but males sing from exposed perches during the breeding season and perform song-flights.

Sites:

BALEARIC IS Formentera*** (summer), Ibiza*** (summer), Mallorca*** (summer), Menorca*** (summer).
BOSNIA-HERZEGOVINA Hutovo blato**.
CANARY IS El Hierro***, Fuerteventura***, Gomera***, Gran Canaria***, La Palma***, Lanzarote***, Tenerife***.
CAPE VERDE IS*.
CORSICA Cap Corse*** (summer).
CROATIA Mljet***, Neretva Delta***.
CYPRUS*.
EGYPT Nile Delta* (winter).
FRANCE Camargue*** (summer), Leucate*** (summer).
GIBRALTAR* (passage).
ISRAEL Arava Valley***, Ein Gedi** (winter), Nizzana***.
ITALY Gargano Peninsula** (summer), Monte Conero* (passage), Orbetello Reserve* (summer), Tuscan archipelago*** (summer).
JORDAN Amman NP** (winter), Azraq* (winter), Wadi Rum** (passage).
MADEIRA*.

MALTA*.
MOROCCO Agadir and the Sous Plain*** (passage, winter), Boumalne***, Goulimime to Tan-Tan***, Oued Massa***, Oukaimeden***, Tafilalt***.
PORTUGAL Baixo Alentejo*** (summer), Cape St Vincent*** (summer), Castro Marim*** (summer), International Douro*** (summer), International Tagus*** (summer), Ria Formosa*** (summer).
SARDINIA Monte Arcuso***, San Pietro I***.
SICILY San Vito Peninsula***, Strait of Messina***, Vendicari***.
SPAIN Aiguamolls de L'Empordá*** (summer), Cabo de Gata***, Cáceres-Trujillo Steppes*** (summer), Coto Doñana***, Ebro Delta*** (summer), Garraf Massif*** (summer), La Serena** (summer), Monfragüe*** (summer), Santa Pola** (summer), Sierra de Gredos*** (summer), Zaragoza Steppes*** (summer).
SYRIA Wadi al-Qarn-Burqush**.
TUNISIA Chott el Djerid***, Kelbia Lake* (winter).

Ménétries's Warbler
Sylvia mystacea   SH (M) Mig

Range: Breeds from the Lower Volga S to Transcaucasia, in E Turkey and at scattered sites in Syria and perhaps Lebanon. A summer visitor, wintering in Arabia and E Africa, arrives in breeding areas in early Apr–May and departs in Sep. Passage birds recorded in Israel and Egypt.

Subspecies: Nominate *mystacea* occurs from Volga River to Transcaucasia and NE Turkey, *rubescens* in SE Turkey and the Middle East to Iraq and *turcmenica* further E.

Tips: Found in scrub, especially tamarisk, saxaul and acacia, in gardens, palm groves and hedgerows, often on hillsides and in mountains, along river valleys and ravines. Very active but skulking, and keeps to cover apart from occasional spells feeding on the ground and during breeding when males sing from atop bushes.

Sites:

ARMENIA Armash Fishponds*** (summer), Lake Sevan** (summer).

ISRAEL Arava Valley* (spring).
LEBANON Aamiq Marshes* (summer).

RUSSIA Kalmykia*** (summer), Volga Delta*** (summer).
SYRIA Baath Lake*** (summer), Bahrat Homs*** (summer), Dayr al-Zawr*** (summer),
Tadmur and Sabkhat Muh*** (summer), Wadi al-Qarn-Burqush** (summer).
TURKEY Birecik-Halfeti*** (summer), Yeşilce** (summer).

Subalpine Warbler
Sylvia cantillans   SH (DF) Mig

Range: Breeds from Iberia (except the Atlantic and Biscay coasts) through S France to Italy, including Mallorca, Corsica, Sardinia and Sicily. Further E breeds in the E Adriatic, from Slovenia to the S Balkans, in Greece and on many Greek islands, and in W Turkey. Also in NW Africa from S Morocco to N Tunisia. Winters on the southern edge of the Sahara, departing breeding range in late Jul–Sep and returning in Mar–Apr.

Subspecies: Nominate *cantillans* is found in SW Europe from Iberia to Italy, *moltonii* on the W Mediterranean islands, *inornata* in NW Africa and *albistriata* in SE Europe. This race has recently been recorded as a vagrant on Menorca and vagrant *moltonii* in Belgium.

Tips: Typically found in maquis, garrigue and open oak woodland on dry, sunny hillsides. Sometimes found in hedgerows and riverine scrub, and occasionally in gardens on passage. Generally common and easily seen over much of range, particularly during the breeding season when males sing from exposed perches.

Sites:
ALBANIA Lake Shkodra*** (summer).
ANDORRA* (summer).
BALEARIC IS Mallorca** (summer, passage).
BOSNIA-HERZEGOVINA Hutovo blato** (summer).
BULGARIA Studen Kladenetz*** (summer), Tissata NR*** (summer).
CANARY IS Fuerteventura** (passage), Lanzarote** (passage).
CORSICA Biguglia Lake*** (summer), Cap Corse** (summer, passage), Scandola*** (summer).
CROATIA Cres*** (summer), Mljet*** (summer), Neretva Delta*** (summer), Paklenica NP*** (summer).
CYPRUS* (passage).
EGYPT Suez area** (passage).
FRANCE Camargue*** (summer), Cévennes NP*** (summer), Gruissan*** (summer), Les Alpilles*** (summer), Leucate*** (summer), Ouessant* (passage), Prats-de-Mollo*** (summer).
GIBRALTAR* (passage).
GREECE Akarnanika Mts*** (summer), Dadiá-Soufli Forest*** (summer), Delphi*** (summer), Lake Kerkini*** (summer), Mikrí Prespa NP*** (summer), Mt Olympus NP*** (summer), Mt Parnassós NP*** (summer), Nestos Delta*** (summer), Porto Lagos area*** (summer), Vikos-Aoos NP*** (summer).
GREEK IS Corfu*** (summer), Crete*** (summer, passage), Kos*** (summer, passage), Lesvos*** (summer, passage), Náxos*** (summer), Rhodes*** (summer, passage).
ISRAEL Arava Valley** (passage), Eilat** (passage).
ITALY Circeo NP*** (summer), Gargano Peninsula*** (summer, passage), Monte

Conero*** (summer, passage), Orbetello Reserve*** (summer), Po Delta*** (summer), Tuscan archipelago*** (summer).
JORDAN Aqaba* (spring), Azraq* (spring), Petra* (spring), Wadi Dana-Fidan* (spring), Wadi Rum* (spring).
MACEDONIA Babuna Gorge*** (summer), Galicica NP*** (summer), Lakes Ohrid and Prespa*** (summer).
MALTA* (passage).
MOROCCO Agadir and the Sous Plain*** (passage), Dayet Aaoua*** (summer), Merja Zerga*** (passage), Oued Massa*** (passage), Oualidia*** (passage), Oukaimeden*** (summer), Tafilalt*** (passage, winter), Zaër*** (summer), Zeida** (passage).
PORTUGAL Baixo Alentejo*** (summer), International Douro*** (summer), International Tagus*** (summer), Montesinho*** (summer), Peneda Gêres NP*** (summer), Ria

Formosa*** (summer), Santo André Lagoon*** (passage), Tagus Estuary*** (summer).
SARDINIA Giara di Gesturi*** (summer), Monte Arcuso*** (summer), San Pietro I*** (summer). **SICILY** San Vito Peninsula*** (summer), Strait of Messina*** (summer).
SPAIN Aiguamolls de L'Empordá*** (summer), Cabo de Gata*** (summer), Cádiz Lagoons*** (passage), Coto Doñana*** (passage), Garraf Massif*** (summer), Jaca*** (summer), La Serena*** (summer), Llobregat Delta*** (summer), Monfragüe*** (summer), Ordesa NP*** (summer), Picos de Europa*** (summer), Serrania de Ronda*** (summer), Sierra de Gredos*** (summer), Zaragoza Steppes*** (summer).
SWITZERLAND Leuk (passage).
TUNISIA Ain Draham** (summer), Lake Ichkeul*** (summer, passage).
YUGOSLAVIA Lake Skadar*** (summer).

Sardinian Warbler
Sylvia melanocephala

SH DF   Mig PMig

Range: Breeds over much of Iberia (except the N coast and C parts), and widely in S France and Italy, on the Balearics, Corsica, Sardinia, Sicily and Malta. Further E found from Slovenia to Greece, on Crete and many other Greek islands, in parts of Bulgaria and Romania, and in N and W Turkey. Has recently reached W Cyprus and may be expanding range N in France. Also breeds in the Canaries, across NW Africa, in coastal Libya and from Syria to N Israel. More widespread in winter in N Africa, Sinai and S Turkey.

Subspecies: Nominate *melanocephala* is found over much of range, replaced by variable *leucogastra* in the Canaries and *momus* in the Middle East.

Tips: A characteristic and common bird of Mediterranean scrubland, found in maquis and garrigue, open woodland with dense undergrowth and bushy hillsides. Often in vineyards, olive groves, gardens and town parks, but skulking and often difficult to see well other than in brief flights between bushes or when singing from an exposed perch.

Sites:
ALBANIA Lake Shkodra***.
ALGERIA El Kala NP***.
ANDORRA.

BALEARIC IS Formentera***, Ibiza***, Mallorca***, Menorca***.
BOSNIA-HERZEGOVINA Hutovo blato***.

BULGARIA Studen Kladenetz***, Tissata NR***.

CANARY IS El Hierro***, Fuerteventura***, Gomera***, Gran Canaria***, La Palma***, Lanzarote***, Tenerife***.

CORSICA Asco Valley***, Biguglia Lake***, Bonifacio***, Cap Corse***, Scandola***.

CROATIA Cres***, Mljet***, Neretva Delta***, Paklenica NP***.

CYPRUS** (mainly winter).

EGYPT Abu Simbel*** (winter), Aswan*** (passage, winter), Faiyum* (winter), Hurghada*** (winter), Luxor*** (passage, winter), Nile Delta* (winter), Sharm el Sheikh*** (passage, winter).

FRANCE Camargue***, Gruissan***, Les Alpilles***, Leucate***.

GIBRALTAR*.

GREECE Akarnanika Mts***, Amvrakikós Gulf***, Avas Gorge***, Axios-Aliakmonas Deltas***, Dadiá-Soufli Forest***, Delphi***, Evros Delta***, Lake Kerkini***, Mikrí Prespa NP***, Mt Olympus NP***, Mt Parnassós NP***, Nestos Delta***, Porto Lagos area***.

GREEK IS Corfu***, Crete***, Kos***, Lesvos***, Náxos***, Rhodes***.

ISRAEL Arava Valley*** (passage, winter), Bet Shean Valley***, Eilat***, Ein Gedi*** (winter), Golan Heights***, Hula Reserve***, Ma'agan Mikhael***, Nizzana*** (winter).

ITALY Circeo NP***, Gargano Peninsula***, Maremma Regional Park***, Monte Conero***, Orbetello Reserve***, Po Delta***, Tuscan archipelago***.

JORDAN Amman NP***, Aqaba* (passage, winter), Azraq* (passage, winter), Petra***,

Wadi Dana-Fidan***, Wadi Rum***, Wadi as Sir***.

LEBANON Aamiq Marshes***.

MALTA*.

MOROCCO Agadir and the Sous Plain***, Essaouira***, Lac de Sidi Bourhaba***, Merja Zerga***, Ouarzazate***, Oualidia***, Oued Massa***, Oukaimeden***, Tafilalt***, Zaër***.

PORTUGAL Baixo Alentejo***, Boquilobo***, Cape St Vincent***, Castro Marim***, International Douro***, International Tagus***, Montesinho**, Ria Formosa***, Sado Estuary***, Tagus Estuary***.

SARDINIA Cagliari wetlands***, Capo Marargiu***, Giara di Gesturi***, Monte Arcuso***, San Pietro I***.

SICILY San Vito Peninsula***, Strait of Messina***, Vendicari***.

SPAIN Aiguamolls de l'Empordá***, Cabo de Gata***, Cáceres-Trujillo Steppes***, Cádiz Lagoons***, Coto Doñana***, Ebro Delta***, Garraf Massif***, Guadalhorce Estuary***, La Serena***, Llobregat Delta***, Monfragüe***, Picos de Europa***, Santa Pola***, Serrania de Ronda***, Sierra de Gredos***, Tablas de Daimiel***.

SYRIA Aqra Mts***.

TUNISIA Ain Draham***, Cap Bon Peninsula***, Chott el Djerid***, Kelbia Lake***, Lake Ichkeul***, Tunis***, Zaghouan***.

TURKEY Dalyan***, Göksu Delta* (winter), İstanbul***, Kızılırmak Delta***.

YUGOSLAVIA Lake Skadar***.

Cyprus Warbler
Sylvia melanothorax   SH (CF) (SD)   PMig

Range: Endemic breeder to Cyprus, where widespread and common. A partial migrant, with some departing higher areas and moving to the coasts, and others migrating in Sep–Oct, mainly to Egypt. Regular on passage and in winter in Israel but rare in Lebanon. Returns to Cyprus in late Feb–early Mar, with occasional overshoots noted in S Turkey.

Tips: Search dense scrub in coastal plains and mountains; the species is often associated with juniper and myrtle, sometimes undergrowth of open pine woodland and orange plantations. Found in semi-desert areas and wadis in winter. Generally skulking but frequently perches prominently in trees when singing.

Sites:
CYPRUS***.
ISRAEL Arava Valley*** (passage, winter), Eilat** (passage, winter), Ein Gedi*** (winter).

JORDAN Wadi Dana-Fidan* (passage, winter), Wadi Rum* (passage, winter).

Rüppell's Warbler
Sylvia rueppellii   SH (DF)   Mig

Range: Endemic breeder to the Western Palearctic: in S Greece, Crete, islands in the Aegean, W and S Turkey, NW Syria and N Israel, perhaps Lebanon. Departs breeding areas in late Aug–Sep, wintering in Chad and Sudan, returning late Mar–Apr. Passage noted in Cyprus, throughout the Middle East, Egypt and Libya, also rarely in Italy.

Tips: Look for this locally common species on rocky hillsides and ravines with dense thorn scrub, and sometimes found in undergrowth of open oak woodland, and in gardens. Occurs to 1,600m. Skulking, often less active than its congeners, but perches conspicuously when singing.

Sites:
CYPRUS*** (passage).
EGYPT Abu Simbel** (passage), Aswan*** (passage), Hurghada** (passage), Luxor*** (passage), Suez area*** (passage), Zaranik** (passage).
GREECE Delphi*** (summer), Mt Parnassós NP*** (summer).

GREEK IS Crete*** (summer, passage), Lesvos*** (summer, passage), Náxos*** (summer).
ISRAEL Arava Valley*** (passage), Eilat*** (passage), Ein Gedi*** (passage), Ma'agan Mikhael*** (summer), Mt Hermon*** (summer).
ITALY Gargano Peninsula (passage).

Desert Warbler
Sylvia nana   D SD (FG)   Res Mig (Dis) (Nom)

Range: Breeds in NW Africa in scattered and isolated pockets in E Morocco, Algeria and C and S Tunisia and on the eastern edge of our region, from the Volga Delta E to Kazakhstan. Largely resident in N Africa with only limited dispersal and possibly nomadic during droughts. Asian birds are migratory, departing breeding areas in Sep–Oct to winter in the Middle East and NE Africa, and returning from late Apr.

Subspecies: Two races occur in the region which are considered full species by some authorities; nominate race in Asian part of range and *deserti* in N Africa.

Tips: Inhabits desert areas and steppe, usually with low bushes, sometimes in more heavily vegetated habitats or sand dunes. Skulks but also feeds on the ground in the open and sings from an exposed perch. Often associates with Desert Wheatear in winter.

Sites:
ISRAEL Arava Valley*** (passage, winter), Eilat*** (passage, winter).
JORDAN Wadi Rum (passage), Wadi Dana-Fidan (passage).

MOROCCO Tafilalt***.
RUSSIA Kalmykia*** (summer), Volga Delta*** (summer).
TUNISIA Chott el Djerid***, Tataouine.

Arabian Warbler (Red Sea Warbler)
Sylvia leucomelaena   SD SH   Res (Dis)

Range: Breeds mainly in Arabia and on the Red Sea coast and Horn of Africa. In the Western Palearctic found only in the Arava Valley of Israel and Wadi Araba in Jordan. Believed resident throughout range, although young birds may wander to some extent in winter.

Tips: Search semi-desert areas with thornbush and acacia bushland, wadis, ravines and rocky hillsides. Skulking and remains within dense foliage except when singing from exposed perch during breeding season.

Orphean Warbler
Sylvia hortensis   CF MF DF SH   Mig

Range: Breeds in E and S Portugal, across much of Spain and S France to Italy, also from Slovenia to Greece and Crete, Macedonia and S Bulgaria. Range continues across Turkey, except the interior, to Transcaucasia. In the Middle East breeds in Lebanon, N Israel and W Jordan, and in N Africa in Morocco, N Algeria and Tunisia, and coastal Libya. Winters on the southern edge of the Sahara, in S Arabia and from Iran to India. Departs breeding areas from late Jul, mainly in Aug–Sep, and returns in Apr–May. Passage noted throughout the Middle East and N Africa, with a winter record from Morocco.

Subspecies: Nominate race occurs in W of range as far as Italy and NW Libya, *crassirostris* in SE Europe and from NE Libya to the Middle East. Race *jerdoni* breeds E of the Western Palearctic but may occur in the Middle East on passage. The three forms are sometimes considered two full species.

Tips: Search for this species in open coniferous and deciduous woodland, usually in taller bushes and smaller trees, in lowlands and foothills. Also in orchards and olive groves, gardens and parks, riverine shrubs and roadside avenues. Keeps within dense foliage and usually sings from cover, rarely using an exposed perch.

Sites:

ALBANIA Lake Shkodra*** (summer).
ARMENIA Meghri Area*** (summer),
BULGARIA Rila Mts*** (summer), Studen Kladenetz*** (summer), Tissata NR*** (summer).
CROATIA Cres** (summer), Mljet*** (summer), Paklenica NP*** (summer).
CYPRUS* (passage).
EGYPT Abu Simbel*** (passage), Aswan*** (passage), Hurghada* (passage), Luxor** (passage), Suez area** (passage), Zaranik** (passage).
FRANCE Camargue*** (passage), Leucate** (summer).
GEORGIA Iori Steppes** (summer).
GIBRALTAR* (passage).
GREECE Amvrakikós Gulf*** (summer), Avas Gorge** (summer), Dadiá-Soufli Forest***

(summer), Delphi*** (summer), Evros Delta* (summer), Mikrí Prespa NP*** (summer), Mt Parnassós NP** (summer), Nestos Delta** (summer), Porto Lagos area*** (summer).
GREEK IS Corfu*** (summer), Crete* (passage), Lesvos*** (summer, passage).
ISRAEL Arava Valley*** (passage), Eilat*** (passage), Mt Hermon*** (summer), Nizzana*** (passage).
ITALY Abruzzo NP*** (summer), Sibillini NP*** (summer).
JORDAN Wadi Dana-Fidan** (spring), Wadi Rum* (spring).
LEBANON Barouk Cedars*** (summer), Qaraoun Lake** (passage).
MACEDONIA Babuna Gorge** (summer), Galicica NP*** (summer), Lakes Ohrid and Prespa*** (summer).

MOROCCO Zeida** (summer).
PORTUGAL Baixo Alentejo*** (summer), Castro Marim*** (summer), International Douro*** (summer), International Tagus*** (summer), Montesinho* (summer), Sado Estuary** (summer), Tagus Estuary*** (summer).
SPAIN Aiguamolls de L'Empordá*** (summer), Cabo de Gata** (summer), Cádiz Lagoons** (passage), Coto Doñana** (passage), Ebro Delta** (summer), Garraf Massif*** (summer), Jaca*** (summer), La Serena*** (summer),

Llobregat Delta*** (summer), Monfragüe*** (summer), Serrania de Ronda** (summer), Sierra de Gredos*** (summer), Zaragoza Steppes* (summer).
SWITZERLAND Leuk (summer, passage).
SYRIA Wadi al-Qarn-Burqush** (summer).
TUNISIA Ain Draham** (summer), Cap Bon Peninsula*** (summer, passage), Lake Ichkeul*** (summer).
TURKEY Akseki*** (summer), Birecik-Halfeti** (summer), Dalyan*** (summer), Soğuksu NP** (passage), Yeşilce*** (summer).

Barred Warbler
Sylvia nisoria   MF DF SH FG Mig

Range: Main breeding range is from E Germany, the Czech Republic and E Austria SE to Bulgaria and E to the foothills of the Urals, the Caspian and Caucasus. Also breeds in scattered pockets in S Sweden (mainly coastal areas and the islands of Öland and Gotland), and the S coast of Finland, in S Switzerland and N Italy, throughout the Balkans and Turkey. Rare and irregular breeder in Denmark. Departs breeding areas in Aug–Sep to winter in E Africa, via the E Mediterranean; returns to N of breeding range in mid–late May, earlier in S. Passage noted throughout E and SE Europe and the Middle East, and is a rare but regular autumn migrant as far W as Britain.
Tips: Found in open deciduous and mixed forest and woodland, plantations and shelterbelts, parks and large gardens. Also bushy hillsides and riverine scrub, hedgerows and grassland with scattered taller trees and shrubs. Usually keeps to dense foliage but uses exposed perches as song-posts in the breeding season. Often nests in close proximity to breeding Red-backed Shrikes.

Sites:
ARMENIA Khosrov Preserve*** (summer), Mt Aragats*** (summer).
AUSTRIA Lake Neusiedl*** (summer), Marchauen-Marchegg Reserve*** (summer), Wienerwald*** (summer).
BELARUS Belovezhskaya Pushcha NP*** (summer), Berezinsky Reserve*** (summer), Pripyatsky NP*** (summer).
BELGIUM Het Zwin* (passage).
(autumn), Orkney Is* (autumn), Pembrokeshire

Is* (autumn), Portland* (autumn), Scilly** (autumn), Shetland Is** (autumn), Spurn Peninsula** (autumn).
BULGARIA Albena-Golden Sands*** (summer), Burgas area** (summer), Cape Emine*** (summer, passage), Cape Kaliakra*** (summer, passage), Lake Shabla*** (summer), Lake Srebarna*** (summer), Rusenski Lom NP*** (summer), Strandja Mts*** (summer), Studen Kladenetz*** (summer), Tissata NR*** (summer).

CYPRUS** (passage).

CZECH REPUBLIC Beskydy Mts*** (summer), Lednice*** (summer), Pálava Hills*** (summer), Pohořelice Fishponds*** (summer), Poodří*** (summer), Soutok*** (summer), Třeboňsko*** (summer), Znojmo*** (summer).

DENMARK Amager** (passage), Bornholm-Christiansø*** (passage), Møn-Falster** (passage, summer), Skagen*** (passage), Skallingen-Blåvandshuk** (passage).

EGYPT Hurghada* (passage), Zaranik** (passage).

ESTONIA Matsalu Bay*** (summer), Vilsandi NP*** (summer).

FINLAND Åland Is** (summer).

FRANCE Ouessant** (autumn).

GERMANY Heligoland*** (passage), Mecklenburg Lakes*** (summer), Oder Valley*** (summer), Rügen*** (summer).

GREAT BRITAIN Flamborough Head** (autumn), Minsmere* (autumn), N Norfolk coast**.

GREECE Dadiá-Soufli Forest*** (summer), Evros Delta* (summer), Mikrí Prespa NP*** (summer).

GREEK IS Lesvos** (passage).

HUNGARY Aggtelek NP*** (summer), Bükk Hills NP*** (summer), Buda Hills*** (summer), Csákvár*** (summer), Danube Bend*** (summer), Hanság*** (summer), Hortobágy NP*** (summer), Kis-balaton*** (summer), Lake Fertö*** (summer), Lake Velence*** (summer), Ócsa*** (summer), Pilis Hills*** (summer), Zemplén Hills*** (summer).

ISRAEL Arava Valley** (passage), Eilat* (passage).

JORDAN Azraq* (passage), Wadi Rum* (passage).

LATVIA Lake Lubana*** (summer).

LEBANON Aamiq Marshes** (passage), Qaraoun Lake* (passage).

LITHUANIA Kirsiu Peninsula** (passage).

MACEDONIA Galicica NP*** (summer), Lakes Ohrid and Prespa*** (summer).

NORWAY Lista*** (passage), Mølen*** (summer, passage), Utsira* (passage).

POLAND Białowieża Forest*** (summer), Biebrza Marshes*** (summer), Bieszczady NP*** (summer), Chełm Marshes*** (summer), Gdańsk Bay*** (summer), Kampinos NP*** (summer), Milicz Fishponds*** (summer), Siemianówka Reservoir*** (summer), Słońsk*** (summer).

ROMANIA Dobrudja*** (summer), Lake Călăraşi*** (summer), Turda Gorge*** (summer).

SLOVAKIA Malé Karpaty*** (summer), Nízke Tatry NP*** (summer), Slanské Hills*** (summer), Slovenský Kras*** (summer), Vihorlatske Hills*** (summer), Záhorie*** (summer).

SLOVENIA Ljubljansko Moor*** (summer).

SWEDEN Falsterbo* (passage), Gotland** (summer, passage), Leuk* (summer), Kristianstad (passage), Öland*** (summer, passage).

TURKEY Dalyan* (passage), Soğuksu NP* (summer), Yeşilce** (summer).

UKRAINE Crimean Mts*** (summer), Dunay Delta** (summer).

YUGOSLAVIA Fruška Gora NP** (summer).

Greenish Warbler
Phylloscopus trochiloides   CF MF DF (SH) Mig

Range: Mainly breeds in S Finland, the Baltic states, Belarus and N Ukraine across Russia to the Urals. Isolated populations exist in NE Germany, N Poland and on the Swedish island of Gotland. Range expanded W in the second half of the 20th century but numbers fluctuate at edges of range. Regular visitor and rare breeder in mainland Sweden and first bred in Norway and the Czech Republic in the 1990s. Has bred on Heligoland (Germany) and attempted to do so in Denmark, and may also breed in S Poland. Winters in India and SE Asia, departing breeding areas in Aug and returning in mid–late May.

Tips: Inhabits coniferous, mixed and deciduous woods, often with aspen and birch and sometimes near streams. On passage and as a vagrant recorded in any habitat with bushes and trees. Often feeds in upper branches, very active and can be difficult to see well.

Sites:
BELARUS Belovezhskaya Pushcha NP* (summer), Berezinsky Reserve** (summer).
CZECH REPUBLIC Krkonoše NP* (summer).
DENMARK Bornholm-Christiansø*** (summer, passage), Møn-Falster** (passage), Skallingen-Blåvandshuk* (passage).
ESTONIA Taevaskoja*** (summer).
FINLAND Åland Is** (summer), Kolvanan Uuro*** (summer), Kuusamo*** (summer), Liminganlahti*** (summer), Linnansaari NP*** (summer), Oulanka NP*** (summer), Patvinsuo NP*** (summer).

FRANCE Ouessant* (autumn).
GREAT BRITAIN N Norfolk coast* (autumn), Shetland Is* (autumn), Spurn Peninsula* (autumn). **LATVIA** Cape Kolka*** (summer, passage). **LITHUANIA** Cepkeliai NR** (summer). **POLAND** Białowieża Forest** (summer), Biebrza Marshes* (summer), Gdańsk Bay** (passage).
SWEDEN Falsterbo* (passage), Gotland** (summer, passage), Holmöarna** (summer, passage), Öland** (passage), Tåkern* (summer).

Green Warbler
Phylloscopus nitidus   CF MF DF Mig

Range: Often considered a race of Greenish Warbler, this form breeds in the Caucasus and Transcaucasia, reaching W to N Turkey, and winters in S India and Sri Lanka. Departs breeding range in Aug–early Oct and returns in early May.

Tips: Found in montane deciduous, coniferous and mixed forests with dense undergrowth, bushes and trees, up to the treeline, often in juniper scrub. In parts of range also occurs in lowland forests. Very active and usually feeds in the canopy.

ARMENIA Arapan Area*** (summer), Lake
Sevan** (passage).
GEORGIA Mt Kazbek*** (summer).

RUSSIA Teberdinskiy Reserve*** (summer).
TURKEY Borçka*** (summer), Sivrikaya***
(summer), Sumela*** (summer).

Arctic Warbler
Phylloscopus borealis　　　　　　　　　　CF MF　Mig

Range: In our region breeds in N Scandinavia and the Kola Peninsula, and from SE Finland across N Russia to the Urals. Rare or scarce in Scandinavia but common in Russia. Winters in SE Asia and departs breeding range in Aug–early Sep, returning mid Jun.

Tips: Coniferous and mixed forests, birch woodland, willows and poplar, often in damp areas and along rivers. Passage birds occur in a wide range of habitats with trees and bushes. Generally stays in upper branches and often perches on walls and fences on passage.

Sites:

FINLAND Kevo NR*** (summer), Kilpisjärvi Saana*** (summer), Kuusamo*** (summer, passage), Lake Inari*** (summer), Lemmenjoki NP** (summer), Oulanka NP** (summer), Pallas-Ounastunturi NP* (summer), Urho Kekkonen NP*** (summer).
GREAT BRITAIN Shetland Is* (autumn).

NORWAY Øvre Pasvik NP* (summer), Varanger* (summer).
RUSSIA Kola Peninsula*** (summer).
SWEDEN Abisko NP* (summer), Padjelanta NP* (summer), Sarek NP* (summer), Tärnasjön* (summer).

Pallas' Leaf Warbler
Phylloscopus proregulus　　　　　　　　CF MF DF　Mig

Range: Breeds from C Siberia to the Himalayas and E to the Pacific, and departs breeding range in late Aug–Sep to winter in S China and SE Asia, returning in late May–Jun. Occurs in our region as a scarce migrant to NW Europe, recorded annually in Great Britain and Scandinavia. More than 50 are recorded in Great Britain most years and over 150 in some, almost all in mid Oct–early Nov, and mostly on Shetland, the E and S coasts, and Scilly.

Tips: Breeds in coniferous forest with dense undergrowth, at edges, in clearings and meadows within coniferous or mixed forests. Passage noted in a range of habitats with trees and bushes, and in Great Britain often seen feeding high in sycamores with other passerine migrants including tits and Goldcrests.

Sites:
DENMARK Bornholm-Christiansø** (autumn).
FINLAND Åland Is* (autumn).
FRANCE Ouessant** (autumn).
GREAT BRITAIN Dungeness (autumn), Flamborough Head* (autumn), N Norfolk coast* (autumn), Portland* (autumn), Scilly**

(autumn), Shetland Is* (autumn), Spurn Peninsula* (autumn).
NETHERLANDS Texel (autumn).
NORWAY Utsira* (autumn).
SWEDEN Falsterbo* (autumn), Gotland** (autumn), Holmöarna** (autumn), Öland*** (autumn).

Yellow-browed Warbler
Phylloscopus inornatus   MF (CF) DF)   Mig

Range: Breeds from the Urals to the Pacific and S to the Himalayas. An uncommon breeder in the extreme NE of the Western Palearctic in the N Urals. Winters from E Arabia to India and SE Asia. Departs breeding areas in Aug–Sep, returning in May. Elsewhere in our region is a scarce passage migrant in NW Europe, being most regular in Great Britain with more than 300 records most years, the majority on Shetland, the E and S coasts, and Scilly. Also regular in Scandinavia, France, the Netherlands and elsewhere.

Tips: Sometimes found in coniferous forest but generally prefers birch, willow and poplar in areas of mixed woodland. Often associates with tits, 'crests' and other *Phylloscopus* on passage, and in Great Britain frequently feeds in sycamores. Best located by distinctive call.

Sites:
DENMARK Bornholm-Christiansø** (autumn).
FINLAND Åland Is* (autumn).
FRANCE Cap Gris Nez* (passage), Ouessant** (autumn).
GERMANY Heligoland** (autumn).
GREAT BRITAIN Dungeness (autumn), Flamborough Head** (autumn), N Norfolk coast** (autumn), Orkney Is** (autumn), Portland* (autumn), Scilly*** (autumn),

Shetland Is* (autumn), Spurn Peninsula** (autumn).
ISRAEL Arava Valley (autumn).
NETHERLANDS Oostvaardersplassen (autumn), Terschelling* (autumn), Texel (autumn).
NORWAY Utsira* (autumn).
SWEDEN Falsterbo* (autumn), Gotland** (autumn), Holmöarna** (autumn), Öland*** (autumn).

Western Bonelli's Warbler
Phylloscopus bonelli   DF Mig

Range: Formerly considered conspecific with Eastern Bonelli's Warbler, this form breeds over much of Iberia (except the SE), and from W and C France E to Austria and Slovenia, including Corsica and the Apennines of Italy, and possibly the Krkonoše Mts of the Czech Republic. Also breeds in NW Africa from the Sous Valley in Morocco to NW Tunisia. Departs breeding grounds in Aug–Oct to winter in W Africa and returns in Apr–early May.

Tips: Search open deciduous woodland with sparse undergrowth, generally prefers oak, sometimes beech or birch. Usually on hillsides and slopes, often in montane areas, particularly in S. Keeps to the canopy and best located by slow trilling song.

Sites:

ALGERIA Djebel Babor*** (summer), El Kala NP*** (summer).

ANDORRA*** (summer).

AUSTRIA Hohe Tauern NP*** (summer), Hohe Wand** (summer), Karwendel Reserve*** (summer), Lake Neusiedl** (summer), Schneeberg Mts*** (summer).

BALEARIC IS Mallorca*** (passage).

CANARY IS* (passage).

CZECH REPUBLIC Krkonoše Mts (summer).

FRANCE Baie de Bourgneuf*** (summer), Cévennes NP*** (summer), Écrins NP*** (summer), Fontainebleau** (summer), Île d'Oléron*** (summer), Leucate** (summer), Prats-de-Mollo*** (summer), Pyrenees NP*** (summer), Queyras NP*** (summer), Vanoise NP*** (summer).

GERMANY Ammer Valley*** (summer), Berchtesgaden NP*** (summer).

GIBRALTAR*** (passage).

ITALY Abruzzo NP*** (summer), Gran Paradiso NP*** (summer), Stelvio NP*** (summer), Sibillini NP*** (summer).

MALTA* (passage, mainly spring).

MOROCCO Boumalne** (passage), Dayet Aaoua*** (summer), Zaër*** (summer).

PORTUGAL Cape St Vincent*** (passage), International Douro*** (summer), Montesinho*** (summer), Peneda Gêres NP*** (summer), Ria Formosa* (passage), Sado Estuary*** (summer), Santo André Lagoon*** (passage), Tagus Estuary** (passage).

SARDINIA San Pietro I** (passage).

SICILY Strait of Messina** (passage).

SPAIN Aigües Tortes NP*** (summer), Coto Doñana*** (passage), Garraf Massif*** (summer), Jaca*** (summer), Llobregat Delta*** (summer, passage), Monfragüe*** (summer), Ordesa NP*** (summer), Picos de Europa*** (summer), Serrania de Ronda*** (summer), Sierra de Gredos*** (summer), Sierra de Guadarrama*** (summer), Tablas de Daimiel*** (summer).

SWITZERLAND Clos-du-Doubs*** (summer), Col de Bretolet*** (summer), Fanel NR*** (summer), Flims*** (summer), Leuk*** (summer), Monte Generoso*** (summer), Swiss NP*** (summer).

TUNISIA Ain Draham*** (summer).

Eastern Bonelli's Warbler
Phylloscopus orientalis   DF MF Mig

Range: Breeds in the S Balkans from Bosnia–Herzegovina, Macedonia and C and S Bulgaria to N Greece, W Turkey and also extreme SE Turkey. May breed in Lebanon and a rare breeder in N Israel. Has bred in Romania and Jordan. Winters in Sudan but true extent of winter range unknown. Present on breeding grounds Apr–Oct and occurs on passage in Cyprus, Turkey, the Middle East and Egypt.

Tips: Look for this species in open deciduous, mixed or coniferous woodland and scrub in dry mountain areas.

Sites:

BULGARIA Rila Mts*** (summer), Strandja Mts** (summer), Trigradski Gorge*** (summer).
CYPRUS** (passage).
EGYPT Abu Simbel** (passage), Aswan** (passage), Luxor* (passage), Suez area** (passage), Zaranik** (passage).
GREECE Amvrakikós Gulf*** (summer, passage), Avas Gorge*** (summer), Dadiá-Soufli Forest*** (summer), Evros Delta* (summer), Mikrí Prespa NP*** (summer), Porto Lagos area*** (summer).

GREEK IS Corfu** (passage), Kos*** (passage), Lesvos*** (summer, passage).
ISRAEL Arava Valley*** (passage), Eilat*** (passage), Ein Gedi*** (summer).
JORDAN Aqaba** (passage), Azraq* (passage), Wadi Rum** (passage).
MACEDONIA Galicica NP*** (summer), Lakes Ohrid and Prespa*** (summer).
MALTA* (passage, mainly spring).
TURKEY Akseki*** (summer), İstanbul*** (passage), Soğuksu NP*** (summer).
YUGOSLAVIA Obedska bara** (summer).

Caucasian Chiffchaff
Phylloscopus lorenzii   CF MF DF SH   AMig PMig

Range: Breeds throughout the Greater and Lesser Caucasus, and in NE Turkey, but exact range little known due to confusion with Common Chiffchaff. An altitudinal or short-distance migrant departing northern breeding areas in Sep and returning in late Apr–May. Winter range is poorly known, thought to be mainly in the Tigris and Euphrates valleys of Iraq and adjacent Turkey, Syria and Iran. This form is sometimes regarded as a race of **Mountain Chiffchaff** *P. sindianus* or as a race of **Common Chiffchaff** *P. collybita*.

Tips: Breeds in montane forest, often willows and poplars, at the treeline and in alpine and subalpine meadows, and rhododendron thickets, often along streams. In winter moves to lower, south-facing slopes but probably completely vacates higher areas. Area of overlap with range of Common Chiffchaff is poorly known but the two certainly occur in close proximity in Armenia and probably elsewhere. In Armenia Caucasian Chiffchaff invariably occurs at higher altitudes and generally prefers lighter woodland or scrub with Common Chiffchaff usually found in more mature deciduous woodland or forest.

Sites:
ARMENIA Arapan Area*** (summer), Khosrov Preserve*** (summer), Lake Sevan*** (summer, passage), Mt Aragats*** (summer), Pambak Mts*** (summer).
AZERBAIJAN Zakataly*** (summer).

GEORGIA Mt Kazbek*** (summer).
RUSSIA Teberdinskiy Reserve*** (summer).
TURKEY Borçka*** (summer), Sivrikaya*** (summer).

Canary Islands Chiffchaff
Phylloscopus canariensis   CF MF   Res

Range: Recently split from Common Chiffchff, this species is endemic to the western Canaries and found on El Hierro, La Palma, Gomera, Tenerife and Gran Canaria, and possibly Lanzarote and Fuerteventura but may have been extinct on these islands since the 1940s.
Subspecies: Extant race is *canariensis*, that from the eastern islands is *exsul* but this race may now be extinct.
Tips: Montane and hill forest including Canarian Pine and Laurel.

Sites:
CANARY IS El Hierro***, Gomera***, Gran Canaria***, La Palma***, Tenerife***.

Iberian Chiffchaff
Phylloscopus ibericus   DF MF   PMig

Range: Until recently this form was considered to be a race of Common Chiffchaff. Breeds in extreme SW France, N and C Spain, in a few scattered upland areas of S Spain and over most of Portugal. Also in coastal N Morocco, N Algeria and N Tunisia. A partial migrant, but extent of winter range in tropical Africa unclear due to difficulties of identification. Passage noted on the Canaries and in N Africa, in Morocco and Algeria.
Subspecies: Recently split into nominate race in the N and *biscayensis* in the S.
Tips: Woodlands and forest, mainly deciduous, and often found in upland areas. Best identified by distinctive song.

Sites:

ALGERIA Djebel Babor***.
CANARY IS Lanzarote* (passage).
GIBRALTAR* (passage).
PORTUGAL Montesinho***, Peneda Gêres
NP***, Ria Formosa***, Sado Estuary***, Santo
André Lagoon***, Tagus Estuary***.
SPAIN Aigües Tortes NP*** (summer), Cabo de
Gata***, Garraf Massif***, Llobregat Delta***,

Monfragüe***, Picos de Europa*** (summer),
Santa Pola*** (passage, winter), Serrania de
Ronda***, Sierra de Gredos*** (summer),
Sierra de Guadarrama*** (summer), Tablas de
Daimiel***.
TUNISIA Ain Draham***.

Canary Islands Kinglet (Tenerife Goldcrest)
Regulus teneriffae   CF MF   Res

Range: Endemic to the Canaries, where widespread and common in forests on La Palma, Hierro, Gomera and Tenerife. Perhaps a short-distance altitudinal migrant, but mainly resident. Formerly considered a race of either Goldcrest *R. regulus* or Firecrest *R. ignicapillus*.
Tips: Montane and hill forest including Canarian Pine and Laurel.

Sites:
CANARY IS El Hierro***, Gomera***, La
Palma***, Tenerife***.

Red-breasted Flycatcher
Ficedula parva   CF DF MF (SH)   Mig

Range: Main breeding range is from E Germany, the Czech Republic and E Austria N to S Finland and E to the Urals. Isolated pockets occur in S Sweden, W Germany, the Balkans, N Turkey and the Caucasus. Most move SE to winter in India and SE Asia, and passage is common through SE Europe, Turkey and Cyprus with small numbers regularly recorded in the Middle East and Egypt. Departs breeding areas Aug to mid Sep, returning late Apr–early Jun. Small numbers regularly seen far to the W of main passage, e.g. in Great Britain over 100 occur in some years, mainly in Sep–Oct, with most on Shetland, the E coast and Scilly.
Tips: Found in mature deciduous and mixed forests, up to 2,000m in the Caucasus. In mountains and N of range also in coniferous forest. Usually near forest edges and clearings, wooded riverbanks, on passage also in orchards, parks and large gardens. Active and often keeps high in trees.

Sites:

ARMENIA Arapan Area*** (passage).

AUSTRIA Lake Neusiedl* (summer), Wienerwald*** (summer).

BELARUS Belovezhskaya Pushcha NP*** (summer), Berezinsky Reserve*** (summer), Pripyatsky NP*** (summer).

BULGARIA Albena-Golden Sands** (passage), Cape Kaliakra*** (passage), Lake Durankulak*** (passage), Lake Shabla*** (passage), Strandja Mts*** (passage), Tzarichina NR*** (summer).

CZECH REPUBLIC Beskydy Mts*** (summer), Jeseníky Mts** (summer), Krkonoše NP*** (summer), Šumava NP*** (summer), Třeboňsko*** (summer).

DENMARK Amager* (passage), Bornholm-Christiansø*** (passage), Møn-Falster** (passage), Skagen*** (passage), Skallingen-Blåvandshuk** (passage).

EGYPT Hurghada* (passage), Santa Katharina Monastery* (passage), Sharm el Sheikh* (passage), Suez area* (passage), Zaranik* (passage).

ESTONIA Lake Endla***, (summer), Matsalu Bay*** (summer), Nigula NR*** (summer), Taevaskoja*** (summer).

FINLAND Åland Is*** (summer), Kolvanan Uuro*** (summer), Patvinsuo NP*** (summer), Vesijako NP*** (summer).

FRANCE Cap Gris Nez* (autumn), Ouessant** (autumn).

GERMANY Ammer Valley*** (summer), Bayerischer Wald NP** (summer), Berchtesgaden NP*** (summer), Heligoland*** (passage), Mecklenburg Lakes*** (summer), Rügen*** (summer), Vessertal*** (summer).

GREAT BRITAIN Dungeness* (autumn), Flamborough Head** (autumn), N Norfolk coast** (autumn), Orkney Is** (autumn), Pembrokeshire Is* (autumn), Portland* (autumn), Scilly** (autumn), Shetland Is** (autumn), Spurn Peninsula** (autumn).

GREECE Amvrakikós Gulf** (passage).

GREEK IS Lesvos** (passage).

HUNGARY Aggtelek NP*** (summer), Börzsöny NP*** (summer), Bükk Hills NP** (summer), Csákvár*** (summer), Kis-balaton** (summer), Pilis Hills** (summer), Zemplén Hills*** (summer).

ISRAEL Arava Valley* (autumn).

JORDAN Azraq (passage).

LATVIA Cape Kolka*** (summer), Lake Engure*** (summer), Lake Pape*** (summer).

LITHUANIA Kirsiu Peninsula*** (passage).

MALTA (autumn).

NORWAY Utsira* (passage).

POLAND Białowieża Forest*** (summer), Biebrza Marshes*** (summer), Bieszczady NP*** (summer), Chełm Marshes*** (summer), Gdańsk Bay*** (summer), Kampinos NP*** (summer), Milicz Fishponds*** (summer), Szczecin Bay area** (summer), Tatra NP*** (summer).

ROMANIA Bicaz*** (summer), Danube Delta*** (summer), Dobrudja*** (summer, passage), Gurghiu Mts*** (summer), Poiana Brașov*** (summer), Retezat NP*** (summer), Turda Gorge*** (summer).

RUSSIA Teberdinskiy Reserve*** (summer).

SLOVAKIA High Tatras NP** (summer), Malá Fatra** (summer), Malé Karpaty*** (summer), Nízke Tatry NP*** (summer), Slanské Hills*** (summer), Slovenský Kras*** (summer), Vihorlatske Hills*** (summer).

SWEDEN Falsterbo* (summer, passage), Färnebofjärden* (summer), Gotland** (summer, passage), Holmöarna*** (passage), Kristianstad* (summer), Öland** (summer, passage), Tåkern*** (summer).

TURKEY İstanbul*** (passage), Kızılırmak Delta** (summer), Sumela*** (summer).

UKRAINE Carpathians*** (summer), Dunay Delta** (passage), Tiligul Liman*** (passage).

Semi-collared Flycatcher
Ficedula semitorquata

DF MF Mig

Range: Main breeding range is in the Caucasus and N Turkey but also breeds in Albania, N Greece and S Bulgaria. Winters in E Africa and passage noted in Cyprus, the Middle East and Egypt. Departs breeding areas in Aug–Sep and return passage through the Mediterranean and Middle East occurs in late Mar–early May.

Tips: Found in deciduous woodland, especially oak and beech, often on hillsides, also in orchards and plantations, valleys and gorges, and sometimes in spruce forest in the Caucasus.

Sites:

ARMENIA Pambak Mts*** (summer).
BULGARIA Albena-Golden Sands*** (summer, passage), Cape Kaliakras** (passage), Lake Shabla** (passage), Ropotamo NP*** (summer), Strandja Mts*** (summer), Studen Kladenetz*** (passage), Trigradski Gorge*** (passage), Tissata NR*** (passage), Tzarichina NR** (summer).
CYPRUS* (passage).
GEORGIA Iori Steppes** (summer), Mt Kazbek*** (summer).
GREECE Amvrakikós Gulf*** (summer, passage), Dadiá-Soufli Forest*** (summer), Mikrí Prespa NP*** (summer), Mt Olympus NP*** (summer), Porto Lagos area*** (summer).

GREEK IS Corfu*** (passage), Lesvos** (passage).
ISRAEL Arava Valley*** (passage), Eilat*** (passage), Ein Gedi*** (passage).
JORDAN Azraq* (spring), Petra (spring), Wadi Rum* (spring).
LEBANON Aamiq Marshes*** (passage).
MACEDONIA Galicica NP*** (summer), Lakes Ohrid and Prespa*** (summer), Mavrovo NP** (summer).
RUSSIA Teberdinskiy Reserve*** (summer).
TURKEY Sivrikaya*** (summer), İstanbul*** (summer), Soğuksu NP*** (passage), Yeşilce*** (passage).
UKRAINE Crimean Mts** (summer).

Collared Flycatcher
Ficedula albicollis

DF MF (SH) Mig

Range: Main breeding range is from S Poland, the Czech Republic, Slovakia and Hungary N to Lithuania and E to C European Russia. Elsewhere, isolated pockets occur in E France, S Germany, S Switzerland, S Italy, the Balkans and, far from main range, on the Swedish islands of Gotland and Öland. A summer visitor arriving in late Apr–early May and departing for E African wintering grounds in Aug–Sep. Passage noted throughout SC and SE Europe, Turkey, the Middle East and Egypt.

Tips: Occurs in deciduous woodland, particularly mature oaks, and at edges or rides and in clearings. Sometimes found in pine woodland, orchards and parks.

Sites:

AUSTRIA Lake Neusiedl*** (summer), Marchauen-Marchegg Reserve*** (summer), Wienerwald*** (summer).

BELARUS Belovezhskaya Pushcha NP*** (summer), Pripyatsky NP*** (summer), Pripyatsky NP*** (summer).

BOSNIA-HERZEGOVINA Sutjeska NP*** (summer).

BULGARIA Albena-Golden Sands** (passage), Cape Kaliakra*** (passage), Lake Durankulak*** (passage), Lake Shabla** (passage), Trigradski Gorge*** (passage).

CROATIA Pokupsko Depression*** (summer).

CYPRUS* (passage).

CZECH REPUBLIC Beskydy Mts*** (summer), Lednice*** (summer), Pálava Hills*** (summer), Pohořelice Fishponds*** (summer), Poodří*** (summer), Soutok*** (summer), Třeboňsko*** (summer).

FRANCE Lorraine NP*** (summer).

GERMANY Schweinfurt*** (summer).

GREECE Amvrakikós Gulf*** (passage), Axios-Aliakmonas Deltas** (passage), Evros Delta* (passage), Nestos Delta** (passage).

GREEK IS Corfu*** (passage), Crete*** (passage, mainly spring), Kos*** (passage), Lesvos*** (passage), Náxos*** (passage), Rhodes*** (passage).

HUNGARY Aggtelek NP*** (summer), Börzsöny NP*** (summer), Buda Hills*** (summer), Bükk Hills NP*** (summer), Csákvár*** (summer), Danube Bend*** (summer), Kis-balaton*** (summer), Lake Fertö*** (summer), Lake Velence*** (summer), Pilis Hills*** (summer), Zemplén Hills*** (summer).

ISRAEL Arava Valley*** (passage), Eilat*** (passage), Urim*** (passage).

ITALY Abruzzo NP*** (summer), Circeo NP** (passage), Monte Conero* (passage), Po Delta*** (passage).

JORDAN Azraq** (passage), Petra (passage).

LEBANON Qaraoun Lake** (passage).

MALTA* (passage).

POLAND Białowieża Forest*** (summer), Biebrza Marshes* (passage), Bieszczady NP*** (summer), Kampinos NP*** (summer).

ROMANIA Danube Delta*** (summer), Dobrudja*** (passage), Gurghiu Mts*** (summer), Retezat NP*** (summer), Turda Gorge*** (summer).

SARDINIA San Pietro I* (passage).

SICILY Strait of Messina** (passage), Vendicari*** (passage).

SLOVAKIA High Tatras NP*** (summer), Malá Fatra*** (summer), Malé Karpaty*** (summer), Nízke Tatry NP*** (summer), Slanské Hills*** (summer), Slovenský Kras*** (summer), Vihorlatske Hills*** (summer), Záhorie*** (summer).

SLOVENIA Kocevje** (summer), Krakovski Forest*** (summer).

SWEDEN Gotland*** (summer), Öland*** (summer, passage).

SYRIA Dayr al-Zawr** (passage).

TUNISIA Cap Bon Peninsula* (passage).

TURKEY Dalyan*** (passage), İstanbul** (passage), Kocaçay Delta*** (passage), Soğuksu NP*** (passage), Yeşilce*** (passage).

UKRAINE Carpathians*** (summer), Dunay Delta*** (passage), Tiligul Liman*** (passage).

YUGOSLAVIA Fruška Gora NP** (summer), Obedska bara** (summer).

Atlas Flycatcher
Ficedula speculigera

DF MF   Mig

Range: Recently split from Pied Flycatcher and confined to NW Africa, breeding in the mountains of C Morocco, N Algeria and extreme NE Tunisia but generally scarce throughout range. Arrives on breeding grounds in late Apr.

Tips: Usually occurs at 1,200–1,800m in oak and cedar forest, and in Aleppo Pine woodland. Fairly easy to see in Morocco.

Sites:
ALGERIA Djebel Babor*** (summer).
MOROCCO Dayet Aaoua*** (summer),
Oukaimeden** (summer), Zaër** (summer).
TUNISIA Ain Draham* (summer).

Bearded Tit
Panurus biarmicus

FW   Res (Irr)

Range: Very patchy range in our region, breeding in widely scattered localities in E and S Britain, at coastal sites from W France to Denmark, more widespread in Germany, including some inland areas and E to Poland and the Baltic states. Further S breeds in parts of C Spain and the Mediterranean coasts of Spain and France, and the N Adriatic coast of Italy. More common and widespread in the E, in Hungary and Romania, parts of Greece and C Turkey, and in the Volga Delta. Most populations are basically sedentary but undergo irruptive movements with birds dispersing to other reedbeds. Some return in spring to their natal sites but others form the basis of a new colony. Winter range similar to but more extensive than breeding range.

Subspecies: Nominate *biarmicus* is found over most of Europe with very similar *russicus* from Austria to S Russia and Turkey and *kosswigi* isolated in S Turkey.

Tips: Main habitat is large reedbeds in fresh or brackish water, sometimes with scattered trees and bushes. Remains out of sight for long periods but occasionally seen in flight over reeds and, in early morning, perches prominently on stems.

Sites:
ARMENIA Armash Fishponds***.
AUSTRIA Lake Neusiedl***.
GREAT BRITAIN Dungeness*, Minsmere***, N Norfolk coast*** , Portland** (winter).

BULGARIA Burgas area***, Lake Durankulak***, Lake Shabla***, Lake Srebarna***, Strandja Mts.

CZECH REPUBLIC Lednice***, Pohořelice Fishponds**, Třeboňsko***.

DENMARK Amager**, Møn-Falster***, Rømø***, Skagen***, Stignæs***.

FINLAND Åland Is*** (summer), Liminganlahti*** (summer), Viikki*** (summer).

FRANCE Camargue***, Cap Gris Nez***, La Brenne***, Gruissan***, Teich Reserve***, Trunvel Reserve***.

GERMANY Federsee***, Mecklenburg Lakes***.

GREECE Lake Kerkini***, Mikrí Prespa NP***, Nestos Delta***.

HUNGARY Biharugra***, Hortobágy NP***, Kis-balaton***, Kiskunság NP***, Lake Fertö***, Lake Velence***, Ócsa***.

ITALY Gargano Peninsula***, Isonzo Regional Park***, Monte Conero*** (passage, winter), Po Delta***.

LATVIA Lake Engure*** (summer), Lake Lubana*** (summer), Lake Pape*** (summer).

MACEDONIA Lakes Ohrid and Prespa***.

NETHERLANDS Lauwersmeer***, Naardermeer***, Oostvaadersplassen***, Terschelling***, Texel***, Zwanenwater***.

NORWAY Lista*** (summer).

POLAND Biebrza Marshes*** (summer), Chełm Marshes*** (summer), Gdańsk Bay*** (summer), Milicz Fishponds*** (summer), Słońsk*** (summer), Szczecin Bay area*** (summer).

ROMANIA Danube Delta***, Dobrudja***, Satchinez***.

RUSSIA Volga Delta***.

SLOVAKIA Záhorie***.

SPAIN Aiguamolls de l'Empordá**, Coto Doñana***, Ebro Delta***, Santa Pola***, Tablas de Daimiel***.

SWEDEN Falsterbo***, Getterön***, Gotland***, Hjälstaviken***, Hornborgasjön***, Kristianstad***, Kvismaren***, Lake Krankesjön***, Öland***, Tåkern***.

SWITZERLAND Fanel NR***, Klingnau Reservoir***.

SYRIA Baath Lake***.

TURKEY Göksu Delta***, Kulu Gölü***, Sultan Marshes***, Van Gölü*.

UKRAINE Dunay Delta***.

Arabian Babbler (Brown Babbler)
Turdoides squamiceps   D SD SH FG Res (Dis)

Range: Breeds in NE Sinai, S Israel and adjacent W Jordan, and in NE Saudi Arabia. Common and perhaps expanding range in Israel and Jordan, but rare in Sinai. Resident, although possibly dispersive in parts of range.
Tips: Mainly seen in acacia bush country, scrubby wadis and desert oases, but also in gardens, vineyards and reedbeds. Highly sociable and gathers in noisy groups in bushes in the evening.

Sites:
ISRAEL Arava Valley***, Eilat***, Ein Gedi***.
JORDAN Aqaba***, Petra***, Wadi Dana-Fidan***.

Iraq Babbler
Turdoides altirostris

FG FW   Res

Range: Breeds in SW Iran and Iraq, and recently found breeding along the Euphrates in Syria. Mainly resident but with local dispersal and seems to be expanding NW.
Tips: Found in reedbeds, riverine scrub and palm groves, sometimes in cultivation close to water. Shy when breeding but outside breeding season forms large noisy parties.

Sites:
SYRIA Baath Lake***, Dayr al-Zawr***.

Fulvous Babbler
Turdoides fulvus

D SD SH   Res

Range: Breeds S of the Atlas Mts in Morocco and in N Algeria, in Tunisia and NW Libya, formerly in S Egypt and probably still does so in the extreme SE.
Subspecies: Four races occur in the Western Palearctic; nominate *fulvus* from N Algeria to NW Libya, *maroccanus* from further W in Morocco and two further races in the far S: Ahaggar race *buchanani* and *acaciae* from Tibesti.
Tips: Scrub-covered sandy plains, semi-desert and desert edge, oases and olive groves. The only babbler in N Africa.

Sites:
MOROCCO Agadir and the Sous Plain**, Goulimime to Tan-Tan***, Tafilalt***.

TUNISIA Chott el Djerid***.

Sombre Tit
Parus lugubris   D SD SH FG   Res (Dis)

Range: Breeds in the Istra Peninsula and Dalmatian coast S to Albania, Greece and Macedonia, Lesvos and Crete, also in S Bulgaria and C and S Romania. In Turkey widespread in the W and S and less common in parts of the N and E. Small and isolated pockets in Transcaucasia and in the Middle East including W Syria, Lebanon and N Israel. Some local wandering in winter but largely resident.

Subspecies: Nominate race is found in the Balkans and N Greece and *anatoliae* in Lesvos, Turkey and S Transcaucasia, and the Middle East. Birds from E Romania and E Bulgaria are sometimes separated as *splendens*. Race *hyrcanus* from SE Azerbaijan and Iran is often regarded as a full species, the **Caspian Tit**.

Tips: Deciduous, mixed and coniferous woodland, in wooded valleys and on rocky hillsides, vineyards, olive groves, scrub and gardens. Shy and unobtrusive, much less sociable than its relatives and uncommon over much of range, usually occurring at low densities.

Sites:
ALBANIA Lake Shkodra***.
ARMENIA Meghri Area*** (summer).
BOSNIA-HERZEGOVINA Hutovo blato**. Sutjeska NP***.
BULGARIA Cape Emine***, Rila Mts***, Rusenski Lom NP***, Strandja Mts**, Studen Kladenetz***, Trigradski Gorge***, Tissata NR***.
CROATIA Neretva Delta***, Paklenica NP***.
GREECE Avas Gorge***, Dadiá-Soufli Forest***, Delphi***, Evros Delta*, Lake Kerkini**, Mikrí Prespa NP***, Mt Parnassós NP***, Valia Kalda NP***, Vikos-Aoos NP***.

GREEK IS Corfu***, Lesvos**.
ISRAEL Mt Hermon***.
LEBANON Barouk Cedars***.
MACEDONIA Babuna Gorge***, Galicica NP***, Lakes Ohrid and Prespa***.
ROMANIA Dobrudja**, Gurghiu Mts***.
SYRIA Wadi al-Qarn-Burqush**.
TURKEY Akseki***, Bafa Gölü***, Birecik-Halfeti***, Dalyan***, Soğuksu NP***, Yeşilce***.
YUGOSLAVIA Durmitor NP***, Lake Skadar***.

Siberian Tit
Parus cinctus   CF MF (DF)   Res (Nom)

Range: Main breeding range is in N Scandinavia, the S Kola Peninsula and across N Russia to the Urals. Small and isolated populations further S in montane Norway and adjacent Sweden. Mainly resident but may be nomadic and undergoes southward movements in winter, when numbers are high.

Tips: Coniferous forest, particularly spruce but also pine and larch, and also deciduous woodland along rivers and birch in mountains. Requires mature forest with decaying trees for nest holes. Uncommon over much of range.

Sites:

FINLAND Kevo NR***, Kilpisjärvi Saana***, Kuusamo***, Lake Inari***, Lemmenjoki NP***, Maltio NR***, Oulanka NP***, Pallas-Ounastunturi NP***, Patvinsuo NP***, Pyhä-Häkki NP***, Pyhätunturi NP***, Urho Kekkonen NP***.

NORWAY Øvre Pasvik NP***, Rondane NP***, Stabbursdalen NP***, Varanger*.
RUSSIA Kola Peninsula***.
SWEDEN Abisko NP*, Ammarnäs***, Muddus NP***, Padjelanta NP**, Ripakaisenvuoma***, Sarek NP***, Tyresta NP***.

Crested Tit
Parus cristatus   CF MF DF   Res (Dis)

Range: Breeds from Iberia and France across Europe to the S Urals and in Scandinavia N to the head of the Gulf of Bothnia. To the S breeds as far as the Mediterranean coasts of Spain and France, N Italy and in the mountains of the Balkans and N Greece. A small isolated population survives in remnants of the ancient Caledonian pine forest in NC Scotland. Mainly resident but some dispersal noted, particularly in the N and E, and range is expanding in some areas due to increased forestation.

Subspecies: Several races occur in our region with widespread nominate *cristatus* over much of the N and E of range, *mitratus* in C and W Europe, and the more restricted *scoticus* in Scotland, *abadiei* in Brittany and *wiegoldi* in W and S Iberia.

Tips: Requires dead wood for breeding and almost confined to pine forest in N of range but found in mixed woodland further S, in beech woods in the Pyrenees and cork oak woodlands in Iberia. Also conifer plantations and in Scotland may occur in rural gardens in winter.

Sites:

ANDORRA*.
AUSTRIA Hohe Tauern NP***, Hohe Wand***, Karwendel Reserve***, Schneeberg Mts***.
BELARUS Belovezhskaya Pushcha NP***, Berezinsky Reserve***, Prypyatsky NP***.
BELGIUM Het Zwin**, Kalmthoutse Heide***, Lesse et Lomme NR***.
BOSNIA-HERZEGOVINA Sujetska NP***.
GREAT BRITAIN Cairngorms and Speyside***.
BULGARIA Rila Mts***.
CROATIA Paklenica NP***, Plitvice***.
CZECH REPUBLIC Beskydy Mts***, Jeseníky Mts***, Krkonoše NP***, Šumava NP***.

DENMARK Ringkøbing Fjord***, Skagen***.
ESTONIA Matsalu Bay***, Nigula NR***.
FINLAND Åland Is***, Kolvanan Uuro***, Kuusamo***, Oulanka NP***, Parikkala***, Patvinsuo NP***, Vesijako NP***.
FRANCE Baie de Bourgneuf***, Cévennes NP***, Écrins NP***, Fontainebleau***, Forêt d'Issaux***, Forêt d'Orient***, Golfe du Morbihan***, Île d'Oléron***, La Brenne***, Lac du Der-Chantecoq***, Les Alpilles***, Lorraine NP***, Marais Poitevin***, Mercantour NP***, Prats-de-Mollo***, Pyrenees NP***, Queyras NP***, Vanoise NP***.

GERMANY Ammer Valley***, Bayerischer Wald NP***, Berchtesgaden NP***, Mecklenburg Lakes***, Rügen***, Vessertal***.

GREECE Mikrí Prespa NP***, Mt Olympus NP***, Mt Olympus NP***, Valia Kalda NP***, Vikos-Aoos NP***.

HUNGARY Aggtelek NP***, Zemplén Hills*** (summer).

ITALY Gran Paradiso NP***, Stelvio NP***.

LATVIA Cape Kolka***.

LITHUANIA Kirsiu Peninsula***.

NETHERLANDS Veluwe***.

POLAND Białowieża Forest***, Biebrza Marshes***, Bieszczady NP***, Gdańsk Bay***, Kampinos NP***, Szczecin Bay area**, Tatra NP***.

PORTUGAL Baixo Alentejo***, Castro Marim***, Montesinho***, Peneda Gerês NP***, Ria Formosa***, Sado Estuary***, Santo André Lagoon***, Tagus Estuary*.

ROMANIA Bicaz***, Poiana Braşov***, Retezat NP***.

SLOVAKIA High Tatras NP***, Malá Fatra***, Nízke Tatry NP***.

SLOVENIA Karst RP***, Kocevje***, Triglav NP***.

SPAIN Aigües Tortes NP***, Coto Doñana***, Garraf Massif***, Jaca***, Llobregat Delta***, Monfragüe***, Ordesa NP***, Picos de Europa***, Serrania de Ronda***, Sierra de Gredos***, Sierra de Guadarrama***.

SWEDEN Färnebofjärden***, Getterön***, Hornborgasjön***, Kristianstad***, Lake Ånnsjön***, Lake Krankesjön***, Stockholm archipelago***, Store Mosse NP***, Tåkern***, Tyresta NP***.

SWITZERLAND Aletschwald***, Clos-du-Doubs***, Fanel NR***, Flims***, Monte Generoso***, Swiss NP***.

UKRAINE Carpathians***.

YUGOSLAVIA Durmitor NP***.

African Blue Tit
Parus teneriffae

CF MF SH Res

Range: Now afforded species status, this group of races from the Canaries and N Africa was formerly considered conspecific with Blue Tit. In the Canaries breeds on all seven main islands and in N Africa from N Morocco to N Tunisia S to the northern edge of the Sahara, with an isolated population in NE Libya. Also occurs on the Italian island of Pantellaria.

Subspecies: This species is split into six races, *ultramarinus* in NW Africa and Pantellaria and *cyrenaicae* isolated in NE Libya, and in the Canaries, *degener* on Fuerteventura and Lanzarote, *teneriffae* on Tenerife, Gomera and Gran Canaria, *palmensis* on La Palma and *ombriosus* on El Hierro.

Tips: Usually found in upland laurel and pine forests in the Canaries, but also in tamarisk scrub on drier islands. In N Africa found in cypress, pine and oak woodland, often at altitude but also in palm groves in dry lowlands and in juniper scrub in Libya.

Sites:

ALGERIA Djebel Babor***, El Kala NP***.

CANARY IS El Hierro***, Fuerteventura***, Gomera***, Gran Canaria***, La Palma***, Lanzarote***, Tenerife***.

MOROCCO Agadir and the Sous Plain***, Boumalne***, Dayet Aaoua***, Oukaimeden***, Zaër***.

SICILY Pelagie Is (Pantellaria)***. **TUNISIA** Ain Draham***, Cap Bon Peninsula***, Lake Ichkeul***, Zaghouan***.

Azure Tit
Parus cyanus
MF DF SH FW   Res (Nom)

Range: Generally rare in our region, with main breeding range from C European Russia E to the Urals, roughly between 50° and 60°N. Also in N Kazakhstan and S Belarus; the first breeding for Ukraine took place in 2001 and has bred in Finland and W of usual range in Russia. Occasionally undergoes sudden expansions of range W towards Europe, followed by equally rapid retreats to usual range. Sometimes hybridises with Blue Tit during such invasions, resulting in birds with mixed characters (formerly known as Pleske's Tit '*P. pleskei*'). Mainly resident with some altitudinal movement in parts of range and is occasionally nomadic.

Subspecies: Nominate *cyanus* occurs over most of Western Palearctic range with *hyperriphaeus* in Kazakhstan, occasionally in winter in S Russia.

Tips: Usually found in willows beside rivers and lakes, sometimes in open conifer forest, poplars, birches, reeds and rushes.

Site:
BELARUS Prypyatsky NP**.

Krüper's Nuthatch
Sitta krueperi
CF (DF)   Res (Dis) (AMig)

Range: Found on the Greek island of Lesvos and perhaps also Khios, but main range is in W and S Turkey and in a narrow band across the N of the country to Georgia, with an isolated population on the N slope of the western Caucasus. Mainly resident but with some dispersal of young birds (has been recorded in the İstanbul area), and an altitudinal migrant in some areas.

Tips: Search spruce and fir forests, also pine, especially Turkish Pine, juniper and cedar. Usually occurs at 1,000–2,000m, but also from sea level to the treeline. Occurs in fir forest, sometimes feeding in broadleaf woodland, in the Caucasus. Rarely feeds on rocks or the ground being usually seen in trees, mainly on branches rather than the trunk, and has characteristic tit-like feeding behaviour. Very vocal and often betrays its presence by calling.

Sites:
GREEK IS Lesvos**.
RUSSIA Teberdinskiy Reserve***.

TURKEY Akseki***, Bafa Gölü***, Dalyan***, Göksu Delta**, İstanbul (passage), Kızılırmak Delta (passage), Soğuksu NP***, Uludağ NP***.

Corsican Nuthatch
Sitta whiteheadi   CF Res (AMig)

Range: Endemic to Corsica, where occurs in the central mountains from Tartagine S to Ospedale and possibly to Montagne de Cagna. Population is probably fewer than 2,000 pairs, mostly in the Natural Regional Park with strongholds in the Cinto, Rotondo, Renoso and Incudine areas. Young birds may undergo some altitudinal movement in severe winters but otherwise resident.

Tips: Found in mature forests of Corsican Pine with plenty of decaying wood and where little or no management occurs. Occurs mainly at 1,000–1,500m, but may occur down to 300m in winter. Not particularly shy but can be difficult to locate due to habit of feeding tit-like in the canopy. The only nuthatch on Corsica.

Sites:
CORSICA Asco Valley***, Restonica Valley***.

Algerian Nuthatch (Kabylie Nuthatch)
Sitta ledanti   MF Res (AMig)

Range: Endemic to N Algeria and only discovered in 1975. Found in a few very small areas of the Petite Kabylie range including Djebel Babor, the Guerrouch Forest in Taza NP, and Tamentout and Djimla Forests. Probably undergoes some altitudinal movement but largely resident.

Tips: Search mixed montane forest with oaks, cedar and fir in the few known localities at 1,500–2,000m. In Taza NP occurs lower (300–1,100m), often in streamside alders and willows. This is not a difficult species to see in its restricted range, but the country's political situation degenerated in the mid 1990s and it is advisable to wait until the current climate improves before making a visit. The only nuthatch known from Algeria.

Site:
ALGERIA Djebel Babor***.

Eastern Rock Nuthatch (Great Rock Nuthatch)
Sitta krueperi   CF (DF) Res (Dis) (AMig)

Range: Breeds across E and SE Turkey from Gaziantep eastwards and in Armenia and S Azerbaijan. Resident with limited altitudinal movement and post-breeding dispersal.

Subspecies: Two races occur in our region; *dresseri* in SE Turkey and N Iraq and *obscura* in NE Turkey and Transcaucasia.

Tips: Search rocky hillsides and gorges, cliffs and boulder-strewn woodland, and often seen near streams and areas with artemisia and pistacio. Sometimes occurs in more wooded areas than Western Rock Nuthatch, especially in winter, and often at lower altitudes where the two species overlap. Nests in rocks and builds a distinctive flask-shaped mud nest like that of Western Rock Nuthatch; occasionally builds in trees. Usually found at 1,000–2,500m, but often found lower in winter.

Sites:
ARMENIA Khosrov Preserve***, Vedi Hills***.   **TURKEY** Birecik-Halfeti***, Doğubeyazit***,
GEORGIA Iori Steppes***.   Yeşilce***.

Western Rock Nuthatch (Rock Nuthatch)
Sitta neumayer   M Res (AMig)

Range: Breeds on the E Adriatic coast from Slovenia to Albania, in scattered parts of the S Balkans and Greece, Corfu, Zakynthos and Lesvos, possibly Crete, and almost throughout Turkey except the Black Sea coast. Also in the S Caucasus and in parts of the Middle East including N Syria, Lebanon and N Israel. Basically resident but with some altitudinal movement and limited post-breeding dispersal.

Subspecies: Three–four races occur in our region differing very slightly in bill-length and depth of colour above and below. Nominate *neumayer* is found in SE Europe, *syriaca* in W and C Turkey S to Israel and *rupicola* in E Turkey, Armenia and Azerbaijan. Birds from W Turkey are sometimes separated as *zarudnyi*.

Tips: Search rocky slopes, gorges and cliffs with occasional bushes, from sea-level to above 2,500m, even over 3,000m. Occasionally feeds in trees. Locally common and often seen around ancient monuments (such as Delphi) and builds distinctive flask-shaped mud nest.

Sites:
ALBANIA Drini Delta***, Lake Shkodra***.   **BULGARIA** Rila Mts***, Studen Kladenetz***,
ARMENIA Mt Aragats***.   Trigradski Gorge***, Tissata NR***.

CROATIA Neretva Delta***, Paklenica NP***.
GEORGIA Iori Steppes***.
GREECE Akarnanika Mts***, Avas Gorge***, Dadiá-Soufli Forest***, Delphi***, Lake Kerkini**, Mikrí Prespa NP***, Mt Olympus NP**, Mt Parnassós NP***, Valia Kalda NP***, Vikos-Aoos NP***.
GREEK IS Corfu***, Lesvos***.
ISRAEL Mt Hermon***.

LEBANON Aammiq Marshes***, Barouk Cedars**.
MACEDONIA Babuna Gorge***, Galicica NP***, Lakes Ohrid and Prespa***, Mavrovo NP***.
SYRIA Wadi al-Qarn-Burqush**.
TURKEY Akseki***, Birecik-Halfeti***, Dalyan***, Demirkazik***, Göksu Delta***, Soğuksu NP***, Van Gölü***, Yeşilce***.
YUGOSLAVIA Lake Skadar***.

Wallcreeper
Tichodroma muraria

M (C) AMig

Range: Widespread but generally uncommon in montane areas across S Europe. Breeds in the Cantabrians and Pyrenees, the Alps, Apennines and on Corsica, in the Tatras and Carpathians, the S Balkans and N Greece, the Taurus Mts of S Turkey, the Pontic Mts of the NE, and the Caucasus and Transcaucasia. May regularly breed in the Jura and Massif Central of France. Mainly an altitudinal migrant but some regularly make longer movements and individuals may return to the same site in successive years. In winter is more widespread in N Spain, S France, Corsica, Italy and the Balkans and sometimes reaches Cyprus.

Tips: Occurs on rocky gorges, cliffs and boulder-strewn slopes, usually in limestone areas at 700–2,000m, but as low as 300m and up to at least 3,000m. In winter descends lower and can be seen on earth banks, quarries and buildings, and sometimes on sea-cliffs and rocky riverbeds. Carefully search large vertical slabs of rock in likely areas for this bird, which is usually seen close to rocks but occasionally in open flight over mountain valleys.

Sites:
ANDORRA.
ARMENIA Arapan Area***, Khosrov Preserve***. Mt Aragats***, Pambak Mts***.
AUSTRIA Hohe Wand*, Karwendel Reserve***, Schneeberg Mts**.
BULGARIA Rila Mts***, Trigradski Gorge***.
CORSICA Asco Valley***. Restonica Valley***.
CROATIA Paklenica NP**.
CYPRUS (winter).
CZECH REPUBLIC Pálava Hills* (winter).
FRANCE Cévennes NP* (winter), Écrins NP***, Forêt d'Issaux* (winter), Les Alpilles* (winter),

Mercantour NP**, Pyrenees NP***, Queyras NP**, Vanoise NP***.
GEORGIA Iori Steppes** (winter), Mt Kazbek***.
GERMANY Ammer Valley**, Berchtesgaden NP**.
GREECE Mt Olympus NP***, Mt Parnassós NP***, Valia Kalda NP**, Vikos-Aoos NP***.
HUNGARY Zemplén Hills*.
ISRAEL Ein Gedi* (winter), Mt Hermon* (winter), Wadi Ammud-Mt Arbel** (winter).
ITALY Abruzzo NP***, Circeo NP** (winter),

Gran Paradiso NP***, Orbetello Reserve (winter), Sibillini NP***, Stelvio NP***, Tuscan archipelago* (winter).
LEBANON Barouk Cedars (winter).
MACEDONIA Babuna Gorge*, Mavrovo NP**.
POLAND Tatra NP***.
ROMANIA Bicaz***, Poiana Braşov***, Retezat NP***, Turda Gorge***.
RUSSIA Teberdinskiy Reserve***.
SLOVAKIA High Tatras NP**, Malá Fatra***, Nízke Tatry NP***.
SLOVENIA Triglav NP***.

SPAIN Aiguamolls de l'Empordá* (winter), Aigües Tortes NP***, Garraf Massif* (winter), Jaca***, Ordesa NP**, Picos de Europa***.
SWITZERLAND Aletschwald***, Clos-du-Doubs** (winter), Col de Bretolet**, Flims**, Leuk*** (winter), Monte Generoso***, Swiss NP**.
TURKEY Birecik-Halfeti (winter), Borćka***, Demirkazik**, Göksu Delta* (winter), Sivrikaya***.
UKRAINE Carpathians*.

Short-toed Treecreeper
Certhia brachydactyla   DF MF (CF) Res (Dis)

Range: Endemic to our region, this species breeds throughout Iberia and France E to S Denmark and Germany, Poland and W Ukraine, the Balkans, Greece and W Turkey. Occurs over most of lowland Italy and on Sicily, Crete and other Greek islands, and there are isolated populations in the N Caucasus and in NW Africa from the Moyen and Haut Atlas of Morocco to NW Tunisia. Also breeds in the Channel Is (common on Guernsey and Jersey), Cyprus and Syria, and possibly in Corsica, where birds of the N African race have been recorded. Resident with very limited post-breeding dispersal but perhaps increasingly recorded in S England.

Subspecies: Five races are recognised but distinctions are minor and there is much intergradation. Nominate *brachydactyla* is found in S Iberia, E France and Denmark eastwards, including Sicily and Crete, *megarhyncha* in the remainder of Iberia, and from W and N France to W Germany, *mauretanicus* in N Africa, *dorotheae* in Cyprus and *harterti* in Turkey.

Tips: Occurs mainly in lowland deciduous forest, especially with oaks, in large gardens, orchards, olive groves and town parks. Also in montane cedar and pine woodlands in the S and may occur up to 1,800m in parts of range. Range overlaps extensively with that of **Common Treecreeper** *C. familiaris* and it is often very difficult to distinguish them. Short-toed replaces Common in lowland forests over much of Europe but occurs at considerable altitude in Turkey.

Sites:
ALBANIA Lake Shkodra***.
ALGERIA Djebel Babor***, El Kala NP***.
ANDORRA*.
AUSTRIA Marchauen-Marchegg Reserve***, Wienerwald***.

BELGIUM Hautes Fagnes Natural Park***, Kalmthoutse Heide***, Lesse et Lomme NR***.
BULGARIA Albena-Golden Sands***, Ropotamo NP***, Strandja Mts***.
CYPRUS*.

CZECH REPUBLIC Lednice***, Soutok***, Třeboňsko***.

FRANCE Baie de Bourgneuf***, Cévennes NP***, La Brenne***, Fontainebleau***, Forêt d'Orient***, Golfe du Morbihan***, Île d'Oléron***, Lac du Der-Chantecoq***, Lorraine NP***, Marais Poitevin***, Romelaere NR***, Trunvel Reserve***.

GERMANY Ammer Valley**, Berchtesgaden NP***, Kuhkopf***, Rügen***, Vessertal***.

GIBRALTAR* (winter).

GREECE Dadiá-Soufli Forest***, Mikrí Prespa NP***, Mt Olympus NP***, Valia Kalda NP***, Vikos-Aoos NP***.

GREEK IS Corfu**, Crete***, Lesvos***.

HUNGARY Aggtelek NP***, Csákvár***, Danube Bend***, Hanság***, Hortobágy NP***, Kis-balaton***, Kiskunság NP*, Lake Fertö***, Lake Velence***, Pilis Hills***, Zemplén Hills***.

ITALY Gargano Peninsula***, Monte Conero***, Po Delta***.

MACEDONIA Babuna Gorge**, Galicica NP***, Lakes Ohrid and Prespa***, Mavrovo NP***.

MOROCCO Dayet Aaoua***, Zaër***.

NETHERLANDS Lauwersmeer***, Oostvaardersplassen***, Terschelling***, Texel***, Veluwe***.

POLAND Białowieża Forest***, Białystok Fishponds***, Biebrza Marshes***, Chełm Marshes***, Gdańsk Bay***, Milicz Fishponds***, Słońsk***, Szczecin Bay area**.

PORTUGAL Baixo Alentejo***, Boquilobo***, Castro Marim***, Montesinho***, Peneda Gerês NP***, Ria Formosa***, Sado Estuary***, Santo André Lagoon***, Tagus Estuary***.

SLOVAKIA Malá Fatra***, Záhorie***, Zlatná na Ostrove***.

SLOVENIA Karst RP***, Kocevje***.

SPAIN Aigües Tortes NP***, Coto Doñana***, Garraf Massif***, Jaca***, Llobregat Delta***, Monfragüe***, Ordesa NP*, Picos de Europa**, Serrania de Ronda***, Sierra de Gredos***, Sierra de Guadarrama***.

SWITZERLAND Klingnau Reservoir***, Niderholz***.

TUNISIA Ain Draham***, Lake Ichkeul***, Zaghouan***.

TURKEY Göksu Delta**, İstanbul***, Kızılırmak Delta***, Soğuksu NP***, Uludağ NP***.

UKRAINE Carpathians***.

YUGOSLAVIA Durmitor NP***, Lake Skadar***, Obedska bara***.

Penduline Tit
Remiz pendulinus　　　　　　　　　　FW BW (SH)　Mig (Res)

Range: Main range extends from S Sweden, Denmark and Germany to the Black Sea and E to the Urals. Also widespread in Iberia, at scattered sites in W and S France, Italy and Sicily, the S Balkans, N Greece and Crete and in Turkey and the Caucasus. First bred recently in Norway and Finland and may have bred in Cyprus. Has declined in some S parts of range but appears to be expanding in the N, and vagrants increasingly recorded in S Britain. Mediterranean and Caucasus populations are resident, more northerly birds are migratory. Winter range more extensive in S Iberia and Greece, and also in the Middle East and Egypt.

Subspecies: Nominate *pendulinus* occurs over most of European range, replaced by *caspius* in the W Caspian region and *menzbieri* in Turkey and Transcaucasia. Race *macronyx* occurs in S Kazakhstan and hybridises with *caspius* at the mouth of the Ural river; this race is now often considered a full species, **Black-headed Penduline Tit.**

Tips: Usually found in reedbeds in fresh or brackish water, often with scrub, particularly willow, alder, tamarisk, and other plants. Also in trees, hedges and bushes close to or over-hanging water. May be seen away from water on passage. Best located by insistent call.

Sites:

ARMENIA Lake Sevan***.

AUSTRIA Lake Neusiedl*** (summer), Marchauen-Marchegg Reserve*** (summer).

BALEARIC IS Mallorca* (winter).

BELARUS Belovezhskaya Pushcha NP*** (summer), Berezinsky Reserve*** (summer), Prypyatsky NP*** (summer).

BULGARIA Albena-Golden Sands*** (summer), Burgas area*** (summer), Lake Durankulak*** (summer), Lake Shabla** (summer), Lake Srebarna*** (summer), Strandja Mts* (summer), Studen Kladenetz*** (summer).

CORSICA Biguglia Lake* (winter), Cap Corse** (passage, winter).

CROATIA Kopački Rit** (summer).

CYPRUS* (winter).

CZECH REPUBLIC Lednice*** (summer), Nové Mlýny*** (summer), Poodří*** (summer), Třeboňsko*** (summer).

DENMARK Amager** (summer), Rømø** (summer).

FRANCE Baie de Vilaine* (passage), Camargue***, La Brenne** (passage), Gruissan***, Teich Reserve* (winter).

GERMANY Mecklenburg Lakes** (summer), Oder Valley*** (summer).

GREECE Axios-Aliakmonas Deltas***, Evros Delta**, Lake Kerkini***, Mikrí Prespa NP***, Porto Lagos area***.

GREEK IS Crete**.

HUNGARY Biharugra*** (summer), Danube Bend** (summer), Hanság*** (summer), Hortobágy NP*** (summer), Kis-balaton*** (summer), Kiskunság NP*** (summer), Lake Fertö*** (summer), Lake Velence*** (summer), Ócsa*** (summer), Tihany*** (summer).

ISRAEL Bet Shean Valley*** (winter), Hula Reserve** (winter), Ma'agan Mikhael*** (winter).

ITALY Circeo NP***, Lake Massaciuccoli***, Orbetello Reserve** (winter), Po Delta***.

JORDAN Azraq* (spring).

LATVIA Lake Engure*** (summer), Lake Lubana*** (summer), Lake Pape*** (summer).

LEBANON Aammiq Marshes** (passage, winter).

MACEDONIA Babuna Gorge*, Lakes Ohrid and Prespa***.

MALTA* (winter).

NETHERLANDS Oostvaardersplassen***.

POLAND Białowieża Forest*** (summer), Białystok Fishponds*** (summer), Biebrza Marshes*** (summer), Chełm Marshes*** (summer), Milicz Fishponds*** (summer), Słońsk*** (summer), Szczecin Bay area** (summer).

PORTUGAL Boquilobo*** (winter), Castro Marim*** (winter), Ria Formosa*** (winter), Sado Estuary*** (winter), Santo André Lagoon*** (winter), Tagus Estuary*** (winter).

ROMANIA Danube Delta*** (summer), Lake Călăraşi*** (summer), Satchinez*** (summer).

RUSSIA Volga Delta*** (summer).

SLOVAKIA Senné Fishponds*** (summer), Záhorie*** (summer), Zlatná na Ostrove*** (summer).

SPAIN Aiguamolls de L'Empordá***, Cádiz Lagoons*** (winter), Coto Doñana*** (winter), Ebro Delta***, Guadalhorce Estuary*** (winter), La Serena*, Llobregat Delta***, Monfragüe* (summer), Santa Pola*** (winter), Tablas de Daimiel***.

SWEDEN Falsterbo** (passage), Getterön*** (summer), Hornborgasjön*** (summer), Kristianstad*** (summer), Kvismaren*** (summer), Lake Krankesjön*** (summer), Öland*** (summer), Tåkern*** (summer).

SWITZERLAND Fanel NR*** (summer), Grangettes** (passage), Klingnau Reservoir** (passage).

SYRIA Dayr al-Zawr*** , Yarmuk Valley** (winter).
TURKEY Dalyan*** (summer), Manyas Gölü*** (summer), Sultan Marshes*** (summer),
Uluabat Gölü*** (summer), Van Gölü** (summer).
UKRAINE Dunay Delta*** (summer).
YUGOSLAVIA Obedska bara** .

Nile Valley Sunbird
Anthreptes metallicus

SH FG Dis

Range: In our region breeds only in the Nile Valley N to Cairo. Disperses or undertakes short-distance movements, becoming more widespread throughout the valley and occurring in the Faiyum and the Suez Canal areas in Oct–Mar. Migrants possible on Red Sea coast.
Tips: Search open acacia woodland and scrub in river valleys, gardens and irrigated farmland.

Sites:
EGYPT Aswan*** , Luxor*** .

Palestine Sunbird (Orange-tufted Sunbird)
Nectarinia osea

SH F Res (Dis)

Range: Western Palearctic breeding range confined to the Middle East, in SW Syria, Israel and adjacent W Jordan, and has recently begun to colonise S Sinai. Has bred in S Lebanon and recorded in N Sinai. Resident or undergoes short-distance dispersal, and mainly occurs in autumn or winter in Lebanon and S Syria. Old records for the far S of Turkey.
Tips: Found in orchards and gardens, along wadis and roadsides and in bushy valleys, sunny hillsides and open dry grassland with scattered bushes and trees. Often in cypress trees and occurs up to 1,500m in Jordan.

Sites:
EGYPT Santa Katharina Monastery*** , Zaranik. **ISRAEL** Arava Valley*** , Eilat*** , Ein Gedi*** , Hula Reserve*** , Ma'agan Mikhael*** , Nizzana*** , Wadi Ammud-Mt Arbel*** .
JORDAN Aqaba*** , Petra*** , Wadi Dana-Fidan*** , Wadi Rum*** , Wadi as Sir*** .
SYRIA Yarmuk Valley*** .

Black-crowned Tchagra (Bush Shrike)
Tchagra senegala   SH DF   Res (Dis)

Range: Widespread in tropical Africa but in our region found only in W and N Morocco, coastal Algeria and extreme N Tunisia (endemic race *cucullata*). Has been recorded in Libya where may breed.

Tips: Inhabits dry scrubby areas with scattered trees, arid open woodland, plantations and gardens. Difficult to see, usually solitary and keeps low in vegetation or hops on ground like a thrush. Best located by loud whistling call and heard more often than seen. Most often observed diving into cover or in low flight between bushes but has a distinctive display flight.

Sites
MOROCCO Agadir and the Sous Plain***, Essaouira***, Oued Massa***, Zaër***.

TUNISIA Ain Draham***, Cap Bon Peninsula***.

Lesser Grey Shrike
Lanius minor   SH FG   Mig

Range: Main range is in SE Europe from Slovenia, Hungary and Romania S to Greece, Turkey and the Caucasus, and from Ukraine across Russia S of 55°N to the Caspian. Also breeds at scattered sites elsewhere in E Europe including S Poland, the Czech Republic, Slovakia and E Austria. Range much reduced further W but still breeds in NE Spain and S France, Italy and Sicily. A summer visitor arriving in mid Apr to mid May and departing late Jul–early Sep, with a peak in the second half of Aug. Passage is mainly through the E Mediterranean and migrants are common on Cyprus and in the Middle East. Spring passage is generally further E than in autumn.

Tips: Found in open areas with scattered trees, hedges or copses. Often in vineyards, orchards, groves or plantations, along roadsides and frequently seen on overhead wires and telephone poles.

Sites:
ALBANIA Drini Delta** (summer), Lake Shkodra*** (summer).
ARMENIA Armash Fishponds*** (summer), Mt Aragats*** (summer).
AUSTRIA Lake Neusiedl* (summer).
BELARUS Belovezhskaya Pushcha NP** (summer).

BOSNIA-HERZEGOVINA Hutovo blato*** (summer).
BULGARIA Albena-Golden Sands* (summer), Belene* (summer), Burgas area*** (summer), Cape Kaliakra*** (summer, passage), Lake Durankulak*** (summer), Lake Shabla** (summer), Lake Srebarna** (summer), Rila Mts***

(summer), Rusenski Lom NP*** (summer), Strandja Mts** (summer), Tissata NR*** (summer).
CROATIA Kopački Rit** (summer), Neretva Delta*** (summer).
CYPRUS** (passage).
CZECH REPUBLIC Znojmo** (summer). **EGYPT** Abu Simbel** (passage), Aswan*** (passage), Hurghada*** (passage), Luxor** (passage), Sharm el Sheikh** (passage), Zaranik*** (passage).
FRANCE Camargue* (summer).
GEORGIA Iori Steppes*** (summer), Mt Kazbek*** (summer).
GREECE Akarnanika Mts** (summer), Axios-Aliakmonas Deltas*** (summer), Dadiá-Soufli Forest*** (summer), Evros Delta** (summer), Lake Kerkini* (passage), Mikrí Prespa NP*** (summer), Mt Parnassós NP** (summer), Nestos Delta*** (summer), Porto Lagos area*** (summer).
GREEK IS Corfu*** (summer, passage), Crete** (passage, mainly autumn), Kos*** (passage), Lesvos*** (passage, rare in summer), Náxos** (passage), Rhodes*** (summer, passage).
HUNGARY Aggtelek NP* (summer). Biharugra*** (summer), Hanság* (summer), Hortobágy NP*** (summer), Kis-balaton* (summer), Kiskunság NP*** (summer), Lake Fertö* (summer), Lake Velence* (summer), Ócsa** (summer), Szeged Fishponds** (summer), Zemplén Hills* (summer).

ISRAEL Eilat** (passage), Jezreel Valley** (passage).
ITALY Circeo NP* (summer), Gargano Peninsula** (summer), Maremma Regional Park** (summer), Po Delta* (summer), San Giuliano Reserve** (summer).
JORDAN Azraq** (spring).
LEBANON Aammiq Marshes** (passage), Qaraoun Lake** (passage).
MACEDONIA Galicica NP* (summer), Lakes Ohrid and Prespa** (summer).
MALTA (passage).
ROMANIA Danube Delta*** (summer), Dobrudja*** (summer, passage).
RUSSIA Kalmykia*** (summer), Teberdinskiy Reserve** (summer), Volga Delta*** (summer).
SICILY Vendicari** (passage).
SLOVAKIA Malé Karpaty*** (summer), Senné Fishponds*** (summer), Slovenský Kras** (summer), Záhorie** (summer).
SPAIN Aiguamolls de L'Empordá*** (summer).
SYRIA Dayr al-Zawr*** (passage).
TUNISIA Cap Bon Peninsula* (passage).
TURKEY Demirkazik*** (summer), Göksu Delta*** (summer), İstanbul** (passage), Sultan Marshes*** (summer).
UKRAINE Askania-Nova*** (summer), Dunay Delta*** (summer).
YUGOSLAVIA Durmitor NP** (summer), Fruška Gora NP** (summer), Obedska bara** (summer).

Southern Grey Shrike
Lanius meridionalis   SH FG SD   PMig

Range: Recently separated from **Great Grey Shrike** *L. excubitor*. Breeds in SW France, over much of Iberia, except the N coast, and across most of NW Africa, in coastal Libya and in Egypt in the Nile Valley and the Red Sea coast. Also found in Sinai, Israel and W Jordan, and N Saudi Arabia. Breeds on Lanzarote, Fuerteventura, Tenerife and Gran Canaria in the Canaries. A partial migrant, with some western birds crossing the Mediterranean at Gibraltar to winter in NW Africa.

Subspecies: Six races are recognised from the Western Palearctic. Nominate race is found in Iberia and SW France, *koenigi* in the Canaries, *algeriensis* in NW Africa, *elegans* in the N Sahara and *aucheri* in NE Africa and Arabia. Central Asian form *pallidirostris*, the **Steppe Grey Shrike**, breeding from the Volga eastwards and occurring in the Middle East on passage and in winter, is sometimes given specific status.

Tips: Found in open areas with trees and bushes including semi-desert and steppes, prefers more cover than Great Grey Shrike but like other shrikes often perches prominently on roadside wires.

Sites:

CANARY IS Fuerteventura***, Gran Canaria***, Lanzarote***, Tenerife***.
EGYPT Abu Simbel**, Aswan***, Hurghada***, Luxor***, Nile Delta* (winter), Sharm el Sheikh***, Zaranik**.
FRANCE Camargue***, Leucate***.
GIBRALTAR*** (passage).
ISRAEL Arava Valley***, Eilat***, Golan Heights***, Hula Reserve***, Nizzana***.
JORDAN Azraq***, Petra***, Wadi Dana-Fidan***, Wadi Rum*.
LEBANON Aamiq Marshes**, Qaraoun Lake*.
MOROCCO Agadir and the Sous Plain***, Boumalne***, Essaouira***, Goulimime to Tan-Tan***, Ouarzazate***, Oued Massa***, Tafilalt***, Zaers***, Zeida***.

PORTUGAL Baixo Alentejo***, Boquilobo***, Castro Marim***, International Douro***, International Tagus***, Montesinho***, Peneda Gerês NP***, Ria Formosa***, Sado Estuary***, Santo André Lagoon***, Tagus Estuary***. **RUSSIA** Kalmykia*** (summer), Volga Delta*** (summer).
SPAIN Aiguamolls de L'Empordá***, Cabo de Gata***, Cáceres-Trujillo Steppes***, Cádiz Lagoons***, Coto Doñana***, Garraf Massif***, Guadalhorce Estuary***, La Serena***, Llobregat Delta***, Monfragüe***, Serrania de Ronda***, Sierra de Gredos***, Sierra de Guadarrama***, Tablas de Daimiel***.
TUNISIA Cap Bon Peninsula***, Chott el Djerid***, Kelbia Lake***, Lake Ichkeul***, Zaghouan***.

Woodchat Shrike
Lanius senator

SH FG Mig

Range: Breeds in Iberia, C and S France and discontinuously across Europe to E Poland and Hungary. In the S found on the Balearics, Corsica, Sardinia, Sicily and much of mainland Italy, the E Adriatic coast, the S Balkans and Greece. Widespread in W and S Turkey and the Caucasus, and also breeds in W Syria, Lebanon, Israel and Jordan. In N Africa breeds in Morocco and across N Algeria to Tunisia and NW Libya. A summer visitor wintering in northern tropical Africa. Departs breeding grounds in Jul–Sep, passage occurring throughout S Europe, N Africa and the Middle East, and returns Apr–May. Declining in N of range.

Subspecies: Four races occur in our region; nominate in Europe N of the Pyrenees, Italy and Sicily, Greece and W Turkey, *badius* on the Balearics, Corsica, Sardinia and Capraia, *rutilans* in Iberia and NW Africa (often lumped with nominate), and *niloticus* in Turkey and Cyprus (has occurred as a vagrant to Spain).

Tips: Usually easy to see in open country with bushes and trees, olive groves and orchards. Often along roadsides, in gardens or hedges in cultivated areas. Generally below 1,000m but higher in S France and Spain.

Sites:

ALBANIA Drini Delta** (summer), Karavasta Lagoon*** (summer), Lake Shkodra*** (summer).

ANDORRA** (summer).

ARMENIA Vedi Hills*** (summer).

AUSTRIA Lake Neusiedl** (summer).

BALEARIC IS Formentera*** (summer), Ibiza*** (summer), Mallorca*** (summer), Menorca*** (summer).

BOSNIA-HERZEGOVINA Hutovo blato*** (summer).

GREAT BRITAIN Portland* (passage), Scilly* (spring). **BULGARIA** Burgas area*** (summer, passage), Strandja Mts*** (summer, passage), Studen Kladenetz*** (summer), Tissata NR*** (summer).

CANARY IS Fuerteventura* (passage).

CORSICA Biguglia Lake*** (summer), Bonifacio*** (summer).

CROATIA Cres*** (summer), Neretva Delta*** (summer), Paklenica NP*** (summer).

CYPRUS** (passage, rare in summer).

EGYPT Abu Simbel** (passage), Aswan*** (passage), Hurghada*** (passage), Luxor*** (passage), Sharm el Sheikh* (passage), Suez area*** (passage), Zaranik*** (passage).

FRANCE Camargue*** (summer, passage), Dombes*** (summer), Gruissan*** (summer), Leucate*** (summer).

GEORGIA Iori Steppes*** (summer).

GERMANY Kuhkopf* (summer).

GIBRALTAR** (passage).

GREECE Akarnanika Mts*** (summer), Axios-Aliakmonas Deltas*** (summer), Dadiá-Soufli Forest*** (summer), Delphi*** (summer), Lake Kerkini*** (summer, passage), Mikrí Prespa NP*** (summer), Mt Parnassós NP***

(summer), Nestos Delta*** (summer), Porto Lagos area*** (summer).

GREEK IS Corfu*** (summer), Crete*** (passage, rare in summer), Kos*** (summer, passage), Lesvos*** (summer, passage), Náxos*** (summer, passage).

IRELAND Saltee Is* (spring).

ISRAEL Arava Valley*** (passage), Bet Shean Valley*** (summer, passage), Eilat*** (passage), Ein Gedi*** (passage), Mt Hermon*** (summer), Nizzana*** (passage), Wadi Ammud-Mt Arbel*** (summer).

ITALY Circeo NP*** (summer), Gargano Peninsula*** (summer), Lake Massaciuccoli*** (summer), Maremma Regional Park*** (summer), Monte Conero*** (summer, passage), San Giuliano Reserve*** (summer).

JORDAN Amman NP*** (summer), Aqaba* (passage), Azraq*** (passage), Wadi Rum* (passage), Wadi as Sir*** (summer).

LEBANON Aammiq Marshes*** (passage), Qaraoun Lake** (passage).

MACEDONIA Galicica NP*** (summer), Lakes Ohrid and Prespa*** (summer).

MADEIRA (passage).

MALTA** (passage).

MOROCCO Agadir and the Sous Plain*** (summer), Essaouira*** (summer, passage), Oued Massa*** (summer, passage), Ouarzazate*** (passage), Oukaimeden*** (summer), Zaër*** (summer), Zeida** (passage).

PORTUGAL Baixo Alentejo*** (summer), Boquilobo*** (summer), Cape St Vincent*** (summer, passage), Castro Marim*** (summer), International Douro*** (summer), International Tagus*** (summer), Montesinho*** (summer), Peneda Gerês NP* (summer), Ria Formosa***

(summer), Sado Estuary*** (summer), Santo André Lagoon*** (summer), Tagus Estuary*** (summer).
ROMANIA Dobrudja*** (summer, passage).
RUSSIA Teberdinskiy Reserve** (summer).
SARDINIA Giara di Gesturi*** (summer), Oristano wetlands*** (summer), San Pietro I*** (summer).
SICILY San Vito Peninsula*** (summer), Vendicari*** (passage).
SPAIN Aiguamolls de L'Empordá*** (summer), Cabo de Gata*** (summer), Cáceres-Trujillo Steppes*** (summer), Cádiz Lagoons*** (summer), Coto Doñana*** (summer), Ebro Delta*** (summer), Garraf Massif*** (summer), Guadalhorce Estuary* (passage), Jaca*** (summer), La Serena*** (summer), Llobregat Delta*** (summer), Monfragüe*** (summer), Picos de Europa*** (summer), Santa Pola*** (summer), Serrania de Ronda*** (summer), Sierra de Gredos*** (summer), Sierra de Guadarrama*** (summer), Tablas de Daimiel*** (summer), Zaragoza Steppes*** (summer).
SYRIA Aqra Mts*** (summer), Tadmur and Sabkhat Muh** (passage).
TUNISIA Cap Bon Peninsula*** (summer, passage), Lake Ichkeul*** (summer, passage), Zaghouan*** (summer).
TURKEY Birecik-Halfeti*** (summer), İstanbul*** (passage), Kocaćay Delta*** (summer).
UKRAINE Dunay Delta* (summer).
YUGOSLAVIA Carska bara** (summer), Lake Skadar*** (summer), Obedska bara** (summer).

Masked Shrike
Lanius nubicus   DF SH FG Mig

Range: Almost confined to the Western Palearctic as a breeder, its range extends outside the region only into W Iran. Breeds in parts of N Greece, S Macedonia, S Bulgaria, W, S and SE Turkey, some E Aegean islands and Cyprus. In the Middle East breeds in Syria, Lebanon, Israel and W Jordan. Winters mainly in E Africa with small numbers in S Arabia and passage occurs across most of the E Mediterranean, notably Cyprus, the Middle East and through the Nile Valley in Egypt. Departs breeding areas in Aug–early Sep, rarely Oct, returning mid Mar–May. Possibly a nocturnal migrant as passage records are scarce.

Tips: Often prefers areas with more cover than other shrikes; a bird of open woodland and light forest, scrub and cultivation with scattered trees, orchards, olive groves, vineyards and gardens. On passage seen in trees and bushes in a wide variety of habitats. More often perches concealed than other shrikes but sometimes on overhead wires.

Sites:
BULGARIA Rila Mts* (summer), Strandja Mts** (summer), Studen Kladenetz*** (summer), Tissata NR*** (summer).
CYPRUS* (summer).
EGYPT Abu Simbel* (passage), Aswan** (passage), Hurghada*** (passage), Luxor** (passage), Santa Katharina Monastery** (passage), Sharm el Sheikh** (passage), Suez area*** (passage), Zaranik* (passage).
GREECE Avas Gorge*** (summer), Axios-Aliakmonas Deltas*** (summer), Dadiá-Soufli Forest*** (summer), Evros Delta** (summer), Porto Lagos area*** (summer).
GREEK IS Lesvos*** (summer).

ISRAEL Arava Valley*** (passage), Eilat*** (passage), Ein Gedi*** (passage), Urim** (passage), Wadi Ammud-Mt Arbel*** (summer).
JORDAN Amman NP*** (passage), Aqaba*** (passage), Azraq*** (passage), Petra* (summer, passage), Wadi Rum** (summer), Wadi as Sir*** (summer).

LEBANON Aammiq Marshes*** (summer, passage), Qaraoun Lake** (summer).
SYRIA Aqra Mts*** (summer), Jabal Slenfeh*** (summer).
TURKEY Akseki*** (summer), Dalyan*** (summer), Göksu Delta*** (summer), İstanbul** (summer, passage), Kocaćay Delta*** (summer).

Siberian Jay
Perisoreus infaustus   CF (MF)   Res (Dis)

Range: Breeds in E and N Norway, C and N Sweden and throughout most of Finland except the S. Also found on the Kola Peninsula and across N Russia to the Urals. Declining in S of range, particularly in Finland.

Subspecies: Three races occur in our region but differences are clinal: nominate *infaustus* in N Scandinavia and the Kola Peninsula with *ostjakorum* to the E and *ruthenus* in further S in C Scandinavia.

Tips: A bird of mature, closed-canopy coniferous forest, sometimes birch in far N of range. Usually shy and secretive but may be seen along forest trails and at picnic sites in some areas, and around villages in winter. Often feeds on outermost branches of trees.

Sites:
FINLAND Åland Is*, Kevo NR***, Kuusamo***, Lake Inari***, Lemmenjoki NP***, Maltio NR***, Oulanka NP***, Pallas-Ounastunturi NP***, Patvinsuo NP***, Pyhä-Häkki NP***, Pyhätunturi NP***, Urho Kekkonen NP***.

NORWAY Øvre Pasvik NP***, Rondane NP***, Stabbursdalen NP***, Varanger**.
RUSSIA Kola Peninsula***.
SWEDEN Ammarnäs***, Lake Ånnsjön***, Muddus NP***, Padjelanta NP***, Ripakaisenvuoma***, Sarek NP***.

Azure-winged Magpie
Cyanopica cyanea   CF MF DF SH FG   Res

Range: This species has an extraordinarily disjunct range, breeding in Iberia with the remainder of the range in E Asia. In our region breeds in S and E Portugal and C and S Spain. Locally fairly common in Iberia, where may be increasing. Resident but may wander outside breeding range in autumn and winter.

Subspecies: Iberian birds belong to race *cooki* which may be treated as a full species in the future.

Tips: Occurs in open woodland and at forest edges, both coniferous and deciduous, in groves of trees and orchards. Often in isolated groups in warmer valleys separated by higher ground. Tends to be secretive and rather shy but often feeds on the ground.

Sites:

PORTUGAL Baixo Alentejo***, Castro Marim***, International Douro**, International Tagus***, Ria Formosa***, Sado Estuary***, Tagus Estuary***.

SPAIN Cáceres-Trujillo Steppes***, Coto Doñana***, La Serena***, Monfragüe***, Sierra de Gredos***, Sierra de Guadarrama***.

Nutcracker (Spotted Nutcracker)
Nucifraga caryocatactes

CF MF   Res (Irr)

Range: Breeds in S Norway, Sweden and Finland and from the Baltic states and NE Poland across Russia to the Urals. Also in montane areas further S in the Alps, Carpathians and SE Europe. Smaller and more isolated populations exist in the Ardennes of Belgium, E France and Germany, established after major invasions. Probably an altitudinal migrant in some areas and occasionally irruptive. In times of food shortage large numbers of Siberian birds move W into Europe, rarely reaching as far as Iberia and N Africa.

Subspecies: European breeding birds belong to the nominate race but irruptions involve mainly Siberian birds of the race *macrorhynchos*.

Tips: Inhabits coniferous forest, often spruce but also fir and pine. Prefers Arolla Pine in the Alps and Macedonian Pine in the Balkans. Also found in mixed forest with hazel and plentiful conifers. Often perches on topmost branch of a tree.

Sites:

AUSTRIA Hohe Wand*, Karwendel Reserve**, Schneeberg Mts**.

BELARUS Belovezhskaya Pushcha NP***, Berezinsky Reserve***, Prypyatsky NP***.

BELGIUM Croix-Scaille NR*, Hautes Fagnes Natural Park*, Lesse et Lomme NR*.

BOSNIA-HERZEGOVINA Sujetska NP***.

BULGARIA Rila Mts***, Trigradski Gorge* (irregular).

CZECH REPUBLIC Beskydy Mts***, Jeseníky Mts***, Krkonoše NP***, Šumava NP***.

ESTONIA Matsalu Bay***, Nigula NR***.

FINLAND Åland Is***.

FRANCE Écrins NP***, Mercantour NP***, Queyras NP***, Vanoise NP***.

GERMANY Ammer Valley***, Bayerischer Wald NP***, Berchtesgaden NP***, Mecklenburg Lakes* (winter), Vessertal***.

HUNGARY Aggtelek NP* (winter), Zemplén Hills* (winter).

ITALY Gran Paradiso NP***, Stelvio NP***.

LATVIA Lake Lubana***.

NORWAY Hardangervidda NP***, Mølen** (autumn).

POLAND Białowieża Forest***, Biebrza Marshes***, Bieszczady NP***, Tatra NP***.

ROMANIA Bicaz***, Gurghiu Mts***, Poiana Braşov***, Retezat NP***.

RUSSIA Kola Peninsula***.

SLOVAKIA High Tatras NP***, Malá Fatra***, Nízke Tatry NP***.

SLOVENIA Triglav NP***.

SWEDEN Falsterbo** (passage, winter), Holmöarna*** (passage), Kristianstad** (passage), Hornborgasjön***, Store Mosse NP***, Tåkern** (passage).

SWITZERLAND Aletschwald***, Col de Bretolet***, Flims***, Monte Generoso***, Swiss NP***.

UKRAINE Carpathians***.

Red-billed Chough
Pyrrhocorax pyrrhocorax

M C (FG)   Res (AMig)

Range: Generally rare and local with a highly fragmented range in our region: coastal Ireland (except the E), W Scotland, especially Islay, the Isle of Man and coastal and some inland parts of Wales, and the Brittany coast. In W Europe found mainly in upland and montane areas over much of Iberia and parts of S France, the W Alps and Pyrenees, Sardinia, Sicily and S Italy. Further E breeds in the S Balkans, Greece and Crete, S and E Turkey and the Caucasus, and probably C Syria. Also breeds on La Palma in the Canaries and in the Atlas Mts of Morocco and Algeria. Generally decreasing throughout range but recently bred in Cornwall for the first time for many decades. Resident with some altitudinal movement in higher mountains.

Subspecies: Four races occur in our region differing mainly in size and to a lesser extent the colour of plumage gloss. Nominate race is found in the British Isles, *erythropthalmus* over most of Europe, *barbarus* in N Africa and the Canaries and *docilis* in Greece and SW Asia.

Tips: Search montane areas with close-cropped fields and meadows, also quarries with suitable cliffs and surrounding pastures. Descends in winter. In the British Islesles and Brittany found mainly on coasts with high rocky cliffs and nearby open grassland.

Sites:
ANDORRA***.

ARMENIA Khosrov Preserve***, Mt Aragats***.

GREAT BRITAIN Anglesey***, Islay***, Pembrokeshire Is***.

CANARY IS La Palma***.

FRANCE Cévennes NP***, Écrins NP***, Mercantour NP***, Ouessant***, Prats-de-Mollo***, Pyrenees NP***, Queyras NP***, Vanoise NP***.

GEORGIA Mt Kazbek***.

GERMANY Berchtesgaden NP***.

GREECE Mikrí Prespa NP***, Valia Kalda NP***, Vikos-Aoos NP***.

GREEK IS Crete***.

IRELAND Akeragh Lough***, Cape Clear Is***, Cliffs of Moher***, Galley Head***, Kinsale***, Saltee Is***.

ITALY Abruzzo NP***, Gran Paradiso NP***, Sibillini NP***, Stelvio NP***.

MACEDONIA Sara Mts***.

MOROCCO Agadir and the Sous Plain***, Boumalne***, Oukaimeden***.

PORTUGAL Baixo Alentejo**, Cape St Vincent***, International Douro***, International Tagus***, Peneda Gerês NP***.
RUSSIA Teberdinskiy Reserve***.
SICILY Strait of Messina***.
SLOVENIA Triglav NP***.
SPAIN Aigües Tortes NP***, Jaca***, La Serena*, Monfragüe NP***, Ordesa NP***, Picos de Europa***, Serrania de Ronda***, Sierra de Gredos***, Sierra de Guadarrama***.
SWITZERLAND Aletschwald**, Leuk* (winter).
SYRIA Tadmur and Sabkhat Muh*.
TURKEY Demirkazik***, Sivrikaya***, Uludağ NP***, Van Gölü***.

Alpine Chough (Yellow-billed Chough)
Pyrrhocorax graculus

M Res (AMig)

Range: Widespread and locally common in montane areas of S Europe, NW Africa and SW Asia. In Europe breeds in the Cantabrians, Sierra de Gredos and Pyrenees, in the Alps and Apennines, on Corsica and Crete and widely in the ranges of SE Europe. Also breeds in S and E Turkey, the Caucasus, and the Rif and Atlas Mts of Morocco. In the Middle East occurs in Syria and probably elsewhere including Al Shouf in Lebanon. Recently seen in S Spain, where perhaps an immigrant from Morocco. Resident with some limited altitudinal movement in winter.

Subspecies: Two similar races occur in the region: nominate over much of range with *digitatus* in Syria and Lebanon.

Tips: Inhabits montane pastures with nearby cliffs and rocky outcrops, also around high-altitude habitation such as ski-resorts. Occurs up to 3,400m in the Alps.

Sites:
ANDORRA***.
ARMENIA Pambak Mts***.
AUSTRIA Hohe Tauern NP***, Hohe Wand**, Karwendel Reserve***, Schneeberg Mts***.
BOSNIA-HERZEGOVINA Sutjeska NP***.
BULGARIA Rila Mts***.
CORSICA Asco Valley***. Restonica Valley***.
FRANCE Mercantour NP***, Prats-de-Mollo***, Pyrenees NP***, Queyras NP***, Vanoise NP***.
GEORGIA Mt Kazbek***.
GERMANY Ammer Valley***, Berchtesgaden NP***.
GREECE Mikrí Prespa NP***, Mt Olympus NP***, Mt Parnassós NP***, Vikos-Aoos NP***.
GREEK IS Crete***.
ISRAEL Mt Hermon**.
ITALY Abruzzo NP***, Gran Paradiso NP***, Sibillini NP***, Stelvio NP***.
LEBANON Barouk Cedars.
MACEDONIA Galicica NP***, Sara Mts.
MOROCCO Oukaimeden***.
POLAND Tatra NP***.
RUSSIA Teberdinskiy Reserve***.
SLOVENIA Triglav NP***.
SPAIN Aigües Tortes NP***, Jaca***, Ordesa NP***, Picos de Europa***, Sierra de Gredos***.
SWITZERLAND Aletschwald***, Col de Bretolet***, Flims***, Monte Generoso***, Swiss NP***.
TURKEY Demirkazik***, Sivrikaya***, Uludağ NP***.

Brown-necked Raven
Corvus ruficollis

D SD M (U) Res

Range: Widespread across N Africa, mainly in the interior and largely absent from coasts. Also occurs in Sinai, S Israel and widely in Jordan, and breeds on the Cape Verde Is, where partial albinism is common. Resident with some wandering in winter.

Tips: Search deserts and semi-deserts, the species being common in artemisia steppe or near jujube trees, around habitation, cultivated areas and oases, and is often found on cliffs and crags in mountains.

Sites:
CAPE VERDE IS*.
EGYPT Abu Simbel***, Aswan***, Hurghada***, Luxor***, Sharm el Sheikh***, Suez area***.
ISRAEL Arava Valley***, Eilat***, Ein Gedi***, Mt Hermon***, Nizzana***.

JORDAN Aqaba***, Azraq***, Ghadir Burqu'***, Wadi Rum***.
MOROCCO Boumalne, Goulimine to Tan-Tan***, Tafilalt***.
TUNISIA Chott el Djerid***, Tataouine***.

Fan-tailed Raven
Corvus rhipidurus

D SD M U Res

Range: Breeds in the Middle East in the Rift Valley of Israel (mainly the S) and W Jordan, and extreme SE Egypt. Formerly bred in S Sinai and vagrants recorded in N Egypt and Syria. Resident with some wandering in winter.

Tips: A bird of cliffs and rocky gorges in mountains, desert and semi-desert from sea level to 3,000m. In parts of range occurs close to man and often seen at refuse tips.

Sites:
ISRAEL Ein Gedi***, Mt Hermon***.
JORDAN Aqaba***, Petra***, Wadi Dana-Fidan***, Wadi Rum***.

Tristram's Starling
Onychognathus tristrami   D SD M U   Res (Dis)

Range: Breeds mainly in W and S Arabia with small populations in S Sinai and S Israel and adjacent Jordan. Mainly resident with some dispersal in winter.

Tips: Found in desert and semi-desert areas on cultivated land, in rocky hills, ravines and wadis. In some areas closely associated with man, nesting on buildings and feeding on refuse tips. Usually in noisy flocks and often very approachable.

Sites:
EGYPT Santa Katharina Monastery***.
ISRAEL Arava Valley***, Eilat***, Ein Gedi***, Mt Hermon***.

JORDAN Aqaba***, Petra***, Wadi Dana-Fidan***, Wadi Rum***.

Spotless Starling
Sturnus unicolor   U FG   Res (PMig) (Dis)

Range: Confined to the Western Palearctic and breeds throughout most of Iberia, on Corsica, Sardinia and Sicily and, in N Africa, from the Sous Valley in Morocco to C Tunisia. Has expanded N in recent years and now breeds in Aude, SW France. In the 1990s the first breeding for the Balearics occurred on Menorca where formerly a vagrant.

Tips: Locally common in towns and villages, on cliffs and rocky outcrops, in open woodland and cultivated land, and associating with cattle in many areas. Forms mixed flocks with **Common Starling** *S. vulgaris* in winter.

Sites:
BALEARIC IS Menorca*.
CORSICA Bonifacio***.
GIBRALTAR*.
SARDINIA Cagliari wetlands***, Capo Marargiu***, Giara di Gesturi***, Oristano wetlands***.
MOROCCO Agadir and the Sous Plain***, Asilah and Oued Loukkos***, Essaouira***, Merja Zerga***, Oualidia***, Oued Massa***, Zeida***.

PORTUGAL Baixo Alentejo***, Cape St Vincent***, International Douro***, Montesinho***, Ria Formosa***, Sado Estuary***, Santo André Lagoon***, Tagus Estuary***.
SPAIN Aiguamolls de l'Empordá***, Aigües Tortes NP**, Cabo de Gata***, Coto Doñana***, Ebro Delta***, Garraf Massif***, Guadalhorce Estuary***, Jaca***, Llobregat Delta*, Monfragüe***, Picos de Europa***,

Santa Pola***, Serrania de Ronda***, Sierra de Gredos***, Sierra de Guadarrama***, Zaragoza Steppes***.

TUNISIA Cap Bon Peninsula***, Chott el Djerid***, Kelbia Lake*** Lake Ichkeul***, Tunis***, Zaghouan***.

Rose-coloured Starling
Sturnus roseus   FG Mig (Irr)

Range: Regular breeding range is from SW Ukraine and across S Russia but breeds further W after irruptions. Departs breeding areas in Jul–Aug to winter mainly in India, on return to breeding areas occasionally irrupts westwards, with breeding occurring regularly in Romania, less so in Hungary, probably also regularly in Turkey and exceptionally as far W as Italy. Large numbers bred in Romania in 1998, 2002 and 2003.

Tips: Found mainly on cultivated land and open grassland with cliffs and rocky outcrops, often nesting in rocks or on buildings. Highly social and breeds colonially.

Sites:
ARMENIA Armash Fishponds*** (summer), Mt Aragats*** (summer).
GREAT BRITAIN Scilly** (autumn).
BULGARIA Burgas area* (irregular autumn), Cape Kaliakra*, Lake Durankulak* (irregular autumn).
GEORGIA Iori Steppes*** (summer).
GREECE Porto Lagos area* (irregular autumn).
GREEK IS Lesvos** (irregular autumn).
HUNGARY Hortobágy NP* (irregular summer, autumn), Zemplén Hills* (irregular summer), Szeged Fishponds* (irregular, autumn).

ISRAEL Arava Valley (autumn).
ROMANIA Danube Delta (irregular summer, autumn), Dobrudja (irregular summer, autumn).
RUSSIA Kalmykia*** (summer), Volga Delta*** (summer).
TURKEY Bulanik, Göksu Delta*, Kızılırmak Delta* (passage), Van Gölü*.
UKRAINE Askania-Nova** (summer), Crimean Mts** (summer).

Spanish Sparrow
Passer hispaniolensis　　　　　　　　　　　　DF SH FG U　Res (PMig) (Dis)

Range: Breeds in E Portugal, C Spain and scattered parts of S Spain and S France, the E Adriatic, Balkans and Greece, across much of Turkey and parts of S Russia and Transcaucasia. In the Mediterranean breeds on Sardinia and Cyprus. Middle Eastern range includes N Syria, Lebanon, Israel and N Sinai. In N Africa breeds from S Morocco to NE Libya and also occurs on Madeira, the Canaries and Cape Verde Is.

Subspecies: Nominate race is found over most of range with *transcaspicus* in SW Asia, Cyprus and N Sinai. Replaced by hybrid Italian Sparrow in Italy, Corsica, Sardinia and Sicily, Malta and Crete.

Tips: Less commensal than House Sparrow but occurs in urban areas where latter is absent. Otherwise found in open woodland, farmland, hedgerows, olive groves and scrub-covered hills with scattered trees. Breeds colonially and is gregarious at all times.

Sites:

ALBANIA Lake Shkodra***.

ARMENIA Armash Fishponds***.

AZERBAIJAN Kyzylagach Bay***.

BOSNIA-HERZEGOVINA Hutovo blato***.

BULGARIA Albena-Golden Sands***, Burgas area***, Cape Kaliakra***, Lake Durankulak***, Lake Shabla***, Strandja Mts***, Studen Kladenetz***, Tissata NR***.

CANARY IS Fuerteventura**, Gomera**, Gran Canaria**, Lanzarote***, Tenerife**.

CAPE VERDE IS*.

CROATIA Mljet***, Neretva Delta***, Paklenica NP***.

CYPRUS* (summer).

EGYPT Abu Simbel*** (passage, winter), Aswan*** (passage, winter), Faiyum*** (winter), Hurghada*** (winter), Luxor*** (passage, winter), Nile Delta*** (winter), Sharm el Sheikh*** (winter), Zaranik**(passage, winter).

GREECE Axios-Aliakmonas Deltas***, Dadiá-Soufli Forest***, Evros Delta**, Lake Kerkini***, Mikrí Prespa NP***, Nestos Delta***, Porto Lagos area***.

GREEK IS Corfu***, Kos***, Lesvos***.

GEORGIA Iori Steppes**.

ISRAEL Arava Valley***, Bet Shean Valley***, Eilat***, Ein Gedi***, Hula Reserve***, Wadi Ammud-Mt Arbel***.

JORDAN Aqaba** (passage), Azraq* (winter), Petra*, Wadi Dana-Fidan** (winter), Wadi Rum* (winter), Wadi as Sir***.

MACEDONIA Galicica NP***, Lakes Ohrid and Prespa***.

MADEIRA*.

MOROCCO Agadir and the Sous Plain***, Asilah and Oued Loukkos***, Dayet Aaoua***, Goulimine to Tan-Tan***, Oualidia***, Ouarzazate***, Oued Massa***, Zaër***, Zeida***.

PORTUGAL Baixo Alentejo***, Cape St Vincent** (autumn), International Douro**, International Tagus***.

ROMANIA Dobrudja**.

SARDINIA Cagliari wetlands***, Capo Marargiu***, Giara di Gesturi***, Oristano wetlands***, San Pietro I***.

SPAIN Cabo de Gata**, Cáceres-Trujillo Steppes***, Coto Doñana***, La Serena**, Monfragüe NP***, Tablas de Daimiel***.

SYRIA Yarmuk Valley***.

TUNISIA Cap Bon Peninsula***, Chott el Djerid***, Lake Ichkeul***, Tunis***.
TURKEY Bafa Gölü***, Birecik-Halfeti***, Göksu Delta***, Kocaçay Delta***, Manyas Gölü***, Ulubat Gölü***, Uludağ NP***, Van Gölü***.

Italian Sparrow
Passer italiae   DF SH FG U   Res

Range: This form has been assigned to both Spanish and House Sparrows in the past but is now generally considered a stabilised hybrid between the two. Breeds throughout most of Italy, in Corsica, Sicily, Malta and Crete, but more southerly populations, e.g. in Sicily and Crete, tend to be closer to Spanish Sparrow.
Tips: often occurs in rocky habitats but strongly tied to human habitation in many areas and generally common.

Sites:
CORSICA Asco Valley***Biguglia Lake***, Bonifacio***, Cap Corse***.
GREEK IS Crete***.
ITALY Lake Massaciuccoli***, Maremma Regional Park***, Po Delta***, Tuscan archipelago***.
MALTA***.

Dead Sea Sparrow (Scrub Sparrow)
Passer moabiticus   SH D SD   Mig PMig

Range: Found in very scattered localities in the SE of the region. Breeds in S Turkey, adjacent N Syria and in S Syria, and the Rift Valley of Israel and Jordan. In the 1970s began to colonise Cyprus but now extinct there. Northernmost breeders in Turkey and N Israel are migratory, others partially migratory or dispersive, but wintering areas poorly known.
Tips: Inhabits scrub, particularly tamarisk, in desert or semi-desert areas, often near water. Breeds colonially, often in poplars, and frequently associates with Spanish Sparrow. Among the most reliable sites is Birecik in Turkey where it nests at the ibis breeding centre, and at Dayr al-Zawr in Syria.

Sites:
ISRAEL Arava Valley***, Bet Shean Valley***, Eilat***, Ein Gedi* (passage), Hula Reserve** (summer).
JORDAN Aqaba* (winter), Wadi Dana-Fidan (winter).

SYRIA Baath Lake***, Bahrat Homs***, Dayr al-Zawr***, Yarmuk Valley*** (mainly winter).
TURKEY Birecik-Halfeti***.

Cape Verde Sparrow (Iago Sparrow)
Passer iagoensis

FG SH U   Res

Range: Endemic to the Cape Verde Is, where it is fairly common on most islands but scarcer on Sal and Branco and absent from Fogo. Sometimes considered a race of **Rufous Sparrow** *P. motitensis*.
Tips: Dry plains, rocky cliffs and gorges, cultivated areas and parks and gardens in towns. Highly social at all times, nests colonially.

Site:
CAPE VERDE IS*.

Desert Sparrow
Passer simplex

D SD SH   Res (Nom) (Dis)

Range: In our region breeds in SE Morocco, parts of C and S Algeria, S Tunisia, and C and S Libya.
Tips: Inhabits desert edges and sandy plains with scattered trees, olive groves, oases and wadis. Usually seen in small flocks, often near habitation. Undoubtedly the best-known site for this species is the Café Yasmina on the edge of the Erg Chebbi in Morocco, where sightings are guaranteed.

Sites:
MOROCCO Tafilalt***.
TUNISIA Chott el Djerid**.

Pale Rock Sparrow (Pale Rockfinch)
Carpospiza brachydactyla

FG SH SD Mig

Range: Breeds in SE Turkey, adjacent N Syria, Lebanon, the Mt Hermon area, Armenia and Azerbaijan, and has bred in Jordan and probably NE Saudi Arabia. Departs breeding areas in Aug–Oct to winter in NE Africa, less regularly in S Iraq and Kuwait, and rarely in S Israel and Sinai, returning in Feb–May.

Tips: Search grass-covered plains and arid, rocky hillsides, semi-deserts and wadis, cultivated land in some areas and is often associated with pistacio trees. Usually seen in flocks, sometimes pairs. Best located by insect-like buzzing voice.

Sites:
ARMENIA Vedi Hills*** (summer).
ISRAEL Arava Valley*** (passage), Eilat*** (passage), Ein Gedi* (passage), Mt Hermon*** (summer).
JORDAN Azraq* (passage), Ghadir Burqu'* (irregular passage, winter), Petra (passage), Wadi Dana-Fidan* (summer), Wadi Rum* (passage, winter).

LEBANON Aammiq Marshes* (summer).
SYRIA Tadmur and Sabkhat Muh*** (passage), Wadi al-Qarn-Burqush** (summer).
TURKEY Birecik-Halfeti*** (summer), Van Gölü* (summer), Yeşlce*** (summer).

Yellow-throated Sparrow
Petronia xanthocollis

SH FG U Mig

Range: Very limited range in our region, breeding in SE Turkey where only discovered in the 1970s, Syria and E Iraq. A summer visitor arriving Mar–Apr and departing Sep–Nov to winter in India.

Tips: Occurs in dry woodland and cultivation, villages, gardens and oases. Gregarious at all times, migrating in flocks and breeding colonially.

Sites:
SYRIA Dayr al-Zawr***.
TURKEY Birecik-Halfeti*** (summer), Van Gölü (summer).

Rock Sparrow
Petronia petronia   M SD (FG) (U Res (PMig) (AMig)

Range: Breeds throughout Iberia and the Balearics, W and S France, S Switzerland, S Italy, on Corsica, Sardinia and Sicily. Further E it is patchily distributed in the S Balkans and Greece, more widespread in Turkey and the Caucasus, S to Israel and Jordan. Also breeds in the Atlantic on Madeira, Porto Santo, the Desertas and W Canaries, and across N Africa from S Morocco to Tunisia and NW Libya. A partial or altitudinal migrant in some parts of range.

Subspecies: Three–five very similar races occur in our region; nominate *petronia* is found from Iberia and Morocco to W Turkey, *barbara* from Algeria to Libya, *exigua* from C Turkey to the Caucasus, and *puteicola* in the Middle East. Atlantic island birds are sometimes separated as *madeirensis*.

Tips: Search for this species on cliffs and gorges, scree slopes and rocky outcrops, semi-desert and desert edge, and barren hillsides up to 2,500m. Also in cultivated areas, on ruins and in villages. Usually in pairs or small flocks, often nests colonially. Presence often revealed by characteristic wheezing call.

Sites:
ANDORRA***.

ARMENIA Lake Sevan***, Mt Aragats**, Pambak Mts**.

BALEARIC IS Formentera**, Ibiza**, Mallorca*.

BULGARIA Tissata NR***.

CANARY IS El Hierro*, Gomera*, Gran Canaria**, La Palma***, Tenerife**.

CORSICA Bonifacio***.

FRANCE Camargue***, Cévennes NP***, Les Alpilles***, Queyras NP***.

GREECE Delphi**, Mikrí Prespa NP***, Mt Olympus NP**.

GREEK IS Corfu***, Lesvos***.

ISRAEL Arava Valley***, Mt Hermon***, Wadi Ammud-Mt Arbel***.

ITALY Abruzzo NP***, Gargano Peninsula***, Sibillini NP***.

JORDAN Amman NP***, Azraq***, Petra***, Wadi Dana-Fidan***, Wadi Rum***, Wadi as Sir***.

MACEDONIA Galicica NP***, Lakes Ohrid and Prespa***.

MADEIRA***.

MOROCCO Agadir and the Sous Plain**, Boumalne***, Dayet Aaoua***, Oukaimeden***.

PORTUGAL Baixo Alentejo***, Boquilobo***, International Douro***, International Tagus***, Montesinho***, Peneda Gerês NP***, Sado Estuary**, Tagus Estuary**.

RUSSIA Teberdinskiy Reserve***.

SARDINIA Giara di Gesturi**, Oristano wetlands***.

SICILY San Vito Peninsula***.

SPAIN Aiguamolls de l'Empordá***, Aigües Tortes NP***, Cabo de Gata***, Cáceres-Trujillo Steppes***, Coto Doñana***, Garraf Massif***, Jaca***, La Serena**, Monfragüe***, Ordesa NP***, Picos de Europa**, Serrania de Ronda***, Sierra de Gredos***, Sierra de Guadarrama**, Zaragoza Steppes***.

SYRIA Tadmur and Sabkhat Muh***.

TUNISIA Chott el Djerid***.

TURKEY Birecik-Halfeti***, Demirkazik***, Soğuksu NP***, Van Gölü***.

Snowfinch (White-winged Snowfinch)
Montifringilla nivalis

M Res (AMig)

Range: A local breeder in the Cantabrians and Pyrenees, the Alps and N Apennines and in the Balkans to N Greece. Also breeds in C and S Turkey, more widely in the E of the country and the Caucasus. Very rare breeder on Corsica. Some move lower in winter but is otherwise resident.

Subspecies: Nominate race occurs in S Europe, replaced by *alpicola* in the Caucasus.

Tips: Search rocky slopes and mountains, edges of glaciers and snowfields, and alpine meadows with nearby rocky outcrops and cliffs. Often seen feeding alongside roads and around buildings in winter.

Sites:

ANDORRA*.

ARMENIA Arapan Area***. Mt Aragats***, Pambak Mts***.

AUSTRIA Hohe Tauern NP***, Hohe Wand*, Karwendel Reserve***, Schneeberg Mts***.

AZERBAIJAN Zakataly**.

BOSNIA-HERZEGOVINA Sujetska NP*.

CORSICA Asco Valley***.

FRANCE Cévennes NP* (winter), Les Alpilles* (winter), Mercantour NP**, Pyrenees NP***, Queyras NP***, Vanoise NP**.

GEORGIA Mt Kazbek***.

GERMANY Berchtesgaden NP**.

GREECE Mt Olympus NP**, Mt Parnassós NP***, Vikos-Aoos NP***.

ITALY Abruzzo NP***, Gran Paradiso NP***, Sibillini NP***, Stelvio NP***.

RUSSIA Teberdinskiy Reserve***.

SLOVENIA Triglav NP***.

SPAIN Aigües Tortes NP***, Jaca***, Ordesa NP***, Picos de Europa**.

SWITZERLAND Aletschwald***, Flims***, Swiss NP***.

TURKEY Demirkazik***, Sivrikaya***, Van Gölü***.

Blue Chaffinch
Fringilla teydea

CF (MF) (FG) Res

Range: A Canarian endemic, fairly common on Tenerife but now rare on Gran Canaria, with a single record from NW Lanzarote. Some limited altitudinal movements occur in winter.

Subspecies: Nominate form occurs on Tenerife and *polatzeki* on Gran Canaria

Tips: Found mainly in forests of Canarian Pine, at 1,000–2,000m but also commonly as low as 300m. Usually found in dense undergrowth and sometimes in laurels and tree heath, rarely seen in non-native trees. Recorded at lower levels during severe weather.

Red-fronted Serin
Serinus pusillus

M FG MF   AMig

Range: Locally common in our region, breeding in parts of S and E Turkey and more widely in the Caucasus. Mainly an altitudinal migrant but some winter on the S coast of Turkey, more rarely in Lebanon and Syria, and increasingly in recent years in N and C Israel, with one recent record from Jordan. Departs breeding areas late Jul–Sep and returns Mar–Apr.

Tips: A bird of scrub and scree-slopes, meadows and open woodland, mainly at 2,000–4,000m in montane areas and high valleys. Often associated with juniper or wild roses and sometimes seen close to habitation.

Sites:

ARMENIA Pambak Mts***.
GEORGIA Mt Kazbek***.
GREEK IS Lesvos* (winter).
ISRAEL Golan Heights* (winter), Mt Hermon* (winter).

LEBANON Qaraoun Lake* (passage, winter).
RUSSIA Teberdinskiy Reserve*** (summer).
TURKEY Demirkazik***, Sivrikaya***, Uludağ NP***, Van Gölü***.

Syrian Serin (Tristram's Serin)
Serinus syriacus

SH FG (SD)   PMig

Range: Confined to the Western Palearctic, in a very limited area of the Middle East, breeding only in the Lebanon and Anti-Lebanon ranges of S Syria, Lebanon and N Israel, with an isolated population at Wadi Dana in Jordan. A partial migrant with some leaving breeding areas in Sep–Oct, when regularly found in S Israel and sometimes Jordan, returning late Mar–early Apr. Also recorded in Sinai and N Egypt at this season.

Tips: Found on wooded and bushy hillsides at 1,000–2,000m, usually in juniper or cedar but also deciduous trees and orchards. In winter occurs in lower and more open areas, often in scrub and semi-deserts.

Sites:

ISRAEL Arava Valley* (passage, mainly spring), Eilat** (passage), Ein Gedi** (winter), Mt Hermon*** (summer), Nizzana*** (winter).

JORDAN Amman NP*, Petra* (winter), Wadi Dana-Fidan***, Wadi Rum* (passage), Wadi as Sir* (passage).

LEBANON Aammiq Marshes* (passage), Barouk Cedars*** (summer), Qaraoun Lake** (passage).

SYRIA Wadi al-Qarn-Burqush*** (summer).

Canary (Island Canary)
Serinus canaria   CF MF SH FG   Res (Dis)

Range: an Atlantic Is endemic breeding throughout the Azores, on Madeira and the Canaries. In the Canaries common on most islands but only recently discovered breeding at a single site on Lanzarote, and only possibly breeds on Fuerteventura. Some Madeiran birds winter on Porto Santo and the Desertas and inter-island movements have been recorded in the Azores.

Tips: Common in pine and laurel forests, open woodland and scrub on hillsides; in lower areas around cultivation, in gardens and orchards. Occurs from sea level to 1,500m.

Sites:
AZORES*.
CANARY IS El Hierro***, Gomera***, Gran Canaria***, La Palma***, Lanzarote*, Tenerife***.

MADEIRA*.

Citril Finch
Serinus citrinella   M CF (FG) AMig

Range: In Iberia breeds in the Cantabrians, Pyrenees and in the Sierra de Gredos, Sierra de Guadarrama and Serrania de Cuenca. Further E breeds in the Massif Central, Vosges and Jura, over much of the Alps as far as S Germany and E Austria and in uplands of N Italy and Slovenia. In winter occurs at lower elevations and is more widespread in Spain and the Alps.

Tips: Search conifer forest, mainly pine, larch and spruce at 800–1,500m. Also found in birch-holly woodland and montane meadows, and in winter lower valleys, woodland edges and more open country.

Sites:
ANDORRA*.
AUSTRIA Hohe Tauern NP***, Hohe Wand**, Karwendel Reserve***, Schneeberg Mts***.

FRANCE Cévennes NP***, Écrins NP***, Forêt d'Issaux***, Mercantour NP***, Prats-de-

Mollo***, Pyrenees NP***, Queyras NP***, Vanoise NP***.
GERMANY Ammer Valley***, Berchtesgaden NP***.
ITALY Gran Paradiso NP***, Stelvio NP***.
SLOVENIA Triglav NP**.

SPAIN Aigües Tortes NP***, Jaca***, Ordesa NP***, Picos de Europa***, Sierra de Gredos***, Sierra de Guadarrama***.
SWITZERLAND Aletschwald***, Col de Bretolet***, Flims***, Monte Generoso***, Swiss NP***.

Corsican Finch
Serinus corsicanus

CF MF DF SH FG AMig

Range: Formerly treated as a race of Citril Finch *S. citrinella*. Confined to Corsica and Sardinia, where widespread and fairly common, and Capraia, Gorgona and Elba in the Tuscan archipelago. Undertakes altitudinal movements in winter and becomes more widespread in lowland areas.

Tips: Occurs in more varied habitats than Citril Finch, in coniferous and deciduous woodland, and in more open areas from sea level to mountains. Often nests in tree heath.

Sites:
CORSICA Asco Valley***, Bonifacio***, Restonica Valley***.
ITALY Tuscan archipelago***.

SARDINIA Capo Marargiu***, Giara di Gesturi***, Monte Arcuso***, San Pietro I***.

Twite
Carduelis flavirostris

Summer **M T** winter **ES FG** **Res PMig Mig AMig**

Range: Found in two widely disjunct areas of the Western Palearctic. Breeds in coastal areas of NW Europe in N Great Britain and from Varanger and the Kola Peninsula to S Norway. The eastern population breeds in the Caucasus and in E and SE Turkey with small isolated populations in S Turkey. Northernmost birds are migratory and winter from E and S Great Britain to S Scandinavia and the southern shores of the Baltic, departing northern breeding areas in late Sep–Oct and returning Mar–Apr. Caucasian birds move lower in winter and it is more widespread in Turkey at this season.

Subspecies: Nominate race occurs in Fenno–Scandia replaced by *pipilans* in the British Isles. More distinct Caucasian birds belong to race *brevirostris*.

Tips: In the N breeds on open moorland, sometimes in mountains, in areas of rocky grassland and dwarf birch. More easily found in winter, in open coastal areas with abundant weeds, sometimes on pastures. Caucasian birds breed on high rocky plateaux at 2,500–3,500m and in winter move to lower plains and valleys.

Sites:

ARMENIA Arapan Area***, Mt Aragats***, Pambak Mts***.
BELGIUM Het Zwin** (winter).
GREAT BRITAIN Minsmere** (winter), N Norfolk coast*** (winter), Orkney Is***, Outer Hebrides***, Rhum***, Shetland Is***, Spurn Peninsula*** (passage).
DENMARK Amager*** (winter), Bornholm-Christiansø*** (winter), Ringkøbing Fjord*** (passage, winter), Rømø*** (passage, winter), Skagen*** (passage, winter), Skallingen-Blåvandshuk*** (passage, winter).
FINLAND Pallas-Ounastunturi NP*** (summer).
FRANCE Baie de Bourgneuf*** (winter), Baie du Mont-St-Michel*** (winter), Cap Gris Nez*** (passage, winter), Somme Estuary*** (winter).
GEORGIA Mt Kazbek*** (summer).

HUNGARY Hortobágy NP** (winter), Kiskunság NP*** (winter).
IRELAND Cliffs of Moher*** (summer), Rathlin Is* (summer), Strangford Lough*** (winter).
NETHERLANDS Lauwersmeer*** (winter), Oostvaardersplassen*** (winter), Terschelling*** (winter), Texel*** (winter).
NORWAY Lofoten Is*** (summer), Slettnes*** (summer), Utsira*** (summer, passage), Varanger*** (summer).
RUSSIA Kola Peninsula* (summer), Teberdinskiy Reserve*** (summer).
SWEDEN Falsterbo** (passage, winter), Getterön*** (passage, winter), Gotland*** (passage, winter), Kristianstad*** (passage, winter), Öland*** (passage, winter).
TURKEY Sivrikaya*** (summer).

Arctic Redpoll
Carduelis hornemanni

T CF SH   Res (PMig) (Nom)

Range: Breeds in the far N of Scandinavia, on the Kola Peninsula, the Arctic coast of Russia from the White Sea E, and in S Novaya Zemlya. Winters S to 60°N in Scandinavia and Russia, irregularly further S. Annual in Great Britain with highest numbers in invasion years, most in autumn with some overwintering. A resident and partial migrant with main autumn movement in Aug–Oct but often rather nomadic in winter, returning mainly in Mar.

Subspecies: Race breeding in our region is *exilipes* (nominate *hornemanni* breeds in the Canadian Arctic and Greenland) but some individuals are not separable in the field from paler races of *C. flammea*. The taxonomy of the redpoll group is confused with some authorities treating *flammea* and *hornemanni* as conspecific, and others regarding *exilipes* and *hornemanni* as two full species.

Tips: Breeds on tundra with stunted bushes, birch and willow scrub, rocks and ravines. In winter found in open woodland and scrub. Search flocks of Common Redpoll for migrants and vagrants of this species.

Sites:

GREAT BRITAIN N Norfolk coast* (autumn, winter), Shetland Is* (autumn).
DENMARK Skagen** (winter).
FINLAND Kevo NR*** (summer).
NORWAY Øvre Pasvik NP*** (summer), Slettnes*** (summer), Varanger*** (summer).

RUSSIA Kola Peninsula***.
SWEDEN Abisko NP** (summer), Ammarnäs*** (summer), Falsterbo* (autumn), Holmöarna** (passage), Lake Ånnsjön***.

Two-barred Crossbill (White-winged Crossbill)
Loxia leucoptera   CF   Res (PMig) (Irr)

Range: Breeds in NE Finland and E across N Russia, and has bred in N Norway and Sweden. Periodically irruptive when large numbers move S or SE to S Scandinavia, the Baltic states and further S in Russia. Most movements occur in late Sep–Dec, sometimes returning as early as Jan but mainly in Mar–Apr.

Tips: Prefers larch, sometimes cedar, spruce or fir. Outside regular range during invasion years search flocks of Common Crossbill for individuals of this species but beware of Common Crossbills with wing-bars.

Sites:

FINLAND Kuusamo***, Lemmenjoki NP***, Oulanka NP***, Pallas-Ounastunturi NP***, Urho Kekkonen NP***.
LATVIA Cape Kolka** (passage).

LITHUANIA Kirsiu Peninsula** (passage).
RUSSIA Kola Peninsula*.
SWEDEN Falsterbo* (autumn), Holmöarna*** (passage).

Scottish Crossbill
Loxia scotica   CF   Res

Range: Currently regarded as Britain's only endemic bird, being confined to the NE and C Highlands of Scotland. Breeds from N Argyll to Inverness, E to Aberdeenshire and S to Perth. However, the current status of crossbills present in parts of Scotland is now confused. A recent study in Abernethy Forest revealed that Parrot Crossbills far outnumbered Scottish Crossbills in the period 1995–2001. If this is a long-established population then many past records of Scottish Crossbills may be erroneous. This form is considered by some to be a race of **Common Crossbill** *L. curvirostra* and by others to be a small-billed race of Parrot Crossbill, and it may soon lose species status.

Tips: Search ancient native Caledonian pinewoods but bear in mind that both Common and Parrot Crossbills may also be present. Also found in mature plantations but not in closed-canopy areas.

Sites:
GREAT BRITAIN Cairngorms and Speyside***.

Parrot Crossbill
Loxia pytyopsittacus

CF Res (PMig) (Irr)

Range: Main range is in C Norway, S and E Sweden and E Finland and E across Russia to the Pechora River. Also breeds irregularly in the Baltic states, Poland and Belarus. Has bred elsewhere in N Europe and the first confirmed breeding in Great Britain was in Norfolk in 1984. However, a recent study found Parrot Crossbills breeding in Abernethy Forest in the Scottish Highlands. This area has long been considered a stronghold of Scottish Crossbill, but the study showed Parrot Crossbills to be far the most numerous of the three crossbill species present. These may be part of a long-established population or the result of a more recent irruption.

Tips: Prefers pine but sometimes seen in spruce and, less often, in larch, often in drier or montane areas. Usually in pairs or small groups, larger during invasions, when often associates with Common Crossbill. In Scotland found in ancient Scots Pine woodlands.

Sites:
DENMARK Skagen** (winter).
ESTONIA Nigula NR*** (irregular).
FINLAND Åland Is***, Kuusamo***, Liminganlahti***, Linnansaari NP***, Oulanka NP***, Pallas-Ounastunturi NP***, Patvinsuo NP***, Pyhä-Häkki NP***, Urho Kekkonen NP***.
GREAT BRITAIN Cairngorms and Speyside**.
LATVIA Lake Pape*** (passage).

NORWAY Lista (passage), Øvre Pasvik NP***, Utsira* (passage).
POLAND Gdańsk Bay* (summer, passage).
RUSSIA Kola Peninsula***.
SWEDEN Ammarnäs***, Falsterbo** (autumn), Färnebofjärden***, Gotland***, Holmöarna*** (passage), Lake Ånnsjön***, Muddus NP***, Store Mosse NP (passage), Tåkern***, Tyresta NP***.

Crimson-winged Finch
Rhodopechys sanguineus   M SH (FG) AMig

Range: A chiefly C Asian bird that breeds in our region in C, SE and E Turkey and the Caucasus, montane S Lebanon and N Israel, probably also Syria, and in the High Atlas of Morocco and Algeria. Moves lower in autumn and winter, when it occurs in Syria and more widely in NW Africa.

Subspecies: The race *alienus* occurs in N Africa and may well be a separate species. The nominate race occurs in remainder of range.

Tips: Search dry scrub-covered montane slopes and rocky ridges, and is often seen in juniper above the treeline. Occurs at 900m but usually above 2,000m and up to 3,000m, descending in winter, when occurs on rocky and bare ground, in dry cultivation and sometimes gardens. Feeds largely on the ground, in small flocks in winter and is often tame and approachable. Uncommon to locally common in our region and is more widespread in Turkey than previously thought.

Sites:
ARMENIA Arapan Area***, Mt Aragats***.
GEORGIA Javakheti Plateau**, Mt Kazbek***.
ISRAEL Mt Hermon***.
LEBANON Barouk Cedars***.

MOROCCO Boumalne**, Oukaimeden***.
TURKEY Demirkazik***, Doğubeyazit***, Sivrikaya***, Van Gölü***.

Desert Finch
Rhodospiza obsoleta   SD FG Res

Range: A mainly C Asian species with isolated populations in our region. Breeds in SE Turkey, adjacent N and C Syria, and parts of Israel and Jordan. Resident with some short-distance dispersal in Oct–Mar. Occasionally wanders further afield in winter.

Tips: Inhabits semi-desert and dry plains with scattered trees and bushes, often at the edges of cultivation or along roads. Loosely colonial when breeding and sociable at all times, spends much time on the ground but also perches in trees.

Sites
ISRAEL Arava Valley***, Bet Shean Valley***, Eilat***, Mt Hermon***, Nizzana***.
JORDAN Azraq***, Wadi Rum.
LEBANON Qaraoun Lake (winter).

SYRIA Bahrat Homs***, Sabkhat al-Jubbal***.
TURKEY Birecik-Halfeti***, Yeşilce***, Van Gölü*.

Mongolian Finch
Bucanetes mongolicus   M   Res (AMig)

Range: A C Asian species that reaches the extreme western edge of its range in E Turkey and the Caucasus. Generally rare in our region, but regular in the Doğubeyazıt area and around Van Gölü. More numerous in parts of the Caucasus, particularly in Nakhichevan, in Azerbaijan, where its breeds sympatrically with Trumpeter Finch. Breeding long suspected in Armenia but confirmed only in 2001 and has been recorded in the Arax Valley. Resident with some altitudinal movement, occurring lower in Oct–May.

Tips: Occurs in upland semi-desert areas at 1,000–4,000m on rocky slopes, ravines and cliff-faces with sparse vegetation. A semi-colonial breeder and sociable outside the

Sites:
ARMENIA Vedi Hills*** (summer).

TURKEY Doğubeyazıt** (summer), Van Gölü** (summer).

Trumpeter Finch
Bucanetes githagineus   D SD SH   Res (PMig) (Nom)

Range: Breeds across N Africa, except the NW coastal strip, and in Sinai and S Israel. Isolated populations exist in the Canaries and in a tiny area of S Spain, mainly in Almería and Murcia but increasing and spreading, and apparently feral birds breed in southern Portugal. Probably also a regular breeder in SE Turkey, the Caucasus and Syria. Resident, partially migratory or nomadic, with birds wandering widely during droughts, but more migratory further E. In winter rare but regular in Lebanon and N Israel, possibly annual on Malta with occasional influxes.

Subspecies: Nominate race occurs in most of the Sahara and Egypt, *crassirostris* from Sinai to Turkey and Iraq. Canarian birds, found on Tenerife, Gran Canaria, Fuerteventura and Lanzarote (a vagrant to Hierro), belong to *amantum*, and *zedlitzi* occurs in Spain and NW Africa.

Tips: Bare rocky deserts and semi-deserts, dry hillsides and stony steppes, cliffs and wadis. Also occurs on shores in the Canaries. Sociable, usually on the ground but occasionally perches on bushes and wires. Best located by its song, likened to a toy trumpet.

Sites:

ARMENIA Khosrov Preserve**, Vedi Hills***.
CANARY IS Fuerteventura***, Gomera**, Gran Canaria**, Lanzarote***, Tenerife**.
EGYPT Hurghada***, Luxor***, Sharm el Sheikh***, Suez area***.
ISRAEL Arava Valley***, Eilat***, Ein Gedi***, Nizzana***.
JORDAN Aqaba***, Azraq***, Ghadir Burqu'***, Petra**, Wadi Rum**.

MALTA (passage).
MOROCCO Boumalne***, Goulimine to Tan-Tan***, Ouarzazate***, Tafilalt***, Zeida***.
SPAIN Cabo de Gata***, Serrania de Ronda (winter).
SYRIA Tadmur and Sabkhat Muh***.
TUNISIA Chott el Djerid***, Tatahouine***.
TURKEY Birecik-Halfeti, Yeşilce**, Van Gölü.

Common Rosefinch (Scarlet Grosbeak)
Carpodacus erythrinus   MF DF SH FG Mig

Range: Main range is from the Netherlands to the Baltic states and S Finland and E across Belarus, Ukraine and Russia to the Urals. Also breeds in very scattered localities across C and SE Europe, in N Turkey and the Caucasus. In recent decades has expanded westwards, although the recently established Dutch population is now in decline, and has also bred in Britain, France, Belgium and Sweden in recent decades. Occurs on passage over much of C and E Europe and is regular W to Great Britain in small numbers. Leaves breeding grounds late Jul–Aug and returns in mid May.

Subspecies: Nominate occurs over most of range with *kubanensis* in N Turkey and the Caucasus.

Tips: Search woodland edges, close to farmland, thickets and hedgerows; often prefers wetter areas.

Sites:

ARMENIA Khosrov Preserve*** (summer), Mt Aragats*** (summer).
BELARUS Belovezhskaya Pushcha NP*** (summer), Berezinsky Reserve*** (summer), Prypyatsky NP*** (summer).
BELGIUM Het Zwin* (passage).
GREAT BRITAIN Flamborough Head** (passage), Minsmere* (spring), N Norfolk coast*** (passage), Orkney Is** (passage), Portland** (passage), Scilly*** (passage), Shetland Is*** (passage), Spurn Peninsula** (passage).
BULGARIA Cape Kaliakra*** (passage).
CZECH REPUBLIC Jeseníky Mts*** (summer), Krkonoše NP*** (summer), Šumava NP*** (summer).

DENMARK Bornholm-Christiansø*** (summer, passage), Hanstholm*** (summer, passage), Møn-Falster*** (summer, passage), Skagen*** (passage), Skallingen-Blåvandshuk*** (summer, passage).
ESTONIA Matsalu Bay*** (passage), Nigula NR*** (summer).
FINLAND Åland Is*** (summer), Kolvanan Uuro*** (summer), Kuusamo*** (summer), Liminganlahti*** (summer), Parikkala*** (summer), Patvinsuo NP*** (summer), Ruissalo*** (summer), Vesijako NP*** (summer).
FRANCE Cap Gris Nez*** (passage), Ouessant*** (passage).
GEORGIA Mt Kazbek*** (summer).

GERMANY Mecklenburg Lakes*** (summer), Oder Valley*** (summer), Rügen*** (summer).
GREEK IS Lesvos* (passage).
ISRAEL Bet Shean Valley*** (passage, winter).
LATVIA Cape Kolka*** (summer), Lake Lubana*** (summer), Lake Pape*** (summer).
LITHUANIA Kirsiu Peninsula*** (summer).
NETHERLANDS Oostvaardersplassen* (summer, passage), Terschelling* (summer, passage), Texel* (summer, passage), Zwanenwater* (passage).
NORWAY Utsira* (passage).
POLAND Białowieża Forest*** (summer), Białystok Fishponds*** (summer), Biebrza Marshes*** (summer), Bieszczady NP*** (summer), Chełm Marshes*** (summer), Gdańsk Bay*** (summer), Milicz Fishponds*** (summer), Siemianówka Reservoir*** (summer), Słońsk*** (summer), Szczecin Bay area** (summer), Tatra NP*** (summer).
RUSSIA Teberdinskiy Reserve*** (summer), Volga Delta*** (passage).
SLOVAKIA High Tatras NP*** (summer), Orava Reservoir*** (summer).
SWEDEN Falsterbo*** (passage), Gotland*** (summer, passage), Hjälstaviken*** (summer, passage), Holmöarna*** (passage), Hornborgasjön*** (summer), Kristianstad*** (summer, passage), Kvismaren*** (summer), Lake Ånnsjön*** (summer), Öland*** (summer, passage), Tåkern*** (summer).
TURKEY Soğuksu NP*** (passage), Sivrikaya*** (summer), Yeşilce*** (summer, passage).
UKRAINE Carpathians*** (summer).

Sinai Rosefinch (Pale Rosefinch)
Carpodacus synoicus   D SD   Res

Range: In our region breeds in S Sinai, Israel, W Jordan and N Saudi Arabia, and elsewhere much further E in Asia. Chiefly resident but may descend lower in winter or become somewhat nomadic. More widespread in Sinai in winter.

Tips: Inhabits rocky deserts, arid foothills and dry mountains up to 2,000m, usually in remote and barren areas with little vegetation but often near a water source. Frequently visits natural and man-made drinking sites both morning and afternoon. Often seen in family parties and larger groups outside the breeding season.

Sites:
EGYPT Santa Katharina Monastery***.
ISRAEL Arava Valley*** (winter), Eilat*** (winter).

JORDAN Aqaba**, Petra***, Wadi Dana-Fidan***, Wadi Rum***.

Great Rosefinch
Carpodacus rubicilla   M (SH) Res

Range: In our region breeds in the C and E Caucasus Mts, but the main range is much further E in Asia. Resident with some altitudinal movement and in winter occurs over a wider area in the Caucasus.

Tips: Usually found at 2,500–3,500m in alpine meadows and on scree-slopes, boulder-strewn hillsides and cliffs above the rhododendron zone. In winter descends to 1,000–1,500m, in ravines and valleys, where it occurs in scrubby habitats.

Sites:
GEORGIA Mt Kazbek***.
RUSSIA Teberdinskiy Reserve***.

Pine Grosbeak
Pinicola enucleator   Summer **CF (SH)** winter **DF (U)**   Res **(PMig) (Irr)**

Range: Breeds in N Norway, N Sweden, N and E Finland, the Kola Peninsula and across N Russia, mainly between 65°N and 70°N. In some years most remain within breeding range but in others virtually all move S, reaching S Scandinavia, European Russia and Germany, and the species may have bred in Ukraine following an invasion in 2001. Most movements occur in late Sep–Oct and late Feb–Mar, but irruptions can occur in midwinter.

Tips: Breeds in pure conifers, favouring spruce and larch, or woods mixed with birch and alder; also Arctic scrub and in winter often in deciduous woodland, sometimes gardens.

Sites:
BELARUS Belovezhskaya Pushcha NP* (winter), Berezinsky Reserve* (winter).
FINLAND Kevo NR***, Kuusamo***, Lake Inari***, Lemmenjoki NP***, Oulanka NP***, Pallas-Ounastunturi NP***, Patvinsuo NP***, Pyhätunturi NP***, Urho Kekkonen NP***.
NORWAY Lista (passage), Øvre Pasvik NP***, Stabbursdalen NP***.

RUSSIA Kola Peninsula***.
SWEDEN Abisko NP***, Ammarnäs***, Holmöarna*** (passage), Lake Ånnsjön***, Muddus NP***, Padjelanta NP***, Ripakaisenvuoma***, Sarek NP***, Tarnasjön***.

Azores Bullfinch
Pyrrhula murina   CF DF MF   Res

Range: Formerly considered a race of Common Bullfinch *P. pyrrhula*. Endemic to the Azores, where now extremely rare with a very restricted range and probably numbers *c.*150 pairs. Breeds on São Miguel, where rediscovered after being thought extinct for nearly 50 years. Restricted to the Pico da Varda area of the E of the island, in the Pico da Varda and Pico Verde mountains and the Ribeira do Guilherme Valley. Some altitudinal movement may occur but otherwise resident.

Tips: Occurs in native laurel forest, and sometimes found in dense stands of the introduced Japanese Red Cedar.

Site:
AZORES*.

Hawfinch
Coccothraustes coccothraustes   MF DF (FG)   Res (Mig) (Dis)

Range: Widespread from Iberia and NW Africa to S Scotland and S Scandinavia and E across Russia to the Urals. In the Mediterranean breeds on Corsica and Sardinia and also from N Greece, across N Turkey to the Caucasus. More widespread around the Mediterranean and Middle East in winter.

Subspecies: Three races occur in our region; nominate over much of Europe with *nigricans* in Ukraine and the Caucasus and *buvryi* in NW Africa.

Tips: Uncommon over much of range and usually shy and elusive, spending much time quietly in deep foliage. Often seen in beech and hornbeam woods, also oak and cherry, in some areas in parks, large gardens and orchards. Most easily seen in winter when flocks feed along hedges and woodland edges, and more often on the ground.

Sites:

ALBANIA Lake Shkodra**.
ALGERIA El Kala NP***.
ANDORRA.
AUSTRIA Marchauen-Marchegg Reserve***, Wienerwald***.
BALEARIC IS Mallorca* (passage, winter).
BELARUS Belovezhskaya Pushcha NP***, Berezinsky Reserve***, Prypyatsky NP***.

BELGIUM Croix-Scaille NR*, Hautes Fagnes Natural Park*, Lesse et Lomme NR*.
BOSNIA-HERZEGOVINA Sujetska NP***.
GREAT BRITAIN Breckland***, N Norfolk coast***, Shetland Is* (passage).
BULGARIA Albena-Golden Sands***, Cape Kaliakra**, Rila Mts***, Ropotamo NP***, Strandja Mts***, Studen Kladenetz**.

CORSICA Asco Valley***, Restonica Valley***.
CYPRUS* (winter).
CZECH REPUBLIC Lednice***, Pálava Hills***, Třeboňsko***.
DENMARK Bornholm-Christiansø***, Skagen***.
ESTONIA Matsalu Bay*** (passage).
FRANCE Fontainebleau***, Forêt d'Orient***, Lac du Der-Chantecoq***.
GERMANY Bayerischer Wald NP***, Berchtesgaden NP**, Vessertal***.
GREECE Avas Gorge**, Dadiá-Soufli Forest***, Mikrí Prespa NP***, Nestos Delta*.
GREEK IS Lesvos*** (passage, winter).
HUNGARY Aggtelek NP***, Börzsöny NP***, Buda Hills***, Csákvár***, Danube Bend***, Pilis Hills***, Zemplén Hills***.
ISRAEL Mt Hermon** (winter).
ITALY Abruzzo NP***, Gargano Peninsula***, Po Delta***, Sibillini NP***.
JORDAN Amman NP* (winter), Wadi as Sir* (winter).
LATVIA Cape Kolka** (passage).
LITHUANIA Kirsiu Peninsula** (passage).
MACEDONIA Galicica NP***, Lakes Ohrid and Prespa***.
MALTA* (passage, winter).
MOROCCO Dayet Aaoua***, Oukaimeden**.
NETHERLANDS Oostvaardersplassen***, Terschelling***, Texel***, Veluwe***.

NORWAY Utsira* (passage).
POLAND Białowieża Forest***, Bieszczady NP***, Chełm Marshes***, Gdańsk Bay**, Kampinos NP***, Milicz Fishponds***, Siemianówka Reservoir**, Słońsk***.
PORTUGAL Baixo Alentejo***, Boquilobo***, International Douro***, International Tagus***, Montesinho**, Ria Formosa**, Sado Estuary***, Santo André Lagoon***, Tagus Estuary***.
ROMANIA Dobrudja***, Retezat NP***.
RUSSIA Teberdinskiy Reserve**.
SLOVAKIA Nízke Tatry NP***, Slovenský Kras***, Vihorlatske Hills***.
SLOVENIA Triglav NP***.
SPAIN Cáceres-Trujillo Steppes***, Coto Doñana***, Monfragüe***, Picos de Europa***, Serrania de Ronda**, Sierra de Gredos***, Sierra de Guadarrama**.
SWEDEN Falsterbo**, Gotland***, Hornborgasjön***, Kristianstad***, Öland***.
SWITZERLAND Niderholz***, Col de Bretolet** (passage).
TUNISIA Ain Draham***.
TURKEY Birecik-Halfeti* (winter), İstanbul**, Soğuksu NP***.
UKRAINE Carpathians***, Crimean Mts**.
YUGOSLAVIA Fruška Gora NP**, Lake Skadar**.

Lapland Bunting (Lapland Longspur)
Calcarius lapponicus   Summer **T** winter **ES FG**   **Mig**

Range: Breeds in upland areas of C and S Norway and in coastal areas of N Norway, N Sweden, N Finland and the Kola Peninsula, and Arctic Russia, including Ostrov Kolguev and Novaya Zemlya. Winters from Ukraine and S Russia eastwards, less commonly in C Europe. Small numbers winter in coastal NW Europe from Denmark and Sweden to N France and on the E coast of Britain, being most numerous in the Waddensee. In Great Britain mainly a scarce passage migrant and winter visitor present Oct–Mar but has bred sporadically in Scotland since the 1970s.

Subspecies: Nominate race breeds in N Europe, birds wintering in Great Britain and north-western Europe include the very similar *subcalcaratus* from Greenland.

Tips: Breeds on shrubby and mossy tundra with dwarf willows, often near lakes. In winter search shores and coastal grassland, pastures and waste ground. Often associates with other buntings, particularly Snow Bunting, sometimes flocks of larks or finches.

Sites:

BELGIUM Het Zwin** (winter).

GREAT BRITAIN Dungeness* (autumn, winter), Flamborough Head* (autumn), Minsmere* (autumn, winter), N Norfolk coast*** (passage, winter), Pembrokeshire Is* (autumn), Portland** (autumn, winter), Scilly*** (autumn, winter), Shetland Is*** (autumn), Spurn Peninsula*** (passage, winter).

DENMARK Bornholm-Christiansø*** (passage, winter), Møn-Falster** (passage), Ringkøbing Fjord** (passage, winter), Rømø*(passage, winter), Skagen*** (passage, winter), Skallingen-Blåvandshuk*** (passage, winter).

FINLAND Kevo NR*** (summer), Kilpisjärvi Saana*** (summer), Lake Inari*** (summer), Lemmenjoki NP*** (summer), Oulanka NP*** (summer), Pallas-Ounastunturi NP*** (summer), Urho Kekkonen NP*** (summer).

FRANCE Baie du Mont-St-Michel* (passage, winter), Cap Gris Nez* (passage, winter), Marais Poitevin* (winter), Ouessant** (passage), Somme Estuary** (passage, winter), Trunvel Reserve* (autumn, winter).

GERMANY Heligoland*** (passage).

HUNGARY Hortobágy NP*** (winter), Kiskunság NP*** (winter).

IRELAND Mullet Peninsula* (passage, winter).

LATVIA Cape Kolka** (passage).

LITHUANIA Kirsiu Peninsula** (passage).

NETHERLANDS Lauwersmeer** (passage, winter), Oostvaardersplassen (winter), Texel* (passage).

NORWAY Dovrefjell NP*** (summer), Fokstumyra*** (summer), Hardangervidda NP*** (summer), Rondane NP*** (summer), Slettnes*** (summer), Stabbursdalen NP*** (summer), Utsira*** (passage), Varanger*** (summer).

POLAND Gdańsk Bay*** (passage, winter).

RUSSIA Kola Peninsula*** (summer), Teberdinskiy Reserve* (winter).

SWEDEN Abisko NP*** (summer), Ammarnäs*** (summer), Falsterbo** (passage), Gotland*** (passage), Hjälstaviken*** (passage), Holmöarna*** (passage), Kristianstad*** (passage), Lake Ånnsjön*** (summer), Öland*** (passage), Padjelanta NP*** (summer), Sarek NP*** (summer).

Snow Bunting
Plectrophenax nivalis   Summer **T M** winter **ES FG** Mig **(AMig) (Res)**

Range: Breeds in Iceland and N Scotland, the uplands and N of Scandinavia and the Kola Peninsula, and across Arctic Russia including Svalbard, Franz Josef Land and Novaya Zemlya. Main wintering range is from E Poland, Belarus and Ukraine eastwards, but smaller numbers winter on the E coast of Great Britain and in coastal NW Europe from the Baltic and S Scandinavia to Brittany.

Subspecies: Nominate race occurs on Arctic islands, the Faroes and Fenno–Scandia intergrading with *vlasowae* in the NE, and *insulae* breeds in Iceland and Scotland.

Tips: Breeds on rocky tundra and coasts, in S of range on barren mountains. In Arctic settlements often nests on buildings. In winter search shingle and sandy shores, open coastal farmland and waste ground. Often occurs with Lapland Buntings and Horned Larks.

Sites:

BELARUS Belovezhskaya Pushcha NP* (winter).

BELGIUM Het Zwin** (winter).

GREAT BRITAIN Anglesey* (autumn, winter), Cairngorms** (summer), Dungeness* (autumn, winter), Islay* (winter), Minsmere* (autumn, winter), N Norfolk coast*** (autumn, winter), Orkney Is** (winter), Outer Hebrides*** (autumn, winter), Pembrokeshire Is** (autumn, winter), Portland* (autumn, winter), Scilly*** (autumn, winter), Shetland Is*** (passage, winter), Spurn Peninsula*** (passage, winter).

DENMARK Bornholm-Christiansø*** (passage, winter), Hanstholm** (winter), Møn-Falster** (passage), Ringkøbing Fjord*** (passage, winter), Rømø*** (passage, winter), Skagen*** (passage, winter), Skallingen-Blåvandshuk*** (passage, winter), Stignæs*** (passage).

FAROE IS* (summer).

FINLAND Kevo NR*** (summer), Kilpisjärvi Saana*** (summer), Lake Inari*** (summer), Lemmenjoki NP*** (summer), Liminganlahti*** (passage), Oulanka NP*** (summer), Pallas-Ounastunturi NP*** (summer), Urho Kekkonen NP*** (summer).

FRANCE Baie du Mont-St-Michel* (passage, winter), Cap Gris Nez** (passage, winter), Ouessant** (passage), Somme Estuary** (passage, winter), Trunvel Reserve* (autumn, winter).

HUNGARY Hortobágy NP*** (winter), Kardoskút*** (winter), Kiskunság NP*** (winter).

ICELAND Breiðafjörður***, Grímsey*** (summer), Northwest Peninsula*** (summer), Jökulsárgljúfur NP*** (summer), Lake Mývatn*** (summer), Olfusar Delta***, Reykjanes Peninsula*** (summer), Skagafjörður***, Thingvellir NP*** (summer).

IRELAND Mullet Peninsula**(passage, winter), North Bull*** (winter).

LATVIA Cape Kolka** (passage, winter), Lake Pape** (passage, winter).

LITHUANIA Kirsiu Peninsula** (passage).

NETHERLANDS Lauwersmeer*** (passage, winter), Oostvaardersplassen** (winter), Terschelling*** (winter), Texel*** (winter).

NORWAY Dovrefjell NP*** (summer), Fokstumyra*** (summer), Hardangervidda NP*** (summer), Lofoten Is*** (winter), Øvre Pasvik NP*** (summer), Rondane NP*** (summer), Slettnes*** (summer), Utsira*** (passage), Varanger*** (summer).

POLAND Gdańsk Bay*** (passage, winter).

ROMANIA Danube Delta** (winter), Dobrudja** (winter).

RUSSIA Kola Peninsula*** (summer), Volga Delta*** (winter).

SVALBARD* (summer).

SWEDEN Abisko NP*** (summer), Ammarnäs*** (summer), Falsterbo** (summer, passage), Getterön*** (passage, winter), Gotland*** (passage), Hjälstaviken*** (passage), Holmöarna*** (passage), Kristianstad*** (passage, winter), Lake Ånnsjön*** (summer), Öland*** (passage, winter), Padjelanta NP*** (summer), Sarek NP*** (summer).

Pine Bunting
Emberiza leucocephalos   CF SH (FG)   Mig

Range: Mainly a rare migrant to our region but breeds in the extreme E on the western slope of the Urals. Departs breeding areas from Aug with main passage in Sep–Oct and winters from Afghanistan to India and China. In the Western Palearctic small numbers regularly occur at this season on Mt Hermon in Israel, and perhaps also Lebanon. Also occurs in NE Italy and S France as a regular migrant and winter visitor in small numbers.

Tips: Breeds in clearings or edges of taiga forest, often in newly cut or burned areas, sometimes in wooded steppe, often close to water. In winter and on passage mainly on farmland and waste ground, and in Italy often occurs on coasts and at river mouths.

Sites:
FRANCE Camargue (passage, winter).

ISRAEL Arava Valley (winter), Golan Heights** (winter), Mt Hermon* (winter).

LEBANON Aammiq Marshes (winter).

Cirl Bunting
Emberiza cirlus   DF SH FG   Res (Dis)

Range: Breeds in SW England, France (except the NE) and Iberia throughout the Mediterranean region to N and W Turkey, as well as in NW Africa from C Morocco to N Tunisia. In the Mediterranean breeds on the Balearics, Corsica, Sardinia, Sicily and Crete.

Subspecies: Usually considered monotypic but birds from Corsica and Sardinia are sometimes separated as *nigrostriata* and those from Portugal as *portucaliae*.

Tips: A common bird over much of its range but in severe decline in the N and in Great Britain now perhaps best seen at Prawle Point in Devon. Found in open deciduous woodland and warm south-facing hillsides with scattered trees and scrub. Also in orchards, vineyards and hedgerows, parkland and generally similar habitats to Yellowhammer but requires more trees.

Sites:
ALGERIA El Kala NP***.

ANDORRA*.

BALEARIC IS Formentera***, Mallorca***.

BULGARIA Albena-Golden Sands***, Burgas area***, Cape Emine***, Cape Kaliakra***, Rila Mts***, Ropotamo NP***, Strandja Mts***, Studen Kladenetz***, Trigradski Gorge***, Tissata NR***.

CORSICA Asco Valley***, Biguglia Lake***, Bonifacio***, Cap Corse***, Restonica Valley***.
CROATIA Cres***, Mljet***, Paklenica NP***.
FRANCE Cévennes NP***. Golfe du Morbihan***, Île d'Oleron***, Les Alpilles***, Marais Poitevin***, Pyrenees NP***.
GREECE Akarnanika Mts***, Avas Gorge***, Dadiá-Soufli Forest***, Delphi***, Lake Kerkini***, Mikrí Prespa NP***, Mt Olympus NP***, Mt Parnassós NP***.
GREEK IS Corfu***, Crete***, Lesvos***, Náxos***, Rhodes***.
ITALY Abruzzo NP***, Circeo NP***, Monte Conero***, Po Delta***, Sibillini NP***, Tuscan archipelago***.
MACEDONIA Galicica NP***, Lakes Ohrid and Prespa***.
MOROCCO Agadir and the Sous Plain***, Dayet Aaoua***, Oukaimeden***, Zaër***, Zeida**.

PORTUGAL Cape St Vincent**, International Tagus***, Montesinho***, Peneda Gerês NP***, Sado Estuary***, Santo André Lagoon***, Tagus Estuary***.
ROMANIA Dobrudja**.
SARDINIA Giara di Gesturi***, Oristano wetlands***, San Pietro I***.
SICILY San Vito Peninsula***.
SLOVENIA Karst RP***.
SPAIN Cabo de Gata**, Cáceres-Trujillo Steppes***, Coto Doñana***, Garraf Massif***, Jaca***, La Serena**, Monfragüe***, Ordesa NP***, Picos de Europa***, Serrania de Ronda***, Sierra de Gredos***, Sierra de Guadarrama***.
SWITZERLAND Leuk***, Monte Generoso***.
TUNISIA Ain Draham***.
TURKEY Dalyan***, İstanbul***, Kocaçay Delta***, Soğuksu NP***.
YUGOSLAVIA Durmitor NP***.

Rock Bunting
Emberiza cia

M SH (FG) Res (AMig) (PMig)

Range: Breeds over much of Iberia (except the Mediterranean coast), S France in the Massif Central and Alps, N into Germany along the Rhine and E into Austria. In Italy breeds in the Apennines and N Sicily and occurs widely but discontinuously in SE Europe from Slovakia and C Hungary to Greece, possibly also Crete. Breeds across much of Turkey to the Caucasus and in S Crimea, in the Middle East S to N Israel and in NW Africa from C Morocco to N Tunisia. A partial migrant in N of range but most are resident or altitudinal migrants.

Subspecies: Nominate *cia* is found over most of range with *par* in the Crimea and Caucasus. Various other races have been described but differences are very slight.

Tips: Characteristic bird of dry, rocky and south-facing hillsides with sparse vegetation, often juniper scrub, sometimes vineyards and olive groves. Usually found below 1,900m in the Western Palearctic and most numerous in Spain.

Sites:
ANDORRA*.
ARMENIA Mt Aragats***.

AUSTRIA Hohe Wand**, Schneeberg Mts*.
BOSNIA-HERZEGOVINA Sutjeska NP**.

BULGARIA Albena-Golden Sands***, Rila Mts***, Rusenski Lom NP***, Strandja Mts**, Studen Kladenetz***, Trigradski Gorge***, Tissata NR***.

CROATIA Cres***, Paklenica NP***.

FRANCE Cévennes NP***, Les Alpilles***, Prats-de-Mollo***, Pyrenees NP***, Vanoise NP***.

GEORGIA Mt Kazbek***.

GIBRALTAR* (winter).

GREECE Dadiá-Soufli Forest***, Delphi***, Lake Kerkini***, Mikrí Prespa NP***, Mt Olympus NP***, Mt Parnassós NP***, Valia Kalda NP***, Vikos-Aoos NP***.

GREEK IS Crete*, Lesvos* (passage, winter), Náxos***, Rhodes*.

HUNGARY Aggtelek NP***, Börzsöny NP**, Bükk Hills NP**, Pilis Hills***.

ISRAEL Mt Hermon***.

ITALY Gargano Peninsula***, Gran Paradiso NP***, Stelvio NP***.

JORDAN Amman NP* (winter), Wadi as Sir* (winter).

LEBANON Barouk Cedars* (winter).

MACEDONIA Galicica NP***.

MOROCCO Boumalne***, Oukaimeden***, Zeida**.

PORTUGAL Baixo Alentejo***, Cape St Vincent**, International Douro***, International Tagus***, Montesinho***, Peneda Gerês NP***.

ROMANIA Dobrudja**, Poiana Braşov***, Turda Gorge***.

RUSSIA Teberdinskiy Reserve***.

SICILY San Vito Peninsula***.

SLOVAKIA High Tatras NP*, Slovenský Kras***, Zemplínská Reservoir**.

SLOVENIA Karst RP***, Triglav NP***.

SPAIN Aiguamolls de l'Empordá***, Aigües Tortes NP***, Cabo de Gata**, Coto Doñana (passage), Garraf Massif***, Jaca***, La Serena**, Monfragüe***, Ordesa NP***, Picos de Europa***, Serrania de Ronda***, Sierra de Gredos***, Sierra de Guadarrama***.

SWITZERLAND Leuk***, Monte Generoso***.

SYRIA Aqra Mts***.

TUNISIA Zaghouan***.

TURKEY Akseki***, Borçka***, Dalyan**, Demirkazik***, Sivrikaya***, Soğuksu NP***.

UKRAINE Crimean Mts***.

YUGOSLAVIA Durmitor NP**.

House Bunting (Striated Bunting)
Emberiza striolata   SD FG U   Res

Range: Occurs over much of C and S Morocco and in Algeria in the Atlas Mts of the N, the Plateau du Tademait in the centre and Ahaggar in the S, also in C Tunisia and NW Libya. Elsewhere breeds in C and S Sinai and locally in S Israel and W Jordan. Resident with some wandering and altitudinal movement in winter.

Subspecies: Nominate race is found in Israel, Jordan and Sinai with *sahari* in most of NW Africa and *theresae* in SW Morocco. The three forms are sometimes considered to be two separate species: **Striated Bunting** *E. striolata* (Middle East) and **House Bunting** *E. sahari* (NW Africa).

Tips: In N Africa is commensal, occurring in villages and towns and cultivation. In the Middle East tends to avoid habitation but may occur around livestock and occurs on dry rocky slopes with sparse vegetation, sometimes wandering to low-level plains in winter.

Sites:
EGYPT Sharm el Sheikh*.
ISRAEL Arava Valley***, Eilat***, Ein Gedi***.
JORDAN Aqaba***, Petra**, Wadi Rum***.

MOROCCO Agadir and the Sous Plain***, Boumalne***, Essaouira***, Oued Massa***.
TUNISIA Chott el Djerid***, Tatahouine***.

Cinereous Bunting
Emberiza cineracea   SH SD (D)   Mig

Range: Very restricted range, breeding on the Greek islands of Lesvos, Khios, Karia and Skyros, probably Samos, and in W and S Turkey, and in SE Turkey from the Gaziantep area eastwards, possibly extending into N Syria. In the 1990s singing males were reported from Corfu. Begins to leave breeding areas in late Jul, with main passage in Aug–Sep. Passage recorded in S Turkey, Syria, Lebanon, Israel and Jordan. Winters on southern Red Sea coasts and returns to breeding areas in late Mar–Apr, with spring migrants regular in S Israel and rare in Cyprus.

Subspecies: Nominate *cineracea* is found in Greece and W Turkey, *semenowi* in SE Turkey.

Tips: Search dry rocky slopes with sparse vegetation up to the treeline. On passage occurs in lower areas, deserts, stony plains and wadis, sometimes in coastal areas and often with other buntings. Rare and local, common only on Lesvos where most numerous in the W, and generally shy during the breeding season.

Sites:
CYPRUS (passage).
GREEK IS Lesvos*** (summer).
ISRAEL Arava Valley** (passage, mainly spring), Eilat* (sp).

JORDAN Azraq (spring), Petra (spring), Wadi Rum (spring).
TURKEY Birecik-Halfeti*** (summer), Yeşilce*** (summer), Van Gölü** (summer).

Ortolan Bunting
Emberiza hortulana   SH FG DF   Mig

Range: Breeds in Iberia and parts of C and S France, the Alps and N Italy and from Slovenia to Romania and S to Greece, Crete, much of Turkey and the Caucasus, perhaps also N Syria. In the N breeds from E Germany and S Scandinavia across Russia to the Urals. Small populations in the Netherlands, S Germany and E Austria. Passage noted throughout S Europe, N Africa and the Middle East. Scarce but regular migrant in Britain, mainly in Shetland and on the E coast in spring, and in SW England, particularly Scilly, in autumn. Leaves breeding areas in Aug–Sep, returning late Mar–Apr reaching N of range in May.

Tips: A bird of open scrubby woodland, forest edge and dry grassy hillsides with scattered trees and bushes, often on farmland, in orchards and along roadsides. Occurs in montane areas to 2,300m in S. On passage mainly on open grassland, in semi-desert areas and steppes. Generally scarce and declining due to changing farming methods but still locally common in some areas.

Sites:

ALBANIA Lake Shkodra*** (summer).

ANDORRA* (summer).

ARMENIA Mt Aragats*** (summer).

AUSTRIA Lake Neusiedl** (summer), Wienerwald** (summer).

BALEARIC IS Mallorca* (passage).

BELARUS Belovezhskaya Pushcha NP*** (summer), Berezinsky Reserve*** (summer), Prypyatsky NP*** (summer).

GREAT BRITAIN Flamborough Head* (passage), N Norfolk coast** (passage), Orkney Is** (passage), Portland* (passage), Scilly** (autumn), Shetland Is** (passage).

BULGARIA Cape Emine*** (summer), Cape Kaliakra*** (summer), Lake Durankulak*** (summer), Lake Shabla*** (summer), Lake Srebarna*** (summer), Strandja Mts*** (summer), Tissata NR*** (summer).

CANARY IS Fuerteventura** (passage).

CROATIA Cres** (summer), Paklenica NP*** (summer).

CYPRUS* (passage).

DENMARK Bornholm-Christiansø*** (passage), Møn-Falster* (passage), Skagen*** (passage), Skallingen-Blåvandshuk** (passage), Stignæs*** (passage).

EGYPT Hurghada** (passage), Sharm el Sheikh*** (passage), Zaranik**(passage).

ESTONIA Matsalu Bay*** (summer).

FINLAND Åland Is*** (summer), Liminganlahti*** (summer), Parikkala*** (summer), Ruissalo*** (summer).

FRANCE Baie du Mont-St-Michel* (passage), Cévennes NP*** (summer), Écrins NP*** (summer), Leucate*** (summer), Ouessant** (passage), Queyras NP*** (summer).

GEORGIA Mt Kazbek** (passage).

GERMANY Heligoland*** (passage), Schweinfurt** (summer).

GIBRALTAR* (passage).

GREECE Dadiá-Soufli Forest*** (summer), Delphi*** (summer), Lake Kerkini*** (summer), Mikrí Prespa NP*** (summer), Mt Olympus NP*** (summer), Mt Parnassós NP*** (summer).

GREEK IS Corfu*** (summer), Crete*** (summer, passage), Kos*** (summer, passage), Lesvos*** (passage).

ISRAEL Arava Valley*** (passage), Bet Shean Valley*** (passage), Eilat*** (passage, mainly sp), Ein Gedi*** (passage), Jezreel Valley*** (passage), Ma'agan Mikhael*** (passage), Nizzana*** (passage).

ITALY Abruzzo NP*** (summer), Monte Conero*** (summer), Orbetello Reserve*** (summer), Po Delta*** (summer), Sibillini NP*** (summer), Tuscan archipelago*** (passage).

JORDAN Amman NP** (passage), Aqaba*** (passage), Azraq** (passage), Ghadir Burqu'** (passage), Petra** (passage), Wadi Dana-Fidan* (passage), Wadi Rum** (passage).

LATVIA Lake Pape** (summer).

LEBANON Aammiq Marshes*** (passage), Barouk Cedars* (passage), Qaraoun Lake** (passage).

MACEDONIA Babuna Gorge** (summer), Galicica NP*** (summer), Lakes Ohrid and Prespa*** (summer).

MALTA* (passage).

NETHERLANDS Oostvaardersplassen (passage), Terschelling* (passage), Texel* (passage).

NORWAY Utsira* (passage).

POLAND Białowieża Forest** (summer), Biebrza Marshes*** (summer), Bieszczady NP*** (summer), Chełm Marshes*** (summer), Gdańsk Bay*** (summer), Kampinos NP** (summer), Milicz Fishponds*** (summer),

Siemianówka Reservoir*** (summer), Słońsk*** (summer).
PORTUGAL Cape St Vincent* (autumn), Castro Marim** (passage), Montesinho** (summer), Peneda Gerês NP** (summer), Sado Estuary* (summer), Santo André Lagoon* (passage), Tagus Estuary* (passage).
ROMANIA Dobrudja*** (summer, passage).
RUSSIA Teberdinskiy Reserve*** (summer), Volga Delta*** (passage).
SPAIN Aiguamolls de L'Empordá*** (summer), Cáceres-Trujillo Steppes*** (summer), Coto Doñana*** (passage), Garraf Massif*** (summer), Jaca*** (summer), Ordesa NP*** (summer), Picos de Europa*** (summer), Serrania de Ronda*** (summer), Sierra de

Gredos*** (summer), Sierra de Guadarrama*** (summer), Tablas de Daimiel*** (summer).
SWEDEN Falsterbo** (passage), Kvismaren*** (summer), Öland*** (passage), Tåkern*** (summer).
SWITZERLAND Fanel NR** (passage), Grangettes* (passage), Leuk*** (summer).
TURKEY Dalyan*** (summer), Demirkazik*** (summer), İstanbul*** (passage), Kocaçay Delta*** (summer), Soğuksu NP*** (summer), Uludağ NP*** (summer), Van Gölü*** (summer).
UKRAINE Carpathians*** (summer).
YUGOSLAVIA Fruška Gora NP** (summer), Lake Skadar*** (summer).

Grey-necked Bunting
Emberiza buchanani   M SH Mig

Range: Main breeding range is in C Asia but with isolated populations in Turkey in E and SE Anatolia, and the Caucasus, breeding in the NW Arax Valley. Leaves breeding areas in Aug–Sep to winter in Pakistan and India, returning in Apr–early May.
Tips: Search arid rocky slopes, gorges, scree slopes and plateaux with sparse vegetation, usually above 1,000m. Highly terrestrial and can be elusive in summer, this species is best looked for in spring when singing, or in autumn when flocks gather. Locally common in the Van area of Turkey but rare in Armenia and Azerbaijan.

Sites:
ARMENIA Vedi Hills*** (summer).
RUSSIA Teberdinskiy Reserve (summer).

TURKEY Doğubeyazit*** (summer), Van Gölü*** (summer).

Cretzschmar's Bunting
Emberiza caesia   SD FG Mig

Range: A Western Palearctic endemic breeder, with a very limited range in the Aegean and E Mediterranean. Breeds in S Albania, W and S Greece, and on most Aegean islands, S Crete and Rhodes. Also in W and S Turkey, Cyprus and, in the Middle East, in W Syria, Lebanon, N Israel and W Jordan. Main passage periods are Aug–early Oct and Mar–Apr. Winters in small numbers in Egypt.

Tips: Best looked for on dry rocky hillsides up to 1,300m with sparse vegetation, rocky gorges and wadis, and sometimes found in cultivation, especially on passage. Usually seen on the ground and often permits close approach. Generally at lower altitudes than Ortolan Bunting in areas where they overlap. Peak passage is generally earlier than Ortolan. Common on Khios.

Sites:

CYPRUS* (summer, passage).
EGYPT Hurghada*** (passage), Sharm el Sheikh** (passage), Zaranik** (passage).
GREECE Akarnanika Mts*** (summer), Dadiá-Soufli Forest*** (summer), Delphi*** (summer), Mt Parnassós NP*** (summer), Valia Kalda NP** (summer), Vikos-Aoos NP*** (summer).
GREEK IS Corfu*** (summer), Kos*** (summer), Lesvos*** (summer), Náxos*** (summer), Rhodes*** (summer).
ISRAEL Arava Valley*** (passage), Eilat*** (passage, mainly sp), Ein Gedi** (passage), Jezreel Valley*** (passage), Ma'agan Mikhael*** (passage), Mt Hermon*** (summer), Nizzana*** (passage).

JORDAN Aqaba (passage), Azraq* (passage), Petra* (passage), Wadi Dana-Fidan*** (summer), Wadi Rum* (summer, passage), Wadi as Sir*** (summer).
LEBANON Aammiq Marshes*** (summer), Barouk Cedars*** (summer), Qaraoun Lake** (passage).
MACEDONIA Galicica NP*** (summer).
SYRIA Aqra Mts*** (summer), Jabal Slenfeh*** (summer), Wadi al-Qarn-Burqush** (summer), Yarmuk Valley*** (summer).
TURKEY Akseki*** (summer), Bafa Gölü*** (summer), Dalyan*** (summer), Demirkazik** (summer), Göksu Delta*** (summer), Yeşilce*** (summer).

Rustic Bunting
Emberiza rustica   CF MF DF (FG) Mig

Range: Breeds in SE Norway, C and N Sweden, most of Finland, the S Kola Peninsula and across N Russia. Has bred in Estonia and Latvia. Departs breeding range in Aug–Sep and returns late Apr–May.

Tips: Breeds in wetter areas with spruce, pine or birch forest and along watercourses. On passage found in a range of wooded and open habitats including woodland edges, farmland and waste ground.

Sites:

GREAT BRITAIN Shetland Is* (passage).
DENMARK Bornholm-Christiansø* (passage).
FINLAND Kuusamo*** (summer), Lake Inari*** (summer), Lemmenjoki NP*** (summer), Oulanka NP*** (summer), Pallas-Ounastunturi NP*** (summer), Patvinsuo NP*** (summer), Pyhä-Häkki NP*** (summer), Urho Kekkonen NP*** (summer).

GERMANY Heligoland** (passage).
NORWAY Øvre Pasvik NP* (summer).
RUSSIA Kola Peninsula*** (summer).
SWEDEN Ammarnäs*** (summer), Falsterbo (autumn), Gotland*** (passage), Holmöarna*** (summer, passage), Muddus NP*** (summer), Öland*** (passage), Ripakaisenvuoma*** (summer).

Little Bunting
Emberiza pusilla   T CF MF FG Mig

Range: Breeds in extreme N Norway, (probably also the far N of Sweden), in NE Finland and the Kola Peninsula and E across Russia to the Urals. Numbers fluctuate in Scandinavia. Departs breeding areas in late Aug–Sep and returns in May–early Jun. Migrates SE but is regular in small numbers in W Europe and annual in Great Britain with 10–30 recorded most years, mainly in autumn.

Tips: Breeds in shrubby wet tundra and open woodland, usually birch, willow or alder. On passage often in coastal areas but also found at woodland edges and beside rivers, on cultivated land and sometimes in reeds.

Sites:

GREAT BRITAIN Scilly* (autumn), Shetland Is* (autumn).
DENMARK Bornholm-Christiansø* (passage).
FINLAND Kuusamo*** (summer), Lake Inari*** (summer), Oulanka NP*** (summer).
FRANCE Ouessant* (autumn).

GERMANY Heligoland** (passage).
NETHERLANDS Oostvaardersplassen (passage), Texel (passage).
NORWAY Øvre Pasvik NP*** (summer), Stabbursdalen NP*** (summer), Utsira* (passage).

RUSSIA Kola Peninsula*** (summer).
SWEDEN Falsterbo (passage), Gotland**
(passage), Holmöarna** (passage), Öland***
(passage).

Yellow-breasted Bunting
Emberiza aureola　　　　　　　　　　　　　　CF MF SH FW　Mig

Range: In our region breeds in C and SE Finland
(although has declined in recent years), on the S Kola
Peninsula S to N Ukraine and E across Russia. Has bred in
Latvia and Norway. Present in breeding range late
May–Jun until late Aug–Sep.

Tips: Breeds close to water in dense shrubs and willow
and birch scrub, also forest edges and peat bogs. On passage occurs in cultivated areas, scrubland, and sometimes reedbeds.

Sites:
GREAT BRITAIN Shetland Is* (autumn).
FINLAND Liminganlahti*** (summer),
Parikkala*** (summer).

RUSSIA Kola Peninsula*** (summer).
SWEDEN Holmöarna** (passage).

Black-headed Bunting
Emberiza melanocephala　　　　　　　　　　　　　　SH FG　Mig

Range: Breeds in the E Adriatic from Slovenia to Greece,
the S Balkans, Greek islands and throughout Turkey and
Transcaucasia. Also breeds from E Ukraine to the
Caspian, Cyprus and, in the Middle East, as far S as N Israel
and W Jordan. Increasing and now fairly widespread in
Italy and records from SE France have also increased in
recent years, culminating in the first proven breeding in
2000. Departs breeding areas in late Jul–Aug and returns
in late Apr–early May.

Tips: Common in open country with scattered bushes, trees and scrub, often in cultivated
areas, especially cereal fields, olive groves and vineyards. A common and characteristic
roadside bird in much of Greece and Turkey, often singing from roadside wires.

Sites:
ALBANIA Drini Delta*** (summer), Karavasta
Lagoon*** (summer), Lake Shkodra***
(summer).

ARMENIA Armash Fishponds*** (summer),
Khosrov Preserve*** (summer), Lake Sevan***
(summer), Mt Aragats*** (summer).

AZERBAIJAN Turianchai Reserve*** (summer).

BOSNIA-HERZEGOVINA Hutovo blato*** (summer).

BULGARIA Albena-Golden Sands*** (summer), Burgas area*** (summer), Cape Emine*** (summer), Cape Kaliakra*** (summer), Lake Durankulak*** (summer), Lake Shabla*** (summer), Lake Srebarna*** (summer), Rila Mts*** (summer), Ropotamo NP*** (summer), Rusenski Lom NP*** (summer), Strandja Mts*** (summer), Studen Kladenetz*** (summer), Tissata NR*** (summer).

CROATIA Cres*** (summer), Mljet*** (summer), Neretva Delta*** (summer), Paklenica NP*** (summer).

CYPRUS** (summer).

EGYPT Zaranik* (passage).

GEORGIA Iori Steppes*** (summer), Mt Kazbek* (passage).

GREECE Akarnanika Mts*** (summer), Axios-Aliakmonas Deltas*** (summer), Dadiá-Soufli Forest*** (summer), Delphi*** (summer), Evros Delta*** (summer), Lake Kerkini*** (summer), Mikrí Prespa NP*** (summer), Mt Parnassós NP*** (summer), Nestos Delta*** (summer), Porto Lagos area*** (summer).

GREEK IS Corfu*** (summer), Kos*** (summer), Lesvos*** (summer), Náxos*** (summer), Rhodes*** (summer).

ISRAEL Golan Heights*** (summer), Mt Hermon*** (summer).

ITALY Gargano Peninsula*** (summer), Orbetello Reserve** (summer).

JORDAN Amman NP*** (summer), Aqaba* (passage), Azraq* (passage), Wadi Rum* (passage), Wadi as Sir*** (summer).

LEBANON Aammiq Marshes*** (summer), Qaraoun Lake** (passage).

MACEDONIA Babuna Gorge*** (summer), Galicica NP*** (summer), Lakes Ohrid and Prespa*** (summer).

ROMANIA Kalmykia*** (summer), Dobrudja*** (summer).

RUSSIA Teberdinskiy Reserve*** (passage).

SYRIA Aqra Mts*** (summer), Jabal Slenfeh*** (summer), Sabkhat al-Jabbul*** (summer).

TURKEY Akseki*** (summer), Birecik-Halfeti*** (summer), Dalyan*** (summer), Demirkazik*** (summer), İstanbul*** (summer), Manyas Gölü*** (summer), Uluabat Gölü*** (summer), Sultan Marshes*** (summer), Yeşilce*** (summer).

YUGOSLAVIA Lake Skadar*** (summer).

Albania

Ornithologically this remains one of the least-known countries in Europe, and given the recent conflicts in the Balkans this situation is likely to remain the case in the near future. Albania possesses mountains and forest, as well as some of the most important wetlands in Europe, but these are undoubtedly suffering the same habitat degradation that has occurred so widely in the Balkans. The large montane lakes of Albania may be among the best birding areas in the country but are more easily visited from neighbouring Macedonia and Greece. Birding would be most productive on a spring visit when the summer visitors have arrived.

1) Drini Delta Bordered by the Barbalush Mountains to the north and the River Drini to the south, this is an area of coastal lagoons, marshes, sandbars and woodland in the north of the country. Important for Pygmy Cormorant, there are also Olive-tree and Eastern Olivaceous Warblers, Lesser Grey Shrike and Black-headed Bunting, with Western Rock Nuthatch and Rock Partridge on nearby hillsides.

2) Karavasta Lagoon Probably the best-known birding site in Albania, Karavasta consists of two main lagoons separated from the sea by a pine-covered sandbar known as the Divjaka Forest. There are extensive fisheries on site but large areas of bare sand and mud remain, with scrub and some deciduous woodland.

Albania's national bird, Dalmatian Pelican, breeds here in small numbers as well as Collared Pratincole, Greater Short-toed and Crested Larks, Red-rumped Swallow, Black-headed Bunting and Woodchat Shrike. Passage birds include Pygmy Cormorant, White Pelican, Great Egret and Pallid Harrier, and possibly Slender-billed Curlew. Greater Spotted Eagle is a rare winter visitor, White-tailed Eagle more regular and wintering waterfowl include White-headed Duck.

Karavasta lies c.100km south-west of Tirana.

3) Lake Ohrid (see Macedonia, page 515).

4) Lake Shkodra (Lake Skadar, Lake Scutari) A large, mainly shallow lake on the border with Montenegro, and an important breeding site for Pygmy Cormorant and Dalmatian Pelican. Squacco and Purple Herons, Glossy Ibis, Ferruginous Duck and Whiskered Tern are also present. Passerines include Orphean and Moustached Warblers and Lesser Grey Shrike, and southeastern specialities such as Eastern Olivaceous and Olive-tree Warblers, Western Rock Nuthatch and Black-headed Bunting. Wintering and passage waterfowl can number as many as 250,000 on the lake as a whole.

5) Mikrí Prespa National Park
(see Greece, page 470).

Algeria

Were it not for the endemic nuthatch there would be little of birding interest in Algeria. Despite an excellent wetland area in the north-east and a broad range of desert species further south, most of Algeria's birds can be seen more easily in Morocco and Tunisia. Algeria is a difficult, and currently very dangerous, country to visit but once entry is gained travel, either by private car or public transport, is fairly easy and accommodation is relatively cheap. Algiers has an international airport; alternatively, the country can be

entered by road or rail from Tunisia, or by ferry from Marseilles. Car hire is available in Algiers, Bejaïa, Constantine or Annaba, and the trip to see the nuthatch, once the political climate improves, can be made in a day from Algiers by road.

1) Djebel Babor Famous ornithologically as the site of the first discovery, in 1975, of the Algerian Nuthatch, Djebel Babor is a 2,000m mountain in the Petite Kabylie range in north-eastern Algeria. Around 80 pairs of the nuthatch are thought to survive here in the summit forest of endemic Algerian Fir, oak and cedar. Other birds include Bonelli's Eagle, Barbary Partridge and Levaillant's Woodpecker.

Once the difficulties of entering the country have been overcome, Djebel Babor is fairly easy to reach and the nuthatches are easily located. The mountain is c.225km east of Algiers: head east to Bejaïa, then south-east to Sétif via Kherrata, and 12km further on a road leads east to the mountain. The best time to visit is May–September, as snow may block roads outside this period.

2) El Kala National Park This National Park in far north-eastern Algeria is one of the most important wetlands in North Africa and lies between Cap Rosa in the west and Cap Mezira in the east, and includes a range of habitats such as dunes and coastal pinewoods, marshes and a system of freshwater and brackish lakes.

Thousands of waterbirds winter in the area including White-headed and Marbled Ducks. Breeders include Squacco Heron and Purple Swamphen, and the surrounding woods and scrub are home to Long-legged Buzzard, Levaillant's Woodpecker, the recently separated African Blue Tit, and warblers such as Western Bonelli's and Sardinian. In 1984 a pair of Lesser Spotted Eagles was found nesting at El Kala, the first Algerian breeding record of this species.

The town of El Kala, 5km west of the park, is a popular holiday area for Algerians and has hotel accommodation. The park headquarters is located at Lake Tonga.

Andorra

This tiny independent state, covering less than 500km², lies on the southern slopes of the eastern Pyrenees. Although it is best known as a popular resort for winter sports enthusiasts, there is a good range of mountain and forest birds to be found. Much of Andorra consists of high mountains with narrow valleys and deep gorges, alpine meadows, broadleaf and coniferous woodlands, and slopes with Mediterranean scrub.

As elsewhere in the Pyrenees, raptors are amongst the greatest attractions for birders, and Lammergeier, Griffon Vulture and Golden Eagle are all seen fairly easily, as well as Northern Goshawk and Short-toed Eagle. Other montane species include Ptarmigan and Dotterel, both choughs, Alpine Accentor, Wallcreeper, Rock Bunting and Snowfinch. Forest birds include Capercaillie, Eagle and Tengmalm's Owls, Black Woodpecker and passerines such as Crested Tit, Western Bonelli's Warbler and Citril Finch. More open areas and woodland edges have breeding Eurasian Scops Owl, as well as Dartford and Subalpine Warblers, and Ortolan Bunting.

In such a small country, a single base can be used to explore most areas and the capital, **Andorra La Vella**, is within easy reach of excellent birding habitat.

Armenia

Only recently 'discovered' by Western birders, Armenia promises to be one of the great destinations of the future, providing the political situation remains stable. Armash is one of the most exciting wetlands in the Western Palearctic and the huge Lake Sevan hosts most of the world's breeding Armenian Gulls. The mountains of Armenia are home to Caucasian specialities such as Caucasian Black Grouse, Caspian Snowcock and Crimson-winged Finch, while semi-deserts and arid mountain slopes hold the eastern race of Red-tailed Wheatear, Upcher's Warbler, Mongolian Finch and Grey-necked Bunting.

1) Aparan area This is one of the best Armenian sites for migrating raptors. It is situated at the north-eastern foothills of Mount Aragats *c.*45km north of Yerevan and surrounded with mountains forming a migratory passageway stretching from north to south. Habitats include mountain steppes with extensive farmland fields at the bottom of the valley and, on gentler slopes, riparian meadows and a reservoir, scrub and isolated patches of woodland.

Passage raptors include Marsh, Pallid and Montagu's Harriers, Levant Sparrowhawk, Long-legged and Steppe Buzzards and Western Honey-buzzard, Golden, Short-toed, Booted, Lesser and Greater Spotted, Eastern Imperial and Steppe Eagles. In addition there is a range of other migrants such as waders and passerines. Higher elevations in nearby mountains hold Shore Lark, *magna* Bluethroat, Caucasian Twite and Crimson-winged Finch.

2) Armash Fishponds are situated in south-central Armenia close to the border with Turkey, Iran and Nakhichevan. The area is privately owned but access is usually allowed after pre-arranged permission.

This area, situated in the arid and salty semi-deserts of Ararat Plain in the Arax Valley, is one of the best birding sites in the country. There is much marginal vegetation around the many ponds and extensive network of channels, where reedbeds provide excellent habitat for a range of waterbirds at all seasons.

Breeders include Pygmy Cormorant, Ruddy Shelduck, Red-crested Pochard, Ferruginous Duck and small numbers of Marbled and White-headed Ducks. Larger wading birds are common and include Glossy Ibis, Eurasian Spoonbill and White Stork, as well as Little Bittern, Black-crowned Night, Squacco and Purple Herons, and Cattle Egret. Breeding waders of the area include Pied Avocet, Collared Pratincole (a recent colonist), White-tailed Lapwing and Kentish Plover. A range of wetland warblers is possible in the reedbeds, with Savi's, Moustached, Paddyfield, 'Caspian' Reed and Great Reed all present. The surrounding farmland is inhabited by the '*armenica*' form of Siberian Stonechat, saltplain banks have Blue-cheeked and European Bee-eaters, European Roller, Lesser Short-toed Lark and Tawny Pipit, in Tamarisk scrub Upcher's Warbler can be found, but the arid-land passerine of most interest is Ménétries' Warbler, which is common in this area. Passage waders include Temminck's Stint, Broad-billed, Terek and Marsh Sandpipers and Red-necked Phalarope, Greater Sand Plover is less frequently seen. Gull-billed, White-winged and Whiskered Terns breed in the area along with Slender-billed Gull, while Pallas' and Armenian Gulls occur on passage and in winter. A wide range of other migrants can be seen throughout the valley including waterfowl, pelicans and storks and raptors including Lesser Kestrel, Steppe Eagle and Pallid Harrier.

3) Khosrov Preserve Some 19 species of raptor breed in this area at the southern end of the Gegham range in central Armenia. Habitats in this 230km^2 reserve include mountain peaks and plateaux, alpine meadows, woodland and scrub, as well as two rivers and a small lake.

Lammergeier, Egyptian, Griffon and Black Vultures are among the raptors present, and others include Short-toed, Golden and Lesser Spotted Eagles, Long-legged Buzzard and Levant Sparrowhawk. Various raptors, including Steppe Eagle, also occur on passage. Other montane specialities include Caspian Snowcock and Chukar Partridge, and passerines such as both rock thrushes, Wallcreeper, Eastern Rock

Nuthatch and Red-billed Chough. In addition to Eurasian Scops and Eurasian Eagle Owls, the area is home to Armenia's only Tengmalm's Owls. Other birds of interest include Middle Spotted Woodpecker, White-throated Robin, Black-headed Bunting and Trumpeter Finch.

Permission from the director of the preserve is needed to enter the territory.

4) Lake Sevan Famous as one of the few breeding sites of the localised Armenian Gull, Sevan is a very large, high-altitude lake in east-central Armenia and the surrounding land is a National Park. As well as the breeding gulls, the area is important for passage and wintering waterfowl.

Although thousands of Armenian Gulls breed at the lake, mainly along the north-west shore, there are a few other breeding birds of interest that include Ruddy Shelduck, Caucasian Chiffchaff, Barred Warbler, Black-headed Wagtail and Common Rosefinch. Passage species include, among various raptors, Red-footed Falcon, and good numbers of Demoiselle Crane, which are usually best seen in the south-east corner of the lake in September. Pallas' Gull occurs from mid autumn and throughout winter, and can usually be seen at Cape Noratoos on the west shore.

The lake, north-east of Yerevan, is something of a tourist attraction and accommodation can be found on the north-west shore with some available on the eastern shore.

5) Meghri Area This area lies in the extreme south of Armenia on the border with Iran. The landscape is dry and subtropical, with gardens and scrubs along the Arax River, and an abundance of crags and rocky outcrops on the southern slopes of Meghri Range covered with open juniper woodland and indented with deep arid gorges. Interesting birds of the area include Levant Sparrowhawk breeding in gardens, Eastern Orphean and Upcher's Warblers found in scrubby habitats, Sombre Tit in juniper woodland and Red-tailed Wheatear attached to rocky outcrop and boulder-scattered open areas in the gorges. Occasionally Black Francolin and See-see Partridge are recorded in the area.

6) Mount Aragats This mountain lies north-west of Armenia's capital, Yerevan, and reaches more than 4,000m. It is an excellent area for montane species and the lower slopes can also be productive.

Shore Lark, Alpine Accentor, Wallcreeper, 'Caucasian' Twite and Snowfinch occur in the higher areas around Lake Karilich, along with more localised high-altitude specialities such as Crimson-winged Finch. Other upland birds include both rock thrushes, Ring Ouzel, Western Rock Nuthatch and Red-billed Chough. Raptors include Lesser Spotted Eagle and Long-legged Buzzard in summer and Pallid Harrier and Steppe Eagle in autumn. The lower slopes and scrub of Dog Rose and Dwarf Juniper hold more of the region's specialities such as Radde's Accentor and White-throated Robin, as well as Barred Warbler, Ortolan Bunting and *magna* Bluethroat. In the foothills around the gardens Lesser Grey Shrike, Eastern Olivaceous Warbler, Black-headed Bunting and Rosy Starling also occur, and among rocky landscapes at the southern foothills of the mountain Black-eared and Finsch's Wheatears can be found. Wooded areas are home to Caucasian Chiffchaff and Syrian Woodpecker.

The area is best explored via the roads leading to Amberd Fortress and to Lake Karilich at more than 3,000m altitude. Mount Aragats is reached by road from Yerevan but accommodation is very limited outside the capital.

7) Pambak Mountains This range is in north-cental Armenia and reaches altitudes of 1,000–3,000m, containing many areas of cliffs, rock-slides and alpine meadows interspersed with forests mainly on the northern slopes.

This is one of the few Armenian sites for Caucasian Black Grouse and other sought after species found here include Caspian Snowcock, Lammergeier and Griffon Vulture, Lesser Spotted and Golden Eagles, Radde's and Alpine Accentors, 'Caucasian' Twite, *magna* Bluethroat, Semi-collared Flycatcher, *samamisicus* Common Redstart, Caucasian Chiffchaff and Red-fronted Serin.

8) Vedi Hills are situated *c.*30km south-east of Yerevan and characterised by an extremely dry landscape of rocky hills indented with dry riverbeds with scrub and semi-desert vegetation, several deep ravines and numerous rocky outcrops. The area's specialities include Upcher's Warbler, Finsch's Wheatear, Woodchat Shrike, Eastern Rock Nuthatch, Pale Rock Sparrow, Mongolian and Trumpeter Finches and Grey-necked Bunting. As the Khosrov Preserve is situated nearby, a good selection of raptors is often encountered in the area.

Austria

Lake Neusiedl in eastern Austria is now one of the most famous birding sites in Europe and a regular destination for bird tour companies and independent birders. An excellent range of wetland birds can be seen here, with steppe and forest species within easy reach. However, much of Austria consists of mountains and most of the alpine specialities are found with relative ease. A visit in late May to early June is

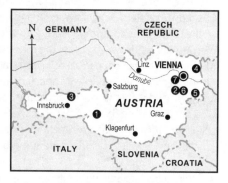

likely to produce the most species, although September is best for passage waders.

1) Hohe Tauern National Park This is a spectacular range of peaks in the eastern Alps with permanent snowfields in the highest parts, hundreds of glacier-fed streams flowing through narrow gorges, fast-flowing rivers, rapids and waterfalls. Most famous are the Krimml Falls, the highest in Europe, and the park also contains Austria's highest peak, Großglockner (3,797m). Much of the area consists of extensive spruce forest with some pine and larch in the higher parts. Above the treeline there are pastures and dwarf-scrub vegetation.

Birds present in the park include typical mountain-dwellers such as Golden Eagle, Ptarmigan, Black Grouse, Alpine Chough and Snowfinch, but a group of non-breeding Griffon Vultures summer here and there is a WWF feeding programme for these birds. This is also the site of a Lammergeier reintroduction scheme, although the birds are difficult to see. Forest birds include Eurasian Pygmy Owl, Three-toed Woodpecker and Citril Finch.

There are marked trails and various cabins within the park and an information centre at Matrei in Osttirol.

2) Hohe Wand This is a very popular tourist area and although it still has some good birds they may require some time and effort to find. The Hohe Wand (meaning High Wall) is an impressive limestone outcrop, 12km long by 3km wide, near Eisenstadt in eastern Austria. A road accesses the top of the escarpment and there are extensive coniferous forests.

The birds are typical of alpine forests with Capercaillie (possibly still Hazel Grouse), Black Woodpecker, Crested Tit, Nutcracker, Western Bonelli's Warbler and Citril Finch. More montane species also occur such as Alpine Accentor, Rock Thrush, Wallcreeper and Rock Bunting.

The site can be covered on a day-trip from Vienna and the less-disturbed western part of the plateau is now the best area to search for the scarcer species.

3) Karwendel Reserve North of Innsbruck in the western Austrian Alps is the largest Nature Protection Area in Austria. Karwendel is famous for its spectacular scenery with lakes, rivers and waterfalls, dense forest and open alpine meadows. There are high, rocky peaks reaching a maximum of 2,700m at Bikkarspitze.

Birds include typical montane species such as Golden Eagle, Rock Partridge and Ptarmigan, Alpine Accentor, Wallcreeper and Snowfinch. The forests hold Hazel Grouse and Capercaillie, woodpeckers including Black, Grey-headed, White-backed and Three-toed, as well as Eurasian Pygmy and Tengmalm's Owls. Passerines include Crested Tit, Western Bonelli's Warbler and Citril Finch.

Reached by road from Innsbruck to the south or Pertisau to the east, there are many minor roads which access the mountains in this area.

4) Marchauen-Marchegg Reserve In eastern Austria on the Slovakia border, this WWF reserve is part of an extremely important area of near-natural riverine and floodplain forest, a habitat that is much reduced throughout Europe. This complex of flooded woodlands and open meadows, backwaters and marshes is the largest stretch of such habitat remaining in Austria and is home to a superb range of birds.

Wetland species include various herons, Eurasian Spoonbill and both storks, crakes and waders. The woodlands are home to various species of owl, possibly including Ural, and seven woodpeckers including Syrian and Middle Spotted, as well as many other species. Raptors include Red and Black Kites, harriers, Lesser Spotted Eagle and possibly still Saker, as well as wintering White-tailed Eagle. Passerines present include Thrush Nightingale, Collared Flycatcher, Penduline Tit and warblers such as River, Savi's and Barred.

The reserve is situated close to the north end of the village of Marchegg, 40km north-east of Vienna on Route 49.

5) Lake Neusiedl (Neusiedler See), Seewinkel and the Austrian Hanság One of the largest lakes in Europe, Neusiedl is vast and shallow, rather salty and lined by dense reedbeds several kilometres wide in places. Although water levels fluctuate, the lake averages only 1–2m deep and is fed by springs through the underlying rock. It remains one of the best birding sites in Europe with over 300 species recorded including many that are rare further W. Most are wetland birds, and particularly those dependent on reedbeds, but the lake is surrounded by agricultural land and wood, which also support a different set of species. Some of the specialities include Great

Egret, Little Bittern and Savi's, River and Moustached Warblers in the reeds and Grey-headed, Black and Syrian Woodpeckers as well as Barred and Icterine Warblers in surrounding trees. Plains in this area are home to a few pairs of Saker Falcon.

The **Seewinkel** is the area of shallow saline lakes adjacent to Lake Neusiedl where the Hungarian steppe or 'puszta' extends westwards. The region forms part of the Lake Neusiedl Ramsar site and includes the reserve of Lange Lacke, which holds important heronries. It shares many of the same birds as Neusiedl, with perhaps fewer breeding species although Ferruginous Duck and Montagu's Harriers nest. Many wetland species are easier to see here than at the large lake. Large numbers of passage birds occur throughout the area including Red-crested Pochard and Lesser White-fronted Goose. Much of the land between the numerous lakes has been lost to agriculture and this is now threatening the wildlife value of much of the area. However, there are still areas of reeds, wet meadows, hayfields and small woodlands in the area.

The **Hanság** is a nearby area under heavy agricultural use that is one of Austria's few sites for Great Bustard. This forms part of the Neusiedl-Seewinkel National Park.

Accommodation can be found in the village of Neusiedl-am-See and many other villages in the area. The entire area is very well covered by organised birding holidays and for independent travellers the lake is less than an hour's drive of Vienna airport.

6) Schneeberg These mountains, south-west of Vienna, have become more popular with birders in recent years, as disturbance to the nearby Hohe Wand has increased and the birds have become harder to find.

The area holds a similar range of species to other montane Austrian sites, with Golden Eagle, Ptarmigan, and passerines such as Alpine Accentor, Wallcreeper, Alpine Chough and Snowfinch all fairly easy to find.

This area lies near the town of Hirschwang and the higher parts can be reached by railway from Puchberg.

7) Wienerwald (Vienna Forest) Close to the Austrian capital and with a range of interesting birds, the scattered patches of woodland known as the Vienna Woods have long been popular with birders. Collared and Red-breasted Flycatchers, Short-toed Treecreeper, Golden Oriole and various woodpeckers are the main attractions and the **Schönbrunn Palace**, within the city itself, has most of these and is easily worked. **Laxenburg Schlosspark** consists of open parkland and woods and has a similar range of species.

Further afield the **Lainzer Tiergarten** to the south-west has deciduous, mixed and coniferous forest, meadows and streams. This former imperial hunting park is now a Nature Protection Area and has Western Honey-buzzard and White-backed and Black Woodpeckers, as well as breeding passerines including Barred Warbler and Ortolan Bunting. These areas are remnants of the once-extensive Vienna Forest, in the north-east foothills of the Alps, which still holds populations of Black Stork, Corn Crake and Eurasian Eagle Owl.

In Vienna take the A21 and follow signs to Altmansdorf, then either head north to the Schönbrunn Palace or south to Laxenburg. Lainzer Tiergarten has an information centre, marked trails and observation points, and is situated in west Vienna and reached via the A1.

Azerbaijan

Azerbaijan is little known ornithologically and will probably remain so for the foreseeable future, as there were still armed conflicts in some areas in the late 1990s. However, with a stable political situation this remote country could become a popular birding destination, with several Caucasian specialities including Caucasian Black Grouse and both snowcocks, as well as raptors including Lammergeier, Egyptian, Griffon and Black Vultures. Currently there is virtually

no tourist infrastructure in Azerbaijan, with accommodation very scarce outside the capital, Baku, and limited public transport. Late May to early June would be the best time to visit for the grouse and snowcocks, but it is essential to check the political situation before contemplating a trip.

1) Kura Valley salt-lakes This site consists of a series of shallow and saline lakes with fluctuating water levels in the valley of the Kura River. Although bird numbers are lower than in the past, this is still the most important inland wetland area in Azerbaijan. All of the lakes have extensive reedbeds and many islands, and are set in the semi-desert landscape of the Mil steppe. Apart from the vast reedbeds the main vegetation is salsola and tamarisk scrub. The area is important for both breeding and wintering birds but suffers from hunting and pollution.

The formerly freshwater **Lake Akgel** (Aggel) is now brackish and covers more than 9,000ha, much of which is reedbeds. Breeders include Pygmy Cormorant, Little Bittern, Great Egret, Glossy Ibis, Eurasian Spoonbill and Purple Swamphen. Marbled Duck also breeds, but in lower numbers than formerly and other breeding birds of interest include Black Francolin, Black-winged Stilt, Black-winged Pratincole and White-tailed Plover. Dalmatian Pelican, Whooper Swan, White-headed Duck and White-tailed Eagle winter here, along with good numbers of many other waterbirds including Red-crested Pochard.

The smaller complex of lakes and channels at **Lake Boz-Koba** has a similar range of breeding birds plus Great Bittern, Ruddy Shelduck and Montagu's Harrier, and was the last breeding site in the country for Dalmatian Pelican, which may still be seen here.

Lake Sarysu is a similar complex of brackish and saltwater with breeding Ferruginous Duck and tens of thousands of passage and wintering waterbirds. Greater Flamingo is a rare visitor throughout the year. The Kura Valley lies inland of Kirov Bay and can be reached by road from Baku.

2) Kyzylagach Bay Although decreasing water levels have reduced the attractiveness of this area for birds, it is still one of the most important for wetland birds in the country. Whereas wintering and passage birds formerly occurred in millions, today's totals are usually in the low hundreds of thousands. The bay is open to the Caspian Sea and includes Little Kyzylagach, which is now an overgrown freshwater reservoir separated from the sea by an artificial dam. As well as salt, brackish and fresh water, habitats comprise large reedbeds and marshy areas surrounded by dry arable land, steppe and semi-desert.

Pygmy Cormorant, Great Bittern, Purple, Black-crowned Night and Squacco Herons, Cattle and Little Egrets, Glossy Ibis and Ruddy Shelduck are among the breeding birds of the area, along with Black-winged Stilt, Blue-cheeked Bee-eater and Spanish Sparrow. However, the area was most famous for its passage and wintering birds, which include most European waterfowl species and Lesser White-fronted Goose, Red-breasted Goose and Marbled Duck are all possible. Purple Swamphen once bred here, but its current status is unclear and there are old records of Siberian White Crane, which could perhaps occur again. White-tailed and Greater Spotted Eagles are both winter visitors.

Kyzylagach Bay forms part of the larger Kirov Bay and lies south of the capital Baku. It can be reached by road from Sal'yany.

3) Turianchai Reserve A reserve on the Bozdag Ridge in the southern foothills of the Greater Caucasus and one of the best sites in Azerbaijan for breeding raptors. Habitats include eroded slopes, steppe and dry juniper woodland, and riverine alder and poplar forest along the Turianchai River.

Breeding raptors include Lammergeier, Egyptian, Griffon and Black Vultures, Short-toed, Lesser Spotted, Eastern Imperial and possibly Bonelli's Eagles, Long-legged Buzzard and Lesser Kestrel. Greater Spotted Eagle occurs on passage. Other breeding birds of interest include Chukar Partridge, Eurasian Eagle Owl. Eurasian Roller, Blue-cheeked Bee-eater and Black-headed Bunting.

Turianchai and the Bozdag Ridge can be reached by road from Baku.

Zakataly This area forms part of the southern Greater Caucasus range and has deep gorges, alpine meadows and extensive beech woodland.

4) Zakataly reserve is important for several montane species including Lammergeier, Griffon and Black Vultures, Golden Eagle, Chukar Partridge, Eurasian Eagle Owl and Snowfinch, as well as specialities of this corner of the Western Palearctic such as Caucasian Black Grouse, Caucasian Snowcock and Güldenstädt's Redstart.

Zakataly lies in the far north of the country and can be reached by road from Yevlakh.

Azores

This archipelago, lying almost 1,500km off the coast of Europe, consists of nine major islands split into three groups; the western Azores, consisting of Corvo and Flores, the central group comprising Graciosa, Terceira, São Jorge, Faial and Pico, and the eastern group of São Miguel and Santa Maria. The main ornithological interest of the archipelago lies in the endemic and very rare Azores Bullfinch and several more widespread species with distinct races. In addition there are breeding seabirds and the islands are potentially the best area in the Western Palearctic for transatlantic vagrants.

1) Western Azores These have colonies of Cory's and Little Shearwaters, Madeiran Storm-petrel and the fast-declining Western Palearctic population of Roseate Tern maintains a stronghold here, with most on Flores. Manx Shearwaters are known to occur on these islands and may breed.

2) Central Azores A similar range of species is found in the central Azores, and islets off Graciosa have the highest numbers of breeding Madeiran Storm-petrel in the archipelago, which curiously nest at two different periods, suggesting that they are genetically distinct populations and are possibly separate species. This island has also hosted the attempted breeding of Red-billed Tropicbirds, at this the only known European site, and Fea's Petrel has also been recorded, although it is not known to breed. Terceira, the easternmost of the central Azores, has a reputation for attracting Nearctic waders and the disused quarry south of the harbour at Praia da Vitoria is especially productive.

3) Eastern Azores São Miguel is home to the critically endangered Azores Bullfinch, which is now generally afforded species status. The one place this species can be found is the Pico da Vara area of eastern São Miguel, where little more than 100 pairs are thought to survive. The laurel forest here is the most extensive and best preserved in the Azores, and covers the Pico da Vara and Pico Verde mountains and the Ribeira do Guilherme Valley. south-east of São Miguel is the island of Santa Maria, which has breeding shearwaters, Madeiran Storm-petrel and Roseate Tern. The islet of Vila, off Santa Maria, holds the same species as well as Bulwer's Petrel at its only Azorean site, and Sooty Tern has also bred here in small numbers in recent years.

Visiting the Azores in autumn will undoubtedly give the serious birder the best chance of finding North American vagrants in the Western Palearctic. More than a dozen species of wader can be expected, if not guaranteed, as well as several waterfowl including breeding American Black Duck. In addition there is the chance of Double-crested Cormorant, Pied-billed Grebe, Great and Little Blue Herons, and Belted Kingfisher; in fact virtually any North American bird recorded in the Western

Palearctic. Passerines are recorded less frequently but certainly occur and greater coverage will undoubtedly produce many more.

Tourism is increasing in the Azores and there are regular flights and plentiful accommodation on the islands. Being a relatively new birding destination there is much left to discover and in autumn there is every possibility of adding a new species to the Western Palearctic list.

Balearic Islands

This group of islands in the western Mediterranean is one of the most popular tourist destinations in the Western Palearctic. They are also ideal for birders and the easiest place in the Mediterranean to combine a cheap package holiday with a birding trip. There are no endemics but there are several sought after resident birds such as Egyptian and Black Vultures, Eleonora's Falcon, Audouin's Gull, Thekla

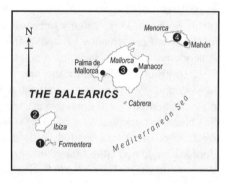

Lark and Moustached and Marmora's Warbler, plus a wide range of migrants. The islands are packed with holidaymakers in summer but less so in spring and autumn, when the greatest diversity of birds can be seen. Mallorca is the best island for resident birds but there can be much of interest on the other islands during passage periods.

1) Formentera is the smallest, driest and southernmost of the four main Balearic Islands, lying c.5km south of Ibiza. The main birding interest is at the Estany Pudent, a brackish lagoon and saltpans, and famous as a site for Black-necked Grebe, which is present all year but numbers thousands in winter. Black-winged Stilt and Kentish Plover are regular, and in the scrubland around the lagoon and saltpans there are Greater Short-toed Lark, Tawny Pipit, and Sardinian and Marmora's Warblers. Estany Pudent is situated in the north of the island and the road from La Savina to Es Pujols follows the north and east shores. Nearby areas include Salinas Marroig, which sometimes attracts Greater Flamingo, and Estany des Peix west of La Savina, which is good for gulls and terns. Many of the headlands of Formentera have breeding birds of interest and are attractive to migrant passerines. Cap de Barbaria is the southernmost point of the island and holds breeding Thekla Lark, Blue Rock Thrush and Woodchat Shrike, a range of passerine migrants, and shearwaters offshore. The easternmost point of the island is La Mola, where small numbers of Audouin's Gull breed. Follow the main road east across the isthmus to El Pilar and on to the lighthouse. Rock Sparrow and Cirl Bunting are common here. Larger numbers of Balearic Shearwaters breed around Formentera than elsewhere in the archipelago and there are colonies of European Storm-petrel and Audouin's Gull on the islets between Formentera and Ibiza. There is no airport and Formentera can only be reached by ferry from Ibiza.

2) Ibiza is principally known as the summer haunt of thousands of night clubbers, but it also has birding interest in the extensive woodlands, high cliffs and salines. Breeding birds are fewer than those of the larger Balearics but include Eleonora's Falcon, Audouin's Gull and Marmora's Warbler, and migrants occur in significant numbers. One of the best-known birding areas is Las Salinas, close to the airport in the far south. Greater Flamingo is regular and Stone-curlew, Kentish Plover and Black-winged Stilt breed. The salines are reached on the PM801 from Ibiza town and by turning south on the PM802 after 4km. Cabo Falco can also be reached from here, where the cliffs have Blue Rock Thrush and Thekla Lark. In the far south-west at Cala d'Hort Eurasian Crag Martin and Marmora's Warbler breed, and there also stunning views of two small islands offshore which host breeding Balearic Shearwater, European Storm-petrel, Eleonora's Falcon and Audouin's Gull.

3) Mallorca is the largest of the Balearics and by far the best for birders with most of the more sought after residents and a wider range of migrants. Most of the best birding areas are conveniently located in the north-east of the island and Puerto de Pollença makes an ideal base. The Albufera and Albufereta Marshes, reached from the C712 south of Alcúdia, constitute one of the best wetland areas in the western Mediterranean with good viewing facilities and a superb range of birds. Albufera supports Little Bittern, Cattle Egret and Black-crowned Night and Purple Herons, with the first breeding by Squacco Heron in 2000. Marbled Duck bred here in 1997 and Red-crested Pochard, White-headed Duck and Purple Swamphen have been reintroduced. Spotted and Little Crakes are also regular, and the reedbeds support Cetti's Warbler and Zitting Cisticola and Spain's largest population of Moustached Warbler. Eleonora's Falcon gathers to feed over the area and Red-footed Falcon is a rare but regular passage visitor. Also hawking insects over the marsh are Red-rumped Swallow, and Pallid and Alpine Swifts. Scrubland around the saltpans to the south holds Stone-curlew, Greater Short-toed Lark and Tawny Pipit. The Bocquer Valley is an easy walk from Puerto de Pollença and very popular with visiting birders. Marmora's Warbler is common here but the main attraction is the variety of passerine migrants that can occur. Shearwaters, Eleonora's Falcon, Audouin's Gull, Blue Rock Thrush and Marmora's Warbler can all be seen at Cap de Formentor in the far north-east of the island, and the Tramuntana Mountains along the north coast hold Black Vulture, which can often be seen at Cuber Reservoir. The quarry at the reservoir is the best site on the island for Rock Thrush. The best birding site in the south of Mallorca is Salinas de Levante, which can be viewed from the PM604 and minor roads. Gull-billed, Caspian and marsh terns are possible here as well as Mediterranean and Audouin's Gulls.

4) Menorca is smaller than Mallorca and has fewer birds, but these include Egyptian Vulture and Dartford Warbler, and Spotless Starling bred here in 1998, the first Balearic record. S'Albufera es Grau, on the east coast 8km north of Mahón, is Menorca's only Parc Naturel and is a brackish lake with small reedbeds surrounded by scrub-covered hillsides. Waders and waterfowl occur on passage and migrant raptors include Red Kite and Booted Eagle. In the north-east the reedbeds at Son Parc may still support Moustached Warbler but there has been much habitat loss at this once important site. The Cap de Cavalleria, the northernmost point of the island, has Stone-curlew, Thekla Lark and Dartford Warbler. The best site in the north-west is Algaiarens Gorge, reached from Ciutadella de Menorca on the Cala Morell road following signs for La Vall. There is a European Bee-eater colony here and Red Kite, Egyptian Vulture and Booted Eagle can be seen. A large colony of Cory's Shearwater, as well as Pallid Swift, Eurasian Crag Martin and Blue Rock Thrush, can be found at Punta de s'Escullar west of Cala Morell, and all these species can also be found further west at Punta Nati. The most scenically attractive birding site on Menorca is surely the Algendar Gorge reached from Cala Santa Galdana on the south coast. The high cliffs are home to Red Kite, Egyptian Vulture and Booted Eagle, and a range of passerines breeds in the dense vegetation in the valley bottom. The largest reedbed on the island is at Son Bou on the south coast where Moustached and other warblers breed.

Bay of Biscay

In recent years it has become clear that one of the easiest and most comfortable ways to see good numbers of highly sought after seabirds (and whales) is from the ferries between England and Spain that cross the Bay of Biscay. The ferries run from Portsmouth to Bilbao or Plymouth to Santander, and both routes round Ouessant before heading south across the eastern half of Biscay.

South of Brittany the ocean floor drops from the relatively shallow continental shelf to the much deeper Abyssal Plain and deep oceanic trenches, before once again meeting the shelf close to the coast of Spain. It is this variety of water depths and seabed topography that gives the region its abundance of wildlife. In addition to the seabirds this is the best area in Europe for cetaceans and there are special trips with guides to cater for those interested in whale-watching.

During the early part of the trip, in the west part of the Channel, Northern Fulmar, Northern Gannet and Kittiwake are numerous, with Great Skua also seen frequently. Smaller numbers of the other three skuas are usually present, as well as European Storm-petrel and shearwaters. Sooty, Manx and Balearic are commonest but Cory's and Great can be seen after strong westerly winds. Heading south into Biscay the numbers of birds increase, especially when approaching the edge of the shelf; Great and Cory's Shearwaters become much more numerous and with the right combination of timing and winds this is one of the most regular areas in Europe for Sabine's Gull. Where the water is deepest the numbers of birds tend to decrease but once the shelf is reached they appear again, and here Little Shearwater and Wilson's Storm-petrel are possible.

Late-summer to early-autumn trips are the best for birders and also whale-watchers, with the optimum period being mid-August to mid-September.

Belarus

Increasingly featured in the brochures of the larger bird tour companies, Belarus is undoubtedly on the way to becoming one of the top birding destinations of the future. With extensive temperate mixed forests and some of the best wetlands in Europe, this country has all that Poland has to offer plus the chance of eastern specialities such as Pallid Harrier and Azure Tit. Tourist infrastructure is improving and roads and public transport are generally good, but it is still far easier to visit Belarus on an organised birding trip. A visit between mid May and mid-June would produce the most species, but as usual owls and woodpeckers are easier to locate earlier in spring.

1) Belovezhskaya Pushcha National Park This is the east part of the forest known across the Polish border as Białowieza and has a similar range of undisturbed forest and marshland habitats, and much the same birdlife. The forest is deciduous, with oak and lime in particular, with large coniferous areas and some very wet areas. As well as Europe's best-preserved primeval forest, the area also has marshes, meadows and large areas of more disturbed woodland.

Around 170 species breed with owls and woodpeckers among the specialities. Owls include Eurasian Eagle, Ural, Eurasian Pygmy and Tengmalm's and the rare Great Grey is present in some years. Woodpeckers include Black, Grey-headed, White-backed, Middle Spotted and Three-toed, and possibly Syrian. Greater Spotted Eagle has been recorded and may breed, and Lesser Spotted certainly does, as well as Booted and White-tailed Eagles. Other raptors include Red and Black Kites, three harriers and Red-footed Falcon. Also breeding are both storks, Hazel and Black Grouse and Capercaillie, which may now be extinct in the Polish sector of the forest. The more open and wetter areas have breeding Corn Crake and Great Snipe. Passerines are varied with Nutcracker, Collared and Red-breasted Flycatchers, and River and Barred Warblers among the most sought after.

The park lies in the west of Belarus and can be reached by road from Brest.

2) Berezinsky Biosphere Reserve This reserve is located 120km north of Minsk and the 1,200km² area consists of vast pine forests, fens, bogs and wet meadows along the floodplain of the Beresina River. Nearly 220 bird species have been recorded in the area.

Great Bittern, Common Crane and Black Stork breed here as well as Corn Crake and raptors including White-tailed Eagle and Montagu's Harrier. The extensive forests have owls such as Ural, Eurasian Pygmy and Tengmalm's, woodpeckers including White-backed and Three-toed, as well as Capercaillie and Black Grouse.

Accommodation is available at a hunting lodge within the reserve and there is also the Reserve Hotel in Domzheritsy.

3) Prypyatsky National Park Although much of this area remains a rarely visited wilderness, the Prypyat Marshes is one of the best wetland areas in the entire Western Palearctic. Situated in the south of Belarus, the Prypyat region covers a vast area of marshes, bogs and lakes, birch woodland, pine forest and agricultural land. Nearly 200 species breed here and over 250 have been recorded in total.

Breeding birds of the marshes include all five European grebes, both storks, Common Crane, Corn Crake and Spotted and Little Crakes. Ducks including Ferruginous breed, as well as White-winged Tern, Terek Sandpiper and Great Snipe. Raptors include Black Kite, White-tailed and Lesser Spotted Eagles, and Pallid Harrier. More wooded areas host Capercaillie, Black and Hazel Grouse, various woodpeckers including White-backed, and owls including Eurasian Eagle. The long list of woodland passerines includes Nutcracker, Barred Warbler and Collared Flycatcher, and the speciality, Azure Tit, a highly sought after species for many birders. Aquatic Warbler is among the various wetland warblers found in the area, which is also an important stopover point for migrating waterfowl, particularly geese, and waders, especially in spring.

The National Park lies c.280km south of Minsk, and the small town of Turov forms an ideal base where accommodation is available.

Belgium

Rarely thought of as a birding destination, Belgium's main interest for British birders lies in its forest species, which can be seen on a short break. These include Eurasian Eagle and Tengmalm's Owls, and Grey-headed, Black and Middle Spotted Woodpeckers. Black Stork is also now possible in Belgium and Hazel Grouse is present in some years. These birds can be seen in the Ardennes, an area of wooded hills in the south of the country.

1) Blankaart Reserve and the Yser Estuary On the east bank of the Yser in western Belgium, the habitats of Blankaart include the shallow and heavily vegetated Lake Blankaart, marshes with extensive reedbeds and wet meadows.

Well known as one of the few Belgian breeding sites for Black-tailed Godwit, Blankaart also has many other nesting species including both bitterns, Kentish Plover, Crested Lark and Savi's Warbler. During passage periods a wide range of waders occurs and large numbers of waterfowl winter here.

To reach Blankaart follow the coastal road west from Oostende to the Yser and then inland to Blankaart near Woumen, c.8km south of Diksmuide and just west of the N369. Entry to the reserve requires a permit but much can be seen from local roads and paths.

2) Croix-Scaille Reserve This area of deciduous woodland forms part of the upland plateau of Croix-Scaille, which is in turn part of the Ardennes plateau. As well as extensive woodlands the area has scrub, grassland and remnant bogs.

In addition to a good selection of woodland species, this area hosts breeding Black Stork, Nutcracker and Hazel Grouse in very small numbers, although these may not be present every year.

Croix-Scaille is situated on the River Semois and can be reached from the town of Gedinne in the south of Belgium.

3) Hautes Fagnes Natural Park Belgium's largest protected area, the Hautes Fagnes (High Fens) lies in the eastern Ardennes on the border with Germany. It consists of a high plateau with dense oak and beech woodland, peat bogs and fens. The most important area of peat bog is protected as a nature reserve.

An important area for Black Grouse, breeding raptors and Common Crane on passage, breeders include a small population of Black Grouse, Corn Crake, Red Kite, with Grey-headed and Black Woodpeckers and both treecreepers in the woodlands. A major attraction for birders is Tengmalm's Owl, which occurs in small numbers in these forests, breeding mainly in nest boxes.

The Hautes Fagnes is popular with tourists and accommodation can be found in all local towns, and there are campsites and marked trails within the park.

4) Het Zwin Belgium's best-known bird reserve is situated on the border with the Netherlands and consists of saltmarshes and mudflats at the former mouth of the River Zwin. Large lagoons have been created to attract breeding birds with some success. Pied Avocet, Kentish Plover and Mediterranean Gull occur in summer and Cattle Egret has bred since the 1990s. Small numbers of feral White Stork and Barnacle Goose also breed.

A wide range of waders occurs on passage and the area is very important for waterfowl, including Smew and Pink-footed, Bean and Greater White-fronted Geese in winter. Raptors hunt over the reserve in winter and Twite, Shore Lark, Lapland and Snow Buntings can be seen on the saltmarshes.

To reach the reserve take Route 67 north from Brugge and turn towards Knokke-Heist, and it is then signposted eastwards on a minor road.

5) Kalmthoutse Heide and the Campine This is one of the best-known reserves in the part of north-east Belgium known as the Campine, a large area of heaths, plantations and woodlands with scattered marshes and lakes. Kalmthoutse lies in the west of this region, on the Belgian-Dutch border. Here, there are inland, mobile sand dunes, heaths, pinewoods and small lakes.

More than 100 species have been recorded breeding including Northern Goshawk and Black Woodpecker, and passerines such as Wood Lark, Bluethroat and Crested Tit. In the wetter areas there are various ducks, Black-necked Grebe and Spotted Crake, and significant numbers of duck pass through the area on migration.

The reserve has marked footpaths and an observation tower, but access to part of the dune area is restricted. To reach the reserve leave Antwerp north on the E10 to Maria-ter-Heide and turn left for Kalmthout. There are also nature reserves at Stiemerbeck Valley, near Genk, and around Herentals, Geel and Kasterlee with a similar range of species.

6) Lesse et Lomme Nature Reserve In a scenically attractive part of southern Belgium, the Lesse et Lomme Nature Reserve is situated close to the confluence of the Lesse and Lomme rivers. Habitats are varied with fertile valleys and densely wooded hillsides, dry calcareous grassland and rocky cliffs.

In addition to the more widespread woodland birds, there are some specialities such as possible Hazel Grouse, which is very rare in Belgium. Other species breeding here include Corn Crake, Black and Middle Spotted Woodpeckers, and Red-backed Shrike. Raptors on passage and in winter include Black Kite.

The reserve has open access and can be reached from the towns of Rochefort to the N, Auffe to the west and Wavreille to the E.

Bosnia-Herzegovina

There is very little recent information on the birds of this country, formerly part of Yugoslavia, and this situation seems unlikely to change in the near future. Although mountain areas are now being opened for skiing and are presumably safe, the threat of landmines will exist in lowland areas for many years to come. Like most of the Balkans this area is still suffering from extensive habitat loss and wetlands are under particular threat. A spring visit would be most productive but all Bosnia-Herzegovina's birds are more easily seen in other, safer countries.

1) Hutovo blato This site adjoins Croatia's Neretva Delta and has probably suffered much the same habitat degradation. What remains of the wet meadows and riverine forest may still hold breeding Pygmy Cormorant, various herons and Ferruginous Duck, but there is little recent information.

Like Neretva, this area may now have lost most of its wetland birds but species such as Black-eared Wheatear, Sombre Tit and Black-headed Bunting, and Woodchat and Lesser Grey Shrikes can still be seen. Warblers probably include Olive-tree, Spectacled, Subalpine, Sardinian and Cetti's, and Zitting Cisticola.

Hutovo blato lies on the coast north-west of Dubrovnik and can be reached by road south of Mostar.

2) Sutjeska National Park The country's highest mountain, Maglic at 2,386m, is situated in this park as well as large areas of mature, and possibly still largely untouched, forests of beech and spruce. At higher levels there are alpine meadows and bare rocks, and the park is split by the Sujetska Gorge.

Golden Eagle, Rock Partridge, Alpine Accentor, Rock Thrush and Alpine Chough are among the birds found in higher areas, and Hazel Grouse and Capercaillie occur in the forests. Eurasian Eagle, Ural and Tengmalm's Owls are also found in these forests, as well as woodpeckers including Grey-headed, Black, Middle Spotted, White-backed and Three-toed. The park also supports Corn Crake, Sombre Tit and Nutcracker.

The park can be explored from the village of Tjentiste on the main Sarajevo-Dubrovnik road, *c.*90km south of Sarajevo.

Bulgaria

With mountains, forest, steppe and some of the best wetlands in Europe, Bulgaria is now one of the most popular countries in the region for travelling birders. Accommodation is plentiful and relatively inexpensive, with ski centres in the mountains and numerous holiday resorts on the Black Sea coast. The latter is on a major migration route and a package holiday is an ideal way to see a large number of species for those on a budget or a family holiday. There are many south-

eastern specialities to be seen in Bulgaria including Pygmy Cormorant, pelicans and raptors, including Levant Sparrowhawk and Long-legged Buzzard, as well as numerous passerines. There is much to see throughout the year, with the greatest variety on spring (late Apr to early May) and autumn passage (late August to late September). Bird tour companies now operate regular winter trips to see the large numbers of Red-breasted and other geese.

1) Albena-Golden Sands With all the facilities of a modern tourist resort, this area on the Black Sea coast offers an ideal introduction to Bulgaria for the birder on a family holiday. As well as eastern specialities the area is on the Black Sea flyway, and at the right time of year all manner of migrating birds can be seen passing through.

Syrian Woodpecker, Eurasian Scops Owl and Crested Lark can be found as well as Red-rumped Swallow, Thrush Nightingale, Olive-tree Warbler and Semi-collared Flycatcher. These species can often be seen around the resort areas and a stretch of cliffs at the northern end of Albena has Pied Wheatear and Rock Bunting. Between Albena and the mouth of the River Batova is Baltata Forest, now much reduced and a reserve with restricted access, but still home to Grey-headed, Black and Middle Spotted Woodpeckers. A marshy area at the river mouth has Black-crowned Night Heron, Little Bittern and Savi's Warbler. Fields and scrub-covered hillsides around the town hold Calandra Lark, Eastern Olivaceous and Barred Warblers, Spanish Sparrow and Black-headed Bunting. N of Albena is Balchik, where Eurasian Eagle Owl may still be present on cliffs south of the town.

Over the sea divers, grebes and Yelkouan Shearwater can be seen on passage, along with gulls and terns, and large numbers of pelicans, storks, waterfowl, raptors and waders can be seen during passage periods.

This is one of the most popular tourist areas in Bulgaria and accommodation and package deals are plentiful. Golden Sands is 15km north of Varna and Albena 15km further N; both are easily reached from the E87.

2) Belene Island This is the most famous birding site along the Bulgarian Danube and consists of riverine woodland and scrub, wet meadows and farmland. The area held important colonies of waterbirds, although habitat changes have reduced numbers in recent decades. Belene is one of several Danube islands that are now nature reserves including Vardim c.20km downstream.

Pygmy Cormorant still occurs, as does Glossy Ibis, but in much-reduced numbers. Other birds present in summer include Eurasian Spoonbill and Squacco, Purple and Black-crowned Night Herons, Whiskered Tern and warblers such as River and Eastern Olivaceous. Lesser Grey Shrike also occurs on farmland but is now rare.

The island is between Belene village and Svishtov, c.70km north-east of Pleven. No attempt should be made to reach the island, as all of the birds can be seen in the surrounding area.

3) Burgas area Despite much habitat loss, this part of the Black Sea coast remains one of the best for wetland birds in the country. The site consists of four lakes: Burgas, with extensive reedbeds, Mandra, now a reservoir, Poda, a brackish lagoon, and Atanasovo, which is now largely saltpans.

The area attracts birds all year, with rare breeders including both bitterns and Black-crowned Night, Squacco and Purple Herons, Great and Cattle Egrets, Ferruginous Duck, Mediterranean Gull and Gull-billed Tern. Corn Crake and Little Crake breed but remain as elusive as ever, and waders include Pied Avocet, Black-winged Stilt and Collared Pratincole. Reedbeds are home to Cetti's, River and Savi's Warblers, as well as Bearded and Penduline Tits, and Barred, Eastern Olivaceous and Olive-tree Warblers breed nearby. Open farmland around the lakes has Long-legged Buzzard, European Roller, Syrian Woodpecker, Lesser Grey Shrike and various larks and other passerines, including Cirl and Black-headed Buntings.

Passage periods can be excellent with both pelicans and both storks, Glossy Ibis, Eurasian Spoonbill and Ruddy Shelduck. Raptor passage is also impressive with Lesser Spotted Eagle numerous, and Pallid Harrier, Levant Sparrowhawk and Short-toed, Eastern Imperial, Steppe, Greater Spotted and Booted Eagles regular. Waders usually include Great Snipe, Temminck's Stint, Broad-billed and Marsh Sandpipers, and Red-necked Phalarope. Slender-billed Curlew has been recorded and may occur again. In winter the lakes and nearby coast attract Black-throated Diver, Bewick's and Whooper Swans, geese including Red-breasted, and ducks, usually including White-headed Duck. White-tailed Eagle is regular in winter.

All of the lakes lie close to the town of Burgas, which has an airport and plentiful accommodation. All major sites can be reached from the E87 coast road.

4) Cape Emine This headland on the Black Sea coast is one of the best migration watchpoints in Bulgaria, second only to Cape Kaliakra to the north. The peninsula is the easternmost extension of the central Balkan range and has rocky cliffs, scrub, oak woodland and dry grassland.

Yelkouan and, sometimes, Cory's Shearwaters can be seen at sea during passage periods, as well as Mediterranean and Slender-billed Gulls and divers. Other migrants include both pelicans, both storks and a wide range of raptors including Short-toed, Lesser Spotted and Booted Eagles. Birds present on the cape in summer include Levant Sparrowhawk, Black-eared and Isabelline Wheatears and Sombre Tit, and the area is one of the best in the country for Olive-tree Warbler.

Cape Emine is situated c.50km north of Burgas and close to the popular holiday resort of Sunny Beach, where accommodation is plentiful.

5) Cape Kaliakra A coastal headland with 60m cliffs, Kaliakra acts as a bottleneck for migrants passing the west shore of the Black Sea, and also has breeding birds of great interest.

The limestone cliffs have the country's only breeding European Shags, as well as Long-legged Buzzard, Black-eared, Pied and Isabelline Wheatears, and possibly Saker Falcon. Yelkouan Shearwater may be seen from the point and terns and gulls are usually present. En route to the point itself are patches of stony steppe with scrub and grassland where Stone-curlew and various shrikes, larks and buntings breed, as well as Spanish Sparrow.

Small numbers of Great Bustard may still winter in this area and possibly also Red-breasted Geese. A wooded valley on the plateau north of the cape has fresh water and reedbeds with a variety of warblers, including Barred, Hawfinch and breeding Eurasian Eagle Owl and Syrian Woodpecker.

It is migrants however, that attract most birders. Regular in autumn are both storks, White Pelican and Pygmy Cormorant. Raptors include Black Kite and all four harriers, Levant Sparrowhawk, and Lesser Spotted, Booted and Short-toed Eagles. Red-footed Falcon and Saker Falcon also occur regularly. Passerines are present in large numbers and include Lesser Grey Shrike and Red-breasted Flycatcher, with Rose-coloured Starling in some years.

There is abundant tourist accommodation on this stretch of coast and an international airport at Varna.

6) Lake Durankulak In the far north-east of Bulgaria, on the Black Sea coast, this lake lies in the Dobrudja and like nearby Lake Shabla holds Red-breasted Goose in large numbers during severe weather. The brackish water and marshland have extensive reedbeds and are surrounded by farmland and plantations.

Summering species include Red-necked and Black-necked Grebes, Pygmy Cormorant, various herons, Ferruginous Duck and, in some years, Red-crested Pochard and Ruddy Shelduck. Whiskered Tern and Collared Pratincole breed and reedbed passerines include Bearded and Penduline Tits, Cetti's and Savi's Warblers, and the species that this site is most famous for, Paddyfield Warbler, which is common here. Surrounding farmland has Montagu's Harrier and Red-footed Falcon, Stone-curlew, Syrian Woodpecker and passerines including Calandra Lark, Eastern Olivaceous Warbler and Lesser Grey Shrike. White Pelican occurs on passage along with many herons, storks, waterfowl, raptors and waders. In winter Greater White-fronted and Lesser White-fronted Geese can be seen with the Red-breasted Geese, ducks include Smew and White-headed Duck, and White-tailed Eagle may occur. The steppe-like grassland around the lake may attract Great and Little Bustards in severe winters.

The lake is situated east of the E87 between Durankulak village and Vaklino, in the far north of the country close to the Romanian border.

7) Lake Shabla This area is best known as a wintering site for Red-breasted Goose when the weather is severe in the usual wintering grounds further north in Romania. However, even without the geese it is still an excellent birding area and consists of two irregularly shaped lakes, joined by a channel, and separated from the Black Sea by a narrow sandbar with a saline pool (Shabla Tuzla) to the S. There are extensive reedbeds, plantations and grassland. To the south is the rocky headland of Cape Shabla.

Other waterfowl include Whooper Swan, Greater White-fronted and Lesser White-fronted Geese, and Ferruginous Duck. Black-throated Diver, Black-necked Grebe, Pygmy Cormorant, Great Bittern and Great Egret are also regular in small numbers. White-tailed Eagle is among the regularly wintering raptors and Pallas' Gull is possible.

During passage periods the site can be one of the best in Europe, with both pelicans, both storks, Glossy Ibis, Eurasian Spoonbill and Common Crane all regular, along with many grebes, waterfowl, raptors and waders. Shabla Tuzla is excellent for waders: Black-winged Stilt, Pied Avocet and Kentish Plover breed, and Broad-billed and Marsh Sandpipers and Jack Snipe occur on passage. Gulls usually include Mediterranean and Slender-billed, and all three marsh terns occur in autumn.

Lake Shabla and the surrounding area has breeding wetland birds including both bitterns, Purple Heron, crakes and, sometimes, Ruddy Shelduck and Ferruginous Duck. Reed warblers include Cetti's, Savi's and even Paddyfield, and away from the water there are Barred and Eastern Olivaceous. Other breeding birds of the woods and farmland include Montagu's Harrier and Red-footed Falcon, Eurasian Scops Owl, European Roller and Syrian Woodpecker. Lesser Grey Shrike is a rare nesting species in open areas, where Calandra Lark, Isabelline Wheatear and Black-headed Bunting are more common.

The lakes lie c.5km north-east of the village of Shabla, in north-east Bulgaria, and can be reached on the main coast road, the E87. Shabla has a campsite and hotels.

8) Lake Srebarna One of Bulgaria's most important wetlands, Srebarna is a 600ha area of fresh water surrounded by reeds and willow scrub, and separated from the Danube by a narrow belt of riparian woodland and farmland. The lake is famous for its waterbirds and, in particular, as a breeding site for Dalmatian Pelican. Following a long decline, the species ceased breeding in the mid 1990s but small numbers have since returned, and it remains one of the most reliable sites for the species in Europe. More than 180 species have been recorded in the area.

Also present in summer are: Red-necked and Black-necked Grebes, Pygmy Cormorant, both bitterns, various herons, and small numbers of Glossy Ibis and Eurasian Spoonbill. White Pelican has recently bred here for the first time in many years but is much commoner on passage. Other breeders include Ferruginous Duck, crakes and marsh terns, European Roller, European Bee-eater and Penduline Tit. Levant Sparrowhawk hunts the nearby woodland and Black Kite and Montagu's Harrier over farmland. A wide variety of raptors, waterfowl and waders occur on passage. The lake is also famous for large numbers of wintering geese, mainly Greater White-fronted, but Lesser White-fronted and Red-breasted are usually also present. White-tailed Eagle formerly bred but now occurs only as a rare winter visitor, at which season it may be joined by Red Kite and Rough-legged Buzzard.

Lake Srebarna is situated 18km west of Silistra and the reserve has a visitor centre and a viewpoint overlooking the pelican colony. Silistra has hotel accommodation or the area can be easily reached by road from the tourist resorts of Bulgaria's Black Sea coast.

9) Rila Mountains This area in south-west Bulgaria is famous for the Rila Monastery, with its murals, and is a popular tourist destination, making it relatively easy to reach for birders in search of montane and forest birds. The lower valleys have some mixed and deciduous woodland, but most of the forests are coniferous, with alpine meadows higher up, and largely bare rock on the peaks.

In the highest areas are Golden Eagle, Rock Partridge, Alpine Accentor and easily seen Wallcreeper, as well as Shore Lark, Alpine Chough and Western Rock Nuthatch. Dense forests on the lower slopes have Lesser Spotted and Booted Eagles, Hazel Grouse and Capercaillie. Woodpeckers are well represented, with Black, Grey-headed, Syrian, Middle Spotted, White-backed and Three-toed all present. Passerines include Sombre and Crested Tits, Eastern Bonelli's Warbler and Nutcracker.

north-east of Rila is the skiing centre of Borovets, which has similar birds but more tourist facilities and a chair-lift to the high tops. Mount Musala is the highest peak in the range at 2,925m and lies 10km south of Borovets.

The lower areas to the south and towards the edge of the Rila Mountains have Short-toed Eagle, Eurasian Scops Owl and European Roller, as well as passerines such as Masked and Lesser Grey Shrikes, Orphean Warbler and Black-headed Bunting.

The area is easily reached by road from Sofia. Most towns in the area have accommodation and there is access to higher areas via ski-lifts. There are numerous hiking trails, many of which are excellent for birding.

10) Ropotamo National Park Where the River Ropotamo enters the Black Sea in south-east Bulgaria is an area of diverse habitats including sandy and rocky beaches, dunes, freshwater marshes, hillside scrub and woodland, and flooded forest. The range of habitats results in an interesting variety of breeding birds and this is one of the most important sites in Bulgaria for Semi-collared Flycatcher.

Both bitterns breed as well as Great Egret, Squacco and Purple Herons, Pygmy Cormorant, Black Stork, and Spotted and Little Crakes. Levant Sparrowhawk, Northern Goshawk and Booted and Lesser Spotted Eagles are among the breeding raptors, and woodpeckers include Grey-headed, Syrian and Middle Spotted. Eurasian Scops and Eurasian Eagle Owls can be found on the wooded hillsides, and passerines include Greater Short-toed Lark and Tawny Pipit on the dunes, Olive-tree Warbler and Cirl Bunting in the scrub, and Short-toed Treecreeper and Hawfinch in the woods. Semi-collared Flycatcher is often seen around the car park. Rufous Bush Robin has been reported from this area. A wide variety of migrants can be seen at Ropotamo, from pelicans and storks to passerines, with Yelkouan Shearwater and divers on the sea. White-tailed and Greater Spotted Eagles are rare winter visitors.

About 20km south of Sozopol, Ropotamo can be reached on the E87. Parts of the reserve require a permit to visit but it is possible to arrange boat trips along the river.

11) Rusenski Lom National Park An important raptor site consisting of a complex of limestone gorges, stream valleys and plateaux, interspersed with meadows, farmland, scrub and forest in the far north of Bulgaria. There is a well vegetated river flowing through the main canyon and small ponds scattered over the farmland.

Short-toed, Lesser Spotted and Golden Eagles, Egyptian Vulture, Levant Sparrowhawk, Long-legged Buzzard, Saker Falcon and Lesser Kestrel all breed here, and the wooded gorges are home to Black Stork, Eurasian Eagle and Eurasian Scops Owls, and woodpeckers including Black, Middle Spotted and Syrian. Farmland nearby hosts White Stork, European Roller, European Bee-eater, shrikes and Tawny Pipit. Rock Thrush and Black-headed and Rock Buntings can be seen on the rockier plateaux, and Ruddy Shelduck has nested in the rocks along the gorge.

Rusenski Lom lies 15km south of the Danube port of Ruse and can be reached from there on the E85 or from the Black Sea coast on the E70. Most of the best gorges are found between the villages of Ivanov in the west and Pisanec in the E.

12) Strandja Mountains This part of Bulgaria is rarely visited by birders but the range of habitats here, including wooded ridges and river valleys, scrub and wetlands, holds a rich variety of breeding birds. In addition, like other sites on the Black Sea coast, a wide variety of migrants passes through the area.

The area is one of the best in the country for raptors, with breeding Black Kite, Egyptian Vulture, Montagu's Harrier, Northern Goshawk and Levant Sparrowhawk, and Short-toed, Lesser Spotted, Golden and Booted Eagles. Also present in summer, and perhaps breeding, are Long-legged Buzzard, Eastern Imperial Eagle and Saker Falcon. Other breeders include Black and White Storks, Chukar Partridge, Great Spotted Cuckoo, Eurasian Eagle and Eurasian Scops Owls. European Bee-eater and European Roller also breed, as well as Grey-headed, Black, Syrian, Middle Spotted and White-backed Woodpeckers. Among the many passerines of interest are Red-rumped Swallow, Isabelline Wheatear, Eastern Olivaceous, Olive-tree, Barred and Eastern Bonelli's Warblers, Sombre Tit and Semi-collared Flycatcher.

The Strandja Mountains lie in extreme south-east Bulgaria and can be explored from the town of Sozopol on the Black Sea coast or the village of Malko Turnovo close to the Turkish border.

13) Studen Kladenetz In the far south of the country, this important site for breeding and passage raptors consists of a reservoir and its surroundings in the Eastern Rodopi Mountains, the deep rocky valley of the River Arda, and the surrounding stony and scrub-covered slopes and rocky cliffs.

This site is exceptional in Bulgaria in hosting three vultures; Black is rare, Griffon much commoner and these residents are joined by Egyptian in summer. Other raptors include Eastern Imperial, Golden, Lesser Spotted, Booted and Short-toed Eagles, and Long-legged Buzzard, Black Kite, Northern Goshawk, Levant Sparrowhawk and Lesser Kestrel. Black Stork also breeds in the area as well as Chukar Partridge, Eurasian Eagle Owl, Syrian Woodpecker and European Bee-eater. Passerines are varied and include such specialities as Western Rock Nuthatch, Sombre Tit, Olive-tree, Eastern Olivaceous and Barred Warblers, and Masked Shrike, as well as Mediterranean birds such as Orphean, Sardinian and Subalpine Warblers, and Woodchat Shrike.

Studen Kladenetz is 40km south of Khaskovo and east of Kardjali. There is a 'vulture restaurant' near the village of Potochnitza but contact the BSPB prior to visiting. The area around the River Arda bridge, near Kotlari, has a similar range of habitats and birds, plus flooded sandpits with breeding Penduline Tit and passage and winter Great Egret and waterfowl.

14) Tissata Nature Reserve The far south-west of Bulgaria is little visited by birders, compared to the Black Sea coast, but there is an interesting mix of eastern and Mediterranean species including several birds hard to find elsewhere in the country.

The valley of the River Struma has rocky, scrub-covered hillsides and cliffs, orchards, vineyards and woodland, and runs through Tissata reserve north of the town of Kresna.

Breeders include raptors such as Long-legged Buzzard, Short-toed and Golden Eagles, and Eurasian Scops and Eurasian Eagle Owls are also present. Eastern birds are represented by Syrian Woodpecker, Masked Shrike, Sombre Tit and Western Rock Nuthatch, and the Mediterranean contingent by Orphean, Subalpine and Sardinian Warblers. Many species typical of dry rocky areas occur including both rock thrushes, Black-eared Wheatear, Lesser Grey Shrike, and Rock, Ortolan and Cirl Buntings. Most of Bulgaria's raptors occur along the valley during passage periods, heading to and from the Aegean, and this migration route is probably the most important flyway in the country after the Black Sea coast.

South of Tissata is the town of Sandanski, where Egyptian Vulture, Lesser Kestrel and European Roller can be found on the rocky hillsides, and this is a good area for Rock Sparrow. North-east are the Pirin Mountains where Lammergeier has been reported.

Kresna makes the ideal base from which to explore the Tissata reserve and is c.110km south of Sofia on the E79. Sandanski and Melnik, further S, are also excellent birding areas.

15) Trigradski Gorge This important raptor site lies in south Bulgaria close to the Greek border in the central Rodopi Mountains. The gorge itself is deep and narrow with steep cliffs up to 200m high in places, conifer-covered slopes and fast-flowing streams.

Golden and Short-toed Eagles breed in or around the gorge as well as Northern Goshawk and Lesser Kestrel. Eurasian Eagle Owl is possible, along with abundant Alpine Swift, Eurasian Crag Martin and Red-rumped Swallow. Black Woodpecker occurs in the conifer forest and rockier areas have Rock Partridge, Rock Bunting, and, one of the specialities of the gorge, Wallcreeper. Passage birds possible along the gorge include Black Stork, European Bee-eater, various warblers and Collared and Semi-collared Flycatchers.

Trigradski Gorge is situated c.65km west of Smolyan and can be reached by road from there or Plovdiv. There are weekly guided tours of the gorge arranged by the BSPB.

15) Tzarichina Nature Reserve The Central Balkan Range, or Stara Planina, spans almost the whole of Bulgaria and includes many national parks, nature reserves and other protected areas. One of the best of these from an ornithological viewpoint is the Tzarichina reserve on the northern slopes, which has ancient mixed forests of beech, fir and pine. In higher areas there are areas of scrub and alpine meadows.

Forest birds found here include a good population of Hazel Grouse, smaller numbers of Capercaillie and woodpeckers including Black, Grey-headed, Middle Spotted and White-backed. The star bird, however, is Ural Owl, which breeds here and elsewhere in this range in very small numbers. Other owls include Tengmalm's, Eurasian Pygmy and Eurasian Eagle. Raptors breeding in the reserve include Northern Goshawk, Golden, Lesser Spotted and Booted Eagles, and possibly Griffon Vulture. Rock Partridge is common and at higher levels there are Shore Lark, Alpine Accentor, Rock Thrush and Ring Ouzel.

Tzarichina reserve can be reached on the E79 north-east of Sofia, then heading east to Etropole and Ribarica.

Canary Islands

In the North Atlantic, c.100km off Morocco, the Canaries are a group of seven volcanic island that hold several endemic species and subspecies. A very popular tourist destination they are ideal for a birding holiday at any time of year. Although the species list is not long the endemics are relatively easy to find, there are seabirds difficult to see elsewhere in the Western Palearctic, and vagrants are frequently recorded.

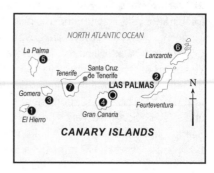

There are two endemic pigeons, Laurel Pigeon and Bolle's Pigeon, Canary is a near-endemic also found on Madeira and the Azores, but the distinctive Blue Chaffinch is found only in the Canaries. Canary Islands Stonechat is a Canarian endemic but Berthelot's Pipit also occurs on Madeira. Plain Swift was once thought to be endemic to the Atlantic Islands but is now known to also occur in Morocco. After a long period in taxonomic limbo, being classified as a race of both Goldcrest and Firecrest, Canary Island Kinglet has recently been generally afforded specific status, and other taxa recently accorded species rank are Canary Island Chiffchaff and the near-endemic African Blue Tit. In addition there are a number of more widespread birds with distinct Canarian races such as Common Kestrel, Common Buzzard, Barn and Long-eared Owls and Great Spotted Woodpecker, as well as passerines including Spectacled and Sardinian Warblers. The one remaining endemic, Canarian Black Oystercatcher, would be the find of a lifetime for any birder, as it has not been seen since 1913. The drier eastern Canaries are home to desert birds akin to those in neighbouring Morocco, such as Houbara Bustard, Cream-coloured Courser, Barbary Falcon and Black-bellied Sandgrouse. In addition, a range of seabirds can be seen from the inter-island ferries. Cory's and Little Shearwaters and Madeiran Storm-petrel and Bulwer's Petrel are common, and Fea's Petrel is frequently seen in autumn. There is also the possibility of vagrants from tropical seas such as tropicbirds or boobies, which are also possible from inter-island ferries, and whale-watching trips are becoming popular, providing further opportunities to see seabirds.

As these are relatively small islands heavily geared towards mass-tourism, the Canaries can offer the birder a cheap package deal with full facilities, car-hire, ferry-trips and internal flights, etc. To see all the endemic species, however, may require visiting three of the islands.

1) El Hierro is the smallest and southwesternmost of the main islands, and reaches more than 1,500 m. It is an island of steep slopes and pine and laurel forests, but is seldom visited by birders. Bolle's Pigeon is present in the Frontera forest of the north and W. The road between Valverde and Frontera runs along a ridge through this area and most of the island's special birds can be seen along it including African Blue Tit of the race *ombriosus*, which is endemic to the island. Also in the north is the Llanos de Nizdafe, an area of scrub and dry farmland with a good range of passerines including the endemic Canarian subspecies of Spectacled and Sardinian Warbler. Seabirds breeding on and around El Hierro include Cory's and Little Shearwaters, Madeiran and European Storm-petrels, Bulwer's Petrel and a small number of Roseate Terns.

2) Fuerteventura is dry and barren and one of the most popular islands of the group for birding visitors, with the main attraction being the endemic Canary Islands Stonechat. Additional draws are Egyptian Vulture, Houbara Bustard, Cream-coloured Courser and Black-bellied Sandgrouse, all found here more easily than on Lanzarote. The plains of Lajares and Tindaya, in the N, are among the best sites for these species, as well as for Barbary Partridge and Stone-curlew. The stony plains around El Cotillo, in the north-east, also support these birds and Spectacled Warbler, Berthelot's Pipit and Lesser Short-toed Lark. The lava fields between El Cotillo and Corralejo hold Barbary Falcon, Canary Island Chat and Trumpeter Finch, and most of these can also be found around La Oliva in the N. The best-known site for the stonechat is the Barranco de Río Cabras (Willis's Barranco) in the east of the island, just 1km north of the airport. Barbary Partridge, Cream-coloured Courser, Houbara Bustard and Black-bellied Sandgrouse are also possible in this area. Los Molinos, in the W, is a dammed valley and the resulting reservoir is the best freshwater area on Fuerteventura. Kentish Plover and Black-winged Stilt occur here and Marbled Duck is regular in small numbers, as well as passage herons. Punta del Jandía forms the south-west tip of the island and most of the specialities, including Egyptian Vulture and Barbary Falcon, can be seen on this rugged peninsula. Cory's and Little Shearwaters, Bulwer's Petrel and European and Madeiran Storm-petrels breed on Isla de Lobos off the northern tip of the island.

3) Gomera is a small circular island with a central volcanic cone rising to 1,484m. It is seldom visited by birders but has both endemic pigeons, Berthelot's Pipit, Canary Island Chiffchaff and Kinglet, and African Blue Tit, all of which can be seen at El Cedro, which is probably the best area for birds on the island. The cliffs in the north-east, at Costa de Majona, have breeding Cory's Shearwater, which also breeds in the south-west, between Punta de la Calera and Playa de Santiago, along with European Storm-petrel and Little Shearwater. The ferry trip between Tenerife and Gomera can be the most productive in the archipelago, with the possibility of Fea's Petrel. Bulwer's Petrel is regularly seen May–September, Little Shearwater in summer and Madeiran Storm-petrel is possible in May and August. Rarities have included Great, Sooty and Balearic Shearwaters, Wilson's and White-faced Storm-petrels, Red-billed Tropicbird and Long-tailed Skua.

4) Gran Canaria Although Blue Chaffinch is present on Gran Canaria, neither of the pigeons occurs there any longer and with the loss of most of the laurel forest the island attracts few birders. However, there are still some areas of Canarian Pine forest, the most important being the Pajonales y La Data National Park in the west of the island, where Berthelot's Pipit, African Blue Tit, Blue Chaffinch and Canary can be found. In the S, the coast between Arinaga and Castillo del Romeral attracts waders, and the scrub around the lighthouse at Punta de Maspalomas holds Southern Grey Shrike, Lesser Short-toed Lark and Berthelot's Pipit. Inland of Puerto de San Nicolás on the west coast is a gorge extending into the mountains with Sardinian Warbler, the Chiffchaff, Rock Sparrow, Canary and Trumpeter Finch.

5) La Palma The avifauna of La Palma, in the north-west Canaries, is little known although it has Red-billed Chough, which occurs nowhere else in the group.

Important areas of laurel forest remain in the N, which support the pigeons as well as Canary Island Chiffchaff and Kinglet, African Blue Tit and Canary, while Plain Swift is common overhead and Berthelot's Pipit is found in more open areas. A similar range of birds is found in the El Canal y Los Tiles reserve, also in the north-east of the island, and this is possibly the best area to see both pigeons in the entire archipelago. To reach it head north from Santa Cruz de la Palma and shortly before Los Sauces there is a left turn signposted Los Tilos, take this and the pigeons can be seen from the road or from the bar at the end of the road. Seabirds breeding on or around La Palma include Bulwer's Petrel and Cory's Shearwater.

6) Lanzarote is the easternmost of the Canaries and famous for its barren, almost lunar, volcanic landscape. For the birder the main attraction is arid-land birds such as Barbary Partridge, Houbara Bustard, Cream-coloured Courser and Stone-curlew, as the forest-dwelling Canarian endemics are absent. Eleonora's and Barbary Falcons breed, but Black-bellied Sandgrouse is now rare. Other breeders include Pallid Swift, Lesser Short-toed Lark, Berthelot's Pipit and Trumpeter Finch. Lanzarote receives more Palearctic migrants than other islands in the archipelago and, in particular, attracts a wider range of passage waders. The Salinas de Janubio, on the west coast, was the best wader spot in the entire archipelago, but recent habitat degradation has meant a reduction in birds. However, Cream-coloured Courser and Kentish Plover can still be seen, sometimes Black-winged Stilt, and Lesser Short-toed Lark, Berthelot's Pipit and Trumpeter Finch occur nearby. Teguise Plain in the centre of the island is now the best site for the declining Houbara Bustard and also supports Cream-coloured Courser and Stone-curlew, Lesser Short-toed Lark, Berthelot's Pipit and Trumpeter Finch. In the north of Lanzarote the spectacular cliffs at Riscos de Famara host Egyptian Vulture, and Eleonora's and Barbary Falcons can be seen from the viewpoints at Guinate and Mirador del Río. There are viewpoints on the cliffs at Mirador del Río and Guinate. The cliffs overlook the island of Graciosa and further offshore are the islets of Montaña Clara, Alegranza, and Roques del Este and Oeste, which hold breeding Cory's and Little Shearwaters, Bulwer's Petrel, European and Madeiran Storm-petrels, and a recently discovered population of White-faced Storm-petrel.

7) Tenerife, with its excellent tourist infrastructure, is perhaps the best base for a birding holiday in the Canaries, and it is also home to most of the group's endemics, which can be seen within a short drive of the main resorts on the south coast. This is the largest island in the group and also has Spain's highest mountain, the 3,718-m Pico del Teide. Although the upper slopes are largely barren, Canarian Pine forest on the lower slopes is home to African Blue Chaffinch and Canary. Pico del Teide is reached via the C821 road, which crosses the centre of the island. The best point for seawatching on the south coast is the Punta de la Rasca lighthouse, where large numbers of Cory's Shearwater can be seen, as well as Little Shearwater, Bulwer's Petrel and European and Madeiran Storm-petrels. The headland is home to Barbary Partridge, Stone-curlew, Plain Swift, Berthelot's Pipit, Spectacled Warbler, Southern Grey Shrike and Trumpeter Finch. The north of Tenerife still has areas of native laurel and juniper forest in the hills, and Erjos in the north-west is famous for the native pigeons, as well as Canary Island Kinglet and Chiffchaff, and African Blue Tit. The best seawatching point on the north coast is Punta de Teno, at the north-west tip of the island, with shearwaters offshore and Barbary Falcon on the cliffs. For better views of seabirds many birders take the Tenerife-Gomera ferry out of Los Cristianos, from which large numbers of Little Shearwaters and Bulwer's Petrels can be seen in mid-late summer. Other species include European and Madeiran Storm-petrels and, later in the year, Great Shearwater and Fea's Petrel.

Cape Verde Islands

At the extreme south-west edge of the Western Palearctic, *c.*500km off the coast of Senegal, the Cape Verdes are remote but increasingly visited by birders due to the presence of several endemics and a selection of seabirds and other species very difficult to see elsewhere. Most of the islands are volcanic in origin with stark landscapes, whilst the three easternmost islands, Sal, Boa Vista and Maio, are flat and sandy.

1) São Tiago (Santiago) is the largest of the islands and, as it supports most of the endemics, is that most frequently visited by birders. The endemic swift, cane warbler and sparrow all occur here, as well as Cream-coloured Courser and Grey-headed Kingfisher. Also found on São Tiago are Black-crowned Finch-lark and Bar-tailed Desert Lark, Brown-necked Raven and Spanish Sparrow. Most of these are generally common and easily seen, even close the island's capital, Praia. The Cape Verde Warbler can be found in the São Domingos Valley, a 30-minute bus journey from the capital. The endemic race of Purple Heron occurs at Banana, Ribeira Montanha, and seabirds offshore include the rarely seen Fea's Petrel, and Cape Verde and Little Shearwaters.

2) Raso Raso Lark is found only on Raso small island of in the north of the archipelago, and is thought to number fewer than 200 birds. Raso is uninhabited and desolate, but can be visited by hiring a fishing boat from the El Faust Pousada in Tarrafal, on São Nicolau, which also provides accommodation. However, permission may be needed to land on the island, as access is now restricted. There are also seabirds on Raso such as Red-billed Tropicbird, Brown Booby, Bulwer's Petrel, Cape Verde Shearwater and Madeiran Storm-petrel.

3) Boa Vista The island of Boa Vista has Bar-tailed Desert Lark, Black-crowned Finch-lark and Hoopoe Lark, as well as courser and Egyptian Vulture. White-faced Storm-petrel can be seen on the Ilhéu dos Pássaros, off the east coast, but they come to land only at night. Madeiran Storm-petrel may also breed here. Magnificent Frigatebird still survives in tiny numbers off the south coast, around the islet of Curral Velho.

As well as endemic species, some of the more widespread birds are represented here by endemic subspecies. The taxonomically problematic Cape Verde Kite, now on the brink of extinction, was thought confined to Santo Antão but none was found in

2001. Two were possibly seen on São Vicente in March 2000 but may have been hybrids, and four were reported on Boa Vista in 2002. The endemic race of Purple Heron, *bournei*, is also now endangered and confined to Ribeira Montanha on São Tiago.

The Cape Verde Is are reached by air from Paris, Amsterdam or Lisbon, or from Dakar in Senegal, and inter-island flights cover most of the islands. Alternatively, the islands can be reached by ferry from Dakar or even the Canaries and there are frequent inter-island ferries, which can provide good views of the seabirds. The bus service on the larger islands is good and car hire is available in Praia. Most landbirds are resident and can be seen all year, but the seabirds have left their breeding grounds by summer and may be hard to find. For these a trip in February-April would be best. Seabirds apart, a good time to visit is at the end of the rains, in October-November.

Corsica

The main ornithological interest in Corsica is, of course, the endemic nuthatch, but this beautiful mountainous island has other attractions, such as Lammergeier and Snowfinch, although both are rare. More common are Spotless Starling, the near-endemic Corsican Finch and Marmora's Warbler. In addition to mountains Corsica has an excellent wetland, at Biguglia, and a good migration watchpoint at Cap Corse. Compared with some other Mediterranean islands, Corsica is expensive but it is home to one of the Western Palearctic's few endemic birds.

1) Asco Valley This 30-km long valley is dominated by Monte Cinto, Corsica's highest peak, at 2,706m. The higher areas have a distinctive subalpine flora, below this are pinewoods and the valley bottom has dense scrub and the bare rocks of the Asco Gorge.

The major attraction is Corsican Nuthatch but the range of habitats supports a variety of breeding species with *Sylvia* warblers and Cirl Bunting in the lower scrub, and the nuthatch and Corsican Finch in the pines. In the highest areas, Lammergeier and Golden Eagle are possible and montane passerines include Wallcreeper, Water Pipit, Alpine Accentor and Snowfinch, the latter a rare species in Corsica. Dotterel is an occasional passage visitor.

To reach the Asco Valley leave Corte north on the N193, take the N197 at Ponte Leccia and then left onto the D147 road signposted Asco.

2) Biguglia Lake This brackish lagoon is one of the largest wetlands on Corsica and one of the island's most important areas for birds. Parts of the shoreline, particularly in the south, have reedbeds with some good breeding birds, and the lake attracts a wide range of passage and wintering birds. More than 120 species have been recorded.

The reedbeds hold Purple Heron, Cetti's Warbler and Zitting Cisticola, and Moustached Warbler, regular in winter, has recently bred. White-headed Duck, a former breeder, has recently been reintroduced. Passage brings various herons, Audouin's Gull and White-winged Tern, with Red-footed Falcon regular in spring. Winter sees the arrival of up to 20,000 waterbirds, which often include Black-throated Diver, Black-necked Grebe and Ferruginous Duck.

The south shore of the lake is the best area for birds and can be reached by road from Bastia on the N193. Turn left at Rorgo-Revinco onto the D207 and park beside the road where the bridge crosses the canal.

3) Bonifacio The town of Bonifacio is situated in the far south of Corsica and its limestone cliffs, maquis-covered plateau and small valleys offer birders a range of Mediterranean species and seabirds offshore.

The town itself has Spotless Starling and Italian Sparrow, and Pallid and Alpine Swifts nest on the cliffs. Birds of the plateau include Blue Rock Thrush, Rock Sparrow and Corsican Finch, and typical Mediterranean scrub warblers such as Sardinian, Dartford and Marmora's. Cory's and Yelkouan Shearwaters can be seen offshore. Eleonora's Falcon occurs on passage throughout the area, and Alpine Accentor in winter.

4) Cap Corse The northern tip of Corsica, Cap Corse, is the island's best migration watchpoint and attracts a wide variety of species. A bird observatory is operated in spring at Barcaggio, where a watercourse has created a small delta with reeds and willow scrub. In addition there is a lagoon and sand dunes, juniper scrub and maquis. The 40-km peninsula has a central ridge of rugged mountains reaching 1,305m at Monte Stello. The coast on the west side is steep and rocky, but the east is gentler with a scattering of small beaches. Seawatching is most productive off the north tip with shearwaters and Audouin's Gull regular.

Spring is the most productive period, when regular migrants include both storks and various herons, raptors including Montagu's Harrier, and both Little and Spotted Crakes. Passerines can be numerous, with a wide range of species including Red-rumped Swallow and Ring Ouzel. Breeding birds include Red Kite, Golden Eagle and Eurasian Scops Owl, and Lammergeier is a non-breeding visitor. Marmora's, Subalpine and Dartford Warblers are common in scrubby areas.

To reach the northern part of Cap Corse take the D80 north from Bastia to Ersa then the D253 to Barcaggio. From the village walk to the observatory and follow the path east to the lagoon and further on to the tower at Pointe d'Agnello for seabirds.

5) Restonica Valley This site is one of the most important in Corsica for the endemic nuthatch, and consists of deep gorges with native conifer woodland and scrub, as well as grasslands, bare cliffs and montane lakes.

Corsican Nuthatch and Corsican Finch can be found with relative ease in this area, as well as the Corsican races of Eurasian Sparrowhawk, Northern Goshawk, Common Buzzard and others. However, of equal attraction for birders is Lammergeier, for which this valley is one of the best sites on the island, and other montane species including Red Kite, Golden Eagle, Wallcreeper and Alpine Chough.

The valley can be reached on the D623 south-west from Corte.

6) Scandola Reserve Near Calvi in north-west Corsica, this scenically attractive reserve has an interesting range of breeding birds.

Famous for breeding Osprey, the cliffs here also have Pallid and Alpine Swifts, Eurasian Crag Martin and Blue Rock Thrush. Inland the main habitat is dense maquis with many passerine breeders, particularly *Sylvia* warblers.

The reserve is best visited by boat, from either Calvi or Porto. Most trips stop at the village of Girolata, and from here the maquis-covered hillsides can be explored.

Croatia

This was the most popular tourist area of the former Yugoslavia before the conflicts of the 1990s and the eventual division of the country, and it now appears to be safe to visit again. The rugged coast and numerous islands are the best-known area ornithologically, with birds such as Eleonora's Falcon and Rock Partridge to be seen as well as south-eastern specialities including Sombre Tit and Western Rock Nuthatch. The current state of habitats and birds of the inland areas, forests and mountains are little known, but there may

still be important populations of wetland birds and raptors. Mid May to mid June is the optimum time for a birding visit, with summer visitors on the breeding grounds and some passage birds still moving through.

1) Cres The dry and rocky island of Cres, off the Istra Peninsula, has deciduous forest and high sea-cliffs. Part of the island is protected as a Special Ornithological Reserve.

Cres is important for breeding raptors, particularly Griffon Vulture and Short-toed and Golden Eagles. Raptors also migrate along the island's central ridge, including kites, harriers, Booted and Bonelli's Eagles, and Lesser Kestrel. Other birds include Eurasian Eagle and Eurasian Scops Owls, and a range of passerines. Shearwaters can be seen offshore, possibly also European Storm-petrel.

Cres can be reached from the mainland at Pula or Rijeka, or from the neighbouring island of Krk.

2) Kopački Rit The Special Zoological Reserve of Kopački Rit, also a Ramsar Site and Nature Park, is in the far east of Croatia, close to the border with Yugoslavia. The reserve covers part of the floodplain of the Danube and Drava rivers, and consists of extensive wet forest with numerous oxbows and channels, large reedbeds and a series of fishponds. This site has long been an important breeding area for waterbirds, herons in particular, and more than 130 species have bred.

Both bitterns, Black-crowned Night, Squacco, and Purple Herons may still breed, as well as Great Egret, both storks and Pygmy Cormorant. Ferruginous Duck and

Whiskered Tern probably still breed, and raptors possible in the area include Black Kite, White-tailed Eagle and Saker Falcon. Passerines include Savi's Warbler and Penduline Tit in the reeds and Lesser Grey Shrike in the farmland. Kopački Rit was an important site for passage Eurasian Spoonbill and Common Crane, and autumn sees the arrival of Bean Geese and other waterfowl. Greater Spotted Eagle was regular in winter and may still occur.

Providing the political situation remains stable, it should be relatively straightforward to visit Kopački Rit, which can be reached from Osijek. Head north to Bilje and follow signs for Kapacevo.

2) Mljet This is one of the most visited of the numerous islands off the Dalmatian coast, and its dry, rocky and scrub-covered slopes are home to many Mediterranean birds.

Breeders include Eurasian Scops Owl, Pallid and Alpine Swifts, Black-eared Wheatear, Olive-tree, Spectacled and Orphean Warblers, and Cirl and Black-headed Buntings. Eleonora's Falcon and Blue Rock Thrush breed on the offshore island of Vis. Shearwaters can be seen offshore in summer and on passage, and Black-throated Diver occurs in winter.

Mljet can be reached by ferry from Dubrovnik, landing at Sovra and there are ferries to Vis from Split.

3) Neretva Delta Much of this formerly extensive wetland has been lost to agriculture and the large numbers of passage waterbirds probably no longer occur, but the area still supports breeding birds of interest.

Rock Partridge, Black-eared Wheatear, Sombre Tit, Western Rock Nuthatch and Black-headed Bunting breed, as well as Woodchat and Lesser Grey Shrikes. Warblers include Olive-tree, Spectacled, Subalpine, Sardinian and Cetti's, and Zitting Cisticola.

The delta lies south of Split on the Dalmatian coast and can be reached via the main coast road.

4) Paklenica National Park This National Park is situated on the southern slopes of the Velebit Mountains and is an area of dramatic scenery. Habitats include valleys with beech-covered slopes, high rocky peaks and two gorges reaching the Dalmatian coast. The larger, 10-km Wern gorge forms the main access into the park. The spectacular limestone walls of these gorges reach 400m in places and there are numerous caves. The 3,600-ha National Park also has forests of oak, hornbeam and Black Pine, and there are large areas of scrub in the lower areas.

Paklenica has long been famous for its vultures and Griffon is still present, although Egyptian no longer occurs. Other raptors include Short-toed and Golden Eagles, and Rock Partridge and Eurasian Eagle Owl are probably still present. Passerines include Blue Rock Thrush, Western Rock Nuthatch, Wallcreeper, Sombre Tit and various warblers and buntings.

Paklenica National Park is located c.46km north-east of Zadar on the Dalmatian coast and there is an information centre at Starigrad-Paklenica.

5) Plitvice Lakes National Park Before the break-up of Yugoslavia and the conflicts of the 1990s this National Park was one of the most visited tourist sites in the country. A World Heritage Site, the park includes a string of 16 lakes connected by waterfalls. Surrounding the lakes are dense beech, fir and pine forests, and subalpine meadows.

Although never renowned for its birds, Plitvice is worth visiting for the scenery alone. There is little information on the birds currently present but this was once, and may still be, a good site for grouse, owls, woodpeckers and other forest birds. Eurasian Eagle Owl was present and perhaps also Ural Owl, and woodpeckers numbered at least eight species. About 126 species of bird have been recorded within the park, which covers nearly 20,000 ha.

Part of the park is a strict nature reserve with restricted access, but most is open. The National Park lies between the towns of Otočac and Bihac. Once attracting more than one million tourists p.a., Plitvice is again becoming popular with visitors and will continue to do so, as long as the political situation remains stable.

6) Pokupsko Depression This area includes the Crna Mlaka Special Ornithological Reserve and several fishpond complexes, riverine deciduous forest and grasslands near Zagreb.

White-tailed and Lesser Spotted Eagles probably still breed, as well as Little Bittern, Squacco and Black-crowned Night Herons, Black and White Storks, Ferruginous Duck and Corn Crake. The area was of even greater importance as a passage stopover for more than 20,000 waterbirds.

Crna Mlaka lies c.30km south-west of Zagreb. Leave the motorway at the Jastrebarsko exit, turn left and the reserve is signposted.

Cyprus

With all the tourist facilities a visitor could wish for, two endemic species and a superb variety of migrants, Cyprus is a deservedly popular destination for birders. Habitats on this large and rugged island include freshwater marshes and salt-lakes, cliffs and rocky headlands, farmland and scrub and pine-clad mountains, which reach almost 2,000 m. The two endemic breeders, Cyprus Pied

Wheatear and Cyprus Warbler, are widespread and common, and can be seen in most parts of the island.

1) Akamas Peninsula Many of the best birding areas are on the west coast between the Akamas Peninsula and Akrotiri. Although the Baths of Aphrodite is one of the busiest tourist attractions in Cyprus, the surrounding area and the adjacent peninsula attract large numbers of migrants, from herons and waterfowl offshore to numerous passerines in the bushes and scrub of the headland. Passage raptors can include Pallid Harrier and Eleonora's Falcon, and European Bee-eater, European Roller and Wryneck are common. Passerine migrants include species such as Greater Short-toed Lark, Eurasian Crag Martin, Thrush Nightingale and Isabelline Wheatear, and warblers can be abundant and include River, Eastern Olivaceous, Olive-tree, Rüppell's, Orphean and Barred. Breeding birds of the peninsula include Griffon Vulture and Blue Rock Thrush on the cliffs, Chukar Partridge and Black Francolin in the grasslands, and

Masked Shrike, Spectacled Warbler and Black-headed Bunting in the scrub, as well as the two endemics.

2) Paphos is in the centre of the west coast. Birders congregate here to exchange news on birds in the area. Large numbers of migrants occur on the headland and, as it is now well watched, rarities are frequently recorded, with Pallas' Gull, Glossy Ibis, Caspian Plover, Bimaculated Lark and Red-throated Pipit all possible.

3) Asprokremmos Dam is inland of Paphos. Finsch's Wheatear is regular here in winter.

4) Dhiarizos Valley is to the south-east. It is possibly the best area on the island for Black Francolin and crakes along the reed-fringed watercourse.

5) Cape Aspro, further east, is the largest Eleonora's Falcon colony in Cyprus.

6) Kensington Cliffs is close to Cape Aspro. These cliffs are famous for Griffon Vulture and wintering Wallcreeper.

7) Phassouri is a well-known birding spot that consists of wet meadows and reedbeds with a few gravel pits. Squacco Heron, Glossy Ibis, Spur-winged Plover, two species of pratincole and Great Snipe are all regular in spring. Red-throated Pipit and Citrine Wagtail are among the many passerines that occur here on passage, and Armenian Gull may be regular in winter.

8) Akrotiri Salt-lake on the southernmost peninsula of Cyprus was considered the best birding site on the island until recent habitat deterioration and the discovery of other 'hotspots'. However, it still attracts passage waders and a variety of passerines, with Bluethroat, Moustached Warbler and Penduline Tit in winter. Dead Sea Sparrow formerly bred but this colony has died out. The area is still worth checking for Demoiselle Crane in late August to early September, and Greater Flamingo still winters here.

9) Larnaca Greater Flamingo also winters at Larnaca on the east coast, where passage Ruddy Shelduck, Greater Sand Plover and Slender-billed Gull may also be found.

10) Akhna Reservoir lies on the border with Turkish-occupied Cyprus but is easily accessible and well worth visiting. Passage birds possible here include Ferruginous and White-headed Ducks, Glossy Ibis, Little and Baillon's Crakes, Black-winged Pratincole, Spur-winged Plover and Marsh Sandpiper, and Pied Kingfisher has been recorded on several occasions.

11) Troodos Mountains are the highest part of Cyprus. Pallid Swift, Eurasian Crag Martin and Short-toed Treecreeper are easily found here.

12) Paphos Forest, to the south-west, has raptors including Northern Goshawk and Bonelli's Eagle, with the chance of passage Long-legged Buzzard, and it is possible that Eastern Imperial Eagle may persist here.

Despite the still-strong hunting tradition in Cyprus, the island is fast becoming one of the Western Palearctic's most popular birding destinations, for both independent travellers and those on organised tours. Much remains to be discovered about the island's birdlife and new species are added to the list each year. Increasing interest from foreign birders will undoubtedly assist the efforts of local conservationists to establish reserves and enforce hunting laws. The Turkish-occupied part of Cyprus is likely to have the same birds and more, as it is much less developed, but much remains to be discovered about this part of the island. It is now possible to travel between Greek and Turkish Cyprus much more freely and hopefully this will encourage birders to explore the island more fully.

Czech Republic

Now popular with bird tour companies, the Czech Republic has a superb range of forest and upland birds, and the fish-ponds are among the best in Europe. As elsewhere, seeing the owls and more elusive woodpeckers often requires local assistance, but independent birding in this country is easy and can be conveniently combined with a trip to eastern Austria. Most of the best birding sites lie in the formerly sensitive border areas, but all are easily reached by road. Spring

is the best time to visit, particularly for the more sought-after owls, woodpeckers and Hazel Grouse, but some areas are blocked by snow until late in the season.

1) Beskydy Mountains Forming part of the west Carpathians, the Beskydy range lies in the far east of the Czech Republic, on the border with Slovakia. Excellent for forest and upland birds this area contains many nature reserves. The hills reach a little over 1,300m and spruce forests dominate many of the slopes. Lower areas have woodlands of beech and fir, and the area is famous amongst birders for its owl and woodpecker populations.

These mountains are the most reliable site in the Czech Republic for Ural Owl and there are also Eurasian Eagle, Tengmalm's and Eurasian Pygmy Owls. White-backed Woodpecker is found here at one of its European strongholds, and other woodpeckers include Black, Grey-headed and Three-toed. Black and Hazel Grouse occur and Capercaillie has been reintroduced. Other forest birds include Crested Tit, Nutcracker, Collared and Red-breasted Flycatchers, and Barred Warbler. Corn Crake breeds in the meadows and breeding raptors include Northern Goshawk and Lesser Spotted Eagle.

Spring is the best time to visit, particularly for the owls and woodpeckers, but heavy snow can persist in the area until late April. The Moravian Beskydy is situated in the north-east of the Czech Republic and can be reached from Frenštát or Rosnov to the west.

2) Jeseníky Mountains This popular skiing area lies in the north of the country, near the Polish border, and consists of mountains with extensive conifer forests and patches of beech, peat bogs and moorland.

Birds are typical of central European forests, with Black Stork, Hazel Grouse, Black Grouse, Capercaillie, Tengmalm's and Eurasian Eagle Owls, and woodpeckers including Grey-headed, Black and Middle Spotted. Woodland passerines include Crested Tit, Red-breasted Flycatcher and Nutcracker, with Water Pipit, Alpine Accentor and Ring Ouzel in more open higher areas. Eurasian Dotterel may breed occasionally but is principally a rare migrant.

As this is a skiing centre, there is plentiful accommodation and chair-lifts to the higher parts. Sumperk, situated *c.*220km from Prague and reached via Route 44, makes a good base.

3) Krkonoše National Park In the north of the country close to the Polish border, this National Park is situated in the high and dramatic Krkonoše Mountain of Bohemia. Much of the area is coniferous forest, mainly spruce and pine on the hillsides, with beech woodland in lower areas, but the entire region has long been affected by acid rain.

Despite this, an excellent range of coniferous forest birds can be found and the additional habitats of peat bogs and alpine meadows add diversity. More than 150 species have bred in the area. Higher levels have Ring Ouzel, Alpine Accentor (at one of its northernmost points) and Water Pipit, and Red-spotted Bluethroat (at its only Czech breeding site) and Black Grouse can be seen in the peat bogs. Eurasian Dotterel formerly bred, but probably occurs now only on passage. In the forests, Lesser Spotted Eagle, Capercaillie, Black Stork and Nutcracker breed. Other forest birds include Red-breasted Flycatcher, Crested Tit and Common Rosefinch, and Greenish Warbler is a recent colonist. Owls include Eurasian Eagle, Eurasian Pygmy and Tengmalm's, and there are Grey-headed, Black, Three-toed, Middle Spotted and White-backed Woodpeckers.

Easily reached by road from Prague, *c.*130km north-east on the E65, this area has a good tourist infrastructure due to its popularity with skiers. Most of the local villages can provide accommodation, and Špindlerův-Mlýn and Harrachov have National Park information centres.

4) Lednice Fishponds One of the best birding areas in the country, the Lednice Important Bird Area consists of a series of fishponds (Sedlec), as well the parkland and woods of the Zámecký Chateau. There are four main fishponds, with reedbeds and broad muddy fringes, especially in autumn when the fish are harvested. Surrounding the ponds are woods, pastures and cultivated land. The River Dyje fringed by meadows flows through part of the park.

The fishponds hold a good selection of breeding wetland birds including both bitterns, Purple Heron and, probably, Great Egret. Also breeding here are passerines including Bearded and Penduline Tits, Bluethroat and Savi's Warblers. Both Red and Black Kites breed in the area. Passage periods are most productive, particularly in autumn when water levels are lowered. Taiga Bean and Greater White-fronted Geese are common, and ducks include hundreds of Red-crested Pochard. A variety of waders occurs in autumn and a couple of White-tailed Eagles regularly winter.

The Zámecký Chateau estate is famous for its heronry on an island in the large fishpond, which supports the largest Black-crowned Night Heron colony in the country. The many mature trees provide ideal habitat for woodpeckers, and as many as seven species occur including Black, Middle Spotted and Grey-headed as well as Wryneck. This area also has Barred and River Warblers, Collared Flycatcher and Hawfinch. To the west are the marshes and reedbeds of Pastvisko reserve with more wetland birds and White Stork. Access to this reserve is prohibited but much can be seen from the surrounding area.

Lednice is in the south of the Czech Republic, close to the Austrian border. To reach the area take the E65 from Brno and leave on the Podivín exit. An alternative is to visit the area from Austria, crossing the border at Mikulov and taking the minor road east towards Lednice.

5) Nové Mlýny Reservoir Once riverine woodland, this area was flooded to form a large reservoir, which is now being divided and drained in an effort to restore the habitat. The middle section of the reservoir is the best for birds.

This is the only regular breeding site in the country for Mediterranean Gull and other breeders include Purple Heron, White Stork, Red-crested Pochard and Ferruginous Duck. Passerines include Bluethroat, Savi's Warbler and Penduline Tit, and woodlands support Wryneck, Grey-headed and Middle Spotted Woodpeckers. Divers, grebes and Great Egret occur on passage, and the area attracts thousands of geese on passage and in winter. White-tailed Eagle is regular all year, with most in winter. This is the most important site for wintering Smew in the country.

The reservoir is about 40km south of Brno and can be reached on the E461 road.

6) Pálava Hills This extensive area in the south of the country contains a range of habitats, dominated by limestone outcrops, in a landscape of rolling hills and low-lands, much of which has deciduous forest cover.

Popular with visiting birders, the area has a good selection of forest birds with woodpeckers such as Grey-headed, Black, Middle Spotted and Syrian, and Eurasian Eagle Owl breeds. Northern Goshawk is resident and Eastern Imperial Eagle may be present in summer. Passerines include Barred Warbler, Collared Flycatcher and Hawfinch. White Stork breeds in local villages and Wallcreeper is an occasional winter visitor to rockier areas.

Access is unrestricted to most of the area and Brno is the nearest major town.

7) Pohořelice Fishponds These fishponds, their associated reedbeds and surrounding land support both bitterns, Purple Heron and White Stork, Red-crested Pochard, Ferruginous Duck, Spotted Crake and Bearded Tit in summer. The area attracts large numbers of passage geese and some waders, and White-tailed Eagle is regular on passage and in winter. Woodland in the surrounding area hosts Grey-headed, Syrian and Middle Spotted Woodpeckers, Barred Warbler and Collared Flycatcher.

The village of Pohořelice lies 25km south of Brno and can be reached on Route 52.

8) Poodří This Protected Landscape Area is part of the floodplain of the River Odra and consists of wet meadows, oxbow lakes and fishponds, reedbeds and forest. Like other Czech wetlands it boasts a fine selection of birds.

This is one of the very few breeding sites for Common Goldeneye in the Czech Republic, and other wetland breeders include Red-necked and Black-necked Grebes, Black Stork, both bitterns, Spotted, Little and Corn Crakes, and passerines including River Warbler and Penduline Tit. Other breeders include Black Grouse, Wryneck, Grey-headed and Middle-Spotted Woodpeckers, Barred Warbler and Collared Flycatcher. White-winged Tern, Bluethroat and Aquatic Warbler occur on passage.

Poodří is situated in the north-east of the country, between Šternberk and Odry.

9) Soutok In the far south of the country, where the Morava (March) and Dyje (Thaya) rivers meet is an area of flooded forest, pools and wet meadows known as Soutok that supports a selection of interesting birds.

Both storks breed as well as Little Bittern, Purple Heron, Eurasian Spoonbill and crakes, and raptors include Black and Red Kites, but the main attraction is the small numbers of Saker Falcon that occur here. Woodpeckers include Grey-headed, Black and Middle Spotted, and there are passerines such as River and Barred Warblers, Collared Flycatcher and Short-toed Treecreeper. White-tailed Eagle occurs on passage.

Soutok is situated south-east of Břeclav in southern Moravia.

10) Šumava National Park In the south-west of the country, these mountains extend along the borders of Germany and Austria, and habitats include spruce forest on the higher hillsides, beech and fir forests in lower areas, and extensive peat bogs. In the valleys are numerous marshes and damp meadows.

Breeding birds of the forest include Hazel and Black Grouse, Capercaillie, owls including Eurasian Eagle, Eurasian Pygmy and Tengmalm's, and Ural Owl bred in 1998 following reintroduction. Woodpeckers include Grey-headed, Black, White-backed and Three-toed. Also breeding are both storks and Corn Crake, and raptors including Lesser Spotted Eagle. A wide variety of passerines breed including Wood Lark, White-spotted Bluethroat, Red-breasted Flycatcher, Common Rosefinch, Nutcracker and Crested Tit. More than 140 species have bred in the area.

From Prague take the N4 south for 130km to Vimperk, where permits and advice are available from the information centre. In the centre of the park is Mount Boubin, one of the best areas for forest birds, and the floodplain of the River Vltavice, south of Horni Vltavice, is excellent for lowland species. Spring is the best time to visit, although the weather may be wet there is more chance of locating the more elusive birds when they are displaying.

11) Třeboňsko The importance of this Protected Landscape Area is reflected in its designation as a Ramsar Site and Biosphere Reserve, and it also includes several state nature reserves. It is also one of the best birding areas in Europe. The terrain is varied, consisting of both wet and dry habitats, including fishponds and rivers, wet meadows and peat bogs, as well as deciduous and coniferous forest and farmland.

More than 150 species have bred in this area, including Black-necked Grebe, Great Bittern and other herons, both storks, Red-crested Pochard and Corn Crake. Wetland passerines include Savi's and River Warblers, and Bearded and Penduline Tits. In the forests are grouse, Grey-headed, Black and Middle Spotted Woodpeckers, and Eurasian Pygmy, Tengmalm's and Eurasian Eagle Owls. Breeding raptors include three harriers, two kites and White-tailed Eagle. Passerines of the wooded areas include Barred Warbler, Collared and Red-breasted Flycatchers, and Short-toed Treecreeper. Also internationally important for passage and winter birds, Třebonsko attracts large numbers of Taiga Bean Goose, many ducks, passage waders, herons including Great Egret, and Eurasian Spoonbill.

This area is in the south of the Czech Republic, close to the Austrian border. The town of Třeboň is c.140km south of Prague and can be reached via the E55.

12) Znojmo Though now heavily cultivated, the grassland around the town of Znojmo is the sole remaining site for Great Bustard and Stone-curlew in the country. Other birds of open grassland here include Tawny Pipit and Lesser Grey Shrike, which are both scarce in the Czech Republic. Red Kite may still breed and Rough-legged Buzzard is often present in winter, sometimes also Saker Falcon. Znojmo is situated close to the Austrian border near the town of Hrádek.

Denmark

Low-lying Denmark is best known as a passage stopover and wintering area for large numbers of waterfowl and waders, particularly the Waddensee on the west coast, which is the most important area for such birds in Europe. In addition there are some superb migration watchpoints in the north and west of the mainland, and on islands in the east, which attract many rarities. As elsewhere in Scandinavia, Denmark is expensive but this can be countered in part by saving on car hire and using the excellent public transport system. Passage periods and winter are the best times to visit for birds.

1) Amager Within easy reach of the Danish capital, the island of Amager has excellent birding with breeding birds of interest, scarce passage waders, and passage and wintering raptors and waterfowl.

Red-necked and Black-necked Grebes, Penduline Tit and Thrush Nightingale can be found in summer, and wintering waterfowl include Whooper Swan, Long-tailed Duck and Velvet Scoter. The large and open former military area of Vestamager attracts raptors in winter, often including Rough-legged Buzzard and sometimes also White-tailed Eagle. This area of grassland and woods, open beaches, marshes and lakes is the best birding area within easy reach of Copenhagen. To the south is the mixed woodland area of Konge-lunden, which is good for passage raptors and where Tengmalm's Owl sometimes winters. Nearby, to the west and south, are saltmarshes that attract passage waders including Broad-billed Sandpiper and Red-necked Phalarope.

Amager is situated on the east side of Copenhagen.

2) Bornholm and Christiansø These rather remote islands have farmland and woodlands with several small nature reserves. Although holding breeding birds absent from the rest of Denmark, the main interest lies in migrants, which include waders, waterfowl, raptors and passerines. Christiansø, 20km east of Bornholm is Denmark's premier rarity hotspot.

Common Crane breeds in small numbers, as well as Black Woodpecker, and Denmark's only breeding Tengmalm's Owls nest at Almindingen. Also present in summer are Greenish Warbler and Common Rosefinch. The only Danish colonies of Common Guillemot and Razorbill can be found on Græsholm, near Christiansø.

Passage geese occur in large numbers, as well as Common Crane and raptors such as Rough-legged Buzzard and Northern Goshawk. Scarcer species seen regularly include Caspian Tern, Bluethroat, Pallas' Leaf and Yellow-browed Warblers, Red-breasted Flycatcher and Ortolan Bunting. Also possible are Subalpine, Blyth's

Reed, Dusky and Radde's Warblers, and Little and Rustic Buntings. Wintering birds include Slavonian Grebe, seaducks, with fairly regular King and Steller's Eiders, and Purple Sandpiper.

Bornholm can be reached by ferry from Denmark, Sweden and Germany.

3) Hanstholm This is one of Denmark's largest fishing ports and as such it attracts gulls in large numbers, which usually include Glaucous and Iceland. The adjacent coasts are also good for seawatching, particularly in autumn with strong westerly winds. Grey Phalarope and Little Auk are possible here. Many birds can be seen from the harbour but better sites can be found to the east, at Roshage, or the west, at Ørhage. The nearby Hansted reserve is a large area of heathland, plantations and ponds, famous for some of Denmark's very few breeding Common Cranes, although they can be difficult to see. Taiga Bean Goose occurs on passage as well as a range of other waterfowl and waders, with Whooper Swan in winter.

Hanstholm can be reached from Ålborg or Thisted on the E11.

4) Hellebæk This area consists of farmland, deciduous woodland, conifer plantations and lakes on the north coast of Zeeland. The area has breeding Northern Goshawk and Black Woodpecker, but the main interest lies in migrants. Passage brings numbers of raptors, including regular Red Kite, White-tailed and Golden Eagles, and Common Crane.

The area can be reached by road from Helsingør.

5) Møn and Falster These islands off the south of Zeeland are famous as migration watchpoints, particularly in spring, and rarities are frequently recorded.

Regular migrants include storks, various waterfowl (sometimes including Lesser White-fronted Goose), waders and seabirds. Raptors are varied with regular White-tailed Eagle, Rough-legged Buzzard and Red-footed Falcon. Passerine migrants include scarce species such as Barred and Greenish Warblers, and Red-breasted Flycatcher, all of which have attempted to breed. Wryneck, Black Woodpecker, Wood Lark and Common Rosefinch also breed. Other scarcer migrants such as Ring Ouzel and Ortolan Bunting are regular. Hoeje-Møn, in the east of the island, has high cliffs and deciduous woodland, attractive to migrant passerines and breeders. The nearby valley of Jydelejet is also an excellent site for passerines. The Ulvshale Peninsula in the north-west has woodland and marshland with breeding Great Bittern, Pied Avocet, passage waders and ducks, and there is a bridge across to Nyord, where the church-yard can be productive for migrants. Busemark Mose in Ostmøn has Spotted Crake, Thrush Nightingale, Savi's Warbler and Bearded Tit.

Gedser on the south coast of the neighbouring island of Falster is another excel-lent migration watchpoint for seabirds, raptors and passerines. Black-throated Diver and Pomarine Skua are regular here as well as Long-tailed Duck in winter. Nearby is Bøtø Nor, an important staging area for geese and a breeding site for Spotted Crake and other marsh birds.

The area is easily reached by road from Copenhagen on the E4.

6) Ringkøbing Fjord Once open to the sea, Ringkøbing Fjord has long been enclosed by a coastal sandbar, and the continued drifting of sand has formed the peninsulas of Tippersande and Værnsande, now vegetated and used for grazing. Much of the land is now under some form of protection and one of the best areas is the Tipperne-Vaernengene-Nymindestrom complex of reserves in the south. The remaining lakes are shallow and brackish, and there are saltmarshes and sandy beaches, more established vegetated areas have extensive conifer plantations where Crested Tit breeds.

Great Bittern, Spotted Crake and Pied Avocet are among the many breeders. During passage periods all of the regular European wader and waterfowl species can be seen. Among the most important are Whooper and Bewick's Swans, and most of the Svalbard population of Pink-footed Goose is present. Nymindestrom reserve, further south, is mainly dunes and has breeding Crested Lark. Shore Lark, Twite and Snow and Lapland Buntings occur on passage and in winter, when raptors include Rough-legged Buzzard and, often, White-tailed Eagle.

Ringkøbing Fjord is a Ramsar site and the entire area is excellent for birds, and although some reserve areas may have limited access much of the area can be seen from local roads. Just inland, the canalised river valley at Skjern has wet meadows with breeding duck and Corn Crake, and passage White Storks often frequent this area. The fishing port of Hvide Sande often attracts Glaucous and Iceland Gulls in winter. Ringkøbing town has hotels and makes an ideal base for exploring the area.

7) Rømø Nature Park In the east of the Waddensee, a series of islands extends from Fanø in the north to the German island of Sylt in the south. One of the central islands in the chain is Rømø, a large sandbank, linked to the mainland by a causeway. The west of the island has a broad open sandy beach and the east has coastal meadows, often flooded, with extensive reedbeds and pine plantations.

Summering birds include Red-necked Grebe, Great Bittern, Spotted Crake, Pied Avocet, small numbers of Kentish Plover and, sometimes, Gull-billed Tern. Montagu's Harrier, Bearded and Penduline Tits also breed. During migration the mudflats attract large numbers of waterfowl including scoter, and a range of waders. Pied Avocet can occur in thousands in autumn. Geese winter in good numbers, when Rough-legged Buzzard also occurs and Shore Lark, Twite and Snow and Lapland Buntings are regular.

Access is unrestricted and the park is reached by road from Skærbæk.

8) Skagen Situated at the northernmost tip of Jutland, Skagen is famous as a migration watchpoint and popular with birders from all over Scandinavia. The most productive time is mid April to late May, with large movements evident during easterly winds. Passerines form the bulk, but raptors occur in good numbers and include both kites, White-tailed Eagle and, sometimes, Pallid Harrier. Along this coast, divers are fairly common (and have included Yellow-billed), as are seaducks, gulls and terns, and flocks of grounded passerines can be seen virtually anywhere along the sandy beaches or the extensive dunes, but particularly at the extreme tip of the peninsula. Glaucous and Iceland Gulls often occur in the harbour.

West of the town of Skagen is Flagbakken hill, from which many migrants can be seen and in the surrounding conifer plantations are Wood Lark, Tawny Pipit and Crested Tit. Like all well-watched migration spots, rarities are frequently found and more than 340 species have been recorded at Skagen. There is a youth hostel just west of Skagen and a campsite to the north-east where birders meet and exchange information. Skagen can be reached by taking the Frederikshavn road from the city of Ålborg, then turning north on Route 40.

9) Skallingen-Blåvandshuk North-west of Esbjerg, Skallingen lies on a sandy peninsula in the Waddensee, a vast area of intertidal mud and sandflats. Skallingen reserve consists of sandy beaches and dunes, backed by marshland on the inland side. The westernmost point is Blåvandshuk, one of Denmark's premier migration watchpoints and the site of a bird observatory.

Pied Avocet, Kentish Plover and terns breed, but the main ornithological interest is the large numbers and variety of passage birds. Geese, ducks and waders occur in spring but there is more variety in autumn when seabird passage during south-westerly or westerly winds can be outstanding. Divers, seaducks, petrels, skuas, gulls, terns and auks all occur in huge numbers, and often include scarce and rare species with Sabine's Gull a possibility. Easterly winds bring greater numbers and variety of landbirds, and increase the chances of Siberian rarities. Rough-legged Buzzard and White-tailed Eagle occur in winter.

Access is unrestricted, and there is accommodation in local towns and camping within the Skallingen reserve, which is reached from Ho, 8km east of Blåvand.

10) Stevns Klint Largely farmland with scattered patches of beech trees, this area is another of Denmark's excellent passage raptor watchpoints. Winds from the west produce the best results, and although the most numerous species are Western Honey-buzzard and Common Buzzard, a range of other species occurs with regular Red Kite, White-tailed Eagle, Rough-legged Buzzard and Red-footed Falcon, and occasional Lesser Spotted and Golden Eagles.

The best observation point is the church at Højerup, reached by road from Køge and Store Heddinge.

11) Stignæs At the south-eastern tip of Zeeland, Stignæs is an important migration watchpoint with waterfowl, raptors and passerines occurring in large numbers in spring and autumn. This is an area of farmland, woodlands and marshes, sheltered sea-bays and islands.

Red-necked Grebe and Bearded Tit breed in the area, but passage periods provide the main interest. Nearly 30,000 raptors pass through each year including small numbers of Red Kite, Northern Goshawk and Rough-legged Buzzard. All of the commoner migrant passerines can be seen, as well as Red-throated Pipit and Ortolan Bunting. Whooper Swan, Taiga Bean Goose and Long-tailed Duck occur in winter as well as Rough-legged Buzzard, Northern Goshawk and White-tailed Eagle.

Stignæs can be reached by road from Skælskør towards Borreby.

12) Vadehavet Bird Sanctuary A continuation of the Waddensee, the Vadehavet is the coastal area from the German border north to Rømø. In the north the coast has a low cliff but from Emmerlev Klev southwards the marshes are protected by a dyke on the landward side. This is the largest bird sanctuary in Denmark and an internationally important site for waterfowl and waders on passage. Common Shelduck gathers here to moult and other ducks, especially Common Eider and scoters, occur in thousands. Geese also roost in large numbers, in particular, Barnacle, Dark-bellied Brent and Pink-footed, and most of the European waders can be seen.

Most of the area is of open access, but the island of Jordsand, south of Rømø, is a nature reserve and closed to the public. The area is easily reached by road from Emmerlev.

Egypt

With birds that can be seen nowhere else within the Western Palearctic and some of the world's most famous ancient monuments, Egypt is the perfect destination for birders with non-birding partners. The Nile hosts an excellent range of birds, many of which are easily seen from cruise ships, and the further south one goes the greater the likelihood of encountering African species. Long-tailed Cormorant, Yellow-billed Stork, African Skimmer and African Pied Wagtail are all

possible at Abu Simbel on Lake Nasser, and this area should be on the itinerary of every birding trip to Egypt. In addition the country supports a range of desert birds, many of which can be seen around or close to ancient monuments, and Hurghada on the coast offers several Red Sea specialities including Sooty and White-eyed Gulls. Suez is one of the top raptor migration watchpoints in the Western Palearctic, and Sharm el Sheikh in southern Sinai, a famous diving centre, is now becoming popular with birders. Zaranik, on Sinai's north coast, is a recently discovered migration site with enormous potential and will surely become a regular haunt of visiting birders. Unlike in some countries, many of Egypt's special birds can be seen close to the main tourist areas, and this is partly why it is so popular with birders. The southern Red Sea coast has long been a sensitive area and is only just becoming accessible to tourists, but there is undoubtedly much to be discovered here for birders willing to venture off the regular tourist trail.

1) Abu Simbel In the south of Egypt, on the very edge of the Western Palearctic, the birdlife of Abu Simbel has a strong African element. During passage periods European migrants are abundant but it is the tropical African specialities that attract birders. Birds such as Yellow-billed Stork, Egyptian Goose, African Skimmer, Long-tailed Cormorant and Pink-backed Pelican are regular here at the northernmost limits of their range, and other species seen along Lake Nasser's shoreline include Senegal Thick-knee, Spur-winged Lapwing and Kittlitz's Plover.

Desert species such as Brown-necked Raven, Cream-coloured Courser and Crowned and Spotted Sandgrouse can be seen in the surrounding area, and African Collared, Laughing and Namaqua Doves, and Blue-cheeked Bee-eater are regular. Desert Eagle Owl and Rock Martin can be seen around the ancient monuments. Sooty Falcon breeds on cliffs not far from Abu Simbel and may hunt over the lake, whilst Lanner and Barbary Falcons also breed in the area as well as Egyptian Vulture, and Lappet-faced Vulture is possible. Vagrants from the south have included Goliath Heron, Bateleur and Sacred Ibis.

Abu Simbel lies on the west shore of Lake Nasser, 280km south of Aswan and is an important tourist attraction. It can be reached by road or air and there is hotel accommodation in the town. Boat trips onto the lake can be arranged.

2) Aswan In recent years Aswan has become an essential part of the itinerary of any birding trip to Egypt. It is conveniently situated at the head of Lake Nasser, roughly midway between the popular birding areas of Abu Simbel and Luxor.

Birds typical of the Nile Valley are common at Aswan and include Striated Heron, Egyptian Goose, Spur-winged Lapwing and Purple Swamphen. Senegal Thick-knee and Kittlitz's Plover also occur. Pied Kingfisher is abundant, as is Little Green Bee-eater, and passerines include Nile Valley Sunbird and Common Bulbul, with a wide range of migrants occurring on passage. Black-shouldered Kite is common in the farmland surrounding Aswan and Cream-coloured Courser, Egyptian Nightjar and Hoopoe Lark are possible in the area. Kitchener's Island is an interesting spot with gardens that attract a variety of birds, and Agilka Island is the home of the Temple of Philae and a popular tourist attraction. It is also excellent for birds with White-tailed Wheatear, Eastern Olivaceous and Graceful Prinias, as well as passerine migrants. The boat trip to the island usually provides views of a variety of waterbirds.

Aswan can be reached by road, rail or air from Cairo and Luxor, and it is possible to take cruises between Aswan and Abu Simbel.

3) Faiyum The large oasis at el Faiyum, and in particular Lake Qarun at the northern end, attracts a good range of migrants including herons, crakes, Pallas' Gull and White-tailed Lapwing, and has some of Egypt's special birds such as Senegal Thick-knee, Spur-winged Plover, Senegal Coucal, and Little Green and Blue-cheeked Bee-eaters. Greater Painted-snipe is also possible.

The Faiyum oasis can be reached by road and is c.110km south-west of Cairo.

4) Hurghada Increasingly popular as a birding destination, Egypt's Red Sea coast is ideal for seeing a range of species very difficult to find elsewhere in the Western Palearctic. Hurghada is the best-known birding site and in recent years has greatly expanded as a tourist resort providing accommodation, car hire and boat trips.

The main attraction is the Red Sea specialities present in summer but almost anything could turn up on passage. In summer Sooty and White-eyed Gulls are common, terns include White-cheeked, Greater and Lesser Crested, Caspian and Bridled. Greater Sand Plover is common, Lesser appears in smaller numbers, Striated Heron and Western Reef Egret breed, and Sooty Falcon can be seen. Crowned Sandgrouse can be seen to the south, at Bir Beida, 10km west of Quseir, and probably elsewhere in the area, whilst Spotted Sandgrouse also occurs in the surrounding desert, along with Sand Partridge, Cream-coloured Courser, Lanner Falcon, Hooded Wheatear, Desert and Bar-tailed Desert Larks, and Trumpeter Finch.

During passage periods the variety of birds can be outstanding with White Pelican, both storks, Greater Flamingo and Eurasian Spoonbill, as well as a wide range of waders, Slender-billed Gull is possible in winter and Pallas' in spring. Brown Booby is regular and Red-billed Tropicbird has been recorded and formerly bred in the area. Passage raptors occur in numbers and passerines such as Thrush Nightingale and Lesser Grey and Masked Shrikes are common.

Many seabirds can be seen from the beaches north of the port but boat trips to the nearby islands are more productive. Gifton Kabir has White-cheeked Tern, White-eyed Gull, Sooty Falcon, Eurasian Spoonbill and herons. Further south, the island of Umm Agawish has Bridled and Lesser Crested Terns and Sooty Gull.

Hurghada can be reached by road from Cairo or Luxor, by air from Cairo or boat from Sharm el Sheikh.

5) Luxor With outstanding ancient monuments, Luxor is one of the top tourist destinations in Egypt and thus easy to reach with plentiful accommodation. In addition to the historical sites the birding here is excellent with a good range of wetland and desert species typical of Egypt.

On the Nile itself, Cattle Egret is common and there are also Striated and Purple Herons, Glossy Ibis and Eurasian Spoonbill, Egyptian Goose and Spur-winged Lapwing, and occasionally African Skimmer and White-tailed Lapwing. Wintering ducks can include Marbled, Ferruginous and Red-crested Pochard. The reedbeds and mudflats viewed from the bridge to Crocodile Island, 4km south of Luxor, have Purple Swamphen, Squacco Heron and Little Bittern, with Little Crake and Greater Painted-snipe infrequently recorded. Passerines include Graceful and Clamorous Reed Warblers and, in winter, Moustached Warbler and Bluethroat. Black-shouldered Kite is common, as are Pied Kingfisher, Little Green Bee-eater, Common Bulbul and Nile Valley Sunbird.

Desert birds can be seen whilst visiting the historical sites, with Rock Martin at Karnak, and Trumpeter Finch, Blue Rock Thrush and wheatears including White-tailed, Desert, Hooded and Mourning in the Valley of the Kings. Sooty Falcon, Barbary Falcon and Lanner are also present in the area, in addition to Long-legged Buzzard, Cream-coloured Courser and Spotted Sandgrouse.

Luxor can be reached by road, rail or air from Cairo.

6) Nile Delta This vast delta, from Alexandria in the west to Port Said in the east, is Egypt's most important farming and fishing area, but remains home to large numbers of breeding, passage and wintering birds.

The best areas for birds are the large brackish lakes in the north of the delta. **Lake Maryut** is south of Alexandria and, unlike the other lakes, has no direct link to the sea. Further east is **Lake Idku**, in the centre of the delta is the much larger **Lake Burullus** and just west of Port Said is **Manzala**, the largest of the lakes: all are surrounded by extensive reedbeds and large areas of salicornia and tamarisk scrub.

Birds present in summer or on passage include various herons, Greater Flamingo, crakes, Purple Swamphen, Senegal Thick-knee, Greater Painted-snipe, Collared Pratincole, Kittlitz's and Spur-winged Plovers, Senegal Coucal, Pied and White-breasted Kingfishers, and Little Green and Blue-cheeked Bee-eaters. Among the passerines are Lesser Short-toed Lark, Zitting Cisticola and Graceful and Clamorous Reed Warblers. Many of these are also present in winter, as well as Black-necked Grebe, Great Bittern, Great Egret, Red-crested Pochard and Ferruginous Duck.

Alexandria and Port Said are both easily reached from Cairo, and the delta has a network of roads and railways.

7) Santa Katharina Monastery Situated in the centre of the southern Sinai Peninsula, this well-known tourist attraction is famous among birders as one of the few reliable sites for Sinai Rosefinch. The monastery lies on the slopes of Mount Sinai and its gardens attract many migrants. Wadis and hills in this area hold a selection of typical Sinai birds and part of the surrounding area has now been designated a National Park.

The rosefinch is fairly common and can often be seen around the car park, and Tristram's Starling is another desert speciality. One of the most sought-after Western

Palearctic birds, Hume's Owl has been found in this area but may not be present annually. Other typical Sinai species include Sand and Chukar Partridges and passerines such as Desert and Bar-tailed Desert Larks, Rock Martin, and Hooded and White-tailed Wheatears. Palestine Sunbird has been recorded and may now be established in the area.

The monastery can be reached by road from Cairo, Suez or Sharm el Sheikh, and can be visited in a day from Eilat in Israel. There is a nearby holiday village providing accommodation.

8) Sharm el Sheikh This town in southern Sinai, very popular with divers, is becoming increasingly popular as a birding destination, with the main attractions being the desert specialities, the sought-after seabirds of the Red Sea and numerous migrants.

Sooty Falcon breeds on small islets just offshore and hunts over the mainland at dusk, and other raptors possible here include Lesser Kestrel and Barbary Falcon, Griffon Vulture, harriers, Long-legged Buzzard, Levant Sparrowhawk and various *Aquila* eagles. Desert specialities include Desert Eagle Owl, Lichtenstein's, Spotted and Crowned Sandgrouse, and passerines such as Blackstart, Scrub Warbler, Brown-necked Raven, Southern Grey Shrike and Trumpeter Finch, with House Bunting possible. However, larks and wheatears are the most characteristic desert passerines and here include Crested, Bar-tailed Desert and Hoopoe Larks, and Red-tailed, White-tailed, Hooded, Mourning and Desert Wheatears.

Western Reef and Striated Herons may occur anywhere along this coast but particularly in mangroves. Sooty Gull and Bridled Tern are among the seabirds and waders occur in great numbers and variety, and include such scarce species as Black-winged Pratincole, Spur-winged Lapwing and Marsh Sandpiper. Greater Painted-snipe has been recorded.

Nabq Protected Area is north of Naama Bay and hosts what may be the world's most northerly mangroves. An excellent area for waders and other waterbirds, migrant passerines can be numerous.

Undoubtedly one of the best areas is the sewage works north of the town, which attracts ducks, waders and terns on passage, and many other migrants including raptors and storks. Any bushes or trees can attract passerine migrants and plantations, gardens and the golf course should be thoroughly searched.

Ras Muhammad National Park is c.25km south-west of Sharm el Sheikh at the southernmost tip of the Sinai Peninsula. Although famed for its reefs, it is worth visiting for Sooty Falcon, waders and seabirds. The Sharm el Sheikh to Hurghada ferry can produce Red-billed Tropicbird and Bridled Tern.

With increasing numbers of birders visiting the area it is inevitable that a long list of rarities is accumulating and undoubtedly more will be recorded. Sharm el Sheikh has accommodation and an international airport, and can also be reached by road or by sea from Hurghada.

9) Suez area One of the best raptor migration watchpoints in the Western Palearctic lies just south of the town of Suez, and this area is also excellent for some of the Red Sea specialities, as well as desert birds.

All the migrant raptors of the region can be seen with Short-toed, Lesser Spotted, Steppe and Booted Eagles particularly numerous. Autumn sees higher numbers passing through but most species also occur in spring. Among rarer raptors seen here are Red Kite, Lammergeier and Bonelli's Eagle. Other regular migrants include White

Pelican, both storks and Eurasian Spoonbill, and Demoiselle Crane has been recorded. The best point to watch for raptors is a ridge south of the town.

The port and beaches are excellent for seabirds, with White-eyed and Slender-billed Gulls, and Caspian, Greater and Lesser Crested Terns. Waders can include Greater Sand Plover and Purple Swamphen, Pied Kingfisher and Clamorous Reed Warbler occur in marshy areas. To the south of Suez is one of the best and most accessible areas of desert in Egypt. Sooty Falcon, Cream-coloured Courser and Spotted Sandgrouse occur in Wadi Hagul, reached from the Cairo to Suez road. Desert passerines include Desert and Hoopoe Larks, Mourning Wheatear, Scrub Warbler, Brown-necked Raven and Trumpeter Finch.

Suez is easily reached by road from Cairo and the best spots for birding can be accessed from the main coast road south of the town.

10) Wadi el Natrun This wetland area in northern Egypt is famous among birders as one of the most reliable sites in the Western Palearctic for Kittlitz's Plover. The area consists of a series of saline lakes surrounded by wet meadows. Other species possible here include Senegal Thick-knee, Greater Painted-snipe and Spur-winged Lapwing, and Great Snipe has been recorded. Blue-cheeked Bee-eater occurs in summer and this area is home to an endemic race of Graceful Prinia.

Wadi el Natrun can be reached from the main Cairo to Alexandria road, north-west of Cairo.

11) Zaranik This relatively recently discovered migration hotspot lies on the north coast of Sinai and comprises a lagoon, beach and desert vegetation at the east end of the saline Lake Bardawil. Autumn is the best time, especially mid August to mid-October. The area is now designated a protected area and Egypt's first bird observatory is based here.

Breeders include Kentish Plover and Spur-winged Lapwing, and Pied Avocet, a rare breeding bird in Egypt. Also present in summer are Slender-billed Gull and Greater Sand Plover as well as Greater Flamingo. Arid land specialities such as Desert Wheatear, Southern Grey Shrike and Hoopoe Lark can also be seen. Huge numbers of migrants occur in autumn and can be seen from the beach. Seawatching regularly produces skuas, including Long-tailed, as well as shearwaters. Audouin's Gull occurs in autumn and various members of the Herring Gull complex appear in winter including Caspian, Armenian and Heuglin's. More than 40 species of wader have been recorded including Black-winged Pratincole, Cream-coloured Courser and Broad-billed Sandpiper, as well as Terek Sandpiper and White-tailed Plover. This is one of the best sites in the Mediterranean for passage Corn Crake. Passage raptors include Steppe and Lesser Spotted Eagles, Pallid and Montagu's Harriers, Long-legged Buzzard and Red-footed Falcon, with spring the peak season. Passerines are varied and include such specialities as Thrush Nightingale, Olive-tree, Rüppell's, Orphean and Barred Warblers, and Ortolan and Cretzschmar's Buntings. Wheatears include Isabelline, Pied, Cyprus Pied, Black-eared and Finsch's. Any areas of vegetation are worth checking but the best areas are around the observatory, the pumping station and the fishing village.

Zaranik is situated c.35km west of El Arish on the main road across northern Sinai and can be reached by bus or taxi from Cairo or El Arish. The bird observatory can provide accommodation for a small number of visitors, for a small fee, but advance booking must be made. A permit is required to enter the protected area.

Estonia

As well as having an excellent range of breeding wetland and forest birds, Estonia is of international importance as a passage stopover for hundreds of thousands of waterfowl and Common Crane. Rare migrants include regular Lesser White-fronted Goose and Steller's Eider, and species such as White-tailed Eagle, Ural Owl and Blyth's Reed Warbler are among the breeders. Estonia now regularly features in bird tour company brochures but independent travellers will find reasonably priced accommodation and car hire, good roads and a reasonable public transport system. As elsewhere, woodpeckers and owls are best seen with local assistance but a spring visit to Estonia could result in a trip list approaching 200 species.

1) Emajõgi Floodplain Around the mouth of the River Emajõgi in the east of Estonia is a large area of lakes, marshes, wet meadows and forest that supports breeding birds of interest, as well as being an important staging area for migrants.

Breeders include Great Bittern, Black Grouse, Common Crane, Spotted and Corn Crakes, and Great Snipe. Raptors include White-tailed and Greater Spotted Eagles. Swans and geese occur on passage.

The area is situated east of Tartu on the shores of Lake Peipus.

2) Lake Endla More than 170 species have been recorded in the forests and wetlands between Torma and Lake Endla, and nearly 150 are known to have bred. Hazel and Black Grouse, Capercaillie, Black Stork and Common Crane are among the breeding birds, and raptors include White-tailed, Golden and Lesser Spotted Eagles.

Torma is situated c.70km north of Tartu.

3) Matsalu Bay A large, shallow bay where the Kasari River meets the sea, Matsalu is a Ramsar site with an internationally important nature reserve. The habitat consists of numerous rocky islands fringing the bay, extensive reedbeds, saltmarshes and flooded meadows in the delta, and woodland, grazing pastures and hay-meadows inland.

Almost 300 species have been recorded, of which 170 have bred including many wetland birds such as Great Bittern, crakes and various ducks, waders and warblers. In addition, a small number of Barnacle Geese have bred since the 1980s, and Temminck's Stint and Great Snipe may be present in summer. Raptors are well represented, with Golden Eagle and Montagu's Harrier breeding. The forests host Grey-headed and White-backed Woodpeckers and Eurasian Eagle Owl. Despite the large number of breeding species the area is perhaps more important as a staging area during passage periods. In spring and autumn large numbers of swans and geese, about one million diving ducks and waders, and thousands of Common Cranes visit the area. Divers also pass through in thousands in spring and autumn, and Steller's Eider is regular.

Permits are required to visit the reserve, available from the headquarters at Penijoe on the south-eastern shore. Matsalu Bay is reached via the A207 road c.110km from Tallinn towards Virtsu.

4) Nigula Nature Reserve In south-west Estonia, close to the Latvian border, this reserve consists of a large lake and associated bog land surrounded by dense conifer forest.

Wet areas have breeding Black-throated Diver and Common Crane but most birders are in search of the forest birds, which include Black Stork, Hazel Grouse, Capercaillie, Nutcracker, woodpeckers, including Black, White-backed and Three-toed, and owls such as Eurasian Eagle, Eurasian Pygmy, Tengmalm's and Ural. Raptors include Golden and Lesser Spotted Eagles with Greater Spotted sometimes present in summer.

From Pärnu take the road to Häädemeeste and continue to Tali. On the Tali to Nurme road stop just past Vanajarve Station and the lake is to the west. A track crosses bog and forest to the reserve centre.

5) Taevaskoja A good range of forest birds can be found in this area of south-east Estonia including Hazel and other grouse, Tengmalm's Owl and White-backed and Three-toed Woodpeckers. Greenish Warbler also breeds here.

Taevaskoja is c.30km south-east of Tartu and the birding is best on the hiking tracks starting at Saesaare Pavilion to the north-east of Taevaskoja.

6) Vilsandi National Park This National Park is situated at the western tip of the island of Saaremaa and covers offshore islands, shallow bays and lakes, and habitats include reedbeds, wet meadows and coniferous forest.

Nearly 250 species have been recorded with over 100 breeding, including Caspian Tern, Barnacle Goose, Common Crane and Barred Warbler. The area is also important for passage and wintering waterfowl including Barnacle Goose and Steller's Eider.

Saaremaa can be reached by ferry from Virtsu and Vilsandi by boat from Papisaare. Permits are required, available from the National Park office in Kihelkonna.

Faroe Islands

This group of islands, a self-governed region of Danish territory, is situated in the north Atlantic midway between Shetland and Iceland. Despite frequent bad weather, these islands are increasingly visited by birders for their important seabird colonies.

Various seabirds breed on the rugged cliffs and steep grassy slopes including internationally important numbers of skuas and auks, Manx Shearwater, and European and Leach's Storm-petrels. Rock Pipit also breeds. The remaining habitat is mainly

FAROE ISLANDS

sheep-grazed grassland, with moorlands and hayfields holding breeding waders. There are small woodlands in some areas, with Redwing and the Faroes race of Winter Wren. The moors have peat bogs and there are also many pools where Red-necked Phalaropes nest, and the mountains, which reach more than 880m, host Purple Sandpiper and Snow Bunting.

Although only *c.*50 species breed, vagrants are frequent and more than 250 species have been recorded. Most of the larger seabird colonies are in the north with **1) Mykines** the best island, but Kallsoy, Vidoy, Fugloy and Svínoy also hold impressive numbers. **2) Streymoy** is the main island, and also has seabird colonies including Great Skua, and **3) Sandoy** to the south is good for wildfowl and waders, whilst **4) Nólsoy** produces many vagrants.

The airport at Vagar has regular flights from Glasgow, Reykjavik and Copenhagen, and the islands can be reached by boat from Norway or Denmark. Internally, public transport is good including regular boats between islands and car rental and boat hire is available. June is generally the best month to visit.

Finland

Owls are one of the main attractions for birders visiting Finland, but this country also has the Western Palearctic's most accessible Red-flanked Bluetails, at Kuusamo, and a good selection of breeding waders in northern areas. Many bird tour companies visit Finland and these trips are often combined with a visit to Varangerfjord in Norway for ducks and seabirds. In addition to the bluetail there are several other species which can be difficult to see elsewhere in this land of forest and lakes. These include Terek and Broad-billed Sandpipers, River, Blyth's Reed and Greenish Warblers, and Little, Rustic and Yellow-breasted Buntings. As in other Scandinavian countries, it has become the norm to enlist the help of local birders to see owls but independent birding is easy, albeit expensive. Although the owls are

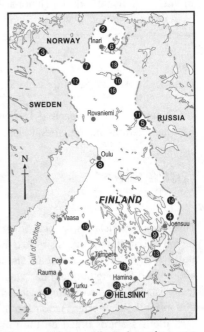

best seen in early spring a later trip in late May to mid Jun will produce the most species. By this time the owls should be feeding young and fairly easy to locate.

1) Åland Islands More than 6,000 islands form this archipelago lying midway between Sweden and Finland. Habitats vary from virtually bare rock on the smaller, outlying islands to woodland and farmland on the larger islands. Many islands have reeds and other vegetation growing on their shores, typical of the brackish and almost tideless Baltic Sea.

Birds here are varied and this is the best area for Steller's Eider and White-tailed Eagle in the country. There are also Northern Goshawk, Eurasian Eagle and Tengmalm's Owls. Others include Capercaillie, Hazel and Black Grouse, many water-fowl, waders and seabirds including Caspian Tern and Arctic Skua. Passerines include Nutcracker, Siberian Jay and Thrush Nightingale, and warblers include Greenish and, on the eastern islands, Barred. Increasingly, River and Blyth's Reed Warblers are seen, and autumn brings regular Pallas' Leaf, Yellow-browed and Dusky Warblers. Others include Red-breasted Flycatcher and Bearded and Crested Tits.

Unfortunately the birds on these islands are well scattered and no single island will produce all the specialities. Thrush Nightingale is found mainly on the western islands, as is Caspian Tern. However, Foglo in the south-east is one of the better areas with regular wintering Steller's Eider and White-tailed Eagle, which winters in larger numbers south of Åland, around the islands of Lågskär and Nyhamn. Signildskär in the west of the archipelago is another important island and the site of Finland's oldest bird observatory. Breeding here are auks, gulls and Caspian Tern.

As these islands are popular with tourists, accommodation is plentiful and the archipelago is easily reached by air or ferry from Turku. Alternatively, the visitor can travel by air or sea from Sweden. There are numerous inter-island boat services.

2) Kevo Nature Reserve A reserve in Finnish Lapland that contains the Kevojoki Canyon, as well as pine woodlands and birch scrub along the banks of the Kevo River.

Breeders include Rough-legged Buzzard, Gyr Falcon, Ptarmigan and Long-tailed Skua, with Temminck's Stint, Jack Snipe, Broad-billed Sandpiper and Red-necked Phalarope in the wetter areas. The scrub and woodland have Red-throated Pipit, Bluethroat and Arctic Warbler, as well as Siberian Tit, Siberian Jay, Arctic Redpoll and Pine Grosbeak.

The reserve is popular with visitors and lies 18km south of Utsjoki or by track 11km east of Karigasniemi, which is on Route 4, 100km beyond Inari.

3) Kilpisjärvi Saana In the far north-west of Finland, a narrow tongue of Finnish territory projects north-west into Sweden and Norway, and at the tip of this is Kilpisjärvi Saana. The habitat is mainly high fjell with alpine vegetation, and the limestone outcrops support a rich and varied flora. Valleys have numerous ponds and streams.

Parts of the area are wooded and these have Siberian Tit, Arctic Warbler, Redwing and Brambling, but the area is best known for its montane and tundra birds. Present in summer are Rough-legged Buzzard, Gyr Falcon and, sometimes, Snowy Owl, Willow and Ptarmigans, Dotterel and Long-tailed Skua, and passerines such as Shore Lark, Red-throated Pipit, Ring Ouzel, and Lapland and Snow Buntings. Waders such as Temminck's Stint and Red-necked Phalarope, and ducks including Smew and Long-tailed Duck nest in wetter areas of the valleys. Lesser White-fronted Goose is possible in summer.

Kilpisjärvi can be reached by road and there are marked nature trails.

4) Kolvanan Uuro Just north of Joensuu in eastern Finland is the small and narrow valley of Kolvanan Uuro, densely wooded and home to typical Scandinavian woodland birds including Greenish Warbler and Thrush Nightingale. Also present are Hazel Grouse and Capercaillie, with Black-throated Diver on a small lake in the valley.

From Joensuu take Route 18 north and turn right after Uuro, signed Kolvanan Uuro.

5) Kuusamo Best known to birders as the premier site in Europe for Red-flanked Bluetail, Kuusamo is also famous for an annual bird race in which as many as 30 teams take part, producing species lists of over 150 in mid Jun.

There are many typical Scandinavian woodland species in the surrounding conifer-covered hills. These include Hazel Grouse, Capercaillie, Tengmalm's and Northern Hawk Owls, Siberian Tit, Siberian Jay, Parrot and Two-barred Crossbills, and Pine Grosbeak. Higher areas have Golden Eagle and Willow Grouse. The lakes close to town hold Black-throated Diver, Red-necked Grebe, Velvet Scoter and Smew and, in the wetlands around them, Temminck's Stint, Jack Snipe and Broad-billed Sandpiper breed as well as Little and Rustic Buntings.

Kuusamo is situated east of Route 5 about 800km north of Helsinki.

6) Lake Inari One of the largest lakes in Finland, this huge waterbody is in Lapland, 250km north of the Arctic Circle. The shores vary from rocky to marshy, and there are many inlets and islands providing nesting habitat for Whooper Swan, Velvet Scoter, Smew, Common Crane and Broad-billed Sandpiper. Much of the surrounding area is forested and Arctic Warbler, Siberian Tit, Siberian Jay and Pine Grosbeak are present. In higher areas, Dotterel and Long-tailed Skua breed, along with Lapland and Snow Buntings.

This is a large area and difficult to cover but there are conveniently spaced huts for hikers. This is one of the worst areas in Europe for mosquitoes and a good repellent is essential. Most visitors reach the area by road from Rovaniemi to the south, although Ivalo has an airstrip with connections to Helsinki.

7) Lemmenjoki National Park This vast wilderness area in north-west Finland has few roads or habitations. Much of the park is flat and open, with birch forest, pine heath and bogs, and most of the main peaks (up to 600m) are on the east side of the park. The Lemmenjoki River winds along one of the valleys, through steep-sided gorges with spectacular falls, and elsewhere forms lakes.

The birdlife is rich and varied with a good range of tundra, coniferous forest and wetland species. Most of the typical Arctic birds occur including Rough-legged Buzzard, Gyr Falcon, and Lapland and Snow Buntings. The forests are home to Northern Hawk and Great Grey Owls, Three-toed Woodpecker and Capercaillie, and many waders breed in the wetter areas. The Naukussuo swamp in the south-west of the park has breeding Jack Snipe, Temminck's Stint and Broad-billed Sandpiper. Open-water birds include Whooper Swan and Smew.

The park has campsites and cabins, an airstrip, marked trails and canoes for hire.

8) Liminganlahti The city of Oulu, on the Gulf of Bothnia, is surrounded by many wetlands with an excellent range of passage waders and waterfowl. Forests nearby hold Ural, Great Grey, Tengmalm's and other owls, although they can be very difficult to find and usually require local assistance.

The best known of the wetlands in the Oulu area is Liminganlahti to the south of the city on the edge of Liminka Bay, which has observation towers, wooden trails and a visitor centre. Habitats include marshland and wet meadows, open water and reedbeds, with some birch woodland. Breeders include Black-throated Diver, grebes, Great Bittern, Common Crane and Red-necked Phalarope. This is perhaps the best site to see Yellow-breasted Bunting in the Western Palearctic, usually found around the bird tower, and is famous as the westernmost point for breeding Terek Sandpiper. Blyth's Reed Warbler is also possible in summer. The area is also important for passage birds with Whooper Swan and Taiga Bean Goose in thousands, regular Lesser Greater White-fronted Goose and a variety of waders.

Oulu can be reached by air or road from Helsinki, and Liminganlahti lies south of the town near Liminka.

9) Linnansaari National Park In south-eastern Finland lies the vast Lake Saimaa, of which part of this is included in Linnansaari National Park. Habitats in the park include open fresh water and numerous islands. The islands vary from small and bare rocky islets to larger forested islands with mixed woodland of conifer and birch.

Breeding birds include Black-throated Diver, ducks and gulls on the lake. Greenish and other warblers breed in the woodlands, as well as Parrot Crossbill. White-backed Woodpecker, scarce in Finland, also breeds here in numbers and White-tailed Eagle occurs on passage.

Access is unrestricted but the park can only be reached by water and there are no regular boat services. Boats can be arranged in Oravi, 40km north-west of Savonlinna, or in Rantasalmi.

10) Maltio Nature Reserve North-east of Pyhätunturi National Park and close to the southern border of Lapland, this reserve has wooded hillsides, high fjell, peat bogs and lakes. Black-throated Diver breeds as well as several duck species and various waders including Whimbrel and Wood Sandpiper. In wooded areas there are Three-toed Woodpecker, Siberian Tit, Siberian Jay and Brambling.

Access to the reserve is only with permission from the National Park office. Situated north-east of Savukoski, the park is reached via Martii.

11) Oulanka National Park In north-east Finland, just outside the Arctic Circle and close to the Russian border, the main feature of Oulanka is the spectacular Oulankajoki River. Flowing east through the park this river rushes through deep valleys and ravines with rapids and waterfalls. In some parts the river flows more slowly and passes through flower-filled meadows and eventually into Russia. The rest of the park is largely forested, mainly with pine and spruce but also birch, rowan and aspen.

Birds of the forests include Hazel and Black Grouse, Capercaillie, owls such as Eurasian Eagle, Great Grey, Northern Hawk and Tengmalm's, and Black and Three-toed Woodpeckers. Passerines include Arctic and Greenish Warblers, Crested and Siberian Tits, Siberian Jay, Two-barred and Parrot Crossbills, and Pine Grosbeak. In the north there are wetter areas, home to breeding waders, waterfowl and Rustic and Little Buntings. The speciality that attracts many birders is Red-flanked Bluetail and nearby Ristikallio Gorge is one of the best areas for this sought-after species.

There is an information centre, marked hiking trails, lodges and campsites within the park.

12) Pallas-Ounastunturi National Park This National Park covers a long upland plateau forming part of the backbone of west Lapland. There are marshes, forests and lakes.

Birdlife includes Rough-legged Buzzard, Golden Eagle, Gyr Falcon, Ptarmigan and Long-tailed Skua, and often Snowy Owl. There are Hazel Grouse, Great Grey Owl and many passerines in the woodlands, and various waterfowl and waders breed in the wetland areas.

This park is very popular with hikers in summer and skiers in winter, there are marked hiking trails and an information centre, and the area can be reached by leaving Route 79 at Sarkijärvi, south of Muonio, on Routes 957 and 9571.

13) Parikkala Known as the Finnish Lake District and lying close to the Russian border, habitats around Parikkala include lakes, reedbeds and marshes, farmland and pine woodland.

Although there is a good range of wetland birds here, the main birding attraction is Blyth's Reed Warbler and this has been a regular site for the species since its expansion into Europe in the mid 20th century. Other eastern birds found here include River Warbler and Yellow-breasted Bunting, and Booted Warbler is possible. The marshes also hold grebes and ducks, Great Bittern, Common Crane and crakes. In wooded areas there are Common Rosefinch and Ortolan Bunting, and White-backed Woodpecker is present but scarce.

Situated just west of Route 6, Parikkala is signed from the main road. The best and most popular area is known as Siikhalati Marsh, just off the E3, which runs east of Parikkala. This reserve covers a shallow bay on Lake Simpele and has a visitor centre, observation tower and logbook. To the north, at Lake Saaperinjärvi, there are also marshland birds and Yellow-breasted Bunting. South of Parikkala, at Lake Vakevanjärvi there is a small hill called Sampolankallio, which overlooks the border and from where Greater Greater Spotted Eagle can be seen.

14) Patvinsuo National Park A moorland and old forest area with lakes and bogs in the east of Finland, Patvinsuo is an excellent site for a variety of bird species.

Capercaillie, Black and Hazel Grouse, and Willow Grouse breed, as well as Ural and Tengmalm's Owls, Three-toed Woodpecker, Red-breasted Flycatcher, Siberian Tit, Siberian Jay and Pine Grosbeak. Lakes have Black-throated Diver, Whooper Swan and Taiga Bean Goose, and waders include Broad-billed Sandpiper and Jack Snipe.

The park is 30km south-east of Lieksa and there is an information centre, nature trails and observation towers.

15) Pyhä-Häkki National Park This National Park protects a small area of primeval forest in central Finland where the dominant trees are spruce and pine, and some may be up to 500 years old. Situated where the wetter, flatter land of the west meets the hill country of central Finland, the few open areas in this park are at the edges of swamps and small woodland pools.

The area is rich in typical Scandinavian woodland birds including Northern Goshawk, Hazel and Black Grouse, Capercaillie and Three-toed Woodpecker. Owls include Ural, Eurasian Pygmy and Tengmalm's, and passerines such as Siberian Tit and Siberian Jay, Parrot Crossbill and Rustic Bunting occur.

There are marked hiking trails in the park, which lies on the road between Saarijärvi and Viitasaari.

16) Pyhätunturi National Park A small National Park lying just inside Arctic Circle on the edge of the uplands that comprise much of northern Finland. The park's main feature is a distinctively shaped, isolated mountain, 540m high, with steep sides, rocky outcrops and deep boulder-strewn ravines. There are some forested areas but much of the park consists of open moss and sedge fenland.

Birdlife is not particularly rich but there are Rough-legged Buzzard, Willow Grouse, Siberian Jay, Siberian Tit and Pine Grosbeak.

There are marked hiking trails within the park, which is accessed by road, 50km north of Kemijärvi. The park has an information centre on the Pelkosenniemi road and from here visitors can take a number of trails or a chairlift to the higher areas.

17) Ruissalo A small island off southern Finland, Ruissalo has open farmland and deciduous forest and there is a bay on the southern shore which attracts waterfowl and waders.

Oak woodland is scarce in Finland and this island is popular with birders for species such as Stock Dove, Tawny Owl and Grey-headed Woodpecker, which are difficult to find elsewhere. Black Woodpecker also occurs, as well as Thrush Nightingale and Common Rosefinch. Barnacle Goose occurs on passage and there is a small breeding population of dubious origin. A variety of waterfowl, raptors, waders, seabirds and passerines pass through on migration.

Ruissalo lies about 7km west of Turku and can be reached by road

18) Urho Kekkonen National Park This area of north-east Finland consists of birch woodland and pine forest, with peat bogs and marshes and open tundra on higher ground.

Upland areas have Golden Eagle and Rough-legged Buzzard, Willow Grouse, Ptarmigan, Shore Lark, and Snow and Lapland Buntings. Forest birds include Capercaillie, Black and Hazel Grouse, Northern Hawk and Great Grey Owls, Three-toed Woodpecker, Arctic Warbler, Siberian Jay, Siberian Tit, crossbills and Pine Grosbeak. Wetland breeders are numerous with Whooper Swan, Smew and Common Crane, and a variety of waders including Broad-billed Sandpiper, Jack Snipe and Red-necked Phalarope. A particularly good area for waders lies just south of the park at Mutenia.

There is an information centre at Tankavaara on the E4 road and nature trails with observation towers. It is also possible to explore this area fully on an extended hike using cabin accommodation.

19) Vesijako Natural Park North-west of Lahti in southern Finland is Vesijako, an area of lakes and mature forest, and a good site for a range of Scandinavian woodland birds.

Forest birds include Capercaillie, Black Grouse and Hazel Grouse, and these woods are home to Ural, Tengmalm's and Eurasian Eurasian Eurasian Pygmy Owls. Passerines are numerous and include Red-breasted Flycatcher, warblers and finches. Black-throated Diver breeds around the lakes.

From Lahti head north on Route 58 until Arrakoski and keep left for the park.

20) Viikki (Vanhakaupunginlahti) Helsinki is a good city for birders and Viikki, *c.*6km to the north-east, is one of the best of many sites in and around the capital. This small wetland lies at the mouth of the Vantaanjoki River and is surrounded by farmland and forest.

Migration periods are the most productive with large numbers of waterfowl and waders passing through in spring, joined by raptors and passerines in autumn. Bearded Tit breeds and Eurasian Eurasian Eurasian Pygmy Owl occurs in winter.

France

The Camargue has long been one of most popular birding destinations in Europe, and is still one of the best wetlands in the country, but France has a great deal more to offer. Although most of the north of the country is flat and rather featureless farmland there are excellent wetlands in the centre, at La Brenne, and the Biscay coast in the west is of international importance for waterfowl and waders. British birders now make regular trips to the lakes of Champagne for White-tailed Eagle and Common Crane, which have recently

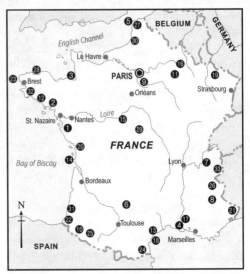

begun to winter there. The uplands of the Massif Central in south-central France have some good birds, but the Pyrenees forming the border with Spain provides the best montane birding in Europe. The Alps have always been less popular with birders than the Pyrenees because they lack vultures but recent introductions have led to the establishment of Lammergeier and Griffon. France is a large country with many and varied habitats but an autumn trip combining the Camargue with the Pyrenees is likely to produce the longest species list.

1) Baie de Bourgneuf and Île de Noirmoutier

The west coast of France has several large and shallow inlets of international importance for birds, and the Baie de Bourgneuf, south of the Loire Estuary, is one of the best. Vast areas of mudflats, in addition to disused saltpans and nearby freshwater marshes, make this highly attractive to a wide range of waders and waterfowl on passage and in winter. The Île de Noirmoutier and the causeway which links it to the mainland provide shelter to the west part of the bay and to the east are extensive polders behind the seawall. The Île de Noirmoutier has a large area of saltmarsh and disused saltpans with breeding waders and terns.

Black-winged Stilt, Pied Avocet and Kentish Plover are among the breeding birds of interest, as well as Black Kite, Montagu's Harrier and passerines including White-spotted Bluethroat and Cetti's Warbler. Dunes and dry pinewoods have Greater Short-toed, Crested and Wood Larks, Tawny Pipit and Western Bonelli's Warbler. Dark-bellied Brent Goose can reach 10,000 on passage with smaller numbers wintering, and all the regular waterfowl and waders also occur.

The Baie de Bourgneuf can be reached on the D751 west from Nantes, turning onto the D758 to Bourgneuf-en-Retz. From here the D758 continues through the marshlands of the Marais de Machecoul to Bouin, and on to Beauvoir-sur-Mer.

2) Baie de Vilaine A range of coastal habitats can be explored in this estuary on the south coast of Brittany including sandy, shingle and rocky beaches, extensive inter-tidal mudflats, saltmarsh and cliffs. The area is important for tens of thousands of waders, waterfowl and seabirds in autumn and winter.

Grebes, divers, and seaducks occur in winter including scoters and Long-tailed Duck. Dark-bellied Brent Goose also occurs at this season, as well as a good range of waders. In autumn three species of skuas can be seen at the estuary mouth as well as Balearic Shearwater, gulls and terns. This estuary is a good site for Sabine's Gull in mid-September after severe weather. Purple Sandpiper is common on rocky shores.

The estuary can be viewed from several points and there is free access to the entire area. To reach Baie de Vilaine head for La Roche-Bernard on the N165 Vannes to Nantes road. From here take the D34 towards Pénestin. It is also possible to view the estuary from the north at Pointe de Penlan, which can be reached via the Arzal Dam.

3) Baie du Mont-St-Michel This huge bay is one of the most important wader haunts in the country and most of the area consists of mudflats with saltmarshes and islands, coastal grasslands and reedbeds, as well as stretches of cliffs and rocky shoreline. The bay attracts in excess of 20,000 birds on passage and in winter including all of the regular north European waders, as well as seaduck and others, and the area receives large numbers of passerine migrants.

Waterfowl in winter include thousands of Dark-bellied and a few Pale-bellied Brent, small numbers of grey geese, and the site is of major importance for scoters. Hirundines, pipits and wagtails, larks and buntings are among the many passerines that move through in spring and autumn. Breeding species include Kentish Plover and Dartford Warbler. The cliffs make a good migration watchpoint, particularly for passerines, and a wide range of species is possible. Balearic Shearwater can also be seen in good num-bers. Shore Lark, Twite and Snow and Lapland Buntings are regular in winter.

The bay can be explored easily by road and the polders and dykes in the west can be viewed from the GR34 footpath which crosses the area.

4) Camargue One of the top ornithological sites in the Western Palearctic which despite loss of habitat and disturbance from tourists remains one of the most popular among independent birders and those on organised trips. In addition to the true Camargue and the Petit Camargue, there is the associated area of Le Crau and together the variety of habitats gives rise to an outstanding range of birds.

At the heart of the Rhône Delta is the Camargue reserve, a large wetland that becomes a virtual desert in March to September when much of the water evaporates, leaving permanent water in just a few lakes. Many of these fresh and brackish waters are fringed by dense reedbeds, offering extensive habitat for many wetland birds. One of the permanent lakes is the huge Étang de Vaccarès where most of the wetland birds of the area can be seen. In addition to various herons there are Greater Flamingo, Pied Avocet, Black-winged Stilt and various waders, gulls and terns. Glossy Ibis has recently returned as a breeder. Further north there are drainage ditches and more varied veg-etation with scrubland warblers, chats and shrikes, and Eurasian Scops Owl breeds in patches of woodland. The habitats and birds of the Petit Camargue, to the north-west, are similar but less varied. Seabirds offshore include Mediterranean and Slender-billed Gulls, Gull-billed, Caspian and marsh terns, with skuas, shearwaters and Razorbill at sea.

The Crau Plain is a former river delta that is now dry, pebble-covered grassland with patches of scrub. Pin-tailed Sandgrouse occurs as well as Stone-curlew and Little

Bustard. Other species to be seen here in summer include Egyptian Vulture, European Roller, Great Spotted Cuckoo, Greater Short-toed Lark and Lesser Grey Shrike.

An area such as the Camargue is bound to attract vagrants and in recent years species such as Western Reef Heron, Terek and Broad-billed Sandpipers, and Pine Bunting have become almost regular. Extreme rarities such as Slender-billed Curlew, Spanish Imperial Eagle and Marmora's Warbler have also been recorded. Scarcer raptors increasingly winter in the area with Greater Spotted and Booted Eagles, Long-legged Buzzard and Lanner Falcon often present.

Although there are good birds throughout the year late summer when the tourist season is at its peak is probably best avoided. The entire area can be explored by road from the town of Arles.

5) Caps Gris Nez and Blanc Nez These two headlands jutting into the English Channel are excellent migration watchpoints and among the best birding sites in northern France. Between the two is Wissant Bay with sand dunes backed by marshland.

Breeding birds include a few of the commoner seabirds and Common Rosefinch has bred. The marshes hold Bluethroat and Cetti's and Savi's Warblers. However, the main draw is the spring and autumn passages offshore. Divers and grebes pass by and shearwaters occur in large numbers with Balearic and Sooty, as well as Manx, and European and Leach's Storm-petrels are possible. Dark-bellied Brent Geese are regular with some staying to winter, and seaduck include scoters and Long-tailed Duck. Sabine's Gull has been seen and skuas, terns and auks are numerous. Passerine migrants are often abundant and the wide variety includes regular appearances by species such as Richard's, Red-throated and Tawny Pipits, and Yellow-browed Warbler and Red-breasted Flycatcher are annual. Snow Bunting and Twite are often present on the dunes from late October and Great Bittern winters in the marshes.

Cap Blanc Nez lies *c.*11km south-west of Calais and Gris Nez *c.*30km, on the D940, and the whole area is within easy reach of the Channel ports for British birders, either as a daytrip or at the start of a longer French tour. Wissant Marsh can be reached on the D940 by turning right onto a track at the south end of the marsh which leads to the reserve.

6) Cévennes National Park This National Park consists of an area of fairly low mountains with spectacular scenery on the south edge of the Massif Central. Habitats are varied with gorges, cliffs and scree, bare plateaux, open heath and alpine meadows, and areas of coniferous, mixed and deciduous woodland. Although very popular with tourists, especially the dramatic Tarn and Jonte Gorges, the area is very important for a number of species and raptors in particular.

Griffon and Black Vultures are once again resident in the area after successful reintroduction and Egyptian Vulture occurs in summer. Golden Eagle, Red Kite and Northern Goshawk are also resident, with Montagu's Harrier, Short-toed Eagle and Black Kite in summer. Eurasian Eagle Owl is present but difficult to see and Eurasian Scops Owl occurs in summer. Higher areas are home to Red-billed Chough, Ring Ouzel and both rock thrushes, although typically high-altitude species such as Alpine Accentor, Wallcreeper and Snowfinch are generally seen only in winter. The Causse Méjean in the central Cévennes is an important area of open grassland with almost steppe conditions, and breeding species such as Little Bustard, Stone-curlew, Greater Short-toed Lark, Tawny Pipit and Ortolan Bunting. Capercaillie and Black Grouse also breed, with Black Woodpecker in forested areas and Hazel Grouse has recently been rediscovered in the Massif Central. Alpine Swift and Eurasian Crag Martin are easily seen throughout the gorges in summer.

Access to the park is unrestricted, but visitors are advised to keep to marked trails; there are guided walks in the summer and information centres.

7) Dombes This is an excellent wetland area with numerous shallow, well-vegetated ponds interspersed with wet meadows in woodland and farmland. As well as a good range of breeders the area is extremely important for passage and wintering birds.

Black-necked Grebe and Red-crested Pochard breed, both bitterns may be present, and herons can include Purple, Black-crowned Night and Squacco. Other wetland breeders include Whiskered Tern, Spotted Crake and Black-winged Stilt. Raptors in summer include harriers, Northern Goshawk and Black Kite. Surrounding woods and farmland hold European Bee-eater, Wryneck and Woodchat Shrike. Passage waterfowl include Ferruginous Duck and waders occur in autumn.

Dombes lies in the Rhône Valley close to the town of Villars and can be reached via the N83 Bourg-en-Bresse to Lyon road, which bisects the region.

8) Écrins National Park Considered by some to contain Europe's finest mountain scenery, more than 10 per cent of this park consists of glaciers and a central group of four peaks, the highest of which is over 4,000m. Beech, birch and fir forests clothe the lower slopes with subalpine heath, meadows and bare rock at higher levels.

Birds are typical of the western Alps with Golden Eagle, Ptarmigan and Rock Partridge. High-altitude passerines include Water Pipit, Wallcreeper and Red-billed Chough. The forests have some coniferous forest and montane specialities such as Hazel Grouse, Capercaillie, Eurasian Pygmy and Tengmalm's Owls, Black Woodpecker, Crested Tit and Nutcracker.

The park has hiking trails and information centres, mountain refuges in the inner zone and campsites in the peripheral zone. The park is reached on the N85 Gap-Grenoble road then the D985a from St-Firmin to La Chapelle-en-Valgaudemar, where the information centre is located.

9) Fontainebleau Forest Within easy reach of Paris, this area of extensive woodlands is heavily used for all kinds of recreation and forestry but remains home to a selection of typical lowland birds. In addition to coniferous, mixed and deciduous forest, the area has open grassland, heath and small patches of wetland.

Woodpeckers are well represented with Black, Grey-headed and Middle Spotted, and raptors include Northern Goshawk. Other breeders include Wryneck and most of the commoner woodland species, plus both treecreepers, Crested Tit, Western Bonelli's Warbler and Hawfinch. Spring is the most productive time to visit this forest, which is a popular stop-off for birders heading south to the Mediterranean.

Fontainebleau lies c.60km south-east of Paris and just east of the Autoroute du Soleil. The forest, covering c.170km², almost surrounds the town and there is a network of roads making exploration easy.

10) Forêt d'Issaux This Pyrenean forest is famous among birders for its isolated population of White-backed Woodpecker, although even here they can be very difficult to locate. Other species include Golden Eagle, Black Woodpecker, Crested Tit and Citril Finch. Nearby Arrete-Pierre-St-Martin has Water Pipit and Ring Ouzel in summer. The forest can be reached on the N134 from Oloron, turning west at Bedous, and the woodpeckers can be searched for on forested slopes from Osse-en-Aspe westwards. Wallcreeper can be seen in winter in a rocky gorge near Lourdios.

11) Forêt d'Orient This area of forest surrounds a huge reservoir, and the Lac d'Orient and the Lac du Der-Chantecoq to the north-east have become among the most popular winter birding sites in France. The forest is a Regional Park and lies amidst rolling farmland and low wooded hills. Although the lake is popular with watersports enthusiasts there is an bird reserve on the north-eastern side. Water levels vary and are generally lower in autumn and winter, thus exposing large areas of mud. Although there is a good range of breeding birds in the woods and around the lake, the main importance of the area lies in the wetland birds attracted on passage and in winter.

White-tailed Eagle and Common Crane are the two species that draw birders from all over Europe to the area. Up to three eagles occur on passage, with sometimes five or more wintering, and the cranes occur on passage in March and November, and can exceed 12,000 birds with smaller numbers wintering. In addition there are winter swans and grey geese among the waterfowl, regular Great Egret and a range of waders on passage.

The area is less visited in summer but there are breeding Little Bittern, Red and Black Kites, Northern Goshawk and woodpeckers including Black, Grey-headed and Middle Spotted. Black Stork is possible in summer or on passage.

The Fôret d'Orient lies c.16km east of Troyes and can be reached on the N19. From the N19 at Lusigny a minor road follows the western shore and there are many viewing points from this road. The D43 gives access to the northern and eastern sides of the lake.

12) Golfe du Morbihan This vast bay on Brittany's south coast is an important stopover and wintering area for waders and waterfowl, and holds tens of thousands of birds in season. Huge mudflats are exposed at low tide and there are saltmarshes and numerous islands, channels and lagoons, as well as arable farmland, shingle beaches and rocky shores nearby. The area is widely used for shellfish farming and shooting is widespread but there is a no-hunting bird reserve at Séné, south-east of Vannes.

Especially important for Dark-bellied Brent Goose in October to March, the area also supports high numbers of other waterfowl, all of the regular waders of north Europe and c.1,000 Black-necked Grebes. Breeding species of interest include Kentish Plover, Black-winged Stilt and Pied Avocet. Eurasian Spoonbill is regular on passage and an introduced population of Sacred Ibis has been present since the 1980s on the mudflats. A passerine speciality is Bluethroat, which breeds at Séné reserve and can also be found at the Marais de Suscinio, south of Sarzeau. The land surrounding the bay has extensive pinewoods with Black Woodpecker, Short-toed Treecreeper and Crested Tit, and Cirl Bunting and Zitting Cisticola can be found on nearby farmland.

To reach the area, take the N165 Vannes to Nantes road turning off towards Sarzeau just south of Vannes. The best areas can all be reached from the D780 by taking minor roads towards the sea between Noyalo and Sarzeau.

13) Gruissan, Campignol and Ayrolle Lagoons Although the Camargue is the best-known birding site on the Mediterranean coast of France there are many other areas with similar birds. One of the best of these is a group of large lagoons south of Narbonne, centred on Île St Martin. This area has the Étang de Gruissan to the north, Campignol to the west and the huge Étang de l'Ayrolle to the south. In addition to the lagoons there are saltpans, sandy beaches and dunes, reedbeds and tamarisk scrub. The Roc de Conilhac, north of Campignol, is a good spot for watching raptor passage.

Greater Flamingo is regular on passage and in winter but can be seen throughout the year, both storks occur on passage as well as Red-crested Pochard. Passage raptors include Short-toed Eagle, Black Kite and Eleonora's Falcon. Cattle Egret is present all year, Purple Heron in summer, and Pied Avocet and Kentish Plover breed. Reedbeds hold Bearded and Penduline Tits and Moustached Warbler in winter. Up to 20,000 waterfowl winter in the area, Mediterranean Gull is fairly common, with Audouin's Gull and Whiskered Tern regular on passage. The drier areas, scrub and vineyards are home to a range of Mediterranean birds including Great Spotted Cuckoo, European Bee-eater, Greater Short-toed Lark, Black-eared Wheatear and warblers such as Dartford, Sardinian and Subalpine.

The town of Gruissan can be reached from Narbonne via the A9 and D32, and the three lakes and Île St Martin can be explored on minor roads from here. The minor road signed Mandirac leads to the Roc de Conilhac.

14) Île d'Oléron Off the Biscay coast, this is a popular area with tourists but there are still several excellent birding areas. A large island now joined to the mainland, the main ornithological interest lies in the marshes, saltpans and mudflats in the north of the island and the northernmost tip is good for seawatching.

Seabirds seen off the Pointe de Chassiron include Balearic Shearwater, Leach's and European Storm-petrels, and various skuas, gulls, terns and auks in September to October. Mediterranean Gull occurs in numbers in winter. Douhet Marsh near St-Georges in the east of the island has breeding Black-winged Stilt and Bluethroat. There are many other mudflats and marshes around the island's coast, all of which can provide good birding. Purple Heron breeds and raptors include Montagu's Harrier, Short-toed Eagle and Black Kite. Species more characteristic of the Mediterranean reach Île d'Oléron in summer including Eurasian Scops Owl, Hoopoe, Crested Lark and Tawny Pipit. Other breeding passerines include warblers such as Zitting Cisticola, Savi's and Western Bonelli's. A wide range of waders occurs on passage, especially in spring.

The Île d'Oléron is easily reached by road from Marennes on the mainland.

15) La Brenne This area of woodland and agricultural land dotted with hundreds of lakes has become a very popular birding destination. Many of the lakes are shallow and fringed with reeds, providing perfect habitat for a large number of wetland birds.

Present in summer are Black-necked and other grebes, various ducks, crakes and marsh terns. Herons are well represented with both bitterns, egrets and Purple and Black-crowned Night Herons. In addition, there are breeding harriers and the woods support kites and Short-toed Eagle. Drier farmland has Little Bustard and Stone-curlew, and European Bee-eater breeds at La Roche Posay and Neons-sur-Creuse.

Passage brings Osprey and other raptors, often Common Crane, many terns and a variety of waders. Winter sees the arrival of waterfowl including a few Ferruginous Ducks. White-tailed Eagle is becoming more regular in winter and Black-shouldered Kite has been recorded.

All of the numerous lakes in this region are worthy of investigation and most can be viewed from surrounding roads. Some have hides and one of the best sites is Chérine Natural Reserve. To reach the region, take the N143 from Tours south-east to Châteauroux and from there head for Mézières-en-Brenne.

16) Lac du Der-Chantecoq This area south-west of Paris has become a regular winter destination for European birders due mainly to the presence of White-tailed Eagle and Common Crane on passage and in winter. The large artificial lake with wet meadows and marshes is set in grazing land and deciduous forest, and a wide range of species occurs throughout the year.

More than 30,000 Common Cranes have been recorded, virtually the entire Scandinavian breeding population. Although some winter, the largest numbers use the area as a stopover and numbers generally peak mid February to mid March and mid-October to mid November. Up to five White-tailed Eagles are usually present in winter. Other species present on passage and in winter include divers and grebes, Bewick's and Whooper Swans, grey geese and most of the commoner ducks, as well as Smew, scoters and sometimes Ferruginous Duck.

Breeders include both bitterns and Purple Heron around the lake and raptors including both kites and Booted Eagle. Black, Grey-headed and Middle Spotted Woodpeckers occur in woodland, along with Short-toed Treecreeper, Crested Tit and Hawfinch.

The lake is 15km south-west of St-Dizier, easily reached by motorway from Paris or the Channel ports via Reims. From St-Dizier the lake is signed, take the D384.

17) Les Alpilles This range of hills is a popular destination for birders visiting the Camargue. Habitats on these limestone hills include cliffs, maquis-covered hillsides, woods and farmland.

Egyptian Vulture is virtually guaranteed in summer and the area also has Bonelli's and Short-toed Eagles, and is probably the best site in France for Eurasian Eagle Owl. Other species include Alpine Swift, Eurasian Crag Martin, Blue Rock Thrush and Rock Bunting, with Alpine Accentor, Rock Sparrow and even Snowfinch and Wallcreeper possible in winter. Typical Mediterranean species including Eurasian Scops Owl and Dartford, Sardinian and Subalpine Warblers can also be seen. Small numbers of Little Bustard can sometimes be found on the lower farmland.

The area is north of Arles and can be explored from St-Rémy-de-Provence on the D5. Within the hills the best spot from which to scan for larger raptors is La Caume, and Wallcreeper and Eurasian Eagle Owl are also possible here.

18) Leucate A limestone plateau overlooking the sea, a lagoon and saltmarshes, Leucate hosts various Mediterranean birds as well as being an important migration watchpoint.

Great Spotted Cuckoo, Crested Lark, Tawny Pipit, both rock thrushes, Woodchat Shrike and Ortolan Bunting can be seen on the plateau, and warblers including Dartford, Sardinian, Subalpine, Spectacled, Orphean and Western Bonelli's. The lagoon supports breeding Pied Avocet, Kentish Plover and Slender-billed Gull, with Greater Short-toed Lark on the saltmarsh and Moustached Warbler in the reeds. Greater Flamingo is regular on passage and in winter but is often present all year, and the area attracts many storks, herons, waterfowl, waders and passerines on passage. More than 15,000 raptors occur annually with Western Honey-buzzard the most numerous, but other regulars include kites, Short-toed and Booted Eagles, harriers and falcons. Audouin's Gull occurs on passage and Black-throated Diver and grebes can be seen offshore in winter.

Leucate is situated on the Languedoc-Roussillon coast c.30km south of Narbonne.

19) Lorraine National Park There are several excellent birding spots within this National Park, which is situated south of Metz and consists of woodland and farmland with lakes, and the area is good for raptors, waterbirds and woodland birds. This is one of the few French breeding sites for Collared Flycatcher.

Lac de Lindre lies east of Nancy near Dieuze and is surrounded by forests, are home to Black Stork, Booted Eagle, Black and Red Kites and six species of woodpecker, as well as Collared Flycatcher. The Tarquimpol peninsula on the southern shore affords views over the lake, which has breeding Black-necked Grebe, both bitterns, Purple Heron, and Spotted and Little Crakes. The lake can also be viewed from Linde-Basse on the western shore and there are reedbeds in the inlet at Guermange in the east. Divers, grebes, swans and geese occur in winter with White-tailed Eagle occasionally present.

In the west of the National Park is Lac de Madine with similar but perhaps fewer breeding birds, although Penduline Tit can occur on passage. The lake lies 20km west of Pont-a-Mousson. To the south of Lac de Madine and north-west of Toul is the Forêt de la Reine, a national forest with Collared Flycatcher, Black, Middle Spotted and Grey-headed Woodpeckers, Short-toed Treecreeper and Hawfinch.

Metz and Nancy are both easily reached by motorway.

20) Marais Poitevin and the Baie de l'Aiguillon This is one of many excellent birding areas on the Biscay coast. The Marais Poitevin Regional Park forms a broad crescent of land north and east of La Rochelle and consists of grassland traversed by numerous drainage channels, with wetter areas and reedbeds attracting a variety of breeding, passage and winter visitors. Two particularly scarce species are regular in this area on passage, Little Bustard and Aquatic Warbler. The park also includes some outlying patches of woodland to the east such as the Forêt de Chize, Forêt d'Aulnay and Forêt de L'Hermitain. The farmland has birds such as Montagu's Harrier, Stone-curlew and Cirl Bunting.

The Baie de l'Aiguillon is the most important site in France for coastal waders during passage periods and in winter, and also attracts large numbers of waterfowl. More than 250,000 waders of a wide range of species gather here in autumn and as many as 100,000 winter. Eurasian Spoonbill and Common Crane occur on passage. Breeders include Little Bittern, Black-crowned Night and Purple Herons, White Stork, Black-winged Stilt, Corn Crake, Black Kite and Short-toed Eagle.

A network of minor roads enables exploration of much of the surrounding marshes and woodland, and the reserve is well signed. Little Bustard can be seen in September to October from a hide at the Poire/Velluire Common reserve, 20km south-east of Luçon.

21) Mercantour National Park On the border with Italy, Mercantour National Park covers an area of diverse habitats with cliffs and screes, coniferous and deciduous woodland, Mediterranean scrub and alpine grassland.

Golden and Short-toed Eagles breed and Lammergeier has been reintroduced to the area. Other alpine species include various grouse, Rock Partridge, Wallcreeper, Alpine Accentor, Snowfinch and both choughs. Forest areas have Black Woodpecker, owls including Eagle, Eurasian Pygmy and Tengmalm's, Nutcracker, Crested Tit and Citril Finch. A particularly good area is around the village of Boréon.

The rugged peaks are very popular with climbers and there are marked hiking trails, guided walks and an information centre. Mercantour can be reached by road from Nice or Barcelonette. The village of Boréon makes an excellent base.

22) Organbidexka The best-known migration watchpoint in the Pyrenees, there is now a bird observatory at Organbidexka, manned by volunteers and attracting thousands of visitors each year. Raptors are the main attraction with more than 20,000 moving through this pass in densely forested mountains.

Black Kite and Western Honey-buzzard are the most numerous species, often with more than 10,000 of each and the peak period is late August to early September. Also seen are Red Kite, harriers, Short-toed and Booted Eagles and, more rarely, Egyptian Vulture and Northern Goshawk. Other migrants include storks, pigeons and passerines, with Common Crane in October. Lammergeier, Red Kite and White-backed Woodpecker breed.

Organbidexka is on the Haute-Soule and lies c.10km west of Larrau on the road to St-Jean-Pied-de-Port.

23) Ouessant (Ushant) This is undoubtedly the premier rarity hotspot in France with a list of vagrants unequalled elsewhere in the country. Situated at the extreme north-west point of France, this small island is ideally located to receive migrants and is now the only permanent coastal bird observatory in the country. More than 370 species have been recorded. The island has grazing land, heath and woodland and is fringed by rocky cliffs, stacks and islets.

As well as migrants, Ouessant has substantial seabird colonies with various gulls plus Manx Shearwater, European Storm-petrel and Puffin. Red-billed Chough, Rock Pipit and Dartford Warbler also breed. Passerine migrants are the birds Ouessant is most famous for and, in addition to the commoner species, the island attracts birds such as Wryneck, Greater Short-toed Lark, Barred, Greenish, Pallas' Leaf and Yellow-browed Warblers, Red-breasted Flycatcher, Common Rosefinch, and Snow and Lapland Buntings. Other birds include waterfowl, raptors and waders. Seabirds include regular Sabine's Gull and Cory's, Sooty, Great, Manx, Balearic and even Little Shearwaters. Real rarities are frequent and have included vagrants from north America and Siberia.

Île d'Ouessant is c.20km off Brittany and can be reached by boat from Brest or Le Conquet, or by air from Brest-Guipavas airport but advance booking is essential. There is a campsite and self-catering can be arranged at the observatory.

24) Prats-de-Mollo Reserve This reserve offers birders staying on the Mediterranean coast the chance to see high-altitude species with relative ease. The 2,784m Pic du Canigou is nearby and habitats include wooded valleys, alpine meadows and cliffs.

Ptarmigan, Water Pipit, Alpine Accentor and Rufous-tailed Rock Thrush all occur in higher areas with Capercaillie, Eurasian Eagle and Tengmalm's Owls, Black Woodpecker, Western Bonelli's Warbler and Citril Finch among the forest birds. Both choughs are common and raptors include Short-toed, Golden and Bonelli's Eagles and occasional Lammergeier. Blue Rock Thrush occurs in the village.

To reach the village of Prats-de-Mollo, take the D115 west from Le Boulou, which is 20km south of Perpignan and once in the village take the minor road to La Preste.

25) Pyrenees National Park Extending more than 100km along the French-Spanish border from the valley of the Aspe to that of the Aure, and less than 15km wide, this park protects a stretch of the Pyrenees including the 3,298m Vignemale. One of the most popular destinations of this area is the glacial Cirque de Gavarnie, which adjoins Spain's Ordesa National Park.

Birds include all the typical Pyrenean species and this is one of the best Wallcreeper sites in the Western Palearctic. Raptors are a speciality and include Golden and Bonelli's Eagles, Griffon and Egyptian Vultures, and Lammergeier. The cliffs near Aste-Beon is the site of a vulture restaurant, where winter carrion is laid out for the birds. Others include Water Pipit, Alpine Accentor and Snowfinch. The forests hold Eurasian Eagle Owl, Black Woodpecker, Crested Tit and Citril Finch.

The park has several roads, marked hiking trails and information centres, mountain refuges in the inner zone and campsites in the outer zone. Many roads in the area are blocked by snow until May.

26) Queyras National Park An ancient steep-sided glacial valley, this National Park has dense pine forests with hay meadows and peat bogs at higher levels.

Ptarmigan is found on the high peaks, alpine meadows and subalpine heath have Rock Partridge, Black Grouse, Water Pipit, Alpine Accentor and Snowfinch, and rockfaces have Eurasian Crag Martin, Alpine Swift, both choughs and Wallcreeper. The forests are home to Crested Tit and Citril Finch.

Some of the best birds are found in the east and south of the park where nature trails offer visitors the opportunity to explore ancient forests and long abandoned farmland. Golden Eagle, Northern Goshawk, Tengmalm's and Eagle Owls are possible in the Guil Valley and Monte Viso areas.

To reach the park follow the D902 to Brunissard and from here a public track leads to a campsite with amenities. Take the marked trail (the GR5) for a 12km hike through woods and open rocky areas to the 2,000m Pra-Premier plateau.

27) Romelaere Nature Reserve Within easy reach of the Channel ports this reserve is popular with British birders and easily covered in a day-trip. The area consists of several lakes originally dug for peat extraction, surrounded by reeds, wet grazing land and woodlands. It is important for waterfowl on passage and in winter and has a good range of breeding wetland birds in summer.

Breeding Bluethroat is a major attraction as are Short-toed Treecreeper and Savi's Warblers and, sometimes, Little Bittern. Great Reed Warbler was once regular but has declined in recent years, whilst other summer warblers include Cetti's, Marsh and Grasshopper, with Golden Oriole in the woods. Great Bittern is a rare in winter.

The reserve is situated close to St-Omer, c.40km south-east of Calais. There is a visitor centre open at weekends all year and on weekdays in summer, and a series of hides along a nature trail.

28) Sept-Îles Nature Reserve This small group of islands off Brittany holds the best seabird colonies in France, with Northern Gannet and Puffin at their southernmost colonies nesting alongside Northern Fulmar, Manx Shearwater, European Storm-petrel, European Shag, gulls, Razorbill and Common Guillemot. Rock Pipit is also present.

Landing is prohibited on the best of the islands but the birds can be seen from boat trips around the islands, which can be arranged at Perros-Guirec.

29) Sologne One of the best birding areas in central France, Sologne combines forest and open country with a variety of wetland habitats. There are deciduous woodlands and mature conifer plantations as well as farmland and heath, lakes, ponds and marshes, many with extensive reedbeds.

Black-necked Grebe breeds and herons include both bitterns, Black-crowned Night and Purple Herons. Raptors in summer include harriers, Black Kite, Short-toed and Booted Eagles, and Northern Goshawk. Whiskered Tern also breeds and the reeds are home to crakes, including Baillon's, and warblers including Cetti's and Savi's. Wood Lark nests on the heath and the woods have Grey-headed, Black and other woodpeckers. In autumn and winter the area is used by waterfowl including Smew and Ferruginous Duck, and Common Crane is regular.

The Sologne can be reached via the N20 south of Orleans, and at Nouan-le-Fuzelier head west on the D923 to St-Viatre.

30) Somme Estuary With a bird collection, information centre and picnic area close by, this is a reserve for all the family. On the northern coast of France, the area has marshes, saltings and extensive mudflats at low tide, and further inland are woods and farmland.

Waders are attracted here in large numbers on passage and in winter, and all of the regular northern European species can be seen. There are waterfowl including Dark-bellied Brent Goose on passage and wild swans and sawbills in winter. Divers, grebes and seaducks occur offshore. Eurasian Spoonbill and Purple Heron are regular on passage and Great Egret may occur in winter. Snow Bunting, Lapland Bunting and Shore Lark can be seen in autumn and winter on sandy shores, and Rough-legged Buzzard sometimes occurs in winter. In summer the beaches are invaded by hordes of holidaymakers but the reserve has Cattle Egret, Pied Avocet and Kentish Plover, sometimes Black-winged Stilt, and Bluethroat.

Baie de Somme reserve is a Ramsar site and situated on the north shore of the estuary adjacent to the Parc Ornithologique du Marquenterre. There is an area of sand dunes to the south at Le Crotoy with Crested Lark. The Somme Estuary is easily reached by road from the Channel ports, by following signs for the bird park from Abbeville.

31) Teich Bird Reserve The Bassin d'Arcachon is ornithologically one of the country's most important areas and the Parc Ornithologique du Teich one of the best birding localities in western France. The reserve consists of large expanses of shallow, brackish water, many of which are managed specifically for birds and have sluices to control water levels. About 80 species breed including herons and egrets, and this area is important as a migration stopover and wintering area. Around 280 species are recorded annually.

Black-crowned Night Heron, White Stork and Kentish Plover breed and raptors in summer include Black Kite and Short-toed Eagle. There are numerous passerines, most notably Bluethroat and Bearded Tit. Wintering waterfowl include large numbers of Dark-bellied Brent Goose as well as include Red-necked and Black-necked Grebes. Eurasian Spoonbill is regular in winter and on passage.

The Bassin d'Arcachon is on the Biscay coast of France and to reach Teich leave Bordeaux towards Bayonne on the A63, turning off at exit 22. There is a bird collection here, hence the small entrance fee, but follow the footpath to the Bassin d'Arcachon. The hedge-lined causeway has 11 hides and the reserve is open all year from 10.00 until 18.00, except July to August, when it stays open until 22.00.

32) Trunvel Nature Reserve The Baie d'Audierne is a site of international importance for breeding, passage and wintering birds, and the Étang de Trunvel lies at its centre. This reserve consists of a lake, marshes, lagoons and sand dunes with scrub and woodland nearby.

The extensive reedbeds support both bitterns, Purple Heron, Zitting Cisticola and Bearded Tit. Other breeders include Kentish Plover and Dartford Warbler. In autumn this is one of the most regular sites in France for Aquatic Warbler.

To reach Trunvel take the D785 south-west from Quimper and turn onto the D156 to Plonéour-Lanvern, heading towards Treguennec and park at Kermabec. Access to the reserve is limited but much can be seen from the perimeter.

33) Vanoise National Park France's first National Park, Vanoise covers a large and scenic area in the south-east of the country, sharing the border for a few kilometres with the Italian Gran Paradiso National Park. Lying between Little St Bernard Pass and Mont Cenis it contains some famous skiing resorts, such as Val d'Isere, but tourist development is largely confined to the peripheral zone, leaving the inner core relatively undisturbed.

Birds are typically mid- to high-altitude species including Golden Eagle, various grouse, Rock Partridge, and passerines such as Rock Thrush, Wallcreeper, both choughs and Snowfinch. Lammergeier has been reintroduced and breeding occurred in 1997. Short-toed Eagle is also present in small numbers and the forests have owls, such as Eagle, Eurasian Pygmy and Tengmalm's, Three-toed Woodpecker and Nutcracker. Corn Crake may still occur in summer.

The park has marked hiking trails from which virtually the whole area can be explored, there are also guided excursions and photo-safaris. The main information centre is at Lanslebourg-Mont Cenis and there are montane refuges in the inner zone and campsites in the outer zone.

Georgia

Although Armenia is now established on the birding scene, neighbouring Georgia has been largely neglected. The political situation seems stable at present, more so than in Azerbaijan, but visiting is still difficult. There is little tourist infrastructure, accommodation is almost non-existent away from the

capital and public transport is far from reliable. Regional specialities in Georgia include both snowcocks, Caucasian Black Grouse, Güldenstädt's Redstart and Great Rosefinch. Organised birding tours have recently recommenced after a gap of more than a decade and this is by far the best way to see Georgia's birds.

1) Iori Steppes Habitats in this large area, the driest part of Georgia, include semi-desert and steppe, scrubland and dry and riparian woodland, and a good selection of sought after birds breeds in the region.

Four species of vulture and White-tailed, Short-toed, Lesser Spotted and Eastern Imperial Eagles are among the raptors, together with very small numbers of Red-footed, Lanner and Saker Falcons. In addition, this is the best Georgian site for Chukar Partridge and the only one for Black Francolin. Other breeders include Black Stork, European Roller, Middle Spotted Woodpecker, White-throated Robin, Finsch's

Wheatear, Eastern Rock Nuthatch and Rose-coloured Starling. Little and Great Bustards occur on passage, as well as Common and Demoiselle Cranes, and Vashlovani is a good raptor migration watchpoint with more than 30 species regular.

This area lies in the far east of Georgia to the south-east of Tbilisi.

2) Javakheti Plateau This high plateau has numerous lakes, scrub-steppe and several dormant volcanoes with boulder-strewn slopes. The lakes attract a wide range of migrants and the area also supports some breeding birds of interest.

Caspian Snowcock, Montagu's Harrier and Golden Eagle breed, along with Radde's Accentor and Crimson-winged Finch, and waterbirds such as Little Bittern, Squacco Heron, Ferruginous Duck, Common Crane, Corn Crake and Kentish Plover. The area is of national importance for breeding White and Dalmatian Pelicans, White Stork, Velvet Scoter, Armenian Gull and Eurasian Eagle Owl. Passage birds include Pygmy Cormorant and Great and Little Bustards, waterfowl such as Lesser White-fronted Goose, Ruddy Shelduck, Marbled Duck and White-headed Duck, and waders including Black-winged Pratincole, Great Snipe, and Marsh and Terek Sandpipers.

The plateau lies south-west of Tbilisi and the most important lakes are Madatapa near Kalinino and Khanchalio near Ninotsminda.

3) Kolkheti A lowland area of farmland, woods and wetlands, Kolkheti is a proposed National Park and an important passage site for waterbirds and raptors.

Little Bittern, Black Stork, White-tailed Eagle and Corn Crake are among the breeders and passage and wintering birds include Black-throated Diver, grebes, Yelkouan Shearwater, storks, Lesser White-fronted and, occasionally, Red-breasted Geese, Long-tailed Duck, Velvet Scoter and Smew. The area is also good for passage raptors with kites, vultures and harriers, Levant Sparrowhawk, Long-legged and Rough-legged Buzzards, and Short-toed, Lesser and Greater Spotted, Steppe, Eastern Imperial and Booted Eagles.

The Kolkheti region is in south-west Georgia, on the Black Sea coast, and includes the lower Rioni River (north of Poti) and Lake Paliastomi.

4) Mount Kazbek (Kazbegi) This mountain, which reaches more than 5,000m, is situated in north-east Georgia, close to the border with Russia, and supports all the Caucasian specialities.

Both Caucasian Black Grouse and Caucasian Snowcock occur here, as well as the highly sought after Güldenstädt's Redstart, Red-fronted Serin and Great Rosefinch. Green Warbler and Caucasian Chiffchaff are also present. More widespread montane birds include Shore Lark and Alpine Accentor, Wallcreeper, both choughs, 'Caucasian' Twite and Snowfinch. The area is good for raptors with Lammergeier, Griffon and Black Vultures and Golden Eagle all present.

Mount Kazbek is three hours by road north of Tbilisi. The Georgian Military Highway bisects the Central Caucasus, and was built as a road-link between Russia and Tbilisi. The road passes through good deciduous woodland in the foothills, but after Pasanauri (where there is a good raptor look-out) the trees give way to the more barren scrub- and scree-covered slopes of the high Caucasus. The area around the Krestovyy Pass is one of the best places for the higher altitude species. Continuing north beyond the pass, the road eventually reaches Kazbegi where there is a modern hotel. Access to the higher slopes is relatively easy both east and west of the town, and it may be necessary to climb to the snowline for the principal specialities. Early morning is best for the snowcock.

Germany

Despite a good range of habitats and some excellent birds, few birders visit Germany. In the north-west the Wattenmeer is part of the most important intertidal area in Europe and the lakes of the north-east, formerly virtually off-limits to Western birders, hold many wetland birds. Inland there are large areas of forest and the south of the country borders the northern Alps, but many of the birds are more easily found in neighbouring countries, where organised tours and independent travellers have located established sites for the more difficult species. Germany undoubtedly has

similar sites, but they remain unknown to most birders outside the country, and the best-known birding site is probably the rarity 'hotspot' of Heligoland. With good roads, public transport and accommodation, Germany should perhaps have a higher profile and there is surely much to be discovered, particularly in the less-visited east.

1) Ammer Valley This area of south Bavaria offers relatively easy access to high-altitude and forest birds, and consists of coniferous and mixed forests on the slopes, and alpine meadows and rocky areas above the treeline.

In lower areas Tawny Pipit and Wryneck can be seen, with Western Bonelli's Warbler, Crested Tit and Nutcracker in the forests. Hazel and Black Grouse, and Capercaillie can also be found, as well Grey-headed, Black, Middle Spotted, White-backed and Three-toed Woodpeckers. Owls include Eagle, Eurasian Pygmy and Tengmalm's. Higher, there are Eurasian Crag Martin, Alpine Accentor, Alpine Chough and Wallcreeper. Raptors include Golden Eagle and Northern Goshawk.

Oberammergau makes an ideal base from which to explore the area and the Karwendel reserve holds most of the sought after species.

2) Bayerischer Wald National Park An undulating forested plateau forms most of this National Park and, with surrounding areas, is one of the largest wooded areas in central Europe. Forests are coniferous and mixed, and there are many wet valleys and bogs adding to the diversity. At higher levels there is bare moorland and there is a lake at the foot of Grosser Rachel, the park's highest peak at 1,453m.

Birdlife is rich and varied with typical forest birds such as Hazel and Black Grouse, and Capercaillie. Owls are represented by Tengmalm's, Eurasian Eagle and Eurasian Pygmy, and Ural Owl has been reintroduced. Woodpeckers include Black, Grey-headed, Three-toed and a few White-backed.

Access to the park is unrestricted and there is an information centre at Neuschönau. The park has marked footpaths, nature trails and refuges, and is reached from Grafenau, 50km north of Passau in south-east Germany.

3) Berchtesgaden National Park Situated in the far south-east of Germany and bordered on three sides by Austria, this area is famous for its superb mountain scenery. Popular with climbers and walkers in summer and skiers in winter, the park consists of four main massifs, of which the most impressive are Watzmann (2,713m) and Hochkalter (2,607m). These are separated by deep valleys, one of which contains the famous Königsee, a 200m-deep glacial lake.

Birdlife is typical of central European uplands with Golden Eagle, Ptarmigan, Eurasian Crag Martin, Alpine Accentor, both choughs, Wallcreeper and Snowfinch. Forests on the lower slopes have Black Grouse, Red-breasted Flycatcher, Nutcracker, Western Bonelli's Warbler and Citril Finch. Tengmalm's, Eurasian Eagle and Eurasian Pygmy Owls can be found by careful searching, and woodpeckers are common and include Black, Grey-headed, Three-toed and White-backed.

The park has marked trails and alpine huts (summer only), as well as information centres at Berchtesgaden and Königsee, and can be reached from Berchtesgaden, 18km south-east of Bad Reichenhall.

4) Dümmer This large shallow lake has extensive reedbeds and is surrounded by bog, open meadows and woodland.

Breeding birds have declined but may still include both bitterns and Spotted and Corn Crakes. An important site for wintering waterfowl with more than 20,000 birds present some years. Montagu's Harrier occurs in summer on Diepholzer Marshes to the north, which also attracts Common Crane on passage.

The lake is 45km north-east of Osnabruck and can be reached on Route 51, turning at Hude.

5) Federsee Nature Reserve A small lake with extensive marshland and reedbeds, over 100 species have bred and many others have been recorded in the area.

Among breeders are Black-necked Grebe, Purple Heron, both bitterns, White Stork and crakes. Raptors breeding in the area include Red Kite and the surrounding woodlands have Black Woodpecker and Black Grouse. Numerous wetland and woodland passerines breed including Bluethroat. Waders and waterfowl occur on passage.

The Federsee is in Baden-Württemberg in south-west Germany, near Reidlingen, to the east of Ulm. The reserve has boardwalks and boats for hire.

6) Heligoland Famous amongst birders for rarities and with a list of over 400 species, this is one of the top rarity spots in Europe. The site comprises two islands, Düne which is popular with tourists, and the larger Oberland, of greater interest to birders.

There is an observatory on Oberland and large numbers of migrants and a wide range of species occur. Among the many passerines are Thrush Nightingale, chats, redstarts and warblers. Autumn regularly produces Richard's Pipit, Yellow-browed and Barred Warblers, and Rustic and Little Buntings. Breeding seabirds include Common Guillemot and Razorbill.

Heligoland lies c.60km off the mainland and there are passenger boats from a number of ports, and also from the islands of Wangerooge to the south and Sylt to the north-east.

7) Kuhkopf There are many good birding areas in the Rhine Valley between Karlsruhe and Mainz, of which perhaps the best is the Kuhkopf reserve. More than 100 species have been recorded breeding on the oxbow lake and in the reedbeds, meadows and oak woodland around it.

Red-necked Grebe, Little Bittern and crakes can be seen in summer as well as Red and Black Kites and Northern Goshawk. Woodpeckers include Grey-headed, Black and Middle Spotted, and there are Bluethroat and Woodchat Shrike.

Take Route 44 to Stockstadt, then head west to Riedstadt-Erfelden and there is a bridge to the reserve.

8) Mecklenburg Lakes This area consists of numerous shallow lakes around the large Lake Müritz; many have reedbeds and are surrounded by mixed pine and beech forest, pasture and cultivated land. In some areas there are juniper heaths and dunes. The mix of habitats results in a diverse avifauna, of which c.150 species have bred.

Present in summer are Red-necked Grebe, both bitterns, both storks, and Red-crested Pochard. Raptors are much in evidence with breeding White-tailed Eagle, both kites, three harriers, Northern Goshawk and Lesser Spotted Eagle. Common Crane and Spotted Crake occur in summer, and the reeds have warblers including Savi's and River, as well as Penduline and Bearded Tits. The varied woodland birdlife includes Black and Middle Spotted Woodpeckers, Thrush Nightingale, Barred Warbler, Red-breasted Flycatcher and Common Rosefinch. The area is also important for an autumn gathering of Common Cranes and the arrival of thousands of wintering geese. Caspian Tern is regular at this season, Whooper and Bewick's Swans winter on the lakes and Rough-legged Buzzard hunts over the area.

Müritz National Park has its headquarters at Waren at the northern end of the lake and this town makes an excellent base to explore the area. Mecklenburg Lakes lie between the A19 Berlin-Rostock road and Route 96 between Berlin and Neubrandenburg. It is best reached from the A24, turning onto the A19 just west of Wittstock.

9) Oder Valley floodplain Between the Oder and a shipping canal on the Polish border is a floodplain with polders and reeds of immense importance to breeding wetland birds.

This is the stronghold of Corn Crake and Spotted and Little Crakes are also relatively common. Also breeding are Black-necked Grebe, both storks, both kites, Lesser Spotted Eagle, Common Crane, Bluethroat, Penduline Tit and Savi's, River, Aquatic and Barred Warblers. Common Crane also occurs on passage, along with tens of thousands of waterfowl including Bewick's and Whooper Swans, both forms of Bean Goose and Greater White-fronted Goose. Smew winters in numbers and Rough-legged Buzzard and White-tailed Eagle are regular. Both bitterns occur at nearby Felchowsee.

The town of Schwedt makes a good base for this area and is c.100km north-east of Berlin.

10) Rügen This Baltic island is joined to the mainland by a causeway and is very popular with tourists in summer. However, Rügen has excellent breeding birds, particularly in the west, with large numbers of Common Crane and geese in autumn. There are several nature reserves, as well as the Jasmund National Park on the east coast. The northern tip, Kap Arkona, is good for migrants.

Udarser Wiek is a traditional stopover for more than 25,000 Common Cranes in September to October, and also attracts waterfowl in good numbers. The Nonnensee, north-west of Bergen, is another excellent area with grebes and various waterfowl species. Red Kite is present and White-tailed Eagle, which breeds on neighbouring Usedom, can also be seen. A wide range of waders occurs, both as breeders and on passage, and seabirds include Caspian Tern, which breeds nearby. The 3,000ha

Jasmund National Park with its spectacular chalk cliffs lies north of Sassnitz and has breeding Thrush Nightingale, Red-breasted Flycatcher, Barred Warbler and Red-backed Shrike. Kap Arkona has breeding Common Rosefinch.

The island is reached via a causeway from Stralsund and the main centre is the town of Bergen.

11) Schweinfurt Parts of the valley of the Main are in a relatively natural state and, like some parts of the Rhine Valley, provide excellent birding. One of the best areas is around Schweinfurt, where there are oxbow lakes, reedbeds and wet woodland.

Both bitterns are present in summer as well as crakes and both kites. Woodpeckers include Grey-headed, Black and Middle Spotted, and there are Collared Flycatcher and Ortolan Bunting.

The best birding sites are the river at Volkach and the area around Dettelbach, and there is easy access from Frankfurt taking the E5 and leaving it at Würzburg.

12) Tiroler Achen Nature Reserve The large, deep Chiemsee, in south-east Bavaria, is fed by the River Ache, which flows from the Alps and enters its south-east corner. The silt deposited by the river has resulted in a delta, which is a designated nature reserve. There are many banks and shoals extending into the lake, reedbeds in the delta and the reserve also has wet meadows, riverine woodland and moorland, and is important both as a breeding and wintering area and as a stopover point during migration.

Breeding species of the delta include Black-necked Grebe, Great Bittern, Red-crested Pochard and Bluethroat, the woodlands have Black and Grey-headed Woodpeckers, and Black Grouse breeds on the moorland.

The Chiemsee lies south-east of Munich, just north of the Munich-Salzburg autobahn, c.10 km west of Traunstein.

13) Vessertal Biosphere Reserve A reserve on the wooded south slope of the Thüringer Wald, this area is important for forest birds with more than 90 species breeding.

Black Stork breeds in small numbers as well as Capercaillie and Black Grouse, Red and Black Kites, Northern Goshawk, Eurasian Pygmy and Tengmalm's Owls, and Black, Grey-headed and Middle Spotted Woodpeckers. Passerines include Red-breasted Flycatcher and Nutcracker.

Take Route 247 north from Schleusingen towards Suhl, turning east to Breitenbach after 2km. There is a trail beside the river from Breitenbach to the village of Vesser.

14) Wattenmeer This vast area forms the German sector of the Waddensee, one of Europe's most important natural habitats, which is shared with the Netherlands and Denmark. Schleswig-Holstein Wattenmeer National Park has coastal islands, vast mudflats and sandbanks, saltmarsh, wet coastal meadows and freshwater marshes. The entire area is of huge importance to the waterfowl and waders of Europe during the breeding season, on passage and in winter.

Breeders include Pied Avocet and Kentish Plover and terns including Gull-billed. A wide range of waterfowl and waders occurs on passage and in winter, with hundreds of thousands of birds often present. More than 100,000 Barnacle and Dark-bellied Brent Geese are recorded on passage, along with similar numbers of various ducks. Katinger Watt is important for passage Lesser White-fronted Goose.

This vast area extends from Denmark to the Netherlands and can be viewed from many points along the German coast.

Gibraltar

Famous as a migration watchpoint, the Rock of Gibraltar rises to more than 420m, with sheer cliffs on the north and east, and gentler slopes on the west side. Much of the area is scrub-covered with open grassy areas where open-country birds occur. Although lower parts of the Rock are now largely developed, the whole of the Upper Rock is a nature reserve.

More than 250,000 raptors of up to 17 species cross the sea to and from Gibraltar to North Africa, just 25km away. Black Kite and Western Honey-buzzard are the most numerous species, but Short-toed and Booted Eagles, Egyptian Vultures, *Accipiter* species and harriers are also common. Many other species also use this route including storks and Common Crane, as well as numerous passerines including 30 species of warbler. At sea shearwaters, gulls, terns and skuas occur. Breeders are few but include Barbary Partridge at its only mainland European locality. One of the best areas for raptors in spring is Jew's Gate, just beyond the entrance to the Upper Rock Nature Reserve, where there is a bird observatory and information centre. In autumn the Upper Galleries and Princess Caroline's Battery, to the north, are more productive but passerine migrants can appear in any well vegetated area. Barbary Partridges can usually be seen from the Mediterranean steps, a footpath on the east side of the Rock. Alameda Botanic Gardens often attract passage and wintering passerines, especially warblers, as does the cemetery in the north. Europa Point, at the southern tip, is an excellent seawatching site at any season and has Pallid Swift in summer and Eurasian Crag Martin in winter.

The best times are March to May and August to October, although there is some passage across the strait at other times. Passerine migration is more prolonged, generally February to May and late July to November, and seabirds pass offshore year-round. Periods of west winds are best for watching raptor migration.

Great Britain (England, Wales and Scotland)

The birds of Great Britain are probably the best watched of any Western Palearctic country and the outlying islands of Shetland in the north and Scilly in the south-west have hosted some of the region's rarest avian visitors. Although some areas are important for waterfowl and waders on passage and in winter, it is seabird colonies for which Great Britain is most famous. These lie mainly on remote northern and western coasts but virtually all are easy to reach. Forest birds cannot compare to those of continental Europe but the mountains and coniferous forests of Scotland hold some interesting birds including Great Britain's only endemic species, Scottish Crossbill, and Red Grouse, which is currently considered a race of Willow Grouse. The RSPB manages a superb network of reserves throughout Great Britain, which cover a wide variety of habitats, and many have excellent viewing facilities.

1) Anglesey One of the most popular areas for birding in Wales, the island of Anglesey has a wide range of habitats and attracts a variety of species. As well as many fresh waters, there are dramatic sea cliffs, rocky shores and muddy estuaries, heaths, farmland and coniferous and deciduous woodlands. In addition to breeding birds the island attracts a variety of passerine migrants, and recent rarities have included Grey Catbird and Black Lark.

Situated on Holy Island, the westernmost headland of Anglesey is **South Stack Cliffs RSPB Reserve** with eroded sea-cliffs topped with maritime heath. Red-billed Chough breeds here alongside Common Guillemot, Razorbill and Puffin. It is also an excellent migration watchpoint, with divers in spring and skuas, shearwaters and storm-petrels in autumn, and this is the one of the best sites in Wales for Sabine's Gull. The reserve is signposted from **Holyhead**, where wintering Black-throated Diver and Black Guillemot often occur in the harbour. Black Guillemot is rare in Wales and breeding is confined to a few pairs at **Fedw Fawr** on the Penmon Peninsula in easternmost Anglesey. Other seabirds breed on the cliffs of the peninsula and Puffin on nearby Puffin Island.

The **Valley Lakes RSPB Reserve** in west Anglesey has regular Great Bittern in winter and a variety of breeding and wintering waterfowl. The largest waterbody on the island, **Llyn Alaw Reservoir,** also attracts waterfowl in numbers in winter, and waders in autumn if water levels are low. **Llyn Cefni** is another reservoir with wintering water-fowl and is a regular site for both wild swans. **Cemlyn Bay** on the north coast has breeding terns with Roseate often present, and a variety of waders occurs in autumn. To the east is **Point Lynas**, the best seawatching point on Anglesey in autumn with large numbers of divers, shearwaters, skuas and auks.

Newborough Warren in south-west Anglesey is one of the finest examples of a sand-dune system in Great Britain and a large area has been planted with Corsican Pine. Nearby is Malltraeth Pool, a good passage wader spot, and the rocky headland of Ynys Llanddwyn, where Purple Sandpiper winters. Roseate Tern can be seen in this area in summer, with divers, grebes and waterfowl in winter.

2) Breckland Also known as the Brecks, this area in the interior of East Anglia, centred on Thetford, covers a large area, roughly from Swaffham in Norfolk south to Bury St Edmunds in Suffolk. Breckland was for centuries a vast plain of heath, grassland and wind-blown sand, but although most has now been lost to development, agriculture and forestation there still remain small patches of open sandy heath, protected as nature reserves.

Stone-curlew is the characteristic Breckland bird and this is still one of the species' strongholds in Great Britain. Wood Lark and European Nightjar are two heathland specialities that are scarce in Great Britain but linger on in Breckland, and this area is also home to other sought after birds in Great Britain such as Western Honey-buzzard, Northern Goshawk and Golden Oriole. There is also a small population of introduced Golden Pheasant in the area and these are sometimes seen on quiet forest rides.

The reserve at **East Wretham** is one of the most interesting for birders with a range of habitats and all the characteristic Breckland birds are found here. Hawfinch is regularly seen in the hornbeams and the conifers have Long-eared Owl and Crossbill. **Weeting Heath** is a National Nature Reserve, and entry is by permit only (obtainable on site). This is undoubtedly the best site in Great Britain for Stone-curlew, which can be seen from well-placed hides without causing disturbance, and is most easily seen early in the season before mid-May. Another reserve with a good range of habitats including heath, bog and woodland is at **Cavenham Heath**, where European Nightjar, Wood Lark, Grasshopper Warbler and Hawfinch breed. One of the best sites for some of Breckland's special birds is the raptor viewpoint at **Mayday Farm**, south of Brandon. Northern Goshawk can be seen from a clearing in the woods and this is one of the best sites in the country for Golden Pheasant, European Nightjar and Wood Lark. Early spring is the best time to see both Northern Goshawk and Golden Pheasant. The 6km **Thetford Forest Bird Trail** accesses a range of wooded and more open habitats, and also has Golden Pheasant, European Nightjar and Wood Lark. The trail begins south of the village of Santon Downham.

Many of the lay-bys and picnic areas on the roads through Breckland give access to good birding habitats and those on the A134 are particularly good.

3) Cairngorms and Speyside The Cairngorms form Great Britain's highest mountain plateau and include the largest nature reserve in the country covering more than 250km^2 of forest and moorland, high mountains, bogs, rivers and lochs.

Birds of the higher parts of the reserve include Golden Eagle, Red Grouse, Ptarmigan, Dotterel, Ring Ouzel and Snow Bunting. In some years a Snowy Owl summers on these high summits. Lower down, **Rothiemurchus** and **Abernethy Forests** are remnants of ancient Caledonian pine forest, which once covered most of the country. The bird specialities of these forests include Scottish Crossbill and Crested Tit, Capercaillie and Black Grouse. **Loch Garten** is famous as the site where Ospreys commenced their recolonisation of Great Britain during the 1950s and the birds can be seen from a well-equipped observation hide.

Aviemore makes an ideal base from which to explore this area, with Abernethy and Loch Garten reached on the B970 to the east. The Cairngorms National Nature Reserve is *c.*10km south-east of Aviemore and is best visited April to August; some areas have restricted access during the deer cull in August to October. There is a visitor centre at Loch an Eilean off the B970 between Inverdruie and Polchar. A 5km nature trail follows the loch side and leads through a selection of habitat types. Visitors planning to wander away from main hiking routes in the higher areas should be prepared for sudden changes of weather.

4) Dungeness This large peninsula on the south-east coast of England was formed by longshore drift and is the largest such structure in Europe. Much of the habitat is open shingle, giving the area an almost desert-like appearance, but some areas have a unique lichen heath community, whilst others have scattered patches of gorse, broom and brambles. Gravel extraction has resulted in many flooded pits with islands providing further habitats.

Dungeness has more than 60 species of breeding bird and over 300 species have been recorded in total. Jutting into the sea on the south coast of England, this is one of the country's finest sites for migrants and passage periods bring thousands of passerines, which are often grounded in bad weather. The bird observatory, between the reserve and the point, attracts many scarce migrants, with Golden Oriole, Hoopoe, Serin and Wryneck recorded annually. There are two rarities for which Dungeness is undoubtedly Great Britain's best site, Penduline Tit and Short-toed Treecreeper. Great Britain's first Audouin's Gull was recorded recently.

Great Cormorant breeds on the islands, with Great Crested and Little Grebes on the pits and other grebes regular in winter. Amongst the commoner gulls Mediterranean is present all year and sometimes breeds, Glaucous Gull is regular on the beach, usually near the fishing boats and occasionally on the reserve, and Yellow-legged and Caspian Gulls are also now regular. All of the commoner terns occur as well as regular Roseate on passage. Ducks winter in large numbers and this is probably Great Britain's best site for Smew, with Red-crested Pochard virtually annual. Bewick's Swan winters on the surrounding farmland, sometimes roosting on the pits, as do Greater White-fronted Geese, and Great Bittern is increasing as a winter visitor.

Off the tip of the peninsula a warm-water outflow from the power station attracts gulls and terns in their hundreds, which in turn attract skuas during passage periods. Many other species can be seen off the point where a hide is situated. Divers, auks, waterfowl and waders can all be seen moving past in spring and autumn.

Dungeness is situated on the south coast of Kent between Hythe and Rye and is reached 3km south of Lydd on the Lydd-Dungeness road. For the RSPB reserve turn off this road at Boulderwall Farm, the observatory is nearer the point, for which turn left by the old lighthouse.

5) Flamborough Head The cliffs at Bempton have long been famous as the site of the only gannetry in mainland Great Britain, but there are also breeding Common Guillemot, Razorbill and Puffin. The cliffs lie on the north coast of the 10km headland, which culminates at Flamborough Head, famous for migrants and rarer passerines in particular. The peninsula is mainly farmland with hedgerows and small woodland patches, grassland and scrub, and is fringed by 75m chalk cliffs. On the south side is South Landing, a densely wooded valley highly attractive to migrants.

It is passage periods that bring birders to Flamborough Head in large numbers. In spring terns pass the head, followed by skuas, including Pomarine and Long-tailed, and all four divers are possible. Easterly winds produce the best results in spring. Autumn passage movements are apparent from late July, but it is August to September during north-west winds that the largest numbers and variety of birds can be seen. Shearwaters include Manx, Balearic and Sooty, sometimes Great and Cory's, and even Little has been recorded. This is undoubtedly one of the best sites in Great Britain for Little Auk, which occurs in thousands after strong northerly gales. Migrant passerines can be abundant and lesser rarities such as Richard's, Tawny and Red-throated Pipits, Bluethroat, Yellow-browed, Barred and other warblers, and Red-breasted Flycatcher are regular, with several true rarities recorded annually.

There is an RSPB reserve at Bempton Cliffs with an information centre and an observation point on the clifftop path. Boat trips to view the cliffs from the sea can be arranged in Bridlington and pelagic trips are also available. Flamborough Head can be reached by road from Bridlington to the south.

6) Islay Although famous for its wintering geese, the Scottish island of Islay has a variety of habitats attracting a wide range of birds year-round. There are extensive moorlands, numerous lochs and smaller lochans dot the landscape, and the north-west peninsula known as the Rhinns is almost separated from the rest of the island by two large sea-lochs, Gruinart in the north and Indaal in the south. In the far south-west of Islay are the spectacular cliffs of The Oa. Most of the island is lowland pasture and moorland but there are also peat bogs and areas of conifer plantations, scrub and mixed woodland.

Up to 20,000 Barnacle Geese winter on Islay, along with Greenland White-fronted Goose and Whooper Swan. Pink-footed and Pale-bellied Brent Geese occur on passage, and divers, grebes and seaduck can be seen on the sea-lochs in winter.

Breeding birds of interest include Golden Eagle, Red and Black Grouse, and Corn Crake, and the cliffs hold breeding Rock Pipit and Red-billed Chough. Breeding seabirds include Razorbill and Common and Black Guillemots.

Loch Gruinart RSPB Reserve in the north-west of Islay is often the best site to view the geese. The westernmost point of the island, Rubha na Faing, on the south-west of the Rhinns is good for seawatching, and Manx and Sooty Shearwaters, European Storm-petrel, divers, grebes and skuas are regular. Glaucous and Iceland Gulls are both regular on Islay, particularly on Loch Indaal and sometimes in Port Ellen harbour.

Accommodation is plentiful and varied, and there is a twice-daily (once on Sundays) ferry service from Kennacraig, 11km west of Tarbert. Alternatively, there are flights from Glasgow.

7) Minsmere One of the RSPB's most famous and popular reserves, Minsmere is also one of the most interesting in terms of the number of species to be seen. The large number of breeders reflects the diversity of habitats that comprise this reserve on the Suffolk coast. As well as lagoons with islands, dunes, beaches and saltmarsh, there are freshwater wetlands with reedbeds, and areas of deciduous woodland, heath and farmland. The various habitats are carefully managed to provide optimum conditions for breeding and visiting birds and disturbance from the public is kept to a minimum.

Over 300 species have been recorded on the reserve, 200 of these annually and c.100 breed, with Great Bittern, Pied Avocet and terns the specialities. Garganey is often present in summer as well as Cetti's and other warblers in the wetland areas. Savi's Warbler was once regular here but has declined, as elsewhere in Great Britain, and is now very rare. Other inhabitants of the reedbeds include Marsh Harrier and Bearded Tit. The woodlands have Tawny Owl and all three British woodpeckers, and European Nightjar and Wood Lark breed on the heathland.

Birders are attracted to Minsmere to see rare visitors such as Purple Heron, Eurasian Spoonbill and Spotted Crake, which turn up regularly, but major rarities also occur with some frequency, including Alpine Accentor and Black Kite in recent years. More than 20 species of wader can be seen in a day in late summer at Minsmere, often including Temminck's Stint in autumn, with Jack Snipe regular in winter.

The reserve is open daily except Tuesdays and is signposted from the village of Westleton in Suffolk.

8) North Norfolk Coast Probably the best birding area in mainland Great Britain, the coast of north Norfolk from the Wash to the Cley-Salthouse area has long been among the most popular destinations for British birders. There are several excellent reserves along this coast and its easterly position makes it ideal for those in search of scarce migrants. The sheer variety of birds to be found in this area is astounding and more than 320 species have been recorded. The Wash is of international importance for passage and wintering waders and waterfowl, and more than 300,000 birds can gather in winter. Divers, grebes and seaducks winter off this coast and scarce waders, raptors and seabirds occur throughout the area on passage, as well as a wide variety of passerines.

Snettisham is an RSPB reserve on the Wash with extensive mudflats and gravel pits that attract Bewick's and Whooper Swans, Pink-footed and Dark-bellied Brent Geese in winter. Shore Lark, Twite and Snow and Lapland Buntings occur here and elsewhere on this coast in winter, and this is possibly *the* mainland site for all four species. To the north is **Holme**, where there are pools, saltmarsh and pinewoods as well as a bird observatory, visitor centre and hides. A regular site for scarce migrants such as Wryneck, Bluethroat and warblers including Icterine, Barred and Yellow-browed, this area also attracts major rarities. Pied Avocet breeds, but there is little else to see in summer. Further east is **Titchwell RSPB Reserve** with hides and a visitor centre. Great Bittern and Bearded Tit are present throughout the year and Marsh Harrier and Pied Avocet in summer. Eurasian Spoonbill is a regular visitor and this is one of the best sites in Great Britain for passage Montagu's Harrier. Jack Snipe occurs in winter and divers, grebes and Long-tailed Duck can be seen offshore. The **Holkham and Wells** area further east is famous for autumn migrants with all the common and scarcer species to be seen, and rare warblers frequently turn up in the Corsican Pines here. Great Britain's first recorded breeding of Parrot Crossbill occurred here in 1984. The large areas of coastal marshland attract winter swans, geese and a variety of waders. Nearby **Blakeney Point** with its large tern colonies can be reached by boat in summer but birders often prefer to walk the 5km shingle bank from Cley. In autumn this can produce excellent seawatching and large numbers of passerine migrants. The **Cley-Salthouse** area has long been a 'Mecca' for British birders and boasts possibly the longest species list of any mainland site. It remains popular and at times can be too crowded with birders for some visitors. However, the large number of watchers means very few interesting birds are missed, and the area has a well-deserved reputation for producing rarities. Habitats include shingle beach and freshwater marshes, reed-fringed pools and wader scrapes, and hides overlook many of the best areas.

Although perhaps best known for rarities and waders in particular, this area also has a good range of regular summer visitors including Pied Avocet, Black-tailed Godwit and Ruff. The reedbeds provide nesting sites for Marsh Harrier, Bearded Tit and Cetti's Warbler, but Savi's Warbler, which was once regular here in summer, is now only a rare visitor. Great Bittern is often present and has recently bred, and Eurasian Spoonbill is often present in spring and summer. A wide range of passage waders occurs, regularly including scarcer species such as Dotterel, Temminck's Stint and Red-necked Phalarope. Montagu's Harrier is a rare but regular migrant. Offshore in autumn skuas can be seen including annual Long-tailed, in addition to Manx Shearwater and Leach's Storm-petrel. In late autumn auks including Little can be seen over the sea, and in winter Glaucous and Iceland Gulls and Black-throated and Great Northern Divers occur. Snow and Lapland Buntings, Shore Lark and Twite frequent the beaches from October.

The entire north Norfolk coast has become fully geared-up for birding visitors and accommodation is plentiful in local villages.

9) Orkney Islands Though less well known as a birding destination than the Shetlands, these green and fertile islands are home to large seabird colonies and attract large numbers of migrants including many rarities. Much of the land is used for raising cattle but there are also cultivated areas and moors, marshes, bogs, lochans and streams, and some islands have dramatic cliffs.

The largest island is Mainland, which boasts extensive tracts of moorland with important breeding populations of Hen Harrier and Short-eared Owl. One of the best areas to see these species is at **Birsay and Cottascarth RSPB Reserve**, where Great and Arctic Skuas, various waders and ducks, and Twite also breed, and Greenland White-fronted Goose occurs in winter. **Hobbister RSPB Reserve** further south has similar moorland breeders, with Black Guillemot on nearby cliffs. In north-west Mainland are two further RSPB reserves; **The Loons**, a marshland with several breeding duck species and wintering Greenland White-fronts, and **Marwick Head** where the thousands of breeding seabirds include Common Guillemot, Razorbill and Puffin. **Loch of Stenness** holds wintering Slavonian Grebe, Whooper Swan and Long-tailed Duck amongst its hundreds of waterfowl, and the seas around Orkney, particularly **Scapa Flow**, are important for Great Northern and Black-throated Divers, grebes and various seaducks. The harbours at Kirkwall and Stromness have regular Glaucous and Iceland Gulls.

The small island of **Copinsay**, to the east of Mainland, is another RSPB reserve and has breeding auks. The island has a good reputation for passerine migrants with regular Bluethroat and Barred Warbler, and can be visited on a day-trip from Mainland.

Hoy is the most rugged of the Orkneys and an RSPB reserve covers a large area of moorland in the north of the island and the world-famous rock stack, The Old Man of Hoy. Great and Arctic Skuas, auks, Manx Shearwater and possibly European Storm-petrel breed, as well as Red Grouse, Rock Pipit and Twite. Barnacle Goose winters in the south of the island. Hoy can be reached by ferry from Mainland.

North of Mainland is **Westray** where one of the most spectacular seabird colonies in Great Britain can be seen at Noup Head. More than 50,000 Common Guillemots can be found on these cliffs as well as thousands of other birds including Razorbill, Black Guillemot and Puffin. The island is also good for passerine migrants during spring and autumn. Westray can be reached by ferry from Mainland.

North Ronaldsay is the northeasternmost of the group and therefore often the best island for migrants, with many scarce passerines and rarities possible. Seawatching can also be excellent with Sooty Shearwater, Leach's Storm-petrel, Long-tailed Skua and Sabine's Gull all recorded.

Papa Westray is the northwesternmost of the islands and also produces excellent seawatching, and there is an RSPB reserve at North Hill. This area consists of maritime heath, a rare habitat confined largely to the Orkneys. Arctic Terns breed here in large numbers and the island has breeding auks and other seabirds.

Corn Crake was until recently a rare breeder on some of the Orkneys, notably Mainland, Copinsay, Westray, Papa Westray and Stronsay. The species has since declined but although breeding may no longer take place the birds still occur.

There are regular ferries from Scrabster to Stromness, and the islands can also be reached by air from Glasgow, Aberdeen or Inverness.

10) Outer Hebrides These islands are the stronghold of the declining British population of Corn Crake and hold some of the highest densities of breeding waders in Europe. One of the most important habitats is the machair, low-lying, flower-rich grassland growing on soil comprising peat and wind-blown sand. Other habitats include upland moor and blanket bog, marshland and lochans, farmland and hay-fields. The coasts have wide sandy beaches backed by dunes in the west and rocky shores with deep marine inlets in the E.

North Uist has many breeding waders but the most important bird is the Corn Crake, which survives due to the traditional farming methods employed here. Whooper Swan is often present in summer, Black-throated Diver breeds as do Red Grouse and Arctic Skua on the moors and Black Guillemot on rocky headlands. Raptors present include Hen Harrier, Golden Eagle and Peregrine Falcon, and passerine breeders include Rock Pipit and Twite. Also important for passage and wintering birds, the island attracts waterfowl such as Pink-footed, Greenland White-fronted and Barnacle Geese, ducks including scoters and Long-tailed, and various waders. Offshore, passage divers are regular, as well as shearwaters, storm-petrels and skuas, and this is one of the best sites in Great Britain for Long-tailed Skua. **Balranald RSPB Reserve** in the north-west of the island is one of the most important areas for birds and where a sighting of a Corn Crake is most likely.

South Uist has similar habitats and species, with excellent seawatching and the freshwater wetlands and sea lochs host important numbers of breeding, wintering and passage waterfowl. **Loch Druidbeg National Nature Reserve** is one of the best areas for breeding waterfowl, with Great Britain's largest surviving colony of native Greylag Goose. Corn Crake also breeds on South Uist as well as Golden Eagle, and White-tailed Eagle is occasionally seen on the east coast, with birds wandering from the reintroduced population on Rhum. **Ardivachar Point** in the north-west and Rubha Ardvule on the west coast are excellent for seawatching, with Grey Phalarope regularly seen. Harbours in the Outer Hebrides often hold Glaucous and Iceland Gulls in winter.

The smaller island of **Benbecula** lies between North and South Uist and has similar habitats. Large numbers of waders can be seen from the north causeway.

Ferries sail to North Uist from Uig on Skye or Tarbert on Lewis, and also to Lochboisdale on South Uist from Oban or Mallaig on the mainland. The three main islands of the southern Outer Hebrides, North Uist, Benbecula and South Uist, are linked by causeways. Accommodation is plentiful on these islands.

11) Pembrokeshire Islands It is the breeding seabirds that draw most visitors to this group of islands off the south-west tip of Wales, and so most make the trip in summer. However, in spring and autumn, migrants occur in large numbers and a wide variety of species can be seen. Divers, skuas and shearwaters occur at sea, a range of waterfowl and waders passes through, and passerines include most of the commoner species plus regular appearances of scarcer migrants and the occasional rarity.

Skomer is the largest island and being closest to the mainland is the most accessible. Breeding seabirds include more than 150,000 pairs of Manx Shearwater and 1,000 pairs of European Storm-petrel, plus Common Guillemot, Razorbill and Puffin. Red-billed Chough and Rock Pipit also breed on the cliffs. The island can be visited from April to mid September by boat from Martins Haven and an overnight stay guarantees seeing the nocturnal shearwaters and petrels. There is limited self-catering accommodation.

The site of Great Britain's first bird observatory, **Skokholm** is considerably smaller than Skomer and has lower sandstone cliffs and less cover. However, the island has many of the same breeding birds as Skomer, with over 40,000 pairs of Manx Shearwater and 6,000 pairs of European Storm-petrel, as well as auks. Skokholm is open to visitors April to October and there is full-board accommodation available, alternatively day-visits can be made June to late August.

Smaller still is **Ramsey** to the N, which is an RSPB reserve famous for its breeding Red-billed Chough, although seabirds are fewer than on the larger islands. Ramsey can be visited by the public between Easter and late October by boat from St Justinians.

Smallest and most remote of the islands is **Grassholm**, another RSPB reserve, which has one of the largest gannetries in the world. Common Guillemot and Razorbill also breed, and Puffin and Manx Shearwater are present offshore. Landing on Grassholm is possible only in calm weather but boat trips around the island are available from April from Martins Haven.

12) Portland Almost an island, Portland is linked to mainland Dorset by the long strip of shingle known as Chesil Beach. The limestone massif of Portland reaches almost 10 km into the Channel and the entire area is excellent for migrants. The north of the island has cliffs and there are disused quarries scattered here and there. The most important areas for birders are Chesil Beach and the Fleet, Verne Common, overlooking Portland Harbour in the N, and the southern, flatter part of the island, especially the tip, Portland Bill. The south of the island is open farmland with small patches of cover, and the observatory is located in an old lighthouse near the point. As well as the migration of passerines and other landbirds, Portland is ideally placed for seawatching and, together with the shore and fresh waters of the Fleet, the range of habitats makes the Portland area one of the most outstanding birding sites on the English south coast.

Breeding and wintering birds are scarce on Portland, but during passage periods the island can attract large numbers of a wide variety of migrants including all the commoner passerines as well as a host of scarcer species. Regular are Hoopoe, Golden Oriole, Woodchat Shrike, European Serin and Ortolan Bunting, and species such as Wryneck, Bluethroat, Richard's and Tawny Pipits, Melodious, Icterine and other warblers, Red-breasted Flycatcher, and Ortolan and Lapland Buntings also occur.

Spring passage begins as early as mid March and continues until early June, with a peak in numbers and variety in late April to early May. Offshore movements can be witnessed from mid March with divers and auks, joined in April to early May by shear-waters, waders, gulls, terns and skuas. Portland Harbour is a winter haunt of all three regular British divers, the scarcer grebes and various seaducks. The northern part is best viewed from Sandsfoot Castle in Weymouth and the western from Ferry Bridge. Autumn passage can occur as early as July, with rarer species peaking in September to early October.

Breeders include Common Guillemot on the West Cliffs along with Razorbill and Puffin, and Peregrine Falcon and Rock Pipit are present all year. In winter there is a regular flock of Purple Sandpiper at Portland Bill.

Like other observatories, Portland has had its share of rarities with records of southern species such Alpine Swift, European Bee-eater, Red-rumped Swallow and Subalpine Warbler, in spring, and more easterly birds such as Calandra Lark, Pechora and Olive-backed Pipits, Greenish and Dusky Warblers, and Pine and Yellow-breasted Buntings, in autumn. Vagrants from North America, such as Yellow-billed Cuckoo, Northern Parula and Savannah Sparrow, have also occurred at Portland.

The brackish lagoon behind the shingle ridge of Chesil Beach is known as **The Fleet** and attracts waterfowl and waders. Dark-bellied Brent can reach 1,000 and Smew and Great Bittern occur in hard winters. Such weather also brings occasional groups of Whooper and Bewick's Swans, and Greater White-fronted Goose. This is one of the best British sites for Kentish Plover, which is annual in spring. Other possible passage species include Eurasian Spoonbill and Roseate Tern. Cetti's Warbler and Bearded Tit occur in the Fleet's reedbeds, mainly in winter, and this may be a regular autumn site for Aquatic Warbler.

The Isle of Portland lies south of Weymouth and most of the area is of open access. A visit to the observatory is essential for the keen birder but ask permission before entering the grounds. The observatory is open March to November and can provide basic accommodation.

13) Rhum Off the west coast of Scotland the island of Rhum is a National Nature Reserve and famous for its well-studied population of Red Deer. Rhum has also been the site of the White-tailed Eagle reintroduction programme, which has led to the successful re-establishment of this species in Great Britain. The island is mountainous with habitats including rocky coasts and cliffs, streams, lochs and bogs, rough grass-land and heather moorland, and small patches of woodland.

Reintroduction of White-tailed Eagle was first attempted in the 1960s, on Fair Isle, but this was ultimately unsuccessful so a new programme was launched on Rhum in the mid 1970s. Whilst many of the young eaglets imported from Norway wandered widely over Scotland, some remained and breeding was first attempted in 1983, the first chick reared in 1985 and the first successful fledging from a British-raised pair occurred in 1996. Although a sighting of White-tailed Eagle cannot be guaranteed, a visit to Rhum certainly provides the best chance of seeing the species in Great Britain.

Golden Eagle is also present in small numbers and the island is also the site of one of Great Britain's largest Manx Shearwater colonies, numbering more than 100,000 pairs and located on Askival, the island's highest hill. Other breeders include Common and Black Guillemots, Razorbill, Puffin and Northern Fulmar, with Red Grouse and Twite on the moorland.

The island can be reached by ferry from Mallaig, those visiting for the day land at Loch Scresort and can freely explore the area around the south side of the loch. Venturing beyond this area or staying overnight requires permission from the warden.

14) St Ives Bay and the Hayle Estuary St Ives is one of the best seawatching points on the British mainland and in the correct weather conditions huge numbers of divers, seabirds and waterfowl are recorded every year, as well as rarities on a regular basis. This large bay on the north coast of Cornwall has sandy beaches, backed by dunes and has rocky headlands at either end. The eastern point is known as the 'island' and this is where most seawatching takes place. The Hayle Estuary lies on the bay and is an important habitat for waders and waterfowl on passage and in winter.

Great Northern and Black-throated Divers are present in winter and occur on passage, Slavonian Grebe is also regular, with occasional Red-necked and Black-necked Grebes. Purple Sandpiper and Rock Pipit occur along the rocky beaches in winter and Water Pipit may winter on Copperhouse Creek.

Spring brings a wider range of species and an increase in gulls brings one or two Glaucous and Mediterranean Gulls to the bay, and Balearic Shearwater regularly appears amongst the Manx flocks. In autumn numbers and variety of birds is greater still. As well as Manx Shearwater there are small numbers of Cory's and Sooty, and European and Leach's Storm-petrels are both likely. Roseate Tern is regular in small numbers and the tern flocks attract skuas in some numbers, with Arctic and Great sometimes numbering 100 per day, Pomarine is seen daily in small numbers, Long-tailed recorded annually and even South Polar Skua has been reported. Gulls at this time include Sabine's, and this is the premier British site for this species and Grey Phalarope. In late autumn auks move past in large numbers, with a few Little Auks in early winter. Much depends on the weather and the area is most productive during northwesterly to northerly winds, following strong southwesterlies associated with an Atlantic depression. However, these are perfect conditions and under some other circumstances there may be very little to see.

The Hayle Estuary is joined from the west by Copperhouse Creek and lies adjacent to an artificial tidal area, the Carnsew Pool. Gulls form an important part of the birdlife here and the area has a good record for attracting rarer species: Glaucous, Iceland and Mediterranean are all fairly regular, and Ring-billed is virtually a permanent resident.

The entire area has a reputation for rarities, and vagrant seabirds, waterfowl and waders are recorded annually. St Ives has produced Black-browed Albatross, Little Shearwater, Wilson's Storm-petrel, Laughing Gull and Bridled Tern, whilst the Hayle Estuary has attracted Black-winged Stilt, Broad-billed Sandpiper and a variety of transatlantic waders. Green-winged Teal and American Wigeon are now regular here, with more than 20 of the latter recorded in some winters.

The 'island' lies north of the town of St Ives in the east of the bay, and the coastguard lookout is the most popular watching point. The Hayle Estuary is just west of the town of Hayle and there is a hide at the head of the estuary. Carnsew Pool and Copperhouse Creek are just north of the town centre and can be viewed from adjacent footpaths.

15) Scilly Every October hundreds of Great Britain's keenest birders descend on this group of islands, scouring them for rare birds, some of which are among the rarest visitors to Europe. The group consists of five inhabited islands and scores of other islets and rocks and lies c.45km south-west of Cornwall. Habitats include farmland and woods, marshes, pools and dunes, cliffs and sandy and rocky beaches.

The main interest is transatlantic vagrants with species such as Red-eyed Vireo and Grey-cheeked Thrush virtually annual, and North American warblers have included Blackpoll, Black-and-white, Magnolia, Yellow-rumped and Hooded, as well as Northern Waterthrush, Northern Parula and Common Yellowthroat. The first British records of Tree and Cliff Swallows have occurred in recent years and undoubtedly there will be other British firsts in the future. Such is the expertise of the many searchers that few rarities go unnoticed on these islands in autumn. There are also waders to be found, with Buff-breasted and Pectoral Sandpipers and American Golden Plover annual. Other transatlantic visitors have included American Black Duck, Common Nighthawk, Black-billed and Yellow-billed Cuckoos, and Chimney Swift.

There are also vagrants from northern Europe and Siberia such as Richard's, Red-throated and Olive-backed Pipits, Radde's and Dusky Warblers, Red-breasted Flycatcher, Bluethroat, and Ortolan, Little and Rustic Buntings. Rose-coloured Starling, Icterine and Melodious Warblers are regular in early autumn. In all, more than 50 rare and sought-after birds appear on the islands each year along with many other scarce and uncommon visitors.

Seawatching in autumn can produce Manx, Great and Sooty Shearwaters, possibly also Cory's, four species of skua, and sometimes Grey Phalarope and Sabine's Gull. These birds can also be seen during the crossing to the islands, and now popular are pelagic trips from Scilly, with target species such as Wilson's Storm-petrel guaranteed and the possibility of such rarities as Black-browed Albatross, Fea's Petrel, Red-billed Tropicbird or Brown and South Polar Skuas.

Fewer birders visit the islands in spring but in addition to the commoner migrants species such as Hoopoe and Golden Oriole, Woodchat Shrike, Mediterranean warblers and rare herons can be expected. With many of the mainland's commoner woodland birds absent, breeding birds can seem sparse in summer. However, the seabird colonies make up for this shortfall with greater numbers and variety than elsewhere in south-west England. Breeders include Manx Shearwater and European Storm-petrel, Razorbill, Puffin and Common Guillemot, and the rare Roseate Tern is usually seen in summer. Winter birders are very few but those that do make the trip can see Great Northern Diver and Long-tailed Duck on the sea, and Purple Sandpiper on rocky shores.

St Mary's is the largest island with excellent birding on the Lower Moors Nature Trail where migrant passerines are numerous, and there is a wader scrape overlooked by hides. Porthellick Pool, on the Higher Moors, also has hides and attracts waders and ducks, as well as regular Spotted Crake. This is probably the best site in Great Britain for good views of Jack Snipe. To the south is the golf course and airport area where the grassland attracts Richard's and Tawny Pipits, sometimes Dotterel, and Buff-breasted Sandpiper is almost annual. The Garrison, close to Hugh Town, is always worth checking for scarce passerines and Porthloo to the north is good for waders.

The island of **Tresco** is north-west of St Mary's and has the best fresh waters in the archipelago, at the Great Pool and the Abbey Pool. Garganey is regular in spring and Spotted Crake in autumn at the Great Pool, and the Abbey Gardens to the south may hold migrant passerines.

St Agnes is the westernmost of the major islands and linked to neighbouring **Gugh** by a sandbar. The Big Pool is one of the major birding interests on St Agnes, but nearby Periglis Beach is worth checking for rare waders. In the south of the island is Wingletang Down, a well-known haunt of rare migrants, especially warblers.

The remaining islands of **Bryher** and **St Martin's** are less visited by birders, except when a rarity is reported. Landing on the Annet and Western Rocks, where most of the seabirds breed, is prohibited but there are boat trips around the rocks from St Mary's.

To visit the Isles of Scilly in October, accommodation, which is mainly on St Mary's but also on the smaller islands, needs to be booked well in advance. Access to the islands is by sea or air from Penzance.

16) Shetland Islands This archipelago of more than 100 islands, islets and rocks off north Scotland is undoubtedly one the best birding areas in Great Britain. Virtually treeless, these islands consist of rough grassland and heather, and cultivated land dotted with bogs and lochans. High cliffs fringe many of the islands and provide homes for some of the most spectacular seabird colonies in the Western Palearctic. In addition, the islands are famous for attracting migrants and some of the rarest visitors to the region have been recorded here. As trees are so scarce, any patch of cover, however small, is worth checking for migrants during passage periods.

As well as the commoner seabirds, European Storm-petrel, Common and Black Guillemots, Razorbill, Puffin, and Great and Arctic Skuas all breed. Other breeding birds of interest include Red-throated Diver, Red-breasted Merganser and various waders including Red-necked Phalarope. Passerines are few but Rock Pipit and Twite breed, and there are two endemic subspecies of Wren found in the islands.

Migrants occur throughout the islands in large numbers and great variety, and include seabirds, waterfowl and waders, owls, raptors and passerines. In addition to the commoner species, the islands regularly attract scarcer migrants such as Wryneck, Bluethroat, Barred Warbler, Common Rosefinch and Ortolan Bunting. Mid May to mid-June is the best time to visit for migrants in spring, whilst the autumn migration is more protracted and passage can be witnessed from mid July to early November. Although rarities often appear in spring it is mainly autumn that brings the rarity hunters to Shetland when vagrants from North America can be seen alongside wanderers from Siberia.

Mainland is the largest island in the archipelago and the capital, Lerwick, hosts Black Guillemot in its harbour all year, joined by Little Auk and Glaucous and Iceland Gulls in winter, and sometimes also King Eider. The plantations at Kergord form the largest patch of woodland in Shetland and regularly hold scarce and rare migrants. Tresta Voe in west Mainland is one of the best of Shetland's many sea inlets, with Great Northern Diver and Long-tailed Duck often present all year, scarcer grebes in winter, and also King Eider. Watsness is the best seawatching point on Mainland, with the rarer skuas regular in spring, sometimes Yellow-billed Diver, and autumn brings Sooty Shearwater. Sumburgh Head in the far south of the island is good for breeding seabirds in summer and one of the best sites for scarce migrants in autumn. The nearby Loch of Spiggie and Loch of Hillwell are the best sites for passage and wintering waterfowl in Shetland, with Whooper Swan and Long-tailed Duck regular. Pool of Virkie also has waterfowl, as well as the chance of rare waders and gulls.

Mousa is a small island off the east coast of Mainland famous for its European Storm-petrel colony. Nocturnal visits can be arranged locally to see these birds. Other breeders include skuas and Black Guillemot.

Boat trips can be arranged around the base of the cliffs at **Noss**, which hold one of the largest seabird colonies in Great Britain, with guillemots, Razorbill, Puffin and skuas. Noss can be reached by boat from the adjacent island of Bressay.

Whalsay is one of the smaller of Shetland's main islands and is 5km off the east coast of Mainland. It is less visited than some other islands but it attracts many migrants due to its position. The ferry trip can produce Little Auk, Great Northern Diver and large numbers of seaducks in winter. The ferry lands at Symbister, a good migrant spot and close to a fish factory attracting regular Glaucous and Iceland Gulls in winter. Skaw in the north-east of the island attracts migrants to its farmed land, gardens and golf course. Whalsay is reached by ferry from Laxo or by air from Lerwick.

Easternmost of the Shetlands and lying 8km off Whalsay are the **Out Skerries**, rocky and exposed islands with little cover, but attractive to migrants due to their position. The largest numbers generally occur during periods of easterly winds and September to October tends to produce most rarities. Given suitable weather conditions all the commoner passerine migrants can be seen, along with scarcer species. At sea in autumn Manx and Sooty Shearwaters, Pomarine Skua and European Storm-petrel can be seen. The Out Skerries can be reached by ferry from Lerwick or Whalsay or by air from Tingwall airport.

The westernmost and remotest island in the group is **Foula**, more than 20km west of Mainland and famous for its internationally important numbers of breeding seabirds, especially Great Skua. Sooty Shearwater is regular in autumn and Purple Sandpiper common in autumn and winter. Passerine migrants appear in small numbers during passage periods. The island can be reached by ferry from Walls or Scalloway on Mainland, and by air from Tingwall. Accommodation on the island must be booked in advance.

Yell is the largest of the northern Shetlands and consists largely of heather moors with lochans and bogs. Lumbister is an RSPB reserve in the west of the island that hosts a combination of moorland, bog and cliff-nesting species. The lochs and sheltered firth have breeding Red-throated Diver, Red-breasted Merganser and Common Eider, whilst these waters are visited by the moorland-nesting skuas for bathing. Also present on the moors and bogs are Golden Plover, Dunlin, Eurasian Curlew and Common Snipe. A car-ferry operates between Mainland and Yell.

Fetlar is the smallest and greenest of the north Shetlands with about one-sixth of the island protected as an RSPB reserve. Birds of the moorland include skuas and nationally important numbers of Whimbrel. However, the most important breeding wader is Red-necked Phalarope, with two-thirds of Great Britain's breeding population found on this island and Loch of Funzie, in the E, the best site. Fetlar is famous in ornithological circles as the former site of Great Britain's only nesting Snowy Owls, but although birds are sometimes present there has been no breeding since 1975. The island can be reached by car-ferry from Unst or Yell.

Unst is the northernmost of the main islands and has some of the largest seabird colonies in Great Britain, and important numbers of waders nesting on the moorland. The northernmost peninsula of the island includes Hermaness, with more than 70,000 pairs of 14 species breeding. On the east coast is Haroldswick Bay, where Great Northern Diver is often present in summer alongside Purple Sandpiper. Further south is Baltasound, where there are gardens and a sycamore plantation, which can be excellent for migrants. Uyeasound on the south coast also attracts divers and seaduck, including occasional Yellow-billed Diver and King Eider. Snowy Owl is an almost annual visitor to Unst and rarities are frequently found. Unst can be reached by ferry from Yell or Fetlar or by air from Tingwall.

Fair Isle is famous as a bird observatory and rarity hotspot, matched in Great Britain only by the Isles of Scilly, and over 350 species have been recorded. This small cliff-fringed island is situated midway between the Orkneys and Shetlands. Although it is so well known for rarities Fair Isle has breeding seabirds such as European Storm-petrel and possibly Leach's, Puffin, Razorbill, guillemots and skuas. Wrens belong to the subspecies *fridariensis*, which is endemic to Fair Isle.

Spring migration begins in March to April but scarcer migrants begin to appear in May. In autumn passage starts in August but peaks in September to October, when the highest numbers of birds occur on east or south-east winds. Lapland and Snow Buntings are regular in October. Rarer migrants that occur with some regularity on Fair Isle in autumn include Greater Short-toed Lark, Richard's, Red-throated and Olive-backed Pipits, Greenish, Yellow-browed and Pallas' Leaf Warblers, Rustic and Little Buntings, and Red-breasted Flycatcher. There are also some rarities that are more likely to appear on Fair Isle than anywhere else in Great Britain (or indeed western Europe), including Pallas' Grasshopper, Lanceolated, Paddyfield and Blyth's Reed Warblers, Pechora Pipit and Yellow-breasted Bunting. The best time for these species is mid- to late September.

Fair Isle lies *c*.40 km south of Sumburgh Head and can be reached by sea or air from Mainland. Accommodation is available at the Fair Isle Lodge and Bird Observatory in April to October and requires advance booking.

17) Spurn Peninsula Surpassing even Flamborough Head to the north and Gibraltar Point to the S, this peninsula is the finest migration watchpoint on the English east coast and the site of Great Britain's first mainland bird observatory. Situated at the entrance to the vast Humber Estuary, this is a long and narrow stretch of unstable sand dunes, which often suffer damage during winter storms. As well as dunes, there is arable and grazing land with hedgerows at the base of the promontory and pools further out. The trees and bushes around the observatory headquarters at Warren Cottage attract numbers of birds in season. Waders occur in large numbers on the outer sandy beach and the mudflats on the Humber side. The area known as the 'Narrows' is probably the best site in the entire area to observe migration, with huge numbers of a wide variety of birds from Goldcrests to Ospreys passing through. At the tip of the peninsula the trees and bushes at 'Point Camp' is another excellent site for passerine migrants.

More than 330 species have been recorded on the Spurn Peninsula and the variety of migrants is astounding. As well as landbirds seawatching can also be spectacular both on the North Sea and Humber Estuary sides. Divers, grebes and Shag are present on passage and in winter, and off the eastern side passage European and

Leach's Storm-petrels are possible. Dark-bellied Brent, Long-tailed Duck and scoters can all be seen and all four regular skuas occur on passage.

Passage raptors include the occasional Montagu's Harrier, but it is passerine migration that is the truly remarkable feature of Spurn. In addition to huge numbers of the commoner migrants, species such as Tawny Pipit, Bluethroat, Ring Ouzel, and warblers including Barred, Pallas' Leaf and Yellow-browed are regular, with Subalpine, Greenish, Arctic, Radde's and Dusky all seen in recent years. Other regular scarce migrants include Red-breasted Flycatcher, Common Rosefinch and Lapland and Snow Buntings. Shore Lark is a rare winter visitor.

The Spurn Peninsula can be reached by road west from Hull to Patrington, then Easington and on to Kilnsea. The road then continues the length of the peninsula.

18) Tregaron Bog (Cors Caron) Originally a lake that has been gradually infilled since the last Ice Age, today Tregaron or Cors Caron is the best remaining example of a raised bog in Wales.

Around 170 bird species have been recorded and the area is important for wintering waterfowl as well as breeding wetland birds. Breeders include ducks, waders and gulls in the wetter areas, and Red Grouse on the moors. Red Kite is often seen hunting over the bog and up to 60 may be present in the area in winter, alongside Hen Harrier. Passage brings waders and waterfowl, and Whooper and, sometimes, Bewick's Swans occur in winter.

Tregaron Bog is c.4km north of the village of Tregaron and an observation tower overlooks the bog.

Greece

The range of habitats in this fairly small country combined with a long bird list and ease of accessibility make mainland Greece difficult to match as a birding destination. Very popular with holidaymakers, much of the country has a good tourist infrastructure with plentiful accommodation and easy travel. However, the north-east corner close to the Turkish border is still a sensitive area, and care should be taken, particularly near airfields and military installations. Much of Greece is mountainous with

extensive forest in the north, and large bird-rich upland lakes on the borders with Macedonia and Albania. Mediterranean scrub and dry farmland are found in lower areas, along with some of the most important wetlands in Europe, although all of these are suffering habitat degradation to some extent. Many south-eastern specialities occur in Greece and a trip in late April to May will produce the longest list, with many migrants passing through. Rare species include both pelicans, Lesser

White-fronted and Red-breasted Geese, and the Evros Delta was once a regular site for Slender-billed Curlew. Despite all these attractions, relatively few birders visit mainland Greece with most opting for a trip to one of the Greek islands. However, there is still much to be discovered in the mountains and more remote forest areas, and the wetlands always offer the chance of rarities.

1) Amvrakikós Gulf Relatively undisturbed compared to many Greek wetlands, the area around this gulf has brackish lagoons and saltmarsh, reedbeds and riverine scrub.

Dalmatian Pelican, Glossy Ibis and Eurasian Spoonbill breed alongside various herons, White Stork and Ferruginous Duck. Other birds present in summer include Black-winged Stilt, Stone-curlew, Collared Pratincole and Gull-billed and Whiskered Terns. Passage is best in spring when a wide range of species from pelicans to passerines can be seen, and winter brings White Pelican, Pygmy Cormorant, Great Egret and Greater Spotted Eagle.

The gulf can be reached on minor roads and tracks from the Arta-Preveza road.

2) Akarnanika Mountains Ranging from the Gulf of Amvrakikós south to the Acheloös Plain, these mountains have scrub and extensive oak woodland on the lower slopes, with Greek Fir *Abies cephalonica* and pastures higher up. Reaching a peak of 1,589m, it is a good area for upland, but not true mountain birds.

The area supports Griffon Vulture, Short-toed, Golden and Bonelli's Eagles, a few pairs of Lesser Kestrel, Rock Partridge, Eurasian Eagle Owl and Middle Spotted Woodpecker. Passerines include Black-eared Wheatear, Blue Rock Thrush, Olive-tree and Subalpine Warblers, Western Rock Nuthatch, Lesser Grey Shrike and Cretzschmar's Bunting.

Access can be gained from the roads between Amfilochia and Agrinio or, nearer the coast, from Vonitsa to Astakos.

3) Avas Gorge Famed for its raptors, this gorge is situated a few kilometres north of Alexandroupolis in north-east Greece and in easy reach of the Evros Delta. A rugged ravine with steep rock-faces and riverine woodland, the area has three species of breeding vulture, four eagles and three buzzards, as well as Black Kite and Lesser Kestrel. Migrant Levant Sparrowhawk passes through in large numbers. In addition the area has Black Stork, Eurasian Eagle Owl and European Roller, south-east specialities such Sombre Tit, Masked Shrike and Isabelline Wheatear, and typical montane birds such as Western Rock Nuthatch, Blue Rock Thrush and Crag Martin.

From Alexandroupolis take the road north to Avandas.

4) Axios-Aliakmonas Deltas The deltas of the Axios and Loudhias rivers were once among the most important Greek wetlands, but like other such areas much has now been lost. In its delta the Axios has been canalised and no longer floods, but there are still pools, coastal lagoons and part of an old branch of the river. In the surrounding area the paddyfields and reedbeds hold a good selection of species all year and the river mouth can be very productive. The Loudhias River to the west has undergone similar habitat loss and is now a canal. Although birds do not occur in the numbers they once did there is still an interesting range of species. The nearby delta of the Aliakmon has much the same habitats but has suffered far less habitat destruction and, with the Kitros saltpans *c.*20km to the south, is now one of the best wetlands in Greece.

Little Bittern, Squacco, Black-crowned Night and other herons breed in this area, as well as small numbers of Eurasian Spoonbill, Glossy Ibis and, probably, crakes. The lagoons have Pied Avocet, Black-winged Stilt, Collared Pratincole, Kentish Plover and Mediterranean Gull. Passage brings a wide variety of birds and scarcer waders include Great Snipe and Broad-billed, Marsh and Terek Sandpipers, and Slender-billed Curlew is possible. Other passage species include Greater Flamingo, Pygmy Cormorant and Dalmatian Pelican. Red-footed Falcon is common in spring and Lanner and Saker Falcons are possible. Winter brings small numbers of White-tailed and Greater Spotted Eagles, and Great Egret is regular, although waterfowl numbers are far lower than once they were.

The main Athens-Thessaloniki road crosses the area.

5) Dadiá-Soufli Forest A forested valley in the far east of Greece, this is one of the best sites for raptors in Europe. More than 30 species are regularly recorded and over 20 breed. Once heavily hunted, the area is now protected and there is a raptor-feeding programme in operation.

The feeding station at Dadiá attracts Black, Griffon and Egyptian Vultures, and Lammergeier is usually present in the area. Eagles include Golden, Lesser Spotted, Booted, Bonelli's, Short-toed, Eastern Imperial and White-tailed, the last two being more numerous in winter, when Greater Spotted may also be present, and Steppe occurs on passage. Also breeding are Black Kite, three *Accipiter* species, Long-legged Buzzard and Lanner Falcon. Red Kite and Saker Falcon occur and Eleonora's Falcon is regular in early summer. There are many other birds of interest including storks, Black-crowned Night Heron, Chukar Partridge, European Roller, European Bee-eater, Middle Spotted and Syrian Woodpeckers, and Eurasian Scops and Eagle Owls. Numerous passerines include Olive-tree, Barred and Orphean Warblers, Semi-collared Flycatcher, Masked and Lesser Grey Shrikes, Sombre Tit, Black-headed Bunting and Spanish Sparrow.

The reserve information centre can be reached on the E5 north of Alexandroupolis, turn off at Lifokos to Dadiá.

6) Delphi One of the most popular archaeological sites in Greece, Delphi has also long been recognised as a good birding site, although an early visit before the crowds arrive may be necessary. Delphi is on the lower slopes of the range that includes the 2,457m Mount Parnassós, and a high crag overlooks the site.

Golden Eagle is regular, especially in spring, high above Delphi with Short-toed Eagle in summer and other raptors such as Levant Sparrowhawk on passage. One of the major attractions for birders is Western Rock Nuthatch, easy to see at Delphi, with Sombre Tit in the pines higher up. Orphean, Rüppell's and Olive-tree Warblers are other eastern Mediterranean specialities found here, as well as Cretzschmar's, Black-headed and Rock Buntings. Eurasian Crag Martin, Red-rumped Swallow and Alpine Swift also breed in the area.

The best time to visit is April to May when summer visitors have arrived, migrants are still passing through and there are fewer tourists. Ancient Delphi lies east of the new town of the same name, c.180km west of Athens and can be reached on the N48 Athens-Levadeia road.

7) Evros Delta Once considered the Greek equivalent of the Camargue or Coto Doñana, this wetland has long suffered from hunting and habitat loss. Situated on the sensitive Greek/Turkish border, access has always been difficult and were it not so, this would have become as popular a birding destination as the other great deltas. Nevertheless, it is still an interesting site with a variety of habitats supporting a range of birds: sand dunes, saline lagoons, freshwater marshes, woodland, scrub and grassland.

Present in summer are Greater Flamingo, both storks, various herons, waterfowl such as Ruddy Shelduck and Ferruginous Duck, and a range of raptors. Breeding waders such as Pied Avocet and Black-winged Stilt are common, but the target species for many is Spur-winged Lapwing at one of its very few European breeding sites. Passerines include such specialities as Isabelline Wheatear, Masked and Lesser Grey Shrikes, and Olive-tree Warbler. Passage is equally, if not more, interesting with Broad-billed, Marsh and Terek Sandpipers, and this was formerly possibly the most regular European site for Slender-billed Curlew, usually recorded in mid April on the saltmarsh south of Drana Lagoon. One was reported in February 2004, one of very few recent reports anywhere in the world. Although scarce, Greater Sand Plover, White-tailed and Sociable Lapwings also occur as migrants. Other regular passage birds are White Pelican, Greater White-fronted and Lesser White-fronted Geese, Glossy Ibis and Eurasian Spoonbill. Internationally important numbers of waterfowl occur in winter and often include Red-breasted Goose and White-headed Duck. Other winterers include Greater Spotted and White-tailed Eagles, Pygmy Cormorant, Dalmatian Pelican and Great Egret, sometimes also Pallas' Gull.

Permits are required for some parts of the area; these are best arranged in advance and must be presented to both police and military before entering restricted areas. The delta is east of Alexandroupolis and reached on the E5 road. The public area is south of the villages of Loutros and Monastiraki, the areas to east of this, which are often the best, require permits.

8) Lake Kerkini This reservoir is now one of the premier wetland sites in Greece. In addition to open water there are reedbeds, particularly on the northern shore, water-lily beds and flooded forest. Around the lake are villages, farmland, woods and the valley of the Strymon River. south and west are hills rich in raptors. The lake and its environs are superb all year and are one of the most important sites in Europe for pelicans.

Dalmatian Pelican is present all year and White Pelican visits in hundreds on passage. Breeders include Pygmy Cormorant and Ferruginous Duck, and there is a heronry in the flooded forest north of the lake with Purple, Black-crowned Night and Squacco Herons, Little Bittern and Eurasian Spoonbill. Glossy Ibis occurs on passage and Great Egret in winter. White Stork is common and Black Storks breeding in nearby hills feed by the lake. In addition to the commoner waterfowl, Lesser White-fronted Goose is possible on passage and White-headed Duck occurs in winter. Whiskered Tern breeds, Pied Avocet and Marsh Sandpiper occur on passage and Great Snipe in winter. The area is remarkable for raptors with Levant Sparrowhawk and Short-toed, Lesser Spotted, Golden and Booted Eagles breeding in the surrounding uplands. Lesser Kestrel occurs on passage and White-tailed and Greater Spotted Eagles winter. An interesting range of birds including Eurasian Eagle Owl and Sombre Tit can be found in the valley behind Sidirokastro.

To reach Lake Kerkini take the N12 north from Thessaloniki towards Serres, and turn left after 60km for Lithotopos.

9) Mikrí Prespa National Park One of the most important wetlands in Greece, this area is becoming increasingly popular with travelling birders. In the far north-west of the country, the park covers most of Mikrí Prespa, which is separated by a narrow strip of land from the larger Megalí Prespa. The lake is shallow and the shores vary from bare rocks to dense reedbeds. Surrounding the lake are bird-rich forests and mountains.

Breeding waterbirds include grebes, Pygmy Cormorant, pelicans and a variety of herons, ducks including Ferruginous, and waders. The surrounding countryside has many raptors, Hazel Grouse, Rock Partridge, woodpeckers including Black, White-backed and Middle Spotted, and numerous passerines. Lesser Kestrel breeds in the town of Agios Germanos. As the lake often freezes in January it is of limited importance to wintering waterfowl. More than 260 species have been recorded.

Mikrí Prespa is best reached from Thessaloniki on the N2 via Florina and from there on the N15. Agios Germanos has an information centre. The best birding is generally along the isthmus between the two lakes and on the eastern shore north of Mikrolimni.

10) Mount Olympus National Park This National Park in the east Olympus Mountains has some of the most dramatic scenery in Greece and is popular with hikers, climbers and skiers, as well as birders. Reaching from the Aegean to over 2,900m the area has habitats ranging from typical Mediterranean maquis on the lower slopes through forests of beech, fir and pine in the higher parts.

Like other Greek mountains, Mount Olympus has a fine selection of raptors including Black and Griffon Vultures, Short-toed, Golden and Booted Eagles, Levant Sparrowhawk, Lanner and Eleonora's Falcons. Lammergeier was regularly seen until recently but may no longer be resident. Other sought-after species include Wallcreeper, Alpine Accentor and Shore Lark, with Eurasian Crag Martin common in gorges. The forests have Grey-headed, White-backed and Three-toed Woodpeckers, Tengmalm's Owl and Crested Tit. Lower down in the maquis *Sylvia* warblers are numerous.

The park is 120km south of Thessaloniki on the N1 Larisa road and on a minor road to the village of Litochoro. Birders usually head for the Spilios Agapitos refuge (open May to October), where food and accommodation is available, although it must be booked well in advance. A trail leads through dense forest to the peak of Skolio. Continuing south on the N1 for a further 30km leads to the Tembi Valley, another area rich in raptors and other species found on Mount Olympus, but with the addition of Black Stork and Lesser Spotted Eagle.

11) Mount Parnassós National Park Parnassós is one of the highest mountains in central Greece at 2,457m, and the National Park has several other high peaks and virtually unspoilt forests of Greek Fir, the best-preserved example of this habitat in Greece. Other habitats include upland meadows, scrub and bare limestone cliffs. The area is especially important for raptors but there is also an excellent range of woodland birds.

Griffon and Egyptian Vulture both breed and Lammergeier may still do so, Short-toed and Golden Eagles are fairly easily seen. The forests hold Northern Goshawk and Lanner Falcon breeds on rocky crags. Woodpeckers are common and include Black, White-backed and Middle Spotted. More open areas support Rock Partridge, Alpine Accentor, Blue Rock Thrush, Alpine Chough, Wallcreeper and Snowfinch. Specialities such as Western Rock Nuthatch, Rüppell's Warbler and Cretzschmar's Bunting can also be found, as well as Olive-tree and Eastern Olivaceous Warblers. Red-rumped Swallow breeds at the ski resort.

The park lies east of Delphi and can be reached via Arachova. Go through the village and after c.15km take either the left fork into the forest or the right, which leads to the ski centre.

12) Nestos Delta Like other Greek wetlands, the Nestos Delta has suffered greatly in recent decades from habitat loss but there are still birds to be found, albeit in smaller numbers, and the total list runs to more than 300 species. Today, the main interest lies in the lagoons beside the river mouth. In addition there are mudflats, saltmarsh, dunes and freshwater marshes. In drier areas there is cultivation, grassland, scrub and poplar woods.

The Nestos Delta has long been famous amongst birders as the Greek stronghold of Spur-winged Lapwing, but there is much else of interest. Pied Avocet, Black-winged Stilt, Kentish Plover, Collared Pratincole and Stone-curlew breed, as well as White Stork and various herons. Mediterranean Gull also nests, alongside terns on the sandbars between the lagoons and the sea. Greater Flamingo and Pygmy Cormorant are usually present, as are Ruddy Shelduck and Ferruginous Duck, and warblers and Bearded Tit breed in the reedbeds. Wooded areas and scrub have Lesser Spotted Eagle, Levant Sparrowhawk, Eurasian Scops Owl and Syrian Woodpecker, and farmland hosts Lesser Grey, Masked and Woodchat Shrikes. The offshore-nesting Eleonora's Falcon hunts the beaches in late afternoon. Passage brings a variety of waders including, on occasion, Slender-billed Curlew, but more regular are Temminck's Stint and Marsh and Broad-billed Sandpipers. Glossy Ibis often appears on passage and raptors include Lesser Kestrel and Red-footed Falcon. White-tailed and Greater Spotted Eagles and Great Egret are present in winter, as well as waterfowl, sometimes including Lesser White-fronted and Red-breasted Geese. Yelkouan Shearwater is common offshore in autumn and winter.

The best areas for birding are the lagoons near the village of Keramotí, reached on the E5 east from Kavála, after 27km turning right towards Chrisoupoli and on to Keramotí. There are beaches and lagoons near the village and towards Monastiraki, where there are also poplar woods. For further lagoons take the airport road on the left fork at the junction just north of Keramotí. A track to the left in the village of Agíasma leads to a reliable lagoon for Spur-winged Lapwing, and closer to the airport another left turn leads to paddyfields and reedbeds, more lagoons and the beach.

13) Porto Lagos and the Thracian Lakes Lake Vistonis is a vast shallow lake on the coast of north-east Greece and the area around Porto Lagos to the south one of the best birding spots in mainland Greece. The village is on a narrow sandy neck of land between the lake and the sea with freshwater lakes, saltpans, coastal lagoons (which may dry out in summer), reedbeds, saltmarsh, scrub and small woodlands. Although there are some exciting breeders, the main interest is in scarce migrants and winter visitors.

Little Bittern, White Stork and Ferruginous Duck breed as well as Pied Avocet, Stone-curlew, Kentish Plover, Collared Pratincole and Mediterranean Gull, although Spur-winged Lapwing is now rare. European Bee-eater, Greater Short-toed Lark and Rufous Bush Robin breed in drier areas, as well as Lesser Grey and Masked Shrikes. Glossy Ibis and Dalmatian Pelican are regular on passage and waders include Broad-billed, Marsh and Terek Sandpipers and, possibly, Slender-billed Curlew. Greater Flamingo can be seen all year. Short-toed Eagle and Lesser Kestrel pass through as well as Eastern Imperial and Bonelli's Eagles. Yelkouan Shearwater is common offshore in autumn and winter, and Slender-billed and Audouin's Gulls occur on passage. In winter thousands of Black-necked Grebe, Pygmy Cormorant and Greater Flamingo are present with smaller numbers of White-headed Duck, Great Egret and geese (including Lesser White-fronted and Red-breasted). Wintering raptors include White-tailed and Greater Spotted Eagles.

Porto Lagos forms an excellent base from which to explore the area and can be reached on the N2 (E90) road from Xánthi. There are salt works and lagoons worth visiting c.5km west of Porto Lagos. Between the town and the sea and along the spit east of the town are pines worth checking for passerine migrants, and there is a channel connecting the lake to the sea that may produce good birds. Heading east to Komotini and then south to Fanari the road passes more lagoons where Dalmatian Pelican and Greater Flamingo occur on passage and in winter. Close to Fanari is Xirolimni Lagoon where Great Egret, Ruddy Shelduck and Ferruginous Duck are possible. Further east is the reed-fringed Lake Mitrikou (Ismarida), south of Pagouria and signed from there, where Whiskered Tern and Eurasian Spoonbill breed. Ferruginous Duck and Ruddy Shelduck are also regular and Dalmatian Pelican occurs in winter. An excellent range of species can be seen throughout the year but the most productive times are passage periods. Slender-billed Curlew was recorded most frequently in September but also in August and in spring.

14) Valia Kalda National Park This National Park is in north-west Greece and covers the forested slopes of part of the Pindos Mountains. Habitats include mountains, reaching 2,177m, dense forests of Black and Bosnian Pine, beech and Greek Fir, and several fast-flowing rivers winding through narrow gorges. Despite much disturbance in recent decades from dam and road construction, it remains a wild and remote area and one of the best in Greece for forest birds.

Well known for raptors, with Griffon and Egyptian Vultures, Eastern Imperial Eagle, Levant Sparrowhawk and Lanner Falcon, there are also Rock Partridge, Wallcreeper and Shore Lark on the peaks. The forests support woodpeckers including Black, White-backed, Middle Spotted and probably Three-toed.

Situated north of the road between Ioannina and Trikkala, the area is seldom visited but there are marked paths. One of the best areas is the Kataras pass, east of Metsovo. The main route through the mountains, the N6, may be blocked by snow until mid May.

15) Vikos-Aoos National Park Close to the Albanian border in north-west Greece, this National Park contains some of the most dramatic scenery in the country. The rivers flow through gorges with sheer limestone walls or densely forested slopes of Black and Bosnian Pine, beech and chestnut. Bare rocky peaks reach more than 2,000m at Tymfi and Smolikas. The Vikos Gorge, with nearly 1,000m-high walls is spectacular and is reached from the village of Monodendri.

Birds include Alpine Accentor, Red-billed Chough and Western Rock Nuthatch, and woodpeckers in the dense forests include Black, Middle Spotted and White-backed. However, it is the raptors that draw most birders to the area. Lammergeier, Griffon and Egyptian Vulture occur, as well as Golden, Booted and Short-toed Eagles, and Lanner Falcon.

North of Ioannina on the N20 road is the village of Konitsa and the National Park is immediately south of here.

Greek Islands

1) Corfu This large island lies off the north-west coast of Greece and is one of the greenest of all the islands. Habitats range from lowland lakes and marshes to the highest point, Mount Pantokratoras at 906m. As well as having interesting residents Corfu attracts many migrants.

Corfu Town (Kerkyra) is home to Alpine Swift and often has Mediterranean Gull in the harbour. Eurasian Scops Owl, Red-rumped Swallow and Spanish Sparrow are common in some villages and Lanner Falcon is sometimes seen on the cliffs at Paleokastritsa. Greater Short-toed and Crested Larks, Tawny Pipit, Lesser Grey and Woodchat Shrikes, and Sardinian, Subalpine and Orphean Warblers are frequent in scrub and farmland. Upland birds found in the Pantokratoras area include Rock Partridge and Bonelli's Eagle, both rock thrushes, Black-eared Wheatear, Western Rock Nuthatch, Rock Sparrow and buntings such as Cirl, Ortolan and Cretzschmar's. On Corfu's northern tip is Andinioti Lagoon where various herons and waders occur on passage, along with breeding Rufous Bush Robin and Olive-tree Warbler. The other famous wetland on Corfu, Lake Korission, lies in the south of the island and attracts passage birds such as Glossy Ibis, Ferruginous Duck and various terns. Further south is the saltpans at Alikes, which are also worth checking for migrants, particularly Collared Pratincole which may also breed. Spring is usually the most productive period on Corfu and migrants can be seen throughout the island. Red-footed and Eleonora's Falcons, Gull-billed, Caspian, Whiskered and White-winged Terns and passerines including Collared and Semi-collared Flycatchers are regular. Cory's and Yelkouan Shearwaters can be seen on boat trips to neighbouring islands.

One of the most popular of the Greek islands with holidaymakers, Corfu can be explored conveniently and cheaply on a package deal.

2) Crete The largest Greek island and one of the best for birders with interesting breeding species and numerous migrants. Although most of the island is mountainous, there are wetlands of interest and offshore islands with seabird colonies and Eleonora's Falcon. Crested Lark, Cetti's and Sardinian Warblers, and Italian Sparrow (currently treated as a race of Spanish Sparrow) are common over much of the island. Eurasian Scops Owl is also widespread, as are Alpine Swift, Black-eared Wheatear, Blue Rock Thrush and Cirl Bunting.

Agia Reservoir in the west is Crete's best wetland and attracts herons, crakes including Baillon's, Collared Pratincole and Moustached Warbler. The Akrotiri Peninsula east of Chania is a good migrant spot where Collared Flycatcher is regular and Chukar Partridge and Rüppell's Warbler are also found. South of Chania is White Mountains National Park where an 11km walk through Samaria Gorge can produce

Golden Eagle, Eurasian Crag Martin, Short-toed Treecreeper and both choughs. These species can also be found on the nearby Omalós Plateau, as well as Lammergeier, Bonelli's Eagle and Alpine Accentor. Further east there is another excellent migrant spot at Rethymno, on the north coast, where the pines attract numerous passerines. south-east of here is the Amari Valley where raptors include Griffon Vulture, Booted and Bonelli's Eagles, Lesser Kestrel and Lanner Falcon.

The Lesithi Plateau in the east is another raptor haunt with Lammergeier, Griffon Vulture, and Golden and Bonelli's Eagles. Other species include Eurasian Crag Martin and Red-billed Chough with Black-eared Wheatear, Woodchat Shrike and Black-headed Bunting lower down. Kato Zakros Gorge in the far east has a spring and attracts a wide range of migrants and breeding birds.

The Dionisiades Is off the far east of Crete are home to Cory's Shearwater, Eleonora's Falcon and Audouin's Gull, and although the islands are difficult to visit, all three species can usually be seen from the adjacent mainland.

Crete is a popular holiday destination and a package deal is an ideal way to explore the island.

3) Kos A Greek island closer to Turkey, Kos is becoming increasingly popular as a birding destination. There is a well-established tourist infrastructure and its position, like Lesvos to the north, is ideal for eastern migrants, particularly in spring.

Migrants aside, Kos has breeding Bonelli's Eagle in the mountains and Lanner is a possibility, Black Woodpecker has recently been discovered and there are also Lesser Kestrel and Long-legged Buzzard. Chukar occurs in agricultural areas and Cape Fokas on the south coast has Blue Rock Thrush and Eleonora's Falcon, and shearwaters can be seen offshore. There are few wetland areas of note, but Alikes Lake in the north is an area of saltpans, reedbeds and open water that attracts herons, passage waders including Broad-billed Sandpiper, Ruddy Shelduck and Greater Flamingo. Similar species occur at Psalidi, a small lake with reedbeds where Zitting Cisticola nests, south-east of Kos town. Open sandy areas are home to Stone-curlew and Tawny Pipit. With further exploration Kos is likely to produce a bird list similar to that of Lesvos, and rarities such as Slender-billed Curlew have been recorded several times at Alikes.

Mount Dikios and its pine-covered slopes is a site for Bonelli's Eagle reached via Zipari. There are good areas for montane and forest birds around the villages of Zia and Pyli high in these hills. Below Pyli, on the coast, is an area of wetlands near Tigaki and the island's only bird reserve. This is another site for waders, herons, crakes and passerines including Olive-tree and Olivaceous Warblers, Cretzschmar's and Ortolan Buntings and other migrants.

There are regular flights to Kos from Athens and the island can also be reached by ferry from Athens, Rhodes and other islands, as well as from Bodrum in Turkey.

4) Lesvos Although a Greek island, Lesvos (Lesbos or Mytilene) lies closer to Turkey and the main attraction for birders is the strongly eastern element in the island's birdlife. Krüper's and Western Rock Nuthatches, Isabelline Wheatear, and Cinereous and Cretzschmar's Buntings occur, along with Ruddy Shelduck and other east Mediterranean specialities. Now well watched in spring, rarities are regularly recorded and Spur-winged Lapwing, Black-winged Pratincole, Citrine Wagtail and River Warbler occur with some frequency. More than 320 species have been recorded and a well-planned trip in spring or autumn will produce an excellent trip list.

Raptors are very well represented with Long-legged Buzzard, Short-toed and Booted Eagles, Levant Sparrowhawk, Lesser Kestrel, and Lanner and Eleonora's Falcons. White-tailed and Greater Spotted Eagles are uncommon winter visitors. Widespread are Crested and Greater Short-toed Larks, Black-eared Wheatear, various buntings and shrikes. In many respects Lesvos is a typical Mediterranean island, dry, rocky and scrub-covered with olive groves in lower areas. However, there are rocky hillsides, densely vegetated gullies and the 950m Mount Olympus, west of the island's only major town, Mytilini. This pine-clad mountain, and the area around the village of Agiasos in particular, is the only site outside Turkey for Krüper's Nuthatch. Also breeding here are Short-toed Treecreeper, Middle Spotted Woodpecker, Sombre Tit and Orphean Warbler. Mount Lepetimnos in the north has Cinereous Bunting, Rüppell's Warbler and Masked Shrike.

In the west of the island, around Eresos, there are rocky slopes perfect for Western Rock Nuthatch and another good site for Cinereous Bunting. There are also Lanner Falcon, Long-legged Buzzard, Chukar Partridge and Cretzschmar's Bunting. Isabelline Wheatear and Rufous Bush Robin also breed in this area and in the 1990s White-throated Robin was found nesting, outside its normal range. Kallonis Bay is a large sea inlet in the south-west with saltpans, river mouths and marshes. This area attracts many waders, waterfowl and others. Various herons occur regularly and the saltpans attract Greater Flamingo, whilst Pygmy Cormorant is usually present in winter. Storks are often seen on passage, as well as Eurasian Spoonbill and Glossy Ibis, especially in spring, and also Ferruginous Duck. Breeders include Stone Curlew, Pied Avocet and Collared Pratincole. In the nearby river mouths there are waders and crakes, and in the east of the bay, in an area known to British birders as 'Derbyshire', there is a pool that regularly attracts Ruddy Shelduck. Rufous Bush Robin breeds close by.

The north coast from Mithymna to Eftalou has breeding Eleonora's Falcon and Yelkouan Shearwater on the cliffs, and Olive-tree Warbler, Sombre Tit, Middle Spotted Woodpecker and Masked Shrike in the olive groves. Ipsilou Monastery should be on the itinerary of any birding visitor to Lesvos for Long-legged Buzzard, Lesser Kestrel, Chukar Partridge, Rock Thrush and Rock Sparrow.

The combination of east Mediterranean specialities, abundant and varied migrants and cheap holidays have made Lesvos one of the most popular birding destinations in the Western Palearctic for both independent travellers, package-deal birders and bird tour companies. Kallonis forms an ideal base with hotels only a few metres from excellent wetland areas. Although there are regular buses to the main centres, the major birding sites are well scattered and hiring a car or motorcycle is probably the best way to see the specialities of the island.

5) Náxos This popular Aegean island is the largest of the Cyclades and the most interesting for birders, with raptors a speciality and a range of migrants. Like most Mediterranean islands, much of Náxos is scrub-covered, with cultivated land and olive groves. Mount Dias (Zeus or Zas), at c.1,000m, is the highest point on the island and has small patches of coniferous and broadleaf evergreen woodland.

Griffon Vulture, Long-legged Buzzard and Bonelli's Eagle breed in the interior with Eleonora's Falcon on coastal cliffs. East Mediterranean specialities include Black-eared Wheatear, Rüppell's Warbler and Cretzschmar's Bunting, the latter common on Mount Diaz, where Rock and Cirl Buntings can also be seen. Cory's and Yelkouan Shearwaters are regularly seen from the inter-island ferries and Audouin's Gull is a scarce but regular visitor. Passage birds include Red-footed Falcon, Red-throated Pipit, Isabelline Wheatear, Lesser Grey Shrike and Collared Flycatcher.

Náxos is easily reached by air or by ferry from Athens.

6) Rhodes This very popular tourist island is rarely thought of as a birding destination but, lying close to the Turkish coast, it has a good selection of east Mediterranean breeding birds and migrants. This large and fertile island has olive groves, vineyards and other cultivated land, as well as scrub and pinewoods.

Breeders include Long-legged Buzzard, Eleonora's Falcon and possibly still Lanner Falcon, as well as Chukar, Alpine Swift, European Bee-eater, Cretzschmar's Bunting and Red-rumped Swallow. Audouin's Gulls are commonly seen from Cape Voudi, north of Faliraki, and Cory's Shearwater on boat trips from Rhodes. During autumn large numbers of passerine migrants move through and a small river mouth, the Loutanis, between Faliraki and Lindos, attracts a variety of waders as well as Glossy Ibis and herons.

Rhodes is one of the most popular of the Greek islands with package-deal tourists and there are frequent flights from most major European cities.

Hungary

Best known for its dry grassland or *puszta*, Hungary is a stronghold for steppe species such as Great Bustard and Saker Falcon. In addition, the Hortobágy is one of Europe's best wetlands and there are numerous fishponds scattered around the country. Raptors, owls and woodpeckers are well represented but local assistance is

often necessary to locate the more elusive species. Bird tour companies regularly visit Hungary but independent birding is easy with accommodation fairly easy to find and travel straightforward. Spring is best for owls, woodpeckers and displaying Great Bustard, but autumn brings large numbers of passage wetland birds. Winter is also a good time to visit for large numbers of waterfowl.

1) Aggtelek National Park Aggtelek lies on the border with Slovakia, on the Gomor-Torna karst plateau. The valleys are now mainly converted to agriculture but the hillsides still have deciduous forest and there are rocky hillsides and gorges, and some wet meadows in the valley bottoms.

This is a good raptor haunt with Golden, Eastern Imperial, Lesser Spotted and Short-toed Eagles, and Northern Goshawk. Ural Owl occurs in variable numbers depending on rodent populations and has bred in good years. In 2001–2002 Eurasian Pygmy Owls held territory in the park. Black Stork is a rare summer visitor, White Stork rather commoner. Forest birds include Hazel Grouse (Hungary's stronghold for this species), and woodpeckers such as Black, Grey-headed, White-backed and Middle Spotted. Nutcracker is a scarce winter visitor. Corn Crake breeds in the valleys and Rock Bunting on the rocky hillsides.

Aggtelek is c.50km north of Miskolc and reached via Route 27 or minor roads from Kazincbarcika.

2) Biharugra Fishponds One of many complexes of fishponds in Hungary that have a good selection of birds, Biharugra is more remote than some but the reedbeds, meadows and puszta here attract an excellent range of species, and are considered by some to be better even than the famed Szeged ponds.

In addition to herons, there are breeding Eurasian Spoonbill, Ferruginous Duck, Little Crake and Whiskered Tern. Reedbed passerines include Savi's and Moustached Warblers, Bluethroat, and Bearded and Penduline Tits. Red-footed Falcon, Lesser Grey Shrike and a few Great Bustards occur on surrounding farmland. Passage periods are also good with waders in spring and waterfowl in autumn. Rough-legged Buzzard and White-tailed Eagle are regular in winter.

These ponds are close to the Romanian border near the village of Biharugra, which is 45km north of the border town of Gyula.

3) Börzsöny Hills Between the Danube and the Slovakian border, these wooded hills have open meadows, vineyards and orchards on the lower slopes, and host a good selection of woodland birds.

Woodpeckers are well represented, as is usual in the hills of north Hungary, with eight species including the nearest White-backed Woodpeckers to Budapest. Other species include Hazel Grouse in very small numbers, Short-toed and Lesser Spotted Eagles, and occasionally Eastern Imperial and Golden in winter. Red-breasted Flycatcher and Barred Warbler are also present, with Rock Thrush and Rock Bunting in rockier areas.

Take Road 2 north from Budapest to the Börzsöny Hills and the road skirts the eastern edge. A network of trails crosses the park.

4) Buda Hills Within easy reach of Budapest, this is an easily accessible site for those with limited time, holding an excellent range of east European birds, particularly those of deciduous woodland. The hills are covered with a mix of mature oak, hornbeam and beech woods, and there are streams, meadows, rocky crags, scrubland and some cultivated areas.

Famous for woodpeckers, the Buda Hills support seven species including Black, Grey-headed, Syrian and Middle Spotted. Other woodland birds include Short-toed Treecreeper, Barred Warbler, Collared Flycatcher and Hawfinch.

The Buda Hills are on the north-east side of Budapest and easily reached from the city centre. The area is accessible by public transport and the hills have a network of paths. Normafa and Hárshegy can be reached by bus from Moszkva-ter and the highest hill, Janos-hegy, has a chairlift from Zugliget. A railway winds through the area linking the various hills from Hüvösvölgy to Széchenyi-hegy. The hills can be busy with day-trippers at weekends but during the week they are much quieter.

5) Bükk Hills National Park Situated north-east of Budapest, the densely wooded Bükk Hills are home to many birds typical of Hungary's north uplands. There are also open meadows and rocky cliffs.

Raptors in summer include Lesser Spotted and Eastern Imperial Eagles and Saker Falcon in more open areas. Eurasian Eagle Owl is also present, as is Hazel Grouse. Grey-headed, Black, Middle Spotted and White-backed are among the eight woodpeckers in these forests, as well as Red-breasted Flycatcher, Short-toed Treecreeper and Hawfinch.

Eger, c.130km from Budapest, makes an ideal base for this area, which can be explored from minor roads to Miskolc.

6) Csákvár and the Vértes Hills The variety of habitats in this area results in a wide range of forest and wetland birds. The hills have rocky outcrops, mixed forest and vineyards, and there are wet meadows and reedbeds close to the town of Csákvár.

Short-toed and Eastern Imperial Eagles and Saker Falcon are present, as are Grey-headed and Middle Spotted Woodpeckers, Red-breasted and Collared Flycatchers, Short-toed Treecreeper and Hawfinch. More open areas have European Bee-eater, Wood Lark and Barred Warbler, and Rock Thrush may summer in the quarries. The marshes at Csákvár have Great Egret, Montagu's Harrier, crakes and wetland warblers and Bean Geese in autumn and winter.

Csákvár is 25km north of Székesfehérvár and can be reached from Budapest on the M1 to Bicske then following minor roads.

7) Danube Bend In winter the stretch of the Danube Bend between Esztergom and Budapest is an important haven for wintering waterfowl, and in summer the banks and islands, particularly Szentendre, hold a range of woodland birds.

Species difficult to see in central Europe such as Black-throated Diver, Slavonian Grebe, Smew and Velvet Scoter are regular here, as well as a range of other waterfowl and White-tailed Eagle in winter. Black Kite can be seen along the river in summer, as well as woodpeckers and warblers.

The stretch between Vác and Göd is often the best area, reached on Road 2 from Budapest.

8) Hanság Grassland, woods, lakes, reedbeds and cultivated land comprise the Hanság and a range of species can be found here, although the most famous bird of the area, Great Bustard, is now very rare.

Montagu's Harrier and Black Kite are among the breeding raptors and there are also Great Egret and Purple Heron, both storks and Corn Crake in summer. Ferruginous Duck is a rare breeder. Passerines include Bluethroat, Savi's, Moustached and Barred Warblers, and Lesser Grey Shrike. Rough-legged Buzzard and White-tailed Eagle occur in winter.

The Hanság is in the far west of Hungary, south of Mosonmagyaróvár and c.160km from Budapest. The area is easily visited by birders based at Neusiedl in Austria. Great Bustard is more easily seen on the Moson Plain to the north.

9) Hortobágy National Park This wetland ranks alongside the Camargue and Coto Doñana as one of the top ornithological areas in Europe and is now designated a Ramsar site and Biosphere Reserve.

Breeders include herons, storks, Glossy Ibis, Eurasian Spoonbill, Black-necked and Red-necked Grebes, Ferruginous Duck and Little and Baillon's Crakes, amongst many others. Pygmy Cormorant has bred in recent years and numbers more than 200 pairs. Waders include Black-winged Stilt, Pied Avocet and Collared Pratincole, sometimes also Black-winged, and breeding raptors include Red-footed and Saker Falcons. Long-legged Buzzard is increasingly present in summer and bred for the first time in 1992. Mediterranean Gull and Whiskered and White-winged Terns also breed. Although most famous as a wetland there is also the puszta nearby, open steppe with Great Bustard, Corn Crake, Stone-curlew and Montagu's Harrier. Numerous passerines breed at Hortobágy with some of the most sought after being Lesser Grey Shrike, Bluethroat, River, Savi's, Aquatic and Moustached Warblers. Rose-coloured Starling breeds in invasion years. White-fronted and both Bean Geese occur on passage, accompanied by Lesser White-fronted and sometimes Red-breasted. Common Crane and various raptors also occur on passage and Slender-billed Curlew has been recorded. White-tailed Eagle and Rough-legged Buzzard occur in winter.

The park is in the far east of Hungary near the town of Debrecen, where the park has its headquarters, and is reached on Route 4 from Budapest, The village of Hortobágy makes an ideal base and Route 33 crosses much of the area giving access to many of the best vantage points. Some of the best areas can only be visited by permit or if accompanied by a warden.

10) Kardoskút A salt-lake set in a landscape of puszta and farmland, Kardoskút is an important passage stopover for waterfowl, Common Crane and waders. In addition it has a reputation for rarities and Slender-billed Curlew has been recorded.

Great Bustard and Greater Short-toed Lark breed in small numbers but there is little else of interest in summer. Autumn brings geese including annual Red-breasted, ducks, and thousands of Common Crane, which may remain several weeks. In winter Rough-legged Buzzard and White-tailed Eagle occur and Shore Lark and Snow Bunting are regular.

To reach Kardoskút take the E47 from Szeged towards Orosháza and follow signs for Kardoskút village. The reserve is about 6km west of the village.

11) Kis-balaton Lake Balaton is one of the largest lakes in central Europe and Kis-balaton at the south-west end provides some of the best wetland birding in Hungary after Hortobágy. The area has reedbeds, sedges and willow scrub at the mouth of the Zala River. Viewing can be difficult but there are fishponds at nearby Boglarlelle, which harbour similar, but more easily seen, birds.

Breeders include both bitterns, Great Egret and Purple, Black-crowned Night and Squacco Herons, Eurasian Spoonbill and occasionally Glossy Ibis. Ferruginous Duck also breeds, as well as Black-necked Grebe, crakes, Pied Avocet and terns. Raptors include White-tailed Eagle and Montagu's Harrier, and there are various woodpeckers in the surrounding woodlands. Passerines are numerous including many warblers, flycatchers and shrikes, Penduline and Bearded Tits. On passage small numbers of Pygmy Cormorant are regular, and it is an important wintering site for waterfowl, especially Taiga Bean Goose, and raptors.

Kis-balaton is 10km south of Keszthely and there is a ringing centre at nearby Fenékpuszta where guides can be arranged. There are two parts to Kis-balaton, the marshland, which requires a permit and guide, and the Kis-balaton Tarozo, a reservoir, part of which needs a permit. Observation towers on Kanyavari I can be visited without a permit.

12) Kiskunság National Park The Kiskunság is a large plain between the Danube and Tisza rivers and seven separate areas of land are protected as the Kiskunság National Park. Although much of the area is farmed there remains areas of deciduous woodland and marshes, and an area of puszta. For birders one of the most interesting areas is the group of salt-lakes between the villages of Szabadszállás and Fülöpszállás. The area is of great importance for breeding, passage and wintering birds.

Collared Pratincole (Black-winged has also bred) breed alongside Black-winged Stilt, Pied Avocet and Kentish Plover at the salt-lakes, with Mediterranean Gull breeding at Kelemen Szék, one of the best of the salt-lakes, where Whiskered Tern also nests. Reedbeds hold both bitterns and other herons, Eurasian Spoonbill and Pygmy Cormorant. All four European crakes occur and waterfowl include Ferruginous Duck. Warblers such as Moustached and Savi's are common, as are Penduline and Bearded Tits. On drier parts of the Kiskunság there are typical grassland species such as Stone-curlew, Tawny Pipit and Crested Lark, with European Roller and Lesser Grey Shrike on overhead wires. This is one of the best sites for Great Bustard with about 400 birds present. Breeding raptors include Montagu's Harrier, and Saker and Red-footed Falcons. Waders and waterfowl occur on passage with thousands of Bean and White-fronted Geese, sometimes accompanied by Lesser White-fronted or Red-breasted Goose. Common Crane is regular on passage and migrating raptors such as Lesser Spotted Eagle are fairly common, with occasional Greater Spotted also seen. Pallid Harrier and Long-legged Buzzard are rare but regular in early autumn.

Kiskunság National Park is centred on the town of Kecskemét, which is easily reached via the main Budapest-Szeged road. Visiting the park requires a permit and there are several observation towers. However, most of the birds can be seen outside the protected areas and driving along the minor roads can be highly productive.

13) Lake Fertö This is the Hungarian part of the large lake known in Austria as Neusiedl, and the birds are much the same, but this part of the lake has suffered less development. Of huge importance to breeding waterbirds, the shallow, rather saline lake and the countryside around attract large numbers of passage and wintering birds. More than 250 species have been recorded and Pygmy Cormorant is regular in some numbers. Drier plains nearby still support Great Bustard.

Red-necked Grebe, various herons, storks and Eurasian Spoonbill breed, as well as Red-crested Pochard and Ferruginous Duck. Reedbeds have Savi's and Moustached Warblers and damp scrub and thickets hold Bluethroat and River Warbler. Raptors in summer include harriers, Black Kite and possibly Lesser Spotted Eagle. In autumn Bean Geese and White-fronts arrive and Barnacle Goose is now regular. Rough-legged Buzzard occurs in winter.

Due to its position, Lake Fertö is easier to reach from Vienna than Budapest, and is only an hour by road via the border crossing at Kinzelbach.

14) Lake Velence and Dinnyés Marshes Close to Budapest and with an outstanding bird list, Lake Velence is a very popular birding destination. This large shallow lake has extensive reedbeds and wet meadows, and the adjacent Dinnyés Marshes, in particular, are of great importance for breeding birds and wintering waterfowl.

Among the many breeders are Red-necked and Black-necked Grebes, Little Bittern, Black-crowned Night, Squacco and Purple Herons, Great Egret and Eurasian Spoonbill. Crakes also breed, as well as Ferruginous Duck and Montagu's Harrier. Bluethroat breeds at Dinnyés and other reedbed passerines include Penduline and Bearded Tits, and warblers such as Savi's and Moustached. Drier areas have European Bee-eater and Lesser Grey Shrike. Both forms of Bean Goose and White-fronts arrive in thousands in autumn and stay for the winter if the weather is not too harsh.

Lake Velence can be reached from Budapest on the M7 to the north shore or Road 70, which leads to the south. However, the lake can be very busy in summer and it is necessary to head for the reserve on the western shore. The northern shore has a peninsula with ferry trips and a nearby café, which provides a good vantage point. The reserve at Dinnyés Marshes and the reserve on Lake Velence require permits. This site is ideal for birders staying in Budapest without the time to visit Balaton or Hortobágy.

15) Ócsa Wetland birds are common and varied in this small area of damp woodlands, wet meadows, reedbeds and ponds within easy reach of Budapest.

Both storks can be seen as well as various herons, crakes and wetland warblers. Ferruginous Duck, Montagu's Harrier and European Roller breed and Saker Falcon is possible, along with passerines such as Lesser Grey Shrike.

Ócsa is c.20km south-east of Budapest and reached on the M5 then Road 50. There is an observation tower and ringing station where entry to restricted areas can be arranged.

16) Pilis Hills These wooded hills adjoin the Buda range at its northern end and stretch north to the Danube.

Another good woodpecker site, like the Buda Hills there are seven species present, as well as Barred Warbler, Collared Flycatcher, Short-toed Treecreeper and Hawfinch. Found here, but not in the Buda Hills, are small numbers of Saker Falcon, Short-toed and Lesser Spotted Eagles, Black and White Storks, European Bee-eater and Red-breasted Flycatcher. Quarries hold Rock Bunting and perhaps Rock Thrush. Eastern Imperial and Booted Eagles are possible on passage.

The Pilis Hills can be reached on Road 11 north from Budapest along the river to Szentendre, then east into the hills, on Road 10 to Esztergom, which passes through the hills, or via Pilisvorosvar on Road 1. Alternatively there are boat trips from Budapest to Viségrad, which are likely to produce Black Kite.

17) Szeged Fishponds This complex of fishponds with associated puszta and salt-marsh is one of Hungary's best-known birding sites and is of great importance for birds throughout the year.

Both bitterns and other herons breed, as well as Eurasian Spoonbill and sometimes Glossy Ibis. This is the best site for Mediterranean Gull in the country and other summering birds include Pied Avocet and Kentish Plover. Black-winged Stilt breeds nearby at Kistelek and drier farmland supports Red-footed Falcon and European Roller. Passerines include Savi's and Moustached Warblers and Lesser Grey Shrike. Eastern Olivaceous Warbler may also occur. Passage waders occur in good numbers and variety, particularly in spring, and late autumn brings geese and Common Crane. White-tailed Eagle occurs in winter and Rose-coloured Starling is an irregular autumn visitor.

The ponds lie just north of Szeged c.170km south-east of Budapest and reached on the E5. Most birds can be seen from surrounding roads or an observation tower, but a permit is required to enter the site.

18) Tihany Although Lake Balaton is a popular summer holiday resort there are a few areas of great interest to birders. One such is Tihany, a small peninsula on the northern shore that is partly a nature reserve and has an interesting range of birds. The peninsula has woodland, vineyards and orchards as well as two ponds and scrub covered sandy areas that give an almost Mediterranean feel. Belsö-tó, or the Inner Lake, is heavily used by anglers and has few birds but Külsö-tó, the Outer Lake, has breeding Little Bittern, Purple Heron and Ferruginous Duck, as well as warblers and Penduline Tit. The woodland and scrub hold Eurasian Scops Owl, Crested Lark and Tawny Pipit. In autumn and winter the lake itself may hold grebes and duck including Smew and sometimes Long-tailed Duck.

Tihany is c.125km from Budapest on the M7, then along the northern shore of Balaton on Road 71. The peninsula has a network of footpaths and tracks, and most is of open access, although permission to enter the vineyards should be sought.

19) Zemplén Hills Hungary's best raptor site is the Zemplén Hills, in the north-east close to the Slovakian border. These rugged hills are bounded to the west and south by the Bodrog and Hernád rivers, and the lower slopes and valleys have vineyards and orchards. Higher on the slopes there are deciduous woodlands, with conifers at higher levels.

Breeding raptors include Eastern Imperial, Lesser Spotted, Short-toed and Booted Eagles, Black Kite and Saker Falcon. This is probably Hungary's best site for Eurasian Eagle Owl, and Tengmalm's and Ural Owls are present some years. White Stork is common in villages, but Black Stork can be very elusive and found only in the remoter areas, as is Hazel Grouse. Woodpeckers include Black, Grey-headed, White-backed, Syrian and Middle Spotted. Hawfinch is common and the orchards and open woodlands have Wryneck, Wood Lark and Lesser Grey Shrike, and breeding warblers include River and Barred. Wetland areas have Great Egret and other herons in summer. Boldogkovar in the Zemplén Hills is a regular site for Wallcreeper.

Zemplén Hills are north of Szerencs, which is c.35km from Miskolc on Road 37. From Szerencs stay on Road 37 to Sátoraljaújhely or take minor roads north into the hills.

Iceland

Waterfowl are the main birding attraction of Iceland, of which two species in particular are very difficult to see elsewhere in the Western Palearctic, Barrow's Goldeneye and Harlequin Duck. In addition there are some truly huge seabird colonies, breeding waders including both phalaropes, and two of the region's most impressive raptors, White-tailed Eagle and Gyr Falcon. Although Iceland is expensive to visit, independent birding is easy and

most of the main sites readily accessible. Mid-July is the best time to visit for waterfowl and when the biting flies are less of a nuisance.

1) Breiðafjörður and the Snæfellsnes Peninsula A vast shallow bay in north-east Iceland between the North-west Peninsula and the Snæfellsnes with numerous islands, grassland and marshes and extensive inter-tidal areas. Snæfellsnes is a narrow peninsula dominated by the Snæfellsjökull volcano and has important seabird colonies.

Breiðafjörður is famous for White-tailed Eagle and the islands support a few pairs of Grey Phalarope. Harlequin Duck can be seen both in the bay and on the southern side of Snæfellsnes. Gyr Falcon, Ptarmigan and Snow Bunting breed on the peninsula and seabird colonies include Black, Common and Brünnich's Guillemots, Razorbill, Puffin, Glaucous Gull and Arctic Skua. Divers, Whooper Swan and Long-tailed Duck also breed, and waders present in summer include Purple Sandpiper and Red-necked Phalarope. Pale-bellied Brent Goose and large numbers of waders occur on passage, and Iceland Gull is present in winter.

In recent years the area has become an important base for whale-watching trips and shorter trips can be arranged to view seabird colonies. There are roads around the perimeter and across the peninsula and also along the shore of the Breiðafjörður enabling the entire area to be easily explored. There are regular boats across the bay from Stykkishólmur to Brjónslækur, on the North-west Peninsula, which stop at some islands including Flatey, which has breeding Grey Phalarope and Black Guillemot.

2) Grímsey This small island off the north coast is famous as the last breeding site of Little Auk in the country, but numbers are now extremely low if the species still breeds at all. However, there are other birds including Common and Brünnich's Guillemots, Razorbill and Puffin, Red-necked Phalarope and Snow Bunting. The island receives few visitors in winter but Little Auk is then common and Ivory Gull a possibility.

Grímsey can be reached by air or ferry from Akureyri.

3) Jökulsárgljúfur National Park In north-east Iceland, north of Lake Mývatn, this National Park is centred on a 0.5km wide, 100m deep canyon on the Jökulsá River. In the south are three impressive waterfalls, in the central area the broad valley has much vegetation and to the north, in the valley of the Vesturdalour, there are high cliffs overlooking grassland.

Gyr Falcon, Ptarmigan and Snow Bunting nest, with Great Northern Diver and Red-necked Phalarope on the lakes and Great Skua in the delta in the north of the park.

The park is 45km north-west of Grímsstaðir and is open mid June to September.

4) Lake Mývatn One of the best waterfowl sites in Europe with 15 species of duck nesting around its shores, as well as divers, Slavonian Grebe and geese. The two specialities, Harlequin Duck and Barrow's Goldeneye, are common and Nearctic species such as American Wigeon and Ring-necked Duck are often present. Glaucous Gull and Arctic Skua breed at the lake, Great Skua is also seen and breeding waders include Red-necked Phalarope. Gyr Falcon, Ptarmigan and Snow Bunting occur in the surrounding area, but Snowy Owl is now only a rare visitor.

In Icelandic, Mývatn means lake of midges and the area is best avoided in June and August, when populations of these insects are at their peak. Late May or mid-July is the best time with plenty of ducks but fewer flies. Lake Mývatn can be reached by air or road from Reykjavík and there is a good bus service from the capital. Parts of the shore are closed to visitors during the breeding season, but most birds can be seen from open areas. Harlequin Ducks are best seen on the Laxá River, which enters the lake at Skjálfandi Bay.

5) North-west Peninsula Remote and rocky, the peninsula is a vast wilderness area, until recently virtually inaccessible but becoming popular with birders as a stronghold of White-tailed Eagle and Gyr Falcon. In addition, there are some of the largest seabird colonies in the Western Palearctic.

Latrabjarg is the best known of the seabird cliffs and is situated on the western-most point of the peninsula. As well as the world's largest Razorbill colony, there are Common and Brünnich's Guillemots and Puffin. Although they do not breed here, there are usually Little Auks present. Other breeding seabirds include Black Guillemot, Arctic Skua and Glaucous Gull, with Iceland Gull in winter. On the many lakes, particularly Lake Vatnsdalsvatn, are breeding Great Northern Diver and Slavonian Grebe, and waterfowl including Whooper Swan and Harlequin and Long-tailed Ducks. Non-breeding King Eiders are often present in summer. Summering waders include Purple Sandpiper and Red-necked Phalarope.

There are regular flights and buses to Ísafjördhur from Reykjavík, and the area can be explored by road.

6) Olfusar Delta This area of south Iceland contains coastal freshwater marshes and is one of the most important sites for breeding waders and passage and wintering waterfowl.

Whooper Swan, Long-tailed Duck and Glaucous Gull are present all year and summering birds include skuas, and Red-necked, sometimes Grey Phalaropes. Pink-footed, Greater White-fronted and Pale-bellied Brent Geese occur on passage, as well as Great Northern Diver and Slavonian Grebe. Harlequin Duck and Barrow's Goldeneye occur in the area. This part of Iceland is also famous for rarities and a number of Nearctic vagrants have been recorded.

This area lies c.40km south-east of Reykjavík.

7) Reykjanes Peninsula Its close proximity to Reykjavík makes this rocky and volcanic peninsula popular with birders. There are high cliffs with breeding seabirds and a few lakes, and the area often attracts Nearctic vagrants.

All three guillemots, Razorbill, Puffin, Arctic Skua and Glaucous Gull breed, with the best seabird cliffs being at Krisuvikurberg. Purple Sandpiper and Snow Bunting also breed and Manx Shearwater and Leach's and European Storm-petrels occur offshore in summer. Sooty Shearwater and Pomarine Skua are regular in autumn and winter brings Great Northern Diver, Harlequin and Long-tailed Ducks, often a few King Eider, and Iceland Gull.

There is an international airport at Keflavík and the entire peninsula is easily explored by road from Reykjavík.

8) Skaftafell National Park Containing some of Iceland's most dramatic scenery, including hot springs, the highest mountain and largest glacier, Skaftafell is also famous for its rich and varied flora, and there are birds of interest.

Both Arctic and Great Skuas breed on the Skeidarársandur, an extensive sand-plain formed by glacial outwash. Ptarmigan and Red-necked Phalarope also breed, as well as waders and a few landbirds, and there are Razorbills on nearby cliffs.

Skaftafell is 15km north-west of Hofn and access is unrestricted. The park has a campsite and marked hiking trails.

9) Skagafjördur This site includes extensive river floodplains with lakes and marshes and a fjord with islands. It is one of the most important areas for breeding waders and passage waterfowl in Iceland.

Summering birds include Great Northern Diver, Slavonian Grebe, Whooper Swan and Pink-footed Goose, with Glaucous Gull and Snow Bunting present all year. The small island of Drangey has more than 10,000 pairs of breeding seabirds including all three guillemots, Razorbill and Puffin. Pink-footed and Barnacle Geese occur on passage.

Sauðárkrókur is the largest town and is easily reached by road or air from Reykjavík, and there are regular boat trips to Drangey in summer.

10) Thingvellir National Park Despite its dramatic scenery with volcanoes, lava fields and the largest lake in the country, this National Park was established for historical reasons, as the site of the early Icelandic parliament. The lake is surrounded by meadows with shrubs and dwarf birches, and moss and lichen on the more exposed areas.

The lake, Thingvallavatn, is deeper than Mývatn and has steep and rocky shores, making it less attractive to waterfowl, although Great Northern Diver breeds, Harlequin Duck can be seen on the nearby River Oxara, and Barrow's Goldeneye on the River Sog, which drains the lake. Whooper Swan and other waterfowl visit on passage. Gyr Falcon, Ptarmigan and Snow Bunting are regular in the area.

Although birds are fewer and less varied than those of Mývatn this lake, only 50km from Reykjavík, is much easier to reach. The route is clearly signed from the capital and buses are frequent.

11) Westmann Islands (Vestmannaeyjar) An archipelago off the south-west coast famous for its immense seabird colonies. Only Heimaey is inhabited but the most famous of the islands is Surtsey, the second largest of the group, which rose from the sea in the 1960s as a result of volcanic activity and is now protected as a Scientific Reserve. The islands are virtually all grassland and rock, with dramatic cliffs and off-shore stacks.

Manx Shearwater and European Storm-petrel breed and the Leach's Storm-petrel colony on Ellidhaey is possibly the largest in Europe. Various gulls breed, including Glaucous, and there are also Great and Arctic Skuas, but it is the auk colonies that have made these islands famous. Razorbill and Common, Brünnich's and Black Guillemots all breed, and the world's largest Puffin colonies are here. Great Northern Diver, Long-tailed Duck and Gyr Falcon are seen in winter. These islands are also well known as a haunt of vagrant Nearctic passerines and there are records of American Robin, Ruby-crowned Kinglet and various warblers.

The archipelago can be reached by daily ferry from Thorlákshöfn or by air from Reykjavík, and boats can be hired to view the seabird colonies.

Ireland (Republic of Ireland and Northern Ireland)

Compared to continental Europe, and even Britain, the birdlife of Ireland seems rather impoverished and many woodland birds, in particular, are missing. However, some waterfowl species winter in internationally important numbers and there are excellent seabird colonies. Red Grouse is widespread and Red-billed Chough breeds on many coasts. Many foreign birders visit Ireland for the seawatching and, due to its position, the country can boast some of the best in the entire region. Shearwaters can occur off the south-west in huge numbers and

vagrant tubenoses are frequently seen. Another attraction is Nearctic vagrants and waders in particular, which occur more regularly here than anywhere else in the Western Palearctic, except perhaps the Azores. Autumn is by far the best time for vagrants.

1) Akeragh Lough On the coast of Kerry in the south-west, Akeragh is famous amongst birders as one of the premier sites for vagrant Nearctic waders and waterfowl on this side of the Atlantic. The lake is brackish and shallow, fringed by reedbeds and surrounded by damp grassland, and dries out to some extent in summer. The waders present depends on water levels and the nearby beach is sometimes more productive.

Although the North American vagrants reaching Akeragh do not match those of a few decades ago there is still an excellent chance of something special in autumn. Pectoral Sandpiper is annual and double figures are reached in some years, and others have included Solitary, Baird's, White-rumped, Western and Least Sandpipers, Long-billed Dowitcher and Stilt Sandpiper. Many European waders also occur here in autumn including occasional Temminck's Stint. Various ducks occur in autumn and winter, and both Bewick's and Whooper Swans are regular. Red-billed Chough feeds in the surrounding fields.

The lough lies south of the village of Ballyheige and is private property, but can be explored on foot or viewed from Route 105 which passes the lake.

2) Belfast Lough Despite heavy industrialisation Belfast Lough has several excellent birding sites along both the northern and southern shores. Close to Belfast, there are artificial lagoons and mudflats remain in the inner lough, with rockier shores and sandy bays towards the mouth. The lough holds nationally important wintering numbers of various species, with more than 20,000 birds regularly present. Waders are the most numerous but the area has good numbers of divers, grebes and seaduck.

Many waders occur at Belfast Lough RSPB Reserve, within Belfast Harbour Estate. Covering the remaining mudflats between Whitehouse and Holywood and a large artificial lagoon, in recent years this has become the best birding spot in the area with c.100 species recorded annually and rarities frequently reported. A small flock of Pale-bellied Brent Goose is regular and gulls include annual Ring-billed, Mediterranean, Iceland and Glaucous. There is a comfortable heated observation room, with toilets, information and telescopes for public use as well as further hides.

Further from Belfast the shore is more accessible from Holywood onwards, with rockier parts towards the mouth of the lough at Bangor holding Purple Sandpiper in winter. Black Guillemot can be seen at Bangor Pier and in winter Great Northern and sometimes Black-throated Divers on the lough, as well as grebes and Long-tailed Duck.

The RSPB reserve is signed from the A2 Belfast-Bangor road and the southern side of the lough can be viewed from several points between Holywood and Bangor, and the northern shore between Newtownabbey and Carrickfergus.

3) Cape Clear Island World famous as a seawatching site, this is a hilly, scrub-covered island, with small wooded patches and gardens, off the south-west tip of Ireland.

Breeders include Common and Black Guillemots, Razorbill and Puffin, as well as Red-billed Chough. However, it is seabirds, and shearwaters in particular, that have made this a birding destination. Manx, Great and Sooty Shearwaters are most numerous, Cory's less so (but has occurred in hundreds) and Balearic is occasional in autumn and winter. Also regular are Sabine's Gull and European and Leach's Storm-petrels, auks and skuas. It is also well known as a site for wind-blown vagrants from North America, which occur annually, as do Siberian vagrants. For seawatching and rarities late summer to autumn is the best time to visit. Rarities such as Black-browed Albatross and Bulwer's Petrel have been seen, and Little Shearwater and Fea's Petrel are increasingly recorded.

There is a bird observatory and up to ten visitors can stay on a self-catering basis, but advance booking is essential. The island is reached by daily mail boat from Baltimore in Co. Cork. Boat trips in search of pelagic species are sometimes possible.

4) Cliffs of Moher At more than 200m high and 10km long the Cliffs of Moher are an impressive sight and the most popular tourist destination in Co. Clare. The structure of the cliffs with layers of different rocks has resulted in ideal nesting sites for various seabirds.

Common Guillemot and Razorbill are among the breeding seabirds, and Red-billed Chough and Twite also nest here. Just offshore and viewable from the visitor centre is Goat Island, where 1,000 pairs of Puffins make their nesting burrows.

Cliffs of Moher are reached by signed roads from Lisdoonvarna or Liscannor. There is a car park and visitor centre as well as clifftop walks.

5) Galley Head Ireland's most famous seawatching point after Cape Clear Island, Galley Head also attracts migrant passerines and waders.

Red-billed Chough breeds on the cliffs, but the main interest is during passage periods. Skuas, shearwaters and petrels pass offshore, particularly in south-westerly winds in autumn, at which time Fea's Petrel is possible amongst other rare seabirds. Passerine migrants also occur and the area has a reputation for turning up Nearctic vagrants.

Galley Head is south-west of Clonakilty and reached by following signs for Red Strand. Much of the promontory can be explored but the tip is private and should not be entered without permission.

6) Ireland's Eye This small island close to Dublin has breeding seabirds including Ireland's most recently established gannetry. The island has grass-covered slopes with steep cliffs and there is a rocky stack offshore.

Among breeding seabirds are Manx Shearwater, Common and Black Guillemots, Razorbill and a few pairs of Puffin. Skuas and European Storm-petrel occur offshore in autumn, and Pale-bellied Brent Goose on the island in winter.

Birds are best seen by hiring a boat at Howth Harbour and rounding the island.

7) Kinsale Old Head of Kinsale is another of Ireland's best seawatching points and the cliffs also host breeding seabirds. Scrub and farmland at the base of the point attract passerine migrants and there is a small marsh nearby which can be good for waders.

Common and Black Guillemots, Razorbill and Red-billed Chough breed on the cliffs, skuas, shearwaters and other seabirds pass in autumn, and divers occur on the sea in winter. Seawatching is best in autumn during strong south-westerly winds and Fea's Petrel is a possibility here.

The town of Kinsale is on the south coast of Ireland, south-west of Cork. The Old Head is west of the town and the marsh just inland.

8) Mullet Peninsula and Islands The Mullet is a long peninsula, almost an island, in north-western County Mayo. The west coast has sandy beaches with dunes and machair and there are rocky cliffs and windswept headlands. There are several sites of interest including Termoncarragh Lake in the north, Annagh Marsh just to the south-west and two lakes further south, Cross Lough and Leam Lough. Offshore there are islands with seabird colonies and the promontories along the peninsula have great potential for seawatching.

The Mullet is of importance for two breeders, Corn Crake, which breeds at Termoncarragh, and Red-necked Phalarope, a few pairs of which still nest at Annagh. Greater White-fronted Goose occurs in winter, as well as Whooper Swan and various ducks and waders. Wintering gulls at Belmullet often include Ring-billed, Glaucous and Iceland. During passage periods the peninsula can be excellent with a wide range of waterfowl and waders passing through. Seawatching can produce Great and Sooty Shearwaters and all four European skuas. The shallow and sheltered Broadhaven Bay to the north and Blacksod Bay to the south attract waders in good numbers. The nearby islands of Inishglora and Inishkeeragh have breeding European Storm-petrel and Black Guillemot. The islands are also important for wintering Barnacle Goose and Purple Sandpiper and Turnstone. Vagrants are inevitable at such a location and various Nearctic waterfowl, waders and passerines have been record-ed. Many more vagrants undoubtedly go unrecorded at this under-watched site.

Belmullet makes the best base and all the mainland birding spots can be reached by road from there. It may be possible to reach the islands by hiring a fishing boat.

9) North Bull A long narrow sandbar in Dublin Bay, North Bull is a popular recreational beach but there are also extensive mudflats and saltmarsh that provide important feeding and roosting sites for waders and waterfowl. Breeding species are few but during passage and winter the birder can expect large numbers of a variety of species.

Pale-bellied Brent Goose is among the most numerous of the waterfowl and various seaducks, divers and grebes occur offshore. Most of the regular European waders occur, with the occasional Pectoral Sandpiper, and the tip has regular wintering Purple Sandpiper. Snow Bunting occurs on the sands in winter. Vagrant waders and waterfowl are frequently recorded and Black Brant is almost regular.

North Bull has an information centre and is within easy reach of Dublin.

10) North Slob Sited in Wexford Harbour, North Slob is one of the best wetland areas in the country. The main habitats are mudflats and wet meadows with numerous drainage channels, ideal for geese and other waterfowl.

The area is most famous for Greenland White-fronted Goose, with *c.*50 per cent the global population wintering here, along with Pink-footed, Pale-bellied Brent and Barnacle Geese. Snow Goose and the smaller races of Canada Goose are also regular and are likely to be genuine vagrants having accompanied migrating White-fronts. Other wintering species include Slavonian Grebe, Bewick's Swan and various ducks and waders. In autumn transatlantic waders are regular. Divers and seaducks occur offshore on passage and in winter.

The best time to visit is October to April when the largest numbers of waterfowl are present, although earlier in the autumn is better for waders. The area is reached via the Wexford-Gorey road and there are hides and an observation tower.

11) Rathlin Island Off the coast of Co. Antrim, Rathlin, part of which is an RSPB reserve, has dramatic cliffs, moors and grassland and several breeding birds of interest. Migrants also occur and around 200 species have been recorded.

Manx Shearwater, Common and Black Guillemots, Razorbill and Puffin breed, as well as Rock Pipit and, although breeding is irregular, Twite occur in summer. Offshore, skuas, petrels and Sooty Shearwaters frequently pass and seaduck including scoters can be seen during the boat trip across the sound.

The island is reached by daily boat service in summer from Ballycastle, depending on the weather. Boat trips to see the seabirds can be arranged and bus tours of the island are available.

12) Saltee Islands About 5km off the coast of County Wexford are the two Saltee islands, the larger of which, Great Saltee, has rocky cliffs and boulder-strewn beaches and a scrub covered interior. There are internationally important numbers of seabirds breeding here and migrants appear in good numbers. Little Saltee has fewer seabirds but probably has migrants of interest.

Breeding seabirds include Manx Shearwater, Common Guillemot, Razorbill and Puffin, as well as Red-billed Chough and Rock Pipit. Passage brings passerine migrants in large numbers and most springs produce scarce migrants such as Hoopoe, Tawny Pipit, Golden Oriole and Woodchat Shrike, with rarer species often recorded. South-easterly winds produce the best birding in spring. Skuas and shearwaters may be seen off the islands during southerly winds in autumn.

Day trips to the islands can be arranged in Kilmore Quay, but permission from the owners is required to stay overnight. The best time to visit is mid-May when migrants will be present and seabirds arriving.

13) Strangford Lough This huge waterbody is connected to the sea by a narrow channel between the villages of Strangford and Portaferry. The lough has rocky shores at the entrance but the most important habitat is the vast areas of mudflats exposed at low tide. In addition there are *Zostera* beds and saltmarsh at the north end of the lough. Quoile Pondage is an artificial freshwater lagoon in the south-west corner of great importance to wintering waterfowl and Pale-bellied Brent in particular.

At peak times Strangford Lough hosts more than 20,000 waterfowl and 40,000 waders, and is one of the most important sites for birds in Ireland. In addition to Pale-bellied Brent there are Greenland White-fronts and a few Whooper Swans. Divers and grebes winter as well as a range of seaducks. Common and Black Guillemots and Razorbill can often be seen near the lough's entrance.

September to October brings peak Brent numbers and the widest range of species. There are roads around many of the lough's shores and numerous viewing points. However, there is a Wildfowl & Wetlands Trust reserve at Castle Espie, which has full visitor facilities including an information centre.

14) Tacumshin and Lady's Island Lakes A shallow coastal lagoon separated from the sea by a ridge of sand and shingle, Tacumshin Lake is well known as a rare wader haunt. The lake has low sandy islands, a small marsh known as 'White Hole' at the south-western corner and reedbeds in the north-west. Nearby Lady's Island Lake has more water but generally fewer birds.

Breeders are few at Tacumshin but Lady's Island Lake has terns including Roseate. The main interest at both lakes is in autumn when most of the regular European waders can be seen and there is the possibility of rarer species such as Broad-billed and Marsh Sandpipers from the east and various North American species. Pectoral Sandpiper is annual and White-rumped and Baird's virtually so. Wintering and passage waterfowl also occur, with Whooper and Bewick's Swans and Pale-bellied Brent Goose regular, and divers occur on the sea.

For Tacumshin take the road from Wexford to Kilmore Quay, turn left following signs for Tomhaggard and from here minor roads lead to the lake. Lady's Island Lake lies about 2km to the east.

Israel

Of all the countries in the Western Palearctic, Israel is one the best for birding in terms of the number of species to be seen. As well as most of the Middle Eastern specialities there is an astounding number of migrants, in particular at Eilat, in the south of the country, which is probably the best single site in the entire region. Travel is generally easy, although this can vary depending on the political situation, and access to the best birding areas is usually trouble-free. Accommodation is plentiful throughout the country and guided trips to see

species such as Hume's Owl can be arranged, particularly at Eilat.

1) Arava Valley A northward extension of the African Rift Valley, the Arava runs north from Eilat to the Dead Sea and covers large areas of cultivated land and gravel desert.

Much of the area can be explored from Route 90 and extensive coverage by birders in recent decades has led to the discovery of well-known 'hotspots', but many species are probably much more widespread than currently known. Larks and wheatears are specialities with numerous species present, and the area attracts large numbers of migrants.

For larks and wheatears the area around the Km 33 post is probably the best in the Western Palearctic. Larks possible include Dunn's and Thick-billed, Bimaculated, Desert and Bar-tailed Desert, Hoopoe and Temminck's Horned. Wheatears include Desert, Mourning, Hooded and Red-tailed. Tristram's Starling, Desert Warbler and Desert Finch are also present. To find this area turn right off Route 90 just past the Km 33 post, park at the pumping station and continue on foot along the track.

Timna Valley is signposted from Route 90 between Km 33 and Km 40. The impressive rocks are a popular tourist attraction but for birders there is the opportunity to see various desert species such as Egyptian Vulture, Sooty Falcon and Sand Partridge, with Lichtenstein's Sandgrouse at dusk at the lake.

One of the most famous areas for migrants is known as Km 40 where date palms and bushy areas attract passerine migrants, and a sewage farm and marshy pools hold passage waders and ducks. Lichtenstein's Sandgrouse may come to drink at dusk. The surrounding desert has Hooded and Isabelline Wheatears. To explore this area turn right off Route 90 shortly after the Km 40 post.

Yotvata is c.40km north of Eilat on Route 90 and has cultivated land that attracts a variety of passerine migrants and has a good selection of resident species. One area worth checking is west of Route 90 opposite the Km 50 post. Arabian Warbler and wintering Cyprus Warbler can be seen here and Barbary Falcon is possible over the nearby hills. Some of the best areas can be found by turning right off Route 90 at Yotvata petrol station. This road leads to fields with large numbers of pipits, wagtails and other migrants. There is also a sewage farm where the Spanish Sparrows are worth checking for Dead Sea Sparrow. The *Acacia* trees around Ye'elim Holiday Village hold regular Arabian Warbler as well as Masked Shrike, Palestine Sunbird and Arabian Babbler. A track to the right at the Km 53 post north of Yotvata leads to more fields with migrant passerines including Spectacled Warbler and Oriental Skylark, and perhaps pratincoles, courser and even Macqueen's Bustard. Still further north, at a sewage farm near Shizzafon on the Beer Sheva road, Crowned Sandgrouse visit to drink in the mornings and other birds include Sand Partridge, Hooded and White-tailed Wheatears.

Kibbutz Lotan is becoming one of the most popular birding areas in the valley and the wide range of habitats attracts a variety of breeding, passage and wintering birds. Among scarcer birds regularly seen here are Citrine Wagtail, Red-breasted and Semi-collared Flycatchers, and Cretzschmar's and Cinereous Buntings. The nearby wadi at Nahal Quetura hosts Desert Eagle Owl and Arabian Warbler all year, and Striated Scops Owl and Cyprus Warbler in winter.

Shizaf Nature Reserve is one of the best birding areas in the north of the valley. Located south of Hazeva off Route 90 the reserve has sandgrouse, Desert Eagle Owl and many birds typical of further south, including Arabian Warbler, Arabian Babbler, Brown-necked Raven, Dead Sea Sparrow and House Bunting. The field school at Hazeva has sewage ponds that regularly attract Spotted and Crowned Sandgrouse.

2) Bet Shean Valley This fertile valley of farmland, fishponds and reservoirs attracts an outstanding range of birds including waterfowl, waders, herons and storks, gulls and terns, as well as many passerines. The best-known area is around Kfar Ruppin kibbutz but the entire valley provides excellent birding.

Pygmy Cormorant and Pallas' Gull are regular in winter and the reservoirs and fishponds also attract herons and storks, Little and Baillon's Crakes, Whiskered Tern and White Pelican. White-breasted and Pied Kingfishers are common and a variety of ducks occur. Passerines include Clamorous Reed Warbler and regular passage Citrine Wagtail. The fields around the kibbutz hold regular wintering Little Bustard, passage pratincoles, Stone-curlew, Spur-winged and possibly Sociable Lapwings. Black Francolin is fairly common and passerines include various larks, pipits and wheatears.

Kfar Ruppin kibbutz lies close to the Jordanian border due east of Bet Shean town, and can be reached on Route 71, then turning onto Route 6688. Neve Eitan kibbutz, also east of Bet Shean, is another excellent birding site.

3) Eilat and surrounding area For sheer variety of species there are few better birding areas in our region than Eilat on the Red Sea coast where over 420 species have been recorded.

During passage periods it is not only variety but also numbers that impress, with more than one million raptors passing annually. Most of the Western Palearctic's migratory raptors can be seen, plus rarities such as Eastern Honey-buzzard, which has become regular in recent years. There are also storks and Greater Flamingo, herons, waterfowl, waders and crakes, and numerous passerine migrants throughout the area, attracted in particular to the farmland around the town. Sited in a largely desert area, any vegetation will attract migrants and there are gardens, palm plantations and scrubby wadis as well as cultivated areas.

The local breeders are of great interest and include Lichtenstein's Sandgrouse and Sand Partridge, numerous larks and wheatears, Tristram's Starling and Brown-necked Raven. Other specialities include Dead Sea Sparrow, Desert Finch, Trumpeter Finch and House Bunting. Two elusive and highly sought-after owls can be seen in the Eilat region, Hume's and Striated Scops, but seeing them often requires local help.

Eilat is visited each year by hundreds of birders and this has led to certain 'hotspots' becoming established. Most visitors begin their birding at North Beach where many of the hotels are situated. At the far north of the Red Sea, Eilat is visited by seabirds difficult to see elsewhere in the Western Palearctic such as Brown Booby and White-eyed Gull. Others, such as Slender-billed Gull and Gull-billed Tern, are regular but with strong southerly winds there is the possibility of rarer birds such as Streaked Shearwater, Red-billed Tropicbird and White-cheeked Tern. Striated and Western Reef Herons are usually present. Crakes often occur along the Sewage Canal, where it empties into the sea at North Beach. Waders can include Greater Sand Plover and the canal is good for White-breasted Kingfisher and Little Green Bee-eater.

Inland and west of the canal are the Saltpans where Greater Flamingo, herons and a range of waders occur. Slender-billed Gull is regular, as are marsh terns and, often, Gull-billed and Caspian Terns. Sooty and Barbary Falcons pass through in autumn and migrant passerines include Red-throated Pipit and Citrine Wagtail. North of the Saltpans are Palm Plantations that attract a host of passerine migrants. Further north but still within walking distance of the town is an area known as the South Fields where large numbers of migrants of all kinds occur. Many common European species can be seen, as well as more eastern birds, and this is a good site for Namaqua Dove. The Eilat Bird Sanctuary and Ringing Station is located on the site of a former refuse tip north of the Saltpans and close to the Jordanian border crossing. The pools and bushes host many migrant passerines and rarities are often trapped.

There is an information centre at the entrance to Kibbutz Eilot with a bird log. The North Fields also attract migrant passerines with regular Oriental Skylark. Desert Finch and Dead Sea Sparrow are also present and Caspian Plover is sometimes seen here in spring. The North Fields are best reached by road, take Route 90 north from Eilat and turn right on the new road to Aqaba, then left on a track beside a date plantation. Continuing north are the Northern Reservoirs or Saltpans where passage terns and waders occur and ducks in winter. Desert and Isabelline Wheatear are found in the surrounding desert, with Crowned Sandgrouse sometimes seen.

Amram's Pillars, reached by turning left off Route 90 at the Km 20 post, has rock formations that attract tourists, but for birders there is a range of desert species including Sand Partridge, Egyptian Vulture and Sooty Falcon, and passerines including Hooded and Mourning Wheatears, Desert Warbler and Brown-necked Raven. This is also a regular wintering site for Sinai Rosefinch.

Lichtenstein's Sandgrouse breeds in the deserts around Eilat but can be regularly seen at the pumping Station north-west of the town. This water also attracts Sand Partridge, Trumpeter Finch, House Bunting, Arabian Babbler and Blackstart. Originally attracted to a small pool, the birds now drink from a specially provided tray. The pumping station is best visited just before dusk, but care must be taken to avoid disturbance. To reach the station head for the top of Jerusalem Street, cross the junction and continue until a sharp left-hand bend, shortly after which there is a track to the right, signed Nahal Netaphim, and the pumping station is on the right. The pumping station track leads into the Eilat Mountains and by keeping right at all junctions it follows Wadi Roded until it reaches Eilot Kibbutz close to Route 90 north of Eilat. A good range of local specialities occurs here including Palestine Sunbird and Tristram's Starling, as well as Scrub Warbler and wheatears, with Cyprus Warbler in winter.

Within easy reach of Eilat, the Eilat Mountains are best known as a raptor migration watchpoint and most of the many species that pass through southern Israel can be seen in good numbers from these hills. Verreaux's Eagle has been seen with some frequency and both Hume's and Desert Eagle Owls are possible. Raptor watching is best from higher areas and in particular on Mount Yoash, reached from the Ovda road west of Eilat and considered by some to be one of the best sites in the world for spring raptor-watching. En Netaphim has a spring, which attracts many of the typical desert species. The spring is signed to the right from the Ovda road just past Mount Yoash. Nahal Shamon, just outside the town on Route 12, is a well known site for Striated Scops Owl, although care must be taken as Eurasian Scops Owl also occurs.

Rarities frequently appear at Eilat, especially on passage and virtually any Palearctic migrant could occur, as well as the occasional wanderer from Arabia or Africa. News of such sightings is spread via the Birdwatching Information Centre on Hatmarin Boulevard, open every evening for the exchange of information on sightings and sites, and from here trips to see birds such as Hume's Owl can be arranged. Eilat is easily reached by air from Europe, and one of the easiest and cheapest ways to visit is on a package holiday.

4) Ein Gedi This wadi on the western shore of the Dead Sea is protected by two nature reserves, Nahal David and Nahal Arugot, and has breeding Middle Eastern specialities, as well as being an important migrant spot.

This was a regular site for Hume's Owl, but although this species may still be seen in the area, it can no longer be guaranteed. However, there are many other birds of interest including Sand and Chukar Partridges, Little Green Bee-eater, Desert Lark and Arabian Babbler. Three species of raven occur here, as well as Tristram's Starling. Griffon Vulture occurs on passage but is also resident, as are Golden and Bonelli's Eagles and Long-legged Buzzard. Lanner, Barbary and Sooty Falcons are also present and Verreaux's Eagle has been recorded. Eagles also occur on passage including Short-toed, Steppe, Lesser Spotted and Eastern Imperial. Passerine migrants include many chats and warblers, Cyprus Warbler winters in the area, and Wallcreeper and Syrian Serin are possible at this season. There is a population of the introduced Indian Silverbill at the Nahal David National Reserve.

Ein Gedi is one hour by road south of Jerusalem and there are other wadis further south worth searching; Wadi en Zafzafa and Wadi n Ze'elim are particularly good.

5) Golan Heights After Mount Hermon this is the most important area for upland birds in Israel and consists of rocky hills and rough pastures with spectacular gorges. The best areas are in the south of the range, to the east of the Sea of Galilee.

The **Gamla Nature Reserve** is one of the best sites in the country for breeding raptors, with Griffon and Egyptian Vultures, Short-toed and Bonelli's Eagles, and Long-legged Buzzard. Eurasian Eagle Owl and Little Swift also occur, and breeding passerines include Long-billed Pipit, Black-eared Wheatear, Blue Rock Thrush, Southern Grey Shrike and Black-headed Bunting. Eurasian Crag Martin and Finsch's Wheatear occur in winter, as well as Black Vulture. This species can be seen throughout the year at Wadi Meizar further south. The Bnei Israel Reservoir has wintering Marbled Duck, Common Crane and Little Bustard, and sometimes Black-bellied Sandgrouse. In the north of the range, around El Rom and Meyrom Golan, there are breeding Calandra and Bimaculated Larks, and Radde's Accentor, Red-fronted Serin and Pine Bunting are possible in winter. Great Bustard has been recorded wintering in the Golan Heights.

Gamla National Reserve is reached from Route 87, then Route 808 at Ha-Mapalim, which also leads to the reservoir, and Wadi Meizar lies east of Mevo Khama and is reached from Route 98.

6) Hula Reserve Hula (Huleh) lies north of the Sea of Galilee and covers one of Israel's most outstanding wetlands consisting of fishponds, papyrus beds and a reservoir set within cultivated land. Recent habitat restoration has increased the reserve area and made it one of the best birding sites in Israel. Much of the surrounding valley has similar habitats and birds.

Major birding attractions are Pygmy Cormorant, White Pelican and Common Crane on passage and in winter, and there are many other Middle Eastern specialities such as Black Francolin, White-breasted and Pied Kingfishers, Clamorous Reed Warbler and Dead Sea Sparrow. Various herons breed and Greater Flamingo is often present, ducks are numerous, particularly in winter and can include Ruddy Shelduck, Red-crested Pochard, Marbled, Ferruginous and White-headed. A wide range of raptors occurs in autumn and winter with Greater Spotted, Eastern Imperial, Steppe, Lesser Spotted, Short-toed, Booted and White-tailed Eagles all regular. Harriers, including

Pallid, roost here in large numbers, along with Black Kite, and Long-legged Buzzard and Saker are also seen. Little Bustard and Red-breasted Goose are possible in winter. Passerines include regular wintering Citrine Wagtail, Moustached Warbler and Penduline Tit.

Hula is reached from Route 90 c.12km north of Rosh Pinna (which has a Lesser Kestrel colony) and is clearly signed. There is a car park and reception centre, well-marked trails, hides, boardwalks and observation towers, it is open 08.00–16.00 (15.00 on Fridays), and there is an entrance fee.

7) Jezreel Valley Only relatively recently has the importance for birds of this part of northern Israel been recognised. This fertile valley is heavily cultivated and there are two large reservoirs, and the area attracts migrant waterbirds and raptors in large numbers.

Tishlovit and neighbouring Kefar Baruch Reservoirs are very attractive to passage and wintering waterfowl, hosting a variety of species including Marbled, Ferruginous and White-headed Ducks and Ruddy Shelduck and Red-crested Pochard. White Pelican and Common Crane occur in winter and various herons, waders and crakes on passage. Large numbers of migrant raptors pass through and there is a survey station 1km south of Kibbutz Ginnegar. Among the most numerous raptors are Short-toed and Lesser Spotted Eagles, Levant Sparrowhawk and Red-footed Falcon, but Steppe, Greater Spotted and Booted Eagles, harriers, Eleonora's Falcon and Lesser Kestrel also occur.

Tishlovit can be reached from Route 73, turning south 1km west of Kibbutz Ginnegar. This leads to a lorry park and from here turn left for Tishlovit or continue straight on to Kefar Baruch. All of the fields in this area are worth checking for migrants, which can include Sociable Lapwing.

8) Ma'agan Mikhael Within easy reach of Tel Aviv and with specialities such as Pallas' and Armenian Gulls, this is a very popular birding site. An area of fishponds close to the Mediterranean coast, this site attracts a wide range of seabirds, waders and other wetland birds. The ponds are situated in an area of orchards and scrubby fields, which also host birds of interest.

Pallas' and Armenian Gulls are winter visitors, generally present October to April, and Slender-billed Gull is also seen. Greater Sand Plover and Spur-winged Lapwing are also regular and Kittlitz's Plover has occurred in winter. Greater Painted-snipe is a possibility and Crab Plover has been recorded. Regular passage waders include Temminck's Stint, and Marsh, Terek and Broad-billed Sandpipers. White Pelican, storks, Greater Flamingo, Glossy Ibis and Eurasian Spoonbill can be seen, as well as various herons and ducks. White-breasted and Pied Kingfishers are easily found and Little and Baillon's Crake are often present. Passerines around the ponds include Clamorous Reed Warbler and, in winter, Moustached Warbler, Bluethroat and Penduline Tit. Scrub and cultivated areas hold Crested Lark, Graceful Prinia and, in summer, Rüppell's Warbler. Yelkouan Shearwaters are common offshore. Vagrants are frequently reported and have included Nearctic waders.

Ma'agan Mikhael lies just north of Nasholim beside the Tel Aviv-Haifa motorway, c.50km north of Tel Aviv and 30km south of Haifa. There are further fishponds to the north, at Mayan Zevi, and further north still is the beach resort of Nasholim, where seawatching from the rocky headlands can produce shearwaters and skuas.

9) Mount Hermon No birding trip to Israel is complete without visiting Mount Hermon in the extreme north-east of the country and, at 2,224m, Israel's highest peak. The summit and the approach have an excellent range of birds, many of which are difficult to see anywhere else in Israel. Mount Hermon has forests and alpine meadows and a ski-centre at about 2,000m.

The approach road, Route 98 from Galilee, passes through stony desert with Isabelline and, possibly, Finsch's Wheatears, Crested and possibly Calandra and Bimaculated Larks. Further on Cretzschmar's Bunting, Upcher's and Rüppell's Warblers are likely, and between Mas'ada and Majdal Shams White-throated Robin is present in summer. Another excellent area is between the Nimrod Fortress and Neve Ativ ski village, on Route 989, which also leads to Majdal Shams. From Majdal Shams to the ski lift Rock Thrush and Rock Sparrow occur on the hillsides, and sometimes Olive-tree Warbler. Pale Rock Sparrow also occurs at mid altitudes on Mount Hermon. Around the ski lift is the best area for Syrian Serin and Western Rock Nuthatch, and Sombre Tit can be found in nearby woodlands. Crimson-winged Finch is usually found only on the summit and to see this species it is necessary to take the ski lift from the ski centre. Alpine Chough can also be seen at the highest levels but is rare, the endemic race of Shore Lark is also possible and Wallcreeper occurs in winter. Raptors include Griffon and Egyptian Vultures, Bonelli's and Short-toed Eagles, Long-legged Buzzard and Levant Sparrowhawk. A winter visit to M Hermon may produce Radde's Accentor, Red-fronted Serin and Pine Bunting, which are all rare in Israel.

Visiting this area has been little problem in the past, despite the presence of army barriers on the road above Majdal Shams, where it may be necessary to obtain permission.

10) Nizzana area In the Negev desert on the sensitive Israeli/Egyptian border, Nizzana has a large military presence at all times and birders have been asked to leave the area. However, the area has some of the best desert birding in the Middle East.

This area is the best site in Israel for Macqueen's Bustard but there are also Sand Partridge, four species of sandgrouse and Cream-coloured Courser. Larks include Short-toed and Lesser Short-toed, also Hoopoe, Temminck's Horned and Bar-tailed Desert, but these are scarcer, and even Thick-billed is possible. Wheatears include Isabelline, Desert, Mourning and Finsch's. Other passerines include Scrub and Spectacled Warblers, Palestine Sunbird, Desert Finch and Trumpeter Finch.

Nizzana is c.55km south-west of Beer Sheva on Route 40; turn west after Telalim following signs for Ashalim, and Nizzana is about 40km further on. On the approach from Telalim, the fields in the Ashalim area are good for sandgrouse and raptors, and along the track to the military camp at Qeziot are some sewage ponds that attract Spotted, Black-bellied, Crowned and, sometimes, Pin-tailed Sandgrouse. Nizzana Castle has Desert Wheatear and Orphean Warbler, in winter also Finsch's Wheatear and Syrian Serin, and the road towards Azzuz runs through a good area for bustards.

11) Tel Shiqmona Israel's best seawatching point lies west of Haifa within easy reach of the city.

In autumn Yelkouan Shearwater occurs in hundreds, with smaller numbers of Cory's Shearwater, Arctic Skua and Slender-billed Gull. Armenian Gull can be seen all year and Pallas' Gull is regular in winter, when Greater Sand Plover also occurs.

Tel Shiqmona can be reached via Route 4 and morning visits are most productive, particularly in strong westerly winds.

12) Urim area The north-western Negev Desert, particularly between Urim and Ze'elim, is probably the best area for wintering raptors in Israel.

Eastern Imperial, Greater Spotted and Steppe Eagles, Long-legged Buzzard, Black Kite and Pallid Harrier are all present, and falcons include Lanner and Saker. As well as raptors there is a wide range of desert birds such as Cream-coloured Courser and two species of sandgrouse, and wintering Sociable Lapwing is regular. Larks are very common and include Greater Short-toed, Bimaculated and Calandra. Other species present in late autumn/winter (the best time for raptors) include Chukar Partridge, Dotterel, Spur-winged Lapwing, and Red-throated and Tawny Pipits. Common Crane occurs on passage and in winter. Macqueen's Bustard is possible and is perhaps best searched for off Route 222, in the Revivim and Retamim areas, and off Route 232 around Moshav Dekel.

To reach Urim take Route 34 from Beer Sheva, turning west onto Route 241 and after 10km turn left towards Urim, and left again heading south towards Ze'elim. A line of electricity pylons crosses this road and this is often the best area for the raptors. All of the open land around here can be productive and various tracks can be followed to explore off-road. Nearby is Wadi Besor, another site worthy of exploration further west on Route 241. The wadi has Eurasian Scops Owl and Syrian Woodpecker, and Desert Eagle Owl can be seen in a quarry on the nearby hillside.

13) Wadi Ammud and Mount Arbel These two sites lies close to the north-western shore of the Sea of Galilee and are popular with birders for several Middle Eastern specialities.

Wadi Ammud is a regular haunt of Long-billed Pipit, Lesser Kestrel, Desert Eagle Owl and Little Swift. Other birds here include Griffon and Egyptian Vultures, Long-legged Buzzard and Chukar Partridge, whilst Eurasian Crag Martin, Graceful Prinia, Palestine Sunbird and Rock Sparrow are common. Wallcreeper has been recorded here. From Tiberias take Route 90 N, turning left onto Route 8077 after c.10km and the valley is 3km further on. Park on the right and walk north into the gorge. An afternoon/evening visit tends to produce the best birds.

Mount Arbel is known to birders as a winter site for Alpine Accentor and Wallcreeper. Other species include Long-billed Pipit, Radde's Accentor has been recorded and is perhaps regular, and Finsch's Wheatear is possible. Spanish Sparrow and Palestine Sunbird are common. Take Route 77 west from Tiberias and turn right after 4km onto Route 7717 towards Arbel, and follow signs for the National Park. There is a marked trail through the various habitats.

Italy

Probably due to the widespread hunting and the supposed consequent lack of birds, few birders visit Italy. However, the conservation movement is now gaining pace and an interest in birds, other than as shooting targets, is growing. Italy has mountains, the Alps in the far north and the Apennines in the centre, as well as some very good wetland areas, notably in the Po Delta. Although a popular country with tourists with plentiful accommodation, car hire and easy travel, Italy is expensive, which is perhaps another reason for the lack of interest among foreign birders. A spring visit would probably be most productive.

1) Abruzzo National Park In the central Apennines, between 700 and 2,200m, Abruzzo is the last stronghold of several rare mammals and also has a good selection of montane and forest birds. Habitats vary but this is very much an upland area with ancient beech woodland mixed with Black Pine on the lower slopes, dwarf pines further up, and meadows and bare rock on the high peaks.

Birds of the higher areas include Golden Eagle, Rock Partridge and Dotterel, and passerines such as both choughs, Alpine Accentor, Wallcreeper and Snowfinch. The forests are extremely rich in birds with Eurasian Eagle and other owls, Northern Goshawk, and woodpeckers including Middle Spotted and the *lilfordi* race of White-backed. In addition there are Hawfinch and Western Bonelli's Warbler.

Pescasseroli, in the centre of the park, has been developed as a ski resort and is home to the park headquarters. The park can be reached on the S83, from the Pescina exit of the A25 motorway linking Rome and Pescara.

2) Circeo National Park Established to protect a remnant of the once-extensive Pontine Marshes this National Park largely consists of lakes and wet meadows and forests of evergreen oak. In addition there is the 540m Mount Circeo and the scrub covered island of Zannone. The wide range of habitats attract a good diversity of birds to a relatively small and easily accessible area.

Typical Mediterranean breeders include Great Spotted Cuckoo, European Roller, Sardinian and Subalpine Warblers, and shrikes. Wetland breeders include Little Bittern, Cetti's Warbler, Zitting Cisticola and Penduline Tit, and Cory's Shearwater breeds on Zannone. This island is also home to small population of the introduced Erckel's Francolin. Grey-headed Woodpecker was reported here in the 1990s, far outside its usual Italian range, but current status is unclear. Passage brings Audouin's Gull, Marsh Sandpiper and Collared Pratincole, as well as Common Crane, Greater Flamingo, Glossy Ibis, Eurasian Spoonbill and both storks. Great Egret is regular with small numbers wintering and other herons include Black-crowned Night and Squacco. Slender-billed Curlew has been recorded on passage in recent years. Caspian, Gull-billed and marsh terns visit the lakes and passage raptors may include Montagu's Harrier, Greater Spotted Eagle, and Lanner and Red-footed Falcons. Moustached Warbler is regular on passage and winter visitors include Black-necked and Slavonian Grebes, Black-throated Diver and a range of waders.

The park is reached from Rome on the S7 towards Terracina, or the S148 Latina road and the Strada Mediana, and there are information centres, nature trails and guided tours.

3) Gargano Peninsula The large limestone headland on the Adriatic coast of southern Italy that forms the Gargano Peninsula is an exceptionally good area for both breeding birds and migrants, and much of the area is now a National Park. As well as the high sea cliffs there are sand dunes and farmland, Mediterranean scrub, woods of beech, oak and pine, gorges, rivers and streams. Included within the National Park are two large lakes to the north, Lesina and Varano, which are important for wintering waterfowl, the saltmarshes of Margherita di Savoia to the south, and the offshore Tremiti Is with breeding seabirds.

Raptors are well represented on the peninsula with Egyptian Vulture, kites, Short-toed Eagle, Lesser Kestrel and Lanner Falcon. In the forests are Black, White-backed and Middle Spotted Woodpeckers, and Eurasian Eagle Owl. Three species of swift nest on the cliffs and Little Bustard, Stone-curlew and European Roller in the grasslands. Passerines include many species typical of Mediterranean scrub and woodland. The Tremiti Is hold breeding Cory's and Yelkouan Shearwaters, and attract migrants such as Eleonora's Falcon, Montagu's Harrier and passerines. Among waterfowl wintering on the lakes and coast to the north are Black-throated Diver, Velvet Scoter, Ferruginous and Long-tailed Ducks, and Slender-billed Curlew was recorded in the 1980s and 1990s at Margherita di Savoia. This is also Italy's most important area for breeding Slender-billed and Mediterranean Gulls.

The Gargano Peninsula is easily reached from the main coast road and provides good birding all year. The Foresta di Umbra at the heart of the peninsula is the best area for woodpeckers and the Margherita di Savoia saltmarshes can be viewed from the S159. The Tremiti Is are reached by ferry from Termoli or Rodi Garganico.

4) Gran Paradiso National Park Situated in the extreme north-west of Italy this National Park adjoins the French Vanoise National Park and was originally established to protect the declining Ibex. Most of the park is above 3,000m and there are lakes and glaciers, alpine meadows and high peaks reaching 4,061m at Cima Gran Paradiso. Much of the forest is pine, larch and fir with smaller areas of deciduous woodland and scrub.

The park is increasingly popular with birders, with many typical forest and montane species to be seen. Golden Eagle, Ptarmigan and Rock Partridge are found in the highest areas, along with choughs, Alpine Accentor, Wallcreeper and Snowfinch. The forests hold Hazel and Black Grouse, Eurasian Eagle, Eurasian Pygmy and Tengmalm's Owls, Black and Three-toed Woodpeckers, Crested Tit, Nutcracker and Citril Finch. Lammergeiers from the French reintroduction project are sometimes seen.

There are marked trails and mountain refuges within the park, which can be reached from Aosta.

5) Isonzo Regional Park Close to the Slovenian border in the far north-east of the Adriatic this former river delta is an important breeding area and migrant staging post. Despite much loss of habitat in recent decades the area still has riparian wood-land, wet meadows, reedbeds, saltmarsh and mudflats, and the open sea. Laguna di Grado, to the west is a river-fed tidal lagoon with islands and sandbanks. More than 280 species have been recorded with nearly 100 known to have bred.

Breeders include Little Bittern and other herons, Black-winged Stilt, Cetti's and Savi's Warblers, Zitting Cisticola and Bearded Tit. However, the area is of greater importance outside the breeding season, with large numbers of waterfowl and waders feeding and roosting here, and seaducks in the nearby Panzano Gulf. Rare but regular in winter are Pygmy Cormorant, Great Bittern and Ferruginous Duck, and in spring Squacco Heron, Glossy Ibis and Eurasian Spoonbill occur.

The area can be approached from either Venice or Trieste, turning south at Monfalcone towards Grado, and then east before the bridge on the Primero Canal. From here the Isola della Cona reserve can be visited, which has an information cen-tre, hides and observation posts, and a ringing station.

6) Lake Massaciuccoli This large shallow lake is one of Italy's best-known birding sites and forms part of the Migliarino-San Rossore Natural Park. LIPU has created board-walks and hides, and over 300 species have been recorded. As well as open water there are extensive reedbeds and marshes, with the remaining land heavily cultivated.

The lake is the country's stronghold for both bitterns and Purple Heron. Also breeding are Ferruginous Duck, Black-winged Stilt, Spotted Crake, Penduline Tit, Zitting Cisticola, and Savi's and Moustached Warblers. Passage brings grebes and divers, various ducks and marsh terns, and waders can include Marsh Sandpiper. Collared Pratincole is regular in spring, as well as Great Egret and Eurasian Spoonbill. Slender-billed Curlew has been seen here in the past and could be recorded again.

Lake Massaciuccoli lies c.4km from the Tuscany coast between the towns of Lucca and Viareggio, north of Pisa, and the best access is from the village of Massaciuccoli where LIPU has a visitor centre and guided boat trips can be arranged.

7) Maremma Regional Park One of the few unspoilt parts of the Tuscan coast, the area around Maremma includes undisturbed beaches and dunes, coastal marshes at Trappola, pines and grassland with scattered olive and oak trees. In addition to an interesting range of breeders the area attracts many passage birds and wintering waterfowl.

In spring the marshes at the river mouth hold Black-winged Stilt, Pied Avocet and migrant waders including Collared Pratincole, Temminck's Stint and Marsh Sandpiper. Spring migrants include Purple Heron, raptors and Great Spotted Cuckoo, as well as a range of passerines. Autumn migrants are fewer and less varied, but Slender-billed Curlew is a possibility. Stone-curlew breeds in the drier areas, as well as European Bee-eater, European Roller and shrikes. Short-toed Eagle breeds in the nearby hills of Monte dell' Uccellina. Winter brings waterfowl including Ferruginous Duck, and off-shore Black-throated Diver and Velvet Scoter are possible.

Situated c.15km south of Grosseto, the area is best explored from Alberese. Access is limited, but on weekends and Wednesdays there is a bus service into the heart of the park from the information centre in Alberese.

8) Monte Conero One of the best birding sites on the northern Adriatic coast, Monte Conero is ideally placed to receive migrants and is well known for raptor passage. Although it covers a relatively small area, there is a good range of habitats on this limestone promontory and many breeding birds of interest. Most of the area consists of maquis but there are also pine and oak woods, rocky cliffs and offshore islets, and two small brackish lakes, Lago Grande and Lago Profondo.

Breeders include Blue Rock Thrush and Alpine Swift on the cliffs, and Sardinian Warbler, Ortolan and Cirl Buntings in scrub throughout the area. Western Honey-buzzard is the most numerous passage raptor but many other species are recorded, such as Black Kite, Pallid Harrier, Lesser Spotted, Short-toed and Booted Eagles, Lesser Kestrel, and Red-footed and Eleonora's Falcons. The lakes attract passage and wintering waterfowl and marsh terns in autumn. Passerine migration brings scarce species such as Red-rumped Swallow, Red-throated Pipit, Black-eared Wheatear and Collared Flycatcher. Winter offers divers, grebes and seaducks.

Monte Conero is c.10km south-east of Ancona and can be reached via the coast road. The lakes at Portonovo lie nestled just below the bulk of Monte Conero and can be reached from the village of Poggia di Ancona.

9) Orbetello-Burano Reserves At Orbetello the Italian WWF has created one of the best birding sites in the country. It is an important site for migrants and the varied habitats support breeding populations of many typical Mediterranean species. Laguna di Orbetello is a large lagoon separated from the sea by woods, and the smaller Lago di Burano c.20km to the south-east is a freshwater lake parallel to the sea. Habitats include fresh, brackish and saltwater, marshes and reedbeds, dunes, cultivated land, scrub and woodland. Almost 300 species have been recorded here and 70 have bred.

Breeders include Montagu's Harrier, Black-winged Stilt, Stone-curlew, European Bee-eater and Great Spotted Cuckoo. Non-breeding Greater Flamingo is usually present all year and various waders and waterfowl occur on passage, joined by grebes in winter. Slender-billed Curlew has been recorded on passage.

Orbetello Lagoon is separated from the sea by the Tombolo della Giannella, which leads to Monte Argentario, a large rocky promontory with cliffs, oak groves and garrigue. Various warblers breed here including Marmora's, as well as Tawny Pipit, Black-eared Wheatear, Ortolan and Black-headed Buntings, and small numbers of Lesser Kestrel and Short-toed Eagle. Audouin's Gull can often be seen offshore.

The town of Orbetello is c.150km north of Rome on the S1 or Via Aurelia. A permit is required for the reserve, which has an information centre and observation hide.

10) Po Delta The vast delta of the Po River is a wetland area on the northern Adriatic coast stretching from Venice south to Ravenna, and as well as marshes and lagoons includes riparian woodland and coastal pinewoods. It is of immense importance for breeding, passage and wintering birds, and contains many reserves.

This is the best area for breeding herons in Italy with both bitterns, Cattle and Great Egrets, and Black-crowned Night, Squacco and Purple Herons. Other breeding waterbirds include small numbers of Pygmy Cormorant, Glossy Ibis, Eurasian Spoonbill, Ferruginous Duck, Spotted and Little Crakes, and Collared Pratincole. More common are Black-winged Stilt, Pied Avocet, Kentish Plover and Whiskered Tern. Wetland passerines include Moustached Warbler and Bearded and Penduline Tits. Many thousands of waterfowl and waders use the delta on passage and in winter, and among the commoner species are Ferruginous Duck, and Marsh and Terek Sandpipers. Aquatic Warbler also occurs in autumn.

There is excellent birding throughout the delta but particularly good spots include the WWF reserve at Punta Alberete, which protects a small area of flooded forest with breeding Pygmy Cormorant and Glossy Ibis. Another recommended site is the Valli di Comacchio, a huge brackish lagoon surrounded by smaller lagoons, salt-marsh and farmland. LIPU have a reserve at Boscoforte, a sandy peninsula projecting into the lagoon, with breeding Collared Pratincole, Gull-billed Tern and Mediterranean Gull, and Lesser Crested Tern has bred here.

The S309 skirts the western side of the delta and minor roads lead into the area from here.

11) San Giuliano Reserve This large artificial lake and some of the surrounding farm-land and woods is a WWF reserve, and the area boasts a range of habitats. Passage periods are generally the most productive and c.170 species have been recorded.

In spring Black-winged Stilt and Pied Avocet appear at the lake, and a range of herons are seen. Raptors include both kites and sometimes Egyptian Vulture, which has bred but is mainly a scarce migrant, and the nearby town of Matera is famous for its large Lesser Kestrel colony. Other regular spring migrants are European Bee-eater and European Roller. Midsummer has fewer birds but with autumn approaching duck numbers begin to increase and thousands are present in winter including Ferruginous Duck. Scarcer migrants in autumn include Glossy Ibis and storks and terns are regular.

To reach the reserve head for Matera on the E844 from Naples, or from Bari on the S96. At Matera take the S7 to Ferrandina, turning left after 10km to follow signs for the WWF reserve. There is a visitor centre and guided tours are available.

12) Sibillini National Park In the central Apennines, this National Park has large areas of deciduous and mixed woodland, alpine meadows and bare rocks, and reaches 2,476m of Monte Vettore.

Mountain birds such as Golden Eagle, Lanner Falcon, Rock Partridge, both choughs, Alpine Accentor, Wallcreeper and Snowfinch occur and Dotterel has bred. In the lower forests are Northern Goshawk, Eurasian Eagle Owl and Middle Spotted Woodpecker, and White-backed is also possible.

The park is reached on the S4 road north of Rieti and the hills can be explored on minor roads off the S396 and S78 roads.

13) Stelvio National Park This is Italy's largest National Park and is situated in the Alps adjoining the Swiss border and the Swiss National Park. Altitudes range from 350m to over 3,900m, and the park includes deep valleys, glaciers and lakes, with larch and spruce forests in lower areas, and Arolla Pine in upland parts.

The birdlife of the park includes Golden Eagle, Ptarmigan, Capercaillie and Black Grouse, and many other typical alpine species, with Black and other woodpeckers, and Eurasian Eagle, Eurasian Pygmy and Tengmalm's Owl in the forests. Lammergeier has been reintroduced to the adjacent Swiss National Park and may wander across the border.

The National Park can be reached by road from Tirano to the south or Merano to the north-east, and there is an information centre at Bormio where the park offices are located.

14) Tuscan archipelago Seven main islands comprise this archipelago between Tuscany and Corsica, off the west coast of Italy. The entire group is now a National Park, but the most interesting island for birders is Capraia, the third largest and the closest to Corsica. Like most Mediterranean islands, the main habitats are garrigue and maquis, with small patches of pine and evergreen oak woodland, and cultivated areas. The islands have extensive rocky coastlines with important numbers of breeding seabirds.

Cory's and Yelkouan Shearwaters nest, as well as Audouin's Gull and Blue Rock Thrush. Scrubland birds are numerous and varied, with Rock Partridge, Rock Thrush, Black-eared Wheatear and *Sylvia* warblers, which include Marmora's and Spectacled. The recently split Corsican Finch occurs on Capraia and Elba, but the attraction for many birders is migrants. Spring is the optimum time on Capraia, with a huge variety of species regularly recorded including raptors, waders, crakes, storks and herons. Passerines include Greater Short-toed Lark, Ortolan Bunting and various warblers, whilst scarcer species such as Red-throated Pipit are also regular. Autumn passage involves fewer birds, but winter brings regular sightings of Alpine Accentor and Wallcreeper on Capraia.

Capraia is reached by a daily, three-hour ferry trip from Livorno and one-day trips can be arranged in high season. Shearwaters are seen from the ferry. For the rest of the year an overnight stay is required, and there are paths leading from the town into the surrounding hills and scrub, which are the best areas for passerine migrants.

Jordan

Though it attracts far fewer birding visitors then neighbouring Israel, Jordan supports most of the Middle Eastern specialities, with Verreaux's Eagle more likely here, and a large number of migrants pass through. Azraq was once one of the most important wetlands in the region and is still well worth visiting, and an excellent range of desert birds can be seen at the most impressive collection on ancient monuments outside of Egypt, at Petra.

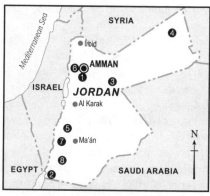

Many desert species can also be seen at Dana, and Aqaba deserves more attention than it has so far received. Most of the birds recorded at Eilat should also be possible there. There are some sensitive sites in border areas but independent birding and travel is fairly easy. Accommodation and car hire are readily available in the major towns, and there is a reasonable public transport system.

1) Amman National Park This National Park largely consists of pine plantations but it is set within an area of orchards, hillsides and wadis that holds a good selection of breeding birds and attracts many migrants.

Breeding species of interest include Chukar Partridge, Calandra Lark, Spectacled Bulbul, Rufous Bush Robin, warblers including Eastern Olivaceous, Upcher's and Spectacled, Masked Shrike and Black-headed Bunting.

The park lies west of the Desert Highway and 13km south of Amman's 7th Circle.

2) Aqaba Compared to well-watched Eilat only a few kilometres across the border in Israel, Aqaba is comparatively rarely visited by birders, although more than 350 species have been recorded and many more undoubtedly go unnoticed. There are gardens, palm groves and small cultivated areas, but overall there is much less vegetation than at Eilat, although the nearby Aqaba Mountains are likely to hold similar species to the hills around Eilat, and the sea should attract the same birds.

Vegetated areas around the town and the sewage plant to the north attract a range of passerine migrants, as well as scarcer birds such as Corn Crake, Namaqua Dove and Blue-cheeked Bee-eater. Little Green Bee-eater, Arabian Babbler and Tristram's Grackle are common in the area, but passage raptors are fewer than at Eilat. Lammergeier has been recorded in the mountains and may still breed, and other possible breeders include Lanner Falcon and Hume's Owl. At sea White-eyed and Slender-billed Gulls are regular, as are Cory's Shearwater and skuas on passage, and rarer species such as Brown Booby and White-cheeked Tern are possible. Striated and Western Reef Herons are present on the beaches, but the best areas for waders are generally south of the port towards the Saudi border, where White-tailed Lapwing, and Caspian and Greater Sand Plovers are possible.

Aqaba can be reached by air or road from Amman.

3) Azraq A Ramsar site and the most famous ornithological spot in Jordan, Azraq is an oasis in a vast area of the stony desert known as hamada, and provides a feeding and resting site for thousands of migrants. Despite much habitat loss and modification in recent decades, this is still an excellent area and provides a good base for trips into the desert for local specialities. Today, the most important area lies outside the reserve in the Qa' al Azraq, a large, flat basin which floods in wet winters. Numbers and variety of breeding birds have declined, but migrants still occur and when water levels are high birds can appear in large numbers.

An astounding variety of migrants pass through the area, with raptors such as Levant Sparrowhawk, Steppe and both Spotted Eagles, Lesser Kestrel and Red-footed Falcon, as well as most of the European waterfowl and waders. Passerines can include such sought-after species as Bimaculated Lark, White-throated Robin, Collared Flycatcher and Masked Shrike. Purple Swamphen has been recorded and Pied Kingfisher has occurred in winter. The area surrounding the Azraq oasis is home to a number of desert specialities including Macqueen's Bustard, Cream-coloured Courser, Egyptian Nightjar, Graceful and Scrub Warblers, Rufous Bush Robin and various larks and wheatears.

Azraq is easily reached by road from Amman, lying c.90km east of the city. The Qa' al Azraq lies to the east of the reserve and between the villages of South Azraq and North Azraq is a left turn leading to the government-run rest house, the gardens of which attract many migrant passerines. About 10km to the south-west is Shaumari Wildlife Reserve, where Macqueen's Bustard occurred until about 1980 and may still do so, and Cinereous Bunting has been recorded.

4) Ghadir Burqu' This site consists of a large near-permanent freshwater pool at the eastern limit of the basaltic desert in eastern Jordan and is one of the most important birding areas in this part of the country. The area attracts large numbers of migrants and there are many desert specialities in the surrounding boulder fields.

Grebes, ducks, raptors and waders occur on passage, as well as passerines, and Common Crane winters in the area. Macqueen's Bustard almost certainly occurs in winter and may still breed in the area, and Finsch's Wheatear winters. Other species probably breeding include Long-legged Buzzard, Golden Eagle, Sand Partridge, Cream-coloured Courser, Greater Sand Plover, Bar-tailed Desert, Thick-billed and Temminck's Horned Larks, and Desert Wheatear.

The area can be reached by 4WD, north-west from the pumping station at Muqat.

5) Petra This famous ancient city, the biggest tourist attraction in Jordan, is on the edge of Wadi Araba in a deep canyon in rugged sandstone hills, entered through a narrow gorge. Despite the crowds, there are many birds, particularly in quieter areas such as Beidha, an ancient village 8km to the north, which attracts far fewer tourists.

Species difficult to see in the Western Palearctic such as Pale Crag Martin, Spectacled Bulbul and Palestine Sunbird occur here, as well as other desert birds such as larks and wheatears, Arabian Babbler, Fan-tailed Raven and Tristram's Starling. However, the site is most famous for Sinai Rosefinch, which is fairly common and often seen drinking at the spring at Qattar ad Dayr. Hume's Owl also occurs but requires a dusk visit, and Syrian Serin is possible in winter. Raptors include Bonelli's Eagle, Sooty and Barbary Falcons, Lesser Kestrel and Long-legged Buzzard, with others on passage.

Easily reached by road from Amman or Aqaba, the journey takes around three hours on the Desert Highway. Petra can thronged with tourists but quietest times of early morning and late afternoon are also the best times for birds.

6) Wadi as Sir This wadi and neighbouring Wadi ash Shita are within easy reach of Amman. The wadi floors are cultivated or covered with dense scrub, but become drier in the lower reaches. There are rocky slopes with scattered shrubs, and the ridges have olive groves, pine plantations and remnants of original oak woodland.

Laughing Dove and Syrian Woodpecker breed in the more wooded areas, as well as Eastern Olivaceous Warbler and Masked Shrike, whilst the wadi floors hold White-breasted Kingfisher, Rufous Bush Robin and Palestine Sunbird. Drier and rockier parts support Chukar Partridge, Desert Lark, Long-billed Pipit, Blackstart and Scrub Warbler.

Wadi as Sir is west of Amman and reached by road from Bayder Wadi as Sir.

7) Wadi Dana-Fidan This wadi and surrounding hillsides form one of Jordan's best known reserves and support a fine selection of Middle Eastern specialities.

More than 20 species of raptor occur here in spring including residents such as Griffon Vulture, Long-legged Buzzard, Bonelli's Eagle and Barbary Falcon, and migrants including Egyptian Vulture and Booted, Eastern Imperial and Steppe Eagles. Eurasian Scops, Desert Eagle and Hume's Owls also occur, and passerines include Rock Martin, Palestine Sunbird, Fan-tailed Raven and Sinai Rosefinch. Pale Rock Sparrow has bred and Cretzschmar's Bunting is present in summer. Sand Partridge, Bar-tailed Desert and Hoopoe Larks, and Arabian Warbler occur in the Fidan area, and Dunn's Lark, Dead Sea Sparrow and sandgrouse are also possible.

Dana village, at the head of the wadi, can be reached by turning off the King's Highway at Al Qadisyya and with 4WD it is possible to continue through the wadi to Feinan, Fidan and, eventually, Wadi Araba.

8) Wadi Rum A huge wadi with steep cliffs, ravines and rock pillars surrounded by arid desert, the Wadi Rum area has many desert birds, particularly larks and wheatears, and also attracts large numbers of migrants.

Desert, Bar-tailed Desert, Hoopoe and Temminck's Horned are among the larks found here, as well as Hooded, Black-eared, Mourning and White-tailed Wheatears. Raptors include Long-legged Buzzard, Sooty and Barbary Falcons, and Verreaux's Eagle is possible, best looked for east of Wadi Rum village. Lappet-faced Vulture and Lammergeier have also been recorded in the area, and Hume's and Desert Eagle Owls are possible. Other desert species include Stone-curlew and Cream-coloured Courser and rockier areas hold Brown-necked and Fan-tailed Ravens and both rock thrushes. The village has Tristram's Starling, House Bunting, Sinai Rosefinch and Masked Shrike, and the surrounding cultivation supports Spectacled Bulbul, Trumpeter Finch, Scrub Warbler, Spanish and Rock Sparrows, and many migrants. Passage wheatears at Wadi Rum can include Isabelline, Northern, Red-tailed and Cyprus Pied, and warblers such as Cyprus, Spectacled, Orphean, Desert, Olive-tree and Upcher's are possible.

Wadi Rum is reached on Route 53 north from Aqaba, turning east after 16km at Ar Rashidiyya to Wadi Rum, and 4WD vehicles with drivers can be hired in the village. Further east is Disi, an area of agricultural land good for migrants.

Latvia

A low-lying land of forests and lakes with a long Baltic coastline, Latvia is rarely visited by birders. Most, if not all, of its species are more easily found in Poland, but there are some excellent birding areas with a wide range of wetland and forest birds, and large numbers of migrants occur along the coast. Major roads are good and accommodation fairly easy to find, but many of the smaller roads are in bad condition,

although the main birding sites can be reached by public transport. Estonia has now become a regular birding destination and the other Baltic states are sure to follow.

1) Cape Kolka An area of varied habitats on the Kurzeme Peninsula in north-west Latvia, Cape Kolka is one of the best migration watchpoints in the country. On the beach are extensive sand dunes, with farmland, bogs and woodlands away from the coast. Part of the area is included in the Sliteres National Reserve.

Breeders include storks, Golden and Short-toed Eagles, three species of grouse, Common Crane and Corn Crake. Various owls and woodpeckers breed and passerines include Wood Lark, Tawny Pipit and Red-breasted Flycatcher. Spring migration is excellent with thousands of raptors, impressive numbers of pigeons and a wide variety of passerines moving through. Offshore, divers and seaducks, seabirds and waders pass the cape in good numbers. Apr–early May is generally the best time for birding this area.

Kolka village is easily reached by road and is *c.*160km from Riga, with daily buses from the capital. The point is *c.*2km from the village and permits for the reserve are available in the village of Mazirbe.

2) Lake Engure This shallow lake close to the Gulf of Riga is one of the most important sites for breeding and wintering waterfowl in the Baltic. The lake has islands, extensive reedbeds and the area is surrounded by mixed and coniferous forest.

All five grebe species breed as well as bitterns and storks, and waterfowl include small numbers of Ferruginous Duck. Also breeding are Common Crane, Corn, Spotted and Little Crakes and, in recent years, Great Egret. Raptors include Lesser Spotted and White-tailed Eagles, and Eurasian Eagle and Tengmalm's Owls breed in the forests, as well as Hazel and Black Grouse. Summer brings Red-breasted Flycatcher, Savi's Warbler and Bearded and Penduline Tits.

The lake is closed to the public in the breeding season but there is an ornithological station 2km east of Berzciems, which allows camping and permits can be obtained here. The area is easily reached by road from Riga and there is a regular bus service.

3) Lake Lubana area Covering more than 30 km², this lake and surrounding fish farms and marshes, farmland and forests, is one of the most important for breeding birds in Latvia. The area also attracts large numbers of passage waders and waterfowl, and is very important for moulting ducks.

Among the many breeders are bitterns, storks, White-tailed and Lesser Spotted Eagles (Greater Spotted Eagle may also breed), crakes and, a recent colonist, Marsh Sandpiper. Another westward-expanding species, Terek Sandpiper has also bred, along with all five European grebes and various ducks, waders, gulls and terns. The forests are home to Black and White-backed Woodpeckers and Nutcracker. On passage Whooper Swan, Bean and Greater White-fronted Geese occur in numbers.

The entire area is interesting, but there are some exceptional sites that are among the best birding spots in Europe. The northern end of the lake can be explored from the Lubana-Grigalava road and further south and east are three groups of fishponds, the first at Idena, east of the lake, and two at Nagli, to the south-east. The latter should not be missed but permission should be sought from the fish farm offices in Nagli or the Orenisi Bird Station in the eastern group of ponds.

4) Lake Pape A shallow lake near the Lithuanian border in south-western Latvia, Lake Pape is connected to the Baltic by a narrow channel. The margins have dense reedbeds and the surrounding area consists of wet meadows with willow scrub and mixed and pine woodlands on sand dunes. This is an important migration watch-point with hundreds of thousands of birds passing through in autumn including raptors, waterfowl, pigeons, owls and passerines.

Bewick's and Whooper Swans occur on passage and geese include small numbers of Lesser White-fronted. White-tailed Eagle is a regular non-breeding visitor. In addition there are breeding birds such as Great Bittern, Corn, Spotted and Little Crakes, and a few pairs of Common Crane. Paddyfield Warbler has bred and may still do so, and Aquatic Warbler has been recorded in summer. Other reedbed birds include Savi's Warbler and Bearded and Penduline Tits, Thrush Nightingale is common in surrounding woods and scrub, and Tawny Pipit occurs on the sand dunes. Passage auks and skuas and other seabirds can be seen offshore.

Leave Riga on the A9, then travel south towards Rucava on the A11. The village of Pape is 12km east on a minor road through the forest. There is an observation tower beside the lake and an ornithological station *c.*3km north of Pape village.

Lebanon

If the political situation permits, Lebanon may once again become a regular tourist destination. Aside from the civil war, the country has suffered from devastating habitat loss and widespread hunting, and it has never been high on the agendas of travelling birders. However, Aammiq Marshes is one of the most important wetlands in the region and recent habitat restoration is maintaining this importance. In addition, huge numbers of migrants pass through the country and there are breeding birds of interest including Syrian Serin and Crimson-winged Finch.

1) **Aammiq Marshes** These marshes in the Bekaa Valley form the most important wetland area between Turkey and Israel. Early in the year the marshes can flood to nearly 300ha with meltwater from the mountains, but by autumn they are often dry. Around the wetland are areas of rough grazing, cultivated land, drainage ditches and woodland, all of which are attractive to passerine migrants. More than 250 species have been recorded in the area.

Great Spotted Cuckoo, Eurasian Scops Owl and Syrian Woodpecker breed in the area, as well as various buntings, wheatears, warblers and shrikes, and rocky gorges host Western Rock Nuthatch and perhaps still Eurasian Eagle Owl. Breeding in the marshes are Little Bittern and warblers such as Graceful, Savi's and Moustached, with Lesser Short-toed Lark in the arid land nearby. Huge numbers of migrants pass over including pelicans, storks and many raptors. Great Snipe is among the waders recorded on spring passage and Pine Bunting is probably regular in winter.

Zahleh, easily reached by road from Beirut, forms a good base from which to explore the Bekaa, with Aammiq Marshes to the north and Qaraoun Lake to the south.

2) **Barouk Cedars** The area known as Barouk Cedars includes the Al Shouf Cedar Reserve, the best surviving stand of cedars in Lebanon. Various Middle Eastern specialities have been recorded and Al Shouf Mountain is a good spot for watching migrant raptors.

Species recorded in summer include Wood and Horned Larks, Finsch's and Black-eared Wheatears, Orphean Warbler, Syrian Serin, Crimson-winged Finch and Cretzschmar's Bunting. Long-legged Buzzard and Booted Eagle have bred in recent years, Chukar Partridge still occurs and Rock Partridge was introduced in the 1990s. Others possible here include Long-billed Pipit, Sombre Tit, Alpine Chough and Rock Bunting. Passage raptors can include Griffon Vulture, Lesser Spotted and Eastern Imperial Eagles, Levant Sparrowhawk and Lesser Kestrel, with rarer species often recorded.

Barouk Cedars is 40km south-east of Beirut.

3) Palm Islands The three, flat and rocky islands that form this group long ago held breeding seabirds including Audouin's Gull and Lesser Crested Tern, but the area has now become popular for recreation and breeding birds are few. However, the islands attract a variety of migrants with over 300 species recorded, and vagrants are always a possibility.

The largest of the islands, Palm, has the most birding potential with scattered patches of fresh water and more vegetation than the other two. Eurasian Crag Martin and Graceful Prinia breed on Palm and Pallid Swift on Ramkine. Long-billed Pipit has been recorded on Palm in winter.

The islands lie 5.5km off the coast north-west of Tripoli.

4) Qaraoun Lake Formed by damming the Litani River, this large reservoir attracts a range of wetland birds on passage and in winter.

Black-necked Grebe, Pygmy Cormorant, White Pelican, herons, storks, Glossy Ibis and Ferruginous Duck are all possible.

The lake lies in the Bekaa Valley and can be visited from Zahleh to the north.

Lithuania

Like the other Baltic states this small country has a good list of breeding wetland and forest birds, and huge numbers of migrants pass along the coast. It is likely to become popular with travelling birders in the future but is currently rarely visited, although accommodation and car hire are readily available in larger towns. A mid-May visit would be most productive, with breeding birds including Greater Spotted Eagle and plenty of migrants, although the

peak time for one of the major attractions, Steller's Eider, is much earlier, in late March.

1) Cepkeliai Nature Reserve This reserve has the largest raised bog in the country, as well as forest patches, lakes and marshes.

The area is important for Black Grouse, Common Crane and Great Snipe and there are also White-tailed Eagle, Corn Crake and Grey-headed, Black, White-backed and Three-toed Woodpeckers. Passerines include Citrine Wagtail and Greenish Warbler.

Cepkeliai is in the far south of Lithuania near Druskininkai and can be reached by road from Vilnius.

2) Kirsiu Peninsula Like the coast of Latvia to the north this area is exceptional for migrants and a huge range of species overfly the area in spring and autumn. Kursiu Lagoon is a huge and shallow brackish lake separated from the Baltic by the narrow, 100-km Kursiu Peninsula, with the ornithological station of Ventes Ragas at its tip. The lagoon regularly attracts more than 20,000 ducks, geese and swans, and one of the most important areas throughout the year is the delta of the Nemunas River, which enters the lagoon just south of Silute on the western shore. Surrounding the lagoon are woodlands, farmland, wet meadows and fishponds.

Breeders include bitterns, White-tailed Eagle, crakes, Great Snipe, River and Aquatic Warblers. The peninsula attracts large numbers of migrants with raptors, storks and passerines occurring in numbers. Tengmalm's Owl and Barred Warbler are fairly regular and rarities such as Azure Tit and Siberian Accentor have been recorded. Offshore, divers, seaducks, seabirds and waders pass the spit during passage periods, and the area is of international importance for wintering Velvet Scoter.

Mid March to early May is generally the best time for birding this area and the peninsula can be reached by ferry from Klaipeda.

3) Lake Kretuonas This is a shallow, island-studded lake surrounded by reeds, wet meadows and woodlands. A range of freshwater and forest birds occur, albeit in small numbers.

Great Bittern, Corn Crake and Great Snipe breed in the wetlands and perhaps also Ferruginous Duck. The woodlands hold Lesser Spotted Eagle and Black Woodpecker, and European Roller is also possible.

Lake Kretuonas can be reached by road north-east of Vilnius.

4) Zuvintas Nature Reserve Habitats include forest and meadows, marshes, raised bog and large lake. One of the best wetland areas in south-west Lithuania.

Breeding species include Great Bittern and Black Stork, three species of crake, Common Crane and Aquatic Warbler, and waterfowl occur on passage.

The reserve is near Marijampole and can be reached by road from Vilnius.

Macedonia

This small mountainous land was one of the best birding areas of Yugoslavia and held raptors and many south-eastern specialities. It appears to be safe to visit at present, although it is advisable to check the situation before contemplating a trip. Accommodation and car hire are readily available in larger towns and Macedonia is likely to become popular with birding tourists.

1) Babuna Gorge This gorge on the Babuna River, along with similar gorges on the nearby Topolka River, is an excellent area for breeding and passage raptors and many other species of rocky areas.

Raptors include Egyptian Vulture, Short-toed and Booted Eagles (perhaps also Golden), Long-legged Buzzard, Levant Sparrowhawk, Lesser Kestrel and Lanner Falcon. Also possible are Griffon and Black Vultures, Lammergeier and Eastern Imperial Eagle. Other species include storks, Rock Partridge, Eurasian Eagle Owl, European Roller and Olive-tree Warbler, possibly also White-backed Woodpecker and Wallcreeper.

The gorge is reached from Titov Veles, following signs for Ohrid for a few kilometres south until the Babuna River is crossed, and from here a track leads to the gorge.

2) Bregalnica Valley Riverine forest is an important habitat at this site in central Macedonia but it is the remnant steppe that makes it of interest to birders.

Little Bustard may still occur with other open-country species such as Long-legged Buzzard, perhaps Saker Falcon, and European Roller. Other species include Black Kite, Egyptian and Griffon Vultures, Short-toed, Eastern Imperial and Golden Eagles, and Eurasian Eagle Owl.

The valley can be reached by road from Titov Veles.

3) Crna Gorge A rocky gorge with high cliffs and scrub-covered slopes, Crna is one of Macedonia's best raptor sites.

Raptors here include Egyptian and Griffon Vultures, Long-legged Buzzard, Short-toed, Golden, Booted and Bonelli's Eagles, Lanner Falcon and Lesser Kestrel, with Lammergeier, Black Vulture and Eastern Imperial Eagle possible. Other birds include Black Stork, Rock Partridge, Eurasian Eagle Owl and European Roller. Hazel Grouse may also occur.

Crna Gorge is in south-eastern Macedonia and can be reached from Bitola.

4) Demir Kapija Gorge Deep gorges, dense forests and remnant steppe form the main habitats in this remote region, which supports a good selection of raptors.

Egyptian and Griffon Vultures are among the raptors here, as well as Levant Sparrowhawk, Long-legged Buzzard and Eastern Imperial Eagle, with the possibility of Lammergeier, Black Vulture and Saker Falcon. Other birds include Black Stork, Rock Partridge, European Roller and Rufous Bush Robin.

This area is situated in south-eastern Macedonia and can be reached from Strumica.

5) Galičica National Park This park in the south-west is between Lakes Ohrid and Prespa, and consists of rugged mountains, forming the southern spur of the Dinaric range. Lower levels have mixed deciduous woodland, higher are dense oak and beech woods and Macedonian Pine forest, and above the treeline are open meadows and the highest point at 2,600m is Mount Galičica.

Raptors include Short-toed, White-tailed and Golden Eagles, harriers, kites, *Accipiter* species and buzzards. There are many south-east species of interest such as Rock Partridge, Syrian Woodpecker, Semi-collared Flycatcher, Sombre Tit and Western Rock Nuthatch. Warblers include Eastern Olivaceous, Olive-tree, Orphean and Eastern Bonelli's, and buntings such as Cretzschmar's, Rock and Black-headed can also be seen.

The towns of Ohrid and Struga on the shores of Lake Ohrid are good bases for exploring this region.

6) Lakes Ohrid and Prespa There are few sites in Europe that can match the mix of montane, forest, Mediterranean and wetland birds found around these two large lakes in south-western Macedonia. Lake Ohrid extends into Albania and Prespa is shared with both Albania and Greece. Much of the surrounding land is farmed, with mixed woodland on the slopes and pines further up. Both lakes are important breeding, passage and wintering sites for waterbirds, and a good range of woodland and montane birds can be seen in the area.

The lakes are important for Pygmy Cormorant and both species of pelican also occur, although breeding is uncertain. Herons thrive here with Purple, Squacco and Black-crowned Night, Great Egret and both bitterns present at various times of the year, as well as Glossy Ibis, Eurasian Spoonbill and storks. Ferruginous Duck occurs all year, joined by Red-crested Pochard, geese and grebes in winter. Little and Baillon's Crakes and Moustached Warbler are among the many reedbed birds, and marsh terns and waders occur on passage. In addition many raptors breed or pass through the area and there are south-eastern specialities such as Rock Partridge, Syrian Woodpecker, Semi-collared Flycatcher and Sombre Tit.

The towns of Ohrid and Struga on the shores of Lake Ohrid are ideal bases for exploring the lakes and the nearby Galičica National Park.

7) Mavrovo National Park This mountainous area, at 600-2,700m, has alpine meadows and extensive areas of forest, and is the country's largest National Park.

Egyptian and Griffon Vultures occur here as well as Short-toed, Lesser Spotted, Eastern Imperial, Golden and Booted Eagles, and Lanner Falcon. Lammergeier is possible. Other forest species include Hazel Grouse and Eurasian Eagle Owl and possible woodpeckers include White-backed, Middle Spotted and Three-toed.

Mavrovo is in north-west Macedonia and reached by road from Debar or Gostivar.

8) Sara Mountains In the far north-west and extending into Kosovo are the Sara Mountains (Sar Planina), an area of rocky hillsides and gorges, forest and alpine meadows. The birdlife is little known but there is probably a good selection of montane and forest birds present.

Griffon Vulture and Golden Eagle are among the raptors known to occur and Hazel Grouse, Rock Partridge, Eurasian Eagle Owl and Red-billed Chough are also present. Other possibilities include Lammergeier, Capercaillie, Ural and Tengmalm's Owls, White-backed and Three-toed Woodpeckers, and Alpine Chough.

The mountains lie west of Skopje, on the border with Kosovo.

Madeira

This Atlantic archipelago lies *c.*350km off the north African coast and consists of two main islands: **1) Madeira** itself, and to the north-east, **2) Porto Santo;** and two groups of smaller islands to the south-east, the nearby **3) Desertas,** and the more remote **4) Selvagems** *c.*160km away.

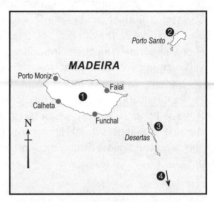

Like the Canaries, Madeira was once covered in laurel forest, and although now much reduced the forest on Madeira is the largest and best-preserved area of such habitat in the world. Much of the main island is cultivated but in higher parts there are areas of scrub and grassland. Coastlines range from open sandy beaches to high sea-cliffs. Porto Santo is much drier than Madeira and the vegetation sparser, whilst the Desertas and Selvagems are even more arid.

Nearly 300 birds have been recorded in the archipelago and more than 40 breed, there is a range of seabirds and some Macaronesian endemics. Trocaz Pigeon is the only endemic species of landbird, but there are endemic races of more widespread birds including Spectacled Warbler. Petrels and shearwaters difficult to see elsewhere in the Western Palearctic are a major attraction. Both Zino's and Fea's Petrels can be seen: Zino's breeds only in the mountains of Madeira and Fea's on Bugio, the most southerly of the Desertas. These two petrels are very similar and often inseparable at sea, and due to the very low population of Zino's it is assumed that the majority of gadfly petrels seen off Madeira are Fea's. Bulwer's Petrel breeds on Selvagem Grande, the Desertas, Porto Santo and on islets off eastern Madeira, and can be seen off the south and east of the island, as well as from inter-island ferries. Cory's Shearwater breeds throughout the archipelago and can be seen year-round, Little Shearwater breeds on islets off eastern Madeira, Porto Santo, the Desertas and Selvagem Grande, and can be seen in summer and autumn. Madeiran Storm-petrel has a similar breeding range and is present throughout the year, and although sometimes seen from boats is rarely seen from shore. European Storm-petrel occurs in these waters as a migrant, White-faced Storm-petrel breeds on the Selvagems but is rarely seen, and Swinhoe's Storm-petrel has been recorded more than once. In addition to petrels and shearwaters, small numbers of Roseate Terns are seen annually and probably breed, and Sooty Tern has bred in the Selvagems. Skuas of four species have occurred on passage. Gulls and terns can be seen off most coasts and in Funchal harbour, but to see the petrels and shearwaters generally requires a trip to one of the promontories.

On Madeira the southernmost point of the island, Porto da Cruz, 3km west of Funchal, is the best site, followed by the westernmost point, Ponta do Pargo. The best seabird site on Porto Santo is Ponta da Calheta in the west. Trocaz Pigeon is today confined to the highlands of Madeira, where only about 1,000 birds remain. The easiest way to see this endemic is to take the Funchal-Santana road to the Poiso crossroads, on towards Ribeiro Frio and into the valley. The pigeons are usually easily found and endemic races of Eurasian Sparrowhawk and Common Buzzard may also be seen. Canary is common in scrubby areas throughout Madeira, and the local race of Spectacled Warbler can be found in eastern Madeira and Porto Santo. In open, arid areas there are Berthelot's Pipit and Spanish and Rock Sparrows. Helmeted Guineafowl is one of several gamebirds introduced to the islands. Migrant passerines occur in varying numbers and vagrant Nearctic waterfowl and waders are frequently recorded.

Madeira is a popular tourist destination and there are flights from most European capitals. Probably the best way to look for seabirds is from a boat and the daily Funchal–Porto Santo ferry, which takes two and a half hours, is excellent. Landing on the smaller islands is strictly limited, but the birds can generally be seen from a boat and sailing and game-fishing trips can be arranged in Funchal harbour.

Malta

This small remote archipelago is in the central Mediterranean c.100km south of Sicily and comprises three main islands: **1) Malta** itself, and the smaller **2) Comino** and **3) Gozo** to the north-west, as well as smaller rocks and islets. There are some seabird colonies but being heavily populated islands with limited habitats, the number of breeding species is very small. Large numbers of migrants occur but unfortunately the Maltese are obsessed with shooting and this remains a major problem. More than 350 species have been recorded in Malta but many only as vagrants.

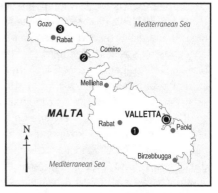

Breeding seabirds include European Storm-petrel, Cory's and Yelkouan Shearwaters, and passerines include Greater Short-toed Lark, Blue Rock Thrush, Cetti's, Spectacled and Sardinian Warblers, Zitting Cisticola and Italian Sparrow. Passage brings herons, waterfowl, raptors, crakes and waders and a wide range of passerines, and there is always the chance of rarities of North African or Middle Eastern origin.

Buskett has the most extensive area of coniferous woodland in Malta and the nearby **Wied Il-Luq** is a small valley with a strip of deciduous woodland. This area attracts many migrant passerines and is a roosting site for passage raptors including occasional Eleonora's Falcon. **Ghadira** in the north-east is a brackish pool surrounded by reeds and tamarisk, and is the most important wetland in Malta. Recent decades have seen habitat restoration at Ghadira and there is now an information centre and observation hide. Most important as a stopover for migrants, the pool attracts various waterbirds and rarities.

On the south coast of Gozo, the cliffs at **Ta'Cenc** have breeding Cory's and Yelkouan Shearwaters, European Storm-petrel and these species also breed at **Filfla**, an islet off the south coast of Malta.

Malta is not usually regarded as a birding destination and some travellers refuse to visit the island as a protest against the hunting. However, there are many interesting passage birds to be seen and the reserves the Malta Ornithological Society have worked so hard to establish deserve to be visited and publicised as much as possible.

Moldova

Moldova is virtually unknown ornithologically and much remains to be discovered, but tourism is still very much in its infancy and birding trips seem a long way in the future. Situated close to the Black Sea and the Dnestr and Danube deltas the birding is likely to be excellent, particularly during passage periods.

1) Balatina This area of riverine woodland and marshes is situated on the Prut River in north-eastern Moldova and frequent flooding makes it ideal for waterbirds.

Breeders include Great Egret, Ferruginous Duck and Lesser Spotted, Greater Spotted and Booted Eagles, and passage brings Pygmy Cormorant, Black Stork, Glossy Ibis, Whooper Swan, Lesser White-fronted Goose, Great Snipe and raptors.

The Balatina area can be reached from the town of Beltsy.

2) Manta Floodplain In the far south of Moldova, this wetland area has lakes, fishponds and wet meadows and is an important stopover site for passage waterfowl.

Pygmy Cormorant and Ferruginous Duck breed and passage visitors include Dalmatian Pelican, Red-breasted Goose, White-tailed and Greater Spotted Eagles, Corn Crake and Great Snipe.

Undoubtedly much remains to be discovered in this very promising area, which lies between the town of Cahul and the village of Slobozia Mare *c.*150km south-west of Moldova's capital, Chisinau.

Morocco

Long one of the most popular winter and spring birding destinations in the region, Morocco is still regularly visited by birders, even though one of the star birds, Slender-billed Curlew, is no longer regularly seen. Several species, such as Dark Chanting-Goshawk, Double-spurred Francolin and African Marsh Owl, can be seen nowhere else in the Western Palearctic, as well as wild Bald Ibis and many other North African and desert specialities. There are

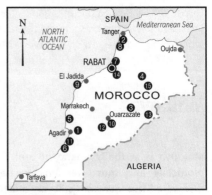

numerous organised bird tours to Morocco but independent birding is also very easy, with plentiful accommodation, good roads and generally easy access to sites.

1) Agadir and the Sous Plain The popular resort of Agadir forms an ideal base from which to explore several excellent birding areas in southern Morocco. There is good seawatching to the north at Cap Rhir, a productive estuary to the south at Oued Sous, and inland the plain of the Sous has many north African specialities.

Agadir itself has Little Swift, Moussier's Redstart, Common Bulbul and House Bunting, with Audouin's Gull regular in the harbour. The cliffs between the city and **Cap Rhir**, 40km north on the P8, have recently discovered colonies of Plain Swift and the cape produces shearwaters, petrels, gulls, terns and skuas during passage periods. About 8km north of Cap Rhir is Tamri, generally considered *the* site for Bald Ibis, as the species can be virtually guaranteed here. If they are not on the lagoon or river at Tamri then they will be somewhere on the cliffs or hillsides along this coast, with 140 recorded *c*.6km north of Tamri in February 2004. The **Sous Plain** is situated between the High and Anti-Atlas, and the foothills of these ranges provide excellent birding habitats. South of Agadir the Sous enters the sea at Oued Sous, and this area is an important stopover for various waders, egrets, Greater Flamingo, Eurasian Spoonbill and White Stork. Terns can include Gull-billed, Caspian and Lesser Crested and all three marsh terns. Ruddy Shelduck often appears in winter and sometimes also Bald Ibis. Brown-throated Crag Martin is resident. The P32 road runs inland from Agadir across the Plain of the Sous to Ouarzazate, a land of orchards, cultivation and remnants of Argan forest, a unique habitat of the area but now much reduced. Dark Chanting-Goshawk, although rare, occurs here, particularly around **Taroudannt** and other raptors found here include Black-shouldered Kite and Tawny Eagle. Stone-curlew, Red-necked Nightjar, Moussier's Redstart, Rufous Bush Robin, Black-headed Tchagra and Fulvous Babbler can also be found. The town of Taroudannt supports Spotless Starling and Pallid and White-rumped Swifts. The foothills of the Atlas have cliffs with raptors including vultures, eagles and Lanner and Barbary Falcons.

Agadir has an airport and is easily reached from most European capitals, and

Taroudannt forms a good base for exploring the inland part of the plain and the Atlas foothills.

2) Asilah and Oued Loukkos In the north of Morocco and close to Tangier, Asilah is well known for Great Bustard and the Oued Loukkos, near Larache, can have some interesting waterbirds.

Up to 50 Great Bustards have wintered in the plains north of Asilah, between Briech on the P2 and the minor road to the east. They can be seen from any vantage point but tend to be most easily found from the small hill near the electricity station. Common Crane also winters here and Little Bustard winters in the marshes at Oued Loukkos, which also support Purple Swamphen, Crested Coot, Marbled and Ferruginous Ducks, and Moustached Warbler.

Asilah is south of Tangier on the P2 and Oued Loukkos further south towards Larache. Take the track to the left immediately after the bridge a couple of kilometres before Larache.

3) Boumalne The area around this town offers birders the opportunity to see upland species in the impressive Todra and Dadès Gorges to the north-east or desert birds along the famous Tagdilt track to the south-east.

Birds of the gorges and high plateaux include Lammergeier, Golden and Bonelli's Eagles, Shore Lark, Moussier's Redstart, Black Wheatear and Crimson-winged Finch. The track from Boumalne to Tagdilt was the best-known desert birding spot in Morocco for many years, until other areas became more accessible. Houbara Bustard may still occur but other birds seen here include Long-legged Buzzard, Lanner Falcon, Cream-coloured Courser, Crowned and Black-belled Sandgrouse, Thick-billed, Hoopoe and Temminck's Horned Larks, and Desert, Mourning, Red-rumped and White-tailed Wheatears.

Boumalne Dadès can be reached on the P32 east of Ouarzazate and this road continues to Tinerhir and the Todra Gorge. The S6902 road runs north from Boumalne into the Dadès Gorge. The Tagdilt track leaves the P32 to the south-west a fewkm east of Boumalne, and there is another southward track a few kilometres further east, where Dupont's Lark has been recorded.

4) Dayet Aaoua One of several montane lakes in the Middle Atlas, Aaoua is surrounded by wooded slopes and the area has several north African specialities.

The site is famous for Crested Coot and this or other lakes in the area also support breeding and passage herons. A tiny population of Demoiselle Crane survived until the mid-1980s but is probably now extinct. The woodlands have Levaillant's Woodpecker, Short-toed Treecreeper and the newly split African Blue Tit and Atlas Flycatcher.

Dayet Aaoua is reached on the P24 north of Ifrane and from there the 4627 leads to nearby Dayet Ifer and Dayet Afourgah. Two other lakes, Dayet Ifrah and Dayet Hachlaff lie to the south-west and can be reached on the 3325.

5) Essaouira This town on the Atlantic coast is famous as a breeding site of Eleonora's Falcon, the larger of only two colonies of this species in Morocco. The surrounding land hosts a wide range of interesting birds including several North African specialities.

The falcons are present from May to October and breed on the Île de Mogador just offshore, although they can be seen from the seafront of Essaouira with a telescope. However, the best birding site in the area is Ksob Wadi *c*.2km south of the town. The falcons regularly visit this river mouth and other species here include Barbary Partridge, Brown-throated Crag Martin and a variety of waders and gulls on passage and in winter. In the dense scrub further up the wadi Black-headed Tchagra and other shrikes can be seen, as well as Rufous Bush Robin and Cetti's and other warblers.

Essaouira lies c.200km north of Agadir and is reached via the main coast road. For Ksob Wadi leave Essaouira southwards and turn right on a sandy track just past the lighthouse.

6) Goulimine to Tan-Tan About 200km south of Agadir the desert between these two towns has a superb range of birds, especially larks and wheatears, excellent raptors, and a range of other species along the Oued Sayed. The best desert birds are south of Goulimine and although they probably occur throughout the area there are certain spots that are guaranteed to produce good birds.

One such area is known as the 'Tan-Tan 100km post', and is c.35km south of Goulimine. Larks in this area include Greater and Lesser Short-toed, Desert and Bar-tailed Desert, Hoopoe, Thick-billed and Temminck's Horned. Wheatears such as White-tailed, Red-rumped and Desert are regularly seen, as well as Trumpeter Finch and Scrub and Tristram's Warblers. Cream-coloured Courser and Black-bellied, Crowned and Spotted Sandgrouse also occur. Raptors include Long-legged Buzzard, Tawny Eagle and Barbary and Lanner Falcons, with Golden Eagle possible in the hills to the E. In the vegetation of the Oued Sayed there are Spectacled Warbler, Thekla Lark and Fulvous Babbler, and the river itself attracts waders. Brown-necked Raven occurs at the refuse tip south of the town.

Goulimine is reached on the main coast road, the P41, south from Agadir.

7) Lac de Sidi Bourhaba (Sidi Bou Ghaba) Like the better known Merja Zerga to the north this lake holds good numbers of a range of waders and waterfowl, and Sidi Bourhaba is of international importance for its wintering Marbled Ducks, which can exceed 1,500 birds. This lake has open water and extensive marshy areas and is surrounded by sand dunes, juniper scrub and eucalyptus woodland.

In addition to Marbled Duck, Sidi Bourhaba also has two of Morocco's specialities, Crested Coot and African Marsh Owl. All three species are usually easy to find, although they can be much scarcer in years of low water levels. The gull roost often includes Audouin's and the surrounding scrub and woodland support Black-shouldered Kite. Slender-billed Curlew has been recorded in this area in the past.

Lac de Sidi Bourhaba is on the Atlantic coast of Morocco, c.30km north of Rabat and can be reached by following signs for Mehdiya Plage from Rabat or the town of Kénitra. There is an information centre and picnic area on the east side of the lake. The reserve area in the southern half is closed to the public but the rest of the lake is of open access and much can be seen from the road and the causeway crossing the northern part. The Marsh Owl is best viewed from the causeway at dusk. A particularly good area is the small marsh at the northern end and seabirds occur at the mouth of Sebou Wadi.

8) Merja Zerga National Park One of the best-known birding sites in Morocco, Merja Zerga is a large shallow lagoon connected to the sea by a narrow channel. The surrounding countryside has cork oak forest, marshes and grassland, and the area as a whole is highly attractive to wading birds and waterfowl.

This was the most reliable site in the world for wintering Slender-billed Curlew, but there have been few confirmed sightings since the mid-1990s. However, the occasional bird may still occur here, along with herons, storks, Glossy Ibis, Eurasian Spoonbill, Greater Flamingo and waders. Merja Zerga holds ornithological interest all year, but most birders visit in autumn or winter when bird numbers are highest. Breeding birds include Collared Pratincole and Red-necked Nightjar, and the campsite at Moulay Bousselham is probably the best site in the Western Palearctic for African Marsh Owl.

Merja Zerga is on the Moroccan coast midway between Tangier and Rabat. The base used by most visitors is Moulay Bousselham, where the channel from the lake meets the sea.

9) Oualidia This site covers a series of lagoons and saltpans on the Atlantic coast between Sidi-Mousa and Oualidia. Although famous for wading birds, a good range of other birds can be seen on passage and in winter.

Greater Flamingo and Eurasian Spoonbill occur on passage and in winter, as well as a variety of migrant herons and waterfowl including Marbled Duck. Slender-billed Curlew has been recorded in the past. To the south of Oualidia is Cap Beddouza where seawatching can produce shearwaters, petrels and skuas.

The S121 south of Sidi-Moussa runs beside the lagoons.

10) Ouarzazate Conveniently situated between the Sous Plain and Boumalne, Ouarzazate is a regular stop-off for birders. Just east of the town is a large reservoir that attracts a range of birds on passage and in winter (the shallower western end is best), and there are desert passerines in the surrounding area.

Eurasian Spoonbill, Greater Flamingo and Ruddy Shelduck occur at the reservoir, as well as Black-winged Stilt and Pied Avocet. Passage raptors include Short-toed and Booted Eagles and a range of passerines occurs. Residents include Long-legged Buzzard, Lanner and, perhaps, Barbary Falcons, sandgrouse, larks and wheatears. Rock Martin has been reported south-east of Ouarzazate, on the P32 towards Zagora and Dark Chanting-Goshawk has been recorded in the area.

Ouarzazate is on the crossroads between the P31 Marrakech-Zagora road and the P32 Agadir-Boumalne road.

11) Oued Massa About 60km south of Agadir is the mouth of Oued Massa, a tidal creek where an excellent range of seabirds, waders and waterfowl can be seen. Nearby, the village of Massa and surrounding desert are home to many North African specialities and this area should be on the itinerary of any birder visiting Morocco. The coastline from Massa to Sous now has National Park status to protect the dwindling population of Bald Ibis.

Gulls, including Audouin's, and terns including Caspian and Gull-billed, are regular at the mouth of the river, and the river itself has Greater Flamingo, Glossy Ibis, Eurasian Spoonbill, herons, Marbled Duck and Ruddy Shelduck. Common Crane is a regular winter visitor to the reedbeds. Raptors include Booted, Bonelli's and Tawny Eagles and Barbary Falcon, and Dark Chanting-Goshawk has been recorded. The village of Massa has Spotless Starling, House Bunting, Moussier's Redstart and Laughing Dove. Desert areas around the village are home to Lesser Short-toed Lark, Cream-coloured Courser and sandgrouse. Black-bellied regularly occurs, visiting the river mouth early morning to drink, and Crowned and Spotted may also be present. Black-headed Tchagra is common in scrubby and cultivated areas closer to the river, and there are also Moustached, Cetti's and Savi's Warblers.

North of the river mouth and village is the campsite of Sidi Rabat where there is a bird log for the area. Seawatching from here can produce shearwaters and skuas, and Bald Ibis and Plain Swift can be seen along this stretch of coast.

Follow the main P30 coast road south from Agadir and turn off at Tiferhal following signs to Massa. The road leads to the centre of the village and turning right at the T-junction leads to the reserve and Sidi Rabat.

12) Oukaimeden Morocco's best-known montane birding site, Oukaimeden is a ski resort at 2,750m in the High Atlas and offers easy access to various upland species, with many others to be seen on the approach through the various habitats.

Montane species include Lammergeier, Golden Eagle, Alpine Accentor, both rock thrushes and both choughs. Black Wheatear, Shore Lark, Rock Sparrow and Crimson-winged Finch also occur, and the foothills hold Little Swift, Wood Lark, Rufous Bush Robin, various warblers and Rock and Cirl Buntings. White-rumped Swift is possible in the area.

Take the S513 south from Marrakech to Vallée de l'Ourika and then the turning to Oukaimeden on the 6035.

13) Tafilalt This area, between Erfoud and Merzouga, is one of Morocco's best known sites for desert birds. There are palm groves along the Ziz Wadi, large areas of stony desert and the Erg Chebbi, Morocco's largest sand dune system. Close to Merzouga is a temporary lake that can attract Greater Flamingo, ducks and waders.

Ziz Wadi hosts breeding Barbary Partridge, Common Bulbul, Rufous Bush Robin, the Saharan race of Eastern Olivaceous Warbler and many migrants. The dunes of Erg Chebbi can appear birdless but support Bar-tailed Desert, Hoopoe and Crested Larks, Desert Warbler and Desert Sparrow, with Tristram's Warbler in winter. Café Yasmina is famous as the best site for Desert Sparrow in the entire Western Palearctic. Among the many species of the stony desert are Spotted and Black-bellied Sandgrouse, larks including Thick-billed and Temminck's Horned, and wheatears such as Desert, Mourning and White-tailed. Other possibilities include Crowned, Brown-necked and Pin-tailed Sandgrouse, Desert Eagle Owl, Egyptian Nightjar, Blue-cheeked Bee-eater, Raven and various raptors. Further east the chances of Houbara Bustard increase (guides can be hired to search for bustards), and there have been reports of Arabian Bustard, which is generally considered extinct in the Western Palearctic.

Erfoud can be reached on the P21 from the north or on the 3454 from Ouarzazate for those with a 4WD vehicle. The 3461 crosses the area from Erfoud to Merzouga and the P21 between Erfoud and Rissani follows Ziz Wadi.

14) Zaër Cork oak woodland and scrub are the major habitats in the Zaër, which form the west part of Morocco's Central Plateau. This area, particularly between Sidi Yahya and Sidi Bettache, is famous as the best site in the Western Palearctic for Double-spurred Francolin, which is fairly easy to locate during a dawn or dusk visit.

In addition to the francolin, Barbary Partridge can be seen and raptors include Black-shouldered and Black Kites, Long-legged Buzzard and Short-toed, Booted and Bonelli's Eagles. Passerines are abundant and include Calandra and Thekla Larks, Rufous Bush Robin, Common Bulbul, African Blue Tit and Black-crowned Tchagra.

The Zaër region can be reached by leaving Rabat south on the motorway, turning off for Témara, and from there take the S202 to Sidi Yahya des Zaër and then the S208 to Sidi Bettache. Much of this area is a royal hunting reserve and it is best to stay on or close to the roads.

15) Zeida Famous as a reasonably reliable site for Dupont's Lark – a difficult bird to find anywhere in the Western Palearctic – with various other larks, wheatears and other species to be seen on the plains south of the town.

Black-bellied Sandgrouse, Thick-billed, Short-toed and Lesser Short-toed, Thekla and Horned Larks, Moussier's Redstart, Red-rumped and Black Wheatears, and Trumpeter Finch all occur here. Dupont's Lark cannot be guaranteed, but the best area was formerly west of the P21 between Zeida and Midelt, reached via the track to the quarry, which leaves the P21 *c.*3.5km south of Zeida. If the plain proves birdless, which it can appear, Moulouya Wadi has a range of birds including European Bee-eater, Rufous Bush Robin and warblers including Western Olivaceous and Orphean.

Zeida can be reached from Fès on the P20 or Er-Rachidia on the P21.

Netherlands

Birding is extremely popular in the Netherlands and the country is also popular with visitors from elsewhere, particularly in winter when impressive numbers of waterfowl occur. Swans and ducks winter here, as well as large numbers of geese including regular Lesser White-fronted and Red-breasted, and White-tailed Eagle and Rough-legged Buzzard are guaranteed. For spring visitors there are breeding wetland birds, with more or less isolated populations of Eurasian Spoonbill, Great Egret and Black-crowned Night and Purple Herons.

Migrants occur in large numbers especially on the North Sea islands, and rarities are frequently recorded. Accommodation is readily available and the public transport system is among the best in Europe.

1) Lauwersmeer A former estuary of the vast Waddensee, the Lauwersmeer is mown fresh water surrounded by arable farmland and open grassland. The area is highly important for large numbers of waterfowl, particularly swans and geese, on passage and in winter.

The area is one of the most important in Europe for wintering Bewick's Swan and smaller numbers of Whooper are also present. Nearly 20,000 Barnacle Geese winter here, as well as thousands of Greater White-fronted, Lesser White-fronted and Red-breasted are regular in small numbers. Lauwersmeer also hosts non-breeding Eurasian Spoonbill and, in recent years, Great Egret has been regular. A wide range of waders occurs on passage and in winter, and Shore Lark and Snow Bunting are present. Rough-legged Buzzard and the occasional White-tailed Eagle occur in winter. Breeders include Great Bittern, Montagu's Harrier and Pied Avocet.

Lauwersmeer is north of Groningen and although are several reserves with limited access much can be seen from adjacent roads, and there are open-access areas in the north. The various woodlands dotted in this area should not be missed and there are several minor roads flanking the eastern and southern shores that give views over the water.

2) Naardermeer Long regarded as an important area for birds, this is the site of one of the oldest Dutch nature reserves, and today consists of lakes and canals, reedbeds and swamp forest.

Although Eurasian Spoonbill no longer breeds there are bitterns and Purple Heron, and Great Egret is increasing. The reeds are home to Savi's Warbler and Bearded Tit.

The Naardermeer is *c.*16km east of Amsterdam on the A1, leaving on the Muiderberg exit. A permit is required, available from Natuurmonumenten, Schaep en Burgh, NL-1243 JJ Graveland, Netherlands (tel. 35 655 9933).

3) Oostvaardersplassen Flevoland is a large area of reclaimed land or 'polders' in the huge and shallow Ijsselmeer, and is now mainly cultivated land with lagoons, reeds and occasional patches of woodland, and several of the more important areas are now reserves. The best of these is Oostvaardersplassen, where a range of birds can be seen at all seasons.

Great Bittern, Great Egret, Purple Heron and Eurasian Spoonbill are among the breeders, which also include Montagu's Harrier, Spotted Crake and Pied Avocet. Breeding passerines include Bluethroat, Savi's Warbler, Bearded and Penduline Tits, and Common Rosefinch. Waterfowl and waders occur on passage, with scarcer birds such as Kentish Plover and Caspian and White-winged Terns regular. Feral Greater Flamingo and Ruddy Shelduck are regular in autumn. Winter brings swans and geese in large numbers including Lesser White-fronted and Red-breasted, as well as Rough-legged Buzzard and sometimes White-tailed Eagle. Northern Goshawk and Black Woodpecker occur in Flevoland's woodlands.

Oostvaardersplassen is easily reached by road from Amsterdam and can be viewed from the Oostvaardersdijk or hides at the east end.

4) Terschelling One of the Friesian chain, Terschelling, like Texel, is an excellent for birding with a good range of breeders and migrants. This long narrow island is largely farmland but there are also woods and conifer plantations, and some built-up areas. Around the fringes are dunes and sandy beaches, saltmarshes and mudflats, and much of the island is protected as nature reserves.

In summer Eurasian Spoonbill, Montagu's Harrier and Spotted Crake can be seen, and passerines include Bluethroat and Bearded Tit. Regular migrants on Terschelling include scarcer species such as Richard's Pipit, Ring Ouzel, Yellow-browed Warbler and Ortolan Bunting. Autumn is the most productive time to visit the island. Winter brings Dark-bellied Brent Goose, Rough-legged Buzzard, Shore Lark and Snow Bunting.

The island is reached by ferry from Harlingen, which must be booked if taking a car. Birding information is available from the nature centre at West-Terschelling.

5) Texel This is the largest and most westerly of the Friesian Islands, which lie between the North Sea and the Waddensee, and more than half of the island has some form of protected status.

The west has extensive sand dunes with shallow lagoons and areas of scrub and woodland. Breeding birds include Pied Avocet and Kentish Plover. Probably the most famous reserve on Texel is De Muy, a reed-fringed lake set amongst the dunes, with breeding Eurasian Spoonbill, Montagu's Harrier and a range of wetland passerines. The east coast of the island borders the Waddensee, the largest intertidal mudflat in Europe, where all of the commoner waterfowl and wader species of Europe occur. Farmland at Zeeburg is managed specifically for Dark-bellied Brents, and woodlands on the island support Short-toed Treecreeper and Hawfinch.

Entry to some of the reserves requires a permit, others can only be visited on guided tours, and details can be obtained from the Texel Tourist Office in Den Burg. The island is reached by a 20 minute ferry trip from Den Helder on the mainland.

6) Veluwe The 1,200km² Veluwe is an area of sandy heath, scrub and pinewoods in the south-central Netherlands, with some good birds, and much of the area is of protected as reserves or National Parks. De Hoge Veluwe National Park and Veluwezoom National Parks cover a large area of the south-west. The area was extensively planted with conifers in the 19th century and there are also mixed and deciduous woodlands.

Raptors in summer include Northern Goshawk and Montagu's Harrier, and other species include Black Grouse, Black Woodpecker, Tawny Pipit, Crested Tit and Short-toed Treecreeper.

De Hoge Veluwe National Park is north-west of Arnhem, with the main entrance on the Otterlo-Hoenderloo road, and Veluwezoom National Park is north-east of Arnhem.

7) Zwanenwater A large shallow lake with extensive reeds, Zwanenwater is situated among coastal dunes and pinewoods close to the coast. As well as the lakes and dunes there are marshes and small patches of pine woodland.

Most famous for its Eurasian Spoonbill colony, Zwanenwater has a good selection of breeding birds including Great Bittern, Spotted Crake and Pied Avocet, with Crested Lark in the dunes.

Zwanenwater is conveniently situated just south of Den Helder and can be visited en route to or from Texel. It is reached by road from Amsterdam, heading for Callantsoog. Although this is a reserve much can be seen from the surrounding dunes.

Norway

The most popular Arctic birding site in the Western Palearctic is Varanger, an essential part of any trip to north Norway and also easily accessible from north Finland. Some of the birds regular here are difficult to see elsewhere in the region and include Yellow-billed Diver, King and Steller's Eiders, Gyr Falcon and Snowy Owl. Elsewhere on the coast are important seabird colonies and some excellent migration watchpoints. Upland breeders, including waders, are well represented in Norway, but Finland is generally better for forest and wetland birds. Norway is expensive and many birders choose to camp or stay within National Parks, but travel is usually easy even in the remote north. Late May to early June is the best time to visit Norway before the emergence of the midges, which make birding unbearable later in the year.

1) Dovrefjell National Park A mountainous area of 250km² in central Norway ranging from 900m to over 2,000m altitude, with marshes, grassland and birch woods.

Birds include several sought-after species such as Red-necked Phalarope, Rough-legged Buzzard and Gyr Falcon, and this is a regular site for Great Snipe. Other breeders include Velvet Scoter, Golden Eagle and Common Crane, with Ptarmigan, Lapland and Snow Buntings, Shore Lark, Dotterel and Purple Sandpiper on the higher peaks.

The park has several hiking trails, cabins and guesthouses, and the E6 road crosses the park, as does the railway, which stops at Kongsvol where there is an information centre.

2) Fokstumyra Nature Reserve A long-established reserve and one of the most popular birding sites in Norway, this small marsh in the valley of the Foksai River near Rondane and Dovrefjell National Parks. As well as marshes, there are patches of birch woodland and scrub and high ground in the immediate area.

Birders are attracted by the range of breeding birds and waders in particular, which include Temminck's Stint, Purple Sandpiper and Great Snipe. Higher peaks near the reserve have Ptarmigan, Rough-legged Buzzard and Dotterel.

A permit is required to enter the reserve, available from the warden, near Fokstua railway station, just outside the reserve, and the area is easily reached by road on the E6 or by rail.

3) Hardangervidda National Park One of the most visited of Norway's National Parks, Hardangervidda consists mainly of a large plateau above the treeline, but there are areas of forest, marshes and meadows, as well as lakes.

The attraction for the birder is the mix of northern breeders at the southernmost point of their range and more southerly species. Waterfowl occur in great variety and include Velvet Scoter and Black-throated Diver, and waders include Dotterel, Purple Sandpiper, Temminck's Stint, Great Snipe and Red-necked Phalarope. Other breeders are Common Crane, Golden Eagle, Gyr Falcon, Long-tailed Skua, Willow Grouse and Ptarmigan. Snowy Owl is frequently seen in higher parts of the park but may no longer breed. In forested areas there are Eurasian Pygmy and Tengmalm's Owls and Black and Three-toed Woodpeckers.

The park is close to the main Bergen-Oslo road and has marked trails and tourist huts offering overnight accommodation and meals.

4) Lista This bird observatory lies at the tip of the Lista Peninsula in the far south of Norway. Best known as a migration watchpoint, Lista attracts a wide variety of passage birds.

Divers, waterfowl, raptors and waders occur, with large numbers of passerines and rarities are frequently seen. Owls and northern finches appear in irruption years. Bearded Tit is among the breeding birds.

Lista is 20km west of Farsund and can be reached on the Rv 463.

5) Lofoten Islands This chain of hundreds of mainly uninhabited islands lies off the coast of Nordland and, despite being inside the Arctic Circle, are green and fertile due to the influence of the Gulf Stream.

The southernmost group holds the main interest for birders, in particular the Røst archipelago, which is grass-covered with steep cliffs and vast seabird colonies including European and Leach's Storm-petrels, Common, Brünnich's and Black Guillemots, Puffin and Arctic Skua. White-tailed Eagle can be seen all year, especially on Vedøya, Rough-legged Buzzard in summer and Gyr Falcon in winter. Also in winter there are Purple Sandpiper and Snow Bunting, with King Eider and Yellow-billed Diver offshore. To the north, the larger islands of Langøya and Andøya have coastal meadows and mudflats, which attract passage Whooper Swan, Pink-footed and Barnacle Geese.

The Røst group is reached by air or regular boat from Bodø on the mainland, which is accessible by road, rail or air from Oslo. Alternatively, visitors can sail from Moskenesøy on the mainland to Værøy and from there to Røst.

6) Mølen A migration watchpoint overlooking the Skagerrak, Mølen is on the Brunlanes Peninsula at the mouth of the Langesundsfjord inlet. Seabirds, raptors, waders and passerines all occur and rarities appear with some frequency.

Shearwaters occur given favourable winds and raptors can include White-tailed and Golden Eagles, Northern Goshawk, Rough-legged Buzzard and Gyr Falcon. Eurasian Pygmy and Tengmalm's Owls appear in invasion years and Nutcracker.

Mølen has a bird observatory and is 115km south-west of Oslo and 10km west of Larvik. It can be reached on the Rv302 to Helgoroa then Nevlunghavn, and Mølen is then signed.

7) Øvre Pasvik National Park Sited on a southward extension of Norway between Finland and Russia, this park and its surroundings consist of lakes, pools and swamps, forest and scrub. The forest here is the westernmost point of the Siberian taiga and the largest area of virgin forest in Norway.

Breeders include divers, Whooper Swan, Taiga Bean Goose and Smew around the lakes and river, and Common Crane, Red-necked Phalarope and Broad-billed

Sandpiper in the marshes. The forests have Great Grey and Northern Hawk Owls, Pine Grosbeak and Siberian Tit. Raptors include White-tailed Eagle, Rough-legged Buzzard and Gyr Falcon.

The National Park is most easily reached by road from Kirkenes on Varanger Fjord south to Gjokasen.

8) Rondane National Park With its dramatic scenery this 580km^2 park in central Norway south-east of the Dovre Massif is popular with tourists, hikers and skiers. There are several peaks above 2,000m, as well as glaciers, canyons and forests.

Rough-legged Buzzard is common in summer, Gyr Falcon breeds in rodent years and Golden Eagle is frequent. Also present are Eurasian Eagle Owl, Capercaillie, Black Grouse, Siberian Tit and Siberian Jay in the forests, and Common Crane and Red-necked Phalarope in wetter areas. Ptarmigan, Dotterel and Lapland and Snow Buntings breed in the more upland parts of the park.

Easily reached by road, on the E6 from Dombås or Otta to the west, or Straumbu to the east, the park has marked hiking trails and visitors can stay in cabins.

9) Runde The island of Runde or Rundoy lies off the coast of More og Romsdal close to the mainland town of Ålesund. The cliffs have the some of the most important seabird colonies in Norway with European Storm-petrel, Common, Brünnich's and Black Guillemots, Razorbill and Puffin. Great Skua occurs in summer and White-tailed Eagle all year.

Runde is accessible by ferry from Ålesund, which can be reached by road or rail from Oslo. May to June is the best time to visit the seabird colonies.

10) Slettnes This area in the far north of Norway is increasingly popular as a spring seawatching site and there are breeding birds of interest.

Breeders include Black-throated Diver, Long-tailed Duck, Red-necked Phalarope and Arctic Skua, and Dotterel, Temminck's Stint and Snowy Owl have also bred in the area. Breeding passerines are few but Red-throated and Rock Pipits, Arctic Redpoll, Twite and Lapland and Snow Buntings are present in summer. Passage can bring four species of diver, Lesser White-fronted Goose, King and Steller's Eiders, and four species of skua.

Slettnes can be reached by car via Gamvik or by air from Tromsø to Mehamn.

11) Stabbursdalen National Park and Valdak The northernmost National Park in Norway, this is a true wilderness consisting of a broad valley at the head of Porsanger Fjord. Through this valley runs the Stabburselva River, but the most notable feature of the park is the world's most northerly pine forest, which has trees perhaps 500 years old.

Birdlife in the forests includes Hazel Grouse, Capercaillie, Three-toed Woodpecker and Siberian Jay, with Lapland and Little Buntings in open areas. Long-tailed Skua may be present in summer in good rodent years. Valdak marshes, at the outlet of the Stabburselva River, attracts regular Lesser White-fronted Goose on passage.

The park is reached by a small road off the main E6 Porsanger Fjord road, 2km south of the bridge over the river.

12) Utsira Primarily an autumn migration spot, Utsira is a small rocky island c.20km off Karmøy in south-western Norway with grassland and heather, cultivated land and conifer plantations.

Passerines are the most numerous migrants, with smaller numbers of various pigeons, owls and other birds. Utsira is the premier rarity site in Norway and has produced many 'firsts' including vagrants from north America and Siberia. Seabirds such as Common Guillemot, Razorbill and Puffin breed on nearby Spannholmene. Offshore during summer and passage periods birds such as Manx Shearwater and Great Skua occur, and tape-luring has produced European Storm-petrel.

The island can be reached by daily boat from Haugesund, at Garpeskjaerskaien on Risoey, and it is possible to stay at the bird observatory. The best time to visit in spring is mid-April until early June and in autumn there is good birding from mid-August until mid-October, with the peak time being early October.

13) Varanger Peninsula and Fjord In the far north-east of Norway, bounded by Tana Fjord to the west, the Arctic Ocean to the east and the famous Varanger Fjord to the south, this area is home to many northerly specialities and attracts birders from across Europe. The northern half and the higher ground of the peninsula is largely bare, but elsewhere there are large areas of crowberry heath with dwarf birch and numerous pools and bogs.

Willow Grouse is found across much of the south of the peninsula and Ptarmigan on higher ground and in the north, but both are scarce. The fjells of the central ridge, such as the 548m Falkefjell, are home to Snow Bunting, skuas and waders including Dotterel, Red-necked Phalarope, Purple Sandpiper and Temminck's Stint. Gyr Falcon and Snowy Owl are sometimes present. In the lower scrub areas are Arctic Redpoll, Bluethroat and Red-throated Pipit, and Siberian Tit and Siberian Jay occur in the south-west of the peninsula. However, most birders visit this region for the birds of Varanger Fjord. Nesseby is a regular site for Red-necked Phalarope, with Black-throated Diver and King and Steller's Eiders on the sea. Further east is Vadsø with shops and accommodation, where Glaucous Gull is usually present. Temminck's Stint breeds here and sometimes Little Stint. Store Ekkerøya is one of the best sites for breeding seabirds and seawatching, and Gyr Falcon and White-tailed Eagle occur here. Offshore, four species of skua are possible, and King and Steller's Eiders and Yellow-billed Diver. Off the easternmost coast of the peninsula is the town of Vardø and east of here are the islets of Hornøya and Reinøya, with breeding auks and Little Auk on passage and in winter. Boat trips can be arranged from Vardø. There are more auk colonies on the northern coast of the peninsula at Syltefjordstauran, which also has the world's northernmost gannetry, and further west at Kongsøy.

The Varanger Peninsula can be reached by road from Sweden or Finland, alternatively, Kirkenes, on the south side of Varanger Fjord, has an airport with flights from Oslo. A car is essential to cover this vast peninsula and can be rented in Kirkenes.

Poland

For wetland and forest birds Poland is difficult to beat, which explains its popularity with bird tour companies and independent birders. Although it is a large country, most of the best birds can be seen in a relatively small area of the east. The Białowieża Forest should be on any birder's itinerary, as well as the Biebrza or Chełm Marshes, preferably both. In the west there are wetlands at Słońsk and in the Barycz Valley, and the Tatras and Bieszczady Mountains in the far south support a

range of forest and upland birds. With slow and unreliable public transport, the independent birder is better off hiring a car, but accommodation is generally easy to find. Mid-May is the most popular time to visit Poland, as all of the summer visitors have arrived and one of the country's star birds, Great Snipe, can be seen in display.

1) Białowieża Forest The largest remnant of the ancient forest that once covered most of Europe, Białowieża is famous as the last home of the European Bison. The forest, made up of oak, lime, alder and pine, has open park-like areas and wet marshes, and the variety of habitats enables more than 170 bird species to breed.

Some forest species are notoriously difficult to locate and assistance from local ornithologists may be necessary. Breeders include storks, Common Crane, various owls and nine species of woodpecker. Great Grey Owl is reported most years and rarer raptors include Greater Spotted, Short-toed and Booted Eagles. Hazel Grouse is common but Black Grouse is now very rare, and Capercaillie may now be extinct in the Polish part of the forest. Smaller woodland birds are abundant and much easier to find, and include specialities such as Collared and Red-breasted Flycatchers, River Warbler and Thrush Nightingale.

The forest is easily reached by road or rail from Warsaw to Białystok, and from there on Route 19 towards Lublin, turning off at Zabludow on Route 685 to Hajnowka and then Route 689 to Białowieża. Most visitors tend to stay in the Hotel Iwa, in the grounds of the Palace Park (Park Palacowy) on the edge of Białowieża village. Here many of the passerines can be found including Hawfinch, Common Rosefinch and River Warbler. The area of forest under National Park status immediately north of the village cannot be entered, except with an official guide, who can be arranged in the village and may be the only way to guarantee some of the more elusive species. However, the majority of birds can be seen in the accessible parts of the forest.

2) Białystok Fishponds One of Poland's best wetland areas, these ponds are close to the industrial city of Białystok and despite much disturbance the area has an excellent selection of breeding birds and attracts a range of passage birds.

Famous as one of the few sites that have all five European grebes breeding, there are also bitterns, Little Crake and Whiskered Tern, and Whooper Swan recently bred for the first time. Passerines include Thrush Nightingale, Penduline Tit and Common Rosefinch.

Białystok is c.190km north-east of Warsaw and the ponds are south-east of the city, between Zascianki and Dojlidy. A road skirts the north of the area to the village of Sobolewo, and there is a network of footpaths across the area.

3) Biebrza Marshes A vast area along the Biebrza River, this area is increasingly popular due to its wealth of breeding birds. The attractions of Biebrza are an easily observed Great Snipe lek, which is the most accessible to the majority of European birders, and the strong population of Aquatic Warbler.

Birds in summer include bitterns, storks and Common Crane, waterfowl including Ferruginous Duck and, as well as Great Snipe, there are Jack Snipe and Marsh Sandpiper. More than a dozen species of raptor occur in the breeding season with Golden, Greater Spotted, Lesser Spotted, White-tailed and Short-toed Eagles among them. There is also Black Grouse, White-winged Tern, Thrush Nightingale and River Warbler. More than 260 species have been recorded, nearly 180 of these breeding in the National Park and adjoining marshes.

The area can be visited independently but it may be easier to join an organised birding trip. The Biebrza Marshes cover a vast area, roughly between Lomza and Augustow in north-east Poland. The town of Goniadz makes an excellent base for exploring the marshes and is close to the best-known Great Snipe lek at Budy.

4) Bieszczady National Park This National Park has been little visited until recently, but is now an increasingly regular part of birding trips to Poland. This range forms part of the eastern Carpathians and the lower parts have rolling grasslands, with forests of beech, pine, spruce and larch at higher levels, and alpine meadows higher still. Many of the typical forest and upland birds of east Europe occur here, but the area is still relatively little known ornithologically.

Breeders include Black Stork, Hazel Grouse and Corn Crake, but the main attractions are raptors, owls and woodpeckers. Golden, Lesser Spotted and Short-toed Eagles breed, and possibly also Booted and Greater Spotted Eagles and Saker Falcon. Ural and Eurasian Eagle Owls are present but elusive and other owls include Eurasian Pygmy and Tengmalm's. Woodpeckers are well represented with nine species, plus Wryneck, and passerines include Red-breasted and Collared Flycatchers, Crested Tit and Nutcracker. Montane birds include Alpine Accentor, Water Pipit, Ring Ouzel and, perhaps, Rock Thrush. Dotterel is an occasional autumn passage visitor.

The National Park is c.90km south-east of Sanok but there are good birds throughout the range. The road through Wetlina, Brzegi Gorne and Ustrzyki Gorne, close to the 1,346m peak of Bieszczady Tarnica, is one of the best areas, with many marked trails into the hills from this road.

5) Chełm Marshes The marshes around Chełm in east Poland have lakes and fish-ponds, peat bogs and wet meadows, and a fine selection of breeding wetland birds.

Breeders include bitterns and storks, Common Crane and crakes, with numerous passerines including Penduline and Bearded Tits and the declining Aquatic Warbler, which is still common here. Raptors include Black Kite, Northern Goshawk, harriers and Lesser Spotted Eagle, and possibly still White-tailed Eagle. The scrubland has Black Grouse and waders including Great Snipe nest in the wet meadows.

The marshes cover a large area between Chełm and the Ukrainian border, and are best explored by road from Chełm, which is 70km east of Lublin. Parts of the marshes are protected as nature reserves, Landscape Parks and Protected Landscape areas. The fishponds at Sosnowica are particularly rich, with breeding Ferruginous Duck and Black Stork, and Eurasian Eagle Owl in nearby woodland.

6) Gdańsk Bay area Away from the highly industrialised city of Gdańsk much of the coastline of this huge bay is good for birds.

Well over 300 species have been recorded in the area, rarities such as Steller's and King Eiders are frequent and species generally scarce in the Baltic such as Dark-bellied Brent and Barnacle Geese are regular. Skuas often appear after stormy weather and Iceland and Glaucous Gulls occur in winter. Citrine Wagtail has bred since the mid-1990s.

The Bay of Puck lies in the north-western corner of Gdańsk Bay and is separated from the open sea by the Hel Peninsula (Mierzeja Helska), a long sand spit with pinewoods and marshes. The bay holds tens of thousands of divers, grebes, seabirds and seaducks, including Long-tailed Duck and Smew, on passage and in winter, and the sandy beaches attract thousands of waders. This is one of Poland's top rarity hotspots and there is a ringing station at Chalupy in spring and autumn. Raptors and passerines on migration occur in huge numbers, Citrine Wagtail and Red-throated Pipit are regular in spring and Broad-billed Sandpiper in autumn. There is a road and railway to the tip of the peninsula. Common Crane and Wood Lark breed in the area and Parrot Crossbill has bred in the pinewoods. Inland, c.30km west of Gdańsk, is an area of marshes, lakes and forest around Kartuzy with breeding birds such as Black Stork, White-tailed Eagle, Red-breasted Flycatcher and River Warbler. On the southern side of the Bay of Puck is the delta of the Reda River, at Rewa, with excellent marshes for waders in autumn. However, probably the best site in the entire area is the Vistula Estuary east of Gdańsk, where the marshes, sandbanks and lagoons hold breeding terns and attract regular Broad-billed and Terek Sandpipers on passage. At times more than 100,000 birds are present in this area. There is a ringing station at Swibno, just west of the river mouth, open August to October. Further east is the Vistula Lagoon, separated from Gdańsk Bay by the Vistula spit (Mierzeja Wislana), another superb area for migrants and rarities. There are extensive reedbeds on the southern side and tens of thousands of waterfowl visit the lagoon in winter and on passage. There are also breeding White-tailed Eagle, Mediterranean Gull and Corn Crake. The spit has a road and the southern shore can be reached via Elblag. Druzno is a reed-fringed lake surrounded by marshes, just south of Elblag, where breeding birds include Ferruginous Duck, Lesser Spotted Eagle, Common Crane and River Warbler, and thousands of geese occur on passage and in winter.

Gdańsk is c.360km north-west of Warsaw and can be reached on the E77 road.

7) Kampinos National Park Very close to Warsaw and with a variety of habitats, this park is an ideal destination for visitors to Poland with limited birding time. Habitats include pine forest, mixed and riverine woodland, scrub and marshland.

The area is important for its population of Corn Crake, but also present in summer are storks, Common Crane, Lesser Spotted Eagle, Black Woodpecker, Wryneck, Collared and Red-breasted Flycatchers and warblers including Barred.

The park lies on the north-western edge of Warsaw, in the Wisla Valley, and the office at Izabelin issues permits and guides for restricted areas can be arranged.

8) Milicz Fishponds and the Barycz Valley Breeding and passage waterbirds thrive at the fishponds around Milicz, in the Barycz River valley, and the surrounding deciduous woodland hold birds of interest.

Both bitterns and storks breed, as well as grebes, crakes, Ferruginous Duck and Common Crane. Poland's only regular breeding site for Purple Heron is here and Whooper Swan has bred. One of the major attractions is breeding White-tailed Eagle and other raptors include Black and Red Kites and Northern Goshawk. Reedbed passerines include Penduline and Bearded Tits and Savi's and River Warblers. Drier areas and woodlands hold European Roller and woodpeckers such as Black, Grey-headed, Middle Spotted and White-backed. Passerines in these areas include Thrush Nightingale, Red-breasted Flycatcher and Bluethroat, and warblers including Barred. Thousands of Bean Geese occur on passage and Lesser White-fronted and Red-breasted Geese are recorded annually. Great Egret is regular in small numbers in autumn, and in winter up to 20 White-tailed Eagles may be present.

Milicz lies c.55km north of Wroclaw and the main fishponds east and west of the town in the Barycz Valley. Many of the ponds and meadows can be viewed from local roads but a permit is required to explore the protected areas. Stawno ponds to the east are generally considered the best for birds. Entry to the central part requires a permit from the ornithological station at Ruda Milicka, 5km east of Milicz. Much useful information about birding in the area is available from the staff here. There are woodlands along the Milicz road and the wooded hills near Skoroszow to the south are good for raptors and woodpeckers.

9) Siemianówka Reservoir Conveniently close to Białowieża, this large reservoir is an ideal addition to a birding trip to the forest. The banks vary from muddy with pools to grass-covered or concrete slopes. The eastern, more vegetated end is the more productive and the wet heathland just beyond is excellent for raptors.

All three marsh terns breed and in summer there are storks, Red-necked and Black-necked Grebes, as well as White-tailed and Lesser Spotted Eagles. However, there are also two species of particular interest, Marsh Sandpiper and Citrine Wagtail, both of which have recently bred. Passerines include Crested Lark, Barred Warbler, Common Rosefinch and Ortolan Bunting.

Siemianówka village is close to the southern shore of the reservoir and can be reached by road from Białowieża via Hajnowka. Alternatively follow the track from Stara Białowieża north to Nareka via Janowo. The best birding areas are the south and east shores, but the northern side can be reached by leaving Siemianówka west to Juskowy Grod and from there east to Ciskowa.

10) Słońsk Reserve One of the best birding sites in western Poland, Słońsk is a large area of marshes where the Warta, Odra and Postomia rivers meet. This area is an extremely important breeding, passage and wintering site for large numbers of waterfowl. Around 160 species have bred, of a total of more than 240 species recorded. The reserve covers more than 4,000ha of rivers, oxbows, lakes and drainage channels with regularly flooded meadows.

Birds in summer include bitterns, Red-necked and Black-necked Grebes, crakes and marsh terns. Black Stork breeds and small numbers of Common Crane nest, with thousands on passage. Lesser Spotted Eagle can be seen in summer, as well as both kites and Montagu's Harriers, with White-tailed Eagle in winter. Breeding passerines include Thrush Nightingale, Penduline Tit and Hawfinch, and warblers include Savi's,

River and, sometimes, Aquatic in the wetlands, and Barred and others in scrub and woodland. Słońsk is an important wintering ground for geese, particularly Greater White-fronted and Taiga Bean, and also for Whooper Swan.

Some of the area is rather inaccessible and much of the reserve requires a permit to visit. However, much can be seen from local roads and there is a dam from Słońsk north towards the Warta River, which gives good views but ask permission at the pumping station before walking it. Słońsk can be reached by road north-east of Poznan or from Berlin via the nearby border crossing at Kostrzyn.

11) Szczecin Bay area A vast estuary on the border with Germany, this area is one of the most important areas for migrant waders in Europe, but the wide range of habitats makes for excellent birding all year. As well as the bay, which holds good numbers of ducks and seabirds, there are deltas, islands, marshes, peat bogs, farmland and deciduous forest. The centre of Wolin Island, at the north-eastern corner of the bay, is protected as the **Wolinski National Park**, and **Karsibór Island** south of Świnoujście was the first reserve to be established by OTOP, the Polish Society for the Protection of Birds. There is an ornithological station at Lake Swidwie, a reed-fringed lake surrounded by wet meadows on the western side of the bay. East of Świnoujście there is some woodland worth exploring and a breakwater with migrant waders.

Breeding birds include raptors such as White-tailed Eagle and Red Kite, which can be seen throughout the area, and Montagu's Harrier, Lesser Spotted and Short-toed Eagles are present in summer. Mediterranean Gull sometimes breeds but more regular are Great and Little Bitterns, and Karsibor holds one of the largest breeding populations of Aquatic Warbler in Europe. The latter can also be found around Kamien Pomorski, along with White Stork, Common Crane and Spotted and Corn Crakes. In winter there can be up to 60 White-tailed Eagles around the bay and passage brings grey geese and other waterfowl, Common Crane, waders and various passerines.

Szczecin, at the southern end of the bay, is c.500km north-west of Warsaw but only 150km from Berlin to the south-west. The area can also be reached from Scandinavia via ferry, docking at Świnoujście. Karsibór is reached over a bridge south of Świnoujście and the reserve has an observation tower. Lake Swidwie is north-west of Szczecin near Stolec.

12) Tatra National Park Reaching almost 2,500m, Poland's highest mountains lie on the border with Slovakia. The range is densely forested, with deciduous woodlands in the lower areas, conifers on the slopes and open meadows and bare rock on the highest peaks.

At the highest levels are Water Pipit, Alpine Accentor, Wallcreeper and Alpine Chough, and the forests support Hazel Grouse, Capercaillie, owls including Eurasian Eagle, Eurasian Pygmy and Tengmalm's, and woodpeckers such as White-backed and Three-toed. Nutcracker and Crested Tit also breed here and lower areas have Thrush Nightingale and River Warbler.

Zakopane makes an ideal base for the area and there are various tracks from the road south of the town leading into the valleys. The high-peak birds can be found by taking the cable car from nearby Kuznice.

Portugal

With an excellent tourist infrastructure and many of the Iberian specialities, Portugal is an ideal destination for the birder on a family holiday. Within a short drive of the Algarve holiday resorts can be found Purple Swamphen, Great Bustard, Red-necked Nightjar and Azure-winged Magpie, amongst many others, as well as seawatching at Europe's south-westernmost point. Although the most popular birding areas are in the south, there are excellent estuaries and wetlands

within easy reach of Lisbon and some very good sites for raptors on the border with Spain, in the north and east of the country. Portugal is notorious for bad driving but a hired car is essential to reach many sites away from the south coast. Spring and autumn passage periods are the optimum time for birds, and also good times to get cheap package deals.

1) Baixo Alentejo One of the best and most popular birding areas in Portugal, the southern Alentejo is an area of plains with scattered limestone outcrops, cork oak woods and olive groves, and in the east there are cliff-lined gorges. The area is important for raptors and steppe birds such as bustards.

The Baixo Alentejo covers a vast area, but there are particular areas that should not be missed. One of the best parts and the easiest to reach from the Algarve is around **Castro Verde**. The grasslands east of the town, and east of **Almodovar** to the S, are home to the country's largest Great Bustard population. Other steppe species include Little Bustard and Stone-curlew, and larks are well represented with Calandra, Greater and Lesser Short-toed, Crested, Thekla and Wood all present. Black-bellied Sandgrouse also occurs and there are Iberian specialities such as Great Spotted Cuckoo, Red-necked Nightjar, Rufous Bush Robin, Azure-winged Magpie and Spotless Starling. European Bee-eater and European Roller are common, as are Southern Grey and Woodchat Shrikes. To the east is the hilltop town of **Mértola**, on the **Guadiana River**, where Portugal's largest Lesser Kestrel colony is found, and just east is **Mina de São Domingos** where White-rumped Swift breeds. Egyptian Vulture, Bonelli's Eagle and Black Stork breed at **Pulo do Lobo** on the Guadiana north of Mértola, and there are important heronries in the central Guadiana valley. Common Crane occurs on the grasslands in winter.

In the north of the Baixo Alentejo the best birding area lies in the triangle between the towns of Mourao, Moura and Barrancos. In addition to steppe species, this area has an excellent raptor list with Red, Black and Black-shouldered Kites and Montagu's Harrier. Rockier areas, particularly near Barrancos, have Egyptian and Black Vultures, Short-toed and Booted Eagles, and small numbers of Spanish Imperial and Golden Eagles. Blue Rock Thrush, Eurasian Crag Martin, Rock Sparrow and Rock

Bunting are found in the gorges. One of the best areas is **Mount Foia** where Rock Bunting and Ring Ouzel occur, with Alpine Accentor in winter. Small Button-quail has been reported from the area but the true status of this extremely rare and very elusive bird in the area is unknown. Black Wheatear has also been reported in the area and may be regular.

The Algarve on Portugal's south coast is one of Europe's most popular holiday areas and makes an ideal base from which to explore this area.

2) Berlenga Islands Portugal's most important seabird breeding area, these rocky islands are home to the southernmost colony of Common Guillemot in Europe. The archipelago is also famous for breeding Madeiran Storm-petrel and Cory's Shearwater, and a variety of migrants can occur including possible Eleonora's Falcon.

The islands are c.10km from the mainland near Peniche, c.100km north of Lisbon on the A8. There are daily boat trips to the main island of Berlenga Grande and it is possible to camp overnight. Madeiran Storm-petrel breeds only in the remote Farilhões, which are difficult to reach as landing is prohibited. However, birds can apparently be heard over Berlenga Grande during the breeding season.

Seawatching from Peniche can produce shearwaters, skuas, gulls, terns and auks, and pelagic trips with local fishermen can be arranged in Peniche.

3) Boquilobo Marsh Open freshwater with extensive marginal vegetation, wet woodlands and cork oak stands are the major habitats of this site within easy reach of Lisbon. Part of the marsh is drained each year, but the inner zone remains flooded and much of the marsh is a nature reserve. Famous for its heronry, one of the largest in Iberia, the area is also important as a wintering site for various species.

Little Bittern, Cattle Egret, Black-crowned Night and Purple Herons all breed, and Squacco Heron is rare in summer. In recent years Eurasian Spoonbill has nested and Purple Swamphen bred in 2002. Other breeders include Whiskered Tern and Baillon's Crake. Black Kite is common and Short-toed and Booted Eagles are usually present, harriers occur on passage and sometimes Black-shouldered Kite. Passerine breeders include Cetti's and Savi's Warblers and the surrounding farmland supports European Bee-eater and Woodchat Shrike. The marsh is of great importance to wintering ducks, and Red-crested Pochard is usually present throughout the year.

Located c.90km north-east of Lisbon, the site is reached via the A1 from Lisbon and by turning off on the IP6 towards Torres Novas. After 10km take the road to Riachos and a right turn after the railway line leads over the river to the reserve headquarters. Part of the marsh is a strict reserve with no public access, but the rest is easily viewed from nature trails and there is a hide overlooking one of the pools.

4) Cape St Vincent-Ponta de Sagres At the extreme south-west tip of the European mainland, these two headlands form the most important migration watchpoint in Portugal. Away from the immediate coast much of the land is used for sheep-grazing or cereal production, but there are woods and scrub-filled valleys.

Although best known as a site for migrants the area has interesting breeding birds, with Lesser Kestrel, Alpine and Pallid Swifts, Blue Rock Thrush and Red-billed Chough on the cliffs, and nearby farmland supports Spotless Starling, Thekla Lark and Spectacled, Sardinian and Dartford Warblers. Little Bustard can be seen along the St Vincent-Sagres road and Eurasian Eagle Owl may still survive in the area. In winter the cliffs often have Eurasian Crag Martin and the rocks below the lighthouse are famous for wintering Alpine Accentor, with Snowfinch in 1999. Seawatching produces shearwaters in good numbers, and in the correct winds skuas and gulls, including Audouin's, can turn up, as well as European and Wilson's Storm-petrels. Madeiran Storm-petrel is possible in strong westerly winds, as are Great Shearwater and Sabine's Gull, and Swinhoe's Storm-petrel has been recorded. Raptor passage is wind-dependent and during easterlies most of the migrant European species can be seen. Booted Eagle and Black Kite are among the most numerous, but there are also Egyptian and Griffon Vultures, Short-toed and Bonelli's Eagles, Red and Black-shouldered Kites, and Eleonora's Falcon is possible. Mid-September to mid-October is the most productive period. Storks also appear in autumn with Black the more numerous, and Dotterel frequently rest on the farmland. Passerines include Red-rumped Swallow, Tawny Pipit, Rufous Bush Robin and Western Bonelli's Warbler.

Sagres forms the ideal base for the area and is reached on the N125 from the international airport at Faro, or from Lisbon south on the A2 to Marateca, the IP1 to Albufeira and the N125 east to Sagres. Offshore shark-fishing trips are available and would undoubtedly increase the chances of seeing the rarer and more pelagic species.

5) Castro Marim One of the best wetlands in southern Portugal lies at the mouth of the Guadiana River, close to the Spanish border. Much of the area is covered by the Reserva Natural do Sapal de Castro Marim e Vila Real de Santo Antonio, and the fresh water, saltpans and saltmarsh and adjacent scrub and pinewoods host a wide variety of breeding, passage and wintering wetland birds.

White Stork, Black-winged Stilt and Pied Avocet are common breeders, Little Bustard and Collared Pratincole occur, and there are six breeding larks including Greater and Lesser Short-toed. Audouin's Gull bred here in 2001, the first record for Portugal. The scrub and woodlands have Red-necked Nightjar, Rufous Bush Robin, Azure-winged Magpie, and Southern Grey and Woodchat Shrikes. Passage bring a range of birds, with Greater Flamingo and Eurasian Spoonbill frequent visitors, waders from stints to godwits and fairly regular Marsh Sandpiper, Caspian, Gull-billed and marsh terns, and raptors such as Booted and Short-toed Eagles and Griffon Vulture. Balearic and Cory's Shearwaters are common offshore on passage and passerines include Red-throated Pipit and Ortolan Bunting. Winters are mild with White Stork and Greater Flamingo often present all year, but colder weather brings waterfowl.

Castro Marim lies on the west bank of the Guadiana and is reached by road from Faro on the IP1, turning south on the N122 just before the river and the Spanish border. There are several areas of particular note around Castro Marim with a good wader spot at the disused saltpans between the village and the river. The area between the saltpans and the bridge over the river is excellent for Stone-curlew, Little Bustard and larks. The N122 between Castro Marim and Vila Real has good birding on either side but particularly to the W. A track heading west off this road leads to the Carrasqueira, a stream which joins the Guadiana, and flows through rough pasture and scrub with pools and saltpans, and an excellent variety of birds, particularly during migration periods. Banco do O'Brill, the breakwater at the mouth of the Guadiana, is good for gulls and terns, sometimes skuas and shearwaters. A few kilometres inland of Castro Marim, the road from Azinhal to Murtal crosses an area of grassland with Little Bustard and Stone-curlew, and woodland and scrub with Wood Lark, Rufous Bush Robin and Orphean Warbler.

6) International Douro The Douro forms part of the border with Spain in north-east Portugal and, like the similar International Tagus to the south, this is an excellent raptor area. The best birding is between Miranda do Douro and Barca d'Alva, and as well the gorge the site covers scrub and farmland and pine and oak woodland.

Raptors include Egyptian and Griffon Vultures, Red Kite and Golden, Booted and Bonelli's Eagles, and other breeders include Black and White Storks and Eurasian Eagle and Eurasian Scops Owls can be seen. There are many passerines such as Thekla Lark, Red-rumped Swallow, Western Bonelli's Warbler and Red-billed Chough.

The area can be explored on minor roads off the N221 and N220 between Miranda do Douro and Barca d'Alva.

7) International Tagus This 40km stretch of the Tagus (Tejo), forming part of the Portuguese-Spanish border, extends from where the Erges joins the Tagus west to Cedillo Dam. It includes steep-sided gorges in places and densely vegetated river-banks, as well as surrounding plains, cork oak woodlands and eucalyptus plantations. Idanha-a-Nova, N of the river, is a particularly good area of open cultivated land with occasional rocky outcrops. This range of habitats in a relatively undisturbed area attracts an excellent variety of birds to breed, some of which are difficult to see else-where in Portugal.

Raptors are well represented with Black, Griffon and Egyptian Vultures, Golden, Booted and Bonelli's Eagles on the cliffs along the river, and Short-toed Eagle, Black, Red and Black-shouldered Kites and Montagu's Harrier in the surrounding farmland. Also breeding along the river and on rocky outcrops are Black Stork, Eurasian Eagle and Eurasian Scops Owls, Eurasian Crag Martin, Red-rumped Swallow, Blue Rock Thrush and, rare in Portugal, Black Wheatear. Birds of the plains include Great and Little Bustards, Stone-curlew and Black-bellied Sandgrouse. Pin-tailed Sandgrouse has been recorded but is commoner on the Spanish side. Spanish Sparrow is abundant in local villages and various larks are common on the farmland, Great Spotted Cuckoo and European Bee-eater breed, and the woodlands hold Azure-winged Magpie and Red-necked Nightjar. In winter Alpine Accentor is a rare but regular visitor.

Most visitors use the town of Castelo Branco, c.40km west, as a base to explore the area. Castelo Branco is reached from Lisbon on the north road towards Santarém, then turn east towards Abrantes and Castelo Branco. The plain of Idanha-a-Nova is reached by leaving Castelo Branco north-east on the N233, turning onto the N240 towards Ladoeiro and then north to Idanha-a-Nova on the N354, which crosses the plain where both bustards are possible. To view the river leave Idanha-a-Nova south-east on the N353 to Rosmaninhal, where White Stork nests, and from there a track leads to Vale da Morena farm, where permission should be sought before proceeding to the river.

8) Montezinho Natural Park This park covers an area of mountains, farmland and woodland with an interesting mix of Mediterranean birds and from further north in Europe.

White Stork and small numbers of Black Stork nest in the park, and raptors include Egyptian Vulture, Montagu's Harrier, Black and Red Kites, and Golden, Bonelli's and Short-toed Eagles. Eurasian Eagle Owl is elusive but Eurasian Scops Owl is common. Great Spotted Cuckoo, Red-necked Nightjar, European Bee-eater and Wryneck also occur, and passerines include Western Bonelli's Warbler, Iberian Chiffchaff, Rock Bunting and Spotless Starling.

Bragança is the nearest major town, has the park headquarters and makes an ideal base from which to explore the park. The centre of the park has uplands, including the Serra de Montezinho, and can be reached via the N103-7 from Bragança. The west of the park is reached on the N103 to Vinhais, then the N316 into the park, and for the east leave Bragança on the N218 to Gimonde, then north on the N308 towards Deilão.

9) Peneda Gerês National Park Portugal's only National Park covers an area of mountains with slopes and valleys densely wooded with oak and pine, lakes, rocky outcrops and high bare peaks.

Breeding birds of the area include Montagu's Harrier, Golden Eagle, Eurasian Scops Owl, Eurasian Crag Martin, Red-billed Chough and Rock Bunting.

The park is best visited in summer when there is a greater range of birds present, and there are marked hiking trails and bridleways and boats and horses can be hired. The information centre is in Braga, 30km south of the park, which can be reached on the N103 or the N203.

10) Ria Formosa The most important birding site in the Algarve is the Ria Formosa, on the coast adjacent to Faro, and despite much loss of habitat most of the area is now a Natural Park. It covers dunes and lagoons, channels and islands, saltpans, pools and river mouths, and is important for a wide range of breeding, passage and wintering birds, and is Portugal's best site for Purple Swamphen.

Little Bittern and Purple Heron breed, as well as egrets, White Stork and Stone-curlew. **Quinta do Lago** in the west of the area has breeding Purple Swamphen and Red-crested Pochard. Dartford Warbler and Short-toed Lark are also common breeders, and Azure-winged Magpie and Short-toed Treecreeper can be seen in pine woodlands. The greatest diversity occurs during passage periods with spring seeing the arrival of Great Spotted Cuckoo, Black-eared Wheatear and Spectacled Warbler. Waders occur in autumn and raptors such as Red Kite, Short-toed and Booted Eagles. In winter Black-necked Grebe, Greater Flamingo, Glossy Ibis and Eurasian Spoonbill are regular, as well as Caspian Tern. Passerines in winter include Water Pipit, Bluethroat and Penduline Tit.

Faro forms the ideal base to explore the Ria Formosa, and there are numerous package deals to this part of Portugal, making a convenient and inexpensive way to visit the area. Quinta do Lago is 18km west of Faro and reached via Almansil, where there is a golf course and lagoons. A nature trail here leads to a hide overlooking a lagoon where Purple Swamphen is virtually guaranteed. Swamphens can also be seen at Dunas Douradas slightly further W. E of Faro is the park headquarters at Quinta do Marim: take the N125 east to Olhão and turn right just before a petrol station on the other side of the town. Cross the railway line and a track to the left leads to the entrance where a small fee is payable.

11) Sado Estuary Despite pollution and habitat loss, this is the most important estuary for birds in Portugal after the Tagus. There are extensive mudflats and saltmarshes, reedbeds and freshwater pools, and the Tróia Peninsula, a scrub-covered and wooded sand spit, separates the estuary from the sea. In addition to a range of breeding birds, the area is of great importance as a passage and wintering site for waterfowl and waders.

Breeders include White Stork, Purple Heron, Cattle Egret, Black-winged Stilt and Kentish Plover. The reeds hold Cetti's Warbler and Portugal's only breeding Great

Bitterns, scrub has Red-necked Nightjar, Dartford Warbler and Cirl Bunting, and the pines support Crested Tit, Azure-winged Magpie and Western Bonelli's Warbler. Booted and Short-toed Eagles occur regularly, as well as Black-shouldered Kite. Black-necked Grebe winters in good numbers and other birds present at this season include Black-winged Stilt, Pied Avocet, Greater Flamingo and White Stork.

The main town of the area, Setubal, is on the north shore of the estuary and reached on the A2 from Lisbon or the IP1 from the S. E of Setubal are extensive salt-pans and those at Gambia are especially worth checking, whilst further along the N10 a minor road towards Zambujal leads to areas of reeds and saltmarsh. From Setubal it is possible to take the car ferry to Tróia on the southern shore. The N253-1 south of Tróia gives good views over the estuary and leads to Comporta, where there are extensive mudflats.

12) Santo André Lagoon The coastal location of this wetland make it one of the most interesting birding sites in this part of Portugal. The lake, which varies seasonally in salinity as well as depth, is separated from the sea by a narrow band of sand dunes covered by scrub and pinewoods. Fringing the lake are reedbeds and willow scrub, and inland there are more pinewoods and cork oak groves.

Breeding birds include Little Bittern, Purple Heron, Black-shouldered Kite, Baillon's Crake and Black-winged Stilt. The pines and oak groves hold Red-necked Nightjar, Great Spotted Cuckoo, Crested Tit and Hawfinch, and the farmland and scrub Crested Lark and European Bee-eater. Outside the breeding season the area is important for Red-crested Pochard in winter and Eurasian Spoonbill, Glossy Ibis and Greater Flamingo on passage. Water Pipit, Penduline Tit and Bluethroat are regular winter visitors. Crested Coot is occasional among the thousands of Common Coot.

Santo André Lagoon can be reached from Lisbon on the A2 via Setubal. From Setubal follow signs to the port and take the Tróia ferry, continuing south through Comporta, then turning west towards Melides. A few kilometres past the latter is the signed turn-off for the lagoon. Various tracks can be used to explore the lake and its surroundings from the road south of Brescos village.

13) Tagus Estuary (Tejo Estuary) Portugal's most important estuary for birds, the Tagus has extensive mudflats, saltmarshes, reedbeds and paddyfields. More than 240 species have been recorded and all of the regular northern European waders either winter or visit on passage.

Breeders include Little Bittern, Purple Heron, Montagu's Harrier, Black-winged Stilt and Collared Pratincole. Small numbers of Red-crested Pochard are present all year, and warblers, Stone-curlew and Calandra Lark breed on adjacent farmland. Little Bustard occurs all year but in larger numbers in winter. Hunting over the farmland are Black-winged Kite and Short-toed and Booted Eagles. Wooded patches have Short-toed Treecreeper, European and Red-necked Nightjars, Azure-winged Magpie and many passerines. Passage birds include Eurasian Spoonbill, Greater Flamingo and Mediterranean Gull, and winter brings Bluethroat and Penduline Tit.

Situated east of Lisbon, the estuary is vast but the best areas are south of the N10 between the Tagus and the Sorraia River, and further south between the estuary and the N118. Further south still is the Paul da Barroca with cork oak woods and rice fields, and among the native birds are feral Yellow-crowned Bishop, Red Avadavat and Village Weaver.

Romania

With the Danube Delta and Dobrudja considered among the best birding areas in Europe, Romania is deservedly one of the most popular of the former Eastern Bloc countries with bird tour companies. It also appeals to independent birders, with cheap package holidays available to the Black Sea coast and ski resorts providing accommodation in the mountains. An outstanding range of breeding birds occurs in the delta and large numbers of

migrants pass coast. The Dobrudja is famous for wintering geese including, at times, the bulk of the world population of Red-breasted Goose. Much of the north and west of the country consists of mountains, with upland and forest birds, and a visit to Romania during the migration periods and covering the whole range of habitats can produce a trip list approaching 200 species.

1) Bicaz This spectacular gorge in the eastern Carpathians has a good range of mountain birds and the forests at nearby Rosu hold grouse, owls and woodpeckers. Lake Bicaz attracts waterfowl on passage and in winter.

Hazel Grouse, Capercaillie and Golden Eagle are fairly common in the area, owls include Eurasian Eagle, Ural and Tengmalm's and woodpeckers include Grey-headed, White-backed and Three-toed. Wallcreeper is found in the gorge and forest passerines include Red-breasted Flycatcher, Crested Tit and Nutcracker. Lake Bicaz is a large mountain reservoir that attracts Greater White-fronted Goose in autumn and Slavonian Grebe in winter.

The town of Bicaz lies c.50km west of Piatra Neamt and the Bicaz-Gheorgheni road passes through the gorge.

2) Danube Delta Considered by some to be Europe's top birding site, the Danube Delta is a vast area of marshes, lakes and islands, wet forests and reedbeds on the Black Sea coast of Romania. Many miles inland, near the regional capital of Tulcea, the Danube splits into the rivers Chilia, Sulina and Sfintu Gheorghe, and these, interconnected by numerous channels and lakes, form the delta. The birds can be difficult to see, except by boat, which is the usual form of transport in the area.

More than 280 species are regular here, and among the many breeders are both pelicans, Pygmy Cormorant, herons, Glossy Ibis and White Stork. Breeding waterfowl include Ruddy Shelduck, Red-crested Pochard, Ferruginous Duck and possibly still White-headed Duck, and among thousands of the commoner species there are Lesser White-fronted and Red-breasted Geese and Smew in winter. Breeding raptors include Booted, Lesser Spotted and White-tailed Eagles, Montagu's Harrier and Red-footed Falcon. Saker Falcon still occurs but is rare. Terns include Caspian and Gull-billed, Whiskered and White-winged, and Mediterranean Gull is numerous on passage. Waders on passage include Broad-billed and Marsh Sandpipers, with Slender-billed Curlew reported. Passerines are abundant in the wetland vegetation and also in the drier areas and woodland. A range of warblers occurs in summer including Savi's, River, Cetti's, Moustached, Paddyfield and Eastern Olivaceous.

Tulcea is the main town of the area, about 280km north-east of Bucharest and served by an airport. It is a major port and the base for ferries downstream into the delta on the three main waterways. Maliuc is further into the delta and boatmen can be hired from here to tour the smaller channels, as well as in Crisan, even deeper into the delta and something of a tourist centre along the Sulina.

The Danube Delta is a difficult area to work and by far the best way to see its many special birds is to join an organised birding tour; most specialist companies arrange trips to this ornithological paradise.

3) Dobrudja Although somewhat overshadowed by the Danube Delta, this part of Romania ranks among the best birding sites in Europe. Many of the birds that breed in the Danube Delta pass through this area on migration and can be very much easier to see here. Dobrudja is on the Black Sea coast between the delta and the Bulgarian border, and is on a major migration route. In addition the area attracts huge numbers of wintering waterfowl.

Most of the world population of Red-breasted Goose winters here, although in severe weather they tend to move into Bulgaria. Greater and Lesser White-fronted Geese also winter, and a huge variety of birds occurs on passage including storks and herons, waterfowl, raptors and waders including Broad-billed Sandpiper. The area also holds many birds of interest in summer: Pygmy Cormorant, Marsh Sandpiper, Pied Wheatear and Paddyfield Warbler.

The **Lake Istria and Nuntasi** area, 45km north of Constanta and reached from the E87, is one of the best sites within the Dobrudja and supports Squacco Heron, Ferruginous Duck, Marsh Sandpiper and Paddyfield Warbler. There are also breeding terns, pelicans on passage and Red-breasted Goose in winter. Sinoie Lagoon is just east of Istria and is an excellent site for waders, with regular Collared Pratincole, Broad-billed Sandpiper and Red-necked Phalarope, and Demoiselle Crane has been recorded. To the N, close to the delta, is the vast Razim Lagoon where summering birds include White Pelican, Ruddy Shelduck and Slender-billed Gull. Pallid Harrier is possible in summer with other raptors further inland at Babadag, on the E87 c.90km north of Constanta. Short-toed, Lesser Spotted, Eastern Imperial and Booted Eagles occur in these hills, as well as Levant Sparrowhawk, Long-legged Buzzard and Red-footed and Saker Falcons. Woodpeckers such as Black, Syrian, Middle Spotted and White-backed can also be found, and passerines include Lesser Grey Shrike and Black-headed Bunting. Lake Techirghiol in the south of the Dobrudja is another excellent wetland area and one of the best sites in the country for wintering White-headed Duck. The lake is c.10km south of Constanta on the E87. Hagieni Reserve, inland of Mangalia, has woodlands, scrub and marshy areas, and attracts crakes, Savi's, River and Barred Warblers, Sombre Tit and Rock Bunting. Close to the Bulgarian border, in the far south of Dobrudja between Lipnita and Baneasa, is the Fetii Valley where raptors include Egyptian Vulture, Levant Sparrowhawk and Long-legged Buzzard, and Eurasian Eagle Owl may be present.

Organised birding tours of the Dobrudja are now commonplace, but it is also possible to tour the area independently. Constanta has an international airport and there are several holiday resorts along this coast. Most of the best birding areas are easily reached from the E87 road.

4) Gurghiu Mountains Ornithologically this densely forested area of the eastern Carpathians is little known, but Hazel Grouse and Capercaillie occur here as well as Grey-headed, White-backed and Three-toed Woodpeckers. Owls include Eurasian Eagle, Ural, Eurasian Pygmy and Tengmalm's. Passerines include Red-breasted and Collared Flycatchers, Sombre Tit and Nutcracker.

The mountains can be explored on minor roads from Reghin, which is north of Tîrgu Mures on Road 15.

5) Lake Cǎlǎraşi Much of this once great wetland area has been converted to fish farms but still holds birds such as White Pelican, Glossy Ibis and various herons Little Bittern, Squacco and Purple Herons. Whiskered Tern and Collared Pratincole breed and during passage periods the area attracts a variety of waders. Passerines include Barred, Moustached and Savi's Warblers and Penduline Tit.

The city of Cǎlǎraşi is 120km south-east of Bucharest on Road 3 and the lake and fish farms c.6km west of the city. There are several other ponds and marshy areas around Cǎlǎraşi, including Ciocǎneşti Fishponds 30km to the W, worthy of investigation.

6) Poiana Braşov Montane and forest birds are relatively accessible at this site in the southern Carpathians where a cable-car can be taken up to 1,960m on Mount Cristianu.

Golden Eagle and upland passerines such as Alpine Accentor, Wallcreeper and Rock Bunting can be seen at the higher levels, and the forests hold Ural and Eurasian Eagle Owls, Three-toed Woodpecker, Crested Tit, Nutcracker and Red-breasted Flycatcher. The ski resort of Poiana Brasov is c.10km south of Brasov.

7) Retezat National Park In the south-eastern Carpathians, this is a mountainous area with many peaks over 2,000m. Most of the area is forested with beech, fir and spruce and dwarf pine scrub in higher areas, as well as glacial lakes and alpine meadows.

Birds include many upland specialities such as Golden Eagle, Water Pipit, Alpine Accentor and Wallcreeper. Lesser Spotted Eagle and Eurasian Eagle Owl are also found here, but it is the forest birds that are the main draw. Owls include Eurasian Pygmy, Ural and possibly Tengmalm's, and there are Grey-headed, Black, Middle Spotted, White-backed and Three-toed Woodpeckers. Other forest dwellers are Hazel Grouse, Capercaillie, Red-breasted Flycatcher, Crested Tit and Hawfinch.

The park can be reached on roads 68 and 66, which follow the northern edge of the range and roads to the mountain resorts leave Piu and Clopotiva.

8) Satchinez This reserve is a remnant of a once vast stretch of periodically flooded wetlands in the far west of Romania. The pools, marshes and wet meadows hold important heronries and other breeders, and the area is an important stopover for migrants. About 150 species have been recorded on the reserve with c.70 breeding.

Breeders include Black-crowned Night, Squacco and Purple Herons, both bitterns, White Stork, Black-necked Grebe and this is a good site for Ferruginous Duck and crakes. Passerines include warblers such as Savi's and River, and Bearded and Penduline Tits. Passage periods bring various waders and all three marsh terns, and in winter Rough-legged Buzzard hunts the marshes. The plains west and north-west of Timisoara are one of the few regular sites for Great Bustard in Romania.

The reserve lies close to Satchinez village, which is c.25km north-west of Timisoara, and spring and summer are the best times to visit with the most species present.

9) Turda Gorge A deep gorge in the Trascau Mountains of Transylvania, this site has many easily seen upland species in an area of outstanding scenery. The gorge, which has high rocky cliffs and riverine woodland, is set in a largely grassland landscape.

Golden Eagle, Eurasian Eagle Owl and Alpine Swift all occur, as well as Black and Grey-headed Woodpeckers. Passerines include Rock Thrush, Red-breasted and Collared Flycatchers, Wallcreeper and Rock Bunting. The gorge lies 8km west of Turda and can be reached on a track from the village of Cheia.

Russia (European Russia)

Although organised birding tours to Siberia and the remote far east of Russia are available, the vast area covered by European Russia is largely ignored, as many of the forest and wetland birds can be seen in more accessible countries, and even the birds of Arctic Russia can be seen in northern Scandinavia, albeit in smaller numbers. In southern Russia the Caucasus has some speciality birds but these can now be seen in Armenia and Georgia. Possibly the best accessible birding in Russia west of the Urals

lies in the south-west, in the Volga Delta and Kalmykian Steppes. The delta is a larger version of the Danube, with many of the same species in much greater numbers, plus birds such as Pallas' Gull. Kalmykia has large areas of dry steppe, a habitat that exists only in scattered fragments further west, and is a stronghold for bustards and Demoiselle Crane. The northern Urals, on the extreme edge of the Western Palearctic, may one day become accessible to birders, but is unfortunately very difficult to visit at present. Several species occur here at the western limits of their range, including Pintail Snipe, Oriental Cuckoo, Lanceolated Warbler and Pallas' Reed Bunting, and the area surely has great potential as a destination for bird tour companies in the future.

1) Volga Delta The Volga River empties into the north-east of the Caspian Sea and forms the largest river delta in Europe, covering more than 6,500km². This vast area has around 100 breeding birds and over 250 species have been recorded. A large area is covered by the Astrakhan Reserve, which includes extensive marshes, riparian woodland and cultivated land. There are numerous lakes and oxbows and the river enters the Caspian through hundreds of channels over a 200km stretch of coast.

Some of the breeding birds are very rare elsewhere in Europe and include Dalmatian Pelican, White-tailed and Greater Spotted Eagles, Purple Swamphen and

Pallas' Gull. Other breeders include various herons, Pygmy Cormorant, Glossy Ibis and Eurasian Spoonbill, and ducks including Ferruginous and Red-crested Pochard. Blue-cheeked Bee-eater also breeds and passerine specialities include Moustached, Paddyfield, Ménétries's and Desert Warblers, and Rose-coloured Starling. Passage is also exceptional, with 10 million waterfowl and waders using the area in autumn. Broad-billed, Marsh and Terek Sandpipers all occur regularly and one of the world's most endangered species, Siberian White Crane, is regular in spring and autumn in very small numbers.

To visit Astrakhan Reserve it is undoubtedly best to join an organised bird tour if possible. In any case, it is necessary to obtain permission from the National Biosphere Reserve of Astrakhan, Nabereshnaja r. Zarew Street 119, RU-414000, Astrakhan. The best times to visit are probably mid-April to mid-June and late August to mid-October. The city of Astrakhan lies in the north of the delta, 90km from the Caspian and is reached by air from Moscow. The usual base for birding trips is the village of Damchik, reached by road (60km) or five hours by boat from Astrakhan. The guest houses here can arrange for experienced local guides to escort visitors into the delta.

2) Kalmykian Steppes north and west of Astrakhan is a vast area of semi-desert with lakes and seasonally flooded depressions that should be on the itinerary of any birder visiting the Volga Delta.

This is the global stronghold of Demoiselle Crane and other steppe birds include bustards, Pallid Harrier, Steppe Eagle and Saker Falcon, as well as larks, wheatears and Rose-coloured Starling. Black Vulture and Black-bellied Sandgrouse are also possible and the area is important for passage and wintering birds.

The most accessible areas are west of Astrakhan along the road to Elista and to the north on the Volgograd road. The area to the south-west, around Liman, is reputed to be the best for Steppe Eagle.

3) Kola Peninsula This vast peninsula in the far north of European Russia consists of tundra, forest and low mountains fringed by rocky coasts. The area has become much more accessible in recent years and there excellent birding opportunities. The Lappland Nature Reserve near Murmansk is good for tundra birds and the Kandalaksha Reserve on the White Sea has important seabird colonies.

Specialities such as Yellow-billed Diver and King and Steller's Eiders can be seen in summer, although they are more numerous as winter visitors, with as many as 16,000 of the latter wintering offshore. Breeding raptors include White-tailed Eagle, Rough-legged Buzzard, Golden Eagle, Northern Goshawk and Gyr Falcon. Willow Grouse occurs throughout the peninsula, Ptarmigan in the N, and Capercaillie and Hazel and Black Grouse in the S. Among waders are Dotterel, Temminck's Stint, Purple and Broad-billed Sandpipers, Jack Snipe and Red-necked Phalarope. Seabirds include Arctic and Long-tailed Skuas, Black, Common and Brünnich's Guillemots, Razorbill and Puffin. Forests of the south support a range of owls including Ural and Great Grey, and Snowy Owl summers on the tundra in the north.

Murmansk, the peninsula's largest town, can be reached by air, rail or road from St Petersburg.

4) Oka Valley Part of the valley of the Oka is a Biosphere Reserve and consists of dry and wet woodland, marshes and small lakes.

Breeders include White-tailed and Greater Spotted Eagles, Corn Crake, White-winged Tern, Eurasian Eagle and Pygmy Owls, and waders such as Great Snipe and

Marsh and Terek Sandpipers. Further east the valley is important for wintering geese and other waterfowl.

Oka Valley reserve lies south of Moscow at Donki, near Serpukhov and can be visited on a day-trip from Moscow.

5) Teberdinskiy Reserve On the northern slope of the Greater Caucasus, this reserve is one of the oldest and most spectacular protected areas in these mountains. Most of the reserve is above 2,000m, and it consists of high ridges and deep valleys, glaciers and streams, forests and alpine meadows. The area is important for breeding birds, with some highly range-restricted species, and also lies on a migration bottleneck where large numbers of storks and raptors can be seen.

Breeders include specialities of the area such as Caucasian Black Grouse and Caucasian Snowcock, and these two species in particular are the main draw for the few Western birders that venture here. Other species of interest include Caucasian Chiffchaff, Green Warbler, Great Rosefinch, Red-fronted Serin and Krüper's Nuthatch. Isabelline Wheatear and Güldenstädt's Redstart may also be possible in this area, and Grey-necked Bunting has been recorded. More widespread upland birds such as Wallcreeper and Alpine Accentor also occur. Raptors include Lammergeier, Griffon Vulture and Golden Eagle. Eastern Imperial, Steppe and Lesser Spotted Eagles and Long-legged Buzzard occur on passage. The forests support Black and Middle Spotted Woodpeckers, and Eurasian Eagle and Tengmalm's Owls.

The ski resort of Dombay makes a good base from which to explore this area, but is undoubtedly much easier to visit reserve with an organised birding tour.

Sardinia

Unlike Corsica, which has its nuthatch, there are no endemic birds on Sardinia but it does have some excellent wetlands and birds such as Greater Flamingo, Eleonora's Falcon and other raptors, Purple Swamphen and Audouin's Gull. Visiting Sardinia is expensive and this undoubtedly puts off some birders, along with the widespread hunting, but accommodation and car hire are widely available. Most of the best birding areas are in the south of the island and there are very good wetlands in easy reach of the capital Cagliari. Sardinia is accessible by air or ferry from mainland Italy or Corsica.

1) Cagliari wetlands Sardinia has some of the best wetland areas in the Mediterranean, some in easy reach of Cagliari, where more than 200 species have been recorded. Molentargius Marsh and Quartu Marshes are to the east, between

Cagliari and Quartu Sant Elena, and to the west are Santa Gilla and Macchiareddu Marshes. Molentargius is part saltpan and part fresh water, whilst Quartu is a long narrow saltpan close to the beach. Macchiareddu is an area of salt works but Laguna di Santa Gilla is fresh water and river-fed.

Regular breeders include Little Bittern, Cattle Egret, Purple Heron, Glossy Ibis, Purple Swamphen, Red-crested Pochard, Black-winged Stilt and Pied Avocet, whilst Greater Flamingo has bred. Also breeding are Slender-billed Gull and Gull-billed Tern. The area is important for passage waterfowl and waders, and Black-necked Grebe, Greater Flamingo, Ferruginous Duck and Pied Avocet occur in winter.

The wetlands east of Cagliari can be reached via the Cagliari-Quartu road. Leave the road at the crossing point of the Terramagni Canal and a path leads to the freshwater Bellarosa Minore and the salt works. Quartu Marsh is reached via a minor road to Villasisimus or the road from Quartu town to Quartu beach. To reach Macchiareddu and Santa Gilla take the S195 coast road to Pula and search the marshes via minor roads.

2) Capo Marargiu The best site for Griffon Vulture in Sardinia, scrub-covered Capo Marargiu lies in the north-west of the island.

In addition to 20 pairs of Griffon Vulture, this area has Red Kite, Bonelli's Eagle and Lesser Kestrel, and passerines including Spotless Starling, Spanish Sparrow and Corsican Finch. The area can be viewed from the Bosa-Alghero road.

3) Giara di Gesturi This largely uninhabited plateau is in southern Sardinia, midway between Cagliari and Oristano, and covers nearly 50km^2 at an altitude of c.500m. The boulder-scattered landscape has large expanses of cork oak forest and Mediterranean maquis.

A range of birds can be seen on the plateau with Barbary Partridge and Little Bustard among the most sought-after, although both are now rare. Calandra Lark is common, as are Wood Lark, *Sylvia* warblers, Woodchat Shrike and Cirl Bunting. The *arrigonii* race of Northern Goshawk is possible and Spotless Starling breeds in villages at the foot of the plateau. During passage periods the area attracts migrant waders and herons, and raptors including Red Kite.

The plateau can be reached on the S197 to Gesturi and then via a signed minor road onto the plateau. Avoid the area on Sundays and holidays, as it is widely used for shooting.

4) Monte Arcuso This WWF reserve is one of Sardinia's best sites for raptors and covers extensive areas of evergreen oak woodland, scrub-covered canyons and mountain peaks reaching nearly 1,000m.

Golden and Bonelli's Eagles occur here, as well as Northern Goshawk of the race *arrigonii*. Corsican Finch is common, as are Marmora's, Dartford, Spectacled and Subalpine Warblers.

Monte Arcuso lies within easy reach of Cagliari, on the S195 heading for Pula. Turn right towards Capoterra and take the minor road at St. Lucia church for the reserve.

5) Oristano wetlands The Gulf of Oristano is on the west coast of Sardinia and, together with the surrounding wetlands, forms one of the best birding areas on the island. Much of the area around the town of Oristano is now used for fish farming or rice-growing but the numbers and variety of birds are of international importance. Among the complex of wetlands are a range of habitats including salt, brackish and freshwater lagoons, extensive reedbeds and grazing land, as well as sandy beaches and dunes and rocky coasts. Sale Porcus is a LIPU reserve and one of the best areas, although the nearby Cabras and Mari e Pauli, S'Ena Arrubia and Mistras areas can be equally good.

Breeding birds include Purple Swamphen, Black-winged Stilt, Pied Avocet, Kentish Plover, Collared Pratincole, Gull-billed Tern and Slender-billed Gull, all at Sale Porcus. In addition, Mari e Pauli has Red-crested Pochard and Ferruginous Duck nests at S'Ena Arrubia. Other species breeding in the area include Stone-curlew, possibly Little Bustard, Montagu's Harrier and Lesser Kestrel. Calandra and Greater Short-toed Larks, Zitting Cisticola, Cetti's Warbler and Rock Sparrow are common in much of the area. Passage brings grebes, waterfowl, herons, raptors, seabirds and waders. Scarcer species recorded regularly include Glossy Ibis and Audouin's Gull, and wintering Greater Flamingo at Sale Porcus has reached 8,000.

Oristano is c.90km north of Cagliari via Route 131. To find Sale Porcus head north from Oristano on the S292, turning off just past Riola Sardo towards Putzu Idu and follow the LIPU signs. Cabras and Mari e Pauli can be seen from the Riola Sardo-Cabras road. Mistras is east of Oristano, follow signs for Torre Grande then Giovanni Sinis. S'Ena Arrubia is c.12km south of Oristano on the Arborea road.

6) San Pietro A scrub-covered, volcanic island off south-western Sardinia, San Pietro has rocky cliffs and offshore islets, but there are also sandy beaches, dunes and brackish lagoons. Since the early 1990s part of the island has been a LIPU reserve, primarily established to protect Eleonora's Falcon, which breeds on the cliffs of the north-west, especially at Capo Sandalo. About 100 pairs breed here and they can be seen best during late afternoon and early evening at Cala Fico and Cala Vina.

Other breeding birds include Cory's and Yelkouan Shearwaters, European Storm-petrel, Audouin's Gull, Alpine and Pallid Swifts, and Blue Rock Thrush. Away from the cliffs the avifauna is typically Mediterranean, with *Sylvia* warblers including Spectacled and Marmora's, Wood Lark and Cirl Bunting. Barbary Partridge also breeds and the recently separated Corsican Finch is common. A wide range of migrants occurs and can include Black-eared Wheatear, Western Bonelli's Warbler and Collared Flycatcher, Greater Flamingo is a regular autumn/winter visitor and Alpine Accentor often occurs in winter.

The port and only town on the island is Carloforte in the east, which can be reached from Cagliari by bus and a half-hour ferry trip.

Sicily

Despite some good wetlands in the south and the presence of breeders such as Eleonora's Falcon and Rock Partridge, it is raptor passage across the Strait of Messina that is of most interest to visiting birders. Tens of thousands of raptors cross the narrow straits here and LIPU have managed to more or less end illegal shooting on the Sicilian side, although it still occurs on the mainland. Among regular raptors are occasional Long-legged Buzzard and Amur Falcon, and storks also pass over.

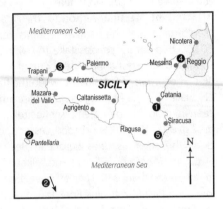

1) Lago di Lentini A brackish wetland with reeds separated from the sea by dunes, this area is one of the best areas for wetland birds in Sicily throughout the year.

Little Bittern, Squacco Heron, White Stork, Ferruginous Duck and Collared Pratincole breed, with Stone-curlew, Calandra and Crested Larks on the surrounding land. Passage periods and winter are also impressive, with up to 1,500 Ferruginous Duck and 400 Glossy Ibis occurring on passage, and good numbers of Great Egret and Eurasian Spoonbill in winter. Passage Slender-billed Curlew has been recorded.

The area is 20km south of Catania but a permit is required from the Consorzio per la Bonifica del Lago di Lentini, in Lentini.

2) Pelagie Islands and Pantellaria Two islands comprise the Pelagie group, Lampedusa and Linosa, which are closer to Tunisia than mainland Italy. Lampedusa is the larger and more southerly of the two, a largely barren limestone rock with high cliffs, whilst Linosa has more vegetation, including cultivated areas and dense bush. The isolated Pantellaria lies to the east off Cap Bon, Tunisia.

Eleonora's Falcon breeds on the cliffs of Lampedusa and Linosa has a large Cory's Shearwater colony in a lava field. Other breeders include European Storm-petrel and Marmora's Warbler. The recently separated African Blue Tit breeds on Pantellaria.

Lampedusa is reached by air daily from Palermo or a ferry from Porto Empedocle, near Agrigento, which also stops at Linosa. The islands are best visited in June, by which time the shearwater colony is at its busiest and the late-breeding Eleonora's Falcon is present.

3) San Vito Peninsula This peninsula lies on Sicily's northern coast and is one of the few undeveloped parts of this coastline. Habitats include sea-cliffs and extensive garrigue with patches of cultivated land and grassland.

One of Sicily's best sites for Bonelli's Eagle, which breeds in very small numbers, Lanner Falcon may still be possible here. Black Kite and Eleonora's Falcon occur on passage. Rock Partridge occurs in the higher rocks, along with Rock Bunting, Rock Sparrow and Blue Rock Thrush. Scrubland warblers include Sardinian, Subalpine and Spectacled Warblers, and Alpine and Pallid Swifts breed on the cliffs.

The easiest part of the peninsula for birding visitors to explore is the reserve at Lo Zingaro on the east side and the best time is spring. The reserve lies north-west of the town of Castellammare del Golfo, on the main coast road from Palermo. Access to the reserve is at Scopello, where guides and maps are available.

4) Strait of Messina Although the majority of European raptors cross the Mediterranean at the narrowest points, i.e. Gibraltar and the Bosphorus, more than 30,000 birds of 17 species take the extremely hazardous Italy-Sicily-Tunisia route: thousands are shot annually, but one of the best areas to observe the passage is the 4km-wide Strait of Messina, between the Italian mainland and north Sicily.

Black Kite and Montagu's Harrier are among the most numerous raptors, but also seen in good numbers are Lesser Kestrel and Red-footed Falcon, and rare but regular are Egyptian Vulture, Short-toed, Lesser Spotted and Booted Eagles. Both storks also cross the strait, as does European Bee-eater and passerines including Collared Flycatcher. At sea both Cory's and Yelkouan Shearwaters are regular spring migrants. In all more than 310 species have been recorded and breeders include Rock Partridge, Pallid Swift, Blue Rock Thrush and Red-billed Chough.

From the Sicilian side of the straits, the best place to watch for migrants is the Monti Peloritani, the wooded and scrub-covered hills above Messina, reached on the Via Palermo. Regular ferries run from Reggio di Calabria on the mainland to Messina. Spring is undoubtedly the best time, with larger numbers in April but greater variety in May.

5) Vendicari Marshland and dunes form the main habitats of this area in south-eastern Sicily, which attracts numbers of waterfowl, waders and seabirds on passage and in winter.

Various herons, storks, Glossy Ibis, Eurasian Spoonbill and Greater Flamingo occur here, as well as Audouin's, Mediterranean and Slender-billed Gulls, and Gull-billed and Caspian Terns. Slender-billed Curlew has been recorded on passage. Passerines include Crested and Greater Short-toed Larks and Spectacled and Sardinian Warblers.

Slovakia

Upland and forest birds, particularly raptors, are the speciality of this small country, and bird tour companies and independent birders often combine a trip to Slovakia with the lowlands of Hungary, resulting in an impressive list. However, Slovakia does have some good wetlands of its own, particularly the Senné

Fishponds in the south-east. The increasing popularity of winter sports has opened up many mountain areas, but it is much easier to join an organised tour, which enlists the help of local ornithologists to locate the more elusive owls and woodpeckers. As early in spring as possible is best for these birds, but snow may block roads in some areas until late spring, by which time these species and Hazel Grouse are more difficult to find.

1) High Tatras National Park This park in northern Slovakia includes the High Tatra and Belanské Tatry ranges, and adjoins Poland's Tatra National Park. The main habitat is spruce and pine forest, with mixed woodland in lower areas and boulder-strewn alpine meadows above the forest.

The birdlife is typical of a central European montane area, with Alpine Accentor, Rock Thrush and Wallcreeper at higher levels, and Crested Tit and Nutcracker in the forest. Among the woodpeckers are White-backed, Middle Spotted and Three-toed, and owls include Eurasian Eagle, Eurasian Pygmy and Tengmalm's, probably also Ural. Raptors are scarce but Lesser Spotted and Golden Eagles occur. Storks, Corn Crake and various passerines occur in the lower valleys.

The closest major town is Poprad, which has an airport and the area is well served by public transport. The area is very popular with skiers in winter and walkers in summer, and is thus geared for tourists. There are cable cars and chair lifts to the more popular slopes, and higher and more remote areas possess well-stocked refuge huts.

2) Malá Fatra This extensive range of high peaks in the north forms part of the western Carpathians. Reaching more than 1,700m, there are river valleys and gorges, impressive forests of beech and oak on the lower slopes, pine, spruce and fir at higher levels, and alpine pastures.

Breeders include Capercaillie, Hazel Grouse and Black Grouse, and owls such as Eurasian Eagle, Tengmalm's and Eurasian Pygmy. Woodpeckers are common in the forests and include Black, Grey-headed, White-backed and Three-toed. Other woodland species such as Nutcracker and Crested Tit are common. Also present, but elusive, is Red-breasted Flycatcher, and there is a small breeding population of Black Stork. Golden Eagle and Wallcreeper breed on the higher crags and the alpine meadows have Water Pipit, Alpine Accentor and Ring Ouzel.

This range, which is partly under National Park status, can be reached from the E50, via the towns of Zilina and Martin. There are ski lifts to the high peaks and the park has a network of hiking trails. The area is popular with skiers in winter and hikers in summer and although disturbance has increased this has made the mountains more accessible.

3) Malé Karpaty This 100km-long range of wooded hills forms the western most sector of the Carpathians, and is very important for raptors, in particular Eastern Imperial Eagle and Saker Falcon.

Other raptors include Lesser Spotted and Short-toed Eagles and Northern Goshawk, and there are many species of interest in the extensive beech, oak and ash woodlands, such as Black Stork, Eurasian Eagle Owl, and Red-breasted and Collared Flycatchers. Unsurprisingly this is excellent woodpecker country with Black, Grey-headed, White-backed, Middle Spotted and Syrian. The warmer southern slopes are home to Wood Lark, Wryneck and European Bee-eater in summer.

Malé Karpaty is a vast area and can be difficult to explore, but Route 61, the Bratislava-Nové Mesto nad Vahom road, skirts the edge of the range and the hills can be explored on minor roads from there.

4) Nízke Tatry National Park This range, with peaks of over 2,000m, extends for 80km across central Slovakia and includes rugged ridges and deep valleys, montane lakes and alpine meadows. The extensive forests consist mainly of spruce and pine with beech on some lower slopes.

Hazel and Black Grouse and Capercaillie breed and raptors include Lesser Spotted and Golden Eagles. Owls are represented by Eurasian Eagle, Tengmalm's and Eurasian Pygmy, and woodpeckers by Black, Grey-headed, White-backed and Three-toed. Other forest birds include Black Stork, Red-breasted Flycatcher, Nutcracker and Hawfinch. More open areas have Corn Crake, Wood Lark and Barred Warbler, and there are Water Pipit, Alpine Accentor, Rock Thrush and Ring Ouzel on the upland meadows.

The E50 road follows the north edge of the mountains and Road 66 runs along the south. The area is very popular with skiers in winter and hikers in summer, and has cable cars enabling visitors to reach the higher zones, and a network of hiking trails.

5) Orava Reservoir This large reservoir is an important stopover for migrants. There are sand and pebble beaches around the reservoir, and marshes, damp woodland, farmland and forests in the surrounding area.

Many species occur in these varied habitats including storks, Lesser Spotted Eagle and Spotted and Corn Crakes. The pine forests support Hazel and Black Grouse, Grey-headed and Black Woodpeckers. In spring and autumn divers and grebes, waterfowl and raptors, herons and waders all pass through in some numbers. The reservoir is north-west of the E77 road to the Polish border, close to the town of Orava.

6) Senné Fishponds One of Slovakia's most popular birding localities with a wide range of breeding, passage and wintering birds, and always a chance of rarities, particularly in autumn when the fishponds are drained. Surrounding the more than 25 ponds are wet grasslands, canals and drainage dykes.

Breeders include bitterns, Black-crowned Night and Purple Herons, Great Egret and Slovakia's only breeding Eurasian Spoonbills. The reeds and wet grasslands have Spotted, Little and Corn Crakes, Black-winged Stilt, Whiskered Tern and ducks including Ferruginous. Pygmy Cormorant has nested in recent years and White Stork breeds in local villages. Aquatic Warbler is an irregular breeder but Savi's Warbler is common and the surrounding farmland has Tawny Pipit, Lesser Grey Shrike, European Roller and Syrian Woodpecker. Raptors in summer include Montagu's Harrier and Red-footed Falcon. Both storks occur on passage, as well as Common Crane and a selection of waders that can include Marsh and Broad-billed Sandpipers and Red-necked Phalarope. Greater White-fronted and both Bean Geese are regular, Lesser White-fronted possible and various grebes occur on passage.

Senné Fishponds are in extreme south-eastern Slovakia c.15km south-east of Michalovce, but can be difficult to find and the access tracks are often waterlogged. From Michalovce head for Inacovce and ask permission to visit the ponds from the fish farm buildings at the west end of the village.

7) Slanské Hills Although famous for raptors these wooded hills interspersed with scrub and open areas also support a range of other birds, particularly owls and woodpeckers.

Among raptors are Short-toed, Booted, Lesser Spotted, Eastern Imperial and Golden Eagles, Northern Goshawk and Saker Falcon. Owls include Eurasian Eagle and Ural, and woodpeckers are represented by Grey-headed, Black, Syrian, Middle Spotted and White-backed. Black Stork and Corn Crake also breed. Passerines include Wood Lark, Barred Warbler, and Red-breasted and Collared Flycatchers.

The north of the Slanské Hills can be explored from Presov and the south from the Kosice-Secovce road.

8) Slovenský Kras Adjoining Aggtelek National Park in neighbouring Húngary, Slovensky Kras is a limestone plateau with gorges, woodlands and scrub, and has an excellent range of birds, with wetland habitats in lower areas.

Raptors are represented by Saker Falcon and Short-toed, Eastern Imperial and Lesser Spotted Eagles, and owls include Eurasian Eagle, Eurasian Scops, Ural and Tengmalm's. Other birds of interest include Hazel Grouse, European Roller, a range of woodpeckers and passerines including Red-breasted and Collared Flycatchers and Rock Bunting.

Slovensky Kras lies south-east of Roznava and can be explored on minor roads and tracks from the E71 road.

9) Vihorlatske Hills In the far east of Slovakia, these are forested hills with occasional deep valleys, rocky outcrops, open and scrubby areas and small lakes.

Both storks breed, among raptors are Short-toed, Lesser Spotted, Eastern Imperial and Golden Eagles, and owls include Eurasian Eagle, Eurasian Pygmy and Ural. Woodpeckers such as Grey-headed, Black, Middle Spotted and White-backed can be seen, as well as passerines including Barred Warbler and Red-breasted and Collared Flycatchers. The hills can be explored on minor roads from Michalovce.

10) Záhorie Close to the Austrian border and the Marchauen-Marchegg Reserve, this site is a Protected Landscape Area and includes several nature reserves. Like the better known Austrian site, Záhorie also has an excellent range of breeding woodland and wetland birds.

Both storks and bitterns breed, as well as Ferruginous Duck and Red-crested Pochard, three crakes, and raptors including Red and Black Kites, Montagu's Harrier and perhaps Saker Falcon. Numerous woodpeckers can be seen and passerines include River and Barred Warblers, Collared Flycatcher, Bearded and Penduline Tits and Short-toed Treecreeper. Jakubovske Fishponds are one of the best areas for breeding wetland birds and attract a range of passage birds such as Eurasian Spoonbill and White-tailed Eagle. In addition there is a dry and sandy area north of Malacky where European Roller, Tawny Pipit and Lesser Grey Shrike occur.

Záhorie is c.20km north of Bratislava between the E65 and the border, and most of the area is of open access.

11) Zemplínská Reservoir Within easy reach of Vihorlatske Hills, this reservoir is an important migration stopover for waterfowl with over 20,000 birds recorded at times.

Both storks, a variety of herons and Common Crane are regular in autumn, as well as large numbers of grey geese including Lesser White-fronted, grebes and the occasional diver There is less interest in summer, as the reservoir is popular with holiday-makers but there is a reserve at the east end where Little Bittern, Ferruginous Duck and Spotted Crake occur, and Great Snipe is regular in autumn. Between Vinne and Kaluza on the north shore are quarries with Eurasian Eagle Owl and Rock Thrush, and woodlands in the area hold Ural Owl.

The reservoir is east of Michalovce and there is easy access to the northern and eastern shores from local roads.

12) Zlatná na Ostrove This largely farmland site bordering the Danube in south-eastern Slovakia is the only area of the country where Great Bustard is likely. Although the original steppe has been lost, the fields, riverine woods and wetlands still support a good selection of birds.

Great Bustard is present all year but only very small numbers now breed. Other birds include White Stork, Montagu's Harrier, Red-footed Falcon and Tawny Pipit. River Warbler, Short-toed Treecreeper and Penduline Tit occur along the river. Rough-legged Buzzard hunts the open areas in winter.

The bustards are generally west of the village of Zlatná na Ostrove, which is *c.*50km south-east of Bratislava. Wetland areas and the Danube can be reached on minor roads between Zlatná na Ostrove and Vel'ké Kosihy.

Slovenia

Now firmly back on the tourist map, Slovenia hosts a good range of birds, combining montane and forest species with wetland birds and Mediterranean specialities. Accommodation and car hire are readily available and it is easy to cover all the important habitats from a single base. Package deals are available and are an ideal way to see around 150 species on a visit in late May to early June.

1) Karst Regional Park A region of limestone hills in south-western Slovenia famous for its geological features, with numerous canyons, sink-holes and caves, Karst also has forest and scrub with interesting breeding birds. Eurasian Scops Owl, Wryneck, Crested Tit, Short-toed Treecreeper and Rock Bunting are among those present in summer.

Postojna is the base for this site in the Dinaric Mountains and can be reached by road from Trieste or Ljubljana.

2) Kocevje The forested hills of the Dinaric plateau above Kocevje are little known ornithologically but cover a vast, largely uninhabited area and are undoubtedly excellent for birds. Forest and grassland cover most of the area but there are high cliffs in the Kolpa Gorge on the Croatian border.

Ural and Eurasian Scops Owls occur in small numbers and the only White-tailed Eagle nest in Slovenia is (or was) in this area. Also present are Wryneck, Black and Grey-headed Woodpeckers, Ring Ouzel, Collared Flycatcher, Crested Tit and Short-toed Treecreeper.

Kocevje is situated in the south of Slovenia and easily accessed by road.

3) Krakovski Forest This important, virtually undisturbed, lowland forest is in eastern Slovenia and part is a nature reserve. The avifauna is little known and undoubtedly much remains to be discovered.

Breeders include Black and White Storks, Lesser Spotted Eagle (at its only Slovenian breeding site), Black and Middle Spotted Woodpeckers, and Collared Flycatcher.

Krakovski Forest is east of Ljubljana in the central Krsko Valley, on the left bank of the Krka River, and the Ljubljana-Zagreb highway runs along the northern side of the forest.

4) Lake Cerknica Although temporary, reed-fringed Cerknica may still support breeding Little Bittern, Ferruginous Duck and Spotted, Little and Corn Crakes. White-tailed Eagle is a non-breeding visitor and White-winged Tern regular on passage. The lake is situated south-west of Ljubljana near the town of Bakek.

5) Ljubljansko Moor Now largely agricultural land, this area still has remnants of original mire habitat with flooded meadows and wet woodland.

This is the most important site for Corn Crake in Slovenia and also supports small numbers of Little Bittern and Lesser Kestrel, as well as Wryneck and Barred Warbler. Black Stork was once a breeding species and may still occur.

This large area, covering more than 150km² and crossed by the Ljubljanica River, is situated on the southern side of Slovenia's capital Ljubljana.

6) Triglav National Park This 840km² area, Slovenia's only National Park, covers limestone mountains of the Julian (Julijske) Alps, reaching more than 2,860m. Habitats include bare mountains and alpine meadows, coniferous, mixed and deciduous woodland on the slopes, and Mediterranean-type scrub in lower areas.

Birds include raptors such as Northern Goshawk and Golden Eagle, and montane species such as Ptarmigan, Rock Partridge, Alpine Accentor, Wallcreeper, both choughs and Snowfinch. The forests support Capercaillie and Hazel and Black Grouse, woodpeckers including Black, Grey-headed and Three-toed, and many passerines. Citril Finch is very rare but possible at Triglav.

The park is situated in the far north-west of Slovenia and has marked hiking trails, an information centre and mountain huts. The nearest major town is Bled to the east.

Spain

Deservedly one of the most popular birding destinations in the Western Palearctic with an excellent range of birds throughout the year and habitats ranging from 3,400m mountains to lowland marshes and virtual semi-desert. More than 200 species are possible on a spring visit, including such Iberian specialities as Marbled and White-headed Ducks, Crested Coot and Purple Swamphen, Black-shouldered Kite, Spanish Imperial Eagle, Black Vulture, Red-necked Nightjar and

Azure-winged Magpie. Spain is also the only country where a sighting of the elusive Small Button-quail is a real possibility. Accommodation and car hire can be found throughout the country with travel and access to birding sites generally easy, and there is a great deal of literature available on birding in Spain.

1) Aiguamolls de L'Empordá and Cap de Creus These marshes on the Golfo de Rosas form one of the best birding areas in north-eastern Spain, second only to the Ebro Delta. The site covers coastal marshes around the mouths of the Muga and Fluvià rivers and includes freshwater pools, brackish lagoons and saltmarshes, wet grassland and riverine woodland. About 300 species have been recorded with nearly 100 of these breeding. A few kilometres to the north is Cabo de Creus, the easternmost point of Spain and a rocky, headland with scrub-dwelling birds and ideal for seawatching. Lesser Kestrel has been reintroduced here.

Various herons breed here, Greater Flamingo occurs on passage and Purple Swamphen and White Stork have been reintroduced. Black-winged Stilt, Pied Avocet and Stone-curlew breed, as do European Bee-eater and European Roller. Passerines include Cetti's, Savi's and Moustached Warblers, Zitting Cisticola, Penduline Tit, Lesser Grey and Woodchat Shrikes. In winter Black-throated Diver can be seen at sea, as well as Velvet Scoter and auks. Waterfowl winter in large numbers and Glossy Ibis is regular. Cabo de Creus holds Bonelli's Eagle, Black Wheatear and Blue Rock Thrush, Rock and Ortolan Buntings. Skuas and shearwaters occur offshore on passage and Wallcreeper and Alpine Accentor can appear in winter.

The Aiguamolls de L'Empordá area is on the Costa Brava and can be reached from the A7 or NII between Barcelona and La Jonquera. There is an information centre at El Cortalet and the reserve has hides and marked trails.

2) Aigües Tortes National Park A wild and rugged area in the central Pyrenees, this park has boulder-strewn hillsides, hanging valleys and high peaks, reaching 2,957m at Contraig. The principal feature of the park are two large valleys, San Nicolau in the north-west and Escrita in the NE, separated by a high mountain pass, the Portarro d'Espot. Lake San Mauricio, a popular summer tourist attraction, lies in the valley of the Escrita River, a steep-sided glacial valley with lakes and pinewoods.

Lammergeier is usually fairly easy to see and other raptors include Griffon Vulture, Golden Eagle and Red Kite. There is a range of other montane birds such as Ptarmigan, both choughs, Wallcreeper and Alpine Accentor, as well as Water Pipit and Rock Bunting. Birds of the pines include Capercaillie, Tengmalm's Owl, Black Woodpecker, Citril Finch and Crested Tit and Short-toed Treecreeper.

The Escrita Valley is best visited from the village of Espot, signed from the C147. The San Nicolau Valley can be reached from Pont de Suert on the N230, heading towards the Aran Valley and turning right after a few kilometres for Caldes de Boí.

3) Cabo de Gata This area of Almería province covers a range of habitats including a rocky headland with seawatching potential, arid scrub covered mountains, steppe-like areas and saltpans. Much of the area is a natural park and adjoins the Campo de Níjar, a larger steppe area to the N. Until recently this was a relatively under-watched part of Spain but it is home to some highly sought-after birds.

European Storm-petrel may breed on the headland, shearwaters occur offshore on passage and Razorbill in winter. The mountains host Bonelli's and Booted Eagles, Lesser Kestrel, Eurasian Eagle Owl, Black Wheatear and Spectacled Warbler. However, the real specialities of the area are Trumpeter Finch and Dupont's Lark. Both occur in the Sierra del Cabo de Gata but are more likely to be found further inland. The finch is most easily found in the desert-like area around the tourist attraction of 'Mini-Hollywood' between Tabernas and the Sierra Almahilla, and the lark in the Campo de

Níjar, a large plain between the Sierra Almahilla and Sierra del Cabo de Gata. Black-bellied Sandgrouse and Little Bustard also occur here. The saltpans attract Greater Flamingo, a range of waders and seabirds including Audouin's Gull, which can be viewed from the comfort of hides. White-headed Duck is possible in winter.

From Almería the N340 leads to Tabernas and the Sierra Almahilla, and the N332 to Níjar. For Cabo de Gata take the N332 from Almería and turn right following signs for San Jose or Cabo de Gata.

4) Cáceres-Trujillo Steppes This part of Extremadura is famous for bustards, but there is also a good range of other species present including a healthy population of Lesser Kestrel in Cáceres town. Much of the once very extensive, undulating plains around and between these two towns have been lost to agriculture, but the remnants support more grassland birds than anywhere else in Spain. The plains consist of dry grassland and farmland with patches of scrub and, in some parts, small pinewoods.

In addition to bustards, these plains support Black-bellied and Pin-tailed Sandgrouse, Stone-curlew and Calandra Lark. In areas of open woodland and scrub there are European Roller, European Bee-eater, Great Spotted Cuckoo, Azure-winged Magpie and Southern Grey Shrike. Raptors include Montagu's Harrier, three species of kite, Spanish Imperial, Booted and Short-toed Eagles, and Black and Griffon Vultures. In the towns there are breeding White Stork and Pallid Swift, and wetter areas have Cattle and Little Egrets and Whiskered Tern. Black Stork is a regular on passage and Common Crane in winter.

Both Cáceres and the smaller Trujillo have good areas of steppe within easy reach, and the N521 road between the two towns can produce Great Bustard. The N523 road from Cáceres to Badajoz also crosses good bustard habitat, but the grasslands are best explored from minor roads and farm tracks. N of the village of Torreorgaz, on the C520 south-east of Cáceres, is a particularly good area, as is the area crossed by the La Cumbre road south-east of Trujillo. There are several small reservoirs in the area, all of which are worth scanning and the grasslands surrounding them often hold bustards. Running south-east from Cáceres is the Sierra de Fuentes, a range of hills with breeding Black Stork and raptors, possibly also Eurasian Eagle Owl. The area is easily reached by road from Madrid on the NV. Although many of the steppe specialities are resident a spring visit is generally most productive.

5) Cádiz Lagoons The numerous lagoons between the town of Jerez de la Frontera and Cádiz Bay in southern Andalucia are home to all the Iberian wetland specialities, as well as a range of other birds. The lagoons are generally shallow with variable amounts of vegetation dependent on season and rainfall, and some dry out in summer. Reeds fringe many of the lagoons, which are surrounded by scrub or farmland.

The water level and extent of vegetation greatly affect the birds present but when wet the lagoons can hold White-headed and Marbled Ducks, Crested Coot and Purple Swamphen throughout the year. Others include Black-necked Grebe, Cattle Egret, Greater Flamingo, herons, Collared Pratincole and Whiskered Tern. Raptors such as Montagu's Harrier, Egyptian Vulture, Black Kite and Short-toed and Booted Eagles occur in summer and Spanish Imperial Eagle in winter. Passerines include Black-eared Wheatear, Woodchat Shrike and warblers such as Cetti's, Savi's and Zitting Cisticola. Passage waders sometimes include Marsh Sandpiper and Ferruginous Duck is regular in winter and spring.

Laguna Medina is the largest lagoon and lies beside the C440 between Jerez and Medina Sidonia. About 6km before this road meets the A4, the lagoon is signed along a track to the right. White-headed and Marbled Ducks, Crested Coot and Purple Swamphen occur here and a smaller pool, known as **Laguna de las Pachecas** or **Laguna Istata**, c.1km to the north on the opposite side of the road is also worth checking. The **Lagunas de El Puerto Santa Maria** (also known as the Lagunas de Terry are c.6km north of El Puerto de Santa Maria and reached from the C440 by turning off to El Portal until the north IV is crossed; after 3km, past the casino, a track on the right follows an irrigation channel to some houses on farmland. Park here and a short walk leads to the lagoons. Laguna Salada is the largest and has artificial islets. Laguna Chica has a reedbed and Laguna Juncosa is usually completely covered in rushes. White-headed and Marbled Ducks, Crested Coot and Purple Swamphen occur here, as well as Collared Pratincole, Red-crested Pochard and Little Bittern. Moustached Warbler is a possible breeder. The **Lagunas de Espera** (Lagunas de Zorilla) are reached from Jerez de la Frontera on the north IV, turning onto the N342 to Arcos de la Frontera. From here take the C343 towards Espera, go through the village and turn left for Las Cabezas de San Juan, and after 2km turn left towards a lagoon known as Hondilla. Greater Flamingo is regular here, as well as the four specialities, which can also be found at **Lagunas de Puerto Real**, reached on a track just past thekm 9 post on the Puerto Real-Paterna de Rivera road. These species are also usually present at the **Lagunas de Chiclana**, E of Chiclana de la Frontera on the N340 close to Cádiz.

Jerez de la Frontera has an airport with domestic and international flights, and most of the local towns and villages provide accommodation. Cádiz Lagoons can also be visited on a day-trip from Gibraltar.

6) Coto Doñana National Park Despite its limited access, this area of over 1,300km^2 is one of the most famous birding destinations in Europe, with a wide range of breeding birds and internationally important numbers of waterfowl in winter and on passage. Much of the park is formed by the marismas of the Guadalquivir River, a large area of shallow lagoons and seasonally flooded salt flats protected from the sea by a large sandbar. Inland there are more dunes, Mediterranean scrub and Stone pine and cork oak woodlands, each habitat having its own characteristic birds.

Breeders include a variety of herons, Eurasian Spoonbill and Iberian specialities such as Marbled Duck, Crested Coot and Purple Swamphen. In drier areas breeding raptors include Red and Black Kites, Short-toed, Spanish Imperial and Booted Eagles, and Lesser Kestrel. Black-shouldered Kite occurs in the El Acebuche area. The scrub has warblers, chats, shrikes and larks, with Azure-winged Magpie, Great Spotted Cuckoo, Crested Tit and Hawfinch among the many woodland birds. In spring and autumn passage seabirds can be seen offshore including Audouin's Gull, and the flooded areas inland hold Common Crane and large numbers of waterfowl. One of the most sought-after of all Western Palearctic birds, Small Button-quail, may still breed in the Coto del Rey area in the north of the park, but due to its highly secretive nature it is rarely seen. Slender-billed Curlew has been reported in winter.

Coto Doñana is worth visiting at any season, but some areas are closed to the public and access is strictly controlled. This usually means it can be visited only as part of an organised minibus/Landover trip, which are not the best way to see birds.

However, all of the specialities can be seen outside the closed areas. The National Park headquarters at El Acebuche has a nearby lagoon overlooked by hides and Azure-winged Magpie and Red-necked Nightjar close by. La Rocina information centre near El Rocío has a nature trail and hides beside a marshy area with Purple Swamphen, Little Bittern and other herons.

7) Ebro Delta Although somewhat overshadowed by the Coto Doñana, the Ebro Delta is one of the finest wetland areas in Spain. Situated on the Mediterranean coast, this delta consists of rice fields, reedbeds, riverine woodland, regularly flooded scrubland, and, closer to the sea, channels and lagoons with saltmarsh, dunes and sandy beaches. Over 300 bird species have been recorded and a range of species can be seen all year.

Breeders include various herons (eight species may be present in summer and this is an important site for Purple Heron), Red-crested Pochard, Purple Swamphen, Audouin's and Slender-billed Gulls and Gull-billed and Whiskered Terns. Black-winged Stilt, Pied Avocet and Collared Pratincole also breed and Greater Flamingo has done so. Summering raptors include Montagu's Harrier, Short-toed and Booted Eagles. Red-necked Nightjar and European Bee-eater are present in summer and passerines include Greater and Lesser Short-toed Larks, Zitting Cisticola, Moustached and Savi's Warblers, Bearded Tit and Spotless Starling. Passage often brings Glossy Ibis, Marsh and Broad-billed Sandpipers and Red-footed Falcon. More than 200,000 birds can winter in the area including grebes, waterfowl, gulls and waders.

The delta is situated on the coast of Catalonia near Amposta and is reached by minor roads east from the N340. Deltebre, in the centre of the delta, has a visitor centre.

8) Garraf Massif Within easy reach of Barcelona, this range of limestone hills with scrub, pinewoods and sea-cliffs provides excellent birding for those on a city-break.

Eurasian Eagle Owl and Bonelli's Eagle are present, as well as Pallid and Alpine Swifts, European Bee-eater, Black and Black-eared Wheatears, both Rock Thrushes, Thekla Lark, Eurasian Crag Martin, Rock Sparrow and Ortolan Bunting. Warblers include Western Bonelli's, but this is ideal *Sylvia* habitat and Dartford, Sardinian, Subalpine and Spectacled all occur. Various raptors occur on passage and Wallcreeper and Alpine Accentor are winter visitors to the higher parts of the range.

To explore the Garraf Massif take the Castelldefels road from Barcelona and turn right towards Palau Novella and Port Ginesta. This road leads through the Rat Penat housing development and to the top of the range. There are various viewpoints and tracks and it is possible to walk to the highest point in the area, the 595m la Morella.

9) Guadalhorce Estuary Despite its unattractive appearance the mouth of the Guadalhorce River is one of the best birding sites in Andalucía, forming an important passage stopover for many species, as well as providing wintering and breeding habitat. In addition to the river there are flooded gravel pits and reedbeds on a scrub-covered plain, riverine woodland and the beach.

Breeders include various herons, Pied Avocet, Black-winged Stilt and Kentish Plover. Audouin's Gull occurs in summer and on passage, and also present in summer are Pallid Swift, European Bee-eater and Greater Short-toed Lark. Greater Flamingo is present all year, and herons, storks, crakes and waders occur as migrants. Collared Pratincole is regular in small numbers, as are Caspian and Gull-billed Terns.

Shearwaters and skuas occur offshore in autumn, and European Roller and White-rumped Swift are regular on passage. Winter brings Black-necked Grebe, Cattle Egret and various waders and waterfowl. Booted Eagle has wintered in recent years and Bluethroat, Penduline Tit and Southern Grey Shrike are regular.

Guadalhorce Marshes can be reached by road from Málaga, taking the N-340 to the west and turning right after 4km, just before the bridge. Continue under the bridge and take the first track towards the beach.

10) Jaca area The area around Jaca is probably the best birding area in the entire Pyrenean range, with most specialities and a range of other birds within easy reach.

One of the best known birding sites is San Juan de la Peña, west of Jaca, where Lammergeier, Griffon and Egyptian Vultures are virtually guaranteed and eagles include Short-toed, Golden, Booted and Bonelli's. These can all be seen from the monastery, as well as both choughs, Rock Sparrow and Rock Bunting. Birds in surrounding forests include Black and Middle Spotted Woodpeckers, Western Bonelli's Warbler, Crested Tit, Short-toed Treecreeper and Citril Finch. About 10km further west is the Hecho Valley, which is one of the lowest parts of the Pyrenees to have regular Wallcreeper, at the Boca del Infierno, as well as many other typical Pyrenean birds. Higher parts of the valley host Ptarmigan, Alpine Accentor and Snowfinch. Griffon Vultures breed on the flat-topped Peña de Oroel, just south of Jaca, and the woods here are good for Black Woodpecker.

Jaca is reached on the N240 from Pamplona or the N330 road from Somport, on the French border, to Huesca. The C125 from Jaca crosses the Oroel to Bernues, and from there a minor road leads to San Juan de la Peña. To reach the Hecho Valley take the C134 from Jaca to Puente de la Reina and from there take the minor road for Hecho.

11) La Serena This area is probably Spain's most important steppe area and although numbers have declined this is still the best bustard site in the country. Most of the area is dry grassland used for grazing sheep, and is bordered in the north by the Orellana and Zujar reservoirs and to the south by the ridge of the Sierra de Tiros.

As well as Great and Little Bustards, La Serena is home to Stone-curlew and Black-bellied and Pin-tailed Sandgrouse. Raptors include Black-shouldered Kite all year, Black Kite, Montagu's Harrier and Lesser Kestrel in summer, and Griffon and Black Vultures in winter. Other grassland birds include European Roller, Calandra and Greater Short-toed Larks, Tawny Pipit and Southern Grey Shrike. The reservoirs and rivers in the north attract Collared Pratincole and Gull-billed Tern in summer, and the woods and rocky ridges between the two reservoirs, and in the Sierra de Tiros in the south, host Black Stork, Eurasian Eagle Owl, Golden and Bonelli's Eagles and many passerines. Common Crane winters in the area in thousands.

La Serena is easily explored from local roads and the best area for bustards is between Castuera and Cabeza del Buey.

12) Llobregat Delta One of the most popular tourist cities in Spain, Barcelona is also well worth visiting for birders, with the superb Llobregat Delta nearby. Although much of the delta has been lost to development there are still some excellent beaches and lagoons, marshes, farmland and pinewoods.

Birds include various herons, waders such as Black-winged Stilt and Kentish Plover, and small numbers of Spotted Crake, perhaps also Little and Baillon's Crakes. Red-crested Pochard is rare but regular. Breeding warblers include Cetti's, Moustached, Savi's and Zitting Cisticola. Audouin's Gull is present in summer and Mediterranean Gull in winter, when Cattle Egret and Penduline Tit also occur. The delta attracts passage waders and wintering waterfowl can include 5,000 ducks of up to 15 species, including Ferruginous Duck and Red-crested Pochard. Raptors, including Booted Eagle, may be present in winter as well as a range of gulls. Hills around Barcelona support a range of birds including Western Bonelli's Warbler and Crested Tit.

The delta is just south of Barcelona and can be explored from the roads around the airport or to the beach. Part of the area is protected as reserves and entry to some areas may be prohibited at times.

13) Monfragüe National Park The best-known raptor site in Spain, Monfragüe covers a stretch of the Tagus Valley in the Extremadura region and has much more besides raptors, making it one of the most popular birding sites in the country. Habitats range from open grassland, wooded valleys and scrub-covered hillsides to high rocky crags. Part of the area has been planted with non-native trees, but much native woodland remains as well as dehesa, a habitat almost confined to Iberia, dry, open pasture with scattered patches of cork and Holm oak.

The raptors of Monfragüe number c.20 breeding species, including three vultures, and this is probably the world's best site for Black Vulture and Spanish Imperial Eagle. There are also four other eagles, three kites and two harriers. One of the best spots is the pinnacle of Peñafalcón where vultures breed alongside other raptors, White-rumped Swift is a recent colonist and there are also Alpine Swift, Red-billed Chough, Blue Rock Thrush, Crag Martin, and the other major birding attraction of the park, Black Stork. Black Vulture and Golden and Spanish Imperial Eagle are probably best seen along the ridge of the Sierra de las Corchuelas. Other birds of the upland areas include Red-rumped Swallow and Black-eared Wheatear, whilst the wooded valleys of this river and the Tagus are home to Great Spotted Cuckoo, Azure-winged Magpie, Southern Grey and Woodchat Shrikes and European Bee-eater. The reservoirs have Cattle Egret and Purple and Black-crowned Night Herons, and the dry plains Little Bustard and Stone-curlew.

Monfragüe is reached from Trujillo via the C524, which leads to Castillo de Monfragüe and Villareal de San Carlos, where the park information centre is located.

14) Ordesa National Park With the adjoining Pyrenees National Park across the French border, this is the largest protected area in the Pyrenees. Long renowned for its exceptional beauty and fascinating range of plants and animals, the area has extensive beech forests and pinewoods, a number of caves, fast-flowing rivers and glaciers.

The area is famous for raptors, particularly Lammergeier, but others include Golden Eagle, Northern Goshawk and, in summer, Egyptian Vulture. Other montane birds include Ptarmigan, Water Pipit, Alpine Accentor, Wallcreeper and Snowfinch. Both choughs occur and Alpine Swift and Eurasian Crag Martin are common. The forests are home to Capercaillie, Black Woodpecker and Citril Finch.

The park has an information centre, marked hiking trails and viewpoints, and can be reached on the C-140 to Torla, then the minor road signed to Ordesa and after 10km there is a car park. The Añisclo Gorge is a less-visited alternative within the park, reached from the C-138 to Ainsa and from there on a minor road towards Bielsa. A further area to visit is the Pineta Valley, reached from Bielsa on the minor road to the

Parador Nacional de Monte Perdido, a luxury hotel at the foot of the valley. Tengmalm's Owl can be found here in the woods on the slopes of Mount Perdido.

15) Picos de Europa This limestone massif in northern Spain is increasingly popular with birders and also has immense botanical interest. Large parts of the Picos de Europa are now under protected: Covadonga on the western flank is a National Park and Saja in the east is the country's largest national reserve. These mountains cover a wide range of habitats including glacial lakes, cliffs and bare peaks at over 2,500m. There are large areas of subalpine grassland, heathland where the forest has been cleared, and lowland hay-meadows. The forests are now much reduced but some beech woodlands remain, replaced by oak lower down.

Birds include a range of breeding raptors such as Griffon and Egyptian Vultures, Golden, Bonelli's and Short-toed Eagles, with Booted Eagle on passage. Eurasian Eagle Owl breeds in gorges and montane birds include Alpine Accentor, Wallcreeper, both choughs and Snowfinch, and the forests have Black and Middle Spotted Woodpeckers, Citril Finch and Iberian Chiffchaff.

The Picos de Europa range is situated midway between Oviedo and Santander. Covadonga National Park can be reached from the village of Cangas de Onis, on the 6312, turning off at Soto de Cangas. There is an information centre at Oviedo and the park has resident wardens, nature trails and refuges. Cabezón de la Sal provides a good base for Saja National Reserve and can be reached via the N634. From here the C625 runs through the Saja River valley to Palombera pass. In the east of the reserve is Fuente De, a popular birding site for high-altitude species, reached by cable-car from nearby Espinama.

16) Santa Pola The Santa Pola area has a range of habitats and birds, and lies conveniently between the tourist centres of Alicante and Torrevieja. Cabo de Santa Pola has typical Mediterranean scrub with numerous Dwarf Fan Palms. About 4km offshore is the island of Tabarca, covered with prickly-pear and attractive to migrants. East of Santa Pola is a series of saltpans with an excellent range of wetland birds.

Rufous Bush Robin, shrikes and warblers are common breeders on the headland and the cliffs are home to Black Wheatear and Blue Rock Thrush. Pallid Swift, Greater Short-toed Lark and Black-eared Wheatear breed on Tabarca, Audouin's Gull is often seen and European Storm-petrel breeds on nearby islets. During passage periods and in winter the headland and island can provide good seawatching with regular shearwaters and Razorbill. What was once a delta is now the Santa Pola saltpans, freshwater pools and reedbeds, saltmarsh and a long sandy beach. Greater Flamingo, Red-crested Pochard and Kentish Plover occur year-round and other residents include Lesser Short-toed Lark, Moustached Warbler and Bearded Tit, joined in summer by herons, Marbled Duck, Black-winged Stilt and Gull-billed and Whiskered Terns. During passage the saltpans may be visited by Slender-billed and Audouin's Gulls and Caspian Tern, and Marsh Sandpiper has been regular in recent years.

Santa Pola can be reached on the N332 south from Alicante, and Tabarca by boat from Santa Pola. Camping is permitted for those wishing to spend more than the usual few hours.

17) Serrania de Ronda Ronda is an ancient town of great historical interest and attracts large numbers of tourists, but has also long been a popular base for birders wishing to explore one of the best areas for montane birds in southern Spain.

The town of Ronda is split in two by a 135m-deep gorge with Lesser Kestrel, Pallid and Alpine Swifts, Eurasian Crag Martin, Blue Rock Thrush and Rock Sparrow. Fields nearby have Cirl and Ortolan Buntings and Woodchat Shrike. Grazalema is a small town c.30km to the west in a mountainous forested area with an excellent range of birds including Egyptian and Griffon Vultures, Golden, Short-toed, Bonelli's and Booted Eagles, and possible Eurasian Eagle Owl and Spanish Imperial Eagle. Other birds in the hills north and west of the town include Red-necked Nightjar, Black Wheatear, Rock Thrush and Western Bonelli's Warbler. White-rumped Swift occurs in some of the higher areas.

The area can be reached by road from the resorts on Spain's Costa del Sol, it is only 35km from Marbella, and there are airports at Gibraltar and Malaga. Ronda can be approached from the south-west on the C341 via Gaucín or from the south-east on the C339 via San Pedro.

18) Sierra de Gredos Part of the Sistema Central in central Spain, this range is in easy reach of Madrid and is heavily visited both during the summer and for skiing. There are many peaks over 2,000m and a good selection of montane birds can be seen.

The area is a stronghold for Black Vulture and there are Egyptian and Griffon Vultures and eagles including Golden, Spanish Imperial, Short-toed and Booted. Both storks breed, as well as Eurasian Eagle Owl, Great Spotted Cuckoo, Red-necked Nightjar, European Bee-eater, Red-billed Chough, Alpine Accentor, Water Pipit, Rock Thrush and Rock Bunting. The pine and oak woods have Citril Finch, Hawfinch, Western Bonelli's Warbler, and Dartford Warbler, Azure-winged Magpie and Ortolan Bunting occur in open country and scrub. White-spotted Bluethroat nests in the broom on these slopes, in larger numbers than elsewhere in Spain.

The southern Sierra de Gredos is reached by road from Madrid on the NV, turning off at Talavera de la Reina on the C502 to Arenas de San Pedro, and the north is best explored from Ávila.

19) Sierra de Guadarrama Like the Sierra de Gredos, this part of the Sistema Central attracts large numbers of tourists but is still home to good populations of large raptors including Spanish Imperial Eagle. The sierra covers a large area with extensive pine and oak forests and scrub.

Around 20 pairs of Spanish Imperial Eagle survive here, as well as Golden, Short-toed, Booted and Bonelli's Eagles, Griffon and Black Vultures and both kites. White Stork is common and a few pairs of Black Stork are present but difficult to locate. Other breeders include Eurasian Eagle Owl, Eurasian Crag Martin, Rock Thrush and Rock Bunting. The Sierra de Guadarrama is a large and difficult area to cover, but historic Segovia provides an excellent base. This town, on a bend of the Eresma River, has breeding White Stork and Red-billed Chough around the cathedral. In the surrounding countryside are Lesser Kestrel, Eurasian Scops Owl and Stone-curlew. For more montane species leave Segovia on the N601 and head for La Granja, a densely wooded montane area excellent for large raptors. True upland species are best looked for at or close to the pass at Puerto de Navacerrada, one of the best birding sites in the Sierra de Guadarrama, reached by leaving Madrid on the A6, turning off at Villalba onto the N601 and continuing for another 60km.

20) Tablas de Daimiel National Park This wetland area consists of a network of channels, islands, lagoons and flooded marshland where two rivers meet.

Of national importance for its waterfowl, Tablas de Daimiel has Black-necked and other grebes, ducks including White-headed and is an important site for Red-crested Pochard. There are various herons, Black-winged Stilt, Collared Pratincole and Gull-billed and Whiskered Terns. The reeds support numerous warblers, Penduline and Bearded Tits. Many other passerines inhabit the tamarisk stands and farmland around the marshes, including Southern Grey and Woodchat Shrikes, Calandra and Wood Larks, and drier steppe-like areas have Great and Little Bustards, and Stone-curlew.

The town of Daimiel is c.30km north-east of Ciudad Real on the N430 road to Manzanares. The park is signed from Daimiel and has an information centre, trails and hides.

21) Zaragoza Steppes Probably the best site in the world for Dupont's Lark, the dry grasslands of the Ebro Valley between Zaragoza and Belchite are also important for a number of steppe species.

Black-bellied and Pin-tailed Sandgrouse occur in large numbers and there are Great and Little Bustards, Montagu's Harrier, Egyptian Vulture, Short-toed and Golden Eagles and Lesser Kestrel. In addition to Dupont's there are Calandra, Lesser Short-toed and Thekla Larks, and Black Wheatear and Blue Rock Thrush.

Dupont's Lark is possible throughout but certain areas are best for this notori-ously elusive bird. Los Monegros is one of these and is also good for sandgrouse, and the part best known for the lark is south-east of Zaragoza and north of Osera. Permits are required to visit Lomazas reserve (but the larks may be visible from the car park), which is east of the C222 Mediana-Belchite road. El Planerón reserve (no permit required) is excellent for sandgrouse and lies on the Z306 Belchite-Quinto road.

Svalbard (Spitsbergen)

Today this once inaccessible high Arctic land of dramatic mountains, glaciers and deep, narrow fjords can be visited with relative ease via plane or by joining one of the cruises to and around the islands. Despite being roughly midway between north Norway and the North Pole, Svalbard has a climate tempered by the effects of the Gulf Stream, which reaches its western shores. Late July to August is the most popular time to visit Svalbard, but a little earlier is better for birds, late

June to early July, when most of the regular species can be seen.

The attraction of Svalbard is the huge seabird colonies and the chance to see some specialities of the far north, which occur only as rare vagrants elsewhere. Breeding seabirds include important numbers of auks such as Brünnich's and Black Guillemots, Puffin and millions of Little Auks, and there is a small colony of Common Guillemot. Ivory Gull is perhaps the one species that draws most birders and it breeds in small numbers at scattered localities on the main island of Spitsbergen, on **Nordausland** to the north-east and the small and more remote **Kong Karls Land** even further east. Sabine's Gull also breeds irregularly in very small numbers, particularly on **Moffen Island**, Ross's Gull may have bred and Glaucous Gull is regular. Arctic Skua is a widespread breeder, Long-tailed and Great breed irregularly in small numbers and Pomarine has also bred. Breeding waders include both phalaropes, although Red-necked is very scarce, Purple Sandpiper and other more widespread species. Breeding waterbirds include Red-throated Diver, Pink-footed, Barnacle and Pale-bellied Brent Geese, King Eider and Long-tailed Duck. Ptarmigan is widespread on the larger islands, and is the only resident landbird. The only breeding passerines are the widespread Snow Bunting and much rarer Northern Wheatear.

Of the non-avian attractions here the greatest must be Polar Bear: around one-fifth of the world population occurs on northern and eastern coasts of Svalbard. The best way to see Svalbard and its wildlife is from the many cruise ships that now visit the archipelago. These can be taken from Tromsø in Norway or by flying to the main settlement at Longyearbyen and joining the ship there. For Polar Bears and to guarantee some of the bird specialities it is necessary to visit the remote east and north shores and islands. There is a limited accommodation in Longyearbyen and a campsite on Hotelneset c.5km away. Guided hiking trips can be arranged on the islands, but visitors should not venture away from settlements due to the risk of a confrontation with bears. Svalbard is a fragile habitat and much of the land is protected, with three National Parks and numerous reserves, bird sanctuaries and botanical reserves.

Sweden

Expensive to visit and lacking the Arctic birds of Norway's Varangerfjord and Finland's Red-flanked Bluetail and Yellow-breasted Bunting, Sweden is rather neglected by foreign birders. However, most of Scandinavia's specialities can be seen in Sweden although, as elsewhere, locating the more elusive owls and woodpeckers usually requires local assistance. Sweden also has some very good wetlands and during passage periods birders from all over Scandinavia gather at certain watchpoints. The best and most popular of these are Ottenby on Öland and Falsterbo. Car hire and accommodation are both very expensive

in Sweden, so many birders take their own cars and either camp or use the refuge huts found in most National Parks.

1) Abisko National Park One of the most popular of Sweden's National Parks, Abisko is no longer the inaccessible place it once was and attracts thousands of tourists each year. The Abiskojakka Valley forms part of the park and runs north to south through it, with spectacular canyons in several places. Much of the rest of the park is bare rock, alpine meadows and boulder fields, with birch scrub and dwarf willows in the lower areas. The National Park also covers part of Lake Torneträsk and the island of Abiskosuolo.

Birds of the uplands include Golden Eagle, Rough-legged Buzzard, Gyr Falcon, Willow Grouse, Ptarmigan and Long-tailed Skua. Many species of wader breed including Purple Sandpiper, Temminck's Stint, Dotterel and Red-necked Phalarope. Scrubby areas have Bluethroat and sometimes Arctic Warbler, and Black-throated Diver, Slavonian Grebe, Long-tailed Duck and Velvet Scoter nest on the lakes. This is one of the best sites in Europe for Northern Hawk Owl and Snowy Owl sometimes breeds.

The park has good visitor facilities, with a tourist and information centre that can provide accommodation, marked trails and a cable-car to My Njulla. Whereas once the only way to visit Abisko was by rail, there is now a road to Narvik in Norway and the park can be toured by car. Insect repellent is essential in this part of Sweden.

2) Ammarnäs This area of forest, lakes and bogs is centred on a delta formed by the Vindelälven and Tjulan rivers, and is part of Vindelfjällens Nature Reserve.

Specialities of Ammarnäs include Willow Grouse, Ptarmigan, Golden Eagle, Rough-legged Buzzard, Gyr Falcon, Broad-billed Sandpiper, Great Snipe and Long-tailed Skua. The forests support Hazel Grouse, Northern Hawk and Tengmalm's Owls, Three-toed Woodpecker and Siberian Jay.

Ammarnäs village can be reached by road from Sorsele, c.90km away. Much visited by Swedish birders, the area is now a regular haunt of foreign visitors.

3) Falsterbo Sweden's premier migration watchpoint, Falsterbo lies on a peninsula in the far south-west of the country, just 20km from the Danish island of Sjælland. It is most famous for raptors and more than 1,000 per day are regularly recorded. Other migrants include seabirds, waders and waterfowl, as well pigeons and passerines, with more than 100,000 birds per day at times. Late August to October is the best time, with the greatest variety in early to mid-September but the highest numbers occur in late September to early October.

More than 340 species have been recorded including 30 raptors, with regular Rough-legged Buzzard, Red Kite, White-tailed and Golden Eagles, Montagu's Harrier and Northern Goshawk. Rarer species recorded almost annually include Greater and Lesser Spotted Eagles, Pallid Harrier, Black Kite and Red-footed Falcon. Black-throated Diver, Red-necked and Slavonian Grebes, Great Bittern and White Stork are regular migrants, and Black Stork almost annual. Winter and passage waterfowl include swans and geese, with occasional records of Lesser White-fronted and Red-breasted Geese. Spotted Crake is regular and hundreds of Common Crane move across the peninsula from mid September to mid-October. Regular waders include Kentish Plover (which also breeds here, its only Swedish site), Temminck's Stint, Broad-billed Sandpiper and Red-necked Phalarope, all four skuas can occur, as well as Caspian Tern and sometimes White-winged in autumn. Common and Black Guillemots and Razorbill occur through most of the year. More unusual migrants include Black Woodpecker, and Tengmalm's Owl is regular in October to November. Among scarcer passerines regularly seen are Shore Lark, Richard's, Tawny and Red-throated Pipits, Citrine Wagtail, Greenish, Pallas' Leaf and Yellow-browed Warblers, Penduline Tit, Nutcracker and Two-barred Crossbill and Parrot Crossbills.

Falsterbo is c.25km south of Malmö and easily reached by road. There are a number of good viewing points but the best are possibly Falsterbo Canal, further west at the heath at Ljungen and the lighthouse and Nabben close to the tip. In easterly winds Skanör harbour is good for seabirds.

4) Färnebofjärden Nature Reserve This extensive wetland complex includes the Dalälven River, where it forms a series of shallow lakes, peat bogs and marshes, and forest that is regularly flooded in spring.

The forest is ancient and undisturbed, and particularly good for woodpeckers with all seven Swedish breeding species. There are grouse, Northern Goshawk and Ural, Tengmalm's and Eurasian Pygmy Owls. Wetter areas have breeding Black-throated Diver and Common Crane, and Whooper Swan occurs in good numbers on passage.

The Nature Reserve is reached by road from Uppsala and from there to Heby. March to early April is the best time for grouse, owls and woodpeckers, and later in the year for breeding wetland birds.

5) Gammelstadsviken Nature Reserve This reserve, near Luleå at the head of the Gulf of Bothnia, consists of a shallow, brackish lake with extensive reedbeds, and provides habitat for breeding waterfowl and waders and feeding sites for migrants.

Breeders include Red-necked and Slavonian Grebes, Great Bittern and ducks and waders such as Jack Snipe and Red-necked Phalarope. Passage visitors include Common Crane and Broad-billed Sandpiper.

The Nature Reserve is reached via Luleå, but access to some areas is prohibited in the breeding season.

6) Getterön Nature Reserve This important area lies on the Kattegat coast of south-eastern Sweden and includes Farehammarsviken Bay, an near-enclosed inlet formed by embankments linking a former island to the mainland. The area is important for passage and wintering geese, ducks and waders, and recent habitat restoration has increased its value for breeders. Improved visitor facilities have made Getterön one of the best places in Sweden and nearly 330 species have been recorded.

As well as commoner breeding ducks, waders and passerines, Great Snipe can be seen at a lekking site, there are Bearded and Penduline Tits, and sometimes River and Blyth's Reed Warblers. Woodlands just inland have owls including Eurasian Eagle, Eurasian Pygmy and Tengmalm's, and Black Woodpecker. In autumn Point Gubbanasan can be one of the best seawatching sites in Sweden with shearwaters, divers, grebes, seaducks and seabirds in good numbers, particularly after westerly winds. Divers (including Yellow-billed) and waterfowl winter in large numbers.

The reserve is north of Varberg and reached on the E6, following signs to Grena. There is a well-equipped visitor centre, open daily spring to autumn and at weekends in winter with shop and cafeteria, as well as hides and observation points with wheel-chair access. Access to some areas is restricted in the breeding season but most of the reserve is easily viewed.

7) Gotland The largest of the Baltic islands, Gotland is popular with holiday-makers and birders, as it has an unusual selection of birds including the northernmost breeding Collared Flycatchers and an isolated population of Barnacle Goose. Other birds present in summer include Golden Eagle, Common Crane, Pied Avocet, Caspian Tern, Thrush Nightingale, Greenish Warbler and Bearded Tit. White-tailed Eagle is a non-breeding visitor and Steller's Eider occurs on the west coast in winter.

Faro, in the far north is a good area for migrants, with Red-throated Pipit, Bluethroat and Little and Rustic Buntings regularly seen. Off the eastern coast are several low-lying, grass-covered islands, traditionally used for grazing but now important reserves. **Lausholmar Nature Reserve** off the south-east consists of three islands, used mainly for military purposes but famous for their breeding Barnacle Geese, of migrant rather than feral origin. Close by on the mainland is **Faludden**, a narrow peninsula that can be good for seabird migration and **Stockviken**, which is on the southern side of the peninsula, with wet meadows and a shallow, eutrophic lake. Breeders include Pied Avocet and Caspian Tern and the area is noted for its rarities. From Burgsvik take the eastern road and fork right after 2km, continue for another 3km to the Stockviken signpost and the observation tower is visible after 2km. **Hoburgen** is the southernmost point of Gotland and another famous migration watchpoint, with regular scarcer passerines such as Richard's Pipit, Pallas' Leaf and Yellow-browed Warblers, as well as seabirds. The most accessible seabird colonies in the Baltic are on the **Karlsö Islands**, a few kilometres off the south-west coast of Gotland. These grass-covered islands hold breeding Common and Black Guillemots and Razorbill. Passerines such as Red-breasted Flycatcher, Barred Warbler and Greenish Warbler are regular on passage. There are daily boat trips and guided tours to these islands from Klintehamn in summer, although the area is a Nature Reserve and access is restricted. **Gothems Storsund** is a lake set in coniferous woodland and has a bird observatory on its southern shore. The lake has much surrounding vegetation and attracts a wide variety of birds in summer and on passage including Common Crane and Caspian Tern. The surrounding woods are home to Black Woodpecker and Northern Goshawk, and White-tailed Eagle occurs on passage. From Visby take Route 147 east and turn onto Route 146 after 35km. From here take the road to Botvaldevik and after a short distance there is a track to a car park on the left.

Gotland is reached by daily ferry from the Swedish mainland towns of Sodertalje, Nyäshamn, Västervik or Oskarshamn, with most arriving at Visby, less often Kappelshamn or Klintehamn. The crossing takes 4-5 hours, or, as an alternative, a flight from Stockholm takes about an hour.

8) Hjälstaviken Nature Reserve This popular birding site was once part of Ekolsund Bay, on Lake Mälaren, but is now an isolated shallow lake with extensive reedbeds and wet meadows. Part of the eastern shoreline is rocky and steep, with coniferous woodland on a hill overlooking the lake and there are also patches of deciduous woodland in the area. The Nature Reserve is noted for its breeding birds, which number c.100, and is also important for passage birds.

One of the specialities is breeding Great Bittern, which is scarce in Sweden, and other birds present in summer are Slavonian Grebe, Common Crane, crakes and Great Snipe. Passage brings waterfowl and waders and there is always the chance of rarities. Golden Eagle and Rough-legged Buzzard occur in winter. Around 250 species have been recorded in total.

The Nature Reserve is reached on the E18 from Stockholm or, alternatively, from Uppsala or Enköping. Access is unrestricted and there is a path around the lake beginning at the car park in the south-east corner just off the E18.

9) Holmöarna Although popular with Swedish birders, this archipelago in the Gulf of Bothnia is a relatively new destination for foreign birders. However, there are some excellent breeding birds and a wide range of migrants to be seen.

Of more than 250 species recorded here, 130 breed including Black-throated Diver, Black Grouse, Common Crane, Black Guillemot, Tengmalm's Owl and Three-toed Woodpecker. Passerines in summer include River, Blyth's Reed and Greenish Warblers and Rustic Bunting. Yellow-billed Diver and King and Steller's Eiders are regular on passage, and large numbers of owls, Nutcracker and crossbills occur on the islands during irruptions.

The main island of Holmön can be reached by boat from Norrfjärden, north-east of Umeå, but no cars are allowed on the island. However, bikes can be hired and the other main island, Ängeön, is reached by bridge. The more remote Stora Fjäderägg, north-east of Holmön, is often the best area for migrants and the bird observatory can provide accommodation and arrange boat trips to reach the island.

10) Hornborgasjön Nature Reserve The habitats around this lake have been extensively restored in recent decades, and the reedbeds and willow swamp are famous for breeding wetland birds and Common Crane on spring passage. Around 130 species breed and more than 280 have been recorded in the area. The land surrounding the lake is mainly farmland with some wooded areas.

Breeders include all five European grebes, Great Bittern, various waterfowl including Whooper Swan, waders and Common Crane. Nearby to the east is Billingen, a wooded hill with Black Grouse, Capercaillie, Eurasian Pygmy and Tengmalm's Owls, and Black Woodpecker.

The reserve is 20km south-west of Skövde, in Skaraborg between Goteborg and Stockholm. It is well equipped to receive visitors with observation towers or viewpoints around the lake. There are two visitor centres, Hornborga Naturum, on the eastern shore near Fågeludden which has a shop and cafeteria, exhibitions and an observation tower with wheelchair access, and on the south shore is Trandansen, the best spot to watch the cranes.

11) Kristianstad area This city, in Skåne, lies in the valley of the Helge River and nearby are some of Sweden's best wetland areas, known as the Vattenrike. South of the city is Lake Hammarsjön, part of which is a Nature Reserve with observation towers, hides and boardwalks to view the birds of this large shallow lake. Many of the haymeadows and grazing marshes are managed for breeding birds, and there are woodlands, sand dunes and scrub, adding to the diversity of habitats and making the area one of the best in southern Sweden for birders.

There are extensive reedbeds and the surrounding meadows are good for breeding waders, in particular the Håslövs Ängar, and other breeders include Great Bittern and various ducks, Corn Crake is regular in summer and White Stork has been reintroduced. Raptors include Red Kite and Montagu's Harrier, and wetland warblers include small numbers of Savi's and River among the commoner species. The sandy shores south of Åhus have heaths with Tawny Pipit and Wood Lark, and pinewoods where Black Woodpecker and Crested Tit nest. Common Crane occurs in thousands in spring and Taiga Bean Goose and Whooper Swan are regular on passage and in winter. White-tailed Eagles gather at the peninsula north of Åhus in winter, when up to 50 can be present, and passage Red-footed Falcon and Caspian Tern are frequent.

Lake Araslövssjön has a similar range of birds and an observation tower on the southern shore near the car park. The area is open at weekends but access may be restricted during the week as this is a military area.

Kristianstad can be reached on Route 15 road from Malmö. Lake Araslövssjön lies west of the city and Lake Hammarsjön to the south-east.

12) Kvismaren This wide valley in south-central Sweden consists of low-lying pasture with open water, reeds and willow scrub. The main wetland area is surrounded by canals and embankments, and there are pine woodlands in some areas.

For breeding wetland birds Kvismaren is one of the best sites in southern Sweden. Great Bittern and Spotted Crake breed, and Little and Baillon's Crakes are also present. There are grebes and ducks and reedbed passerines including River Warbler and Penduline Tit. Farmland nearby has Ortolan Bunting, Common Rosefinch and Thrush Nightingale. Passage brings waders and waterfowl including Lesser White-fronted Goose, and in winter Golden Eagle and Northern Goshawk hunt over area.

To reach Kvismaren leave Örebro south-east on Route 207 for 15km, then turn right towards Norrbyas, from here continue another 3km to the Kvismare canal.

13) Lake Ånnsjön This large shallow lake and its surroundings in west-central Sweden is very important for 90 species of breeding bird and large numbers of migrants. In the upper part of the Indal River system, the lake has extensive marshes where rivers enter the lake, and there are large areas of forest in the surrounding hills.

Black-throated Diver breeds, as well as ducks including Velvet Scoter and Long-tailed Duck, Taiga Bean Goose breeds occasionally and Lesser White-fronted has done so. Among the many breeding waders are Temminck's Stint, Purple Sandpiper and Red-necked Phalarope, sometimes Broad-billed Sandpiper, and Common Crane nests. Forest supports Hazel Grouse, Capercaillie, Northern Hawk Owl, Three-toed and Black Woodpeckers, and Siberian Jay. Nearby high ground has Willow Grouse, Ptarmigan, Long-tailed Skua, and Lapland and Snow Buntings.

The area c.100km west of Östersund and can be reached from there on the E75 to Ann or Handöl. The site has trails, hides and observation towers.

14) Lake Krankesjön A Nature Reserve in the far south of Sweden, Krankesjön is a large shallow lake surrounded by reeds, flooded meadows, scrub and woodland.

The area boasts a wide range of breeders including Great Bittern, Black-necked Grebe and various waterfowl and waders. Also important for passage birds, there are good numbers of Whooper Swan and Greater White-fronted Goose in autumn, and many waders. Wintering raptors often include Red Kite, White-tailed and Golden Eagles.

The area is only a short distance inland of Falsterbo, between the villages of Revinge and Silvåkra, and can conveniently be combined with a visit there.

15) Muddus National Park A large park in the far north of Sweden, Muddus consists of forests, lakes and marshes on a plateau bisected by a valley, broad in the north but passing through narrow gorges in the S.

There are three bird sanctuaries within the National Park to which access is restricted during the breeding season, and an observation tower open all year. Wetlands have Black-throated Diver, Slavonian Grebe, Whooper Swan and various ducks and waders. In the forest owls include Ural, Northern Hawk, Eurasian Eagle and Tengmalm's, and raptors can be seen such as Golden Eagle and Northern Goshawk. Other birds here include Capercaillie, Pine Grosbeak and Rustic Bunting.

The National Park has campsites and cabins for tourists, there are marked hiking trails and the observation tower at Lake Muddusluobbal. The easiest approach is from Ligga, 20km north of Jokkmokk. Alternatively, the park can be reached on foot from Nattavara to Solaure Lake or from Sarkavare.

16) Öland This long narrow island off the east coast of Sweden has forest, heaths and farmland, and an interesting range of breeders, but is most famous for migrants and is the most popular birding area in the country. Öland is linked to the mainland at Kalmar and there are also regular ferries.

Although migrants can be seen throughout the main focus is Ottenby, at the southern tip where many birders exchange news. Rarities are frequently seen, from the south in spring and the east in autumn, and there have been more firsts here than anywhere else in Sweden, with c.350 species recorded in total. Spring migration peaks in mid April to mid-May, but rarer species tend to occur mid May-early June. Mid October is the peak time for autumn rarities. Virtually any Scandinavian migrant can occur here with regular appearances by Lesser White-fronted and Red-breasted Geese, Temminck's Stint and Broad-billed Sandpiper, and an astounding range of passerines. Yellow-billed Diver is possible in winter, along with King and Steller's Eiders and raptors such as White-tailed and Golden Eagles and Gyr Falcon. There are also breeders of interest in the Ottenby area including Thrush Nightingale, Barred Warbler and Red-breasted and Collared Flycatchers. Ottenby Nature Reserve has marked footpaths and observation towers, and although some areas are closed during the breeding season, most of the area is open access. A new visitor centre was opened in 1997.

On the western coast of Öland, around an old causeway, **Beijershamn** has marshes and reedbeds with a range of summering birds including Caspian Tern, and passage waders such as Temminck's Stint and Broad-billed Sandpiper. To reach there travel south from the ferry terminal at Färjestaden and turn left at Vickleby church. **Kapelludden** is on the east coast of Öland and has shallow bays and coastal meadows. Pied Avocet and Caspian Tern occur in summer, along with small numbers of Montagu's Harrier, Common Crane and Corn Crake. Around 330 species have been recorded including almost annual Red-breasted Goose. To reach Kapelludden take the road east at the church in the village of Bredsätra, north-east of Borgholm.

17) Padjelanta National Park Between the Norwegian border and Sarek, this is the largest National Park in Sweden and a vast area of wilderness with mountains, glaciers, lakes and forests. Much of the land consists of alpine meadows, dwarf willow scrub and grassy heath. Padjelanta adjoins both Sarek and Stora Sjöfallets National Parks.

Breeders include Golden Eagle, Rough-legged Buzzard and Gyr Falcon in the uplands, as well as Long-tailed Skua and Snow Bunting. On lower ground and in marshy areas there are Taiga Bean and Lesser White-fronted Geese and woodlands have Siberian Jay and Pine Grosbeak. Snowy Owl may be present in lemming years.

There are marked hiking trails and cabins in the park, but walking here should only be undertaken by those experienced in such conditions. There is also a small landing field for aircraft. Access is from Kvikkjokk via Såmmarlappa and Tarraluoppar to Staloluokta. The area is best visited in June to August.

18) Ripakaisenvuoma This area lies in the far north of Sweden, 120km above the Arctic Circle and c.50km east of Kiruna. The main habitat is a large mire complex with swampy woodlands, coniferous forest, lakes and marshes.

Breeders include Whooper Swan, Taiga Bean Goose, Common Crane and waders including Temminck's Stint, Broad-billed Sandpiper and Jack Snipe. The forests have Hazel Grouse, Siberian Tit, Siberian Jay and Pine Grosbeak. White-tailed and Golden Eagles occur in summer.

The industrial town of Kiruna is easily reached by road or rail from Stockholm. Ripakaisenvuoma can be reached on Route 396, the Vittangi-Karesuando. road

19) Sarek National Park One of the largest National Parks in Europe and, with the adjacent Padjelanta and Stora Sjöfallet, the largest protected wilderness area in Europe. The National Park consists of a vast area of mountains, reaching more than 2,000m at Sarektjåkkå, gorges, including the spectacular Rapa Valley and many glaciers. Another feature is the Luottolako Plateau, snow-covered most of the year and an important breeding site for arctic birds.

Golden Eagle, Rough-legged Buzzard and Gyr Falcon hunt the mountains, with Ptarmigan, Dotterel and Long-tailed Skua breeding in the uplands, and sometimes Snowy Owl. Other breeders include Red-necked Phalarope, Purple Sandpiper, Arctic Warbler and Bluethroat. Lesser White-fronted Goose is possible.

Visitors to Sarek should be fully equipped and experienced in coping with harsh conditions, as there is no accommodation. Access is unrestricted but the park is best visited June to September, and is reached by track from Kvikkjokk. There are some hiking trails and a small number of bridges within the park.

20) Stockholm archipelago Thousands of islands form this archipelago east and north-east of Stockholm, where Lake Mälaren meets the Baltic and many areas are protected as reserves. Vegetation ranges from virtually none to forest. Angso in the north has traditionally managed meadows with abundant wild flowers, but the 400 rocky islets of Stora Nassa have little vegetation except birch and juniper scrub on the largest and wet grassland on others. The Lilla Nassa group has virtually no vegetation but the Gilloga Is have abundant cover and Svenska Hogarna juniper scrub, grassland and heather.

The archipelago is important for breeding seabirds including gulls, Arctic Skua, Caspian Tern, Razorbill and Black and Common Guillemots. Waterfowl include Velvet Scoter and Long-tailed Duck. Some of the larger islands have woodlands with Black Grouse, Black and Three-toed Woodpeckers, and Crested Tit.

Bullerö reserve, one of the best areas, is only 35km from Stockholm and can be reached via Stavsnas. Access to some areas is restricted in the breeding season but full details can be obtained from the field centre on Bullerö. Some of the outer islands are difficult to reach and should not be unduly disturbed.

21) Store Mosse National Park This large area of peat bog is situated in central Småland, in south Sweden, and includes marshes and lakes with scattered pinewoods and dwarf shrubs more typical of further north. This mix of northern and southern elements is reflected in the avifauna: more than 220 species have been recorded with around 100 breeding.

Black-throated Diver breeds, along with Red-necked Grebe, Whooper Swan, crakes, Common Crane and Jack Snipe, among many others. Forest birds include Hazel and Black Grouse, Capercaillie, Tengmalm's and Eurasian Pygmy Owls, and Black and Three-toed Woodpeckers. Golden and White-tailed Eagles hunt the area in winter.

One of the best areas is the oligotrophic Lake Kävsjön, which has observation towers (one with wheelchair access). The park has well-marked trails, hides and access is unrestricted. The park is c.15km from Värnamo, which is on the E4 c.50km south of Jonköping. The Värnamo-Hillerstorp road crosses the park. A few kilometres south-west of Store Mosse, near Reftele, is Lake Draven, another excellent lake with observation towers.

22) Tåkern Nature Reserve A lake with extensive reedbeds, Lake Tåkern is in south-central Sweden east of the vast Lake Vättern. The shallow, eutrophic water and its surroundings attract large numbers of birds, making it a favourite site for Swedish and visiting birders. Around 270 species have been recorded, with 120 of them breeding.

Famed for both breeders and migrants, the lake is notable for having all five European grebes nesting and for the tens of thousands of passage geese, which sometimes include Lesser White-fronted. One of Europe's densest populations of Great Bittern is found here and other breeders include Spotted Crake, Common Crane, and Bearded and Penduline Tits. In addition to geese, the lake is important for passage swans, ducks and raptors, and White-tailed Eagle and Rough-legged Buzzard hunt the area in winter.

During the breeding season access to some parts of the reserve is restricted, although the observation towers, hides and most trails are open and there is good wheelchair access. Tåkern is reached by leaving the E4 at Ödeshog, if coming from the south, or Vaderstad from the north, with a network of minor roads around the lake. Kvarnstugan, in the south-west, has a field station where accommodation may be available. Forest at Omberg, between Lakes Tåkern and Vättern, supports Black Woodpecker, Nutcracker, Red-breasted Flycatcher and Greenish Warbler.

23) Tärnasjön Nature Reserve This Nature Reserve consists of a long narrow lake and a delta where the Tärna River enters Lake Tärnasjön. There is seasonally flooded marshland, birch and spruce forest, and the Vindalfjällen Mountains are nearby.

Whooper Swan and many ducks breed around the lake, including Velvet Scoter, also waders such as Purple Sandpiper, Great Snipe and Red-necked Phalarope. Raptors include Golden Eagle and Gyr Falcon, and White-tailed Eagle may breed. The woodlands have Eurasian Eagle and Great Grey Owls, Arctic Warbler and Pine Grosbeak.

Access to the reserve is unrestricted and it can be reached from Tärnaby.

24) Tyresta National Park Only recently afforded National Park status, this forested area with mires and lakes is on the outskirts of Stockholm and is one of the largest intact blocks of coniferous forest in southern Sweden.

Breeding birds include Black-throated Diver, Capercaillie, Hazel and Black Grouse, Tengmalm's and Eurasian Pygmy Owls, Black Woodpecker, Nutcracker and Parrot Crossbill.

To reach the park leave Stockholm on Motorway 73 and turn off on Route 227 at Handen, then head for Tyresta village.

Switzerland

This land of lakes and mountains is not a regular destination for birders. For those in search of montane birds the Pyrenees have always been more popular because they hold vultures. However, Lammergeier and Griffon can now be seen in the Alps and there are also Rock Partridge, Eurasian Pygmy Owl and Nutcracker, which are absent from the Pyrenees. The large Swiss lakes

are important for wintering divers and waterfowl. Switzerland is very expensive but is one of the few countries in Europe where most of the birds can be seen using public transport, and there are numerous cable cars giving easy access to the highest areas.

1) Aletschwald area This beautiful area in the Upper Valais borders the Great Aletsch Glacier and consists of coniferous forest, scree slopes and alpine meadows. It is important for many alpine and subalpine birds, and the tourist facilities make access a simple matter.

Ptarmigan, Black Grouse and Rock Partridge can be found as well as raptors such as Northern Goshawk and Golden Eagle. The forests have elusive owls, including Eurasian Pygmy and Tengmalm's, and woodpeckers such as Black and Three-toed. Open areas host Water Pipit, Alpine Accentor, Rock Thrush, Eurasian Crag Martin and Snowfinch. Wallcreeper can be seen as well as both choughs, Alpine being the more numerous. Passerines include Nutcracker, Crested Tit and Citril Finch.

Most visitors begin from Mörel, from where there are cable cars to Greicheralp and Reideralp opposite Mörel railway station. There are also chair lifts to the Hohflüe and Mossfluo. From Greicheralp there are hiking trails covering the range of habitats, and there is a Pro Natura visitor centre on the Reiderfurka.

2) Clos-du-Doubs Nature Reserve This is one of the most popular areas in Switzerland, but despite the pressure from tourism the site is excellent for birds. The Clos-du-Doubs is formed by a meander in the Doubs River and habitats include the river itself and steep rocky cliffs, wooded hillsides and scrub.

Breeders include Black and Red Kites, Northern Goshawk, Grey-headed and Black Woodpeckers, and Western Bonelli's Warbler. Eurasian Crag Martin breeds on the cliffs and Wallcreeper can be seen in winter.

St-Ursanne makes an ideal base to explore this area and the 15km footpath following the river and ending at the village of Soubey provides good birding.

3) Col de Bretolet This mountain pass, with the neighbouring Col de Cou, is the best known migration watchpoint in the Alps, being particularly renowned for raptors. The area consists of alpine meadows and spruce forest with pastures in lower areas.

Birds in summer include Golden Eagle, Black Grouse, Tengmalm's Owl, Nutcracker, Alpine Chough and Citril Finch, with Rock Thrush and Wallcreeper possible. Passage raptors include Black and Red Kites, Montagu's Harrier and Northern Goshawk. Many other birds occur in addition to raptors, with regular Black Stork and numerous passerines including Citril Finch in large numbers.

Col de Bretolet can be reached from Lausanne, leaving the motorway for Monthey and taking the Val d'Illiez road to Champéry and then Barme. From Barme the Col is a further 5km on foot.

4) Flims Popular with skiers in winter, the Flims area is excellent in summer with most of the high-mountain specialities found in the Alps. Large areas of higher ground are rock-strewn meadows and the lower slopes have extensive spruce forests.

Golden Eagle and Ptarmigan occur in the higher areas, along with Alpine Accentor, Ring Ouzel, Alpine Chough and Snowfinch. Alpine Swift, Eurasian Crag Martin and Wallcreeper can also be found in this area, and the forests are rich in birds including Hazel and Black Grouse, Eurasian Pygmy and Tengmalm's Owls, Three-toed Woodpecker, Nutcracker and Citril Finch. Dotterel occurs in small numbers in autumn.

Flims is reached by road from Chur and there is a cable-car to the summit of Cassonsgrat. From here it is possible to search for the high-top specialities on the walk to Naraus. The best area for forest birds is from the nearby village of Falera, where the hiking trail to Ruschein provides opportunities for owls and woodpeckers.

5) Fanel Nature Reserve The vast Lake Neuchâtel in western Switzerland is one of the most important ornithological areas in the country and boasts large numbers of diving ducks in winter. One of the best areas is the Fanel Nature Reserve in the north-east corner of the lake, with marshes, reedbeds, islands and sandbanks, and the neighbouring reserve of Chablais de Cudrefin has deciduous woodland. Wintering waterfowl are the main interest but there is also an excellent range of breeders and a wide variety of migrants.

Breeders include Black-necked Grebe, Little Bittern, Purple Heron, Bearded and Penduline Tits, and Savi's Warbler. In nearby woodlands, Black Kite, Grey-headed Woodpecker, Western Bonelli's Warbler and Crested Tit nest. Winter brings waterfowl in tens of thousands with numbers of Red-crested Pochard and regular Smew.

Fanel Nature Reserve is between Zihl and Broye canals, close to the town of Ins and at the east edge of a large reed swamp, the Grande Caricaie. From Ins head for La Sauge and park just before the bridge. Various footpaths cover the area and there are two observation towers, although access to both is limited to members of the major Swiss ornithological societies.

6) Grangettes The reedbeds, marshes and riverine forest in the delta of the Rhône at Villeneuve is the best birding area around Lake Geneva. Of most importance during passage periods and winter, more than 265 species have been recorded in the Les Grangettes area.

Wintering birds include Black-throated Diver, grebes, and ducks which can include Red-crested Pochard, Ferruginous and Long-tailed Ducks, Velvet Scoter and Smew. On passage a wide range of herons, waterfowl and waders can be seen, with occasional rarities such as skuas. Breeders include Black Kite and Savi's Warbler.

Les Grangettes can be reached on foot from Villeneuve.

7) Klingnau Reservoir This is one of the most important areas for wetland birds in Switzerland and lies on the Aare River between Koblenz and Klingnau. More than 270 species have been recorded in the reedbeds, mudflats and riverine woodlands.

Although better known for passage and wintering birds, there are Red Kite, Grey-headed Woodpecker, perhaps also Middle Spotted, and Short-toed Treecreeper in summer. Passage brings a wide range of birds including storks and herons, waterfowl, raptors, crakes and waders.

Klingnau is north-east of Brugg in northern Switzerland. The reservoir has a footpath (suitable for wheelchairs) on the western shore, which can be reached on foot from Klingnau and followed into Koblenz.

8) Leuk The farmland, woods, grassland and ponds around Leuk support breeding species difficult to find elsewhere in Switzerland, and the area attracts a wide range of migrants.

Little Bittern breeds and passage herons include Black-crowned Night, Squacco and Purple. Other species in summer include Wood Lark, Eurasian Crag Martin, Tawny Pipit, Rock Thrush, Western Bonelli's Warbler and Cirl, Rock and Ortolan Buntings. Passage birds often include scarcer species such as Short-toed Eagle, Red-footed Falcon, Greater Short-toed Lark and warblers such as Subalpine, Orphean and Barred. High-altitude birds such as Rock Partridge and Red-billed Chough occur in winter, particularly in the Feschelbach Gorge c.2km east of Leuk and this is an excellent year-round site for Wallcreeper.

Leuk is east of Sierre and reached on Route 9. A footpath runs east from Leuk on the bank of the Rhone to the Feschelbach Gorge. The top of the gorge can be reached on the Leuk-Erschmatt road. Across the river is farmland and a series of ponds worth checking.

9) Monte Generoso Between Lake Lugano and Lake Como and close to the Italian border, Monte Generoso reaches more than 1,700m and has rocky crags and alpine pastures, and coniferous and deciduous forests. More than 130 species have been recorded.

At higher levels birds such as Golden Eagle, Rock Partridge and Alpine Swift can be seen, as well as Eurasian Crag Martin, Alpine Accentor, Rock Thrush, Wallcreeper and Rock Bunting. Forested areas have Eurasian Eagle Owl, Nutcracker and Citril Finch, as well as more widespread species.

This is a very popular area with tourists in summer and early morning visits are recommended. The ideal way to see a range of birds is to stay at the hotel on the summit, which has a rack railway up to it.

10) Niderholz This ancient woodland between the Rhine and the town of Marthalen has a range of forest birds and is probably the best site in Switzerland for Middle Spotted Woodpecker.

Other birds include Black and Red Kites, Northern Goshawk, Black and Grey-headed Woodpeckers, and Short-toed Treecreeper. Alpine Swift occurs over some of the local villages.

Marthalen is the ideal base from which to explore the Niderholz, and a marked trail leads from there through the Niderholz via Hornlispitz hill and Chachberg plateau, and back to the village.

11) Swiss National Park Established in 1914, this National Park is one of the most beautiful in Europe, as well as being one of the best studied. In contrast to much of Switzerland, the area is relatively undisturbed and well protected, and these factors have led to it being chosen as a site for the reintroduction of Lammergeier to the

Alps. Sited in the Engadine in eastern Switzerland, the park adjoins Italy's Stelvio National Park. Reaching 3,165m at Piz Quattervals this is a high-mountain area with deep valleys and hillsides densely forested with conifers, and above the treeline are alpine meadows.

Birds of the park include typical European montane species such as Golden Eagle, Ptarmigan and Rock Partridge, as well as the reintroduced Lammergeier. Passerines include Alpine Accentor, Wallcreeper, Alpine Chough and Snowfinch. Dotterel sometimes occurs on passage in the high meadows. The forest zone has Eurasian Eagle and other owls, Hazel Grouse, Capercaillie, Nutcracker and woodpeckers including Black and Three-toed.

Access is unrestricted but visitors should keep to the numerous marked paths, and most of the park is inaccessible in winter. To reach the area by road cross the Flüela or Julier Pass, or take the train to Zernez and then the postbus to the Ofen Pass.

Syria

This country has been little visited until recently but has enormous potential and will surely become a regular birding destination in the future, providing the political situation allows. Syria supports many Middle Eastern specialities in its large desert areas, but of most interest is the recent discovery at Dayr al-Zawr, a town on the Euphrates with a superb selection of wetland birds nearby, of two species that appear to be recent invaders from Iraq, White-cheeked Bulbul and Iraq Babbler. Of enormous conservation importance is the recent discovery of Bald Ibis breeding in central Syria, but this tiny population should not be disturbed. Brown Fish Owl, another highly sought after bird, may still occur, although there are no recent records. Accommodation is fairly easy to find in most towns, there is a good bus service between towns, and the best birding areas can usually be reached by taxi.

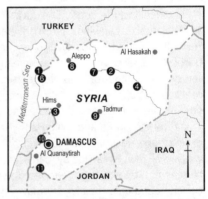

1) Aqra Mountains This area of far north-western Syria has the country's best remaining woodlands and is home to many breeding birds of interest.

Golden and Short-toed Eagles occur, probably with other raptors such as Griffon Vulture and Northern Goshawk, and Eleonora's Falcon is a regular non-breeding visitor to the coast at Umm al-Tuyyur. Passerines include Olive-tree and Rüppell's Warblers, and Rock, Cretzschmar's and Black-headed Buntings.

To reach the area head north from Al-Ladhiqiyah (Latakia) towards Kassab, close to the Turkish border, and most of the area will produce good birding. The Important Bird Area of Umm al-Tuyyur is c.30km north of Al-Ladhiqiyah.

2) Baath Lake One of the most important wetland sites in the country, Baath Lake is a shallow reservoir formed by the damming of the Euphrates.

Breeders include various herons, Blue-cheeked Bee-eater, Bearded Tit and warblers including Savi's, Eastern Olivaceous and Ménétries's. Iraq Babbler occurs here at the westernmost point of its known range. Wintering birds include Greater White-fronted Goose and Pied Kingfisher.

The lake is situated on the Euphrates near Raqqa and only 10km from the eastern end of Lake Assad, and can be reached from Al-Mansurah.

3) Bahrat Homs An important site for waterfowl, with more than 20,000 wintering birds, Bahrat Homs is a reservoir that varies considerably in size, increasing in spring with meltwater and shrinking again through the summer.

Wintering birds include Black-necked Grebe, various herons, Ruddy Shelduck, Marbled and Ferruginous Ducks, and Red-crested Pochard. Great Bittern, White Pelican, waders and marsh terns occur on passage. Glossy Ibis, Purple Swamphen and Spur-winged Lapwing have been recorded in summer, and the surrounding land supports Ménétries's Warbler, Dead Sea Sparrow and Desert Finch.

The reservoir lies 15km south-west of Homs and just west of Qattine.

4) Dayr al-Zawr This town in the Euphrates Valley is only one of probably a number of excellent birding sites along the Syrian stretch of the river.

Breeders include Ruddy Shelduck, Marbled Duck, Squacco Heron, Spur-winged and White-tailed Lapwings, and Whiskered Tern. The surrounding area supports Black Francolin, Striated Scops Owl, Blue-cheeked and European Bee-eaters, Upcher's Warbler and, recently discovered here, Yellow-throated Sparrow. Dead Sea Sparrow can be seen in the town, as well as two recent colonisers, Iraq Babbler and White-cheeked Bulbul. The valley is also an important passage route for storks and waders, probably also raptors and passerines including Lesser Grey Shrike. Black Stork, Greater White-fronted Goose and Pallid Harrier occur in winter. Macqueen's Bustard is possible in steppe areas around the town.

Dayr al-Zawr is reached by road from Aleppo (Halab) or Damascus. Many birds can be seen in the town and the footbridge is a popular spot, but there are several particularly good areas nearby. Shumaytiyah is an oxbow lake 20km north-west of the town, off the Haqqa-Dayr al-Zawr road, with excellent breeding birds. Others include Mayadin Pool, 2km south-east of Mayadin between the river and the Dayr al-Zawr road, and Halabiyat Zulbiyat c.40km north-west of Dayr al-Zawr on the right bank of the river.

5) Jabal al-Bishri This isolated mountain is situated in semi-desert c.80km west of Dayr al-Zawr in central Syria and has cliffs and scattered trees.

Birds include Egyptian and Griffon Vultures, Sand Partridge, Macqueen's Bustard and Pin-tailed Sandgrouse. Little Bustard probably occurs in winter. Little else is known about this region's avifauna but a variety of larks and wheatears is likely to occur.

The site can be reached from the Damascus-Dayr al-Zawr road.

6) Jabal Slenfeh Wooded mountainsides are the main habitat on the western slopes of the Jibal al-Nusayriyah range in north-west Syria. Woodlands are scarce in Syria and this area holds many breeders of interest, as well as being the country's best raptor migration watchpoint.

Griffon Vulture, Chukar Partridge, Alpine Swift, Wood Lark, Masked Shrike and

Cretzschmar's and Black-headed Buntings are among the breeders. Migrant raptors include Egyptian Vulture, Levant Sparrowhawk and Short-toed and Lesser Spotted Eagles, and White Stork occurs in thousands.

The site is 20km north-east of Al-Ladhiqiyah (Latakia), which is reached by road from Hama.

7) Lake Assad A vast reservoir occupying 80km of the Euphrates, Lake Assad (Buhayrat al-Assad) was originally created to produce hydroelectricity but also forms the most important site for passage and wintering waterfowl in Syria.

Although the avifauna is still little known, breeders include Griffon Vulture and, at the north-westend of the lake, See-see Partridge. The lake supports Slender-billed and probably Mediterranean Gulls. Passage can bring Black-necked Grebe, pelicans, Pygmy Cormorant, Great Egret and Sociable Lapwing, with Greater White-fronted Goose in winter.

The lake can be explored from the town of Raqqa.

8) Sabkhat al-Jubbal At times this salt-lake can be 20km long and 5km wide and, with the run-off from nearby irrigation projects, now holds water on a more permanent basis. Reedbeds have developed on the south and south-eastern shores, and the surrounding area is mainly shrubby steppe.

The lake is important for passage and winter waterbirds, but breeders include Black-winged Stilt, Pied Avocet, Greater Sand Plover, Gull-billed and Caspian Terns, and Slender-billed Gull. Surrounding steppe supports Chukar Partridge, Macqueen's Bustard, Cream-coloured Courser, Pin-tailed Sandgrouse and Desert Finch. Striated Scops Owl may occur and Black-winged Pratincole is a former summer visitor but its current status is unclear. Wintering birds may include Greater Flamingo, Common Crane and Pied Kingfisher, but recent information is sketchy. White Pelican occurs on passage and may still winter here, and Red-breasted Goose has been recorded. Other passage birds include Black-necked Grebe, Eurasian Spoonbill, and Marbled and White-headed Ducks.

Sabkhat al-Jubbal is 35km south-east of Aleppo (Halab) and just south of the village of Jabbul, and can be reached from the Aleppo-Raqqa road, turning off at Sfire.

9) Tadmur (Palmyra) and Sabkhat Muh In central Syria, this area of steppe-desert supports various specialities and there is an oasis and Sabkhat Muh, a seasonally flooded salt-lake to the S, which attract migrants.

The area is ideal for bustards and although Little, Macqueen's and Great all occur their status is unclear. Other species probably include Egyptian Vulture, Long-legged Buzzard, Golden Eagle, Cream-coloured Courser, Greater Sand Plover, Pin-tailed Sandgrouse and Desert Eagle Owl. Larks include Desert, Hoopoe and Temminck's Horned and wheatears Desert and Mourning. White-cheeked Bulbul has also been recorded here, far from its main range in Iraq, and Namaqua Dove has been reported. Migrants have been little studied but a wide range is likely at this isolated oasis. Raptors certainly occur and include Black Kite, Pallid and Montagu's Harriers and Saker Falcon. Greater Flamingo and Common Crane have been recorded in winter and numbers of Dotterel are regular. The tiny and recently rediscovered Syrian population of Bald Ibis breeds in mountains near Tadmur but should not be searched for. Birders wishing to see these birds should contact the relevant Syrian conservation bodies.

The ruins at Tadmur are a popular tourist attraction and can be reached from the main Damascus-Dayr al-Zawr road.

10) Wadi al-Qarn and Burqush This wadi north-east of Jdeideh on the Syria/Lebanon border has cliffs, steep rocky hillsides and a small reservoir. Burqush, with similar habitats, is on the slopes of Jabal al-Shaykh (Mount Hermon), 10km north-west of Qatana.

The avifauna is not well known but birds that probably occur here include raptors such as Egyptian and Griffon Vultures, Short-toed Eagle and Long-legged Buzzard, with Lanner Falcon on passage. Passerines thought present include Wood and Horned Larks, Blue Rock Thrush, White-throated Robin and Finsch's Wheatear, warblers such as Upcher's, Spectacled and Ménétries's, and Sombre Tit, Western Rock Nuthatch and Syrian Serin.

The main Damascus-Beirut road runs through the wadi.

11) Yarmuk Valley The Yarmuk River forms part of the Syria/Jordan border and consists of narrow, steep-sided wadis with densely vegetated bottoms that cut through a fertile and irrigated plateau. The site also includes Lake Muzayrib, a spring-fed lake 12km north-west of Dar'a.

Birds likely include Griffon Vulture, White-breasted Kingfisher, Long-billed Pipit, Blackstart, Moustached and Clamorous Reed Warblers, Zitting Cisticola and Palestine Sunbird. Finsch's Wheatear and Penduline Tit winter in the valley and Dead Sea Sparrow occurs in winter and may also breed.

The valley can be reached by road south of Damascus.

Tunisia

With numerous package deals available, Tunisia is a cheap alternative to Morocco, although some of the North African specialities are absent. There are, however, birds such as Barbary Partridge, Moussier's Redstart and various larks and wheatears. There are some important wetlands and Cap Bon is excellent for migrants, but the desert species require travelling some distance inland. Predictably, all the resort areas are on the coast but car hire is readily available and the Chott el Djerid and other inland areas are easily reached by road.

1) Ain Draham This village is surrounded by cork oak woodland, which forms one of the largest stretches of deciduous woodland in the country and many of the birds here are difficult to see elsewhere in Tunisia.

Breeders of interest include Levaillant's Woodpecker, Moussier's Redstart, Atlas Flycatcher, African Blue Tit, Hawfinch and various warblers. Raptors in summer include Black Kite, Long-legged Buzzard and Short-toed and Booted Eagles.

Ain Draham lies just inland of the popular resort of Tabarka on the P17 Tabarka-Djendouba road.

2) Cap Bon Peninsula Cap Bon is little visited by birders, which is rather surprising as it is the best migration watchpoint in Tunisia and attracts a wide range of raptors, waterbirds, passerines and others. Although numbers of passage raptors do not compare with those at the Bosphorus or Gibraltar, those using the Sicily-Cap Bon route can reach around 1,000 per day in peak periods. Much of the peninsula is green fields and rocky coastlines, with the peak of Djebel Abiod providing good raptor-watching, and there are several lagoons.

Passage raptors include regular Black Kite, Egyptian Vulture, Pallid Harrier and Red-footed Falcon, and Long-legged Buzzard, Bonelli's Eagle and Black-shouldered Kite may also be seen on the peninsula. Large numbers of White Stork and a few Black Storks and Common Cranes also use this crossing, whilst Cory's and Balearic Shearwaters, Mediterranean, Slender-billed and Audouin's Gulls, and Caspian and Gull-billed Terns can be seen. Offshore Zembra holds the largest breeding colony of Cory's Shearwater in the Mediterranean, as well Audouin's Gull. The various lagoons and salines on the peninsula can be good for waterfowl, attracting herons, Glossy Ibis, Greater Flamingo and Marbled, Ferruginous and White-headed Ducks. Other birds include North African specialities, such as Barbary Partridge, Black-headed Tchagra and Moussier's Redstart, and others of interest include Thekla Lark, Spotless Starling, Laughing Dove and Common Bulbul.

Cap Bon is easily reached by road from Tunis and the area can also be explored with ease from the popular tourist resort of Hammamet. The village of El Haouaria, close to Cap Bon itself, has a wildlife information centre.

3) Chott el Djerid This area is now a popular birding destination due to an excellent range of easily accessible desert and semi-desert species. Djerid is a vast saltpan covering almost 500 km² but is dry for most of the year.

Greater Flamingo and Ruddy Shelduck have bred, but the area can appear completely birdless at times. However, the oases at Tozeur and Nefta on the northwest edge of the chott have Laughing Dove and House Bunting, and there are similar birds around Kebili on the eastern edge and at Douz further S. Like similar habitats elsewhere, this desert is rich in larks (Desert, Bar-tailed Desert, Hoopoe, Crested and Thekla) and wheatears (Red-rumped, Black, White-tailed, Desert and Mourning). In addition there is Cream-coloured Courser and possibly still Houbara Bustard. Raptors usually present include Long-legged Buzzard and Lanner Falcon. Brown-necked Raven is common at Douz refuse tip, Egyptian Nightjar can be seen at a small marsh 5km to the west and Desert Sparrow (although not guaranteed) at nearby El Hessai oasis, 4km south of Douz. The Saharan race of Eastern Olivaceous Warbler breeds in the Douz area. Along the Douz-Sabria road, at Ghidma, are pools with Marbled Duck, also Fulvous Babbler and House Bunting. Seldja Gorge, near Metlaoui on the Tozeur-Gafsa road, has Little Swift, the two 'black wheatears' and Thick-billed Lark has been reported in the nearby desert.

The towns of Tozeur and Nefta in the west and Douz in the east can be reached on a day-trip from the coast, but also offer accommodation and a stay for a couple of days should guarantee most of the desert specialities. The Tozeur-Kebili road is constructed on a causeway across the middle of the chott.

4) Kelbia Lake Kelbia varies greatly in size and can be completely dry or a large shallow lake with dense emergent vegetation. In wet years it has an excellent range of breeding birds and attracts large numbers of passage waders, but it may be dry for years at a time. At peak times the lake has attracted more than 250,000 birds but has frequently been dry in recent years. Surrounding land is good for various desert birds.

Specialities include Purple Swamphen, Marbled Duck and White-headed Duck, all of which breed on a more or less regular basis. Also breeding are Squacco Heron, Collared Pratincole, Black-winged Stilt and Pied Avocet, with Gull-billed Tern on occasion and Greater Flamingo rarely. Passerines include Zitting Cisticola, Moustached Warbler, various larks and Spectacled Warbler, with Marmora's Warbler in winter. Further afield, in the arid land around the lake, Stone Curlew, Black-bellied Sandgrouse and Cream-coloured Courser are possible. Passage birds include Glossy Ibis, Greater Flamingo, Common Crane, Dotterel, Temminck's Stint and Marsh Sandpiper. In wet years waterfowl can include Ferruginous Duck.

The lake is best viewed at the north-western corner near the junction of the GP2 and MC48 and walking S. The lake is easily reached by road from the tourist centres of the Gulf of Hammamet and is only 35km from Sousse.

5) Lake Ichkeul National Park A large shallow lake near Bizerte on the coast, this is one of the country's most popular birding sites. The lake is connected to the sea, the water level highest in autumn and gradually drops over the following months.

Specialities include breeding Marbled and White-headed Ducks, as well as herons, Purple Swamphen and Moustached Warbler. During passage periods the area attracts a variety of waders, which have included Slender-billed Curlew, as well as Greater Flamingo, Audouin's Gull and raptors including Eleonora's Falcon. There is also much of interest in winter with large numbers of waterfowl and Barbary Falcon. The North African endemic Moussier's Redstart occurs south of the lake on Djebel Ichkeul a 450m mountain that also has Black Kite, Short-toed and Booted Eagles in summer and Long-legged Buzzard in winter. Passerines include Blue Rock Thrush, Orphean and Subalpine Warblers.

Bizerte, a popular resort, makes an ideal base and the lake can be reached by road. Roads fringe the north and east shores of the lake.

6) Tataouine For those seeking desert birds an alternative to the Chott el Djerid is the town of Tataouine, in south-east Tunisia, where the oases and semi-desert areas north and south of the town support many of the same species.

Long-legged Buzzard and Lanner Falcon are among the raptors and larks include Desert, Hoopoe and Temminck's Horned. Trumpeter Finch and Brown-necked Raven also occur, as well as Scrub and Tristram's Warblers, perhaps also African Desert Warbler. Dupont's Lark has been reported in the area.

Tataouine is 50km south of Medenine on the GP19, and one of the best birding areas is a track east from the road between the Kilometre 23 and 24 posts north of Tataouine. This area is good for larks but the best-known site for warblers is 25km south of the town, where the Oued Dekouk crosses the GP19.

7) Tunis The capital of Tunisia has breeding Pallid and Little Swifts but the main birding attraction Tunis Lake. Although the north shore is now much degraded, the south half still has excellent wetland birds during passage periods and in winter. It is most famous for wintering Greater Flamingo, but there are also Black-necked Grebe, waders including Pied Avocet and Kentish Plover, and gulls including Slender-billed.

Tunis Lake can be reached by road along the north shore or through the lagoon towards Carthage.

8) Zaghouan Famous for its Roman aqueduct, constructed to supply Carthage with water, this town at the foot of the 1,295-m Mount Zaghouan is now a regular destination for birders.

Moussier's Redstart can be seen at the Temple d'Eau and the surrounding area is good for Barbary Partridge, larks, wheatears and Blue Rock Thrush. Pallid and Alpine Swifts and Eurasian Crag Martin also occur. The area is also excellent for raptors with Red and Black Kites, Egyptian Vulture, Long-legged Buzzard, Short-toed, Golden, Booted and Bonelli's Eagles, Lesser Kestrel and Lanner Falcon all possible.

Zaghouan is c.55km south of Tunis off the C133. For the Temple d'Eau turn left in the town centre and there is a track just inside the temple gates which leads into good birding country.

Turkey

Certainly one of the best birding countries in the region, Turkey has habitats ranging from mountains at more than 5,000m to desert, and some of the best wetlands in the entire region. There are many species either impossible or difficult to see elsewhere in the

region and, with a great deal of travelling, particularly in the east, a trip list in excess of 250 species is possible. Turkey has long been popular with birders and over the years certain 'stake-outs' have become established for otherwise difficult species. Examples include Birecik for Bald Ibis, Bulanik for Demoiselle Crane and Demirkazik for Caspian Snowcock, and with so many birders scouring these areas various other scarce species are found. Turkish wetlands can be frustrating, as so much depends on water levels, but in good years the variety and number of sought-after species can be outstanding. Raptor migration is also much in evidence with large numbers passing the Bosphorus in the north-west and Borçka in the north-east. Package deals are commonplace but few are near good birding areas, and it is necessary to travel extensively to really do Turkey justice. Accommodation is readily available almost everywhere, except in the extreme east, and there are sensitive border areas in the south-east, but independent birding is relatively easy in Turkey.

1) Akseki The mountain village of Akseki is a popular birding site with a number of easily accessible eastern Mediterranean specialities, and is also good for migrants. The village has rocky and scrub-covered hillsides and is close to extensive pine forests.

This is probably Turkey's best-known site for White-backed Woodpecker, which occurs in pinewoods north of the village but can be very difficult to find. Wryneck, Grey-headed, Syrian and Middle Spotted Woodpeckers also occur here, as well as Krüper's Nuthatch and Sombre Tit. Open areas support Olive-tree, Rüppell's and Orphean Warblers, Masked Shrike, and Cretzschmar's and Black-headed Buntings.

Akseki is in the Taurus Mountains just off the 695 road between Beysehir and Manavgat on the coast. In addition to the pinewoods there are two other spots worth checking, including a walled plantation good for migrants reached from the south on a track on the left signed Ibradi. Akseki graveyard in the south-eastern corner of the village is also good for migrants and breeding Olive-tree Warbler.

2) Bafa Gölü (Camiiçi Gölü) Like many Turkish wetlands this site can be among the best birding areas in the country or virtually birdless, depending on water levels. This large lake is rather saline and can cover more than 6,000ha with extensive marshes on the western shore. The surrounding area is largely cultivated, with Salicornia flats close to the lake, and to the south are wooded hills with breeding raptors. The lake is an important stopover for migrant waterfowl and waders, and a wide variety of species occurs in winter.

Breeders include Black-winged Stilt, Collared Pratincole and Spur-winged Plover. Non-breeding Dalmatian Pelican and White-tailed Eagle are present most of the year, and Pied Kingfisher is occasionally recorded. Rufous Bush Robin, shrikes and Black-headed and Ortolan Buntings are common in farmland, as well as Spanish Sparrow and Eastern Olivaceous Warbler. Wooded hills to the south hold Cretzschmar's Bunting, Krüper's Nuthatch and Sombre Tit. Passage brings pelicans and Pygmy Cormorant, Glossy Ibis and various herons, in addition to waders including Broad-billed Sandpiper. Mediterranean Gull and marsh terns are common in spring and autumn. Raptors occur in some numbers and can include Black Kite and harriers, in spring Lesser Kestrel, Red-footed Falcon and Eleonora's Falcon can all be seen. Bonelli's Eagle, Short-toed Eagle and Long-legged Buzzard breed in the nearby hills.

Bafa Gölü is c.150km south of Izmir on the southern side of the Büyük Menderes Valley. It can be reached via Route 525, the Izmir-Milas road, which follows the western shore of the lake. The lake is within easy reach of Kusadasi, now a popular tourist resort.

3) Birecik-Halfeti Birecik is a small village on the Euphrates close to the Syrian border, long famous as a site for Bald Ibis. The colony once bred on cliffs above the village and although free-flying birds can still be seen it is generally thought that there are no truly wild birds present. Land along the river is heavily cultivated, but there are patches of dense scrub on sandbanks in the river. Away from the river the land is mainly rocky hillsides and semi-desert with wadis.

Birders attracted here by the ibis have discovered a wealth of other species, including specialities on the limits of their range and difficult to see elsewhere in the Western Palearctic. One such is Striated Scops Owl, which occurs in the tea-gardens south of the town, along with Eurasian Scops Owl. Spotted Sandgrouse has been recorded in this area twice and may be regular. Pied Kingfisher occurs along the river and in early morning sandgrouse come to drink, albeit in much smaller numbers than formerly. Stone-curlew and Spur-winged Lapwing can be seen on the river, as well as terns. N of the town is a large wadi where Dead Sea, Rock, Pale Rock and Yellow-throated Sparrows have occurred. Ménétries's Warbler also occurs here and Eagle Owl is present. Other birds include Chukar and See-see Partridges, Blue-cheeked Bee-eater, Graceful Prinia and Desert Finch. Wheatears include Black-eared and Desert and larks Greater Short-toed and Lesser Short-toed, Desert and Bimaculated. Long-legged Buzzard is common and Short-toed Eagle and Lesser Kestrel also occur. Sooty and Barbary Falcons have also been recorded, as has Cream-coloured Courser.

The village of Halfeti is 40km north of Birecik, where the Euphrates flows through a deep gorge with sheer cliffs. Egyptian Vulture and Bonelli's Eagle breed here, as well as Little Swift, but the areas formerly occupied by Red-tailed Wheatear, White-throated Robin, Rufous Bush Robin, both rock nuthatches and Cinereous Bunting were recently flooded.

Birecik is on the Gaziantep-Urfa road where it crosses the Euphrates. It is easily reached from Adana, which has an airport. May is by far the best month to visit, any earlier and some of the migrants are not yet be present and any later is often very hot.

4) Borçka Although the Bosphorus is the most famous migration bottleneck for raptors in Turkey, Borçka in the north-east of the country at the eastern end of the Pontics, sees passage of raptors in far larger numbers. More than 400,000 birds were discovered using this easterly corridor in the 1970s. In the Çoruh Valley, c.10km from the border with Georgia, Borçka sees the passage of a large proportion of the Russian raptor populations, as they cross the Caucasus and before they begin to spread out over the Middle East.

Short-toed, Steppe, Lesser Spotted and Booted Eagles occur, as do harriers including Pallid, and Levant Sparrowhawk. Small numbers of Egyptian Vulture, Long-legged Buzzard and Eastern Imperial and Greater Spotted Eagles pass through regularly, and Saker and White-tailed Eagle also occur. The forests here are good for woodpeckers including White-backed, and there is a selection of montane species such as Wallcreeper, rock thrushes and Alpine Accentor. The mixed woodlands of lower slopes have Green Warbler and Caucasian Chiffchaff. Artvin is a village c.30km south of Borçka with regular Lammergeier, often around the refuse tip, and Grey-headed Woodpecker in surrounding forest.

Borçka is reached by taking the northerly road from Erzurum, which follows the Çoruh Valley or, from Trabzon on the Black Sea coast. Trabzon and Erzurum have airports and car hire is available. Basic accommodation can be found in Borçka, but there is more choice at Arhavi on the coast or inland at Artvin. September to early October is the best time to visit Borçka but migrants pass through from August until November. For a spring visit April to May is best. All the hilltops in the Borçka area provide good views and raptors also pass over Arhavi in some numbers.

5) Bulanik This village in the Murat Valley north-west of Lake Van in eastern Turkey is famous as one of the few reasonably reliable sites in the Western Palearctic for Demoiselle Crane. However, even here the birds are not guaranteed; they can be difficult to locate and numbers are very small. The floodplain of the Murat, bordered to the north by hills and with a gorge at the western end, is wide and flat, largely cultivated land with areas of wet grassland, and the river has islands and sandbanks.

Although the crane is the main target for birders, other breeding birds include Pygmy Cormorant, Eurasian Spoonbill, Ruddy Shelduck, Common Crane and Gull-billed Tern. Montagu's Harrier breeds on the floodplain and Black-winged Pratincole and Caspian Tern have bred. Black-bellied Sandgrouse probably breeds, the area is important for Great Bustard, and Little Bustard has occurred in autumn. Collared Pratincole and Spur-winged Lapwing have recently been found breeding here. Passage waders include Great Snipe in spring and Black-winged Pratincole in large numbers in autumn. Rose-coloured Starling is an irregular visitor.

Bulanik is on Route 280, the Mus-Patnos road, c.65km from Patnos but most bird-ers access the floodplain via the village of Yoncali about 8km to the west. The road into the village leads to a ridge, from which the floodplain can be viewed. A track to the south from Yoncali, beside a petrol station, leads to an area of marsh, good for Glossy Ibis and waders. For the Demoiselle Cranes continue past Yoncali to the turn-off for Balutu (Balatos) on the left. Opposite this is a track towards the river, c.4km to the N, which can be driven depending on water levels. Close to the river it usually becomes necessary to walk. Head west along the bank and the cranes can often be seen on islands in the river. The cranes are present from mid May until late August. On higher ground between Bulanik and Lake Van is Haçli Gölü, a stream-fed lake worth visiting during passage for birds feeding on its shallow, muddy margins and in the surrounding marshes, and Saker Falcon occurs in nearby hills. It is located c.12km south of Bulanik on the Ovakisla road.

6) Cizre This town on the border with Syria is the only known site in Turkey for Red-wattled Lapwing, but it is a notoriously sensitive area and birders are advised not to venture from the road.

Fortunately, Red-wattled Lapwing is easy to see, usually on islands in the river or in pools and scrub on the eastern bank. The area can be viewed from the bridge or the police station, or from behind the garage on the road to Iraq east of the town centre. Black Francolin and Pied Kingfisher also occur here. Pale Rock Sparrow is another difficult species found in this area. About 25km west of Cizre, before the town of İdil, a wadi crosses the road. Pale Rock Sparrow occurs here, as well as See-see Partridge, Rufous Bush Robin and Finsch's Wheatear. Black-bellied and Pin-tailed Sandgrouse can also be seen in this area, Eleonora's and Saker Falcons occur, and Brown-necked Raven and Yellow-throated Sparrow have been recorded.

7) Dalyan The popular Dalyan area is an ideal base for the birder on a family holiday with a wide range of habitats in a relatively small area close to good tourist facilities. In addition to the beach there are estuarine and freshwater marshes and the Calibis River, which links the brackish reed-fringed Köycegiz Gölü to the sea. Surrounding the area are pinewoods, Liquidambar forests and scrub-covered slopes, as well as farm-land with higher hills further afield. The site is good for birds all year, but there is much disturbance in summer.

Although waterfowl are scarce, it is other waterbirds that provide most of the interest, with Pygmy Cormorant and Dalmatian Pelican regular, various herons and White-breasted Kingfisher. Raptors are well represented with Long-Legged Buzzard and Short-toed, Lesser Spotted, Golden, Booted and Bonelli's Eagles all in the surrounding hills, as well as Northern Goshawk, Lesser Kestrel and Eleonora's Falcon. Passage raptors include all four harriers, Red-footed Falcon and White-tailed Eagle. Eurasian Eagle and Eurasian Scops Owls also occur. The scrub-covered and rocky hills around the town have a range of passerines such as Western Rock Nuthatch, Rufous Bush Robin, Black-eared Wheatear and Black-headed and Cretzschmar's Buntings, as well as warblers including Eastern Olivaceous, Orphean and Rüppell's. The pines host Wood Lark, Krüper's Nuthatch and Sombre Tit, and the Liquidambar forest virtually endemic to this part of Turkey has Syrian and Middle Spotted Woodpeckers, European Roller and Masked Shrike. Around the lake and other wetter areas are breeding Zitting Cisticola and Penduline Tit.

Dalyan can be reached from the main coastal road between Muğla and Fethiye, the Route 400. Follow signs for Kaunos, the ruins close to Dalyan. Although car hire is relatively expensive, local public transport is cheap and easy to use and there are boats for hire to explore the lake and marshes. The ancient site of Kaunos is *c*.2km south of Dalyan and has *Sylvia* warblers and Western Rock Nuthatch.

8) Demirkazik area A high mountain in the Aladağ range of the Taurus Mountains, Demirkazik is famous as one of the best sites in the world for Caspian Snowcock. It also has a range of other interesting species, but can be a difficult to work without local help. The scenery is spectacular with high rocky crags, deep gorges and alpine grassland.

As well as the snowcock, there are Bimaculated Lark, Radde's Accentor, Western Rock Nuthatch, Red-fronted Serin and Crimson-winged Finch. Isabelline and Finsch's Wheatears, White-throated Robin and Cretzschmar's Bunting occur in summer, Upcher's Warbler has recently been discovered breeding in the area. Typical montane birds such as both choughs, Alpine Accentor, Wallcreeper, Snowfinch and Rock Bunting occur. Raptors include Lammergeier, Griffon Vulture, Golden Eagle and Saker Falcon.

The area is best visited in May to June, the earlier the better for snowcock but later visits are likely to produce a broader range of species. To reach the mountain take the Tarsus-Ankara E90 road, turn off for Çamardi and follow signs for Demirkazik and the Mountain and Ski Centre. The centre can provide accommodation and there is a small hotel nearby, but visitors need to take their own food. Local guides are available. The snowcock can be difficult to see but leaving the centre before dawn and ascending the small gorge on the right just behind the centre is the usual procedure. After an hour or so you reach the terraces, where the snowcock can be heard. Soon after first light they move to the higher crags and can be virtually impossible to see. The grassy depression at the top of the second gorge is a good area for Radde's Accentor and the descent via this gorge often produces Wallcreeper. From early June the snowcock are higher in the mountains and a trip to a recently discovered site is necessary. About 3km north of the mountain centre a track to the right, just before Pinarbasi village, leads to some nomad camps and the higher mountains. After *c*.7km there is track to the right, suitable for 4WD only, which eventually leads to an abandoned mine where the snowcock can be seen, even in August, as well as many other upland species difficult at Demirkazik in summer. Trips to this site by tractor can be arranged with the Safak brothers, who run the pension just outside Çukurbağ village.

9) Doğubeyazit This area is famous for Mongolian Finch, which was discovered here in the early 1990s. This is a central Asian species with an outlying population in the Caucasus, which in recent years has been found in Turkey. The area was already a popular tourist destination for the Işak Pasa Palace, but is now becoming a regular feature on birders' itineraries.

Although Mongolian Finch is not guaranteed, the area provides the best chance of seeing this species in Turkey, with records in May to August on the slopes above the palace. Other birds here include Eurasian Crag Martin, Eastern Rock Nuthatch, Crimson-winged Finch and Grey-necked Bunting.

Doğubeyazit is in the far east of Turkey, NE of Van Gölü and on the main trade route into Iran, and the Işak Paşa Palace is 6km east of the town.

10) Göksu Delta Now a Specially Protected Area, this is one of the best birding areas in the Western Palearctic. Where the Göksu River enters the Mediterranean a large delta has developed and although much has been lost to agriculture the remainder hosts an outstanding collection of species.

In the north of the delta is the town of Silifke, where the Göksu flows through a gorge with vultures and eagles usually present, possibly also Eurasian Eagle Owl. Other birds here and in the hills behind the delta include Spectacled Bulbul, Upcher's Warbler and, in winter, Wallcreeper. Woodland birds include Syrian Woodpecker and Krüper's Nuthatch. W of the river mouth is Paradeniz lagoon, surrounded by dunes and salicornia steppe, but retaining a connection to the sea and usually frequented by gulls, terns and waders. Further west is Akgöl, a larger lagoon with lower salinity and fringed by reedbeds, which has better birds but can be difficult to view. The scrub-covered dunes provide cover for Black Francolin and many migrants. Much of the rest of the delta is cultivated and large areas north of the lakes and east of the river are paddyfields, which attract herons and other wetland birds.

Over 330 species have been recorded including scarce species such as Marbled and Ferruginous Ducks, Ruddy Shelduck, Black Francolin, Spur-winged Lapwing and Purple Swamphen. White-breasted Kingfisher occurs and raptors include Egyptian Vulture and Lesser Kestrel. Various herons breed in the reedbeds of Akgöl, along with Glossy Ibis, Eurasian Spoonbill, Black-winged Stilt, Pied Avocet and Collared Pratincole, and White-tailed Lapwing has bred. White Pelican and Pygmy Cormorant occur mainly on passage. The many other migrants include White Stork, crakes, Common Crane, marsh terns, gulls including Slender-billed, and waders including Greater Sand Plover and Marsh, Terek and Broad-billed Sandpipers. Greater Flamingo is regular in winter, Lanner and Saker Falcons can turn up at any time and Cyprus Pied Wheatear is regular in spring. Birds seen at sea include Cory's Shearwater and Audouin's Gull, which is also regular off the pier at Taşucu. Masked Shrike and Spectacled Bulbul can be seen in Taşucu.

This is a large and difficult area to work, but the variety of excellent birds makes the effort worthwhile. Many birders stay in Taşucu, touring the delta from here and there is an information office next to the ferry booking office where news of the latest sightings and maps of the area are available. To visit the delta, take the Silifke road out of Taşucu and after 2km turn right by a paper factory and head to the beach passing the holiday village of Denizkent and an old airstrip. Continue to the dunes with Akgöl on your left and the sandy promontory to the right. Following a track around the southern edge of Akgöl leads to Paradeniz. To reach the rice fields north of Akgöl take the track around the back of Denizkent. The delta area is reached on the E24 west from Adana where there is an airport.

11) İstanbul and the Bosphorus Straddling the Bosphorus, İstanbul is a classic migration bottleneck where many thousands of migrant birds from Europe pass into the Middle East.

Raptors are the main attraction for the many birders that visit İstanbul each year and most European species pass through, although some peak at different times. In addition both storks occur in thousands, along with many smaller birds such as European Bee-eater and Wryneck and passerines. Yelkouan and Cory's Shearwaters can be seen on the Bosphorus and in the city of İstanbul Laughing Dove and Pallid and Alpine Swifts are common.

The most popular watchpoints are the hills of Çamlica on the Asiatic side of the Bosphorus, reached by taking the southerly suspension bridge and following signs to Çamlica. Kuçuk Çamlica is straight on and Büyük Çamlica to the left, the latter is the most popular watchpoint and there is a conveniently situated cafe on the hill. On the European side the hill of Sariyer, 15km north of the city centre is another excellent watchpoint and there are also Syrian and Middle Spotted Woodpeckers, Short-toed Treecreeper and Olive-tree Warbler there.

On the outskirts of İstanbul and linked to the Sea of Marmara is Büyük Çekmece Gölü, another good site for migrants and wintering birds. Although largely surrounded by built-up areas and farmland, the lake holds good numbers of grebes and waterfowl, including Smew, and marsh terns and Mediterranean Gull occur in autumn. North of İstanbul, where the Bosphorus meets the Black Sea, is the fort of Rumelifeneri where seawatching in autumn and winter will produce divers.

The best times to visit are undoubtedly spring and autumn, and the greatest variety of raptors occurs in September. Storks generally pass through in August to early September. Spring has much the same species but in rather smaller numbers. Mid morning to mid afternoon is the peak time.

12) Kızılırmak Delta The wide delta of Turkey's longest river is the most important wetland for birds on the Black Sea coast. Habitats consist of lakes and vast reedbeds, dunes, scrub and farmland, with small patches of flooded forest. The area is important for breeding, passage and wintering birds, and more than 300 species have been recorded.

Dalmatian Pelican and Great Bittern are present all year and breed in small numbers. Other breeders include Black and White Storks, Eurasian Spoonbill, Redcrested Pochard, Ferruginous Duck, Common Crane, Stone-curlew, Collared Pratincole and Gull-billed Tern. Glossy Ibis and White-headed Duck occur on passage and wintering birds include Great Egret, Greater Spotted Eagle and large numbers of waterfowl, with Black-throated Diver, Yelkouan Shearwater and Velvet Scoter offshore.

Bafra is the main town of the delta and most of the best birding areas lie to the east, with Balik Gölü and Uzun Göl and their surrounding woodlands particularly good. To reach this area leave the main Sinop-Samsun road north at Engiz, east of Bafra. Head for Yörükler and at the village crossroads turn left for the lakes and right for the woodlands. Cernek Gölü and Liman Gölü lie further north and can be reached on a track from Yörükler forest. Karabogaz Gölü is in the west of the delta and can be reached from the Sinop-Samsun road, 15km west of Bafra, heading for Emenli.

13) Kocaçay Delta The lakes, woods and scrub where the Kocaçay River meets the Sea of Marmara support a good range of breeding, passage and wintering birds.

Black Stork and Lesser Spotted Eagle breed in the forest, along with Syrian Woodpecker and perhaps White-backed. Open land supports European Bee-eater, European Roller, Rufous Bush Robin, Rüppell's Warbler, Masked Shrike and Cirl and Ortolan Buntings. Lakesides and beaches have Ruddy Shelduck, Ferruginous Duck, Collared Pratincole and Kentish Plover. Pygmy Cormorant, White Pelican and Eleonora's Falcon occur on passage.

The delta can be reached from Karacabey on the road to Bayrandere. About 25km north of Karacabey the road bends sharply left away from the river and a track leaves the road here, following the west bank of the river to Dalyan Gölü. It is possible to walk along the beach from Dalyan Gölü as far as Yeniköy. The woodlands east of Dalyan Gölü can be explored from the Karacabey-Bayrandere road. Arapçiftliği Gölü is in the east of the delta and can be reached by turning right c.10km north of Karacabey towards Hayırlar and Harmanlı.

14) Kulu Gölü One of the most accessible wetland birding sites in Turkey and although rather small, it has a good range of species and is among the country's most important sites for White-headed Duck. Rather saline and set in open flat country it has good breeding species and is an important site for migrants.

Birds in summer include Black-necked Grebe, herons, Glossy Ibis and Greater Flamingo, and ducks include Ruddy Shelduck, White-headed Duck and Red-crested Pochard, sometimes Marbled Duck. Also breeding are Gull-billed Tern and Mediterranean and Slender-billed Gulls. This is also one of the few Western Palearctic breeding sites for Greater Sand Plover. Much of the surrounding land is rather featureless but may have Great Bustard and Black-bellied Sandgrouse, as well as various larks. Passage brings a variety of waders including Broad-billed, Terek and Marsh Sandpipers and Red-necked Phalarope. Migrant passerines include Red-throated Pipit and Citrine Wagtail breeds.

Kulu is c.100km south of Ankara and reached via the E5, turning off to Konya on the E35. Turn left in Kulu town just before the main minaret and continue through the town to the lake. Probably the best part of the lake is the reed-fringed pool at the southern end where the greatest variety of species occurs.

15) Manyas Gölü Over 200 species have been recorded and more than 90 breed at Turkey's longest-established reserve. Also known as Kuşcenneti (Bird Paradise), the reserve consists of a wooded area in the north-east of the lake, established to protect breeding herons, Eurasian Spoonbill, Pygmy Cormorant and Dalmatian Pelican. There is also a selection of breeding passerines including Savi's and Eastern Olivaceous Warblers and Penduline Tit. Passage birds include White Pelican, White Stork, Red-footed Falcon, ducks and terns. Smew is regular in winter.

Manyas Gölü is situated in north-western Turkey 14km south-east of Bandırma on the Sea of Marmara. Kuşcenneti is signposted from the Bandırma-Balıkesir road. The reserve has a small entrance fee but has a car park, information centre, a museum and an observation tower. Access is restricted to marked paths but boat trips are available.

16) Sivrikaya This small village high in north-eastern Turkey is famous as the only site of relatively easy access to see Caucasian Black Grouse. This very local species is found only in a small area of Turkey and in the Caucasus, and currently Sivrikaya is the easiest place to find them.

This area reaches over 3,700m and the scree slopes, alpine meadows and rhodo-dendron scrub also support the equally sought after Caspian Snowcock and Grey-necked Bunting. Other birds include Lammergeier and Griffon Vulture, and passerines such as choughs, Shore Lark, Alpine Accentor and Snowfinch. Lower areas have Caucasian Chiffchaff (common in woods around the village), Green Warbler, Red-fronted Serin and Rock Bunting.

The best time to visit Sivrikaya for the grouse is May to June, although they are most active at dawn and dusk. For the best chance of seeing them leave the village before dawn and reach the rhododendron scrub above the village as early as possible. Undoubtedly the best views will be achieved by hiring local guide, although the steep climb can be made unaided. The snowcock is best looked for on the high crags south of the village. Sivrikaya is situated on the Erzurum-Rize road north of İspir on the northern side of the Pontic Mountains. The road is bad and may still be blocked by snow at the end of June. Basic accommodation is available in Sivrikaya and camping is possible, but there is also a reasonable hotel further north, towards Ikizdere, which is the preferred option for most birders.

17) Soğuksu National Park The wooded hills and mountains of the northern Anatolian Plateau possess a superb range of breeding woodland birds and attract many passage migrants. The rocky hills, forested slopes and deep valleys of Soğuksu are ideal for raptors, with virtually all the species occurring in Turkey being recorded here.

The most notable species is perhaps Black Vulture, but Lammergeier, Egyptian and Griffon Vultures can also be seen. Lesser Kestrel breeds, as well as Golden and Short-toed Eagles, and perhaps Eastern Imperial. During passage periods kites, harriers and White-tailed Eagle may be present, as well as Steppe and Lesser Spotted Eagles. The forested slopes are home to Black Stork and owls including Eurasian Scops and Eurasian Eagle, with Tengmalm's also recorded, a very rare and local bird in Turkey. Woodpeckers include Black and Grey-headed is also present. Other species here include Western Rock and Krüper's Nuthatches, Sombre Tit and Western Bonelli's Warbler.

Soğuksu National Park is just west of Kizilcahamam, which is c.80km north of Ankara and can be reached on the E89 road to Gedere.

18) Sultan Marshes Another of Turkey's superb wetlands, this area covers fresh and saltwater marshes, reedbeds and temporary pools, beneath the mountain of Erciyes Daği, which reaches almost 4,000m.

Like other wetlands in the area much depends on water levels, but in good years the area supports breeding birds of interest, a wide range of migrants and up to half a million wintering birds. Among the breeders are Pygmy Cormorant, herons, grebes, Red-crested Pochard and Marbled, Ferruginous and White-headed Ducks. Waders include Black-winged Stilt, Pied Avocet, Spur-winged Lapwing and Greater Sand Plover, and Slender-billed Gull and Gull-billed Tern also occur in summer. Reedbeds support Moustached Warbler and Bearded and Penduline Tits. Passage periods bring Dalmatian Pelican and a wide range of waterfowl and waders, and winter attracts large numbers of ducks and geese.

Sultan Marshes are c.60km south of Kayseri and are reached from Route 805, the Kayseri-Niğde road. To explore the marshes turn off Route 805 c.10km south of Yesilhisar-Ovaçiftlik, where the marshes are signposted. Guides are available here and boat trips can be arranged. There is also a road across the north of the marshes to the villages of Çayirözü and Soysallı.

19) Sumela The monastery at Sumela is a popular tourist attraction and in recent years has become a regular destination for travelling birders. Situated in north-eastern Turkey the Byzantine monastery is set into a cliff-face high above the Altindere Valley. The area has rushing streams and dense, damp woodland. For birders the main attraction is a range of montane and forest birds difficult to see elsewhere in Turkey.

Red-breasted Flycatcher is a regular breeder in the valley below the monastery, where Green Warbler is also found, being especially easy to find in spring. Black Woodpecker occurs here, but as elsewhere in Turkey it can be very difficult to locate, and Tengmalm's Owl has been recorded, a very scarce and local bird in Turkey.

Sumela Monastery is c.55km south of Trabzon, near Maçka. To reach it leave Trabzon on Route 885 (E97) towards Maçka. Just before Maçka turn off on the road to Meryem Ana Monastiri and continue for 25km to the monastery. It is very popular with tourists and so there are some facilities and a car park. The monastery itself is high above the car park: follow the path past the cafe, and from there a path leads south through the valley and eventually meets a track back to the car park. The walk is easily completed in three hours and should provide views of most of the typical birds of the area, although the more elusive ones require patience and considerable luck.

20) Uluabat Gölü (Lake Apolyont) A large shallow lake with small islands and extensive reedbeds, Uluabat is on the south side of the Sea of Marmara and has excellent wetland birds in summer and during passage periods. The reedbeds are mainly on the western and north-western shores of the lake, with olive groves, tamarisk scrub, marshes and wet meadows around the remainder.

Breeders include Pygmy Cormorant, herons, Eurasian Spoonbill and harriers, as well as Savi's Warbler and Penduline Tit. On shores and islands there are marsh terns, Collared Pratincole and Spur-winged Lapwing, and grebes and Ferruginous Duck also occur in summer. The surrounding land has Lesser Kestrel, and Rüppell's and Eastern Olivaceous Warblers. Both pelicans can be seen but are not known to breed, whilst regular passage birds include storks, Red-footed Falcon, waders, gulls and terns. In winter large numbers of waterfowl occur, including Smew, and Great White Egret is regular.

The nearest major town is Bursa, 35km to the E, which is easily reached by road from İstanbul. Head east from Bursa and take the road to Akçalar, where the lake comes into view, and leads to the eastern side of the lake. Following the shore eventually leads to a raised track, which runs from the village of Uluabat along the western shore.

21) Uludağ National Park A mountain of over 2,500m and the highest area in west Anatolia, habitats range from maquis on the lower slopes, through deciduous wood-land and beech and fir forest, to alpine meadows at the highest levels.

Fairly close to İstanbul, this is an ideal site to look for birds like Lammergeier and other vultures, Golden Eagle and more than 20 other raptors. Other high-altitude species include Alpine Accentor, both rock thrushes and choughs. The area is also good for specialities such as Isabelline Wheatear and, at almost the westernmost points of their range, Red-fronted Serin and Krüper's Nuthatch. The fir forest holds Tengmalm's Owl, a very local bird in Turkey, and White-backed Woodpecker has been seen.

The park is c.22km south of Bursa and signed from there. Take the road just west of Bursa to the ski-resort, a long twisting road, on which it is well worth making a few stops. Bursa is easily reached from İstanbul and the easiest way to reach Uludağ is the cable car from Bursa, which has an intermediate stop in the alpine meadows of Kadiyayla at about 1,000m and ends at Sarıalan at about 630m.

22) Van Gölü The vast saline Van Gölü in eastern Anatolia supports few birds but marshy areas on its fringes, where freshwater enters the lake, provide excellent birding. Rising water levels in the mid 1990s temporarily flooded some of these areas but most are cur-rently extant. In addition, the surrounding hills are home to some eastern specialities.

One of the most popular areas for visiting birders is Bendimahi Delta in the far north-east of the lake. Breeding birds here include White-headed Duck, Gull-billed Tern, Citrine Wagtail and Rose-coloured Starling. Passage birds include White Pelican, Broad-billed Sandpiper and Caspian Tern.

The marshes between the town of Van and the lake support Ruddy Shelduck, Marbled and Ferruginous Ducks and Moustached and Paddyfield Warblers. Overlooking the marshes is a fortress with breeding Lesser Kestrel and Alpine Swift, and Yellow-throated Sparrow has recently been recorded around the town. Erçek Gölü, E of the main lake and north of the Van-Özalp road, is good for passage waders with regular Broad-billed, Marsh and Terek Sandpipers, and Red-necked Phalarope. Other birds regular here in late summer include Greater Flamingo and Ruddy Shelduck. The road to Özalp leads into the hills where Egyptian Vulture and Long-legged Buzzard breed. About 8km from Van is a quarry with Grey-necked Bunting and the gorge behind the quarry has Eurasian Crag Martin, Rock Thrush and Rock Sparrow, whilst Eurasian Eagle Owl formerly bred and still occurs, Mongolian Finch is frequently seen and Pied Wheatear may be regular. The higher hills east of the gorge support Finsch's Wheatear, Snowfinch and Crimson-winged Finch. The crater lake of Nemrut Daği west of Van Gölü supports Shore Lark, White-throated Robin, Red-fronted Serin and Desert Finch, but is most famous as one of the few breeding sites for the very isolated Turkish population of Velvet Scoter. Eurasian Eagle Owl also occurs here, as well as Alpine and Radde's Accentors and Grey-necked and Cinereous Buntings. Nemrut Daği can be reached on the Ahlat road north of Tatvan. Sodali Gölü is soda lake between Van Gölü and Suphan Daği, a mountain reaching more than 4,000m. The lake is important for passage Black-necked Grebe and White-headed Duck, and many waders, but there is more interest in the surrounding uplands where Lammergeier, Golden Eagle and Saker Falcon are all possible. The lake is south of Route 965, about 30km east of Adilcevaz, on the northern side of Van lake and is reached by following signs for Gölduzu. The mountain can be reached by a long walk from the village of Hormantepe, north of Route 965.

The town of Van can be reached by road or air and Tatvan by rail. Ferries cross the lake from Tatvan.

23) Yeşilce The hills west of Gaziantep are famous as an easily accessible site for a number of species that can be difficult to find elsewhere. The area around Yeşilce, and particularly the valleys of Işikli and Durnalik, are now commonly on the itineraries of birders visiting Turkey.

Specialities include White-throated Robin, Red-tailed Wheatear, Upcher's Warbler, Eastern Rock Nuthatch, Pale Rock Sparrow and Cinereous Bunting. More widespread species include Rufous Bush Robin, Olive-tree Warbler, Sombre Tit, Western Rock Nuthatch and Cretzschmar's and Black-headed Buntings. Chukar and See-see Partridges also occur, and Trumpeter Finch has bred. Collared and Semi-collared Flycatchers occur on passage and Radde's Accentor may be regular in winter.

Yeşilce is located on the Adana-Gaziantep road about 20km west of Gaziantep. Işikli is signposted from Yeşilce: park in Işikli village and search the hillsides on foot, which are a particularly good area for Red-tailed Wheatear. For Durnalik return to the main road and head west turning south opposite a lime-kiln. Park before the village and explore the valley to the right, especially for White-throated Robin. These are two well known sites but the same birds are likely to occur throughout these hills.

Ukraine

Birding has immense possibilities in the Ukraine, although the tourist infrastructure is still rather primitive. Undoubtedly this country will become a regular feature on the itineraries of bird tour companies in the near future, and for some time this will be by far the easiest way to see its birds. Although the Carpathians reach the west of the country, Ukraine is largely low-lying, with

large areas of former steppe, now farmland, and extensive wetlands, with the northern part of the Danube Delta in the south-west. The large peninsula of Crimea is one of the best birding areas, with mountains in the south and some excellent wetlands in the north supporting Demoiselle Crane and Pallas' Sandgrouse.

1) Askania-Nova Reserve This famous reserve in the southern Ukraine covers $c.110km^2$ of open steppe, cultivated land and artificial ponds, and is an important site for steppe birds. Birds of this area include many species difficult to see further west in Europe.

Steppe specialities such as Demoiselle Crane, Great and Little Bustards and raptors including Pallid Harrier, Long-legged Buzzard occur here, perhaps still Steppe Eagle. The wetland areas attract Greater White-fronted and Red-breasted Geese on passage, and Ruddy Shelduck in winter. European Bee-eater and European Roller are present and passerines include Calandra Lark, Lesser Grey Shrike and Pied and Isabelline Wheatears. Rose-coloured Starling can be seen but as elsewhere this is an unpredictable species.

Askania-Nova lies between Odessa and the Crimea, near Kherson, which has an airport. Southern Ukraine can also be reached by road from Romania or by sea from other Black Sea countries.

2) Carpathians This range crosses the south-west corner of Ukraine and is one of the best areas in the country for forest and mountain birds.

Capercaillie, Hazel and Black Grouse, and Black Stork occur in these mountains, as well as owls such as Eurasian Eagle, Eurasian Pygmy, Tengmalm's and Ural, and woodpeckers including Grey-headed, Middle Spotted, White-backed and Three-toed. Among raptors are Northern Goshawk, Short-toed, Lesser Spotted and Golden Eagles. Passerines include Red-breasted and Collared Flycatchers, Crested Tit and Nutcracker.

The highest part of the range in Ukraine is a designated National Park and is situated c.55km south-west of Kolomyya, and can be explored from Yaremcha in the north or Yasinya in the south.

3) Crimean Mountains The forested mountains along the south coast of the Crimean Peninsula, which reach 1,500m, hold breeding raptors including Black Vulture, Short-toed and Eastern Imperial Eagles, and Saker Falcon. Egyptian and Griffon Vultures may still occur and passerines include Pied Wheatear, Rock Thrush, Barred Warbler and perhaps Semi-collared Flycatcher.

Yalta makes a good base, but this is a popular holiday area and accommodation is available all along this coast. There is a good network of hiking trails through the area and one of the best areas is the Karadag Reserve just east of Shchebetovka.

4) Dunay Delta (see also **Danube Delta, Romania**) Many of the birds of the Romanian Danube Delta also occur in the northernmost part, which extends into the south-western Ukraine, where it is known as the Dunay.

Both pelicans can be seen here, as well as Pygmy Cormorant and Paddyfield Warbler, which is more numerous in this part of the delta. Black Stork and a wide range of waders occur on passage, including scarcer species such as Broad-billed Sandpiper and Red-necked Phalarope. Slender-billed Curlew has been recorded.

The delta is c.3 hours by road from Odessa and Izmayil is the main town.

5) Shatsk National Park In far north-western Ukraine, Shatsk National Park includes lakes, forest and steppe, and is important for migrating waterbirds and raptors.

Great Bittern, Ferruginous Duck, Montagu's Harrier and Lesser Spotted Eagle are among the breeders, along with crakes, Eurasian Eagle Owl and Aquatic Warbler. Passage birds include Taiga Bean and Greater White-fronted Geese, Common Crane and raptors including Black Kite, White-tailed, Short-toed and Booted Eagles, and Saker Falcon.

The park is c.200km north of Lvov and can be explored from Kovel.

6) Syvash Bay This shallow bay and its associated lagoons, marshes and surrounding steppe form one of the most important areas for birds in Ukraine, with many species difficult to see further west in Europe. The bay is almost enclosed by the 110km sand-pit of Arabatskaya Strelka and is the largest area of saltwater and brackish lagoons in Europe.

Specialities of the area include Demoiselle Crane and Great Bustard (rare breeder but larger numbers on passage), both pratincoles, Pallas' and Slender-billed Gulls, and Paddyfield Warbler. The area also supports large numbers of more widespread species, with breeding herons, Glossy Ibis, Black-winged Stilt, Pied Avocet, gulls such as Pallas', Mediterranean and Slender-billed, and Gull-billed and Caspian Terns. Among the many thousands of passage birds are Lesser White-fronted Goose, Common Crane, marsh terns, and waders including Broad-billed and Marsh Sandpipers and Great Snipe.

Syash Bay is in the north-east of the Crimean Peninsula, on the shores of the Sea of Azov, and can be explored from the towns of Feodosia in the south or Dzhankoy in the N. One of the best areas for bustards is Kuyuk-Tuk Island.

7) Tiligul Liman On the Black Sea coast this site is a former river delta and a haven for wetland birds. Habitats include freshwater streams, brackish and saltwater lagoons, reed islands and saltmarsh, with associated areas of steppe scrub.

Squacco Heron, Glossy Ibis and Gull-billed Tern are among the breeders and passage birds include White Pelican, Great Egret, Slender-billed Gull, marsh terns and various waders. The area holds significant numbers of Greater White-fronted Goose in winter and occasionally Red-breasted Goose. The delta has a range of passerines including Calandra Lark, Citrine Wagtail and Tawny Pipit, with Red-breasted and Collared Flycatchers on passage. Lesser Kestrel, Red-footed Falcon, European Bee-eater and European Roller hunt insects over the more open, drier habitats.

Tiligul Liman is 35km east of Odessa between the Odessa-Nikolaev road and the coast.

Yugoslavia (Serbia)

Before the ethnic conflicts of the 1990s Yugoslavia was popular with tourists and birders. Since the break-up there have been few visitors and very little is known regarding the birds that still occur. Mountain birds may survive but wetlands are being lost throughout the Balkans, probably including Yugoslavia. This is unlikely to become a safe destination for birders for some time to come, but there are no species found which cannot be seen in more easily visited countries.

1) Biogradska Gora National Park Formerly one of the best-preserved forests in the Balkans, little is known of the present state of this area. In addition to the virgin forest there are several lakes and peaks of over 2,000m.

Birds here probably still include Short-toed and Golden Eagles, Rock Partridge, Eurasian Eagle Owl, Grey-headed Woodpecker, Wood Lark, Ring Ouzel, Sombre Tit and Rock Bunting. The park is situated 93km north of Podgorica.

2) Carska bara Once one of Yugoslavia's top wetland sites, this area of marshes, fishponds, meadows and woods between the Tisa and Begej rivers may still support some birds of interest.

Great Bittern, Squacco Heron and Great Egret were still present in good numbers in the early 1990s, along with smaller numbers of Pygmy Cormorant, Ferruginous Duck and White-tailed Eagle. Eurasian Spoonbill was regular on passage and both Lesser White-fronted Goose and Slender-billed Curlew have been recorded.

This area is north of Belgrade and can be reached on a minor road west from Ečka, on the Belgrade-Zrejanin road.

3) Đerdap (Iron Gates) National Park Covering one of the largest canyons in Europe, this park on the border with Romania stretches more than 100km along the Danube. The site includes 300-m cliffs, a large reservoir and extensive areas of beech and oak woodland.

Pygmy Cormorant probably still breeds, as well as White-tailed, Lesser Spotted and Booted Eagles, and Eurasian Eagle Owl. The area is also important for passage storks, raptors and other birds, and large numbers of waterfowl occur in winter.

The park extends from Golubac, c.100km east of Belgrade, downstream to Tekija and can be explored from Turni-Severin or Požarevac.

4) Durmitor National Park This park, a designated World Heritage Site, covers a mountainous area reaching more than 2,500m, several lakes and a 30km stretch of the Tara Gorge. There are (or were) extensive areas of mixed and deciduous forest, alpine grasslands and inland cliffs.

Little is known of the birdlife of the park and even before the conflict the area was not well studied. However, birds that may still occur include Rock Partridge, raptors such as Short-toed and Golden Eagles, Eurasian Eagle and Eurasian Scops Owls, and woodpeckers including Grey-headed and Syrian. Passerines probably include Rock Thrush, Sombre and Crested Tits, Lesser Grey Shrike and Cirl and Rock Buntings.

The park can be explored from the ski-resort town of Žabljak, which is 65km south-west of Pljevlja.

5) Fruška Gora National Park Within easy reach of Belgrade this was a popular recreational area before the conflict. The park lies on the edge of the Pannonian Plain and follows the Danube for about 80km. Habitats include farmland, remnant steppe and wooded hillsides.

The area was formerly important for raptors, with breeding Lesser Spotted, Eastern Imperial and Booted Eagles and Saker Falcon, as well as storks and Eurasian Eagle Owl. Smaller birds such as Eurasian Scops Owl, Syrian and Middle Spotted Woodpeckers, Wood Lark, Barred Warbler and Lesser Grey Shrike are likely to survive here. Greater Spotted Eagle is possible on passage.

The park can be visited from Novi Sad, about 70km north-west of Belgrade.

6) Lake Skadar (see Lake Shkroda, Albania, page 382) The Yugoslavian part of this lake, known in Albania as Shkroda, can be viewed from the Podgorica-Petrovac road.

Birdlife is much the same as in the Albanian sector with Pygmy Cormorant and Dalmatian Pelican (Yugoslavia's only breeding site), various herons and Ferruginous Duck. Breeding landbirds include Rock Partridge, Olive-tree Warbler, Sombre Tit and Western Rock Nuthatch. To the south is Lake Sasko with a similar range of breeding waterbirds plus Glossy Ibis, and the saltpans at nearby Ulcinj may still support breeding Collared Pratincole.

7) Obedska bara Even before the conflict of the 1990s the birds of this once important area were in decline, but it may still be worth visiting. The reserve is on the northern bank of the Sava and consists of large areas of regularly flooded marshes, meadows and woods.

Breeding here in the mid 1990s were Little Bittern, Black-crowned Night Heron, storks, Ferruginous Duck and Spotted and Little Crakes. Raptors formerly included Black Kite, White-tailed and Lesser Spotted Eagles and Saker Falcon, but which of these remain, if any, is uncertain. Syrian and Middle Spotted Woodpeckers, Savi's Warbler, Collared Flycatcher and Lesser Grey Shrike probably still occur in the woods and farmland.

The reserve can be visited from Obrež, which is on the E94 west of Belgrade.

Bibliography

Europe

Aulén, G. 1996. *Where to Watch Birds in Scandinavia*. Hamlyn, London.

Basque, R. 1994. *Les Oiseaux du Golfe du Morbihan*. Coop Breizh, Vannes.

Brooks, R. 1998. *Birding on the Greek Island of Lesvos*. Brookside, Fakenham.

Carlson, K. & Carlson, C. 2001. *A Birdwatching Guide to the Algarve*. Arlequin Press, Chelmsford.

Coghlan, S. 2001. *A Birdwatching Guide to Crete*. Arlequin Press, Chelmsford.

Coghlan, S. 2003. *A Birdwatching Guide to Brittany*. Arlequin Press, Chelmsford.

Crozier, J. 1998. *A Birdwatching Guide to the Pyrenees*. Arlequin Press, Chelmsford.

de Juana, E. A. (ed.) 1994. *Where to Watch Birds in Spain*. Lynx Edicions, Barcelona.

Evans, L. G. R. 1999. *The Ulimate Site Guide to Scarcer British Birds*. 2nd edition. Birdguides, Sheffield.

Finlayson, C. 1991. *Birds of the Strait of Gibraltar*. T. & A.D. Poyser, London.

Garcia, E. & Paterson, A. 1994. *Where to Watch Birds in Southern Spain: Andalucía, Extremadura & Gibraltar*. Christopher Helm, London.

Gooders, J. 1994. *Where to Watch Birds in Britain & Europe*. Hamlyn, London.

Gorman, G. 1996. *The Birds of Hungary*. Christopher Helm, London.

Gorman, G. 1994. *Where to Watch Birds in Eastern Europe*. Hamlyn, London.

Gosney, D. 1994. *Finding Birds in Bulgaria*. Birdguides, Sheffield.

Gosney, D. 1994. *Finding Birds in Eastern Austria*. Birdguides, Sheffield.

Gosney, D. 1994. *Finding Birds in Greece*. Birdguides, Sheffield.

Gosney, D. 1996. *Finding Birds in Finland*. Birdguides, Sheffield.

Gosney, D. 1996. *Finding Birds in Hungary*. Birdguides, Sheffield.

Gosney, D. 1996. *Finding Birds in Mallorca*. Birdguides, Sheffield.

Gosney, D. 1996. *Finding Birds in Northern France*. Birdguides, Sheffield.

Gosney, D. 1996. *Finding Birds in Northern Spain*. Birdguides, Sheffield.

Gosney, D. 1996. *Finding Birds in Poland*. Birdguides, Sheffield.

Gosney, D. 1996. *Finding Birds in Romania*. Birdguides, Sheffield.

Gosney, D. 1996. *Finding Birds in Southern France*. Birdguides, Sheffield.

Gosney, D. 1996. *Finding Birds in Southern Spain*. Birdguides, Sheffield.

Hagemeijer, W. J. M. & Blair, M. J. (eds.) 1997. *The EBCC Atlas of European Breeding Birds: Their Distribution and Abundance*. T. & A.D. Poyser, London.

Harrap, S. & Redman, N. 2003. *Where to Watch Birds in Britain*. Christopher Helm, London.

Hearl, G. 1996. *A Birdwatching Guide to Menorca, Ibiza and Formentera*. Arlequin Press, Chelmsford.

Hearl, G. 2002. *A Birdwatching Guide to Mallorca*. Arlequin Press, Chelmsford.

Heath, M. F. & Evans, M. I. (eds.) 2000. *Important Bird Areas in Europe*. BirdLife International, Cambridge.

Hora, J. et al. 1992. *Important Bird Areas of Europe: Czechoslovakia*. Czechoslovak ICBP Section, Prague.

Hutchinson, C. 1994. *Where to Watch Birds in Ireland*. Christopher Helm, London.

Iankov, P. 1996. *Where to Watch Birds in Bulgaria*. Pensoft, Sofia.

Knystautas, A. 1987. *The Natural History of the USSR*. Century Hutchinson, London.

Kren, J. 2002. *Birds of the Czech Republic*. Christopher Helm, London.

La Ligue Française pour la Protection des Oiseaux, 1992. *Where to Watch Birds in France*. Christopher Helm, London.

Lega Italiana Protezione Uccelli, 1994. *Where to Watch Birds in Italy*. Christopher Helm, London.

Madders, M. 2002. *Where to Watch Birds in Scotland*. 4th edition. Christopher Helm, London.

Moore, C. C., Elias, G. & Costa, H. 1997. *A Birdwatcher's Guide to Portugal and Madeira*. Prion, Huntingdon.

Palmer, M. 1994. *A Birdwatching Guide to the Costa Blanca*. Arlequin Press, Chelmsford.

Palmer, M. 2002. *A Birdwatching Guide to Southern Spain*. Arlequin Press, Chelmsford.

Rebane, M. 1999. *Where to Watch Birds in North and East Spain*. Christopher Helm, London.

Rose, L. 1995. *Where to Watch Birds in Spain and Portugal*. Hamlyn, London.

Saunders, D. 2000. *Where to Watch Birds in Wales*. 3rd edition. Christopher Helm, London.

Sultana, J. & Gauci, C. 1982. *A New Guide to the Birds of Malta*. Malta Ornithological Society, Valletta.

Sultana, J. 1993. *Important Seabird Sites in the Mediterranean*. Malta Ornithological Society, Valletta.

Thibault, J.-C. & Bonaccorsi, G. 1999. *The Birds of Corsica*: BOU Checklist No. 17. British Ornithologists' Union, Tring.

van den Berg, A. & Lafontaine, D. 1996. *Where to Watch Birds in Holland, Belgium & Northern France*. Hamlyn, London.

Welch, H., Rose, L., Moore, D., Oddie, W. & Sigg, H. 1996. *Where to Watch Birds in Turkey, Greece and Cyprus*. Hamlyn, London.

Wheatley, N. 2000. *Where to Watch Birds in Europe & Russia*. Christopher Helm, London.

For more detailed birding site-guides in England consult the extensive *Where to Watch Birds* series from Christopher Helm which now covers the entire country.

North Africa & the Atlantic Islands

Bergier, P. & Bergier, F. 1990. *A Birdwatcher's Guide to Morocco*. Prion, Huntingdon.

Clarke, A. & Collins, D. 1996. *A Birdwatcher's Guide to the Canary Islands*. Prion, Huntingdon.

Combridge, P. & Snook, A. 1997. *A Birdwatching Guide to Morocco*. Arlequin Press, Chelmsford.

Goodman, S. M. & Meininger, P. L. 1989. *The Birds of Egypt*. Oxford University Press, Oxford.

Gosney, D. 1996. *Finding Birds in the Canary Islands*. Birdguides, Sheffield.

Gosney, D. 1997. *Finding Birds in Northern Morocco*. Birdguides, Sheffield.

Gosney, D. 1996. *Finding Birds in Southern Morocco*. Birdguides, Sheffield.

Sargeant, D. E. 1997. Cape Verde: *A Birder's Guide to the Cape Verde Islands*. Birders' Guides & Checklists, Holt.

Wheatley, N. 1995. *Where to Watch Birds in Africa*. Christopher Helm, London.

Middle East

Adamian, M. S. & Klem, D. 1999. *Handbook of the Birds of Armenia*. AUA, Yerevan.

Andrews, I. J. 1995. *The Birds of the Hashemite Kingdom of Jordan*. Privately published, Musselburgh.

Evans, M. I. (compiler) 1994. *Important Bird Areas of the Middle East*. BirdLife International, Cambridge.

Flint, P. R. & Stewart, P. F. 1992. *The Birds of Cyprus: An Annotated Checklist*. British Ornithologists' Union, Tring.

Gosney, D. 1994. *Finding Birds in Eastern Turkey*. Birdguides, Sheffield.

Gosney, D. 1996. *Finding Birds in Cyprus*. Birdguides, Sheffield.

Gosney, D. 1996. *Finding Birds in Israel*. Birdguides, Sheffield.

Gosney, D. 1996. *Finding Birds in Turkey: Ankara to Birecik*. Birdguides, Sheffield.

Gosney, D. 1996. *Finding Birds in Western Turkey*. Birdguides, Sheffield.

Green, I. & Moorhouse, N. 1995. *A Birdwatcher's Guide to Turkey*. Prion, Huntingdon.

Paz, U. 1987. *The Birds of Israel*. Christopher Helm, London.

Roselaar, C. S. 1995. *Songbirds of Turkey: an Atlas of Biodiversity of Turkish Passerine Birds*. Pica Press, Robertsbridge.

Shirihai, H. 1996. *The Birds of Israel*. Academic Press, London.

Shirihai, H., Smith, J., Kirwan, G. & Alon, D. 2000. *A Guide to the Birding Hot-spots of Northern Israel*. Society for the Protection of Nature in Israel, Tel-Aviv.

Shirihai, H., Smith, J., Kirwan, G. & Alon, D. 2000. *A Guide to the Birding Hot-spots of Southern Israel*. Society for the Protection of Nature in Israel, Tel-Aviv.

Wheatley, N. 1996. *Where to Watch Birds in Asia*. Christopher Helm, London.

Yosef, R. 1995. *Birdwatching in Eilat*. Privately published, Eilat.

Index of scientific names

English names of birds are listed in taxonomic order on pages 5–9.

Index of sites